The Concise
Oxford Companion
to American Literature

THE CONCISE
OXFORD COMPANION
TO
AMERICAN
LITERATURE

JAMES D. HART

New York   Oxford
OXFORD UNIVERSITY PRESS
1986

Oxford University Press

Oxford   New York   Toronto
Delhi   Bombay   Calcutta   Madras   Karachi
Petaling Jaya   Singapore   Hong Kong   Tokyo
Nairobi   Dar es Salaam   Cape Town
Melbourne   Auckland

and associated companies in
Beirut   Berlin   Ibadan   Nicosia

Library of Congress Cataloging-in-Publication Data

Hart, James David, 1911-
The concise Oxford companion to American literature.

An abridged ed. of: The Oxford companion to
American Literature.
Includes index.
1. American literature—Dictionaries.   2. American
literature—Bio-bibliography.   I. Hart, James David,
1911-   Oxford companion to American literature.
II. Title
PS21.H32   1986   810′.9   86-8510
ISBN 0-19-503982-3

1 3 5 7 9 8 6 4 2

Printed in the United States of America
on acid-free paper

Preface

The first edition of *The Oxford Companion to American Literature* was begun fifty years ago. Its first printing was over forty-five years ago. During the intervening years it has undergone many changes in several editions and many printings. The most recent was the thoroughgoing revision for the fifth edition issued in 1983. The first edition was printed on 888 very tightly packed double-column pages. The most recent one, with a more spacious format, runs to 896 larger pages. From first to last these editions extend beyond the central essentials of their subject to present a good deal of rather specialized or even esoteric material on the literature of America and even much information that lies on the periphery of the literature itself. Now, at last, here is an abbreviated text, reduced nearly by half. Although much has been pared away, this latest version continues to be so closely guided by the general principles of the basic book's fifth edition that I think it appropriate and helpful to reprint here much of the text that first appeared three years ago as the introduction to that volume.

Berkeley, California   J.D.H.
March 1986

From the Preface to the Fifth Edition of
The Oxford Companion to American Literature

Designed to serve as a useful companion for students and general readers, this volume provides ready references, first of all, to the authors and writings, past and present, that are included in the area of American literature. In addition, some references extend to the written word in America outside conventional literary criteria but relevant to them. The volume treats certain major nonliterary aspects of the American mind and the American scene as these are reflected in and influenced by American literature. The scope of the work also embraces far more than belles letters, yet, it excludes some forms of publication, such as cookbooks and comic books. It is a companion to reading rather than to literature alone, but literature is its focus.

In alphabetic arrangement, the work includes short biographies and brief bibliographies of American authors, with information regarding their style and subjects. It also includes some selected separate entries printing summaries of important American novels, stories, essays, poems (with verse forms noted), plays, biographies, and autobiographies, tracts, narratives, and histories, to provide a brief sense of the original works, and, occasionally, including succinct but salient quotations. Other subjects include definitions and historical outlines of literary schools and movements, literary awards, literary societies, scholarly organizations, magazines, newspapers, anthologies, and cooperative publications. Literary terms that are sufficiently defined in dictionaries are not cited unless they have a distinctive history in the United States or warrant definition by American examples. Thus there are no entries on the conventional terms of prosody, but existentialism, free verse, impressionism, polyphonic prose, and stream of consciousness are all treated, and there are full entries on such subjects as the ballad, local color, romanticism, and the tall tale.

As indicated even by a glance at the column of Literary History in the Chronological Index that concludes this book, much of the writing that is discussed in these pages may not be distinguished as literature, but it is all important for a comprehensive review of expression in America. The written word does not exist in a vacuum, and the author of this book has therefore constantly kept in mind the idea that the fullest understanding of major works in literature, let alone lesser pieces of writing, depends upon an informed knowledge of the social and cultural atmosphere of their place and time.

The work continues to include some biographies of persons who are not authors but who have been important in the nation's social history and culture, brief articles on religious sects, Indian tribes, and other subjects that may seem outside the purview of literature but whose relationships with it are genuine and significant. Entries will be found on subjects that range alphabetically from Abolitionist to the Zuñi Indians, the former entry, for example, including references to authors as various as Samuel Sewall, Franklin, Crèvecœur, Richard Hildreth, Harriet Beecher Stowe, Hinton Helper, Lowell, and Whittier, and the latter including a reference to an author as current as Edmund Wilson.

Just as American materials that lie on the periphery of literature are treated, so some foreign materials that are relevant to this country's writings are also represented. Foreign authors are also given attention when they have written important books about the United States or when they bear some other relation of consequence to American literature and life. One will find entries on Charles Dickens, Frank Harris, and Rudyard Kipling, among others, but the entries tell only of their American associations.

Every precaution, within the limits of time and energy at the disposal of one man, has been taken to make the book comprehensive, balanced, and accurate. The fact that both the plan and the writing are entirely the work of one man has made for a carefully considered proportion in the entries, so that authors past and present, literary movements of earlier times and of this moment, are all assessed in relation to one another in an attempt to achieve a proper balance in which antiquarianism will not overwhelm appreciation of the present and contemporaneity will not seem so attractive as to depreciate previous eras.

The length of an article should, nevertheless, not be considered as precisely marking the relative importance of its subject. Many matters have upset the use of exact standards of length, although an attempt has constantly been made to allot space according to a judgment of what is significant in American literary and social history as considered both by me and by general scholarship on the whole field here treated. However, even among authors, such considerations must be recognized as the duration of their careers, the scholarly controversies about them, the differences between those who were recluses and those who entered actively into the life of their times, and the distinctions between those who wrote books on different subjects and in varying forms and those whose books were all cut on the same pattern. This is true also of the descriptions and plot summaries,

which, irrespective of the literary quality of the books, may be lengthened or shortened according to the diffusion or simplicity of the subject matter. The same forces operate in the general articles.

Over forty years have passed since the first edition of this book was printed. During that time new authors and new subjects have come to prominence, and, indeed, new attitudes toward the study of literature have been developed. This book was written in its first version during the 1930s, which were still the formative years for the academic study of American literature. Not only was there relatively little scholarship and criticism addressed to the subject, but many authors now highly esteemed were then little known. In that time the colonial poet Edward Taylor was only in the process of being discovered, while Faulkner, though in mid-career, was little read or valued. Now, nearly a half-century later, the situation is very different. Furthermore, the book attempts to keep up-to-date, so that authors not yet born when this book was first begun now appear in this latest edition. Such matters have affected the book, and it is much altered from the first edition of 1941. But it is certainly not an entirely new book, for happily it appears to have stood the test of time well. Where it has changed, it has not changed all at once. Some significant alterations have been made in each of the four preceding editions and minor modifications and additions have been made quietly in each of their several printings.

This fifth edition has been entirely reset in a somewhat changed format and thus has allowed freedom for a fresh and thoroughgoing revision, without the need to follow the pagination of the past or to be constrained by text already in type. Probably every page has undergone some changes from the earliest edition. The alterations are so many and of such different kinds that they cannot be readily described, but attention can be drawn to basic changes from the fourth edition.

The fifth edition contains full-scale entries on more than 240 authors not in the last edition. It also contains over 115 new entries devoted to detailed summaries of books that were either not in the fourth edition or but briefly noted in it. Of the authors and other subjects previously treated, in this edition over 590 have had extensive changes beyond merely updating made in the entries devoted to them.

Berkeley, California   J.D.H.
March 1983

Note

CHARACTERS and REAL PERSONS are entered under their surnames, the former in ordinary bold type, the latter in captials (e.g. Natty Bumppo under **Bumppo,** NATTY, and Henry James under **JAMES,** HENRY), unless the surname is little known, or the two names are generally considered an indissoluble whole (e.g. **John Henry** and **Little Eva**). For the sake of convenience, a few famous characters are also entered under their Christian names.

AUTHORS and other persons are entered under their proper names rather than their pseudonyms (e.g. **CLEMENS,** SAMUEL, rather than Mark Twain, and **Cody,** WILLIAM, rather than Buffalo Bill). In all cases the pseudonym is entered with a cross reference to the proper name. Upon rare occasions, when the real name is forgotten or little known, the entry is under the pseudonym (e.g. **TRAVEN,** B. rather than **TORSVAN,** BERICK TRAVEN).

FULL NAMES are given; those parts not ordinarily used are enclosed in brackets (e.g. **CATHER,** WILLA [SIBERT], and **MENCKEN,** H[ENRY] L[OUIS]). Variant spellings and originals of altered names are enclosed in parentheses (e.g. **FAULKNER** (or FALKNER) and **O'SHEEL** (SHIELDS).

When more than one member of a family is mentioned, the entry is under the name that is most celebrated (e.g. **Grimké,** SARAH, followed by ANGELINA EMILY). When several members of a family are equally famous, separate entries are made (e.g. the James family).

A TITLE consisting of a Christian name and a surname is entered under the Christian name (e.g. *Tom Sawyer*). The TITLE OF A BOOK OR PAMPHLET is italicized; at the head of an article it is given in bold italics (e.g. *Mosses from an Old Manse*). The title of a work not separately issued, i.e. printed in a periodical or as part of a book, is enclosed in quotation marks (e.g. "Young Goodman Brown"); at the head of an article it is given in bold italic type.

All publication DATES, except as otherwise indicated, are American. Plays are dated in reference to first production rather than publication, although both dates are given for plays which are separately summarized. All dates are based on the New Style Calendar.

The symbol ♦ is used to indicate a cross-reference.

The Concise
Oxford Companion
to American Literature

A

ABBOTT, Lyman (1835–1922), son of Jacob Abbott, was the successor of Henry Ward Beecher both in the pulpit of his Plymouth Church (Congregational) in Brooklyn and as editor of *The Outlook* (originally *The Christian Union*).

Abie's Irish Rose, comedy by Anne Nichols, produced in 1922. Its sentimental plot is concerned with the love of a Jewish youth and an Irish girl in New York's Lower East Side. The play is credited with being one of the most popular ever produced in the U.S., having had a New York run of 2327 performances.

Absalom, Absalom!, novel by Faulkner,♦ published in 1936.

The story of Thomas Sutpen and the intricate patterns of other lives involved with his are narrated mainly through Quentin Compson, the grandson of Sutpen's befriender, General Compson. Born to a poor-white family in the West Virginia mountains in 1807, Sutpen runs away at 14 and makes his way to Haiti. There he later marries Eulalia Bon, a planter's daughter, and they have a son, Charles. Discovering his wife's partial black ancestry, Sutpen leaves her and the child, and two years later (1833) appears in Yoknapatawpha County, Mississippi, with a band of wild Haitian blacks. He obtains 100 acres of land questionably from the Chickasaw Indians, creates a plantation, and builds a large house on "Sutpen's Hundred." As a further part of his grand design to achieve aristocracy, Sutpen marries Ellen Coldfield, of a respectable family, and they have children, Henry and Judith. Years later, at the University of Mississippi, Henry meets and admires Charles Bon, Sutpen's Haitian son, who has grown to manhood in New Orleans. When Bon comes home with Henry for Christmas, he falls in love with Judith, but Sutpen forbids their marriage. To Henry he reveals that he is Bon's father (but conceals the black background), and Henry reacts by renouncing his birthright and leaving with Bon, and upon the outbreak of the Civil War, the two go off to fight. During the war Ellen dies but the men survive. Although Bon will not repudiate his octoroon mistress and their son, he still wants to wed Judith, being willing to leave only if Sutpen will acknowledge him as "Bon, my son." Learning of Bon's Negro blood, Henry murders him to prevent the marriage, and then disappears himself. Intent on begetting an heir and founding a dynasty, Sutpen gets engaged to his sister-in-law Rosa Coldfield, who leaves him when he suggests that they try to have a son before marrying. Attempting "to replace that progeny the hopes of which he had himself destroyed," Sutpen has relations with the granddaughter of Wash Jones, a poor-white squatter on Sutpen's Hundred. When he casts off Milly Jones and the child because it is a girl, Wash kills Sutpen with a scythe. Bon's son by his mistress, Charles Etienne De Saint-Valery Bon, is brought to the plantation by Clytemnestra (Clytie), another daughter of Sutpen by one of his slaves. Charles Etienne in turn marries a full-blood black woman and fathers an idiot son, Jim Bond. After Judith and Charles Etienne die of yellow fever, only Sutpen's black heirs, Clytie and Jim Bond, remain on the decaying plantation. In 1910, shortly before her death, Rosa, aided by Quentin, finds Henry, now aged and wasted, returned and hidden in the house, and when Rosa sends for an ambulance, Clytie, thinking it a police car come to arrest Henry for the old murder, sets fire to the house, violently ending the "doom" of Sutpen's own destructive career on a "land primed for fatality and already cursed with it."

Acres of Diamonds, see *Conwell, Russell.*

ADAMS, Abigail [Smith], (1744–1818), wife of John Adams, from whom she had to be separated for long periods during the Revolution, occasioning her frequent, loving, lively, and outspoken letters. She also engaged in much correspondence with other family members. Her charming letters were published by her grandson Charles Francis Adams as *Letters of Mrs. Adams . . .* (2 vols., 1840) and *Familiar Letters of John Adams and His Wife* (1876). Better-edited texts appear in the Adams Papers.♦

ADAMS, ALICE (1926–   ), Virginia-born author, educated at Radcliffe, long resident in San Francisco, whose novels include *Careless Love* (1966), *Families and Survivors* (1974), *Listening to Billie* (1978), *Rich Rewards* (1980), and *Superior Women* (1984), sensitive studies of women—young to middle-aged—and their relations to family, friends, husbands, and lovers. She is also known for stories, collected in *Beautiful Girl* (1979), *You Can't Keep a Good Woman Down* (1981), and *To See You Again* (1982).

ADAMS, ANDY (1859–1935), born in Indiana, moved to Texas to become a cowboy, and during the mining boom went to Colorado, where he later wrote his stories of the cattle kingdom. He is one of the few authors of cowboy stories who are considered to have achieved high literary merit. Among his books are *The Log of a Cowboy* (1903), a semi-autobiographical novel of a five-month-long cattle drive from Texas to Montana, and *Cattle Brands* (1906), stories of frontier life in the 1880s.

ADAMS, CHARLES FRANCIS (1807–86), son of John Quincy Adams, entered politics as a "conscience" Whig, founded the *Boston Whig,* and in 1848 ran for the vice-presidency as a Free-Soil candidate. He later entered Congress as a Republican, and in 1861 was appointed minister to England, where he served during the Civil War. His diplomacy prevented England from continuing to furnish ironclad vessels to the Confederacy, and he was an arbitrator of the Alabama Claims. He edited the *Works of John Adams* (1850–56), the letters of Abigail Adams,♦ and the *Memoirs of John Quincy Adams* (12 vols., 1874–77). Henry, Brooks, and Charles Francis Adams, Jr., were his sons.

ADAMS, FRANKLIN P[IERCE] (1881–1960), columnist, radio performer, and humorist, began his journalistic career in Chicago (1903). He worked on various New York papers and was best known for his column, "The Conning Tower."

ADAMS, HANNAH (1755–1831), is generally considered the first professional woman author of America. Her popular works included *Alphabetical Compendium of the Various Sects . . . from the Beginning of the Christian Era to the Present Day* (1784); *A Summary History of New England* (1799); *The Truth and Excellence of the Christian Religion Exhibited* (1804); and *The History of the Jews* (1812).

ADAMS, HENRY [BROOKS] (1838–1918), great-grandson of John Adams and grandson of John Quincy Adams, claims in his autobiography that his conventional education was defective, despite the best Boston and Quincy background, Harvard, German postgraduate training, and his position as secretary to his father (Charles Francis Adams) when he represented the U.S. as minister to England during the Civil War. Henry Adams's first publication, an article on Captain John Smith (1867), was followed by other contributions to periodicals, including a review of Lyell's *Principles of Geology* (1868), clearly showing his belief in the importance of the evolutionary theory in human history and Adams's own divorce from the absolute standards of his ancestors. Returning from England to Washington, D.C. (1868), he continued to write carefully considered articles, and, completely out of sympathy with Reconstruction politics, abandoned former ideas of a political career to teach history at Harvard (1870–77), for most of this period also editing *The North American Review.* He next went to Washington to write history and to seek the companionship of such men as Secretary of State Evarts, John Hay, and Clarence King, for he said ironically, "So far as [I] had a function in life, it was as stable-companion to statesmen." There he wrote *Democracy*♦ (1880), an anonymous novel on Washington politics, and *Esther* (1884), a pseudonymous novel of New York society. In 1872 he married Marian Hooper, whose suicide in 1885 tragically affected his life. Although he never mentions her in his writings, she probably served as a model for the heroine in *Esther.* Adams commissioned his friend Saint-Gaudens to design for her grave in Washington a symbolic statue, which he called "The Peace of God." When he could no longer endure life at Washington, he made a long trip through the Orient, from which he returned to complete his *History of the United States During the Administrations of Thomas Jefferson and James Madison* (9 vols., 1889–91), portraying politics and diplomacy in the early republic. He "drifted back to Washington with a new sense of history" after a summer in Normandy (1895) and a visit to the Paris Exposition (1900), where he saw the huge dynamo that in his autobiography he was to take as a symbol of mechanistic power and energy in the multiplicity of the

20th century as contrasted to the force of the Virgin, "the ideal of human perfection," representing the unity of the 13th century, which he treated in *Mont-Saint-Michel and Chartres*♦ (1904). This scholarly descriptive work, interpretively studying a unified world, was Adams's first attempt to measure the life and thought of an era in terms of Force. In 1910 he published "A Letter to American Teachers of History," reprinted in *The Degradation of the Democratic Dogma* (1919) by his brother Brooks Adams. This work sets forth Henry Adams's dynamic theory of history. The second law of thermodynamics posits a universal tendency to dissipate mechanical energy and thus vitiates the idea of human history as evolving toward a state of perfection. On the contrary, according to Adams, human thought is a substance passing from one phase to another through critical points determined by attraction, acceleration, and volume (equivalent to pressure, temperature, and volume in mechanical physics), and he contends that history must be studied in the light of these principles. The complementary work to *Mont-Saint-Michel* is a study of 20th-century multiplicity, *The Education of Henry Adams*♦ (1907). The skepticism and cynicism in the account of his self-termed failures pass beyond autobiography to a study of the garment of education draped on the "manikin" Henry Adams, a figure used to measure motion, proportion, and human conditions. In later chapters the use of his dynamic theory of history is made explicit. Other books include *Chapters of Erie and Other Essays* (1871), written with his brother Charles Francis Adams, Jr.; *The Life of Albert Gallatin* (1879); *John Randolph* (1882); and *The Life of George Cabot Lodge* (1911). His letters, printed in various collections, are being edited in 6 volumes (1982–), and those of his wife were published in 1936.

ADAMS, JOHN (1735–1826), 2nd President of the U.S. (1797–1801), was born in Braintree (now Quincy), Mass., graduated from Harvard (1755), was admitted to the bar (1758), and soon entered public life. He opposed the Stamp Act and the Boston Port Act, and was a delegate to the first Continental Congress, where he aided in drafting a petition to the king and a declaration of rights, and to the second Congress, in which he proposed Washington for military commander, hoping to draw Virginia into greater support of Revolutionary policies. He worked for inde-

pendence, but disliked Paine's plan of government suggested in *Common Sense,* and set forth his own ideas in *Thoughts on Government* (1776), one of his several energetic publications on current questions. He helped draft the Declaration of Independence and, according to Jefferson, was "the pillar of its support on the floor of Congress," where he also served on many important committees. From 1777 to 1779 he was a commissioner to France, and unsuccessfully consulted the French government concerning peace negotiations with England, but his negotiations with the Dutch to secure a treaty and loan were ultimately successful. In 1782–83 he accompanied Jay and Franklin to England, where they negotiated the treaty of peace, and in 1785 he was appointed envoy to the Court of St. James's. During his residence in England, Adams wrote a three-volume *Defence of the Constitutions of Government of the United States of America against the Attack of Mr. Turgot* (1787). Upon his return (1788) he was elected the first Vice-President of the U.S., and, although his office was mainly a matter of routine, he worked without party alignment on the side of the Federalists. His *Discourses on Davila* (1791), drawing a moral for the U.S. from the history of France, alienated Hamilton, who thought the work tended to weaken the government, while Jefferson considered it as leaning toward hereditary monarchy and aristocracy. After another term as Vice-President, Adams was elected to the presidency in 1796, despite the opposition of Hamilton. Jefferson was antagonistic to Adams's administration, and Hamilton, with a strong influence in the cabinet, particularly opposed Adams's conciliatory policy toward France, by which war was averted. Hamilton's animus, as displayed in his *Letter Concerning the Public Conduct and Character of John Adams* (1800), played into the hands of the Jeffersonians, and after he failed of reelection Adams retired to private life in Quincy. His *Works* were collected in ten volumes (1850–56), and many separate volumes of his correspondence have been issued, of which the most important are the letters addressed to his wife Abigail and the communications with Jefferson. His diary, autobiography, and family correspondence have been published as part of the Adams Papers. ♦

ADAMS, JOHN QUINCY (1767–1848), 6th President of the U.S. (1825–29), son of John and Abigail Adams, was born in Braintree (now Quincy), Mass., and received his early training by accompanying his father on diplomatic missions to France and Holland. He graduated from Harvard (1787), was admitted to the bar (1790), and entered politics; his answer to Paine's *Rights of Man,* signed "Publicola" (1791), and similar essays, led Washington to appoint him minister to the Netherlands (1794). In 1797 his father appointed him minister to Berlin, and he remained abroad until 1801. Literary results of this residence were his translation of Wieland's poetic romance *Oberon* (first published 1940) and his *Letters on Silesia* (1804). In 1803 Adams was elected to the Senate, where his want of allegiance to Federalist tradition caused his resignation (1808). He had already been appointed Professor of Rhetoric and Belles-Lettres at Harvard, and his college lectures were published (1810). In 1809 he was appointed minister to Russia, and six years later minister to England, to remain until Monroe invited him (1817) to be secretary of state. In this capacity he postponed the Oregon boundary question by treaty with England, secured Florida from Spain, and recognized the rebelling Spanish colonies. The principles underlying his policies were drafted by him in the Monroe Doctrine (1823). After four years of independent policies as President, he was elected to Congress (1831) without any definite party support, and continued to serve until his death 17 years later. He was considered to be without peer as a parliamentary debater, and worked hard to oppose the extension of slavery and consequently the admission of Texas and the Mexican War. All his actions were characterized by an independence of party. His *Memoirs* (12 vols., 1874–77) cover half a century, and are valuable both as political commentary and as a study in American letters; they have been described by Allan Nevins in his edition (1928) as written "with malice towards all." His independent mind is indicated by the diversity of his other writings, which include the minor *Poems of Religion and Society* (1848), which he himself treasured, and the celebrated *Report on Weights and Measures* (1821), in which the subject is examined with the exactness of mathematical science, the sagacity of statesmanship, and the wisdom of philosophy.

ADAMS, LÉONIE [FULLER] (1899–), New York poet, whose books, *Those Not Elect* (1925), *High Falcon* (1929), *This Measure* (1933), and *Poems* (1954), have been described as works of a modern metaphysical

poet because of their sensitivity, austere intensity, and emphasis on intellect. She taught English at New York University, Bennington College, and Columbia University. In 1969 and the '70s she received several major awards and grants for her poetic achievements.

Adams Papers, archives of the Adams family, housed in the Massachusetts Historical Society, originally made available to scholars in a microfilm collection. A letterpress edition being prepared under the editorship of Lyman Henry Butterfield draws also upon public and private collections for its selective but scholarly gathering of documents. Series I contains the diaries of the Adams family statesmen, 1755–1880; Series II deals with the family correspondence, 1761–1889; and Series III prints general correspondence and other papers of the statesmen.

ADDAMS, JANE (1860–1935), reformer and sociologist, founded the Chicago social settlement, Hull-House, in 1889. Among her books are *Democracy and Social Ethics* (1902), *A New Conscience and an Ancient Evil* (1912), *Twenty Years at Hull-House* (1910), *Peace and Bread in Time of War* (1922), and *The Second Twenty Years at Hull-House* (1930).

Adding Machine, The, expressionistic play by Elmer Rice,♦ produced and published in 1923.

ADE, GEORGE (1866–1944), Indiana author, whose books are noted for their racy use of vernacular and sympathetic portrayal of country characters. His *Fables in Slang* (1899) is often credited with being one of the most acute literary examples of the language of the common American. The satire and speech of this book appear also in *People You Know* (1903) and *Hand-Made Fables* (1920). Ade was the author of several musical comedies, notably *The Sultan of Sulu* (1902), and such plays as *The College Widow* (1904) and *Just Out of College* (1905), farcical satires on student life.

ADLER, RENATA (1938–), after graduation from Bryn Mawr and further education at Harvard and the Sorbonne, wrote social and political essays for *The New Yorker* and literary criticism collected in *Toward a Radical Middle* (1970). Her film reviews for *The New York Times* were collected in *A Year in the Dark* (1970). *Speedboat* (1976) is a short, episodic novel about the education and experiences of a young woman journalist, and *Pitch Dark* (1983) is a similarly constructed novel about a woman journalist breaking off her long-standing affair with a married man.

Adulateur, The, satirical play by Mercy Otis Warren, ♦ published in 1773.

Adventures of Augie March, The, see *Augie March, The Adventures of.*

Advertisements for the Unexperienced Planters of New England . . . , work by Captain John Smith. ♦

Advice to the Privileged Orders, work by Joel Barlow. ♦

Afloat and Ashore, romance by Cooper ♦ (1844). *Miles Wallingford* ♦ is a sequel.

After the Fall, two-act play by Arthur Miller, ♦ produced and published in 1964.

Age of Anxiety, The, long poem by Auden. ♦

Age of Fable, The, see *Bulfinch, Thomas.*

Age of Innocence, The, novel by Edith Wharton, ♦ published in 1920. It received a Pulitzer Prize, and in 1928 was dramatized by Margaret Ayer Barnes.

In the highest circle of New York social life during the 1870s, Newland Archer, a young lawyer, is the fiancé of May Welland. Before their engagement is announced, he meets May's cousin Ellen Olenska, the wife of a dissolute Polish count, from whom she is separated although she does not divorce him because of the conventional taboo. The taboo extends so far that she is nearly ostracized by her former friends, and only the efforts of Archer and his mother save her position. She wins the toleration of her grandmother, Mrs. Manson Mingott, but even then she is distrusted. Archer's taste and intelligence distinguish him in this dogmatic society, and he discovers in Ellen the companion spirit he has sought but not found in May, who is the product of her strict, formal environment. The two fall in love, but it is too late for Archer to withdraw from his engagement. He marries May but is dissatisfied with their convention-bound relationship. Ellen moves to Washington, then returns to care for her grandmother, and her relation with Archer is rekindled. When May reveals to Ellen that she is pregnant, the situation becomes intol-

erable for the Countess, who goes to live in Paris. Archer is never sure how much his wife knows until after her death, many years later, when he visits Paris with his son Dallas. Ellen invites them to visit her, but at the last moment Archer sends Dallas alone, feeling that, though they are now free to marry, he prefers his ideal vision of Ellen to the reality.

Age of Reason, The, deistic work by Thomas Paine, ♦ published in two parts (Paris, 1794–95). Between the writing of the first and second parts, Paine spent 11 months in prison because of his activities in the French Revolution.

Part I affirms the existence of God and offers proofs from the arguments of design and first cause. The knowledge of God has been obscured, according to the author, by the calumnies of the Bible and all national institutions of churches, which are no more than "human inventions set up to terrify and enslave mankind, and monopolize power and profit." Man's moral duty should be to observe the real and ever-existing word of God in the creation, and to strive to imitate this beneficence. Part II is mainly an attack on the Bible, pointing out the cruelty of Moses, the folly of Solomon, the exaggerations of the prophets, the improbability of Jesus' miraculous birth, and the general inconsistency that renders the Bible fallible.

AGEE, JAMES (1909–55), Tennessee-born author, after graduation from Harvard (1932) began his literary career with *Permit Me Voyage* (1934), a work issued in the Yale Series of Younger Poets. He served on the staffs of *Fortune* and *Time,* and for the former wrote a study of Alabama sharecroppers during the Depression, which when found inappropriate for the magazine was issued with photographs by Walker Evans as *Let Us Now Praise Famous Men* ♦ (1941). *The Morning Watch* (1951), a novella sensitively depicting a day in the life of a 12-year-old boy in a Tennessee school, was a prelude to his major work of fiction, *A Death in the Family* ♦ (1957), a partly autobiographical and poetic story of a happy, secure Tennessee family whose good life is shattered by the father's death in an auto accident. His motion picture reviews for *Nation, Time,* and other journals were posthumously collected as *Agee on Film* (1958). *Agee on Film: II* (1960) contains five of his own screenplays, including Stephen Crane's *The Bride Comes to Yellow Sky* and *The Blue Hotel. A Death in the Family* was dramatized as *All the Way*

Home (1960) by Tad Mosel and won a Pulitzer Prize. Agee's letters to his old schoolteacher and friendly mentor from his sixteenth year to his death were published as *Letters to Father Flye* (1962).

Aggawam, see *Simple Cobler of Aggawam.*

Agrarians, name applied to certain Southern writers, including J.C. Ransom, J.G. Fletcher, R.P. Warren, Allen Tate, and Donald Davidson, who championed an agrarian economy for the South and the more general movement known as Regionalism. ♦

Ah, Wilderness!, play by Eugene O'Neill. ♦

Ahab, CAPTAIN, character in *Moby-Dick.* ♦

AIKEN, CONRAD [POTTER] (1889–1973), was born in Georgia but reared in Massachusetts, from which his parents' families had come, and educated at Harvard (A.B., 1911), so that a strong sense of a New England heritage is evident in his writing. In his maturity he lived for many years in England but returned to make his home in Massachusetts. His early poetry is marked by subtle musical rhythms and is concerned with the problem of personal identity, what it is that constitutes one's own consciousness, how to achieve self-knowledge, and how to transcend the self so as to understand the world at large. The volumes that collect this early poetry include *Earth Triumphant* (1914); *Turns and Movies* (1916); *The Jig of Forslin: A Symphony* (1916); *Nocturne of Remembered Spring* (1917); *The Charnel Rose, Senlin: A Biography, and Other Poems* (1918); *The House of Dust: A Symphony* (1920); *Punch: The Immortal Liar* (1921); *Priapus and the Pool* (1922); and *The Pilgrimage of Festus* (1923). A more metaphysical expression is developed in *John Deth* (1930), *The Coming Forth by Day of Osiris Jones* (1931), *Preludes for Memnon* (1931), *Landscape West of Eden* (1934), and *Time in the Rock* (1936), philosophic poems dealing with consciousness and time. *And in the Human Heart* (1940) is a sequence of 43 sonnets extending the concern with consciousness to the intensity of love. *Brownstone Eclogues* (1942) picks up the setting and subject of *The House of Dust:* the city and the quest of the individual for identification with its good and evil. *The Soldier* (1944) traces the common soldier through history in treating the wars of armies and the wars of the spirit. In *The Kid* (1947) Aiken uses the figure of William Blackstone, an individualistic and very early New En-

gland settler, as a symbol for the American character which is developed in the guise of such diverse later figures as Thoreau, Johnny Appleseed, and Whitman. Later poetry showing great musical quality and setting forth his essentially existentialist position appears in *Skylight One* (1949), *A Letter from Li Po* (1955), *Sheepfold Hill* (1958), and *The Morning Song of Lord Zero* (1963). He published *Selected Poems* (1929, Pulitzer Prize), *Collected Poems* (1953), and another *Selected Poems* (1961). He is also known for his critical writing in *Scepticisms* (1919), commenting on contemporary poets, his introduction to an edition of Emily Dickinson's poems (1924), which had much to do with establishing her reputation, and *A Reviewer's ABC* (1958). In 1927 appeared his first novel, a fantasy titled *Blue Voyage,* which treats some of his poetic themes as it tells in stream-of-consciousness prose of a dramatist's voyage to England, supposedly for reasons of his career and his love for a girl, but actually in his quest for self-knowledge. Later novels are *Great Circle* (1933), another tale of a voyage and of the quest to discover oneself; *King Coffin* (1935), the story of a neurotic criminal; *A Heart for the Gods of Mexico* (1939), about a dying woman's last love as it takes her from Boston to Mexico; and *Conversation; or, Pilgrims' Progress* (1940), dealing with crises in a man's life as husband, father, and artist. His stories have appeared in *Bring! Bring!* (1925), *Costumes by Eros* (1928), and *Among the Lost People* (1934), the last-named including "Mr. Arcularis," dramatized by the author and published as a play in 1957, about a sad old man who is dying, as he lived, alone, and who imagines himself on a recuperative sea voyage while he is actually outward bound toward death on an operating table. *Ushant* (1952), subtitled "an essay," is a psychological autobiography, reissued (1971) with the names of actual people replacing the original pseudonyms. *Selected Letters* was published in 1978.

AIKEN, GEORGE L. (1830–76), actor, and author of many plays, who dramatized Harriet Beecher Stowe's *Uncle Tom's Cabin* and acted in its first performance at Troy, N.Y. (Sept. 27, 1852), where it ran for 100 nights.

Air-Conditioned Nightmare, The, U.S. travel account by Henry Miller, ♦ published in 1945.

Airways, Inc., play by Dos Passos, ♦ published 1928, produced 1929.

AKINS, ZOË (1886–1958), born in Missouri, began writing for *The Mirror* of W.M. Reedy, and came to New York to write plays for the Washington Square Players, achieving her first professional success with *Déclassée* (1919), a play showing the social decline of an English lady. This was followed by *Daddy's Gone A-Hunting* (1921), the story of a man who forsakes his wife to pursue his dream of becoming a great painter. Several less successful plays were produced during the next ten years, among them *The Varying Shore* (1921), tracing in reverse chronology the career of a woman from her death as a gambler and demimondaine to her unhappy shy girlhood, and *The Texas Nightingale* (1922), revived as *Greatness* (1923), the story of an opera singer. Miss Akins returned to her full power with *The Greeks Had a Word for It* (1930), a satirical comedy of three unscrupulous girls whose only loyalty is to one another. In 1935 she won the Pulitzer Prize with *The Old Maid,* ♦ adapted from a novelette by Edith Wharton. *O, Evening Star* (1936) is the story of an aging actress whose burlesquing of serious drama in a motion picture reestablishes her career. *Forever Young* (1941), her first novel, deals with a Midwestern girls' school in the early 1900s.

Al Aaraaf, allegorical poem by Poe,♦ published in *Al Aaraaf, Tamerlane, and Minor Poems* (1829) and revised in later printings.

ALBEE, EDWARD [FRANKLIN] (1928–), after a troubled youth, in his early thirties quickly became a leading figure of the new drama of the absurd that mingles the realistic with fantasy to present a savagely satirical attack on spiritual sterility, blandness, conformity, and hypocrisy, and to summon up with deep feeling the tragedy of alienation. His first play, *The Zoo Story* (Berlin, 1959; New York, 1960), a one-act drama, presents a young homosexual who, hating both the world he can't live in and the one he does inhabit, manages to trick an ordinary, middle-aged, and innocent stranger whom he encounters in New York's Central Park into killing him. Another short play, *The Death of Bessie Smith* (Berlin, 1960; New York, 1961), treats the agonizing death of the black woman singer of blues counterpointed with a horrid fight involving a nurse, an intern, and an orderly in the all-white hospital to which she is brought after an auto accident. *The Sandbox* (1960) symbolically treats family relationships as Mommy and Daddy, tired of Grandma, an unusually vital person, leave her on a beach to be picked up by a young man representative of Death. *The American Dream* (1961), another play in one act, again presents a grotesque comedy about a middle-class Mommy and Daddy who tortured their adopted son to death because he seemed unlikely to grow up into the clean-cut "American Dream" type of young man. *Who's Afraid of Virginia Woolf?* ♦ (1962), Albee's first three-act play, presents an all-night drinking bout of a middle-aged professor and his wife, joined by a vacuous instructor and his silly wife, in which through horrid verbal torturing of one another they eventually achieve catharsis by exorcising their fixation about a nonexistent son, which the older couple had created to sustain themselves, an illustration of what Albee has called the need to "try to claw our way into compassion." *Tiny Alice* (1965) is a more obscure and symbolic drama that presents the richest woman in the world corrupting a Catholic lay brother, whom she seduces, marries, and arranges to have murdered. In 1963 he dramatized Carson McCullers's *The Ballad of the Sad Café.* ♦ His other adaptations are: James Purdy's *Malcolm* (1965), Giles Cooper's *Everything in the Garden* (1967), and Nabokov's *Lolita* (1981). *A Delicate Balance* ♦ (1966; Pulitzer Prize, 1967) depicts a family unhappily questing for love and purpose without success. In 1968 Albee produced *Box* and *Quotations from Chairman Mao Tse-tung,* the former presenting a huge box on stage while the sole voice is an offstage monologue, and the latter presenting four characters who speak banal lines from Mao and the sentimental American poet Will Carleton, the two linked dramas suggesting the lack of significant values in human relations. *All Over* (1971) treats the attitudes toward life of the diverse hangers-on who gather at the deathbed of a so-called great man. *Seascape* (1975) is a two-act play abstractly presenting a seemingly average man and wife who on a deserted beach encounter a humanoid couple in an earlier stage of evolutionary development and through conversation gain insights into curiosities of human behavior and beliefs. *The Lady from Dubuque* (1979) presents three fiercely captious couples to whom the Lady from Dubuque (Death) will come. *Counting the Ways* (1977) and *Listening* (1977) are short plays in which respectively two and three characters discuss their relationships.

ALCOTT, [AMOS] BRONSON (1799–1888), born in Connecticut, had little formal education, and early attempted to support himself as a peddler in the Southern states and as a schoolteacher in New England and Pennsylvania (1823–33). His educational ideas, in his Temple School at Boston (1834–39) and later in his work as school superintendent at Concord and elsewhere, attempted to create the harmonious development of the physical, intellectual, aesthetic, and moral natures, with stress placed on imagination. To achieve this end, he favored a conversational method of instruction, attempted to beautify the school surroundings, to give study and instruction the aspect of recreation, and introduced such innovations as gymnastics, organized play, and the honor system. His philosophy, mediating between the extreme idealistic and materialistic positions, was summed up in the term Personalism. Alcott was an extreme Transcendentalist,♦ yet he was opposed to its doctrine of individualism and believed that all seemingly separate minds are linked by a common relation to a central Mind; that is, as he said, "all souls have a Personal identity with God and abide in Him." His philosophy, his theory of infant education founded "on the great principle that every infant is already in possession of the faculties and apparatus required for his instruction," his later emphasis on birth or heredity as more important than education and environment in determining character, and his social conscience were all bound up with his own integrated and benevolent personality. In 1835 Alcott's assistant at the Temple School, Elizabeth Peabody, edited his *Record of a School, Exemplifying the General Principles of Spiritual Culture;* and this was followed by two volumes of his *Conversations with Children on the Gospels* (1836–37). These books, setting forth his theory and practice of education, won Alcott the support of such friends as Channing and Emerson, but lost him many pupils, whose parents considered his ideas dangerous and improper, so that the school was finally abandoned. In 1840 he moved with his wife and children to Concord, where he attempted to live by farming an acre of land, but this also failed. He then went to England (May–Oct. 1842), where an Alcott House had been founded to experiment with his educational ideas, and met Carlyle, who found the voluble American tiresome, but "like a venerable Don Quixote, whom nobody can laugh at without loving." In the U.S. again, in the company of a group of mystics, Alcott made plans for a cooperative community, which resulted in the ill-fated experiment at Fruitlands.♦ This transcendental, communal,

vegetarian organization persisted for only seven months, and in January 1845 the family returned to Concord. There and elsewhere, Alcott continued to lecture and to hold informal "conversations" to disseminate his ideas, meanwhile being supported mainly by the labors of his wife and his daughter Louisa May Alcott.♦ Not until 1868 did they become financially independent, when Louisa published *Little Women,* based on the family life during her childhood. In 1859 Alcott became superintendent of Concord schools, where he introduced the teaching of singing, dancing, reading aloud, and such novel subjects as physiology. This work and his endeavors in higher education that culminated in the Concord School of Philosophy (1879–88), a profound influence on U.S. education through his disciple W.T. Harris and others, embodied not only his philosophic ideas but also his genius for conversation and his personal influence. His serene unworldliness, his idealism in the midst of a material world, and his preoccupation with his own ideas and innumerable reforms made his practical relations with his family and friends difficult, although he considered the Family a golden mean between the hermit's cell and the phalanstery, and his home life was beautiful and generally happy. Emerson said, "As pure intellect I have never seen his equal"; and Thoreau agreed that he was "the sanest man I ever knew." As an apostle of Transcendentalism, his medium was "conversation," in which he informally developed his ideas and personality. In this spontaneous art, Alcott exhibited the most lucid and brilliant aspects of his thought, but after his death his reputation waned when he could be approached only through the colder medium of his writings. Among his early books on education were *Observations on the Principles and Methods of Infant Instruction* (1830) and *The Doctrine and Discipline of Human Culture* (1836). Later writings include the mystical "Orphic Sayings,"♦ published in *The Dial* (1840–41); *Tablets* (1868); *Ralph Waldo Emerson* (1865, 1882); *Concord Days* (1872), a work based on his journals; and *Table Talk* (1877). *New Connecticut* (1887) is a poetical autobiography of his youth, and *Sonnets and Canzonets* (1882) is a volume written in memory of his wife. A selection from his *Journals* was published in 1938 and from his *Letters* in 1969.

ALCOTT, LOUISA MAY (1832–88), a daughter of Bronson Alcott, reared in Boston and Concord, and educated by her father, receiving instruction and guidance also from such friends as Thoreau, Emerson, and Theodore Parker. She worked at various tasks to help support her family, and at the age of 16 wrote a book, *Flower Fables* (1854), followed by poems and short stories, some of which were published in the *Atlantic Monthly*. She was a nurse in a Union hospital during the Civil War until her health failed; her letters of this period were published as *Hospital Sketches* (1863). She issued her first novel, *Moods,* in 1865, and toured Europe as a lady's companion the same year. Between 1863 and 1869 she published anonymous and pseudonymous Gothic romances and thrilling tales, like "Pauline's Passion and Punishment," in popular journals. These were discovered and collected by Madeleine B. Stern in *Behind a Mask* (1975) and *Plots and Counterplots* (1976). In 1867 she became editor of a juvenile magazine, *Merry's Museum. Little Women* ♦ (1868–69), her charming and immensely popular story for children, presents a cheerful account of her own early life in New England; in it she portrays herself as Jo, and her sisters May, Elizabeth, and Anna respectively as Amy, Beth, and Meg. This work brought the financial security she had been trying to achieve for her family, and she continued to write in the same vein in *An Old-Fashioned Girl* (1870), *Little Men* (1871), and *Work* (1873). She revisited Europe (1870–71), returning to Boston to continue her participation in such reform movements as temperance and woman suffrage and her writing of moralistic fiction for children. Her later works include *Eight Cousins* (1875); *Rose in Bloom* (1876); *Silver Pitchers and Independence* (1876), containing "Transcendental Wild Oats," about her father's experiments at Fruitlands; *Under the Lilacs* (1878); *Jack and Jill* (1880); *Aunt Jo's Scrap-Bag* (6 vols., 1872–82); *Jo's Boys* (1886); and *A Garland for Girls* (1888).

ALDRICH, THOMAS BAILEY (1836–1907), born in Portsmouth, N.H., lived there and in New Orleans and New York during his childhood. His birthplace is the scene of his semi-autobiographical novel, *The Story of a Bad Boy* (1870). He had planned to enter Harvard, but when his father died in 1852 he took a business position instead, and soon began to write poetry for magazines. After the publication of his first collection, *The Bells* (1855), he held various posts on N.P. Willis's *Evening Mirror* and *Home Journal,* the *Tribune* at the outbreak of the Civil War, and the *Illustrated News*. In 1865 he began his

permanent residence in Boston, the mecca of his ambition and home of the New England group of authors who were the objects of his lifelong veneration. He was editor of *Every Saturday* (1866–74), during which period he published refined, delicately finished, but shallow verses, mainly in the *Atlantic Monthly,* which he collected in various volumes. His novels, written during the same years, were also marked by technical skill and charm, though they lack depth of understanding. They include *Prudence Palfrey* (1874), a romantic tale set in a small New England town; *The Queen of Sheba* (1877), a fantastic story of a young man's meeting with a girl who thinks she is the Queen of Sheba, their second meeting years later after she has recovered her sanity, and their falling in love; and *The Stillwater Tragedy* (1880), a detective mystery, partly concerned with an employer's triumph in quelling a strike. His best-known short stories appeared in *Marjorie Daw and Other People* (1873), *Two Bites at a Cherry, with Other Tales* (1894), and later volumes. Aldrich's editorship of the *Atlantic Monthly* (1881–90) was noted for his conservative policy and his adherence to "Boston-plated" traditions, which also appear in his collected essays, *From Ponkapog to Pesth* (1883), *An Old Town by the Sea* (1893), and *Ponkapog Papers* (1903).

Alexander's Bridge, novel by Willa Cather. ♦

ALFRED, WILLIAM (1922–), New York City-born author and educator, after graduation from Brooklyn College and previous service in the army went to Harvard on a GI scholarship, remaining there as a faculty member (1954–) after receiving an M.A. and a Ph.D. His first play, *Agamemnon* (1954), is an adaptation of Aeschylus' drama in verse, with a modern setting and situation. *Hogan's Goat* (1966), also a verse play, is a lively treatment of Irish-American life and politics in Brooklyn during the 1890s and was adapted by Alfred as a musical, *Cry for Us All* (1970). *The Curse of an Aching Heart* (1982) is a play also located in Brooklyn but during the 1940s.

ALGER, HORATIO, JR. (1832–99), born in Massachusetts, was reared by strict Puritan parents. He graduated from Harvard (1852) and its Divinity School, but it has been said that he rebelled by going to Paris to live a bohemian life, upon his return suffering a breakdown before he became a Unitarian minister (1864). He quit his pulpit (1866), perhaps ousted for questionable relations with his choirboys, and moved to New York to begin his literary career. While associated with the Newsboys' Lodging House as chaplain and philanthropist, he wrote nearly 130 popular books for boys, all based on the principle that a struggle against poverty and temptation inevitably leads a boy to wealth and fame. His most noted hero was the central figure in the Ragged Dick series (1867ff.), while the Luck and Pluck (1869ff.) and Tattered Tom (1871ff.) series were only second in popularity. He also wrote biographies of self-made statesmen. It is estimated that more than 20,000,000 copies of Alger's novels were published.

Algerine Captive, The; or, The Life and Adventures of Dr. Updike Underhill, novel by Royall Tyler, ♦ published in 1797.

Algonquin (or ALGONKIN) **Indians,** name applied to nomadic hunting tribes in Quebec and Ontario, and later to the entire Algonquian linguistic family to which they belong. Located originally near Ottawa, the Algonquian tribe was driven northward by 17th-century wars with the Iroquois and British, whom they, as allies of the French, opposed. They had the characteristic attributes of a Plains tribe. ♦ The linguistic family, whose primitive culture preceded those of the Mound Builders and Iroquois, included the Arapaho, Blackfoot, and Cheyenne of the northern Plains; the Ojibway, Cree, Shawnee, Delaware, Mohegan, Narragansett, and Pequot of the eastern U.S.; and tribes as far south as the Powhatan. Longfellow uses Algonquian legends in his poem on the Mohawk hero Hiawatha.

Algonquin Round Table, informal meeting place in the dining room of the Algonquin Hotel (New York City), mainly from the 1920s through the 1940s, of a lively, witty group, whose participants included Franklin P. Adams, Robert Benchley, Heywood Broun, Marc Connelly, Russel Crouse, George S. Kaufman, Dorothy Parker, Robert E. Sherwood, Frank Sullivan, and Alexander Woollcott.

ALGREN, NELSON (1909–81), born in Detroit and reared in Chicago slums, grew up in poverty and insecurity. His career as a writer of realistic novels of social protest began with *Somebody in Boots* (1935), about a poorwhite Texas boy's vagabondage and criminality during the Depression, and was continued

in *Never Come Morning* (1942), about a Polish hoodlum in Chicago who dreams of a better life as a prizefighter. *The Man with the Golden Arm* (1949) depicts the life of Frankie Machine (the Americanized version of his Polish name, Majcinek), a stud-poker dealer in a Chicago gambling club who becomes a dope addict and commits suicide, and places him in a panorama of the corrupt and violent lives of Chicago's underdogs who, like Frankie, are frustrated by their slum environment. *A Walk on the Wild Side* (1956) presents a somewhat similar underworld in New Orleans during the Depression, emphasizing the erotic and bohemian. The stories of *The Neon Wilderness* (1947) are less violent treatments of lower-class life. *Who Lost an American?* (1963) collects sketches of a lighter sort about life in New York and Chicago and on his travels abroad. *Conversations* (1964) issues tape-recorded recollections, *Notes from a Sea Diary* (1965) collects stories and a commentary on Hemingway, and *The Last Carousel* (1973) gathers short prose and poetry. *The Devil's Stocking* (1984; published in Germany as *Calhoun,* 1980) is the fictive treatment of the actual case of a black boxer convicted (1967) of murder.

Alhambra, The, 41 sketches by Irving, ♦ published in 1832 and revised and enlarged in 1852, the result of the author's residence (1829) in the ancient Moorish palace at Granada in Spain. His purpose was "to depict its half Spanish, half Oriental character; . . . to revive the traces of grace and beauty fast fading from its walls; to record the regal and chivalrous traditions . . . and the whimsical and superstitious legends of the motley race now burrowing among its ruins." Tales of medieval Moorish Spain are interspersed with architectural and other descriptions, and anecdotes of the author's experiences among the native residents.

Alice Adams, novel by Booth Tarkington, ♦ published in 1921 and awarded a Pulitzer Prize.

All God's Chillun Got Wings, play by Eugene O'Neill, ♦ produced and published in 1924.
　　Jim Harris, clumsy, intelligent, and ambitious, is a black reared in a New York slum district, where he adores Ella Downey, a white girl who spurns him when she begins to feel the force of race prejudice. She lives for a time with the ruffian Mickey, but he deserts her and their illegitimate child dies. Ella in despair accepts Jim's proposal of marriage,

and they live awhile in France, returning to New York so that Jim may study law. Ella is inferior in mind and feeling to her husband, and, in conflict with his mother and sister, is unable to conceal her dislike of his race. The strain of their life affects her mind, and to maintain her illusion of superiority she so harasses Jim that he fails in his bar examinations. He remains loyal and kind, and when Ella, becoming insane, believes that they are children again, he prays to God to "let this fire of burning suffering . . . make me worthy of the child You send me for the woman You take away."

All the King's Men, novel by Robert Penn Warren,♦ published in 1946, winner of a Pulitzer Prize. The protagonist is said to be based on Huey Long.

Willie Stark, a self-educated Southern backcountry man, infatuated with power and dreams of public service, is elected governor of his state. Vital, unscrupulous, and demagogic, he attracts into his employ Jack Burden, a newspaperman and "student of history" in search of truth; Sadie Burke, an intense and intrepid secretary, who becomes his mistress; and Tiny Duffy, a fat yes-man. Willie sends Jack to Burden's Landing, his childhood home, to find something with which to blackmail Judge Irwin, a dignified, honorable, old family friend and former attorney general, who reneged on a promise to the Boss. In his "excursion into the past," Jack renews old friendships with Adam Stanton, an idealistic surgeon, and his sister Anne, the unmarried patrician who was his first love. Through Jack they become involved with the Boss, who fascinates and repels them and fulfills an incompleteness in their characters: Anne eventually replaces Sadie as his mistress and Adam becomes director of the hospital Willie built as an altruistic act. Jack gets evidence that Irwin took a bribe, but the Judge won't submit to Willie and commits suicide. From his grief-stricken mother Jack learns that Irwin was his father. Adam, after receiving news of Anne's affair by an anonymous telephone call instigated by Sadie, gets into the Capitol and, in shooting Willie, is himself killed. Jack returns to Burden's Landing, marries Anne, and comes to realize that Willie was corrupted by success and destroyed by a conflict between the will to power and the desire to perform good works. At last able to understand his own past and aware of the infinite consequences of a single act and the common guilt of men, Jack prepares to "go into the

convulsion of the world . . . and the awful responsibility of Time."

ALLEN, ETHAN (1738–89), hero of the Revolutionary War, was earlier a leader of the Green Mountain Boys in their opposition to the rule of New York state in the New Hampshire Grants. In an expedition against Montreal, he was captured and imprisoned by the British (Sept. 1775–May 1778), an experience described in his blunt, egotistical, and amusing *Narrative of Colonel Ethan Allen's Captivity* (1779). The deistic book *Reason the Only Oracle of Man* (1784) is sometimes called "Ethan Allen's Bible," but most of it was written by the free-thinker Dr. Thomas Young (1732–77).

Almanac in America followed much the same development as in England, where it began as a calendar with the addition of some astronomical data. The first American work of this nature, *An Almanack for New England for the Year 1639,* was compiled by William Pierce (or Peirce) and printed by Stephen Daye, and, with the exception of a broadside, was the first work printed in the British colonies. Until the close of the 17th century, this press, associated with Harvard, continued to issue annual almanacs, and together with other presses caused Boston to become a center of almanac-making. The first humorous almanac was compiled in 1687 by John Tulley, of Saybrook, Conn. Subsequently all American almanacs, like their English counterparts, contained not only calendars but compendiums of popular science, notices of remarkable events and dates, problems, proverbs, jests, and practical information of various kinds, illuminated by illustrations. Among important early almanacs were the *Astronomical Diary and Almanack* issued from Dedham, Mass., by Nathaniel Ames and his son, 1725–75; *The Rhode Island Almanac,* issued 1728–58 by James Franklin; and *Poor Richard's Almanack*♦ and *The Farmer's Almanack.*♦ The Crockett almanacs♦ were a popular 19th-century series, noted for their tall tales of frontier heroes. Many religious sects and reform organizations issued almanacs, which have also been used by advertisers of medicines and other products. Several modern almanacs and books of facts are issued annually in large paperback editions.

Ambassadors, The, novel by Henry James,♦ published in 1903.

Lambert Strether, an intelligent, conscientious American editor, is sent by his wealthy fiancée, Mrs. Newsome, a rigorously conventional Massachusetts widow, to Paris to bring home her son Chad, who has spent several years in Europe and is now required to take charge of the family's business interests. She has been unable to learn why Chad chooses to remain abroad, and when Strether arrives he discovers the young man much changed by his Old World environment and his relations with the charming, cultured Countess de Vionnet, who later appears to be Chad's mistress. Gradually Strether comes to realize the fascinations and satisfactions that life offers in Paris but not in Woollett, Mass., and he virtually gives up his mission. Then a new group of ambassadors is sent after him, including Chad's aggressively proper sister Mrs. Pocock; her husband, Jim; and Jim's appealing but inexperienced young sister Mamie, who has been expected to marry Chad. Their arguments are suplemented by those of Strether's American friend Waymarsh, and the situation becomes comic, for none of these people can comprehend the education that has reformed Chad and Strether. Chad's determination to remain in Paris is unmoved, but Strether's conscience is reawakened, and he is persuaded to return to America, even though this will end his attachment to the quiet, kindly Maria Gostrey, an expatriate who has been a sympathetic spectator of his cultural adventure and the comedy of contrasted manners it has involved.

Ambitious Guest, The, allegorical tale by Hawthorne,♦ published in *The Token* (1835) and in *Twice-Told Tales* (1837).

America, name first applied to the present continent of South America (1507).

"America," patriotic hymn written by Samuel Francis Smith,♦ was first sung at a Boston Fourth of July meeting (1831) and published in *The Choir* (1832), a collection edited by Lowell Mason. The tune is the British "God Save the King," often erroneously attributed to Henry Carey (1690?–1743), but actually a traditional air whose earliest known version is by John Bull (1563–1628). Smith's hymn is frequently known as "My country, 'tis of thee," its opening line.

"America the Beautiful," patriotic hymn by Katherine Lee Bates,♦ written in 1893 and published in *The Congregationalist* (July 4, 1895). A revision was published in 1904, and

in the author's *America the Beautiful and Other Poems* (1911). Of the 60 tunes composed for it by various musicians, those most frequently used are by W.C. Macfarlane and S.A. Ward.

American, The, novel by Henry James,♦ published in 1877 and dramatized by the author in 1891.

Christopher Newman, a wealthy American on a visit to Paris, meets Claire de Cintré, a widow of noble birth, half French and half English. On his first call at her home, Newman is turned away by her ungracious brother Marquis Urbain de Bellegarde, but later he meets others of the family, Urbain's wife, the charming younger brother Count Valentin, the shrewd, proud old Marquise, and her maid, the sympathetic Englishwoman Mrs. Bread. The American becomes a close friend of Valentin, who encourages his courtship of Mme de Cintré, but the others tolerate him only because of his wealth. Finally his proposal is accepted, the engagement is formally announced, and the Marquis reluctantly introduces Newman to his aristocratic friends. Meanwhile the American comes to know Mlle Noémie Nioche, a copyist of paintings, whose meek, shabby-genteel father is Newman's French teacher. Newman benevolently orders a number of Noémie's paintings in order to provide her a dowry, and introduces her to Valentin. Although the young man realizes she is mercenary and unscrupulous, he continues to see her, and she is the cause of a duel in which he is fatally wounded. Before learning of this, Newman receives word that Mme de Cintré, influenced by her mother and brother, has broken their engagement. Summoned to Valentin's deathbed, he hears the young man's disgust with his family, and is told that Mrs. Bread knows a guilty secret about them that Newman may use to further his own ends. After Valentin's funeral, Mme de Cintré announces that she intends to become a nun. Through Mrs. Bread, Newman discovers that the Marquise killed her husband, and he threatens to expose the evidence, but Urbain and his mother still refuse to allow the marriage. At first Newman determines to fulfill his revenge, but in a revulsion of feeling he destroys the evidence of the murder.

American Academy and Institute of Arts and Letters, organization that amalgamated (1976) the Institute (founded 1898), modeled on the French Academy, with 250 members divided into sections in Art, Literature, and

Music, and the Academy (founded 1904), an honorary circle of 50 members within the Institute. Both were chartered by acts of Congress. The Academy's purpose is to promote American literature, art, and music by honoring prominent persons in these fields, presenting public addresses, bringing representatives of foreign academies to the U.S., and organizing conferences, publications, collections, and awards. Authors among the original Academy members included Henry Adams, Aldrich, Burroughs, Clemens, Hay, Howells, J.C. Harris, Henry James, C.E. Norton, and Stedman.

American Academy of Arts and Sciences, scholarly society of about 1800 elected Fellows, founded in 1780, and representing all areas of learning. It holds frequent meetings at which papers are delivered, makes some grants, publishes *Daedalus,* a quarterly journal, and since 1956 has annually presented its Emerson-Thoreau Medal for distinguished achievement in literature. Its headquarters have always been in or near Boston.

American Antiquarian Society was founded by Isaiah Thomas at Worcester, Mass. (1812). Its collections of Americana extend to 1876 and the holdings prior to 1821 are preeminent. A private institution, it has some 300 elected members.

American Claimant, The, story by S.L. Clemens,♦ written under his pseudonym Mark Twain and published in 1892. It is based on the play *Colonel Sellers,* written by Clemens with Howells (1883) and produced unsuccessfully (1886). The character of Sellers first appeared in *The Gilded Age.* ♦

Viscount Berkeley is an earnest young man who desires a just trial of the rights of American claimants to his father's earldom, and he goes to America to investigate the matter, as well as to see the democratic institutions he admires. The current claimant is Colonel Mulberry Sellers, in his old age still "the same old scheming, generous, goodhearted . . . failure he always was," and still on the trail of easy wealth. By a number of complicated coincidences, Berkeley, believed to have died in a hotel fire, disguises himself to seek work and test the institutions of Western democracy. Although disappointed in both quests until he is employed as a painter of chromos, he discovers Sellers, with whose beautiful and sensible daughter Sally he falls in love. Berkeley summons his father, who comes to America, is won over by Sally,

and consents to a marriage. The families plan to return to England together, but as the ship is about to leave the colonel is missed. He has gone off on a scheme to control the sunspots, leaving a message that asks the others to watch for a vast sunspot which will mean: "Mulberry Sellers throws us a kiss across the universe."

American Commonwealth, The, political and social survey by James Bryce, ♦ published in two volumes in 1888, and supplemented and revised in 1910.

American Crisis, The, see *Crisis, The American.*

American Democrat, The, or Hints on the Social and Civic Relations of the United States of America, critical work by Cooper,♦ published in 1838.

Returning from Europe in 1835, the author was struck by "a disposition in the majority to carry out the opinions of the system to extremes, and a disposition in the minority to abandon all to the current of the day," and he writes in order to express "the voice of simple, honest and . . . fearless truth" on the peculiarities of the American system in theory and practice. Following an introduction and general chapters on government and republican theories, he discusses government in the U.S., especially with regard to the doctrine of state rights. The 43 brief chapters that follow are concerned with "Distinctive American Principles," "Equality," "Liberty," "Advantages of a Democracy," "Disadvantages of a Democracy," "Prejudice," "The Private Duties of Station," "Language," "Demagogues," "The Press," "Property," and similar subjects, all discussed from the point of view of a conservative thinker who is convinced of the value of an aristocratic system.

American Dream, An, novel by Norman Mailer,♦ published in 1965.

Stephen Richards Rojack, a former congressman from New York, friend of Jack Kennedy, World War II hero, and television star, a "personality . . . built upon a void," is torn between an urge to suicide and a desire to see Deborah Kelly, the society heiress wife from whom he has long been separated, although she remains "the armature of [his] ego." His nighttime visit to Deborah leads to a quarrel; he strangles her, and after making love to her maid he throws Deborah's body out of her apartment window, telling the

15

police who take him into custody that she committed suicide. Her father, Oswald Kelly, arranges Rojack's release and he continues his dark night of adventure, including an attack upon Shago Martin, a black jazz singer patronized by Deborah, a brief romantic interlude with Cherry, an appealing blonde nightclub entertainer, and an encounter with Deborah's father, who attempts to push him off a skyscraper parapet. Returning to Cherry's apartment and finding her murdered by a friend of Shago Martin, Rojack leaves New York for Las Vegas, where he fantasizes an affectionate telephone conversation with Cherry.

American Dream, *The,* one-act play by Edward Albee,♦ produced in 1961.

In a serio-comic vein of absurdity, two middle-class Americans, Mommy and Daddy, are presented as torturing and dismembering their adopted son because he gives no promise of growing up to be a clean-cut young man who typifies the American Dream. After his death they send for another adopted son. This one satisfies his Mommy because he is handsome and athletic, though it is also obvious that he lacks emotions, intelligence, morality, and virility.

American Farmer, see *Letters from an American Farmer.*

American Language, *The,* study by H.L. Mencken,♦ published originally in 1919, in revised editions in 1921 and 1923, and corrected, enlarged, and rewritten for its fourth edition, 1936, with supplementary volumes in 1945 and 1948. This "inquiry into the development of English in the United States" was begun in articles in the Baltimore *Evening Sun* as early as 1910 to investigate the differences between American and English, but by 1936 Mencken was convinced that the influence of American had become so strong that in "some not too remote tomorrow" the language of Englishmen will be "a kind of dialect of American, just as the language spoken by the American was once a dialect of English." In his investigation Mencken first treats his subject chronologically, then takes up specific elements, such as pronunciation, spelling, grammar, and slang. He also deals with proper names and with non-English dialects in the U.S.

American Literature (1929–), journal of literary history, criticism, and bibliography, published quarterly by the Duke University Press with the cooperation of the American Literature Group of the Modern Language Association.

American Mercury, *The* (1924–), monthly magazine founded by H.L. Mencken♦ and George Jean Nathan♦ as a successor to their *Smart Set,* "to attempt a realistic presentation of the whole gaudy, gorgeous American scene," with all phases of American culture and institutions treated in a spirit of boisterous skepticism. The subject matter included not only lusty critical commentaries, but also short stories, poems, plays, and reviews of the arts, in keeping with the full-blooded editorial policy. After the first year Nathan ceased to be co-editor, and in 1930 he silently disappeared from the magazine. The many noted contributors included Dreiser, O'Neill, Sherwood Anderson, Cabell, Hergesheimer, Sandburg, Van Vechten, Sinclair Lewis, and Edgar Lee Masters. Among several celebrated departments, "Americana" was devoted to clippings from newspapers, ironically reflecting the alleged stupidity of the American mass mind. In 1934 Mencken left the magazine, but his decade and the next were memorialized in *The American Mercury Reader* (1944). In 1946 it absorbed *Common Sense,* but it underwent more drastic changes of ownership and views until in 1952 it became a right-wing journal with no relation to the original magazine except for name. Since 1968 it has been published from Orange County, Cal.

American Notes for General Circulation, travel account by Dickens,♦ published in 1842. Dickens visited the U.S. (Jan.–May 1842) in a tour that took him from Boston and New York to Canada and as far west as St. Louis. His book is almost wholly descriptive, and does not attempt to analyze institutions. He wrote in a complimentary fashion about much of America, but antagonized many readers by criticizing the penal system, the lack of copyright and hence the pirating of English works, and the entire system of slavery and its adherents.

American Philosophical Society, first scientific society in America, founded at Philadelphia (1743) by Franklin, its first president. His successors were Rittenhouse and Jefferson. The Society issues *Transactions, Proceedings* (since 1838), and *Memoirs* (since 1900) and makes research grants. It has some 600 elected members.

American Quarterly (1949–　), scholarly journal of American civilization studies, founded at the University of Minnesota, moved (1951) to the University of Pennsylvania.

American Renaissance, seminal critical study by F.O. Matthiessen,♦ published in 1941, analyzing Emerson, Thoreau, Hawthorne, Melville, and Whitman in their concern with the relation of the individual to society, conceptions of good and evil, attitudes toward nature, relations to their times, predecessors, and successors, relation to other arts, symbolism, and language.

American Scene, The, descriptive and interpretive work by Henry James,♦ published in 1907. The author toured the U.S. (1904) after an absence of "nearly a quarter of a century," and writes from a point of view that he claims to be almost as fresh as that of an "inquiring stranger" and as acute as that of an "initiated native." He describes his dramatic adventure in rediscovering an America occupied by "a society reaching out into the apparent void for the amenities, the consummations, after having earnestly gathered in so many of the preparations and necessities." The chapters of sensitive and cultivated appreciation include discussions of New England, New York, and Newport; the foreign aspects of New York City; "social notes" on upper-class life; and places associated with such authors as Hawthorne, Emerson, Thoreau, and Irving. The general impression is in keeping with his attitude as an expatriate:

> You touch the great lonely land—as one feels it still to be—only to plant upon it some ugliness about which, never dreaming of the grace of apology or contrition, you then proceed to brag. . . . You convert the large and noble sanities that I see around me . . . one after the other to crudities, to invalidities, hideous and unashamed. . . .

American Scholar, The, address by Emerson♦ delivered before the Phi Beta Kappa Society of Harvard (Aug. 31, 1837), published separately in 1837, and reprinted in *Nature, Addresses, and Lectures* (1849). Called "our intellectual Declaration of Independence" by Holmes, the work was immediately influential and remains important as an idealistic appeal for the active leadership of American society by native thinkers, developed through contact with the best products of former cultures and through free intercourse with nature and their fellow men.

The author announces that "Events, ac-tions arise, that must be sung, that will sing themselves." The original unit, man, has been "minutely subdivided and peddled out," however, and "in this distribution of functions, the scholar is the delegated intellect . . . he is *Man Thinking.*" The scholar, following "the ancient precept 'Know thyself,' and the modern precept, 'Study Nature,' " must interpret the distinctive new culture, for "Each age must write its own books." Yet he must act, as well as think and write. His duties are all implied in the term "self-trust"; knowing himself and his function, he must be self-reliant and free of bondage to the "popular cry." Society's purpose is to produce perfect individuals, and the scholar's idealistic mission is both to embody this perfection in himself and to make use of his divine inspiration for the highest good of his fellows.

American Scholar, The (1932–　), quarterly journal published by the United Chapters of Phi Beta Kappa and aimed at embodying and furthering the purposes and implications of Emerson's address from which its title is derived. In addition to articles and book reviews it occasionally publishes poetry.

American Taxation, On, speech by Edmund Burke, delivered in the British Parliament (April 19, 1774), urging repeal of the duty on tea imports of the British colonies in America.

American Tragedy, An, novel by Dreiser,♦ published in 1925 and dramatized by Patrick Kearney in 1926. The plot is based on an actual New York murder case.

Clyde Griffiths, son of street evangelists in Kansas City, wants to escape his family's drab life and to get wealth and social position. Becoming a bellboy in a hotel, he plunges into the worldly society of his fellow employees, but this life ends as the result of an automobile accident for which he is legally culpable. Providentially he meets his wealthy relative Samuel Griffiths, who is attracted by the youth's engaging manner and employs him in his collar factory in New York state. Here Clyde enters into a liaison with Roberta Alden, a working girl, and almost simultaneously falls in love with Sondra Finchley, who seems to him to represent the dazzling "four hundred" of the small town. Roberta discloses that she is pregnant and demands that Clyde provide for her. In a frenzy he plans to murder her, and takes her to a deserted lake resort. They row out on the lake, where, though Clyde lacks the courage to complete his plan, the boat is overturned, possibly by accident. He swims away, leaving Roberta to drown. After a lengthy trial, he is condemned to death.

AMES, FISHER (1758–1808), son of Nathaniel Ames (1708–64), an almanac editor, after graduation from Harvard was admitted to the bar (1781). His political essays in Boston newspapers and a powerful speech in the Massachusetts convention that ratified the Constitution made him the leading orator and pamphleteer of New England Federalism.

AMMONS, A[RCHIE] R[ANDOLPH] (1926–   ), North Carolina-born poet, after graduation from Wake Forest College and study at the University of California, Berkeley, where he was encouraged by Josephine Miles, wrote poetry while working in a glass factory before publishing his first small book, *Ommateum, with Doxology* (1955), whose title refers to the vision that insects have with compound eye structure. A move to teaching creative writing as a professor at Cornell (1964–   ) preceded his next book, nearly a decade later, *Expressions of Sea Level* (1964). With it began his career as a major poet. Writing in his own voice, he also relates clearly to the American transcendental tradition, recalling Emerson's concern with the relations of the One and the Many, Thoreau's isolation and concentration on nature, and Whitman's democratic sensibility and use of lengthy monologue. While waiting for the publication of his second volume, Ammons wrote a personal poetic journal, *Tape for the Turn of the Year* (1965), whose brevity in line and length in form were the result of his typing it, without revision, on a roll of adding machine paper. His collection of lyrics was quickly followed by another, *Corsons Inlet* (1965), in one of whose poems he wrote of "eddies of meaning . . . running like a stream through the geography of my work . . . but Overall is beyond me." In these works and those that followed, including *Northfield Poems* (1966), *Uplands* (1970), *Briefings* (1971), *Collected Poems* (1971, National Book Award), *Sphere: The Form of a Motion* (1974), *Diversifications* (1975), *The Snow Poems* (1977), *Highgate Road* (1977), *A Coast of Trees* (1981), *Wordly Hopes* (1982), and *Lake Effect Country* (1983), he confirmed his position as a leading American writer of his time (he won a Bollingen Prize, 1973–74), whose poems are marked by a tension between specific observations and philosophic

abstractions framed in an ecological context, often expressed in meditations inspired by solitary walks along a shoreline.

Anarchiad, The, 12 papers in mock-heroic verse, jointly composed by the Connecticut Wits. ♦

ANDERSON, MAXWELL (1888–1959), born in Pennsylvania, was reared in North Dakota, from whose state university he graduated in 1911. He received his M.A. from Stanford (1914), taught school in California and North Dakota, and became a New York journalist until 1924. His first play was *White Desert* (1923), a tragedy of repressed lives in North Dakota, and his second, written with Laurence Stallings, was the immensely successful comic play about U.S. soldiers at war, *What Price Glory?* (1924). With Stallings he also wrote *First Flight* (1925), about an episode in the youth of Andrew Jackson, and *The Buccaneer* (1925), about the pirate Sir Henry Morgan. These were collected in *Three American Plays* (1926). Anderson published his only book of poems as *You Who Have Dreams* (1925). *Outside Looking In* (1925) was a dramatization of Jim Tully's *Beggars of Life,* and *Saturday's Children* (1927) a comedy of modern marital relations. His next play, written with Harold Hickerson, was *Gods of the Lightning* (1928), dealing with the Sacco-Vanzetti case, and he turned to blank-verse drama with *Elizabeth the Queen* (1930), concerned with Elizabeth's love for the Earl of Essex. *Night Over Taos* (1932), also in verse, dramatizes the end of the feudal era in New Mexico in 1847. *Both Your Houses* (1933, Pulitzer Prize) is a prose satire of political corruption in Congress. With *Mary of Scotland* (1933), the author returned to verse and to English and Scottish history, but *Valley Forge* (1934) has a distinctly American theme, as do many of his later plays, which include *Winterset* (1935), a verse tragedy suggested by the Sacco-Vanzetti case; *The Wingless Victory* (1936), an adaptation of the Medea theme, set in Salem in 1800; *The Masque of Kings* (1936), a verse play concerning the Mayerling affair; *High Tor* (1937), a satirical fantasy on the encroachments of industrialism on personal liberty; *The Star Wagon* (1937), a prose fantasy about an inventor who controls time; and *Knickerbocker Holiday* (1938), a musical comedy (with Kurt Weill) satirizing the New Deal through a story of Stuyvesant's New Netherland. Later verse plays include *Key Largo* (1939), about an idealistic American in the Spanish Loyalist army; *Journey to Jerusalem* (1940), about the young Jesus; and *The Eve of St. Mark* (1942), about an American farm boy killed in World War II. Two other plays concerned with this war are *Candle in the Wind* (1941) and *Storm Operation* (1944), the latter about U.S. soldiers in North Africa. After a lesser play, *Truckline Café* (1946), he wrote three historical dramas; *Joan of Lorraine* (1947), interpreting Joan of Arc as a mystic through a drama about the production of a play concerning different conceptions of her; *Anne of the Thousand Days* (1948), about Anne Boleyn and Henry VIII; and *Barefoot in Athens* (1951), about Socrates. *Lost in the Stars* (1948) was a dramatization of Alan Paton's *Cry, the Beloved Country* for a musical production, and *The Bad Seed* (1955) was a dramatization of the last novel by William March, ♦ concerning an evil child. *Eleven Verse Plays* (1940) collects some of his dramas. His radio plays include *The Feast of Ortolans* (1938), set in France in 1789. Essays are printed in *The Essence of Tragedy* (1938) and *Off Broadway* (1940).

ANDERSON, ROBERT W[OODRUFF] (1917–), New York City-born playwright, after receiving his A.B. and M.A. from Harvard and navy service in World War II taught playwriting and began writing his own dramas, including *All Summer Long* (1953); *Tea and Sympathy* (1953), about an unhappy preparatory school boy accused of homosexuality; *Silent Night, Lonely Night* (1959), about the effect of Christmas Eve on a man and woman who meet then by chance; *The Days Between* (1965), produced in small theaters throughout the nation by the American Playwrights' Theatre; *You Know I Can't Hear You When the Water's Running* (1967), four one-act plays; *I Never Sang for My Father* (1968), about a man's struggles with his domineering father; and *Solitaire/Double Solitaire* (1971). He has written two novels: *After* (1973), about a man trying to find himself after the death of his beloved wife, and *Getting Up and Going Home* (1978).

ANDERSON, SHERWOOD (1876–1941), born in Ohio, at the age of 14 began his restless career, drifting from job to job and serving in the Spanish-American War. For a time he settled in his native state, was married, and became the manager of a paint factory; but he suddenly walked out of the factory, left his family, and made his way to Chicago. It was there, while writing advertising copy, he met Carl Sandburg and

Floyd Dell, who encouraged him to publish his first book, *Windy McPherson's Son* (1916), a novel dealing with a boy's life in a drab Iowa town, his rise to success as a manufacturer, and his renunciation of this life to "find truth." This was followed by another novel, *Marching Men* (1917), set in the Pennsylvania coal region and showing the failure of a mystical movement to organize the workers in order to free them from oppressive routine. He also published a book of poems, *Mid-American Chants* (1918), but it was not until 1919, when *Winesburg, Ohio* ♦ appeared, that he first attracted wide attention. These stories of small-town people voice the philosophy of life expressed in all his later works. Adopting a naturalistic interpretation of American life, he believed that the primal forces of human behavior are instinctive and not to be denied, as he supposed they are, by the standardization of a machine age. His characters are puzzled, groping, baffled, and possess no vision of order or channel for directing their energies against the frustrations of contemporary existence. Primarily through sex, which he endowed with a mystical significance, Anderson conceived man as having an opportunity to escape from the confinement of this regulated life. Similarly, he placed stress on the mystical identification of man with the primal forces of nature. In *Poor White* (1920), a novel of the Midwest, "the town was really the hero of the book. . . . What happened to the town was, I thought, more important than what happened to the people of the town." What happens is that the machine comes to the town, destroying whatever beauty and significance it once possessed. The same themes and attitude of mind are evinced in subsequent books: *The Triumph of the Egg* ♦ (1921), stories and poems depicting frustration and maladjustment in typical American backgrounds; *Horses and Men* (1923), stories mainly about horse racing; and *Many Marriages* (1923), a novel about a businessman's attempt to escape routine. In *Dark Laughter* (1925), a novel contrasting the laughter and song of unrepressed blacks with the spiritual sterility of the whites, he reached artistic maturity both in his style—simple, direct, consciously naïve, and admittedly indebted to Gertrude Stein—and in his mastery of form. *Tar: A Midwest Childhood* (1926) is a fictional treatment of his own life, which he had begun to describe in *A Story Teller's Story* (1924). After issuing two volumes of sketches, *The Modern Writer* (1925) and *Sherwood Anderson's Notebook* (1926), and a volume of poetry, *A New Testament* (1927), he retired to a small Virginia town to edit two newspapers, one Republican and the other Democratic. His next book, *Hello Towns!* (1929), is a narrative of visits to small towns, and *Nearer the Grass Roots* (1929) sets forth his reasons for retirement, to be "in close and constant touch with every phase of life in an American community every day of the year." *Perhaps Women* (1931) is a critical work, placing hope for salvation from the sterility of mechanized life in the leadership of women. *Beyond Desire* (1932), his first novel in seven years, shows a shift of scene to the industrialized South, but is still concerned with the problem of modern frustrations. A book of stories, *Death in the Woods* (1933), and a survey of the U.S. during the Depression, *Puzzled America* (1935), were followed by another novel, *Kit Brandon* (1936), showing the author's characters still trapped in a situation with which they cannot cope. *Home Town* (1940) is a collection of essays. *Memoirs* (1942) and selected *Letters* (1953; 1984) were posthumously issued.

André, blank-verse tragedy by William Dunlap, ♦ produced and published in 1798. The author's revision was produced in 1803 as *The Glory of Columbia* (published 1817).

Androboros, the first American play to be printed (1714), was written by Robert Hunter, governor of New York (1710–19), and is a political satire that was reprinted from its rare first edition in the *Bulletin of the New York Public Library* (March 1964).

Anecdote of the Jar, poem by Wallace Stevens, ♦ published in *Harmonium.* ♦ In three four-line stanzas the speaker tells of placing a jar on a Tennessee hillside, illustrative of the way a work of art brings order to a slovenly wilderness.

ANGELOU, MAYA (1928–   ), St. Louis-born author, singer, dancer, playwright, and stage and screen actress, long resident in California, has achieved most success with her frank and warm-hearted autobiographical accounts of her life as a young black woman in America, *I Know Why the Caged Bird Sings* (1970), *Gather Together in My Name* (1974), and *Singin' and Swingin' and Gettin' Merry Like Christmas* (1976). She has also published collections of her poems: *Just Give Me a Cool Drink of Water 'fore I Diiie* (1971), *Oh Pray My Wings Are Gonna Fit Me Well* (1975), *And Still I Rise* (1978), and *Shaker, Why Don't You Sing* (1983).

Angle of Repose, novel by Wallace Stegner. ♦

Animal Kingdom, The, play by Philip Barry, ♦ produced and published in 1932.

"Anna Christie," play by Eugene O'Neill, ♦ produced in 1921 and published in 1922, when it received a Pulitzer Prize. It is a revision of his unsuccessful play *Chris Christopherson* (1920).

Chris Christopherson, Swedish-American captain of the coal barge *Simeon Winthrop,* awaits the arrival of his daughter Anna in the saloon of Johnny-the-Priest on the New York waterfront. Several years before, he sent her to relatives on a Midwestern farm, away from the baneful influence of "dat ole davil sea," and he pictures her as an innocent country girl; but when she enters it is obvious to all except Chris that Anna is a coarse, hardened woman of the underworld. She confesses to her father's mistress, Marthy, that she was seduced by a cousin when she was 16, lived as a prostitute in St. Louis, was ill in a prison hospital, and has acquired a deep-seated hatred of men. Father and daughter leave New York on a voyage of the barge, and the sea that Chris hates proves to be the means of Anna's regeneration, until the *Winthrop* picks up a boatload of shipwrecked sailors, one of whom is the rough Irishman Mat Burke. In love with Anna, Mat wants to marry her, but when she discloses her history, he and Chris go off separately to get drunk, and sign for a voyage on the same ship. But Mat's love is stronger than his sense of Anna's shame, and both men go back to Anna, who promises to make a home for them when they return.

Annabel Lee, lyrical ballad by Poe, ♦ posthumously published in the New York *Tribune* (Oct. 9, 1849). In six stanzas of alternate four- and three-stress lines, the poem has been called "the culmination of Poe's lyric style" in his recurrent theme of the loss of a beautiful and loved woman.

Annie Kilburn, novel by Howells, ♦ published in 1889.

Another Country, novel by James Baldwin, ♦ published in 1962.

Anthology Club, Boston literary society (*c.*1804–11), devoted to raising the standards of American literature.

ANTHONY, Susan B[rownell] (1820–1906), was a leader in the movement for woman suffrage and an ardent lecturer on abolition and temperance. Her test (1872) of the 14th Amendment as allowing women the vote led to a famous trial. With others she wrote a *History of Woman Suffrage* (4 vols., 1881–87, 1900). She is the heroine of Gertrude Stein's opera *The Mother of Us All* (1949).

ANTIN, Mary (Mary Antin Grabau) (1881–1949), born in Russian Poland, was brought to Boston (1894), where she attended public school and began to write poems which were published in local papers. While still a child, she wrote in Yiddish *From Plotzk to Boston,* an impressionistic description of life inside the Jewish Pale in Poland and the emigration of her family, which she translated into English for publication in 1899. She married a Columbia professor, and attended college at Columbia and Barnard (1901–4), but left before receiving a degree to become a settlement worker at Hale House in Boston. In 1912 she extended her early book to make *The Promised Land,* a full account of the customs and hardships of European Jews, as contrasted with the enlightenment and free opportunity they found in the U.S. A later work is *They Who Knock at Our Gates* (1914).

Antinomianism, any theory that holds that moral law as such, or the Old Testament legal system specifically, is not binding upon Christians. In America the Antinomian controversy was precipitated by Anne Hutchinson,♦ who was supported, in her protest against the legal system of the Massachusetts Puritans, by her brother-in-law John Wheelwright, Governor Vane, and other Bostonians. She was opposed by John Winthrop and by the people and clergy of the rural districts.

ANTONINUS, Brother, see *Everson, William.*

Apache Indians, group of tribes or bands related to the Navaho, characteristically unsettled, predatory, and ferocious.

Apple-Tree Table, *The, and Other Sketches,* ten prose pieces by Melville,♦ collected in 1922. Originally published in *Harper's Maga-* zine and *Putnam's* (1850–56), the sketches range from the critical "Hawthorne and His Mosses" to the title story, an allegory of the appearance of two beautiful living insects in the dead wood of an ancient piece of furniture.

APPLESEED, Johnny, see *Chapman, John.*

Arbella, flagship of the small fleet that arrived at Salem, Mass. (June 12, 1630), carrying some 600–700 persons from England to found a Puritan colony.

archy and mehitabel, humorous verses by Don Marquis♦ collected (1927) from his columns in the New York *Sun* and later from the New York *Tribune.* They present the adventures of archy, a literary cockroach, who writes free verse because he cannot manipulate a typewriter shift key, and of his friend mehitabel, a cat, whose motto is "toujours gai," as they consider and comment on contemporary U.S. life. First gathered in *archy and mehitabel;* there were several sequels.

ARENDT, Hannah (1906–75), German-born scholar, emigrated to the U.S. (1941), where she held several major academic posts and published influential works of political theory, including *Origins of Totalitarianism* (1951) and *The Human Condition* (1958).

Arikara Indians, Plains tribe♦ devoted to bison hunting and maize agriculture, are considered a branch of the Pawnee. They appear in Neihardt's *Song of Hugh Glass* and *Song of the Indian Wars.*

Armies of the Night, *The,* book by Norman Mailer,♦ published in 1968. The work is divided into two parts in keeping with its concern with the nature of its genre. The first, titled "History as a Novel," records Mailer's reactions as he recounts his participation in an anti-Vietnam march on the Pentagon in October 1967; the second, "The Novel as History," treats in more generalized fashion the sociopolitical background of the march.

Arminianism, doctrine developed by the followers of Jacobus Arminius (1560–1609), a Dutch theologian and critic of Calvinism. These followers, frequently called Remonstrants, differed from orthodox Calvinists on the following points: (1) predestination is conditional rather than absolute; (2) atonement is universal; (3) regeneration requires the Holy Spirit; (4) divine grace is needed for human effort, but it does not act irresistibly in man; (5) believers can resist sin but may fall from grace. These liberal ideas inclined toward a belief in the freedom of man's will. The Remonstrants later became an independent church, and among those who shared their views were the Methodists, against whose doctrines Jonathan Edwards was led to write his *The Freedom of the Will,* defending the orthodox Calvinist view.

ARNOLD, BENEDICT (1741–1801), Revolutionary War general who, with Ethan Allen, captured Fort Ticonderoga (1775) and marched through the Maine woods in an attempt to seize Quebec. As commander of Philadelphia in 1778 he got in trouble with civil authorities and was tried at a court-martial. At this time he began to make treasonable reports to Clinton, the British general. In 1780 he accepted the command of West Point, and plotted to deliver the garrison to André. When the plot failed because of André's capture, Arnold fled to the British army, later leading devastating raids against Virginia and his native Connecticut. The latter part of his life was spent in England and New Brunswick. He appears as a character in Brackenridge's play *The Death of General Montgomery,* dealing with the Quebec campaign, and in such plays on the affair of André as those by William Dunlap, Samuel Woodworth, W.W. Lord, and Clyde Fitch; and also in D.P. Thompson's novel *The Green Mountain Boys,* F.J. Stimson's novel *My Story,* ostensibly an autobiography, and Harold Sinclair's *Westward the Tide.* Source materials concerning his expedition to Quebec were edited by Kenneth Roberts as *March to Quebec* (1938) and employed in the same author's novel *Arundel* (1930).

ARNOLD, MATTHEW (1822–88), English poet, critic, and educator, visited the U.S. in 1883 and again in 1886, at which times he delivered the lectures collected in *Discourses in America* (1885) and gathered the impressions on which he based his essays in *Civilization in the United States* (1888), finding America to have industry, conduct, and equality but also "a middle class of stunted religion, intellect, and manners."

ARNOW, HARRIETTE (1908–), Kentucky author of novels set in her Cumberland Mountains region, and of *The Dollmaker* (1954), contrasting the values of her native

area with those she experienced in Detroit during World War II.

Arrow and the Song, The, poem by Longfellow, ♦ published in *The Belfry of Bruges and Other Poems* (1845). In three quatrains of four-stress iambic lines, the poet likens his art to the shooting of arrows into the air. As he finds an arrow imbeded in an oak, long after losing it, so it is with his song, which ". . . from beginning to end, I found again in the heart of a friend."

Arrowsmith, novel by Sinclair Lewis, ♦ published in 1925 and awarded a Pulitzer Prize, which Lewis declined.

Martin Arrowsmith attends the University of Winnemac, in a Midwestern state, where he is influenced by Max Gottlieb, a sincere though sardonic bacteriologist. At college he marries Leora Tozer, a nursing student. They settle in Wheatsylvania, N.D., but his medical practice there is so small that he is forced to accept a post in the health department of Nautilus, Iowa. Disillusioned by the charlatanry of his superior, Dr. Almus Pickerbaugh, Martin leaves this post to enter a fashionable Chicago clinic. After further disappointment, he joins Gottlieb at the McGurk Institute in New York, hoping to find in altruistic research the relief he desires from publicity-seeking and money-grabbing commercial medicine. Martin is now tolerably happy, disturbed only by the patronizing visits of Capitola McGurk, wife of the founder, and by the demand that he turn out results to make newspaper copy. His actual discovery of an "X Principle," an organism that preys on bacteria, is not publicized until a Frenchman has announced a similar discovery. When an epidemic breaks out on the West Indian island of St. Hubert, Gottlieb urges Martin to seize this opportunity to test the efficacy of his "bacteriophage." With Leora and Gustaf Sondelius, a titanic Swedish scientist, he goes to the stricken settlement. Leora and Sondelius die of the plague, after which Martin, instead of maintaining rigid scientific controls, administers the serum indiscriminately, thus destroying the results of his experiment. He returns to New York to marry a rich widow, whose social life interferes with his work. Finally, with Terry Wickett, an uncouth but conscientious chemist, he leaves the McGurk Institute and his wife, establishing himself on a Vermont farm to manufacture serum and pursue his research.

Artemus Ward, pseudonym of Charles Farrar Browne. ♦

ARTHUR, TIMOTHY SHAY (1809–85), author of nearly 100 moral tales and tracts, including *Temperance Tales* (1843); *Agnes; or, The Possessed. A Revelation of Mesmerism* (1848); and *The Debtor's Daughter; or, Life and Its Changes* (1850). His novel *Ten Nights in a Barroom and What I Saw There* ♦ (1854) was dramatized with great success by William W. Pratt in 1858. Arthur was also the editor of several magazines devoted to the cause of temperance.

Artist of the Beautiful, The, allegorical tale by Hawthorne, ♦ published in the *Democratic Review* (1844) and in *Mosses from an Old Manse* (1846).

Owen Warland, a youthful watchmaker, obsessed with a desire to create something ideally beautiful, loves Annie Hovenden, daughter of his former master. She is unsympathetic toward his aspirations and his delicate nature, and Peter Hovenden and the blacksmith, Robert Danforth, both rough and unimaginative, oppress Owen and destroy his inspiration. Annie marries Danforth, and for a time Owen forsakes his dreams for grosser practical activities, but then devotes himself to creating a mechanical butterfly, fragile, lovely, and endowed with living qualities. When he exhibits his work to Annie and her family, Danforth and Hovenden seem to oppress the insect as they do its creator, while Annie prefers to admire her child. The child, who resembles his grandfather, rudely crushes the butterfly, but Owen looks on calmly; "he had caught a far other butterfly than this."

As I Lay Dying, stream-of-consciousness novel by Faulkner, ♦ published in 1930.

Addie Bundren lies dying, and her children prepare to fulfill her desire to be buried in her native Jefferson (Miss.), far from the crude backcountry surroundings of her married life. Cash, one of her sons, makes her coffin, and when she is dead the family unites to carry out the one wish of hers it has ever respected. Another son, Vardaman, still a child, in shock confuses the excitement of catching a big fish and of his mother's death so that he says "my mother is a fish," just as, remembering how he was stifled in a shut corn crib, he bores holes through the coffin so that she can breathe. Led by their mean, simple-minded, whining father, Anse, the family sets off in a mule-drawn wagon. Floods have washed out a bridge, and while fording a river they lose their team. Jewel, Addie's illegitimate son, also nearly loses his beloved horse as it too is plunged in the river, and as Cash is dragged out, he breaks his leg. But although the horse is saved from the river, it is lost to Jewel when Anse trades it for a new team. During the gruesome ten-day trek, although the body begins to decay, Cash rests on the coffin, his leg in a homemade cast that permanently cripples him. One night Darl, the most imaginative and intense of the sons, sets fire to a barn where the coffin is lying so as to cremate his mother and end the horrid pilgrimage, and Jewel, helping to rescue the animals, is badly burned. Arrived in Jefferson, Darl is seized by the authorities and sent to the insane asylum, and Cash is taken to a doctor. Dewey Dell, their sister, buys a "cure" for her pregnancy, paying the drug clerk by giving herself to him. Having fulfilled his duty to Addie, Anse "borrows" money from Dewey Dell, buys a set of false teeth, and, "kind of hangdog and proud, too," returns with a strange woman, saying, "Meet Mrs. Bundren."

ASCH, SHOLEM (name also spelled SHALOM or SHOLOM) (1880–1957), Polish-born novelist, came to the U.S. in 1914 and later lived in New York City and in London. His books are written in Yiddish or German, and among those which have been translated into English are *Uncle Moses, Chaim Lederer's Return,* and *Judge Not,* republished as *Three Novels* (1938); *The Mother* (1930, new translation 1937), the story of a Polish family in New York City; *Three Cities* (1933), a realistic trilogy of 20th-century Jewish life in Russia and Poland; *Salvation* (1934), a novel of Polish Jews of the 19th century; *The War Goes On* (1936), a plea for tolerance and humanity set in a story of Jews in postwar Germany; *East River* (1946), a novel of Jewish life in New York at the opening of this century; *A Passage in the Night* (1953), about a Jewish businessman discovering faith on approaching death; and a trilogy, *The Nazarene* (1939), presenting Jesus as the last and greatest Jewish prophet, *The Apostle* (1943), about St. Paul, and *Mary* (1949), about the Virgin. *The Prophet* (1955) is a novel about Isaiah. His many Yiddish plays include *Mottke the Vagabond* (1917), new translation, and *Mottke the Thief* (1935). *What I Believe* (1941) is a testament of faith.

Ash-Wednesday, poem by T.S. Eliot,♦ was published in 1930 as a profession of his faith in the Church of England and represented a statement of the faith which he had called for at the end of *The Waste Land.* By employing certain portions of Dante's *Divine Comedy* and a sermon of Lancelot Andrewes in the frame of reference within which this poem of doubt and faith is constructed, Eliot manages to objectify the emotions he desires to evoke, concerning the security, the emotional satisfaction, and the profound truth that he can find only by accepting the traditions of the Church.

ASHBERY, JOHN [LAWRENCE] (1927–   ), poet born in Rochester, N.Y., after an A.B. from Harvard and graduate study of French literature at Columbia and New York University became an art and literary critic in France. His first poems, *Turandot* (1953) and *Some Trees* (1956), the latter in the Yale Series of Younger Poets, appeared before his expatriation. The later works have been influenced by French surrealism and relate to the abstractions of New York action painters, including Jackson Pollock and Robert Motherwell. They are melodious, dream-like, and ever-shifting meditations that do not order the exterior world but in solipsistic fashion present the poet's personal associations and sensory responses to it. Opposed to conventional logic, realism, and the idea of a usable past, the poetry cannot be explicated in a traditional way. Ashbery's evocative images and musicality make fragments sensually beautiful, but the entirety of a work is opaque, lacking sequential development in syntax or theme. His collections include *The Poems* (1960), *The Tennis Court Oath* (1962), *Rivers and Mountains* (1966), *Selected Poems* (1967), *Three Madrigals* (1968), *Sunrise in Suburbia* (1968), *77, Fragment* (1969), *The Double Dream of Spring* (1970), *Three Poems* (1972), *Self-Portrait in a Convex Mirror* (1975, National Book Award, National Book Critics Circle Award, Pulitzer Prize), *Houseboat Days* (1977), *As We Know* (1979), *Shadow Train* (1981), and *A Wave* (1984). He has also published a novel (written with James Schuyler♦), *A Nest of Ninnies* (1969), a parody of modern U.S. life as seen through the experiences of two vacuous suburban families; and has written two one-act plays, *The Heroes* (1952), a light-hearted presentation of classical mythology in modern times, and *The Philosopher* (1962), a travesty of conventional detective story drama, and a three-act play, *The Compromise* (1956). In 1974 Ashbery became a professor of English at Brooklyn College.

ASIMOV, ISAAC (1920–   ), born in Russia, brought to New York City at age three, was graduated from Columbia University at 19 and after military service returned there to receive a Ph.D. in 1948. Although nominally on the faculty of Boston University's School of Medicine since 1949, his life is devoted to his career of prodigious authorship, which began with his sale of a science fiction story at age 18 to *Amazing Stories,* though it did not lead to book publication until the appearance of his novel *Pebble in the Sky* (1950), when he was 30. It has since been phenomenal as he turns out book after book in diverse genres on a wide variety of subjects. He is well known for his science fiction stories and novels, particularly for his Foundation trilogy, *Foundation* (1951), *Foundation and Empire* (1952), and *Second Foundation* (1953), and his other works include nonfictional studies for adults and for teenagers on numerous scientific and technological subjects, essays on many topics, histories, Biblical studies, humor, and mysteries and fantasies for children and adults. He publishes numerous works every year, reaching his hundredth in 1969 and his *Opus 200* in 1979. The latter year was also the date of publication of his autobiography, *In Memory Yet Green,* telling of his life to age 34, continued in *In Joy Still Felt* (1980).

Aspern Papers, The, novelette by Henry James,♦ published in 1888.

An American editor with an enthusiasm for the works of Jeffrey Aspern, a romantic poet of the early 19th century, goes to Venice to acquire the letters that Aspern wrote to his mistress, a Miss Bordereau, whom he called "Juliana." Under an assumed name he rents a suite in the ancient palace where she lives in poverty and seclusion with her niece, Miss Tina. He finds that the old lady is shrewd and haughty and accepts him as a lodger only to put aside money for the future of Miss Tina, a timid, unattractive spinster much in awe of her aunt. During his residence with them, the editor wins the friendship of Miss Tina, to whom he reveals his mission. Miss Bordereau falls ill and he attempts to rifle her desk, but she surprises him and frightens him off before suffering a relapse. Leaving Venice for a fortnight, he returns to find the old lady dead. Miss Tina welcomes him expectantly, and he realizes that she is in love with him. She says that she could give him the papers only if he were "a relative," and, alarmed at this proposal, he leaves. At their next interview he learns that she has destroyed the letters. Her suffering has matured and ennobled her, and she dismisses him with tact and restraint.

Assignation, The, story by Poe,♦ published as "The Visionary" in *Godey's Lady's Book* (1834) and under its present title in *Tales of the Grotesque and Arabesque* (1840). It contains the poem "To One in Paradise."

Passing at midnight near the Bridge of Sighs in Venice, the narrator sees an acquaintance rescue the child of the young Marchesa Aphrodite from drowning, while her aged husband, Di Mentoni, a conniving aristocrat, looks on indifferently. He overhears the Marchesa's whispered "Thou hast conquered," and her promise to meet the rescuer one hour after sunrise. The latter, a young man known throughout Europe for his fabulous wealth and solitary nature, asks the narrator to join him, which he does, arriving shortly after sunrise. He finds his host in a mood of eccentric gaiety, desirous of exhibiting his objects of art and discoursing on his aesthetic theories and tastes. Among the paintings is a portrait of the Marchesa, and the visitor guesses his host's unfulfilled love for her. At the hour after sunrise a page arrives with news of the Marchesa's death; and he finds his host not asleep from an excess of wine, as he supposed, but dead by the same poison that killed his beloved.

Assiniboin Indians, northern Plains tribe, many of whom migrated in the 17th century from Dakota to Lake Winnipeg, and later to the upper Saskatchewan and Assiniboin rivers. The Assiniboin figure in Neihardt's *Song of Three Friends.*

Assistant, The, novel by Bernard Malamud,♦ published in 1957.

Morris Bober, a 60-year-old Jewish owner of a small grocery store in Brooklyn, hoping to sell out before competition, theft, and illness overwhelm him, is instead wounded by robbers. Good fortune comes his way when Frank Alpine, a stranger caught up in the robbery, assists Bober as he recuperates. Alpine is also a threat to Bober and his wife Ida because he falls in love with their daughter Helen but is unsuitable for her since he is not Jewish. When he pilfers from the cash register he is fired, but after Bober's death he returns to work and hopes to win Helen by converting to her faith.

ATHERTON, GERTRUDE [FRANKLIN] (1857–1948), California author, whose many novels include a series depicting life in her native state from Spanish times to the present, in such volumes as *Before the Gringo Came* (1894), revised as *The Splendid Idle Forties* (1902), romantic short stories; *The Californians* (1898, revised 1935); *Rezánov* (1906); *The Sisters-in-Law* (1921); and *The Horn of Life* (1942). She also wrote a fictional biography of Alexander Hamilton, *The Conqueror* (1902), and several society novels which include *Julia France and Her Times* (1912) and the sensational *Black Oxen* (1923), about an aging woman's rejuvenation by a glandular operation. Other works are essays, short stories, and a history of California, *Golden Gate Country* (1945), in the American Folkways series, and several novels on classical themes. *Adventures of a Novelist* (1932) is her autobiography.

Atlantic Monthly (1857–), magazine of literature, art, and politics, was founded at Boston by leading New England literary figures. It was named by Holmes, who contributed his *Autocrat of the Breakfast-Table,* and the editor for the first four years was Lowell, who wrote for the magazine himself and also obtained contributions from Emerson, Longfellow, Motley, Whittier, Harriet Beecher Stowe, and other prominent authors. Although the editors denied that it was meant to be an organ of Bostonian or New England opinion, the *Atlantic* was generally accused of Brahminism and failure to recognize writers outside of its region. In politics they contended that it was "the organ of no party or clique," but it was considered to be strongly antislavery. It was, however, relatively uninterested in current affairs until purchased by the publishers Ticknor and Fields (1859), and edited by J.T. Fields (1861–71). During the Civil War there were articles on contemporary matters by Sumner, Carl Schurz, and others prominent in politics, and the *Atlantic* published such stirring verses as "The Battle Hymn of the Republic," "Barbara Frietchie," and the second series of *The Biglow Papers,* as well as *The Man Without a Country.* Under the editorship of Howells (1871–81) the magazine was less concerned with politics and, without ceasing to be representative of New England, drew its authors from farther afield. Nevertheless, the greatest success of his editorship was the publication of Aldrich's "Marjorie Daw." He added new departments, including book reviews, and sections on science, music, and education. Under Aldrich's editorship (1881–90), the Brahmin standards were returned to; contributors included Fiske, Henry James, Parkman, Mary N. Murfree, Sarah Orne Jewett, and George Edward Woodberry. H.E. Scudder's editorship (1890–98) emphasized social subjects in articles like those of Theodore Roosevelt on civil service; and his assistant W.H. Page, who succeeded him (1898–99), brought the magazine even more into the national scene. Under Page and Bliss Perry (1899–1909) contributors included J.J. Chapman, Woodrow Wilson, Jacob Riis, Booker T. Washington, Cleveland, and William Allen White. The later *Atlantic* preserves its heritage as an intelligent literary journal with a keen interest in contemporary affairs. *Jubilee* (1957) is an anthology from its first 100 years collected by its editor (1938–66), Edward Weeks.

ATTAWAY, WILLIAM (1911–), Mississippi-born black author, reared in Chicago, graduated from the University of Illinois, and held various jobs before writing his two novels, *Let Me Breathe Thunder* (1939), about two tough young white hoboes, and *Blood on the Forge* (1941), about Southern black farmworkers trying to compete in Pennsylvania steel-mill jobs. His only other book, *Hear America Singing* (1967), is for children.

AUCHINCLOSS, LOUIS [STANTON] (1917–), graduate of Yale with a law degree from the University of Virginia, is a New York lawyer whose polished fiction about high society began with several volumes issued under the pseudonym Andrew Lee. His novels include *The Indifferent Children* (1947), about a dilettante during World War II; *Sybil* (1952), portraying an Edith Wharton kind of heroine; *A Law for the Lion* (1953); *The Romantic Egoists* (1954), stories told by one character; *The Great World and Timothy Colt* (1956), about a disillusioned New York lawyer; *Venus in Sparta* (1958) and *Pursuit of the Prodigal* (1959), portraying different kinds of rich, upper-class New Yorkers who leave their wives and move out of their usual world; *The House of Five Talents* (1960), tracing one of his kind of family from 1873 to 1948; *Portrait in Brownstone* (1962), about a New York society woman; *The Rector of Justin* (1964), a study of the founding headmaster of an Episcopalian boys' school in New England; *The Embezzler* (1966), about a socialite who misappropriates some bonds; *A World of Profit* (1968), presenting a young

Jewish entrepreneur of New York and the WASP family whose estates he buys; *A Writer's Capital* (1974), characterizing a lawyer who comes to write satires of the elite; *The Dark Lady* (1977), presenting a social climber in New York; *Watchfires* (1982), treating the values and standards of an upper-class New York lawyer during the Civil War era; and *The Book Class* (1984), about a group of upper-class women who meet for monthly luncheons and literary discussion throughout their lives. Stories with similar themes have appeared in several volumes beginning with *The Injustice Collectors* (1950). He has also written books on Henry James (1961 and 1975), Shakespeare (1969), Edith Wharton (1971), and Richelieu (1973), and *False Dawn* (1984), on women in the 18th century. *Life, Law and Letters* (1979) collects essays and sketches.

AUDEN, W[YSTAN] H[UGH] (1907–73). British-born poet, educated at Oxford. During the Depression of the 1930s he and other English authors—Spender, Isherwood, and C. Day Lewis, among them—were deeply affected by Marxism, an interest that Auden called "more psychological than political." His works of that period include *Poems* (1930) and *The Orators* (1932), prose and poetry, bitter and witty, on the impending collapse of British middle-class ways and a coming revolution. During this decade he also experimented with lively plays using verse and the vernacular in the vein of Brecht; and after his own *The Dance of Death* (1933), a verse play, he collaborated with Christopher Isherwood on *The Dog Beneath the Skin* (1936), a fanciful prose and verse play satirizing the middle class, *The Ascent of F6* (1936), and *On the Frontier* (1938), all with incidental music by Benjamin Britten. His experiences as a traveler during the Spanish Civil War are reflected in the poem *Spain* (1937), and other travels gave rise to *Letters from Iceland* (1937), verse and prose in collaboration with Louis MacNeice, expressing a holiday mood in temporarily escaping Europe; and *Journey to a War* (1939), a sad survey of the contemporary situation, issuing out of a voyage to China, with Isherwood's prose balancing Auden's verse. This decade and this period of ideas ended in 1939 with Auden's coming to live in the U.S., confirmed by his naturalization as a citizen in 1946. Although he tried an American theme in *Paul Bunyan,* a choral operetta written with Benjamin Britten and produced in 1941, his shift in this period was more in views and attitudes than in nationalism. New collections of poetry were *Another Time* (1940) and *The Double Man* (1941), a title showing he was cleft in his intense search for a belief or logic, while the English title, *New Year Letter,* comes from the longest poem in a collection including prose too. Having moved away from the Marxism of the 1930s, he came in the 1940s to the heritage of his Anglo-Catholic faith and to a Christian existential view. Books included *For the Time Being* (1945), a Christmas oratorio confronting the present day with a religious view, and containing "The Sea and the Mirror," a commentary on *The Tempest* concerned with the relations of art and society; and *The Age of Anxiety: A Baroque Eclogue* (1948, Pulitzer Prize), an ironic idyll, set in a cheap New York bar, on man's isolated condition, intensified in an era without tradition or belief. In 1950 he issued his *Collected Shorter Poems, 1930–44,* and later lyrics were gathered in *Nones* (1951), a volume which opened themes that were developed in *The Shield of Achilles* (1955), *Homage to Clio* (1960), and *About the House* (1965), which in their contrast of human qualities and natural forces, and the treatment of the relation of nature to history, displayed great technical skill. In 1968 and 1970 he reassessed respectively the shorter and the longer poems he wished to preserve and issued new editions of them. These volumes were followed by poetry in *City Without Walls* (1969); *Epistle to a Godson* (1972); *Academic Graffiti* (1972), 61 clerihews about famous people; *Thank You, Fog* (1974), his last lyrics; and *Collected Poems* (1976), a final selection, often with revisions. His later prose included *The Enchafèd Flood: The Romantic Iconography of the Sea* (1951), lectures on the Romantics' attitudes toward man, God, and nature; an edition of *The Living Thoughts of Kierkegaard* (1952); *Making, Knowing and Judging* (1956), his inaugural lecture as Professor of Poetry at Oxford (1956–61); and *The Dyer's Hand* (1962), a major work collecting lectures, essays, musings, and aphorisms. His final prose works appeared in *Secondary Worlds* (1968), lectures on poetry, history, and music; *A Certain World* (1970), extracts with comments from Auden's reading; and *Forewords and Afterwords* (1973), a collection of minor commentary. In 1972 Auden returned to England to live out his last years at Oxford.

AUDUBON, JOHN JAMES (1785–1851), born in Haiti, was educated in France, where Rous-

seau's and Buffon's works led to nature study. After training by David, the French artist, he lived in 1804 on his father's estate near Philadelphia. In the next years he traveled and tried business, portrait painting, drawing instruction, decorating porcelain, taxidermy, and depicting the birds of Kentucky and neighboring wild areas, leading to his *The Birds of America*♦ (1827–38). His narrative gifts and knowledge of the frontier are better seen in the extracts published as *Delineations of American Scenery and Character* (1926) and *Audubon's America* (1940). With the American naturalist John Bachman he worked on *Viviparous Quadrupeds of North America,* completed by his two sons (2 vols., plates, 1842–45; 3 vols., text, 1846–54). He painted many portraits but his fame rests on his bird paintings, whose scientific accuracy may be challenged but whose fresh vitality is unquestioned. His *Journal* was published in 1929 and his *Letters* in 1930.

Augie March, *The Adventures of,* novel by Saul Bellow,♦ published in 1953.

Augie March, a young Chicago Jew, leaves his charity-supported mother, tyrannical grandmother, and mentally retarded brother George, and with his opportunistic older brother Simon ventures into the world to make a living. He manages to graduate from high school but learns about life and himself through diverse jobs and experiences. He first works as a "man at arms" for the crippled William Einhorn, a learned but inept and dishonest businessman who instills in him a love of books; then he becomes a salesman in an elegant saddle shop, leaving when Mrs. Renling, the owner's wife, tries to refine and adopt him. He takes part in a robbery, tries to smuggle immigrants over the Canadian border, steals and sells expensive books, and is briefly a union organizer. Unlike Simon, Augie remains emotionally involved with his family, is deeply upset when his mother and George are institutionalized, and grieves when Grandma Lausch dies. Unwilling to emulate Simon, who married Charlotte Magnus for her money, he leaves his job with Simon and stops courting Charlotte's cousin Lucy, persisting in searching for his own fate in his own way. His love affair with Thea Fenchel, on their iguana hunt in Mexico, convinces him that independence and love are irreconcilable but, sometime later, back in the U.S., he marries Stella, an actress he aided in Mexico. Considering the shambles of Simon's marriage and reflecting on his own unachieved desires for a stable life, Augie recognizes that "everyone got bitterness in his chosen thing," but retains his optimism, humor, and amazement at man's "refusal to lead a disappointed life."

Aunt Polly, character in *Tom Sawyer* ♦ and its sequels.

AUSTIN, MARY [HUNTER] (1868–1934), born in Illinois, moved to California at the age of 18, and lived for many years in the desert, engaged in the study of Indian life. She was a member of the artist colony at Carmel, and later moved to Santa Fe, N.M., to teach and continue her study of the Indians. Her first book, *The Land of Little Rain* ♦ (1903), is a sympathetic description of the beauties of Western desert life. After *The Basket Woman* (1904), a book of short stories, she wrote her first novel, *Isidro* (1905), a romance of California in the days of the Franciscan missions and Mexican rule. *The Flock* (1906) is a factual but poetically conceived narrative of shepherd life. *Santa Lucia: A Common Story* (1908), her first writing concerned with contemporary city life, tells of three women's different adjustments to typical marital problems, while *A Woman of Genius* (1912) is a novel about a woman who attempts to escape from her restricted life through a stage career. *The Green Bough* (1913) tells the story of Jesus' progress from the passion to the ascension, and *The Lovely Lady* (1913) is an idyl concerned with a boy's dreams, his disillusion, and his ultimate triumph. *The Ford* (1917), a realistic novel of social injustice and reform, is set in central California. After *The Trail Book* (1918), stories for children dealing with primitive life, and *Outland* (1919), a mystical romance exalting the primitive values, she wrote *No. 26 Jayne Street* (1920), a novel concerned with contemporary radical activities in New York City. The subjects of her other works are divided between life in the West and the position of the individual in an increasingly standardized machine culture. These include *California, the Land of the Sun* (1914); *The American Rhythm* (1923), studies of American Indian songs, and original poems expressing the same spirit and movement; *Everyman's Genius* (1925), a "personal research into the nature and processes of genius"; *A Small Town Man* (1925), a revision of *The Man Jesus* (1915), presenting the author's concept of Christ as a human being and great mystical genius; and *Children Sing in the Far West* (1928), Indian songs and original poems, written with the "help" of the children in her

classes, and preserving their youthful approach. Mrs. Austin recorded her sympathetic understanding of the West, her mystical attitude, and her personal rebellion for the freedom of the individual in an autobiography, *Earth Horizon* (1932).

Authors League of America, founded in 1912 to protect copyright material. Its categories of membership have changed over the years, and in 1964 its structure added to the League an Authors Guild and a Dramatists Guild. Matters of concern to members in both Guilds (e.g. copyright, freedom of expression) remain the League's province, but matters in which their interests differ (e.g. contract terms, subsidiary rights) are the province of the respective Guilds.

Autobiography of Alice B. Toklas, The, personal narrative by Gertrude Stein. ♦

Autobiography of an Ex-Colored Man, The, novel by James Weldon Johnson. ♦

Autocrat of the Breakfast-Table, The, by Holmes, ♦ was published in 1858, although the germ of the idea may be seen in two papers published (1831–32) in *The New England Magazine* and never reprinted. These rambling Addisonian essays describe imaginary table talk at a Boston boarding house, and include a number of the author's poems: "The Deacon's Masterpiece," ♦ "The Chambered Nautilus," ♦ "Contentment," "The Living Temple," and others. The conversation comprehends many topics and expresses Holmes's urbane philosophy and his concept of the New England character in an easy, genial, witty style. Among those who participate are the Autocrat; the Schoolmistress, to whom he becomes engaged; the Landlady and her Daughter; the Old Gentleman Opposite; the Divinity Student; and the Poor Relation. The success of the *Autocrat* led the author to write three other series: *The Professor at the Breakfast-Table* (1860), *The Poet at the Breakfast-Table* (1872), and *Over the Teacups* (1891).

Avon's Harvest, blank-verse narrative by E.A. Robinson, ♦ the title poem of a volume published in 1921.

Awake and Sing!, play by Clifford Odets, ♦ produced and published in 1935.

Awakening, The, novella by Kate Chopin, ♦ published in 1899.

Edna Pontellier, still in her 20s, is

vaguely discontented in her marriage to Léonce Pontellier, a 40-year-old stockbroker of New Orleans, whose main interests are business and bourgeois respectability. While at a vacation resort at Grand Isle, joined only on weekends by her husband, she begins to awaken from the submissiveness he expects of her as she discovers the freer, romantic society of Creoles and also becomes enamored of young Robert Lebrun. After he leaves suddenly for Mexico her life is empty when she returns to the city. She grows more estranged from her husband, turning frenetically to friends from Grand Isle. Upon Robert's return, they admit their love for one another, but when he says "Good-by— because I love you," she goes to the resort, deserted in off season, and naked swims suicidally far out from the shore, buoyed by "the touch of the sea . . . sensuous, enfolding the body in its soft, close embrace."

Awkward Age, The, novel by Henry James,♦ published in 1899.

The "awkward age" of Nanda Brookenham follows her emergence from childhood segregation to her mother's London salon. The girl and her mother are both in love with Vanderbank, a young government official, although Nanda is also fond of Mitchett, who wishes to marry her. Mrs. Brookenham's friend, the Duchess, wants Mitchett to marry her fragile, innocent niece Aggie, and the two older women wage a diplomatic battle over the match, using as weapons Mrs. Brookenham's relations with Vanderbank and the Duchess's liaison with Lord Petherton. Mr. Longdon, just reentering London society after 30 years' seclusion, sees in Nanda a resemblance to her grandmother, whom he once loved, and, interesting himself in her affairs, is converted to her modern point of view. He realizes that, though she wants Vanderbank, the young man is not anxious to marry her because of her sophistication and frank display of affection. He thereupon gives her a large dowry as bait, but even then the ambitious Vanderbank fails to propose. Mitchett, finally discouraged, marries Aggie, and Mrs. Brookenham overplays her hand by demanding Nanda's return from a visit at Longdon's home. This alienates Vanderbank, and Nanda establishes herself in a separate suite at home. Longdon and Mitchett, who has found his marriage unsatisfactory, decide, and Nanda later agrees, that she should live permanently at Longdon's country place, since he can meet her on her own modern terms.

Axe-Helve, The, blank-verse dramatic narrative by Robert Frost,♦ published in *New Hampshire* (1923).

Axel's Castle, critical essays on symbolism by Edmund Wilson,♦ published in 1931 with the subtitle "A Study in the Imaginative Literature of 1870 to 1930." The authors treated are Yeats, Valéry, Eliot, Proust, Joyce, Gertrude Stein, Rimbaud, and Villiers de l'Isle-Adam. The poetic prose drama *Axel* by the last-named author gives the work its title, for it treats a character, Count Axel, and has a setting that suggests the subjective and symbolic quality of the literature with which Wilson deals.

B

Babbitt, novel by Sinclair Lewis,♦ published in 1922.

George Folansbee Babbitt, an enterprising, moral, stereotyped, and prosperous real-estate broker of the typical Midwestern city of Zenith, has been trained to believe in the virtues of home life, the Republican party, and middle-class conventions. Suddenly tiring of his life, he takes a vacation with Paul Riesling, an artist who has been forced into the role of a businessman. His return to Zenith is at first difficult, but he shortly discovers pleasure in campaigning for a friend for mayor, in several profitable real-estate deals, in the vice-presidency of the Boosters' Club, and in speeches before prominent local gatherings. During his wife's absence, he again tries to find an outlet from Zenith standards. After an unsuccessful and lonely trip to Maine, he enters into a liaison with Mrs. Tanis Judique, an attractive widow who fails to be the "fairy child" of his dreams when he sees her in clear light in relation to her group of nondescript would-be bohemians, "The Bunch." He next turns to liberalism, when impressed by Seneca Doane, a socialist lawyer. For this added heresy he is ostracized by all right-minded citizens. He is not again able to return to Zenith's outlook until his wife Myra is suddenly taken ill, and he once more feels a spiritual union with her and a sympathy with his city's point of view.

BABBITT, IRVING (1865–1933), professor of French at Harvard (1894–1933), as a leader of the New Humanism♦ was a trenchant critic of romanticism and its arch-apostle, Rousseau. His books include: *Literature and the American College* (1908), a plea for the humanities; *The New Laokoön* (1910), on the romantic confusion in the arts; *Rousseau and Romanticism* (1919).

Backward Glance o'er Travel'd Roads, A, Whitman's prose epilogue to *Leaves of Grass,*♦ which served as a preface to *November Boughs* (1888), and appeared in the collected volume in 1889 for the first time.

Leaves of Grass, according to the essay, is intended "to articulate . . . uncompromisingly my own physical, emotional, moral, intellectual, and aesthetic Personality, in the midst of, and tallying, the momentous spirit and facts of . . . current America—and to exploit that Personality, identified with place and date, in a far more candid and comprehensive sense than any hitherto poem or book." Whitman abandons conventional themes, ornaments, euphemism, and rhyme so as "to conform with and build on the concrete realities of the universe furnish'd by science," and to root himself "in the emotional and imaginative action of the modern times." His purpose is to write "poems of realities and science and of the democratic average and basic equality," but he points out his literary influences, which might have come to naught had not the Civil War given a final reason for "an autochthonic and passionate song."

BACON, DELIA SALTER (1811–59), was among the first to propound the theory that Shakespeare's plays were written by a group headed by Bacon and including Raleigh and Spenser, and that a great system of thought was concealed in them by ciphers. Emerson and Carlyle encouraged her for a time, and Hawthorne, who describes her in *Our Old Home,* wrote a preface for her *Philosophy of the Plays of Shakspere Unfolded* (1857). She also wrote such fiction as *Tales of the Puritans* (1831) and *The Bride of Fort Edward* (1839), a closet drama on the Revolution. She was violently insane during her last two years.

BAKER, DOROTHY (1907–68), Montana-born novelist, attended Whittier College, and graduated from the University of California, Los Angeles. Her novels are *Young Man with a Horn* (1938), inspired by the music of Bix Beiderbecke; *Trio* (1943), dramatized (1944) with her husband Howard Baker (1905–), novelist and poet; *Our Gifted Son* (1948); and *Cassandra at the Wedding* (1962), a psychological study of two sisters and their family.

BAKER, GEORGE PIERCE (1866–1935), was instrumental in encouraging and inspiring many little theaters, stage designers, directors, and dramatists. His 47 Workshop at Harvard (1905–25) served as a laboratory for the staging of plays by such students as

Edward Sheldon, Eugene O'Neill, Philip Barry, John Dos Passos, S.N. Behrman, Sidney Howard, and Thomas Wolfe. After 1925 he continued his work at Yale. Baker is the prototype of Professor Hatcher in Wolfe's *Of Time and the River.*

BAKER, RAY STANNARD (1870–1946), a leading contributor to *McClure's Magazine* during its muckraking period, became an intimate of President Wilson, about whom he wrote several volumes. Under the pseudonym David Grayson, he wrote seven volumes of familiar essays.

BALDWIN, FAITH (1893–1978), popular author of more than 75 books, mainly romantic and light fiction for women, some inspirational poems, and a few books for children. Her first novel, *Mavis of Green Hill* (1921), was followed by many others, including *Office Wife* (1930), *White Collar Girl* (1933), *Men Are Such Fools!* (1936), *Temporary Address: Reno* (1941), *He Married a Doctor* (1943), and *The Lonely Man* (1964). *Testament of Trust* (1960) is an autobiography.

BALDWIN, JAMES (1924–), born in Harlem, where for a short time in his youth he followed his father's footsteps as a preacher, and, as he says, "the rhetoric of the storefront church" has been among the influences on his prose. He left home at the age of 17 and subsequent travels included long expatriation in France. His first novel, *Go Tell It on the Mountain*♦ (1953), about a day in the lives of various members of a Harlem church and, through flashbacks, about their forebears, was immediately hailed as a major treatment of black life in the U.S. and helped to establish Baldwin as the leading black novelist since Richard Wright. His second novel, *Giovanni's Room* (1956), was set in his new residence of Paris and concerned a man torn between homosexual love and love of a woman. His third novel, *Another Country*♦ (1962), is a lengthy tale of complex human relations between races and sexes. His next novel, *Tell Me How Long the Train's Been Gone* (1968), about a black actor recalling his youth in Harlem and his dramatic career, is by implication an assessment of the situation of American blacks. *If Beale Street Could Talk* (1974) is a novel about a pregnant young woman's struggle to free her falsely imprisoned fiancé. *Just Above My Head* (1979), Baldwin's sixth novel, retrospectively treats the life of a Harlem gospel singer as he and his family search for their identities and for

salvation. Baldwin's nonfiction includes *Notes of a Native Son* (1955), containing personal essays, reminiscences of Harlem life, his harsh view of Richard Wright, and consideration of the situation of Northern black intellectuals; *Nobody Knows My Name*♦ (1961), intense personal essays; *The Fire Next Time* (1963), two "letters" vigorously describing the state of the black in the U.S. through his own youthful experiences and his encounter with the Black Muslim movement; *No Name in the Street* (1972), autobiographical fragments and an assessment of race relations in the U.S.; and *The Devil Finds Work* (1976), an essay about blacks and American films and *The Evidence of Things Not Seen* (1985), about murders of black children in Atlanta. He has also written plays, including *Blues for Mister Charley* (1964), about the antagonism between the Negro and the white man (generically called "Mr. Charley"), which depicts a black boy who has become a successful singer in New York but also a drug addict and who, upon returning to his Southern home to start life anew, is murdered by a white man; *The Amen Corner* (1964) is concerned with a woman evangelist torn between religious fanaticism and love of her footloose, jazz-playing husband. *Going To Meet the Man* (1965) is a collection of short stories.

Ballad, narrative poem of communal origin, transmitted by a process of oral tradition among people usually free from literary influences. Folk ballads frequently deal with common people, are presented with simplicity, have little description, and depend mainly on dialogue and incremental repetition, i.e. structural repetitions of a preceding stanza with some variation to advance the story. Metrically, the ballad is usually composed of long seven-stress lines, conventionally printed as two lines of four and three stresses each, rhyming *abcb.* Among the classifications of American folk ballads are those dealing with occupations ("Casey Jones" of the railroad workers, "Git Along, Little Dogies" of the cowboys, and "The Jam on Gerry's Rock" of the lumberjacks), with regions ("The Roving Gambler" of the Kentucky and Tennessee mountains, "The Buffalo Skinners" of the Western plains, and "The Erie Canal Ballad"), with wars ("Yankee Doodle" of the Revolution, and "The Battle of Shiloh Hill" of the Civil War), with racial groups ("John Henry" of the blacks), and with desperadoes ("Sam Bass" and "Billy the Kid"). Many of the ballads are of

English origin, some of these surviving almost intact in the Southern mountains. Variations of the most popular ballads constitute cycles or groups, for example, those concerned with Jesse James,♦ Frankie and Johnny,♦ John Henry,♦ Casey Jones,♦ and Yankee Doodle.♦ The many collections of American folk ballads include Louise Pound's *American Ballads and Songs* (1922), Sandburg's *The American Songbag* (1927), Lomax's *American Ballads and Folk Songs* (1934), and Hudson's *Folksongs of Mississippi* (1936). Among literary adaptations of the ballad form are Longfellow's "Wreck of the Hesperus," Hay's *Pike County Ballads,* Whittier's "Skipper Ireson's Ride," Harte's "The Heathen Chinee," and Lindsay's "The Chinese Nightingale."

Ballad of the Sad Café, The, novella by Carson McCullers,♦ title piece of a book published in 1951. It was dramatized by Edward Albee in 1963.

In a small Georgia town the hardest working and best business person is Miss Amelia Evans, at 30 a tall, strong woman, able to outfight any man, and the owner of a store and a still that produces the best whiskey in the area. She had been married, for ten days only, to Marvin Macy, the town's toughest criminal, who doted on her. When she refused to sleep with him and threw him out of her house he went on a rampage of crime that led to his imprisonment. While he was in prison Miss Amelia was attracted by a distant relative, Cousin Lymon Willis, a dwarfish hunchback, whom she befriended and under whose spell she opened her store at night as the town's café. But after Marvin Macy is released and returns to the town, Cousin Lymon becomes fascinated by him, and it is clear that Miss Amelia will have to fight physically with her one time husband for leadership and for Lymon too. Soon a wrestling match does occur. Amelia is about to win when Lymon jumps on her back and she is downed in defeat. Marvin and Lymon vandalize the store, destroy the still, and leave town, also leaving Miss Amelia a physically and psychologically broken woman, huddling in her closed café.

Balloon Hoax, The, story by Poe,♦ published in the New York *Sun* (April 13, 1844) in the guise of an actual article of news. According to the author, the *"jeu d'esprit . . .* subserved the purpose of creating indigestible aliment for the *quidnuncs* during the few hours intervening between a couple of the Charles-

ton mails." It is an account of a fictitious crossing of the Atlantic in 75 hours (April 6–9) by eight men in "Mr. Monck Mason's Flying Machine . . . the Steering Balloon 'Victoria.' " The balloon, inflated with coal gas, is supposed to have started from a place in north Wales, headed out over the ocean, and then been caught in a powerful gale that lasted two days, driving the craft at great speed until it was landed on Sullivan's Island, S.C.

BALLOU, ADIN (1803–90), founder of the Hopedale Community,♦ was originally a believer in Universalism, but withdrew to expound the doctrine of Restorationism, that all men will be ultimately restored to happiness in the future life. He published a magazine, the *Independent Messenger* (1831–39), and wrote such books as *Practical Christian Socialism* (1854) and *Primitive Christianity and Its Corruptions* (1870).

BANCROFT, GEORGE (1800–1891), Massachusetts statesman and scholar, while holding various government posts obtained material for his monumental *History of the United States* (1834–76). As secretary of navy under Polk, he was instrumental in establishing Annapolis as the U.S. Naval Academy, and as secretary of war *pro tem* (May 1845) he sent General Taylor across the Texas border, precipitating war with Mexico. His standing order to Sloat to occupy California ports in case of war led to the early occupation of that territory. Bancroft was minister to Great Britain (1846–49) and minister to Germany (1867–74). His ten-volume *History* was revised in 1876 to six volumes. A final revision (6 vols., 1883–85) includes the *History of the Formation of the Constitution* (1882). Although the work is now outmoded, it is still important as an example of the aggressive yet spiritual nationalism of America's mid-19th century. Some of Bancroft's many orations and essays are collected in *Literary and Historical Miscellanies* (1855).

BANCROFT, HUBERT HOWE (1832–1918), born in Ohio, came to California (1852) to be a miner and bookseller. In San Francisco he later founded the West's leading bookstore and publishing firm. In 1859 he began to collect a great library of regional source materials, now known as The Bancroft Library.♦ On this collection he based his history of the *Native Races* (5 vols., 1874–75), *History of the Pacific States* (34 vols., 1882–90), *Chronicles of the Builders* (7 vols., 1891–

92), and other works which establish him as the first great historian of the West Coast. Although all the books bear Bancroft's name alone, he depended upon assistants whose work included the preparation of drafts, some of which he altered only slightly in making the final texts. His books for general readers include *California Pastoral* (1888) and *California Inter Pocula* (1888), respectively on the Spanish and gold-rush eras, and the autobiographical works, *Literary Industries* (1890) and *Restrospection, Political and Personal* (1910).

Bancroft Library, THE, formed by Hubert Howe Bancroft, ♦ sold by him to the University of California, Berkeley (1905), which continues to concentrate on his collecting fields: the western part of North America, emphasizing California, and Mexico and Central America. In 1969 it became the major library of rare materials of all sorts on the campus, including the manuscripts and other papers of Mark Twain, the basis of a major publishing program.

Band of Angels, novel by R.P. Warren, ♦ published in 1955.
  Amantha Starr tells the story of her life, beginning in the 1850s as the pampered daughter of a Kentucky plantation owner educated in Ohio until upon her father's death she learns that her mother was a slave. To defray her father's debts, as a 16-year-old girl she is sold to Hamish Bond, an old man in New Orleans, who first makes her his mistress, then frees her. During the Civil War, when Union troops occupy New Orleans, Amantha meets and is married to Captain Tobias Sears, a proper New Englander who commands black soldiers, the most heroic of whom is Lieutenant Oliver Cromwell Jones, once known as Rau-Ru on Hamish's plantation. After the war, while separated from Sears, Amantha takes up with Rau-Ru/Jones, who causes the hanging of Hamish. Reunited, Amantha and Tobias in their middle age during the 1880s drift to Missouri and Kansas, living uneasily as he pursues his career as an idealistic lawyer opposed to the Gilded Age standards. But finally both achieve security with some money but, more importantly, through an understanding of their own identities.

BANGS, JOHN KENDRICK (1862–1922), lecturer, editor of *Puck* (1904–5) and other humorous magazines, who is best known for collections of extravagantly farcical tales,

Tiddledywink Tales (1891), *The Idiot* (1895), *Mr. Bonaparte of Corsica* (1895), and *A Houseboat on the Styx* (1896). In the last he gathers together such diverse characters as Shakespeare, Delilah, Lucrezia Borgia, and Artemus Ward and plays freely with the absurd situations that ensue. It is illustrated by Peter Newell, of whom he wrote a biographical sketch. *The Pursuit of the Houseboat* (1897) is a sequel. With F.D. Sherman he wrote *New Waggings of Old Tales* (1888).

BARAKA, IMAMU AMIRI, see *Jones, LeRoi.*

Barbara Frietchie, poem by Whittier ♦ in four-stress couplets, published in *In War Time and Other Poems* (1864). It relates a supposedly historic incident of Stonewall Jackson's entry into Frederick, Md. The 90-year-old heroine raises the Stars and Stripes:

> Shoot if you must, this old gray head,
> But spare your country's flag, she said.

Her courage impresses the general, who orders his troops to march on. Barbara Frietchie is the subject of a play (1899) by Clyde Fitch, ♦ who makes her a youthful heroine. The name is also spelled Fritchie.

Barefoot Boy, The, poem in tetrameter couplets by Whittier, ♦ collected in *The Panorama* (1856). It recounts the adventures of rural boyhood, with a nostalgic sense of their innocent sensuous enjoyments.

BARLOW, JOEL (1754–1812), one of the Connecticut Wits, ♦ graduated from Yale (1778), taught school, managed a business, preached, entered military service, was admitted to the bar (1786), contributed to *The Anarchiad*, a mock-heroic statement of New England conservatism, and wrote a new version of the Psalms, all of which occupations were incidental to his lifelong ambition to write the great American epic. This work, *The Vision of Columbus* (1787), was finally revised as *The Columbiad* ♦ (1807), which he considered his masterpiece. He went to Europe (1788) and during 17 years of residence abroad changed from a conservative Connecticut Puritan to a cosmopolitan Democrat. As a reward for *A Letter to the National Convention of France* (1792) he was made a French citizen. Inspired by his friend Paine, he next wrote his *Advice to the Privileged Orders* (1792), in which he sets forth the thesis that the state is the responsible agent of all society rather than of any one class, and that its duty is to safeguard the social heritage as a common asset held in trust for future generations. It was during this residence in France that Barlow wrote his charming little poem *Hasty Pudding* ♦ (1796), for which he is best remembered. In 1795 he was appointed consul to Algiers, where he effected important treaties. Upon his return to the U.S. (1805) he published a *Prospectus of a National Institution to be Established in the United States* for research and instruction in the arts and sciences. He lived the quiet life of a scholar for six years, and in 1811 was appointed minister to France. He died near Cracow, Poland, on his way to meet Napoleon, with whom he hoped to consummate a treaty.

BARNES, Djuna (1892–1982), New York-born author long resident in Europe. Her first major work was *A Book* (1923) of short plays, stories, and poems, introspective analyses of people whose temperamental sympathies lie with the simple lives of animals. It was reissued with three new stories as *A Night Among the Horses* (1929), and the stories were somewhat refashioned as *Spillway* in her *Selected Works* (1962). *Ryder* (1928) is a satirical novel in the stream-of-consciousness style, concerned with a man's relations with his mother, his wife, and his mistresses. *Nightwood* (1936), a novel of the relationships of five psychopathic people, has been described by T.S. Eliot as having "a quality of horror and doom very nearly related to that of Elizabethan tragedy." *The Antiphon* (1958) is a blank-verse play. Other publications are *The Book of Repulsive Women* (1948), poems and drawings created in 1915, and *Vagaries Malicieux* (1975), two essays based on life in Paris of the 1920s but described as stories. *Smoke and Other Early Stories* (1982) collects juvenilia.

BARNUM, P[hineas] T[aylor] (1810–91), Connecticut-born impresario, began his career (1835) by exhibiting an aged black woman fraudulently claimed to have been George Washington's childhood nurse. His American Museum (founded 1842) combined sideshows, stage entertainment, and exhibition of curios, attracting crowds by extravagant publicity and advertising. His international reputation began with his first European tour (1844) with his dwarf, "General Tom Thumb," and was extended when he brought to the U.S. foreign stars, such as the "Swedish nightingale" Jenny Lind, whose tour he man-

aged in 1850–52. In 1871 he organized his circus, advertised as "the greatest show on earth." Barnum's books include his *Life* (1855, frequently revised) and *The Humbugs of the World* (1865).

Barren Ground, novel by Ellen Glasgow, ♦ published in 1925.

Dorinda Oakley, daughter of a land-poor farmer in Virginia, at 20 goes to work in Nathan Pedlar's store. She falls in love with Jason Greylock, weak-willed son of the village doctor, and forgets her purpose of helping her father to rebuild the farm, but the day before their planned wedding Jason is forced to marry a former fiancée. Bitterly disillusioned, Dorinda seeks work in New York. At her father's death, Dorinda returns to the family farm, which is impoverished and overgrown with broomsedge. Having studied scientific agriculture, she introduces progressive methods, gradually returning the "barren ground" to fertility and creating a prosperous dairy farm. Her mother becomes an invalid, and her brother Rufus is lazy and selfish, so that Dorinda must carry on unaided. After her mother's death she marries Nathan Pedlar, to provide a home for his children, and after he dies she shelters Jason, now penniless and ill from excessive drinking. He soon dies, and to the suggestion that she might marry again, Dorinda replies with an ironic smile, "Oh, I've finished with all that . . . I am thankful to have finished with all that."

BARRY, Philip (1896–1949), born in Rochester, N.Y., graduated from Yale (1919), and studied in the 47 Workshop of G.P. Baker at Harvard, where he wrote *You and I* (1923), in which a father, trying to guide his son into an artistic career, reveals his own thwarted ambition. Following *The Youngest* (1924), a satirical play concerning the revolt of a youngest son from the bourgeois standards of his family, and *In a Garden* (1925), a sophisticated comedy, he wrote *White Wings* ♦ (1926), an ironic fantasy. His next play, *John* (1927), based on the life of John the Baptist, was unsuccessful, but *Paris Bound* (1927) was a popular comedy concerned with contemporary moral standards. After collaborating with Elmer Rice in writing a fanciful mystery play, *Cock Robin* (1928), Barry returned to his earlier theme of a child's revolt against the standards of her parents in *Holiday* (1928). *Hotel Universe* (1930) was a mystical play, and he further showed his interest in psychological investigation in *Tomorrow and To-*

morrow (1931) and in *The Animal Kingdom* (1932), plays concerned with modern marital relations. After two unsuccessful plays, *The Joyous Season* (1934) and *Bright Star* (1935), and *Spring Dance* (1936), an adaptation, he wrote *Here Come the Clowns* (1938), also published as a novel, *War in Heaven* (1938), in which an "illusionist's" hypnotic powers reveal the inner tragedies of a group of vaudeville actors. *The Philadelphia Story* (1939) is a drawing-room comedy about a young heiress and an author; *Liberty Jones* (1941) is an allegory of the threats to democracy in the modern world; *Without Love* (1942) is a comedy of platonic marriage; and *Second Threshold* (1951) is a play left in manuscript and revised by Robert Sherwood.

BARTH, JOHN [SIMMONS] (1930–), Maryland-born novelist, educated at Johns Hopkins, whose fiction set on the Eastern Shore of his native state includes *The Floating Opera* (1956), the experiences of a man recalled on the day in 1937 when he debates suicide, and *The End of the Road* (1958), another existential and nihilistic view of experience set in a travestied conventional love triangle. Although placed in the same setting, his third novel, *The Sot-Weed Factor*♦ (1960), is more fantastic and funnier in its lusty parody of an 18th-century picaresque tale re-creating the life and times of Ebenezer Cooke. This was followed by *Giles Goat-Boy*♦ (1966), another lengthy, complex, and comic novel full of ingenious parody in its satirical allegory of the modern world conceived in terms of a university campus. *Lost in the Funhouse* (1968) consists of 14 pieces of fiction related in part by their concern with what happens when a writer writes (he makes himself a persona) and a reader reads. *Chimera* (1972) is also a volume of short fiction, retelling in elaborate style tales of Scheherazade, Perseus, and Bellerophon dealing with social and psychological problems of modern life, also introducing the author Barth along the way. The last-named work won a National Book Award. Barth returned to the long novel in *Letters* (1979), an unusual development of epistolary fiction, in which seven more or less parallel narratives are revealed through correspondence written by seven characters from his earlier fiction, including the Author himself as just another imaginary figure, the intricate story comprising an inquiry into the patterns into which the characters have been previously set and the degree of freedom they may possess. *Sabbatical: A Romance* (1982) tells of the

adventures and ideas occasioned by a long cruise of a college professor and her husband, an aspiring novelist. *The Friday Book* (1984) collects essays and other nonfiction.

BARTHELME, DONALD (1931–), author of stories collected in *Come Back, Dr. Caligari* (1964), *Unspeakable Practices, Unnatural Acts* (1968), *City Life* (1970), *Sadness* (1972), *Guilty Pleasures* (1974), *Amateurs* (1976), *Great Days* (1979), and *Overnight to Many Distant Cities* (1984), all possessed of a fantastic humor marked by a straightforward presentation of absurdly grotesque, illogical, and meaningless matters as if to indicate that their world, and therefore our own, is wholly irrational. The same attitudes and parodic style mark his novels, *Snow White* (1967), an oblique, incongruous version of the fairy tale in episodic form, and *The Dead Father* (1975), telling of 19 children hauling their father, both a living man and a gigantic carcass, across a city to his death.

Bartleby the Scrivener: *A Story of Wall Street,* symbolic tale by Melville♦ published anonymously in *Putnam's Magazine* (1853) and reprinted in *The Piazza Tales* (1856). One view is that it reflects Melville's futility at the neglect of his novels ("Dead Letters") and his uncertainty about how to relate to society.

A Wall Street lawyer hires Bartleby, a curious, wraith-like figure, as a copyist. Bartleby refuses to mingle with the other employees, and, when asked to do anything besides copying documents, invariably says, "I would prefer not to." Some inner dignity or pathos in him prevents his being discharged, even when he ceases to work and uses the office for living quarters. The lawyer moves to another building, and the new tenant has Bartleby arrested. Visited in prison by the lawyer, he is silent and refuses favors. Soon he dies, and the lawyer hears a rumor that Bartleby was formerly a clerk in the Dead Letter Office, whose strange atmosphere affected his attitude toward life to the end.

BARTLETT, JOHN (1820–1905), owner of the University Book Store in Cambridge, a meeting place for Harvard professors and students. "Ask John Bartlett" was the customary saying when anyone sought a book or quotation. His reference book *Familiar Quotations* was first published in 1855.

BARTRAM, JOHN (1699–1777), first native American botanist, established the Philadelphia gardens described, along with a sketch of their creator, in Crèvecœur's *Letters from an American Farmer.*

BARTRAM, WILLIAM (1739–1823), John's son, was also a Quaker and a botanist and accompanied his father on exploring trips. His fame rests on his *Travels Through North and South Carolina, Georgia, East and West Florida, the Cherokee Country, the Extensive Territories of the Muscogulges, or Creek Confederacy, and the Country of the Chactaws* (1791), which Coleridge called a work of "high merit." His philosophic vision of the idea of the "natural" man, and his rich descriptions influenced, among others, Chateaubriand, Coleridge, Wordsworth, and Lafcadio Hearn.

BASSO, [JOSEPH] HAMILTON (1904–64), Louisiana-born novelist who was a chronicler of Southern society in moods that ranged from the satirical to the sunny, but that were generally temperate. His novels are *Relics and Angels* (1929); *Cinnamon Seed* (1934); *In Their Own Image* (1935); *Courthouse Square* (1936); *Days Before Lent* (1939); *Wine of the Country* (1941); *Sun in Capricorn* (1942), about a power-mad politician like Huey Long; *The Greenroom* (1949); *The View from Pompey's Head* (1954), about a Southerner, long resident in New York, called back by a legal case to his hometown, whose mores he rediscovers, and *Light Infantry Ball* (1959), another view of the same town, this time during the disintegration caused by the Civil War; and *A Touch of the Dragon* (1964), a modern comedy of manners. *Beauregard* (1933) is a biography; *Mainstream* (1943) studies great Americans from Mather to F.D. Roosevelt; and *A Quota of Seaweed* (1960) contains travel sketches.

BATES, KATHERINE LEE (1859–1929), Massachusetts author, professor at Wellesley (1885–1925), whose writings include scholarly works, children's books, and poems, of which the most famous is "America the Beautiful" ♦ (1893).

"Battle Hymn of the Republic, THE," song popular among Union partisans in the Civil War, was written by Julia Ward Howe ♦ at the suggestion of J.F. Clarke, ♦ when both were visiting McClellan's troops in December 1861. The words, whose chief message Mrs. Howe described as "the sacredness of human liberty," were to be sung to the tune of "John Brown's Body," which is ascribed to William Steffe (*c.*1856). James T. Fields is said to have named the "Battle Hymn," and he was responsible for its publication in the *Atlantic Monthly* (Feb. 1862).

Battle of the Kegs, The, Revolutionary War ballad by Francis Hopkinson, ♦ was published in 1778, immediately after the Americans under David Bushnell had prepared certain "infernal machines" that were floated down the Delaware River in the form of kegs, intended to destroy British shipping at Philadelphia. The British opened a furious cannonade upon everything floating on the water. Hopkinson describes in rollicking verse the panic into which the British were thrown and their supposed belief that the kegs were filled with armed rebels.

Battle-Pieces and Aspects of the War, poems by Melville, ♦ published in 1866. An appendix contains a prose supplement pleading for a humane and charitable Northern attitude toward Reconstruction.

BAUM, L[YMAN] FRANK (1856–1919), journalist, dramatist, and writer of juvenile tales, best known for his fantasies for children about the land of Oz, ♦ of which the first was *The Wonderful Wizard of Oz* (1900), the story of a little girl, Dorothy, and her dog Toto whisked away on a cyclone from their drab Kansas home to a land of adventure and achievement inhabited by such creatures as a Cowardly Lion, a Tin Woodman, an animate Scarecrow, a witch, and the Wizard himself. The success of this book and Baum's musical extravaganza adapted for the stage (1901) led to his 13 sequels, including *Ozma of Oz* (1907), *The Road to Oz* (1909), and *The Lost Princess of Oz* (1917), as well as many additions to the series by other authors after Baum's death. He himself wrote about 60 books, mostly for children, including 18 for girls, written under the pseudonym Edith Van Dyne.

Bay Psalm Book, name generally given to *The Whole Booke of Psalmes Faithfully Translated into English Metre,* the accepted hymnal of the Massachusetts Bay Colony. The translation was made by Richard Mather, John Eliot, and Thomas Weld, with the stated intention of sacrificing elegance to accuracy. It was published at Cambridge (1640) by Stephen Daye, ♦ and except for a broadside and a brief almanac was the first work printed in the colonies. John Cotton wrote the Preface.

Bayou Folk, 23 stories and anecdotes of Louisiana local color by Kate Chopin,♦ published in 1894.

"A No-Account Creole" is the story of selfish, vain Placide Santien, whose faults are redeemed by his giving up his wealthy fiancée the day before their scheduled marriage, when he learns that she loves another man. "Désirée's Baby" tells of a Louisiana aristocrat who marries an orphan girl. Their son shows evidence of black ancestry, and Armand turns Désirée and the child out of his house. She disappears, and some weeks later he discovers an old letter of his mother, revealing that the Negro blood is in his own family. "La Belle Zoraïde" tells of a beautiful quadroon slave who goes mad because she is not allowed to marry the black father of her child. The child is taken from her, and she transfers her affection to a doll, which she refuses to give up even in return for her own infant.

BEACH, REX [ELLINGWOOD] (1877–1949), Michigan novelist, spent several years in the Klondike and wrote a number of novels concerned with the region, including *The Spoilers* (1906), based on a Nome gold-mining case; *The Silver Horde* (1909), a tale of the salmon fisheries; and *The Iron Trail* (1913). He later turned to other backgrounds, such as the Canal Zone, in *The Ne'er-do-well* (1911); New York City, in *The Auction Block* (1914); and Florida, in *Wild Pastures* (1935). *Personal Exposures* (1941) is an autobiography.

BEADLE, ERASTUS (1821–94), famous publisher of dime novels, began his career by issuing ten-cent song books and game manuals. *Malaeska, the Indian Wife of the White Hunter* (1860) by Ann S. Stephens was the first of his series advertised as "a dollar book for a dime." It is said to have sold 300,000 copies during its first year, and was followed by hundreds of similar works dealing with the desperate adventures of frontiersmen. Among Beadle's writers were "Bruin" Adams, W.F. Cody, Edward S. Ellis, Mayne Reid, and Fred Whittaker. After 1880, train robbers and detectives supplanted Indians and hunters, and the dime novel acquired the opprobrious reputation that has clung to it.

BEAGLE, PETER S[OYER] (1939–   ), novelist born in New York City, resident in northern California, whose works include *A Fine and Private Place* (1960), whose protagonist returns from his burial to join living people; *I See By My Outfit* (1965), about two young Beatniks motor-scooting across the continent to California; and *The Last Unicorn* (1968), presenting a female unicorn transformed into a human and back again as symbolic of the wonder and beauty of love. He has also written *The California Feeling* (1969), a nonfictional travelogue, and *The Garden of Earthly Delights* (1982), a study of the Flemish artist Hieronymous Bosch. In addition, he has written for films and television.

Bear, The, novelette by Faulkner,♦ published in *Go Down, Moses* in 1942. Early versions of parts of the work are "Lion" (*Harper's,* Dec. 1935) and "The Bear" (*Saturday Evening Post,* May 9, 1942), and an abbreviated form, without section 4, which treats of Isaac's dispossessing himself of his lands, appeared in *Big Woods* (1955).

One December day in the 1880s the 16-year-old Isaac McCaslin, heir of one of the good old families of Yoknapatawpha County, is taken to hunt the great bear Old Ben so that the boy may show his courage and be initiated into the ranks of men. Since the age of ten he has learned the woods and the ways of hunters on annual autumnal outings with other McCaslins, Major de Spain, General Compson, and men of Indian blood, like Boon Hogganbeck and Sam Fathers. When Ike was 13 Sam Fathers "had marked his face with the hot blood" of the first buck he had killed, and "in the next November he killed a bear." Now he faces more dangerous game, for Old Ben, who has killed dogs, a fawn, and a colt, is the prime subject of an annual quest by mature men. For this purpose Sam Fathers has trained a huge, almost wild dog, Lion, to hold the beast, but in their first encounter both the bear and the dog are killed. Boon too is ripped by the bear, but he survives to act on Sam's unspoken request, killing the exhausted man, who has lost his will to live. Five years later, when he is 21 and married, Ike makes clear the great meaningfulness of this experience as he tells his older cousin, McCaslin Edmonds, that he plans to give up the plantation he has inherited so as to free himself from the ownership of property, further cursed because it was dubiously acquired and was the site of his grandfather's incestuous relations with his slaves. Ike has come to love the wild beauty of nature, represented by Old Ben. This sacramental feeling he has learned from Sam, rather than from the land, which is only the object of human possession and is now typically despoiled by men.

BEARD, CHARLES A[USTIN] (1874–1948), historian and educator, after graduating from DePauw University (1898) attended Oxford, where he founded Ruskin College (1899) to train labor leaders, and became professor of political science at Columbia (1904–17). He wrote a number of textbooks on European history, but, deciding "that American history is more interesting," he next published *An Economic Interpretation of the Constitution* (1913) and *Economic Origins of Jeffersonian Democracy* (1915), volumes that established him as a liberal historian, and profoundly affected the study of American history but, alienated many traditionalists. Beard resigned from Columbia (1917) to protest the dismissal of pacifist professors, and the next year helped found The New School for Social Research. With his wife, Mary R. Beard,♦ he wrote *The Rise of American Civilization* (2 vols., 1927), an analysis of U.S. institutions, emphasizing social and economic backgrounds; *America in Midpassage* (1939), a continuation; *The American Spirit* (1942), about the "idea of civilization" in the U.S.; and *A Basic History of the United States* (1944).

BEARD, MARY R[ITTER] (1876–1958), is known for historical studies written with her husband, Charles A. Beard,♦ for her work in the woman suffrage and labor movements, and for *A Short History of the American Labor Movement* (1920, revised 1925), *On Understanding Women* (1931), *America Through Women's Eyes* (1933), *Woman: Co-Maker of History* (1940), and *Woman as a Force in History* (1946).

Beare and Ye Club, Ye, first play performed in English in America, was composed by Cornelius Watkinson, Philip Howard, and William Darby, three citizens of Accomac County, Va., in 1665.

Beat movement, a bohemian rebellion against established society which came to prominence about 1956 and had its centers in San Francisco and New York. The term "Beat" expressed both exhaustion and beatification in that the writers, tired of conventional society, and disgusted by it, believed that thoroughgoing disaffiliation from all aspects of the manners and mores of what they saw as a corrupt, crass, commercial world would bring its own kind of blissful illumination, aided by drink and drugs. Writers of the movement expressed their views in their own "hip" vocabulary, combined with phrases from Buddhism, by which they were influenced, but there is a personal statement and power that goes beyond this jargon in the works of the leading literary figures, who include the poets Allen Ginsberg♦ and Gregory Corso♦ and their San Francisco publisher Lawrence Ferlinghetti♦ and the novelist Jack Kerouac.♦ Older writers who related to the movement included Norman Mailer,♦ Henry Miller,♦ and Kenneth Rexroth.♦ Close to them and yet removed in part from the Beat movement because of his greater violence is William Burroughs.♦

BEATTIE, ANN (1947–   ), born in Washington, D.C. Her first novel, *Chilly Scenes of Winter* (1976), presents a man in his twenties lonely and yearning for love, a frustrated, bewildered figure of the 1960s; and her second, *Falling in Place* (1980), set in the late 1970s, treats the loveless marriage of an advertising executive aged 40. *Distortions* (1976), *Secrets and Surprises* (1978), and *The Burning House* (1982) collect stories.

Beauchamp family, characters in Faulkner's fiction, related to the McCaslin family,♦ of whom the most prominent was Lucas, who figures in *Intruder in the Dust.*♦

Beauchampe: or, The Kentucky Tragedy, novel by Simms,♦ published in 1842 as a fictional account of the Kentucky Tragedy.♦ In 1856 the first part was expanded into an independent novel, *Charlemont; or, The Pride of the Village.* In this part Warham Sharpe, a young attorney, assumes the name of Alfred Stevens and the guise of a theological student, to woo Margaret Cooper. After seducing her and failing to keep his promise of marriage, he departs; her illegitimate child dies, and she swears to kill the father.

The revised *Beauchampe,* the former second part, opens five years later, when Margaret, living in seclusion under the name Anna Cooke, accepts the proposal of a young lawyer, Beauchampe. She warns him that he "clasps a dishonoured hand," and requires him to kill her seducer. After their marriage, Beauchampe's friend Sharpe visits them.

When he again attempts to seduce Margaret, Beauchampe discovers his identity, stabs him, and later is condemned to death. On the eve of the execution, he and his wife attempt suicide. Although she succeeds, he is hanged, proclaiming at the last, "Daughters of Kentucky! you, at least, will bless the name of Beauchampe!"

Beauties of Santa Cruz, The, poem by Freneau, ♦ written in the West Indies in 1776 and printed in his *Poems* (1786). This piece, in iambic pentameter quatrains, extols the beauties of the tropics and describes the horrors of slavery, which blot the country's native charms.

Beaver, TONY, giant hero of tall tales told by lumberjacks of the Southern mountains, was "a sort of relative" of Paul Bunyan, ♦ whose mythical exploits he equals.

Bech: A Book, novel by John Updike, ♦ published in 1970. *Bech Is Back* (1982), a sequel, presents the author in his fifties breaking out of a writer's block to create a best seller but no happier or more personally fulfilled.

In seven episodes presented in the guise of lectures with a spurious bibliography, the work reveals the literary and personal life of Henry Bech, a distinguished Jewish author of New York. Revelatory incidents include Bech's travels in the 1960s as a kind of cultural ambassador in Russia and Eastern Europe, his visit as a lecturer to adulatory pupils at a girls' school, his diverse romantic affairs, his difficulties in writing as he ages, and his ultimate enshrinement as a major American author.

Becky Thatcher, character in *Tom Sawyer.* ♦

BEECHER, CATHARINE E[STHER] (1800–1878), daughter of Lyman Beecher and sister of Henry Ward Beecher and Harriet Beecher Stowe. Her work as an educator and reformer included the founding of schools for young ladies at Hartford (1824) and Cincinnati, and main responsibility for the founding of women's colleges in Iowa, Illinois, and Wisconsin. Her writings include *An Essay on Slavery and Abolitionism* (1837); *The Evils Suffered by American Women and . . . Children* (1846); *Women Suffrage* (1871), on a movement she opposed; and *Educational Reminiscences and Suggestions* (1874).

BEECHER, HENRY WARD (1813–87), son of Lyman Beecher and brother of Catharine Beecher and Harriet Beecher Stowe, was a celebrated Congregational minister, moral crusader, and lecturer. At his Plymouth (Congregational) Church in Brooklyn, he became the outstanding pulpit orator of his day, being immensely popular for his sentimental and high-flown rhetoric in sermons on political, social, and religious subjects. He was an ardent champion of antislavery and during the Civil War delivered a popular series of lectures in England on behalf of the Union cause. His sermons were published in many volumes, and his other books include *Norwood; or, Village Life in New England* (1867), a sentimental novel; *The Life of Jesus, the Christ* (1871); *Yale Lectures on Preaching* (1872–74); and *Evolution and Religion* (1885). His reputation was seriously injured by the suit (1874) of Theodore Tilton, who accused Beecher of adultery with Mrs. Tilton. Although the jury disagreed, the scandal turned Beecher from a respected to a notorious figure for some years.

BEECHER, LYMAN (1775–1863), born in New Haven, after graduation from Yale (1797) became a Presbyterian minister on Long Island, at Litchfield, Conn., and at Boston, noted for his fiery and vigorous denunciation of liquor and his strongly anti-Catholic sermons. In 1832 he went to Cincinnati to become the first president of Lane Theological Seminary. There he was the defendant in a noted heresy trial, in which he was acquitted, although he resigned in 1850. His sermons and magazine articles were published in his *Works* (1852), and an *Autobiography* appeared in 1864–65. His children included Catharine Beecher, Henry Ward Beecher, and Harriet Beecher Stowe.

Before Adam, novel by Jack London, ♦ published in 1906.

Beggar on Horseback, satirical play by George S. Kaufman ♦ and Marc Connelly ♦ with music by Deems Taylor. Produced and published in 1924, it was suggested by a German play, Paul Apel's *Hans Sonnenstössers Höllenfahrt.*

Neil McRae, a penniless composer, is maneuvered by his friend Dr. Albert Rice and by the rich but vulgar Cady family into a proposal of marriage to Gladys Cady, although he really loves Cynthia Mason. On the verge of a breakdown from overwork, he is given a sedative by the doctor and dreams of his life with the Cady family as contrasted with that he might have with Cynthia. This dream is enacted on the stage, in the manner of an expressionist drama: Neil goes to work in his father-in-law's "widget" manufacturing business; surrounded by an atmosphere of vulgarity, he finds creative work impossible; and suddenly he murders the entire family. Brought to trial in a comic-opera court, of which Mr. Cady is judge, Neil defends his action by producing his pantomime *A Kiss in Xanadu*, but the jury sentences him to hard labor in the Cady Consolidated Art Factory, where he is forced to produce worthless songs. Awakened from his dream, Neil is accepted by Cynthia after Gladys, realizing their incompatibility, releases him.

BEHRMAN, S[AMUEL] N[ATHANIEL] (1893–1973), graduated from Harvard (1916), where he studied in the 47 Workshop, did graduate work at Columbia under Brander Matthews and St. John Ervine, and contributed to newspapers and magazines, winning his first success as a playwright with a comedy of manners, *The Second Man* (1927). Later plays, mainly in the same genre, include *Serena Blandish* (1929), adapted from a novel published anonymously but attributed to Enid Bagnold, about a naïve Mayfair society girl; *Meteor* (1929); *Brief Moment* (1931), about marital difficulties of a young patrician and a nightclub singer; *Biography* (1932), about a portrait painter and the celebrities she attracts; *Rain from Heaven* (1934); *End of Summer* (1936); *Amphitryon 38* (1937), adapting Jean Giraudoux's version of a Greek legend; *No Time for Comedy* (1939), about a playwright tempted by a lover to serious writing who returns to his wife and witty comedies; *The Talley Method* (1941), a surgeon's education in humanity; *The Pirate* (1942); *Jacobowsky and the Colonel* (1944), with Franz Werfel; *Dunnigan's Daughter* (1945); *Fanny* (1954), with Joshua Logan; *Lord Pengo* (1962); and *But for Whom Charlie* (1964). He also wrote motion-picture scripts; a life of the art dealer Duveen (1952); *The Worcester Account* (1954), stories about his youth which he dramatized as *The Cold Wind and the Warm* (1958); *Portrait of Max* (1960), an intimate memoir of Max Beerbohm; *The Suspended Drawing Room* (1965), presenting profiles; *The Burning Glass* (1968), a novel about a young playwright; and *People in a Diary* (1972), a memoir.

BEIN, ALBERT (1902–), proletarian author, whose plays include *Little Ol' Boy* (1933); *Let Freedom Ring* (1935), adapted from Grace Lumpkin's novel *To Make My Bread;* and *Heavenly Express* (1940), based on firsthand knowledge of hobo life, depicting the afterlife imagined by railroad tramps. His novels are *Road Out of Hell* (1929), from which his first play was adapted; *Love in Chicago* (1929), written under the pseudonym Charles Walt; and *Youth in Hell* (1930), a semi-autobiographical novel about a reform school.

Being There, novel by Jerzy Kosinski, published in 1971.

A man named Chance, adopted by the Old Man when a boy, remains illiterate and a complete innocent as an adult, having spent all his life tending a walled-off garden or watching television in his isolated room. When Chance is made homeless by the death of the Old Man he encounters a new protector, Mrs. Benjamin Rand, who, misunderstanding his name and occupation, calls him Chauncy Gardener. She takes him to the Rand mansion, where he meets the President of the U.S., who interprets Chance's comments on gardening as brilliant metaphors on finance. As a result Chance is catapulted to international prominence, which he accepts with calm detachment.

BELASCO, DAVID (1853–1931), born in San Francisco, where he first achieved recognition as actor, playwright, and producer, was intermittently associated with the New York stage during his youth, and after 1882 was constantly identified with it. He was famous not only for his plays, but also for his managership, discovery, and development of such actors as David Warfield and Mrs. Leslie Carter, his realistic stage settings, and his ability to obtain novel effects with newly invented electric lights. Many of his plays were written with collaborators: *Hearts of Oak* (1879), adapted from an English melodrama, with James A. Herne; *Lord Chumley* (1888), a domestic drama, with Henry C. De Mille; *The Girl I Left Behind Me* (1893), with Franklin Fyles; *The Return of Peter Grimm* (1911), with Cecil B. De Mille; *Madame Butterfly* ♦ (1900), *Adrea* (1904), and *The Darling of the Gods* (1902), with John L. Long; and many other plays with these and other writers. Belasco's own plays include *The Heart of Maryland* (1895), a Civil War drama; *Zaza* (1898), adapted from the French; *DuBarry* (1901); and *The Girl of the*

Golden West♦ (1905). Six of his plays were collected and edited by M.J. Moses (1928).

Belfry of Bruges, The, and Other Poems, volume of poems by Longfellow, ♦ published in 1845, which contains "The Arsenal at Springfield," "The Bridge," and "The Arrow and the Song."♦ "The Belfry of Bruges," in rhymed couplets of eight-stress lines, recalling the ancient glories of the Belgian city, is prefaced by a "Carillon" in four-stress lines, describing the chimes as the poet heard them during a restless night.

BELITT, BEN (1911–), poet born in New York, after receiving an A.B. and M.A. from the University of Virginia became a professor of English at Bennington. His poems have been published in *The Five-Fold Mesh* (1938), *Wilderness Stair* (1955), *The Enemy Joy* (1964), *Nowhere But Light* (1970), and *The Double Witness* (1977). He wrote *Adam's Dream* (1977), about translation, and has translated poems of Rimbaud, Lorca, and Neruda.

BELKNAP, JEREMY (1744–98), Congregational clergyman and historian, was the author of a *History of New Hampshire* (3 vols., 1784, 1791, 1792), noted for its research, impartiality, and literary merit. His humorous allegory *The Foresters* (1792) narrates the founding and growth of British colonies in America, and his *American Biography* (2 vols., 1794–98) is the prototype of many later works.

Bell for Adano, A, novel by John Hersey♦ (1944, Pulitzer Prize), dramatized (1944) by Paul Osborn.

Bell Jar, The, novel by Sylvia Plath, ♦ published (1963) under the pseudonym Victoria Lucas, and under her own name in 1966. The story is based on the author's own experiences.

Esther Greenwood, a 19-year-old Smith College student, during a summer internship working for a fashion magazine in New York undergoes a series of experiences that leave her unable to cope with competition, professional and personal, and cause her to attempt suicide. Assisted to a private institution by Philomena Guinea, the woman who had provided her college scholarship, she recovers, makes peace with a high-school boyfriend, is liberated by a sexual experience, and returns recovered to college.

BELLAMY, EDWARD (1850–98), born in Massachusetts, had a public school education, toured Europe in 1868, returned to study law, but, though admitted to the Massachusetts bar, never practiced. He entered journalism, edited the Springfield *Union,* and in 1880 founded the Springfield *Daily News.* He had already begun writing fiction, publishing *The Duke of Stockbridge* as a serial in 1879. This novel, completed after his death by a cousin and published in 1900, was a sort of proletarian romance dealing with Shays's Rebellion. Other novels included *Six to One: A Nantucket Idyl* (1878), the result of a voyage to Hawaii; and *Dr. Heidenhoff's Process* (1880) and *Miss Ludington's Sister* (1884), romances showing his interest in psychic phenomena. These were overshadowed by the immensely popular *Looking Backward: 2000–1887*♦ (1888), a Utopian romance predicting a new social and economic order, which led to the founding of a Nationalist party that advocated its principles. To aid this cause and further his social theories, he founded the *New Nation* (1891), lectured widely, and wrote *Equality* (1897), a sequel to *Looking Backward* but much more of a theoretical tract. Bellamy's only other writings were *The Blindman's World and Other Stories* (1898) and *The Religion of Solidarity* (a fragment, published 1940). His early death from tuberculosis ended a career of social reform in which he set forth a theory of state capitalism that has greatly affected U.S. economic thinking and the proletarian movement.

BELLOW, SAUL (1915–), born in Canada of parents recently emigrated from Russia, was reared in Chicago and educated at the University of Chicago and at Northwestern (B.S., 1937). He has taught at Minnesota, Princeton, New York University, and elsewhere, but his career is that of a writer. His first two novels, presenting a Kafka-like atmosphere, are *Dangling Man*♦ (1944), a psychological study of a man waiting to be inducted into the army and living in limbo between civilian and military life, and *The Victim* (1947), about the agonizing, equivocal relations of Jew and Gentile. His next novel, *The Adventures of Augie March*♦ (1953), which won a National Book Award, is naturalistic in treating the picaresque adventures of a young Chicago Jew. *Seize the Day* (1956) includes a novella, stories, and a one-act play. *Henderson the Rain King*♦ (1959) opens with a realistic depiction of an intense middle-age Connecticut millionaire whose inner urge for fulfillment of self—"I want, I want"—drives him to primitive Africa, where in a symbolic tragi-comedy he encounters fantastic experiences. *Herzog* ♦ (1964) is an intense revelation of the life and experiences of a middle-aged Jewish intellectual, presenting his involvements with two wives and other women, with his children, with a friend who betrays him, and with his careers of teaching and writing. He is led through neurosis almost to suicide and emerges "pretty well satisfied to be, to be just as it is willed." *Mr. Sammler's Planet* (1969) is a fictive critique of modern society as seen by a survivor of a Nazi concentration camp resident in New York. *Humboldt's Gift* ♦ (1975, Pulitzer Prize) depicts a crisis in the life of the narrator that is resolved by his friend, the poet Humboldt. Bellow did not publish another novel until *The Dean's December,* ♦ issued seven years later, whose protagonist is in part an autobiographical figure. *Mosby's Memoirs* (1968) and *Him with His Foot in His Mouth* (1984) collect stories, *The Last Analysis* (1964) is a comic play, and *To Jerusalem and Back* (1976) deals with his visit to Israel. In 1976 he was awarded a Nobel Prize.

Bells, The, poem by Poe, ♦ published in 1849. The four irregular stanzas, of varied meter, depict onomatopoetically, by means of reiterated alliteration, assonance, and phonetic imitation, four ways in which the sounds of bells influence moods: the merry tinkle of sleigh bells; the mellow, golden notes of wedding bells; the terrible shriek of alarm bells; and the solemn, melancholy roll of funeral bells. Poe's first version of this *tour de force* of "tintinnabulation" consisted of only 18 lines, suggested by his friend Mrs. M.L. Shew, but in its complete form the poem contains 113 lines. Its origin has been traced to a passage in Chateaubriand's *Le Génie du christianisme.*

Ben Bolt, popular ballad by T.D. English, ♦ first published in the *New-York Mirror* (1843).

Benbow family, characters in Faulkner's fiction, figure prominently in *Sartoris* ♦ and *Sanctuary.* ♦ In the former novel, Horace ("Horry") Benbow and his sister Narcissa ("Narcy") Benbow are introduced as members of an old but less extensive and less important family than the Sartoris clan, to which they are related. Horace comes home to Jefferson in 1919 from World War I, a

lawyer by training and a lonely man, seeking tranquillity in art and poetry. Partly to escape his possessive sister he drifts into an affair with the coarse Belle Mitchell, whom he marries when she gets a divorce. Narcissa marries young Bayard Sartoris, also recently returned from the war and himself disoriented, but her resentment of his indrawn desperation and her exasperation at the recklessness of Sartoris men become an expression of deep-seated resentment of men generally. Bayard abandons her and on the day of his death in a plane crash in 1920 she gives birth to a son, naming him Benbow Sartoris, as if to fend off the destructiveness she associates with the Sartoris family name. In *Sanctuary* Horace becomes aware of Belle's shallow nature, leaves her, and gets enmeshed with bootleggers, idealistically defending one against a false murder charge. The widowed Narcissa, concerned for her social position, wants Horace to return to Belle, and contrives to thwart his handling of the case so that he loses it. The Benbows disappear from direct involvement in Faulkner's work after *Sanctuary,* although they are mentioned in *Absalom, Absalom!* and *The Unvanquished.*

BENCHLEY, ROBERT [CHARLES] (1889–1945), drama critic, humorist, and actor, after graduating from Harvard (1912) wrote for New York newspapers and magazines, and was theater critic of *Life* (1920–29) and *The New Yorker* (1929–40). His sketches of the tribulations of the average man are collected in *Of All Things* (1921), *Love Conquers All* (1922), *Pluck and Luck* (1925), *The Early Worm* (1927), *20,000 Leagues Under the Sea; or, David Copperfield* (1928), *The Treasurer's Report* (1930), *No Poems* (1932), *From Bed to Worse* (1934), *My Ten Years in a Quandary* (1936), *After 1903— What?* (1938), *Inside Benchley* (1942), and *Benchley Beside Himself* (1943). He also played in motion pictures and on the radio.

BENÉT, STEPHEN VINCENT (1898–1943), brother of W.R. Benét, was born in Pennsylvania, and graduated from Yale (1919). As an undergraduate he wrote two books of poetry, *Five Men and Pompey* (1915), dramatic monologues, and *Young Adventure* (1918); shortly after graduation he wrote his first novel, *The Beginning of Wisdom* (1921), a college story in the vein of F. Scott Fitzgerald. He reached his full poetic power with *John Brown's Body* ♦ (1928, Pulitzer Prize), a long narrative poem of the Civil

War. His *Ballads and Poems, 1915–30* were collected in 1931. *Western Star* (1943, Pulitzer Prize), a section of a projected epic poem on the westward migration, depicts the settling of Jamestown and Plymouth. He wrote librettos for two one-act folk operas, *The Headless Horseman* (1937) and *The Devil and Daniel Webster♦* (1939), with music by Douglas Moore, and other poems, stories and novels.

BENÉT, WILLIAM ROSE (1886–1950), New York poet and critic, who wrote exuberant, romantic verse, ranging from Oriental fantasy to cowboy balladry. *Rip Tide* (1932) and *The Dust Which Is God* (1941, Pulitzer Prize) were verse novels, the latter autobiographical. He was wed to Elinor Wylie,♦ whose works he collected, and he was a brother of S.V. Benét.

Ben-Hur: *A Tale of the Christ,* novel by Lew Wallace,♦ published in 1880 and dramatized by William Young in 1899.

Benito Cereno, story by Melville,♦ published in *The Piazza Tales* (1856). Its source is a chapter in Amasa Delano's *Voyages and Travels* (1817). Robert Lowell adapted Melville's story in a one-act verse play of the same title in *The Old Glory* (1965).

In 1799 Captain Delano puts in for water at an uninhabited island off Chile, where he encounters a Spanish merchantman in ruinous condition, commanded by Benito Cereno, a sensitive young Spaniard now gravely ill and enabled to pursue his duties only with the solicitous care of his black servant Babo. Cereno tells the American that he sailed from Buenos Aires for Lima, with a crew of 50 and a cargo including 300 Negroes owned by Alexandro Aranda. Off Cape Horn, he says, many of the crew were lost in a storm, and disease destroyed most of the other whites and blacks. Delano offers aid, but is uneasy at the insubordination of the slaves and the careless seamanship and seeming ingratitude of Cereno. He is about to return to his ship when Cereno jumps into his boat, precipitating an attack by the Negroes from which they barely escape. Cereno explains that the blacks had mutinied, led by Babo, and wanted to be carried to Africa. Delano seizes the slave ship, and takes it with his own to Lima, where Babo is executed. Cereno enters a monastery, but soon dies.

BENJAMIN, PARK (1809–64), editor and publisher, is best known for his *New World* (1839–45), a literary journal that reprinted British works without remunerating their authors.

BENNETT, JAMES GORDON, see *New York Herald.*

Berenice, tale by Poe,♦ published in the *Southern Literary Messenger* (1835) and reprinted in *Tales of the Grotesque and Arabesque* (1840).

Egaeus, gloomy and unhealthy, grows up with his cousin Berenice, who is "agile . . . overflowing with energy" until she contracts a form of epilepsy that causes frequent trances. The youth's mind becomes diseased, and although he never loved Berenice while she was normal, he now madly proposes marriage. As the wedding approaches, he sees her as she is, pale and shrunken, but her white teeth fascinate him, and he feels insanely certain that to possess them would cure his own malady. When she is stricken with epilepsy and entombed as dead, Egaeus, unconscious of what he does, draws her teeth. He returns to the library, and there a servant makes him aware of what he has done, telling him that Berenice has not been dead but in a trance.

BERGER, THOMAS [LOUIS] (1924–　), Cincinnati-born author, long resident in New York, whose works include *Crazy in Berlin* (1958), the beginning of a comic saga about Carlo Reinhart, a happy GI in occupied Germany at the end of World War II, whose fantastic picaresque tale is continued in *Reinhart in Love* (1961), with the anti-hero back in his conformist Midwest home, and concluded in *Vital Parts* (1970), in which Reinhart's curiously old-fashioned style appeals to the salesman Bob Sweet, who wants to preserve him through cryonics. *Little Big Man* (1964) is a fanciful parody of the Old West myth presented through the life of the ancient frontiersman Jack Crabb, kidnapped by Indians from an emigrant wagon and eventually a participant in Custer's last stand. *Killing Time* (1967) presents through the tale of a mass murderer many questions about sanity and madness, crime and legality. *Regiment of Women* (1973) fictively treats the dominance of women in the 22nd-century U.S. *Sneaky People* (1975) comically depicts the diverse involvements and deceptions of a Midwestern family in the 1930s. *Who Is Teddy Villanova?* (1977) is a parody of the detective novel; *Arthur Rex* (1978) is a satiric and parodic retelling of Arthurian legendry; *Neighbors* (1980) is a fantastic account of violent relations, real and imagined, between neighboring families; and *Feud* (1984) is a fantastic view of life and sudden death in middle American towns of the 1930s. *Reinhart's Women* (1981) is another novel about his unheroic protagonist, now in his fifties.

BERKELEY, GEORGE (1685–1753), Irish-born bishop of the Church of England, is famous as an idealistic philosopher. By 1723 he had conceived the project of founding a college in Bermuda and wrote a poem to favor the cause, with the prophetic opening line "Westward the course of Empire takes its way." While waiting to obtain funds for this project, he came to America (1729) and settled at Rhode Island for nearly three years. There he formed a Literary and Philosophical Society, and wrote *Alciphron* (1732), a series of Platonic dialogues opposing deism and finding proof of God's existence in Berkeley's own theory of vision. William Byrd and others pointed out the defects of the Bermuda plan, which failed completely, although King's College (now Columbia) was largely based on Berkeley's model. Berkeley Divinity School at New Haven is named in his honor, as is the city of Berkeley, the site of the original University of California campus.

BERRIGAN, TED (EDMUND J.M. BERRIGAN, JR.) (1934–82), poet whose experimental works, very diverse in style but often parodic, include *A Lily for My Love* (1959), *The Sonnets* (1964), *In the Early Morning Rain* (1971), and *Red Wagon* (1976). *Galileo; or Finksville* (1964) is a play, and *Bean Spasms* (1967) is a medley of poems and prose pieces written with Ron Padgett. Berrigan's poems, old and new, are collected in *So Going Around Cities* (1980).

BERRY, DON (1932–   ), Minnesota-born novelist, long resident in Oregon, the setting of *Trask* (1960), depicting Indian and white relations in the mid-19th century; *Moontrap* (1962), dealing with mountain men; and *To Build a Ship* (1963), the last volume of this loosely related trilogy. *A Majority of Scoundrels* (1961) is an informal history of the Rocky Mountain Fur Company.

BERRY, WENDELL (1934–   ), Kentucky-born author and professor at his alma mater, the state university. His poems, redolent of the region and its people, are collected in *The Broken Ground* (1964), *Openings* (1968), *Findings* (1969), *Farming: A Handbook*

(1970), *The Country of Marriage* (1973), *Clearing* (1977), and *The Wheel* (1983). His novels, also set in his native state, are *Nathan Coulter* (1960), about a boy growing up in the tobacco-farming land; *A Place on Earth* (1967; revised, 1983), about a Kentuckian at home whose only son is missing in action during World War II but who returns home; *The Memory of Old Jack* (1974), in which a 92-year-old farmer recalls the ways of life of his earlier days. He has also written essays collected in *The Long-Legged House* (1969), *The Unforeseen Wilderness* (1971), *A Continuous Harmony* (1972), *The Unsettling of America: Culture and Agriculture* (1977), and *Standing by Words* (1983). *The Hidden Wound* (1970) contains recollections of childhood and the effect of racism on him. *A Part* (1980) contains translations and poems.

BERRYMAN, JOHN (1914–72), born in Oklahoma, educated in the U.S. and England, a professor of humanities at the University of Minnesota, wrote a study of *Stephen Crane* (1950) for the American Men of Letters Series, but is best known for his poetry. His early works are *Poems* (1942); *The Dispossessed* (1948); *Homage to Mistress Bradstreet* (1956), a biographical ode, richly allusive, moving and relevant to the present day in its inquiry into the personal and spiritual life of the colonial poet Anne Bradstreet♦; and *His Thought Made Pockets and the Plane Buckt* (1958). In 1964 he published *77 Dream Songs* (Pulitzer Prize), the opening of a series of 18-line poems that reached to 385 in all, presenting his own persona of Henry, who lives through personal and social crises and survives. It is a work complex in themes, celebrating a kind of negative courage with ironic humor, and employing diction and syntax that are very American and often derive from the stereotyped minstrel-show Negro. The poem is completed in *His Toy, His Dream, His Rest* (1968) and *The Dream Songs* (1969). Prior to the collection of the entirety of this major work, *Berryman's Sonnets* (1967) published 115 Petrarchan sonnets telling of a summer love affair, *Short Poems* (1967) gathered lyrics, and *Love and Fame* (1970) brought together autobiographical poems showing Berryman returning to his parents' faith of Catholicism. Despite this turn to religion, Berryman took his own life. *Delusions, etc.* (1972) posthumously gathers late poems, and *Henry's Fate* (1977) prints unpublished parts of the *Dream Songs* and other fragments. *The Freedom of the Poet* (1976) collects stories and essays, and *Recov-*

ery (1973) is an incomplete autobiographical novel about an intellectual man's addiction to alcohol.

Best sellers, term for books that are remarkably popular, for a brief time or over a period of many years. Seldom of great literary significance, such works are often ephemeral and dependent upon temporary tastes and interests. Nevertheless, the best-selling book in the U.S., as in other Christian lands, has been the Bible. Publications of special sects, like the *Book of Mormon* and *Science and Health,* have also been widely circulated. Best sellers of colonial times included the *New England Primer* and *The Day of Doom,* followed later by political tracts like *Common Sense,* by chapbooks like Weems's life of Washington, and by almanacs. In the mid-19th century gift books had huge sales, as did dime novels♦ and children's literature.♦ Widely read poems included *Hiawatha, Nothing To Wear,* and "Plain Language from Truthful James," and later poets with great followings included Ella Wheeler Wilcox, James Whitcomb Riley, Robert Service, and Edgar Guest. Texts that have been popular include the *Spelling Book* and dictionary of Noah Webster, the school primers of Caleb Bingham, the *Eclectic Readers* of William H. McGuffey, and cookbooks.

The novel has been the most popular literary genre in the U.S., and widely read works include *Charlotte Temple* (1794), *The Spy* (1821), *Uncle Tom's Cabin* (1852), *The Lamplighter* (1854), *St. Elmo* (1867), *The Gates Ajar* (1868), *Barriers Burned Away* (1872), *Tom Sawyer* (1876), *Ben-Hur* (1880), *Looking Backward* (1888), *In His Steps* (1896), *Hugh Wynne* (1897), *When Knighthood Was in Flower* (1898), *David Harum* (1898), *Richard Carvel* (1899), *The Call of the Wild* (1903), *The Little Shepherd of Kingdom Come* (1903), *The Clansman* (1905), *The Winning of Barbara Worth* (1911), *Riders of the Purple Sage* (1912), *Dere Mable!* (1918), *The Covered Wagon* (1922), *Gentlemen Prefer Blondes* (1925), *Anthony Adverse* (1933), *Gone with the Wind* (1936), *The Robe* (1942), *The Naked and the Dead* (1948), *From Here to Eternity* (1951), *The Caine Mutiny* (1951), *Lolita* (1958), *The Group* (1963), and *War and Remembrance* (1978). The first American novel to sell over 1,000,000 copies was *Uncle Tom's Cabin. In His Steps* has been the most popular work with a religious theme, and *Gone with the Wind* has been fastest selling.

Very popular types of fiction, although not always represented by single books, are detective stories♦; novels of Western adventure by such authors as Harold Bell Wright, Zane Grey, Max Brand, and Louis L'Amour; science fiction, like that of Isaac Asimov and Ray Bradbury; and novels by women, ranging from the moral and sentimental, like those of Kathleen Norris and Frances Parkinson Keyes, to the toughly realistic and frankly sexual, like the works of Jacqueline Susann and Erica Jong. In recent years authors whose works almost consistently appear on bestseller lists have included O'Hara, Steinbeck, Michener, Irving Stone, Uris, Vidal, and Wouk. Popularity on first publication in hardbound editions is usually repeated in paperback reprints, but some authors, like Erskine Caldwell, find their large public only in reprints, as do works of certain desirable genres, such as the lushly romantic pseudo-historic novels called Gothic romances. Selection by major book clubs usually assists bookstore sales and popularity of reprints. Popular plays may be considered in the category of best sellers, even if they do not always sell very well when put into print. The greatest stage successes in the U.S. have included *The Drunkard, A Trip to Chinatown, The Old Homestead, Our American Cousin, Under the Gaslight, East Lynne, Rip Van Winkle, Sherlock Holmes, The Squaw Man, Lightnin', Abie's Irish Rose, The Green Pastures, Tobacco Road, Life with Father, Oklahoma!, My Fair Lady, Hello, Dolly!, Guys and Dolls,* and *A Chorus Line.*

BEVERLEY, ROBERT (*c.*1673–1722), Virginia planter and minor statesman, wrote *The History and Present State of Virginia* (1705, enlarged 1722) to replace the work of John Oldmixon and other English historians whom he regarded as superficial.

Beyond the Horizon, play by Eugene O'Neill,♦ produced and published in 1920, when it won a Pulitzer Prize.

Robert Mayo, of poetic nature, dislikes work on his father's farm, and plans to seek adventure as a seaman. His brother Andrew, better adapted to farm life, has been his rival for the love of Ruth Atkins, but when she reveals that she loves Robert, Andrew goes to sea instead. In the next three years Ruth's passion fades, and Robert fails as a farmer. Persecuted by the complaints of his wife and his mother, he is consoled only by his daughter and his books, while Ruth hopes that Andrew still loves her and will return. Andrew, home for a day, shows that travel has made him hard and commonplace, and he reveals to Ruth that his love for her soon passed. Disillusioned and poverty-stricken, the family passes another five years on the farm. Robert's daughter dies, his wife is apathetic, and Andrew returns only when Robert is dying of consumption. Escaping from his bed, he watches the sunrise from a hill: "It isn't the end. It's a free beginning . . . beyond the horizon!"

Bible in Colonial America, originally brought from England and Europe in various versions, was first partially translated and published in the English colonies with the issuance of the Bay Psalm Book♦ (1640). The first publication of the complete Bible was the translation of John Eliot♦ into the language of the Massachuset Indians (New Testament, 1661; Old Testament, 1663). The British monopolistically refused to let an English-language Bible be printed in the colonies and so none was issued until after the Revolution, when Robert Aitken of Philadelphia printed the New Testament in 1777 and the complete Bible in 1782.

Bibliography of American Literature, compiled by Jacob Blanck and sponsored by the Bibliographical Society of America, is planned to provide a detailed physical description of all first editions (books, pamphlets, broadsides, etc.) by some 300 authors who lived between the Federal period and 1930, with emphasis on writers of belles lettres. Seven volumes of the eight projected appeared between 1955 and 1983.

BIERCE, AMBROSE [GWINETT] (1842–1914?), born in Ohio, served in the Civil War and became a brilliant and bitter journalist in San Francisco. In England (1872–75) he was on the staff of *Fun,* contributed to *Tom Hood's Comic Annual,* edited two issues of *The Lantern* for the exiled Empress Eugenie, and published under the pseudonym Dod Grile three collections of his vitriolic sketches and witticisms, *The Fiend's Delight* (1873), *Nuggets and Dust Panned Out in California* (1873), and *Cobwebs from an Empty Skull* (1874). Returning to San Francisco, he wrote for Hearst's *Examiner,* and his wit and satire made him the literary dictator of the Pacific coast, strongly influencing many writers, including his friend George Sterling. Many of his works were potboilers, but in 1891 he issued *Tales of Soldiers and Civilians,* ♦ stories reminiscent of Poe's tales of horror and marked by an ingenious use of the surprise

ending, a sardonic humor, and a realistic study of tense emotional states. This was followed by *The Monk and the Hangman's Daughter* (1892), a medieval romance translated with a collaborator from the German of Richard Voss, and *Black Beetles in Amber* (1892), witty satirical verses. Later poems are collected in *Shapes of Clay* (1903). *Can Such Things Be?♦* (1893) is a second volume of tales, also dealing with episodes of the Civil War and the California frontier, with the supernaturalism, horror, and sardonic humor of the earlier volume. In 1897 Bierce went to Washington as correspondent for the Hearst newspapers, and there he collected his *Fantastic Fables* (1899), Aesop-like tales about contemporary economics and politics, whose temper is also observable in *The Cynic's Word Book* (1906), which he retitled *The Devil's Dictionary♦* (1911), a volume of ironic definitions. *The Shadow on the Dial* (1909) is a series of disillusioned essays on contemporary civilization. For several years Bierce was occupied with editing his *Collected Works* (1909–12), 12 volumes of his better prose and verse, interlarded with journalism. Tired of American civilization, in 1913 he disappeared into war-torn Mexico, to seek "the good, kind darkness." Although weird stories have been told concerning his fate, it is probable that in Mexico he found the euthanasia he desired.

A brief book, *Write It Right* (1909), "a blacklist of literary faults," was not included in his *Works.* Posthumously collected books include *The Letters of Ambrose Bierce* (1922), *Ambrose Bierce's Civil War* (1956), and *The Enlarged Devil's Dictionary* (1967).

Big Money, The, novel by Dos Passos,♦ published in 1936. It is the last of the trilogy *U.S.A.* (collected 1938), following *The 42nd Parallel♦* (1930) and *1919♦* (1932). Interspersed in the narrative are brief biographies of Frederick Taylor, Ford, Veblen, Isadora Duncan, the Wright brothers, Valentino, Frank Lloyd Wright, Hearst, and Samuel Insull.

The war hero Charley Anderson returns to New York, is disillusioned in his aim to produce good airplanes regardless of profits, takes to drink and stock market gambling, marries an heiress, has an affair with Margo Dowling, is divorced, enters into a real estate fraud, and is killed in an auto accident.

Margo becomes a New York chorus girl after a sad and seamy youth and desertion by her husband. After her affair with Charley she uses the last of his money to get work in Hollywood movies but later sinks into obscurity.

Mary French, onetime Vassar student and an idealistic labor reporter, is discouraged by the arrest of her lover, Ben Compton, a Communist, and by the outcome of the Sacco-Vanzetti case but continues to work for labor causes.

Richard Ellsworth Savage is alone able to cope with the era, accepting its standards and opportunistically serving the "public relations" firm of J.W. Moorehouse, whose successor he promises to become.

The final character is a "vag," hitchhiking across the continent, who thinks of the comfort of the passengers in a plane overhead, and of his youthful beliefs: "went to school, books said opportunity, ads promised speed, own your own home, shine bigger than your neighbor. . . ."

Big Sky, The, novel by A.B. Guthrie,♦ published in 1947. *Fair Land, Fair Land* (1982) is a sequel carrying Dick Summers to the age of 70 in a changed West.

Big Sur and the Oranges of Hieronymus Bosch, personal narrative by Henry Miller,♦ published in 1957.

BIGGERS, Earl Derr (1884–1933), born in Ohio, educated at Harvard, became a journalist in Boston and later won fame as a popular novelist and playwright. He is best known for his *Seven Keys to Baldpate* (1913), a melodramatic story set in a lonely mountain inn, and a series of detective novels whose hero is the enigmatic Chinese sleuth Charlie Chan. Among these are *The Chinese Parrot* (1926), *Behind That Curtain* (1928), and *The Black Camel* (1929).

Biglow Papers, The, two series of satirical verses in Yankee dialect by Lowell,♦ the first written in opposition to the Mexican War and the second in support of the North during the Civil War. The first of the verses appeared in *The Boston Courier* (1846), and the first series was published in book form in 1848, while the second appeared in the *Atlantic Monthly* during the Civil War and was collected in 1867. Both are purportedly written by the young New England farmer Hosea Biglow, and edited with a complicated pseudo-critical apparatus by Homer Wilbur, "Pastor of the First Church in Jaalam."

Of the nine "letters" in the first series, three represent versified epistles from Hosea's friend Birdofredom Sawin, "Private in the Massachusetts Regiment," who swallows the propaganda of "manifest destiny" but comes to disappointment and disillusion. ("Nimepunce a day fer killin' folks comes kind o' low fer murder.") The remaining six are Hosea's satirical portrait of a recruiting sergeant; his satire of a hypocritical politician, "What Mr. Robinson Thinks"; his parody of an address by a State Street stump speaker; "The Debate in the Sennit," burlesquing a speech by Calhoun; the pusillanimous "Pious Editor's Creed"; and the declaration of principles by a supposed presidential candidate, which leaves him uncommitted, "frontin' South by North."

The second series, with a critical introduction over Lowell's signature, includes "The Courtin'," a humorous narrative in dialect verse, and 11 satirical "letters," including two from Birdofredom Sawin, now resident in the South and gulled by Confederate propaganda; "Mason and Slidell: A Yankee Idyll"; malicious burlesque speeches by Jefferson Davis and a hypocritical man of wealth, "Honourable Preserved Doe"; an appeal to sentiment, "Sunthin' in the Pastoral Line"; a demand that the Confederate "system" be crushed ("Conciliate? it jest means *be kicked*"); "Kettleopotomachia," macaronic Latin verses by Parson Wilbur; an idyllic depiction of the approaching peace; and a view of Reconstruction, "Mr. Hosea Biglow's Speech in March Meeting."

Bill Arp, pseudonym of Charles H. Smith.♦

BILLINGS, Josh, pseudonym of H.W. Shaw.♦

Billy Budd, novelette by Melville,♦ was written during the five years before his death and published in 1924. The much revised manuscript, left without definitive form, was reissued in a very careful edition in 1962. A dramatization was made by Louis O. Coxe and Robert H. Chapman as *Uniform of Flesh* (1949), revised as *Billy Budd* (1951).

Billy Budd is the typical Handsome Sailor of 18th-century balladry, and because of his innocence and beauty is hated by Claggart, a dark, demon-haunted petty officer. In his simplicity, Billy cannot understand why Claggart should hate him, why evil should desire to destroy good. Claggart concocts a fantastic story of mutiny, supposedly plotted by Billy, whom he accuses to the captain. Billy, unable to speak, in his only act of rebellion strikes Claggart a fatal blow. Captain Vere, who sympathizes with Billy and recognizes his essential innocence, is nevertheless forced to condemn him, and though Billy is hanged he lives on as a legend among sailors.

Billy the Kid, sobriquet of William H. Bonney (1859–81), desperado of the Southwest, who was a leader in the Lincoln County cattle war in New Mexico. His subsequent career of wholesale cattle stealing brought his score of murders to 21 before he was finally killed by a sheriff. The Kid is the subject of many stories and ballads, and he has been apotheosized in dime novels and serious fiction.

Birches, blank-verse lyric by Robert Frost,♦ published in *Mountain Interval* (1916). The poet describes his boyhood pleasure in climbing birch trees, swinging from the tops until the supple trunks bent in a curve to the ground. He dreams of being again "a swinger of birches," and finds in this occupation a symbol for his desired surcease from "considerations," in which he might

> go by climbing a birch tree . . .
> *Toward* heaven, till the tree could bear no
>   more,
> But dipped its top and set me down again.
> That would be good both going and coming
>   back.

BIRD, ROBERT MONTGOMERY (1806–54), born in Delaware, became a physician in Pennsylvania but is remembered as a novelist and dramatist. His early comedy of Philadelphia life, *The City Looking Glass* (1828, published 1933), was followed by his most popular play, *The Gladiator* (1831, published 1919), a blank-verse tragedy about the revolt of Spartacus, a Thracian, against his Roman captors. Edwin Forrest, who acted in it over 1000 times, in 1832 produced *Oralloossa*, a tragedy concerned with the assassination of Pizarro, which he followed with Bird's best play, *The Broker of Bogotá* (1834, published 1917), a domestic tragedy set in Colombia. Bird revised John Augustus Stone's *Metamora* (1836), a romantic tragedy depicting King Philip as a noble savage, also a starring vehicle for Forrest, but when the actor broke a financial agreement with him Bird turned to writing fiction. In 1834 he published anonymously *Calavar; or, The Knight of the Conquest,* a tale of the Mexican conquistadors, which was later praised by Prescott. *The Infidel; or, The Fall of Mexico* (1835) is a sequel. *The Hawks of Hawk-Hollow* (1835), a romance of the Revolution, deals with a prominent Pennsylvania family's decline because of disloyalty to the patriot cause. *Sheppard Lee* (1836)

uses a psychological study of metempsychosis to satirize contemporary social conditions, and reflects Bird's Whig sympathies in regard to slavery. His finest novel, *Nick of the Woods; or, The Jibbenainosay* (1837), was an anti-noble savage treatment of Indians in its story of a Quaker who brutally kills the "savages" to avenge their murder of his family. This was followed by *Peter Pilgrim; or, A Rambler's Recollections* (1838), a series of realistic travel sketches, and *The Adventures of Robin Day* (1839), a picaresque novel.

Birthmark, The, allegorical tale by Hawthorne,♦ published in *Mosses from an Old Manse* (1846).

Aylmer, a scientist, marries Georgiana, a beautiful woman whose single physical flaw is a tiny crimson birthmark on her left cheek, resembling a hand. The mark repels Aylmer, who determines to use his scientific knowledge to remove it. Assisted by his rude, earthy servant, Aminadab, he unsuccessfully tries every known method, finally using a powerful potion which, although it causes the birthmark to fade, causes her death also. Aminadab laughs, and the author concludes:

> Thus ever does the gross fatality of earth exult in its invariable triumph over the immortal essence which, in this dim sphere of half-development, demands the completeness of a higher state.

BISHOP, ELIZABETH (1911–79), born in Massachusetts, graduated from Vassar (1934), long resident in Brazil, wrote spare, colloquial poetry published in *North & South* (1946), reprinted with additions as *North & South—A Cold Spring* (1955), for which she received a Pulitzer Prize; *Brazil* (1962); *Questions of Travel* (1965); *Complete Poems* (1969, National Book Award); *Geography III* (1976); and *That Was Then* (1980). The posthumous *Collected Prose* (1984) brings together memoirs (one of Marianne Moore) and stories, some previously unpublished.

BISHOP, JOHN PEALE (1892–1944), West Virginia-born author who lived on Cape Cod, whose poems are collected in *Green Fruit* (1917); *The Undertaker's Garland* (1922), written with Edmund Wilson; *Now with His Love* (1933); and *Minute Particulars* (1936). *Many Thousands Gone* (1931) is a book of stories, and *Act of Darkness* (1935) is a novel. Bishop is said to be the prototype of Tom D'Invilliers in *This Side of Paradise.* His *Collected Essays* and his *Collected Poems* were published in 1948. His correspondence with Allen Tate was printed in 1981.

Black April, novel by Julia Peterkin,♦ published in 1927.

Black Boy, autobiography of Richard Wright,♦ published in 1945.

This story of the author's life to the age of 19, when he went north, incorporates an evocation of the South, rural and urban, as he moved from place to place, living mainly in Jackson, Miss., and Nashville, Tenn., with a succession of relatives after his father abandoned the family and his mother was incapacitated by paralyzing strokes. In addition to summoning up a sense of the sights, sounds, smells, and ways of life in the South, Wright explores the genesis of an artist, an individual who rebels against the beliefs and mores of pietistic relatives and against schoolmasters and schoolmates, finally finding a larger world in his voracious reading of Mencken, Dreiser, Sinclair Lewis, and other authors. The book also vividly presents racial conflict in the South, with its physical, political, social, and spiritual violence against blacks.

Black Cat, The, story by Poe,♦ published in 1843, collected in *Tales* (1845).

A condemned murderer tells of his crime and its discovery. For years he cherished a pet black cat, Pluto, until intemperate drinking led him to destroy one of its eyes during a fit of malevolence. The cat recovered, but its master's perverse mood continued, and he tied it by the neck to a tree. The same night, his home was destroyed by fire, except for a newly plastered wall that bore the image of a cat with a noose about its neck. Now poverty-stricken and degenerate, the man was haunted by this image, but nevertheless brought home a stray one-eyed cat, which had a single white mark on its black breast, resembling a gallows. He came to hate the animal, and one day attempted to kill it with an axe; murdering his wife when she interfered, he placed her body in a cellar recess that he concealed with plaster. When police came to make a search, they found nothing until a ghastly scream from the walled recess caused them to open it and discover the cat seated upon the head of the corpse.

Black Mountain College, experimental liberal arts institution, near Asheville, N.C., founded (1933) by dissident faculty and students of Rollins College (Florida) for innova-

tive and improvisory learning. Although it foundered (1956), its teachers, including Josef Albers, and its journal, *The Black Mountain Review* (1954–57), had a great effect far beyond its campus. The major figure was Charles Olson,♦ for a time the chancellor, whose important students include Creeley, Duncan, Levertov, and John Wieners. Creeley edited the *Review,* concentrating on the college's poets but including also Ginsberg, Kerouac, and Zukofsky.

Black Riders, The, and Other Lines, volume of free verse by Stephen Crane,♦ published in 1895. Influenced by reading Emily Dickinson, Crane in these concise, intense unrhymed poems foreshadows the work of the Imagists. Elliptical renderings of his naturalistic philosophy, they show his bewildered bitterness of youth buffeted by the great impersonal forces of the world.

Blackfoot Indians, group of bison-hunting Algonquian tribes in Alberta and Montana, of which the Blackfoot proper are the most prominent. They once ranged from the Yellowstone River to the Rocky Mountains, and they figure in diaries of 19th-century plainsmen, being noted for their constant warfare with the Crow, and their unwavering hostility toward whites. In Irving's *Adventures of Captain Bonneville* and the *Life* of Beckwourth they appear as horse thieves and ruffians.

BLACKMUR, R[ICHARD] P[ALMER] (1904–65), poet and critic, although without formal education after high school, was not only a learned critic but served as a resident fellow (1940–48) and professor (1948–65) at Princeton. His books include *From Jordan's Delight* (1937) and *Second World* (1942), poems; *The Double Agent* (1935), *The Expense of Greatness* (1940), *Language as Gesture* (1952), *The Lion and the Honeycomb* (1955), essays on literature; *Form and Value in Modern Poetry* (1957) and *Eleven Essays in the European Novel* (1964). *Henry Adams* (1980) is a posthumous gathering of studies of the historian.

BLECHMAN, BURT (1932?–), New York novelist and New York University Medical School faculty member, whose works include the fantastic and satirical treatment of Jewish family life *How Much?* (1962), adapted for the stage by Lillian Hellman as *My Father, My Mother and Me* (1963); *The War of Camp Omongo* (1963), satirizing the values of middle-class children at summer camp; *Sta-*

tions (1964), a metaphorical story of homosexuality; *The Octopus Papers* (1965), a satirical view of the New York art world and pseudo-bohemians; and *Maybe* (1967), treating the loneliness of a Park Avenue widow whose only solace is to spend money.

BLEECKER, ANN ELIZA (1752–83), born in New York City, after her marriage at the age of 17 lived in Poughkeepsie and later in a frontier village near Albany. Her epistolary novel, *The History of Maria Kittle* (1797), deals with the capture of an American woman by Indians during the French and Indian War. Her melancholy verse was collected in *The Posthumous Works of Ann Eliza Bleecker* (1793), to which was added *A Collection of Essays, Prose and Poetical* by her daughter Margaretta Faugères (1771–1801).

Blithedale Romance, The, romance by Hawthorne,♦ published in 1852. Blithedale was suggested by Brook Farm, and the character Zenobia by Margaret Fuller, while Miles Coverdale is a fictional self-portrait.

Coverdale visits Blithedale Farm, near Boston, a socialized community for the betterment of mankind. He meets Silas Forster, a farmer, and his wife; Zenobia, a passionate and queenly woman; Hollingsworth, a former blacksmith, who brings his sledgehammer method to bear upon the evils of society but lacks the spark of spiritual light; and Priscilla, a delicate girl said to be a city seamstress. Zenobia and Priscilla both fall in love with Hollingsworth, who, however, loves mankind in the aggregate too fiercely to be gentle to individuals. Returning to the city, Coverdale meets the people of the community in a different atmosphere. Zenobia is again a wealthy woman of fashion, and actually Priscilla's half-sister, although this remains unknown. Priscilla falls under the mysterious influence of the mesmerist Westervelt, from whom she is rescued by Hollingsworth, and upon their return to Blithedale Hollingsworth gives his love to Priscilla, although he has previously wooed Zenobia to get money for his philanthropic work. Unable to bear defeat, Zenobia drowns herself. Hollingsworth marries Priscilla, but his energy and peace of mind are lost, and Priscilla is now the sole prop of his broken spirit. Coverdale remains skeptical concerning human progress.

Blix, novel by Frank Norris,♦ published in 1899. The story is partly autobiographical.

Blockade, The, unpublished play by General John Burgoyne,♦ was performed in Boston (1775) while the British army occupied the city. It ridicules the valor of the rebel soldiers and makes light of the situation in which the British found themselves.

Bloudy Tenent of Persecution, The, tract by Roger Williams,♦ written primarily as an attack on John Cotton, was published in London (1644). The treatise is in the form of a dialogue between two fugitive angelic characters, Truth and Peace, who, after a long separation, are still unable to find a home in the civilized world and meet in a dark refuge. Their conversation, on intellectual freedom in civil and ecclesiastical governments, is an argument for democratic liberty and tolerance, and attacks persecution for cause of conscience. The "bloudy and slaughterous conclusions" of Cotton and the other persecutors are answered, according to the author, in "spiritually white milk." Cotton's reply, *The Bloudy Tenent Washed and Made White in the Bloud of the Lamb* (1647), was answered by another tract on liberty of conscience, *The Bloudy Tenent Yet More Bloudy, by Mr. Cotton's Endeavour To Wash It White in the Bloud of the Lamb* (1652).

Blue Hotel, The, story by Stephen Crane in *The Monster and Other Stories.* ♦

Blue laws, term applied to colonial legislation, especially in New England, which restricted personal action in order to improve community morality. A collection of such laws was made by the Rev. Samuel Peters in his derogatory *General History of Connecticut* (London, 1781), and he was the first to popularize the term. His hatred of republicanism and nonconformity led him to make gross misrepresentations about the stringency of these laws, but his discredited statements have generally found their way into the popular mind.

Blue Voyage, novel by Conrad Aiken. ♦

BLY, NELLY, pseudonym of Elizabeth C. Seaman. ♦

BLY, ROBERT [ELWOOD] (1926–), Minnesota-born poet, whose first volume, *Silence in the Snowy Fields* (1962), contains spare poems of the native farm scene in which he continues to live, direct but also marked by striking imagery. The poems in *The Light Around the Body* (1967) differ in that some are more mystical, others more political in his intense hatred of the Vietnam War. The work was selected for a National Book Award, and Bly gave the prize money to an antidraft organization. Later poems, some prose poems, appear in *Sleepers Joining Hands* (1973), *Old Man Rubbing His Eyes* (1975), *The Morning Glory* (1975), *This Body Is Made of Camphor and Gopherwood* (1977), *This Tree Will Be Here for a Thousand Years* (1979), *The Man in the Black Coat Turns* (1981), and *A Man Loves a Woman in Both Worlds* (1983). He has also translated some fiction of Selma Lagerlöf and of Knut Hamsun, as well as poetry from German, Spanish, and Swedish, including that of Trakl, Neruda, and Lorca, who have influenced him. His periodical, originally *The Fifties,* which changes its title with each decade, has printed some of these authors, as well as Americans. *Leaping Poetry* (1975) is a critical work.

Bobbsey Twins, series of books for girls by Edward Stratemeyer.♦

BODENHEIM, Maxwell (1893–1954), born in Mississippi, moved to Chicago and then to New York, where he published *Minna and Myself* (1918), a volume of poems using the sharply pictorial technique of Imagism. The highly mannered use of language and the author's posturing as an aesthetic misanthrope is also evident in later verse. Bodenheim's novels, including *Crazy Man* (1924), *Replenishing Jessica* (1925), and *Naked on Roller Skates* (1931), show a similar vivacious cynicism, iconoclasm, and jazz-age paganism. He wrote several plays, including *The Master-Poisoner* (1918), with Ben Hecht, ♦ who later attacked him in his fiction. Always a bohemian drifter and drinker, he spent his last years in squalor and was murdered.

BOGAN, Louise (1897–1970), Maine-born poet who lived in New York, whose books include *Body of This Death* (1923); *Dark Summer* (1929); *The Sleeping Fury* (1937); *Poems and New Poems* (1941); *Collected Poems* (1954); and *The Blue Estuaries* (1968). Her volume of *Selected Criticism* (1955) was extended in *A Poet's Alphabet* (1970), a posthumous collection. *What the Woman Lived* (1973) prints her letters. Her spare, sensitive poetry, mostly in traditional forms, is marked by intensity of personal expression and incisive imagery.

BOK, Edward William (1863–1930), born in Holland, came to the U.S. at the age of 7,

and at 26 became editor of the *Ladies' Home Journal.* ♦ *The Americanization of Edward Bok* (1920, Pulitzer Prize) is the best known of his books.

BOKER, George Henry (1823–90), Philadelphia playwright, whose major romantic dramas were *Leonor de Guzman* (1835), concerning Leonor, the mistress of Alfonso XII, 14th-century monarch of Castile, and his Queen Maria, and *Francesca da Rimini* (1855), treating in verse the story of Paolo and Francesca.

Bollingen Poetry Translation Prize, awarded (1961–68) by the foundation responsible for the poetry prize. After 1963 both became biennial.

Bollingen Prize in Poetry, established (1948) by the Bollingen Foundation, financed by Paul Mellon and named by him for the Swiss home of the psychoanalyst Jung. The award ($1000 to 1960, $2500 to 1964, $5000 thereafter) was given annually for the highest achievement in American poetry issued the preceding year, but became a biennial award after 1963. The first award (1949), to Pound's *Pisan Cantos,* recommended by the Fellows in American Letters of the Library of Congress, precipitated a controversy spearheaded by Robert Hillyer and led the Library to discontinue all prizes under its auspices. The Prize has since been administered by the Yale University Library and later winners are Wallace Stevens (1950), J.C. Ransom (1951), Marianne Moore (1952), MacLeish and W.C. Williams (1953), Auden (1954), Léonie Adams and Louise Bogan (1955), Aiken (1956), Tate (1957), Cummings (1958), Roethke (1959), Delmore Schwartz (1960), Yvor Winters (1961), J.H. Wheelock and R. Eberhart (1962), Frost (1963), Horace Gregory (1964–65), R.P. Warren (1966–67), Berryman and Mona Van Duyn (1968–69), no award (1969–70), James Merrill (1971–72), A.R. Ammons (1973–74), David Ignatow (1975–76), W.S. Merwin (1977–78), May Swenson and Howard Nemerov (1979–80), Anthony Hecht and John Hollander (1981–82).

Bonifacius, essay by Cotton Mather, ♦ published in 1710 with the subtitle *An Essay Upon the Good, That Is To Be Devised and Designed . . . ,* often reissued as *Essays To Do Good.* Franklin liked it because it anticipated his practical Yankee view of good deeds.

BONTEMPS, ARNA [WENDELL] (1902–73), Louisiana-born author, educated in California, received an M.A. from the University of Chicago, and was librarian of Fisk University. His novels about his black people include *God Sends Sunday* (1931), about a jockey, dramatized with Countee Cullen as *St. Louis Woman* (1946); *Black Thunder* (1936), about a slave revolt in Virginia in 1800; *Drums at Dusk* (1939), about the slave revolt and emancipation in Haiti; and many children's books, including *Sam Patch* (1951), written with Jack Conroy. His nonfiction includes another work written with Conroy, *They Seek a City* (1945); *The Story of the Negro* (1948); *Chariot in the Sky* (1951), about the Jubilee Singers of Fisk University; and *One Hundred Years of Negro Freedom* (1961). His correspondence with Langston Hughes was published in 1979.

Book of Annandale, The, blank-verse narrative by E.A. Robinson,♦ published in *Captain Craig* (1902).

Book of Common Prayer, A, novel by Joan Didion,♦ published in 1977.

Grace Strasser-Mendana, a 60-year-old American woman, formerly an anthropologist, is a longtime resident of the equatorial country Boca Grande, and widow of a member of its leading political family. She is fascinated by Charlotte Douglas, a 40-year-old Californian, who has turned up in Boca Grande, traveling aimlessly and alone. She recently suffered a nervous breakdown because Marin, the daughter she and her second husband Lloyd had hoped to raise as a teenager playing tennis at the local country club, instead fled underground when she was found to be a member of a radical group that had bombed a San Francisco office building and hijacked a plane. Charlotte has an affair with Grace's son Gerardo, who is planning a coup to seize the government. When the revolution breaks out Charlotte refuses to flee Boca Grande with Grace and Gerardo, and she is soon killed by a soldier for no reason.

BOONE, DANIEL (1734–1820), born in Pennsylvania, moved to North Carolina, made an extended exploration of Kentucky (1769–71), and as an agent of the Transylvania Company led a band of colonists along the Wilderness Road♦ through the Cumberland Gap to the site of Boonesborough, where a fort was erected in 1775. After the region was made a county of Virginia (1776), he held many local offices, but when he lost his land by suits he moved to West Virginia and then to Missouri. The legend of Boone as the discoverer of Kentucky and the greatest of frontiersmen was begun with the biography written by John Filson♦ and extended by Byron in the eighth canto of *Don Juan* (1823), as well as by many laudatory references in contemporary literature and tall tales. Audubon, who met Boone in Missouri, retold one of his adventures in the *Ornithological Biography*. He is a frequent figure in fiction, as in Churchill's *The Crossing,* Elizabeth Madox Roberts's *The Great Meadow,* and Caroline Gordon's *Green Centuries.*

BOORSTIN, DANIEL J. (1914–), Atlanta-born educator and author, after an A.B. from Harvard, Rhodes scholarship, and law degree from Yale had a distinguished academic career teaching American history, mainly at the University of Chicago, before becoming Director, National Museum of History and Technology, Smithsonian Institution, and then Librarian of Congress (1975–). His books include: *The Americans: The Colonial Experience* (1958), *The Americans: The National Experience* (1965), *The Americans: The Democratic Experience* (1973, Pulitzer Prize), and *The Discoverers* (1983), the first part of a world history.

BOOTH, PHILIP (1925–), New Hampshire-born poet, graduated from Dartmouth, has taught at Bowdoin, Wellesley, and Syracuse (1961–). His first book, *Letter from a Distant Land* (1957), contains a blank-verse autobiographical address to Thoreau. Later works which show his deeply ingrained feeling for the New England coast and the tough, terse turn of mind of the region, along with a Yankee wit, are published in *The Islanders* (1961), *Weathers and Edges* (1966), *North by East* (1967), *Beyond Our Fears* (1968), *Margins* (1970), *Available Light* (1976), and *Before Sleep* (1980).

BOOTHE, CLARE (CLARE BOOTHE LUCE) (1903–), has written the plays *The Women* (1936), satirizing wealthy women in the U.S.; *Kiss the Boys Goodbye* (1938), ridiculing Hollywood's star system; and *Margin for Error* (1940), a melodrama about the murder of a Nazi consul. *Europe in the Spring* (1940) recounts travels in Allied countries and recommends an American crusade for world democracy. She was married to Henry Robinson Luce (1898–1967), the publisher of *Time,* and served as U.S. representative from

Connecticut (1943–47) and U.S. ambassador to Italy (1953–56).

BORDEN, LIZZIE (1860–1927), was accused of hacking to death her aged father and stepmother in Fall River, Mass. (Aug. 4, 1892). The trial of the spinster Lizzie was a national sensation. Since there was only circumstantial evidence, she was acquitted, but her supposed crime won her a place in American popular legend. In addition to ballads and contemporary literature, the case has been the subject of several novels; of some plays, including John Colton's *Nine Pine Street* (1933); and a ballet, *Fall River Legend* (1948) by Agnes De Mille.

Border Romances, series of novels by W.G. Simms♦ dealing with colonial and 19th-century life in the South. The romances are *Guy Rivers, The Yemassee, Richard Hurdis, Border Beagles, Beauchampe, Helen Halsey, Charlemont, The Cassique of Kiawah, Voltmeier,* and *The Cub of the Panther.*

Boston Athenaeum, association of Boston literary men, was founded in 1805 as an outgrowth of the Anthology Club♦ and patterned after the Liverpool Athenaeum in England. A corporation was organized (1807), and a library, a museum, and a laboratory were founded. Although the institution underwent trying times and was criticized as being limited to the wealthy, the library became valuable and in 1845 was provided with its own large building. The society has continued to influence Boston's literary life, and it is mentioned in such journals as Hawthorne's *American Notebooks.* It serves as the setting of Hawthorne's posthumous story "The Ghost of Doctor Harris."

Bostonians, The, novel by Henry James,♦ published in 1886. Miss Birdseye is believed to represent Elizabeth Peabody. ♦

Basil Ransom, a Mississippi lawyer, comes to Boston to seek his fortune, and becomes acquainted with his cousins, the flirtatious widow, Mrs. Luna, and her neurotic sister, Olive Chancellor. He is taken by Olive, a radical feminist, to a suffragette meeting, where he meets Miss Birdseye, an aged, altruistic worker for lost causes. They hear an address by beautiful young Verena Tarrant, whose gift of persuasion interests Olive as an instrument for her own use. Olive removes the girl to her own luxurious home, converts her to the feminist cause, and even urges her

to vow that she will never marry. Fleeing the attentions of Mrs. Luna, Ransom attempts to win Verena to his belief that her proper sphere is a home and a drawing room, not a career as lecturer for a preposterous political movement, and there is open hostility between Ransom and the jealous Olive. Their struggle reaches a climax when Verena is about to begin her lectures, for she loses confidence, especially after the death of Miss Birdseye. Completely unnerved by Ransom's presence at her initial appearance, she consents to marry him, and Olive, who must announce her protégée's defection, is left desolate.

BOUCICAULT, DION (1820–90), Irish-born dramatist and actor, came to the U.S. (1835), where he turned out musical interludes, melodramas, adaptations from the French, dramatizations of Dickens's novels, and *The Poor of New York,* a "superficial but graphic picture" of the panic of 1857. His melodramatic play about slavery, *The Octoroon; or, Life in Louisiana* (1859), adapted from Mayne Reid's *The Quadroon,* created a sensation. *The Colleen Bawn* (1860) began a long series of Irish comedy dramas which brought him his greatest fame, although his collaboration with Joseph Jefferson on *Rip Van Winkle* (1865) was unusually successful. Except for a decade in London (1862–72), and shorter journeys abroad, he continued his declining dramatic career in New York, where most of his 132 plays were produced.

Bound East for Cardiff, one-act play by Eugene O'Neill,♦ produced and published in 1916.

In mid-Atlantic on the British tramp steamer *Glencairn,* the seaman Yank has been injured in a fall and lies moaning in his bunk. His friend, the Irishman Driscoll, and the other seamen encourage him with rough expressions of good will, but Yank realizes that he is dying. Since he fears to be alone, Driscoll remains with him, and they discuss old adventures and their mean life at sea. Yank considers that "this sailor life ain't much to cry about leavin'," and refuses to accept his friend's comfortable piety. Before the night fog lifts he dies, with a vision of "a pretty lady dressed in black."

BOURJAILY, VANCE [NYE] (1922–), Ohio-born writer, after service in World War II wrote *The End of My Life* (1947), a novel about a young man's collapse in the war, and *The Hound of Earth* (1954), about a scientist who runs away from his army job and his family after the bombing of Hiroshima. Bourjaily then became the editor of *discovery*, ♦ a distinguished departure in little magazines, and after its demise returned to fiction, writing *The Violated* (1958), a long novel of character analysis; *Confessions of a Spent Youth* (1960), about a young man's life and loves before, during, and after World War II; *The Man Who Knew Kennedy* (1967), treating the era of the President; *Brill Among the Ruins* (1970), depicting sociocultural turmoil of the 1960s as it affects a middle-aged man; *Now Playing at Canterbury* (1976), a kind of *Canterbury Tales* set in the U.S. of the '60s and '70s; and *A Game Men Play* (1980), a panoramic social history and adventure tale of the 20th century. *The Unnatural Enemy* (1963) and *Country Matters* (1973) are nonfictional works about rural life.

BOURNE, RANDOLPH SILLIMAN (1886–1918), while a student at Columbia, from which he graduated in 1913, and during the remainder of his short life, established himself as a spokesman of his generation through his critical examination of American institutions, attacks on big-business civilization, and criticism of sentimental ideas in literature and elsewhere. His books, *Youth and Life* (1913), *The Gary Schools* (1916), and *Education and Living* (1917), show him to be a disciple of John Dewey although he felt pragmatism failed to direct a war-torn world. His pacifist articles were posthumously collected as *Untimely Papers* (1919), and his philosophical and critical views are summed up in *The History of a Literary Radical* (1920), edited by Van Wyck Brooks.

Bowery, THE, street in New York City, situated in lower Manhattan, whose name derives from the fact that it once ran through Peter Stuyvesant's farm, or *bouwerie,* as it was called by the Dutch settlers. The 19th-century-stage type of the Bowery boy, representing the characteristic exuberant, impudent rascal of the district, in the plug hat, red shirt, and turned-up trousers of the volunteer fire department, was introduced in the play *A Glance at New York* (1848). The Bowery was long notorious for its dance halls, gambling houses, and other criminal resorts, which were fliply commented upon in a song ("The Bowery! I'll never go there any more!") by a bumpkin recounting his misadventures in Charles Hoyt's play *A Trip to Chinatown* (1891). Fiction about the squalid slum life there includes Stephen Crane's *Maggie* and *George's Mother* and Edward W. Townsend's *Chimmie Fadden, . . . and Other Stories* (1895).

BOWLES, JANE (1917–73), New York-born author, resident abroad for long periods as a child with her family and as an adult after marriage (1938) to Paul Bowles. ♦ She created a reputation among the avant-garde with *Two Serious Ladies* (1943), an experimental novel about two women, one rich and prosperous, the other sensuous and sinful, whose lives touch only twice. A play, *In the Summer House* (1954), and her stories, *Plain Pleasures* (1966), were issued together as her *Collected Works* (1966). *Feminine Wiles* (1976) collects stories and sketches, another play, and letters.

BOWLES, PAUL (1910–84), born in New York City, after study with Aaron Copland and Virgil Thomson became a composer, writing scores for ballets and motion pictures, an opera, *The Wind Remains* (1943), and incidental music for plays by Saroyan and Tennessee Williams. His later career was that of an author and his setting Morocco, where he was long expatriated. His works include *The Sheltering Sky* (1949), *Let It Come Down* (1952), and *The Spider's House* (1955), novels about Occidentals in the Arab world, having as themes isolation, lovelessness, and the loss of tradition. He issued *Collected Stories* (1979), and *The Thicket of Spring* (1972) collects poems. *Their Heads Are Green and Their Hands Are Blue* (1963) chronicles his journeys through Hindu, Mohammedan, Buddhist, and Central American lands. *A Life Full of Holes* (1964) is a novel by an illiterate house servant in Morocco, tape recorded and translated from an Arabic dialect by Bowles. *Without Stopping* (1972) is his autobiography.

BOYD, JAMES (1888–1944), born in Pennsylvania, was reared in North Carolina, graduated from Princeton (1910), studied at Cambridge, served in World War I, and returned to North Carolina to write. His two major novels, *Drums* (1925) and *Marching On* (1927), use his experience of war, but are set respectively in Revolutionary and Civil War times, in keeping with his theory that a writer needs "perspective of years." His other novels are *Roll River* (1935), set in his native Harrisburg; and *Long Hunt* (1930) and *Bitter Creek* (1939), about the frontier West. *Eighteen Poems* (1944) is a posthumous collection.

BOYESEN, HJALMAR HJORTH (1848–95), born in Norway, came to the U.S. (1869), and was a professor of German at Cornell and Columbia, as well as an author influenced by Howells. Denouncing the subservience of writers in the U.S. to the standards of the young American girl, "the Iron Madonna who strangles in her fond embrace the American novelist," his own fiction includes *The Mammon of Unrighteousness* (1891), a realistic treatment of American city life, contrasting two brothers, one a social idealist, the other a ruthless politician; *The Golden Calf* (1892), portraying the disintegration of a young man's ideals when he is tempted by wealth; and *The Social Strugglers* (1893).

BOYLE, KAY (1903–   ), born in Minnesota, was long an expatriate in France, returning to the U.S. in 1941. Her impressionistic stories have appeared in *Wedding Day* (1930), *First Lover* (1933), *The White Horses of Vienna* (1936), *The Crazy Hunter* (1940), *Thirty Stories* (1946), *The Smoking Mountain* (1951), *Nothing Ever Breaks Except the Heart* (1966), and *Fifty Stories* (1980). Her novels include *Plagued by the Nightingale* (1931), dealing with an American girl and her French husband, torn between the need to have a child so as to receive his legacy and the desire to avoid transmitting his hereditary disease; *Year Before Last* (1932), *Gentlemen, I Address You Privately* (1933); *My Next Bride* (1934); *Death of a Man* (1936); *Monday Night* (1938); and *The Youngest Camel* (1939). *Primer for Combat* (1942), *Avalanche* (1943), a tale of espionage; *A Frenchman Must Die* (1946); and *His Human Majesty* (1949) are set in France during World War II. *Generation Without Farewell* (1959) depicts Germans and Americans just after World War II; and *The Underground Woman* (1975) is about a woman jailed for anti-Vietnam War protest and her concern for her daughter involved in a cult. Poems are published in *A Glad Day* (1938); *American Citizen* (1944), about her Austrian refugee husband who became a U.S. soldier; *Testament for My Students* (1970), works written in the 1920s and '30s; and the selections mistitled *Collected Poems* (1962). *The Long Walk at San Francisco State* (1970) prints essays on social and political issues. She expanded the autobiography of Robert McAlmon♦ as *Being Geniuses Together* (1968) by interspersing her own memoirs with his.

Boy's Will, A, first book of poems, published in 1913 by Robert Frost,♦ the title derived from the refrain of Longfellow's "My Lost Youth."♦

BRACE, GERALD WARNER (1901–   ), received his A.B. from Amherst and graduate degrees from Harvard, and has taught at various New England colleges, chiefly Boston University (1939–68). His novels, all dealing with New England people and scenes, include *The Islands* (1936), set in Maine; *The Wayward Pilgrims* (1938), about a chance meeting in a Vermont depot; *Light on a Mountain* (1941); *The Garretson Chronicle* (1947), depicting changing ways in three generations of a Massachusetts family; *A Summer's Tale* (1949); *The Spire* (1952); *The World of Carrick's Cove* (1957); *Winter Solstice* (1960); *The Wind's Will* (1964); and *Between Wind and Water* (1966). *The Department* (1968) is a novel about a professor recalling 40 years in an English department. *The Age of the Novel* (1957) and *The Stuff of Fiction* (1969) are critical works. *Days That Were* (1976) presents memories of his youth.

Bracebridge Hall; or, The Humorists: A Medley, 49 tales and sketches by Irving,♦ published in 1822 under the pseudonym Geoffrey Crayon, Gent. Resembling its predecessor, *The Sketch Book,* the collection includes stories with English, French, and Spanish settings, but is chiefly remembered for "Dolph Heyliger" and its sequel, "The Storm-Ship," which recount the adventures of a New York lad who undertakes to discredit the legend of a haunted house, but encounters its ghost and recovers a fabulous buried treasure, as well as marrying an heiress. Americanized versions of the Flying Dutchman theme are presented in "The Storm-Ship," and other stories in the volume are also based on European folklore.

BRACKENRIDGE, HUGH HENRY (1748–1816), born in Scotland, was brought to a Pennsylvania farm at the age of five, and entered Princeton in 1768, where he became intimate with Freneau and Madison, and collaborated with the former on *The Rising Glory of America* (1772), a poetical expression of ardent national consciousness. He studied theology, and in 1774 received his M.A., writing *A Poem on Divine Revelation.* During the Revolutionary War he served as a chaplain, and wrote two patriotic plays for amateur production, *The Battle of Bunkers-*

Hill (1776) and *The Death of General Montgomery* (1777), neoclassical dramas in rather stilted blank verse. His more pungent contributions to the cause are included in his sermons, *Six Political Discourses* (1778), and in his work as editor of the patriotic *United States Magazine.* Repelled by strict dogma, he gave up the ministry to practice law, and in 1781 settled in the frontier village of Pittsburgh. There he had an active political career and showed himself to be an aristocratic democrat, attempting to mediate between the federal government and the local insurrectionists during the Whiskey Rebellion, as described in his *Incidents of the Insurrection in the Western Part of Pennsylvania* (1795). His satirical contributions to the local paper mirrored his political and social ideas, which are more completely treated in his novel *Modern Chivalry♦* (1792–1815). In 1799 he was appointed justice of the Pennsylvania Supreme Court.

BRADBURY, RAY [DOUGLAS] (1920–), born in Illinois, long resident in Los Angeles, began to publish in pulp magazines, but after 1945 became known for serious stories. These include works of both fantasy and science fiction, now macabre, now humorous, collected in volumes including *Dark Carnival* (1947); *The Martian Chronicles* (1950, titled *The Silver Locusts* in England), about Mars a century hence; *The Illustrated Man* (1951); *The Golden Apples of the Sun* (1953), satirical sketches; *October Country* (1955); *A Meditation for Melancholy* (1959); *R Is for Rocket, S Is for Space* (1962); *The Machineries of Joy* (1964); *Twice Twenty-Two* (1966); *Any Friend of Nicholas Nickleby's Is a Friend of Mine* (1968); and *I Sing the Body Electric* (1969). His novels include *Fahrenheit 451* (1953), presenting a future totalitarian state in which supertelevision presents all that people are to think or know, and the ownership of books is cause for the state to burn both volumes and owners; and *Dandelion Wine* (1957) and *Something Wicked This Way Comes* (1962), about boyhood experiences in the Midwest. He has written many plays, including *The Meadow* (1947), *The Anthem Sprinters* (1962), *The Wonderful Ice Cream Suit* (1965), *The Halloween Tree* (1968), *Pillar of Fire* (1975), and film scripts, including *Moby Dick* (1954). His poems appear in *When Elephants Last in the Dooryard Bloomed* (1973) and *Where Robot Men and Robot Women Run Round in Robot Towns* (1977).

BRADFORD, ROARK (1896–1948), author of stories about blacks and their folklore, whose books include *Ol' Man Adam an' His Children* (1928), from which the play *The Green Pastures♦* (1930) was adapted; *This Side of Jordan* (1929); *Ol' King David an' the Philistine Boys* (1930); *John Henry* (1931), about the legendary hero, dramatized by the author in 1940; and *How Come Christmas* (1934), a one-act "modern morality."

BRADFORD, WILLIAM (1590–1657), as a boy joined the Separatist group of William Brewster, with whom he emigrated to Amsterdam (1609) and then to Leyden. He came to America on the *Mayflower* (1620), and the following April was elected governor of Plymouth Colony, an office to which he was reelected every year from 1622 to 1656, with the exception of 1633, 1634, 1636, 1638, and 1644, when he was an assistant, having "by importunity gat off" from the position of leadership. Bradford's life was inseparably bound with the settlement, of which he was long the outstanding authority in all executive, judicial, and legislative matters. In 1627 Bradford and seven leading Pilgrims, with four London merchants, assumed the £1800 debt to the original merchant adventurers. Although these "Undertakers" held a monopoly of fishing and trading, the land and cattle were distributed equally among the "Old Comers." Bradford willingly aided all common enterprises, including the New England Confederation, but considered his colony as a compact community. About 1630 he began to write his *History of Plimmoth Plantation,♦* which he completed in 1651. A fragment of his letter-book (1624–30) as well as his letters to Winthrop have been published in the *Collections* of the Massachusetts Historical Society. Other works printed by this organization and the Colonial Society of Massachusetts include his *Dialogue between some young men born in New England and sundry ancient men that came out of Holland;* a long descriptive poem of 1654; *A Word to New Plymouth; A Word to New England;* and *Of Boston in New-England.* He is also considered to be the author of the first half of *Mourt's Relation,♦* which chronicles the events from September 6, 1620, to March 23, 1621.

BRADSTREET, ANNE [DUDLEY] (*c.*1612–72), daughter of Thomas Dudley, governor of the Massachusetts Bay Colony, was born in England, where at age 16 she married Simon Bradstreet, also a governor of the colony.

Two years later she left her comfortable home to accompany both men on the voyage of the *Arbella,* settling first at Ipswich and later in North Andover, Mass. In the intervals of arduous household tasks and the care of her eight children, she found time for her literary interests, and in 1650 the first edition of her poems was published in England as *The Tenth Muse Lately Sprung Up in America,* the manuscript having been taken without her knowledge to a London publisher by an admiring brother-in-law. A posthumous second edition, with her own additions and corrections, was issued at Boston (1678), and a scholarly edition with some additional material was published in 1867. Mrs. Bradstreet's literary influences were obvious and acknowledged, for she was enamored of Quarles, Joshua Sylvester's translation of Du Bartas's *Divine Semaine,* Spenser, and Sir Philip Sidney, although she reproaches the latter "miracle of wit" for his *Arcadia.* Cotton Mather in the *Magnalia* praised her highly, and Nathaniel Ward and others were equally lavish in the commendatory verses that prefaced her poetry. Her longer work consists of poetic discourses on the four elements, the four humors, the four ages of man, the four seasons, and "A Dialogue between Old England and New." The long, rhymed history, "The Four Monarchies," is based closely on Raleigh's *History of the World* and treats the Persian, Greek, and Assyrian kingdoms and the Roman Commonwealth. Her current reputation is based on the later and shorter poems, in which she looked into her heart or out upon a real New England world, and was less dependent on stock poetic conventions. These include "The Flesh and the Spirit"; "Contemplations," her nature poem on the transiency of man's life; "On the Burning of Her House"; "To My Dear and Loving Husband," showing a moving use of the Donnean conceit; "On My Son's Return Out of England"; and "The Author to Her Book." In the prose "Meditations Divine and Morall," written for her son, she composed simple, pithy, and sincere aphorisms, and in her short spiritual autobiography, "Religious Experiences," she also employs a sweet and simple prose. A moving biographical poem, *Homage to Mistress Bradstreet* (1956), was written by John Berryman.

Brahma, poem by Emerson,♦ published in 1857 and reprinted in *May-Day and Other Poems* (1867). In alternately rhymed tetrameter quatrains, the poem reflects the author's interest in Hindu religious thought,

in which Brahma personifies the universal creative force, embodying his concept of an eternal, all-inclusive divine power.

Brahmins, name humorously applied to upper-class New England society, derived from the name of the highest or priestly caste among the Hindus. In *Elsie Venner,* Holmes speaks of "the harmless, inoffensive, untitled aristocracy" of New England, and specifically of Boston, "which has grown to be a caste by the repetition of the same influences generation after generation," so that it has acquired a distinct organization and physiognomy.

BRAITHWAITE, William Stanley Beaumont (1878–1962), black author and editor, whose poetry, first published in *Lyrics of Life and Love* (1904) and *The House of Falling Leaves* (1908), was gathered in *Selected Poems* (1948). He also wrote *Frost on the Green Tree* (1928), stories; *The House Under Arcturus* (1941), an autobiography; and *The Bewitched Parsonage: The Story of the Brontës* (1950). He was well known for his annual *Anthology of Magazine Verse and Year Book of American Poetry* (1913–29).

BRAND, Max, pseudonym of Frederick Faust (1892–1944) used for his prodigious output of adventure fiction, including cowboy novels like *Destry Rides Again* (1930) and a series about Dr. Kildare.

BRAUTIGAN, Richard (1935–84), San Francisco author, whose loosely conceived short "novels" composed of comic, whimsical, and surrealistic sketches of gently anarchic, unselfish, and Beat♦ ways of life include *A Confederate General from Big Sur* (1964), *Trout Fishing in America* (1967), *In Watermelon Sugar* (1968), *The Abortion: An Historical Romance* (1971), *Revenge of the Lawn* (1971), *The Hawkins Monster: A Gothic Western* (1974), *Willard and His Bowling Trophies: A Perverse Mystery* (1975), and *Sombrero Fallout: A Japanese Novel* (1976). *Dreaming of Babylon: A Private Eye Novel* (1977) and *So the Wind Won't Blow It All Away* (1982) are novels. *The Pill Versus the Springfield Mine Disaster* (1968), *Rommel Drives on Deep into Egypt* (1970), *Loading Mercury with a Pitchfork* (1976), and *June 30th, June 30th* (1978) collect brief poems.

Breakfast at Tiffany's, short novel by Truman Capote,♦ published in 1958.

An unnamed narrator, a onetime resident

in the 1940s of an old brownstone apartment building in the East 70s of New York City, reminisces about a glamorous fellow tenant, Holly Golightly, with "a face beyond childhood, yet this side of belonging to a woman," and not yet 19. Independent since age 14, fay, and very appealing, she has already had a life for herself, including refusal of a Hollywood film career. Her background is as unusual as her life in New York: as a teenage hillbilly she married an older veterinarian in Texas, but she later became an uninhibited playgirl of café society. By a series of misadventures she is arrested as a go-between of a drug-smuggling gang and therefore flees to Brazil, never to be seen again by the admiring friend who writes her story as she passes into modern legendry.

Bricks Without Straw, novel by A.W. Tourgée,♦ published in 1880. Intended to demonstrate the fallacy of freedom for Southern blacks without the "straw" of an adequate social and economic basis for free development, the story is concerned with Reconstruction days on the North Carolina tobacco plantations.

Bride Comes to Yellow Sky, The, story by Stephen Crane in *The Open Boat.* ♦

Bridge, The, long poem by Hart Crane,♦ published in 1930.

Opening with a proem, "To Brooklyn Bridge," in which the structure, both "harp and altar," is conceived as lending "a myth to God," the eight succeeding sections begin with "Ave Maria," in which Columbus dedicates himself to the new world, and "Powhatan's Daughter," envisioning Pocahontas as an earth goddess but also drawing upon the legend of Rip Van Winkle, the author's own boyhood experiences, the movement of Americans flowing like a river, a dance of life and death associated with an Indian chief, and the farewell of a pioneer mother to her son who is leaving Indiana to go to sea. "Cutty Sark," the third section, presents a kaleidoscopic view of life at sea, at the Panama Canal, and in the Bowery. It is followed by "Cape Hatteras," hovered over by the spirit of Whitman and guided by him as elements of America, such as the achievements of the Wright brothers, are evoked. "Three Songs," treating the power of woman as Venus and Virgin, precede "Quaker Hill," which summons up the sense of degradation in American culture, a theme intensified in "The Tunnel," in which Poe is

the author's Virgil in a Hell conceived as a modern subway. The work concludes in its eighth section, "Atlantis," with an affirmative vision that returns to the symbolism of the opening view of Brooklyn Bridge "iridescently upborne Through the bright drench and fabric of our veins. . . ."

Bridge of San Luis Rey, The, novel by Thornton Wilder,♦ published in 1927 and awarded a Pulitzer Prize.

British Prison Ship, The, poem by Freneau♦ in four cantos of heroic couplets was published in 1781. In a revision the poem was recast in three cantos. It describes the author's experiences when seized by the British during the Revolutionary War. The first canto tells of his capture; the second describes with bitter satire the horrors of the prison ship *Scorpion,* where the combination of foul air, rotten food and water, and bad treatment soon made him violently ill; and the third tells of his transfer to a so-called hospital ship, the *Hunter,* where the treatment was equally inhumane.

BRODSKY, JOSEPH (1940–), born and reared in Leningrad, imprisoned for two years, then exiled by the Soviet government (1972), presumably for writing apolitical poetry. He has been a visiting professor (1972 ff.) at several U.S. universities. His lyric poetry published in English treating universal or often religious themes includes elegies for Donne and T.S. Eliot and has been collected in *Selected Poems* (1973) and *A Part of Speech* (1980). *Less Than One* (1981) contains essays.

Brom Bones, character in "The Legend of Sleepy Hollow."♦

BROMFIELD, LOUIS (1896–1956), born in Ohio, served in World War I, became a New York journalist and foreign correspondent, and long made his home in France. His first novel, *The Green Bay Tree* (1924), opens a tetralogy, *Escape,* including *Possession* (1925), *Early Autumn* (1926, Pulitzer Prize), and *A Good Woman* (1927), about efforts of individuals to escape the domination of family and tradition in different eras of American life. His twelve other novels include *The Farm* (1933), about a century in the life of an Ohio family. Story collections include *Awake and Rehearse* (1929), and plays include *The House of Women* (1927), dramatizing *The Green Bay Tree.* Bromfield's conservative social views are set forth in *A Few Brass Tacks* (1946). *From My Experience* (1955) treats the pleasures and miseries of his farming in Ohio and Brazil.

Brook Farm, cooperative community (1841–47) near West Roxbury, Mass., nine miles from Boston. Under George Ripley, the Transcendental Club established the community to apply its theories, forming a stock company under the name Brook Farm Institute of Agriculture and Education. Among those interested in it were Hawthorne, Charles Dana, John S. Dwight, George W. Curtis, Theodore Parker, Orestes Brownson, Margaret Fuller, Elizabeth Peabody, C.P. Cranch, Bronson Alcott, W.E. Channing, and Emerson. Of these, only Hawthorne, who wrote about it in *The Blithedale Romance,* and Dana and Dwight lived there. Among the objectives were the promotion of the great purposes of human culture and brotherly cooperation, in order to secure the highest benefits of physical, intellectual, and moral education. The life of the community was simple, all members sharing in the work and the educational and social advantages, and receiving similar pay. Occupations included the tilling of the farm, industrial employments, and school teaching. In 1843 it came under the influence of Albert Brisbane, an influential New York journalist, and soon turned into a Fourierist phalanx. As the U.S. center of Fourierism it issued *The Phalanx* (1843–45) and *The Harbinger* (1845). When an incomplete central phalanstery was burned, enthusiasm waned and the group dissolved (Oct. 1847). The Fourierist period is described in the *Letters* (1928) of Marianne Dwight Orvis.

BROOKS, GWENDOLYN (1917–), poet reared in Chicago's slums, whose works include *A Street in Bronzeville* (1945), lyrics; *Annie Allen* (1949, Pulitzer Prize), a verse narrative about a black girl's life to maturity in World War II, treating her race's isolation as both spiritual and social; *The Bean Eaters* (1960), about contemporary black life in the U.S.; and *Selected Poems* (1963). Later volumes of poetry, more militant in tone but continuing to treat the lives and problems of blacks, include *In the Mecca* (1968), *Riot* (1969), *Family Pictures* (1970), and *Aloneness* (1971). *Maud Martha* (1953), a novelette about a black woman's romance, is set in Chicago; *Bronzeville Boys and Girls* (1956) is a book for children; and *Report from Part One* (1972) collects autobiographical pieces.

BROOKS, PHILLIPS (1835–93), from the pulpit of Trinity Church in Boston, the stronghold of Episcopalianism, won an international reputation as a vigorous leader of his faith, being made a bishop in 1891. Although he published such books as *Lectures on Preaching* (1877), *The Influence of Jesus* (1879), and *Essays and Addresses* (1892), his best-loved contribution is his Christmas hymn "O Little Town of Bethlehem."

BROOKS, VAN WYCK (1886–1963), born in New Jersey of an upper-class, cultivated family, after graduation from Harvard (1904) entered upon his literary career. In biographies and criticism, beginning with *The Wine of the Puritans* (1909), he first developed the thesis that the Puritan tradition crushed American culture and placed an undue emphasis on material values, neglecting the aesthetic side of life. This theory is illustrated in *America's Coming-of-Age* (1915), *Letters and Leadership* (1918), *The Ordeal of Mark Twain* (1920), and *The Pilgrimage of Henry James* (1925). He strikingly altered this belief in his later books, which, in addition to a revision of the Mark Twain study, include the very appreciative analyses of American life, *Emerson and Others* (1927) and *Sketches in Criticism* (1932). His "history of the writer in America," titled *Makers and Finders,* includes *The Flowering of New England* (1936, Pulitzer Prize), on the period 1815–65; *New England: Indian Summer* (1940), continuing to 1915; *The World of Washington Irving* (1944), concerning 1800 to the 1840s outside New England; *The Times of Melville and Whitman* (1947); and *The Confident Years* (1952), about the era 1885–1915. All of these present a rich, impressionistic, and anecdotal view of the American literary scene with its writers, great and small, all treated knowingly and appreciatively. His life was devoted to interpreting the literary and cultural life of the U.S. in numerous other books which show a steadfast humanism, a Jeffersonian liberalism, and an appreciation of the American past. His views of literature and antipathy to many 20th-century movements appear in *On Literature Today* (1941), *Opinions of Oliver Allston* (1941), *The Writer in America* (1953), and *From a Writer's Notebook* (1958). His own impressionistic reminiscences appeared in *Scenes and Portraits: Memories of Childhood and Youth* (1954); *Days of the Phoenix* (1957), about the 1920s; and *From the Shadow of the Mountain: My Post-Meridian Years* (1961), from 1931 to his seventy-fifth birthday—all collected in *An*

Autobiography (1965). His correspondence with Lewis Mumford was published in 1970.

Brother Jonathan, sobriquet applied to America and the American people, which has been largely supplanted by the name Uncle Sam.

BROWN, CHARLES BROCKDEN (1771–1810), after a brief career as a lawyer in his native Philadelphia, moved to New York to become the first professional author of the U.S. Under the influence of William Godwin, he wrote *Alcuin: A Dialogue* (1798), a treatise on the rights of women. Further stimulated by Godwin's *Caleb Williams* and his own critical ideas of fiction, Brown in two frenetic years composed his four best novels, *Wieland*♦ (1798); *Arthur Mervyn* (1799–1800), a complex tale of intrigue, terror, and romance set in plague-stricken Philadelphia; *Ormond; or, The Secret Witness* (1799), a similarly melodramatic romance, also set in Philadelphia; and *Edgar Huntly; or, Memoirs of a Sleep-Walker* (1799), an epistolary romance about the fantastic adventures of a somnambulist. These were quickly followed by *Clara Howard* (1801), which was published in England as *Philip Stanley,* and *Jane Talbot* (1801). These Gothic romances were carefully documented in fact and pseudo-science, and influenced by the moral purpose of Godwin, the sentimentalism and psychology of Richardson, and above all the horrors of the school of Mrs. Radcliffe. After this brief burst of fiction, Brown entered business, although he also edited *The Monthly Magazine and American Review* and *The Literary Magazine and American Register* and did such hackwork as the *Memoirs of Carwin, the Biloquist.* He held high critical standards concerning American literature and believed in using distinctively American materials and in writing novels whose ideas would stir thinkers while their plots would attract ordinary readers. Although Brown was appreciated by Keats, Shelley, and Scott, and even influenced his own master, Godwin, he failed to achieve his aims because of his haste, immaturity, stilted language, fascination by the pathological, and inability to master completely the Godwinian plot structure. Despite his failings, his Gothic romances transferred to an American setting have a dark emotional intensity that gives his work more than historical significance. William Dunlap wrote a biography of Brown (1815). A scholarly edition of his works began publication in 1977.

BROWN, HARRY [PETER MCNAB, JR.] (1917–), first wrote humorous sketches about a Brooklyn GI in Britain during World War II, collected in *Artie Greengroin, Pfc.* (1945). His other writing about the war is serious, including *A Walk in the Sun* (1944) and *A Sound of Hunting* (1946), respectively a novelette and a play about U.S. soldiers in Italy. Other fiction includes *The Stars in Their Courses* (1960), set in the Western U.S. of the 1870s but written as a parallel to the story of the *Iliad.* His poetry has been collected in *The End of a Decade* (1941), *The Poem of Bunker Hill* (1941), *The Violent* (1943), and *The Beast in His Hunger* (1949).

BROWN, JOHN (1800–1859), Abolitionist leader, in 1855 moved with his five sons from Ohio to Osawatomie, Kan., following the passage of the Kansas-Nebraska Bill. Believing himself to be the special instrument of God intended to destroy proslavery settlers, he deliberately murdered five of his Southern-minded neighbors, and this, and similar acts, together with his previous reputation as an operator of the Underground Railroad, made him nationally celebrated as "Brown of Osawatomie." In 1859 he and his followers moved to Harpers Ferry, Va., where, on the night of October 16, he and 21 others captured the U.S. armory, with the intention of establishing a base from which they might free slaves by armed intervention. A force of U.S. marines under R.E. Lee attacked the armory, killed ten of Brown's men, and wounded and captured Brown. With the insurrection quelled, Brown was hanged (Dec. 2, 1859). His sincerity and dignity when on trial led many liberals to treat him as a martyr, e.g. Thoreau's *The Last Days of John Brown.* He is also lauded in Benét's *John Brown's Body,* ♦ the title too of a Civil War song, in Whittier's "John Brown of Osawatomie," Stedman's "How Old Brown Took Harpers Ferry," and Leonard Ehrlich's novel *God's Angry Man* (1932).

BROWN, STERLING A[LLAN] (1901–), born in Washington, D.C., educated at Williams College and Harvard and long a professor at Howard University, is known for poetry celebrating his black people through the use of folk themes and dialect. These were first published in *Southern Road* (1932) and gathered in *Collected Poems* (1980). He has also written books about black poetry, fiction, and drama.

BROWN, WILLIAM HILL (1765–93), author of "the first American novel," *The Power of Sympathy* (1789), an epistolary romance of seduction and suicide long attributed to Mrs. Sarah Morton. Another novel by Brown, *Ira and Isabella; or, The Natural Children* (1807), uses a similar plot, with a happy ending. He also wrote verse fables, a comedy, and *West Point Preserved* (1797), a tragedy about André.

BROWN, WILLIAM WELLS (1816?–84), black leader, born in Kentucky, reared in St. Louis, where he worked for Lovejoy's press until he found freedom in Ohio, where he aided fugitive slaves. His works include an autobiographical *Narrative* (1847); *The Anti-Slavery Harp* (1848), poems; *My Three Years in Europe* (1852); *Clotelle; or, The President's Daughter* (London, 1853), said to be the first novel by a black; this tale of a mulatto born to Jefferson's housekeeper was issued in the U.S. without references to the President as *Clotelle: A Tale of the Southern States* (1864); *The Escape* (1858), a play; and *The Black Man: His Antecedents, His Genius, and His Achievements* (1863), expanded as *The Rising Son* (1874).

BROWNE, CHARLES FARRAR (1834–67), humorist born in Maine, is better known under his pseudonym Artemus Ward. In 1857 he began to contribute to the Cleveland *Plain Dealer* the series of "Artemus Ward's Sayings," a record of the imaginary adventures of an itinerant showman. He capitalized on the traits of backwoods and Down East characters, and attracted attention with comic misspellings. He often wrote on current events and jibed at insincerities and sentimentality. For a short time he was editor of *Vanity Fair.* He was at the height of his fame as a London lecturer and contributor to *Punch* when he died of tuberculosis. A selection from his books was made by A.J. Nock (1924).

BROWNE, J[OHN] ROSS (1821–75), born in Ireland, was brought to Kentucky when 11, and as a young man began his life of traveling, which furnished material for books. His first book, *Etchings of a Whaling Cruise* (1846), was influenced by Dana and in turn influenced *Moby-Dick.* His trip around the Horn to California, where he served as official reporter for the first Constitutional Convention (1849), and other Far Western experiences as a customs house inspector, special inspector of Indian affairs, and com-

missioner of mines furnished material for *Crusoe's Island . . . with Sketches of Adventures in California and Washoe* (1864) and *Adventures in Apache Country* (1869), which anticipate the attitude and materials of Mark Twain's *Roughing It.* His frontier humorist's view of Europe in *Yusef . . . a Crusade in the East* (1853), the first of several foreign travel books, preceded Twain's *Innocents Abroad.* Browne also wrote governmental reports and was U.S. minister to China.

BROWNSON, ORESTES AUGUSTUS (1803–76), New England clergyman and liberal thinker, originally a Presbyterian, became successively a Universalist, an independent, a Unitarian minister, and a Roman Catholic. He was an ardent advocate of various liberal and socialistic projects, supported the Workingmen's party, and was interested in Transcendentalism and Brook Farm. He set forth his ideas in several magazines that he edited, in *Charles Elwood, or the Infidel Converted* (1840), a semi-autobiographical novel; *The Convert* (1857), an account of his conversion to Catholicism, which created a contemporary sensation; and *The Spirit-Rapper* (1854), a romance concerning spiritualism, which the author attributed to Satanic influence.

BRYANT, WILLIAM CULLEN (1794–1878), born at Cummington, Mass., was educated at home, at the district schools, and at Williams College. After writing *The Embargo* (1808), at the age of 14, indignant satires against Jefferson's administration, he wrote *Thanatopsis*◆ and "To a Waterfowl,"◆ but left them unpublished while continuing a legal career that lasted to 1825. His fame as a poet dates from the printing of *Thanatopsis* (1817). In 1821 he read "The Ages" at Harvard as a Phi Beta Kappa poem and published his first mature book of *Poems.* In 1824–25 he wrote poems for the *United States Literary Gazette,* including "A Forest Hymn,"◆ "Monument Mountain," "Rizpah," and "An Indian at the Burial Place of His Fathers," which established him as the leading poet of the U.S. Early in 1825 he became co-editor of the New York *Evening Post,* whose full editorship he assumed in 1829 and held for almost 50 years. By 1840 he had become one of the leading Democratic editors, but his vigorous opposition to slavery brought him into the new Republican party. In 1832 he published a new collection of *Poems,* which included "The Death of the Flowers," "To the Fringed Gentian,"◆ "Mutation," and "The Song of Marion's Men." Although new additions and other books continued to appear, this edition contains all of the essential Bryant. Throughout he shows certain ideas growing always out of a limited range of emotional responses, and reporting a few aspects of man and nature. He was a poet of nature, and his work is often compared with that of Wordsworth, who profoundly influenced him, but Bryant's God remained ever a Divine Being distinct from His creation. Nature is simply the visible token of God's transcendent beauty and awful power, and thus nature influences man for good. There is a pervading sense of the transiency of earthly things, but he thinks of the somber certainty of the grave, rather than the earlier Puritan obsession with the terrors of hell. Although Bryant's themes were few and his thought not profound, he possessed a simple dignity and an impeccable, restrained style. The Doric nobility and dignity of the poet fitted him well for his translation of the *Iliad* (1870) and the *Odyssey* (1871–72), blank-verse renditions plain in style and simple in movement. His other publications include *The Fountain* (1842), *The White-Footed Deer* (1844), *A Forest Hymn* (1860), *Thirty Poems* (1864), *Hymns* (1869), *Among the Trees* (1874), and *The Flood of Years* (1878). His best prose is found in his *Letters of a Traveller* (1850; 2nd series, 1859), and in the collected *Orations and Addresses* (1873).

BRYCE, JAMES (1838–1922), English historian and diplomat, after a career as an Oxford professor, a member of Parliament, and in various political posts, became ambassador to the U.S. (1907–13). His great work *The American Commonwealth*♦ was published in 1888, after five visits to this country and wide reading on American history and institutions.

BUCK, PEARL [SYDENSTRICKER] (1892–1973), born in West Virginia, reared in China, where her parents were missionaries. Educated at Randolph-Macon and Cornell, she returned to be a missionary and teacher at Chinese universities. Of her many novels about China the best known is *The Good Earth*♦ (1931, Pulitzer Prize), the first of a trilogy, *The House of Earth,* also including *Sons* (1932) and *A House Divided* (1935). Other novels include *East Wind, West Wind* (1930), *The Mother* (1934), *This Proud Heart* (1938), *Dragon Seed* (1942), *Pavilion of Women* (1946), *Come, My Beloved* (1953), *Imperial Woman* (1956), about the last Chinese empress, and *The Living Reed* (1963),

about an upper-class Korean family from 1881 to the end of World War II. She also wrote stories; children's books; essays, mainly asking for U.S. understanding and support of China; *Fighting Angel* (1936) and *The Exile* (1936), biographies of her father and mother, collected in *The Spirit and the Flesh;* and *My Several Worlds* (1954) and *A Bridge for Passing* (1962), autobiographical narratives. She won a Nobel Prize in 1938.

BUECHNER, [CARL] FREDERICK (1926–   ), novelist and clergyman, after graduation from Princeton (1947) taught English at Lawrenceville School (1948–53) until ordained to the Presbyterian ministry (1958), after which he became a teacher of religion and school minister at Phillips Academy, Exeter, until 1967. His first novel, *A Long Day's Dying* (1949), is an elaborately contrived and strenuously symbolic work which deals with the tensions in the relations among a widow, her son, and her mother when she is discovered to have had sexual relations with the boy's young college instructor and, to save her reputation, accuses the teacher of a homosexual relationship with her son. The psychological analysis of the first novel, as well as its Jamesian mannerisms and baroque syntax, is also observable in *The Seasons' Difference* (1951), a novel about the responses of a group of children and adults to a vision seen by the youngsters' tutor. *The Return of Ansel Gibbs* (1958) is a story more plainly told of the private and public life of a liberal man appointed to a U.S. cabinet post. *The Final Beast* (1965) draws religious meaning from its tale of a minister whose attempt to aid a member of his congregation leads to a tragic misinterpretation of his actions. *The Entrance to Porlock* (1970) is a strangely symbolic novel, again in an elaborate style, of an octogenarian and his family as he becomes involved with a mystic and his queer charitable community. *Lion Country* (1971), *Open Heart* (1972), *Love Feast* (1974), and *Treasure Hunt* (1977) form a series of novels that create a parable related to individual involvement in evangelical religion. *The Magnificent Defeat* (1966) prints sermons; *The Hungering Dark* (1969), *The Alphabet of Grace* (1970), and *Wishful Thinking* (1973) contain meditations and prayers; *The Faces of Jesus* (1974) studies artists' interpretations of Christ; and *Telling the Truth* (1977) collects essays on the Gospel. *The Sacred Journey* (1982) is a memoir animated by the author's religious convictions, and *A Room Called Remember*

(1984), subtitled "Uncollected Pieces," contains sermons.

Buffalo Bill, see *Cody, W.F.*

Building of the Ship, The, ode in four-stress trochaic verse by Longfellow,♦ published in *The Seaside and the Fireside* (1849). A long narrative describes the construction and launching of a sailing ship. It concludes with the famous apostrophe to the Federal Union, beginning: "Thou, too, sail on, O Ship of State!"

BUKOWSKI, CHARLES (1920–   ), born in Germany, son of a U.S. soldier and German woman, reared in the U.S., worked mainly as an unskilled laborer until, aged 35, he began to write poetry. His prolific output, published in many limited-edition booklets, begun with *Flower, Fist and Bestial Wail* (1960), includes larger collections: *It Catches My Heart in Its Hands* (1963), *Burning in Water, Drowning in Flame* (1974), *Love Is a Dog from Hell* (1977), and *Dangling in the Tournefortia* (1981). In them his attitude is that of a tough, lowbrow outsider, egocentric and very masculine, whose personal interests and literary subjects are drink and sex and violence. He has also written stories: *Erections, Ejaculations, Exhibitions and General Tales of Ordinary Madness* (1972), *Life and Death in the Charity Ward* (1973), and *South of No North* (1973). *Notes of a Dirty Old Man* (1969) is partly memoir and partly fiction, while other novels are *Post Office* (1971), *Factotum* (1975), *Women* (1978), and *Ham on Rye* (1982), about the seedy life of the quasi-autobiographical Henry Chinaski. Wholly autobiographical works include *Confessions of a Man Insane Enough To Live with Beasts* (1965) and *Shakespeare Never Did This* (1979).

BULFINCH, THOMAS (1796–1867), son of Charles Bulfinch (1763–1844), a noted Boston architect, was the author of *The Age of Fable* (1855), a popular treatment of classic myths and also Scandinavian, Celtic, and Oriental myths. Other works include *The Age of Chivalry* (1858) on Arthurian and Welsh legends, *Shakespeare Adapted for Reading Classes* (1865), and *Oregon and Eldorado* (1866), treating a sea expedition to the Pacific Northwest which his father helped to organize.

Bulwark, The, novel by Dreiser,♦ posthumously published in 1946.

Solon Barnes is the son of a Quaker farmer and tradesman who brings his family from Maine to a Quaker suburb of Philadelphia, where his quiet faith and integrity make him a "bulwark" of the community. Despite his increasing wealth his faith is sorely tried when his children grow up to suffer, or, as he sees it, to sin. The death of Solon's wife is the final blow, and it seems that his religious faith may be shattered. Under the influence of these emotional shocks, however, he undergoes a deep religious conversion. In humility he blames his own lack of understanding for his children's errors, and expresses a philosophy of love for all creatures, faith in divinity and personal revelation, and acceptance of his sufferings.

Bumppo, NATTY, see *Leather-Stocking Tales.*

Bunker Hill, in Boston, was the approximate site of the first severe engagement of the Revolutionary War (June 17, 1775). The British attacked the newly constructed American fort on Breed's Hill, but were twice routed by the American defenders, who capitulated on the third charge, being out of powder. Although the battle was a British victory, American morale was strengthened by the demonstration of their small force. The battle is a frequent subject in American literature, as in Brackenridge's play *The Battle of Bunkers-Hill,* Cooper's novel *Lionel Lincoln,*♦ and J.W. De Forest's novel *A Lover's Revolt.*

BUNNER, H[ENRY] C[UYLER] (1855–96), edited *Puck* (1878–96), to which he contributed much of the familiar verse which appeared in such books as *Airs from Arcady and Elsewhere* (1884). Bunner's craftsmanship and urbanity are best seen in "*Short Sixes*" (1891), light stories and sketches about New York foreshadowing the work of O. Henry.

Bunyan, PAUL, giant hero of many tales told by lumberjacks of the Great Lakes region and the Pacific Northwest. Originally, the stories may have described a French Canadian, "Bon Jean," but in their later form they are pure mythology. They tell of the exploits of the greatest of all boss loggers, which include such fantastic feats as the creation of the Grand Canyon and Puget Sound, and the invention of the double-bitted axe and of a gigantic hotcake griddle, greased by flunkies who skate on it with sides of bacon strapped to their feet. Bunyan's crews included the one that logged on the Big Onion River during the winter of the blue snow, when it was so cold that cuss words froze in the air, thawing out the next Fourth of July with a great din. Among his companions were Babe the blue ox, who measured 42 axe handles and a plug of Star tobacco between the eyes; Sourdough Slim, the cook; and Johnny Inkslinger, the clerk. A similar hero of the South is Tony Beaver.♦ Books by Esther Shephard, T.G. Alvord, R.L. Stokes, and James Stevens collect Bunyan tales. Frost wrote a poem, "Paul's Wife," Louis Untermeyer wrote a verse version of many tales in *The Wonderful Adventures of Paul Bunyan* (1945), and the choral operetta *Paul Bunyan* by Auden and Benjamin Britten was produced (1941) but never published, except for three songs in Auden's *Collected Poems*.

BURGESS, GELETT [FRANK] (1866–1951), Massachusetts-born author, identified with San Francisco, where he led a literary group, Les Jeunes, in editing *The Lark* (1895–97), in which appeared his quatrain, "The Purple Cow," and his drawings of "goops."

BURKE, KENNETH [DUVA] (1897–), literary and philosophic critic, whose books include *Counter-Statement* (1931); *Permanence and Change: An Anatomy of Purpose* (1935), a philosophic investigation of the evolution of ethical ideas; *Attitudes Toward History* (2 vols., 1937), a psychological interpretation of historical events and characters; *The Philosophy of Literary Form* (1941), *A Grammar of Motives* (1945), and *A Rhetoric of Motives* (1950), linguistic analyses interpreting human motives; *The Rhetoric of Religion* (1961), further "studies in logology"; *Perspectives by Incongruity* (1964); *Language as Symbolic Action* (1966) and *Dramatism and Development* (1972). *Towards a Better Life* (1932) contains fictive "epistles and declamations"; *The White Oxen* (1924) prints stories; and poems are gathered in *Book of Moments* (1955) and *Collected Poems* (1968). He was awarded the National Medal for Literature♦ in 1980.

BURNETT, FRANCES [ELIZA] HODGSON (1849–1924), born in England, came to the U.S. (1865) and published *That Lass o' Lowrie's* (1877), a popular novel of the Lancashire coal mines. This was followed by romantic stories and novels, many of them for children, of which the most famous is *Little Lord Fauntleroy* (1886), about a kindly young American boy whose mother keeps

him in long curls, lace collars, and velvet suits when she takes him to England where he is the heir to a peerage and wins the affection of his crusty uncle, an earl. Mrs. Burnett dramatized the novel (1888) with great success.

BURNS, JOHN HORNE (1916–53), born in Massachusetts, educated at Andover and Harvard, served in the army during World War II, and as a teacher at a boys' school. Before his early death he wrote the novels *The Gallery* (1947), about the conquering American army in World War II; *Lucifer with a Book* (1949), a sensational view of a boys' boarding school; and *A Cry of Children* (1952).

BURROUGHS, EDGAR RICE (1875–1950), author of popular and fantastic adventure stories about Tarzan, the son of a British nobleman, deserted in the African jungle in infancy and reared by apes. *Tarzan of the Apes* (1914) is the first in a lengthy series of tales about the boy, who grows up to wed and have a son, and a grandson in the many sequels. He also wrote many works of science fiction.

BURROUGHS, JOHN (1837–1921), through keen observation of his native Catskills and under the influence of Emerson and Thoreau, became the greatest writer of nature essays after his two Transcendentalist masters. Although all his writing is characterized by a distinctive charm and simplicity, his first works, such as *Wake-Robin* (1871) and *Birds and Poets* (1877), are the most poetic in manner. *Locusts and Wild Honey* (1879) and *Squirrels and Other Fur-Bearers* (1900) are products of a period of more scientific observation, which lasted until *c*.1908. During his final years Burroughs held the belief that the salvation of society depends upon "the great teachers and prophets, poets and mystics," rather than upon cold scientific reason, and he expressed this creed in such books as *The Breath of Life* (1915) and *Accepting the Universe* (1920). He was a friend of Whitman, and his early appreciation of the poet may be seen in *Notes on Walt Whitman as Poet and Person* (1867), a book written in part by the subject. *My Boyhood* (1922) is autobiographical; *The Heart of John Burroughs's Journals* appeared in 1928.

BURROUGHS, WILLIAM S[EWARD] (1914–), born in St. Louis, long expatriated in Paris and elsewhere, best known for his frank accounts of his life as a drug addict, begun under the pseudonym of William Lee in

Junkie (1953) and continued in *The Naked Lunch* (Paris, 1959; New York, 1962), a bitter, existential account of an addict's life and a surrealistic evocation of the subjective horrors involved. Other works, showing a relation to the Beat movement, include *The Exterminator* (1960); *The Soft Machine* (Paris, 1961); *The Ticket That Exploded* (Paris, 1962); *Nova Express* (1964), fiction about interplanetary gangsters that satirizes modern life; *The Wild Boys* (1971), a fantasy about revolutionary homosexuals; *The Last Words of Dutch Schultz* (1975), fiction about a real gangster, whose deathbed talk is recorded; *Port of Saints* (1980), a quasi-autobiographical novel; *Cities of the Red Night* (1981), a novel about a Utopian settlement; and *The Place of Dead Roads* (1984), a kind of science fiction fantasy involving a 19th-century writer of wild west stories.

Bury the Dead, play by Irwin Shaw,♦ produced and published in 1936.

BUSHNELL, HORACE (1802–76), religious thinker, as pastor of the North Church (Congregational) of Hartford, Conn. (1833–59), propounded a gospel attacking the harshness of Calvinism, upholding the oneness of deity and the goodness of man, accepting intuition as a basis of theological knowledge, and emphasizing the New Testament. His books include *Christian Nurture* (1847); *God in Christ* (1849); *The Age of Homespun* (1851), depicting the rural New England of his youth; *Nature and the Supernatural* (1858), attacking Transcendentalism; and *The Vicarious Sacrifice* (1866). His writings were collected (1876–81), and *The Spirit in Man* was published in 1903.

Busy-Body Papers, 32 articles in the form of letters contributed to Bradford's *American Weekly Mercury* during 1729. Six of these (1–5, 8) are definitely ascribed to Franklin, and the others are supposed to be the work of his friends. The papers follow the Addisonian form in their homely comments on social, moral, and religious conduct, and other topics. The character Critico is evidently a satirical portrait of Franklin's rival, Samuel Keimer, and the entire series was begun as an attempt to win readers from Keimer's *Pennsylvania Gazette*.

By Blue Ontario's Shore, poem by Whitman,♦ first published in the 1856 edition of *Leaves of Grass* as "Poem of Many in One." Formed partly from the prose preface of 1855, it was reprinted in 1867 as "As I Sat Alone by Blue Ontario's Shore," and under its present title in 1881.

At the command of a Phantom, "Chant me the poem that comes from the soul of America," the poet sings of "These States . . . the amplest poem" and "the great Idea, the idea of perfect and free individuals . . . that is the mission of Poets." He calls for poets freed from past conventions, coteries, schools, and religions, celebrates himself "a man before all—myself, typical before all," and declares "These States—what are they except myself?" "Thrilled with the Power's pulsations and the charm of my theme," he announces, "Bards for my own land, only, I invoke."

By Love Possessed, novel by James Gould Cozzens,♦ published in 1957.

Between the time that an ornate French gilt clock inscribed "amor vincit omnia" strikes three o'clock one afternoon and its striking of four o'clock two days later, Arthur Winner, Jr., a conservative, middle-aged lawyer, undergoes a series of crises and discoveries that force him to alter the view he takes of himself, the rational standards of his revered late father (in whose living room the clock is situated), and his world, centered on his well-to-do and well-born family's community.

BYRD, WILLIAM (1674–1744), Virginia planter, resided at Westover on the James River, and in 1737 had the city of Richmond laid out on his lands. His library of more than 4000 volumes was reputedly the largest in the English colonies, and his cultural interests resulted in his membership in the Royal Society. He was a colonial agent in England (1697–1705, 1715–26). His commission as a surveyor of the boundary line between North Carolina and Virginia, reported in his *History of the Dividing Line,* and *Journey to the Land of Eden* and *Progress to the Mines,* posthumously published journals found among his Westover Manuscripts, are lively and witty accounts of an urbane patrician in a frontier setting. *The Secret Diary of William Byrd of Westover* (1941) and *Another Secret Diary* (1942) are later discovered accounts written in shorthand in the years 1709–12, 1739–41, as is *The London Diary* (1958) concerning part (1717–21) of his second residence in England.

C

CABELL, JAMES BRANCH (1879–1958), Virginia novelist and a man of letters best known for his series of urbane, highly mannered, pseudo-erudite romances of Dom Manuel, set in the mythical medieval country of Poictesme. *Beyond Life* (1919) and *Straws and Prayer-Books* (1924), critical works, are prologue and epilogue to the Poictesme series, composed of novels, stories, and poems, whose sequence of action, as distinct from sequence of publication, is: *Figures of Earth* (1921), *The Silver Stallion* (1926), *Domnei* (1920), *The Music from Behind the Moon* (1926), *Chivalry* (1909), *Jurgen* (1919), *The Line of Love* (1905), *The High Place* (1923), *Gallantry* (1907), *Something About Eve* (1927), *The Certain Hour* (1916), *The Cords of Vanity* (1909), *From the Hidden Way* (1916), *The Jewel Merchants* (1921), *The Rivet in Grandfather's Neck* (1915), *The Eagle's Shadow* (1904), and *The Cream of the Jest* (1917).

CABLE, GEORGE WASHINGTON (1844–1925), born in New Orleans, served in the Confederate army, studied engineering, and was a warehouse clerk before he turned to writing as a career. His early sketches were published in the New Orleans *Picayune,* and his stories of Louisiana local color appeared in *Scribner's* and *Appleton's* at intervals from 1873 to 1879. In the latter year he published a collection of romantic short stories, *Old Creole Days* (1879), which was followed by a novel about feuding and intrigues among 19th-century Creoles in Louisiana, *The Grandissimes* (1880). Other books include *Madame Delphine* (1881), a novelette about a quadroon woman; *Dr. Sevier* (1885), a novel set in New Orleans before and during the Civil War; *Bonaventure* (1888), concerned with a Creole among the descendants of Acadian exiles; *John March, Southerner* (1894), a novel of the Reconstruction, about an amiable old judge and his dealings with Northern intrigues in a small town; *Strong Hearts* (1899), a collection of stories; *The Cavalier* (1901), a story of the Civil War; and *Bylow Hill* (1902), treating the unhappy marriage of a New England clergyman and a Southern girl. Cable, who continued to write until 1918, was a leader of the local-color movement, and his stories depicting the charm of New Orleans society, though slight in narrative value, are distinguished by their style and an appreciation of the locality, although there were those who attacked his treatment of the Creoles.

CAHAN, ABRAHAM (1860–1951), who came to the U.S. from Russia (1882), was long the editor of the *Jewish Daily Forward.* Besides works in Yiddish he wrote realistic fiction in English, including *Yekl, a Tale of the New York Ghetto* (1896), *The Imported Bridegroom and Other Stories* (1898), and *The Rise of David Levinsky* (1917), a novel of the good and bad in a Jew's Americanization in New York. He also wrote an autobiography (5 vols., 1916–36).

CAIN, JAMES M[ALLAHAN] (1892–1977), novelist and journalist, known for his novels of racketeers and others on the criminal fringe. His books include *The Postman Always Rings Twice* (1934; dramatized, 1936; made into a film, 1946, 1981; adapted as an opera, 1982), a tough story, written in a popularization of Hemingway's style, about the plotting of a voluptuous girl and her lover, a young drifter, to murder her husband; *Double Indemnity* (1936); *Serenade* (1937); *Mildred Pierce* (1941); *Love's Lovely Counterfeit* (1942); *Past All Dishonor* (1946), set in Nevada during the Civil War; *The Butterfly* (1947); *The Moth* (1948); *Galatea* (1953); *Mignon* (1962), set in New Orleans just after the Civil War; *Rainbow's End* (1975); and *The Institute* (1976). *The Baby in the Icebox* (1981) collects stories.

Caine Mutiny, The, novel by Herman Wouk,♦ published in 1951. Part of the plot was dramatized by the author as *The Caine Mutiny Court-Martial* (1954).

Entering the navy as a midshipman in December 1942, Willie Keith, a wealthy, spoiled Princeton graduate, in love with a spirited nightclub singer, May Wynn, grows to manhood through his experiences in the South Pacific on the minesweeper *Caine.* When Philip Queeg comes aboard the wretched, filthy ship as commander he soon incurs the men's enmity because of his obsessive meticulousness, demonic orders and punishments, extreme emotional instability, and monomaniacal ambition. Tom Keefer, a clever intellectual, convinces the uneducated but loyal and capable executive officer, Steve Maryk, that Queeg is a classic paranoid who is too sick to hold command. During a typhoon, with Willie, now officer of the deck, Maryk takes command. He is court-martialed but acquitted, thanks to his shrewd lawyer, Barney Greenwald, who reveals at a triumphal dinner that Keefer, the author of the mutiny, had lied in order to keep his own future secure. Returning to the *Caine,* Willie becomes executive officer under Keefer, who shows cowardice at a decisive moment, when Willie saves the ship. Keefer is discharged, Willie becomes commanding officer on the *Caine's* final voyage, and, the war ended, he looks forward to marriage with May and preparation for a university teaching career.

Calamus, section of Whitman's *Leaves of Grass*♦ containing 45 poems first published in the 1860 edition. Its theme of the spiritual love of man for man complements that of "Children of Adam." ♦

The calamus, a plant generally known as the sweet flag, serves as a threefold symbol. Its leaves symbolize mortality; its fascicles, which cling together for support, represent "adhesive" love or friendship; and its perennial pink-tinged aromatic root is symbolic of immortal life, from which bloom successive transient forms. This mystical group of poems, frequently considered a reflection of the author's homosexuality, was said by Whitman to have "Political significance" in celebrating the "beautiful and sane affection of man for man" which would "make the continent indissoluble" and weld the states into a "Living Union."

The title was used by Richard Maurice Bucke♦ for his edition (1897) of letters written between 1868 and 1880 by Whitman to his friend Peter Doyle, a Washington streetcar conductor.

CALDWELL, Erskine [Preston] (1903–   ), Georgia-born prolific author of fiction whose best-known novels are *Tobacco Road* (1932), depicting the squalid, ignorant but sexually active lives of back-country sharecroppers, and *God's Little Acre* (1933), a somewhat more melodramatic tale of Georgia "crackers" that also displays rich folk humor, indignation at social inequities, and lusty bawdiness. *Tobacco Road* was dramatized by

Jack Kirkland (1933) with enormous success. Beginning in the 1930s Caldwell also wrote many volumes of short stories, long very popular in paperback reprints.

CALDWELL, [Janet] Taylor (1900–85), English-born novelist, reared in the U.S., began her career of writing very popular and dramatic novels, usually set in the past, with *Dynasty of Death* (1938), about wealthy families of munitions manufacturers, a saga continued in *The Eagles Gather* (1940) and *The Final Hour* (1944). Other novels include *The Earth Is The Lord's* (1941), about Genghis Khan; *Time No Longer* (1941), about Nazi Germany, and written under the pseudonym Max Reiner; *The Arm and the Darkness* (1943), set in 16th-century France; *This Side of Innocence* (1946), about rich and powerful New York families in the Gilded Age; *Dear and Glorious Physician* (1959); *A Prologue to Love* (1961); *A Pillar of Iron* (1965), a fictive life of Cicero; and *Answer as a Man* (1981), her thirty-sixth novel, about a rags-to-riches American at the beginning of the 20th century. *Dialogues with the Devil* (1967) comments on the modern world, revealing her conservative views and religious bent.

CALISHER, Hortense (1911–   ), born in New York City, graduated from Barnard, has taught English at various universities, and is known for her stories that subtly interpret character, collected in *In the Absence of Angels* (1951), *Tale for the Mirror* (1962), and *Extreme Magic* (1964). *False Entry* (1961) is a novel about a character known only by his pseudonym Pierre Goodman and his involvement in an Alabama trial, testifying against racists in the murder of a black. *Textures of Life* (1963) is a novel about relationships between parents and adult children and their respective marriages. *Journal from Ellipsia* (1965) is comic science fiction, and *Mysteries of Motion* (1983) is a serious novel involving space travel. *The Railway Police and The Last Trolly Ride* (1966) are two novellas. Other novels include *Queenie* (1971), *Eagle Eye* (1973), and *On Keeping Women* (1977), all depicting modern New Yorkers in family relationships. *Herself* (1972) is an autobiography.

Call of the Wild, The, novel by Jack London, ♦ published in 1903.

Buck, offspring of a St. Bernard and Scotch shepherd dog, lives on a California estate until he is stolen and shipped to the Klondike.

There he is trained as a sledge dog, and wins the leadership of the team from Spitz. He gives his entire allegiance to his master, John Thornton, even breaking the ice and dragging a 1000-pound load on a sledge so that Thornton may win a wager. After Thornton is murdered by Indians, Buck responds to the call of the wild, and abandons human civilization to lead a wolf pack.

CALLAGHAN, MORLEY (1903–), Canadian-born author, whose novels include *Strange Fugitive* (1928), the story of a bootlegger; *It's Never Over* (1930), tracing the effects of disgrace upon the family and friends of a murderer; *A Broken Journey* (1932); *Such Is My Beloved* (1934); *They Shall Inherit the Earth* (1935), a study of an average family during the Depression; *More Joy in Heaven* (1937); *The Loved and the Lost* (1951); *The Many-Colored Coat* (1960); *A Passion in Rome* (1961); *A Fine and Private Place* (1975); and *A Time for Judas* (1984), the story of Jesus as seen by Judas. *A Native Argosy* (1929) and *Close to the Sun Again* (1977) collect stories. *No Man's Meat* (1931) and *Now That April's Here* (1936) are novelettes. *That Summer in Paris* (1963) prints his "memories of tangled friendships with Hemingway, Fitzgerald, and some others."

Calvinism, system of theological thought found in the doctrinal expressions of the Reformed and Presbyterian churches, which derives its name from John Calvin (1509–64), the French Protestant reformer. In Calvin's own day, the element of his teaching that involved him in most conflict was his interpretation of Holy Communion, which differs from that of Luther, but his followers have been mainly distinguished by their emphasis upon predestination. The distinctive characteristics of Calvinism were formulated at the Synod of Dort (1618–19), in opposition to the Five Articles (1610) of the Arminians,♦ and are known as the Five Points: (1) total depravity, man's natural inability to exercise free will, since through Adam's fall he has suffered hereditary corruption; (2) unconditional election, which manifests itself through God's wisdom to elect those to be saved, despite their inability to perform saving works; (3) prevenient and irresistible grace, anticipatory grace available only to the elect; (4) perseverance of saints, predetermined elect inevitably persevere in the path of holiness; and (5) limited atonement, man's hereditary corruption, partially atoned for by Christ, and provided to the elect through the

Holy Spirit, gives them the power to attempt to obey God's will as revealed through the Bible. These five dicta were embodied in the beliefs of those whose church polity was Presbyterian, Baptist, and Congregational, and in the beliefs of certain other groups. In New England both Puritans♦ and Pilgrims♦ agreed with Calvinism in their creation of a theocratic state, but the Covenant theology♦ became as important as the original Calvinist doctrine. New Englanders tended to study Calvin less than such later formulators of Protestant opinion as William Perkins and William Ames. In addition to reading Augustine and other church fathers, they emphasized above all the Bible. Expressions of 17th-century Calvinist thought in New England may be found in such works as *The Wonder-Working Providence of Sions Saviour in New England,* ♦ *The Simple Cobler of Aggawam,* ♦ the *Magnalia Christi Americana,* ♦ and *The Day of Doom.* ♦ Later, Calvinism in the Congregational Church was considerably modified and softened by the Half-Way Covenant,♦ although under evangelical stress the earlier doctrines were temporarily revived in the Great Awakening. ♦ The doctrinal framework has been less successful in withstanding the changes in intellectual climate than have the ethical teachings, which have affected both orthodox Calvinists and such diverse thinkers as Franklin and the Transcendentalist writers.

Cambridge (originally NEWE TOWNE), Mass., is situated on the bank of the Charles River opposite Boston. It was founded (1636) by members of the Massachusetts Bay Company, and renamed (1638) in honor of the English university town, following the establishment of Harvard College. It has always been an intellectual center, and was the home of the first printing press in the English colonies, established by Stephen Daye. Craigie House, a colonial mansion occupied by Washington (1775) and later the home of Longfellow (1837–82), is situated there. Since Harvard, Radcliffe, and the Massachusetts Institute of Technology are all located there, it is not only a great center of higher education but a major axis for research in all fields of knowledge. Between the Harvard Yard and the campus of MIT is the district called "The Unknown City," a leading industrial and manufacturing center in New England. During the 19th century, Cambridge was the home of many literary figures, including Longfellow, Lowell, Dana, Margaret Fuller, Holmes, Howells, John Fiske,

C.E. Norton, and John Bartlett. Later authors, in addition to those associated with the university faculties, have included Samuel Crothers, Margaret Deland, Conrad Aiken, David McCord, and May Sarton.

Cambridge Platform, basic statement of New England Congregationalism♦ until the adoption of the Saybrook Platform (1708) in Connecticut. The Cambridge Platform was drafted by Richard Mather, amended and adopted by a church synod at Cambridge (1648), and printed as *A Platform of Church-Discipline* (1649).

Can Such Things Be?, 24 stories by Ambrose Bierce,♦ published in 1893. Mainly concerned with episodes of the Civil War and the California frontier, they are marked by a psychological realism, sardonic humor, and clever use of surprise endings and effects of supernatural horror, exhibited in such titles as "The Realm of the Unreal," "Some Haunted Houses," "Bodies of the Dead," and "Mysterious Disappearances."

"My Favorite Murder" is a perversely humorous narrative which concludes: "Altogether, I cannot help thinking that in point of atrocity my murder of Uncle William has seldom been excelled." "The Famous Gilson Bequest," anticipating Clemens's "The Man That Corrupted Hadleyburg," tells of a hanged California horse-thief who leaves his wealth to the man who convicted him, maliciously stipulating that anyone who can prove that Gilson robbed him shall receive the property instead. This results in years of litigation, the wrecking of moral conscience in the community, and the premature aging and death of his victim. "One Kind of Officer," a Civil War story, tells of Captain Ransome's fire on his own troops, owing to the mistaken orders of a general who is killed in battle, leaving Ransome to be punished for his superior's error.

Cane, work by Jean Toomer,♦ published in 1923, is a major product of the Harlem Renaissance. A brief book incorporating stories, poetry, and a play, the first third presents black people, mainly women, in the South in prose and verse sketches; the next group of tales deals with light-colored persons in the North, uncertain about themselves and their place in society; and the last third of the work contains one story, "Kabnis," about a black of that name from the North who goes to the South as a teacher,

meets blacks of diverse views, and is frustrated in his search for a way of life.

Cannery Row, novel by John Steinbeck,♦ published in 1945.

On Cannery Row in Monterey, California, live Doc, the sympathetic, wise, lonely owner of the Western Biological Laboratory; Dora, the tough-minded but warm-hearted madam of a brothel, the Bear Flag Restaurant; Lee Chong, the shrewd, kind proprietor of a remarkably well-stocked grocery store; and Mack and his five happy-go-lucky friends, compounded of "Virtues and graces and laziness and zest." Since they like and admire Doc, these pleasant, philosophic bums engage in a great expedition to catch frogs for which Doc will pay and thus finance a surprise party they plan for him. Fortified by liquor got from Lee, they begin their party at Doc's laboratory, of which they accidentally make a shambles and from which their innumerable frogs escape long before Doc arrives. Ashamed of the disaster, the men settle into gloom until months later, forgiven by Lee and Doc, and with Dora's aid, they plan a birthday party for Doc, who locks up his valuables for a party that has "all the best qualities of a riot and a night on the barricades."

Cantos, The, long, fluid body of poetry by Ezra Pound.♦ Begun with the publication of the first three segments in *Quia Pauper Amavi* (1919), the work occupied Pound for most of the rest of his life. Succeeding volumes adding to the work are *A Draft of XVI Cantos . . . for the Beginning of a Poem of Some Length* (1925), *A Draft of Cantos XVII to XXVII* (1928), *A Draft of XXX Cantos* (1933), *Eleven New Cantos, XXXI–XLI* (1934), *The Fifth Decad of Cantos* (1937), *Cantos LII–LXXI* (1940), *The Pisan Cantos* (1948)—a particularly unified segment of ten sections based on Pound's incarceration in an Italian prisoner-of-war camp, in which he views himself as a romantic hero whose sensibility will bring order to a world of chaos, *Section: Rock-Drill, 85–95 de los Cantares* (1956), *Thrones; 96–109 de los Cantares* (1959). The writing begun in 1915 was finally collected in *The Cantos of Ezra Pound* (1970), but the work was not brought to any conclusion and simply trails off with fragments of Cantos 110 to 117.

In kaleidoscopic manner, lacking any evident overall plan or continuing narrative, the cantos move with very free association over diverse aspects and eras of history, American, European, and Oriental, for all time is treated as contemporary. Similarly there is no distinction made in the use of diverse languages, and the English is often peppered with Greek, Latin, Provençal, Italian, and Chinese, according to the subject of the passages of frequently shifting topics. Not only are subject and language very varied, but the elliptical style ranges from laconic and esoteric juxtapositions to lengthy allusive associations. Among all this variety there are, however, relationships which apparently are meant to evaluate history by comparison, and to present a morality for the individual based on Confucian thought and one for society depending upon the ostensibly humanitarian use of state-controlled credit and money. The *Cantos* are filled with esoteric lore, recondite theories, personal allusions, and the author's own crotchets so that they are extremely difficult to follow in their entirety, no matter how evocative or effective limited passages or particular images may be, with the result that the whole body of work breaks into fragments that are often not only pedantic but confusing. Nevertheless, the work, particularly in its earlier sections, has had a tremendous impact on modern poetry.

Cape Cod, descriptive work by Thoreau,♦ posthumously published (1865) and edited by the younger W.E. Channing, after chapters had been printed in *Putnam's Magazine* (1855) and the *Atlantic Monthly* (1864). Describing the natural environment and people of "the bare and bended arm of Massachusetts," the account is based on the author's experiences during three short visits to Cape Cod (Oct. 1849; June 1850; July 1855) and includes ten essays on the history and character of the inhabitants, "The Highland Light," Nantucket, the sea, the beach, and other aspects of the Cape.

CAPOTE, TRUMAN (1924–84), New Orleans-born author whose novels are *Other Voices, Other Rooms*♦ (1948), about a homosexually inclined boy painfully groping toward maturity; and *The Grass Harp* (1951, dramatized 1952), about innocent people, old and young, escaping social restraint by living in a tree house. *Breakfast at Tiffany's*♦ (1958) is a novella about a light-hearted, amoral playgirl of New York, Holly Golightly. *Tree of Night* (1949) contains stories, and *Local Color* (1950) collects travel sketches. *House of Flowers* (1954) is a musical play set in a West Indies bordello. *The Muses Are Heard* (1956)

is a witty account of his travels with the black cast of *Porgy and Bess* through Russia. *In Cold Blood*♦ (1966) examines a notorious multiple murder. *A Christmas Memory* (1966), *The Thanksgiving Visitor* (1969) and *One Christmas* (1983) are memoirs of childhood; *The Dogs Bark* (1973) collects essays and other short pieces; and *Then It All Came Down* (1976) contains interviews and comments on current criminal justice. *Music for Chameleons* (1980) is another collection of pieces, a true murder tale, some recollections, and short stories.

Captain Craig, blank-verse narrative by E.A. Robinson,♦ the title poem of a volume published in 1902.

Captain of the Gray-Horse Troop, The, novel by Hamlin Garland.♦

Captains Courageous, novel by Kipling,♦ published in 1897.

Captivity Narrative, account of kidnapping by Indians of white persons, usually women, taken by long journeys into the wilderness. The tale of Mary Rowlandson♦ (1682), the earliest example, is representative of New England colonial texts concentrating on the Indians as sons of the Devil removing a daughter of Zion into Satan's lands, often considering it a judgment or test of the Lord. Later accounts, like that of John Williams♦ (1707), telling of the seizure of a man, represent an 18th-century shift to a political point of view in presenting the French allies of the Indians as evil in trying to convert a captive to Catholicism. The genre passed into fiction with Ann Bleecker♦ (1797). In the 19th century the popular account about Mary Jemison♦ (1824) sentimentalized a white woman's romantically happy adjustment to primitive life. Later narratives were like melodramatic penny dreadfuls, as in R.B. Stratton's *The Captivity of the Oatman Girls* (1857), dealing with Far Western Indians.

CAREY, HENRY CHARLES (1793–1879), son of Mathew Carey, in whose publishing firm he was a partner until he retired to write his *Essay on the Rate of Wages* (1835), which mainly accepted the doctrine of laissez-faire, believing that natural laws tend toward a universal harmony of interests. His other works include *Principles of Political Economy* (3 vols., 1837–40) and *The Past, the Present, and the Future* (1848), championing a protective tariff. His *Harmony of Interests* influenced the high U.S. Tariff Act of 1861. In later works he prescribed manufactures for the South, lamented the low tariff, and reiterated his idea of harmony. *The Principles of Social Science* (3 vols., 1858–59) contains the summation of his doctrines, stressing the analogy between natural and social science.

CARMAN, [WILLIAM] BLISS (1861–1929), Canadian-born poet, after 1888 made his home in New York and Connecticut. He edited *The Chap-Book* and published his first notable poetry in *Low Tide on Grand Pré: A Book of Lyrics* (1893), whose youthful buoyancy and pagan love of nature won it immediate success. In collaboration with Richard Hovey♦ he wrote *Songs from Vagabondia* (1894), which, being marked by a carefree gypsy spirit, helped to initiate a revolt against the scholarly and anemic poetry of the time. The collaboration was continued in *More Songs from Vagabondia* (1896) and *Last Songs from Vagabondia* (1901).

CARNEGIE, ANDREW (1835–1919), Scottish-born industrialist, began work in a cotton factory after his family moved to Pennsylvania (1848). By 1873 he was engaged in the steel industry, in which he showed remarkable organizing ability and shrewd judgment, as in the selection of such lieutenants as Henry C. Frick. His career was climaxed (1901) when the U.S. Steel Corporation purchased his interests for $250,000,000. During his retirement he wrote an essay, *The Gospel of Wealth* (1889), setting forth the idea that rich men are trustees for the public benefit, which he put into practice in large endowments to educational institutions, including the Carnegie Institute at Pittsburgh (since 1967 Carnegie-Mellon University), and in gifts for the erection of libraries throughout the U.S. His books include *Triumphant Democracy* (1886), *The Empire of Business* (1902), and an *Autobiography* (1920).

Carolina Playmakers, writing and producing group founded at the University of North Carolina (1918) by Frederick Henry Koch (1877–1944), who had founded the Dakota Playmakers in 1910. The North Carolina group, now called the Playmakers Repertory Company, in their own theater and during frequent tours through the Southern states has been influential in the little-theater movement as a leader in regional and folk drama. Plays by student writers, including Thomas Wolfe and Paul Green, have been published in a series of *Carolina Folk-Plays.*

CARRUTH, HAYDEN (1921–), Connecticut-born poet whose works, employing traditional forms, include *The Crow and the Heart* (1959), *Nothing for Tigers* (1965), *For You* (1970), *From Snow and Rock, for Chaos* (1973), *If You Call This Cry a Song* (1983), and *The Sleeping Beauty* (1983). *The Bloomingdale Papers* (1975) is an early long poem chronicling his experiences in a mental hospital. *Appendix A* (1963) is a novel, and *Working Papers* (1982) collects essays and reviews.

CARRYL, CHARLES EDWARD (1842–1920), New York financier, was an author of juvenile fantasies in the tradition of Lewis Carroll. These include *Davy and the Goblin* (1886) and *The Admiral's Caravan* (1892), which are interspersed with such verses as "The Plaint of the Camel" and "Robinson Crusoe's Story."

CARRYL, GUY WETMORE (1873–1904), son of Charles Edward Carryl, was also an author of light verse, published in such volumes as *Fables for the Frivolous* (1898), *Mother Goose for Grown-Ups* (1900), and *Grimm Tales Made Gay* (1903).

CARVER, RAYMOND (1939–), Oregon-born author, on the faculty of Syracuse University, is best known for his short stories, often treating the bleak lives of blue-collar people, published in *Will You Please Be Quiet, Please* (1976), *What We Talk About When We Talk About Love* (1981), and *Cathedral* (1983). Poems are collected in *Winter Insomnia* (1970) and *At Night the Salmon Move* (1976). *Fires* (1984) is a selection of poems, stories, and essays.

CARY, ALICE (1820–71), Ohio-born author whose quasi-autobiographical stories and sketches, *Clovernook; Or Recollections of Our Neighborhood in the West* (1852), give a good sense of a woman's life on the frontier. A "Second Series" (1853) introduced the coming of cities and commerce. With her sister Phoebe (1824–71) she moved to New York, gained a reputation for their *Poems* (1849), and became the subject of Whittier's poem "The Singer."

Casey at the Bat, mock-heroic poem by Ernest Lawrence Thayer, first published in the San Francisco *Examiner* (June 3, 1888). The poem, which soon became enormously popular and was a favorite piece in the repertory of DeWolf Hopper, tells of the dramatic defeat of the Mudville baseball team when its hero, the great Casey, struck out.

Cask of Amontillado, The, tale by Poe,♦ published in *Godey's Lady's Book* (1846).

During the excitement of the carnival in an Italian city, Montresor determines to seek revenge for "the thousand injuries" inflicted on him by Fortunato, a wine connoisseur. He inveigles the drunken Fortunato to his underground vault to taste a choice Amontillado he claims to have stored there. When they reach a crypt at the end of a passage, Montresor shackles the stupefied Fortunato and proceeds to wall him up with stone and mortar. Fortunato cries for help, but there is no one to hear, and Montresor completes his work, the last sound from his victim being a faint jingling of bells on his carnival motley.

Cassandra, poem in iambic tetrameter quatrains by E.A. Robinson,♦ published in *The Man Against the Sky* (1916). This prophetic satire of thoughtless American ideals denounces the modern trinity of "Dollar, Dove, and Eagle," and predicts their defeat by "the merciless old verities," asserting that "the power is yours, but not the sight":

> You have the ages for your guide,
> But not the wisdom to be led.

CASSILL, R[ONALD] V[ERLIN] (1919–), born in Iowa, educated at the University of Iowa, where he has taught creative writing. His novels include *Eagle on the Coin* (1950), treating personal and political involvements in a black's campaign for a small-town school board; *Clem Anderson* (1961), about the degradation and death of a promising young author; *The President* (1964), about a psychotic, power-seeking college president; *La Vie Passionée of Rodney Buckthorne* (1968), a comic work about academia and Greenwich Village culture; *Dr. Cobb's Game* (1970), a lively tale drawing on Britain's Profumo case of 1963 to treat sexual and social motivations; *The Goss Women* (1974), another story of sex and society; *Hoyt's Child* (1976); and *Labors of Love* (1980), presenting a failing author who overcomes his writer's block and begins to analyze women when deserted by his wife and his mistress. *The Father* (1965) collects stories. He has also issued popular paperback novels under his own name and that of Owen Aherne.

Cat on a Hot Tin Roof, play by Tennessee Williams,♦ produced and published in 1955 and awarded a Pulitzer Prize.

On his sixty-fifth birthday, Big Daddy Pollitt, vulgar, fat, ruthless, and the richest cotton planter of the Mississippi Delta, is surrounded by his family: Brick, his favorite son, a withdrawn, alcoholic ex-football hero, and Brick's wife Maggie, the passionate, vital "cat" who is unrelenting in her struggle to get what she wants; Gooper, the hypocritical, avaricious elder son whose wife Mae is about to produce their sixth "no-neck monster" child; and Big Mama, his loud, garrulous wife of 40 years. Maggie, determined to have marital relations with her remote husband and to produce an heir for the plantation, turns on Brick to tell him that she and his closest friend, Skipper, now dead, had slept together because each needed the warmth that Brick's "godlike" superiority and ideally pure relationship would not provide, and that in forcing Skipper to face the truth of his latent homosexuality she drove him to drink, drugs, and destruction. Soon after, Big Daddy makes Brick see that his alcoholism stems not from a noble disgust with the "mendacity" of the world, but from disgust with himself for refusing to help Skipper when the basic nature of their relationship became evident. Faced by his own truth, Brick retaliates by telling Big Daddy that he is dying of cancer. Aware that there is no will and anxious to inherit the rich plantation, Gooper and Mae tell Big Mama the truth about her husband's health and are surprised by her outraged revulsion toward the trusteeship they have had prepared. Wanting to make Big Daddy happy and determined not to be disinherited, Maggie announces that she and Brick are expecting a child, and later that evening, having locked away the liquor, she sets about attempting to make the lie come true, hoping both to rekindle Brick's desire and to save him from his cold detachment and death-in-life.

Catch-22, novel by Joseph Heller,♦ published in 1961.

On the Mediterranean island of Pianosa during the last months of World War II, Captain John Yossarian of the U.S. air force attempts to avoid further combat after having experienced grisly events and observing his fellow officers being ridiculous in their lust for promotion. Trying to be grounded as insane, he turns up naked at the ceremony in which General Dreedle is to award him a

DFC. His commander, Captain Cathcart, drives his men to more and more combat, so that he may look impressive, and General Peckham makes them fly in formations that will make his aerial photos look good, while Lieutenant Milo Minderbinder ignores the whole matter of war and enemy forces as he goes about making a fortune and gaining power in black-market schemes. But fantastic bureaucratic rulings, extending to a Catch-22, prevent Yossarian from achieving his objective, and he deserts to seek a saner world in neutral Sweden.

Catcher in the Rye, The, novel by J.D. Salinger,♦ published in 1951.

Holden Caulfield, a lonely, compassionate, and quixotic 16-year-old boy, plagued by the "phoniness" of his moral environment, leaves Pencey, the Pennsylvania preparatory school from which he has been expelled, for New York City. Having said goodbye to his conceited athletic roommate Stradlater and the "pimply, boring" Ackley, and fearful of confronting his parents, he checks into a depressing, cheap hotel. Unable to see or telephone his innocent, affectionate sister Phoebe, of whom he is very fond, he goes in desperation to nightclubs. Returning to the hotel, he accepts the elevator operator's offer of a prostitute, but depressed by and sorry for the girl, he retains his virginity, only to be confronted soon by the girl and her pimp, Maurice, who demands more money and fights with Holden. The next morning he meets Sally Hayes, an old girl friend, takes her ice skating, tells her that he is tired of the ubiquitous hypocrisy that he encounters, and asks her to run away with him to the New England countryside. Righteously angered by his impractical scheme, the pseudo-sophisticated Sally refuses, they fight, and Holden leaves her. After becoming drunk and making a nostalgic visit to Central Park, he sneaks home that evening to see Phoebe, who is distressed by his negativism and challenges him to name one thing he would like to be. Holden replies that he would like to be "the catcher in the rye." Mistaken in his recollection of Burns's poem, he says, "Anyway, I keep picturing all these little kids playing some game in this big field of rye and all. Thousands of little kids, and nobody's around—nobody big, I mean—except me. And I'm standing on the edge of some crazy cliff. What I have to do, I have to catch everybody if they start to go over the cliff—I mean if they're running and they don't look

where they're going . . . ," a persistent image indicative of his desire to preserve innocence. Leaving his parents' apartment, he spends the night at the home of Mr. Antolini, his former English teacher, whose homosexual advances repel Holden and set him in flight. "Confused and frightened and even sickened by human behavior," he decides to see Phoebe once more before running away to the West, but suddenly filled with love for her and the world, he knows he cannot leave. After going home, Holden has a nervous breakdown, but recovers to tell in his own vivid vernacular of these two dramatic days and of the experiences and feelings that lie behind them, as he is filled with sympathy for everyone he has known, "even . . . that goddam Maurice."

Cathedral, The, blank-verse poem by J.R. Lowell,♦ published Christmas 1869. A revised edition (1877) includes the "Ode Recited at the Harvard Commemoration."

CATHER, WILLA [SIBERT] (1873–1947), born in Virginia, as a child moved with her family to Nebraska, where she was reared among the immigrants who are the subjects of many of her novels. After graduation from the University of Nebraska (1895), where her study of Latin may have influenced her graceful Virgilian style, and a period of journalism and high-school teaching, she published a book of poems, *April Twilights* (1903, enlarged 1923), and a book of short stories, *The Troll Garden* (1905). She was on the staff of *McClure's* (1906–12), leaving to devote herself to creative writing after the publication of her first novel, *Alexander's Bridge* (1912), the story of an engineer torn between love for his wife and the woman he had loved during his youth. With *O Pioneers!*♦ (1913) she turned to the Nebraska prairies to tell of the heroic and creative qualities of the passing frontier. *The Song of the Lark*♦ (1915) is again a study of a woman's character; and *My Ántonia*♦ (1918), episodic in construction like her other novels, tells of a Bohemian immigrant girl's life on the frontier, and the pioneer strength that preserves her through numerous adversities. *One of Ours* (1922), which won a Pulitzer Prize although it is not considered to rank with her best work, tells of a young man's escape from his oppressive life on a Midwestern farm to vitalizing experiences as a soldier in France during World War I. *A Lost Lady*♦ (1923) differs from Cather's previous studies of women in the Middle West in that the heroine's grace, charm, and cultivated taste place her above and apart from the new grasping generation that succeeds the era of pioneers. *The Professor's House*♦ (1925) is partly the story of an idealistic scholar's adjustment to middle age, and partly that of his favorite student's discovery of an ancient cliff city in New Mexico, the description of which foreshadows the setting of *Death Comes for the Archbishop. My Mortal Enemy* (1926) is a short novel concerned with a selfish and strong-willed woman who brings about her own downfall. The author's idealism and love of the past reach a climax in *Death Comes for the Archbishop*♦ (1927), her celebration of the spiritual pioneering of the Catholic Church in New Mexico. Catholicism is also at the core of *Shadows on the Rock*♦ (1931), which deals with 17th-century Quebec. *Lucy Gayheart* (1935) is the story of a Midwestern girl who gives up an early love affair to study music, then abandons her career to become the mistress of an egotistical concert singer and meets an accidental death after he deserts her. *Sapphira and the Slave Girl* (1940) is a novel based on a story recalled from her Virginia childhood. *Obscure Destinies* (1932) contains three novelettes set in small communities of the Middle West, and *Youth and the Bright Medusa* (1920) is a volume of stories dealing with the careers of artists. *Not Under Forty* (1936) is a collection of essays presenting the author's theory of fiction, and describing literary encounters with writers who influenced her, such as Sarah Orne Jewett.

CATLIN, GEORGE (1796–1872), self-taught painter of Indian life, lived in Pennsylvania until 1832, when he made an eight-year expedition to various Indian tribes from the Yellowstone River to Florida, resulting in the 300 engravings and descriptive text of *The Manners, Customs and Condition of the North American Indians* (2 vols., 1841). From 1852 to 1857 he traveled in Central and South America and explored the Far West, as recorded in *Last Rambles Amongst the Indians of the Rocky Mountains and the Andes* (1867) and *Life Among the Indians* (1867). He also aroused interest in Indian culture by bringing troupes of Indians to the East and Europe, before the period of the shows of Buffalo Bill and P.T. Barnum. His artistic work, though uneven in quality and primitive in style, possesses the charm,

sincerity, and documentary value of authentic records of American Indian life.

Cat's Cradle, novel by Vonnegut, ♦ published in 1963.

Jonah, a journalist, goes to Ilium, N.Y., the manufacturing city where the late Felix Hoenikker lived, to write a book about that eccentric scientist and his invention of an atom bomb and of a crystal named ice-nine that will freeze anything aqueous with which it comes in contact. On a magazine assignment Jonah next goes to the Latin American island nation of San Lorenzo. There he learns of the black adventurer and ex-soldier Earl McCabe, who was the land's autocratic ruler until superseded by Papa Monzano, a dictator, who has been aided by Hoenikker's son Franklin. Jonah learns too of another black ex-soldier, Lionel Boyd Johnson, who has become the people's spiritual leader by the creation of a religion called Bokononism and the preaching of "foma," useful lies. Papa Monzano kills himself with a bit of ice-nine that he got from Franklin Hoenikker, and when by accident his frozen body slides into the sea, all the surrounding water is congealed and all the San Lorenzans are killed, save Bokonon, Jonah, and a few others.

Caulfield, HOLDEN, hero of *The Catcher in the Rye.* ♦

Cave, The, novel by R.P. Warren. ♦

Cavender's House, dramatic narrative in blank verse by E.A. Robinson, ♦ published in 1929.

Cawdor, narrative poem by Robinson Jeffers, ♦ the title piece of a volume published in 1928.

Using a powerful unrhymed five- and ten-stress line, the poet sets his story in the farming country of the California coast in 1909–10. After a fire destroys their farm, Fera Martial and her blind father go to live with their neighbor Cawdor. When Cawdor desires her for her beauty, Fera marries him, but she falls in love with Cawdor's young son Hood. The lad refuses her advances, and for revenge Fera tells her husband that his son has raped her. Infuriated, Cawdor quarrels with Hood and accidentally kills him. Later, after Fera tells Cawdor the truth, he blinds himself in a passion of guilt.

Cayuga Indians, see *Iroquois Indians.*

***Celebrated Jumping Frog of Calaveras County,
The,*** sketch by Clemens♦ written under his
pseudonym Mark Twain, was published in
the New York *Saturday Press* (1865) and
reprinted as the title piece of a series of
sketches that formed his first book (1867).
Although his source was an old folk tale that
had been in print in California as early as
1853, Clemens was catapulted into fame by
his version, which tells of the jumping frog
Dan'l Webster, pet of gambling Jim Smiley,
which is defeated when a stranger fills its
gullet with quail shot while Smiley's attention
is distracted.

Celestial Railroad, The, allegorical tale by
Hawthorne,♦ published in 1843 and collected in *Mosses from an Old Manse* (1846).

The narrator travels the way of Christian in
Pilgrim's Progress, from the City of Destruction to the Celestial City. Instead of going
afoot, he finds that modern achievement has
made possible an easy, convenient Celestial
Railroad, on which he rides in the company of
affable, bluff Mr. Smooth-it-away, who scoffs
at the difficult path of old-fashioned pilgrims.
The ancient landmarks and institutions are all
changed, and on arriving at the end of the line,
the passengers expect to cross the river by
steam ferryboat. But here Mr. Smooth-it-
away deserts them, laughing and showing his
identity by breathing smoke and flame. About
to drown, the narrator suddenly awakens to
"thank Heaven it was a Dream!"

Centaur, The, novel by John Updike,♦ published in 1963.

During three winter days of 1944 George
Caldwell, a 50-year-old high-school teacher
of science in Olinger, Pa., and his teenage
son Peter have experiences that, though
realistically told, are parallel to classic myths.
Olinger is Olympus; the senior Caldwell is
Chiron, the centaur who was a teacher of
heroes, famed for surrendering his immortality and accepting death to be released from
the pain of a wound; and Peter is not only an
uneasy adolescent troubled by a skin disease,
infatuated by a sweet girl, Penny, and envious of boys who are better athletes or more
appealing, but he is Prometheus in love with
Penelope and envious of Daedalus. While
Caldwell copes with his wife Cassie (Ceres),
who is eager to develop their property into a
farm, and with his father-in-law, Pop Kramer
(Kronos), he moves restlessly through life as

he encounters a veritable pantheon of deities:
the garage mechanic Al Hummel (Hephais-
tos), who helps him when he is wounded, as
does Doc Appleton (Apollo); the school
principal Zimmerman (Zeus), a petty tyrant
enjoying an affair with a school-board member, Mrs. Herzog (Hera); and the lascivious
physical education teacher, Vera (Venus),
who is attracted to the local minister, the
Rev. March (Ares).

Center for Editions of American Authors,
organized by the Modern Language Association (1963) to promote textual and bibliographical study and to oversee the creation of
approved texts for definitive editions of
classic American authors, including Cooper,
Stephen Crane, John Dewey, Emerson,
Hawthorne, Howells, Irving, Melville,
Simms, Thoreau, Mark Twain, and Whitman. Its publication program was later directly overseen by the National Endowment
for the Humanities.

Century of Dishonor, A, treatise by Helen
Hunt Jackson.♦

Chainbearer, The, novel by Cooper,♦ published in 1845 as the second part of his
Littlepage Manuscripts.♦

Chambered Nautilus, The, poem by
Holmes,♦ included in *The Autocrat of the
Breakfast-Table* (1858) and in later collections of poems. It consists of five seven-line
stanzas, in the pattern of three iambic pen-
tameters, three trimeters, and a final alexan-
drine: $a5a3b3b5b5c3c6$.

A chambered nautilus is a mollusk that
begins life in a small shell and builds larger
ones as it grows. In the poem this symbolizes
human endeavor, and the reader is exhorted
to build a broader and more comprehensive
life, growing with his age and experience.

Chan, CHARLIE, detective hero of a number
of mystery novels by Earl Derr Biggers.♦

Chance Acquaintance, A, novel by Howells,♦
published in 1873.

CHANDLER, RAYMOND (1888–1959), born
in Chicago, reared in England, moved to
southern California (1912) but did not begin
to write his famous mystery stories until he
was in his forties. He soon became the prime
figure of the school of hard-boiled detective
fiction, also distinguished for his presentation
of the seamy side of his Los Angeles setting.

His tough sleuth, Philip Marlowe, became a cult figure. Chandler's major works are *The Big Sleep* (1939), *Farewell, My Lovely* (1940), *The Lady in the Lake* (1943), and *The Long Goodbye* (1954), all of which were made into very popular films.

CHANNING, WILLIAM ELLERY (1780–1842), born in Rhode Island, became pastor of a Boston Congregational church (1803) but broke with its tenets and by 1819 was considered the "apostle" of Unitarianism and the leading opponent of Calvinism. As a stimulating force in the intellectual life of Massachusetts, he did much to prepare the way for Transcendentalism and other advanced social and cultural movements. In his *Remarks on American Literature* (1830), he asks for a literary Declaration of Independence. His pamphlets on pacifism, antislavery, temperance, public education, and labor conditions are included in his collected *Works* (6 vols., 1841–43).

Chantey, sailors' song, whose stanzas, subject to occasional extemporization, were sung by a leader while others joined in the rhythmical refrain, intended to make easier such work as pulling ropes or moving the capstan. Many chanteys originated among American sailors, and others among lumbermen in the forests of Maine and the Northwest. "The Rio Grande," "Shenandoah," and "Blow the Man Down" are well-known examples of the type.

Chanting the Square Deific, poem by Whitman, ♦ published in the *Sequel to Drum-Taps* (1865–66) and added to the 1867 edition of *Leaves of Grass.*

This expression of Whitman's religious thought is presented in four stanzas, each dealing with an aspect of the deity. The first side of the square deific is Jehovah, or the relentless, inexorable laws of nature. The second is Christ, the affectionate "consolator." The third is Satan, the spirit of individual freedom in opposition to the omnipotent. The fourth is the feminine Santa Spirita, the soul which mystically pervades all, giving direction and form to the divine energies.

Chap Book, The (1894–98), semi-monthly little magazine, was founded at Cambridge as a house organ of the publishers Stone and Kimball. Moved with the firm to Chicago after six months, it had already become a separate publication, printing works by

Henry James, Hamlin Garland, Eugene Field, Bliss Carman, and Julian Hawthorne, in addition to contributions from such foreign authors as Wells, Beerbohm, Stevenson, Henley, and Yeats. In typography, illustrations, and literary content, the magazine was faintly suggestive of the English *fin de siècle* publications, and in its turn affected *The Lark* ♦ and other American periodicals. It was increased in size (1897) and later lost much of its charm and naïveté.

Chapbooks, pamphlet editions of popular literature, widely distributed in the early U.S., especially during the first quarter of the 19th century. Like the English publications of the same type, they included such various materials as jokes, ballads, marvelous accounts, fables, Gothic tales, biographies of popular heroes, model letters, moral stories, and orations. Mason Weems ♦ was an author and peddler of chapbooks, and among the prominent publishers was Isaiah Thomas. Chapbooks shared with almanacs and newspapers the most important place in the dissemination of popular literature in their time.

CHAPMAN, JOHN JAY (1862–1933), literary critic, translator, essayist, whose eclectic criticism was based on an "essentially aristocratic" and Emersonian appreciation of individualism.

CHAPMAN, MARIA WESTON (1806–85), was associated with Garrison as treasurer of the Massachusetts Anti-Slavery Society and as an editor of the *Liberator.* She wrote many abolitionist articles, and her *Life of Harriet Martineau* (1877) was the result of a long personal friendship. She sponsored the publication of *The Liberty Bell* ♦ (1839–58).

Character and Opinion in the United States, essays by Santayana, ♦ published in 1920.

Chautauqua movement, an outgrowth of the lyceum movement, ♦ originated at Lake Chautauqua, N.Y., where annual Methodist Episcopal camp meetings had been held until they were reorganized (1874) as assemblies for religious study. The program was extended to include other branches of education, as well as musical and dramatic entertainments. The resulting Chautauqua Institution offered correspondence courses, published books, issued *The Chautauquan* (1880–1914), and held an annual summer school. Its success caused other communities throughout the U.S. to imitate the venture, and "chautauqua" became a generic name for programs given by troupes of lecturers and entertainers, operated in the manner of traveling theatrical companies, and performing in rural settlements.

CHAYEFSKY, PADDY (1923–1981), writer of television dramas and a producer of films and legitimate plays. His works include *Marty* (1953, TV; 1955, film), a direct, sympathetic treatment of the romance of a lonely Bronx butcher and a spinster schoolteacher. *The Bachelor Party* (1954, TV; 1957, film) and *The Catered Affair* (1955, TV; 1956, film) also blend reportorial realism about commonplace people with a sentimental attitude toward their problems. A dedication to Judaism is seen in *The Tenth Man* (1959), a play using the theme of the Dybbuk but set in the Bronx, and in *Gideon* (1961). Another stage play, *The Passion of Josef D.* (1964), is a morality with music, depicting Stalin, Trotsky, and Lenin during the Russian Revolution. Six of his works are collected in *Television Plays* (1955). Later works include *The Latent Heterosexual* (1968), a play; *Network* (1975), a film he wrote and produced; and *Altered States* (1978), a science fiction novel.

CHEEVER, JOHN (1912–1982), Massachusetts author whose formal schooling ended and literary career began with expulsion from Thayer Academy, the subject of his first story, published in 1930. His many later stories, frequently dealing satirically with affluent New Englanders living in suburbia, often appeared in *The New Yorker* and have been collected in *The Way Some People Live* (1943), *The Housebreaker of Shady Hill* (1958), *Some People, Places and Things That Will Not Appear in My Next Novel* (1961), *The Brigadier and the Golf Widow* (1964), and *The World of Apples* (1973). *The Wapshot Chronicle♦* (1957), an episodic novel about the comically raffish lives of a wealthy Massachusetts family during the first half of the 20th century, was given a National Book Award. Its sequel, *The Wapshot Scandal♦* (1964), continues the tale of the family decline in their hometown, St. Botolph. His third novel, *Bullet Park* (1969), also depicting a suburban family, is a firmer-structured work, more satirical and more of a morality story. *Falconer♦* (1977), a later novel, deals with an ex-professor's experiences as an inmate in Falconer Prison, and is a story of

human redemption. *Oh What a Paradise It Seems* (1982) is a novella about an aging man who is rejuvenated by an unusual romance and who uses his new energies to save the landscape of the area where he lived as a boy.

Cherokee Indians, large tribe that formerly occupied the mountains of Georgia, Alabama, Tennessee, and Carolina. They aided the British both against the French and in the Revolutionary War, when they attacked frontier settlers. In 1827 they adopted a government modeled on that of the U.S., after which, although the U.S. Supreme Court upheld their autonomy, they were forcibly deported (1838–39) to Oklahoma. Disbanded (1906) they became U.S. citizens. The high state of their culture is represented in such individuals as Sequoyah,♦ who created their alphabet. Elias Boudinot, an educated Cherokee, edited the *Cherokee Phoenix* (1828–35), the first newspaper for an Indian tribe, and wrote *Poor Sarah; or, The Indian Woman* (1833). The "Deathsong of a Cherokee Indian," sometimes attributed to Freneau, appears as a song in Tyler's play *The Contrast.* Cherokee Indians of the colonial period appear in the novels of Mary N. Murfree,♦ and those of later times in stories by W.G. Simms,♦ who gained first-hand knowledge by a sojourn among them. *The Cherokee Night* is a play by Lynn Riggs. John R. Ridge, an early California poet and journalist, was of Cherokee descent.

CHESNUT, MARY BOYKIN [MILLER] (1823–86), daughter of a U.S. senator from South Carolina and married to the scion of a great plantation owner of the state, also a senator, was a passionate believer in states' rights. During the Civil War she kept a lively, sharp-eyed diary of life in the Confederacy, also expressive of sympathy for black people. *A Diary from Dixie* (1905) was reissued in an enlarged, revised text by Ben Ames Williams. The complete text of some 400,000 words was edited by C. Vann Woodward as *Mary Chesnut's Civil War* (1981) and awarded a Pulitzer Prize, although some historians questioned its authenticity since Mrs. Chesnut rewrote the work substantially during Reconstruction. *The Private Mary Chesnut* (1984) edited by Woodward and Elisabeth Muhlenfeld draws on more personal journals.

CHESNUTT, CHARLES W[ADDELL] (1858–1932), black author, best known for *The Conjure Woman* (1899), a series of dialect stories about incidents of slavery, told by an old black gardener to his Northern employers. This was followed by a biography of Frederick Douglass (1899) and a second collection of stories, *The Wife of His Youth* (1899), dealing with a free black's conflicting loyalties to the wife he had married in slavery and to the more refined black woman whom he later meets. His less successful novels are *The House Behind the Cedars* (1900), concerned with a light-complexioned black woman who is undecided whether to enjoy comfort as a white man's mistress or the sincere love of a black man; *The Marrow of Tradition* (1901), about the struggles of black and white half-sisters; and *The Colonel's Dream* (1905), telling of an idealist's unsuccessful attempt to root race hatred out of a Southern town.

Cheyenne Indians, Plains tribe♦ of the Algonquian family, inhabited a region near the Black Hills and then migrated to the headwaters of the Platte River, where in 1830 they divided into northern and southern bands. Treaties with the southern group were constantly violated, and, after an indiscriminate massacre by U.S. troops, there began the bitter war which culminated in Custer's annihilation of a great number of the Cheyenne in 1868, and the revenge of others, who joined Sitting Bull in the Battle of Little Big Horn. The Cheyenne are the subject of a study by G.B. Grinnell and figure in the novels of Hamlin Garland, in Howard Fast's *The Last Frontier,* and in a fanciful form in *Little Big Man* by Thomas Berger.

Chicago, free-verse poem by Carl Sandburg,♦ published in 1914 and collected in his *Chicago Poems* (1916). This ode to the city, which the poet accept as "wicked . . . crooked . . . brutal," but acclaims as proud . . . flinging magnetic curses amid the toil . . . fierce," is a celebration of its

> Laughing the stormy, husky, brawling laughter of Youth, half-naked, sweating, proud to be Hog Butcher, Tool Maker, Stacker of Wheat, Player with Railroad and Freight Handler to the Nation.

Chickasaw Indians, war-like tribe that originally inhabited northern Mississippi. During the colonial period they sided with the English against the French, and they continued to be friendly with the whites, aiding the U.S. against the Creek in 1793. They migrated to Oklahoma in accordance with later treaties, and served in the Confederate army. Ikkemotubbe♦ and other Indian characters in Faulkner's Yoknapatawpha saga belong to the tribe.

CHILD, LYDIA MARIA (1802–80), Massachusetts Abolitionist, whose *Appeal in Favor of that Class of Americans Called Africans* (1833) won many to the antislavery cause, as did her widely circulated *Correspondence* (1860) with the governor of Virginia. Her fiction, humane and didactic rather than creative, includes *Hobomok* (1824), a romance set in Massachusetts during Endecott's governorship and glorifying the "noble savage"; *The Rebels; or, Boston Before the Revolution* (1825), concerned with the Stamp Tax agitation; and *Philothea* (1836), a romance of classical Greece. She was a sister of Convers Francis.

Children of Adam, section of Whitman's *Leaves of Grass,* ♦ first published in the 1860 edition as "Enfans d'Adam," and given its present title in 1867. It contains 16 poems, all concerned with physical love, identifying the sexual impulse with the spiritual force of the universe. Among the poems in the section are "I Sing the Body Electric,"♦ "Spontaneous Me,"♦ "Once I Pass'd Through a Populous City,"♦ and "Facing West from California's Shores."♦ "Calamus,"♦ a section concerned with the spiritual love of man for man, forms a complement.

Children of the Night, The, poems by E.A. Robinson.♦

Children's Hour, The, poem by Longfellow,♦ published in *Birds of Passage* (1860). Ten jocund quatrains describe the nightly descent upon the poet's study of his three "blue-eyed banditti" daughters, "grave Alice, and laughing Allegra, and Edith with golden hair."

Children's Hour, The, play by Lillian Hellman.♦

Children's literature in America first consisted of aids to piety, seemingly addressed to miniature adults. The earliest examples include Cotton's *Milk for Babes, Drawn out of the Breasts of Both Testaments* (1646) and the perennial *New England Primer* (1683?). In the colonial era most books for children were imported from England or, like the popular *Songs from the Nursery* (1719), were republished by American printers such as Isaiah

Thomas. Since the early 19th century, many adult books, particularly humorous fiction and adventure tales, have been adopted by children, some of the earliest including works on American subjects by Irving, Cooper, and Dana. The trend away from the religious to the generally moral and didactic as suited to a child began in mid-19th-century works by Hawthorne and in the Peter Parley tales. The more modern desire to entertain as well as instruct is also found in the novels by Jacob Abbott. Other works of his time include new versions and additions to Old World fairy tales, folklore, and stories of chivalry. Popular verse included C.C. Moore's "A Visit from St. Nicholas," Sarah Josepha Hale's "Mary Had a Little Lamb," and Longfellow's poems. Separate traditions of works for boys and girls grew up, but several generations of both sexes made best sellers of Harris's Uncle Remus stories, Howard Pyle's tales of pirates and medieval heroes, Seton-Thompson's animal books, Palmer Cox's Brownies, Bennett's *Master Skylark,* Baum's Oz books, Gelett Burgess's Goops, the novels of Frank Stockton, and Thornton Burgess's stories of animal characters.

Among the most popular books for girls have been Mary Mapes Dodge's *Hans Brinker,* Louisa May Alcott's *Little Women,* Isabella Alden's Pansy series, Frances Baylor's *Juan and Juanita,* Harriet Lothrop's *Five Little Peppers,* Frances Hodgson Burnett's *Little Lord Fauntleroy,* Alice Hegan Rice's *Mrs. Wiggs of the Cabbage Patch,* Kate Douglas Wiggin's *Rebecca of Sunnybrook Farm,* L.M. Montgomery's *Anne of Green Gables,* and the novels about Nancy Drew by Edward Stratemeyer and his syndicate. Boy readers, reputedly enamored of dime novels and adult stories of manly adventures, like those by Jack London, also probably read many of these works, just as girls frequently read such popular books for boys as D.P. Thompson's *The Green Mountain Boys,* Trowbridge's *Cudjo's Cave,* the stories of Mayne Reid, Aldrich's *The Story of a Bad Boy,* Noah Brooks's *The Boy Emigrants,* Eggleston's *The Hoosier Schoolboy,* the popular series of C.C. Coffin and Horatio Alger, Clemens's *Tom Sawyer* and *Huckleberry Finn,* Tarkington's *Penrod,* and the various series concerned with the Rover Boys, Tom Swift, Frank Merriwell, and the Hardy Boys.

Works in these veins continue popular, but later vogues include the flashily illustrated and diverse subjects of so-called comic books; highly imaginative science fiction novels with fantastic heroes like Tarzan and some supermen; quieter fantasies; histories, biographies, and studies of adult subjects (including scientific concepts and frank treatments of social and sexual issues), generally well written and illustrated for young people. Recent popular authors include those who write just for children, like Dr. Seuss (Theodore Geisel), Maurice Sendak (equally noted for his illustrations), and Walter Farley, the creator of a series about a black stallion, and those who also write for adults, like Asimov, Bemelmans, Pearl Buck, Ray Bradbury, Mary Ellen Chase, Marchette Chute, Elizabeth Coatsworth, Walter Edmonds, Howard Fast, Rachel Field, Esther Forbes, Will James, MacKinlay Kantor, Phyllis McGinley, Sandburg, Saroyan, Steinbeck, Thurber, Van Loon, and E.B. White. Each year since 1921 the book judged best receives the Newbery Medal, named for an 18th-century chapbook publisher, and since 1938 the work considered to have the best illustrations receives a Caldecott Medal. Since *The Children's Magazine* (1789) there have been many periodicals edited exclusively for children, including *The Youth's Companion* (1827–1929), *Parley's Magazine* (1833–41), *Merry's Museum for Boys and Girls* (1841–72), *St. Nicholas* (1873–1940), *American Boy* (1899–1941), *Boy's Life* (1911–   ), and *Cricket* (1973–   ).

Chillingworth, ROGER, character in *The Scarlet Letter.* ♦

Chingachgook, Indian chieftain also known as John Mohegan, character in Cooper's Leather-Stocking Tales. ♦

Chippewa Indians, see *Ojibway Indians.*

CHIVERS, THOMAS HOLLEY (1809–58), born in Georgia, early abandoned medicine for a career as author, publishing *The Path of Sorrow* (1832), poems about his unhappy first marriage; *Conrad and Eudora* (1834), a verse drama based on the Kentucky Tragedy, a celebrated contemporary crime; and *Nacoochee* (1837), which has a preface on the transcendental nature of poetry. He is principally known for his association with Poe (1840–49), although the two were never actually friends. Charges of plagiarism followed the publication of Chivers's *Eonchs of Ruby* (1851), to which he replied with counter charges, and critics believe that his previously published "Isadore" and other poems influenced the writing of "The Raven" and "Ulalume." The title poem of *The Lost Pleiad* (1845) and "To Allegra Florence in Heaven" are elegies for his daughter, and after the death of three other children Chivers became increasingly interested in various mystical movements, writing a prose work on the *Search After Truth; or, A New Revelation of the Psycho-Physiological Nature of Man* (1848). Several later volumes of poetry exhibit his sentimentality, lack of critical judgment, and finally his unbalanced mind.

Choctaw Indians, agricultural tribe of southern Mississippi, who served against the British in the French and Indian Wars and in the Revolution. They later aided the U.S. against the Creek, and after ceding their lands to the national government moved to Oklahoma. The Choctaw of Louisiana inspired affectionate tributes in the poetry of the brothers Adrien Rouquette♦ and François Rouquette. ♦

CHODOROV, EDWARD (1904–), and JEROME (1911–), his brother, are noted as playwrights, scenarists, and directors. Edward's plays include *Wonder Boy* (1932), *Kind Lady* (1935), and *Those Endearing Young Charms* (1943). Jerome's plays, in collaboration with Joseph Fields, include *My Sister Eileen* (1940), *Junior Miss* (1941), *Anniversary Waltz* (1954), and *The Ponder Heart* (1957), adapted from Eudora Welty's novel. Other plays include *Culture Caper* (1975), based on Updike's *Bech*.

CHOPIN, KATE [O'FLAHERTY] (1851–1904), St. Louis author, from her marriage to a Louisiana Creole until his death (1882) lived in New Orleans and on a Louisiana cotton plantation. Returning to her native city, she began to write tales for children and the local-color stories for which she is noted. *At Fault* (1890) is an undistinguished novel of Creole life in the Cane River section of central Louisiana. Her importance in the local-color movement depends primarily, however, on her interpretations of Creole and Cajun life in her collections of short stories and anecdotes, *Bayou Folk*♦ (1894) and *A Night in Acadie* (1897). These carefully polished tales are delicately objective in treatment and marked by a poignant restraint of which perhaps the greatest example is "Désirée's Baby" in the former volume. Mrs. Chopin's last novel, *The Awakening*♦ (1899), caused a storm of criticism that ended her

literary career because readers of the time were shocked not only by the story of a Southern lady's revolt against her husband and love of a young man but by the frank sense of sexuality.

Christian Science, religion founded upon principles formulated by Mary Baker Eddy♦ from New Testament teachings, in her book *Science and Health with Key to the Scriptures*♦ (1875). According to this text, science is Christ's revelation of the Eternal Mind, the source of all being, and his message is that the power of Mind (Truth, God, Spirit) overcomes illusions of sin, sickness, and death. The followers of Christian Science attempt to end the illusory conflict of mind and body by unceasing prayer and "the understanding of Truth and Love," which will dispel the belief in disease or the supposition that any evil can emanate from God. The Church of Christ, Scientist, founded at Boston (1879), since 1892 has been known as the Mother Church. Other churches are self-governing and self-supporting, but all accept Mrs. Eddy's tenets. The churches do not have pastors, and services are conducted by two persons, one reading from the Scriptures, the other from *Science and Health*.

Christmas, JOE, character in Faulkner's novel *Light in August*. ♦

Churches Quarrel Espoused, The, controversial work by John Wise,♦ was published in 1710 as an answer to the *Questions and Proposals* (1705) propounded by Increase and Cotton Mather in their project to substitute a central association of clergy for the system of lay-controlled independent churches. With earnest logic and annihilating invective, Wise shows the danger or folly of each proposal, which he opposes with the theory of democracy. Because its democratic theme transcends the specific issues, the book was republished (1772) and widely read prior to the Revolution and again before the Civil War.

CHURCHILL, WINSTON (1871–1947), novelist popular in his day for his historical romances: *Richard Carvel* (1899), about an officer under John Paul Jones; *The Crisis* (1901), depicting his native St. Louis in the Civil War era; and *The Crossing* (1904), presenting the frontier, mainly Kentucky, during the Revolutionary War. His other fiction includes *Coniston* (1906) and *Mr. Crewe's Career* (1908), treating the political scene of his own time.

CIARDI, JOHN (1916–   ), born in Boston, educated at Bates and Tufts, was poetry editor (1956–72) of *The Saturday Review.* His own poetry, often marked by vernacular diction and homely wit, includes *Homeward to America* (1940); *Other Skies* (1947); *Live Another Day* (1949); *From Time to Time* (1951); *As If, Poems New and Selected* (1955); *I Marry You* (1958), love poems; *In Fact* (1963); and *Lives of X* (1971), about his youth. He translated Dante's *Inferno* (1954).

Cisco Kid, character in O. Henry's "The Caballero's Way" of *Heart of the West,* who was transmuted into an almost mythic figure, a romantic Latin cowboy and Robin Hood of the U.S. Southwest, through a series of films and television serials.

Civil Disobedience, essay by Thoreau, originally delivered as a lecture and first printed as "Resistance to Civil Government" in Elizabeth Peabody's *Aesthetic Papers* (1849).

Asserting that "That government is best which governs not at all" and that "Government is at best but an expedient," the author points to such injustices and abuses as the prosecution of the Mexican War, the treatment of native Indians, and the institution of slavery. To cooperate with government, even to the extent of paying taxes, he says, is to condone its crimes and participate in them, and an "honest man" must "withdraw from this copartnership." Individual conscience, not law, is the moral arbiter; "under a government which imprisons any unjustly, the true place for a just man is also a prison." He cites his own refusal to pay a tithing or poll tax, in order "to refuse allegiance to the State, to withdraw and stand aloof from it effectually." He will participate only in those governmental activities that he approves:

> any man more right than his neighbors constitutes a majority of one already. . . . There will never be a really free and enlightened State until the State comes to recognize the individual as a higher and independent power, from which all its own power and authority are derived. . . .

Clansman, The, novel by Thomas Dixon,♦ published in 1905 as the second volume of a trilogy including *The Leopard's Spots* (1902) and *The Traitor* (1907), melodramatic and extremist Southern depictions of the Reconstruction era, violently racist in their characterizations of blacks, and Klux Klan as potenti[ ] Confederate region. popular, as was Di[ ] touring companies (1[ ] adapted by D.W. Griffith [   ] *Birth of a Nation* (1915).

CLAPPE, LOUISE AMELIA KNAPP SMITH (1819–1906), came to California from her native Massachusetts with her husband in 1849, and, over the pseudonym Dame Shirley, wrote letters (1851–52), ostensibly to her sister, which give a witty, feminine view of the gold rush. They were issued in San Francisco's *Pioneer Magazine* (1854–55) and as a book, *The Shirley Letters,* in 1922.

Clarel: A Poem and Pilgrimage in the Holy Land, poem in 150 cantos by Melville,♦ published in two volumes in 1876. Using the setting he observed on a trip to Palestine (1857), Melville treats the problems of a modern culture not based on religion, and the resultant spiritual and psychological turmoil of its peoples. The narrative describes the experiences of a young American theological student, Clarel, who, while visiting Jerusalem, falls in love with Ruth, a Zionist, and recounts his travels with various pilgrims to the great sites of the region. His fellows include a man deformed in body and spirit who doubts his Roman Catholic faith, an Anglican clergyman with easy belief in the goodness of man and nature, a cynic who feels the emulation of Christ leads but to destruction, an apostate Jew whose scientism is used to attack religion, and an American of great moral qualities and aesthetic sensitivity but without clear commitments. Despite lengthy philosophic conversations, Clarel is unable to resolve his religious uncertainties, and he returns on Ash Wednesday to the grief of finding Ruth dead.

CLARK, ELEANOR (1913–   ), author of *Rome and a Villa* (1952) and *The Oysters of Locmariaquer* (1964), local-color studies summoning up the sense of the Italian capital and of Brittany respectively, and *Tamrart* (1984), about a camelback excursion in the Sahara. She also wrote *Eyes, Etc.* (1977), about her loss of vision, and three novels: *The Bitter Box* (1946), *Baldur's Gate* (1971), and *Gloria Mundi* (1979). She is married to Robert Penn Warren.

CLARK, WALTER VAN TILBURG (1909–71), born in Maine, reared in Nevada, was a

essor of English and the author of *The
x-Bow Incident* (1940), a psychological
novel about a lynching in Nevada's cattle
country; *The City of Trembling Leaves* (1945;
in England *Tim Hazard,* 1951), about a Reno
boy whose ambition is to be a composer; and
The Track of the Cat (1949), a symbolic tale
of hunting a panther in the Sierra. *The
Watchful Gods* (1950) collects stories.

Clean, Well-Lighted Place, A, story by
Hemingway, published in *Winner Take Nothing.* ◆

At a sidewalk table of a Spanish café an
old, deaf man sits drinking brandy late at
night as the two waiters discuss him, the older
one with sympathy because he too is lonely,
fearful, confident of nothing, and also in need
of the security of a clean, well-lighted place.

CLEMENS, SAMUEL LANGHORNE (1835–
1910), born in Florida, Mo., was the son of a
Virginian imbued with the frontier spirit and
grandiose dreams of easy wealth, who had
married in Kentucky and spent the rest of his
life in a restless search for profits from land
speculation. The family settled in Hannibal,
Mo. (1839), where Samuel grew up under the
influence of this attitude, and passed the
adventurous boyhood and youth that he
recalls in *Tom Sawyer* and *Huckleberry Finn.*
After his father's death (1847), he left school
to be apprenticed to a printer, and was soon
writing for his brother Orion's newspaper.
He was a journeyman printer in the East and
Middle West (1853–54), and in 1856 planned
to seek his fortune in South America, but
gave up this idea to become a steamboat pilot
on the Mississippi, a position that he considered the most important discipline of his
life. When the Civil War began, the riverboats ceased operation, and, after a brief trial
of soldiering with a group of Confederate
volunteers, Clemens went to Nevada with his
brother, who had been appointed secretary to
the governor. In *Roughing It* he describes the
trip west and his subsequent adventures as
miner and journalist. After he joined the staff
of the Virginia City *Territorial Enterprise*
(1862), he adopted the pseudonym Mark
Twain, ◆ by which he was thereafter known,
and began his career as a journalistic humorist in the frontier tradition. His articles of the
time are collected in *Mark Twain of the
Enterprise* (1957).

During this period he met Artemus Ward
and others who encouraged his work, collaborated with Bret Harte in San Francisco,

and wrote "The Celebrated Jumping Frog" ◆
sketch (1865), which won him immediate
recognition. He increased his popularity with
letters and lectures about his trip to the
Sandwich Islands, went East to lecture, published *The Celebrated Jumping Frog of Calaveras County and Other Sketches* (1867), and
made the tour of the Mediterranean and the
Holy Land that he describes in *The Innocents
Abroad* ◆ (1869), a humorous narrative that
assured his position as a leading author and
shows his typical American irreverence for
the classic and the antique. In 1870 Clemens
married Olivia Langdon, with whom he
setted in Hartford, Conn. The effect of this
marriage upon his career has been responsible for two divergent interpretations of his
work. Mrs. Clemens belonged to a genteel,
conservative society, and it has been claimed
(mainly by Van Wyck Brooks) that the
puritanical and materialistic surroundings
into which Clemens was thrust frustrated his
potential creative force for fierce revolt and
satire. Others (principally Bernard De Voto)
posit the idea that Clemens began as a
frontier humorist and storyteller, and that his
later work shows the unthwarted development of these essential talents.

In *Roughing It* ◆ (1872) he continues the
method of *The Innocents Abroad,* seasoning
the realistic account of adventure with humorous exaggerations in his highly personal
idiom. Next he collaborated with C.D.
Warner in *The Gilded Age* ◆ (1873), a satirical novel of post-Civil War boom times that
gave a name to the era. *A Tramp Abroad* ◆
(1880) is another travel narrative, this time of
a walking trip through the Black Forest and
the Alps. England during the reign of Edward VI is the scene of *The Prince and the
Pauper* ◆ (1882), while *A Connecticut Yankee
in King Arthur's Court* ◆ (1889) is a realistic-
satirical fantasy of Arthurian England. During this period, however, Clemens was dealing with the background of his own early life
in what are generally considered the most
significant of his characteristically American
works. In *The Adventures of Tom Sawyer* ◆
(1876) he presents a nostalgic tale of boyish
adventure in a Mississippi River town, and in
Life on the Mississippi ◆ (1883) and *The
Adventures of Huckleberry Finn* ◆ (1884) he
celebrates the flowering of Mississippi valley
civilization, in terms of its own pungent tall
talk and picaresque adventure.

External events soon interfered with the
even flow of Clemens's creative activity.
During his residence in Hartford, he had been
a partner in the publishing firm of Charles L.

Webster and Company, which reaped a fortune through the sale of Grant's *Memoirs* and Clemens's own writings, but bad publishing ventures and the investment of $200,000 in an unperfected typesetting machine drove him into bankruptcy (1894). To discharge his debts he made a lecturing tour of the world, although he had come to dislike lecturing, and the record of this tour, *Following the Equator♦* (1897), has an undercurrent of bitterness not found in his earlier travel books. During this decade, although he wrote *The Tragedy of Pudd'nhead Wilson♦* (1894) and the *Personal Recollections of Joan of Arc♦* (1896), most of his work is uneven in quality, and *The American Claimant♦* (1892), *Tom Sawyer Abroad♦* (1894), and *Tom Sawyer, Detective♦* (1896) are feeble echoes of earlier work. In 1898 he finished paying off his debts, but his writings show that the strain of pessimism he formerly repressed was now dominating his mind. *The Man That Corrupted Hadleyburg* (1900), *What Is Man?♦* (1906), and *The Mysterious Stranger♦* (1916) demonstrate this attitude. He continued to travel widely, lectured and wrote articles on contemporary events and such controversial works as *Christian Science* (1907) and *Is Shakespeare Dead?* (1909), but his bitterness was deepened by the loss of his wife and two daughters. His pessimism was perhaps no more profound than the optimism of his own Colonel Sellers, but his feeling that it was too mordant for publication caused him to instruct that certain of his works be published posthumously.

Since 1906 he had been engaged in dictating his autobiography to his secretary, A.B. Paine, who later became the first Literary Editor of the Mark Twain Estate, and issued a collection of *Letters* (1917), the authorized biography (3 vols., 1912), and the *Autobiography* (1924). The second editor, Bernard De Voto, created volumes of material from the papers left by Clemens, including *Letters from the Earth* (1963). Drawing on the same sources, the third editor, Dixon Wecter, collected *The Love Letters of Mark Twain* (1949); and the fourth editor, Henry Nash Smith, edited with William M. Gibson, *Mark Twain–Howells Letters* (2 vols., 1960). A scholarly edition of his *Works* began publication by the University of California Press in 1972, which also began issuing (1967) a scholarly edition of his previously unpublished *Papers,* most of whose originals are in the University's Bancroft Library.

An important early estimate of his work is *My Mark Twain: Reminiscences and Criticisms* (1910), by his friend and adviser Howells. The prevalent critical attitude has come to consider Clemens's most distinctive work as summing up the tradition of Western humor and frontier realism. Beginning as a journalist, he assumed the method and point of view of popular literature in the U.S., maintaining the personal anecdotal style that he used also in his capacity of comic lecturer. In travel books, he digresses easily from factual narrative to humorous exaggeration and burlesque. The novels are episodic or autobiographical, and not formed by any larger structural concepts. He wrote in the authentic native idiom, exuberantly and irreverently, but underlying the humor was a vigorous desire for social justice and a pervasive equalitarian attitude. The romantic idealism of *Joan of Arc,* the bitter satire of feudal tyranny in *A Connecticut Yankee,* the appreciation of human values in *Huckleberry Finn,* and the sense of epic sweep in *Life on the Mississippi* establish Clemens's place in American letters as an artist of broad understanding and vital, although uneven and sometimes misdirected, achievement.

Clements Library (THE WILLIAM L. CLEMENTS LIBRARY OF AMERICANA), donated to the University of Michigan (1923), is a collection of rare books and manuscripts on early America and the Revolution. R.G. Adams was the director (1923–51). Carl Van Doren's *Secret History of the American Revolution* is based on the manuscript materials there.

Clock Without Hands, novel by Carson McCullers,♦ published in 1961.

COATES, ROBERT M[YRON] (1897–1973), after graduation from Yale (1919) became an expatriate in France, where he wrote *The Eater of Darkness* (1929), a surrealist novel. Returning to the U.S., he turned to the American background in *The Outlaw Years* (1930), a history of the Natchez Trace pirates. Later fiction includes *Yesterday's Burdens* (1933), about a "modern Everyman" in New York City; *Bitter Season* (1946), about New York during World War II; *Wisteria Cottage* (1948), concerning a man with a Messiah complex; and *Farther Shore* (1955), about the pathetic love affair of a Hungarian resident in New York. *All the Year Round* (1943) and *Hour After Westerly* (1957) collect stories. *The View from Here* (1960) is a work of reminiscences.

COATSWORTH, Elizabth [Jane] (1893–), New York poet, whose works include *Fox Footprints* (1923), employing Oriental themes in the manner of Imagism; *Atlas and Beyond* (1924) and *Compass Rose* (1929), verses about many lands; and *The Creaking Stair* (1949). Her most popular children's book is *The Cat Who Went to Heaven* (1930). *Here I Stay* (1938), a novel for adults, and *Country Neighborhood* (1944), sketches, are set in Maine. *Personal Geography* (1976) is subtitled "Almost an Autobiography."

COBURN, D[onald] L[ee] (1938–), born in East Baltimore, long resident in Dallas as an advertising writer, wrote his first play, *The Gin Game,* had it successfully produced in a small Los Angeles theater (1976) and then on Broadway (1977). It was awarded a Pulitzer Prize for drama (1978), and published (1979). The two-character, two-act play depicts a series of gin rummy games between a man and a woman living in a home for old people, whose contests (always won by her) reveal their characters, their loneliness, and their relationships of a geriatric sexual sort.

Cocktail Party, The, verse play by T.S. Eliot,♦ produced in 1949, published in 1950.

At his cocktail party, Edward Chamberlayne tries to conceal the fact that his wife Lavinia has left him, but he is found out by his mistress Celia; talented, lonely Peter Quilpe; and a mysterious stranger, the psychiatrist Sir Henry Harcourt-Reilly. Harcourt-Reilly arranges Lavinia's return, and although Edward still finds her his "angel of destruction," Sir Henry makes him see that they are bound together by "the same isolation," as her former lover Quilpe has now fallen in love with Celia, and if Edward is incapable of giving love, Lavinia cannot be loved. Celia too feels alone, and craving "the intensity of loving in the spirit" refuses to be reconciled to the human condition accepted by the others and chooses to journey in quest of faith. Two years later at a cocktail party given by Edward and Lavinia for the same guests, they learn that Celia, having become a nurse in a heathen country, has been crucified and is now worshipped as a goddess. Harcourt-Reilly tells the Chamberlaynes they should not feel guilt since the saintly way was right for Celia and another way is for them, since "there are two worlds of life and death."

Code, The, blank-verse dramatic narrative by Robert Frost,♦ published in *North of Boston* (1914).

An experienced farmhand tells a "town-bred farmer" of the pride his fellows take in their competence, and the resulting code:

The hand that knows his business won't be told
To do work better or faster—those two things.

For illustration he describes an incident that took place when he worked for a certain Sanders, of Salem, a prodigious worker himself. They were engaged in unloading a wagon of hay, and Sanders made the mistake, while standing below to pile the load, of saying to the hand on the wagon, "Let her come!" Offended at this breach of the code, the hand dumped the entire load down on the helpless farmer, regardless of the danger of suffocating him. Sanders extricated himself, and showed that he recognized the justice of his employee's act:

"Discharge me? No! He knew I did just right."

CODY, William Frederick (1846–1917), known by his sobriquet Buffalo Bill, served as a frontier scout during the Civil War, and again from 1868 to 1872, as well as in the battles against the Sioux. In 1883 he started his famous "Wild West" show, the prototype of many later ones, and he had previously acted in Western melodramas. The dime novels of Ned Buntline and Prentiss Ingraham are partially responsible for his popular reputation. He acted for two years in Buntline's play *The Scouts of the Plains* (1873). His autobiography (1904) is unreliable. E.E. Cummings wrote a poem about him.

Colonel Sellers, play by Clemens♦ and Howells,♦ featuring the hero of *The Gilded Age.*♦ Unsuccessfully produced in 1886, it was the basis of Clemens's story *The American Claimant.*♦

Columbiad, The, epic poem in heroic couplets by Joel Barlow,♦ was published in 1807 as a revision of his *The Vision of Columbus* (1787). It is a tedious and turgid work modeled on Milton and influenced by Shenstone and Timothy Dwight.

According to the preface, Barlow's purpose is "to inculcate the love of national liberty, and to discountenance the deleterious passion for violence and war; to show that on the basis of republican principle all good morals, as well as good government and hopes of permanent peace, must be founded." The poem is concerned with the vision revealed by a "radiant seraph" to Columbus, an old man dying in prison. Columbus sees the future glories of America, and a distant vision of a league of all nations, "assembled to establish the political harmony of mankind."

Come-outers, name applied to those 19th-century New Englanders who, believing that ministers and creeds were unnecessary, found the only source of divine truth in what God said directly to their hearts. Members of this vigorous mystic movement came originally from Cape Cod.

Common Sense, pamphlet by Thomas Paine,♦ published anonymously at Philadelphia (Jan. 10, 1776). At a time of rising passion against the British government, the work was the first unqualified argument for complete political independence, and helped turn colonial thought in the direction that, six months later, culminated in the Declaration of Independence. Over 100,000 copies were sold by the end of March, and it is generally considered the most important literary influence on the movement for independence.

The argument is presented in four parts entitled: "Of the Origin and Design of Government in General; with Concise Remarks on the English Constitution"; "Of Monarchy and Hereditary Succession"; "Thoughts on the Present State of American Affairs"; and "Of the Present Ability of America. . . ." The most cogent points of the closely reasoned discussion may be summarized in these extracts:

> Here then is the origin and rise of government; namely, a mode rendered necessary by the inability of moral virtue to govern the world; here too is the design and end of government, viz. freedom and security. . . . Of more worth is one honest man to society, and in the sight of God, than all the crowned ruffians that ever lived. . . . We have boasted the protection of Great Britain, without considering, that her motive was *interest* not *attachment*. . . . I challenge the warmest advocate for reconciliation to show a single advantage that this continent can reap by being connected with Great Britain. . . . Our corn will fetch its price in any market in Europe, and our imported goods must be paid for buy them where we will. . . . Everything that is right or reasonable pleads for separation. The blood of the slain, the weeping voice of Nature cries, 'TIS TIME TO PART. . . . The republican form of government is the best because it is founded on the most natural principles. . . . 'Tis not in numbers but in unity that our great strength lies; yet our present numbers are sufficient to repel the force of all the world.

Compensation, essay by Emerson,♦ published in *Essays, First Series* (1841); also, a poem by Emerson, published the same year.

The idea of compensation is implicit in Emerson's thought, and involves his concept of the "Over-Soul"♦: "An inevitable dualism bisects nature, so that each thing is a half, and suggests another thing to make it whole." Although the malicious are apparently rewarded rather than punished, the view that justice will be meted out in an afterlife is erroneous, for it "is not postponed. . . . What we call retribution, is the universal necessity by which the whole appears wherever a part appears. . . . Every act rewards itself." The necessary conditions that life involves may not be avoided: "Our action is overmastered and characterised above our will by the law of nature. . . . Our strength grows out of our weakness." But the author does not counsel indifference. "Under all this running sea of circumstance . . . lies the aboriginal abyss of real Being." Wisdom and virtue involve no penalty, but are qualities of being; "in a virtuous action, I properly *am*." The individual, trusting instinct, acts in accord with a divinely balanced justice, and "the changes which break up at short intervals the prosperity of men, are advertisements of a nature whose law is growth."

Compson family, characters in Faulkner's fiction, an old family centrally involved in Jefferson history from the town's earliest years, figures most prominently in *The Sound and the Fury*♦ and more briefly in *Absalom, Absalom!,*♦ *The Town,*♦ and *The Mansion.*♦ The family is traced back to Quentin MacLachan Compson, who comes to Carolina from Scotland in the 18th century and who, while his son Charles Stuart Compson is fighting with the British in Georgia in 1778, takes his infant grandson Jason Lycurgus Compson to Kentucky. In 1811 Jason Lycurgus goes to the Chickasaw Agency in Mississippi, where he wins money racing horses against Ikkemotubbe, a Chickasaw chief from whom he obtains a square mile of land, on which he builds an estate, while the town of Jefferson begins to grow around it. Jason Lycurgus's son Quentin MacLachan II becomes governor of Mississippi, and *his* son Jason Lycurgus II becomes a Confederate general, later helping to build the railroad to Jefferson. His son Jason III (Jason Richmond, Sr.), a lawyer, becomes a recluse who spends his time drinking, reading the classics, and exercising his cynical wit in the years after he marries Caroline Bascomb and fathers four children: a daughter, Candace (Caddy), and three sons, Quentin III, Benjamin (Benjy), originally named Maury, and Jason IV, whose sad stories are the subject of *The Sound and the Fury.* The last generation of the Compson family is Caddy's illegitimate daughter Quentin, for Jason remains a bachelor, Quentin commits suicide, and the idiot Benjy is castrated and, according to *The Mansion,* dies in the fire he sets to the family house.

COMSTOCK, ANTHONY (1844–1915), was head of a YMCA campaign against obscene literature, special agent for the Post Office Department, founder of the Society for Suppression of Vice, and a leader of Boston's Watch and Ward Society. He was the father of the so-called Comstock law (1873) to exclude vicious matter from the mails. In his various campaigns, he caused the arrest of more than 3000 persons and destroyed 50 tons of books, 28,400 pounds of stereotyped plates for printing objectionable books, and nearly 4,000,000 pictures. He wrote several books on immorality in art and literature. *Anthony Comstock: Roundsman of the Lord* (1927) is a biography by Heywood Broun and Margaret Leech.

Confessions of Nat Turner, The, novel by William Styron,♦ published in 1967 and awarded a Pulitzer Prize. It stirred much controversy, mainly from blacks, who considered the interpretation of Turner to be inaccurate.

Told in the first person, yet, in the author's view, "less an 'historical novel' in conventional terms than a meditation on history," the account of an actual person and event is based on the brief contemporary pamphlet of the same title presented to a trial court as evidence and published in Virginia a year after the revolt of fellow slaves led by Turner in 1831. Imagining much of Turner's youth and early manhood before the rebellion that he headed at the age of 31, Styron in frequently rhetorical and pseudo-Biblical style has Turner recall his religious faith and his power of preaching to other slaves. Embittered and frustrated by the evils of slavery, including the failure to obtain the freedom promised by his first master, Turner is portrayed as unable to find surcease in human relations, black or white, sexually or spiritually. Impelled by supernatural visions, the basically kind Turner becomes the leader of a small band of Southampton County slaves, who raise a violent insurrection in which many white men and women are killed but which is put down with great speed and brutality so that more than twice as many blacks die. Those captured and hanged include Turner.

Confidence-Man, The: His Masquerade, unfinished satirical novel by Melville,♦ published in 1857. This last novel printed during the author's life shows a pessimistic view best described by the title of a handbill that figures in the story: "Ode on the Intimations of Distrust in Man, Unwillingly Inferred from Repeated Repulses, in Disinterested Endeavors to Procure His Confidence."

A deaf-mute boards the Mississippi steamboat *Fidèle,* bound from St. Louis for New Orleans, and displays to the passengers a slate on which he writes: "Charity thinketh no evil; suffereth long, and is kind; endureth all things; believeth all things; and never faileth." This is regarded as a proof of lunacy, although the passengers consider the barber's "No Trust" sign as wise and well expressed. Optimistic, faith-seeking mankind then appears in a variety of other disguises, as the "Masquerade" continues, and distrust replaces confidence in the course of each episode.

Congo, The (*A Study of the Negro Race*), poem by Vachel Lindsay,♦ published in *The Congo and Other Poems* (1914). With a sensational use of varied syncopated rhythms, occasional rhymes, and frequent alliteration, the poet presents this "roaring, epic, ragtime tune" on the traits of blacks: "Their Basic Savagery"; "Their Irrepressible High Spirits"; and "The Hope of Their Religion."

Congregationalism, system of church government in which each congregation is autonomous and democratic. No hierarchy exists, since Christ is in principle the head of each church, and the various congregations are related as fellow participants in the common family of God. This form of church polity in America was inaugurated by the Pilgrim Fathers, who were Separatists,♦ and by the later stream of Puritan colonists.♦ It was virtually the established religion in New England (*c.*1631–1833), and its basic statement was the Cambridge Platform (1648). Increasing liberalism during the 17th century caused the adoption of the Half-Way Covenant. ♦ In 1705, the proposal that higher church assemblies be created, similar to those of the Presbyterians, failed to be accepted in Massachusetts, largely because of the opposition of John Wise, ♦ but the Saybrook Platform (1708) in Connecticut tended toward Presbyterianism. The Great Awakening♦ (1734ff.) revitalized the religious life of New England for a time, but eventually led to the breakdown of Congregationalism and the rise of Unitarianism during the mid-19th century. Most of the New England Congregationalists who went west became Presbyterians. In 1871 a National Council was formed, although local churches still remain independent.

Coniston, novel by Winston Churchill, ♦ published in 1906.

Connecticut Wits, literary group of the late 18th century, centered at Hartford (known also as the Hartford Wits), whose origin is ascribed to the quickening interest in literature at Yale during this period, when most of the group were tutors or students there. They patterned themselves after the Augustan wits, but preserved the intellectual and spiritual conservatism of Connecticut. Aiming to modernize the rigidly scholastic curriculum of Yale, they also wished to supply poetry that would celebrate America's literary independence by extolling native history and society. Although they copied London modes, after the Revolution they clung to their orthodox Calvinism and Federalism, bitterly opposing deism and equalitarianism. Their collaborations included *The Anarchiad* (1786–87), *The Echo* (1791–1805), and *The Political Greenhouse* (1799). Members included John Trumbull, Timothy Dwight, Joel Barlow, Lemuel Hopkins, David Humphreys, Richard Alsop, and Theodore Dwight.

Connecticut Yankee in King Arthur's Court, A (1889), realistic-satirical fantasy of Arthurian England by Clemens ♦ under his pseudonym Mark Twain.

An ingenious Yankee mechanic, knocked unconscious in a fight, awakens to find himself at Camelot in A.D. 528. Imprisoned by Sir Kay the Seneschal and exhibited before the knights of the Round Table, he is condemned to death, but saves himself by posing as a magician like Merlin, correctly predicting an eclipse, and becoming minister to King Arthur. He increases his power by applying 19th-century knowledge of gunpowder, electricity, and industrial methods; but when he attempts to better the condition of the peasantry he meets opposition from the church, the knights, Merlin, and the sorceress Morgan le Fay. He accompanies the king in disguise on an expedition among the common people, and, when they are captured, they are rescued by the Yankee's trained troop of 500 knights on bicycles. His daughter Hello-Central becomes ill, and with his wife Alisande (Sandy) he takes her to France. Back in England, he finds his work undone, Arthur killed, the land in civil war. Gathering friends in a cave with modern armed defenses, he declares a republic, fights off an attack, but is wounded. Merlin, pretending to nurse him, puts him asleep until the 19th century.

CONNELL, Evan S[HELBY], Jr. (1924–), born in Kansas City, educated at Dartmouth and, after naval aviation service, at the University of Kansas, has long lived in California. *Mrs. Bridge* (1959) is a humorous, ironic, and sad series of sketches about a suburban society matron who lives a life of quiet desperation. *The Patriot* (1960), with a similar tone but a more conventional novelistic technique, treats the maturing of an idealistic boy in World War II naval air force service. His other novels include *The Diary of a Rapist* (1966), on sexual violence; *Mr. Bridge* (1969), a companion piece to his first book; *The Connoisseur* (1974), a sensitive study of a man's aesthetic development through appreciation of Mayan art; and *Double Honeymoon* (1976), about a romance of the protagonist of his previous novel. Stories are collected in *The Anatomy Lesson* (1957), *At the Crossroads* (1965), and *St. Augustine's Pigeon* (1980). *Notes from a Bottle Found on the Beach at Carmel* (1963) and *Points for a Compass Rose* (1973) are long philosophic poems. *A Long Desire* (1979) and *The White Lantern* (1980) are nonfiction treatments of great acts of exploration, anthropology, and archaeology; and *Son of the Morning Star* (1984) is a study of Custer's Last Stand.

CONNELLY, Marc[us Cook] (1890–1980), Pennsylvania-born journalist and playwright, is best known for his play *The Green Pastures* ♦ (1930, Pulitzer Prize), based on Roark Bradford's stories of the black's conception of Old Testament history. With George S. Kaufman he wrote plays including *Dulcy* (1921), satirizing a well-meaning, stupid woman who jeopardizes her husband's chances; *To the Ladies* (1922), about a brilliant woman who saves her husband from his stupidities; *Merton of the Movies* (1922), dramatizing H.L. Wilson's novel; and *Beggar* *on Horseback* (1924), satirizing the repression of the artist by bourgeois society.

Conqueror Worm, The, poem by Poe,♦ published in *The Raven and Other Poems* (1845) and later included in "Ligeia."

Conquest of Canaan, The, epic poem in 11 books of conventional heroic couplets, by Timothy Dwight,♦ published in 1785. Written between 1771 and 1773, the work is claimed by the author to be "the first epic poem to have appeared in America." Shuttling with sonorous declamation between Canaan and Connecticut, it is an allegory in which Joshua's conquest of Canaan suggests the struggle under Washington.

Conquest of Granada, A Chronicle of the, history by Irving,♦ published in 1829 and revised in 1850. Praised by Prescott and others for its careful documentation, the work is the result of research in Spanish archives and in the library of Obadiah Rich, but is presented within a frame of humorous and romantic fiction, and purports to be based on a work by the fictitious "Fray Antonio Agapida," who is "intended as a personification of the monkish zealots" of its period (1478–92). Through this chronicler, Irving emphasizes the barbarity of the Christian conquerors, the prejudices and ignorance of the court, and the heroism of the Moorish leaders in their hopeless struggle to retain Granada.

Conquest of Mexico and *Conquest of Peru,* histories by W.H. Prescott. ♦

Contrast, The, social comedy by Royall Tyler,♦ produced in 1787 and published in 1790.

Maria is affianced by her American father, Van Rough, to wealthy Billy Dimple, Anglomaniac disciple of Chesterfield. Colonel Manly, a serious-minded Revolutionary officer, loves Maria but honorably forswears her. Losing his fortune by gambling, Dimple decides to break with Maria and marry the wealthy Letitia. When Van Rough discovers Dimple's duplicity he favors the officer's suit. Letitia spurns Dimple when he is discovered flirting with another girl. The subplot is concerned with Jonathan, Manly's servant, whose homespun shrewdness is contrasted with the wiliness of the popinjay Jessamy, servant of Dimple.

CONWELL, RUSSELL HERMAN (1843–1925), Massachusetts-born Philadelphia Baptist minister, founded Temple University (1888) and was its first president. His book *Acres of Diamonds* (1888) was delivered thousands of times as a lecture, and set forth his gospel of the reconciliation of orthodox Christianity with the dominant capitalist spirit, stressing individual initiative and the Christian responsibility of the wealthy class to society.

COOKE, JOHN ESTEN (1830–86), Virginia author, best known for his romances of colonial Virginia, *Leather Stocking and Silk* (1854), *The Virginia Comedians* (1854), and *Henry St. John, Gentleman* (1859). He served in the Confederate army throughout the Civil War, and in the intervals of campaigning wrote a *Life of Stonewall Jackson* (1863). The war also prompted another series of romances in which its events are seen through the eyes of a fictitious aide to Stonewall Jackson.

COOKE, ROSE TERRY (1827–92), Connecticut short-story writer and poet, whose best tales, *Huckleberries Gathered from New England Hills* (1891), are homely incidents of New England rural life, told in a simple, spontaneous, humorous manner.

Cool Tombs, free-verse poem by Carl Sandburg,♦ written in 1915 and collected in *Cornhuskers* (1918). Meditating upon death's negation of human ambition and turmoil, the poet concludes:

> . . . tell me if the lovers are losers . . .
> tell me if any get more than the lovers
> . . . in the dust . . . in the cool tombs.

COOPER, JAMES FENIMORE (1789–1851), born at Burlington, N.J., was reared on a manorial estate at Cooperstown on Otsego Lake, west of Albany, N.Y. Educated at the local school and in Albany, Cooper went to Yale, from which he was dismissed (1806). During the next five years he served at sea as a foremast hand, was a midshipman in the navy (1808–11), and left to marry and settle as a country gentleman at Mamaroneck.

At 30 he was suddenly plunged into a literary career, when his wife challenged his claim that he could writer a better book than the English novel he was reading to her. The result was *Precaution* (1820), a conventional novel of manners in genteel English society. His second book, *The Spy*♦ (1821), was an immediate success and established Cooper's typical attitude toward plot and characterization, being significant for its use of the American scene as the background of a romance. In *The Pioneers* ♦ (1823) he began his series of Leather-Stocking Tales, ♦ but in his rapid quest for unusual subjects he turned to the sea in *The Pilot* ♦ (1823), intending to prove that a sailor could write a better novel than the landsman Scott had done in *The Pirate* (1822).

To further his position as the outstanding American novelist, he planned to write 13 national romances, one for each of the original states, but wrote only *Lionel Lincoln* (1825), dealing with Revolutionary Boston. Encouraged by the success of *The Pioneers* and the growing interest in the clash between savagery and civilization on the frontier, he continued his history of the pioneer scout Natty Bumppo in *The Last of the Mohicans* ♦ (1826) and *The Prairie* ♦ (1827). While traveling abroad (1826–33), nominally as U.S. consul at Lyons, he published *The Red Rover* (1827), *The Wept of Wish-ton-Wish* (1829), and *The Water-Witch* (1830), romances about America and life on American ships. In addition, he wrote *The Bravo* (1831), *The Heidenmauer* (1832), and *The Headsman* (1833), a trilogy intended to dispel the glamor of feudalism and to show its decline before the rise of democratic liberalism. *A Letter . . . to General Lafayette* (1831) champions republics against monarchies, and *Notions of the Americans* (1828) is an answer to English critics of U.S. society and government.

Upon his return, Cooper in turn was repelled by the absence of what he considered to be public and private virtue, the abuses of democracy, and the failure to perceive the best elements of the life he had conjured up in his novels. *A Letter to His Countrymen* (1834), petulantly expressing his conservatism, was followed by his satire, *The Monikins* (1835), and four volumes of *Gleanings in Europe* (1837–38), containing brilliant descriptions and pungent social criticism. *The American Democrat* ♦ (1838), a full statement of his aristocratic social ideals, was followed by *Homeward Bound* (1838) and *Home as Found* (1838), fictional statements of these themes.

During the ensuing years, the press attacked his books and personal character, and he brought suits for libel against various Whig papers, arguing his own cases so successfully that he was regularly victorious. He returned to live at Cooperstown, where he carried his war with the press over to a war with the people concerning property rights, in which,

although he was consistently vindicated, he stood alone and unpopular.

Meanwhile he wrote a scholarly *History of the Navy* (1839), whose simplicity and gusto were overlooked in a controversy centering on his treatment of the Battle of Lake Erie. With the publication of *The Pathfinder* ♦ (1840) and *The Deerslayer* ♦ (1841) he completed the epical Leather-Stocking series, and in a burst of creative energy wrote 16 works of fiction, a great amount of controversial literature, and some scholarly and factual works. *Mercedes of Castile* (1840) deals with the first voyage of Columbus; *The Two Admirals* (1842) is a story of the British navy before the Revolutionary War; and *Wing-and-Wing* (1842) is concerned with a French privateer in the Mediterranean. *Ned Myers* (1843) is the fictional biography of a former shipmate, and the *Lives of Distinguished American Naval Officers* (1846) supplements the *History of the Navy*. *Wyandotté* (1843) deals with the outbreak of the Revolution in New York; *Le Mouchoir* (1843), republished as the *Autobiography of a Pocket-Handkerchief*, is a short romance of New York society and class distinctions; *Afloat and Ashore* (1844) and its sequel *Miles Wallingford* (1844) seem to present a self-portrait of Cooper; *The Crater* (1848) is a Utopian social allegory; and *Jack Tier* (1848), *The Oak Openings* (1848), and *The Sea Lions* (1848) are all swift-moving historical romances. Cooper's last novel, *The Ways of the Hour* (1850), concerned with the perversion of social justice, is a forerunner of the modern mystery novel. Another late work is an unpublished comedy, *Upside Down, or Philosophy in Petticoats,* produced in New York. Of the novels written after 1840, the most important are those in the trilogy known as the Littlepage Manuscripts: *Satanstoe* (1845), *The Chainbearer* (1845), and *The Redskins* (1846), tracing the growing difficulties between propertied and propertyless classes in New York. A collection of *Letters and Journals* (6 vols., 1960–68) by James F. Beard gathers all known previously unpublished manuscripts.

Cooper's achievement, although uneven and the result of brilliant improvisation rather than a deeply considered artistry, was nevertheless sustained almost to the close of a hectic, crowded career. His worldwide fame attests his power of invention, for his novels have been popular principally for their variety of dramatic incidents, vivid depiction of romantic scenes and situations, and adventurous plots. But a more sophisticated view caused a revival of interest in the mid-20th century concentrating on Cooper's novels in their creation of tension between different kinds of society, between society and the individual, between the settlement and the wilderness, and between civil law and natural rights as these suggest issues of moral and mythic import.

COOVER, ROBERT [LOWELL] (1932–), Iowa-born author, winner of a Faulkner Award for the best first novel in 1965 with *The Origin of the Brunists,* which fuses realism, satire, and fantasy in telling of a mystic cult founded by the survivor of an accident in a coal mine. It was followed by another fanciful novel of multilevel character, *The Universal Baseball Association, Inc., J. Henry Waugh, Prop.* (1968), about a lonely accountant who fantasizes a rich, warm life in the imaginary baseball league he has invented and avidly follows. *The Public Burning* (1977) is an even more surrealistic and satirical novel in its depiction of the U.S. at the beginning of the Eisenhower administration as Vice-President Nixon and Uncle Sam go golfing together while Ethel and Julius Rosenberg are condemned to death for espionage. *A Political Fable* (1980) is a novella about politics, first issued in a journal in 1968, and *Spanking the Maid* (1982), another novella, satirically treats the use of sadism in fiction. *Pricksongs and Descants* (1969) contains short fictional pieces juxtaposing famous legends with his own inventive stories, and other slight, short pieces are gathered in *In Bed One Night* (1983). Coover has also written plays, *A Theological Position* (1972) and *The Water Pourer* (1972), and a film, *On a Confrontation in Iowa City* (1969).

CORMAN, CID (SIDNEY CORMAN) (1924–), Boston-born writer, graduated from Tufts University (1945), was much influenced by Charles Olson, edited *Origin* (1951–71), to which many Black Mountain♦ authors contributed. His own spare poems, suggestive of the Orient, appeared in 49 slight collections from 1944 through 1975, including *Thanksgiving Eclogue* (1954) and *Livingdying* (1970). *Aegis* (1984) contains selected poems, 1970–1980. Long expatriated in Japan, he has also translated from the Japanese and written essays.

CORSO, GREGORY [NUNZIO] (1930–), poet of the Beat movement♦ from New York City and friend of Allen Ginsberg, has led a

checkered life in several lands and spent three years in prison. His poems of protest, now intensely bitter, now amusingly irreverent, appear in *The Vestal Lady of Brattle* (1955), *Gasoline* (1958), *Bomb* (1958), *The Happy Birthday of Death* (1960), *Long Live Man* (1962), *Elegiac Feelings American* (1970), and *There Is Yet Time To Run Back Through Life and Expiate All That's Been Sadly Done* (1965). *This Hung-Up Age* (1955) is a play, and *The American Express* (1961) is a novel.

COTTON, JOHN (1584–1652), as dean of Emmanuel College, Cambridge, became interested in Puritanism. He emigrated to the Massachusetts Bay Colony (1633) and became a religious leader. Once close to the antinomianism of Anne Hutchinson, he joined those who adjudged her a heretic. He wrote many works on the church, and a catechism for children, *Milk for Babes, Drawn out of the Breasts of Both Testaments* (1646). *The Keyes of the Kingdom of Heaven* (1644) was the standard Congregational guide in New England until the publication of the Cambridge Platform (1648). Cotton also wrote a second volume of *A Survey of the Summe of Church-Discipline* (1648), continuing the work of Thomas Hooker.♦ His autocratic views on civil and religious government provoked Roger Williams to write *The Bloudy Tenent of Persecution*♦ (1644), which was answered by Cotton's *The Bloudy Tenent Washed and Made White in the Bloud of the Lamb* (1647). He wrote the preface to *The Bay Psalm Book.* ♦ He was the father-in-law of Increase Mather.

Cotton Boll, The, ode by Henry Timrod,♦ published in his *Poems* (1873). Written during the Civil War, it embodies the author's observations on the "small sphere" of a single boll of cotton, which symbolizes the cotton fields of the South in their "soft white fibres,"

> That, with their gossamer bands,
> Unite, like love, the sea-divided lands.

Country of the Pointed Firs, The, local-color sketches by Sarah Orne Jewett,♦ published in 1896.

A woman who spends her summers in the isolated seaport town of Dunnet, Me., describes the region in these portraits and anecdotes. She lives as a boarder with kindly Mrs. Almira Todd, through whose gossip she comes to know the lives and idiosyncrasies of the people. On a visit to Green Island, she meets Mrs. Todd's charming old mother, Mrs.

Blackett, and her shy brother William. Other acquaintances are aged Captain Littlepage, who tells a fantastic story of discovering Purgatory in the Arctic; Abby Martin, the "Queen's Twin," born in the same hour as Victoria; old Mrs. Fosdick, "the best hand in the world to make a visit," who tells of her childhood on her father's ship; and the gentle shepherdess Esther Hight, who, though courted by William Blackett for 40 years, continues to live with her invalid mother. A visit from Mrs. Fosdick leads Mrs. Todd to tell of her cousin, "Poor Joanna," who became a hermit on Shell-heap Island when "crossed in love." Later events are the death of old Mrs. Hight and the happy marriage of William and Esther.

Couples, novel by John Updike,♦ published in 1968.

In Tarbox, Mass. (a town like Ipswich), during the 1960s the young married set of stylish suburbanites is composed of men and women trying to find their own identities, often through finding themselves in bed with somebody else's mate. Frank and Albert Appleby and Herbert and Marcia Smith exchange partners and thus become known as The Applesmiths, while Ben and Irene Saltz, silently smarting over the community's alleged anti-Semitism, become involved with the Constantines, Eddie, a swinging airline pilot, and Carol, the town's sharpest gossip, and thus become The Saltines. Piet Hanema, a red-headed, well-built contractor and restorer of old houses, is proud of his Dutch heritage but as free and easy as any of his WASP neighbors. Among the women with whom he becomes involved is the well-bred Foxy Whitman, wife of a Boston University scientist, who becomes pregnant by Piet. She gets an abortion from the dentist Freddy Thorne, though his price for the operation is a night with Piet's pretty wife Angela. In time the couples drift apart from their marriages, their liaisons, and the town. Among them, Piet and Foxy, each divorced, later get married and move to Lexington, where they come to be accepted as just another couple in that town.

Courtin', The, dialect verse narrative by Lowell, in *The Biglow Papers.* ♦

Courtship of Miles Standish, The, narrative poem in unrhymed English hexameters by Longfellow,♦ published in 1858. The central theme is apocryphal, although material is drawn from early New England histories and tradition.

Miles Standish, captain of the Plymouth Colony, calls upon his better-educated friend John Alden to woo the maid Priscilla for him. Alden, also in love with the girl, yields to the duty of friendship and blurts out Standish's message, at which Priscilla makes her famous arch inquiry, "Why don't you speak for yourself, John?" Infuriated by Alden's failure, which he attributes to a betrayal of trust, Standish leaves on an Indian campaign without bidding farewell to his friend. During his absence, Alden and Priscilla are constantly together, and, receiving news of his death, plan to marry. The news proves to be false, Standish returns to attend the wedding and beg forgiveness for his anger, and the three are reunited as friends.

Coverdale, MILES, character in *The Blithedale Romance.* ♦

Cowboy, name given during the Revolution to lawless marauders who pillaged neutral territory and were supposedly favorable to the English. Those who favored the rebels were known as Skinners. Both figure in fiction about the Revolutionary War, particularly Cooper's *The Spy.* ♦ The term "cowboy" has since been applied, particularly in the West, to cattle herders, and there are distinctive cowboy ballads♦ and tall tales.♦ Popular romancing about the cowboy dates back to dime novels and other pulp fiction beginning in the 1870s, preceding infrequent realistic reminiscences like *A Texas Cowboy* (1885) by Charles Siringo. Owen Wister's *The Virginian*♦ (1902) became the classic handling of the type, far surpassing in popularity the literary works of writers who had more experience of cowboy life, such as Andy Adams's *The Log of a Cowboy* (1903) and E.M. Rhodes's *Good Men and True* (1910). The mythology of the masculine and heroic cowboy has been continued in a large body of fiction from the time of Clarence E. Mulford (*Hopalong Cassidy,* 1910), Zane Grey (*Riders of the Purple Sage,* 1912), and Max Brand (*Destry Rides Again,* 1930) to the present-day paperback publications of Louis L'Amour. The works of these authors and others in their vein have been further popularized in numerous film versions by stars who have included William S. Hart, Tom Mix, Gene Autry, Roy Rogers, and John Wayne. Cowboys have also been the subject of television programs.

COWLEY, Malcolm (1898–   ), born in Pennsylvania, served in World War I, graduated from Harvard (1920), and later became an expatriate in France. *Blue Juniata* (1929) prints semi-autobiographical poems tracing his mental and emotional development during this period, to his final facing of the American scene. *A Dry Season* (1942), further poems, is partly about the "lost generation." Prose works, concerned with social and intellectual forces in contemporary society, include *Exile's Return: A Narrative of Ideas* (1934; revised, 1951), partly autobiographical, analyzing the postwar generation; *The Literary Situation* (1954), about the sociology of contemporary American authorship; *Think Back on Us* (1967), collecting his writings during and on the 1930s; *A Many-Windowed House* (1970), *A Second Flowering* (1973), and *And I Worked at the Writer's Trade* (1978), essays on modern American literature; and *The Dream of the Golden Mountains* (1980), a memoir of the '30s. He edited *After the Genteel Tradition* (1937) and many works by major American writers. *The View from 80* (1981) contains reflections on the life of an octogenarian.

COXE, Louis O[sborne] (1918–   ), born in New Hampshire, after graduation from Princeton (1940) and naval service has taught English at Lawrenceville, Harvard, Minnesota, and Bowdoin (1955–   ). His poetry has been collected in *The Sea Faring* (1947), *The Second Man* (1955), *The Wilderness* (1958), *The Last Hero* (1965), and *Nikal Seyn and Decoration Day* (1966), whose sense of tradition, lofty subjects, and disciplined craftsmanship may be reasons why he has called himself "the first neo-Victorian." *The Middle Passage* (1960) is a book-length blank-verse narrative poem on the depravity of the slave trade. With Princeton classmate Robert H. Chapman he wrote the dramatic adaptation of *Billy Budd* (1951), first produced in an earlier version as *Uniform of Flesh* (1949). He is also the author of a critical book, *Edwin Arlington Robinson* (1969), and *Enabling Acts* (1976), critical essays.

COZZENS, James Gould (1903–78), born in Chicago but reared on Staten Island and educated at Harvard (1922–24), where he wrote his first novel, *Confusion* (1924), the story of an aristocratic, rebellious French girl. Leaving college to become a tutor in Cuba, he wrote *Michael Scarlett* (1925), a historical romance, and gathered background for *Cock*

Pit (1928), set on a Cuban sugar plantation, and *The Son of Perdition* (1929), about a despotic American company official in Cuba. His more mature work begins with the novelette *S.S. San Pedro* (1931), based on the mysterious sinking of the *Vestris,* followed by *The Last Adam* (1933), published in England as *A Cure of Flesh,* introducing a representative Cozzens figure and setting in the story of a crusty, heterodox doctor in a rigid Connecticut town. *Castaway* (1934) is an atypical fantasy, presenting, with seeming realism, New York after a disaster that leaves the sole surviving man wandering in a great department store. The most characteristic novels begin with *Men and Brethren* (1936), a study of a liberal clergyman; *Ask Me Tomorrow* (1940), about an American in Europe; and *The Just and The Unjust* (1942), about a murder trial, for they deal with mature professional men in a stratified society who are called upon to resolve a conflict between the ideal and the possible and who acquiesce in the way things are, without complete loss of principle. This point of view and the tone of detached disenchantment appear most markedly in *Guard of Honor*♦ (1948, Pulitzer Prize), about the clash between human and military values at an air force base in World War II; and *By Love Possessed*♦ (1957), depicting a lawyer, one of the men of reason, and his involvements in love. Cozzens's last novel, *Morning, Noon, and Night* (1968), in presenting the recollections of one man in his sixties also gives a sense of upper-middle-class New England life in the 20th century. *Children and Others* (1964) collects stories, half of them about boys' views of their teachers, parents, and other adults. His *Selected Notebooks: 1960–1967* was published in 1984, and his wartime memoranda and Air Force diary were issued as *A Time of War* (1984).

Cracker-barrel humor, originally associated with the native American wise saws involved in the swapping of gossip, information, and social and political views around the cracker barrel of New England general stores, but later extended to all shrewd, homespun, idiomatic Yankee wit, such as that of Jack Downing, Sam Slick, the characters in Lowell's *Biglow Papers,* the Widow Bedott, and Mrs. Partington, and further extended to all horse-sense folk humor of the U.S., regardless of region.

CRADDOCK, Charles Egbert, pseudonym of Mary N. Murfree. ♦

CRANE, [HAROLD] HART (1899–1932), Ohio-born poet, although he published only two books during his lifetime, is recognized as an outstanding poet of his era. *White Buildings* (1926), despite its lack of a single theme to synthesize the author's experience of the American scene, is distinguished by a sonorous rhetoric and concrete imagery, revealing by tangential suggestion an acute mystical perception. The promise of this early work is fulfilled in *The Bridge*♦ (1930), a long mystical poem concerned with the American background and the modern consciousness to which it gives rise. Crane finds in America a principle of unity and absolute faith, through the integration of such symbols as Columbus, Pocahontas, Rip Van Winkle, Poe, Whitman, the subway, and, above all, Brooklyn Bridge, an image of man's anonymous creative power unifying past and present. The lack of discipline in the poet's personal existence, and his belief that his creative ability had been dissipated, caused him to commit suicide by jumping from a ship that was bringing him home from a year's residence in Mexico. His *Collected Poems* (1933) incorporate previously unpublished West Indian sketches and other new poems. His *Letters* were published in 1952, and his correspondence with Yvor Winters was printed in 1978.

Crane, ICHABOD, hero of "The Legend of Sleepy Hollow."♦

CRANE, STEPHEN (1871–1900), born in New Jersey, spent most of his youth in upstate New York; he attended Lafayette College and Syracuse University, each for a year, before moving to New York City to become a struggling author and do intermittent reporting for the *Herald* and *Tribune*. His first book, *Maggie: A Girl of the Streets*♦ (1893), was too grim to find a regular publisher, and remained unsold even when Crane borrowed from his brother to issue it privately. Early in 1893, with no personal experience of war, deriving his knowledge primarily from reading Tolstoy and *Battles and Leaders of the Civil War*, he wrote *The Red Badge of Courage*♦ (1895), his great realistic study of the mind of an inexperienced soldier trapped in the fury and turmoil of battle.

The success of this book led to the reissue of *Maggie*, and Crane's reputation was established. In quick succession appeared his book of free verse, influenced by Emily Dickinson, *The Black Riders*♦ (1895); *The Little Regiment*♦ (1896), naturalistic Civil War stories,

issued in England as *Pictures of War; George's Mother* (1896), the story of the dull lives of a young workingman and his mother in New York; and *The Third Violet* (1897), a conventional novelette about the romance of a young artist.

Because of his successful treatment of war in his masterpiece, Crane was thrust for most of his brief remaining life into war reporting. After a period as a correspondent in the Southwest and in Mexico, he was sent with a filibustering expedition to Cuba at the end of 1896. The sinking of the ship and his subsequent 50-hour struggle with the waves furnished the theme of his best-known short story, "The Open Boat." Inexperience and illness made his trip to Greece, to report the Turkish war, almost futile. Following a short residence in England, he went to Cuba to report the Spanish-American War, and his journalistic sketches and stories of this period are collected in *Wounds in the Rain* (1900). His observation of the Greco-Turkish War resulted in *Active Service* (1899), a satirical novel about a war correspondent.

Upon his return to New York, Crane's health was already broken by the hardships he had endured, and, possibly owing to his early treatment of squalor in *Maggie* and rumors about the immorality of his common-law wife, a myth now arose to the effect that he was a drunk, a drug addict, and generally depraved. Disgusted by unpleasant notoriety, he returned to England, having meanwhile published two collections of short stories, *The Open Boat*♦ (1898) and *The Monster*♦ (1899), and a second volume of free verse, *War is Kind* (1899). *Whilomville Stories*♦ (1900) is a collection of tales concerned with typical childhood incidents in a small New York town. Crane's last work shows a decrease in power, for he was broken in health and soon died of tuberculosis in Germany, where he had gone to seek a cure. Posthumously published volumes include *Great Battles of the World* (1901), an uninspired historical study; *Last Words* (1902), a collection of his early tales and sketches; *The O'Ruddy* (1903), an unfinished romance, completed by Robert Barr; and *Men, Women, and Boats* (1921), a selection, including several stories never before published. His *Letters* were collected in 1960, and the University of Virginia issued a scholarly edition of his works (10 vols., 1969–75).

CRAWFORD, FRANCIS MARION (1854–1909), son of noted sculptor Thomas Crawford

(1813–57), and nephew of Julia Ward Howe, was born in Italy, educated in the U.S. and abroad. His literary career, extending over 25 years, more than 40 novels, and several plays, made him popular and famous in his own time for his romances of cosmopolitan and sophisticated life. He also wrote historical tales and a novel about political corruption in the U.S. of the Gilded Age.

CREELEY, ROBERT [WHITE] (1926–   ), Massachusetts-born poet, graduated from Black Mountain College, where he became close to Charles Olson, whose *Selected Writings* he edited (1966), and where he was editor of *The Black Mountain Review* ♦ (1954–57). He subsequently traveled widely and became a faculty member (1963) of the State University of New York at Buffalo. With *Le Fou* (1952) he began publication of numerous brief collections of poetry, selected in *For Love* (1962), marked by terse, laconic treatments of love, presented with great immediacy. Later volumes—*Words* (1967), *Pieces* (1969), *The Finger* (1970), *St. Martin's* (1971), *A Day Book* (1972), *Thirty Things* (1974), *Away* (1976), *Later* (1978), *Mirrors* (1983), and *A Calendar* (1983), 12 poems, one for each month, among others—show him continuing a stripped-down style and diction in presenting the problems of understanding in dealing with personal feelings and relations. He has also written stories, *The Gold Diggers* (1954, enlarged 1965); a quasi-autobiographical novel, *The Island* (1963), about a young American writer living on Majorca; and critical essays, *A Quick Graph* (1970) and *Was That a Real Poem* (1979). *The Collected Poems, 1945–75* appeared in 1983 and *The Collected Prose* in 1984.

Creole, name applied to American-born descendants of the French and Spanish settlers of Latin America. The term did not originally mean persons of mixed white and Negro blood, although this is one of its various connotations in popular usage. In Louisiana it is used to distinguish descendants of the original French settlers from the "Cajun" heirs of the exiles from Acadia. ♦ Creole life in Louisiana has been depicted by such local-color authors as Cable, Hearn, Grace King, and Kate Chopin, and been the subject of critical comment by a descendant, Adrien Rouquette.

CRÈVECŒUR, MICHEL-GUILLAUME JEAN DE (1735–1813), known as J. Hector St. John de Crèvecœur, was born in France, and emi-grated to Canada during the last of the French and Indian Wars. He served under Montcalm, and later seems to have explored near the Great Lakes and the Ohio River. He landed at New York (1759), took out naturalization papers (1765), traveled extensively in Pennsylvania and New York, and settled with his American wife in Orange Country, N.Y. His travels are described in his later book, *Voyage dans la Haute Pensylvanie et dans l'état de New-York* (3 vols., 1801), translated as *Journey into Northern Pennsylvania and the State of New York* (1963). He spent idyllic years on his New York farm until the Revolution, when, as a Loyalist, he was forced to flee to New York and then to France (1780). During the quiet decade prior to the Revolution, he probably wrote most of the charming *Letters from an American Farmer* ♦ (1782) on which his reputation rests. Other informative and vivid essays written during this period have been published in *Sketches of Eighteenth-Century America* (1925), which also includes a play, "Landscapes," six scenes showing the hypocrisy, inhumanity, cupidity, and abuse of power which underlay the Revolution. In 1783 Crèvecœur returned to America only to discover that his wife was dead, his home burned, and his children had disappeared, as a result of an Indian raid. Eventually he found his children, and settled in New York, where as French consul he attempted to cement the friendly relations of the two countries. He returned to France (1790), where he passed the rest of his life. Although he did not consider himself a man of letters, the French thought of him as a true "man of feeling," and when his *Lettres d'un cultivateur Américain* appeared in France (1783), it was adulterated with artificial sentimentality and redundant rhetoric. For this and other reasons, Crèvecœur has often been considered merely a sentimental Rousseauistic romancer, but current criticism looks upon him as being a fresh and vigorous recorder of events and scenes in early American rural life.

Crisis, The American, series of 13 regular and three specially issued pamphlets by Thomas Paine, ♦ published between Dec. 19, 1776, and April 19, 1783. The first pamphlet appeared at a time of gloom and uncertainty, when the Revolutionary army faced defeat because of its retreat across New Jersey and the imminent defection of some of the colonies, and Washington the day before had written ". . . if every nerve is not strained to the utmost to recruit the new army with all possible expedition, I think the game is pretty near up." Paine's direct, incisive style, and his stirring opening, "These are the times that try men's souls," created an immediate reaction in favor of the patriotic cause, and Washington had the pamphlet read before every regiment. The subsequent crossing of the Delaware and the victories at Trenton and Princeton were partly credited to its influence. Later issues continued to oppose defeatism and compromise, and were influential in maintaining morale and a unified spirit in the colonies.

CRISTOFER, MICHAEL (1945–), New Jersey-born actor and dramatist, whose plays include *The Mandala* (1967), *Rienzi* (1968), *Dorian* (1969), *Plot Counter Plot* (1971), *Americomedia* (1972), and *The Shadow Box* (1977, Pulitzer Prize), which presents three separate persons dying of cancer and the ways each meets the end of life. Other plays include *Ice* (1974), presenting two men and a woman living in an isolated Alaskan cabin; and *Black Angel* (1976), about the later life of a World War II German officer responsible for the deaths of many French civilians.

CROCKETT, DAVY (DAVID) (1786–1836), born in Tennessee, spent a shiftless youth until his political career began (*c.*1816) with his appointment as justice of the peace. He boasted that none of his decisions was ever reversed because of his dependence on "natural-born sense instead of law learning." After being twice elected to the state legislature, he accepted a humorous proposal that he run for Congress, and to his surprise was elected, serving from 1827 to 1831, and again from 1833 to 1835. Because of his opposition to Jackson, the Whigs adopted him as a convenient tool through whom to draw the backwoods democracy to its standard. Davy was soon turned by skillful politicians into a frontier hero, whose picturesque eccentricities, backwoods humor, tall tales, shrewd native intelligence, and lusty pioneer spirit were all aggrandized. Whig journalists in short order turned out such books, attributed to Davy, as *Sketches and Eccentricities of Col. David Crockett* (1833), *An Account of Col. Crockett's Tour to the North and Down East* (1835), *The Life of Martin Van Buren* (1835), and *Col. Crockett's Exploits and Adventures in Texas* (1836). With the exception of the last, which is posthumous, he may have had a hand in all these works, and he gladly claimed the *Tour* and life of Van Buren. Swallowing the Whig bait, he enjoyed his sudden rise to fame and was glad to aid in propagating the

myth, which, however, removed him from office, since his constituents would not tolerate his desertion of Democratic principles. Piqued, he left Tennessee to participate in the war for Texan independence, and a few months later died in the heroic defense of the Alamo, adding a final dramatic chapter to his career. *A Narrative of the Life of David Crockett, of the State of Tennessee* (1834) passes as his autobiography, although the claim has often been disputed. In any case the book has the robust manner attributed to Crockett, and contains fine examples of the farce and exaggeration of the tall tale.

Crossing, The, historical romance by Winston Churchill,♦ published in 1904.

Crossing Brooklyn Ferry, poem by Whitman,♦ published in the 1856 edition of *Leaves of Grass* as "Sun-Down Poem" and given its present title in 1860. Based on the author's reminiscences of life in Brooklyn and the trip across the East River to Manhattan, it is a rhapsody of the daily crowds and of the panorama of the city as seen from the river, in which he mystically identifies himself with everybody and everything: "great or small, you furnish your parts toward the soul."

Crow Indians, Plains tribe of the Sioux family, which once ranged along the upper Yellowstone and Big Horn rivers of Wyoming and Montana. The Crow were nomadic hunters and warriors, conducted a constant warfare with the Blackfoot, and aided the U.S. army against the Sioux. They are described as predatory ruffians in *The Adventures of Captain Bonneville* and in Beckwourth's *Life,* but F.B. Linderman's *American* gives a more favorable view of them.

Crying of Lot 49, novel by Thomas Pynchon,♦ published in 1966.

When Mrs. Oedipa Mass learns that the will of her onetime lover, a real estate mogul, Pierce Inverarity, has made her an executor of his estate, she leaves her husband Mucho to investigate Inverarity's property. The investigation leads to the discovery of what she takes to be a conspiratorial underground communications system dating from the 16th century. As she travels through California on her new quest she encounters the system's symbol, the Tristero, a muted post horn, in many odd places and meets such curious people as Professor Bortz, editor of a 17th-century drama that treats the Tristero.

Finally she believes she will solve the enigma through a mysterious bidder eager to buy Inverarity's stamp collection, but the novel concludes as Oedipa awaits the crying out at the auction of the salient lot numbered 49.

CULLEN, COUNTEE (1903–46), black author, a major figure of the Harlem Renaissance♦ of the 1920s, was educated at New York University (A.B., 1925) and Harvard (M.A., 1926). While he was only in his twenties, his poetry won prizes in journals and was collected in *Color* (1925), *Copper Sun* (1927), *The Ballad of the Brown Girl* (1927), and *The Black Christ* (1929). As the titles indicate, the themes were racial, but he was also criticized for being unduly influenced by the romanticism of Keats and for failing to use black rhythms and idioms. A later collection, *The Medea and Some Poems* (1935), opens with a translation of Euripides' tragedy. His other works include *One Way to Heaven* (1932), a novel about Harlem life; *Caroling Dusk* (1927), an anthology of verse by black writers; an adaptation of Arna Bontemps's novel *God Sends Sunday* as a musical play, *St. Louis Woman* (1946); and two books for children.

CUMMINGS, E[DWARD] E[STLIN] (1894–1962), born in Cambridge, Mass., after receiving his A.B. (1915) and M.A. (1916) from Harvard joined the service of the American volunteer Norton Harjes Ambulance Corps in France before the U.S. entered World War I, and in 1917 was confined for several months in a French concentration camp on an unfounded charge of treasonable correspondence. This experience provided the basis for his first book, *The Enormous Room*♦ (1922), a prose narrative of a poetic and personal perception. His first book of poetry, *Tulips and Chimneys* (1923), followed by *&* (1925), *XLI Poems* (1925), and *is 5* (1926), clearly established his individual voice and tone. The poems show his transcendental faith in a world where the self-reliant, joyful, loving individual is beautifully alive but in which mass man, or the man who lives by mind alone, without heart and soul, is dead. The true individual Cummings praised, often reverently and with freshness of spirit and idiom, but the "unman" was satirized as Cummings presented witty, bitter parodies of and attacks on the patriotic or cultural platitudes and shibboleths of the "unworld." This poetry is marked by experimental word coinages, shifting of grammar, blending of established stanzaic forms and free verse, flamboyant punning, typographic distortion, unusual punctuation, and idiosyncratic division of words, all of which became integral to the ideas and rhythms of his relatively brief lyrics. These he continued to write with subtlety of technique and sensitivity of feeling and to publish in *ViVa* (1931), *No Thanks* (1935), *1/20* (1936), *Collected Poems* (1938), *50 Poems* (1940), *I x I* (1944), Χαῖρε (1950), *Poems: 1923–1954* (1954), *95 Poems* (1958), and the posthumously collected *73 Poems* (1963). His other works are *him* (1927), an expressionist drama in verse and prose, with kaleidoscopic scenes dashing from comedy to tragedy; a book which bears no title (1930); *Eimi* (1933), a travel diary utilizing the techniques of his poetry and violently attacking the regimentation of individuals in the U.S.S.R.; *Tom* (1935), a satirical ballet based on *Uncle Tom's Cabin; CIOPW* (1931), drawings and paintings showing his ability in charcoal, ink, oil, pencil, and watercolor; *Anthropos, The Future of Art* (1944); *Santa Claus* (1946), a morality play; and *i* (1953), "six nonlectures" delivered at Harvard.

CUMMINS, MARIA SUSANNA (1827–66), Massachusetts author, contributor to the *Atlantic Monthly,* wrote the popular moralistic romance *The Lamplighter* (1854), concerned with the life of a Boston orphan girl who is befriended by the lamplighter Trueman Flint, grows up under his protection, and is rewarded for her goodness and purity when she marries a childhood sweetheart.

CUNNINGHAM, J[AMES] V[INCENT] (1911–85), poet of the school of Yvor Winters, received his A.B. and Ph.D. from Stanford, and taught at Brandeis beginning in 1953. His disciplined poetry, often abstract and epigrammatic, sometimes witty, and marked by fine craftsmanship, is printed in six volumes beginning with *The Helmsman* (1942) and gathered in *Collected Poems and Epigrams* (1971). *Collected Essays* was issued in 1977.

D

DAHLBERG, EDWARD (1900–1977), born in Boston, the illegitimate son of the Junoesque owner of the Star Lady Barbershop of Kansas City, as he describes in his autobiography, *Because I Was Flesh* (1964). This work also tells of his years in a Jewish orphan asylum in Cleveland, his education at the University of California (1922–23) and at Columbia (B.S.). For some time after 1926 he was an expatriate in Europe. His novels include *Bottom Dogs* (England, 1929), about a boyhood like his own, giving a sense of the horror of orphanage, slum, and hobo experiences; *From Flushing to Calvary* (1932), depicting the sordid lives of slum dwellers in New York City; and *Those Who Perish* (1934), treating the effects of German Nazism upon American Jews. His prophetic, mystical literary criticism, in the vein of his friend D.H. Lawrence, is printed in *Do These Bones Live?* (1941), revised as *Sing O Barren* (1947) and *Can These Bones Live?* (1960). Other works include *Flea of Sodom* (1950), essays and parables indignantly attacking contemporary civilization; *The Sorrows of Priapus* (1957), on the dichotomy of mind and body in Hellenic, Hebraic, and pre-Columbian cultures; *Truth Is More Sacred* (1961), correspondence with Herbert Read about modern literature; *Cipango's Hinder Door* (1966), poems; *The Carnal Myth* (1968), subtitled "A Search into Classical Sensuality"; and *The Olive of Minerva* (1976), a comic novel about sex and cuckoldry. *Epitaphs of Our Times* (1967) collects his letters, and *Confessions* (1971) contains reminiscences.

Daisy Miller: A Study, novel by Henry James,♦ published in 1878 and dramatized by the author in 1883.

Frederick Winterbourne, an American expatriate visiting at Vevey, Switzerland, meets commonplace, newly rich Mrs. Miller, from Schenectady, N.Y., her mischievous small son Randolph, and her daughter Daisy, an "inscrutable combination of audacity and innocence." The Millers have no perception of the complex code that underlies behavior in European society, and Winterbourne is astonished at the girl's innocence and her mother's unconcern when Daisy accompanies him to the Castle of Chillon. Some months later he meets the family in Rome, where

Daisy has aroused suspicion among the American colony by being seen constantly with Giovanelli, a third-rate Italian. Ostracized by former friends, who think her "intrigue" has gone too far, Daisy denies to Winterbourne that she is engaged to Giovanelli, with whom the American meets her one night in the Colosseum. When he comments on her indiscretion in exposing herself to the danger of "Roman fever," Giovanelli says, "but when was the Signorina ever prudent?" A few days later she falls ill with malaria, and a week afterward dies. At her funeral Giovanelli tells Winterbourne that Daisy was "the most beautiful young lady I ever saw, and the most amiable . . . and the most innocent." He says that he had hoped to marry her, but believes she would not have accepted him.

Dakota Indians, see *Sioux Indians.*

DALY, [JOHN] AUGUSTIN (1838–99), author or adapter of more than 90 plays, most of which were radically altered from the original French or German, and often given an American setting. His own best plays were *Horizon* (1871), a romantic drama of the West; and *Divorce* (1871), a problem play; but he was also the author of melodramas such as *Under the Gaslight* (1867), in which heroes were tied to logs about to be sawed in two, or bound to railroad tracks in the paths of onrushing trains. The most successful of his ventures as a producer were in the theater in New York City that bore his name.

Damnation of Theron Ware, The, novel by Harold Frederic,♦ published in 1896. Its title in England is *Illumination.*

Theron Ware, simple, handsome, and eloquent, is a Methodist preacher at Octavius, N.Y. Desiring wealth and fame, and being ignorant of his own limitations, he plans to write an epoch-making book. His damnation occurs through his growing enlightenment, which makes him conscious of his ignorance and of the mean emotionalism of his church, as well as of his inability to enter into the saner and wider outlook of those he admires. He is attracted by Celia Madden, daughter of a rich Irish immigrant, who, with her pastor, Father Forbes, and her agnostic friend, Dr.

Ledsmar, makes him realize a fullness of life he has never imagined. Misled by his passion for Celia, Ware wrongly accuses her of illicit relations with Father Forbes, and she dismisses him, telling him he is a fool and a bore. He is at last saved from complete ruin by the emotional revivalist Sister Soulsby, whose common sense he can understand.

DANA, RICHARD HENRY, JR. (1815–82), son of a Massachusetts poet and essayist, was reared according to conventional New England standards. He suffered serious eye trouble as a sophomore at Harvard, and to regain his health shipped to California as a common sailor (1834). On the Pacific coast he worked for more than a year gathering hides, after which he returned to Boston and completed his education at Harvard law school. In fulfillment of his vows "to redress the grievances and suffering of that class of beings with whom my lot had so long been cast," his first publication was an article in the *American Jurist* (1839) on "Cruelty to Seamen." In 1840, the year of his admission to the bar, he published the famous account of his voyage, *Two Years Before the Mast,* ♦ which won immediate popularity, created many imitators and followers of its realistic approach, and permanently influenced the literature of the sea. His second book, *The Seaman's Friend* (1841, called in England *The Seaman's Manual*), was designed to show common sailors their legal rights and duties, and constitutes a reference book of sea terms, customs, and laws. Dana was active in Free-Soil politics, and provided legal assistance without charge to slaves captured under the Fugitive Slave Law, thereby antagonizing those of his own class of Brahmins in Boston whose cotton mills were dependent on the Southern plantations. During the Civil War he was U.S. attorney for the district of Massachusetts, and succeeded in convincing the U.S. Supreme Court, despite its Democratic leanings, that the Northern blockade was legal. Although he held several minor offices, he never attained the diplomatic heights of which he was ambitious. His edition of *Elements of International Law by Wheaton* (1866) made him the object of an invidious and protracted suit for plagiarism, and the slanders involved caused the Senate to refuse his appointment as minister to England (1876). Wearied by many abortive attempts to obtain public office, he declared bitterly, "My life has been a failure compared with what I might and ought to have done," and "My great success—my book—was a

boy's work, done before I came to the Bar." He went to Europe (1878) to rest and to write further books, but died before completing any of his proposed writings on international law, which he hoped might establish his reputation in this field. One of his several later voyages is described in *To Cuba and Back* (1859), which lacks, however, the qualities for which his first book is admired. Some of his addresses were collected as *Speeches in Stirring Times* (1910).

Dangling Man, novel by Saul Bellow, ♦ published in 1944.

At 27, a Chicagoan named Joseph, a university graduate, an intellectual, five years married, leaves his job with a travel bureau, and under the pressure of waiting to be taken to war as a draftee feels himself alienated from society. In his diary between Dec. 15, 1942, and April 9, 1943, he objectively describes his quarrels with friends, in-laws, his wife Iva, by whom he is supported in their mean rooming house, and his brother Amos, a go-getting success, as he undergoes intense self-analysis dedicated only to the belief "I must know what I myself am." Talks with his alter ego, "Tu As Raison Aussi," finally convince him that man creates his own destiny and send him to volunteer in the army rather than continue to wait indefinitely to be inducted.

Daring Young Man on the Flying Trapeze, The, first book by William Saroyan, ♦ issued in 1934. It collects 26 stories, all brief, and some only a page long, in the author's own idiosyncratic vein, written with great speed during a time when he claimed to have written a story a day for 30 days. The title work presents a poor, jobless, aspiring young author in San Francisco as he makes his way through a day conceiving, among many other things, of a "flight with grace . . . to some sort of eternity."

Dark Laughter, novel by Sherwood Anderson, ♦ published in 1925.

John Stockton, a Chicago reporter, leaves his wife and his routine life to travel down the Illinois and Mississippi rivers, dreaming of the epic Mark Twain might now write, "of song killed, of laughter killed, of men herded into a new age of speed, of factories, of swift, fast-running trains," and his story is accompanied by a chorus of "dark laughter" and song by the unrepressed blacks, contrasted with the spiritual sterility of machine civilization.

DARROW, CLARENCE SEWARD (1857–1938), Ohio-born lawyer, mainly associated with Chicago, was noted for his defense of labor organizations, acting as counsel for Debs in the case resulting from the Pullman strike; for William D. Haywood, accused of instigating the murder of the governor of Idaho; and for the McNamara brothers, accused of dynamiting the Los Angeles *Times* building. He was also known as a criminal lawyer in such cases as the trial of Loeb and Leopold (1924) and the Fortescue-Massie case in Honolulu. His agnosticism was strikingly revealed in the Scopes trial.♦ He wrote several books, including *A Persian Pearl* (1898), literary essays; *Farmington* (1904), a novel about his own youth; *An Eye for an Eye* (1905), a novel concerned with the fallacy of the Mosaic law; *Crime: Its Cause and Treatment* (1922); and *The Story of My Life* (1932). *Attorney for the Damned* (1957) collects 13 major speeches.

DAVIDSON, DONALD [GRADY] (1893–1968), Tennessee author, professor at Vanderbilt University, is one of the exponents of regionalism♦ who founded *The Fugitive*♦ and contributed to the group's symposia. His own books include *The Tall Men* (1927), a blank-verse poem; *The Attack on Leviathan* (1938), essays opposing centralization of political and economic power in the North; *Lee in the Mountains* (1938), short narrative poems on Southern heroes; *The Tennessee* (2 vols., 1946–48), a history of the river and valley; *Still Rebels, Still Yankees* (1957), essays; *Southern Writers in the Modern World* (1958); *The Long Street* (1961), poems written over a long period of time; and *The Spyglass* (1963), early essays. His collected *Poems* appeared in 1966 and his correspondence with Allen Tate in 1974.

DAVIS, H[AROLD] L[ENOIR] (1896–1960), Oregon author whose novels are *Honey in the Horn* (1935, Pulizer Prize), about Oregon in the homesteading era; *Harp of a Thousand Strings* (1947), contrasting French and American ways of life; *Beulah Land* (1949), a picaresque tale of Indian and white frontier life; *Winds of Morning* (1952), set in the Columbia River area of the 1920s; and *Distant Music* (1957), about three generations of a pioneer Oregon family. *Team Bells Woke Me* (1953) is a collection of stories; *Kettle of Fire* (1959) contains essays and articles about the Pacific Northwest; and *Proud Riders* (1942) is poetry about people in the Far West.

DAVIS, REBECCA [BLAINE] HARDING (1831–1910), lived most of her life in Philadelphia, the background of several of her books. She first came into prominence with her realistic story "Life in the Iron Mills" (*Atlantic Monthly,* 1861). *Margaret Howth* (1862), a novel of life in a mill town, is somewhat marred by an undue stress on moral contrasts, but shows her purpose "to dig into this commonplace, this vulgar American life, and see what is in it." *Waiting for the Verdict* (1868) is a novel strongly in favor of blacks, and *John Andross* (1874), about the Whiskey Ring and Pennsylvania corporation lobbying, shows the effect of political corruption. Mrs. Davis was the author of several other novels, an autobiography, and many short stories, some of which are collected in *Silhouettes of American Life* (1892). Some of her later writing drifts into sentimentality and prevailing literary conventions, but she is adept at character portrayal.

DAVIS, RICHARD HARDING (1864–1916), son of Rebecca H. Davis, was born in Philadelphia, where in 1886 he began the journalistic career that was to make him the leading reporter of his time. Letters reporting his journalistic tours of this period were collected in *The West from a Car Window* (1892), *The Rulers of the Mediterranean* (1894), *Our English Cousins* (1894), *About Paris* (1895), and *Three Gringos in Venezuela and Central America* (1896). As correspondent for New York and London papers, he reported the Spanish war in Cuba, the Greco-Turkish War, the Spanish-American War, the Boer War, the Russo-Japanese War, and World War I, whose vividly dramatized accounts were collected in several books. Beginning with *Gallegher and Other Stories* (1891) and *Van Bibber and Others* (1892) he published 11 volumes of stories which show adept craftsmanship but are journalistic, with more stress on effect and form than on substance. He also wrote slick, lively, and melodramatic novels and plays.

DAVISON, PETER [HUBERT] (1928–), New York City-born poet and editor, graduated from Harvard, was a Fulbright Scholar at Cambridge University, and won the award of the Yale Series of Younger Poets with *The Breaking of the Day* (1964). Later collections include *The City and the Island* (1966), *Pretending To Be Asleep* (1970), *Dark Houses* (1971), *Walking the Boundaries* (1974), *A Voice in the Mountain* (1977), *Barn*

Fever (1981), and *Praying Wrong* (1984). *Half Remembered* (1973) is an autobiography. He became poetry editor of the *Atlantic Monthly* in 1972.

DAY, CLARENCE [SHEPARD] (1874–1935), essayist, best known for his autobiographical works, *God and My Father* (1932), *Life with Father* (1935), *Life with Mother* (1937), and *Father and I* (1940), in which, with affectionate humor, he characterizes his family's Victorian traditions and typical upper-class life in 19th-century New York. *Life with Father*, dramatized (1939) by Howard Lindsay and Russel Crouse, once held the record of having the longest continuous run of any American play.

Day of Doom, The, theological poem in ballad meter by Michael Wigglesworth,♦ published in 1662. The subject is indicated by the subtitle, *A Poetical Description of the Great and Last Judgment.* Few stanzas approach the poetic, and the work is now interesting only as a historical document, but in its own day it was immensely popular in both America and England. It is estimated that a copy was sold for one in every 20 persons then in New England, or one in every 45 in the colonies. Other versified theology of the same nature is annexed to the work as preface and postscript, while "Vanity of Vanities" serves as a "Song of Emptiness To Fill Up the Empty Pages Following."

Day of the Locust, The, novel by Nathanael West,♦ published in 1939.

Tod Hackett, a recent Yale graduate in the 1930s, moves to Hollywood to make set and costume designs for a film studio while also pursuing his own painting. There he meets Faye Greener and her father, Harry, a down-and-out actor reduced to selling homemade silver polish door to door. One of his customers, Homer Simpson, a bland 40-year-old bookkeeper, becomes enamored of Faye and in a "business arrangement" offers her lodging in his cottage just to aid her. She in turn houses a cowboy from Arizona and a young Mexican in the garage, stages a drunken party at Homer's house, and goes to bed with Miguel, the Mexican. Disillusioned, Homer walks to the railroad station to return to Utah but on the way is attacked by a pesky boy and knocks him down. Then Homer is attacked by a swarming crowd of people who had gathered to see the arrival of stars at a premiere and out of boredom were seeking any excitement they might find. In a frenzied scene, reminiscent of Tod's surrealistic painting, *The Burning of Los Angeles,* the mob overwhelms Homer and Tod loses his own self-control.

Days, blank-verse poem by Emerson,♦ published in the *Atlantic Monthly* (1857) and reprinted in *May-Day and Other Pieces* (1867). When the Days come to offer gifts "to each . . . after his will," the poet hastily chooses only "a few herbs and apples," realizing too late the scorn of the departing Day.

Days Without End, play by Eugene O'Neill. ♦

Deacon's Masterpiece, The; or, The Wonderful "One-Hoss Shay," poem by Holmes♦ in *The Autocrat of the Breakfast-Table,* was first published in the *Atlantic Monthly* (1858). In its rhymed four-stress couplets, anapests are frequently substituted for iambs, and a humorous effect is derived from the monotonous rhyme and absurd rhythm. A parable of the breakdown of Calvinism, the poem tells of a deacon who wanted a carriage that would never break down, so that he built all of its parts with equal strength. Exactly a century after the construction of this masterpiece, the whole work fell apart at once.

Deadwood Dick, sobriquet of Richard W. Clarke (1845–1930), English-born frontiersman in South Dakota, noted as an Indian fighter and express guard for Black Hills gold shipments. A series of dime novels was written about his exploits, mainly by Edward L. Wheeler, although they were later attributed to Clarke.

Dean's December, The, novel by Saul Bellow,♦ published in 1982.

Albert Corde, dean of men at a Chicago college, accompanies his Rumanian-born wife Minna, an astronomer, to Bucharest to be with her dying mother. Communist authorities deny visiting rights as a means of punishing the old woman, a lapsed Communist, and the young one because she defected to the West. This example of the state's control of individuals is balanced by the anarchy that the Dean witnesses in his home city when a campus murder case leads him to write articles dealing with the violent ways of life to which black people are driven, both those on the streets and those in jails.

Dear Judas, narrative poem by Robinson Jeffers.♦

Death Comes for the Archbishop, novel by Willa Cather,♦ published in 1927.

Bishop Jean Latour and his vicar Father Joseph Vaillant together create pioneer missions and organize the new diocese of New Mexico. Youthful friends in France, they are lifelong comrades, united by a love of their native country, as well as by their common purpose, but their characters are sharply contrasted. Latour is an intellectual and a patrician, highly sensitive but tolerant and possessed of an indomitable resolution and courage, remaining solitary in the midst of his people's love and his friend's devotion. Vaillant is practical, humane, companionable, and vigorous. The two combine to triumph over the apathy of the Hopi and Navajo Indians, the opposition of corrupt Spanish priests, and adverse climatic and topographic conditions. They are assisted by Kit Carson and by such devoted Indians as the guide Jacinto. When Vaillant goes as a missionary bishop to Colorado, they are finally separated, but Latour dies soon after his friend, universally revered and respected, to lie in state in the great Santa Fe cathedral that he himself created.

Death in the Afternoon, discursive work by Hemingway,♦ published in 1932. In it he describes the rearing and fighting of bulls in Spain, and depicts the bullfight as a kind of microcosmic tragedy, in which the death of the bull is inevitable but must be achieved by the observance of ritual, which gives the animal a maximum chance to destroy the matador. The discussion includes lengthy digressions, in the form of conversations between the author and an old lady, presenting his philosophy through consideration of various aspects of life and death.

Death in the Family, A, quasi-autobiographical novel by James Agee,♦ left incomplete at his death, pieced together by others and published in 1957. It received a Pulitzer Prize. A play by Tad Mosel,♦ *All the Way Home,* was based on the novel. Produced in 1960, published in 1961, it also won a Pulitzer Prize.

The intimacies of the life of Jay Follet in Knoxville, Tenn., are interrupted when he has to visit his ailing father, and they come to an end when he is killed in an auto accident. His wife Mary, his four-year-old daughter Catherine, and especially his six-year-old son Rufus grapple with the meaning of death, of faith, and of maturity.

Death of a Salesman, play by Arthur Miller,♦ produced and published in 1949, won a Pulitzer Prize.

Willy Loman, a bewildered, well-intentioned, unsuccessful traveling salesman aged 63, is pleased by the return home for a visit of his sons Biff and Happy, but they are upset by his peculiar behavior and hallucinatory conversations with figures of a happier past, and they worry about the effect on Linda, their compassionate mother, who loves her husband and recognizes that his actions stem from the disparity of his "massive dreams" and a disappointing reality. Wanting desperately to be successful and well liked, Willy had fallen victim to the false values of society and cannot cope with his failure or that of Biff, once a high-school football hero, now moody and jobless. Linda persuades Biff to try for a good job to make his father proud, but when, with Happy, he meets his father in the restaurant where they intend to treat him to a celebration dinner, Biff tells the truth about his ill-fated appointment and destroys Willy's hopes. In confusion Willy goes to the washroom and relives the awful time when Biff, desperately needing his help, traveled to Boston, where he discovered him with his mistress. Realizing his responsibility for Biff's aimlessness and disillusionment, Willy stumbles back to the table, only to find that the boys have deserted him for two chippies. Humiliated and stunned, he returns home, fights with Biff, and then is touched by Biff's tears of concern and love. In a final hallucinatory talk with his brother Ben, a successful self-made man, Willy decides on suicide to provide Biff with insurance money. At the funeral, which none of his business acquaintances attend, a friend points out "Willy was a salesman . . . a man . . . riding on a smile and a shoeshine. . . . Nobody dast blame this man. A salesman is got to dream, boy. It comes with the territory."

Death of the Hired Man, The, blank-verse dramatic narrative by Robert Frost,♦ published in *North of Boston* (1914).

Warren and Mary, a farmer and his wife, discuss the return of Silas, an aged farmhand who has worked for them often in the past, always wandering off when other employment offered itself, and coming "home" at times of difficulty. Warren wants to dismiss him, but Mary describes the poignant contrast between his former proud competence and his present broken health, loneliness, and pitiful eagerness to serve. She tells of his infirm mind, which she thinks a sign of approaching death, and her husband is moved to reconsider. When he enters the house to talk with Silas, he discovers the old man dead.

DE BOW, JAMES DUNWOODY BROWNSON (1820–67), born at Charleston, first won prominence as editor of the *Southern Quarterly Review,* which he left to found his own monthly, *De Bow's Review* (1846–80), issued with differing titles from New Orleans, Columbia, Nashville, and Washington. Mainly written by the editor, the magazine was influential in molding Southern opinion in antebellum days, through its violently partisan championing of Calhoun, the protective tariff, and slavery. After the Civil War, it was sympathetic to the Reconstruction.

Declaration of Independence, formal proclamation of the 13 colonies, announcing their separation from Great Britain, was adopted July 4, 1776. In the second Continental Congress on June 7, Richard Henry Lee, a Virginia delegate, proposed a resolution of independence, and four days later Jefferson, Franklin, Adams, Roger Sherman, and Robert Livingston were appointed as a committee to draft the declaration. The actual writing was done by Jefferson, although corrections were made by Franklin, Adams, and the Congress at large. The document is based on the natural-rights theory of government, derived from Locke and 18th-century French philosophers, and proclaims that the function of government is to guarantee the inalienable rights with which men are endowed. These include "Life, Liberty, and the pursuit of Happiness." The declaration contended that, since George III had willfully violated these rights, revolution was justifiable and necessary. The document was signed (Aug. 2) by 56 colonial representatives.

Deephaven, local-color sketches by Sarah Orne Jewett,♦ published in 1877.

Deephaven, described by Helen Denis, who accompanies her friend Kate Lancaster on a summer visit to the Maine seaport town, is isolated and poor because of the decline of its port since the early 1800s. Its peculiar distinction, deriving from its decayed grandeur and fading memories, makes the place seem "more like one of the lazy little English seaside towns. . . . It was not in the least American." The population mainly consists of poor fishermen and farmers, and retired sea captains and their families, except for such relics of aristocracy as old Miss

Chauncey, the lonely, half-insane resident of East Parrish, whose mind dwells still in her distant youth. "The Captains" are usually to be found "sunning themselves like turtles on one of the wharves," exchanging anecdotes of seafaring days. Life moves in a slow rhythm of reminiscence, and perhaps the busiest of the townspeople are such shrewd, methodical housewives as Mrs. Kew, wife of the lighthouse keeper, "peart" old Mrs. Bonny, and the Widow Jim, tenderly faithful to the memory of her brutal husband.

Deerslayer, The, romance by Cooper,♦ published in 1841. An anonymous dramatization was produced the same year. The romance is the first in plot sequence of the Leather-Stocking Tales. ♦

At Lake Otsego, during the 1740s, early in the French and Indian Wars, lives the trapper Thomas Hutter, with his daughters Judith and Hetty. The frontiersmen, giant Hurry Harry and Natty Bumppo, known as Deerslayer among the Delaware Indians, help Hutter to resist an Iroquois attack and return to his log fortress. There Deerslayer is joined by his friend, the Mohican chief Chingachgook, and they attempt to ransom Hutter and Hurry Harry, who have been captured. Feeble-minded Hetty slips away to the Iroquois camp, where she is unharmed because of the Indians' veneration for the demented, and before her return she sees her father and Harry, as well as Chingachgook's bride Hist, also a captive. The trapper and Harry are released, but Deerslayer, who helps his friend rescue Hist, is captured, and Hutter is later killed. Judith, who discovers that she and Hetty are not Hutter's children but are actually of noble birth, tells Deerslayer, when he is released on parole, that she loves him. She tries to prevent his return to the Iroquois, but he keeps his word, returns, and is about to be tortured. Judith appears, delaying the executioners until Chingachgook arrives with a troop of British soldiers. Hetty is killed, and Judith disappears. Although Deerslayer later learns that Judith married one of the titled British officers, he always treasures romantic memories of the affair.

DE FOREST, JOHN WILLIAM (1826–1906), Connecticut-born novelist, utilized his experiences as a Civil War captain to write the first realistic novel of that conflict, *Miss Ravenel's Conversion from Secession to Loyalty*♦ (1867), which gives a vivid picture of a soldier's feelings in battle, the sordid corruption and inefficiency during the war, and the subtleties of the feminine mind. *Kate Beaumont* (1872) is a realistic study of South Carolina life and manners, which De Forest had observed as a district commander of the Freedmen's Bureau. Further examples of his vigorous realism and study of character are *Honest John Vane* (1875) and *Playing the Mischief* (1875), political novels set in the corrupt Washington of Grant's administration. Other, lesser novels are "Witching Times" (serialized in *Putnam's Magazine* 1856–57, not separately published), about the Salem witchcraft trials; *Seacliff or The Mystery of the Westervelts* (1859), concerning a domestic tragedy in Connecticut; *Overland* (1871), set in frontier New Mexico and California; *The Wetherel Affair* (1873), a mystery story; *Justine's Lovers* (1878); *Irene the Missionary* (1879), set in Syria, where he had traveled in the 1850s; *The Bloody Chasm* (1881), dealing with the post-Civil War era; and *A Lover's Revolt* (1898), a romance of the Revolution. De Forest also wrote a scholarly *History of the Indians of Connecticut . . .* (1851), *Oriental Acquaintance: or, Letters from Syria* (1856), *European Acquaintance: Being Sketches of People . . .* (1858), and *Poems* (1902). *A Volunteer's Adventures* (1946) and *A Union Officer in the Reconstruction* (1948) collect letters and articles written during and after the Civil War.

Deism, trend of religious thought, characterized by belief in the existence of a God who rules natural phenomena by established laws, not by miracles, and in the rational nature of men, who are capable of understanding these laws and of guiding their lives by them. In America, deism evolved partly as a protest against Calvinism, partly as an attempt to reconcile religious belief with scientific thought. The former attitude appears in the writings of Charles Chauncey and Jonathan Mayhew, and the latter in Cotton Mather's *The Christian Philosopher♦* (1721), which attempts to give proof of benevolent design in the universe. A more positive deism, advocating a belief in a natural universal religion and having a more utilitarian basis, appears in the writings of Franklin and the eclectic philosophy of Jefferson. The political liberalism of the Revolution was related to the attitude exhibited in such deistic works as Ethan Allen's *Reason the Only Oracle of Man,* and the books of Elihu Palmer (1764–1806), who attempted to establish a republican religion. The most extreme expression of deism is Paine's *The Age of Reason♦* (1794–95). By about 1810 its force was arrested by

the emotional reaction of revivalism. The emphasis on the perfectibility of man and of human institutions engendered by the Revolution gave way to renewed concern with the preparation for immortality. Deism thus declined as a movement, but its views continued to appear sporadically, in such authors as Abner Kneeland, the two Owens, Orestes Brownson, and Frances Wright, and it is a source of later rational and skeptical philosophic thought, as well as of the liberalism of Unitarianism, Universalism, and other movements.

DELANO, Alonzo (1802?–74), born in Albany, N.Y., emigrated to Illinois, is known for his narrative of his overland voyage to California (1849) and residence there, *Life on the Plains and Among the Diggings* (1854), one of the most interesting accounts of the great migration, supplemented by 36 letters to newspapers collected in *Alonzo Delano's California Correspondence* (1952). As a frontier humorist resident in the mines, Delano made a great local reputation with works that include *Pen-Knife Sketches, or Chips of the Old Block* (1853), *Old Block's Sketch Book* (1856), *A Live Woman in the Mines* (1857), a play, and *A Sojourn with Royalty* (1936).

DELANY, Martin R[obinson] (1812–85), free-born black of the present West Virginia, who published a newspaper in Pittsburgh, assisted Frederick Douglass with his journal, attended Harvard Medical School for a year before issuing *The Condition, Elevation, Emigration, and Destiny of the Colored People of the United States* (1852), which argues for emigration of blacks to a state of their own creation. His novel *Blake: or The Huts of America,* serialized partly (1859) and fully (1861–62), was first issued as a book in 1970. It deals with a West Indian kidnapped into U.S. slavery who escapes to plot an insurrection in his homeland. Delany was the first black major in the U.S. army during the Civil War. *Principia of Ethnology* (1878) is a defense of blacks' intelligence and achievements.

Delaware Indians, confederacy of Algonquian tribes, were given their present name by colonists who found them in the Delaware River valley, but their own name is Leni-Lenape. Their early history and migration to North America are told in their tribal chronicle, the *Walam Olum*. In 1682 they made their famous treaty with Penn, which they retained for 50 years. Defeated by the Iroquois (1720), they moved into Ohio, where they sided with the French in the French and Indian War, and against the Americans in the uprising of Pontiac and the Revolution. The whites attacked a peaceful Delaware settlement in 1782, causing the remainder of these Christian Indians to flee to Ontario. Others ceded their lands to the U.S. and moved to Oklahoma. The Delaware figure as noble, wise, and just in the Leather-Stocking Tales, and appear also in Freneau's "Prophecy of King Tammany," Brown's *Edgar Huntly,* Paulding's *Koningsmarke,* Nicholas Hentz's *Tadeuskund,* and outside of literature, in studies by Rafinesque, E.G. Squier, and D.G. Brinton. They are mentioned in Irving's *Tour of the Prairies,* but the most comprehensive early account of them was in Schoolcraft's six-volume *History, Conditions, and Prospects of the Indian Tribes in the United States* (1851–57), used as a source by Thoreau and Longfellow. A fictional view of them in modern life occurs in *The Light in the Forest* (1953) by Conrad Richter.

Delicate Balance, A, play by Edward Albee,♦ produced and published in 1966 and awarded a Pulitzer Prize.

DELL, FLOYD (1887–1969), born in Illinois, after a career in Chicago journalism moved to New York (1913), and for the next ten years was a prominent radical, serving as an editor of *The Masses* and *The Liberator.* He wrote one-act plays, such as *The Angel Intrudes* (1918), and also wrote a study of child psychology, *Were You Ever a Child?* (1919). His first novel, *Moon-Calf♦* (1920), won acclaim as a representative document of the disillusioned postwar generation. This was followed by a sequel, *The Briary-Bush* (1921), and by *Janet March* (1923), *Runaway* (1925), and other novels concerned with the hopelessness of youth in a confused world, the spirit of the jazz age, and the revolt against convention typified by the residents of Greenwich Village.

DELMAR, VIÑA (1905–   ), New York City author, whose novels, *Bad Girl* (1928; dramatized, 1930) and *Kept Woman* (1929), and short stories, *Loose Ladies* (1929), were sensations of the day for their sleek, hard-boiled treatments of jazz-age girls. Later works include two fictional treatments of Confederate heroes, *Beloved* (1956), about Judah P. Benjamin, and *The Big Family* (1961), about John Slidell. *The Becker Scandal* (1968) is a memoir about an event of 1912

that touched her parents. *A Time for Titans* (1974) is a novel featuring Jefferson, Napoleon, and Toussaint L'Ouverture.

DEMBY, WILLIAM (1922–   ), Pennsylvania-born novelist, after education at West Virginia State College for Negroes and Fisk University was long an expatriate in Rome, writing for Italian films. His first novel, *Beetlecreek* (1950), depicts evil in the relations between blacks and whites in a West Virginia town. *The Catacombs* (1965) is a novel about a novelist in Rome named William Demby caught up in the immoralities and crises of the times. *Love Story Black* (1978) and *Blueboy* (1980) are shorter novels.

Democracy: An American Novel, by Henry Adams,♦ was published anonymously in 1880. "Old Granite" is believed to represent President Hayes.

Madeleine Lee, a young New York widow, moves to Washington to investigate "the tremendous forces of government, and the machinery of society, at work. What she wanted was POWER." With her sister Sybil, she creates a salon, attends Senate debates, and entertains legislators and diplomats. Through her admirer John Carrington, a lawyer, she captures as her guest the political boss, Senator Ratcliffe of Illinois, whose party has just elected the new President, "Old Granite." The President-elect, an unsophisticated Indiana lawyer, is lost among the capital's intrigues, and, though he hates and distrusts Ratcliffe, is forced to place control of patronage in his hands, and to appoint him secretary of the treasury. During the months before the inauguration, Ratcliffe falls in love with Madeleine, who is first repelled by his coarse vanity, then fascinated by his self-command and position. Carrington, who undertakes with Sybil a secret campaign against the senator, is sent to Mexico on business, but through Sybil he reveals to Madeleine that Ratcliffe is guilty of selling his influence. Disillusioned, she now refuses his proposal, at which Ratcliffe calls her a heartless coquette and departs wrathfully. Having learned enough of the mechanism and instruments of power, Madeleine deserts Washington for a tour of Europe, and Sybil writes Carrington that he may yet hope to win her sister's hand.

Democratic Vistas, prose pamphlet by Whitman,♦ published in 1871, incorporating earlier essays. It was reprinted in *Two Rivulets* (1876).

The main themes are the ideals of democracy and individualism, which the author does not consider to be incompatible, and he outlines a new cultural order for the U.S. He condemns the degradation of democracy and the growth of cankerous wealth during the post-Civil War period, prophesies a future greatness, and announces that there must be a declaration of cultural independence to achieve a truly national indigenous literature.

DERLETH, AUGUST [WILLIAM] (1909–71), Wisconsin author, noted for his regional writings and prolific literary career. After graduation from the state university (1930) he averaged nearly three published books annually, including a long series of novels about Sac Prairie, whose prototype is Sauk City.

Descent into the Maelström, A, story by Poe, ♦ published in *Graham's Magazine* (1841) and reprinted in *Prose Tales* (1843).

A Norwegian sailor and his brother are trapped in their fishing boat when a hurricane draws it into the fearful Moskoe-ström, a whirlpool that periodically forms and subsides. Whirled about the inner verge of the gulf, they face death, and the elder brother becomes insane. The other sees that of the many objects in the grasp of the whirlpool, small cylindrical ones are least likely to be destroyed, and, lashing himself to a cask, he jumps into the sea. When the Moskoe-ström subsides, he floats to safety and is rescued by fellow fishermen. They do not recognize him or believe his story, for his hair has turned white and his expression is completely altered.

Description of New England, A, autobiographical narrative by John Smith. ♦

Desire Under the Elms, play by O'Neill, ♦ produced and published in 1924.

Ephraim Cabot, in his elm-shaded New England farmhouse in 1850, is a decadent Puritan, harsh and miserly. He acquired the farm from his dead second wife, mother of his son Eben, who works it with his elder half-brothers, Simeon and Peter. Eben, who resembles his gentle mother, hates Ephraim for having mistreated her, and the other sons are kept from joining the gold rush to California only by their avaricious interest in inheriting the farm. When Ephraim, despite his 75 years, takes a third wife, Simeon and Peter sell their shares to Eben and leave for California. Ephraim's third wife is Abbie Putnam, a young widow, greedy and sensual, whose only purpose is to gain her husband's wealth, and she seduces Eben in order to have a child who will inherit it. Ephraim exults over the birth of his supposed son, and when he reveals that the new child will inherit the property, Eben repudiates Abbie's love, which is by now genuine. She kills the child and in a rage confesses her crimes. Eben informs the police, but, overcome by love for Abbie, admits a part in the murder, and is arrested with her.

De Spain, MAJOR CASSIUS, character in the Yoknapatawpha saga of Faulkner. After service in the Confederate cavalry, he becomes the sheriff who, in *Absalom, Absalom!,* kills Wash Jones after Jones has murdered Thomas Sutpen. Some of Sutpen's land becomes his, and to it he annually invites hunting parties as described in "The Bear." In *The Hamlet* his barn is burned, presumably by Ab and Flem Snopes. His son Manfred, a West Point graduate and veteran of the Spanish-American War, becomes mayor of Jefferson and president of the Sartoris Bank. In *The Mansion,* when Will Varner discovers that Eula Varner Snopes, his daughter, is De Spain's mistress, Manfred has to sell his bank stock to Eula's husband Flem and to leave Jefferson.

Detective story, form of fiction whose main structural characteristic is a reversal of the sequence of events: the catastrophe, generally a murder, is typically presented first, followed by the introduction of suspected criminals and of a series of clues whose significance the reader is not supposed to grasp until the story is ended by a climax of explanation, in which the detective hero shows how the crime was committed, the motives for it, and finally the identity of the criminal. Poe's "The Murders in the Rue Morgue," ♦ "The Purloined Letter," ♦ and "The Mystery of Marie Rogêt" ♦ are considered the first modern detective stories. In them there appears the prototype of fictional detectives, C. Auguste Dupin, an intellectual amateur who demonstrates an astounding ability to solve crimes by analyzing clues unobserved or misinterpreted by the police and his simple friend, the narrator of the tales. Some dime novels featured detectives like Nick Carter, but the detective novel did not become widely popular until the work of such foreign authors as Gaboriau, Wilkie Collins, and Conan Doyle was published in the U.S. The first full-length detective novels of the U.S. of importance were those of Anna

Katharine Green, the most popular being *The Leavenworth Case* (1878). The vogue of detective fiction has become tremendous in the 20th century and American authors include Earl Derr Biggers, Raymond Chandler, Erle Stanley Gardner, Dashiell Hammett, Frances Noyes Hart, John D. MacDonald, Ross Macdonald, J.P. Marquand, Elliott Paul, Ellery Queen, Mary Roberts Rinehart, Mickey Spillane, Rex Stout, and S.S. Van Dine. Detective plays of the American theater include Gillette's *Sherlock Holmes,* Elmer Rice's *On Trial,* and Mary Roberts Rinehart's *The Bat.*

DE TOCQUEVILLE, see *Tocqueville.*

DEUTSCH, BABETTE (1895–1982), New York poet, noted for her sensitive intellectual verse, highly charged with emotion and concerned with social questions and attitudes. Her reputation was established by her early volumes, *Banners* (1919), *Honey Out of the Rock* (1925), and *Fire for the Night* (1930). *Epistle to Prometheus* (1931) is on the Promethean spirit throughout the ages; *One Part Love* (1939), a protest against the spiritual darkness of today; *Take Them, Stranger* (1944), poems of war; *Animal, Vegetable, Mineral* (1954) and *Coming of Age* (1959), new and selected earlier poems and translations; and *Collected Poems* (1969). Besides novels, *A Brittle Heaven* (1926), *In Such a Night* (1927), *Mask of Silenus* (1933), and *Rogue's Legacy* (1942), she wrote a biography of Whitman (1941) for children. Critical works include *Potable Gold: Some Notes on Poetry and This Age* (1929), *This Modern Poetry* (1935), revised as *Poetry in Our Time* (1954), and anthologies of Russian and German poetry.

Devil and Daniel Webster, The, one-act folk opera by Stephen Vincent Benét♦ and Douglas Moore, produced in 1939. It is based on a short story by Benét, published in *Thirteen O'Clock* (1937). *Scratch* (1971) is a prose dramatization by MacLeish.

Jabez Stone, a New Hampshire farmer, sells his soul to the devil in return for ten years of prosperity. When the devil comes to his wedding to collect, Jabez appeals to a guest, Daniel Webster, to defend him before the devil's jury of American villains. Appealing to them as men, Webster's eloquence touches their memories of freedom and wins an acquittal.

Devil's Dictionary, The, by Ambrose Bierce,♦ was first published as *The Cynic's Word Book* (1906) and retitled in 1911. Collected from newspaper contributions (1881–1906), and addressed to "enlightened souls who prefer dry wines to sweet, sense to sentiment, wit to humor, and clean English to slang," the volume contains witty, concise "definitions" reflecting Bierce's bold social criticism, pessimism, and skeptical philosophy.

DE VOTO, BERNARD [AUGUSTINE] (1897–1955), Utah-born professor of English at Northwestern University (1922–27) and Harvard (1929–36), later edited *The Saturday Review of Literature* (1936–38), and occupied the "Easy Chair" of *Harper's* (1935–55). As Literary Editor of the Mark Twain Estate he issued previously unpublished manuscripts as *Mark Twain in Eruption* (1940) and *Letters from the Earth* (1962). His own studies of the writer include *Mark Twain's America* (1932) and *Mark Twain at Work* (1942). His study of "the continental experience," a trilogy on the impact of the West on the American mind, is contained in *The Course of Empire* (1952), about discovery and exploration from the 16th century to the 19th; *Across the Wide Missouri* (1947, Pulitzer Prize), about the Rocky Mountain fur trade; and *The Year of Decision: 1846* (1943). Other studies of American ideas include *Forays and Rebuttals* (1936), *Minority Report* (1940), and *The Easy Chair* (1955), collections of forthright essays; and *The Literary Fallacy* (1944), criticizing American authors of the 1920s for holding aloof from vital experience. His novels include *The Crooked Mile* (1924); *The Chariot of Fire* (1926); *The House of Sun-Goes-Down* (1928); *We Accept with Pleasure* (1934); *Mountain Time* (1947); and lesser fiction under the name John August. A collection of *Letters* (1975) was edited by Wallace Stegner, who also wrote a biography (1974).

DE VRIES, PETER (1910–), born in Chicago, long resident in Connecticut, for a time an editor of *Poetry,* later on the staff of *The New Yorker* (1944–), is known for his humorous, sophisticated novels, beginning with *But Who Wakes the Bugler?* (1940), often about suburban Connecticut life, as in *Tunnel of Love* (1954), adapted with Joseph Fields as a play (1957); *Comfort Me with Apples* (1956); *The Mackerel Plaza* (1958); *The Tents of Wickedness* (1959), indulging not only in his exuberant punning but travestying the styles of Faulkner, Hemingway, and

Fitzgerald; *Through the Fields of Clover* (1961), about the reunion of a fantastic New England family; and *Reuben, Reuben* (1964), presenting outsiders' views of an ex-urbanite community. Regardless of setting, his lively comedies of manners, though farcical and peopled with fantastic characters, have some serious concern with matters of religion or morality. His fiction also includes *Let Me Count the Ways* (1965), concerning a man converted to religion after paradoxically suffering a sudden sickness at Lourdes; *The Vale of Laughter* (1967), a sardonic comedy narrated by a stockbroker and his former philosophy professor; *The Cat's Pyjamas and Witch's Milk* (1968), two related novellas of pathos told comically; *Mrs. Wallop* (1970); *Into Your Tent I'll Creep* (1971), satirizing women's liberation in relation to marriage; *Forever Panting* (1975); *The Glory of the Hummingbird* (1974), about a small-town Indiana boy's success through a television quiz show; *I Hear America Swinging* (1976), treating the effect of the new sexual liberation on an Iowa farming community; *Madder Music* (1977), portraying an author who comes to think of himself as Groucho Marx; *Consenting Adults, or The Duchess Will Be Furious* (1980), a tale with a light, lively plot set again in Illinois; *Sauce for the Goose* (1981), fliply presenting the love affair of a feminist journalist; and *Slouching Towards Kalamazoo* (1983), a comic story of an affair between a boy and his eighth-grade teacher. *The Handsome Heart* (1943) and *The Blood of the Lamb* (1962) are more sober novels. *No, But I Saw the Movie* (1952) and *Without a Stitch in Time* (1972) collect stories.

DEWEY, JOHN (1859–1952), philosopher and educator at the universities of Minnesota, Michigan, Chicago, and after 1904 at Columbia. His influence on education and thought came also from his books, leadership of many learned societies, connection with the Socialist party, and work as adviser to foreign governments. His most important writings on education, following his *Psychology* (1887), include *The School and Society* (1899), *The Child and the Curriculum* (1902), *Moral Principles in Education* (1909), *Interest and Effort in Education* (1913), *Experience and Education* (1938), and *The Public Schools and Spiritual Values* (1944).

In these works he emphasizes the changes in educational needs due to the industrial revolution, the democratic point of view, and the concept of man as a biological entity required to adjust himself to his environment and the complex structure of modern society. His scientific realism, the basis of this attitude, springs from pragmatism, of which Dewey was the leading exponent after the death of William James, but he shifted the emphasis of pragmatic thought from religion and the will to believe to practical problems of social reconstruction, calling his philosophy "instrumentalism."

Dial, The (July 1840–April 1844), quarterly magazine of literature, philosophy, and religion, was the organ of the New England Transcendentalist movement, and grew out of the informal meetings of the Transcendental Club. ♦ Although Alcott, who gave the magazine its title, thought it insufficiently transcendental, it was considered obscure by the general public, and savagely attacked by the press. Margaret Fuller, the editor, was assisted by George Ripley, but she failed to give the magazine unity, admitting many contradictory articles. Among the early contributions were Thoreau's "Friendship"; Emerson's "The Problem" and "Man the Reformer"; Alcott's "Orphic Sayings"; Miss Fuller's "Goethe"; Theodore Parker's "German Literature"; Elizabeth Peabody's "Christ's Idea of Society"; and writings by George Ripley, C.P. Cranch, and W.H. Channing. Emerson succeeded as editor (July 1842), and gave *The Dial* a more unified attitude, publishing extracts from Oriental religious writings entitled "Ethnic Scriptures," his own "Lectures on the Times," and further writings by W.H. Channing, Miss Fuller, Parker, Charles Lane, Jones Very, J.F. Clarke, Lowell, and C.A. Dana.

Dial, The (1880–1929), monthly journal of literary criticism, was founded at Chicago as a conservative review. In 1892 it became a fortnightly, continuing the original policy until 1918, when it was moved to New York. New contributing editors, including Conrad Aiken, H.E. Stearns, Randolph Bourne, and Van Wyck Brooks, made it a radical journal of opinion, publishing such previously taboo authors as Dewey, Veblen, Laski, Beard, and R.M. Lovett. Under Scofield Thayer, after 1920, *The Dial* became the most distinguished literary monthly in the U.S. to champion modern artistic movements. It drew contributors from many nations and had as associates Thomas Mann, T.S. Eliot, James Stephens, and Paul Morand. It printed virtually all the distinguished authors of the period, and was noted also for its fine reproductions of modern graphic art. Marianne Moore was editor after 1926.

Diamond as Big as the Ritz, The, story by F. Scott Fitzgerald,♦ published in *Tales of the Jazz Age* (1922).

John T. Unger, a teenager from Hades, Miss., becomes a friend of Percy Washington at their Massachusetts preparatory school and goes to spend the summer holiday at the Washington mansion in the wilds of Montana. It is located on isolated land that conceals a diamond mine and a single gem one cubic mile in extent, discovered by Percy's grandfather and concealed from the world. The summer ends when the diamond mountain is located from planes by aviators who land to scale its great peak. With his father and mother Percy disappears into the mine but the mountain disintegrates, burying them and the aviators, while John and Percy's two sisters contemplate the scene of the disaster.

Diamond Lens, The, story by Fitz-James O'Brien. ♦

DICKENS, CHARLES (1812–70), English novelist, whose first tour of the U.S. (Jan.–May 1842) is described in his *American Notes for General Circulation*♦ (1842), and furnished the background for portions of *Martin Chuzzlewit*♦ (1843–44). He visited the U.S. again (Nov. 1867–April 1868), when he presented a popular series of readings in Eastern cities.

DICKEY, JAMES [LAFAYETTE] (1923–), Georgia-born poet, on the faculty of the University of South Carolina (1969–). His first volumes of poetry, *Into the Stone* (1960), *Drowning with Others* (1962), *Helmets* (1964), and *Buckdancer's Choice* (1965, National Book Award), were the sources from which he selected his *Poems* (1967). In the same year that he issued his next volume of poetry, *The Eye-Beaters, Blood, Victory, Madness, Buckhead and Mercy* (1970), he also published a novel, *Deliverance.* A thrilling adventure story about four Georgia businessmen going by canoe down a rugged river on a hunting trip and fighting for their lives against the wilderness and malevolent mountaineers, it became a best seller and he later adapted it for a film version. His next poetry, *The Zodiac,* a lengthy work in 12 parts, did not appear until 1976. Meanwhile he had published prose works, *The Suspect in Poetry* (1964), frank, often polemical reviews of contemporary poets, followed by the

similar *Babel to Byzantium* (1968), *Self-Interviews* (1970), based on tape-recorded commentary on his poetry, and *Sorties* (1971), extracts from his journals and essays on poets. Dickey returned to poetry with a new collection, *The Strength of Fields* (1979), whose title work was written for President Carter's inaugural, while other poems, like those written before, often deal with masculine adventure and violence. *The Early Motion: "Drowning with Others" and "Helmets"* (1980) and *The Central Motion* (1983) collect previously published poems. *Puella* (1982) is a long poem about a girl developing from a child to a woman. *Night Hurdling* (1983) collects miscellaneous minor writing.

DICKINSON, EMILY [ELIZABETH] (1830–86), the daughter of Edward Dickinson, a prominent lawyer of Amherst, Mass., was educated at Amherst Academy and for one year at Mount Holyoke Female Seminary. Her life was outwardly eventless, for she lived quietly at home and for the last 25 years secluded herself from all but the most intimate friends. Though never married, she cultivated intense intellectual companionships with several men in succession, whom she quaintly called her tutors. The first was Benjamin F. Newton, a law student in her father's office, who introduced her to stimulating books and urged her to take seriously her vocation as poet. Religious questionings prompted by his early death led her to appeal for guidance to the Rev. Charles Wadsworth of Philadelphia, whom she met in 1854. She soon came to regard him as her "dearest earthly friend," and for purposes of poetry created in his image the "lover" whom she was never to know except in imagination. From the time of Wadsworth's removal to San Francisco, in the spring of 1862, may be dated her withdrawal from village society and her increasing preoccupation with poetry. She initiated a literary correspondence with T.W. Higginson, whom she knew only through his papers in the *Atlantic Monthly,* and his kindly encouragement was a support to her through years of loneliness. Besides Higginson, the circle of friends to whom she occasionally showed a few of her poems included Samuel Bowles, Dr. J.G. Holland, and Helen Hunt Jackson. For the most part, however, she wrote in secret and guarded her poems even from her family.

Before her death, she had composed well over 1000 brief lyrics, her "letter to the world," records of the life about her, of tiny ecstasies set in motion by mutations of the seasons or by home and garden incidents, of candid insights into her own states of consciousness, and of speculations on the timeless mysteries of love and death. Her mind was charged with paradox, as though her vision, like the eyes of birds, was focused in opposite directions on the two worlds of material and immaterial values. She could express feelings of deepest poignancy in terms of wit. Like Emerson, her preference for the intrinsic and the essential led her often to a gnomic concision of phrase, but her artistry in the modulation of simple meters and the delicate management of imperfect rhymes was greater than his.

Publication, in Emily Dickinson's unworldly view, formed no part of a poet's business. Only six of her poems, not counting an early verse valentine, were printed during her lifetime, and none with her consent. From the chaotic mass of manuscripts found after her death, some carefully revised, others carelessly jotted down on odd scraps of paper, six volumes have been selected: *Poems* (1890) and *Poems: Second Series* (1891), edited by Mabel L. Todd and T.W. Higginson; *Poems: Third Series* (1896), edited by Mrs. Todd; *The Single Hound♦* (1914), edited by Emily's niece Martha Dickinson Bianchi; *Further Poems* (1929) and *Unpublished Poems* (1936), edited by Mrs. Bianchi and Alfred Leete Hampson. A collection was issued as *Poems: Centenary Edition* (1930). Posthumous publication kept the poems from being presented in any effective order. Trifling pieces and fragments were included with major lyrics and the text was often inaccurate, badly punctuated, or poorly displayed on the page. However, *Bolts of Melody* (1945), poems long suppressed because of a family feud, was carefully edited by Mabel L. Todd and Millicent Bingham, and a complete *The Poems of Emily Dickinson* was issued in a scholarly edition (3 vols., 1955) including variant readings by Thomas H. Johnson, who, in addition to this definitive work, edited the poet's *Letters* (3 vols., 1958). *The Manuscript Books of Emily Dickinson* (1982) reproduces in facsimile the manuscripts of the canon of 1147 poems in the fascicles into which the author gathered them.

DICKINSON, JOHN (1732–1808), Philadelphia lawyer, led the conservative group in the Pennsylvania legislature during the debates on proprietary goverment. He wrote *Protest against the Appointment of Benjamin Franklin* (1764), and the Sugar Act and proposed Stamp Act caused him to write *The Late Regulations Respecting the British Colonies on the Continent of America . . .* (1765). When England continued to assert its rights of taxation, he began to publish in the *Pennsylvania Chronicle* his *Letters from a Farmer in Pennsylvania* (1768), contending that England's acts violated the social compact to protect property and should therefore be resisted by petition to be followed, if necessary, by boycott and arms. A member of both Continental Congresses, he wrote other addresses and petitions and "A Song for American Freedom" (the Liberty Song); he hoped for reconciliation and voted against the Declaration of Independence. After the war, he represented Delaware in Congress and wrote two series of *Letters of Fabius* (1788, 1797) in favor of the Constitution.

Dictionary of American English, based on historical principles, was compiled at the University of Chicago under the editorship of Sir William Craigie and James R. Hulbert.

DIDION, JOAN (1934–   ), California author whose novels include *Run River* (1963), depicting deteriorating ways of life in her native Sacramento Valley; *Play It as It Lays♦* (1970), presenting a woman caught in the social disintegration of southern California; *A Book of Common Prayer♦* (1977), treating the growing self-awareness and shattering life of a California woman in Central America; and *Democracy* (1984), presenting an old American family of Hawaii in the 1970s caught up in the era's moral and political corruption. *Slouching Towards Bethlehem♦* (1968) and *The White Album♦* (1979) are nonfictional works on contemporary life, mainly related to California, her synecdoche for a deteriorating modern world. *Salvador* (1983) presents her first-hand view of El Salvador's civil war. She and her husband, John Gregory Dunne,♦ also write film scripts.

Diedrich Knickerbocker, see *Knickerbocker.*

DILLARD, ANNIE (1945–   ), Pittsburgh-born author of *Pilgrim at Tinker Creek* (1974, Pulitzer Prize), a sensitive view of the natural surroundings in which she lives. She has also written *Tickets for a Prayer Wheel* (1974), poetry; *Holy the Firm* (1977); and *Teaching a Stone To Talk* (1982), further essays on nature. *Living by Fiction* (1983) collects essays on contemporary literature. She also wrote a little book, *Encounters with Chinese Writers* (1984).

DILLON, GEORGE (1906–68), while an undergraduate at the University of Chicago became an editor of *Poetry.* The poems in *Boy in the Wind* (1927), published the year of his graduation, have a soft musical quality. *The Flowering Stone* (1931), a more vigorous work, won a Pulitzer Prize (1932). His later works are translations, of Baudelaire's *Flowers of Evil* (1936) with Edna St. Vincent Millay, and of Racine's *Three Plays: Andromache, Britannicus, Phædra* (1961).

Dilsey, character in Faulkner's novel *The Sound and the Fury.* ♦

Dime novel, popular name for cheap thrilling tales of history, romance, warfare, or any violent action, many of which were set in America during the Revolution, Civil War, or frontier period. They attained an immense popularity in the U.S. from the publication of *Malaeska: The Indian Wife of the White Hunter* in 1860 by Ann Sophia Stephens to about 1895, at which time they began to be superseded by pulp magazines and such series as those concerning Frank Merriwell, the Rover Boys, and Tom Swift. Many of the novels, whose major publisher was Beadle and Adams of New York, cost only five cents. Although the development of plot closely followed conventional moral patterns, stern critics mistakenly called dime novels immoral. They probably fostered a nationalistic attitude, emphasizing as they did the democratic vigor and individualism of the American people. Among the most famous authors were E.Z.C. Judson, Prentiss Ingraham, Edward L. Wheeler, who created "Deadwood Dick," and J.R. Coryell, who created "Nick Carter."

Dimmesdale, ARTHUR, character in *The Scarlet Letter.* ♦

Dinsmore, ELSIE, character in novels for children by Martha Finley. ♦

Divinity School Address, name commonly given to the address delivered by Emerson ♦ before the senior class of Divinity College, Harvard (July 15, 1838), published that year, and reprinted in *Nature, Addresses, and Lectures* (1849). The discourse provoked a strong reaction among the faculty, and Andrews Norton attacked it as irreverent and atheistic in *On the Latest Form of Infidelity* (1839). Received with enthusiasm by W.E.

Channing and Theodore Parker, the address had no immediate effect on the church, but caused Emerson's virtual ostracism from strict Unitarian circles.

In "The American Scholar," the author appeals for a return to original intellectual experience; here he appeals for a return to original spiritual experience. Truth is attainable only through intuition, "it cannot be received at second hand." Since historical Christianity has fallen into errors, its influence is baneful. By emphasizing past revolution, it limits and discourages the direct exploration of Moral Nature, which alone communicates spiritual greatness and the divine spirit. The formal church is dry, false, and moribund; the "great and perpetual office of the preacher is not discharged." Young men entering the ministry must search their own hearts, preach their own message:

> speak the very truth, as your life and conscience teach it, and cheer the waiting, fainting hearts of men with new hope and new revelations.

DIXON, THOMAS (1864–1946), born in North Carolina, was a Baptist minister and lyceum lecturer before he became an author. His most sensational novels are the trilogy *The Leopard's Spots* (1902), *The Clansman* ♦ (1905), and *The Traitor* (1907), extremist Southern views of the Reconstruction era, vigorously antiblack and strongly supportive of the original Ku Klux Klan. Of his 20 novels, all are tracts for his social views, and many concerned with contemporary issues, opposing feminism, socialism, and pacifism, among other matters. After the success of D.W. Griffith's adaptation of *The Clansman* as *The Birth of a Nation* (1915), Dixon made five films at his own Los Angeles studio, all based on his novels.

Dr. Grimshawe's Secret, romance by Hawthorne, ♦ posthumously edited from an unfinished manuscript by his son Julian and published in 1883.

Dr. Heidegger's Experiment, allegorical tale by Hawthorne, ♦ published in *Twice-Told Tales* (1837).

The doctor, an aged physician and scientist, invites four of his venerable, eccentric acquaintances to take part in a test of some water from the Fountain of Youth. Medbourne, an impoverished former merchant, Gascoigne, a ruined politician, Colonel Killigrew, a gouty old wastrel, and the Widow Wycherly, a faded beauty, see the doctor restore a dried rose by applying the water, and are eager to try it. Dr. Heidegger declares he merely wishes to see the results, and does not drink, but serves his guests full glasses. They become increasingly younger until they reach gay and reckless youth, when the three men vie for the favors of the Widow. They accidentally upset the table, and spill the water. Then the doctor notices that his rose has faded again, and gradually his guests resume their aged appearances. He says that he has learned from the experiment not to desire the delirium of youth, but his friends resolve to make a pilgrimage to Florida in search of the Fountain.

DOCTOROW, E[DGAR] L[AWRENCE] (1931–), New York City-born author and faculty member at Sarah Lawrence College. *The Book of Daniel* (1971) is a fictive biography of a boy recalling his parents, who, like their models, Ethel and Julius Rosenberg, were executed for providing secret information to an enemy nation. He won great popularity and a National Book Critics Circle Award with another novel, *Ragtime* (1975), a jazzily written view of early-20th-century America that fuses tales of fictional characters and such real people as Henry Ford, Scott Joplin, Emma Goldman, and J.P. Morgan. *Loon Lake* (1980) is a picaresque novel about a Midwestern American's experiences in the 1930s and post-World War II U.S. Other works include *Essays and Conversations* (1983) and *Lives of the Poets* (1984), stories and a related novella that they illuminate.

DODGE, MARY [ELIZABETH] MAPES (1831–1905), New York City author and editor of juvenile fiction, is best known for her popular *Hans Brinker; or, The Silver Skates* (1865), a story of youthful adventures in a Dutch setting. She became editor of the magazine *St. Nicholas* in 1873, and in this position was the most important influence of the time on children's literature.

Dodsworth, novel by Sinclair Lewis,♦ published in 1929, was dramatized by Sidney Howard and the author (1934).

Samuel Dodsworth, automobile manufacturer of the Midwestern city of Zenith, retires to devote himself to cultural pursuits and a trip to Europe. During their time abroad he and Fran, to whom he has long been married, drift apart as she has affairs with sophisticated foreigners while he learns from an American widow a true appreciation of European culture.

Dogood Papers, essays in the manner of the *Spectator,* contributed by Franklin♦ to *The New England Courant* (March–Oct. 1722). Published anonymously when the author was only 17, the 14 papers purport to have been written by Silence Dogood, widow of a parson, and their range of subjects is indicated by such titles as "Pride and Hoop Petticoats," "Freedom of Thought," "Drunkenness," and "Receipt for a New England Funeral Elegy."

Dolliver Romance, The, unfinished novel by Hawthorne,♦ posthumously published in the *Atlantic Monthly* (1864, 1871) and in book form in 1876. The author's last work, it was an attempt to develop the theme of the elixir of life also essayed in *Septimius Felton.*

Domain of Arnheim, The, descriptive tale by Poe,♦ published in 1847. It incorporates "The Landscape Garden" (1842), and "Landor's Cottage" is a "pendant."

Domestic Manners of the Americans, descriptive work by Frances Trollope.♦

DONLEAVY, J[AMES] P[ATRICK] (1926–), was born in Brooklyn and served in the U.S. navy, but went to Trinity College, Dublin, in his parents' native Ireland, and has since lived there and in England. *The Ginger Man* (Paris, 1955; U.S., 1958) is a lusty comic novel about a red-bearded ex-GI and the grubby life he and his wife lead in Ireland and in London. Donleavy dramatized the work, produced in England (1959) and New York (1963), and published in New York (1961), and wrote another play, *Fairy Tales of New York* (1961), reworked as a novel, *A Fairy Tale of New York* (1973), a satire on contemporary America. Other broadly comic novels include *A Singular Man* (1963), *The Saddest Summer of Samuel S.* (1966), and *The Beastly Beatitudes of Balthazar B.* (1968), all dramatized by the author; *The Onion Eaters* (1971), a more surrealistic tale; *The Destinies of Darcy Dancer, Gentleman* (1977), another picaresque story; *Schultz* (1979), a farce about an American impresario in England; and *Leila* (1983), further adventures of Darcy Dancer. Donleavy collected stories in *Meet My Maker, the Mad Molecule* (1964) and wrote a parody of etiquette books, *The Unexpurgated Code* (1975).

Dooley, MR., character in a series of books by F.P. Dunne.♦

DOOLITTLE, HILDA (1886–1961), known by her initials, was born in Pennsylvania, went to Europe in 1911, married English author Richard Aldington in 1913, and lived in England thereafter. An early member of the school of Imagism, she is frequently considered the outstanding poet consistently practicing its principles. *Sea Garden* (1916), her first collection, shows the classically chiseled, objective method for which she became famous, and *Hymen* (1921) indicates her interest in the Hellenic tradition. Her later volumes, *Heliodora and Other Poems* (1924) and *Hippolytus Temporizes* (1927), a drama in classic form, foreshadowed her translation of the *Ion of Euripides* (1937). Editions of her *Collected Poems* appeared in 1925 and 1940, but later verse includes the trilogy, *The Walls Do Not Fall* (1944), *Tribute to Angels* (1945), and *Flowering of the Rod* (1946), while *By Avon River* (1949) contains both poetry and prose about Shakespeare and Elizabethan literature, and *Helen in Egypt* (1961) is a posthumously issued long poem. Her *Collected Poems 1912–1944* was published in 1983. Her prose fiction is published in *Palimpsest* (1926), *Hedylus* (1928), *The Hedgehog* (1936), and *Bid Me to Live* (1960), the last being a stream-of-consciousness novel of Bloomsbury life in 1917, an obvious *roman à clef*. *Tribute to Freud* (1956) is a prose work on the psychoanalyst, whose patient she was. Other late works include *End to Torment* (1958), a memoir of Pound. *Hermetic Definition* (1972), a personal statement cast in philosophic terms, and *HERmione* (1981), an autobiographical novel about a young woman torn between love for a man (obviously based on Pound) and for a woman, are posthumously issued works.

DORN, ED[WARD MERTON] (1929–), Illinois-born poet, studied at Black Mountain College under Charles Olson, about whose work he wrote a critical study, *What I See in the Maximus Poems* (1960). His own poetry, often loose and idiomatic, appears in many collections, including *Gunslinger,* whose four "Books" were gathered in 1975, and in *Selected Poems* (1978). *Views* (1980) contains essays, some reminiscing about Black Mountain, and *Interviews* (1980) prints tape-recorded conversations.

DOS PASSOS, JOHN [RODERIGO] (1896–1970), born in Chicago, was educated abroad and in the U.S. After graduation from Harvard (1916), he went to Spain, nominally to study architecture, but he soon entered World War I as a member of the French ambulance service, later joining the U.S. medical corps. Experiences of this period furnished the material for his first book, *One Man's Initiation—1917* (1920, reissued with a new preface as *First Encounter,* 1945), a novel about an ambulance driver. This was followed by *Three Soldiers* (1921), showing the effects of war on three types of character. After publishing a volume of poetry, *A Pushcart at the Curb* (1922), and *Rosinante to the Road Again* (1922), essays on the art and culture of Spain, he returned to fiction with *Streets of Night* (1923), which has been characterized as a typical "art novel" of the time, and deals with a sensitive boy's attempt to escape from the crass conventions of his world. With *Manhattan Transfer* (1925), a collective portrait in hundreds of fictional episodes of the sprawling, diversified life of New York City, Dos Passos reached maturity both in his outlook upon the world and in his stylistic technique. His next book, *Orient Express* (1927), a travel diary, also shows a broadening point of view and a greater interest in social problems, as do the works collected as *Three Plays* (1934): *The Garbage Man*♦ (1926), produced as *The Moon Is a Gong* and dramatizing the distressed lives of a representative New York couple; *Airways, Inc.* (1929), contrasting the atmosphere of big business with the oppressed lives of workers, and showing the background of a building trades strike; and *Fortune Heights* (1933), showing a real-estate development during boom times, and its ruin in the Depression. In 1930 Dos Passos published *The 42nd Parallel,*♦ the first novel in his *U.S.A.* trilogy (collected 1938), which also includes *1919*♦ (1932) and *The Big Money*♦ (1936). These novels, which tell the story of the first three decades of the 20th century in the U.S., have as their protagonist the social background of the nation, and as their major theme the vitiation and degradation of character in a decaying civilization based on commercialism and exploitation. The trilogy employs several distinctive fictional devices. Its basis is a number of episodes from the lives of diverse characters, whose actions either converge or run parallel. The panoramic background is the "Newsreel," a selection from contemporary headlines, advertisements, popular songs, and newspaper articles, which suggest the general atmosphere at the time of each episode. Among the narrative episodes are interspersed brief biographies of prominent Americans of the period, whose lives form a counterpart, often ironic, of the lesser figures of the fiction. A third device is "The Camera Eye," presenting the author's point of view toward the subject matter, through impressionistic stream-of-consciousness passages. The wide panorama of American life is interpreted as being marked by corruption, futility, frustration, and defeat.

This view of the contemporary world is also exhibited in a travel book of this period, *In All Countries* (1934), which deals with such subjects as the Sacco-Vanzetti case, communism in Russia, and Mexican agrarian socialism. Excerpts from this book and from his two previous travel books are combined with new material on the Spanish Civil War in *Journeys Between Wars* (1938). *Adventures of a Young Man* (1939), about Glenn Spotswood, a naïve, idealistic Communist, betrayed by the party when he does not follow its program, is the first of a trilogy continued in *Number One* (1943), about Glenn's brother Tyler, who works for a demagogue like Huey Long, and *The Grand Design* (1949), about the boy's father, a disillusioned liberal in Washington during the New Deal and World War II. The trilogy was collected as *District of Columbia* (1952).

His later fiction includes *The Prospect Before Us* (1950), a novel in the form of lectures on the contemporary world as Dos Passos gloomily saw it; *Chosen Country* (1951), a panoramic view of the U.S. from the mid-19th century to the Depression; *Most Likely To Succeed* (1954), a novel satirizing bohemians and Communist followers between the wars; *The Great Days* (1958), a novel about a former war correspondent's unhappy recollections; and *Midcentury* (1961), a novel about contemporary America in which the techniques of *U.S.A.* and its faith in individualism now celebrate free enterprise. Nonfiction of these years includes *The Ground We Stand On* (1941), biographies of men who influenced American liberty; *Men Who Made the Nation* (1957), on American leaders from the end of the Revolution to Hamilton's death; and *Prospect of a Golden Age* (1959), other selected biographical sketches. *State of the Nation* (1944) and *Tour of Duty* (1946) describe wartime travels, while *Brazil on the Move* (1963) treats travels abroad. *The Theme Is Freedom* (1956) and *Occasions and Protests* (1964) collect essays also representative of his later, conservative views, while *Mr. Wilson's War* (1963) treats U.S. history from 1901 to 1921 from a point of view different from the liberalism of *U.S.A.*, the trilogy that covered the same era. *The Best Times* (1966) is an informal memoir,

and *The Fourteenth Chronicle* (1973) collects letters and diaries.

DOUGLASS, FREDERICK (1817–95), born into slavery in Maryland, escaped to Massachusetts (1838), where he was employed as a lecturer by antislavery societies. He published a *Narrative of the Life of Frederick Douglass* (1845, revised 1892). Fearing capture as a fugitive slave, he spent several years in England and Ireland, returning to purchase his freedom and establish the antislavery newspaper *North Star.* Since he favored political methods for freeing the slaves, he became a follower of J.G. Birney rather than of Garrison. He organized two regiments of blacks in Massachusetts during the Civil War, and continued to labor for his people during the Reconstruction, later serving as secretary of the Santo Domingo Commission (1871), marshal of the District of Columbia (1877–81), recorder of deeds for the District (1881–86), and minister to Haiti (1889–91). Although his first book is his most famous, he wrote two other autobiographies: *My Bondage and My Freedom* (1855) and *Life and Times of Frederick Douglass* (1881). He is also the subject of biographies by C.W. Chesnutt and Booker T. Washington.

DOWNING, MAJOR JACK, pseudonym of Seba Smith. ♦

Drake, TEMPLE, character in Faulkner's *Sanctuary* ♦ and its sequel, *Requiem for a Nun.*

Dred: A Tale of the Great Dismal Swamp, novel by Harriet Beecher Stowe, ♦ published in 1856. It complements *Uncle Tom's Cabin* by showing the demoralizing influence of slavery on the whites. Dred is modeled on Nat Turner. There were three dramatizations of *Dred,* including one by Brougham.

DREISER, THEODORE [HERMAN ALBERT] (1871–1945), born at Terre Haute, Ind., of a poor and intensely religious family, who taught him to shun many human experiences as degrading or destructive. He early developed a yearning for wealth, society, and the kind of life which he later gave to his hero Cowperwood, an unscrupulous magnate of big business, who is the subject of an exhaustive character study in *The Financier* ♦ (1912), *The Titan* ♦ (1914), and *The Stoic* (1947).

After a period of newspaper reporting in St. Louis, Chicago, Pittsburgh, and New York, stimulated by reading Balzac, and released from his crass success-worship by studying Huxley, Tyndall, and Spencer, he came to see life as a strangely magnificent composite of warring energies, having no plan or purpose. His journalism and hackwork were temporarily interrupted by the writing of *Sister Carrie* ♦ (1900), the story of a working girl and her life as the mistress of a man who descends the social scale as she rises to success as an actress. The publishers withheld the novel from circulation because they were disturbed by its amoral treatment of Carrie's life, and so Dreiser did not earn enough royalties or gain a wide enough reputation to allow him to retire from commercial activities, including the editing of pulp magazines and women's fashion journals, until the publication of *Jennie Gerhardt* ♦ (1911), the story of a woman who sacrifices her own interests rather than jeopardize her lover's social and economic security by opposing his marriage.

In *The "Genius"* ♦ (1915), the story of a gifted but weak artist, and *An American Tragedy* ♦ (1925), the story of a youth of unstable character trapped by circumstances that lead to his execution for murder, Dreiser sets forth his naturalistic concept of American society. This view, developed in the four previous books, concludes that, since the chaotic nature of life precludes spiritual satisfactions, it is normal and right to take the most one can from the economic grab bag. Dreiser has been acclaimed for this sincere and profound consciousness of the tragedy of life as he saw it in America, despite the ugliness of his heavy style, and his structural incompetence, chaotic verbosity, and sometimes confused character drawing. Often bogged down by clumsy writing, his books nevertheless are endowed with power by sheer force and an honest massing of details. In *Dreiser Looks at Russia* (1928), *Tragic America* (1931), and *America Is Worth Saving* (1941), he expressed hopeful belief in socialism, as opposed to his former confused naturalism, while *The Bulwark* ♦ (1946) emphasized the place of spiritual values in the life of the modern individual.

His many other writings include *Plays of the Natural and Supernatural* (1916); *The Hand of the Potter* (1918), a tragedy; *Free* (1918), *Chains* (1927), and *A Gallery of Women* (2 vols., 1929), short story collections; *Moods, Cadenced and Declaimed* (1926, enlarged 1928), a book of poetry; *Hey Rub-a-Dub-Dub* (1920), essays setting forth his philosophic views; *The Color of a Great City* (1923) and *My City* (1929), vignettes of

New York; *Twelve Men* (1919), studies of actual persons, including one of his brother, Paul Dresser, whom he is said to have assisted in writing "On the Banks of the Wabash"; and the autobiographical works, *A Traveler at Forty* (1913), *A Hoosier Holiday* (1916), *A Book About Myself* (1922), which was republished as *Newspaper Days* (1931), and *Dawn* (1931). *An American Laborer* (1983) is an unfinished memoir of his unhappy, impoverished period after the publication of *Sister Carrie. His Letters* was published in 1959 (3 vols.), and his *American Diaries, 1902–1926* was printed in 1982.

Drum-Taps, poems by Whitman, ♦ published in 1865, containing descriptive scenes at the front and in Washington hospitals during the Civil War, as well as "Pioneers! O Pioneers!" ♦ A small supplement, issued after Lincoln's assassination as *Sequel to Drum-Taps* (1865–66), contained "When Lilacs Last in the Door Yard Bloom'd," ♦ "O Captain! My Captain!," ♦ "Chanting the Square Deific," ♦ and other poems. Both volumes were incorporated in the 1867 edition of *Leaves of Grass.*

DRURY, ALLEN [STUART] (1918–   ), Texas-born journalist and novelist, after graduation from Stanford (1939) worked on California newspapers and as a Washington correspondent for *The New York Times* and *Reader's Digest* before writing his popular and sensational novel *Advise and Consent* (1959, Pulitzer Prize), about the political and personal machinations in the Senate upon the occasion of considering confirmation of a secretary of state. The novel was successfully dramatized (1960). In 1962 Drury published *A Shade of Difference,* employing some of the same characters in a novel about conflicts between the new African nations and white prejudice as they appear in United Nations and U.S. policies. Later political novels include *Capable of Honor* (1966) and its sequel *Preserve and Protect* (1968), *The Throne of Saturn* (1971), *The Promise of Joy* (1975), *The Hill of Summer* (1981), and *The Roads of Earth* (1984), a two-part novel on a confrontation between the U.S. and the U.S.S.R. in the late 1980s, and *Decision* (1983).

DU BOIS, W[ILLIAM] E[DWARD] B[URGHARDT] (1868–1963), after graduation from Fisk (1888) and a Ph.D. from Harvard (1895) became a professor of economics and history at Atlanta University (1897–1910) and a dynamic leader of social reform activities on behalf of his fellow blacks. He opposed the views of Booker T. Washington as too conservative and limited, organized young black intellectuals in a Niagara Movement, helped to found the National Association for the Advancement of Colored People (1909), which he later disavowed (1948) as too conservative, and was an editor of the magazine *Crisis* (1910–34). Meanwhile he wrote *The Souls of Black Folk♦* (1903) and *Darkwater* (1920), essays, sketches, and verses about the life of blacks in the U.S. His significant historical and sociological studies dealing with black people in Africa and the U.S. and over a long period of time include *The Suppression of the African Slave Trade to the U.S.A.* (1896), his doctoral thesis; *The Philadelphia Negro* (1899); *John Brown* (1909); *The Negro* (1915); *The Gift of Black Folk* (1924); *Black Reconstruction* (1935); and *Color and Democracy: Colonies and Peace* (1945), a tract against imperialism and for the independence of small nations. *Dusk of Dawn* (1940) he described as "not so much my autobiography as the autobiography of a concept of race." He also wrote novels: *The Dark Princess* (1928) and *The Black Flame: A Trilogy,* which incorporates *The Ordeal of Mansart* (1957), *Mansart Builds a School* (1959), and *Worlds of Color* (1961). In 1958 he was awarded the Lenin International Peace Prize and in 1961 he joined the Communist party. The year before his death he moved to Ghana and became a citizen of that nation. His *Correspondence* was published in 3 volumes (1979).

DUGAN, ALAN (1923–), achieved great success with his first volume of *Poems* (1961), issued in the Yale Series of Younger Poets, which won a Pulitzer Prize and a National Book Award. *Poems 2* (1963), *Poems 3* (1968), *Collected Poems* (1970), *Poems 4* (1974), and *New and Collected Poems* (1983) are also directly stated, dry, bleak views of life.

DUNBAR, PAUL LAURENCE (1872–1906), born in Dayton, Ohio, of parents who had been slaves in Kentucky, and resided in that city most of his short life, early displaying his talents as a poet. Under the auspices of the Moravian Church but with his own funds he issued a booklet of his lyrics, *Oak and Ivy,* in 1893, followed by *Majors and Minors* (1895), both treating black themes with both pathos and humor. He supported himself by menial jobs, including one that Frederick Douglass arranged at the Haiti Building in the Colum-

bian Exposition at Chicago, but when Howells gave the second collection of poems a long and enthusiastic review, Dunbar's reputation was established. The best of the earlier poetry and some new works were then printed by a major publisher as *Lyrics of Lowly Life* (1896) with a preface by Howells. He became a popular reader of his poetry on a lecture circuit in the U.S. and England and held a job at the Library of Congress until sickness forced him to leave. Meanwhile he wrote further poems using folk materials and situations of plantation life set forth in dialect and exhibiting the influence of Burns and James Whitcomb Riley, and even the sentimental views of white interpreters of the Old South. These appeared in *Lyrics of the Hearthside* (1899), *Lyrics of Love and Laughter* (1903), and *Lyrics of Sunshine and Shadow* (1905). He also wrote a one-act musical play, *Uncle Eph's Christmas* (1900), and four novels: *The Uncalled* (1896), *The Love of Landry* (1900), *The Fanatics* (1901), and *The Sport of the Gods* (1902), melodramatic stories, the first three about whites, respectively concerning an orphan, an American aristocrat roughing it in Colorado, and conflicts between Southerners and Unionists in the Civil War era, while the last novel treats a black family from the South caught up in crime in Harlem.

DUNCAN, ROBERT [EDWARD] (1919–), poet associated with the San Francisco Bay area, studied at the University of California and taught at Black Mountain College.♦ Influenced by Pound and holding to the belief of Charles Olson in an "open field" of composition in which a poem not only treats a theme but picks up associations of the moment of composition, Duncan's writing tends to be rhapsodic and orphic. His ongoing "Passages" relate to Pound's *Cantos* and Olson's *Maximus* poems. Duncan's collections include *Heavenly City, Earthly City* (1947); *Medieval Scenes* (1950); *Letters* (1958), containing poetry and prose; *The Opening of the Field* (1960); *Roots and Branches* (1964); *The Years as Catches* (1966), his early poems; *Passages 22–27* (1966); and *Bending the Bow* (1968). *Faust Foutou* (1960) and *Medea at Kolchis* (1965) are plays.

DUNLAP, WILLIAM (1766–1839), born in New Jersey, began his versatile career at 16 as a professional portrait painter, among his early subjects being George and Martha Washington. He returned to New York after three years of study in London under Benjamin West, but had only a moderate success as a painter. Inspired by the success of Royall Tyler's *The Contrast,* he wrote *The Father; or, American Shandyism* (1789), a successful comedy of manners. He followed it with 30 original plays and many adaptations from the French and German, particularly Kotzebue. His best plays include *André* (1789), a blank-verse tragedy about the British spy in the Revolutionary War, and *The Italian Father* (1799), based on Dekker's *The Honest Whore.* He also wrote biography, fiction, and history, including a *History of the Rise and Progress of the Arts of Design in the United States* (2 vols., 1834) and *The History of the American Theatre* (1832).

DUNNE, FINLEY PETER (1867–1936), Chicago journalist, editor of *Collier's* (1918–19), is best known as the author of a series of books in which Mr. Dooley, an Irish saloon keeper, criticizes current events, leaders, and aspects of the social scene, with a rich brogue and shrewd native humor. *Mr. Dooley in Peace and in War* (1898) was the first of this series, which concluded with *Mr. Dooley on Making a Will* (1919).

DUNNE, JOHN GREGORY (1932–   ), Connecticut-born writer resident in southern California since 1964, author of *True Confessions* (1977), a tough police novel in the vein of Raymond Chandler, and *Dutch Shea, Jr.* (1982), a novel of a similar nature. His nonfictional works include *Delano* (1967), about the labor movement of Cesar Chavez; *The Studio* (1969), about the film industry; *Vegas* (1974), depicting Nevada's gambling city; and *Quintana and Friends* (1978), essays and reviews. He and his wife Joan Didion♦ also write film scripts.

Dupin, C. AUGUSTE, hero of "The Murders in the Rue Morgue,"♦ "The Purloined Letter,"♦ and "The Mystery of Marie Rogêt,"♦ and prototype of the intellectual amateur who is often the main character in the detective story.♦

DWIGHT, THEODORE (1764–1846), Massachusetts lawyer, grandson of Jonathan Edwards and brother of Timothy Dwight, is remembered as one of the Connecticut Wits,♦ of whom he was probably the most vehemently Federalist member.

DWIGHT, TIMOTHY (1752–1817), born in Massachusetts, was a grandson of Jonathan Edwards and brother of Theodore Dwight. He showed precocious brilliance by entering Yale at the age of 13, and as a tutor there (1771–77) worked and studied so excessively that he precipitated a physical breakdown. To recuperate, he turned to an equally disproportionate amount of hiking and horseback trips, and his observations furnished much of the material for his later *Travels in New England and New York* (4 vols., 1821–22). His literary interests at Yale and his attempts with John Trumbull to introduce contemporary English literature into the curriculum may be considered the genesis of the Connecticut Wits. ♦ His major poems are *The Conquest of Canaan*♦ (1785); *Greenfield Hill* (1794), lauding American principles and landscape; and *The Triumph of Infidelity* (1788), a heavy-handed satire in defense of Calvinism. He was president of Yale (1795–1817), where, despite his narrow political, social, and religious views, he proved a great teacher and college leader.

E

Each and All, poem by Emerson,♦ published in 1839 and reprinted in his *Poems* (1847). In couplets of four-stress verse, it expresses his apprehension of the beauty of complete nature, "the perfect whole," despite passing disappointments and the realization that isolated facts may be ugly:

> All are needed by each one;
> Nothing is fair or good alone.

East Lynne, sentimental melodramatic novel by the English author Mrs. Henry Wood, published in 1861. Its dramatic version was extremely popular on the American stage during the later part of the century for its sensational and lachrymose plot about crime and licentious behavior in English high society.

East of Eden, novel by John Steinbeck,♦ published in 1952.

In the late 1890s Adam Trask marries Cathy Ames, a beautiful but viciously evil former prostitute, and moves from his family farm in Connecticut to the Salinas Valley, California. There, aided by Sam Hamilton, a warm-hearted Irishman, he develops a large ranch, and Cathy gives birth to their twin sons. Hating her situation and her husband, Cathy shoots Adam when he tries to prevent her leaving, and under the name of Kate Albey joins a house in Salinas run by a madam whom she slowly poisons so as to get a place of her own to cater to men's darkest and most perverted desires. Adam, withdrawn and detached, has the help of kindly Sam and of his educated servant Lee, a Chinaman, in rearing his children, Caleb and Aron, whom he had considered naming Cain and Abel, particularly since Lee interpreted the Biblical story to show that although God exiled Cain to the land east of Eden, He said to him, "if thou doest well . . . thou mayest rule over sin." The boys grow up, Aron as a naïve, open-hearted, and religious young man innocently loving a girl named Abra, while Caleb has a stormy adolescence, torn between desires for innocence and for adventures in evil, conceived by him to be a heritage from his mother, whom he comes to know. To hurt Adam, who dotes on Aron, Caleb takes his brother to meet their mother, and Aron is so shocked by the experience that he gives up Abra and enlists in the army during World War I. Kate commits suicide, bequeathing her wealth to Aron, whose own death in war leads to Adam's paralysis by a stroke. Caleb is guilt-ridden by the sequence of events he set in motion, but Adam on his deathbed recalls Lee's Biblical interpretation, and in forgiving Caleb he gives him the chance, like that given Cain, to make a moral choice and thus to create of his life what he will.

EASTLAKE, WILLIAM (1917–   ), born and reared in New York City, after army service and residence in Paris moved to a New Mexico ranch. His novels include *Go in Beauty* (1956), about rivalry between brothers; *Bronc People* (1958), again a contrast of brothers, but these younger, also set in New Mexico; *Portrait of an Artist with Twenty-Six Horses* (1963), a story of fantasy and suspense involving a white man about to die and his Navajo friend; and *Castle Keep* (1965), concerning American soldiers seizing a European castle in World War II. Eastlake is also known for his many short stories.

EASTMAN, MAX [FORRESTER] (1883–1969), social critic, whose writings are devoted to literary criticism, the relation of art to life, and problems of economic inequality. He is best known for his social criticism, although his first book, *Enjoyment of Poetry* (1913), had a success unsurpassed by any of his later works. His own verse was collected in *Poems of Five Decades* (1954). He was a founder and editor of *The Masses* and *The Liberator.* Among his later books are *Marx, Lenin, and the Science of Revolution* (1926); *The Literary Mind: Its Place in an Age of Science* (1931); *Artists in Uniform* (1934); a translation of Trotsky's *History of the Russian Revolution* (3 vols., 1932–33); *Enjoyment of Laughter* (1936); *Marxism: Is It Science?* (1940); *Stalin's Russia* (1940), showing his hostility to the orthodox Communist party line; and *Reflections on the Failure of Socialism* (1955). Reminiscent works are *Heroes I Have Known* (1942), sketches of people including Debs, Isadora Duncan, Clemens, Chaplin, Anatole France, Trotsky, Freud, and John Dewey;

Great Companions (1959), essays on 12 friends, including Hemingway, Millay, and Santayana; and *Love and Revolution* (1965), an autobiography.

EBERHART, RICHARD [GHORMLEY] (1904–), Minnesota-born poet, educated at Dartmouth and Cambridge, has taught at various schools and colleges, and since 1956 has been a professor of English and poet in residence at Dartmouth. His poetry assumes a variety of forms, ranging from romantic description to allegory, and is marked by intensity, honesty, and precision of diction. It includes *A Bravery of Earth* (1930), partly about his world tour on a freight steamer; *Reading the Spirit* (1937); *Song and Idea* (1942); *Burr Oaks* (1947); *Brotherhood of Man* (1949); *An Herb Basket* (1950); *Undercliff* (1953); *Great Praises* (1957); *The Quarry* (1964); *Thirty One Sonnets* (1967), written in his youth; *Shifts of Being* (1968); *Fields of Grace* (1972); *Poems to Poets* (1976); *Collected Poems* (1976); and *Florida Poems* (1981). "The Visionary Farms" (1952) is one of his *Collected Verse Plays* (1962). He has also published *Selected Prose* (1978) and *Of Poetry and Poets* (1979). Among many honors he has received a Bollingen Prize, Pulitzer Prize, and National Book Award.

EDDY, MARY BAKER (1821–1910), discoverer and founder of Christian Science,♦ was born in New Hampshire. She was married three times, although for a long time an invalid. In 1862 she became a patient of Phineas P. Quimby, a mental healer of Portland, Me., with whom she had contact until 1865 and in whom for a time she had much confidence. To the spiritual enlightenment she received with recovery from a serious injury (1866) she attributed her discovery of Christian Science. She began to work out her own metaphysical system and her students and followers increased rapidly after the publication of *Science and Health with Key to the Scriptures*♦ (1875). The following year the Christian Science Association was formed, and in 1879 the various associations were merged in the Church of Christ, Scientist. She founded (1883) and for a time edited the *Journal of Christian Science,* which won more recruits to her Metaphysical College and church. Although she retired in 1889 to a secluded home at Concord, N.H., and made few appearances thereafter at the Mother Church in Boston, Mrs. Eddy never ceased to be the actual leader of the Christian Science movement and the chief author of its writings.

EDEL, [JOSEPH] LEON (1907–), born in Pittsburgh but educated at McGill University, Toronto (M.A., 1928), and the University of Paris (Litt.D., 1932), served as a journalist before entering an academic career in 1950 as a professor at New York University. He is particularly known for his scholarly work on Henry James, including various editions such as *The Complete Plays* (1949) and the *Complete Tales* (12 vols., 1963–65) and selected *Letters* (2 vols., 1974–75), but particularly for his authoritative *Life* (5 vols., 1953–72), which won a Pulitzer Prize and National Book Award for two of its volumes. Edel's other works include a study of Joyce (1947), *The Psychological Novel* (1955), *Literary Biography* (1957), *Bloomsbury, A House of Lions* (1979), *Stuff of Sleep and Dreams: Experiments in Literary Psychology* (1982), and, with E.K. Brown, *Willa Cather* (1953). Works he has edited include the *Papers* (1972) of Edmund Wilson.

Edict by the King of Prussia, satire by Franklin,♦ published in the Philadelphia *Public Advertiser* (1773). It is written in the form of a royal proclamation, claiming that England belongs to Prussia because of its original settlement by Anglo-Saxons from that country. Having established English dependence upon Prussia, the king imposes a long list of political and legal restrictions upon the English people. In this fashion, Franklin satirizes the British attitude toward the American colonies.

Education of Henry Adams, The, autobiography of Henry Adams,♦ privately printed (1907) and posthumously published (1918). Subtitled "A Study of Twentieth-Century Multiplicity," the work complements *Mont-Saint-Michel and Chartres*♦ (1904), in which Adams interprets the 13th century in Europe as "the point of history when man held the highest idea of himself as a unit in a unified universe." In *The Education,* embodying his theory of the acceleration of historical force, he describes the modern world as a "multiverse," leading to a metaphysics and science of multiple aspects and reactions. Using himself "for purpose of model, to become a manikin on which the toilet of education is to be draped in order to show the fit or misfit of the clothes," he asserts that his formal education, at Harvard and elsewhere, failed to prepare him for the conflicts he had to meet. The narrative is incomplete, for it omits any mention of his marriage, or other events between 1871 and 1892, but there are vivid descriptions of his encounters with Harvard education, as both student and teacher; with diplomacy in England during the Civil War; with the theories of Darwin; and with other intellectual influences. The chapter "The Dynamo and the Virgin" expresses his view that the mechanical dynamo, symbol of electrical energy, corresponds to the central symbol of the Virgin that unified the thought of medieval Europe. The concluding chapters are a more explicit discussion of the dynamic theory of history and the law of acceleration.

EDWARDS, HARRY STILLWELL (1855–1938), Georgia journalist and author, whose books include a novel, *Sons and Fathers* (1896), and two popular stories about blacks, *Æneas Africanus* (1919) and *Æneas Africanus, Defendant* (1921).

EDWARDS, JONATHAN (1703–58), born in Connecticut, entered Yale before he was 13 and graduated in 1720. His interest in scientific observation was manifested at the age of 11 in an account "Of Insects," on phenomena related to the flying spider (*Andover Review,* Jan. 1890), and a group of acute comments on "The Soul," "The Rainbow," "Being," and "Colours." While at Yale he read Locke's *Essay Concerning Human Understanding* with more delight than a "greedy miser" finds in "some newly discovered treasure," and began to combine reflections on the mind with his observations of natural science. He made a precocious venture into Berkeleyan idealism, evidently without knowing Berkeley, and, in his "Notes on the Mind," decided: "That which truly is the substance of all Bodies, is the infinitely exact, and precise, and perfectly stable Idea, in God's mind, together with his stable Will, that the same shall gradually be communicated to us, and to other minds, according to certain fixed and exact established Methods and Laws."

After two additional years of theological study at Yale, and a year of tutoring there, he became (1726) the colleague of his grandfather Solomon Stoddard in the Congregational pastorate at Northampton, Mass. He had made a series of formal "Resolutions" for his spiritual progress, but it is in his "Personal Narrative" (written *c.*1740) that he rehearses his spiritual autobiography. Here one sees his intense absorption in the idea of God's infinite will throbbing through the universe. Edwards married Sarah Pierpont (1727), whom he had described four

years earlier in a famous lyrical passage. Upon the death of his grandfather (1729), he became the sole pastor of the Northampton church. With stern discipline and exalted fervor he fought the growing Arminianism and the weakening of Congregational churches through the Half-Way Covenant, writing a *Treatise Concerning Religious Affections* (1746) and *A Vindication of the Gospel Doctrine of Justifying Faith* (1746). His discourse *God Glorified in . . . Man's Dependence upon Him* (1731) attacked those who relied for salvation solely on moral effort, and his sermon on *Divine and Supernatural Light* (1734) argued that saving grace came solely from the mind's supernatural illumination by the loveliness of divine holiness. There ensued a tremendous revival of religious fervor, the Great Awakening, in which the community, lacking its pastor's iron will, gave way to a wave of emotionalism and morbid belief in God's absolute justification in condemnation. Edwards's sermons ranged from those on *Charity and Its Fruits* (1738) to the notorious *Sinners in the Hands of an Angry God* (1741). Although he criticized the hysterical excitement that accompanied the Awakening, he defended it as a vitally important crisis in *A Faithful Narrative of the Surprising Work of God* (1737), *The Distinguishing Marks of a Work of the Spirit of God* (1741), *Some Thoughts Concerning the Present Revival of Religion in New England* (1742), and *An Humble Attempt To Promote Visible Union of God's People* (1747). He explained that the two activities of the mind—understanding and inclination or will—are indispensable for true religion. Man wills what he loves, and, instead of depending upon mere understanding of God and obedience to worldly morality, he shares directly in the divine light.

When Edwards applied this criterion to admission to the Lord's Supper, excluding those who wished to ally themselves to the church without supernatural conversion, his parishioners grew resentful, and this and other matters led to his dismissal (1750). After preaching his dignified *Farewell Sermon* (published 1751), he became a missionary to the Housatonic River Indians and pastor of a small congregation at Stockbridge. He had meanwhile published his apologia, *An Humble Inquiry into the Rules of the Word of God* (1749), and *An Account of the Life of the Late Reverend Mr. David Brainerd* (1749), an example of piety. In his next attack on Arminianism, Edwards reverted to the "Notes on the Mind," developing his ethical point of view in *A Careful and Strict Enquiry into the Modern Prevailing Notions of . . . Freedom of Will♦* (1754), his greatest work, which became a primary Calvinistic document. In *The Great Christian Doctrine of Original Sin Defended* (1758), he argues that depravity is inevitable, since an identity of consciousness and a continuity of divine action make all men as one with Adam. "The Nature of True Virtue," in *Two Dissertations* (1765), upholds virtue as moral beauty, which, in the form of love, seeks the highest good of all being. Since God is the supreme object, truly disinterested love will be directed toward Him. The lower form of natural virtue rests on self-love, and those not enlightened by saving grace will only perceive and approve justice and benevolence, rather than the essential and primary beauty of virtue. In the second of the *Dissertations,* "Concerning the End for Which God Created the World" (written 1755), he returned to the mystic pantheism of his youth, declaring the world to be an emanation of God's infinite fullness, created to express His glory. Since He is the supreme excellence, He loves the world as He is infused into it. In this, Edwards's tendency to negate the personal, Hebraic concept of God and to view Him as an infinite being foreshadows Transcendentalism. After his work in Stockbridge, he became president of the College of New Jersey, an office he held from January 1758 until his death in March.

EGGLESTON, EDWARD (1837–1902), born in Indiana, received a strict Methodist rearing and was educated in country schools. Both influences are important in his later writing. He was successively a Bible agent, a circuit-riding Methodist minister, a pastor of small churches, and a writer and editor of Sunday school and juvenile magazines. His novels include *The Hoosier Schoolmaster* (1871), marked by a pious sentimentalism but distinguished for its realism in depicting the backwoods country of Indiana; *The End of the World* (1872), an Indiana love story, whose background is concerned with the belief of the Millerites in an approaching day of doom; *The Circuit Rider* (1874), about a Methodist preacher in Ohio during the early 19th century, distinguished for its realistic exposition of the lawlessness of frontier society; and *Roxy* (1878), which is set in Indiana during the same period, and vividly contrasts pioneer and "poor-white" types.

Eimi, travel narrative by E.E. Cummings♦ of his 36-day visit to the Soviet Union, published in 1933. This long prose work employs the techniques of his poetry and, like it, also celebrates the individual of the title (Greek, "I am"), and with wit and vigor attacks the regimentation of people in the U.S.S.R.

Eleonora, story by Poe,♦ in *The Gift* (1842). This brief romance tells of a youth reared with his cousin Eleonora in the beautiful Valley of the Many-Colored Grass. They fall in love, but she dies after he pledges never to wed "any daughter of Earth." Grieving, he goes to a strange city to serve at the gay court of the king, where he falls in love with and weds "the seraph Ermengarde." One night he hears a "familiar and sweet voice" absolve him of his vow "for reasons which shall be made known to thee in Heaven."

ELIOT, CHARLES W[ILLIAM] (1834–1926), president of Harvard (1869–1909), made the university the leading American institution of higher learning through his improvement of the graduate and professional schools, the distinguished scholars he attracted, the raising of undergraduate standards, and such reforms as the "elective system." After his resignation, he interested himself in civil service reform, peace organizations, and public affairs. He edited *The Harvard Classics* (1910), a 50-volume selection from world literature, popularly known as "Dr. Eliot's Five-Foot Shelf of Books," for self-education of persons without college training. His books include *The Religion of the Future* (1909) and *The Durable Satisfactions of Life* (1910).

ELIOT, JOHN (1604–90), English-born missionary, educated at Cambridge, came to Boston (1631), where, as the first to preach to the Indians in their native tongue, he obtained the sobriquet "Apostle to the Indians." His translation of the Bible into the language of the Massachuset Indians (New Testament, 1661; Old Testament, 1663) was the first complete Bible printed in the English colonies.

ELIOT, T[HOMAS] S[TEARNS] (1888–1965), born in St. Louis, graduated from Harvard (1910) and studied at the Sorbonne and at Merton College, Oxford. For a year he was an instructor in philosophy at Harvard, and his first articles were on this subject. In 1914 he went to Europe, and he did not return to the U.S. until 1932, when he held a lectureship at Harvard. In the intervening years he did some schoolteaching in England, became a London bank clerk, wrote reviews and poems, assisted in editing a literary journal, and in 1923 became editor of the quarterly review *Criterion.* In 1927 he became a British subject because of his interest in the English church and state.

His first volume of criticism, *The Sacred Wood* (1920), emphasized the importance of tradition, both in creative writing and in criticism, and through further critical work he was partly responsible for a revival of interest in Donne and Dryden, in whom he found a fusion of thought and feeling that gave a unified sensibility to their poetry. *For Lancelot Andrewes♦* (1928) showed that in the Church of England he found the symbol and expression of meaningful form and discipline that he judged necessary to adequate fulfillment of his own life and service to letters. In *After Strange Gods* (1934), lectures delivered at the University of Virginia, he revealed his increasing preoccupation with tradition as it relates to the expression of moral problems in contemporary literature.

Not only was his poetry in harmony with his critical standards, but it also showed his understanding and skillful use of the works of earlier authors in the presentation of his ideas. His first volume of verse, *Prufrock and Other Observations* (1917), had a tone of flippant despair, but he employed the rhythms and technique of ironic contrast of some of the French Symbolists in "The Love Song of J. Alfred Prufrock"♦ and other poems. A second volume, *Poems* (1920), contained a brilliant series of quatrains, including "Sweeney Among the Nightingales," "Sweeney Erect," "The Hippopotamus," and "Mr. Eliot's Sunday Morning Service," in which he further indicated that he felt life to be ignoble, sordid, or stultifying, while it had once been otherwise, using the figure of Sweeney,♦ among others, to show this. In this volume he also displayed the inanition of modern life in "Gerontion,"♦ and he reached the fullness of his poetic expression during this period of despair in *The Waste Land♦* (1922).

After "The Hollow Men" (1925), which indicated this trend, he issued *Ash-Wednesday♦* (1930), and made clear his allegiance to the Church of England. In this context he wrote the dialogues and choruses of *The Rock* (1934), a pageant representing the past and present difficulties of the Church and its ultimate triumph, and *Murder in the Cathedral♦* (1935), a latter-day morality play concerning the assassination of Thomas à Becket

and affirming the value of the Church as a medium for social action. Later verse plays were *The Family Reunion♦* (1939), a drama of sin and expiation, two symbolic comedies on faith and the quest for personal identity, *The Cocktail Party♦* (1950) and *The Confidential Clerk* (1954), and *The Elder Statesman* (1958), about a distinguished old man who sees not only the nature of his youthful follies but his son's imitations of them. In 1943 he collected *Four Quartets,♦* poetic considerations of time and place, memory and consciousness. In 1948 he was awarded a Nobel Prize.

His poetry illustrated also two critical formulas expressed in his prose. In *The Sacred Wood* he declared, "The only way of expressing emotion in the form of art is by finding an 'objective correlative'; in other words, a set of objects, a situation, a chain of events which shall be the formula of that particular emotion," and in "Tradition and the Individual Talent," an essay also from *The Sacred Woods,* he declared, "Poetry is not a turning loose of emotion, but an escape from emotion; it is not the expression of personality, but an escape from personality."

His other works include *Ezra Pound: His Metric and Poetry* (1917); *Ara Vos Prec* (1919); *Homage to John Dryden* (1924); *Shakespeare and the Stoicism of Seneca* (1927); *The Journey of the Magi* (1927); *A Song for Simeon* (1928); *Dante* (1929); *Animula* (1929); *Marina* (1930); *Triumphal March* (1931); *John Dryden, the Poet, the Dramatist, the Critic* (1932); *The Use of Poetry and the Use of Criticism* (1933), his Harvard lectures; *Old Possum's Book of Practical Cats♦* (1939); *The Idea of a Christian Society* (1940); *Notes Toward a Definition of Culture* (1949); and *On Poetry and Poets* (1957). His *Poems Written in Early Youth* (1904–10) was privately issued (1950) and for sale (1967).

Eliza, character in *Uncle Tom's Cabin.♦*

ELKIN, STANLEY [LAWRENCE] (1930–), novelist whose fiction is marked by black humor, symbolism, rich prose, and a satiric view of contemporary American life. His novels are *Boswell* (1964), a comic depiction of a young man who attaches himself to prominent people, including the Queen of England; *A Bad Man* (1967), about a department store owner who ends up in prison; *The Dick Gibson Show* (1971), describing the adventures, sometimes surreal, of an early-day radio announcer; *The Franchiser* (1976), depicting an American businessman who creates chains of motels and restaurants; *The Living End* (1979), about the death of an ordinary man and how God judges him in the afterworld; and *George Mills* (1982), about a man's 1000 years of reincarnations. *Criers and Kibitzers, Kibitzers and Criers* (1966) collects stories, and *Searches and Seizures* (1973) prints three novellas. Born in New York City, Elkin has been a professor at Washington University, St. Louis, since 1959.

ELLIOTT, GEORGE P[AUL] (1918–80), born in Indiana, reared in California, after receiving an A.B. and M.A. (1941) from the University of California taught English and creative writing at his alma mater, Cornell, Barnard, Iowa, and St. Mary's College (California). His novels include *Parktilden Village* (1958), set in a California apartment-house development; *David Knudsen* (1962), about the son of a nuclear physicist who develops radiation sickness; *In the World* (1965); and *Muriel* (1972), a portrait of a narrow, possessive woman. His stories are collected in *Among the Dangs* (1961) and *An Hour of Last Things* (1968). His poems are in *Fever and Chills* (1961) and *From the Berkeley Hills* (1969). *A Piece of Lettuce* (1964) and *Conversions* (1971) are essays on literature and society.

ELLISON, RALPH [WALDO] (1914–   ), Oklahoma-born author, a student at Tuskegee Institute (1933–36), has been a visiting professor of creative writing, black culture, and humanities at various major universities, but is best known for his naturalistic novel, *Invisible Man*♦ (1952), winner of a National Book Award, tracing the life of a young black man trying to find himself as an individual as well as in relation to his race and society. He also wrote *Shadow and Act* (1964), essays.

Elmer Gantry, see *Lewis, Sinclair.*

Elsie Dinsmore, see *Finley, Martha.*

Elsie Venner; A Romance of Destiny, novel by Holmes,♦ published in 1861, was previously serialized as *The Professor's Story.* The prototype of the heroine is said to be Margaret Fuller. The author's intention was "to test the doctrine of 'original sin' and human responsibility," and he spoke of the work as "a medicated novel," since it was an early instance of scientific analysis of character and of the concept of a pattern of heredity.

A professor of medicine tells the story of Elsie Venner, a New England girl whose snake-like nature is traced to the prenatal influence of a snakebite that her mother suffered. Elsie loves Bernard Langdon, one of the professor's students, but Bernard does not return her affection, though she saves his life when he is almost killed by a rattlesnake. Her peculiar quality, which sets her apart from others and fascinates Helen Darley, a teacher in the academy where Bernard teaches temporarily, is lost during her illness following Bernard's rejection, but she dies as a result.

EMERSON, RALPH WALDO (1803–82), born in Boston, the son of a Unitarian minister who was a member of an old Puritan family. After his father's death, he was raised by his mother and an aunt, Mary Moody Emerson, a zealously pious woman who expressed her sardonically critical mind in a style her nephew admired and imitated. At Harvard in 1820 he began to keep the voluminous journals that he continued throughout his life, and that formed the basis of most of his essays and poems. After graduation (1821) he took over his brother's Boston school for young ladies, although with some misgivings, and when he moved to Canterbury with his family in 1823 he expressed his relief at returning to the natural beauties of the countryside in the poem "Good-bye."♦ He taught for two more years, then entered the Divinity School at Harvard, where ill health and doubts on dogma made him a desultory student. Although approved as a candidate for the Unitarian ministry (1826), he had to go to Georgia and Florida for the winter because of a pulmonary disease. He married in 1829, but his wife died in 1831. A year later came the great turning point in his life; he resigned his pastorate of the Second Church of Boston, where he had been an effective and popular preacher, because he could not conscientiously administer the Lord's Supper.

During a tour of Europe (1832–33), he met Carlyle, Wordsworth, and Coleridge, through whom he became intimately associated with transcendental thought and its sources in German idealism. Other influences on Emerson's later thinking included his own Unitarian-Yankee background, his admiration for Plato and the neo-Platonists, his study of the sacred books of the East, the skepticism of Montaigne, the new republican tradition, the line of British philosophy that ran through Berkeley, Hume, and Locke, and the mystical metaphysics of Swedenborg. On his return to Boston he did some preaching, but turned more and more to lyceum lecturing, for which he drew materials from his journals. His addresses, presented in such series as "The Philosophy of History," "Human Culture," "Human Life," and "The Present Age," in turn furnished the basis for his later essays, which, without formal unity, are bound together by pithy, stimulating sentences that contain the quintessence of his philosophy. Among these are "Self-Reliance,"♦ "The Over-Soul,"♦ "Compensation"♦ "Spiritual Laws," "Love," and "Friendship."

In 1835 Emerson remarried and settled in Concord,♦ the home of his forefathers, which was thereafter the center of his own activity. Here he was intimate with Thoreau, Alcott, Jones Very, Margaret Fuller, Brownson, Hawthorne, and others who shared in the movement of Transcendentalism.♦ His first book, *Nature*♦ (1836), is the fundamental document of his philosophy, and expresses also his constant, deeply felt love for the natural scenes in which he passed so much of his time. His Transcendental ideas were next applied to cultural and national problems in his oration *The American Scholar*♦ (1837). A year later, in his "Divinity School Address,"♦ he attacked formal religion and championed intuitive spiritual experience. As a result, it was 30 years before he was again invited to speak at Harvard.

To promulgate his ideas further, in 1840 he joined with other Transcendentalists in publishing *The Dial,*♦ and, though he did not sympathize with the communal experiments at Brook Farm and Fruitlands, he became interested in many contemporary reform movements and extended the sphere of his lecturing. Some of these lectures received their final form in the first series of *Essays* (1841), whose 12 pieces were "History," "Self-Reliance," "Compensation," "Spiritual Laws," "Love," "Friendship," "Prudence," "Heroism," "The Over-Soul," "Circles," "Intellect," and "Art." With the second series of *Essays,* which appeared three years later, these works established Emerson's reputation throughout the U.S. and abroad. In 1845 he delivered the series of lectures published as *Representative Men*♦ (1850). His first volume of *Poems* (1847), together with *May-Day and Other Pieces* (1867), included such poems as "Threnody,"♦ "Compensation,"♦ "Each and All,"♦ "The Rhodora,"♦ "The Sphinx,"♦ "Days,"♦ "The Humble-Bee,"♦ "Voluntaries,"♦ "Concord Hymn,"♦ "May-Day,"♦ and "Brahma."♦ His poetry is intellectual, gnomic, and metaphysical.

During 1847–48 he visited England and France, renewed the friendship with Carlyle that had been maintained in their notable correspondence, and made new friends among the most distinguished European thinkers and writers. His lectures on England the following season formed the basis of his book *English Traits* (1856). A collection of *Addresses and Lectures* was published in 1849, and *The Conduct of Life*♦ (1860) and *Society and Solitude*♦ (1870) contain the materials of the lectures in his lyceum circuit, which took him as far west as the Mississippi. He contributed, with Channing and Clarke, to the *Memoirs* of Margaret Fuller (1852), and in 1855 helped found the Saturday Club. During the 1850s, Emerson's journals exhibit his great interest in antislavery, and he was an active sympathizer with the Northern struggle in the Civil War, but by 1866 realized that his career was nearly at its end. In the poem "Terminus" he declared:

> Fancy departs; no more invent;
> Contract thy firmament
> To compass of a tent.

Thereafter, although in 1870 he gave a series of lectures at Harvard, published as *Natural History of Intellect* (1893), and continued to lecture and write, issuing *Letters and Social Aims* (1876), his mental capacities showed a slow but sure decline. He made journeys to California (1871) and to Europe (1872), but gradually slipped into a serene senility in which his mind finally became a calm blank. His son Edward Waldo Emerson (1844–1930) edited his *Complete Works* (1903–4), along with the *Journals* (10 vols., 1909–14), and several collections of correspondence. A complete edition of previously unpublished *Letters* was edited by R.L. Rusk (6 vols., 1939). *Early Lectures* appeared in three volumes (1959–64). Publication of a complete edition of the *Journals* and *Notebooks* (16 vols.) was begun (1960–), as was a scholarly edition of *Collected Works* (1972–).

Emerson, whose thought is often considered the core of Transcendentalism, stood apart from much of the activity of the movement, and, though he summed up the major development of romanticism in America, his philosophy is rooted in the Puritan background and tempered by the many systems of thought that converged in him. He had no complete philosophical system, but with a style now vibrant, now flinty, preached the great doctrine of a higher individualism, the spiritual nature of reality, the importance of self-reliance, the obedience to instinct, the obligation of optimism and hope, and the existence of a unifying Over-Soul which explains the many diverse phenomena of life.

Emperor Jones, The, expressionist play by O'Neill,♦ produced in 1920 and published in 1921. An operatic version by Louis Gruenberg was produced in 1933.

The giant black Brutus Jones, former Pullman porter and ex-convict, becomes in two years the feared, autocratic "emperor" of a West Indian island. Exploiting the superstition of the primitive natives, claiming that only a silver bullet can kill him, he enriches himself at their expense, and brags to a cockney trader, Smithers, that when the inevitable rebellion comes he will escape to France, where he has sent a fortune. The uprising suddenly begins, but he is unable to locate his hidden supplies in the forest, where he loses his way. The incessant thumping of a tomtom undermines his courage, and a series of brief, symbolic scenes shows his mental return to earlier phases of his own and his race's history: his murder of another black, Jeff, in a gambling altercation; his escape from a prison chain gang; the slave auction block; the slave ship; the witch doctor and crocodile god in the Congo jungle. In each episode he fires a shot from his pistol, the last silver bullet being fired at the sacred crocodile. During this imaginative retrogression to a savage state, he circles through the forest; emerging where he had entered, he falls riddled by the silver bullets of the rebel tribesmen.

Emperor of Ice Cream, The, poem by Wallace Stevens,♦ published in *Harmonium.*♦ Presenting the body of a slatternly woman at her wake attended by a man who represents pleasure and by wenches who are apparently fellow prostitutes, the refrain declares that the only ruling power is the emperor of ice cream, or physical satisfaction, but it is evident that death is the real ruler and that with it all pretense or seeming must yield to actuality.

Encantadas, The, or Enchanted Isles, sketches by Melville,♦ published under the pseudonym Salvator R. Tarnmoor in *Putnam's Magazine* (1854) and reprinted in *The Piazza Tales* (1856). Seven of the ten sketches are descriptions of the uninhabited Galápagos Islands in the Pacific, "a group rather of extinct volcanoes than of isles; looking much as the world at large might, after a penal conflagration." The remaining

three are narratives of people who lived temporarily in the islands. These include a Creole adventurer from Cuba, who acquires title to Charles's Isle, brutally rules his colonists, and is overthrown and banished by them; a half-breed woman who is stranded on Norfolk Isle while searching for tortoise oil, and finally rescued by an American ship; and the hermit of Hood's Isle, who enticed and then enslaved deserting sailors, until he in turn was imprisoned by their captains.

Encyclopaedia Britannica, The, founded in Edinburgh in 1768, has grown from the three-volume first edition to 30 volumes (1977). It was first popular in the U.S. in pirated versions, and its first American contributor was Edward Everett on George Washington. Purchased in 1901 by Horace Hooper, an American bookseller, it was for a time conducted under the sponsorship of the London *Times.* Sears, Roebuck, and Co. bought and brought it to Chicago (1920), and in 1943 its ownership passed to William Benton, affiliated with the University of Chicago, which he made the beneficiary of the publication's profits. In 1974 it was revised into a one-volume *Propaedia* (an outline of entries), ten volumes of *Micropaedia* (short entries), and 19 volumes of *Macropaedia* (long entries by authorities).

ENDECOTT, JOHN (*c.*1589–1665), emigrated from England (1628), and was governor of the Massachusetts Bay Colony (1629–30) until the arrival of Winthrop. He held other important posts in the colony and was several times governor. Although an able administrator, he was stern and intolerant, and persecuted Quakers, followers of Thomas Morton, and others who differed in creed. In "Endicott and the Red Cross,"♦ Hawthorne tells the story of his tearing the sign of the cross from the British ensign because he considered it to smack of popery. Robert Lowell made a verse adaptation in "Endicott and the Red Cross" in *The Old Glory* (1965). The first of Longfellow's *New England Tragedies*♦ deals with his persecution of Quakers. Endicott is a variant spelling.

Endicott and the Red Cross, story by Hawthorne,♦ published in *Twice-Told Tales* (1837). It is a brief account of the rebellious gesture of the Puritan governor John Endecott, who, when Charles I decided to send an Anglican governor to England, tore the Red Cross from the British ensign, because he wish to demonstrate the dislike of the Massachusetts Bay colonists for "the idolatrous forms of English Episcopacy." A passage in the tale describes the punishment of an adulteress, later the theme of *The Scarlet Letter.*

ENGLE, PAUL [HAMILTON] (1908–), Iowa poet and member of the faculty of the University of Iowa, whose *American Song* (1934) won acclaim as the heir of the tradition of *Leaves of Grass,* more because the poet aimed at Whitman's vitality and American quality than because he approached his achievement. While at Oxford as a Rhodes Scholar, Engle wrote in similar verse *Break the Heart's Anger* (1936), protesting against American materialism. In *Corn* (1939) his thought and technique became more controlled, and he was content to express aspects of the simple life of Iowa farmers, while *West of Midnight* (1941), celebrating the "light in American sky" while Europe was blacked out, contains poems in his early manner as well as brief, taut lyrics. *American Child* (1945) is a sonnet sequence about his daughter, enlarged (1956) upon the birth of another daughter; and other lyrics appeared in *The Word of Love* (1951), *Poems in Praise* (1959), *A Prairie Christmas* (1960), *A Woman Unashamed* (1965), and *Embraced* (1969). *Always the Land* (1941) is a novel about conflicts between two generations of Iowa farmers, and *Golden Child* (1962) is a prose tale of Christmas, originally a libretto for a television opera.

Enormous Room, The, autobiographical narrative by E.E. Cummings,♦ published in 1922.

As members of an American ambulance corps in France during World War I, the author and a friend are erroneously suspected of treasonable correspondence, and imprisoned by the French (Aug. 1917–Jan. 1918) in a concentration camp at La Ferté Macé, 100 miles west of Paris. Their fellow prisoners include the hyper-refined Count Bragard, the belligerent Fighting Sheeney, the tragic gypsy Wanderer and his family, the inarticulate but expressive Zulu, the servile, clownish Surplice, and the childish giant Jean le Nègre. All suffer under the needlessly cruel stresses of captivity, inhumane treatment by the officials and *plantons* (jailers), and the extremely filthy surroundings. Nevertheless they maintain the idiosyncratic beauties and humors of individual character, which the author exalts as the highest human values. The narrative is set in

the form of a pilgrimage, and the intended resemblance to Bunyan's *Pilgrim's Progress* appears in the presentation of the *Directeur* as the fiend Apollyon, and of certain remarkable prisoners as the Delectable Mountains.

Essays To Do Good, see *Bonifacius.*

Esther, novel by Henry Adams,♦ published in 1884 under the pseudonym Frances Snow Compton. The character of the heroine is modeled on the author's wife, and that of Wharton on the sculptor Saint-Gaudens.

Esther Dudley, a young painter, is introduced to Stephen Hazard, preacher at St. John's in New York City, whom she at first dislikes because he is absorbed in religious work, while she shares the free-thinking of her invalid father. When Esther is commissioned to work on the decoration at St. John's, under the direction of the prominent artist Wharton, she uses as a model her friend Catherine Brooke. During the progress of the work, Wharton falls in love with Catherine, while Esther becomes friendly with Stephen, who is enthusiastic about her painting and visits her father. After the latter's death she becomes engaged to the clergyman but soon realizes that their views of life are incompatible. In spite of their love, attempts at reconciliation fail, and Stephen announces that he will not trouble her again until she stands in need of his and the church's consolations.

Ethan Brand: A Chapter from an Abortive Romance, story by Hawthorne,♦ published in *The Snow-Image* (1851).

Ethan Brand, formerly a lime-burner, has sought the Unpardonable Sin, and now returns to his New England home, announcing that he has found it in his own soul, in intellectual pride and in the separation of mind and heart. The townspeople do not understand him and consider him mad. He takes the place of his successor at the limekiln, and during the night lies down to perish in the furnace. When the other lime-burner returns in the morning, he finds the lime all burnt snow-white, and on its surface a human skeleton within whose ribs is a piece of marble in the shape of a heart.

Ethan Frome, novelette by Edith Wharton,♦ published in 1911. It was dramatized by Owen and Donald Davis (1936).

This grim story is told by a middle-aged engineer, who pieces together the history of the inhabitants of a bleak Massachusetts farm. Zenobia (Zeena) is a whining slattern who hugs imaginery ailments to her barren breast, and spends upon quacks and patent medicines the scant substance her husband, Ethan Frome, manages to wring from the grudging earth. Her cousin Mattie Silver is left destitute and comes to live with them. The friendship of Ethan and Mattie arouses Zeena's jealousy, and after a year Mattie is ousted to make way for a strong hired girl. On their way to the railroad station, Ethan and Mattie realize that they cannot bear to part, and when they are coasting down their favorite snow slide he purposely steers their sled into a great elm. Intead of being killed, they are crippled for life, and spend the remainder of their unhappy days on the barren farm under Zeena's surveillance.

Ethnogenesis, ode by Timrod, ♦ written in 1861 during the meeting of the first Confederate Congress, and published in his *Poems* (1873). It enthusiastically hails the new nation, optimistically proclaiming its inevitable victory in the war, and celebrates the character of the Southern people and the perfection of soil and climate in the South.

Eureka: A Prose Poem, metaphysical work by Poe, ♦ published in 1848.

Based on the author's reading in Newton, Laplace, and others, the work accepts intuition, as well as induction and deduction, among legitimate paths to knowledge. Unity and diffusion are truths, because they are felt to be so, and "irradiation, by which alone these two truths are reconciled, is a consequent truth—I perceive it." The universe, composed of atoms radiated outward from a primary divine unity to an almost infinite variety, is conceived to be governed by the complementary laws of attraction and repulsion, in terms of which all phenomena are explicable. This is shown by mathematical proof, and by reference to the principles of heat, light, and electricity. This view of a harmoniously ordered, perfect universe is then extended in a discussion of literary criticism, especially applied to fiction. "In the construction of plot . . . we should aim at so arranging the incidents that we shall not be able to determine, of any one of them, whether it depends from any one other or upholds it." The view has also an ethical application: "God—the material *and* spiritual God—*now* exists solely in the diffused Matter and Spirit of the Universe," and the regathering of these elements will reconstitute "the *purely* Spiritual and individual God," so that the operations of "Divine

Injustice" or "Inexorable Fate" may at last be understood. We "no longer rebel at a *Sorrow* which we ourselves have imposed upon ourselves," and "in this view alone the existence of Evil becomes intelligible . . . it becomes endurable."

Europeans, The: A Sketch, novel by Henry James, ♦ published in 1878.

Eugenia, Baroness Münster, an expatriated American, is the morganatic wife of a German prince, who is about to repudiate her in favor of a state marriage. With her artist brother Felix Young she goes to Boston to visit relatives whom she has never before seen, in hopes of making a wealthy marriage. Mr. Wentworth, their uncle, establishes Eugenia and Felix in a nearby house, and his children, Gertrude, Charlotte, and Clifford, soon become intimate with them. Felix, gay and debonaire, enriches himself by painting flattering portraits of the Bostonians, and is involved in a love affair with Gertrude. Mr. Acton, a friend of the Wentworths and himself somewhat a man of the world, is attracted to Eugenia, who also makes a near-conquest of Clifford, an awkward youth suspended from Harvard for drunkenness. She overplays her hand with Acton, who realizes her deceitfulness and attempts to stay away from her. Clifford, too, is not to be snared, and becomes engaged to Acton's sister Lizzie. Gertrude weds Felix, after refusing the minister, Mr. Brand, who marries Charlotte. Eugenia returns to Europe, feeling that her fortune-hunting scheme is impractical in unsusceptible America.

Evangeline, A Tale of Acadie, narrative poem in unrhymed English hexameters, by Longfellow, ♦ published in 1847. Material was drawn from works by T.C. Haliburton, Schoolcraft, and possibly Chateaubriand, while Goethe's *Hermann und Dorothea* was a strong influence on the verse and manner of treatment. The subject was known to Hawthorne, who suggested it to Longfellow. A dramatization was made in 1860 by Sidney Frances Bateman.

Evangeline, daughter of Benedict Bellefontaine, is about to be married to Gabriel Lajeunesse, son of Basil, the blacksmith of the Acadian village of Grand Pré, when, during the French and Indian War, the English exile the French residents to safer British colonies. The lovers are separated, and Gabriel and Basil make their way to Louisiana, while Evangeline continues to seek them. Finding Basil, she goes with him on further quests and alone to the Michigan woods. Years of fruitless wandering cause her to become prematurely old, and she settles in Philadelphia as a Sister of Mercy. There, during a pestilence, she recognizes a dying old man as her former lover. The shock of his death kills her, and, united at last, they are buried together in the Catholic cemetery.

EVERSON, WILLIAM (1912–), California poet whose career has been in part influenced by the pantheism and long poetic line of Jeffers, later celebrated in an elegy, *The Poet Is Dead* (1964), and a critical study, *Robinson Jeffers: Fragments of an Older Fury* (1968). Everson's early poems (1934–40) were collected in *Single Source* (1966). During World War II he was a conscientious objector and while at a camp in Waldport, Ore., issued his own *War Elegies* (1943) and *Waldport Poems* (1944), the printing a crude forerunner of his distinguished handpress printing of the late 1940s to '70s. Later poems, some of his own printing, include *The Residual Years* (1948), *A Privacy of Speech* (1949), *Triptych for the Living* (1951), *The Crooked Lines of God* (1959), and *The Hazards of Holiness* (1962), marked by rhapsodic, mystic, and erotic power as well as by regional imagery, and particularly by the religious exaltation that took him into the Catholic church. From 1951 to 1971 he was a Dominican lay brother, writing under the name of Brother Antoninus further poems collected in *The Rose of Solitude* (1967), *The Last Crusade* (1969), and other volumes. In 1974 appeared *Man-Fate*, his swan song of religious life. Later works, written while he taught both poetry and printing at the University of California, Santa Cruz, include the long and powerful poem of human love *River-Root* (1976), with explicit erotic imagery.

Excelsior, poem by Longfellow,♦ published in *Ballads and Other Poems* (1841). In four-stress iambic couplets, with the title as a refrain, the poem figuratively depicts the life of a man of genius, as he maintains his individualistic purpose, resisting temptations and ignoring warnings. Climbing the mountain of his career, he passes beyond the village and the monastery, repeating his idealistic motto, until he is found dead on the highest glacier. Even then a voice is heard from the sky, proclaiming the motto as a promise of immortality.

Executioner's Song, The, fictive biography by Norman Mailer.♦

Exile's Return, a partly autobiographical narrative of the "lost generation" by Malcolm Cowley.♦

Existentialism, European philosophic movement with various schools or attitudes of different eras, including the Christian concepts of Kierkegaard and Maritain, but affecting American literature primarily in terms of an atheistic view shared with or influenced by Sartre and Camus. Holding that there are no accepted bases to explain the mysteries of human existence and that the individual must develop his being free of society, existentialism contends that solitariness makes the right condition for freedom of choice. However, it also brings anguish to the individual as he recognizes the futility of attempting to treat the paradoxes of a meaningless universe and an absurd world and to achieve self-mastery in an atmosphere of entire freedom. Such views and such a sense of metaphysical isolation in the consideration of the individual in the present moment are found in the fiction of Saul Bellow, Paul Bowles, Ralph Ellison, William Styron, and Richard Wright. Frequently using the monologue to show the protagonist's growing consciousness of the human condition, since thought rather than action is dominant in existential fiction, their novels deal with depersonalization, alienation from society and belief in divinity, and an individual search for identity.

Expressionism, aesthetic movement in which the artist expresses inner experience through the free representation of objective facts. Since it emphasizes the creator's mood and attitude, the movement is a development of Impressionism,♦ from which it differs by being more concerned with individual intellectual conceptions, and less with the structure of exterior facts. Both movements belong to the later phase of romanticism. Expressionism originated in European painting, and was brought to the U.S. by painters. Although exemplified in literature by T.S. Eliot and other poets, it has been more influential in the theater, in the work of such stage designers as R.E. Jones and in the dramatic technique of such plays as *"The Hairy Ape," The Emperor Jones, The Adding Machine,* and *Beggar on Horseback.*

Fable, A, novel by Faulkner,♦ published in 1954 and awarded a Pulitzer Prize.

Under the pacifist influence of a corporal and his 12 followers in 1918, a French regiment refuses to attack the Germans, who for the same reason do not counterattack. The commander, concerned with his military record, requests that the entire regiment be executed, but the supreme French general, who knows the corporal to be his natural son and who heads the tribunal considering the case, sees war as "so long ingrained in man as to have become an honorable tenet of his behavior and the national altar for his love of bloodshed and glorious sacrifice." Having been warned of the pacifist plan by a betrayer among the corporal's 12 men, he collaborates with the German command to resume the war. Among the idealists killed in an ensuing barrage is a black lay preacher, whose remarkable adventure in America with a superb, stolen racehorse is a long interpolated tale. As the local populace turns against the corporal, fearing that the whole regiment will be shot because of him, a reenactment of the Passion of Christ develops and becomes ramified. Wed to a woman named Magda, and already betrayed, the corporal is denied by the betrayer as he conducts a "last supper" in prison, and then is taken by the old general to a hilltop fortress to be tempted with life at the expense of his exalted hope for man's repudiation of war and urged to abandon "that aberrant and futile dream" that "man . . . will prevail." Unrelenting, the corporal is shot along with two criminals and given surreptitious but decent burial. But the resumption of war, in the form of an explosion near the grave, "resurrects" him, and through a combination of chance and the greed of men assigned to get the body of an unknown soldier, he is entombed beneath the everlasting flame in Paris.

Fable for Critics, A, verse satire by Lowell,♦ published anonymously in 1848. Its eccentric "slap-dash" rhythm has been characterized as a "genial anapestic gait," and the rhymes are equally careless, but besides the humor there are shrewd critical estimates of such contemporary authors as Emerson ("A Greek head on right Yankee shoulders"); Longfellow ("Why, he'll live till men weary of Collins and Gray"); Bryant ("A smooth, silent iceberg, that never is ignified"); Margaret Fuller ("She always keeps asking if I don't observe a Particular likeness 'twixt her and Minerva"); Poe (". . . with his raven, like Barnaby Rudge, Three-fifths of him genius, and two-fifths sheer fudge"); Hawthorne ("His strength is so tender, his wildness so meek . . . He's a John Bunyan Fouqué, a Puritan Tieck"); Cooper ("He has drawn you one character, though, that is new . . . He has done naught but copy it ill ever since"); and Lowell himself (". . . who's striving Parnassus to climb With a whole bale of *isms* tied together with rhyme . . ."). A disputed passage concerning two anonymous authors is considered to deal with Thoreau and W.E. Channing ("Fie, for shame, brother bard; with good fruit of your own, Can't you let Neighbor Emerson's orchards alone?"). The fable in which these comments are set deals with a gathering of the gods on Olympus, whereat a critic, worshiper of Apollo, attempts to satisfy the god's desire for a lily. The critic searches assiduously, passing the various authors in review, and at last produces a thistle. Apollo, disgusted, speaks of the happy period before the advent of critics, and the gods disperse. A similar plan is followed by Amy Lowell in her *Critical Fable.*

Fables for Our Time, and Famous Poems Illustrated, by James Thurber,♦ published in 1940.

Twenty-eight brief, wry, witty fables in the style of a modern Aesop, illustrated by the author, whose indicative titles include "The Fairly Intelligent Fly" and "The Rabbits Who Caused All the Trouble." The nine poems, so popular as to be platitudinous, like "Excelsior" and "Curfew Must Not Ring To-Night," are printed with illustrative embellishments by Thurber. In 1956 he published *Further Fables for Our Time.*

Facing West from California's Shores, poem by Whitman,♦ published in the "Children of Adam" section of *Leaves of Grass* (1860), and given its present title in the 1867 edition.

The poet, "a child, very old . . . long having wander'd," represents himself as symbolic of mankind looking backward "towards the house of eternity," the mystic Orient, from the vigorous utilitarian West, and questioning where he is to find fulfilled his search for the complete man. The poem thus foreshadows the theme of "Passage to India."♦ Its being placed in the "Children of Adam" section indicates that Whitman believed the instinct of sex to be both the physical and the spiritual force of creative progress in man and nature.

Falconer, novel by John Cheever,♦ published in 1977.

Ezekiel Farragut, descended from a wealthy, aristocratic New England family that fell on hard times, by the age of 48 is confined to Falconer State Prison in Connecticut for the murder of his older brother Eben, who had taunted him with being their parents' unwanted child. In prison he is cured of his drug addiction but becomes involved homosexually with another inmate, Jody, until his friend escapes. Some time later a cellmate dies. Farragut removes the body from its shroud, zips himself in its place, and upon being carried out of the prison faces his future with a fearless sense of freedom.

Fall of the House of Usher, The, story by Poe,♦ published in 1839, and reprinted in *Tales of the Grotesque and Arabesque* (1840). It contains the poem "The Haunted Palace."♦

A childhood companion of Roderick Usher, who has not seen him for many years, is summoned to the gloomy House of Usher to comfort his sick friend. The decayed mansion stands on the edge of a tarn, and is fungus-grown and dreary. Roderick and his twin Madeline are the only surviving members of the family, and both suffer serious physical and nervous maladies. Roderick entertains his friend with curious musical and poetic improvisations, indicating his morbid tastes by his choice of reading. Madeline, in a cataleptic trance, is thought to be dead, and her body is placed in the family vault. During a storm, Roderick is overcome by a severe nervous agitation, and his friend reads aloud from a medieval romance, whose horrifying episodes coincide with strange sounds from outside the room. Finally Madeline appears, enshrouded, and she and her brother fall dead together. The friend rushes from the house, and, as he looks back in the moonlight, sees the whole House of Usher split asunder and sink into the tarn.

F.kamily Reunion, The, verse play by T.S. Eliot,♦ produced and published in 1939.

Harry, Lord Monchensey, returns to his English country home, after eight years abroad following the death at sea of his young wife. The occasion is the birthday of his mother, Amy, imperious matriarch of the family, which also includes her sisters, Ivy, Violet, and Agatha. Harry shows his neurotic, guilt-ridden condition by a blurted confession that he murdered his wife. He has returned in search of inner peace, but the avenging spirits (Eumenides) now become visible. From Agatha Harry learns that his father had loved her, not Amy, who had used him merely to have the children and home she desired. The father's frustrated desire to murder his wife seems to have been inherited by the son. Harry departs to complete his "pilgrimage of expiation," and the shock kills Amy.

Fanshawe, romance by Hawthorne,♦ published anonymously in 1828. It was probably written during the author's college years, and the background resembles Bowdoin.

Fantasy literature, see *Science fiction.*

Farewell to Arms, A, novel by Hemingway,♦ published in 1929, and dramatized by Laurence Stallings (1930).

Frederic Henry, an American lieutenant in the Italian ambulance service during World War I, falls in love with an English nurse, Catherine Barkley. She returns his feeling, and when Henry, wounded during a bombardment, is sent to a hospital at Milan, Catherine comes to nurse him. They spend a happy summer together while he recuperates, and in the autumn Catherine confesses that she is pregnant, but will not marry him, fearing to be sent back to England. Henry returns to his post, finds his comrade Rinaldi depressed by the monotonous horrors of the war, and shares the suffering during the disastrous retreat from Caporetto. He deserts, learns that Catherine has been transferred to Stresa, and joins her there. Although he is in civilian clothes, he is suspected, and forced to flee with Catherine to Switzerland. They go to Lausanne for the birth of their child, but both mother and baby die, leaving Henry desolate and alone in a strange land.

Farmer's Almanack (1793–   ), Massachusetts almanac, founded by Robert Bailey Thomas (1766–1846), and still published with his name as editor. It has later been called *The*

Old Farmer's Almanac, to distinguish it from its many imitators, and issued from New Hampshire. Its importance as a source of information on New England life and manners appears in G.L. Kittredge's *The Old Farmer and His Almanack* (1904).

FARRELL, JAMES T[HOMAS] (1904–79), Chicago novelist in the naturalist tradition, studied at the University of Chicago, and held several jobs as clerk, salesman, and newspaper reporter. His experiences as a baseball enthusiast and pupil of Catholic schools on the city's South Side are the basis of *Young Lonigan*♦ (1932). This naturalistic stream-of-consciousness study of an adolescent in a squalid urban environment shows Farrell's chief influences to be Dreiser, Joyce, and Proust, but also exhibits his interest in the common facts of U.S. life, and his indignation at social and economic inequalities. *Gas-House McGinty* (1933) depicts the activities of employees in a city express office, but *The Young Manhood of Studs Lonigan*♦ (1934) follows the hero through his moral disintegration as the result of contact with the Chicago underworld, and *Judgment Day* (1935), completing the trilogy, tells of his defeat and death.

A new series of novels telling the story of Danny O'Neill, a sensitive youth with a background like Lonigan's, includes *A World I Never Made* (1936), *No Star Is Lost* (1938), *Father and Son* (1940), *My Days of Anger* (1943), and *The Face of Time* (1953). Other novels are *Tommy Gallagher's Crusade* (1939), about a boy who joins a priest's anti-Semitic campaign; *Ellen Rogers* (1941), about a selfish, middle-class girl; *Bernard Clare* (1946), about a frustrated New York author in the late 1920s, and its sequels, *The Road Between* (1949) and *Yet Other Waters* (1952); *This Man and This Woman* (1951), about the breakup of a long marriage. *The Silence of History* (1963) begins a tetralogy about Eddie Ryan, a University of Chicago student in 1926, who loses his faith in Catholicism and searches to find his own way; continued in *What Time Collects* (1964), about an unhappy marriage; *Lonely Future* (1966); and *When Time Was Born* (1967). Later novels include *Boarding House Blues* (1961); *New Year's Eve, 1929* (1967); *Childhood Is Not Forever* (1969); *Invisible Swords* (1971), depicting the relationship of a New York publisher and his wife upon discovering their child is retarded; *A Brand New Life* (1972); *The Dunne Family* (1976), about the lives and fates of a Chicago Irish family; and

The Death of Nora Ryan (1978) and *Sam Holman* (1983).

His many stories, similar in attitude and subject to the longer fiction, are collected in *Calico Shoes* (1934), *Guillotine Party* (1935), *Can All This Grandeur Perish?* (1937), *$1,000 a Week* (1942), *To Whom It May Concern* (1944), *When Boyhood Dreams Come True* (1946), *The Life Adventurous* (1947), *An American Dream Girl* (1950), *French Girls Are Vicious* (1956), *A Dangerous Woman* (1957), *Side Street* (1961), *Sound of the City* (1962), and *Judith* (1974), portraits of aging people, presumably based on actual friends.

Farrell's literary credo is set forth in *A Note on Literary Criticism* (1936), describing his views as Marxist but not of the usual "crass and oversimplified" sort; *The League of Frightened Philistines* (1945), defending the social value of naturalistic realism; *Literature and Morality* (1947); and *Reflections at Fifty* (1954). Other writings include *My Baseball Diary* (1957), reflections on his love of the national pastime; *It Has Come To Pass* (1958), about a visit to Israel; and *Collected Poems* (1965).

Fashion: *or, Life in New York,* comedy of manners by Anna Mowatt,♦ produced in 1845 and published in 1850.

FAST, HOWARD M[ELVIN] (1914–   ), New York author of historical fiction. Some of his works are set during the American Revolution, including *Two Valleys* (1933); *Conceived in Liberty* (1939), about a private at Valley Forge; *The Unvanquished* (1942), depicting Washington's development as a leader; *Citizen Tom Paine* (1943), a fictional biography; *April Morning* (1961), a boy's view of the beginnings of battles; *The Crossing* (1971), about Washington crossing the Delaware; and *The Hessian* (1972), telling of an innocent drummer boy tried for an atrocity, a victim of war's passions. Other fiction includes *The Children* (1937), about New York slums; *The Last Frontier* (1941), treating an Indian campaign of 1878–79; *Freedom Road* (1944), about a Southern black who becomes a congressman during Reconstruction; *The American* (1946), the story of Altgeld; *Clarkton* (1947), about a mill strike; *My Glorious Brothers* (1948), about Israel's ancient freedom; *Spartacus* (1952), treating the Roman slave revolt; *Moses, Prince of Egypt* (1958); *The Winston Affair* (1959), set in World War II; *Power* (1963), dealing with American labor during the days of a John L. Lewis-like figure; *Agrippa's Daughter* (1964);

Torquemada (1966); a four-volume series set in San Francisco: *The Immigrants* (1977), *Second Generation* (1978), *The Establishment* (1979), and *The Legacy* (1981); *Max* (1982), about the making of a Hollywood movie mogul; and *The Outsider* (1984), presenting the life of a rabbi in post-World War II U.S. *The Naked God* (1957) is an account of his membership in the Communist party (1943–56), during which time he won a Stalin International Peace Prize (1953), wrote propagandistic works, and was ostracized in some quarters, including film studios, though novels of this period (e.g. *Spartacus*) were filmed after he left the Party. Fast's other writings include children's books, short stories, plays, biographies, and, under the pseudonym E.V. Cunningham, detective and police novels, but his greatest success has been as a historical novelist.

FAULKNER (originally FALKNER), WILLIAM [HARRISON] (1897–1962), grew up in Oxford, Miss., a member of a family like that of the Sartoris clan in his novels centered on "Jefferson" in his mythical Yoknapatawpha County. ♦ After desultory education he joined the British Royal Air Force in Canada because he was too slight for U.S. requirements, but World War I ended before he was commissioned or saw service beyond training. Following the war he took some courses at the University of Mississippi and published *The Marble Faun* (1924), pastoral poems. Drifting to New Orleans, where he worked on a newspaper and also wrote the fiction collected in *New Orleans Sketches* (1958), he met Sherwood Anderson, who helped him publish *Soldiers' Pay* ♦ (1926), his first novel, about the homecoming of a dying soldier, in the vein of the "lost generation." Following a brief stay in Europe (1925), he issued *Mosquitoes* (1927), a satirical novel set in New Orleans, later the site of his minor novel *Pylon* (1935), about aviators at a Mardi Gras.

With the publication of *Sartoris* ♦ (1929) he found his own themes and setting, for it is the first novel in his long, loosely constructed Yoknapatawpha saga, whose themes include the decline of the Compson, ♦ Sartoris, ♦ Benbow, ♦ and McCaslin ♦ families, representatives of the Old South, and the rise of the unscrupulous Snopes ♦ family, which displaces them. The life of the region is treated from the days of Indian possession, through the pre-Civil War era, down to modern times. The saga of macabre violence and antic comedy is written in a sensitive but often baroque style and depicts its region as a microcosm in which its subjects often achieve mythic proportions. *The Sound and the Fury* ♦ (1929) introduces the significant but decadent Compson family in a remarkably structured story. *As I Lay Dying* ♦ (1930) reveals the psychological relationships of a subnormal poor-white family on a pilgrimage to bury their mother. *Sanctuary* ♦ (1931) is a sadistic horror story, ostensibly written to make money but carefully reworked before publication as a serious novel. *Light in August* ♦ (1932), although also filled with horrors, is a more balanced contrast of positive and negative forces of life in its presentation of violent adventures involved in the relations between men and women, black and white. *Absalom, Absalom!* ♦ (1936), set in early 19th-century Jefferson, shows the tragic downfall of the dynastic desires of the planter Colonel Sutpen. *The Unvanquished* ♦ (1938) uses earlier short stories to create a novel about the Sartoris family in the Civil War. *The Wild Palms* (1939) shows the effects of a Mississippi flood on the lives of a hillbilly convict and a New Orleans doctor and his mistress. *The Hamlet* ♦ (1940), the first volume of a trilogy, shows the rise to power of the depraved Snopes family. *Intruder in the Dust* ♦ (1948) is a more compassionate tale of a black man on trial and the concomitant growing moral awareness of a white boy. *Requiem for a Nun* (1951), a sequel to *Sanctuary*, combines the forms of play and novel to treat the tortured redemption of Temple Drake. *A Fable* ♦ (1954, Pulitzer Prize) is a lengthy parable of the Passion of Christ set in a framework of false armistice and actual mutiny in World War I. *The Town* ♦ (1957) carries on the story of the white trash Flem Snopes and his coming to Jefferson, while *The Mansion* ♦ (1960) concludes the Snopes story by treating the family in the first half of the 20th century. *The Reivers* ♦ (1962, Pulitzer Prize), published just before the author's death, is an amusing fictive "reminiscence" of a boy's various misadventures in 1905. Many of the novels' characters, settings, and themes appear in stories collected in *These 13* (1931); *Idyll in the Desert* (1931); *Miss Zilphia Gant* (1932); *Dr. Martino* (1934); *Go Down, Moses* (1942), including the symbolic novelette "The Bear" ♦; *Knight's Gambit* (1949); *Big Woods* (1955), hunting tales; and *Uncollected Stories* (1979). *Salmagundi* (1932) gathers early essays and poems, and *A Green Bough* (1933) collects poems. Other works include *Early Prose and Poetry* (1962), *Essays, Speeches and Public Letters* (1965), *Flags in the Dust* (1973), the original uncut text of *Sartoris;* and *Vision in Spring*

(1984), 14 love poems written (1921) to his wife.

During the 1930s he was off and on in Hollywood as a script writer, but his works for film are not accounted as being of much consequence. Critical views stated while teaching in Japan, at the University of Virginia, and at West Point appear in *Faulkner at Nagano* (1956), *Faulkner in the University* (1959), and *Faulkner at West Point* (1964). Lesser works include posthumously published juvenilia, *Marionettes: A Play in One Act* (1975) and *Mayday* (1976), while *The Wishing Tree* (1967) is a book for children. *Selected Letters* appeared in 1977. For his literary accomplishments Faulkner was awarded a Nobel Prize in 1950 and in acceptance made a brief but important statement about his belief "that man will not merely endure: he will prevail . . . because he has a soul, a spirit capable of compassion and sacrifice and endurance" and "the writer's duty is to write about these things."

FAUSET, JESSIE REDMON (1882–1961), born in New Jersey of a long-established family of free blacks, was probably the first black woman to become a member of Phi Beta Kappa, upon her graduation from Cornell (1905). After graduate study at the University of Pennsylvania and the Sorbonne she became a high-school teacher of French and Latin and an editor of DuBois's *The Crisis,* which she opened to new young writers of the Harlem Renaissance. She herself wrote four novels: *There Is Confusion* (1924), a love story concerning an educated black woman who wants to be a concert singer and a black man whom she helps in his fight to become a doctor; *Plum Bun* (1929), presenting two sisters, one who passes for white while living in Greenwich Village, where she has an unhappy love affair with a white man, the other admitting her race and living affirmatively in Harlem; *The Chinaberry Tree* (1931), another story about black women and the need for them to accept their heritage; and *Comedy: American Style* (1934), depicting an insecure, frustrated black woman.

FEARING, KENNETH (1902–61), poet and novelist, born in Chicago, resident in New York after graduation from the University of Wisconsin. *Angel Arms* (1929), *Poems* (1935), *Dead Reckoning* (1938), *Afternoon of a Pawnbroker* (1943), and *Stranger at Coney Island* (1949) are verse satires of disintegrating, contemporary, middle-class life. His *New and Selected Poems* appeared in 1956. His

novels include *The Hospital* (1939), about a moment in the big institution; *Clark Gifford's Body* (1942), a modern parallel of John Brown's raid; *The Big Clock* (1946), a fast-paced tale of murder and a manhunt; and *The Crozart Story* (1960).

Federalist, *The,* 85 essays in support of the Constitution, signed by the pseudonym Publius, and written mainly by Hamilton, ♦ assisted by Madison ♦ and Jay. ♦ First printed (1787–88) in the form of letters to the New York *Independent Journal, Packet,* and *Daily Advertiser,* they were collected and revised by Hamilton (2 vols., 1788). There are many critical editions, including those of P.L. Ford and H.C. Lodge. The latter summarizes the long controversy over the authorship by attributing 51 essays to Hamilton, 14 to Madison, 5 to Jay, 3 to Hamilton and Madison in collaboration, and 12 to either Hamilton or Madison.

At the time of writing, the purpose was principally to persuade New York voters to accept the Constitution, but the collected essays have come to be considered an authority on abstract principles of American government, and many Supreme Court decisions have been based in part on statements in *The Federalist.* The first paper, written by Hamilton, outlines the intention of numbers 1 to 51: "to discuss the following interesting particulars:—The utility of the UNION to your political prosperity—The insufficiency of the present Confederation to preserve that Union—The necessity of a government at least equally energetic with the one proposed, to the attainment of this object—The conformity of the proposed Constitution to the true principles of republican government—its analogy to your own State constitution—and lastly, The additional security which its adoption will afford, to the preservation of that species of government, to liberty, and to property." Specific subjects include "Dangers from Foreign Force and Influence" and "from Dissensions between the States"; "The Union as a Safeguard against Domestic Faction and Insurrection"; "Commercial Relations and a Navy"; "Revenue"; "Economy in Government"; "The Powers Necessary to the Common Defense"; "Militia"; "Power of Taxation"; and "Restrictions on the Authority of the Several States." Numbers 52 to 83 proceed to a detailed analysis of the governmental functions as defined by the Constitution, while the last two essays refute objections and summarize the general argument.

FEIBLEMAN, PETER S[TEINAM] (1930–), novelist born in New York City, reared in New Orleans, for seven years resident in Spain, whose novels include *A Place Without Twilight* (1958) and *The Daughters of Necessity* (1959), treating families in the South, respectively black and wealthy white; and *The Columbus Tree* (1972), about Americans in Spain. *Tiger Tiger Burning Bright* (1963) is his dramatization of his first novel. *Strangers and Graves* (1966) collects four novellas.

FEIKEMA, FEIKE, see *Manfred, Frederick.*

Feminism, reform movement aiming at the social, educational, and political equality of women with men, which arose during the late 18th century. The first great document of feminism was the *Vindication of the Rights of Woman* (1792), by the English author Mary Wollstonecraft. American women, including Abigail Adams and Mercy Otis Warren, were just as early in agitating that the Constitution specifically state the rights of women. Later prominent leaders in America included Emma Willard, who wrote a *Plan for Improving Female Education* (1819); Margaret Fuller, who wrote *Woman in the Nineteenth Century* (1845); and Harriet Farley, who edited the *Lowell Offering.* As an early result of feminist agitation, Oberlin College was the first institution of higher learning to grant degrees to women (1837). After the convention led by Elizabeth Stanton, Lucretia Mott, and others (1848), the movement became a predominantly political one for woman suffrage. With suffrage gained by the 19th Amendment (1920), further work for women's rights moved spasmodically and, on the whole, slowly. It finally became dynamic in the 1960s with the creation of the National Organization for Women (NOW) as a leader of the cause of feminism, thereafter called Women's Liberation. A major thrust was toward passage of an Equal Rights Amendment (ERA) to the Constitution, although it failed, but that was only part of a large movement for social changes rather than mere political action as women worked for full equality in every way, socially, legally, educationally, commercially, and sexually. Outstanding expositions of the so-called Women's Lib include *The Feminine Mystique* (1963) by Betty Friedan and *Sexual Politics* (1970) by Kate Millett, but there are many other champions of the cause and journals for it, like *Ms.,* founded in 1971 by Gloria Steinem and others. Aspects of the feminist dynamic have become more evident in diverse ways by women writers of very various sorts, ranging, for example, over the warm-hearted autobiographies of Maya Angelou, the sociopolitical essays and fiction of Renata Adler, the personal poetic statements of Anne Sexton, and the frank expressions of sexuality and individual independence of Erica Jong.

FERBER, EDNA (1887–1968), Michigan-born novelist and playwright, resided in New York City. After her first novel, *Dawn O'Hara* (1911), she wrote the short stories about the business woman Emma McChesney, collected in *Roast Beef, Medium* (1913), *Personality Plus* (1914), and *Emma McChesney and Co.* (1915). Besides other collections of stories, including *Mother Knows Best* (1927), she was the author of successful novels: *Fanny Herself* (1917); *The Girls* (1921), a study of three generations of women; *So Big* (1924, Pulitzer Prize), about Selina, a truck gardener, and her sacrifices for her son Dirk; *Show Boat* (1926), the romantic story of Magnolia Hawks, leading lady of her father's showboat troupe, who marries Gaylord Ravenal, a gambler, and after he deserts her becomes a successful singer; *Cimarron* (1930), about the 1889 land rush in Oklahoma and the region's later development; *American Beauty* (1931), about Polish immigrants in Connecticut; *Come and Get It* (1935), about the Wisconsin logging industry; *Saratoga Trunk* (1941), about a Creole adventuress and a cowboy gambler at a Saratoga (N.Y.) spa in the 1880s; *Great Son* (1945), about four generations of a Seattle family; *Giant* (1950), set in Texas; and *Ice Palace* (1958), set in modern Alaska but presenting its past too. *Show Boat* was made into an operetta (Kern and Hammerstein, 1927); and with George S. Kaufman she wrote plays, including *Minick* (1924), based on one of her stories; *The Royal Family* (1927), lampooning the Barrymores; *Dinner at Eight* (1932); and *Stage Door* (1936). *A Peculiar Treasure* (1939) and *A Kind of Magic* (1963) are autobiographies.

FERLINGHETTI, LAWRENCE (1920–), New York-born poet and publisher resident in San Francisco, with whose Beat movement◆ he is identified. He was the publisher of Ginsberg's *Howl* and his City Lights Bookshop was a center for many writers and artists in the late '50s. His own works include *Pictures of the Gone World* (1955), *A Coney Island of the Mind* (1958), *Starting from San Francisco* (1961), *After the Cries of the Birds* (1967), *The Secret Meaning of Things* (1969), *Tyrannus Nix* (1969), *Open*

Eye, Open Heart (1973), *Who Are We Now?* (1976), and *Endless Life* (1981), colloquial poems, often topical in subject, and suited to public reading; *Her* (1960), a novel about an artist's search for the ideal in the guise of a woman; *Unfair Arguments with Existence* (1962), experimental plays; and *Routines* (1963), proposals for happenings. With Nancy Peters he created *Literary San Francisco* (1980), a pictorial history.

Few Figs from Thistles, A, satirical poems by Edna St. Vincent Millay. ◆

FIEDLER, LESLIE A[ARON] (1917–), professor at State University of New York, Buffalo, whose lively and often very witty literary criticism appears in his works of "literary anthropology," *Love and Death in the American Novel* (1960); *Waiting for the End* (1964), on 20th-century American literature and culture; *The Return of the Vanishing American* (1968), on the Western as genre; *The Stranger in Shakespeare* (1972); and *Collected Essays* (1971), often pursuing archetypal myths and making psychic explorations. *What Was Literature?* (1982) suggests that the popular products of mass society, literary and other, are more important than the high art of sophisticated culture. He has written stories, *The Last Jew in America* (1966) and *Nude Croquet* (1969), and a novel, *The Messengers Will Come No More* (1974). *Being Busted* (1969) deals with his arrest for possession of marijuana, and *Freaks* (1978) surveys myths about and social responses to physical abnormality.

FIELD, EUGENE (1850–95), filled his column "Sharps and Flats" in the Chicago *Daily News* (1883–95) with whimsical humor and with verse—often in real or imaginary dialects—that appealed to the popular taste in humor and sentiment. Among his best-known poems are the sentimental "Little Boy Blue" and the "Dutch Lullaby" ("Wynken, Blynken, and Nod"), both set to music by Reginald DeKoven and also by Ethelbert Nevin. His collections of newspaper contributions include *A Little Book of Western Verse* (1889), *A Little Book of Profitable Tales* (1889), *With Trumpet and Drum* (1892), *A Second Book of Verse* (1892), *The Holy Cross and Other Tales* (1893), *The Love Affairs of a Bibliomaniac* (1896), and *The House* (1896).

FIELD, RACHEL [LYMAN] (1894–1942), Massachusetts author of such children's books as *The Cross-Stitch Heart and Other One-Act*

Plays (1927) and *Hitty, Her First Hundred Years* (1929), and novels for adults, including *Time Out of Mind* (1935), *All This, and Heaven Too* (1938), and *And Now Tomorrow* (1942).

Fifty Grand, short story by Hemingway, in *Men Without Women.* ◆

Figure in the Carpet, The, tale by Henry James, ◆ collected in *Embarrassments* (1896).

Considered to be a self-revelation of the author, this is the narrative of an earnest young critic's study of the works of the brilliant novelist Hugh Vereker—his search for "the figure in the carpet," which Vereker tells him cryptically is the key to an appreciation of his books, although no one has yet understood it. The young man repeats this to his friend Corvick, an experienced critic, who dedicates himself to discovering the secret figure, and claims to have done so when he marries Gwendolyn Erme, who has been equally anxious to know the solution. Corvick is accidentally killed before writing his projected essay, and the young critic can elicit from Gwendolyn only the assertion that her husband told her the secret. Later she marries another critic, Drayton Deane. After both Gwendolyn and Vereker have died, the young man meets Deane and implores him to divulge the secret. The astonished Deane knows nothing of it, and the disappointment of the young man is mitigated by the torment of the second husband, who thinks his wife may have considered him unworthy of sharing the sacred confidence.

Financier, The, novel by Dreiser, ◆ published in 1912 and revised in 1927. The story and its sequel *The Titan* ◆ are based on the career of C.T. Yerkes, a flamboyant financier of Philadelphia, Chicago, and London.

Frank Algernon Cowperwood, son of a steady, unimaginative Philadelphia bank clerk, grows to manhood in the years before the Civil War, and early demonstrates shrewdness, personal magnetism, self-command, and ability at leadership. By the outbreak of the war, he is operating a successful note-brokerage business, is married to Lillian Semple, an attractive widow several years his senior, has a son and daughter, and a few years later seems firmly established as a millionaire business leader and art collector. His ambition is unsatisfied, however, and he becomes associated with Edward Butler, a wealthy contractor, one of the "Big Three" in local politics, with whom he manages deals in stocks and the building of streetcar lines. Butler's daughter Aileen, ten years younger than Cowperwood, attracts him by her beauty, intelligence, and spirit, and the two form a liaison which they conceal for a period of years. Although he now has prestige, power, and personal happiness, the financier overreaches himself in manipulations with city money, and is caught short in the panic of 1871. When Butler refuses to aid him, Cowperwood is indicted for grand larceny, and imprisoned. His father, now president of his bank, is ruined by the scandal, but Cowperwood remains calm and confident. Released a year later, he obtains a divorce, and marries Aileen, whose father has died. In the panic of 1873 he acquires millions by clever trading, and leaves Philadelphia for a wider field of activities in Chicago.

FINEMAN, Irving (1893–   ), author of novels which include *This Pure Young Man* (1930), a story of adolescent development; *Lovers Must Learn* (1932), concerned with American expatriates in Paris; *Hear, Ye Sons* (1933), a story of life in Russian Poland in the 19th century; *Doctor Addams* (1939), about the contrast between the laboratory work of a research scientist and the disorder in his personal life; *Jacob* (1941), an autobiographical novel; *Ruth* (1949), a version of the Biblical story; and *Helen Herself* (1957), a modern novel. *Woman of Valor* (1961) is a biography of Henrietta Szold, the founder of Hadassah.

FINK, Mike (1770?–1823?), keelboatman on the Ohio and Mississippi rivers, noted for tall tales of his exploits, which made him as fabulous as Paul Bunyan. Accounts of his adventures appeared as early as 1829, when tales derived from oral sources found their way into print. There are 11 versions of his death, and his daughter Sal is probably an entirely mythical creation. He figures in works by many writers, including Emerson Bennett. T.B. Thorpe, J.M. Field, and John Neihardt.

FISHER, Vardis [Alvero] (1895–1968), Idaho author, for a time taught English at the University of Utah (1925–28) and at New York University (1928–31), but is best known for his fiction concerned with his region, his own experiences, and man's civilization. After his early works, *Toilers of the Hills* (1928) and *Dark Bridwell* (1931), novels dealing with the repressive effects of frontier life, he wrote his tetralogy concerned with the

life of Vridar Hunter, his not too subtly named alter ego. The first of these, *In Tragic Life* (1932), published in England as *I See No Sin* (1934), is the story of the boyhood and adolescence of the hypersensitive Vridar, who is terrified by the hardships of life on a Western farm, and by the Puritan rigidity of family standards. *Passions Spin the Plot* (1934) deals with his disillusion at failing to discover the meaning of life through attending college at Salt Lake City, and his marriage to the half-Indian girl Neloa. *We Are Betrayed* (1935) tells of his attempt to escape inner confusion by going to war, his return to college, and the conflicts between his Mormon background and the doctrines of Freud. In this state of mind, his mental cruelty drives Neloa to suicide. *No Villain Need Be* (1936) shows Vridar as a professor at a Mormon college and as a struggling author among New York bohemians, and his eventual discovery that there can be no peace for the individual until all men reach "a splended fellowship."

Fisher next wrote several independent novels: *April, A Fable of Love* (1937), about a girl's escape from the monotony of Idaho ranch life; *Forgive Us Our Virtues* (1938), the story of a psychology professor's discovery of the way lives are affected by sexual inhibitions; *Children of God* (1939), a historical novel of the Mormon movement; *City of Illusion* (1941), a story of the Comstock Lode; *The Mothers: An American Saga of Courage* (1943), about the Donner Party; *Pemmican* (1956), about the Hudson's Bay Company; *Tale of Valor* (1958), about the Lewis and Clark expedition; and *Mountain Man* (1965), about the Rocky Mountain fur trade.

The Testament of Man, a series of 12 novels on human development, includes *Darkness and the Deep* (1943), about primitive apemen; *Golden Rooms* (1944), about Neanderthal man; *Intimations of Eve* (1946), about the period when men were hunters, and women tillers of the soil; *Adam and the Serpent* (1947), about the beginning of social institutions and a developing patriarchy; *The Divine Passion* (1948), about the era recorded in the Old Testament; *The Valley of Vision* (1951), about Solomon's times; *The Island of the Innocent* (1952), about Greek and Jew in the time of the Maccabees; *A Goat for Azazel* (1956), about the origins of Christianity; *Jesus Came Again* (1956), the life of a man named Joshua, which parallels that of Jesus; *Peace Like a River* (1957), about the asceticism of early Christianity; *My Holy Satan* (1958), subtitled "a novel of

Christian twilight," about medieval Christianity and the Inquisition; and *Orphans in Gethsemane* (1960).

Other works include a revision and extension at great length of the Vridar Hunter tetralogy; *Sonnets to an Imaginary Madonna* (1927); *The Neurotic Nightingale* (1935), essays; *God or Caesar? The Writing of Fiction for Beginners* (1953); *Love and Death* (1959), collected stories; *Suicide or Murder? The Strange Death of Governor Meriwether Lewis* (1962); and *Thomas Wolfe as I Knew Him* (1973).

FITCH, [WILLIAM] CLYDE (1865–1909), author of more than 30 popular plays, usually vehicles for specific stars. *Barbara Frietchie* (1899) was written for Julia Marlowe, *Nathan Hale* (1899) for Nat Goodwin, *Beau Brummell* (1890) for Richard Mansfield, and *Her Great Match* (1905) for Maxine Elliott. Fitch was extremely versatile, writing farces, society dramas, historical plays, and problem plays, always with an understanding of what would be effective on the stage. Serious studies of the social, financial, and political aspects of New York City are contained in *The Climbers* (1901) and *The City* (1909). His popular farce, *Captain Jinks of the Horse Marines* (1901), was revised in 1925 as a musical comedy. *The Girl with the Green Eyes* (1902), a psychological study of jealousy, is generally considered to be his most important work. His collected plays were edited by M.J. Moses (1915).

FITTS, DUDLEY (1903–68), instructor of English at Phillips Academy, Andover, was well known for colloquial metrical translations of Aristophanes' plays, *Lysistrata* (1954), *The Frogs* (1955), *The Birds* (1957), and *Ladies' Day* (1959), a version of *Thesmophoriazusae*. With Robert Fitzgerald he translated Euripides' *Alcestis* (1935) and Sophocles' *Oedipus* (1949), and he also wrote other translations as well as original poetry. He edited the Yale Series of Younger Poets (1960–68).

FITZGERALD, F[RANCIS] SCOTT [KEY] (1896–1940), born in St. Paul, Minn., where part of his youth was spent until he went to Princeton (1913). There he was a friend of Edmund Wilson♦ and John Peale Bishop♦ and was a leader in theatrical and literary activities until he left because of academic difficulties, and then, after a brief return, to enter the army (1917). While being trained in U.S. camps he wrote the initial draft of his first novel, *This Side of Paradise*♦ (1920), set

at his alma mater and an expression of a new generation and its jazz age. His book having caught the flavor and interests of the changing era, his stories were in great demand by both the popular *Saturday Evening Post* and the critical *Scribner's* as he became a chronicler of the manners and moods of the time. From these journals came his next works, *Flappers and Philosophers* (1920) and *Tales of the Jazz Age* (1922), the latter including "The Diamond as Big as the Ritz."♦ In keeping with the tone of the stories, he himself became a character of the period, the handsome, witty, charming author married to a glamorous girl named Zelda, and both living life as though it were one great party. His lesser, second novel, *The Beautiful and Damned* (1922), was a minor work telling of a rich, aristocratic young artist and his wife foundering in dissipation, suggesting something of the Fitzgeralds' own extravagant life. This was followed by his satirical play, *The Vegetable; or, From President to Postman* (1923), reissued (1976) with previously cut scenes. Then came *The Great Gatsby*♦ (1925), his finest novel, a sensitive and symbolic treatment of themes of contemporary life related with irony and pathos to the legendry of the "American dream." Although he continued to write stories, collected in *All the Sad Young Men* (1926) and later in *Taps at Reveille* (1935), and worked ahead on his most extensive novel, *Tender Is the Night*♦ (1934), his personal life suffered the tragedies of his wife's nervous breakdown and his own loss of security as he became sick and saw his critical esteem and public reception deteriorate, leading him to write the touching essays posthumously collected by Edmund Wilson in *The Crack-Up* (1945). His view of the psychological and spiritual malaise of modern life in *Tender Is the Night* he tried to clarify by a revision not published until after his death. He managed to pick up pieces of his life as a motion picture scenarist in Hollywood, about which he wrote his impressive final novel, *The Last Tycoon*♦ (1941), portraying a studio mogul and his industry, a work not completed because of the author's death by heart attack. *Afternoon of an Author* (1958) collects lesser stories and essays, and *The Pat Hobby Stories* (1962) are 17 tales, written just before his death, about a Hollywood hack writer down on his luck. A great resurgence of popularity led to several new collections of his magazine contributions, including *The Apprentice Fiction* (1969), *In His Own Time* (1971), *The Basil and Josephine Stories* (1976), and *The Price Was High* (1979). His correspondence, beyond that in *The Crack-Up,* appears in *Letters* (1963) and *As Ever, Scott Fitz-* (1972). His *Poems* were collected in 1981.

FITZGERALD, Robert Stuart (1910–85), after graduation from Harvard became a writer for *Time* (1936–49) and a professor of creative writing, after 1965 at Harvard. In addition to his own poetry collected in *A Wreath for the Sea* (1943), *In the Rose of Time* (1956), and *Spring Shade* (1971), he translated the *Odyssey* (1961), for which he received a Bollingen Prize, the *Iliad* (1974), and, with Dudley Fitts, plays of Sophocles and Euripides. *Enlarging the Change* (1984) is a book on literary criticism.

FITZGERALD, Zelda (1899–1948), wife of F. Scott Fitzgerald, whose turbulent life and marriage are reflected in his *Tender Is the Night* and her novel, *Save Me the Waltz* (1932), her version of their life together.

Five Nations, see *Iroquois.*

Fixer, The, novel by Bernard Malamud,♦ published in 1966, winner of a National Book Award and a Pulitzer Prize.

Yakov Bok, a middle-aged Jew, eking out a living as a handyman or "fixer" in Czarist Russia about 1910, after an unhappy marriage leaves his home province for Kiev. There he chances to rescue a man named Lebedev who was undergoing some kind of physical seizure. As a reward he is made an accountant at Lebedev's brickworks and has to live in an area closed to Jews. When a local Christian boy is found murdered in a grisly way, Yakov is arrested as a scapegoat by officials who want a reason to start a pogrom. After two years in prison, often in solitary confinement, he is finally brought to trial, innocent but aware that there is "no such thing as an unpolitical man, especially a Jew."

Flammonde, poem in iambic pentameter couplets by E.A. Robinson,♦ published in *The Man Against the Sky* (1916). It describes the mysterious elderly citizen of Tilbury Town, Flammonde, who, although outwardly a failure, is a constant source of sympathy for the town's troubled and needy.

Flathead Indians, name applied to several Northwestern tribes that practiced occipital flattening on their children, and even to such other tribes as the Nez Percé. The Salish of western Montana, the only tribe now known

by the name, actually never employed this practice. The Flatheads figure in the *Journals of Lewis and Clark, The Adventures of Captain Bonneville,* and James Hall's *The Wilderness and the War Path.*

FLETCHER, John Gould (1886–1950), Arkansas author, was influenced by Southern traditions, although from 1908 to 1933 he lived mainly in Europe. In England he was a leader of the Imagists, whose poetic theory is exemplified in *Irradiations: Sands and Spray* (1915) and *Goblins and Pagodas* (1916), and he experimented with polyphonic prose. His later work, beginning with *Breakers and Granite* (1921) and including *Branches of Adam* (1926), *The Black Rock* (1928), *XXIV Elegies* (1935), *The Epic of Arkansas* (1936), *South Star* (1941), and *The Burning Mountain* (1946), shows a return to the American scene, a more mystical tone, and a tendency toward classic forms. After his return to Arkansas he became a leader of the Agrarians. ♦ He won a Pulitzer Prize for his *Selected Poems* (1938). His prose works include *Paul Gauguin* (1921); *John Smith—Also Pocahontas* (1928); *The Two Frontiers* (1930), about Russia and the U.S.; *Arkansas* (1947), a social history; and his autobiography, *Life Is My Song* (1937).

Floating Opera, The, novel by John Barth.♦

Flowering Judas, title story of a collection by Katherine Anne Porter,♦ issued with five others in 1930 and with still another four in 1935.

Laura, a 22-year-old American resident in Mexico, has an uneasy relationship with the revolutionary leader Braggioni, who courts her, and with the principles of the revolution that she vaguely assists. When Braggioni returns to his wife one evening, Laura falls asleep, dreaming of Eugenio, another revolutionary leader, who killed himself in prison with sleeping pills she had brought him. In the dream he asks her to eat the flowers of a Judas tree so as to travel with him to the land of death, but when he accuses her of being a murderer, she awakens herself, crying aloud "No," in negation of the nameless disaster that she has long feared.

Flowering of New England, The, literary history by Van Wyck Brooks.♦

Folger Shakespeare Memorial Library, Washington, D.C. (dedicated 1932), is the gift of Henry Clay Folger (1857–1930) and his wife and is administered by his alma mater, Amherst. It contains the greatest collection in the U.S. of Shakespeareana, including 79 copies of the First Folio, and a great collection dealing with English culture before 1800.

Following the Equator, autobiographical narrative by Clemens, ♦ published in 1897 under his pseudonym Mark Twain. Describing the Australian section of his lecture tour around the world (1895), he works up, in a rather pedestrian way, second-hand materials concerning the aborigines, early settlers, and local animals. Although there are witty interludes, vivid accounts such as the one of the Sepoy Mutiny, and satirical disquisitions on the Boer War and imperialistic morality, the book has little of the inspiration that distinguishes Clemens's other travel accounts. In India, he is oppressed by the overpopulation, superstition, plagues, famines, and disasters, and by the disillusioned society resigned to the constant repetition of barren and meaningless processes, which foreshadows the pessimism of the books he wrote in 1898.

FOOTE, MARY HALLOCK (1847–1938), New York-born author, married a civil engineer (1876), and spent her later life in Colorado, Idaho, and California. Her novels of Western life include *The Led-Horse Claim* ♦ (1883), *The Chosen Valley* (1892), and *Cœur d'Alene* ♦ (1894). Among her later works of fiction are *Edith Bonham* (1917) and *Ground-Swell* (1919). Her reminiscences were edited by Rodman Paul as *A Victorian Gentlewoman in the Far West* (1972). *Angle of Repose* (1971) by Wallace Stegner is partly based on her life.

For Lancelot Andrewes, critical essays by T.S. Eliot, ♦ published in 1928. The title essay is an examination of the style and thought of the 17th-century Anglican bishop, whom Eliot finds to be not only important in the history of the church, but also distinguished for his prose and his vital thought. In "The Humanism of Irving Babbitt," Eliot questions the possibility of a long life or significance for the New Humanism, since it is presented as an alternative to religion. He demonstrates that Babbitt's faith in civilization must have as discipline a center of dogmatic moral reference, derived from religious authority.

For the Union Dead, collection of poems by Robert Lowell, ♦ published in 1964.

The last of the 35 poems of the book is the title poem, first published with a different title in the paperback edition (1960) of *Life Studies.* In 17 unrhymed, meterless quatrains it treats with bitter irony an example of degradation in New England as symptomatic of modern life, presenting the Boston Common dug up for an underground garage so that its monument to the noble, idealistic Colonel Shaw and his black regiment in the Civil War has to be propped up by a plank while "giant finned cars nose forward . . . a savage servility slides by on grease." Other poems deal with the Puritan heritage, the threat of nuclear war, the corruption of modern society, and personal relations, of which the most intense is the double sonnet, "Night Sweat," presenting the poet's own emotional turmoil.

For Whom the Bell Tolls, novel by Hemingway, ♦ published in 1940. The title is derived from a sermon by Donne: "No man is an *Iland,* intire of it selfe; every man is a peece of the *Continent* . . . And therefore never send to know for whom the *bell* tolls; It tolls for *thee.*"

Robert Jordan, an American, has entered the Loyalist army during the Spanish Civil War of the 1930s, and has been sent to join a guerrilla band in the mountains near Segovia to blow up a strategic bridge at the exact minute that will help a Loyalist advance. During the three days and nights that he spends in the guerrillas' cave, he awaits with a romantic opposition to heroism what he suspects will be his own destruction and that of his companions. He falls in love with Maria, daughter of a Republican mayor, who has seen her parents killed and was herself raped by Falangists. Her close-cropped hair is a symbol of her tortures; Jordan helps her to regain her desire to live. Their passionate love is abetted by the powerful woman Pilar, who dominates the group by her force of character, gusto, and love of the Republic. Her man Pablo is wily but lacks belief and hence courage. The others include foul-mouthed Agustín; pedantic, dignified Fernando; the gypsy Rafael; and the adoring Andrés. A sense of impending disaster develops, with smoldering opposition within the group, a Falangist attack on the guerrilla leader El Sordo on a neighboring hill, acts of cowardice by Pablo, and a mission by Andrés to Loyalist headquarters to carry a note from Jordan saying the advance is likely to fail, with the messenger impeded by the Communists' bureaucracy and suspicion. The generals finally realize they should have cancelled the attack, but it is too late. Leaving the retreat, Jordan successfully blasts the bridge. In the attempt to flee he is wounded, and forces the others to leave him. He lies on the hillside almost delirious, restraining himself from suicide so that he may shoot the leader of the Fascists, and thinks, "I have fought for what I believed in for a year now. If we win here we will win everywhere. . . ."

FORD, JESSE HILL (1928–), Alabama-born author, graduated from Vanderbilt University, for some time was a resident of Tennessee, the region where his fiction is set. *Mountains of Gilead* (1962), *The Liberation of Lord Byron Jones* (1965), *The Feast of St. Barnabas* (1969), and *The Raider* (1975) are novels, the last about a pre-Civil War period marked by violence, part of it between blacks and whites. *The Conversion of Buster Drumwright* (1963) is a play, and Ford was co-author of a film version (1969) of his second novel. *Fishes, Birds and Sons of Men* (1967) collects stories.

Foregone Conclusion, A, novel by Howells,♦ published in 1875.

Forest Hymn, A, blank-verse poem by Bryant,♦ published in 1825, and reprinted as the title piece of a volume (1860).

Expressing a concept of nature akin to that of Wordsworth, Bryant proclaims, "The groves were God's first temples," where He raised shrines for beauty before the advent of human religion, and the flower still seems "an emanation of the indwelling Life" which pervades all things. The poet communes in the forest with "the perpetual work of thy creation, finished, yet renewed forever," and prays that men, in meditation there, may

... to the beautiful order of thy works
Learn to conform the order of our lives.

Fort Barthold Indians, see *Arikara* and *Mandan.*

Forty-niners, emigrants to California in the gold rush of 1849, which followed the discovery of gold by James Marshall (Jan. 1848). By June 1848, the local rush to the gold fields was in full course, and President Polk's message to Congress (Dec. 5), incorporating news of the possibilities of great wealth, inaugurated the international excitement. Ships were diverted from their usual routes to carry gold seekers from European countries, China, Australia, and the South Seas. Many

Mexicans came by overland routes, and it is believed that a total of nearly 100,000 persons had entered the territory by the end of 1849. The thousands of emigrants from the eastern U.S. used three principal routes: by ship around Cape Horn; a combination of sea and land travel, crossing Central America by the Panama or Nicaragua route; and in wagon trains across the Plains. The common goal was the Mother Lode region. Innumerable diaries, letters, and other writings of the period have been published, including those by Alonzo Delano,♦ "Dame Shirley,"♦ and Bayard Taylor,♦ and the forty-niners figure frequently in literature, the earliest major fictional interpretation being by Bret Harte.

42nd Parallel, The, novel by Dos Passos,♦ published in 1930. It is the first of the trilogy *U.S.A.* (collected 1938), including *1919*♦ (1932) and *The Big Money*♦ (1936). Interspersed in the narrative are brief biographies of Debs, Burbank, Haywood, Bryan, Minor Keith, Carnegie, Edison, Steinmetz, and La Follette. (For critical discussion, see *Dos Passos.*)

Fainy ("Mac") McCreary, a social idealist, bums across the continent, works for an anarchist printer in San Francisco, edits an I.W.W. paper, marries, deserts his wife and children, and goes to Mexico with a revolutionist.

J. Ward Moorehouse becomes a shrewd, ruthless trader, enters Pittsburgh journalism and advertising, divorces his wife, marries a steel heiress, Gertrude Stagle, and fosters a plan of "co-operation" between capital and labor at the outbreak of World War I.

Eleanor Stoddard, an interior decorator in Chicago, decorates the Moorehouse home, and becomes intimate with the capitalist.

Janey Williams, left friendless when her brother Joe enlists in the navy, becomes Moorehouse's secretary, and goes with him to Mexico in a vain attempt to "buy" Mac; again in New York, she quarrels with her brother over U.S. participation in the war, which he denounces as the plot of munitions makers. She becomes intimate with G.H. Barrow, a dishonest labor leader, when Moorehouse concentrates his ardor on Eleanor.

Charley Anderson, a poor North Dakota boy, is attracted to socialism and the I.W.W., travels through the U.S., meets Ben Compton, brother of Janey's roommate Gladys, and learns of Moorehouse's big business propaganda. Disillusioned by the suppression of socialism, and craving action, he and his friend Doc Rogers join a French ambulance corps.

Fountainhead, The, novel by Ayn Rand,♦ published in 1943. It celebrates the achievements of an architect (presumably suggested by Frank Lloyd Wright) who is fiercely independent in pursuing his own ideas of design and who is therefore an example of the author's concept of Objectivism, which lauds individualism and "rational self-interest."

Four Million, The, 25 short stories by W.S. Porter,♦ published in 1906 under his pseudonym O. Henry. A preface explains the title: "Not very long ago some one invented the assertion that there were only 'Four Hundred' people in New York City who were really worth noticing. But a wiser man has arisen—the census taker—and his larger estimate of human interest has been preferred."

"The Gift of the Magi" is a tale of two New Yorkers who sell their most valued possessions to buy Christmas gifts for each other. Unknown to her husband, the wife sells her hair in order to purchase a chain for his watch, while he secretly sells the watch to buy her a pair of combs. "Of all who give and receive gifts, such as they are wisest. . . . They are the magi. . . ." "The Furnished Room" tells of a cheap boardinghouse room haunted by the "ghosts" of unfortunate residents. An attractive girl, penniless and despairing of her career as a singer, commits suicide in it. A week later her former sweetheart rents it. When he scents a trace of the mignonette she used to wear but can find no clue of her presence, he too commits suicide.

Four Quartets, cycle of poems by T.S. Eliot,♦ collected in 1943. These religious and philosophic meditations have a musical structure implied by their title, and are composed of four long lyrics titled by place names: "Burnt Norton," the site of an English country house; "East Coker," the English village that was the Eliot family's ancestral home; "The Dry Salvages," a group of rocks off Cape Ann, Massachusetts; and "Little Gidding," the British site of a 17th-century Anglican community. The dominant themes are time present, time past, time future, timelessness, identity, memory, consciousness, and place.

Four Saints in Three Acts, opera with libretto by Gertrude Stein♦ and music by Virgil Thomson.

Fourierism, communistic Utopian system for the reorganization of society, devised by Charles Fourier (1772–1837), French socialist author. He argued that the universe was so created that there is a harmonious connection between the organic and inorganic, between man and God, man and the world, and the world and the universe. Human passions are unchangeable, but, with due allowance for the variety of individual aptitudes and abilities, they may be brought to an equilibrium or harmony. For this purpose, Fourier wished to create phalansteries, social units of some 1600 persons, who would divide their labor according to their natural inclinations and abilities. Thereby the artificial restraints of ordinary civilized life would be destroyed, while a systematic agricultural society would be created in which all could live as one family, and yet retain many individual rights. Albert Brisbane, Horace Greeley, and Parke Godwin were the principal figures in developing Fourierism in the U.S. The best-known colony was the North American Phalanx. ♦ Brook Farm♦ was for a time Fourierist, and a colony was founded in Texas by Fourier's chief disciple, Victor Considérant.♦ The movement had a temporary vogue among U.S. reform groups, but declined after the 1850s.

FOX, PAULA (1923–), born in New York City, a professor of English at C.W. Post University, and author of the novels *Poor George* (1967), concerning the unhappy life of a Manhattan schoolteacher; *Desperate Characters* (1970), depicting the relatively undramatic but loveless life of a middle-aged married couple in New York City; *The Western Coast* (1972), presenting a young New York woman trying to find herself by moving to California, and then to England; and *The Widow's Children* (1976), about the relationships and lack of affection among family members. She has also written books for children.

FOX, WILLIAM PRICE (1926–), Illinois-born author, reared in South Carolina, the setting for his stories collected in *Southern Fried* (1962) and *Southern Fried Plus Six* (1968) and his novel *Moonshine Light, Moonshine Bright* (1967), the salty tale of two teenaged boys involved in a variety of skulduggery. *Ruby Red* (1971), another novel, whose setting is extended to Nashville, presents the seamy life of girls trying to get into country-singer show business. *Dr. Golf* (1963) collects humorous articles on golf.

FRANKLIN, BENJAMIN (1706–90), born in Boston, at the age of ten began to work with his father, a tallow chandler and soap boiler, and from 12 to 17 was apprenticed to his half-brother James Franklin, to whose *New England Courant* he contributed his Dogood Papers♦ (1722). He had little formal education, but read widely, being particularly influenced by Locke, Shaftesbury, Xenophon, the *Spectator,* and some of Cotton Mather's works. After a quarrel with his brother (1723), he ran off to Philadelphia, where he entered the printing shop of Samuel Keimer. Under the patronage of Governor Keith, he was sent to England to buy equipment for his own press, but, failing to receive the necessary money, he worked in a London printing house. While abroad he wrote *A Dissertation on Liberty and Necessity, Pleasure and Pain* (1725) to refute Wollaston's *Religion of Nature Delineated,* which he had set in type.

He returned to Philadelphia (1726), and four years later had his own press, from which he issued *The Pennsylvania Gazette* (1729–66), contributing such pieces as the letters of Anthony Afterwit and Alice Addertongue, and "A Witch Trial at Mount Holly." He also wrote, at this time, the Busy-Body Papers♦ and "Dialogues between Philocles and Horatio" (1730). He made a common-law union (1730) with Deborah Read, daughter of his first landlady, by whom he had two children. He was also the father of two illegitimate children. By frugality, industry, and native shrewdness he established a successful business. His popularity and prestige were enhanced by his *Poor Richard's Almanack♦* (1733–58) and the Junto Club♦ (1727).

In his pragmatic way, he devised at 22 a "religion" for the attainment of useful virtues, holding firmly to the belief that the most acceptable service to God is doing good to men. When he had kept his shop so well that it kept him, he became a leader in philanthropic, scientific, and political affairs. He initiated projects for establishing city police, for paving, cleaning, and lighting the streets, and for the first circulating library. He also founded the American Philosophical Society, a city hospital, and an Academy for the Education of Youth, which was the forerunner of the University of Pennsylvania. For a time he published the second monthly magazine issued in America, *The General Magazine* (1741), and some of his diverse interests are reflected in *A Proposal for Promoting Useful Knowledge* (1743), *Plain Truth, or*

Serious Consideration on the Present State of the City of Philadelphia (1747), and *Proposals Relating to the Education of Youth in Pensilvania* (1749). He was interested in every sort of natural phenomenon, and made many scientific experiments, including the famous one with a kite to show the identity of lightning and electricity (reported in *Experiments and Observations on Electricity,* 1751–54). He had already invented the Franklin Stove (described in his *Account of the New Invented Pennsylvania Fire Place,* 1744), as well as a new kind of clock.

After holding minor public offices, he was made deputy postmaster-general for the colonies (1753–74), and was Pennsylvania's representative at the Albany Congress (1754), at which his "Plan of Union" was seriously considered. In 1757 he was sent to England to attempt to secure better governmental conditions for the colony, and he remained abroad, with brief interruptions, until 1775. There he was intimate with Burke, Hume, Adam Smith, Chatham, and other thinkers; received degrees from three British universities; continued his scientific interests; wrote a pamphlet that anticipated the Malthusian theory of population; and published *An Historical Review of the Constitution and Government of Pennsylvania* (1759) and an influential argument for the retention of Canada, *The Interest of Great Britain Considered with Regard to Her Colonies* (1760). He protested against the Stamp Act, and in his examination before the House of Commons (1766) increased his prestige by his lucid replies, which showed that the tax was contrary to custom.

When Georgia, New Jersey, and Massachusetts joined Pennsylvania in designating him as their agent, Franklin's position assumed virtually ambassadorial importance, Meanwhile he published his *Cool Thoughts on the Present Situation of Our Public Affairs* (1764) and a *Preface to the Speech of Joseph Galloway* (1764), asking for the replacement of the proprietary government of Pennsylvania by a royal charter. He demanded no colonial rights except those already possessed by all British subjects, and his admiration for England lessened in proportion to his increasing loyalty to the colonies. He strongly opposed the Townshend acts, and expressed his feeling in two satires, the "Edict by the King of Prussia"♦ (1773) and "Rules by Which a Great Empire May Be Reduced to a Small One"♦ (1773).

Because of his connection with the affair of the *Letters* of Thomas Hutchinson♦ (1772), he was dismissed from his postal position. Feeling that Lord North was driving the colonies into rebellion, he returned to America to serve in the Continental Congress, become postmaster-general, and aid in drafting the Declaration of Independence, after which he was sent to France to negotiate a treaty. Enthusiastically welcomed by the French as a witty and benign backwoods sage, a sort of Rousseauistic Socrates who was going to restore the Golden Age, he succeeded in securing a treaty of commerce and defensive alliance (Feb. 1778), after Burgoyne's surrender inspired confidence in America's prospects. In this year he was appointed plenipotentiary to the French court, obtained repeated loans from France, and negotiated commercial treaties with Sweden and Prussia. He also found time for scientific matters, for a frivolous correspondence with Mme Helvetius and Mme Brillon, and for amusing his friends by such urbane bagatelles from his private press at Passy as *The Ephemera* (1778), *The Morals of Chess* (1779), *The Whistle* (1779), and *The Dialogue Between Franklin and the Gout* (1780). He was a member of the commission that signed the Treaty of Paris (Sept. 1783), and in 1785 he returned home. After serving three years as president of the executive council of Pennsylvania, he became a member of the Federal Constitutional Convention, in which capacity he signed the Constitution, although he did not entirely approve of it. His last public act was the signature of a memorial to Congress for the abolition of slavery, and less than a month before his death he wrote an ironic letter "On the Slave Trade" to *The Federal Gazette*, as brilliant as the similar "Edict by the King of Prussia," which he had composed 17 years before.

His *Autobiography*, commenced in 1771, was never finished, and breaks off abruptly during the account of the year 1757, with a few random comments on the years 1757–59. It was published in England, France, and Germany before the American edition of 1818, but the complete work did not appear in English until 1867. This account is the epitome of Franklin's spirit. In it one sees him as a typical though great example of 18th-century enlightenment, a Yankee Puritan who could agree with Rousseau and Voltaire, and use the language of Defoe and Addison with a genial homely twang. His style, perfectly adapted to the ends to which he devoted it, is lucid, precise, and salty, revealing both his mental and moral temper. His mind was pragmatic, and though his greatest enthusiasm was reserved for science, he had a mellow tolerance for all types of thought. With candor and common sense, he relished the various turns in his life and took them easily, understanding and sharing the Gallic spirit while remaining pungently American. A definitive, scholarly edition of his *Papers* (1959–   ) under the editorship of Leonard W. Labaree (vols. 1–14) and William B. Willcox (vols. 15–40) is planned.

Franny and Zooey, stories by J.D. Salinger. ♦

FREDERIC, HAROLD (1856–98), New York author, at 19 was a reporter on the *Utica Observer* and three years later became its editor. He was next editor of the *Albany Evening Journal* and London correspondent of *The New York Times*. His first novel, *Seth's Brother's Wife* (1887), is a realistic picture of New York farm life, local politics, and the less glamorous aspects of journalism. *The Lawton Girl* (1890) is the story of a girl who tries to live down a tarnished reputation in her native New York town. After a fantasy, *The Return of the O'Mahony* (1892), he wrote *The Copperhead* (1893), his first significant work, depicting the intolerant attacks upon Abner Beach, a New York farmer who opposes Abolitionism when this movement is sweeping the North during the Civil War. *The Damnation of Theron Ware* ♦ (1896), a realistic story of the fall of a Methodist minister, was his most popular work. He also wrote a historical novel, *In the Valley* (1890), dealing with the Revolution, and *Marsena and Other Stories* (1894), about the Civil War. *March Hares* (1896), *Gloria Mundi* (1898), and *The Market Place* (1899) are romantic stories based on his knowledge of English life. A scholarly edition of his *Major Works* began publication in 1978.

Freedom of the Will, The, treatise by Jonathan Edwards, ♦ published in 1754. The full title is *A Careful and Strict Enquiry into the Modern Prevailing Notions, of that Freedom of Will which is supposed to be Essential to Moral Agency, Vertue and Vice, Reward and Punishment, Praise and Blame*. Written to uphold the doctrine of necessity against Arminianism, the work was frequently translated and reprinted, became a primary document in Calvinistic theology, and won Edwards eminence among American philosophers.

Defining the will as "that by which the mind chooses anything," and freedom or liberty as "the power, opportunity, or advantage, that any one has to do as he pleases, or conducting in any respect, according to his pleasure," the author bases his case for predestined necessity on the postulate that every event must have a cause. "That whatsoever begins to be which before was not, must have a Cause why it then begins to exist, seems to be the first dictate of the common and natural sense which God hath implanted in the minds of all mankind. . . ." Since volitions are events, they must have causes: "It is that motive, which, as it stands in the view of the mind, is the strongest, that determines the Will." Human motives impel us in the direction of what seems most agreeable, and this direction is determined entirely without independent activity on the part of the individual will. There is, then, no liberty of choice; liberty consists in the ability to act as one chooses. Having established this fundamental position, the author proceeds to refute the fallacies of "the Arminian notion of Liberty of Will," to answer possible objections, and to assert that his necessitarian position is the basis of Calvinistic doctrine.

FREEMAN, Mary E[leanor] Wilkins (1852–1930), was born in Randolph, Mass., and spent most of her life there until her marriage in 1902, when she moved to New Jersey. The scenes she knew in eastern Massachusetts form the background for most of her tales of New England rural life. Her early work is a dispassionate observation of local character and constitutes an important contribution to the local-color school by its study of repressed people in a decaying social system, capturing their spirit through their dialect. Her first collections of tales, *A Humble Romance* (1887) and *A New England Nun*♦ (1891), established her reputation and contain her finest work. The novels, *Jane Field* (1893), *Pembroke* (1894), and *Jerome, a Poor Man* (1897), show that her forte was not the novel but the short tale revealing a dominant characteristic. Mrs. Freeman was also the author of works in other forms, including *Giles Corey, Yeoman* (1893), a play about the Salem witchcraft trials; *The Heart's Highway* (1900), a historical novel; *The Portion of Labor* (1901), a social novel; and *The Wind in the Rose Bush* (1903), stories of the supernatural. *Edgewater People* (1918) is a collection of short stories of the type and nearly of the caliber of her early work.

FRENCH, Alice (1850–1934), born in Massachusetts, lived most of her life in Arkansas and Iowa, which provided the settings for her fiction written under the pseudonym Octave

Thanet. A conventional figure in the local-color movement, she added nothing to its traditions except a certain interest in labor problems in the West. She is best known for her short stories, which are collected in such volumes as *Knitters in the Sun* (1887), *Stories of a Western Town* (1893), *The Missionary Sheriff* (1897), *The Captured Dream* (1899), and *Stories That End Well* (1911). Among her novels are *Expiation* (1890), *The Man of the Hour* (1905), and *A Step on the Stair* (1913).

FRENCH, Marilyn (1929–), New York City-born author, received an A.B. from Hofstra and a Ph.D. from Harvard, leading to her first book, *The Book as World—James Joyce's "Ulysses"* (1976). She has also written novels, *The Women's Room* (1977), a feminist view of a woman's life, and *The Bleeding Heart* (1980), about an affair between two Americans in their forties, resident in England.

FRENEAU, Philip [Morin] (1752–1832), born in New York of Huguenot ancestry, was educated privately and at the College of New Jersey (Princeton). There he was a classmate of Madison and Brackenridge, and with the latter wrote the poem *The Rising Glory of America,* which was read at the graduation exercises (1771) and published the following year. While at college he also wrote "The Power of Fancy" and other poems. At the outbreak of the Revolution he wrote eight satirical, anti-British poems, but left the country to become a secretary in the home of a prominent planter on the island of Santa Cruz in the West Indies, where he wrote "The Beauties of Santa Cruz,"♦ "The Jamaica Funeral,"♦ and "The House of Night," romantic poems inspired by the lush tropical atmosphere. On his voyage home (June 1778) he was captured by the British, but was soon set free. After a short stay at home, he set out again for the West Indies (1780), only to be captured and, after a questionable trial, remanded to the British prison ship *Scorpion* in New York harbor. After a period of brutal treatment and starvation he was exchanged as a prisoner of war (July 1780). His experiences inspired the poem *The British Prison Ship*♦ (1781). During the next three years he was employed in the Philadelphia post office, and in his leisure poured forth a steady stream of satirical poetry that confirmed his title of "the poet of the American Revolution." From 1784 to his marriage in 1790 he was master of a brig, leading him to write poems on life at sea. He published his first collection, *Poems* (1786), a volume of *Miscellaneous Works* (1788), and his journal, *National Gazette* (1791–93), a lively Jeffersonian paper that attacked Hamilton, who accused him of being Jefferson's mouthpiece, and even Washington called him "that rascal Freneau." He published *Poems Written Between the Years 1768 and 1794* (1795) and essays titled *Letters on Various Interesting and Important Subjects* (1799). In 1809, he published a two-volume edition of his collected poems, and in a final edition of 1815 included the patriotic and satirical poems prompted by the War of 1812. *Last Poems* (1946) contains 50 poems, mainly on topics of the day, originally published in periodicals between 1815 and 1832. Among his best-known short poems of freedom are "Libera Nos, Domine," the ode "God Save the Rights of Man," "To the Memory of the Brave Americans," "On the Memorable Victory of John Paul Jones," and "To My Book," while among his noteworthy poems of romantic fancy are "The Indian Burying Ground,"♦ "The Wild Honey Suckle,"♦ "The Indian Student,"♦ "On a Honey Bee," "On Retirement," and "To a Caty-did."

FRIEDAN, BETTY (1921–), born in Illinois, graduated from Smith College (1942), and has been a leader of feminist activities. Her major writing, *The Feminine Mystique* (1963), was followed by *It Changed My Life: Writings on the Women's Movement* (1976) and *The Second Stage* (1981).

FRIEDMAN, BRUCE JAY (1930–), New York City author, whose first novel, *Stern* (1962), presents a neurotic Jewish man with black humor, characteristic of later novels including *A Mother's Kisses* (1964), comically portraying a Jewish mother who not only chaperons her son Joseph at college but is an erotic figure in her own right; *The Dick* (1970), dealing with a Jewish public relations man in police headquarters; and *About Harry Towns* (1974), portraying a middle-aged screenwriter. His other works include the plays *Scuba Duba* (1968), *Steambath* (1970), and *Foot in the Door* (1979); stories collected in *Far from the City of Class* (1963), *Black Angels* (1966), and *Let's Hear It for a Beautiful Guy* (1984); and a comic self-help manual, *The Lonely Guy's Book of Life* (1978).

From Here to Eternity, novel by James Jones,♦ published in 1951.

Private Robert E. Lee Prewitt reports to a

U.S. army base in Hawaii in 1941 and is subjected to psychological and physical harassment because, though known as a boxer in civilian life, he refuses to fight in the division championship since he had once accidentally blinded a friend in the ring. He breaks under "the treatment" and hits a noncom, for which he is sent to the stockade; there he experiences the brutality of Fatso Judson, the sergeant in charge, a sadist responsible for the death of his fellow prisoner Blues Berry, but from whom his friend Angelo had escaped by discharge after feigning madness. Prewitt kills Judson in a knife fight and runs off to hide with Lorene, a prostitute he loves. When the Japanese attack Pearl Harbor, Prewitt is killed by an M.P. as he tries to return to his company.

Frontier, in America the wilderness region marked by the farthest advance of white colonization. The most popular conception of the significance of the frontier is derived from F.J. Turner,♦ although his theory has been attacked as "poetic," contradictory, and oversimplified. He contended that "the existence of an area of free land, its continuous recession, and the advance of American settlement westward, explain American development. . . ." This development is said to result from a return to primitive conditions on a continually advancing frontier, which is the meeting point of savagery and civilization. American democracy, according to Turner, came out of the American forest, whence it gained strength each time it touched a new frontier.

. . . To the frontier the American intellect owes its striking characteristics. That coarseness and strength, combined with acuteness and acquisitiveness; that practical, inventive turn of mind, quick to find expedients; that masterful grasp of material things, lacking in the artistic but powerful to effect great ends; that restless, nervous energy; that dominant individualism, working for good and for evil, and withal that buoyancy and exuberance which comes with freedom— these are the traits of the frontier, or traits called out elsewhere because of the existence of the frontier.

The frontier has helped to shape some distinctive aspects of American literature, affecting the ballad,♦ the tall tale,♦ and the local-color movement.♦ It has less directly influenced American writing in so many ways as to defy concise summary. The physical frontier, which had a beginning at the Atlantic coast and moved westward until free land was exhausted (*c.*1890), during its progression may be said to have had some influence on virtually every American author, and especially formed the attitude and manner of such writers as Crèvecœur, William Byrd, Timothy Flint, Caroline Stansbury Kirkland, Irving, Cooper, Simms, Longstreet, Crockett, Edward Eggleston, Clemens, Harte, Joaquin Miller, Garland, Frank Norris, E.W. Howe, Rölvaag, Jack London, E.L. Masters, Sinclair Lewis, and Willa Cather. Successive frontiers likewise had their folk idols, among whom may be named Samuel Brady (Pennsylvania), Simon Kenton (Ohio), Lewis Wetzel (West Virginia), Davy Crockett (Tennessee and Texas), Sam Houston (Texas), Billy the Kid (New Mexico), Hugh Glass (Missouri), Kit Carson and Jim Bridger (the Great Plains), Wild Bill Hickok (Kansas), Daniel Boone (Kentucky), Mike Fink (the Mississippi River), and Paul Bunyan (the lumber frontier).

FROST, ROBERT [LEE] (1874–1963), member of a New England family, was born in San Francisco and taken at the age of ten to the New England farm country with which his poetry is identified. After a brief attendance at Dartmouth, where he disliked the academic attitude, he became a bobbin boy in a Massachusetts mill. A short period at Harvard was followed by further work, making shoes, editing a country newspaper, teaching school, and finally farming. This background of craftsmanship and husbandry had its effect upon his poetry in more than the choice of subjects, for he demanded that his verse be as simple and honest as an axe or hoe. After a long period of farming, he moved to England (1912–15), where he published his first book of poems, *A Boy's Will* (1913), whose lyrics, including "Into My Own," "Revelation," "Mowing," and "Reluctance," are marked by an intense but restrained emotion and the characteristic flavor of New England life. He returned to the U.S. to settle on a New Hampshire farm, having achieved a reputation as an important American poet through the publication of *North of Boston* (1914), described by the author as "a book of people," and showing brilliant insight into New England character and the background that formed it. Among the poems in this volume are "Mending Wall,"♦ "The Death of the Hired Man,"♦ "The Code,"♦ "The Wood-Pile,"♦ "Home Burial," and "A Servant to Servants."♦ The same expressive idiom and brilliant observation appear in *Mountain Interval* (1916), containing such characteristic poems as "The Road Not Taken,"♦ "Birches,"♦ "Bond and Free,"♦

"A Time To Talk," "Snow," "Putting in the Seed," and "An Old Man's Winter Night."

The shrewd humor and Yankee understatement that distinguish such poems as "The Cow in Apple Time," "A Hundred Collars," and "Brown's Descent" are exhibited also in Frost's witty self-critical remarks, such as "I might be called a Synecdochist; for I prefer the synecdoche in poetry—that figure of speech in which we use a part for the whole." In both emotion and language he was restrained, and conveyed his messages by implication. Although his blank verse is colloquial, it is never loose, for it possesses the pithy, surcharged economy indigenous to the New Englander. His genre pieces, in the form of dramatic idylls or monologues, capture the vernacular of his neighbors north of Boston. Frost explained his realism by saying, "There are two types of realist—the one who offers a good deal of dirt with his potato to show that it is a real one; and the one who is satisfied with the potato brushed clean. . . . To me, the thing that art does for life is to clean it, to strip it to form." His next book, *New Hampshire* (1923, Pulitzer Prize), shows his ability to deal with genial, informal subjects, as in "The Star-Splitter,"♦ "Maple,"♦ "The Axe Helve,"♦ "New Hampshire,"♦ and "Paul's Wife," and to concentrate emotional impact into a few clean-stripped lines, as in "To Earthward,"♦ "Two Look at Two,"♦ "Stopping by Woods on a Snowy Evening,"♦ "Gathering Leaves," "Fire and Ice," and "Fragmentary Blue." In 1928 he issued a fifth new volume, *West-Running Brook,* with the same warm lyric quality that had characterized his first book. His *Collected Poems* (1930, Pulitzer Prize) assembled in one volume the work that has a lifelong continuity in its rhythms, its clear focusing on the individual, and its observation of the native New England background.

After collecting his poems, although he held positions as an affiliated teacher at Amherst, Harvard, and Michigan, he continued his literary career and in 1936 published *A Further Range* (Pulitzer Prize), whose lyrics, though more playful in blending fact and fantasy, have beneath their frivolity a deep seriousness. A new edition of *Collected Poems* (1939) was followed by *A Witness Tree* (1942, Pulitzer Prize); two blank-verse plays, *A Masque of Reason* (1945), about Job, and *A Masque of Mercy* (1947), in which Biblical characters in modern setting discuss ethics and man's relation to God; and *Steeple Bush* (1947) and *In the Clearing* (1962), later lyrics. Some of his correspondence appears in *Letters to Louis*

Untermeyer (1963) and *Selected Letters* (1964).

Fruitlands, cooperative community led by Alcott♦ (June 1844–Jan. 1845) at Harvard, Mass. In his original plan for a "Concordium," Alcott proposed an institution in the country, where members would labor on the land and live a vegetarian life, basing their unity on religious love, with education and mutual labor leading to "the harmonic development of their physical, intellectual, and moral natures." The experiment died mainly because of the conflict between Alcott's love of family life and his admiration for the ideas of the English "Alcott House" of Charles Lane, who desired to submerge the individual in a communistic society. Louisa Alcott's *Transcendental Wild Oats* is a fictional account of Fruitlands.

FUCHS, DANIEL (1909–), New York City writer whose *Summer in Williamsburg* (1934), *Homage to Blenholt* (1936), and *Low Company* (1937) attracted little attention until republished as *Three Novels* (1961), when they were praised as a moving depiction of the humor and pathos of Lower East Side Jewish life. During his later years as a Hollywood script writer he published a fourth novel, *West of the Rockies* (1971), set in Hollywood, and collected stories and sketches in *The Apathetic Bookie Joint* (1979).

Fugitive, The (1922–25), bimonthly little magazine published at Nashville, Tenn. It contained poetry and criticism championing regionalism and attacking "the highcaste Brahmins of the Old South." Most of the contributors were associated with Vanderbilt University, among them being Donald Davidson, Andrew Lytle, Merrill Moore, John Crow Ransome, Laura Riding, Allen Tate, and Robert Penn Warren. A collection from the magazine was issued as *Fugitive Anthology* (1928).

FULLER, CHARLES (1939–), Philadelphia-born playwright whose themes draw upon his experiences as a black and in the army (1959). His works include *The Perfect Party* (1968), an ironic view of a community of racially mixed couples; *In the Deepest Part of Sleep* (1974); *Candidate!* (1974), concerning the election of a black mayor in a northern city; *The Brownsville Raid* (1976), about black soldiers dishonorably discharged because of racial prejudice during the era of

Theodore Roosevelt; *Zooman and the Sign* (1980), depicting a tough teenager in Philadelphia; and *A Soldier's Play* (1981, Pulitzer Prize), a murder mystery presenting issues about relations between blacks and whites.

FULLER, HENRY BLAKE (1857–1929), Chicago novelist whose writing varied between the two genres of realistic depiction of the Middle West and fanciful portrayals of courtly Europe, which he knew through his travels. His first novel, published under the pseudonym Stanton Page, was *The Chevalier of Pensieri-Vani* (1890), an episodic work contrasting American and European cultures. *The Châtelaine of La Trinitée* (1892) is in the same cosmopolitan spirit. His most successful realistic work, *The Cliff-Dwellers* (1893), a highly dramatic story of social and financial life in Chicago centered on the activities of office workers in a skyscraper, was followed by *With the Procession* (1895), a story of social strivings in Chicago. *The Last Refuge* (1900) is an idealistic and fanciful Sicilian romance, while *Under the Skylights* (1901) contains stories about Chicago artist life, one of which, "The Downfall of Abner Joyce," is a fictional treatment of Hamlin Garland. After *Waldo Trench and Others* (1908), stories set in Italy and contrasting American and continental standards, he returned to the Chicago scene in *On the Stairs* (1918), portraying two men who go up and down the stairs of economic and social life. *Bertram Cope's Year* (1919) deals with a University of Chicago instructor. *Gardens of This World* (1929), a continuation of his first book, and *Not on the Screen* (1930), a satire on motion pictures as well as a realistic account of Chicago, were both posthumously published, and show Fuller to have been still preoccupied with two contrasting types of fiction.

FULLER, [SARAH] MARGARET (1810–50), born at Cambridgeport, Mass., was educated by her father, read Ovid at the precocious age of eight, and as a young woman developed friendships with the Transcendentalists, who accepted her as their intellectual equal. From 1839 to 1844 she held a series of conversational classes at Elizabeth Peabody's home, and had a strong influence on the most cultivated circle of Boston society. In her discussions with this group originated the material of her book *Woman in the Nineteenth Century* (1845), the first mature consideration of feminism by an American touching every aspect of the subject, intellectual, economic, political, and sexual. She edited *The Dial*♦ (1840–42) and in 1844 published her *Summer on the Lakes in 1843,* an optimistic view of Western life based on a visit to Chicago. During her two years in New York, on the staff of the *Tribune,* she established a wide reputation as a critic, and in the summer of 1846 she visited Europe, writing letters which appeared on the front page of the *Tribune.* She had intended to publish a book on the Roman revolution of 1848–49, but this was not completed. After *Papers on Literature and Art* (1846), her works were posthumously published. They are *At Home and Abroad* (1856) and *Life Without and Life Within* (1859). In Italy she was an ardent adherent of Mazzini, and married one of his followers, the Marquis Angelo Ossoli. The ship that brought them to the U.S. was wrecked in a storm off Fire Island, near New York. The body of her child was the only one recovered, and her manuscript on the Roman revolt was lost. Her *Memoirs* (1852) were written by Emerson, W.H. Channing, and J.F. Clarke. Because of her dynamic personality, she figures frequently in literature, being probably the prototype of Elsie Venner,♦ and of Zenobia in *The Blithedale Romance.*♦ In Lowell's *Fable for Critics,* as Miranda,

She always keeps asking if I don't observe a
Particular likeness 'twixt her and Minerva.

Fundamentalism, conservative religious movement of various Protestant denominations during the 20th century, embodying a protest against the incursions of science into revelation. Its object is to maintain traditional interpretations of the Bible and fundamental doctrines of Christian faith. The five points of the doctrine whose literal acceptance is demanded are the Virgin birth, physical resurrection of Christ, inerrancy of the Scriptures, vicarious atonement, and the physical second coming of Christ. The struggle against the teaching of evolutionary theories, which are considered to threaten orthodoxy, became a national issue in the Scopes trial in Tennessee (1925), in which Clarence Darrow defended J.T. Scopes, a public-school teacher who expounded evolution, while William Jennings Bryan upheld the Fundamentalist point of view, winning the case for the prosecution. The trial was the subject of the play *Inherit the Wind* (1955) by Jerome Lawrence and Robert E. Lee. Fundamentalist views have been widely revived and extended during the 1970s and 1980s by some ministers in their churches and allied institutions and on their television programs, becoming a political force under the rubric "The Moral Majority." As in the past, the theory of evolution is challenged while they fulminate against or urge censorship of books, films, and the media whose expression or values they disapprove of.

G

GADDIS, WILLIAM (1922–), born in New York City, after four years at Harvard and much foreign travel published *The Recognitions* (1955), a long, elaborate, experimental, satirical novel with settings as diverse as the author's travels, treating a Yankee artist whose original talent is overwhelmed by his career as a copyist of old masters. His second novel, *J R* (1975, National Book Award), again a rich parodic treatment of hypocrisy and corruption, centers on an ambitious young man's success in business.

GAINES, ERNEST J. (1933–), Louisiana-born author, since age 13 resident in the San Francisco Bay area, has drawn on his background for stories of blacks in his native state. His novels include *Catherine Carmier* (1964); *Of Love and Dust* (1967); *The Autobiography of Miss Jane Pitman* (1971), a saga of black history in the South seen through the reminiscences of a 110-year-old woman; *In My Father's House* (1978); and *A Gathering of Old Men* (1983). *Bloodline* (1968) collects stories of children's views of adult life.

GALE, ZONA (1874–1938), Wisconsin author, known for her short stories in the local-color tradition, collected in such volumes as *Friendship Village* (1908), *Yellow Gentians and Blue* (1927), and *Bridal Pond* (1930). She won a Pulitzer Prize for her dramatization of her novel *Miss Lulu Bett* (1920), a study of a woman repressed by the bleak life of the Middle West. Other novels include *Birth* (1918), dramatized as *Mr. Pitt* (1924), the story of a similarly repressed man, whose simple honesty is scorned by the wife who deserts him and the son who is ashamed of his insignificance; *Faint Perfume* (1923), a character study of a poor relation; and *Papa La Fleur* (1933), the story of a country girl whose ideas of liberty for the younger generation hurt the feelings of both her father and her sweetheart. *The Secret Way* (1921) is a book of poems. *Portage, Wisconsin* (1928) completes the autobiographical narrative begun in *When I Was a Little Girl* (1913). *Still Small Voice* (1940), a biography, was written by August Derleth.

GANN, ERNEST K[ELLOGG] (1910–), Nebraska-born author, whose works include the popular novel *The High and the Mighty* (1953), about the passengers of a disabled plane flying from Hawaii to San Francisco, and *Fate Is the Hunter* (1961), a memoir of his experiences as a flyer, including service as an airline pilot and during World War II in the Army Air Transport Command.

Gant, EUGENE, hero of *Look Homeward, Angel*♦ and *Of Time and the River.*♦

Garbage Man, The: A Parade with Shouting, play by John Dos Passos,♦ produced in 1925 as *The Moon Is a Gong,* and published under the present title in 1926. Experimental in form, the play is a poetic arraignment of oppressive forces in contemporary society.

GARDNER, ERLE STANLEY (1889–1970), California lawyer and writer of detective fiction whose central figure is the lawyer Perry Mason, who serves as sleuth. Earliest in his lengthy series were *The Case of the Velvet Claws* (1933) and *The Case of the Sulky Girl* (1933). In the 30 years following publication of these works, sales of his books in the U.S. totaled 135,740,861 copies.

GARDNER, ISABELLA [STEWART] (1915–), Massachusetts-born poet, whose lively and loving lyrics written in diverse forms appear in *Birthdays from the Ocean* (1955), *The Looking Glass* (1961), and the collection *West of Childhood* (1965). Edith Sitwell said, "the poems arise from her personality," and the author herself said, "they are the poems of a poet who is woman first and poet second. . . . My poems celebrate and affirm life, but they are also elegiac. My central theme is the . . . failure of the I–Thou relationship." She was married to Allen Tate (1959–66) and was an associate editor of *Poetry* (1952–56).

GARDNER, JOHN [CHAMPLIN, JR.] (1933–82), after graduation from Washington University, St. Louis, and a Ph.D. from Iowa State University, became a professor of English at several universities and, beginning in the 1960s, a prolific and popular author.

His novels include *The Resurrection* (1966), about a professor of philosophy who returns to his upstate New York childhood home when he is dying; *The Wreckage of Agathon* (1970), a metaphysical analysis of civilization through the dialogue of a dying Greek philosopher and his disciple; *Grendel* (1971), a *tour de force* in telling the story of *Beowulf* from the sympathetic viewpoint of the monster; *The Sunlight Dialogues* (1972), a multicharactered philosophic and allegorical tale set in his birthplace, Batavia, N.Y.; *Nickel Mountain* (1973), a pastoral set in the Catskills characterizing a man through his relationships; *October Light* (1976, National Book Critics Circle Award), about the conflicts between an elderly brother and sister over political and philosophical issues; *Freddy's Book* (1980), a novel within a novel, ostensibly written by a monstrous 20th-century author, treating 16th-century Scandinavian history and related moral dilemmas; and *Mickelsson's Ghosts* (1982), about a philosophy professor caught up in emotional problems, personal and academic, and even in a violent Mormon mystery. Gardner also wrote *The King's Indian* (1974) and *The Art of Living* (1981), stories; *Dragon, Dragon* (1975), fairy tales for children; *A Child's Bestiary* (1977), in verse; and *In the Suicide Mountains* (1977), a fairy tale. *Jason and Medeia* (1973) is his epic poem of the classic story. His scholarly works include a biography of Chaucer (1977) and a study of his poetry (1977). His critical writings include *The Forms of Fiction* (1961) and *On Moral Fiction* (1978), a cantankerous consideration of modern American novels and their lack of moral content.

GARLAND, [HANNIBAL] HAMLIN (1860–1940), born in Wisconsin, after sharing the oppressive labor of farm life there and in Iowa and South Dakota went to Boston, where he came under the influence of Howells. Returning to the farmland of the Middle Border, he chose the hardships of the farmer for the subject of his stories, which are characterized by objective realism and ethical romanticism. They were collected in *Main-Travelled Roads*♦ (1891), *Boy Life on the Prairie* (1899), and *Other Main-Travelled Roads* (1910), the last containing stories from two previous books, *Prairie Folks* (1893) and *Wayside Courtships* (1897). The writing of these stories, all of which were completed before 1890, led Garland to believe that something besides realistic fiction was needed to ameliorate agricultural conditions. Ac-

cordingly, he wrote *Jason Edwards: An Average Man* (1892) as propaganda for the single-tax theories of Henry George, and *A Spoil of Office* (1892), a novel that, in exposing political corruption, also campaigned for the Populist party. After *A Member of the Third House* (1892), a novel showing the legislative power of the railroads, he wrote *A Little Norsk* (1892), depicting the bleak life of a Dakota farm girl, and *Rose of Dutcher's Coolly* (1895), telling of a girl's revolt against this life. *Crumbling Idols* (1894), a book of essays, sets forth the author's theory of "veritism," combining realism for a democratic purpose with individualism, stemming from Whitman and flavored by local color. *The Captain of the Gray-Horse Troop* (1902) deals with the unjust treatment of the Indians by frontiersmen and cattlemen, and *Cavanagh, Forest Ranger* (1910) with the conflict between cattle ranchers and representatives of the government attempting to conserve natural resources. After the force of his youth had partially been spent, he wrote his comparatively mellow autobiography, *A Son of the Middle Border* (1917), continued in *A Daughter of the Middle Border* (1921, Pulitzer Prize), and the thinner, semi-fictional works, *Trail-Makers of the Middle Border* (1926) and *Back-Trailers from the Middle Border* (1928). Subsequent volumes, *Roadside Meetings* (1930), *Companions on the Trail* (1931), *My Friendly Contemporaries* (1932), and *Afternoon Neighbors* (1934), dwindled into the category of garrulous memoirs. His last books were concerned with psychic research.

GARRETT, GEORGE [PALMER, JR.] (1929–   ), born in Florida, educated at Princeton, to which he returned as a professor after teaching writing and criticism at Hollins College and the University of South Carolina. His first publication was poetry, continued in *The Sleeping Gypsy* (1958), *Abraham's Knife* (1961), *For a Bitter Season* (1967), *Welcome to the Medicine Show* (1978), and *Love's Shining Child* (1981). He is also known for his fiction, his stories being collected in *King of the Mountain* (1958), *In the Briar Patch* (1961), *Cold Ground Was My Bed Last Night* (1964), *A Wreath for Garibaldi* (1969), and *The Magic Striptease* (1973). His novels include *The Finished Man* (1959), about Florida politics; *Which Ones Are the Enemy?* (1961); *Do, Lord, Remember Me* (1965), concerning religious revival show people; *Death of the Fox* (1971), a fictional biography of Sir Walter Raleigh; and *The Succession* (1984), about Queen Elizabeth and her successor, James I. *Sir Slob and the Princess* (1962) is a play for children.

GARRIGUE, JEAN (1914–72), Indiana-born poet, educated at the University of Chicago, published her poetry in *The Ego and the Centaur* (1947), *The Monument Rose* (1953), *A Water Walk by Villa d'Este* (1959), *Country Without Maps* (1964), *New and Selected Poems* (1967), and *Studies for an Actress* (1973). The poems are marked by glittering imagery influenced by Wallace Stevens and by sensitivity to the natural scene and to art. She also wrote a novel, *The Animal Hotel* (1966).

GARRISON, WILLIAM LLOYD (1805–79), spearhead of New England Abolitionism,♦ was born in Newburyport, Mass. During 1829–30 he edited *The Genius of Universal Emancipation* with Benjamin Lundy at Baltimore, but after imprisonment for libel, he returned to his home to pursue policies that were too radical for Lundy. In 1831 he began to publish *The Liberator,*♦ which he continued for 34 years. An ascetic, moralistic, pacifist, and noble agitator, Garrison constantly demanded immediate and complete emancipation of the slaves. Although the circulation of his paper was small, it drew wide attention because of the direct, forcible expression of its owner's passionate beliefs. He attacked the moderate elements who opposed him, disliked the actions of the Anti-Slavery Society, which he split asunder, and his own vituperation was equaled only by that of the slaveholders. He outdid the Southerners in advocating secession, since the Constitution, which permitted slavery, was to him a "Covenant with Death and an Agreement with Hell." After the Civil War, he retired from public activity. His books include *Thoughts on African Colonization* (1832), *Sonnets* (1843), and *Selections* (1852) from his speeches and writings. He was the subject of many works, including one of Whittier's finest poems.

GASS, WILLIAM H[OWARD] (1924–), graduated from Kenyon College, received a Ph.D. from Cornell and became a professor of philosophy while carrying on a literary career. His fiction includes *Omensetter's Luck* (1966), a novel; *In the Heart of the Heart of the Country* (1968), stories and novellas, evoking small-town life in the Midwest; and *Willie Masters' Lonesome Wife* (1970), a lively novella about a stripteaser's recollec-

tions and activities, which is a commentary on art in general. His essays appear in *Fiction and the Figures of Life* (1970) and *The World Within the Word* (1978). *On Being Blue* (1976) is a brief, fanciful meditation on the significance, sexual and other, of the color blue.

Gatsby, JAY, see *Great Gatsby, The.*

GELBER, JACK (1932–), Chicago-born author, whose first and most successful play, *The Connection* (1959), gives a sense of the lives of drug addicts by presenting their story as though it were real, with the heroin shots said to be real doses and the actors ostensibly drifters paid for their performances by the drugs received on stage. Later plays include *The Apple* (1961), a plotless series of confrontations among actors supposedly trying to devise a play; *Square in the Eye* (1966), a more conventional play about a man frustrated by family in his attempt to be a painter; *The Cuban Thing* (1969), on Castro's revolution; *Sleep* (1972); and *Rehearsal* (1976). A novel, *On Ice* (1964), treats the life of the Beat generation.

GELLHORN, MARTHA (1908–), foreign correspondent for *Collier's* (1937–45), whose war reports from the Spanish Civil War, Finland, China, Europe in World War II, and Java appear in *The Face of War* (1959). Her fiction includes *The Trouble I've Seen* (1936), about urban workers on relief during the Depression; *Two by Two* (1958), stories about marriage; *Pretty Tales for Tired People* (1965), stories; *The Lowest Trees Have Tops* (1969), a novel set in Mexico; and *The Weather in Africa* (1980). She was married to Hemingway (1940–45). *Travels with Myself and Another* (1979) is an autobiography.

General William Booth Enters into Heaven, title poem of a volume by Vachel Lindsay,♦ published in 1913. Intended to be sung to the music of the hymn "The Blood of the Lamb," its vigorous drumbeat rhythms describe the apotheosis of the Salvation Army founder, who enters the gates of Paradise at the head of a troop of criminals and slum dwellers:

> Christ came gently with a robe and crown
> For Booth the soldier, while the throng knelt
> down.

"Genius," The, novel by Dreiser,♦ published in 1915.

Handsome Eugene Witla, son of a middle-class family in an Illinois town, cherishes his bent toward drawing and writing, and is looked upon as a dreamer. Then, ambitious and curious about the world, he goes to work in Chicago, spending his spare time in art study. Engaged to Angela Blue, a school-teacher older than himself, he is employed in the art department of a Chicago paper, after which he goes to New York to achieve fame as an illustrator. Sincere but restless, he has affairs with several women, and marries Angela, who is incapable of understanding his tastes or his essential amorality. Eugene's paintings make him famous, but he suffers a nervous collapse, due to overwork and an intemperate sexual life. His savings gone and unable to paint even after a year's rest, he works for some time as a laborer. Then he rapidly climbs the ladder of business success to become managing director of a great publishing firm. Angela, jealous of his philanderings, attempts to win him back by becoming pregnant. He falls in love, however, with a society girl, Suzanne Dale, whose mother ends the affair by causing Eugene to lose his position. Angela dies at the birth of their daughter, and Eugene, belatedly penitent, devotes himself to the care of the child and to his true vocation of realistic painting.

Gentlemen Prefer Blondes, novel by Anita Loos. ◆

GEORGE, HENRY (1839–97), left his middle-class, devoutly Episcopalian Philadelphia home (1855) to sail as a foremast boy to Calcutta, where he was struck by the contrast between poverty and wealth. In 1857 the promise of work drew him to San Francisco, where he struggled against want, observing the rich new country come gradually under the control of a few land-hungry speculators. During the depression and labor troubles of 1877 he began writing his great work, *Progress and Poverty*◆ (1879), which attributes poverty to rent, and proposes a tax on land as the remedy for social ills. This doctrine of a single tax, developed in six other books, numerous periodicals, and his own weekly, *The Standard* (1886–92), won national prominence for its author, as well as the support of labor in his two unsuccessful New York mayoralty campaigns.

GERNSBACK, HUGO, see *Science fiction.*

Gerontion, poem by T.S. Eliot,◆ published in his *Poems* (1920), presents the fragmented thoughts of "an old man in a dry month," who without vital experience of faith is representative of the inanition of modern life and who, by means of images and allusions, yet shows his longing for spiritual rebirth and the expression of emotion.

Gettysburg Address, delivered by Lincoln at the dedication of a national cemetery (Nov. 19, 1863) on the site of the Pennsylvania battlefield where there occurred (July 1–3, 1863) the action that is considered the turning point of the Civil War. Lincoln's speech of three brief paragraphs, following a two-hour address by the principal orator, Edward Everett, was considered unimportant at the time, but has come to be viewed as one of the noblest and most significant expressions of American democracy. Calling for "increased devotion to that cause" for which the Gettysburg dead "gave the last full measure of devotion," he stated that the aim of the Civil War was to make possible "a new birth of freedom . . . that government of the people, by the people, for the people, shall not perish from the earth."

Giants in the Earth: A Saga of the Prairie, novel by Rölvaag,◆ published in Norway (1924–25) and in translation in the U.S. (1927). *Peder Victorious*◆ and *Their Fathers' God*◆ are sequels. The novel formed the basis for an opera (1951) by Douglas Moore.

GIBSON, WILLIAM (1914–), New York City-born dramatist, whose popular plays include *Two for the Seesaw* (1958), a comedy about the brief romance between a sweet girl from the Bronx and a Nebraska lawyer; *The Miracle Worker* (1960), about Helen Keller; and *Golda* (1977), about Golda Meir. Other works include *The Seesaw Log* (1959), about the production of his play with that title; *A Mass for the Dead* (1968), family memoirs; a musical adaptation of Odets's *Golden Boy* (1965); and poems.

Gift books, annual miscellanies widely distributed (*c.*1825–65), contained stories, essays, and poems, usually with a polite or moral tone, and were lavishly printed and adorned for use as Christmas or New Year gifts. Beginning with *The Atlantic Souvenir* (1825–32), the gift books contained some of the best art and literature of the period, when the popular monthly magazine was not yet fully developed. With the coming of the Civil War, some organizations employed the gift book as a medium of propaganda. Before the vogue spent itself, it was responsible for the publication of more than 1000 different volumes, ranging in format from muslin-bound 32mos at 37½¢ to magnificent folios at $20.

Gilded Age, The: A Tale of To-day, novel by Clemens♦ and C.D. Warner,♦ published in 1873 but dated 1874. It was dramatized by G.S. Densmore (1874), and Clemens revised the play the same year. The theme is that of unscrupulous individualism in a world of fantastic speculation and unstable values, and the title has become a popular name for the era depicted in the book, the boom times of post-Civil War years, when unbridled acquisitiveness dominated the national life.

"Squire" Si Hawkins moves, with his wife and family, from Tennessee to a primitive Missouri settlement, the current speculative project of his visionary friend, Colonel Beriah Sellers. During the journey, Hawkins adopts two unrelated orphans, Clay and Laura. Ten years pass, Sellers's optimism costs Hawkins several fortunes, and the children grow in constant expectation of great wealth. When the Squire dies, his family moves to Sellers's new promotion center, Hawkeye, where Laura is attracted by a philanderer, Colonel Selby, who abandons her after a mock-marriage. Her beauty impresses Senator Dilworthy, who invites her and her foster brother to Washington, and there they and Sellers are involved in the intrigues and financial deals of the unscrupulous senator. When Selby reappears, Laura resumes her liaison with him, later murdering him when he attempts to desert her again. She is acquitted after a spectacular court trial, but dies of a heart attack when her career as a lecturer is a failure.

GILDER, RICHARD WATSON (1844–1909), was an assistant editor of *Scribner's Monthly* after 1870, and when it was succeeded by *The Century* (1881) remained as editor until his death. In this position he was a leader of New York artistic, civic, and social life. The best of his 16 volumes of poetry is *The New Day* (1875), a cycle of love sonnets. He characterized his verse as "insufficient but irrepressible," and called himself a "squire of poesy."

Giles Goat-Boy; or, The Revised New Syllabus, novel by John Barth,♦ published in 1966.

In the metaphoric world called the University, control is held by a computer, WESAC, which is able to run itself and to tyrannize people, for it has the ability to subject them to a radiating and disintegrating force, that is, to EAT them, an acronym for its power of

"Electroencephalic Amplification and Transaction." WESAC is so out of hand that one of its developers, Max Spielman, believes it can be controlled only through reprogramming by a Grand Tutor, a prophet, who will bring a "New Syllabus," that is, a new philosophy. For this role and this purpose he selects George Giles, whom he had raised among goats as a goat, though he is actually a human found as an infant in the tapelift of WESAC. George enters the computer to destroy it, and learns to confound WESAC by answering its questions through paradoxes that paralyze the machine. When George emerges, authorities eager to put WESAC back into operation seize him and send him back to the animal site of his boyhood, for he is now the University's scapegoat.

GILMAN, CAROLINE HOWARD (1794–1888), born and reared in Massachusetts, came to know and love the South when her husband Samuel (also a New Englander and author of the hymn "Fair Harvard") accepted a Unitarian pulpit there. Her first book, *Recollections of a Housekeeper* (1834), a light narrative of domesticity, looked back to her old home in the North, but with her sense of a dual allegiance she followed it with *Recollections of a Southern Matron* (1838), another domestic narrative. They illustrated her belief that a common faith in the homely morality of family life shared by women North and South was more important than the societal and political beliefs that divided the men of these increasingly antagonistic regions. A similar attitude informs her autobiographical *The Poetry of Travelling in the United States* (1838). Other lesser works include *Tales and Ballads* (1839), prose stories and verses, and *Verses of a Life Time* (1849), as well as books for children.

GILROY, FRANK D[ANIEL] (1925–), Bronx-born playwright, educated at Dartmouth and the Yale Drama School, began his career with *Who'll Save the Plowboy?* (1962). His first Broadway production, *The Subject Was Roses* (1964), treating an Irish-American family of the Bronx, won a Pulitzer Prize. Later plays include *That Summer—That Fall* (1967), *The Only Game in Town* (1968), and *Present Tense* (1972), the last dramatized from his novel of the same title. He has published several other novels.

Ginger Man, The, novel by J.P. Donleavy,♦ published in Paris in an unexpurgated edition (1955), in the U.S. in an expurgated edition

(1958) and then complete (1965). The author dramatized it for London and Dublin production (1959) and U.S. publication (1961) and production (1963).

Sebastian Dangerfield, a red-headed American studying law at Trinity College, Dublin, after U.S. naval service in World War II, is living in poverty with his wife Marion and their baby because, contrary to his hopes, she receives no money from her wealthy father and because Sebastian squanders whatever cash he can get on liquor. While his friend Kenneth cannot lose his virginity, much as he tries to, Sebastian has constant affairs with women, sometimes, as with Miss Frost, their spinster roomer, to borrow funds, but mostly for fun. Marion leaves him but in time she lets him come to her, and he looks forward to temporary comfort from her and eventual inheritance from his father.

GINSBERG, ALLEN (1926–), New Jersey-born poet, after graduation from Columbia and work at odd jobs found his voice in San Francisco during the time of the Beat movement♦ with the publication of *Howl and Other Poems* (1956), which became famous when its publisher, Lawrence Ferlinghetti,♦ was tried and acquitted for issuing that allegedly obscene work. Its rhapsodic, passionate, Whitmanesque view of modern corruption brought Ginsberg a great reputation, enhanced by *Kaddish and Other Poems* (1961), whose title work was a moving, lyrical lament for his recently dead mother. He issued other, lesser collections with great rapidity, including *Empty Mirror* (1960), early poems; *Reality Sandwiches* (1963), written between 1953 and 1960; *Planet News* (1968), poems of the '60s; *T.V. Baby Poems* (1968); and *Ankor Wat* (1968). He also traveled widely, freely expressing his antiauthoritarian views as well as his new belief in Zen Buddhism, which made him the guru of a new generation, a cult figure for "drop-outs" of all ages who espoused the romantic, mystic, and pacifistic idea of "flower power," a phrase Ginsberg coined. A special sort of spokesman of the '60s, Ginsberg received formal honors in the next decade when *The Fall of America: Poems of These States* (1973) was granted a National Book Award. Other later collections include *The Gates of Wrath* (1973), rhymed poems written 1948–51; *First Blues* (1975); *Mind Breaths* (1977); *Plutonian Ode* (1981); and *Collected Poems 1947–1980* (1984). His prose includes *The Yage Letters* (1963), correspondence with William Bur-

roughs♦; *Indian Journals* (1970); *Allen Verbatim* (1974), lectures; and *Journals* (1977), texts of the 1950s and '60s. *As Ever* (1977) gathers the correspondence with Neal Cassady.

GIOVANNI, NIKKI (YOLANDE CORNELIA GIOVANNI, JR.) (1943–), born in Tennessee, educated at Fisk (A.B., 1967), is best known for her poetry, the early work often militantly black and socially conscious, the later, more personal and mellow. It has been published in *Black Feeling, Black Talk* (1968), *Black Judgement* (1968), *Re: Creation* (1970), *Poem of Angela Yvonne Davis* (1970), *My House* (1972), *The Women and the Men* (1975), *Cotton Candy on a Rainy Day* (1978), and *Those Who Ride the Night Winds* (1983). Her poems for younger readers appear in *Spin a Soft Black Song* (1971) and *Ego Tripping* (1973). *Gemini* (1971) collects essays, many autobiographical and others socially revolutionary or literary criticism. *A Dialogue* (1972) transcribes a tape-recorded talk with James Baldwin on racial and literary subjects, and *A Poetic Equation* (1974) is a similar dialogue with Alice Walker.

Girl of the Golden West, The, play by Belasco,♦ produced in 1905 and published in 1925. It became the libretto of an Italian opera by Puccini (1910).

"The Girl," saloon keeper and schoolmistress in a Far Western mining community, falls in love with Dick Johnson, an outlaw who loves her too. Johnson, wounded, is tracked to her cabin by the sheriff, Jack Rance, who also loves the Girl but accepts her offer to decide by a game of poker whether he shall have her or, if he loses, discontinue his search for her lover. The sheriff is bested by her cheating, but Johnson is captured when he leaves the cabin. When the miners see how much she loves her outlaw, they free him, and Johnson and "The Girl" start eastward to a new life.

GLASGOW, ELLEN [ANDERSON GHOLSON] (1874–1945), born in Richmond, Va., of an aristocratic Southern family, in 1897 published her first novel, *The Descendant. The Freeman, and Other Poems* (1902) is her only volume of verse. *The Voice of the People* (1900) was the first of a long series of novels recording the social and political background of her state from 1850 to the 1940s, and represented her revolt from the sentimental tradition of Southern fiction in depicting the genteel code of the Old South at bay before the new industrial revolution. This study, concerned with the rise of a farm boy to political prominence, and his death in a mob riot, was followed by such contrasts of life in the old and new social classes of the South as *The Battle-Ground* (1902), *The Deliverance* (1904), *The Wheel of Life* (1906), *The Ancient Law* (1908), *The Romance of a Plain Man* (1909), and *The Miller of Old Church* (1911). In *Virginia* (1913) and *Life and Gabriella* (1916) she wrote novels of Southern women victimized by a decaying code of chivalry. Three realistic studies of political and social conflicts followed: *The Builders* (1919); *Old Man in His Time* (1922); and *Barren Ground*♦ (1925). At this time she declared that "what the South needs now is—blood and irony," and she proceeded to write three satirical novels of manners, *The Romantic Comedians* (1926), *They Stooped to Folly* (1929), and *The Sheltered Life* (1932). In *Vein of Iron* (1935) she returned to the study of rural life in Virginia. *In This Our Life* (1941, Pulitzer Prize) is a novel of an aristocratic Virginia family fallen into decadence. *The Shadowy Third* (1923) collects stories; her *Works* were collected in 1938. *A Certain Measure* (1943) collects essays prefatory to her novels. *The Woman Within* (1954) is her autobiography. Her *Letters* were collected in 1958; and an edition of her *Collected Stories* appeared in 1963.

Glass Menagerie, The, play by Tennessee Williams,♦ produced in 1944 and published in 1945.

Laura Wingfield, who wears a leg brace because of a crippling childhood illness and is hypersensitive about it, lives with her mother Amanda and brother Tom in a St. Louis tenement. Her father has long since deserted them, though a dashing photo remains as a reminder of his charm. Amanda, a victim of illusions about her past as a Southern belle and about Laura's future, persists in preparing her daughter for hypothetical secretarial work and for nonexistent "gentlemen callers." She likewise wants Tom to get ahead in his warehouse job, which largely supports the family, but as a poetic dreamer his thoughts, like his father's, are often about escape from the family, as he turns to compulsive movie-going or plans for merchant-marine service. Amanda persuades Tom to invite a friend from the warehouse for dinner, and lets herself leap to romantic conclusions concerning a relationship between the visitor and Laura, even though the

pathetically withdrawn girl is only at home in her private world, which centers on a collection of glass animal figurines. On the appointed evening Tom arrives with Jim O'Connor, who turns out to be a high-school acquaintance whom Laura admired and who has since been part of her dream life. Her shy, nervous confusion is eased by Jim's warmth and she shows him her favorite animal, a tiny unicorn, but when he later teaches her a few dance steps while trying to build up her self-confidence, they bump the table and the unicorn's horn is broken. She discounts the accident, saying that now the unicorn will "feel less—freakish," and Jim is moved to tell her that she herself is different from others "in a nice way," like "Blue Roses," his high-school nickname for her. He tells her that she is pretty and kisses her. He is sincere but casual and, suddenly embarrassed, explains that he cannot call again because he is engaged to another girl. Furious at Tom for bringing home an engaged man, Amanda goads him beyond the breaking point, and he leaves home, haunted by the memory of his sister, who now retreats even further into herself.

Go Down, Moses, collection of seven stories by Faulkner,♦ published in 1942, which treat the McCaslin family,♦ white and black, from the time of Lucius, the founder at the opening of the 19th century, to the mid-20th century, all together representative of Southern history. Hunting and rituals of initiation are basic metaphors. The longest and most significant of the stories is "The Bear."♦

Go Tell It on the Mountain, novel by James Baldwin,♦ published in 1953.

On his fourteenth birthday in 1935, John Grimes faces the issue of religious conversion in the storefront Temple of the Fire Baptized while he wrestles with boyhood problems of sex and anger at his parents. His father, Gabriel, like other relatives and ancestors of young John, is revealed through flashbacks that illuminate John's own problems. John is the illegitimate son of Gabriel's third wife, adopted by him after their marriage. Guilt, bitterness, a sense of doom, and spiritual strivings affect young John, as they have his family before him.

Godey's Lady's Book (1830–98), monthly miscellany founded at Philadelphia by Louis Antoine Godey (1804–78). Sarah J. Hale, the editor from 1837 to 1877, exerted an important influence on fashions and manners, for the magazine was considered a criterion of taste. Among the articles and pictures of fashions were included stories and other contributions from Emerson, Longfellow, Holmes, Hawthorne, Harriet Beecher Stowe, Poe, W.G. Simms, and Paulding, although most of the writers were of a far lower caliber, conforming to the sentimental, moral, and didactic standards of the day. In 1892 the magazine was moved to New York, where as *Godey's Magazine* it published novelettes by Gertrude Atherton, Julian Hawthorne, H.H. Boyesen, and others. It was absorbed by Munsey's *Puritan.*

GODKIN, EDWIN LAWRENCE (1831–1902), came to America from Ireland at the age of 25, and founded *The Nation*♦ (1865), a liberal weekly which he merged with the New York *Evening Post* that he edited (1883–1900). His fearless independence, zeal, and wide knowledge made it an extremely influential newspaper, consistently liberal. His books include *Problems of Democracy* (1896) and *Unforeseen Tendencies of Democracy* (1898).

God's Little Acre, novel by Erskine Caldwell,♦ published in 1933.

God's Trombones, volume of poetry by James Weldon Johnson.♦

GOLD, HERBERT (1924–), Cleveland-born author, long resident in San Francisco, whose novels include *The Man Who Was Not With It* (1956), about a carnival barker who is a dope addict; *Therefore Be Bold* (1960), a light-hearted view of Jewish adolescents in the Midwest; *Fathers* (1967), "a novel in the form of a memoir" about Gold's father and his own experiences as a father; and *Family* (1981), a saga of an immigrant Jewish family in the U.S. He has also written stories and essays and *My Last Two Thousand Years* (1972), an autobiography of himself as a Jew.

GOLD, MICHAEL, pseudonym of Irwin Granich (1893–1967), born and reared on New York's Lower East Side. His experience of the slums and as a worker led him to become a Communist. He was an editor of *The Liberator.* His writings include *120 Million* (1929), sketches of American workers; *Jews Without Money* (1930), a semi-autobiographical work; *Change the World* (1937), articles from the *Daily Worker* and the *New Masses; The Hollow Men* (1941), critical articles on literature; and *Life of John Brown* (1960), the

subject also of a play, *Battle Hymn* (1936), written with Michael Blankfort. He also wrote several plays of his own, some unpublished.

Gold-Bug, The, tale by Poe,♦ published as a prize story in the Philadelphia *Dollar Magazine* (1843) and reprinted in *Tales* (1845). The cryptograph on which the story depends is a development of the interest that prompted Poe's essay "Cryptography" (*Graham's Magazine,* 1841).

William Legrand, an impoverished Southern gentleman, lives in seclusion on Sullivan's Island, South Carolina, his only companion being the black servant Jupiter. One day, when they capture a rare golden scarab beetle, marked with a sort of death's-head, they come upon a curious piece of parchment, which when heated proves to contain a secret cipher and a drawing of a death's-head. Legrand ingeniously decodes the cipher, which directs them to the buried treasure of Captain Kidd. With the aid of a friend and the superstitious Jupiter, both of whom he deliberately mystifies, Legrand locates an indicated tree, in which a skull is nailed, and, by dropping the beetle through an eye of the skull, they are able to establish a line on the position of the cache. Besides several skeletons, they exhume a fortune in old coins and jewels, with which Legrand reestablishes himself in society.

Golden Bowl, The, novel by Henry James,♦ published in 1904.

Charlotte Stant, a daring, intelligent, but penniless American, has a brief affair in Rome with Prince Amerigo, an impoverished Italian aristocrat. After they recognize that life together without money would be fatal to their love, the Prince falls in love with Maggie Verver, who, with her wealthy father, Adam, represents the best qualities of American culture: enthusiasm, moral fineness, the ability to assimilate new values, and a refreshing innocence and delicacy of outlook. Charlotte, a close friend of Maggie, while shopping one day in London with the Prince, considers as a possible gift for Maggie a gilded crystal bowl, perfect except for an invisible flaw. She is persuaded not to buy it, but the bowl becomes a symbol of the Prince's character and the various flawed relationships in the narrative. Maggie marries the Prince and Charlotte marries Adam but the happy relations of the couples are damaged when Maggie by chance buys the golden bowl and learns something from the shopkeeper that makes her suspect the Prince's liaison with

Charlotte. Both the Prince and Adam, realizing that she knows about the affair, appreciate the tact and delicacy with which Maggie handles the situation. Adam takes Charlotte to America, never to return, and the Prince recognizes that, though losing his mistress, he has gained a depth of character and an appreciation of the qualities of his wife.

GOLDMAN, EMMA (1869–1940), Russian-born exponent of anarchism, came to the U.S. (1886) and soon began to write and lecture in behalf of various reform movements, including feminism and birth control. Her anarchist speeches, and the magazine *Mother Earth,* which she founded in 1906, attracted wide attention. She was twice jailed, once for advocating pacifism during World War I. In 1919 she and an associate, Alexander Berkman, were deported to Russia, but their dislike for the Bolshevist regime and their criticism of it led to their leaving the country. Miss Goldman's autobiography, *Living My Life* (1931), was published from her home in France, and her other works include *Anarchism and Other Essays* (revised edition, 1911), *The Social Significance of the Modern Drama* (1914), and *My Disillusionment in Russia* (1925).

Gone with the Wind, novel by Margaret Mitchell,♦ published in 1936 and awarded a Pulitzer Prize. A tremendously popular and frequently revived film was created (1939) from a script written by Sidney Howard.

Set in Georgia during the Civil War and Reconstruction, this long romantic tale centers in the adventures of Scarlett, a high-spirited willful girl, daughter of Gerald O'Hara, an Irish immigrant who has become owner of Tara, a large plantation. Sixteen years old at the outbreak of the war, and in love with their neighbor Ashley Wilkes, she learns that Ashley plans to marry his cousin, the gentle Melanie Hamilton. Out of spite, Scarlett marries Melanie's brother Charles, youthful suitor of Honey Wilkes, Ashley's sister. Charles soon dies in the war, and Scarlett, living in Atlanta with her aunt "Pittypat," is plunged into poverty by the city's fall to the Northern invaders. In the struggle to survive after the war, Scarlett must carry the load of supporting her own family and also Ashley's, for her mother has died, her father has lost his mind, and Ashley, an idealistic aristocrat, is unable to adjust himself to the harsh realities of the new South. Scarlett is determined to keep Tara and to win financial security at any cost.

She works in the fields, does other menial tasks, and, to get money for taxes, marries Frank Kennedy, her sister's fiancé. With Frank's money and her own unscrupulous determination, she establishes a lumber business in Atlanta, and forces Ashley to become manager of one of her mills. Frank is killed in avenging an insult to her, and Scarlett, now 27, marries the war profiteer Rhett Butler, who attracts her by qualities similar to her own. Her selfishness and continuing infatuation for Ashley destroy Rhett's love, however, and he deserts her. When Melanie dies, and Ashley rejects Scarlett's sympathy, she realizes too late that Rhett is the one man she has ever really loved.

Good Earth, *The,* novel by Pearl Buck,♦ published in 1931, awarded a Pulitzer Prize, and dramatized by Owen and Donald Davis (1932). With *Sons* (1932) and *A House Divided* (1935), it forms a trilogy, *The House of Earth.*

Wang Lung, a Chinese peasant, and his plain wife O-lan, once a kitchen slave, by ceaseless labor and dedicated reverence for the soil become rich landowners, many of whose acres are bought from the declining House of Hwang. Their own children, removed from the land, begin to show a loss of the vigor that brought the family to power.

Good Gray Poet, sobriquet of Whitman, first applied to him by W.D. O'Connor.♦

Good-bye, poem by Emerson,♦ written in 1823 and published in *The Western Messenger* (1839). In couplets of four-stress lines, it is an early expression of the theme of *Nature.*♦ The poet rejects the traditional institutions of the "proud world," in favor of "going home" to the untrammeled solitude of nature, where "man in the bush with God may meet."

Good-Bye, My Fancy, poems and prose by Whitman,♦ published in 1891. The verse is reprinted in the final edition of *Leaves of Grass*♦ and the prose in the *Complete Writings* (1902).

GOODMAN, PAUL (1911–72), New York psychoanalyst and author, whose writings include *Growing Up Absurd* (1960), an intense personal and sociological attack on the "eclectic, sensational, . . . phony" U.S. culture and its baneful effect on youth; *The Community of Scholars* (1962) and *Compulsory Mis-Education* (1964), which criticize contemporary U.S. education; *New Reformation* (1970), advice to young dissidents; several volumes of poetry, gathered in *Collected Poems* (1974); plays; novels, including *The Grand Piano* (1949), *The Dead of Spring* (1950), and *Making Do* (1963), experimental in form but setting forth the same nonconformist views as his nonfiction; and literary criticism in *The Structure of Literature* (1954). He had a great following among youth in the 1960s.

Goops, characters in pictures and text created by Gelett Burgess♦ for his journal, *The Lark*, as boneless, quasi-human figures divided by their creator into two types: sulphites, independent thinkers, and bromides, platitudinous bores. In *Goops and How To Be Them* (1900), the first of a long series of amusing books intended to teach manners to youngsters, Burgess reincarnated the term but not the types, now presented as naughty, balloon-headed children.

GORDON, CAROLINE (1895–1981), Kentucky-born author of novels and short stories. Her novels include *Penhally* (1931), about four generations of a Kentucky family; *Aleck Maury, Sportsman* (1934), about a Southerner who is both scholar and sportsman; *None Shall Look Back* (1937), about a Kentucky family during the Civil War; *The Garden of Adonis* (1937), concerning Southern social and economic conflicts; *Green Centuries* (1941), about 18th-century Southern frontier life; *The Women on the Porch* (1944), a psychological analysis of a woman's life; and *The Malefactors* (1956), a sensitive study of an aging, frustrated poet. *The Southern Mandarins* (1984) collects letters.

GORDONE, CHARLES (1926–), Cleveland-born actor, director, producer, and playwright whose plays include *No Place to Be Somebody* (1969, Pulitzer Prize), a dark comedy about blacks in a rundown Greenwich Village saloon, whose owner is determined to be free of the local white Mafia; *The Last Chord* (1976), a melodrama with a related plot; and *Gordone Is Muthah* (1970), almost a one-man show.

GOREY, EDWARD [ST. JOHN] (1925–), after graduation from Harvard began publishing his numerous hand-lettered books, whose brief cryptic narratives and morbidly comic pen-and-ink illustrations are marked by a fey Gothic humor that has created a cult for works bearing such titles as *The Unstrung Harp* (1953), *The Hapless Child* (1961), *The Broken Spoke* (1976), and *The Doubtful Guest* (1978). *Amphigorey* (1972) is a collection of 15 of his small books.

Gospel of Wealth, The, essay by Andrew Carnegie. ♦

Gotham, sobriquet of New York City, derived from the jocular reputation of the "wise men" of Gotham, England, noted for their foolish actions. The name was first so used in Irving's *Salmagundi* (1807–8).

Gothic romance, variety of fiction widely popular in 18th-century England, whose use of medievalism, sensationalism, and supernatural horrors was developed by Walpole's *Castle of Otranto* (1764), set in a background of romantic "Gothic" architecture; Beckford's *Vathek* (1786); M.G. Lewis's *The Monk* (1795); *The Mysteries of Udolpho* (1795) and other romances of horror by Ann Radcliffe; and later by Godwin and Mary Wollstonecraft Shelley. In the U.S., Charles Brockden Brown♦ was the leading early author of Gothic romances, succeeded in the mid-19th century by such writers about the mysterious and the supernatural as Poe♦ and Hawthorne,♦ although Poe's statement, "the terror of which I write is not of Germany, but of the soul," is applicable to both of them. In the 1970s and '80s the term was applied to a very different kind of fiction, generally published in paperback editions, addressed to women, broadly but simply plotted stories of sensual relations between a hero and heroine, often also period pieces set in distant and ostensibly romantic periods or places.

GOYEN, [CHARLES] WILLIAM (1915–83), Texas-born author, educated at Rice, after service in the navy taught writing at the University of Houston and elsewhere. His works include *The House of Breath* (1950), a lyric novel about a boy's life in a Texas town; *In a Farther Country* (1955), a fanciful romance about a Spanish-American woman who in her mean New York room receives real and fancied visitors whose troubled lives she purges of conflict; *Ghost and Flesh* (1952), stories with a Texas setting; *The Faces of Blood Kindred* (1960), a novella and stories; *The Fair Sister* (1963), expanding an earlier story about a black woman evangelist and the world of store-front churches; *Come the Restorer* (1974), a comic fantasy partly set in Texas. *A Book of Jesus* (1973) is a nonfictional work; and *Arcadio* (1984), the tale of a hermaphrodite who is a wandering outcast. He also wrote plays: *The House of Breath* (1956), *The Diamond Rattler* (1960), *Christy* (1964), and *The House of Breath Black/White* (1971).

Graham's Magazine (1826–58), monthly literary journal founded at Philadelphia as *Atkinson's Casket,* was an unimpressive miscellany until 1839, when it was purchased by George Rex Graham (1813–94). After he merged it with *Burton's Gentleman's Magazine* (1840), it became one of the best periodicals in the country. Poe was literary editor of *Graham's Magazine* (1841–42), and increased its circulation from 5000 to 37,000. Among his contributions were such acute criticism as his review of the *Twice-Told Tales;* stories including "The Murders in the Rue Morgue," "A Descent into the Maelström," and "The Masque of the Red Death"; and poems including "To Helen." R.W. Griswold supplanted Poe (1842–43), and later editors included Bayard Taylor and C.G. Leland. The success of the magazine demonstrated the feasibility of paying liberally for contributions, so that it had such contributors as Lowell, N.P. Willis, Bryant, Cooper, Longfellow, C.F. Hoffman, Paulding, and Simms. It was also noted for its colored fashion plates and the engravings of John Sartain.

Grandissimes, The: *A Story of Creole Life,* novel by G.W. Cable,♦ published in 1880.
During the early 19th century there is a feud between the Grandissimes and the De Grapions, aristocratic Louisiana families. A reconciliation finally occurs with the marriage of the widow of the last De Grapion and the head of the Grandissime family.

Grapes of Wrath, The, novel by Steinbeck,♦ published in 1939 and awarded a Pulitzer Prize. The narrative chapters alternate with panoramic essays that show the social significance of the migrant labor problem.
The Joads, expropriated Oklahoma farmers from the Dust Bowl region, set out in a dilapidated automobile for California, which they believe is a land of plenty. The family includes Grampa, a lusty old man who was never "house broke"; Granma, weary and fanatically religious; lonely Uncle John; Pa, who has tacitly surrendered the rule of the family to his wife; Ma, brave, strong, and patient, who dreams and plans for the others; dull-witted Noah; Tom, just released from a jail term for killing a man in a fight; Al, a cocky youth who admires Tom's calm

strength; Rose of Sharon, absorbed in love for her weak husband Connie, with her unborn child; and the children, Ruthie and Winfield. The caravan also includes Casy, an ex-preacher and rustic socialist. During the hard journey, Grampa and Granma die and Noah deserts, but the Joads drive on ("It don't take no nerve to do somepin when there ain't nothin' else you can do."). In California they are hounded by sheriffs and labor contractors, Casy is jailed, and Connie runs away. Haunted by starvation, they spend some time in a government camp, but leave reluctantly to pick fruit at a blacklisted orchard. Tom meets Casy, who is leading the strikers, and during an attack by vigilantes Casy is killed, and Tom in turn kills his murderer. The Joads escape, and, while hiding Tom, work at picking cotton. Exhausted and fearful, Ma finally sends Tom away, and he plans to continue Casy's work as a labor organizer. During a storm, Rose of Sharon gives birth to a stillborn child. Jobless, the Joads face starvation, but Ma cries, "We ain' gonna die out. People is goin' on—changin' a little, maybe, but goin' right on."

GRAU, SHIRLEY ANN (1929–), New Orleans novelist whose works include *The Hard Blue Sky* (1958), presenting the life of an isolated Louisiana island community; *The House on Coliseum Street* (1961), set in her native city and treating the sad, loveless experience of a young girl there; *The Keepers of the House* (1964, Pulitzer Prize), portraying personal and political problems of a Southern family with a background of miscegenation; *The Condor Passes* (1971), chronicling three generations of a Louisiana family and its corrupt patriarch; and *Evidence of Love* (1974), about the tortured relations between father, son, and daughter-in-law. *The Black Prince* (1955) and *The Wind Shifting West* (1973) collect stories.

Graustark, romance by G.B. McCutcheon.♦

Gravity's Rainbow, novel by Thomas Pynchon,♦ published in 1973.
Lieutenant Tyrone Slothrop, toward the end of World War II, is stationed in London as part of the intelligence unit ACHTUNG (Allied Clearing House, Technical Units) to monitor V-2 rocket attacks. He is also under surveillance by the PISCES (Psychological Intelligence Schemes for Expediting Surrender) section of the Firm, a mysterious shadow government within the military, since Teddy Bloat and Pirate Prentice of the Firm have

discovered that the sites of Slothrop's numerous romantic liaisons in London correspond exactly to the locations subsequently hit by rockets. Ned Pointsman of PISCES is convinced that the relationship is associated with the experiments with Imipolex G that were inflicted upon Slothrop as a child by a German scientist, Laszlo Jamf, once at Harvard, now a developer of the V-2. Slothrop himself, always victimized by others, quests for the meaning of such matters, naïvely believing there is a way to understand events, past and present. Therefore he determines to learn about Jamf, and while engaged in an ever-shifting but phantasmagorically related search Slothrop is caught up in great power struggles that, among other affairs, involve a mysterious Captain Blicero (the Nazi officer Weissman) and some Herero tribesmen from Africa who have been trained as German rocket technicians. Slothrop also encounters Major Marvey of U.S. Army Ordnance, a black marketeer named Schnorp, some hashish runners, the director of a pornographic horror film, and diverse other strange men and women. They all appear to be involved somehow in a great conspiratorial cartel. As Oberst Enzian, a leader of the Herero command, says, the "War was never political at all, the politics was all theatre, all just to keep the people distracted . . . secretly, it was being dictated instead by the needs of technology." The rocket takes on metaphoric and mythic significance, answering "to a number of different shapes in the dreams of those who touch it—in combat, in tunnel, on paper" for "each Rocket will know its intended and hunt him . . . shining and pointed in the sky at his back . . . rushing in, rushing closer . . ." like a rainbow arched downward, as if by a force of gravity that is dragging mankind to death.

Great Awakening, THE, series of religious revivals, which began (*c.*1734) with the evangelicalism of Jonathan Edwards.♦ Revivalism was soon spread by such leaders as Theodore Frelinghuysen of the New Jersey Dutch Reformed Church; Gilbert Tennent, a New Jersey Presbyterian; and such lesser men as Benjamin Colman, Joseph Bellamy, George Whitefield, and James Davenport. Although the movement centered in New England, it extended throughout the colonies (*c.*1740–50). After the emotional fervor had spent its force in New England, a controversy developed between the New Lights of western Massachusetts, who held to the theology of Edwards, and the Old Lights of Boston, who were led by Charles Chauncy, and developed a liberalism that culminated in Unitarianism. A similar division in the Presbyterian Church split into a New Side and an Old Side, the former led by William and Gilbert Tennent, being instrumental in the founding of Princeton University. The original frenzied revival occasioned renewed missionary work among the Indians, in which Eleazar Wheelock was active, and which led to the founding of Dartmouth College.

Great Gatsby, The, novel by F. Scott Fitzgerald,♦ published in 1925. It was dramatized by Owen Davis (1926).

Nick Carraway, a young Midwesterner who sells bonds in New York, lives at West Egg, Long Island, which is separated from the city by an ashdump, whose distinctive feature is an oculist's faded billboard with a pair of great staring eyes behind yellow spectacles, symbolic of an obscenely futile world. Nick's neighbor is mysterious Jay Gatsby, whose mansion and fabulous entertainments are financed by bootlegging and other criminal activities. As a poor army lieutenant, Gatsby had fallen in love with Nick's beautiful cousin Daisy, who later married Tom Buchanan, an unintelligent, brutal man of wealth. Through Nick, he manages to meet Daisy again, impresses her by his extravagant devotion, and makes her his mistress. Her husband takes as his mistress Myrtle Wilson, sensual wife of a garageman. When her husband becomes jealous and imprisons her in her room, Myrtle escapes, runs out on the highway, and is accidentally hit by Daisy, who drives on. Gatsby tries to protect Daisy, and Tom, to whom she has become reconciled, brings his hatred of her lover to a climax by telling Myrtle's husband that it was Gatsby who killed her. Wilson shoots Gatsby and then himself. At the end Nick broods over the setting whose

> big shore places were closed now . . . until gradually I became aware of the old island here that flowered once for Dutch sailors' eyes—a fresh, green breast of the new world. . . . I thought of Gatsby's wonder when he first picked out the green light at the end of Daisy's dock. . . . his dream must have seemed so close that he could hardly fail to grasp it. He did not know that it was already behind him, somewhere back in that vast obscurity beyond the city, where the dark fields of the republic rolled on under the night.

Great God Brown, *The,* play by Eugene O'Neill,♦ produced and published in 1926. The concept of multiple personality is expressed in the changeable masks worn by the characters, removed only when they are alone or in the presence of sympathetic persons.

The plot concerns the conflict between William A. Brown, a "visionless demigod of our new materialistic myth . . . inwardly empty and resourceless," and Dion Anthony, representing the "creative pagan acceptance of life."

Great Stone Face, *The,* allegorical tale by Hawthorne,♦ published in *The Snow-Image and Other Twice-Told Tales* (1851). "Old Stony Phiz" is said to represent Webster.

In a mountain valley dominated by a towering rock formation that resembles a noble, majestic face lives the boy Ernest, who learns from his mother the legend that some day a great man bearing the features of the Face will visit the community. He eagerly awaits the coming of this man, but, though he grows to old age and sees Mr. Gathergold the banker, Old Blood-and-Thunder the general, and Old Stony Phiz the statesman, all reputed to resemble the Face, his expectations are disappointed. He has meanwhile lived an honest, helpful life, communing with the spirit of the landmark, and has come to be honored and revered. A poet visits him, in whom again Ernest hopes to see the features of the image but fails. At an outdoor meeting where Ernest preaches, the poet sees that it is Ernest himself who resembles the Stone Face. The simple, venerable old man, unconscious of this, continues to await his hero.

GREELEY, HORACE (1811–72), at the age of 23 founded the *New Yorker,* a critical weekly which he continued until 1841. He also founded the *New-York Tribune,*♦ which he edited for 30 years. His chief assistant (1849–62) was Charles A. Dana.♦ The great influence of the paper was due to Greeley's trenchant editorials, which attacked monopolies and advocated labor organization, a protective tariff, temperance, and a homestead law, supporting the last with the famous phrase "Go West, Young Man!" He also championed Fourierism and opposed all aids to slavery, particularly the Mexican War, the Compromise of 1850, and the Kansas-Nebraska Bill. He exerted his influence in behalf of Lincoln's election, and after the Civil War favored giving blacks the right to vote. In

1872 he was the presidential candidate of the Liberal Republican and Democratic parties, but was defeated. This disappointment and the death of his wife caused him to become insane, and he soon died. His books include *Recollections of a Busy Life* (1868).

Green Grow the Lilacs, folk comedy by Lynn Riggs,♦ produced and published in 1931. It is intended "to recapture in a kind of nostalgic glow . . . the great range of mood which characterized the old folk songs and ballads." An adaptation, *Oklahoma!* (1943), by Richard Rodgers and Oscar Hammerstein II, is a musical play that won an outstanding success and was awarded a special Pulitzer Prize.

Green Pastures, *The,* play by Marc Connelly,♦ produced and published in 1930, and awarded a Pulitzer Prize, is based on Roark Bradford's *Ol' Man Adam an' His Chillun* (1928).

Mr. Deshee, a black preacher in Louisiana, gives a Bible lesson to his country Sunday school class, and the action of the play dramatizes his narratives, presenting black people's anthropomorphic conception of God and Heaven, and representing Old Testament history in terms of Southern black life.

Greenwich Village, district of New York City, situated in lower Manhattan, during the colonial period was a separate village and later became an exclusive residential district. Paine wrote *The Crisis* in Greenwich Village, and Poe later lived there, but it was not until the end of the 19th century that it became famous for its bohemianism as an artistic and literary colony. Among those who lived in the Village, and among those who contributed to its long succession of little magazines, including *The Little Review, The Masses, The Seven Arts,* the *Bohemian,* the *Pagan,* the *Quill,* and the *Playboy,* were E.E. Cummings, Floyd Dell, Mabel Dodge, Max Eastman, Donald Evans, Emma Goldman, Edna St. Vincent Millay, Eugene O'Neill, and Carl Van Vechten. The Greenwich Village Theatre was an outgrowth of the Provincetown Players.♦ Authors and artists have continued among the area's residents, including Edward Albee and Gregory Corso, and among its recent playhouses has been the Caffe Cino, where plays of Lanford Wilson♦ were produced. The Village has a lively nightlife, including jazz clubs, and is a great tourist attraction. Students from nearby New York University and other young people live there, but in large part Village residents are now professional people and business executives, with some successful writers and artists.

GREY, ZANE (1872–1939), writer of Western fiction, the 20th-century heir of the dime novel, whose more than 60 books sold over 13,000,000 copies during his life. His stories, chiefly dealing with cowboy life, are melodramatic and lack characterization, presenting life as a struggle between ruthless villains and self-reliant, brawny heroes who are loyal to their friends and the fictional ethics of the frontier and chivalrous toward their naïve heroines. Grey's most popular novel was *Riders of the Purple Sage* (1912), but all his fiction was widely read and many of his works have been adapted for motion pictures.

Griffiths, CLYDE, character in *An American Tragedy.* ♦

GRIMKÉ, SARAH MOORE (1792–1873) and ANGELINA EMILY (1805–79), daughters of a wealthy South Carolina planter, converted to the Quaker faith and its opposition to the slavery of blacks. Moving to Philadelphia in their twenties, they never returned to the South, but their writings for the American Anti-Slavery Society were addressed in part to readers in their ancestral region. These included *An Appeal to the Christian Women of the South* (1836) and *Appeal to the Women of the Nominally Free States* (1837) by Angelina and *Epistle to the Clergy of the Southern States* (1836) by Sarah. Their pamphleteering and public lecturing next led them into the field of women's rights, a cause for which Sarah wrote *Letters on the Equality of the Sexes and the Condition of Woman* (1838). Sarah married the antislavery orator Theodore Dwight Weld, ♦ moving with him to New Jersey and then to Massachusetts. The two compiled *American Slavery as It Is: Testimony of a Thousand Witnesses* (1839), used by Harriet Beecher Stowe as a source for *Uncle Tom's Cabin.*

Guard of Honor, novel by James Gould Cozzens, ♦ published in 1948 and awarded a Pulitzer Prize.

Landing at his Florida air force base, the plane of Major General Ira N. ("Bus") Beal, a boyish hero of "simple-minded integrity,"

is almost hit by a B-26 piloted by black 2d Lieutenant Stanley Willis, who is angrily thrashed by Beal's friend and pilot, the brave but arrogant Lieutenant Colonel Benny Carricker. The same day, Al James, a black journalist writing an article about the base, discovers that it illegally practices segregation and that there is a mystery about Willis's hospitalization and the arrest of some black officers who had protested against discrimination. The original problems are just being settled when at maneuvers honoring Beal, seven parachutists miss their target and drown in a lake. Col. Ross, a judicious older officer, reflects that since good and bad are inextricably bound together in the human condition, one can expect no more than that "a man must stand up and do the best he can with what there is."

Gullah, corrupt dialect of blacks of the South Carolina and Georgia coast and northeast Florida. It employs an African intonation. Examples may be found in the novels of Julia Peterkin.

GUTHRIE, A[LFRED] B[ERTRAM], JR. (1901–), born in Indiana, reared in Montana, from whose state university he graduated (1923), has since lived in Kentucky, where he was a journalist (1926–47) before he began writing fiction. His novels are *The Big Sky* (1947), about a mountain man from Kentucky, who traps beaver and lives with the Indians in the West during the 1830s and 1840s; *The Way West* (1949, Pulitzer Prize), about an overland caravan from Missouri to Oregon in 1846; *These Thousand Hills* (1956), set in Montana in the later 19th century; *Arfive* (1971), about a new high-school principal's struggles in the Montana town of Arfive around the turn of the century; *Wild Pitch* (1973), *The Genuine Article* (1977), and *No Second Wind* (1980), light mysteries set in a modern cattle town; *The Last Valley* (1975), presenting life in Arfive around the time of World War II; and *Fair Land, Fair Land* (1982), a sequel to *The Big Sky,* carrying one of its characters to the age of 70 in a changed West. *The Big It* (1960) collects stories. *The Blue Hen's Chick* (1965) is an autobiography.

H

H.D., pseudonym of Hilda Doolittle. ♦

"Hairy Ape, The," expressionist play by O'Neill, ♦ produced and published in 1922. It is symbolic of the perversion of human strength by technological progress.

In the cramped forecastle of a transatlantic liner, Yank—brutal, stupid, and profane—is the recognized leader of the stokers, who are the ultimate products of a society subservient to machines. When Mildred Douglas, daughter of the ship's owner, makes a slumming visit to the stokehole, she is shocked by the lurid atmosphere, and faints at encountering Yank's unashamed brutality. Although he is completely adapted to this environment, he now discovers that there is a world in which he does not belong, and "the Hairy Ape," as his friend Paddy calls him, becomes sullen and morose, beginning to think of his position. In New York on Easter Sunday, he swaggers in dirty dungarees up Fifth Avenue, trying in vain to insult the aristocratic strollers, who politely ignore him. Arrested, he is sent to Blackwell's Island, where the prisoners, misunderstanding his rebellion, advise him to join the I.W.W. Rejected by the labor organization, he goes to the zoo to see the ape, the only creature with whom he can now feel kinship. When he liberates it, to help him wreak destruction, the beast crushes him to death.

HAKLUYT, RICHARD (1552?–1616), British geographer and compiler of narratives of exploration. Among his valuable publications dealing with America, preserving original accounts that would otherwise have been lost, are *Divers Voyages Touching the Discoverie of America* (1582); *A Notable Historie Containing Foure Voyages Made by Certayne French Captaynes into Florida* (1587), including the narrative of Laudonnière; *Virginia Richly Valued* (1609), including the account of De Soto's discoveries; and his greatest work, *The Principall Navigations, Voyages, Traffiques, and Discoveries of the English Nation* (1589; 3 vols., enlarged, 1598–1600). The work of Hakluyt was continued by Samuel Purchas, ♦ who collected his unpublished papers in *Hakluytus Posthumus* (4 vols., 1625).

HALE, EDWARD EVERETT (1822–1909), nephew of Edward Everett and great-nephew of Nathan Hale, was a Boston Unitarian clergyman, philanthropist, and popular author. He wrote prolifically on many subjects, but is principally remembered for his tale *The Man Without a Country* ♦ (1865).

HALE, SARAH JOSEPHA [BUELL] (1788–1879), is celebrated as the author of "Mary Had a Little Lamb," ♦ published in *Poems for Our Children* (1830). In addition to her work in behalf of child welfare, feminine education, and other humanitarian movements, she edited *Godey's Lady's Book* (1837–77), and wrote many works typical of Victorian feminine productions.

HALEY, ALEX [PALMER] (1921–), born in Ithaca, N.Y., after service with the coast guard (1939–59), in which he was a journalist, became the aid or ghost writer of *The Autobiography of Malcolm X* (1965). Then, intrigued by a desire to discover his own black heritage, through research involving oral traditions in Gambia, he traced his family back seven generations to an African, Kunta Kinte, enslaved and brought to Annapolis in 1767. Of these facts, and many fictive inprovisations, he created the family chronicle *Roots* (1976), awarded a special Pulitzer Prize (1977).

Half-Way Covenant, doctrinal revision of New England Congregationalism, ♦ drafted by Richard Mather and approved by a church synod (1662). First-generation Congregationalists were admitted to full membership in the church only after a personal experience of conversion, but their children shared in the privileges of full membership except for the Lord's Supper. The Half-Way Covenant proposed to extend this same status of baptism to the children of second-generation members, even though the latter may have confessed no experience of conversion to bring them into full communion.

HALL, DONALD [ANDREW] (1928–), Connecticut-born poet, educated at Harvard and Oxford, where his "Exiles" won the Newdigate Prize (1952). He was a professor at

Michigan (1957–77). His early poetry in *Exiles and Marriages* (1955) was marked by traditional meters and rhythms and formalism as well as ironic wit. *The Dark Houses* (1958), poems about suburban and small-town life, is freer and more emotional. This change is further developed in later works, which are more subjective and rich in sensuous imagery: *The Alligator Bride* (1969), new poems and revised earlier ones; *A Roof of Tiger Lilies* (1964); *The Yellow Room* (1971), about a romance; *The Town of Hill* (1975), a small collection; *A Blue Wing Tilts at the Edge of the Sea* (1975); and *Kicking the Leaves* (1978). He has collaborated in two prose works about baseball, *Playing Around* (1974) and *Dock Ellis in the Country of Baseball* (1976), as well as writing critical studies of the sculptor Henry Moore (1966) and the poet Marianne Moore (1970). *String Too Short To Be Saved* (1961) recalls in prose his youthful summers on a New Hampshire farm, and *Remembering Poets* (1978) contains reminiscences and assessments of Dylan Thomas, Frost, Eliot, and Pound. *Goatfoot Milktongue Twinbird* (1978) collects interviews, essays, and notes on poetry, as does *The Weather for Poetry* (1982). Hall edited the *Oxford Book of American Literary Anecdotes* (1981) and *Claims for Poetry* (1982), by 43 poets on the nature of poetry.

HALL, OAKLEY (1920–   ), California novelist, whose works include *Corpus of Joe Bailey* (1953) and its sequel, *Report from Beau Harbor* (1971), wry depictions of generational and ideological conflicts in California families; *Warlock* (1958), set in a Southwest frontier mining town during the 1880s; *The Downhill Racers* (1963), about skiing enthusiasts; *The Adelita* (1975), concerning an American's involvement in the Mexican Revolution; *The Bad Lands* (1978), portraying conflicts between cattlemen and farmers in South Dakota during the 1880s; and *Lullaby* (1982), the story of dreadful events in the life of a family in Hawaii, perhaps attributable to an ancient curse. Hall also wrote the libretto for the operatic version (1976) of Stegner's *Angle of Repose.*

Hall of Fame, shrine in New York established in 1900 to honor fifty notable Americans with memorial busts and tablets. Every five years (after 1970, every three) a committee of 100 chose additions from persons dead more than 25 years. In 1977 the project was ended for lack of funding. Of the 102 persons honored through 1976, 18 are au-

thors: George Bancroft, Bryant, Clemens, Cooper, Emerson, Hawthorne, Holmes, Irving, Lanier, Longfellow, Lowell, Motley, Parkman, Poe, Harriet Beecher Stowe, Thoreau, Whitman, and Whittier.

HALLECK, FITZ-GREENE (1790–1867), born in Connecticut, was a leading member of the Knickerbocker Group♦ and co-author with J.R. Drake of the "Croaker Papers" (1819), which catapulted him to fame.

HALPER, ALBERT (1904–   ), Chicago-born proletarian novelist, whose *Union Square* (1933), about economic pressures on workingmen, artists, and agitators, tended to satirize radicalism, toward which his later books are sympathetic. *On the Shore* (1934) contains semi-autobiographical sketches of Chicago. *The Foundry* (1934) deals with workers in a Chicago electrotype foundry during the year preceding the 1929 stock market crash, and *The Chute* (1937) deals with workers in a mail-order house. *Sons of the Fathers* (1940) depicts the strain of America's entrance into World War I upon a Jewish immigrant who hoped his sons would never know war; *Only an Inch from Glory* (1943) deals with the frustrations of four New Yorkers; and *The Golden Watch* (1953) tells of a boy growing up in Chicago before World War I. *Little People* (1942) contains stories about Chicago clothing-store employees. Later novels include *Atlantic Avenue* (1956), about physical and emotional violence in Brooklyn and along New York's waterfront, and *The Fourth Horseman of Miami Beach* (1966), about lonely, middle-aged men. *Good-Bye, Union Square* (1970) is a memoir.

Hamlet, The, novel by Faulkner,♦ published in 1931, the first of a trilogy including *The Town*♦ and *The Mansion.*♦
In the 1890s, Will Varner, the mild-mannered economic power of Frenchman's Bend, Yoknapatawpha County, Mississippi, rents some land to Ab Snopes, whose grotesque, ruthlessly greedy son Flem is installed by the 30-year-old Varner heir Jody as a clerk in the Varner store to dissuade Ab from burning the barn, his usual way with landlords. Instead, Flem takes over Varner positions, property, and power as his relatives, including the shrewd, weasly I.O., the idiot Ike, and the primitive Mink, begin to dominate or demoralize the town. When Varner's daughter Eula, a mindless, sensual female, becomes pregnant, she is married off to Flem in return for cash and the deed to

the crumbling pre-Civil War mansion, Frenchman's Place. A different passion overwhelms Ike, who falls in love with a cow, and their daily relationship is made another subject of profit as Lump Snopes sells secret viewing places of the encounters. Flem mulcts the townspeople by inducing them to buy Frenchman's Place as the site of buried treasure on the basis of some gold he had salted there, another example of the way in which the whole community is bilked and corrupted by the Snopeses.

HAMMETT, [SAMUEL] DASHIELL (1894–1961), born in Connecticut, went to San Francisco as a Pinkerton detective and soon drew upon the city's atmosphere and his own business for the novels he began to write. Cool, tough, and hard-boiled in attitude, his works employ Hemingway's mood and spare, realistic dialogue in the genre of the detective story. He took murder out of the settings of polite society and put it into a corrupt urban environment where, as his follower, Raymond Chandler, said, he gave it "back to the people that commit it for reasons, not just to provide a corpse." Hammett's major novels, including *Red Harvest* (1929) and *The Maltese Falcon* (1930), also introduced a new kind of sleuth, the cynical, tough Sam Spade. These works, along with *The Thin Man* (1932), became very popular films, and Hammett himself moved to southern California to write scripts. When he refused to testify about so-called un-American activities in Hollywood he was sent to prison. His friend Lillian Hellman wrote about his stand and his era in *Scoundrel Time* (1976).

Hans Brinker, story for children by Mary Mapes Dodge. ♦

HANSBERRY, LORRAINE (1930–65), Chicago-born dramatist, became the first black woman to have a play produced on Broadway with *A Raisin in the Sun* (1959), an easy-going comedy of a family of black Chicagoans who plan to move into a white neighborhood, illustrative of Langston Hughes's poem: "What happens to a dream deferred, Does it dry up like a raisin in the sun?" She followed this success with *The Sign in Sidney's Brustein's Window* (1964), depicting Jews and other whites as well as blacks in Greenwich Village. After her early death her husband assembled from her plays, letters, diaries, and other writings a dramatic presentation, *To Be Young, Gifted and Black* (1969). For *The Movement* (1964) she wrote wry captions

for photographs of blacks in their struggle for equality. *Raisin* (1973) was a musical adaptation of her first play by others.

HARDWICK, ELIZABETH (1916–), Kentucky-born author of novels, including *The Ghostly Lover* (1945), presenting a Kentucky family as seen by a young girl member; *The Simple Truth* (1955), a character study related to the trial of a college student accused of murdering his sweetheart; and *Sleepless Nights* (1979), a "meditation" on a woman's life. *A View of My Own* (1962) and *Bartleby in Manhattan* (1983) print essays on literature and society, the former mostly from the *Partisan Review,* the latter mainly from the *New York Review of Books;* and *Seduction and Betrayal* (1974) collects essays on women writers. She was married (1949–72) to Robert Lowell.

HARIOT, THOMAS (1560–1621), English mathematician and geographer, accompanied Grenville on his second expedition to Virginia (1586). The two-year sojourn resulted in his *Briefe and True Report of the New-Found Land of Virginia* (1588), which was accompanied in the 1590 edition by the imaginative drawings of a fellow colonist, John White, and was republished by Hakluyt. Raleigh was indebted to Hariot in *The History of the World* for points of chronology and geography. The name is also spelled Harriot and Harriott. Muriel Rukeyser♦ wrote *The Traces of Thomas Hariot* (1971), a study.

Harlem, section of upper Manhattan, whose central area had 275,000 blacks in 1970 and over 161,000 in 1980. It was originally an independent village of Dutch settlers who named it for Haarlem, and was later a residential section for whites until it became predominantly black (c.1914–18). The section figured in literature as early as J.W. Johnson's *The Autobiography of an Ex-Colored Man* (1912), and was widely exploited in the fiction and poetry of the 1920s, the era of the so-called Harlem Renaissance. Leading authors of the period included Countee Cullen, Jessie Redmon Fauset, Langston Hughes, James Weldon Johnson, Claude McKay, Wallace Thurman, and Jean Toomer, and a major commentator on the blacks' situation was W.E.B. DuBois. Writings by whites about the era include Van Vechten's *Nigger Heaven,* O'Neill's *All God's Chillun Got Wings,* and Bodenheim's *Naked on Roller Skates.* Later black authors associated with Harlem include

James Baldwin, Ralph Ellison, Zora Neale Hurston, and LeRoi Jones.

Harmonium, first volume of poetry by Wallace Stevens,♦ published in 1923, when he was almost 44, although some of the poems were printed in journals as early as 1915. The 74 poems include "Sunday Morning,"♦ "The Emperor of Ice Cream,"♦ "Thirteen Ways of Looking at a Blackbird,"♦ "Anecdote of the Jar,"♦ "Le Monocle de Mon Oncle," "The Comedian as the Letter C," and "Peter Quince at the Clavier." In 1931 the work was reissued with three poems (none of the above) omitted and 14 added.

Harper's Monthly Magazine (1850–), founded at New York by Harper and Brothers, with Henry J. Raymond as editor during the first six years. This eclectic literary periodical at first drew widely on British authors, including Dickens, Thackeray, Charles Lever, Trollope, Wilkie Collins, and Hardy, but under the editorship (1869–1919) of Henry M. Alden it printed an increasing amount of American material, including contributions by such diverse authors as Melville, De Forest, Nordhoff, Elizabeth S. Phelps, Henry James, C.D. Warner, Howells, Garland, E.E. Hale, Sarah Orne Jewett, Brander Matthews, and Owen Wister. Among the popular serials were Du Maurier's *Trilby* (1894) and Clemens's *Joan of Arc* (1895–96); featured illustrations were by such artists as E.A. Abbey, A.B. Frost, Howard Pyle, and Winslow Homer. A separate English edition published abroad was edited by Andrew Lang. After 1900, the American publication devoted more space to contemporary politics and social problems, with articles by public figures including Wilson, Theodore Roosevelt, and H.C. Lodge, and following World War I its policy became more notably liberal. The best-known department is the "Editor's Easy Chair," whose occupants have included D.G. Mitchell (1851–53), G.W. Curtis (1853–92), Howells (1901–21), E.S. Martin (1921–35), and Bernard De Voto (1935–55).

Harper's Weekly (1857–1916), illustrated political and literary journal. Although it always published serials, including works by Dickens, Wilkie Collins, Elizabeth Gaskell, and Bulwer-Lytton, it was best known for its engravings and woodcuts, which constitute a pictorial history of the times. In 1862 Thomas Nast joined the staff, and made the magazine notable for its war pictures and political cartoons. His bitter caricatures of the corrupt

Tweed Ring did much to shape public opinion, as did his cartoons, which created the accepted symbols of the Tammany tiger, the Republican elephant, and the Democratic donkey. The magazine was later noted for its photographs and wash drawings, and the writings of such contributors as Kipling, Conan Doyle, Henry James, Howells, H.B. Fuller, R.H. Davis, and Hamlin Garland. Among the editors were G.W. Curtis (1863–92), Carl Schurz (1892–94), and J.K. Bangs (1898–1901). It was absorbed by *The Independent.* ♦

HARRIS, FRANK (1856–1931), born in Ireland, came to the U.S. (1870), where he worked at jobs ranging from boot-blacking to cow punching, the latter occupation being described in *My Reminiscences as a Cowboy* (1930). After attending the University of Kansas, he became an American citizen and was admitted to the state bar (1875). He drifted to Europe for further education, and in England became editor of various magazines and an intimate of such men as Beerbohm, Wilde, and Shaw. He attained a literary reputation for books of short stories such as *Elder Conklin* (1894) and *Montes the Matador* (1900), his novel *The Bomb* (1908), dealing with the Haymarket Riot, and his play *Mr. and Mrs. Daventry* (1900), which critics have contended was mainly written by Wilde. Of this London period, Wilde said, "Frank Harris has been received in all the great houses—*once.*" He returned to the U.S., where he edited *Pearson's Magazine,* but his pro-German views during World War I caused him to retire to Nice. Meanwhile he had won notoriety through his biography *Oscar Wilde: His Life and Confessions* (2 vols., 1916), which has been called maliciously inaccurate; his five volumes of *Contemporary Portraits* (1915–27), impressionistic and frequently scandalous sketches of acquaintances; and his very frank *My Life and Loves* (3 vols., 1923–27).

HARRIS, GEORGE WASHINGTON (1814–69), Tennessee River steamboat captain, later became a political writer and contributed humorous sketches to local newspapers and *The Spirit of the Times.* He is best known for his *Sut Lovingood Yarns* (1867), a collection of broadly funny tales about a rough young Tennessee mountaineer.

HARRIS, JOEL CHANDLER (1848–1908), born and reared in a small town in Georgia, worked on the *Atlanta Constitution* (1876–

1907), in which he printed some of the tales gathered in *Uncle Remus: His Songs and His Sayings* (1881) and other collections setting forth a whimsical, lovable former slave's traditional fables of his race, many of them about animals like Brer Rabbit and Brer Fox who are endowed with human qualities.

HARRIS, MARK (1922–), New York-born author, received his Ph.D. in American Studies from the University of Minnesota and has taught at San Francisco State College (1954–68) and elsewhere. His novels include four wryly humorous works about a big-league baseball player, *The Southpaw* (1953), *Bang the Drum Slowly* (1956), *A Ticket for a Seamstitch* (1957), and *It Looked Like for Ever* (1979). Other works include studies of Vachel Lindsay (1952) and Saul Bellow (1980) and memoirs.

HART, Moss (1904–61), New York playwright, was best known for his collaborations with George S. Kaufman,♦ on comedies which include *Once in a Lifetime* (1930), *You Can't Take It with You* (1936, Pulitzer Prize), and *The Man Who Came to Dinner* (1939).

HARTE, [FRANCIS] BRET[T] (1836–1902), born in Albany, N.Y., went to California (1854), where he engaged in various occupations, including a brief attempt at mining in the Mother Lode. In 1860 he settled in San Francisco, where he became a printer and journalist, and through his contributions to the *Golden Era* and the *Californian* became a prominent literary figure, whose successes included tales about Spanish California in the vein of Washington Irving and a novelette, "M'liss," (1860) about a young girl's adventures in the gold-rush mining country. *Outcroppings* (1865), an anthology of local verse; *The Lost Galleon* (1867), a collection of his poems; and *Condensed Novels and Other Papers* (1867), distinguished for its satirical parodies of famous authors, were his first books. The following year Harte became editor of the newly founded *Overland Monthly,* in which he published his local-color stories, mainly concerned with moral contrasts, including "The Luck of Roaring Camp,"♦ "The Outcasts of Poker Flat,"♦ "Tennessee's Partner,"♦ "Miggles," and "Brown of Calaveras." His famous comic ballad, "Plain Language from Truthful James,"♦ (1870), often called "The Heathen Chinee," also appeared at this time, and, with the collection of *The Luck of Roaring*

Camp and Other Sketches (1870), he was swept into popular favor throughout the U.S. He immediately made a triumphal trip east, where he received a contract from the *Atlantic Monthly* for $10,000 for 12 contributions. He fulfilled the contract with mediocre writing, and his short-lived popularity came to an end. During subsequent years, Harte collected his magazine contributions in numerous volumes, but none approached the success of his earliest writings. He became U.S. consul at Crefeld, Rhenish Prussia (1878), and at Glasgow (1880–85). He lived the remainder of his life in London, where editors accepted his stories more readily than did the American magazines. During his last years he was little better than a hack writer, turning out imitations of the California stories that had won him fame.

Hasty Pudding, The, mock-epic in three cantos of heroic couplets, composed in 1793 by Joel Barlow,♦ published in 1796. While in France, the poet was served a steaming dish of boiled Indian meal (hasty pudding). It reminded him of Connecticut and caused him to write his merry epic on this native dish, ranking "simplicity of diet among the virtues."

HAWKES, JOHN [CLENDENNIN BURNE, JR.] (1925–), Connecticut-born novelist, a graduate of Harvard, has taught English at Brown University (1958–). His fiction includes *The Cannibal* (1949), two related stories presenting almost surrealistically the horrors of devastation in postwar Germany; *The Beetle Leg* (1951), a novel about a construction worker buried alive during the building of a dam and the psychological effect of his death upon friends and co-workers; *The Goose on the Grave* (1954) and *The Owl* (1954), two short novels set in Italy; *The Lime Twig* (1961), about the psychopathic effects on a man of life during and after the London blitz; *Second Skin* (1964), about an aging former navy officer who sheds his old life of violence, horror, and sadness to live a new one that is joyous and sensuous; *The Blood Oranges* (1971), about a contemptible American couple in Greece who destroy a friendly visiting couple; *Death, Sleep and the Traveler* (1974), a man's phantasmagoric view of events that involve himself, his wife, and his friend who is her lover; *Travesty* (1976), a Frenchman's monologue that serves as a suicide note while he prepares to kill his daughter, a friend, and himself; *The Passion Artist*

(1979), presenting a middle-aged widower's fantastic encounters in a European city; *Virginie* (1982), about a girl who has experienced two previous lives in France, both marked by bizarre sexual experiences; and *Adventures in the Alaskan Skin Trade* (1985). *The Innocent Party* (1966) collects four short plays, and *Lunar Landscapes* (1969) collects stories and novellas. The plots of Hawkes's fiction are often oblique, set in a nightmare or a dream kind of world, told in an intricate, highly personal style that frequently verges on the abstract, and marked by a macabre humor.

HAWTHORNE, NATHANIEL (1804–64), was born at Salem, Mass., of a prominent Puritan family, which had spelled the name Hathorne and included a judge at the Salem witchcraft trials, who figures as the accursed founder of *The House of the Seven Gables.* Nathaniel's father, a sea captain, died of yellow fever in Dutch Guiana in 1808, leaving his widow to mourn him during a long life of eccentric seclusion, and this influenced her son's somber and solitary attitude. During his childhood, he read extensively in poets and romancers, and spent an impressionable year at a remote Maine lake, after which he attended Bowdoin College, graduating in 1825. Returning to Salem, he began to write historical sketches and allegorical tales, dealing with moral conflicts in colonial New England.

In 1828 he published anonymously, at his own expense, an immature novel, *Fanshawe,* whose hero resembles the author at this period. The work went practically unnoticed, but interested S.G. Goodrich, who then published many of Hawthorne's stories in *The Token.* These were reprinted in *Twice-Told Tales*♦ (1837, enlarged 1842) and included "The Maypole of Merrymount,"♦ "Endicott and the Red Cross,"♦ "The Minister's Black Veil,"♦ "Mr. Higginbotham's Catastrophe,"♦ "Dr. Heidegger's Experiment,"♦ "The Gray Champion,"♦ "The Ambitious Guest,"♦ and the "Legends of the Province House," containing "Lady Eleanore's Mantle"♦ and "Howe's Masquerade."♦ These tales, which the author said had "the pale tint of flowers that blossomed in too retired a shade," deal with the themes of guilt and secrecy, and intellectual and moral pride, and show Hawthorne's constant preoccupation with the effects of Puritanism in New England. In imaginative, allegorical fashion, he depicts the dramatic results of a Puritanism that was at the roots of the culture

he knew, recognizing its decadence in his own time.

In 1836 he emerged from his seclusion at Salem to begin a career of hack writing and editing. He was also employed in the Boston Custom House (1839–41), and spent six or seven months at Brook Farm, where his sensitiveness and solitary habits, as well as his lack of enthusiasm for communal living, unfitted him for fruitful participation. He married Sophia Peabody, an ardent follower of the Concord school, but even this marriage, although it was a happy turning point in his life, did not bring Hawthorne to share the optimistic philosophy of Transcendentalism. Settling in Concord at the Old Manse, he continued his analysis of the Puritan mind in the tales that were collected in *Mosses from an Old Manse*♦ (1846), including "Young Goodman Brown,"♦ "The Celestial Railroad,"♦ "Rappaccini's Daughter,"♦ "The Artist of the Beautiful,"♦ "The Birthmark,"♦ and "Roger Malvin's Burial."

As Surveyor of the Port of Salem (1846–49), he wrote little, but satirically observed his associates, as he described in the introduction to *The Scarlet Letter*♦ (1850). This novel, written after Hawthorne's dismissal from his post owing to a change of administrations, proved to be his greatest work, and indeed summed up in classic terms the Puritan dilemma that had so long occupied his imagination. Other books of this period include *The House of the Seven Gables*♦ (1851), another great romance, concerned with the decadence of Puritanism; *The Blithedale Romance*♦ (1852), in which he turned to the contemporary scene and his Brook Farm experiences; *The Snow-Image and Other Twice-Told Tales*♦ (1851), containing "The Snow-Image,"♦ "The Great Stone Face,"♦ and "Ethan Brand"♦; and *A Wonder Book*♦ (1852) and *Tanglewood Tales*♦ (1853), stories for children.

During these years, he lived for a time in the Berkshires, where he was friendly with his admirer, Melville. After he wrote a campaign biography of his college friend Franklin Pierce (1852) he was rewarded with the consulship at Liverpool. His departure for Europe (1853) marks another turning point in his life. The ensuing years abroad were filled with sightseeing and keeping a journal, and, although his new cultural acquirements had little influence on his writing, they throw significant light on his character of mind. After his consular term (1853–57), he spent two years in Italy, returning to settle again in Concord (1860). *Our Old Home*♦

(1863), shrewd essays on his observations in England, and *The Marble Faun*♦ (1860), a romance set in Italy, were results of his European residence.

His last years, during which he continued to contribute to the *Atlantic Monthly,* were marked by declining creative powers. His attempts to write a romance based on the themes of an elixir of life and an American claimant to an English estate resulted only in four posthumous fragments: *Septimius Felton* (1872); *The Dolliver Romance* (1876); *Dr. Grimshawe's Secret* (1883); and *The Ancestral Footstep* (1883). Other posthumous publications include *Passages from the American Notebooks* (1868), *Passages from the English Notebooks* (1870), and *Passages from the French and Italian Notebooks* (1871), all edited by his wife. The *English Notebooks* were newly edited from original manuscripts (1942) by Randall Stewart.

Hawthorne has long been recognized as a classic interpreter of the spiritual history of New England, and in many of his short works, as well as in *The Scarlet Letter* and *The House of the Seven Gables,* he wrote masterpieces of romantic fiction. Like Poe, but with an emphasis on moral significance, he was a leader in the development of the short story as a distinctive American genre. The philosophic attitude implicit in his writing is generally pessimistic, growing out of the Puritan background, although his use of the supernatural has an aesthetic rather than a religious foundation, for he presented New England's early Puritanism and its decay in terms of romantic fiction. Emphasis on allegory and symbolism causes his characters to be recalled as the embodiment of psychological traits or moral concepts more than as living figures.

HAY, JOHN [MILTON] (1838–1905), Indiana-born statesman and author, as a law student at Springfield met Lincoln, whose assistant secretary he became. With John Nicolay, another secretary, who also served the President until his assassination, he gathered material for *Abraham Lincoln: A History* (10 vols., 1890). After holding minor posts in foreign legations, he wrote *Castilian Days* (1871) and *Pike County Ballads* (1871), dialect poems about the Illinois frontier. He moved in the circle which included Henry Adams, H.C. Lodge, and Clarence King, and wrote an anonymous novel, *The Bread-Winners* (1884).

HAYES, ALFRED (1911–85), English-born author and scenarist, reared in New York City. His novels, written after army service in Italy, include *All Thy Conquests* (1946), about differences between American troops and Roman citizens; *Shadow of Heaven* (1947), about an aging labor organizer; *The Girl on Via Flaminia* (1949), about a bittersweet affair between a lonely American soldier and a respectable Italian girl, adapted as a play by Hayes (1954); and *The Stockbroker, the Bitter Young Man, and the Beautiful Girl* (1973), an ironic novella. He has also published poems.

HAYNE, PAUL HAMILTON (1830–86), South Carolina author, called "the last literary cavalier," was known before the Civil War for his nature poetry. During the war he was too ill to serve in the army, and lived in poverty after his home was destroyed, but won fame for his martial lyrics. His fragile, charming poetry finds its best expression during the postwar period in his *Legends and Lyrics* (1872). He edited the poems of his friend Timrod (1873) with a pathetic and penetrating introduction, and wrote a life of H.S. Legaré (1878). His own *Collected Poems* was published in 1882.

Hazard of New Fortunes, A, novel by Howells,♦ published in 1890. Basil March also figures in *Their Wedding Journey* (1871), *An Open-Eyed Conspiracy* (1897), and *Their Silver Wedding Journey* (1899).

Basil March becomes editor of a magazine promoted by slangy, affable little Fulkerson and financed by Dryfoos, a farmer who has become a millionaire through the discovery of natural gas on his farm and who backs the magazine in order to give practical business experience to his son Conrad. March engages on his staff a German socialist, Lindau, whose point of view antagonizes Dryfoos. The capitalist orders March to discharge Lindau, but March refuses, and Fulkerson sides with him. During a strike of streetcar employees, Conrad is killed and Lindau is fatally injured while trying to pacify the strikers. Prostrated by the death of his son, Dryfoos magnanimously provides for Lindau's funeral, and sells the magazine to Fulkerson and March.

HAZZARD, SHIRLEY (1931–), Australian-born author, in foreign service and later the United Nations, settled in New York City. Her books include *The Evening of the Holi-*

day (1966), a novella about an unhappy romance, set in Italy; *People in Glass Houses* (1967), subtitled "Portraits from Organization Life," witty views of fictional bureaucrats; *The Bay of Noon* (1970), a novel about romantic entanglements in Italy; *The Transit of Venus* (1980), a novel treating the complex emotional relationships experienced by two expatriate Australian sisters; *Cliffs of Fall* (1963), stories collected from *The New Yorker*. She is married to Francis Steegmuller.

HEARN, Lafcadio (1850–1904), born in the Ionian Islands, of Irish-Greek parentage, was educated in France and England, and emigrated to the U.S. in 1869. Handicapped by poverty, semi-blindness, a morbid inferiority complex, and a scandal resulting from his relations with a mulatto woman, he lived for a time in New Orleans, where he wrote weird newspaper sketches. His early books include *One of Cleopatra's Nights* (1882), stories translated from Gautier, *Gombo Zhêbes* (1885), Negro-French proverbs, *Two Years in the French West Indies* (1890), sketches of his life in Martinique, and *Youma* (1890), the story of a black woman slave in Martinique. In 1890 he moved to Japan, married into a samurai family, became a Japanese citizen with the name Koizumi Yakumo, taught English literature at the Imperial University in Tokyo, and wrote numerous sensitive and sympathetic works about his adopted land.

Heart Is a Lonely Hunter, The, novel by Carson McCullers, ♦ published in 1940.

In a small Georgia town, an intelligent and sympathetic deaf-mute, John Singer, is lonely and saddened when his only friend, another mute, Spiros Antonapoulos, is committed to an institution. He takes a room in the Kelly family home and eats his meals at Biff Brannon's café, but lives only for visits to Antonapoulos, the one person with whom he can communicate. Biff, a warm-hearted, magnanimous, impotent man, and Jake Blount, an intense, alcoholic wanderer, obsessed by a desire to convert others to Marxism, both feel that Singer somehow has a superhuman understanding that brings calm. They visit Singer in his room to tell him their innermost feelings, as do Mick Kelly, a sensitive adolescent tomboy with an intense spiritual hunger, and Dr. Benedict Copeland, an intellectual black man passionately devoted to the improvement of his people's lot. Singer becomes an important and mysterious figure in the town, as "everyone described

the mute as he wished him to be," although he himself feels isolated. Each of his admirers meets tragedy, and Singer himself, upon discovering that Antonapoulos has died, commits suicide. Confused and deeply saddened, each of Singer's four admirers feels the loss of peace and understanding he seemed to offer.

Heathen Chinee, The, see *Plain Language from Truthful James.*

HECHT, Anthony [Evan] (1923–), New York-born poet, whose infrequent volumes are carefully crafted, formal in manner but moving in their treatment of personal and philosophic subject matter. *A Summoning of Stones* (1954) was in part reprinted with new poems in *The Hard Hours* (1967, Pulitzer Prize). Other collections include *The Seven Deadly Sins* (1958), *A Bestiary* (1960), *Millions of Strange Shadows* (1977), and *The Venetian Vespers* (1979). His skill in metrics and his wit are seen in *Jiggery-Pokery: A Compendium of Double Dactyls* (1967), written and edited with John Hollander. He also translated Aeschylus' *Seven Against Thebes* (1973) with Helen Bacon.

HECHT, Ben (1894–1964), born in New York, reared in Wisconsin, was a bohemian member of the literary group that flourished in Chicago just after World War I. He was known as an ironical, cynical, ultra-romantic writer, who was variously dubbed an "intellectual mountebank" and "Pagliacci of the Fire Escape." He drew attention to himself in various ways, such as having a well-publicized literary feud with his friend Maxwell Bodenheim, with whom he wrote *The Master Poisoner* (1918) and other plays; publishing the *Chicago Literary Times* (1923–24), a gaudy iconoclastic little magazine; and vociferously espousing the cause of art-for-art's-sake. His attitude of mind was revealed in his novels, including *Erik Dorn* (1921), and stories. With Charles MacArthur he wrote a popular play, *The Front Page* (1928), a lively, tough treatment of life on a metropolitan newspaper staff. *A Child of the Century* (1954) is his autobiography.

HECKER, Isaac Thomas (1819–88), born in New York, early came under the influence of Orestes Brownson, visited Brook Farm and Fruitlands, and was intimate with the Transcendentalists. He entered the Roman Catholic Church (1844) and was expelled from the

Redemptorist order 13 years later, but was permitted by the pope to found the Paulist Fathers, of which he was the superior until his death. *The Catholic World,* an eclectic monthly magazine that he founded (1865) and edited until his death, is still in existence, having become a bimonthly and changing its name to *New Catholic World* in 1971.

HEGGEN, THOMAS [ORLO] (1919–49), on the basis of naval service in the Pacific during World War II and a knowledge of the interests of a mass audience gained through his prior career with *Reader's Digest,* wrote the very popular novel *Mister Roberts* (1946), about the dull day-to-day life aboard a cargo ship, its stupid captain, and its decent cargo officer. It was also successfully adapted as a play.

HEINLEIN, ROBERT A[NSON] (1907–), graduated from Annapolis, served in the navy (1929–34), and did graduate work in physics at the University of California, Los Angeles, before beginning his career as a writer of science fiction, of which he had published 35 books to 1980. His very popular and influential works deal mostly with the future, outer space, and eugenic breeding of humans but are also often tinged with mysticism and marked by sociopolitical views variously called rightist or anarchistic. His Future History, composed of relatively short fictive sketches, includes *The Man Who Sold the Moon* (1950), *The Green Hills of Earth* (1951), *Revolt in 2100* (1953), *Methuselah's Children* (1958), and *Orphans of the Sky* (1963). Of his numerous longer novels the most popular is *Stranger in a Strange Land* (1961), whose hero is a human born of space travelers from earth and raised by Martians. He is brought to the totalitarian post-World War III world that is in many ways depicted as a satire of the U.S. in the 1960s, marked by repressiveness in sexual morality and religion. The plot, which tells how the heroic stranger creates a Utopian society in which people preserve their individuality but share a brotherhood of community, made Heinlein and his novel cult objects for young people dedicated to a counterculture. Heinlein has continued to publish prolifically other novels, including *The Moon Is a Harsh Mistress* (1967), *Time Enough for Love* (1973), *The Number of the Beast* (1980), and *Friday* (1982); works of nonfiction; many books for children; stories for magazines not collected into volumes; and film and television scripts.

HELD, JOHN, JR. (1889–1958), illustrator known for his woodcuts and drawings imitating this technique, which burlesqued the style and subject matter of the 1890s. Both as author and as artist, in such books as *Grim Youth* (1930) and *The Flesh Is Weak* (1931), he was considered a leading interpreter of the younger generation of the jazz age.

HELLER, JOSEPH (1923–), New York author who served in the air force in World War II. Later he received an A.B. from New York University, an M.A. from Columbia, studied at Oxford, and taught briefly before writing *Catch-22*♦ (1961). This grotesquely comic tale of a madcap bombardier's resistance to his fanatic commander's ambition for promotion at the expense of his American squadron on a Mediterranean island satirizes military illogicality and glorification. It became enormously popular, particularly among younger readers during the Vietnam era, and its title became a catch phrase. Heller's next novel, *Something Happened* (1974), is a dark view of the life of a business executive, disgusted with what he does and is. *Good as Gold* (1979) is a long novel more in the comic vein of his first in its farcical treatment of Jewish family life and of the Washington political scene. *God Knows* (1984) is a lively first-person novel of the Biblical David. *We Bombed in New Haven* (1968) and *Clevinger's Trial* (1974) are plays.

HELLMAN, LILLIAN (1905–84), New York dramatist whose plays include *The Children's Hour* (1934), a tragedy of a malicious child accusing the owners of her boarding school of lesbianism; *Days To Come* (1936), about a strike; *The Little Foxes* (1939), about a reactionary Southern family's struggle to retain wealth and power despite internal feuds and the encroachments of modern society; *Watch on the Rhine* (1941), about an anti-Nazi in the U.S., with his American wife, who is forced to murder to fight against Hitlerism; *The Searching Wind* (1944), about the family of a former U.S. ambassador in wartime Washington and prewar Europe; *Another Part of the Forest* (1946); *The Autumn Garden* (1951), about middle-aged people trying to recapture a sense of youth; and *Toys in the Attic* (1960), set in New Orleans and treating the theme of miscegenation. *My Mother, My Father and Me* (1963) is an adaptation of the novel *How Much?* by Burt Blechman. She collaborated with Richard Wilbur on the comic opera *Candide* (1957), based on Voltaire's work. Her memoirs appeared as *An Unfinished Woman* (1969), emphasizing her personal experiences rather than her literary career; *Pentimento* (1973), about interesting persons she knew; *Scoundrel Time* (1976), an account of her experiences and those of friends during the McCarthy era's hunt for "un-American activities," all brought together as *Three* (1979); and *Maybe* (1980).

HELPER, HINTON ROWAN (1829–1909), North Carolina author, spent three years in California during the gold rush, and wrote his impressions in *Land of Gold: Reality Versus Fiction* (1855). He then became interested in the problem of slavery, and wrote *The Impending Crisis of the South: How To Meet It* (1857), discussing the question from an economic point of view and advocating free labor, although only in the interest of the whites, since he despised blacks. Unpopular in the South, this antislavery argument was widely distributed by Republicans and Abolitionists and won Helper the post of U.S. consul at Buenos Aires. After his return (1866), he wrote three passionate books denouncing the very existence of‑colored races, the first of these being *Nojoque: A Question for a Continent* (1867), a furious satire demanding the extinction of blacks and prophesying a happy "golden age" to be inaugurated by "the total absence of all the swarthy and inferior races of men." He devoted most of the rest of his life to an unsuccessful project that is described in *The Three Americas Railway* (1881).

HEMINGWAY, ERNEST [MILLER] (1899–1961), born in Illinois, while attending school made frequent hunting and fishing expeditions in northern Michigan, which helped condition his later primitivistic attitude. After working as a Kansas City reporter, he joined a volunteer ambulance unit in France, was seriously wounded on the Italian front, returned to the U.S. (Jan. 1919), and then went to Toronto to write for the *Star*. As its foreign correspondent in Paris (1921) he became an expatriate.

Influenced by Ezra Pound and particularly by Gertrude Stein, whose style strongly affected him, he published *Three Stories & Ten Poems* (Paris, 1923) and *In Our Time*♦ (U.S., 1925). These early stories already exhibited the attitude of mind and technique for which he later became famous. As the leading spokesman for the "lost generation" he expressed the feelings of a war-wounded people disillusioned by the loss of faith and

hope, and so thoroughly defeated by the collapse of former values that, their atrophied nerves not permitting them to attack their betrayers, they could turn only to a stoic acceptance of primal emotions. The stories are mainly concerned with "tough" people, either intelligent men and women who have dropped into an exhausted cynicism, or such primitives as frontiersmen, Indians, and professional athletes, whose essential courage and honesty are implicitly contrasted with the brutality of civilized society. Emotion is held at arm's length; only the bare happenings are recorded, and emphasis is obtained by understatement and spare dialogue.

After Hemingway returned to New York and wrote the lesser satirical novel *The Torrents of Spring* (1926), he carried the style and attitude of his short stories into the novel *The Sun Also Rises*♦ (1926), which tells of the moral collapse of a group of expatriated Americans and Englishmen, broken by the war, who turn toward escape through all possible violent diversions. Success in fictional craftsmanship and in portraying the mind of an era was again achieved in *A Farewell to Arms*♦ (1929), the poignant love story of an English nurse and an American ambulance lieutenant during the war. Besides further distinguished collections of short stories, *Men Without Women*♦ (1927) and *Winner Take Nothing*♦ (1933), he wrote only two lesser books during the next few years, although his work continued to exercise a great influence on the literature of the period. *Death in the Afternoon*♦ (1932), a book on bullfighting, and *Green Hills of Africa* (1935), an account of big-game hunting with digressions on literary matters, show a further cultivation of the primitive and brutal levels, contrasted with the hollow culture that had cheated his generation.

In *To Have and Have Not*♦ (1937), Hemingway for the first time showed an interest in a possible solution of social problems through collective action. This attitude continued in newspaper articles from Spain about its civil war, whose espionage was the subject of his realistic play, *The Fifth Column*, adapted for the stage (1940) by Benjamin Glazer, and printed in *The Fifth Column and the First Forty-Nine Stories* (1938), in which appeared two of his finest stories, "The Short Happy Life of Francis Macomber"♦ and "The Snows of Kilimanjaro."♦ *For Whom the Bell Tolls*♦ (1940), his longest novel, on an incident in the Spanish Civil War, has universality in its thesis that the loss of liberty in one place means a loss everywhere. He edited an anthology, *Men at War* (1942), but issued no new novel until *Across the River and into the Trees* (1950), which was considered to show that Hemingway had become bitter and defeatist like his tale's protagonist, an aging colonel. With *The Old Man and the Sea*♦ (1952), a parable of man against nature in a poignant novelette, he recaptured his critical acclaim, recognized in a Nobel Prize (1954).

In his last years he published nothing, and he had been seriously ill for some time before his death as a suicide by gunshot. However, several posthumous works followed, most notably *A Moveable Feast*♦ (1964), sketches of his life and acquaintances in Paris, 1921–1926, and *Islands in the Stream* (1970), a novel in three parts about a painter's unhappy marriage, his affection for his sons, their deaths, his bravery in war, his pleasure in deep-sea fishing, and his loneliness. Later compilations include *The Wild Years* (1962), his journalism for the Toronto *Star; By-Lines* (1967), selected journalism of four decades; *The Nick Adams Stories* (1972), eight of them previously unpublished; and three collections of verse, the last and most inclusive being *88 Poems* (1979). *Selected Letters* was issued in 1981.

Henderson the Rain King, novel by Saul Bellow,♦ published in 1959.

Gene Henderson, an intense, vital millionaire, leaves his Connecticut home for Africa in quest of wisdom, and to satisfy his inner voice's cry, "I want, I want." With Romilayu, a loyal guide, he visits the Arnewi, a humane, cattle-loving people suffering from drought. He makes friends with the king Itelo and his aunts, Mtalba and Queen Willatale, serene, wise women, tries to aid them by cleansing the polluted water supply, but accidentally destroys it, and leaves, disgraced and saddened. Traveling to the island of the Wariri, he finds drought again and he wagers the king, Dahfu, that there will be no rain, but, overwhelmed by a tremendous "wish to *do* something . . . to work the right stitch into the design of destiny before it was too late," he persuades Dahfu to let him try to move an immense idol, the statue of the goddess of clouds. He succeeds, a deluge follows, and although he is made Sungo, the rain king, he is also delivered into the power of the ruler to whom he lost the bet. From Dahfu he learns the fate of Wariri kings: when one weakens, he is killed and his spirit becomes a lion cub that the king's successor must catch within two years. Dahfu, still in his period of trial, has yet to capture Gmilo, the lion spirit of his father, but his uncle Horko, the Queen Mother, and Bunam, the high priest, force him to his obligation, and in his attempt he is clawed to death. As Sungo, Henderson succeeds Dahfu, into whose tomb he is placed near the cub that symbolizes the late king's spirit. Sure that Horko and Bunam effected Dahfu's death, Henderson and Romilayu escape, taking the cub. His inner voice at last quieted, and with an understanding of himself, Henderson and the cub, named Dahfu, take off for his home, after a life "discontinuous with civilization."

HENLEY, BETH (1952?–), Mississippi-born playwright, attended Southern Methodist University, had her first full-length play, *Crimes of the Heart,* performed (1979) in Louisville, where it won a major local prize, and then, after an off-Broadway production, won a Pulitzer Prize (1980). With Gothic humor it presents the antics of three eccentric sisters in a small Mississippi town. *The Miss Firecracker Contest* (1980), produced in her new home in southern California, concerns other bizarre characters and situations in a small Mississippi town.

HENRY, O., pseudonym of W.S. Porter. ♦

HERBST, JOSEPHINE [FREY] (1892–1969), Iowa-born proletarian author, graduated from the University of California (1918). Her major fiction is a trilogy about an American family, the Trexlers: *Pity Is Not Enough* (1933) tells of a son who loses health, wealth, and faith during the Gilded Age; *The Executioner Waits* (1934) shows the family during the years 1918 to 1929, typifying the era's social conflicts and personal frustrations; and *Rope of Gold* (1939) follows the younger Trexlers through the economic chaos of the 1930s. Other novels include *Nothing Is Sacred* (1928), *Money for Love* (1929), *Satan's Sergeants* (1941), and *Somewhere the Tempest Fell* (1947). *The Unknown Americas* (1939) is a social study of Latin America; *New Green World* (1954) depicts John Bartram and other early American naturalists.

HERFORD, OLIVER (1863–1935), English-born humorist, reared in Boston and educated at Antioch College, in his twenties began to contribute to popular journals, and by the turn of the century began to publish his long series of books of prose and verse, many illustrated by his pen-and-ink caricatures. In both media he was an accomplished craftsman possessed of a pleasant wit. His volumes include *The Bashful Earthquake* (1898), *A Child's Primer of Natural History* (1899), *A Little Book of Bores* (1906), *Confessions of a Caricaturist* (1917), *Excuse It, Please* (1929), and *The Deb's Dictionary* (1931). He also wrote plays.

HERGESHEIMER, Joseph (1880–1954), author of romantic character studies frequently treating long-established American families in novels that include *Mountain Blood* (1915), contrasting newly rich and established Virginians; *The Three Black Pennys* (1917), treating the rise and fall of a family of Pennsylvania industrialists; *Java Head* (1919), portraying a Chinese woman married into an old family of Salem sea captains; and *The Limestone Tree* (1931), about Kentucky pioneers and their descendants. He also wrote biographies, essays, travel sketches, and an autobiography.

HERLIHY, James Leo (1927–), Detroit-born author, educated at Black Mountain College, has written novels including *All Fall Down* (1960), depicting the disintegration of a middle-class American family; *Midnight Cowboy* (1965), presenting an ingenuous cowboy who goes to New York City, where he participates in its seamy nightlife and lovingly takes up with a crippled pickpocket; and *The Season of the Witch* (1971), about a young girl who runs away from home and also finds refuge among New York's drifters. He has written plays, including *Blue Denim* (1958), *Crazy October* (1958), and *Stop, You're Killing Me* (1968), and stories collected in *The Sleep of Baby Filbertson* (1959) and *A Story That Ends with a Scream* (1967).

HERSEY, John [Richard] (1914–), born in Tientsin, China, of American missionary parents, was educated in China, the U.S. (Yale, 1936), and England. He was Sinclair Lewis's secretary (1937), became a correspondent for *Time,* and wrote books about events in World War II: *Men on Bataan* (1942), *Into the Valley* (1943), and *Hiroshima* (1946). Some of his novels also use a documentary technique, like *A Bell for Adano* (1944, Pulitzer Prize), about the early days of Allied rule in a Sicilian village; and *The Wall* (1950; dramatized, 1961, by Millard Lampell), about the ill-fated uprising in Warsaw's ghetto against the Nazis. Others have a symbolic character, like *The Marmot Drive* (1953), a tale of depraved New Englanders ridding a valley of woodchucks; *The Child Buyer* (1960), a satirical parable about modern education, dramatized by Paul Shyre

(1964); *White Lotus* (1965), a parable of race relations, treating a mythical Oriental land in which white people are enslaved; and *Under the Eye of the Storm* (1967), a tale of two couples aboard the boat *Harmony* as a hurricane sweeps them to sea. *Here To Stay* (1963) collects *Hiroshima* and eight other "studies in human tenacity." Later nonfiction includes *The Algiers Motel Incident* (1968), about an episode in the Detroit racial riots of 1967; *Letter to the Alumni* (1970), a discussion of dissidence and other problems of students at Yale, where he has been affiliated with the faculty since 1950.

Herzog, novel by Saul Bellow,♦ published in 1964.

Moses Herzog, a professor of history in New York City, undergoes a crisis when his wife Madeline divorces him. To find surcease he goes to Martha's Vineyard and occupies himself composing letters in his mind and on paper, addressed to friends and public figures, living and dead, on issues that plague him. Told that Madeline and her lover, Valentine Gersbach, once Herzog's best friend, are neglecting his daughter June, he rushes to Chicago to get custody of the girl and even plans to murder his former wife and onetime friend. Serio-comic misadventures frustrate his plans, and he goes back to Massachusetts "pretty well satisfied to be, to be just as it is willed . . ." with "no messages for anyone."

HEYWARD, DuBose (1885–1940), South Carolina author, began his career with *Carolina Chansons* (1922), poems written with Hervey Allen, and is best known for his novel about blacks in Charleston, *Porgy*♦ (1925), whose dramatic version, written with his wife Dorothy, won a Pulitzer Prize and was made into an opera by George Gershwin, as *Porgy and Bess* (1935).

Hiawatha, The Song of, narrative poem by Longfellow♦ in unrhymed trochaic tetrameter, published in 1855. Its novel and facile meter has led to many parodies and imitations. The meter derives from the Finnish epic *Kalevala,* which the poem resembles in spirit as well as in several striking passages.

Hiawatha is reared by his grandmother, Nokomis, daughter of the Moon, among the Ojibway on the southern shore of Lake Superior. He learns the language of the birds and animals, secures magic mittens that will crush rocks and magic moccasins that enable him to take mile-long strides, and he seeks vengeance on his father, Mudjekeewis, the West Wind, for a wrong committed against his mother, Wenonah. The fight ends in a reconciliation, and Hiawatha returns as the defender and civilizer of his people. Later he defeats Mondamin, the Corn Spirit, from whose buried body springs the maize, after which he builds a birchbark canoe, has a contest with Nahma, the sturgeon, who swallows both canoe and warrior, and destroys Pearl-Feather, sender of disease and death. The youth then marries Minnehaha, lovely daughter of an arrow-maker of the once hostile Dakotah. The wedding feast and Song of the Evening Star inaugurate an idyllic time of peace and culture, over which Hiawatha rules until the death of his friends, Chibiabos the musician and Kwasind the strong man. Although he kills Pau-Puk-Keewis, who had insulted him, famine and fever visit the people and claim Minnehaha. Golden swarms of bees appear as forerunners of the whites, whose coming Hiawatha prophesied. Telling his people to heed a missionary offering a new religion, he departs for the Isles of the Blest in Keewaydin to rule the kingdom of the Northwest Wind.

HICKS, GRANVILLE (1901–82), a leading Communist critic and editor of *The New Masses,* wrote a Marxist interpretation of American literature since the Civil War, *The Great Tradition* (1933). With John Stuart he wrote a biography of John Reed (1936), and with Ella Winter edited the *Letters of Lincoln Steffens* (1938). *Figures of Transition* (1939), published the year he resigned from the Communist party, is a Marxist study of British literature at the end of the 19th century. He also wrote novels, a book on James Gould Cozzens (1967), essays titled *Literary Horizons* (1970), and *Part of the Truth* (1965), an autobiography.

HIGGINSON, FRANCIS (1586–1630), English nonconformist clergyman, emigrated to Salem (1629), where he was elected pastor, but died from the hardships of the winter. Part of his journal was published in England as *New-Englands Plantation* (1630), and the complete journal in the *Life* (1891) by T.W. Higginson.

HIGGINSON, THOMAS WENTWORTH (1823–1911), born at Cambridge, graduated from Harvard (1841) and Harvard Divinity School, and became a Unitarian minister. During the Civil War, he was colonel of the first regiment of black soldiers, and his war experi-

ences are described in *Army Life in a Black Regiment* (1870). After being wounded, he retired to Newport, later returning to Cambridge to devote himself to writing, teaching, and social reform, being particularly interested in equal rights for blacks and in the woman suffrage movement. His books include *Malbone* (1869), a novel; sketches, including *Oldport Days* (1873) and *Old Cambridge* (1899); the lives of Whittier (1902) and Longfellow (1902) for the Men of Letters series; biographies of Margaret Fuller (1884) and of his ancestor, Francis Higginson (1891); and an autobiographical account, *Cheerful Yesterdays* (1898), valuable for its information about his contemporaries. Higginson was the first to encourage Emily Dickinson, although he tended to "correct" her poems. He edited two volumes of her verse with Mabel L. Todd (1890–91).

HIMES, CHESTER [BOMAR] (1909–84), Missouri-born novelist about the life of fellow blacks in the U.S., attended Ohio State University but began his literary career while in Ohio State Penitentiary (1929–36) for armed robbery. His first novel, *If He Hollers Let Him Go* (1945), depicts with fury the prejudice met by a black worker in California defense plants, an experience he suffered. It was followed by *Lonely Crusade* (1947), about a black laborer meeting discrimination in unions and the Communist party; *Cast the First Stone* (1952), a naturalistic novel about blacks and whites in prison; and *Third Generation* (1954), a saga of a black family from slavery to the mid-20th century. The year of the last publication he became an expatriate in Europe, and his next novel, *The Primitive* (1955), is quasi-autobiographical in its story of a black author and his white mistress. In France he published Harlem murder tales featuring black detectives. He also published *Black on Black* (1973), a collection of shorter works, and a two-volume autobiography, *The Quality of Hurt* (1972) and *My Life as Absurdity* (1976).

History of New York, A, From the Beginning of the World to the End of the Dutch Dynasty, by Diedrich Knickerbocker, burlesque history by Irving,♦ published in 1809 and revised in 1812, 1819, and 1848. It satirizes the methods of contemporary historians, the heroic style of epic poetry, and men and events during the Dutch administration as well as during its own period. Although Irving follows the history of New Netherland as then known, his satirical intention causes him to alter or disregard facts, as when, in the figure of William the Testy (William Kieft), he draws a Federalist caricature of Jefferson. According to the preface, the fictitious chronicler was "a small brisk looking old gentleman . . . a very inquisitive body . . . although a little queer in his ways."

Book I contains a cosmogony and description of the world, parodying contemporary histories, and a burlesque account of the discovery and peopling of America. Book II chronicles the voyage of Hudson, early Dutch colonization, and the founding of New Amsterdam, and gives traditional portraits of Dutch colonial types. Book III describes the "golden reign" of the stolid governor Wouter Van Twiller, who was "exactly five feet six inches in height, and six feet five inches in circumference," and whose head was "a perfect sphere"; the profound deliberations of his burgomasters over their pipes; conditions in early New Amsterdam; the hostility of the neighboring Yankees of Connecticut; and the establishment of Fort Goed Hoop. Book IV tells of the governorship of William the Testy, so learned that he was "good for nothing"; his pugnacity; his war "by proclamation" with the Yankees; his many laws, partisan quarrels, and border disputes. Books V, VI, and VII chronicle the reign of Peter Stuyvesant (Peter the Headstrong): his political reforms and military adventures in Delaware; and his unsuccessful defense of New Amsterdam against the conquering British force.

History of Plimmoth Plantation, see *Plimmoth Plantation, History of.*

History of the Dividing Line, journal of William Byrd♦ during 1728, found among his Westover Manuscripts and first published in 1841. These offhand daily jottings about Byrd's survey of the Virginia-North Carolina border begin with a sparkling sketch of Virginia history, and proceed to caustic comments upon the residents of North Carolina. This vivacious account and its various digressions show Byrd to be a witty, observant, and graceful writer. A variant, *The Secret History of the Line,* was published in 1929.

HOAGLAND, EDWARD (1932–), New York City-born author, graduated from Harvard. His novels include *Cat Man* (1956), about circus life; *The Circle Home* (1960), dealing with prizefighters; and *The Peacock's Tail* (1965), set in a city's slums. Other works include a book about travel in British Colum-

bia, *Notes from the Century Before* (1969), and *The Courage of Turtles* (1971), *Walking the Dead Diamond River* (1972), *Red Wolves and Black Bears* (1976), and *The Tugman's Passage* (1982), essays on rural and urban life, ecology, and animals.

HOFFMAN, DANIEL [GERARD] (1923–), New York City-born author, educated at Columbia, is a professor at the University of Pennsylvania. His first book of poetry, *An Armada of Thirty Whales* (1954), was selected for the Yale Series of Younger Poets. Later volumes include *A Little Geste* (1960), *Striking the Stones* (1968), and *Brotherly Love* (1980), a long poem celebrating the city of Philadelphia. Hoffman has also written critical works on Stephen Crane (1957) and Poe (1972).

HOLLANDER, JOHN (1929–), New York City-born poet, received his A.B. from Columbia and Ph.D. from Indiana University and since 1959 has been a member of Yale's faculty, except 1966–77, when he was at Hunter College. *A Crackling of Thorns* (1958), sophisticated poems, was selected by Auden for the Yale Younger Poets Award, and Auden has been an influence on him, along with the metaphysicals and the tradition of English song represented by Campion and Jonson. Hollander is himself an accomplished musician and wrote the scholarly study *The Untuning of the Sky: Ideas of Music in English Poetry, 1500–1700* (1961). These two earliest books were followed by *Movie-Going* (1962) and *Visions from the Ramble* (1965), poems whose inspirations came from his native city's Broadway and Central Park. His next book, *Types of Shape* (1968), further displayed his virtuosity through its shaped poems reminiscent of Quarles and Herbert. *The Night Mirror* (1971), *Town and Country Matters: Erotica and Satirica* (1972), and *The Head of the Bed* (1973) are further collections showing his remarkable variety, ranging from the philosophic to the sprightly, as well as his command of accented syllabic versification, which in *Tales Told of the Father* (1975) became purely syllabic. *Reflections on Espionage* (1976) contains his witty poetic commentary on contemporary poets and his own concepts of poetry. *Spectral Emanations* (1978) contains selected poems; *Jiggery-Pokery* (1967) is a collection of double-dactylic poems created with Anthony Hecht♦; and *Powers of Thirteen* (1983), the poet's 13th collection, contains 169 (13 × 13) poems of

13 lines, each containing 13 syllables. *Various Owls* (1963) contains nonsense poems for children; and *The Quest of the Gole* (1966) is a mock-epic written for young people. Other works include a masque, *An Entertainment for Elizabeth* (1972), and critical works: *Images of Voice* (1969), *The Figure of Echo* (1981), and *Rhyme's Reason* (1981), a guide to English verse forms, illustrated by Hollander's own witty examples.

Hollingsworth, character in *The Blithedale Romance.* ♦

Hollow Men, The, poem by T.S. Eliot. ♦

Hollywood, district of Los Angeles, situated eight miles northeast of the city's downtown and long famous as the center of motion-picture production for the world. Because of this association the area became synonymous with the flamboyance and glamour attached to the industry and its stars. Besides inspiring a great quantity of romantic fiction as well as serious sociological studies, the place has been the subject of much satirical treatment, e.g. Kaufman's plays, *Once in a Lifetime* and *Stage Door,* and such novels as H.L. Wilson's *Merton of the Movies,* Van Vechten's *Spider Boy,* Fitzgerald's *The Last Tycoon,* Elmer Rice's *A Voyage to Purilia,* John O'Hara's *Hope of Heaven,* Nathanael West's *The Day of the Locust,* Schulberg's *What Makes Sammy Run?,* and Bemelmans's *Dirty Eddy.* Among the dramatists and novelists who have spent time in Hollywood writing for films are Maxwell Anderson, Ray Bradbury, Bromfield, Joan Didion, Dreiser, John Gregory Dunne, Faulkner, F. Scott Fitzgerald, Daniel Fuchs, Ben Hecht, Sidney Howard, George S. Kaufman, Jeremy Larner, Charles MacArthur, Thomas McGuane, David Mamet, Odets, Dorothy Parker, S.J. Perelman, Robert Sherwood, Phil Stong, and Nathanael West. In the post-World War II era of vigorous anticommunism a group labeled the Hollywood Ten (including the writers Alvah Bessie, Ring Lardner, Jr., John Howard Lawson, Albert Maltz, and Dalton Trumbo) were indicted for refusing to testify before the Congressional Committee on Un-American Activities and as a result were blacklisted by film studios for a long time.

HOLMES, JOHN CLELLON (1926–), born in Massachusetts, after navy service in World War II and studies at Columbia and The New School for Social Research began to publish poetry in magazines. *The Bowling Green Poems* (1977) and *Death Drag* (1979) are collections. He is best known for his novels, *Go* (1952), about Beat intellectual drifters in New York City; *The Horn* (1958), presenting the sad latter days of a black saxophonist; and *Get Home Free* (1964), about the misalliance of a bohemian couple. *Nothing More To Declare* (1967) is an autobiographical backward look at Beat writers. His early works were signed by his middle name and surname.

HOLMES, OLIVER WENDELL (1809–94), was born at Cambridge, reared in the traditions of the Brahmin class, and graduated from Harvard in the class of 1829, which he helped to make famous by his long series of reunion poems. His first verse to bring him popularity was "Old Ironsides" ♦ (1830). While studying medicine at Harvard and in Boston, he published in *The New-England Magazine* (1831–32) two papers entitled "The Autocrat of the Breakfast-Table," which were precursors of his later famous work. After two years of study in Paris hospitals, he received his M.D. from Harvard (1836), and his collection of witty occasional *Poems* (1836) was his last literary contribution for some time, since he turned to his chosen profession. From 1847 until his retirement in 1882, he was Parkman Professor of Anatomy and Physiology at Harvard, and for the first six years also served as dean of the Harvard Medical School.

His stimulating qualities as a lecturer soon brought him before the public in the lyceums. As a witty, urbane conversationalist, he reigned supreme in Boston society and club life and became the unofficial poet laureate of all important gatherings in the intellectual "hub of the Universe." As a reformer he was simply a scientific rationalist opposing the Calvinistic dogmas by which he had been reared. He was probably the most militant Unitarian among Boston laymen, and he attacked the religion of his fathers consistently in prose and poetry, notably in "The Deacon's Masterpiece" ♦ (1858) and the more vituperative "The Moral Bully," which satirizes a preacher's hypocritical virtues.

When the *Atlantic Monthly* was founded (1857), Holmes not only named it but also, as a leading contributor, was influenced to become primarily a man of letters. He contributed *The Autocrat of the Breakfast-Table* ♦ (1858), which he followed with *The Professor at the Breakfast-Table* (1860), *The Poet at the Breakfast-Table* (1872), and *Over the Teacups*

(1891), all reflections of the original. Selections from his endless flow of poetry peppered these volumes, notably "The Chambered Nautilus"♦ and "The Deacon's Masterpiece"♦ in the first volume. He also turned to fiction, and in *Elsie Venner*♦ (1861) wrote the best of his three "medicated novels." All exhibit his theological and biological views and are studies of abnormal psychology, but *The Guardian Angel* (1867) and *A Mortal Antipathy* (1885) show diminishing ability. He reprinted from the *Atlantic* two collections of essays, *Soundings from the Atlantic* (1864) and *Pages from an Old Volume of Life* (1883), wrote biographies of Motley (1879) and Emerson (1885), and collected a volume of *Medical Essays* (1883). His addresses, lectures, and minor essays would constitute a large collection.

Besides the several enlarged editions of his *Poems,* his verse was issued in many volumes, including *Songs in Many Keys* (1826), *Songs of Many Seasons* (1875), *The Iron Gate* (1880), and *Before the Curfew* (1888). Although most of his poems were written for specific occasions, some have transcended their occasional nature. Among the best known are "The Ballad of the Oysterman" (1830), a parody of romantic balladry; "The Last Leaf"♦ (1831), on an aged survivor of the Boston Tea Party; "My Aunt" (1831), on the "sad, ungathered rose" of his ancestral tree; "The Boys," written for the thirtieth reunion of his Harvard class; "Bill and Joe" (1851), another reunion poem; "A Sunday Hymn" (1860), which begins "Lord of all being! throned afar"; "Contentment," a humorous poem on "simple pleasures," from the *Autocrat;* "The Living Temple," also from the *Autocrat,* a hymn on man's "wondrous frame"; "Brother Jonathan's Lament for Sister Caroline" (1861), a patriotic poem on the secession of South Carolina; and "Dorothy Q." (1871), a sentimentally humorous piece on a family portrait.

HOLMES, OLIVER WENDELL, JR. (1841–1935), son and namesake of the well-known writer and professor of medicine, was himself professor of law at Harvard, chief justice of the Massachusetts supreme court (1899–1902), and associate justice of the U.S. Supreme Court (1902–32). His writings include *The Common Law* (1881), *Speeches* (1891, 1913), and *Collected Legal Papers* (1920), all exhibiting his distinction of mind and liberal views. Felix Frankfurter wrote *Mr. Justice Holmes and the Constitution* (1927). *Touched with Fire* (1946) collects his

Civil War diary and letters. His correspondence with Sir Frederick Pollock was published in 1941, and his letters to and from Harold J. Laski, in 1953. He is the subject of more popular treatment in Catherine Drinker Bowen's biography, *Yankee from Olympus* (1944), and Emmet Lavery's play *The Magnificent Yankee* (1946).

Home as Found, novel by Cooper,♦ published in 1838 as a sequel to *Homeward Bound.* ♦

Homeward Bound; or, The Chase, novel by Cooper,♦ published in 1838. *Home as Found*♦ is a sequel.

HOOKER, THOMAS (1586–1647), English-born Congregationalist, emigrated to Massachusetts (1633). He was pastor at Newe Towne (Cambridge) for three years, and then, because of his democratic views, took his entire congregation of some 100 families to found the Connecticut Colony. In *A Survey of the Summe of Church Discipline* (1648), he defended New England Congregationalism and postulated the principle of divine absolutism, making temporal absolutism unnecessary. The sovereign will of God, he held, was represented by no ecclesiastical hierarchy, but was communicated directly to the individual believer. The people, walking together in the fellowship of faith, communicate power by voluntary subjection to the governing pastor. A second volume of this work was written by John Cotton.♦

Hoosier Schoolmaster, The, novel by Edward Eggleston,♦ published in 1871. It is based on experiences of his brother George.

Hopi Indians (also called MOQUI or MOKI), agricultural tribe inhabiting a group of pueblos on the mesas of northeastern Arizona. First known to the Spaniards in 1540 through Coronado's expedition, they were made vassals by Juan de Oñate in 1598. Missionary work among them was carried on precariously from 1629 to 1700, when their hostility compelled its abandonment. After the Pueblo Revolt of 1680, their villages were built on mesas for defense against the Spaniards. The Hopi are noted for their mythology and ceremonial dances, including the biennial snake dance. They figure in Willa Cather's *Death Comes for the Archbishop* and in Edna Dean Proctor's *Song of an Ancient People.*

HOPKINSON, FRANCIS (1737–91), Philadelphia patriot, statesman, musician, and poet, was the first graduate of the College of Philadelphia. He was a signer of the Declaration of Independence and a lively political satirist, particularly known for his rollicking poem, "The Battle of the Kegs,"♦ and the lively prose allegory, *A Pretty Story* (1774), treating the events that led to the first Continental Congres.

HORGAN, PAUL (1903–   ), born in Buffalo, N.Y., reared there and in New Mexico. His novels include *The Fault of Angels* (1933), about professional musicians; *The Habit of Empire* (1939), about 16th-century New Mexico; *A Distant Trumpet* (1960), set on an Arizona army post of the 1880s; and *Things as They Are* (1964), beginning a trilogy about the life and early death of a rich young man in Philadelphia and New Mexico, continued in *Everything To Live For* (1968) and *The Thin Mountain Air* (1977). *Figures in a Landscape* (1940) and *The Peach Stone* (1967) collect stories, the former with essays. *Great River* (1954), a history of the Rio Grande, earned him a Pulitzer Prize, as did *Lamy of Santa Fe* (1975), a study of a pioneer bishop. Lincoln figures in *Yours, A. Lincoln* (1942), a play, *Citizen of New Salem* (1961), an essay, and *Songs After Lincoln* (1965), poetic tributes. Historical studies include *Centuries of Santa Fe* (1956) and *Conquistadors in North American History* (1963).

Hound and Horn (1927–34), little magazine, founded as a "Harvard Miscellany" by Lincoln Kirstein and Varian Fry. The title came from Ezra Pound's "The White Stag": " 'Tis the white stag Fame we're hunting, bid the world's hounds come to horn." R.P. Blackmur and Bernard Bandler II became editors (1929), and the following year the magazine moved to New York, losing its association with Harvard. Kirstein became the sole editor, and the quarterly vacillated thereafter among humanism, Southern regionalism, Marxism, and the neoclassicism of its Western editor, Yvor Winters. In its attempt to publish the best avant-garde authors, *Hound and Horn* printed works by Katharine Anne Porter, Kenneth Burke, Allen Tate, Ezra Pound, Gertrude Stein, T.S. Eliot, and many others, whose reputations it helped to establish. *The "Hound and Horn" Letters* (1982) collects correspondence of editors and contributors.

House of Mirth, The, novel by Edith Wharton,♦ published in 1905.

Lily Bart, beautiful, charming, and related to prominent New York families, at 29 is searching for a rich husband with an important social position. She loves Lawrence Selden, a lawyer, who lacks the money she wants. While gambling at a house party she loses a large sum to Gus Trenor, who tries to get her to satisfy his passion by way of repayment. She escapes him and goes on a Mediterranean yachting party led by George Dorset, whose wife conceals a meeting with her lover by accusing Lily of being George's mistress. This ends Lily's life in fashionable society. She reveals her love to Selden but when he comes to her boarding house hoping that she will marry him, he finds that she has committed suicide, having put aside a bequest from her aunt to pay her debt to Trenor.

House of the Seven Gables, The, romance by Hawthorne,♦ published in 1851. It is based on the tradition of a curse pronounced on the author's family when his great-grandfather was a judge in the Salem witchcraft trials.

In Salem stands the ancestral home of the Pyncheons, cursed by Wizard Maule when the first Colonel Pyncheon despoiled him of his wealth. In the mid-19th century, the house is owned by hypocritical Judge Jaffrey Pyncheon, whose studied benevolence makes him an honored citizen. He does not live in the dilapidated mansion, whose occupants are his poor cousin Hepzibah, reduced to operating a cent-shop; a country relative, Phoebe; a single lodger, the young daguerreotypist Holgrave, who falls in love with Phoebe; and Hepzibah's brother Clifford, ill and feeble-minded, just released from prison after a term of 30 years for the supposed murder of a rich uncle. Jaffrey, who had obtained Clifford's arrest, now harasses him in an attempt to find the missing deeds to their rich uncle's property, and threatens to have Clifford confined in an insane asylum. Hepzibah attempts to aid her brother and circumvent the judge, but the latter's sudden death frees them and makes them his heirs. Holgrave reveals that he is actually the last of the Maules, and that the judge, like the rich uncle, died by the curse on the house. Revealing the location of the missing deeds, he marries Phoebe, leaving the House of the Seven Gables, freed of its curse, to Hepzibah and Clifford.

HOVEY, RICHARD (1864–1900), graduated from Dartmouth (1885), went to England and France (1891–1892), where he was influenced by the French Symbolists and translated Maeterlinck's plays. Then, with Bliss Carman, he wrote the exuberant *Songs from Vagabondia* (1894) and two sequels that reveled in ideas of the open road, of joyous youth and good companionship. His poem "Spring" (1898) contained a popular interlude, "A Stein Song," with the refrain, "For it's always fair weather/When good fellows get together."

HOWARD, RICHARD [JOSEPH] (1929–), Ohio-born poet, after an A.B. and M.A. from Columbia and study at the Sorbonne published his first collections, *Quantities* (1962) and *The Damages* (1967), followed by the Pulitzer Prize-winning *Untitled Subjects* (1969), written in syllabic verse and presenting 15 dramatic monologues of 19th-century writers, artists, and composers. *Findings* (1971) and *Fellow Feelings* (1976) present further dramatic monologues, while *Two-Part Inventions* (1974) consists of six fictitious dialogues, such as one between Oscar Wilde and Whitman in the latter's home. *Misgivings* (1979) contains commentaries of Sarah Bernhardt, Victor Hugo, and other subjects on their portraits by the French photographer Nadar, and *Lining Up* (1984) contains further dramatic monologues and dialogues. *Alone with America* (1969) is a prose work on 41 contemporary U.S. poets, and *Preferences* (1974) is his edition with commentary on works chosen by 51 contemporary American poets from their own writings and from favorite works of the past. Howard has also translated (1982) Baudelaire's *Les Fleurs du mal.*

HOWARD, SIDNEY [COE] (1891–1939), California-born playwright, graduated from the state university (1915), studied at Harvard in the 47 Workshop of G.P. Baker, served in World War I, established his reputation with *They Knew What They Wanted* (1924, Pulitzer Prize), about the bitter-sweet lives of an aging Italian winegrower of California and his mail-order bride. This was quickly followed by other successes, including *The Silver Cord* (1926), about a pathologically possessive widowed mother who destroys her son's life. With Charles MacArthur, he wrote *Salvation* (1928), a play about a woman revivalist. Howard's next play was *Alien Corn* (1933), the story of a music teacher in a small college, who forsakes her dream of becoming a

concert pianist because of her love for the married college president, and, when their affair ends, stifles her feelings and continues her teaching. Later plays include *Dodsworth* (1934), in collaboration with Sinclair Lewis.

HOWE, E[DGAR] W[ATSON] (1853–1937), born in Indiana, reared in Missouri and Nebraska, whose most famous novel, *The Story of a Country Town*♦ (1883), is a powerful, melodramatic tale of the narrow life of a Midwestern community, which was privately printed after being rejected by numerous publishers, but has come to be recognized as a significant pioneering work of naturalistic fiction and, in spite of the stilted dialogue and the author's pessimism, has been widely read and frequently republished.

HOWE, IRVING (1920–), professor at Hunter College (1963–) and literary and social critic. His books include *Sherwood Anderson: A Critical Biography* (1951); *William Faulkner: A Critical Study* (1952, revised 1962); *Politics and the Novel: A World More Attractive* (1963); *Steady Work* (1966), essays on the politics of democratic radicalism; *Thomas Hardy* (1967); *The Decline of the New* (1969), a study of the decline of modernism in literature; *The Critical Point* (1973), literary essays; *World of Our Fathers* (1976, National Book Award), about the experiences of East European Jews in the U.S.; *Leon Trotsky* (1978); and *Celebrations and Attacks* (1979), a collection of occasional writings. *A Margin of Hope* (1982) is subtitled "An Intellectual Biography."

HOWE, JULIA WARD (1819–1910), poet and lecturer on social reform, was particularly interested in Abolitionism and woman suffrage. With her husband, Samuel G. Howe, she edited the Boston *Commonwealth,* an antislavery paper, and among her books are *Sex and Education* (1874), *Modern Society* (1881), and a life of *Margaret Fuller* (1883). She is famous as the author of "The Battle Hymn of the Republic"♦ (1862).

HOWELLS, WILLIAM DEAN (1837–1920), born in Ohio, began at the age of nine to set type in his father's printing office. As he tells in *My Year in a Log Cabin* (1893) and "The Country Printer" in *Impressions and Experiences* (1896), his formal education was very slight and he had to school himself in the pressroom and from his father's bookcase. The family life in Hamilton, one of several Ohio towns to which they migrated, is revealed in the autobiographical *A Boy's Town* (1890). After many moves, the family settled in Columbus, where from 1856 to 1861 Howells wrote for the *Ohio State Journal,* and with J.J. Piatt published the *Poems of Two Friends* (1860). Meanwhile he was passionately studying languages and reading what literature he could obtain, activities which in later life he described in such volumes as *My Literary Passions* (1895), *Literary Friends and Acquaintance* (1900), *Years of My Youth* (1916), and others.

In 1860 he wrote a campaign biography of Lincoln, which won him the consulate at Venice. During his four years there he found time to write a pleasant observation of *Venetian Life* (1866) and *Italian Journeys* (1867), and his study of the language and literature later bore fruit in *Modern Italian Poets* (1887). Returning to America (1865), he was associated briefly with *The Nation,* and then accepted the subeditorship of the *Atlantic Monthly,* ♦ a post he held for five years, until he became editor in chief (1871–81). During these years, he lived in and near Boston, and, although he retained the democratic equalitarianism of the Ohio frontier, he also became an adopted son of Brahmin culture.

His first novel, *Their Wedding Journey* (1872), grew naturally out of his travel sketches, as did *A Chance Acquaintance* (1873) and *A Foregone Conclusion* (1875), the latter depicting an Italian background. *The Lady of the Aroostook* (1879) and *A Fearful Responsibility* (1881) both contrast American and Venetian characters and deal with conflicts between love and social rank. Other works of this first period were "Private Theatricals" (*Atlantic,* 1875–76; in book form as *Mrs. Farrell,* 1921); *The Undiscovered Country* (1880), a study of the sordidness of spiritualism and the true spirituality of the Shakers; and *Dr. Breen's Practice* (1881), which deals with the incompetence of a society woman as a physician.

In 1881 Howells forsook the *Atlantic* and began serializing his stories in the *Century Magazine.* At the same time, he departed from his earlier comedies of manners and studies of contrasting types to begin a series of realistic character studies, particularly of characters grappling with ethical problems. The first of these, *A Modern Instance* ♦ (1882), was followed by *A Woman's Reason* (1883), which in its study of feminine nature and Boston social values lacked the breadth of its predecessor and of the masterpiece on Boston and the self-made man that followed it, *The Rise of Silas Lapham* ♦ (1885). *Indian*

Summer (1886), the subtle portrait of a middle-aged widow and her problem of romance, is considered second only to the portrait of Silas Lapham. *The Minister's Charge* (1887) presents the theme that one cannot disclaim complicity with lives that surround one, while *April Hopes* (1888) shows a return to the comedy of manners, although it includes a tragic presentation of young love.

In *Annie Kilburn* (1889), Howells deals with the contrasts among the "summer people," the substantial inhabitants, and the laboring class of a New England town, and his consideration of false charity as against true justice shows an indictment of the existing economic system. This novel marked the change that now came to Howells's life. He moved to New York as a member of the editorial staff of *Harper's,* where he ranged more widely than he had under the Boston influence, and became interested in the larger problems of industrialism. A New York street railway strike, the conviction of the anarchists of the Haymarket Riot, the influence of Tolstoy, and the reading of such social reformers as Henry George, all caused him to turn toward socialism and to adapt his realistic fiction to the problems of the machine age. This transition is reflected in his first novel about New York, *A Hazard of New Fortunes* ♦ (1890), followed by the *Quality of Mercy* (1892), a study of the ramifications of a crime for which the economic order is primarily responsible. These were followed by *An Imperative Duty* (1893), a slight treatment of the problem of miscegenation; *The World of Chance* (1893), a record of New York literary life; and *The Coast of Bohemia* (1893), dealing with a young woman art student.

In *A Traveler from Altruria* ♦ (1894) and again in its sequel *Through the Eye of the Needle* (1907), he returned to his study of social and economic problems, through the medium of a Utopia. Several minor novels followed, which revert to earlier themes: *An Open-Eyed Conspiracy* (1897) and *Their Silver Wedding Journey* (1899) reintroduced the Marches from his first novel; *Ragged Lady* (1899) is a story of American rusticity and European sophistication; *The Landlord at Lion's Head* (1897), with its portrait of Jeff Durgin, is one of the author's great works of character study; and *The Son of Royal Langbrith* (1904) is a dramatic handling of a moral problem. In his last novel, *The Leatherwood God* (1916), he deals with the Ohio frontier of his youth, which is also the scene of *New Leaf Mills* (1913), the chronicle of a year of his childhood.

Throughout his life, Howells wrote short stories, of which two volumes are concerned with the supernatural, but all are less important than his novels. He was also the author of 31 dramas, ranging from farce to blank-verse tragedy, of 11 travel books, of several autobiographical works, and of a few volumes of verse. A scholarly *Selected Edition* of his writings (32 vols.) began publication in 1968, and *Selected Letters* was projected in four volumes.

During his later life, Howells was frequently considered the preeminent American man of letters, and he received many honors both in the U.S. and abroad, as well as the offer of many academic posts. In addition to advising his friend Clemens, he used his important position to aid and encourage such authors as Boyesen, Garland, Stephen Crane, Frank Norris, and Robert Herrick, who were following the trail he had blazed. Both in his articles in the "Easy Chair" of *Harper's Monthly* and in such volumes as *Criticism and Fiction* (1891), *My Literary Passions* (1895), and *Literature and Life* (1902), he was an important critical force. His own literary credo was summed up in *Criticism and Fiction,* in which he championed realism and its truthful delineation of the motives, the impulses, and the principles that shape the lives of actual men and women. The sources of this realism he ascribes not only to science but to democracy, since the realist "feels in every nerve the equality of things and the unity of men." To this concept he also attached certain dicta of his age: that art must serve morality, that it should teach rather than amuse, and that truthfulness to American life would inevitably picture the smiling aspects of experience.

HOWES, BARBARA (1914–), New York-born poet, reared near Boston, educated at Bennington, where she was influenced by Genevieve Taggard, is married to the poet William Jay Smith.♦ Her own lyrics, often quite formal, appear in *The Undersea Farmer* (1948), *In the Cold Country* (1954), *Light and Dark* (1959), *Looking Up at Leaves* (1966), *The Blue Garden* (1972), and *A Private Signal* (1977).

Howe's Masquerade, story by Hawthorne,♦ published in *Twice-Told Tales* (1842).

At the Boston tavern, the Old Province House, once headquarters of the royal governors, the proprietor tells a visitor this legend:

When Governor Howe gave an entertainment, the night before the patriots' victory in the siege of Boston, the guests were costumed as figures of history and fiction, with comic individuals in rags representing Washington and his generals. Late in the evening, a funeral march was heard, and a solemn procession of ancient figures passed through the ballroom. Colonel Joliffe, an aged patriot detained during the siege, was present with his granddaughter, and identified the apparitions as early Puritan governors, "summoned to form the funeral procession of royal authority in New England." According to legend, the procession reappears on each anniversary of the occasion.

Howl, poem by Allen Ginsberg,♦ issued as the title work of a booklet (1956) for which Lawrence Ferlinghetti♦ was tried and acquitted of publishing and selling obscene work. In long Whitmanesque lines, opening with "I saw the best minds of my generation destroyed by madness, starving hysterical naked," part 1 presents these figures living and dying intensely in a modern hell which, in the briefer part 2, is denounced as the destructive product of Moloch's materialism, mechanization, and conformism. The concluding part 3 is a lyrical address of empathy from the poet to a friend confined in a madhouse as the victim of this society.

HUBBARD, ELBERT (1856–1915), founded an art colony at East Aurora (near Buffalo, N.Y.), where his Roycroft Press imitated with more enthusiasm than success the typography of William Morris's Kelmscott Press. He also edited an inspirational magazine, the *Philistine* (1895–1915), whose platitudinously "arty" content was mainly written by himself. A similar magazine, *The Fra* (1908–17), whose title derived from the sobriquet he conferred upon himself, never attained the enormous popularity of the earlier publication. Among his numerous writings is the series of 170 Little Journeys to the homes of great men. His best-known work is the narrative essay *A Message to Garcia* (1899), a typical, timely, Hubbard-inspirational account of an incident in the Spanish-American War, which appealed to industrial magnates so poignantly that they distributed countless copies to promote greater efficiency among their employees. Hubbard died in the sinking of the *Lusitania.*

HUBBARD, WILLIAM (*c.*1621–1704), born in England, graduated from Harvard in the first class (1642) and became active in colonial affairs, entering the ministry at Ipswich (1656). *A General History of New England from the Discovery to MDCLXXX* depended greatly upon Morton's *Memorial* and Winthrop's *Journal,* just as later historians, such as Prince and Cotton Mather, in turn depended upon Hubbard's manuscript, first printed in 1815.

Huckleberry Finn, *Adventures of,* novel by Clemens,♦ written under his pseudonym Mark Twain. A sequel to *Tom Sawyer,*♦ it was begun in 1876 and published in 1884, omitting the chapter included in *Life on the Mississippi.* Although it carries on the picaresque story of the characters in *Tom Sawyer,* the sequel is a more accomplished and a more serious work of art as well as a keener realistic portrayal of regional character and frontier experience on the Mississippi.

Narrated by Huck, the sequel begins with its unschooled hero under the motherly protection of the Widow Douglas and her sister, Miss Watson. When his blackguard father appears to demand the boy's fortune, Huck tricks him by transferring the money to Judge Thatcher, but his father kidnaps him and imprisons him in a lonely cabin. During one of the old man's drunken spells, Huck escapes to Jackson's Island, where he meets Miss Watson's runaway slave, Jim. They start down the river on a raft, but, after several adventures, the raft is hit by a steamboat and the two are separated. Huck swims ashore, and is sheltered by the Grangerford family, whose feud with the Shepherdsons causes bloodshed. The boy discovers Jim, and they set out again on the raft, giving refuge to the "Duke of Bridgewater," itinerant printer and fraud, and the "Dauphin," "Louis XVII of France," actor, evangelist, and temperance faker. At stopping places, the "King" lectures as a reformed pirate, and they present, as "Kean" and "Garrick," dramatic performances culminating in the fraudulent exhibition of the "Royal Nonesuch." Huck witnesses the murder of a harmless drunkard by an Arkansas aristocrat, whose contempt discourages a mob of would-be lynchers. The rogues learn of the death of Peter Wilks and claim legacies as his brothers. Huck interferes in behalf of the three daughters, and the scheme is foiled by the arrival of the real brothers. Then he discovers that the "King" has sold Jim to Mrs. Phelps, Tom Sawyer's Aunt Sally, and at the Phelps farm he impersonates Tom in an attempt to

rescue Jim. When Tom arrives, he masquerades as his brother Sid, and concocts a fantastic scheme to free Jim. In the "mixed-up and splendid rescue," Tom is accidentally shot, and the slave is recaptured. While Tom is recuperating, he reveals that Miss Watson has died, setting Jim free in her will, and that the rescue was necessary only because he "wanted the *adventure* of it." It is also disclosed that Huck's fortune is safe, since his father is dead, but he concludes: "I reckon I got to light out for the territory ahead of the rest, because Aunt Sally she's going to adopt me and sivilize me, and I can't stand it. I been there before."

Hudson Review, *The* (1948–   ), quarterly literary journal, published in New York. Contributors include William Arrowsmith, Saul Bellow, Blackmur, Kenneth Burke, Eliot, Herbert Gold, Richmond Lattimore, W.S. Merwin, Marianne Moore, Pound, Schorer, W.D. Snodgrass, Tate, Eudora Welty, and Yvor Winters. Frederick Morgan was a founder and editor.

Hugh Selwyn Mauberley, poem by Ezra Pound,♦ published in 1920.

The poem begins with an ironic "ode" on Pound's poetic career as seen by his critics at the end of his London period, and continues through 12 parts of the opening section, which presents with complex allusions and varied rhythms the "tawdry cheapness" and degradation of culture in modern civilization, stigmatized as corrupt, commercial, mechanical, and lacking in cultural distinctions. The sources of degradation and sterility are traced from the aesthetics of the Pre-Raphaelites and the *fin de siècle* writers, and the effects are related to five characters variously symbolic of the times. After an "Envoi" that acts as summation, the themes of the first section are ironically employed in the second section to reveal Mauberley, a passive aesthetic poet, as distinct from Pound, an active creative force, for in this second section Mauberley, the lover of beauty, only drifts through life without a vital understanding of relations to past or present, and leaves as legacy but one poem, "Medallion," a precise, pedantic, passionless imagistic work.

HUGHES, [JAMES] LANGSTON (1902–67), Missouri-born major figure of the Harlem Renaissance,♦ had a nomadic life in the U.S. and Europe until he began his prolific literary career with *The Weary Blues* (1926), poems on black themes in jazz rhythms and idiom, whose success made possible his college career at Lincoln University, Pa. (A.B., 1929). His subsequent publications were in diverse media, but he is most widely known for his poetry issued in more than ten books and pamphlets, including *Fine Clothes to the Jew* (1927), *Dear Lovely Death* (1931), *The Negro Mother* (1931), *The Dream Keeper* (1932), *A New Song* (1938), *Shakespeare in Harlem* (1941), *Fields of Wonder* (1947), *One-Way Ticket* (1949), *Montage of a Dream Deferred* (1951), and *Ask Your Mama* (1961). His concern with his race, mainly in an urban setting, is evident in these works, as is his social consciousness, evident also in the topical *Scottsboro Limited* (1932), four poems and a one-act play on the Scottsboro Case, a *cause célèbre* in which nine black men were charged with the rape of two white girls on a freight train in Alabama. He also wrote two novels, *Not Without Laughter* (1930) and *Tambourines to Glory* (1958), and collections of stories including *The Ways of White Folks* (1934) and *Something in Common* (1963), but his major prose writings are those concerned with his character Jesse B. Semple, satirical sketches of a shrewd but supposedly ignorant Harlem resident who, under his nickname Simple,♦ appears in five volumes. For the stage Hughes wrote several plays, including *Mulatto* (1936), revised as a musical drama, *The Barrier* (1950); a musical version of *Tambourines to Glory* (1963); and *Simply Heavenly* (1963), also a musical play, based on his stories about Simple. He wrote two autobiographical volumes, *The Big Sea* (1940), about his youth and his life in the 1920s, and *I Wonder as I Wander* (1956), carrying on his experiences to 1938. Other writings include *Fight for Freedom* (1962), about the NAACP, while his correspondence with Arna Bontemps, with whom he also collaborated on the musical *Tambourines to Glory,* was published in 1979.

HUGO, RICHARD [FRANKLIN] (1923–82), Seattle-born poet and the director of creative writing at the University of Montana (1964–82). His poetry concentrates on bleak views of derelict towns in his native Northwest, yet in his first book, *A Run of Jacks* (1961), he apostrophizes the region's fish and in his third, *Good Luck in Cracked Italian* (1969), he recalls the Italy he knew in the air corps during wartime. Other books include *Death of the Kapowsin Tavern* (1965), *The Lady in Kicking Horse Reservoir* (1973), *What Thou Lovest Well, Remains American* (1975), *31 Letters and 13 Dreams* (1977), which is partly

epistles addressed to other contemporary poets, *Selected Poems* (1979), *White Center* (1980), *The Right Madness on Skye* (1980), *Sea Lanes Out* (1983), and *Making Certain It Goes On* (1984), his collected poems. *The Triggering Town* (1979) prints lectures and essays on poetry. He also wrote under his own name a detective story, *Death and the Good Life* (1981).

Huguenots, French Protestants, whose church was Calvinistic in doctrine and Presbyterian in government. They were bitterly persecuted until the Edict of Nantes granted them freedom of worship (1598). Upon its revocation (1685), many of them fled to America. Some had previously made settlements in Florida and South Carolina, and many of the settlers of New Amsterdam were Huguenots. They became an important element in the society of Virginia and South Carolina, and also settled in Rhode Island, Connecticut, New York, Delaware, Maryland, and Pennsylvania. The only surviving church is in Charlestown.

Humanism, THE NEW, philosophical and critical movement that flourished in the U.S. during the 1920s, under the leadership of Irving Babbitt♦ and P.E. More. It stresses human elements of experience as distinguished from supernatural or animal elements, assuming that the essential quality of human experience is ethical, that there is a dualism of man and nature, and that man's will is free. The New Humanists desire a discriminating, harmonious cultivation of every part of human nature, based upon a universal scale of values rather than the temporary codes of any particular society. They transcend the scientific method, finding their ultimate ethical principle in restraint, recognizing freedom as the "liberation from outer constraints and subjection to inner law." They turn to the Hellenic doctrine of reason, and away from romanticism; although they draw upon Christianity, Oriental philosophy, and certain modern thinkers and tend to make intellect rather than formal theology the universal test. T.S. Eliot♦ and Norman Foerster are among the important followers of this school, although Eliot criticized some of its basic concepts. S.P. Sherman was an early popular spokesman for its philosophy, but later adopted different standards. *Humanism and America* (1930), a symposium by its proponents, was answered by the symposium *The Critique of Humanism*

(1930), and also by Santayana's *The Genteel Tradition at Bay* ♦ (1931).

Humble-Bee, The, poem by Emerson, ♦ published in 1839 and reprinted in *Poems* (1847). In six stanzas of irregular four-stress couplets, the verses celebrate the wisdom and virtues of the "yellow-breeched philosopher," who mocks at care, "sipping only what is sweet," and taking account of only what is cheerful and excellent.

Humboldt's Gift, novel by Saul Bellow, ♦ published in 1975 and awarded a Pulitzer Prize.

The saga of Charlie Citrine begins with him as a bright, bookish, ambitious young man from the Midwest intent on literary success, coming, by way of Chicago, to Greenwich Village. There he becomes the friend and disciple of the visionary poet Von Humboldt Fleisher, obviously modeled on Delmore Schwartz. In time the vexatious Humboldt dies alone, poor and mad, but he continues to affect the life of the middle-aged Charlie, who recapitulates some of the dead poet's folly while also striving for his wisdom. Worldly success comes to Citrine with the winning of two Pulitzer Prizes, respectively for a play and a biography, and an honorary award from the French government. But financial problems plague him and bring a variety of serio-comic difficulties in personal relations with his greedy divorced wife and his voluptuous girlfriend. Most troublesome of all is Ronald (Rinaldo) Cantabile, a minor hoodlum to whom Charlie owes money and whose wife, oddly enough, is writing a dissertation on Fleisher, about whom she seeks information as she pursues Citrine through Chicago and even across the Atlantic. From these difficulties Citrine is saved by money from the tremendously popular film whose fantastic script, written many years ago by Humboldt and Charlie, is a comedy of sorts about cannibalism, a recurrent metaphor in Bellow's novel.

HUMES, H[AROLD] L[OUIS] (1926–), New York-born novelist, educated at Massachusetts Institute of Technology and Harvard, a founder of the *Paris Review,* ♦ whose novels are *Underground City* (1958), a story of personal conflicts of an American and others involved with the Resistance movement and politics in France during the 1940s; and *Men Die* (1959), treating the relationships of black and white survivors of an explosion of a naval ammunition dump.

HUMPHREY, WILLIAM (1924–), born in the east Texas area of the Red River, the setting of most of his fiction. His novels are *Home from the Hill* (1958), about a family whose men are hunters and live and die by the bloody code of their region; *The Ordways* (1965), a larger family chronicle of four generations from Tennessee to Texas; and *Proud Flesh* (1973), portraying the matriarch of a cotton-raising family. *The Last Husband* (1953) and *A Time and a Place* (1968) collect stories. *The Spawning Run* (1971) and *My Moby Dick* (1978) are accounts of Humphrey's fishing for sport, and *Farther Off from Heaven* (1977) is a memoir of his youth.

HUMPHRIES, [GEORGE] ROLFE (1894–1969), graduated from Amherst (1915), to which he returned as a lecturer in English (1957) after a long career of teaching Latin in high school. He wrote poetry published in several volumes and gathered in *Collected Poems* (1965), and verse translations, including Lorca's *The Poet in New York* (1940), *The Aeneid* (1951), and Ovid's *Metamorphoses* (1955). Late poems appear in *Coat on a Stick* (1969).

HUNEKER, JAMES GIBBONS (1857–1921), after studying piano in Paris, where he was affected by the romanticism of contemporary painters, writers, and musicians, wrote for the New York *Sun* on matters concerned with art, literature, drama, and music, and his wit, lush phrasing, and connoisseur's gusto made his criticism stand far above that of other journalists of the time. His sonorous style and love for the voluptuous and colorful are also exhibited in his novel, *Painted Veils* (1920), concerned with New York artists.

Huntington Library, properly titled the Henry E. Huntington Library and Art Gallery, is situated at San Marino, Cal., near Pasadena, on the estate of its founder, a railroad financier, who between 1910 and his death in 1927 accumulated vast collections of books, including the Beverly Chew, Robert Hoe, and Bridgewater libraries, and fine English paintings, particularly from the 18th century. These collections, valued at $30,000,000 upon Huntington's death, have been operated as a public trust with a large endowment. From its incunabula, book and manuscript collections of English and American literature, Americana, and Spanish-American history have come many important scholarly studies. The library's publications are an outgrowth of its research program.

Huron Indians (properly, WANDOT or WYANDOT), confederacy of nomadic Iroquoian tribes, which originally inhabited Ontario, where Champlain visited them (1603). They were bitter enemies of the Iroquois proper, who virtually destroyed them (1648–49). Some survivors fled to Quebec and descendants of others settled in Michigan and Ohio. They fought against the U.S. in the Revolution and the War of 1812, but later moved to Oklahoma. In the Leather-Stocking Tales♦ the Hurons are depicted as treacherous and cruel, and they figure also in *Satanstoe.*

HURSTON, ZORA NEALE (1901?–60), born in Florida, after graduation from Barnard continued her study of anthropology, as evidenced in *Tell My Horse* (1938), about her research into folkways of Haiti and the West Indies; and *Mules and Men* (1935), stories of voodoo among blacks of the South. Her novels include *Jonah's Gourd Vine* (1934), about a black preacher's loves; *Their Eyes Were Watching God* (1937), about a black woman finding happiness in simple farm life; *Moses: Man of the Mountain* (1939), a black folk interpretation of Biblical Jews; and *Seraph on the Suwanee* (1948), about the marrying and civilizing of a Florida cracker woman. *Dust Tracks on a Road* (1942) is her autobiography. She taught at North Carolina College for Negroes. An anthology of her writings was edited by Alice Walker (1979).

HUTCHINSON, ANNE (1591–1643), emigrated from England to Massachusetts (1634), where her vigorous intellect soon led her to hold informal weekly meetings of women, in which she discussed the sermons of the previous Sunday and advocated a "covenant of grace" based on the individual's direct intuition of God's grace, as opposed to the orthodox belief in a "covenant of works" based on obedience to the statutes of church and state. She was called an Antinomian,♦ was said to be "traducing the ministers and their ministry," and, although Governor Vane, her brother-in-law John Wheelwright, and others supported her views, a synod of churches excommunicated her, and Govenor Winthrop banished her from the colony. She and her family went to Rhode Island (1638), then to New York (1642), where Indians massacred all but one of them.

Hymns have been collected by all American Protestant sects and sung in their church services. The scruples of the Puritans forbade original hymns, and they created only new versions of the Psalms. Although the 16th-century English versions of Henry Ainsworth, John Hopkins, and Thomas Sternhold were probably brought over on the *Mayflower,* the first American collection was the *Bay Psalm Book*♦ (1640). Cotton Mather, in his *Psalterium Americanum* (1718), made another translation, as did Thomas Prince (1758), while Thomas Walter gave further impetus to psalmody through his discourse on "singing by note" (1721), and William Billings introduced other reforms in his musical settings (1770). During the late 18th century, Congregationalists began to admit hymns as well as psalms, and, besides the amended versions of Isaac Watts's *Psalms and Hymns* by Joel Barlow (1785) and Timothy Dwight (1800), original religious songs were written by Mather Byles. Later Congregational hymnodists included J.G.C. Brainard and Ray Palmer, and H.W. Beecher's *Plymouth Collection* (1855) was an important Congregational compilation. The Presbyterians, like the Congregationalists, long used versions of Watts, the first of their original hymnodists being Samson Occom. During the 19th century, hymnody was stimulated by Thomas Hastings and by Lowell Mason, whose settings included those for "From Greenland's Icy Mountains" and "Nearer, My God, to Thee." Mason's collection, *The Choir* (1832), included S.F. Smith's "America," and other prominent Baptist hymnodists were Adoniram Judson and Lydia Huntley Sigourney. Members of the Protestant Episcopal church known for their hymns include Francis Scott Key, Sarah Josepha Hale, J.W. Eastburn, and Harriet Beecher Stowe. Other hymnodists of the time included Hosea Ballou, Alice and Phoebe Cary, Lucy Larcom, and Whittier. The Unitarians contributed more to American hymnody than any other sect, their authors including J.Q. Adams, Bryant, J.F. Clarke, Emerson, E.E. Hale, Holmes, Higginson, Longfellow, John Pierpont, and Jones Very. The evangelists Moody and Sankey made hymns more popular in the mid-19th century.

I

I Sing the Body Electric, poem by Whitman, ♦ untitled in the 1855 edition of *Leaves of Grass,* later called "Poem of the Body" as a section of "Children of Adam," and given its present title in 1867. It celebrates the anatomy and the form of men, women, and children, declaring, "These are not the parts and poems of the Body only, but of the Soul, O I say now these are the soul!"

Iceman Cometh, The, play by Eugene O'Neill, ♦ produced and published in 1946.

Harry Hope's run-down New York saloon and rooming house harbors a group of guilt-ridden, unsuccessful alcoholics, who eagerly await a visit from Hickey, a cheerful salesman they consider one of them, though he is outwardly more successful. Upon his arrival Hickey's traditional joke about his wife and the iceman is not forthcoming, and he threatens the men's pipe dreams with talk of bringing to others the peace he claims to have found through having given up drink and discarded all illusions. With hard, humorless cynicism he confesses that he killed his wife out of hatred and summons the police. The idea that Hickey is insane slowly develops as a new pipe dream, allowing the others to resume their old relationships, banter, and illusions, although one of them, who perceives Hickey as the "Iceman of Death," remains truly and despairingly aware of reality.

Ichabod, poem by Whittier, ♦ published in 1850. In quatrains of alternate four- and two-stress lines, the work, whose Hebrew title means "inglorious," expresses the disappointment of the antislavery factions when Webster supported the compromise of 1850 in his "Seventh of March Speech." In "The Lost Occasion" (1880), Whittier, praising Webster's "nobler self," condones his "sad concessions" in this episode.

Ichabod Crane, hero of *The Legend of Sleepy Hollow.* ♦

IGNATOW, DAVID (1914–), Brooklyn-born poet of immigrant parents, whose hard struggles in youth and through the Depression are the stuff from which he has made his poetry, briefly told in Brooklynese speech.

This has appeared in *Poems* (1948), *The Gentle Weight Lifter* (1955), *Say Pardon* (1962), *Figures of the Human* (1964), *Earth Hard* (1968), *Rescue the Dead* (1968), *Poems, 1934–69* (1970), *Facing the Tree* (1975), *Tread the Dark* (1978), and *Whisper to the Earth* (1981). His *Notebooks* (1973) treats both his personal life and his aims as poet.

I'll Take My Stand, anthology published in 1930 by 12 Southerners to set forth their concept of regionalism ♦ as members of the Agrarians. ♦ The contributors to the symposium, actually called a manifesto, included Donald Davidson, John Gould Fletcher, John Crowe Ransom, Allen Tate, R.P. Warren, and Stark Young, most of them former contributors to *The Fugitive.* ♦

Imagism, poetic movement of England and the United States, flourished from 1909 to 1917. Its credo, expressed in *Some Imagist Poets* (1915), included the use of the language of common speech, precision, the creation of new rhythms, absolute freedom in choice of subject matter, the evocation of images in hard, clear poetry, and concentration. Originating in the aesthetic philosophy of T.E. Hulme, the movement soon attracted Ezra Pound, who became the leader of a small group opposed to the romantic conception of poetry and inspired by Greek and Roman classics and by Chinese, Japanese, and modern French poets. In the U.S., the group was represented in *Poetry: A Magazine of Verse* by Pound, H.D., John Gould Fletcher, and Amy Lowell, and by such English poets as F.S. Flint, Richard Aldington, and D.H. Lawrence. Pound collected some of their work in *Des Imagistes: An Anthology* (1914), after which his interest began to wane; Amy Lowell then assumed active leadership, advocating that the group subscribe to a fixed program and hold together for at least three years. Under her guidance were published several anthologies, all entitled *Some Imagist Poets.*

Imp of the Perverse, The, story by Poe, ♦ published in *Graham's Magazine* (1845). A condemned murderer explains his confession, which followed years of safe concealment, in terms of a perverse impulse, and states that perversity is an unrecognized major motive for men's actions.

Impressionism, aesthetic movement in which the artist attempts to present the impressions an object makes upon him, rather than a realistic version of the object itself. Impressionists are thus more concerned with moods or sensations than with the observation of details. The name derives from the French school of painting of the late 19th century, whose exponents included Degas, Monet, Manet, Renoir, and Pissarro, and which was brought to the U.S. by such painters as J.A. Weir, Maurice Prendergast, and Childe Hassam, who were similarly concerned with transitory effects of light and with capturing a momentary luminous atmosphere. Their theories were taken up by writers, especially Baudelaire and other followers of Poe, and Symbolists such as Mallarmé, who attempted to capture the fleeting impressions of a moment, or held that the personal attitudes and moods of an author were more important than any objective depiction of character, setting, and action. In music, the leading impressionist is Debussy, whose American followers include such composers as Griffes and Loeffler. Impressionistic art was most influential at the end of the 19th century and during the early decades of the 20th, when its leading proponents in American criticism included Huneker, Vance Thompson, and G.J. Nathan. In poetry the movement is exemplified in Pound, Sandburg, Amy Lowell, Conrad Aiken, Marianne Moore, and Wallace Stevens, who were influenced by a mingling of trends, including Imagism. ♦ Impressionists in prose include such diverse writers as Van Vechten, Huneker, Gertrude Stein, E.E. Cummings, and Thomas Beer. Expressionism♦ is both an extension and a negation of this point of view.

In Cold Blood, work by Truman Capote, ♦ published in 1966. Described by its author as a "non-fiction novel," it tells of the murder of a well-to-do farmer of Holcomb, Kan., his wife, and two children, by two ex-convicts in the process of committing a robbery of their home in 1959. The aftermath of the criminals' escape to Mexico, capture, trial, appeals to the Supreme Court, and hanging in April 1965 is followed, in a fashion that opens larger social issues.

In Dubious Battle, novel by Steinbeck,♦ published in 1936.

Jim Nolan, a young man whose "whole family has been ruined by this system," joins the Communist party in San Francisco, meets Mac, who "knows more about field work than anybody in the state," and goes with him to Torgas Valley to take part in a strike of fruit pickers. Jim grows in assurance and practically assumes leadership until he is led out of camp by a ruse and brutally murdered. In desperation, Mac places his friend's corpse on a platform and harangues the men: " 'Comrades! This guy didn't want nothing for himself—' "

In His Steps, novel by C.M. Sheldon. ♦

In Our Time, 15 short stories by Hemingway♦ with vignettes serving as interchapters, published in the U.S. in 1925. *in our time* (Paris, 1924) contains only the vignettes. Most stories treat life in the Middle West, but the interpolated sketches describe war in Europe and bullfights.

"Indian Camp," "The Doctor and the Doctor's Wife," "The Three Day Blow," and others tell of the boyhood experiences of Nick, the author's counterpart, who grew up in the Great Lakes region, learning the bitter as well as the beautiful facts of existence through the work of his father, a physician, and through his association with Indian guides and their families. Such stories as "Mr. and Mrs. Elliot," "Out of Season," and "Cross Country Snow" are brief, poignant tales of American expatriates in Europe and their complex loves and friendships. "My Old Man" is the story of a boy's loyalty to his father, an American jockey forced to work in Europe because of unsportsmanlike conduct at home, and of the boy's disillusion following his father's death. The author's enthusiasm for sport and the American wilderness is shown in "Big Two-Hearted River," an account of a trout-fishing expedition.

In the American Grain, essays by William Carlos Williams, ♦ published in 1925.

In 20 impressionistic essays on significant persons of the western hemisphere, chronologically from Eric the Red to Lincoln, and including Cotton Mather, Franklin, and Poe among writers, Williams treats the ways in which these men viewed new worlds, often employing their own words so as to convey their ways of vision and expression. The emphasis on discovery, the idealistic conception of liberty and freedom, and the opposition to Puritanism as a doctrine of denial mark the book as a precursor of elements of

Paterson, White Mule, and other later writings by Williams.

In the Cage, novelette by Henry James,♦ published in 1898.

A girl telegraph clerk in a London department store despises her complacent suitor, Mr. Mudge. Curious about the lives of her wealthy patrons, she is particularly fascinated by the liaison of Lady Bradeen and young Captain Everard, details of which are revealed through their frequent telegrams. Although she "hates" the frivolous rich, she comes to have a tender interest in the affairs of Everard, and the two recognize a certain mutual understanding. When her friend Mrs. Jordan asks her to become a business partner, the girl postpones accepting either this offer or Mr. Mudge's proposal. She helps Everard to avoid a scandal by producing a copy of an intercepted telegram, and her brief association with him ends when Lord Bradeen dies and the lovers are able to marry. Mrs. Jordan's offer is withdrawn, and the girl quickly settles her problems by accepting Mr. Mudge.

Indian Bible, see *Eliot, John.*

Indian Burying Ground, *The,* poem by Freneau,♦ published in his *Miscellaneous Works* (1788). In ten iambic tetrameter quatrains, it portrays sympathetically the spirit of the nomadic Indian hunters, who were traditionally buried in a sitting posture and with images of the objects they knew in life. Freneau's treatment of the immortal "children of the forest" appealed strongly to Scott and Thomas Campbell, who echoed his images in their poetry.

Indians, in addition to creating literary works of their own, like the *Walam Olum,*♦ appear in American literature from the time of the earliest exploration and colonization, e.g. in Captain John Smith's accounts of Pocahontas♦; in New England histories like those by Bradford,♦ Captain Edward Johnson,♦ Daniel Gookin, and the later works on the war led by King Philip; in many captivity narratives, like that by Mary Rowlandson♦; and in studies of their tongues and customs, which were made as early as the 17th century by John Eliot and Roger Williams, among others. More literary and more romantic treatment began with the poetry of Freneau,♦ Sarah Wentworth Morton, J.W. Eastburn, and Robert Sands, and although Indians had appeared in novels by Brackenridge, Charles Brockden Brown, and Gilbert Imlay, they came to great prominence in the fiction of Lydia Maria Child, J.K. Paulding, Cooper, R.M. Bird, and Simms. Indian culture, legendry, and relations with whites also figured prominently in 19th-century poetry, including that by Bryant and Whittier and, most notably, Longfellow's *Hiawatha,* while the popular drama about Indians that began with Major Robert Rogers flourished with plays by James N. Barker, G.W.P. Custis, John A. Stone, and R.M. Bird. More personal and usually more accurate views of various tribes came from explorers, mountain men, and other visitors to the trans-Missouri West, like Irving,♦ Parkman,♦ Frémont, Garrard, and Ruxton. Anthropological studies included the works of Heckewelder, Lewis Morgan, and Schoolcraft, all concentrating on Indians of the eastern U.S. Later champions of the Indians remaining in the western U.S. included writers of fiction as various as Bret Harte, Helen Hunt Jackson, Adolf Bandelier, Mary Austin, Hamlin Garland, J.G. Neihardt, Oliver La Farge, and A.B. Guthrie, while more popularized treatments included those of Stewart Edward White and Zane Grey. (See also *individual entries for each tribe and for prominent figures,* e.g. *Canonchet; Pontiac; Sitting Bull; Tecumseh.*)

INGE, WILLIAM (1913–73), Kansas-born dramatist, whose plays about seemingly ordinary Midwestern people include *Farther Off from Heaven* (1947); *Come Back, Little Sheba* (1950), about a drunkard's dreadful marriage; *Picnic* (1953, Pulitzer Prize), about a simple young girl and boy who entertain fatuous and frustrating dreams of glamorous lives; *Bus Stop* (1955), depicting a diverse group of snowbound people who represent the varied and fluid society of the U.S.; *The Dark at the Top of the Stairs* (1957), a symbolic treatment of loneliness in a family; *A Loss of Roses* (1959), about the Oedipal relation of a 21-year-old son and his widowed mother; *Natural Affection* (1963); and *Where's Daddy?* (1966), a comedy about the quest of a young couple to find values. *Good Luck, Miss Wyckoff* (1970) is a novel about a small-town Kansas schoolteacher involved with a black college football player, and *My Son Is a Splendid Driver* (1971) is a novel about a Kansas boy in the 1930s.

INGERSOLL, ROBERT GREEN (1833–99), practiced law in Illinois and entered Democratic politics before the Civil War, in which he served as a colonel of cavalry and turned to the Republican party. In 1876 he nominated Blaine for the presidency with the famous epithet "the plumed knight." He himself was known as "the great agnostic," because of his long campaign in behalf of free-thinking, including celebrated antireligious lectures on "Superstition," "The Gods," "Some Mistakes of Moses," and similar subjects, criticizing theology and the Bible from a rationalist point of view. His lectures, which had an important influence on American thought during the late 19th century, were published in several collections, and his complete *Works* appeared in 12 volumes (1900).

Innocents Abroad, The; or, The New Pilgrim's Progress, travel narrative by Clemens,♦ published in 1869 under his pseudonym Mark Twain. It is based on letters written during 1867 to the San Francisco *Alta California* and the *New-York Tribune* and *Herald,* describing the tour of the steamship *Quaker City* to Europe, Egypt, and the Holy Land. In this autobiographical account, Clemens has an opportunity to ridicule foreign sights and manners from the point of view of the American democrat, who scorns the sophisticated, revels in his own national peculiarities and advantages, and is contemptuously amused by anything with which he is unacquainted. Characteristic passages are concerned with the comical difficulties of "innocent" tourists, their adventures among deceptive guides, inefficient hotels, and misunderstood customs; a comparison of Lake Como with Lake Tahoe, to the general advantage of the latter; a burlesque account of the ascent of Vesuvius; experiences of various Turkish "frauds"; an awestruck meeting with the Russian royal family; and a naïvely sentimental description of Biblical scenes in Palestine.

International Episode, An, novelette by Henry James,♦ published in 1879.

Lord Lambeth and his friend Percy Beaumont come to America for a visit and at Newport they meet Mrs. Westgate and her sister Bessie Alden. The latter fascinates Lord Lambeth, being bold, intelligent, and typically American, and he is on the verge of falling in love with her when he is suddenly recalled to England. Later the situation is reversed, when Bessie and Mrs. Westgate visit London. The older woman discourages her sister from notifying Lord Lambeth of their arrival, but they meet accidentally, and Lambeth, increasingly charmed by Bessie's independence and frankness, is about to

propose to her. His mother and sister, alarmed, call on the Americans and make plain their disapproval of the match. Bessie keeps her own counsel, but, when Lambeth proposes, she surprises everyone by refusing him.

Intruder in the Dust, novel by William Faulkner,♦ published in 1948.

Lucas Beauchamp, an aging black farmer whose grandparents were the white Carothers McCaslin and a slave woman, is arrested for the murder of Vinson Gowrie, one of a clan of hillsmen known for administering their own violent law. Charles ("Chick") Mallison, County Attorney Gavin Stevens's 16-year-old nephew, visits Lucas in jail, recalling the old man's kindness some years earlier. Lucas asks Gavin to defend him but will tell only Charles that an examination of Vinson's body will prove that his gun was not the murder weapon. When Vinson's body is found it turns out that he was shot by his brother Crawford Gowrie in such a way as to implicate Lucas when Lucas threatened to reveal that Crawford was stealing lumber from Vinson. Crawford is arrested and commits suicide in jail. Lucas is exonerated and the proud, dignified, and courageous black man, who will accept no white man's charity, pays Gavin his fee of two dollars, painstakingly counted out in pennies, as the last act in the events have made him "now tyrant over the whole county's white conscience."

Invisible Man, novel by Ralph Ellison,♦ published in 1952.

The nameless black narrator living in an underground "hole" in New York City, brilliantly lighted by electricity he taps from Monopolated Light and Power, is invisible because people with whom he comes in contact "see only my surroundings, themselves, or figments of their imagination." Such vision is illustrated by his reminiscences of the Kafkaesque pilgrimage he has made from his beginnings in the South. As a bright high-school student he is invited by his town's most important men to deliver an oration to them on the virtues of humility. Before he is allowed to speak he must watch ribald entertainment and is forced to join other "niggers" in a blindfold fistfight. When he finally delivers his speech he mistakenly speaks of "social equality" instead of "social responsibility" and has to apologize abjectly so as to retain his prize of a scholarship to a college for blacks. At the college he finds the head to be a tyrannical hypocrite in his treatment of the students and fawningly humble to the white community. Expelled from the college, he goes to New York and soon falls in with the ruthless Brother Jack, leader of the Communist Brotherhood, more concerned with party politics and an authoritarian platform than with true aid to blacks. He is equally disillusioned by Ras the Exhorter, a West Indian rabble-rousing street leader, basically a self-promoter, and the Rev. B.P. Rinehart, "spiritual technologist" and preacher and a petty criminal as well. His experiences are climaxed by a surrealistic view of a Harlem race riot and its arson and looting. From this he retreats to his hideaway hole, reflecting upon the dehumanization visited not only on blacks but on all modern men.

Iron Heel, The, novel by Jack London,♦ published in 1908.

Purportedly written in 1932, this "Everhard Manuscript" tells of events said to take place between 1912 and 1918, when, by a process of evolutionary development, the great capitalistic monopolies of the U.S. band together in a fascistic organization, the Iron Heel, which seizes control of the country. Stamping out all democratic forms and free institutions, the Iron Heel creates a caste system with a plutocratic aristocracy at the top, supported by secret police, a military oligarchy, and a few powerful subsidized unions that aid in suppressing the majority of organized labor. Originally motivated by fear of the growing revolutionary Socialist party, the Iron Heel succeeds in driving the equalitarian movement underground, but there it continued to militate against the "Oligarchs" and their barbarous tyranny. One of the Socialist leaders is Ernest Everhard, a Californian, whose wife Avis, converted by him to the cause, tells their story in this manuscript. For 20 years they maintain their secret, partially terrorist, organization, which averts war with Germany by a general strike in collaboration with German Socialist unions, instigates armed revolts, and in general advocates the use of force against force. The manuscript breaks off, following Everhard's execution, but footnotes written 700 years later inform the reader that the Iron Heel retained power for 300 years, was overthrown, and was succeeded by a golden age of collectivism.

Iroquois Indians, confederacy of war-like but highly cultured tribes in western New York (united *c.*1570), which consisted originally of Five Nations: Seneca, Cayuga, Onondaga, Oneida, and Mohawk. Among the chiefs who supposedly effected this league was the Mohawk immortalized as Hiawatha by Longfellow. The trade relations of the Iroquois with the Dutch led to their obtaining firearms, with which they became great conquerors of other tribes in the mid-17th century. During the French and Indian Wars they were allies of the British, and in the American Revolution most of the chiefs supported the Loyalists. The Tuscarora Indians joined the confederacy (1715), which became the Six Nations. Besides *Hiawatha* and the Leather-Stocking Tales, the Iroquois figure in such works as Alfred B. Street's *Frontenac, or the Atotarho of the Iroquois* (1849), a metrical romance based on Frontenac's expedition of 1696 against the confederacy. Cadwallader Colden's *History of the Five Indian Nations* (1727) was the first careful study of the subject. Among later works, L.H. Morgan's *League of the Ho-dé-no-sau-nee, or Iroquois* (1851) superseded Schoolcraft's *Notes on the Iroquois* (1847). Edmund Wilson's *Apologies to the Iroquois* (1960) tells of the modern situation of the confederacy.

IRVING, JOHN [WINSLOW] (1942–), New Hampshire-born author, whose first seriocomic novels, *Setting Free the Bears* (1968), a tale of two young men's adventures motorcycling through Austria; *The Water-Method Man* (1972), about an Iowa graduate student's fantastic misadventures; and *The 158-Pound Marriage* (1974), presenting two couples who engage in mate-swapping, were followed by the enormously popular *The World According to Garp*♦ (1978), a fanciful story of a wonderfully talented novelist whose life and works are rich and various but who is murdered at 33; *The Hotel New Hampshire* (1981), portraying an exotic family; and *The Cider House Rules* (1985).

IRVING, WASHINGTON (1783–1859), was born in New York City, the youngest of 11 children of a wealthy merchant. The boy was early influenced by the literary interests of his brothers William and Peter, but in 1798 concluded his education at private schools and entered a law office. His legal studies soon lost their appeal, although he continued in various offices until 1804. For the *Morning Chronicle* edited by his brother Peter, he wrote the "Letters of Jonathan Oldstyle, Gent.," a series (1802–3) of youthful satires on New York society, which won him recognition. To restore his failing health and to further his education, he traveled in Europe (1804–6), where he collected material later used in stories and essays.

Although he was admitted to the bar upon his return, he lost interest in the law and turned seriously to literature. *Salmagundi; or, The Whim-Whams and Opinions of Launcelot Langstaff, Esq., and Others* ♦ (1807–8) is a series of satirical miscellanies concerned with New York society. The leading essays were written by Irving, his brothers, and William Irving's brother-in-law, J.K. Paulding, all members of the group known as the "Nine Worthies" or "Lads of Kilkenny" of "Cockloft Hall." Federalist in politics, conservative in social attitude, and humorous in intention, these early essays represent the position and manner to which Irving was to cling throughout his career. He was now famous as author, wit, and man of society, and, to further his reputation, turned to the creation of the comic Dutch-American scholar Diedrich Knickerbocker, on whose burlesque *History of New York* ♦ he was occupied until 1809. This work, called "the first great book of comic literature written by an American," although ostensibly concerned with the history of the Dutch occupation was also a Federalist critique of Jeffersonian democracy and a whimsical satire on pedantry and literary classics.

Before its completion, Irving suffered a tragic loss in the death of his fiancée, Matilda Hoffman. According to sentimental biographers, who disregard later love affairs, he remained a bachelor to be faithful to her memory. Certainly he was profoundly affected at the time. In spite of the success of the *History,* he deserted creative literature during the next six years, when he was occupied in business with his brothers, in collecting the poems of Thomas Campbell (1810), in editing the *Analectic Magazine* (1813–14), a popular miscellany of reprints from foreign periodicals, and in social and political activities in New York, Philadelphia, and Washington. Toward the end of the War of 1812, he served as an aide-de-camp to the governor, and in 1815 he planned a cruise to the Mediterranean with Decatur; but, when this became impossible, he sailed alone for Liverpool, to take charge of the family business there.

During the next two years, he tried desperately to maintain the failing business, but in 1818 it went into bankruptcy, and he was forced to write for a living. He had already been impressed by the beauties of the English countryside as interpreted by the romantic poets, and, encouraged by Scott, now returned to writing his most successful work, *The Sketch Book* ♦ (1819–20), containing familiar essays on English life, and Americanized versions of European folk tales in "Rip Van Winkle" ♦ and "The Legend of Sleepy Hollow." ♦ As Geoffrey Crayon, the pseudonym by which the book was signed, Irving was now a celebrity, lionized in English and French society, and the intimate of such men as Scott, Byron, and Moore. In Paris (1820) he wrote plays with J.H. Payne, ♦ a collaboration to which he occasionally returned for several years. *Bracebridge Hall* (1822) is another book of romantic sketches, less important than *The Sketch Book,* but equally well received.

Continuing his search for fictional materials, Irving now traveled in Germany (1822–23), spending the winter at Dresden, where he fell in love with an English girl, Emily Foster, who seems to have refused his proposal of marriage. After a year in Paris, he returned to England and published *Tales of a Traveller* (1824), so adversely criticized that Irving was nearly discouraged from further literary activity. After two unproductive years in France, during which he is supposed to have vied with Payne for the affections of Mary Wollstonecraft Shelley, he became a diplomatic attaché in Spain (1826–29), living for a time in Madrid at the home of bibliographer Obadiah Rich and engaged in research for his scholarly but popular *History of the Life and Voyages of Christopher Columbus* (1828), based principally on the work of the Spanish scholar Navarrete. This was followed by *A Chronicle of the Conquest of Granada* (1829), and a "Spanish *Sketch Book,*" *The Alhambra* ♦ (1832), recounting Spanish legends and describing the famous monument.

Irving was secretary of the U.S. legation in London (1829–32), and then returned to New York, after an absence of 17 years, to be welcomed enthusiastically as the first American author to achieve international fame. Again seeking picturesque literary backgrounds, he made an adventurous trip to the Western frontier. This was described in *A Tour on the Prairies,* ♦ published as a part of *The Crayon Miscellany* ♦ (3 vols., 1835). The tour also resulted in *Astoria* (1836), an account of the fur-trading empire of John Jacob Astor, written with his nephew Pierre Irving; and *The Adventures of Captain Bonneville, U.S.A.* ♦ (1837). Irving's *Western Journals* were published in 1944.

After a few years at his Hudson River home, Sunnyside, during which he declined the nomination for mayor of New York City and the secretaryship of the navy offered him by Van Buren, as well as giving up a plan to write a *Conquest of Mexico* in favor of Prescott, Irving returned to his favorite place of exile, becoming minister to Spain (1842–45). His position was made difficult by the Spanish insurrection (1843), and after his resignation two years later he spent a year in London on a diplomatic mission concerning the Oregon Question. Again at Sunnyside, he passed the remaining 13 years of his life in the company of his beloved nieces and innumerable friends, acknowledged as the leading American author, in spite of his waning powers, as evidenced in *Oliver Goldsmith* (1840), a biography of one of his literary masters; *A Book of the Hudson* (1849) and *Wolfert's Roost* (1855), collections of sketches; *Mahomet and His Successors* (2 vols., 1849–50), conventional biographies; and the monumental *Life of Washington* (5 vols., 1855–59), planned as early as 1825, but completed in the last year of his life, just before his health finally failed. Bare of the graces of his early writing, this triumph of scholarship crowned an erratic career that seldom retained its literary focus for more than a few years at a time, but which served in many ways to consolidate the culture of the U.S. and Europe. Unlike his contemporary, Cooper, Irving saw the European past in an aura of romance, and, except for the gentle satire of his early works, consistently avoided coming to grips with modern democratic life. His graceful, humorous, stylistically careful writing is in the tradition of Addison, Steele, and Goldsmith. In subject and method he sought the traditional and the picturesque. A scholarly edition of his *Complete Works* began publication in 1969.

ISHERWOOD, CHRISTOPHER (1904–   ), English-born author, studied at Cambridge, collaborated with Auden♦ on three satirical prose and verse plays, *The Dog Beneath the Skin* (1936), *The Ascent of F6* (1936), and *On the Frontier* (1938), and with him also wrote about their voyage to China in *Journey to a War* (1939). He had already published his first novel in 1928 and had lived in Berlin for four years, the city which was the setting of his novel *The Last of Mr. Norris* (1935) and the sketches *Goodbye to Berlin* (1939), the latter involving a fictive character bearing the author's name, and therefore retitled *I Am a Camera* when dramatized (1951) by John Van Druten. After residence elsewhere in Europe, Isherwood came to the U.S. (1939),

settled near Los Angeles, and was naturalized in 1946. He has worked intermittently as a screenwriter, taught at colleges, and become active in the Vedanta movement, which has led to his translation of three classics of Hindu philosophy, including the *Bhagavad-Gita*. His fiction written in the U.S. includes *Prater Violet* (1945), a symbolic novelette involving the story of an Austrian motion-picture director who produces a film about Vienna in London; *The World in the Evening* (1954); *Down There on a Visit* (1962), the frank, autobiographical story of the quest for selfhood by a character called by the author's name; *A Single Man* (1964), about a day in the sad, lonely life of a middle-aged homosexual professor in a California university after the death of the man he loved; and *A Meeting by the River* (1967), a philosophic tale of brothers with different values who meet in India, one to become a Hindu monk, the other to find a site to film a motion picture. Three very personal books are *Kathleen and Frank* (1972), an account of his parents and their influence on him; *Christopher and His Kind* (1976), about his own life and male lovers from 1929 to 1939; and *My Guru and His Disciple* (1980), about both worldly and spiritual experiences. *The Condor and the Cows* (1949) deals with a trip to South America, and *Exhumations* (1966) collects stories, verse, and articles.

Israel Potter: His Fifty Years of Exile, romance by Melville,♦ published in 1855. It is largely based on an anonymous *Life and Remarkable Adventures of Israel Potter* (1824).

Israel Potter, a New England boy, after youthful experiences as a farmer, surveyor, and peddler becomes a sailor on whaling ships. He joins the Revolutionary army in time to participate in the Battle of Bunker Hill, but is captured by the British and taken to England. There he escapes, goes to London as a laborer, is befriended by rebel agents, and joins them in secret activities. Traveling between London and Paris, he meets Horne Tooke, Franklin, and John Paul Jones, and, becoming a friend of the last, takes part in naval affairs, including the battle between the *Bonhomme Richard* and the *Serapis*. In England again, Israel is associated with Ethan Allen, flees to London in fear of apprehension, and becomes a workman again, marrying and living in alternate want and moderate plenty. Finally, 45 years after his departure, he returns to America, infirm and impoverished, to seek a pension. He is refused, dictates his memoirs, and dies in poverty.

Israfel, poem by Poe,♦ published in *Poems* (1831) and several times revised in later editions. It is prefaced by an altered quotation from the Koran: "And the angel Israfel, whose heart-strings are a lute, and who has the sweetest voice of all God's creatures." In eight stanzas of great metrical variety, ranging from four- to two-stress lines, the poem contrasts the ideal dwelling place of the angel with the poet's own "world of sweets and sours," and concludes that if they were to change places

> He might not sing so wildly well
> A mortal melody,
> While a bolder note than this might swell
> From my lyre within the sky.

It Can't Happen Here, novel by Sinclair Lewis,♦ published in 1935. It was dramatized by the author and John C. Moffitt (1936) for simultaneous presentation by all units of the Federal Theatre.

Doremus Jessup, liberal editor of a Vermont paper, is one of the few in his small town to oppose the nomination and election (1936) of his fellow townsman Berzelius (Buzz) Windrip to the presidency. Upon assuming office, Buzz, who is fascistic and dictatorial, obtains control of the legislature and judiciary, divides the U.S. into eight provinces governed by his henchmen, stifles labor unions, quells riots with machine guns, suppresses racial and political minorities, and jails all his opponents. Doremus is temporarily arrested, his press is taken from him, and his son-in-law is shot for defending him. Walt Trowbridge, an honest ex-senator who had been Buzz's rival for the presidency, flees to Canada, where he sets up a New Underground movement, which Doremus aids by secretly printing a paper in its favor. Two years later, Buzz is deposed by his former friend Lee Saranson, who in turn is soon ousted by Secretary of War Haik. Doremus escapes to Canada, where he joins Trowbridge and his many followers. During the war that Haik declares on Mexico (1939), Doremus takes part in the widespread revolt, converted by necessity from his former liberalism to revolutionary activity.

Ivory Tower, The, unfinished novel by Henry James.♦

J

JACKSON, HELEN [MARIA] HUNT (1830–85), was born at Amherst, Mass., and in 1863 began to write poetry for publication, which was collected in *Verses by H.H.* (1870) and *Sonnets and Lyrics* (1886). Later she wrote a travel book, stories for children, many magazine contributions, and several novels. *A Century of Dishonor* (1881) is a historical account of governmental injustice in the treatment of the Indians. Her indictment was stated even more strongly in the romance *Ramona* (1884), inspired by her work in a government investigation of the Mission Indians of southern California and telling also of avaricious Americans seizing the lands of old Spanish settlers. Her novel *Mercy Philbrick's Choice* (1876) is said to be a fictional study of her friend Emily Dickinson. Many of her early writings were published under the pseudonym Saxe Holm.

JACKSON, SHIRLEY [HARDIE] (1916–65), California-born author, educated at Syracuse University, lived in Vermont, where her husband, Stanley Edgar Hyman (1919–70), a literary critic, taught at Bennington College. Her novels include *The Road Through the Wall* (1948), *Hangsaman* (1951), and *The Bird's Nest* (1954), all depicting adolescents in disturbed states of mind. Other novels are *The Sundial* (1958), about people who believe the end of the world is near; *The Haunting of Hill House* (1959), concerning occult experiences; *We Have Always Lived in the Castle* (1962), presenting a woman writer who poisons her family; and *Come Along with Me* (1968), a posthumously published fragment. *The Lottery* (1949) collects stories of weird or psychopathic subjects placed in direct, realistic settings. *Life Among the Savages* (1953) and *Raising Demons* (1957) are amusing accounts of her life with her children. *The Witchcraft of Salem Village* (1956); *The Bad Children* (1959), a play; and *Nine Magic Wishes* (1963) are works for children.

JAMES, ALICE (1848–92), sister of Henry James, Jr., and William James, reared, like her four brothers, to find her own values without neighborhood, school, or church affiliations, from the age of 16 suffered recurrent psychosomatic sicknesses that were capped by a severe depression during the last 14 years of her life. Bedridden in her later years, in 1889 she began a work variously printed as her *Journal* (1894, 1934) and, complete, as her *Diary* (1964), marked by perceptive observation and psychological understanding.

JAMES, HENRY, SR. (1811–82), father of Henry James, Jr., William James, and Alice James, was a lecturer and writer on religious, social, and literary topics. Born of a wealthy and rigidly orthodox family of Albany, N.Y., he revolted against Calvinism and felt that the social order was unjust. An accident that happened to him as a schoolboy resulted in the amputation of a leg, and drove him further upon his mental resources. After his graduation from Union College (1830), he entered Princeton Theological Seminary (1835), but withdrew after two years, finding himself out of sympathy with orthodox theology. On a visit to England (1837) he became influenced by Robert Sandeman, a Scottish opponent of Calvinism, one of whose books he edited (1838). During the 1840s and '50s, James lived in New York, and traveled abroad frequently, until in 1864 he settled in Boston. In the 1840s he was introduced to the doctrines of Swedenborg, and underwent a kind of religious conversion. Although he never literally embraced these doctrines, they affected his whole later thought and gave him a strongly mystical bias. He was a friend of Emerson and Carlyle, and frequently lectured on them. After 1847 he was an intimate of Parke Godwin, C.A. Dana, Albert Brisbane, and George Ripley and found his social philosophy in the doctrines of Fourierism. Most of his writings were devoted to expressing his religious doctrine, "the immanence of God in the unity of mankind." Among his books are *Christianity the Logic of Creation* (1857); *Substance and Shadow; or Morality and Religion in Their Relation to Life* (1863); *The Secret of Swedenborg, Being an Elucidation of . . . Divine Natural Humanity* (1869); and *Society the Redeemed Form of Man, and the Earnest of God's Omnipotence in Human Nature* (1879). He figures in his son Henry's books *A Small Boy and Others* and *Notes of a Son and Brother.*

JAMES, HENRY, JR. (1843–1916), son of Henry James, Sr., was born in New York City, and, with his brothers William, Garth (1845–83), and Robertson (1846–1910), received a remarkably cosmopolitan, eclectic education. The father, desiring his sons to be citizens of the world, believed that they should avoid forming definite habits of living or of intellect, until prepared to make wise choices of their own. Accordingly, Henry was privately educated by tutors until 1855, when the family went to Europe for a three-year stay. He also lived for a time in Newport (1858, 1860–62) before he entered Harvard Law School (1862). After 1866, although he lived mostly in Europe, his American home was at Cambridge. His conception of himself as a detached spectator of life was maturing, as was his idea that the American scene was hostile toward creative talent and offered no adequate subject matter.

For the time being, however, he divided his interest between European and American materials. During the late 1860s, encouraged by Howells, C.E. Norton, and others, he wrote critical articles and reviews, exhibiting admiration for the technique of George Eliot, and also produced short stories, frequently showing the influence of Hawthorne, one of his masters; a realistic novelette, "Watch and Ward" (*Atlantic Monthly,* 1871; in book form, 1878), concerned with a guardian who loves and marries his ward; and a farce, "Pyramus and Thisbe" (1869). His first important fiction was "A Passionate Pilgrim" ♦ (1871), in which he deals with the first of his great themes, the reactions of an eager American "pilgrim" when confronted with the fascinations of the complex European world of art and affairs.

The author himself during this period was often a pilgrim to the transatlantic world, which he came to regard as his spiritual fatherland, moving there permanently in 1875. During a year in Paris he associated with such masters of his art as Turgenev and Flaubert, but after 1876 he made his home mainly in London, with which much of his writing is concerned. His first novel, following *A Passionate Pilgrim and Other Tales* (1875) and *Transatlantic Sketches* (1875), mainly treating his views of England and Italy, was *Roderick Hudson* ♦ (1876), concerned with the failure of an American sculptor in Rome, resulting from a lack of inner discipline. Other novels and tales of this early London period, when James's course of life was still for him a matter of doubt and self-questioning, include *The American* ♦ (1877), contrasting French

and American standards of conduct; *The Europeans* ♦ (1878), reversing the situation by bringing Europeans into a New England background; *Daisy Miller* ♦ (1879), whose wide popularity is probably owing to its portrayal of a charming, ingenuous American girl; *An International Episode* ♦ (1879), a novelette showing the reactions of Englishmen to the American scene and of an American heiress to aristocratic Britain; *The Madonna of the Future and Other Tales* (1879); and *Confidence* (1880), a romantic, melodramatic novelette about a group of expatriated Americans.

In *Washington Square* ♦ (1881), James again revealed American character, this time in its native environment, but after *The Bostonians* ♦ (1886), a satirical novel of New England reformers and philanthropists, he devoted himself to British and continental themes. *The Portrait of a Lady* ♦ (1881), the first of his mature masterpieces, is a triumph of his method of psychological realism, analyzing the relations of a young American woman with a group of Europeans and expatriated Americans, who objectify her conscientious moral attitude, her sensitive appreciation, and her endurance under suffering. In nearly all of James's fiction, the environment is one of affluence and leisure, in which the preoccupations are with manners and the appreciation of character and the arts, including that of conversation. He treats this society with an infinite refinement of particulars, and in a prose style considered to be unapproached in English for subtlety of phrase and rhythm.

Following *The Portrait of a Lady,* James temporarily turned from the writing of novels. He collected his fiction (14 vols., 1883), and published several new works: a dramatization of *Daisy Miller* (1883); *The Siege of London* ♦ (1883), short stories; *Portraits of Places* (1883), a travel book; *Tales of Three Cities* (1884); *A Little Tour in France* (1885); and *Stories Revived* (3 vols., 1885), reprinting earlier tales.

He returned to the novel with *The Princess Casamassima* ♦ (1886), a melodramatic story of revolutionaries and lower-class life in London, told, as all of James's later fictions are, through the observations and reactions of one character, who usually remains outside the events. This was followed by *The Reverberator* (1888), a novelette concerned with American travelers on the Continent; *The Aspern Papers* ♦ (1888), a novelette which tells of the attempt of a critic to gain a celebrated poet's letters; *A*

London Life (1889), short stories; *The Tragic Muse*♦ (1890), a novel dealing with the lives of artists in English society; *The Lesson of the Master* (1892), short stories; *The Real Thing and Other Tales* (1893); *The Private Life* (1893) and *The Wheel of Time* (1893), collections of tales. At this time he also wrote four comedies, collected in *Theatricals* (2 vols., 1894–95), but none of them was successful in the theater, owing perhaps to his essentially cerebral attitude toward life, his extreme refinement of motive and situation, and his unlifelike dialogue and inability to create dramatic simplifications.

His next series of fictional works includes *Terminations* (1895) and *Embarrassments* (1896), books of stories, the latter containing "The Figure in the Carpet"♦; *The Other House* (1896), an unsuccessful melodramatic novel; *The Spoils of Poynton*♦ (1897), a tragic novel of mean passions magnified by the excellence of their object, a household of precious objects of art; *What Maisie Knew*♦ (1897), a novel told through the medium of a little girl's mind; *In the Cage*♦ (1898), in which a telegraph clerk observes her aristocratic patrons; *The Two Magics* (1898), containing the fine tale of the supernatural "The Turn of the Screw"♦; *The Awkward Age*♦ (1899), portraying a British society girl between adolescence and marriage; *The Soft Side* (1900), a collection of tales; *The Sacred Fount*♦ (1901), a novelette that seems to satirize the typical "detached observer" of James's novels; *The Wings of the Dove*♦ (1902), another of his masterpieces in subtle character portrayal; *The Better Sort* (1903), short stories; *The Ambassadors*♦ (1903), a novel that shows the author's genius for formal structure, as well as his discernment of the values of Old World culture; and *The Golden Bowl*♦ (1904), his last completed novel, which also exhibits him at the height of his artistry.

With the addition of two volumes of stories, *The Altar of the Dead* (1909) and *The Finer Grain* (1910), and two unfinished novels, *The Ivory Tower* (1917) and *The Sense of the Past* (1917), this completed his prolific output of fiction. He edited a second collection of his novels and tales (1907–9), including valuable critical prefaces in which he scrutinized his own fiction in a detached manner, presenting self-judgments as subtle and well formed as the creative works that they assessed. Other writings of his last decade include *William Wetmore Story and His Friends* (2 vols., 1903); *English Hours* (1905), essays; *The Question of Our Speech,*

and *The Lesson of Balzac* (1905), two lectures delivered in the U.S.; *The American Scene*♦ (1907), a descriptive work written after a long journey through the U.S.; *Views and Reviews* (1908), essays; and the autobiographical books, *A Small Boy and Others*♦ (1913), *Notes of a Son and Brother*♦ (1914), and *The Middle Years* (1917). He also returned to playwriting, but of three plays only *The High Bid* was produced (1908).

These last years were troubled ones, saddened by deaths, including that of his brother William, and at the outbreak of World War I he was particularly agitated. To show allegiance to the Allied cause, he became a British subject in 1915. Always strongly conscious of the formal and theoretical phases of his work, he kept *Notebooks* (published 1948) and wrote criticism of his own practice and that of other masters of fiction. Even his *Letters* (3 vols., 1974, 1975, 1980), edited by Leon Edel, display his creative and critical turn of mind. His formal critical writings, sufficient in themselves to establish an author's reputation, were published in *French Poets and Novelists* (1878); *Hawthorne* (1879); *Partial Portraits* (1888), including the essay "The Art of Fiction"; *Picture and Text* (1893); *Essays in London and Elsewhere* (1893); *Notes on Novelists* (1914); *Within the Rim and Other Essays* (1918); and *Notes and Reviews* (1921).

His artistry was conscious at every point, but his intellectual perceptivity in later life seemed to make him a rarefied observer, apparently largely out of touch with many of the more commonplace realities of his times. His eminence in the realm of his choice, however, is unquestioned, as is his influence in the history of the novel, in which he was a pioneer of psychological realism and formal architectonics, and the master of a rich, highly complex prose style and an extremely sensitive apprehension of values of character.

JAMES, WILLIAM (1842–1910), son of Henry James, Sr., was born in New York City, and spent his boyhood, with his brother Henry and two other brothers, in private study in Europe and at Newport. In 1860–61 he tested one of his apparent aptitudes by studying painting under W.M. Hunt at Newport, but abandoned this career to study at Lawrence Scientific School, Harvard (1861–64), and then at Harvard Medical School, which he left to accompany Agassiz on an expedition to collect zoological specimens in Brazil (1865–66). After another year in the Medical School, and a year abroad, he received his M.D. (1869). Physical weakness and a nervous condition that prevented his entering practice or laboratory research caused a period of pessimistic self-doubt, which ended in 1870, partly owing to his reading of Renouvier, whose psychological theories convinced him of the possibility of moral freedom. His long career of teaching at Harvard began in 1872, when he became an instructor in physiology. This work led him into problems of psychology and philosophy, and he soon became interested in the hypotheses of Darwin and Spencer, in 1879 commencing a course on "The Philosophy of Evolution." He had already transferred his instruction to the department of philosophy, and in 1876 had inaugurated a pioneering laboratory of psychology.

From the year of his marriage (1878) until 1890, James's chief occupation outside of his teaching was the writing of *The Principles of Psychology* (1890; abridged as a school text, 1892). This "positivistic" treatise, carefully documenting contemporary psychological knowledge and embodying its author's discoveries and hypotheses, remains a classic text, although somewhat superseded by later investigations, which it helped to inspire. Among the chapters previously published in periodicals is "What Is an Emotion?" (*Mind,* 1884), first stating the so-called James-Lange theory, which suggests that emotions do not cause behavior, but are, rather, collateral results of bodily reactions.

James's many trips to Europe and close association with leading Continental psychologists and philosophers influenced his entry into the wider realm of philosophic problems. During the '80s and '90s, he was also active in the Society for Psychical Research, increasing the prestige of this organization and reinforcing his own impartial speculative attitude. Other activities demonstrating his altruistic idealism and championing of truth regardless of its source included opposing legislative discrimination against Christian Scientists and Spiritualists, campaigning against the Spanish-American War and other imperialist policies of the U.S., advocacy of temperance though not of prohibition, and criticism of the Dreyfus case. At the same time he was publishing many lectures and articles on philosophic subjects, and in 1897 issued *The Will To Believe,* a collection of essays defining his position as a "radical empiricist" and asserting the right to accept metaphysical hypotheses on grounds beyond the possibility of experimental proof. A lecture tour in 1896, made to spread these and similar ideas among influential audi-

ences, resulted in the publication of *Talks to Teachers on Psychology; and to Students on Some of Life's Ideals* (1899), while another phase of his interest in human values appears in *Human Immortality: Two Supposed Objections to the Doctrine* (1898), defending the possibility of life after death.

James's international reputation was further strengthened by his appointment as Gifford Lecturer on Natural Religion at the University of Edinburgh (1901–2). There he delivered the two series of lectures printed in *The Varieties of Religious Experience*♦ (1902), in which he considers religion as an area of psychological facts and treats it, in his brilliant expositional style, from the points of view of science and common sense. He indicates the practical values of religious belief in terms of action and of happiness, and concludes with a statement of his personal dualistic belief.

As early as 1898, while lecturing at the University of California, James had used the term and concept of "pragmatism," adopted from C.S. Peirce, to express his philosophic attitude. During the intervening years, he continued to develop this concept of the mind and its relation to action, and in *Pragmatism*♦ (1907) he defined and amplified this eminently modern philosophic position, according to which an idea has meaning only in relation to its consequences in the world of feeling and action. This pragmatism, differing from that of Peirce, immediately won followers, including John Dewey, but also precipitated attacks, which were answered by James in *The Meaning of Truth* (1909). He had retired from Harvard (1907), but during his last years continued to write and to lecture, and was honored as the foremost American philosopher of his time.

His late and posthumous publications include "The Energies of Men" (1907) and "The Moral Equivalent of War" (1910), expressing his abhorrence of warfare and proposing a substitute, the conscription of youth for projects of manual labor in order to secure discipline and liberate the martial impulses; *A Pluralistic Universe* (1909), defining his metaphysical tenets, in a series of lectures delivered at Oxford in 1908; *Some Problems of Philosophy. A Beginning of an Introduction to Philosophy* (1911), edited by H.M. Kallen; *Memories and Studies* (1911), edited by his brother Henry; *Essays in Radical Empiricism* (1912), edited by R.B. Perry; *The Letters of William James* (2 vols., 1920), edited by his son Henry; and *Collected Essays and Reviews* (1920), edited by Perry.

A scholarly edition of his *Works* was published (7 vols., 1975–78). *Selected Letters* (1961) was edited by Elizabeth Hardwick. A sketchy biography is contained in his brother's *A Small Boy and Others* and *Notes of a Son and Brother,* and Santayana's *Character and Opinion in the United States* includes a study of James and his philosophy.

Jamestown, capital of Virginia (1607–98), situated on what is now an island but was formerly a peninsula in the James River, about 40 miles above Norfolk. The first permanent English settlement within the boundaries of the present U.S., Jamestown was founded (May 13, 1607) on what may once have been the site of a Spanish colony by some hundred colonists under the command of Sir Christopher Newport. During the winters of 1608 and 1609, the colony was threatened with extinction by disease, starvation, and Indian attacks, and it was preserved only by the leadership of such men as John Smith.♦ Fear of Spanish attack was also almost constant. Newport, Sir Thomas Gates, and Sir George Somers reached Jamestown with 150 colonists (1610), but found conditions so deplorable that they were about to give up the settlement. Lord De la Warr arrived unexpectedly at this juncture, bringing more colonists and supplies, and hope was renewed. In 1611, 650 additional colonists were brought. The rapid expansion of tobacco cultivation soon made the community self-supporting. An outstanding example of the acceptance of the whites by the Indians is the marriage of Pocahontas♦ to John Rolfe. America's first legislative assembly was held at Jamestown (1619), and slavery was introduced on this continent that year. Never prosperous, the town had several severe fires, one deliberately set by insurgents in Bacon's Rebellion (1676). Abandoned after Williamsburg became the capital (1699), its ruined buildings were partly restored (*c.*1900). Contemporary treatments of early Jamestown include those by Captain John Smith, Richard Rich, and George Sandys, and later historical novels include John Davis, *The First Settlers of Virginia* (1806), J.E. Cooke, *My Lady Pokahontas* (1885), and Mary Johnston, *To Have and To Hold* (1900).

JARRELL, RANDALL (1914–65), Tennessee-born author, graduated from Vanderbilt (1935), and taught at various colleges. From poems published in *Blood for a Stranger* (1942), *Little Friend, Little Friend* (1945),

Losses (1948), and *The Seven-League Crutches* (1951) he chose his *Selected Poems* (1955). Later poetry and translations appear in *The Woman at the Washington Zoo* (1960, National Book Award) and in *The Lost World* (1965). His other works include *Poetry and the Age* (1953), critical essays; *A Sad Heart at the Supermarket* (1962), essays on literature, the arts, and mass culture; and three posthumous volumes: *The Third Book of Criticism* (1969), *The Complete Poems* (1969), and his translation of *Part One of Goethe's Faust* (1973). *Jerome* (1971) prints his worksheets for an incomplete poem. *Kipling, Auden & Co.* (1980) gathers uncollected essays and reviews. *Pictures from an Institution* (1954) is a satirical novel about faculty at a progressive college for women. His *Letters* were published in 1985.

Java Head, novel by Hergesheimer,♦ published in 1919.

Jazz Age, epithet applied, often invidiously, to the era of the 1920s in the U.S., whose frenetic youth of the postwar period were conceived as more juvenile and hedonistic than the contemporary "lost generation" of expatriates. F. Scott Fitzgerald's *Tales of the Jazz Age* (1922) was a classic representation of the period, as was Percy Marks's *The Plastic Age* (1924). The manners of the times were also depicted in the caricatures of John Held. Treatments of jazz music, as distinct from the jazz-age ethos, occur in many works, including Vachel Lindsay's poem *The Daniel Jazz* (1920) and Dorothy Baker's novel *Young Man with a Horn* (1938).

J.B., poetic drama by Archibald MacLeish♦ treating the theme of Job's trials in a modern setting and idiom.

JEFFERS, [JOHN] ROBINSON (1887–1962), born in Pittsburgh, traveled widely on the Continent until his family settled in California when he was 16. After graduation from Occidental College (California) and desultory graduate study of medicine and other subjects in the U.S. and abroad, he settled with his wife in the town of Carmel, whose surrounding country is the setting of his poetry. After two undistinguished volumes, *Flagons and Apples* (1912) and *Californians* (1916), containing his first California narratives and descriptive pieces, he published *Tamar and Other Poems*♦ (1924), including two long works: the title narrative, adapting the Biblical legend to modern experience in a California scene, and "The Tower Beyond Tragedy,"♦ his own version of the legend of Orestes and Electra, in which Orestes finds salvation from the madness of self-centered humanity by "falling in love outward" with his nonhuman surroundings. Other characteristic poems in the volume include the lyric "Night"♦; "Boats in a Fog" and "Granite and Cypress," expressing Jeffers's love of the spare enduring beauty of the rocky coast on which he made his home; "Shine, Perishing Republic," advising his sons to "be in nothing so moderate as in love of man . . . When the cities lie at the monster's feet there are left the mountains"; "The Coast-Range Christ," a tragically ironic narrative of California mountain people at Christmas; and the apostrophe "To the Stone-Cutters," comparing the poet's work to that of the stone-cutter, both being conscious of ultimate futility, "Yet stones have stood for a thousand years, and pained thoughts found The honey peace in old poems." These were reprinted with additions, the following year, in *Roan Stallion, Tamar, and Other Poems,* the new title piece♦ being an allegorical legend of pantheism.

In *The Women at Point Sur*♦ (1927), through the mad preacher Barclay, the poet again sets forth his conception of the need "to uncenter the human mind from itself," while yet indicating the dangerous aspects of action in accordance with such a philosophic attitude. "Cawdor,"♦ in *Cawdor, and Other Poems* (1928), is a bitterly tragic narrative, in which Jeffers considers "human affairs . . . looking eastward against the earth, reclaiming a little dignity from that association. . . ." Also included in this volume is "Hurt Hawks," expressing the poet's concept of "the wild God of the world . . . intemperate and savage . . . beautiful and wild . . . ," whom the "communal people" have never known, or have forgotten. In 1929 he published *Dear Judas, and Other Poems,* whose title piece retells the story of the betrayal of Christ, describing Judas's motive as one of love. "The Loving Shepherdess," in the same collection, is a parable of self-sacrifice in its story of a girl who, knowing herself doomed to die, wanders over the countryside, devotedly caring for the dwindling flock of her dead father. *Descent to the Dead* (1931), written in England and Ireland, is a volume of elegies in the manner and often in the mood of their Greek models, forming a concise expression of Jeffers's poetic themes, the desire for an end of life, the breaking of the human mold, and the escape to nonhu-

man nature. In *Thurso's Landing, and Other Poems* (1932), the title narrative♦ describes the fatally violent struggle of a California farmer and his rival for his wife's love. *Give Your Heart to the Hawks, and Other Poems* (1933) is a collection whose title narrative♦ deals with the poet's frequent subject of a man who violates a human code, in this case by murdering his brother, and then finds himself alone in a world, beyond humanity, which is inhabited only by the fierce hawks of freedom and soaring flight. The title narrative of *Solstice, and Other Poems* (1935) is a retelling of the Medea legend, while "At the Birth of an Age," in the same volume, is a drama set in the time of Attila. In *Such Counsels You Gave to Me, and Other Poems* (1937), the title narrative♦ is a modern tragedy based on the old Scottish ballad "Edward, Edward." The *Selected Poetry of Robinson Jeffers* was issued in 1938.

Later books include *Be Angry at the Sun* (1941); *Medea* (1946), including a free adaptation of Euripides' drama to fit the modern theater; *The Double Axe* (1948); *Hungerfield and Other Poems* (1945), including a version of Euripides' *Hippolytus;* and a posthumous collection, *The Beginning and the End* (1963). *"What Odd Expedients"* (1981) prints uncollected and unpublished poems.

Jeffers's plots have a realistic setting of the granite cliffs, surf-beaten shore, and towering redwoods of California, yet Jeffers never obscured the symbolism in his use of this background. Accepting a scientific view of the universe, in which man appears to be of but trivial importance, he made the core of his thought the renunciation of humanity and the reliance upon nature. Thus the melodramatic subjects of his narratives have an allegorical significance, and the frequent use of the incest theme symbolizes man regarding man exclusively and leading himself to destruction. From this stemmed his intense revulsion from society, expressed in such statements as "Cut humanity out of my being, that is the wound that festers." He looked forward to the time when man would be driven from the universe, and the grass and the cliff would

. . . enjoy wonderful vengeance and suck
The arteries and walk in triumph on the faces.

In this profound contempt for "the animals Christ was rumored to have died for," and belief that solace will come to the earth only when, freed from humanity, it has attained a "white and most clean, colorless quietness," he found war or any other negative force to be good, in that it cleansed civilization and led back to "the primal and the latter silences."

JEFFERSON, THOMAS (1743–1826), 3rd President of the U.S. (1801–9), was a member of a prominent Virginia family, studied at William and Mary, and practiced law (1767–74). After he entered the House of Burgesses (1769), he was almost constantly in the political service of Virginia and of the nation until his retirement from the presidency. Identified with the aggressive anti-British group, he made an important contribution to the Revolutionary cause in *A Summary View of the Rights of British America* (1774), a brilliant exposition contending that Parliament had no authority in the colonies, whose only bond with England was allegiance to the same king.

As a member of the Continental Congress (1775–76), he was almost wholly responsible for the spirit and phrasing of the Declaration of Independence, his great monument in literature and political theory. In the Virginia House of Burgesses (1776–79) and as governor (1779–81) he attempted to translate the ideals of this document into reality, by advocating laws which would make impossible the maintenance of a landed aristocracy or an established church.

When the British invaded Virginia, he virtually resigned his governorship, and used his leisure to write his *Notes on the State of Virginia* (1784), an unpretentious compendium of information on the geography, natural history, and social and political life of his native land. Again in the Continental Congress (1783), he headed the committee that debated the peace treaty, suggested the plan of the present monetary system, and prepared a report (March 1784) that formulated the plan of government of western territories later embodied in the Ordinance of 1787.

After traveling in Europe and serving as minister to France (1784–89), he returned to the U.S. to become the first secretary of state (1789–93). He championed states' rights, individual liberties, and the ascendancy of the agrarian faction—all in opposition to the Hamiltonian attitude—and objected to the Bank of the United States, the protective tariff, and other measures that would ally the federal government with the monied interests. To further his views, which made him the leader of the anti-Federalist Democratic Republican party then in process of forma-

tion, he backed Freneau's *Federal Gazette,* which attacked the Hamiltonian *Gazette of the United States.*

He retired from office (1793–96), but in 1796 was the Democratic Republican candidate for the presidency, and, running second to Adams, became Vice-President (1797–1801). His most important contribution during this period was his drafting of the Kentucky Resolutions (1798), complementing Madison's Virginia Resolutions in reply to the Federalist Alien and Sedition acts. In 1800 Jefferson and Burr, both Democratic Republican candidates, received equal electoral votes for the presidency. In the congressional election to determine which should be chief executive, Hamilton placed his influence on the side of Jefferson, who was elected. During his two terms, he authorized the Louisiana Purchase, commissioned the expedition of Lewis and Clark, dispatched the naval force of Decatur against the Tripolitans, prosecuted Burr for his unwarranted and bellicose expedition into the Spanish Southwest, and was responsible for the Nonimportation Act and the Embargo Act in retaliation for foreign interference with American trade.

After he left the presidency he was primarily interested in the University of Virginia, which he founded and planned as a modern, broad, and liberal institution of higher education. His designs for his home, Monticello, and for the Virginia state capitol and part of Washington, D.C., stimulated the classical revival in U.S. architecture. Besides his importance in politics and political history, he influenced American culture by his scholarship in sciences and languages, and as a connoisseur and patron of the arts. The variety of his interests and attainments is indicated by his nonpolitical writings, which include *An Essay Towards Facilitating Instruction in the Anglo-Saxon and Modern Dialects of the English Language,* prepared for the University of Virginia and printed by it in 1851, and *The Life and Morals of Jesus of Nazareth,* his personal polyglot compilation of the Gospels, published in facsimile in 1904. He composed his own epitaph: "Here was buried Thomas Jefferson, Author of the Declaration of American Independence, of the Statute of Virginia for Religious Freedom, and Father of the University of Virginia," summing up his lifelong quest of liberty, political, religious, and intellectual. His papers are being published in a projected 60-volume edition (1950–), of which the first 20 were edited by Julian P. Boyd (1903–80).

JEMISON, MARY (1743–1833), "the White Woman of the Genesee," was captured by Indians from her western Pennsylvania home at the age of 15, and, developing a deep affection for them, married into the Delaware tribe and remained with them for the rest of her life. James E. Seaver's *A Narrative of the Life of Mrs. Mary Jemison* (1824), although a late example of the accounts of Indian captivities, is one of the most popular.

Jennie Gerhardt, novel by Dreiser,♦ published in 1911.

As a poor young girl in Columbus, Ohio, Jennie Gerhardt has an affair with Senator Brander, who dies before he can marry her. With their child Vesta she moves to Cleveland and there, attracted by the kindliness and domineering personality of Lester Kane, son of a rich manufacturer, becomes his mistress, although she insists he leave her when she learns that the elder Kane's will provides that Lester receive only a small legacy as long as he remains with Jennie. Lester does leave Jennie to marry Letty Gerald, a woman of his own social class and interests, but installs Jennie in a modest home where she lives with two adopted children after Vesta dies. When Lester falls ill during his wife's absence, he summons Jennie and confesses that she has been his only true love, and she nurses him until he dies.

Jerry of the Islands, novel by Jack London,♦ published in 1917.

Jerry, an Irish setter pup, idolizes his master, Van Horn, who operates a ship to obtain indentured labor from the Solomon Islands. When Van Horn is killed by cannibals, Jerry is taken by the native chief and trained to act as a sentinel. He escapes to the jungle, and ends his quest for a white master when he is found by a California couple who are yachting in the South Seas. Following further adventures, they take Jerry back to the Pacific coast with them.

JEWETT, SARAH ORNE (1849–1909), was born and reared in South Berwick, Me., near York, which resembles "Deephaven." She was early stimulated by Harriet Beecher Stowe's sympathetic depiction of her state's local color, and determined to follow her in recording the life of the dwindling farms and deserted, shipless harbors. Her keen perception led to the *Atlantic Monthly*'s accepting a story when she was 19. In 1873 it also printed "The Shore House," beginning the series gathered as *Deephaven*♦ (1877), which estab-

lished her reputation, although she far exceeded it in her later writing. Her books include *A Country Doctor* (1884), a novel about a New England girl who refuses marriage so as to become a doctor; *A Marsh Island* (1885), a novel depicting the love of a rich painter and the daughter of a New England farmer; *A White Heron* (1886), a collection of stories whose title piece deals with the conflict in the heart of a little girl between her adoration of a young ornithologist and her desire to protect the white heron for which he is searching; and further collections, *The King of Folly Island* (1888), *A Native of Winby* (1893), and *The Life of Nancy* (1895). Her masterpiece is *The Country of the Pointed Firs*♦ (1896), a series of closely knit sketches of a Maine seaport town during the era of its decay from the grandeur of West Indian trading days. Her precise, charmingly subdued vignettes of the gently perishing glory of the Maine countryside and ports have won her a place among the most important writers of the local-color school, and she was a significant influence on the writing of Willa Cather, as the latter tells in *Not Under Forty*. In 1901 Miss Jewett turned to historical romance in *The Tory Lover*, concerned with a young American officer during the Revolution and his conflicting duty to his king and to his native land. Her poems were collected in *Verses* (1916), and she also wrote three books for children.

Joad, family name of the principal characters in *The Grapes of Wrath.* ♦

Joan of Arc, Personal Recollections of, fictional biography by Clemens,♦ published in 1896. To conceal his authorship, so that the book might be received without bias, Clemens invented "The Sieur Louis de Conte," Joan's supposed "page and secretary," whose work is "freely translated by Jean François Alden." The biography follows the known facts in the life of the 15th-century French heroine but amplifies them with several fictional characters and interprets such documents as those relating to the ecclesiastical trial at Rouen in the light of Clemen's lifelong idealistic reverence for "the noble child, the most innocent, the most lovely, the most adorable the ages have produced." Her traits have been said to resemble those of women in the author's family. Other figures, like the comically boastful Paladin and laughing Noël Rainguesson, are related to characters in his earlier fiction. In general, the mood is that of serious, although romanticized, history, but there are characteristic Clemens touches in the use of European folklore, humor, and American tall talk.

John Brown's Body, verse narrative of the Civil War by Stephen V. Benét,♦ published in 1928 and awarded a Pulitzer Prize.

John Henry, hero of a cycle of Negro ballads♦ and tall tales,♦ a "natchal man," born in the "Black River country, where the sun don't never shine," who is sometimes a steel driver in the building of the "Yaller Dog" or "Yaller Ball" railroad line for "Mister Billie Bob Russell," sometimes a roustabout on riverboats. Other figures in the ballads and tales include John Hardy, the gambler; innumerable rivals of John Henry, all named Sam; and the women, Poor Selma, Julie Ann, and Ruby. John Henry's chief exploit is his competition with a steam drill in driving steel, in which he drives faster than the machine, but dies, "with his hammer in his hand," as a result of the exertion. In some versions, the contest is with a steam winch in loading cotton on a riverboat. The legend seems to have originated *c.*1870, when an actual John Henry of such a contest may have existed. The ballads about John Hardy may have arisen from the same source, but their hero differs from John Henry in that he comes to a bad end, murdering a man and dying on the gallows. Roark Bradford's *John Henry* (1931) combines and reconciles the various tales, while Guy B. Johnson's *John Henry: Tracking Down a Negro Legend* (1931) is a collection of variants of the ballads.

John Marr and Other Sailors, poem by Melville,♦ published in 1888. Besides the vigorous title piece, the collection includes such sea pieces as "Bridegroom Dick," "Tom Deadlight," and "Jack Roy." *John Marr and Other Poems* (1922) is a selection from all of Melville's poetic works.

JOHNSON, DIANE [LAIN] (1934–　), born in Illinois, long resident in California, where she earned a Ph.D. from the University of California, Los Angeles, and teaches at the University of California, Davis. Her novels include *Fair Game* (1965), a comic portrayal of four men variously involved with the same woman; *Loving Hands at Home* (1968), a farcical treatment of a Mormon family; *Burning* (1971), an apocalyptic view of lives in Los Angeles; *The Shadow Knows* (1972), portraying the terrifying experiences of a victim-

ized woman; and *Lying Low* (1978), depicting a young woman hiding out as a fugitive in a small California town. *Lesser Lives* (1972) is a biography of the daughter of Thomas Love Peacock, who was the wife of George Meredith, and she also wrote *Dashiell Hammett: A Life* (1983). *Terrorists and Novelists* (1982) collects book reviews.

JOHNSON, EDWARD (1598–1672), colonial Massachusetts chronicler and captain of militia, came to Boston in 1630 to trade with the Indians, and after a short stay sailed for England to bring his family, with whom he returned in 1636. He was a founder of Woburn (1640), and until his death was active in the affairs of that town. As a devout and stalwart Puritan, in 1650 he commenced writing *A History of New-England,* better know by its running title, *The Wonder-Working Providence of Sions Saviour in New-England* (1654). In this anonymously published work, intended to suppress the calumniations of English critics and celebrate the Puritan religious commonwealth in America, Johnson writes with vigor both of homely facts and of great events, and rhapsodizes with an epic view of the founding of New England as a spiritual crusade by soldiers of Christ at war with unbelievers and the wilderness.

JOHNSON, JAMES WELDON (1871–1938), black educator, civil rights leader, and author, was born in Jacksonville, Fla., educated at Atlanta University, and became the first of his race to be admitted to the Florida bar (1897), before moving to New York City and a wider area of activities. With his brother John Rosamond Johnson (1873–1954) he created a song-and-dance act for which they composed such songs as "Under the Bamboo Tree" (popularized by Lillian Russell and later drawn upon by T.S. Eliot in *Sweeney Agonistes*), as well as the so-called black anthem, "Lift Every Voice and Sing," and contributed to the musical comedy *The Shoo Fly Regiment* (1907). In New York he also became active in Republican party politics, leading to appointments as U.S. consul in Nicaragua and Venezuela. He next became the field, later the executive, secretary (1916–30) of the NAACP, increasing its membership enormously (from three to 131 branches in the South), investigated and publicized the brutal U.S. occupation of Haiti, and fought valiantly against lynching. During the period of these diverse careers he became a leader of the Harlem Renaissance,♦ distinguished for both his prose and his poetry. *The Autobiography of an Ex-Colored Man* (1912) is a novel about a light black man who passes as a white and thereby is able to see further into the injustices suffered by his people in the U.S. Other prose writings include *Black Manhattan* (1930), a historical study of New York City; *Negro Americans, What Now?* (1934), his lectures at Fisk University; and *Along This Way* (1933), his autobiography. His poetry appears in *Fifty Years and Other Poems* (1917); *God's Trombones: Seven Negro Sermons in Verse* (1927); *Saint Peter Relates an Incident of the Resurrection Day* (1930), a satire on racial prejudice; and *Selected Poems* (1935). He also edited *The Book of American Negro Poetry* (1922, enlarged 1931) and, with his brother, two collections (1925, 1926) of black spirituals.

JOHNSON, JOSEPHINE [WINSLOW] (1910–   ), Missouri author, whose works include *Now in November* (1934, Pulitzer Prize), a realistic novel of drudgery on a Midwestern farm; *Winter Orchard* (1935), a collection of short stories; *Jordanstown* (1937), the story of a young Midwesterner who during the Depression edits a newspaper in a vain attempt to help the oppressed; *Year's End* (1937), a volume of poetry; *Wildwood* (1946), a novel of a frustrated young girl's upbringing in the home of relatives; *The Dark Traveler* (1963), about the rehabilitation of a schizophrenic young man; and *The Sorcerer's Son* (1965), stories. *The Inland Island* (1969), observations about nature, is also a critical view of contemporary America. *Seven Houses* (1973) is a memoir.

JOHNSON, SAMUEL (1696–1772), was a Congregationalist minister until 1712, when he joined the Church of England, becoming its acknowledged leader in New England. He was the first president of King's College (1754–63) and, as a friend and disciple of the English philosopher Berkeley, became the leading American exponent of Berkeley's idealism, which he made palatable by his pleasing style, while rendering Calvin ridiculous by satirical paraphrase. His principal book, *Ethices Elementa* (1746), was enlarged as *Elementa Philosophica,* published by Franklin in 1752.

JONES, JAMES (1921–77), Illinois-born author, served in the Pacific with the army (1939–44), his experiences furnishing background for *From Here to Eternity* ♦ (1951), a naturalistic novel about army life in Hawaii on the eve of the Pearl Harbor attack. His later

fiction includes *Some Came Running* (1957), a long, panoramic novel set in a Midwestern town between World War II and the Korean War; *The Pistol* (1959), a novella about an army private who accidentally obtains a pistol that comes to be his symbol of safety in war; *The Thin Red Line* (1962), a novel about a U.S. infantry company on Guadalcanal in 1942–43, a sequel to his first novel; *Go to the Widow-Maker* (1967), presenting a successful playwright's quest for manhood through his experiences in learning to skin-dive; *The Merry Month of May* (1971), depicting crises, personal and political, of an American family in Paris during the riots of May 1968; *A Touch of Danger* (1973), a detective tale set on a Greek island; and *Whistle* (1978), the final volume of Jones's World War II trilogy, treating the difficulties four wounded soldiers have in adjusting to civilian life. *The Ice-Cream Headache* (1968) collects stories and a novella, and *Viet Journal* (1974) describes his trip to Vietnam in 1973.

JONES, LEROI (1934–   ), New Jersey-born militant black author, reared in a middle-class environment, attended Rutgers and Howard University (A.B., 1954), served in the Strategic Air Command (1954–57), and studied philosophy and German literature respectively at Columbia and The New School for Social Research before becoming a revolutionary spokesman for his people. He turned his back on Greenwich Village, on the personal and romantic expression that marked his first poetry, *Preface to a Twenty Volume Suicide Note* (1961), divorced his white wife, took the name Imamu Amiri Baraka (1965) as part of his commitment to Afro-Americanism, and founded a black community center, Spirit House, in Newark. An intense black nationalist, he lashes out at whites in his violent one-act plays, *Dutchman, The Slave,* and *The Toilet* (1964). His bitterness and frustration are also evident in his episodic novel *The System of Dante's Hell* (1965), equating Newark slums and the Inferno. Anguish, violent response, and lyrical appreciation of the black spirit mark succeeding volumes of poetry: *The Dead Lecturer* (1964), *Black Magic . . .* (1969), and *In Our Terribleness* (1971). Further plays include *A Recent Killing* (1964), about an aviator intent upon becoming a poet, and the one-act *Four Black Revolutionary Plays* (1969). His stories, some of them clearly autobiographical, are collected in *Tales* (1967). His nonfiction includes *Blues People* (1963), on jazz as an expression of the black people in white America; *Black Music* (1967);

Black Art (1967); and *Black Magic* (1969). Essays are collected in *Home* (1966), powerful social statements for a black nation, and *Raise Race Rays Raze* (1971), written in a black idiom. He has also published *A Black Value System* (1969), *Spirit Reach* (1972), and *African Revolution* (1973). His *Selected Plays and Prose* and *Selected Poetry* were both published in 1979. *The Autobiography of LeRoi Jones* appeared in 1984.

JONG, Erica [Mann] (1942–), born in New York City, graduated from Barnard College (1963). Her books include *Fear of Flying* (1973), about an intense, neurotic New York woman in her thirties enjoying a lively sexual experience for two weeks with an existentialist Englishman; *How To Save Your Own Life* (1977), a sequel in which the woman's first novel becomes a best seller and she prepares to write another while enjoying sexual encounters with a man and a woman; and *Parachutes & Kisses* (1984), continuing the life of her heroine verging on forty. *Fanny* (1980) is a picaresque novel in a pseudo-18th-century style, written from the point of view of a woman. Her poems appear in *Fruits and Vegetables* (1971), *Half-Lives* (1973), *Loveroot* (1975), *At the Edge of the Body* (1979), and *Ordinary Miracles* (1983).

JOSEPHSON, Matthew (1899–1978), New York author, known for a time as a member of the postwar expatriate group and an editor of *Secession* (1922–24), achieved prominence upon publishing the study *Zola and His Time* (1928). His *Portrait of the Artist as American* (1930) presents such Americans as Henry James, Whistler, and Bierce to support the thesis of Van Wyck Brooks that industrial America frustrates artistic creation. Later works include *Rousseau* (1931); *The Robber Barons* (1934), a study of the rise to power of 19th-century American industrialists; *The Politicos* (1938), a companion volume dealing with the political background of this era; *The President Makers* (1940), concerned with political maneuvers from the time of McKinley to that of Wilson; *Empire of the Air* (1944), an account of the growth of an airline; *Stendhal* (1946), *Sidney Hillman* (1952), and *Edison* (1959), biographies; *Union House, Union Bar* (1957), a history of the hotel, restaurant, and bartenders' union; and *Among the Surrealists* (1962) and *Infidel in the Temple* (1967), memoirs. With his wife he wrote a life of Al Smith (1969).

Journal of Julius Rodman, The, fictional travel narrative by Poe,♦ published anonymously in *Burton's Gentleman's Magazine* (1840). It purports to be an account of "the first passage across the Rocky Mountains of North America ever achieved by civilized man," as accomplished in 1792 by an English emigrant, Julius Rodman, with several companions, and described in a diary discovered by his heirs. The character of Rodman and the dates are fictitious, but the adventures and descriptions are based on fact, being largely paraphrased from Irving's *Astoria* and the accounts of Lewis and Clark and Sir Alexander Mackenzie.

Journey to the Land of Eden, A, journal written by William Byrd♦ during 1733, was found among his Westover Manuscripts, from which it was published in 1841. An account of his trip "to the land of Eden," his tract of land near the River Dan in North Carolina, the journal contains urbane and witty observations by a patrician Virginian concerning the boorish backcountry people and the Indians.

Judgment Day, novel by James T. Farrell,♦ published in 1935 as the concluding part of his naturalistic trilogy concerned with the Chicago youth Studs Lonigan. ♦

At 27, Studs contemplates the failure and unhappiness of his family and friends. Worried and suffering because of his weak heart, he fears loneliness, yet almost against his will is involved in an affair with Catherine Banahan, whom he asks to marry him. Events rapidly conspire to defeat him: he loses his savings by an unwise investment in stocks; is unable to buy insurance because of his heart ailment, which has been aggravated by unwholesome living; cannot persuade Catherine to have an abortion when she becomes pregnant; is unemployed during the business depression; and dies, after a brief illness, at the age of 29.

Jumping Frog, see *Celebrated Jumping Frog.*

Jungle, The, novel by Upton Sinclair,♦ published in 1906. This exposé of the Chicago meat-packing industry prompted the investigation by Roosevelt and the federal government that culminated in the pure-food legislation of 1906.

Jurgis Rudkus, a Slav immigrant, marries frail Ona Lukoszaite and seeks security and happiness as a workman in the Chicago stockyards. Foremen abuse him, real-estate sharks filch his meager savings, and at every turn he is beset by misfortunes arising from the poverty, brutality, and disease that are the conditions of his employment. At the birth of a second child, amid direst want, Ona dies. Jurgis's morale temporarily disintegrates and he becomes successively a tramp, common thief, highwayman, and pawn of a corrupt politician. Then, having thought his way through this morass of chicanery and brutality, and despairing of the individual's capacity to face modern society alone, he arrives at a belief in socialism.

Jurgen: A Comedy of Justice, romance set in mythical medieval Poictesme by Cabell,♦ published in 1919.

JUSTICE, Donald [Rodney] (1925–), Florida-born poet, professor at the University of Iowa, has published gentle, well-controlled poems in *The Summer Anniversaries* (1960), *Night Light* (1967), *Departures* (1973), and *Selected Poems* (1979, Pulitzer Prize). He also edited the poems of Weldon Kees (1962).

Juvenile literature, see *Children's literature.*

K

KAEL, PAULINE (1919–), California-born film critic for *The New Yorker* whose reviews are collected in *I Lost It at the Movies* (1965), *Kiss Kiss Bang Bang* (1968), *Going Steady* (1970), *Deeper into Movies* (1975), *Reeling* (1976), *When the Lights Go Down* (1980), and *5001 Nights at the Movies* (1982).

KANIN, GARSON (1912–), New York-born actor, producer, director of plays and motion pictures, whose own stage plays include *Born Yesterday* (1946), a farce about wartime Washington; and *Smile of the World* (1949), about a brilliant young lawyer who becomes a pompous, reactionary Supreme Court justice. He has also written novels: *Do Re Mi* (1955), *Blow Up a Storm* (1959), *A Thousand Summers* (1973), *A Hell of an Actor* (1977), and *Moviola* (1979), and *Cordelia?* (1982), as well as memoirs of people he has known and *Hollywood* (1974).

KAPLAN, JUSTIN (1925–), literary historian, born in New York City, long resident in Cambridge, Mass., is the author of *Mr. Clemens and Mark Twain* (1966, Pulitzer Prize, National Book Award), *Lincoln Steffens, A Biography* (1974), and *Walt Whitman* (1980).

KAUFMAN, GEORGE S[IMON] (1889–1961), New York journalist, playwright, and director, wrote popular plays and musical comedies in collaboration with many authors. Among these were Marc Connelly,♦ with whom he wrote *Dulcy* (1921), *To the Ladies* (1922), *Merton of the Movies* (1922), and *Beggar on Horseback* (1924); Ring Lardner,♦ with whom he wrote *June Moon* (1929); Edna Ferber,♦ with whom he wrote *Minick* (1924), *The Royal Family* (1927), *Dinner at Eight* (1932), *Stage Door* (1936), and *The Land Is Bright* (1941); Morrie Ryskind and George Gershwin, with whom he wrote such musical comedies as *Of Thee I Sing*♦ (1931, Pulitzer Prize) and *Let 'Em Eat Cake* (1933), satirizing revolutionaries; Katherine Dayton, with whom he wrote *First Lady* (1935), a comedy of Washington political and social life; Moss Hart,♦ with whom he wrote *Once in a Lifetime* (1930), a satire of Hollywood, *Merrily We Roll Along* (1934), a play

in reverse chronology, tracing the hero from his failure in middle age back to his youthful promise, *I'd Rather Be Right* (1937), a travesty of the F.D. Roosevelt administration, *You Can't Take It with You*♦ (1936, Pulitzer Prize), *The American Way* (1939), a patriotic panorama of recent history, *The Man Who Came to Dinner* (1939), a farce about an author like Alexander Woollcott, and *George Washington Slept Here* (1940); J.P. Marquand, with whom he wrote an adaptation of *The Late George Apley* (1944); and Howard Teichmann, with whom he wrote *The Solid Gold Cadillac* (1953).

KAZAN, ELIA (1909–), Turkish-born theatrical and motion-picture director, graduated from Williams College (1930), and after study at Yale became an actor with the Group Theatre. Plays he has directed include *The Skin of Our Teeth, A Streetcar Named Desire, Death of a Salesman, Cat on a Hot Tin Roof,* and *J.B.;* motion pictures he directed include *On the Waterfront* and *East of Eden.* He has written novels: *America, America* (1962), somewhat in the form of a screenplay (and made into a film, which he directed, 1963), about a Greek youth escaping poverty and persecution in Turkey by coming to the U.S. at the opening of the 20th century; *The Arrangement* (1967), *The Assassins* (1972), *The Understudy* (1974), *Acts of Love* (1978), and *The Anatolian* (1982), a sequel to his first novel.

KAZIN, ALFRED (1915–), literary critic, has taught at many American universities, but is best known for his critical works, *On Native Grounds*♦ (1942), a study of American prose literature after Howells; *The Inmost Leaf* (1955), essays on European and American literature; *Contemporaries* (1962), essays on American authors, past and present; *Bright Book of Life* (1973), treating American fiction from Hemingway to Mailer; and *An American Procession* (1984), on American authors from 1830 to 1930. His moving autobiographical writings have been issued as *A Walker in the City* (1951), a lyrical treatment of his youth in Brownsville, then a Jewish immigrant section of Brooklyn; *Start-*

ing Out in the Thirties (1965), reminiscences of his young manhood; and *New York Jew* (1978), considering his life into the 1970s.

KELLER, HELEN [ADAMS] (1880–1968), author and lecturer, who, though blind and deaf from the age of two, graduated with honors from Radcliffe (1904) and became a prominent worker for social reforms. Her books include *The Story of My Life* (1902); *The World I Live In* (1908); *Out of the Dark* (1913); *My Religion* (1927); *Midstream: My Later Life* (1929); and *Let Us Have Faith* (1940). Van Wyck Brooks wrote *Helen Keller: Sketch for a Portrait* (1956).

KELLEY, WILLIAM MELVIN (1937–   ), New York-born novelist, inspired to write by John Hawkes and Archibald MacLeish, his teachers at Harvard, has since become a leading black author. His first novel, *A Different Drummer* (1962), is a mythic tale of a black sharecropper who in destroying his farm and discarding his heritage inspires others to seek a better future. Later fiction includes *A Drop of Patience* (1965), about a blind black jazz musician who turns to his people's evangelical religion; *dem* (1967), a satirical and sometimes surrealistic story of a white Madison Avenue advertising executive as he searches for the father of the black baby to which his wife has given birth; and *Dunfords Travels Everywhere* (1970), contrasting a Harvard-educated black in France and a Harlem swindler. *Dancers on the Shore* (1964) collects stories.

KEMBLE, FRANCES ANNE (FANNY KEMBLE) (1809–95), member of a famous English stage family, had a successful career as an actress in London, and came to America (1832), acting for two years before retiring to marry Pierce Butler, owner of a Georgia plantation. Her *Journal* of Frances Anne Butler (2 vols., 1835) is a record of her theatrical tour, freely criticizing many American customs. Her *Journal of a Residence on a Georgian Plantation,* written during the winter of 1838–39, was not published until 1863, when it was meant to influence British opinion against the South, whose slavery she detested. In 1846 she left her husband, returned to the London stage, wrote *A Year of Consolation* (1847), and a year later became involved in a notorious divorce suit. Afterward, in the U.S., she gave public readings of Shakespeare and wrote plays, volumes of poetry, criticism, and autobiography, and *Far Away and Long Ago* (1889), a rambling novel of the Berkshires,

where she made her home. Owen Wister was her grandson.

KENNEDY, JOHN PENDLETON (1795–1870), born in Baltimore, graduated from Baltimore College (1812) and began to practice law. Disliking this profession, he soon entered politics, educational affairs, and literature. *The Red Book* (1818–19) was a publication in the manner of Irving's *Salmagundi. Swallow Barn* (1832, revised 1851), 49 related sketches with a slight plot, pleasantly depicts life in the "Old Dominion" of Virginia during the first quarter of the 19th century. *Horse-Shoe Robinson* (1835) and *Rob of the Bowl* (1838) are full-bodied romances, respectively about conflicts between Tories and patriots during the Revolutionary War in Virginia and concerning plots against Lord Baltimore in 17th-century Maryland. His literary associations at this time included contacts with most of the leading U.S. authors, and he was a patron of Poe, awarding first prize in a short story contest to "MS. Found in a Bottle." In 1838 Kennedy's political career began with his election to Congress as a Whig. He was reelected (1840, 1842), and wrote a satire of Jacksonian democracy, *Quodlibet: Containing Some Annals Thereof . . . by Solomon Second-Thoughts, Schoolmaster* (1840). After the death of President Harrison, Kennedy wrote *A Defense of the Whigs* (1843), attacking Tyler's political defection. His last important literary work was a two-volume biography of William Wirt (1849). In 1852 he became Fillmore's secretary of the navy and urged the expedition to Japan under Commodore Perry, as well as the second Arctic voyage of Kane. Kennedy met Thackeray during the English author's visit to the U.S. (1855–56) and furnished him information later used in *The Virginians.* He supported the Union cause during the Civil War, about which he wrote *Mr. Ambrose's Letters on the Rebellion* (1865). Posthumous publications include *Political and Official Papers* (1872), *Occasional Addresses* (1872), and *At Home and Abroad* (1872).

KENNEDY, WILLIAM (1928–   ), born in Albany, N.Y., where he has continued to live and where he has set his novels: *The Ink Truck* (1969), about a journalist; *Legs* (1975), about an actual gangster; *Billy Phelan's Greatest Game* (1978), portraying Irish and other lively characters of his hometown; and *Ironweed* (1983, Pulitzer Prize), presenting a baseball player who becomes a murderer.

Not only the setting but characters recur in the novels.

KENT, ROCKWELL (1882–1971), New York author and artist, whose books, illustrated by himself, are accounts of sea voyages and residences in the Arctic and South America. They include *Wilderness* (1920), concerning his experiences in Alaska; *Voyaging Southward from the Strait of Magellan* (1924), about his journey to Tierra del Fuego; *N by E* (1930) and *Salamina* (1935), dealing with his life in Greenland; and *This Is My Own* (1940) and *It's Me, O Lord* (1955), autobiography. In addition to illustrations for many books, he is known for his work as a painter, primarily of landscapes distinguished for a use of simple masses of color, and as a pen-and-ink artist and lithographer who used a striking, stark line in a highly stylized manner.

Kentucky Tragedy, celebrated crime known also as the Beauchamp case. Ann Cook, after having been seduced by Colonel Solomon P. Sharp, solicitor-general of Kentucky, married an attorney, Jeroboam O. Beauchamp (1824), making him swear to kill Sharp. Several times challenged, Sharp refused to fight, and Beauchamp's murder plans were equally unsuccessful. Finally Beauchamp, in disguise, stabbed Sharp to death (Nov. 5, 1825). He pleaded not guilty after his arrest, but was convicted after a long trial marked by corruption on both sides. Beauchamp was refused a pardon by the governor, and the night before the execution, Ann joined him in his cell, where both took laudanum. When this did not kill them, they stabbed themselves. Ann died, but Beauchamp was hanged. The affair has been written about in Beauchamp's *Confession* (1826), containing poems by Ann, in plays by Chivers ♦ and Charlotte Barnes, ♦ R.P. Warren's *World Enough and Time,* and Poe's *Politian,* ♦ Hoffman's *Greyslaer,* ♦ and Simms's *Beauchampe.* ♦

Kenyon Review (1939–70, 1979–   ), quarterly journal edited to 1959 by J.C. Ransom from Kenyon College, Ohio. It included many former contributors to *The Southern Review,* ♦ carrying on its program of close textual scrutiny of modern poetry, and the printing of essays on aesthetics along with important new fiction and poetry. Robie Macauley was editor (1959–67), shifting emphasis to essays on contemporary culture. In 1970 the journal ceased publication, but it was revived in 1979, again addressing itself to

literature but not of any one school. Ransom and Macauley edited anthologies of its publications, respectively of criticism (1951) and fiction (1966).

KEROUAC, JACK (1922–69), Massachusetts-born writer who attended Columbia University (1940–42) and roamed about and took odd jobs before he became associated with the Beat movement. ♦ His fiction, very loose in style and structure, includes *The Town and the City* (1950), tracing the Martin family from 1910 in Lowell, Mass., through the war years and the dispersal of the eight children; *On the Road* ♦ (1957), a quasi-autobiographical tale of Beat people ranging around America seeking experience and fulfillment; *The Dharma Bums* (1958), a similar novel but with more emphasis on the discovery of truth or "dharma" through Zen Buddhism; *The Subterraneans* (1958), about a love affair between a Beat writer and a black girl; *Doctor Sax* (1959), an early novel fictively re-creating the author's youth; *Maggie Cassidy* (1959), about the adolescent Jack Duluoz searching for love and identity; *Tristessa* (1960), portraying the morphine addiction of a Mexico City prostitute; *Big Sur* (1962), a sequel to *On the Road,* about the crack-up and withdrawal to the Carmel area of a leader of the Beat movement; *Visions of Gerard* (1963), about the great grief of a French-Canadian family of Lowell, Mass., when its religious young son dies; *Desolation Angels* (1965), treating the Beat generation just prior to the time of *On the Road;* and *Vanity of Duluoz* (1968), again drawing on his youth in a tale of "moral death and resurrection." *Pic* (1971), a posthumously published novel, tells of a black jazz musician making his way from the South to Harlem. *Mexico City Blues* (1959) collects poems, *Lonesome Traveler* (1960) gathers travel sketches, *Book of Dreams* (1960) recounts his dreams in stream-of-consciousness style, *Satori in Paris* (1966) describes his French travels in quest of his ancestry and of illumination, or satori, and *Visions of Cody* (1960, in part; 1970, in full) gathers recollections, some about Neal Cassady, his traveling companion.

KESEY, KEN (1935–   ), born in Colorado, graduated from the University of Oregon, later studied at Stanford, and once worked as a ward attendant in a mental hospital which provided background for his comic macabre novel *One Flew Over the Cuckoo's Nest* ♦ (1962), whose tone also animates his second novel, *Sometimes a Great Notion* (1964), about a feud between two brothers in an Oregon lumber town. *Kesey's Garage Sale* (1973) collects diverse writings, mainly autobiographical. His loose life-style during the '60s, touring around in a bus with his so-called Merry Pranksters, was the subject of an essay by Tom Wolfe♦ in his *Electric Kool-Aid Acid Test.*

KEY, Francis Scott (1779–1843), author of "The Star-Spangled Banner"♦ (1814), was known in his own time as a Maryland lawyer, temporarily associated in practice with his brother-in-law, R.B. Taney, and for his other songs and devotional pieces, posthumously published in *Poems* (1857). He also wrote *The Power of Literature and Its Connection with Religion* (1834).

KILMER, [Alfred] Joyce (1886–1918), poet, journalist, and critic, whose best-known work is the title piece in *Trees and Other Poems* (1914). He died in the second Battle of the Marne, becoming a symbol of courageous poetic idealism destroyed by war. His other books of poetry are *Summer of Love* (1911) and *Main Street* (1917).

Aline Kilmer (1888–1941), his widow, was known as a poet in her own right, having published *Candles That Burn* (1919), *Vigils* (1921), and other books.

KING, Clarence (1842–1901), born at Newport, graduated from Yale (1862), after which he made a horseback trip across the continent to work in the mines of the Comstock Lode and California. He was next engaged (1866–77) in a geological survey of the Cordilleran ranges from eastern Colorado to California, whose results were published in the cooperative *Report of the Geological Exploration of the Fortieth Parallel* (7 vols., 1870–80). This is said to have been the most thorough and the most exact government survey published to that date. After heading the U.S. Geological Survey (1878–81), he continued his own important writings on geological and geophysical problems. His most popular work was the series of sketches *Mountaineering in the Sierra Nevada♦* (1872), scientifically accurate as well as charmingly descriptive of the region. His ability as an author is further seen in "The Helmet of Mambrino" (*Century,* May 1886), and in the discussions with his friends John Hay and Henry Adams, which are said to have been partly responsible for the novels *The Bread-Winners* and *Democracy.*

KING, Grace Elizabeth (1851–1932), New Orleans author, whose short stories and novels of that city were a late development of the local-color movement. Her books include *Monsieur Motte* (1888); *Tales of a Time and Place* (1892); *Balcony Stories* (1893); *The Pleasant Ways of St. Médard* (1916), a novel of Reconstruction days in New Orleans; and historical and biographical works concerning the region.

KINGSLEY, Sidney (1906–), New York playwright and actor, whose plays include *Men in White* (1933), on the medical profession; *Dead End* (1935), about New York's slums; *Ten Million Ghosts* (1936), about munitions makers; *The World We Make* (1939), dramatizing Millen Brand's novel *The Outward Room,* about the cure of a psychopathic girl through sharing in the life of the poor; *The Patriots* (1943), written with his wife Madge Evans, about Jefferson and Hamilton's struggle over the future of the U.S.; *Detective Story* (1949); *Darkness at Noon* (1951), based on Arthur Koestler's novel; *Lunatics and Lovers* (1954), a farce; and *Night Life* (1962).

KINGSTON, Maxine Hong (1940–), California-born author, resident in Hawaii as a schoolteacher, wrote *The Woman Warrior* (1976), a partly fictional work about her girlhood as it was affected by the beliefs of her Chinese family, and *China Men* (1980), again blending family history and legendry in treating the lives of men in her family who left their Oriental culture to live and work in the U.S.

KINNELL, Galway (1927–), born in Rhode Island, after receiving his A.B. from Princeton (1948) and an M.A. from the University of Rochester, has taught at various universities. Early poems, published in *First Poems, 1946–1954* (1970), *What a Kingdom It Was* (1960), and *Flower Herding on Mount Monadnock* (1964), are marked by vivid observation and religious and social consciousness presented in pure, though idiomatic, language. Later poems, often darker and more symbolic, appear in *Body Rags* (1966); *The Lackawanna Elegy* (1971); *The Book of Nightmares* (1971), a sequence of ten intense and personal poems; *The Avenue Bearing the Initial of Christ into the New World* (1974), whose title poem presents Whitman-like religious feelings about the ordinary people encountered on New York's Avenue C; *Mortal Acts, Mortal Words* (1980); *Selected*

Poems (1982, Pulitzer Prize); and *There Are Things I Tell to No One* (1982). Kinnell has translated poems by Yves Bonnefoy, Yvan Goll, and Villon and has written a taut novel, *Black Light* (1966), set in Iran, where he taught for a year. *Walking Down the Stairs* (1978) contains his views on poetry set forth in interviews.

KIPLING, RUDYARD (1865–1936), British poet, novelist, and writer of short stories, resided for several years after 1892 at Brattleboro, Vt. With his brother-in-law, Wolcott Balestier, he wrote *The Naulahka* (1892). *Captains Courageous* (1897) is Kipling's own work concerned with the American scene in telling of life aboard a fishing schooner out of Gloucester.

KIRKLAND, CAROLINE STANSBURY (1801–64), born in New York City, became one of the first settlers of Pinckney, Mich. Her ideas of the West, formed by such works as Chateaubriand's *Atala*, were considerably altered when she went to live on the frontier, as indicated in *A New Home—Who'll Follow?♦* (1839), written under the pseudonym Mrs. Mary Clavers, and reissued (1874) as *Our New Home in the West.*

KITTREDGE, GEORGE LYMAN (1860–1941), authority on Shakespeare and early English literature, professor at Harvard (1888–1936) whose teaching and writing had a profound influence on American scholarship. His works include *The Old Farmer and His Almanack* (1904); *Chaucer and His Poetry* (1915); *Shakspere* (1916); *A Study of Gawain and the Green Knight* (1916); and *Witchcraft in Old and New England* (1929).

KNICKERBOCKER, DIEDRICH, fictitious chronicler of Irving's humorous *History of New York♦* (1809) and in shorter tales and sketches dealing with the Dutch background of the state. Owing to Irving, the name became synonymous with the Dutch in respect to New York. The real Knickerbocker family came to America *c.*1674 and lived chiefly in Albany County.

Knickerbocker Group, school of writers whose association was primarily geographical and due to similar literary tastes. The name was a tribute to Irving's *Knickerbocker's History of New York* (1809), and the members attempted to carry his Addisonian spirit into their superficially sophisticated work.

Besides Irving, Bryant, and Paulding, the writers most generally identified with this group included Hoffman, Drake, Halleck, Verplanck, Sands, Willis, Lydia M. Child, and Epes Sargent. This New York City group was represented in *The Knickerbocker Magazine,♦* but may be said to have waned after its founding. Most of the writers were pilloried in Poe's "The Literati."

Knickerbocker Magazine, The (1833–65), monthly literary magazine, published at New York, was edited by Lewis G. and Willis G. Clark (1834–61). The name was a tribute to Irving, who was a contributor during its heyday, as were Longfellow, Parkman, Paulding, Hoffman, Halleck, Willis, Hawthorne, Whittier, Holmes, Bird, and Bryant. C.G. Leland was editor (1861–62), writing most of the contents himself, although Howells, Aldrich, and Fitz-James O'Brien also contributed. *The Knickerbocker Gallery* (1855) was an anthology selected from the magazine.

KNIGHT, SARAH KEMBLE (1666–1727), known as Madam Knight, was a Boston teacher, also employed in the recording of public documents. She is said to have been an early teacher of Benjamin Franklin. Entrusted with some family business, during the winter of 1704–5 she made an unaccompanied trip from Boston to New York City and back, which occupied five months. During the pauses of her horseback journeys, she kept a journal, which records events in a most amusing fashion and comments entertainingly upon the rough roads, river crossings, intolerable inns, and the manners and speech of the inland rustics. The diary was first published by Theodore Dwight (1825), and has since been frequently reprinted, although the original manuscript is now lost.

Knight's Gambit, collection of closely related stories by Faulkner,♦ published in 1949, in which Gavin Stevens,♦ the county attorney of Yoknapatawpha, solves various crimes and sees that justice is done.

KNOWLES, JOHN (1926–   ), West Virginia-born author, educated at Yale, whose novels include *A Separate Peace* (1960), reminiscences of the unhappy experiences of boys at a New England boarding school; *Morning in Antibes* (1962), depicting Americans on the French Riviera; *Indian Summer* (1966), presenting the uneasy relations of two men; *The Paragon* (1971), a portrait of a brilliant, iconoclastic college student during the Korean War; *Spreading Fires* (1974), a psychological thriller set in the south of France; *A Vein of Riches* (1979), about the waning fortunes of a West Virginia family made rich by coal mining; *Peace Breaks Out* (1980), a sequel to his first novel, treating malevolence that leads to murder at a boys' boarding school; and *A Stolen Past* (1983), a reminiscent tale of college friendships. *Phineas* (1968) collects stories, and *Double Vision* (1964) is a travel book.

Know-Nothing movement sponsored secret societies that flourished in the 1840s and '50s, whose purpose was to oppose the political influence of foreign-born groups, especially those who were Roman Catholics. Although not an actual party, the several organizations within the movement had considerable influence on local and state elections through the American Republican party and similar groupings, and in 1854 they abandoned secrecy to become the American party with Fillmore as their presidential candidate (1856). Carleton Beals's *Brass-Knuckle Crusade* (1960) treats the movement.

KOBER, ARTHUR (1900–1974), was born in Poland and brought to New York as a child. He was the author of *Having a Wonderful Time* (1937), a comedy of New York City office workers at a summer camp in the Catskills, and of another comedy written in collaboration, *Wish You Were Here* (1952); vernacular sketches of life in the Bronx, collected in *Thunder Over the Bronx* (1935), *My Dear Bella* (1941), *Bella, Bella, Kissed a Fella* (1951), and *Ooh, What You Said!* (1958); and *Pardon Me for Pointing* (1939) and *That Man Is Here Again* (1947), sketches of Hollywood. In addition to another play, *A Mighty Man Is He* (1959), he wrote many film scripts.

KOCH, KENNETH [JAY] (1925–), Cincinnati-born author, educated at Harvard (A.B., 1948) and Columbia (Ph.D., 1959), has been on Columbia's faculty since 1959. He is associated with the so-called New York school of poetry of John Ashbery and Frank O'Hara, and his early *Poems* (1953) are marked by a surrealistic use of language. *Ko, or A Season on Earth* (1960) is a long comic poem of complex plots written in Byronic ottava rima. Later collections of poems, including *Thank You* (1962), *The Pleasures of Peace* (1969), and *The Art of Love* (1975), all

marked by an exuberant wit, were followed by *The Duplications* (1977), another capricious Byronic epic, *The Burning Mystery of Anna in 1951* (1979), combining poetry and prose, and *Days and Nights* (1982), also combining long poems and some prose, more sober in tone. *Bertha and Other Plays* (1966) and *A Change of Hearts* (1973) collect his many very short plays. *The Red Robins* is a novel of fantasy that he dramatized (1980). His very successful teaching of poetry to children is treated in *Wishes, Lies, and Dreams* (1970) and *Rose Where Did You Get That Red?* (1973). Similar teaching to sick, aged people in a nursing home is the subject of *I Never Told Anybody* (1977).

KOPIT, ARTHUR L. (1937–), born in New York and educated at Harvard (A.B., 1959), where he wrote and directed several plays, culminating with *Oh Dad, Poor Dad, Mama's Hung You in the Closet and I'm Feelin' So Sad* (1960). This work, published in 1960 and professionally produced in 1962, is subtitled "a pseudoclassical, tragifarce in a bastard French tradition," and presents in wildly farcical but moving style a fantastic treatment of the "silver cord" theme. *Indians* (1969) presents scenes from the lives of Buffalo Bill and Sitting Bull to denounce U.S. treatment of Indians. *End of the World with Symposium To Follow* (1983) deals with the nuclear arms race. Six shorter plays are gathered in *The Day the Whores Came Out To Play Tennis* (1965), and he also wrote the book for a musical play, *Nine* (1982).

KOSINSKI, JERZY [NIKODEM] (1933–), Polish-born, Russian-reared author, came to the U.S. (1957), where he was a graduate student at Columbia and began to write in English. His first novel, *The Painted Bird* (1965), presents a six-year-old Polish boy trapped during the German occupation, in which he suffers endless brutalities. It was followed by further spare fiction treating other violent or perverse situations: *Steps* (1968) presents an anonymous narrator's account of diverse cruelties; *Being There* (1971) is an ironic fable with a different tone in its tale of a gentle, illiterate gardener who achieves national leadership in the U.S. by chance; *The Devil Tree* (1973) is another fable, this one about a very rich young man seeking to find himself; *Cockpit* (1975) is like his other novels in avoiding a sequential plot as it tells of an ex-spy's violent acts of vengeance and quest for intimacy, mainly sexual; *Blind Date* (1977) is an amoral picaresque story, whose protagonist, an antihero, indulges in wild, perverse, and horrid activities; *Passion Play* (1979) depicts another picaresque figure, an impassioned horseman who is also an esoteric novelist; and *Pinball* (1982) is about a seedy musician's quest to learn the true identity of a very popular rock star. Kosinski has written two nonfictional books about people in the USSR, *The Future Is Ours, Comrade* (1960) and *No Third Path* (1962), under the name Joseph Novak. Kosinski taught at Yale (1970–73).

KREYMBORG, Alfred (1883–1966), New York City poet and playwright, whose first collection, *Mushrooms* (1916), was an attempt to achieve direct simplicity in poetry. He next turned to poetic drama, writing *Plays for Poem-Mimes* (1918), *Plays for Merry Andrews* (1920), and *Puppet Plays* (1923), many of which were first presented by the Provincetown Players. ◆ *Less Lonely* (1923) shows the juxtaposition of personal themes and conventional verse forms; *Manhattan Men* (1929) represents a midway point between his early experimentation and his later more conventional poetry. His *Selected Poems* was published in 1945. *Troubadour* (1925) is the autobiography of his youth on the Lower East Side and his later life in Greenwich Village and elsewhere. His other books include novels and a radio drama, *The Planets* (1938), a modern pacifist allegory.

KRONENBERGER, Louis (1904–80), born in Cincinnati, long the drama critic for *Time* (1938–61) and also for *P.M.* (1940–48), was a professor of theater arts at Brandeis (1953–70) and its librarian (1963–70), as well as lecturer at other universities. His books, in addition to various anthologies, include the novels *The Grand Manner* (1929), about an autocratic monarch ruling a democratically inclined people; *Grand Right and Left* (1952), a farcical comedy of manners about people of great wealth and great wit; and *A Month of Sundays* (1961), the bizarre story of a luxurious mental institution that amusingly comments on contemporary absurdities. Other books include *Kings and Desperate Men* (1942), about the manners and tastes of 18th-century England; *The Thread of Laughter* (1952), essays on comic drama from Jonson to Maugham; *Company Manners* (1954), lively essays on American behavior; *The Republic of Letters* (1955), literary history and criticism; *Marlborough's Duchess* (1958), a biography subtitled "a study in

worldliness"; *The Cart and the Horse* (1964), sharp essays on failures in contemporary American culture from the universities to advertising; *The Polished Surface* (1969), essays on worldly literature; *No Whippings, No Gold Watches* (1970), reminiscences; *The Last Word* (1972), on authors of aphorisms; and studies of John Wilkes (1973) and Oscar Wilde (1976).

KRUTCH, Joseph Wood (1893–1970), born in Tennessee, graduated from the state university (1915), served in World War I, and received his Ph.D. from Columbia (1923). He was long on the faculty of Columbia (1925–31, 1937–52) and on the editorial staff of *The Nation* (1924–52) mainly as a drama critic. His books include *Edgar Allan Poe: A Study in Genius* (1926), an analytical biography employing psychoanalysis; *The Modern Temper* (1929), a pessimistic analysis of contemporary life, by a "modern intellectual" who finds that science has destroyed his faith in a beneficent universe, and psychology his belief in his own nobility, so that he "finds only in the pursuit of knowledge that which makes life worth living"; *Five Masters: A Study in the Mutations of the Novel* (1930), an analysis of Boccaccio, Cervantes, Richardson, Stendhal, and Proust, to determine whether their greatness springs from the life of their times or from an essential universality; *Experience and Art* (1932); *Was Europe a Success?* (1934); *The American Drama Since 1918* (1939); scholarly biographies, *Samuel Johnson* (1944) and *Thoreau* (1948); *"Modernism" in Modern Drama* (1953); and *The Measure of Man* (1954), a return to the themes of *The Modern Temper,* with a humanistic plea for "Moral Discourse." After he moved to Arizona many of his books dealt with natural history, the Western scene, and a humanist's view of man and his environment, including *The Desert Year* (1952), *The Best of Two Worlds* (1953), *The Great Chain of Life* (1957), *Human Nature and the Human Condition* (1959), and *The Forgotten Peninsula; A Naturalist in Baja California* (1961). *More Lives Than One* (1962) recalls his varied experiences.

Ku Klux Klan, secret terrorist society widespread in the South during Reconstruction. It intended to keep freed blacks subservient, and used various methods of instilling fear, ranging from masks, flowing white robes, and horseback parades to raids by night, whippings, and tarring and feathering. It figures in Thomas Dixon's *The Clansman,* Evelyn

Scott's *A Calendar of Sin,* and Robert Lewis Taylor's *A Voyage to Matecumbe.* The more recent Ku Klux Klan movement has been nationwide, originating in Georgia (1915) but spreading, as an outgrowth of World War I emotionalism, to many Northern regions. Based on a program of white supremacy, native Americanism, fundamentalism, anti-Semitism, and anti-Catholicism, it had considerable political influence, especially in the early 1920s. The opposition of many Southerners to civil-rights legislation caused the Klan's revival in the 1960s, and it was joined by other extremist organizations that adopted some variation of its name.

KUMIN, MAXINE [WINOKUR] (1925–), born in Philadelphia, where her father was the city's major pawnbroker, was educated at Radcliffe (A.B., 1946; M.A., 1948). Her first novel, *Through Dooms of Love* (1965), titled with a line from Cummings, dealing with the conflict between a radical Radcliffe girl and her pawnbroker father, was followed by *The Passions of Uxport* (1968), with a setting like that of Updike's *Couples,* which presents stormy married life in a Boston suburb. *The Abduction* (1971) and *The Designated Heir* (1974), portrayals of different kinds of women, are later novels. Stories are collected in *Why Can't We Live Together Like Civilized Human Beings?* (1982). Her poetry, collected in *Halfway* (1961), *The Privilege* (1965), *The*

Nightmare Factory (1970), *Up Country: Poems of New England* (1972, Pulitzer Prize), *House, Bridge, Fountain, Gate* (1975), *The Retrieval System* (1978), and *Our Ground Time Here Will Be Brief* (1982), is described by Philip Booth as "memorial rather than confessional," possessing "a resonant language, an autobiographical immediacy, unsystematized intelligence, and radical compassion," and she herself sees all her writing as "private experience giving rise to elegy and celebration." Her essays are collected in *To Make a Prairie* (1979), and she has written many children's books, two with Anne Sexton.

KUNITZ, STANLEY J[ASSPON] (1905–), poet and editor of reference books, graduated from Harvard (1926), and has frequently been a teacher of poetry at colleges and literary workshops. His modern metaphysical poetry appears in *Intellectual Things* (1930); *Passport to War* (1940); *Selected Poems* (1958, Pulitzer Prize), a third of them new; and *The Testing-Tree* (1971), marked, as he says, by "a more open style, based on natural speech rhythms." He has also translated several contemporary Russian poets. *A Kind of Order, A Kind of Folly* (1975) prints essays and other prose. His reference works include *American Authors 1600–1900* (1938), with Howard Haycraft.

L

Lady Eleanore's Mantle, allegorical tale by Hawthorne,♦ published in 1838 and reprinted in *Twice-Told Tales* (1842).

Lady Eleanore Rochcliffe comes to live at the Boston Province House, in the family of her guardian, Colonel Shute. Her haughty beauty distracts Jervase Helwyse, whose love she scorns, and affects all who see her. The curious mantle she wears is said to have supernatural powers and to have some influence in the epidemic of smallpox that soon breaks out, striking first the aristocratic circle of Lady Eleanore, and then the common people she despises. At last she herself is stricken, and as she is dying confesses, "I wrapped myself in Pride as in a Mantle, and scorned the sympathies of nature; and therefore has nature made this wretched body the medium of a dreadful sympathy." Helwyse takes her mantle, which is burned by a mob, and the pestilence begins to subside.

Lady or the Tiger?, The, short story by Frank Stockton,♦ which was sensationally popular when it was published in *The Century* (Nov. 1882). It was reprinted in a collection (1884) and was the subject of an operetta (1888).

LA FARGE, CHRISTOPHER (1897–1956), author, painter, and architect. His verse novels are *Hoxie Sells His Acres* (1934), set in New England; *Each to the Other* (1939), about a young man trying to find his place in the modern world; and *Beauty for Ashes* (1953), about social responsibility and personal independence. *The Sudden Guest* (1946), a prose novel about a New England spinster's disregard for fellow citizens during a hurricane, is an oblique comment on U.S. international relations. *Mesa Verde* (1945) is a verse drama about the cliff dwellers. Collections include *Poems and Portraits* (1941); *East by Southwest* (1944), stories and a poem about the war in the Pacific; and *All Sorts and Kinds* (1949), stories.

LA FARGE, OLIVER [HAZARD PERRY] (1901–63), ethnologist and author, after graduation from Harvard (1924) conducted archaeological investigations in Arizona, Mexico, and Guatemala, and with Frans Blom wrote *Tribes and Temples* (2 vols., 1925, 1927).

Laughing Boy (1929, Pulitzer Prize) is a novel of life among the Navajo Indians, and his later novels include *Sparks Fly Upward* (1931), set in Central America; *Long Pennant* (1933), a story of 19th-century New England seamen; *The Enemy Gods* (1937), about Navajo inability to adapt to white civilization; and *The Copper Pot* (1942), about a New England painter in New Orleans. *As Long as the Grass Shall Grow* (1940) surveys the history and conditions of American Indians, and other works of nonfiction include *Behind the Mountains* (1956), sketches of New Mexico village life in an earlier day, and *Santa Fe: The Autobiography of a Southwestern Town* (1959), collecting local newspaper comments with a commentary. *The Eagle in the Egg* (1949) deals with his wartime service as an officer of the air corps, and *Raw Material* (1945) contains reminiscences of his intellectual development. He was the brother of Christopher La Farge.

LAMANTIA, PHILIP (1927–), San Francisco poet whose works are often surrealist and marked by a rapture, now religious, now inspired by drugs. His books include *Erotic Poems* (1946), *Ekstasis* (1959), *Touch of the Marvelous* (1966), *The Blood of the Air* (1970), and *Becoming Visible* (1981).

Land of Little Rain, The, 14 sketches by Mary Austin,♦ published in 1903. Based on long personal observation, this familiar account of the land, the people, and the animals and plants is concerned with the California region "between the high Sierras south from Yosemite—east and south . . . beyond Death Valley and on illimitably into the Mojave Desert."

"The Pocket Hunter," "Shoshone Land," and "The Basket Maker" are quiet portraits of representative residents in this region of high mountains and vast deserts: a gold miner who spends his life in an infrequently successful search for stray "pockets" of precious metal; an ancient Shoshone medicine man, homesick in exile among the Paiute; and a widowed Paiute woman who devotes herself to rearing her son and to weaving beautiful willow baskets "for the satisfaction of desire." "The Scavengers" is a study of the carrion creatures of the desert—vultures, buzzards, ravens, and coyotes—embodying the author's sense of the delicate economy of nature. "Jimville—A Bret Harte Town" is a genial depiction of a mountain town whose life contains all the themes of Harte's sentimental fiction.

LANIER, SIDNEY (1842–81), born in Macon, Ga., was educated at Oglethorpe University, where he early showed an inclination toward a musical career. Plans for further study were interrupted by his service in the Civil War and his four months' imprisonment at Point Lookout, Md. Seriously ill with consumption, and suffering from poverty, he said that in the eight years after his return in 1865 "pretty much the whole of life had been merely not dying." His novel *Tiger-Lilies* (1867), about his experiences in the Civil War, helped him to decide that he would not settle "down to be a third-rate struggling lawyer for the balance of my little life." Accordingly, he turned to the writing of poetry, published his *Poems* (1877), became a flutist in the Peabody Orchestra at Baltimore, and supplemented his small income by delivering lectures, which were posthumously published as *Shakspere and His Forerunners* (2 vols., 1902). These talks brought him the position of lecturer in English literature at Johns Hopkins in 1879, and the work for his classes resulted in *The Science of English Verse* (1880) and *The English Novel* (1883). In his book on prosody he illuminates his own method by his thesis that the laws governing music and verse are identical, and that time, not accent, is the important element in verse rhythms. Lanier's complete *Poems* were collected in 1884 and are noted for the ballads and lyrics that embody his attempt to produce in verse the sound patterns of music. His arrangements of lines and rhythms were frequently strained as well as novel, in both the emphasis on pattern-making and the interest in metaphysical conceits, and the imagery is often vague as a result of the attention to musical quality. Nevertheless, the poet's theories were successfully practiced in some of his works, outstanding among which are "The Song of the Chattahoochee,"♦ "The Symphony,"♦ and "The Marshes of Glynn."♦ New editions of his *Poems* (1884) were issued with slight additions in 1891 and 1916. A full critical edition of his works was published in ten volumes (1945).

LARDNER, RING[GOLD] [WILMER] (1885–1933), born in Michigan, was known as a sports writer and columnist in Chicago and New York before the great success of his short stories. His first collection, *You Know Me, Al: A Busher's Letters* (1916), employs the racy idiom of the baseball diamond and describes the career of a novice on a professional team. Other books of this early period displaying the author's talent for the humorous use of the vernacular in portraying typical Americans include *Bib Ballads* (1915), a collection of verse; *Gullible's Travels* (1917), satirical stories; *Treat 'Em Rough* (1918); and *The Big Town* (1921), a humorous novel. The publication of *How To Write Short Stories* (1924), a collection, first attracted critical attention to Lardner as a sardonic humorist exposing follies and vices through his characters' conversational speech. Though they seem to follow traditional methods of American humor, his stories are actually cynical and mordant treatments of the subjects. The boxers, baseball players, salesmen, stockbrokers, songwriters, barbers, actresses, stenographers, and other "average" characters whom he depicts are reduced by the author's implied bitterness to their essential commonplaceness, cruelty, viciousness, dullness, and stupidity. This pessimistic view, as well as his ability to reproduce the idioms and habits of mind of everyday people, continued to appear in Lardner's later collections of short stories: *What of It?* (1925); *The Love Nest* (1926); *Round Up* (1929); and *First and Last* (1934). "The Love Nest" was dramatized by Robert Sherwood in 1927, and *June Moon* (1929), written by Lardner in collaboration with George S. Kaufman, is a comedy satirizing the songwriters of Tin Pan Alley. *The Story of a Wonder Man* (1927) is a satirical "autobiography."

Lark, The (1895–97), little magazine published by Les Jeunes, a San Francisco group of literary aesthetes led by Gelett Burgess, ♦ who contributed drawings of "Goops" and nonsense verses, including his "Purple Cow," first pastured there. Although influenced by *The Chap Book* and English *fin de siècle* magazines, it had "no more serious intention than to be gay," and was stopped because Burgess "wanted it to die young and in its full freshness."

LARNER, JEREMY (1937–), author of the novels *Drive, He Said* (1964) and *The Answer* (1968), treating college students attempting to cope with an irrational society, in the latter book by resorting to drugs. He wrote the screenplay of his first novel and of *The Candidate.* His other works include edited, tape-recorded interviews with heroin users, *The Addict in the Street* (1965), and *Nobody Knows* (1970), reflections on the presidential campaign of Eugene McCarthy, for whom he was a speech writer.

Last Leaf, The, poem by Oliver Wendell Holmes,♦ first published in *The Amateur* (1831) and reprinted in his *Poems* (1836), and, according to the poet, "suggested by the appearance in one of our streets of a venerable relic of the Revolution, said to be one of the party who threw the tea overboard in Boston Harbor." The subject is Major Thomas Melville, Herman Melville's grandfather, and the poet's smile leveled at him is not meant disrespectfully,

> But the old three-cornered hat,
> And the breeches, and all that,
> Are so queer!

Last of the Mohicans, The, romance by Cooper,♦ published in 1826, is the second of the Leather-Stocking Tales. ♦

While the French and Indians besiege Fort William Henry on Lake George (1757), Cora and Alice Munro, daughters of the English commander, are on their way to join their father, accompanied by Major Duncan Heyward, Alice's fiancé, the singing teacher David Gamut, and the treacherous Indian Magua, who secretly serves the French. Magua's plan to betray the party to the Iroquois is foiled by the scout Hawkeye (Natty Bumppo) and his companions, old chief Chingachgook and his son Uncas, only survivors of the Mohican aristocracy. Escaping, Magua obtains Iroquois aid and returns to capture the girls. He promises them safety if Cora will become his squaw, but she refuses, and Hawkeye arrives to rescue them. Reaching the fort, they remain until Munro surrenders to Montcalm, who gives them a safe-conduct. When they leave they are set upon by Indians, and the sisters are captured. Hawkeye pursues them, finding Cora imprisoned in a Delaware camp and Alice in a Huron camp. Uncas is captured by the Hurons, and Heyward enters the camp in disguise, rescues Alice, and with Uncas escapes to the Delaware camp, where they are cordially received. Old chief Tamenund, learning Uncas's identity, hails him as his destined successor. Magua then claims Cora as his rightful property, and Uncas is unable to object, but, joined by the English, leads

his tribe against the Hurons. When Magua attempts to desert, Uncas follows, and tries to rescue Cora. Uncas and Cora are killed, and Hawkeye shoots Magua, who falls from a precipice to his death. The others return to civilization, except for Hawkeye, who continues his frontier career.

Last Puritan, The: A Memoir in the Form of a Novel, by Santayana,♦ published in 1936.

Last Tycoon, The, novel by F. Scott Fitzgerald,♦ published in 1941. Left unrevised and incomplete at the author's death, it was edited for publication by Edmund Wilson.

Cecilia Brady, the daughter of a great motion-picture producer, reminisces about events that began five years earlier when she was an undergraduate at Bennington College, starting with a flight home to Hollywood on a plane whose other passengers include Wylie White, a script writer down on his luck, Manny Schwartz, once an influential film producer, and Monroe Stahr, another producer and a partner of Cecilia's father, Pat Brady. Cecilia becomes much attracted to Stahr, but he is caught up in an affair with an English woman. When the woman marries her fiancé, Stahr turns to Cecilia at the very time that he has a falling out with her father and each of the partners conceives the idea of murdering the other. On the way to New York to establish an alibi, Stahr repents and decides to revoke his orders that will result in Brady's death, but his plane crashes before he can carry out his new plans, and Cecilia is deprived of both her father and the man she loves.

Late George Apley, The, novel by J.P. Marquand,♦ published in 1937 and awarded a Pulitzer Prize. A dramatization by Marquand and George S. Kaufman♦ was produced in 1944 and published in 1945.

Mr. Willing, contemporary and friend of the late George Apley, is requested by Apley's son John to describe his life in a book so that the conventional public eulogy may be amplified and humanized. The biography by Willing, based on family letters, adheres to the conventional attitudes it describes. It opens with Apley's birth in 1866 to a wealthy and socially prominent Boston family. His childhood is secure and serene, as he learns to move with the "right people" and to accept a family tradition of protective unity, as well as familial financial, charitable, and cultural responsibility. Apley displays a certain "erratic strain" of rebellion in school and at Harvard, but generally the "essential, undeviating discipline of background" prevails. He is taken into his father's club, works for a summer in the Apley textile mills, is admitted to the Law School, and emerges socially unscathed from an affection for a girl "from Central Square" by bowing to his father's opposition. He marries Catharine Bosworth, the girl of his family's choice, and becomes the father of John and Eleanor Apley. As they develop, his advice to and expectations of them increasingly resemble those of his father toward him. Personal inclinations are more and more subdued by a Puritan sense of duty, and even the desire to escape convention takes a conventional form as his retreat of Pequod Island becomes an exclusive resort. Apley's idealism leads him to attack civic corruption, but social prudence makes him accept a compromise when he is falsely implicated in a scandal. World War I and the Depression alter the tenor of American life and widen the gulf between Apley and his children, but he continues to find refuge in insularity as in a "safe . . . harbour."

LATTIMORE, Richmond [Alexander] (1906–84), after graduation from Dartmouth (1926) and a Rhodes scholarship did graduate work, and was a member of the Bryn Mawr faculty (1935–71). He is known for his translations, including *The Odes of Pindar* (1947), *The Iliad* (1951), *The Oresteia* of Aeschylus (1953), Aristophanes' *The Frogs* (1962), and Euripides' *Iphegenia* (1973), and for scholarly writings as well as his own poetry, including *The Stride of Time* (1966), *Poems from Three Decades* (1972), and *Continuing Conclusions* (1983).

Laus Deo!, poem by Whittier,♦ published in 1865. In six-line stanzas of predominantly four-stress lines, the work is the poet's joyous celebration of the passage of the 13th Amendment abolishing slavery, and was inspired by the "clang of bell and roar of gun" that announced the news (Dec. 18, 1865).

LAWRENCE, D[avid] H[erbert] (1885–1930), English novelist, poet, and critic, in 1915 began to consider U.S. sites for an ideal community, "Rananim." Interest in American culture led to his trenchant *Studies in Classic American Literature* (1923), essays on "The Spirit of Place" and eight authors from Franklin to Whitman. Early versions of the essays have been collected in *The Symbolic Meaning* (1962). In 1922 Lawrence and his wife Frieda moved to a ranch near Taos,

N.M., and lived there until 1925, except for a long visit to Mexico. At Taos he finished *Kangaroo* (1923), wrote another novel, *The Plumed Serpent* (1926), the novelettes *St. Mawr* and *The Princess* (1925), "The Woman Who Rode Away" (1928) and other stories with American settings, and most of the essays in *Mornings in Mexico* (1927) and *Reflections on the Death of a Porcupine* (1934). Views of Lawrence in New Mexico are to be found in many memoirs, including *Lorenzo in Taos* (1932) by Mabel Dodge Luhan and *Journey with Genius* (1951) by Witter Bynner.

LAZARUS, Emma (1849–87), New York poet, best known for her *Songs of a Semite* (1882), which includes the poetic drama "The Dance to Death," about 12th-century Thuringian Jews and constitutes an impassioned answer to the persecution of her people in Russia. She also wrote *Admetus and Other Poems* (1871); *Alide* (1874), a romance based on the life of Goethe; and *By the Waters of Babylon* (1887). She translated the *Poems and Ballads of Heine* (1881), and her collected *Poems* appeared in 1889. Lazarus's love of the U.S. as a refuge for the oppressed is expressed in her sonnet to the Statue of Liberty, which was carved on the pedestal of the statue.

Lazarus Laughed, poetic drama by O'Neill,♦ produced in 1928 but published in 1927. This mystic affirmation of life employs masked choruses.

Leather-Stocking Tales, series of five novels by Cooper,♦ depicting the life of the early American frontier, and deriving its title from the nickname of the hero Natty Bumppo, so called because of his long deerskin leggings. The novels in order of composition are *The Pioneers* (1823), *The Last of the Mohicans* (1826), *The Prairie* (1827), *The Pathfinder* (1840), and *The Deerslayer* (1841). Their sequence in relation to plot is *Deerslayer,*♦ *Last of the Mohicans,*♦ *Pathfinder,*♦ *Pioneers,*♦ *Prairie.*♦ The hero is known by the following names: "Bumppo" or "Deerslayer" in *Deerslayer;* "Hawkeye" in *Last of the Mohicans;* "Pathfinder" in *Pathfinder;* "Natty Bumppo" or "Leather-Stocking" in *Pioneers;* and "the trapper" in *Prairie.* His character remains strikingly consistent throughout the series, which treats his life and adventures from youth to old age and death. The perfect woodsman, who dislikes the restraints and destructiveness of settlements, he understands and loves the forest, and his moral qualities are as great as his understanding. Generous both to friends and to enemies, he possesses a simple, staunch morality, and a cool nerve and never-failing resourcefulness.

Leaves of Grass, poems by Whitman, ◆ the first edition of which (1855) contained 12 poems, including those later entitled "Song of Myself," ◆ "I Sing the Body Electric," ◆ and "There Was a Child Went Forth." ◆ The first edition was anonymous and had a preface, later omitted, in which the author declares that the ideal poet must be a complete lover of the universe, draw his materials from nature, as a seer reveal the cosmic plan which harmoniously unites past, present, and future, be commensurate with his nation, and in America serve as representative of the common people, differing from them only in his superior vision. He is to discover what is permanent in flux, explain its development, and be a realist in his art. His style is to be simple and natural, without such ornamentation as conventional rhyme or meter, since it must have an organic growth like that of a perfect animal or tree, in which each part is in proportion and harmonious with the whole.

The second edition (1856) contained 33 poems, including "Salut au Monde," ◆ "By Blue Ontario's Shore," ◆ "Crossing Brooklyn Ferry," ◆ "Spontaneous Me," ◆ and "Song of the Broad-Axe," ◆ as well as an overblown reply to the author's "dear Friend and Master," Emerson, in acknowledgment of a laudatory letter which is reprinted.

The third edition (1860) was enlarged to 456 pages, containing 122 new poems, including "Starting from Paumanok" ◆ and "Out of the Cradle Endlessly Rocking" ◆ and two new sections, "Calamus" ◆ and "Children of Adam." ◆ The latter contains "Facing West from California's Shores" ◆ and "Once I Pass'd Through a Populous City." ◆

The fourth edition (1867) reprints, in the copies that came last from the press, those poems published as *Drum-Taps* ◆ (1865) and *Sequel to Drum-Taps* (1865–66), including the poems on the death of Lincoln, "When Lilacs Last in the Door Yard Bloom'd" ◆ and "O Captain! My Captain!" ◆; the statement of religion, "Chanting the Square Deific" ◆; and "Pioneers! O Pioneers!" ◆ and "One's-Self I Sing." ◆

The fifth edition (1871) was a reprint, with some copies having as annexes "After All Not

To Create Only," published separately as an ode for the American Institute; and "Passage to India." ◆

The sixth edition (1876), known as the Author's or Centennial Edition, was in two volumes, the first a reprint of the 1871 edition without the annexes, and the second entitled *Two Rivulets,* ◆ containing the annexes to the 1871 edition and other poems and prose. This edition contained a new preface, not later retained, expounding the plan and purpose of the poems.

The seventh edition (1881–82), containing 20 new poems and organizing all poems in groups that represent his final order, was first published in Boston, but, because of official protests against asserted indecency, was withdrawn and reissued by a Philadelphia publisher.

The eighth edition (1889), a special pocket edition, reprinted the poems of *November Boughs* (1888) as "Sands at Seventy," and, as epilogue, the prose preface of that book, "A Backward Glance o'er Travel'd Roads." ◆

The final edition under the author's supervision (1891–92) included "Old Age Echoes," as well as two annexes, "Good-Bye, My Fancy" (separately issued, 1891) and "A Backward Glance o'er Travel'd Roads."

The standard edition was prepared by the author's executors as part of his *Complete Writings* (10 vols., 1902).

LEE, [Nelle] Harper (1926–), Alabama author, educated at the state university, won a Pulitzer Prize with the publication of her first novel, *To Kill a Mockingbird* (1960). The plot turns on the sensational trial of a black man charged with raping a white woman, as seen through the eyes of the young daughter of the white defense lawyer.

LEFFLAND, Ella (1931–), born and reared in the backwater area east of San Francisco Bay, the setting of some of her fiction, whose novels include *Mrs. Munck* (1970), the story of a woman in her forties meanly victimized by a double standard; *Love Out of Season* (1974), presenting a woman's experiences in San Francisco's frenetic Beat world of the 1960s; and *Rumors of Peace* (1979), depicting a girl of grammar-school age growing up during World War II. *Last Courtesies* (1980) collects stories.

LE GALLIENNE, Richard (1866–1947), English journalist, essayist, poet, and novelist, was originally associated with the *fin de siècle* aesthetes. His early verse and epigrammatic prose show the influence of Oscar Wilde. After settling in the U.S. (1903), he modified his early preciosity, although his work continued to indicate his allegiance to the English school of the 1890s. His books include *My Ladies' Sonnets* (1887) and *The Lonely Dancer* (1913), poems; *The Quest of the Golden Girl* (1896), a prose fantasy; *Orestes* (1910), a tragedy; *The Romantic Nineties* (1925), his literary reminiscences; and anthologies exhibiting the tastes of his own period.

EVA LE GALLIENNE (1899–), his daughter, was born in London, where she made her stage debut in 1915. She founded (1926), managed, directed, and acted at New York's Civic Repertory Theatre. *At 33* (1934) and *With a Quiet Heart* (1953) are memoirs.

LEGARÉ, HUGH SWINTON (1797–1843), South Carolina lawyer and statesman, served as U.S. attorney general under Tyler, and as secretary of state *ad interim* (1843) upon the resignation of Webster. He was the great champion of Charleston literature, and his critical opinions had a profound effect upon the Southern cultural renaissance, which was partly expressed in his *Southern Review* (1828–32). His miscellaneous writings were collected in two volumes (1845–46).

Legend of Sleepy Hollow, The, short story by Irving,♦ possibly based on a German source. It was published in *The Sketch Book* (1820). An operetta, *The Headless Horseman* (1936), with music by Douglas Moore and libretto by Stephen Vincent Benét, is based on it.

Ichabod Crane, an assertive, ingenuous Yankee schoolmaster, lanky and angular in appearance, lives among the Dutch folk of Sleepy Hollow on the Hudson, in post-Revolutionary days. He loves Katrina Van Tassel, daughter of a rich farmer, and is the victim of many pranks by the friends of his chief rival for her affections, Brom Van Brunt or Brom Bones, a reckless horseman and neighborhood hero. At an autumn quilting party at Van Tassel's, the guests entertain themselves with stories of ghosts and witches, and Brom tells of the headless horseman said to haunt the region. Ichabod is discouraged in his suit for Katrina, and on his way home, late at night, riding a borrowed plow horse, is frightened by a headless apparition that rides after him and throws a round object at his head. Ichabod is never again seen in Sleepy Hollow, although the next morning the round object is discovered to be a pumpkin. Brom

marries Katrina, and Ichabod's tale becomes a legend of the countryside.

Legree, SIMON, character in *Uncle Tom's Cabin.* ♦

LeGUIN, URSULA K[ROEBER] (1929–), author of novels of fantasy akin to science fiction in their settings on different planets with strange creatures and various time spans but concentrating also on social, cultural, philosophic, and personal issues. These works include a Hainish cycle concerning ur-humans on the planet Hain in *Rocannon's World* (1966), *Planet of Exile* (1966), and *City of Illusions* (1967), and an Earthsea trilogy: *A Wizard of Earthsea* (1968), *The Tombs of Atuan* (1971), and *The Farthest Shore* (1972). She has also written stories, essays, and poems.

Lenore, lyrical ballad by Poe,♦ published as "A Paean" in *Poems* (1831) and considerably revised in later versions (1836, 1843). In four stanzas of seven-stress lines, preserving the fundamental ballad rhythm, it celebrates the death of the poet's beloved:

Ah, broken is the golden bowl!—the spirit flown forever!
Let the bell toll!—a saintly soul floats on the Stygian river.

LENOX, JAMES (1800–1880), heir to one of New York's greatest fortunes, spent much of his mature life in philanthropy, including the creation of the Lenox Library for his great collection of incunabula, Bibles, English literature, and for other sources of scholarship, including his own historical and bibliographical studies. Samuel Allibone was his librarian, and the library itself has become part of the New York Public Library. Henry Stevens, the bookseller, wrote *Recollections of Mr. James Lenox of New York and the Formation of His Library* (1886).

Let Us Now Praise Famous Men, nonfictional work by James Agee♦ with photographs by Walker Evans, published in 1941. Commissioned (1936) by *Fortune* magazine, it was rejected because the collaborators could not treat their subject in a conventional journalistic fashion. Instead they converted and expanded their assignment on cotton tenantry in the U.S. to reveal the ways of life and the personalities of the members of three families in warm, personal terms.

Letters from a Farmer in Pennsylvania *to the Inhabitants of the British Colonies,* by John Dickinson,♦ published in the *Pennsylvania Chronicle* (1767–68) and reprinted as a pamphlet (1768).

Letters from an American Farmer, 12 essays by Crèvecœur,♦ published in London in 1782 under the pseudonym J. Hector St. John. These charming and informative essays sketch the physical and social conditions of American rural life. The author fluctuates between the lover of nature and Rousseauistic idealist, and the realistic farmer writing of hard, unpleasant facts. As a theorist, he was ecstatic concerning America as an asylum for the oppressed and a melting pot for many races; as a farmer he described the frontier as it actually was, the difficulties of agriculture, and the warfare between different parts of animal nature. Half of the letters are concerned with the education, employment, manners, and customs of Americans at Nantucket, Martha's Vineyard, Charleston, and elsewhere. The third answers the question "What is an American?" by stating that, as the product of the melting pot, he is a man who acts on new principles, and must therefore entertain new ideas. The eleventh letter describes a visit to John Bartram, and the last depicts the difficulties of a "frontier man," menaced on one side by savages, and on the other by the unsettled conditions of a Revolution in which he agrees with neither of the opposed groups.

LEVERTOV, DENISE (1923–), born in England of a Welsh mother and a Russian-Jewish father who became an Anglican clergyman, was educated at home and came to the U.S. in 1948 after marriage to an American. Her earlier poems were published in *The Double Image* (1946), and since coming to this country she has issued *Here and Now* (1957), *Five Poems* (1958), *Overland to the Islands* (1958), *With Eyes at the Back of Our Heads* (1959), *The Jacob's Ladder* (1961), *O Taste and See* (1964), *The Sorrow Dance* (1967), *Relearning the Alphabet* (1970), *To Stay Alive* (1971), *Footprints* (1972), *The Freeing of the Dust* (1975), and *Candles in Babylon* (1982), whose free verse presents compact and intensely immediate perceptions of people, things, and feelings. *The Poet in the World* (1973) collects essays on poetry, on teaching, and on the Vietnam War, whose tragedy affected her poetry.

LEVIN, MEYER (1905–81), Chicago author, graduated from the University of Chicago (1924) before becoming a journalist, which career formed the background of his first novel, *Reporter* (1929). His other novels are *Frankie and Johnny* (1930); *Yehuda* (1931), dealing with life on a Zionist farm commune in Palestine; *The New Bridge* (1933), about a family evicted from its tenement home; *The Old Bunch* (1937), a realistic story of the children of Russian-Jewish immigrants in Chicago from 1921 to 1934; *Citizens* (1940), an analysis of the Chicago Little Steel strike and Memorial Day battle of 1937 as seen by a doctor who figured in *The Old Bunch; My Father's House* (1947), about a boy's escape from Poland to Palestine; *Compulsion* (1956), a tense psychological tale based on the Loeb-Leopold case, of which he published his dramatized version (1958), which differed from the Broadway production; *Eva* (1959), about a Jewish girl's escape during World War II from Poland and a German concentration camp to Israel; and *The Fanatic* (1964); about an American-Jewish author's dramatization of philosophic fiction by a victim of the Nazis and the attacks upon the playwright by followers of the Communist line, which the play opposes. This novel reflects Levin's own problems related to his dramatization of *The Story of Anne Frank,* whose rejection he dealt with again in *The Obsession* (1973). Later novels include *The Stronghold* (1965), about post-World War II Germany; *Gore and Igor* (1968), presenting comic adventures of an American and a Russian in Israel during the Six Day War; *The Settlers* (1972), depicting a Russian immigrant family in Palestine, c.1904–18; *The Harvest* (1978), a sequel; *The Spell of Time* (1974), a novella set in Jerusalem; and *The Architect* (1982), a novel based on the life of Frank Lloyd Wright. *The Search* (1950) is an autobiography.

LEVINE, PHILIP (1928–), Detroit-born poet, long resident in California as a professor at the state university campus, Fresno (1958–80), whose volumes of verse, including *On the Edge* (1963), *Red Dust* (1971), *They Feed, They Lion* (1972), *1933* (1974), *The Names of the Lost* (1976), *Seven Years from Somewhere* (1979), *Ashes* (1979), *One for the Rose* (1981), and *Selected Poems* (1984), have as major subjects the oppressed working class of the U.S. and the Spanish Civil War. *Don't Ask* (1981) contains interviews with Levine.

LEWIS, JANET (1899–), born in Chicago and educated at the University of Chicago, has long been a resident of California. Like her husband, Yvor Winters, she is a poet, and her verse has been published in *The Indians in the Woods* (1922); *The Wheel in Midsummer* (1927); *The Earth-Bound* (1946), collecting earlier work; and *Poems Old and New, 1918–1978* (1981). Her fiction, marked by a pure, quiet style, includes *The Invasion* (1932), a novel about an upper Michigan family of Irish and Ojibway heritage; *The Wife of Martin Guerre* (1941), a novella dealing with a famous legal case of 16th-century France; *Against a Darkening Sky* (1943), a novel portraying the dignified character of a woman in a contemporary California setting; *The Trial of Sören Qvist* (1947), another fictive character study, set in 17th-century Denmark and treating the unjust execution of an innocent pastor for an alleged murder; *The Ghost of Monsieur Scarron* (1959), set in the France of Louis XIV; and *Good-Bye, Son* (1946), short stories.

LEWIS, [HARRY] SINCLAIR (1885–1951), born in Sauk Centre, Minn., graduated from Yale (1907), although he left college for a time to work at the Helicon Home Colony, Upton Sinclair's socialist experiment in New Jersey. After engaging in hack writing, travel in the U.S., and editorial positions in New York, he wrote several minor novels, including *Our Mr. Wrenn* (1914), *The Trail of the Hawk* (1915), and *The Innocents* (1917). *The Job* (1917), a realistic novel of life in New York, was his first distinguished work of fiction, and with the publication of *Main Street*♦ (1920) he achieved wide recognition. This story, which contrasts cosmopolitan and Midwestern small-town culture, was followed by the two novels usually considered his best work: *Babbitt*♦ (1922), a satirical portrayal of an "average" American businessman; and *Arrowsmith*♦ (1925), on the career of a man of science. The latter was awarded a Pulitzer Prize in 1926, which Lewis declined. *Elmer Gantry* (1927) is a satirical novel concerned with religious shams and hypocrisy in the U.S., and *The Man Who Knew Coolidge* (1928) is a depiction of a mediocre businessman. These books, although inferior as fiction, are examples of the author's popular iconoclasm, influenced by the criticism of H.L. Mencken. *Dodsworth*♦ (1929), generally ranked with his better novels, is a sympathetic portrayal of a retired manufac-

turer who seeks new interests in European travel.

In 1930 Lewis became the first American author to be awarded the Nobel Prize for distinction in world literature. His later books are *Ann Vickers* (1933), about a woman social reformer; *Work of Art* (1934), the story of a successful businessman; *It Can't Happen Here*♦ (1935), concerned with a future fascist revolt in the U.S.; *Selected Short Stories* (1935); *The Prodigal Parents* (1938), on family relations; *Bethel Merriday* (1940), about a girl in a theatrical touring company; *Gideon Planish* (1943), an exposé of organized philanthropy; *Cass Timberlane* (1945), about the marital problems of a middle-aged Minnesota judge and his young wife; *Kingsblood Royal* (1947), on race prejudice as met by a Midwestern banker who finds he has some black blood; *The God Seeker* (1949), about a New England missionary to Minnesota Indians; and *World So Wide* (1951), about the romances of a Coloradan in Italy with young American girls. *From Main Street to Stockholm* (1952) collects letters, and *The Man from Main Street* (1953) collects essays and ephemera.

Lewis is an ingenious satirist of the American middle class, mimicking its speech and actions with what seems to be photographic realism but is actually more or less good-humored caricature. Critics have accused him of romanticism in overstressing his effects, and often declared that he was himself proof that his charges against American culture were just. *It Can't Happen Here* shows his shift from large-scale social analysis to a more immediate political concern, with a bias seemingly in favor of middle-class liberalism. His plays include *Dodsworth* (1934), written with Sidney Howard; *Jayhawker* (1934), about Free-Soil battles in Kansas before the Civil War, written with Lloyd Lewis; and *It Can't Happen Here* (1930), with John C. Moffitt. Mark Schorer wrote a comprehensive biography, *Sinclair Lewis: An American Life* (1961).

LEWISOHN, LUDWIG (1882–1955), novelist and critic, was born in Berlin and brought as a child to the U.S. Among his many writings, *Upstream* (1922) and *Mid-Channel* (1929) are autobiographical treatments of the problems of Jews in America. His novels include *The Broken Snare* (1908), *Don Juan* (1923), *Roman Summer* (1927), *The Case of Mr. Crump* (1926), *The Island Within* (1928), *Stephen Escott* (1930), *Trumpet of Jubilee* (1937), *For Ever Wilt Thou Love* (1939), *Renegade* (1942), *Breathe Upon These*

(1944), *Anniversary* (1948), and *In a Summer Season* (1955). *Expression in America* (1932) studies the American spirit in literature, using Freudian analysis to attack the Puritan tradition. Besides many translations, his works include critical studies, among them *The Modern Drama* (1915), *The Drama and the Stage* (1922), *The Creative Life* (1924), and *Cities and Men* (1927), marked by idealistic individualism. Sociological studies of Jews, advocating Zionism, include *Israel* (1925), *The Answer: The Jew and the World* (1939), and *The American Jew* (1950). *Haven* (1940), written with his wife, presents matched diaries of a honeymoon.

Liberal Imagination, The, work by Lionel Trilling,♦ published in 1950, collects essays on literature and society in the intellectual tradition of liberalism in the U.S. Marked by the variety that is said to be representative of that tradition, the subjects include considerations of Freud and Literature, Art and Neurosis, Manners, Morals and the Novel, and studies of works by Sherwood Anderson, Henry James, Mark Twain, Kipling, Wordsworth, and F. Scott Fitzgerald.

Liberator, The (1831–65), Abolitionist weekly, was founded at Boston by W.L. Garrison. ♦ Its editorial policy was of a militant-pacifist type, denouncing slavery, calling for its immediate abolition and the enfranchisement of all American blacks, but having no specific program for attaining these ends. For years its editor proved the sincerity of the statement in the first issue: "I am in earnest—I will not equivocate—I will not excuse—I will not retreat a single inch—*and I will be heard.*" The paper inevitably attracted much opposition. Garrison was mobbed, his press destroyed, a law passed prohibiting its circulation to free blacks, a reward offered for the apprehension of anyone who circulated it in South Carolina, and a resolution passed in the Georgia senate offering a reward for the arrest of Garrison. In 1835 a South Carolina mob broke into the U.S. mails and burned copies of *The Liberator,* along with effigies of its editors. Garrison also aroused enmity by his espousal of liquor prohibition and pacifism. The paper printed the writings of the more educated free blacks as well as those of leading Abolitionists, but its circulation has been estimated as being about 1400 in 1837, and never more than 3000. The last issue of *The Liberator* was published upon the ratification of the 13th Amendment.

Library of America, The, collection begun in 1982 of major writings by leading American authors (Literary Classics of the United States) in a series of well-made, readable volumes addressed to a general public rather than to scholars. In keeping with a proposal made in 1968 by Edmund Wilson, each volume contains several works by one author in authoritative texts, introduced by a brief essay and a basic chronology but with a minimum of annotation and editorial apparatus. Approximately 100 volumes are projected, some to contain the writing of more than one author and some to include works of literary significance by historians, philosophers, social and religious thinkers, travelers, explorers, and nature writers.

Library of Congress, U.S. national library at Washington, D.C., established by act of Congress (1800), and housed until 1897 in the Capitol. The purchase (1815) of Jefferson's library of 6457 volumes formed the nucleus of the present collections. Other great early purchases included the manuscripts of Jefferson, Washington, Hamilton, and Madison, and the collection of Peter Force. The library is located in three large buildings near the Capitol, containing 64.6 acres of floor space. In 1980 it contained over 74,000,000 items, including more than 18,000,000 books and pamphlets; great collections of bound newspapers; pieces and volumes of music; maps and views; photographic negatives, prints, and slides; motion-picture reels; phonograph recordings; reels and strips of microfilm; and a vast assemblage of manuscript pieces, including the originals of the Declaration of Independence and the Constitution. After 1846 the copyright law required a copy of every book copyrighted in the U.S. to be deposited in the library, and since 1870 two copies have been required. Most U.S. libraries use its printed catalogue cards. Since 1937 it has annually appointed a Consultant in Poetry in English. Librarians include Herbert Putnam (1899–1939), Archibald MacLeish (1939–45), Luther Evans (1945–53), L. Quincy Mumford (1954–74), Daniel Boorstin (1975–   ).

Lie Down in Darkness, novel by William Styron,♦ published in 1951.

In Port Warwick, a ship-building city of tidewater Virginia, during the last days of World War II, Milton and Helen Loftis and their family are met to bury their daughter Peyton, who committed suicide in New York City. The parents have long been alienated, in part because Milton, an unsuccessful lawyer, has been a kind of dependent of Helen, a bitter woman, in whose family house they live, in part because of tensions created by the fact that their eldest daughter, Maudie, was a retarded cripple, dead in her twentieth year. Milton had an almost unpaternal affection for Peyton, long ago took to drink, and has long had a mistress, Dolly Bonner, who accompanies him to the funeral. Peyton was sent to the proper college, Sweet Briar, but, affected by her unhappy home life, left it to live in New York, to marry Harry Miller, a struggling artist, to separate from him, and to take lovers in a frustrated search to find her own way. Finally she threw herself from a skyscraper. Even her funeral does not go smoothly. The hearse breaks down and during the humid day the procession to the cemetery is interrupted by a traffic jam caused by a revival meeting of blacks. In it are servants of the Loftis family, ecstatic because of their redemption by Daddy Faith, in contrast to the hopeless despair of Milton and Helen Loftis.

LIEBLING, A[BBOTT] J[OSEPH] (1904–63), after study at Dartmouth, from which he was expelled for refusing to attend chapel, became a newspaperman and was with *The New Yorker* after 1935, writing its "Wayward Press" column and other articles. His books include *The Telephone Booth Indian* (1942), about raffish New York City characters; *The Road Back to Paris* (1944), about experiences as a war correspondent; *The Wayward Pressman* (1947), about early newspaper experiences; *Mink and Red Herring* (1949), New Yorker columns; *Chicago: Second City* (1952); *The Honest Rainmaker* (1953), about a racing columnist; *The Sweet Science: A Ringside View of Boxing* (1956); *The Jollity Building* (1962), combining tales from the two preceding books; *Normandy Revisited* (1958), on battle sites he had known; *The Earl of Louisiana* (1961), about Governor Earl Long; *Between Meals: An Appetite for Paris* (1962); *The Press* (1962); *Molly and Other War Experiences* (1964); and *Liebling at Home* (1982).

Life (1883–1936), magazine founded by J.A. Mitchell and E.S. Martin, young Harvard graduates, was intended to be a satirical weekly "of higher artistic and literary merit" than *Puck* and *Judge*. *Life* played the role of *arbiter elegantiarum*, and its early volumes represent the school of genteel humor. Among its artists were F.W. Attwood, E.W.

Kemble, Palmer Cox, Peter Newell, Oliver Herford, and C.D. Gibson, who created his "Gibson Girl" for it; and such authors as J.K. Bangs, Agnes Repplier, and Brander Matthews wrote stories and articles. Besides being the outstanding humorous magazine of the U.S., *Life* was known for its reviews of books and the theater, and its editorial campaigns against vivisection, the Hearst newspapers, and other matters, as well as against Germany during World War I. After the war it was purchased by Gibson, who had Robert Sherwood edit it (1924–28), continuing the dual policy of humor and editorial crusades, now in behalf of its fresh-air camps for poor children and in opposition to the 18th Amendment. Eventually, however, the magazine lost its subtlety and was eclipsed by *The New Yorker*. In 1933 it became a monthly, and in 1936 *Judge* bought its "humorous traditions and features."

Life (1936–72, 1978–), a weekly issued by the publishers of *Time*, ♦ who purchased the title of the humorous journal *Life* (1883–1936), presents news and feature articles mainly through photographs, with editorial standards akin to those of *Time*. The journal ceased publication in 1972, although a few "Special Report" issues appeared occasionally thereafter. In 1978 it was revived as a monthly with less emphasis on current news and more on personalities, although each January issue features "The Year in Pictures."

Life on the Mississippi, autobiographical narrative by Clemens, ♦ published under his pseudonym Mark Twain (1883). The book opens with a brief history of the Mississippi River since its discovery, and Chapters 4 to 22 deal with Clemens's life as a boy on the river. These chapters, originally published in the *Atlantic Monthly*, give a vivid account of his participation in the steamboat age, the science of steamboat piloting, and the life of the river as seen by the pilot. Chapter 3 also contains a lively passage written for *Huckleberry Finn* but never used in the novel. The second part of the book, written some seven years after the first, is an account of Clemens's return to the river as a traveler, 21 years after he had been a pilot. During his trip from St. Louis to New Orleans, he finds that the glamour of the river has been destroyed by railroad competition. Interspersed with his descriptions of the river, his accounts of meeting Cable and Joel Chandler Harris, and

Horace Bixby, who first taught him piloting, are anecdotes of the past, and a vigorous attack on Scott's romanticism and its effect on Southern thought. The second part of the book lacks the unity of the first, has none of its verve and gusto, and is more descriptive and reminiscent.

Life Studies, collection of poetry and prose by Robert Lowell,♦ published in 1959.

Divided into four parts, the volume opens with a section whose religious and social themes develop from Lowell's earlier works. Part Two contains prose recollections of family and youth, set forth in an ironically level tone. Part Three invokes four authors— Ford Madox Ford, Santayana, Delmore Schwartz, and Hart Crane—whose experiences and writings affect Lowell. Part Four, which gives the book its title, opens with recollections in poetic form of the author's family and his childhood, and concludes with four poems about Lowell's mature experiences of marriage, imprisonment for conscientious objection to service in World War II, and hospitalization for mental problems.

Life Without Principle, essay by Thoreau,♦ posthumously published in the *Atlantic Monthly* (1863).

Modern American culture is criticized as being excessively preoccupied with acquisition, at the expense of an awareness of values. "The aim of the laborer should be, not to get his living . . . but to perform well a certain work. . . . An efficient and valuable man does what he can, whether the community pay him for it or not. . . ." Most men dwell thoughtlessly on the surface of existence, obsessed by the need for busyness, small gossip, and conformance to convention. They lack independence and self-expression, as appears in such phenomena as the gold rush to California: "The philosophy and poetry and religion of such a mankind are not worth the dust of a puffball."

All of us have desecrated ourselves:

> the remedy will be by wariness and devotion to reconsecrate ourselves, and make once more a fane of the mind. . . . Even the facts of science may dust the mind by their dryness, unless they are . . . rendered fertile by the dews of fresh and living truth.

Ligeia, tale by Poe,♦ published in 1838 and reprinted in *Tales of the Grotesque and Arabesque* (1840). The poem "The Conqueror Worm"♦ was not included in the tale until 1845.

An aristocratic young man marries Ligeia, a woman of strange, dark beauty and great learning. They are deeply in love, and share an interest in the occult, until a wasting illness triumphs over Ligeia's passionate will to live, and she dies. In melancholy grief, her husband leaves his lonely home on the Rhine to purchase an English abbey, where he grows mentally deranged under the influence of opium. He marries fair-haired Lady Rowena Trevanion, although they are not in love, and Rowena soon dies in a strange manner. Her husband watches by the bier and sees signs of returning life in the body, but considers these to be hallucinations. At last she rises to her feet and loosens the cerements from her head so that masses of long black hair stream forth. When she opens her eyes, he realizes that the lost Ligeia's will to live has triumphed, for she has assumed what was formerly the body of Rowena.

Light in August, novel by William Faulkner,♦ published in 1932.

Joe Christmas is orphaned when his mother dies in childbirth and her father, Eupheus Hines, murders her husband, believing him to be black. The elder Hines leaves the infant at a white orphange on Christmas night (the source of Joe's surname) but from the age of five until he is 18 the boy is reared austerely by a puritanical farmer. Striking and perhaps killing this guardian, Joe embarks on 15 years of compulsive wandering among blacks and whites, hating both, until he settles near Jefferson, Miss., as the lover of Joanna Burden, a reclusive white woman from New England who considers blacks to be "the white race's doom and curse for its sins." In time her attempts to convert Joe to her intense religious beliefs so infuriate him that he cuts her throat and attempts to conceal the murder by burning down her house. Lucas Burch, Joe's white partner in a bootlegging business, is thought to be the murderer but turns off suspicion by telling the sheriff that Joe is black and successfully accusing him of the crime. Joe's grandfather Hines, who fanatically thinks of himself as an avenging angel of the white race, stirs up a lynch mob from which Joe temporarily escapes, but when found he is shot and castrated.

LINCOLN, ABRAHAM (1809–65), 16th President of the U.S. (1861–65), was born in a log cabin in Kentucky, of a typically illiterate and shiftless frontier family. They soon migrated to another place in Kentucky, then to the Indiana woods, where the boy labored on the homestead, garnered a little learning in frontier schools, avoided church membership, and pursued his bent for reading in what books he could obtain. In 1830 the Lincolns moved to Illinois, where Abraham temporarily helped to build the new cabin, split fence rails, and otherwise assist in the tasks of homesteading. After navigating a flatboat to New Orleans, he returned to New Salem, Ill., where he spent six formative years (1831–37) working at odd jobs, studying, reading law, making a wide personal acquaintance, and serving as surveyor, postmaster, captain of volunteers in the Black Hawk War, and in the state legislature (1834–41). Meanwhile Lincoln courted Ann Rutledge, whose father kept the inn where he boarded. Her sudden death (1835), while Lincoln's suit was unsettled, has led to a great deal of sentimental conjecture. His peculiar courtship of and marriage to Mary Todd has also become part of the Lincoln legend.

He was a practicing attorney, beginning in 1836 at New Salem and then at Springfield, and served in Congress (1847–49), opposing the Mexican War as a Democratic-fomented campaign for the extension of slave territory, and consequently becoming unpopular in his home state. In his legal practice he now had as a partner William H. Herndon, whose papers afford an important source of information on the future President. Not only as a circuit-riding lawyer, but also in the higher courts, he was noted for his thoroughness, shrewdness, common sense, and ability to argue a case. He became a good stump speaker, known for his clear, pithy, and witty statements, brilliant by contrast with the trite verbosity then common.

After an unsuccessful campaign for the senatorship (1855), he became a Republican at the formation of the new party, and at the state convention (1856) was a leading figure because of his adroit and earnest dealing with the problem of slavery. As the Republican nominee for the U.S. Senate (1858), he delivered in the party convention his famous speech declaring, "A house divided against itself cannot stand." His fame was greatly increased by his debates with Stephen Douglas, even though the Democrat won the election. In his Cooper Union speech (Feb. 27, 1860), as a potential presidential candidate, he spoke against slavery in the territories, and through his conservative and dignified attitude increased his power in the East. He was elected to the presidency in 1860 by a considerable electoral majority over Douglas and Breckinridge, although he lacked the popular vote.

From the outbreak of the Civil War until the convening of Congress (July 1861), he treated the conflict as a huge insurrection to be met by executive measures. Although faced with dissension in his cabinet and his own party, with radical Abolitionism on one side and defeatist cries for peace on the other, and despite maladjusted governmental and military functions, he managed to steer a middle course, favoring a war policy that was as little vengeful as possible. In military affairs there was confusion, ignorance, personal ambition, political pressure, lack of morale, and experimentation, which brought the pressure of military duties directly upon him. He nevertheless remained tolerant, selfless, and moderate.

The most famous of his executive acts was the Emancipation Proclamation (1862), which freed slaves in rebellious territory, while those in loyal or conquered states were to be freed by later legislation. As it was naturally ineffective in Confederate-controlled areas, the Proclamation was largely an announcement of Lincoln's aims and policies, and had a great moral effect. He made few public addresses, except for his inaugurals, the Gettysburg Address♦ (1863), and the speech on Reconstruction (April 1865). To express his attitude, he depended greatly upon letters addressed to individuals or delegations, intended for public consumption.

His second inaugural address loftily declared, "With malice toward none; with charity for all, let us strive on to finish the work we are in . . . to do all which may achieve and cherish a just and lasting peace. . . ." He advocated a fair restoration of the Southern states to the Union, pardoning Confederates who would swear allegiance and promoting loyal governments in the Southern states, and, though he insisted on reunion and the abolition of slavery, he was generous concerning collateral issues. He was shot by John Wilkes Booth (April 14, 1865) and died the following morning. Stanton's comment, "Now he belongs to the ages," separates the real Lincoln, who encountered calumny, hatred, and misinterpretation of his plans, from the legendary Lincoln, who has been raised to the status of a symbol of American democracy and the Union.

The President's writing, in speeches and letters, is famous for its homespun dignity, lucidity of thought, trenchancy of expression, richness of idea, flexibility of style, adaptability to the audience, and peculiarly American flavor. He was close to the homely idiom of the common man, and his pungent provincialisms and native humor derive from his frontier education and account for his enthusiasm for such humorists as Artemus Ward. There are many collections of anecdotes attributed to him; his letters, speeches, and state papers have been frequently published; and his *Complete Writings* was edited by John Hay and J.G. Nicolay (2 vols., 1894, enlarged to 12 vols., 1905). But to this compilation have been added many others, such as *New Letters and Papers of Lincoln* (1930), edited by Paul Angle; *The Lincoln Papers* (2 vols., 1948), from family-owned documents given to the Library of Congress; and the *Collected Works* (9 vols., 1953), edited by Roy P. Basler.

Biographies began with lives written for presidential campaigns, including one by William Dean Howells in 1860. Later lives include *Herndon's Lincoln* (1889); Nicolay and Hay's *Abraham Lincoln: A History* (10 vols., 1890), based on the papers of his secretaries and some of the President's; Ida Tarbell's *Life* (2 vols., 1900), using a wide variety of sources; Lord Charnwood's *Abraham Lincoln* (1916), a British interpretation; Sandburg's six-volume study (1926, 1939); Beveridge's *Life* (2 vols., 1928), emphasizing the early career; Edgar Lee Masters's *Lincoln, the Man* (1931), which attacks its subject as it praises Douglas; James G. Randall's scholarly account (4 vols., 1945–55); and compilations including an *Autobiography* (1926), drawn from various sources, and a day-by-day calendar.

Lincoln figures frequently in literature. Poems honoring him include Whitman's "O Captain! My Captain!" and "When Lilacs Last in the Dooryard Bloom'd," Lowell's "Commemoration Ode," Edwin Markham's "Lincoln," Robinson's "The Master," and Vachel Lindsay's "Abraham Lincoln Walks at Midnight." The historical fiction in which he figures is less distinguished although it is plentiful, including Edward Eggleston's *The Graysons* (1888), Winston Churchill's *The Crisis* (1901), Upton Sinclair's *Manassas* (1904), Mary Raymond Shipman Andrews's *The Perfect Tribute* (1906), Irving Bacheller's *A Man for the Ages* (1919), and Honoré Wilson Morrow's trilogy, *Forever Free* (1927), *With Malice Toward None* (1928), and *The Last Full Measure* (1930). The best treatments in drama are John Drinkwater's *Abraham Lincoln* (1919) and Robert Sherwood's *Abe Lincoln in Illinois* (1938).

LINDBERGH, ANNE MORROW (1906–), wife of Charles A. Lindbergh (1902–74), who made the first solo flight across the Atlantic (1927), has written *North to the Orient* (1935) and *Listen! the Wind* (1938), narratives of her flights with her husband (1933), exploring routes for commercial aviation. *The Wave of the Future* (1940), a "confession of faith," advocates U.S. domestic reforms in keeping with her husband's isolationist views of the time. *Steep Ascent* (1944) is an introspective novelette of a flight over the Alps by an American woman and her British flyer husband. *Gift from the Sea* (1955) contains musings on modern problems, particularly those of married women. *The Unicorn* (1956) collects her poems. *Dearly Beloved* (1962) is a novel that by means of flashbacks tells of the tangled lives of relatives and friends gathered at a wedding. *Earth Shine* (1969) prints two essays. *Bring Me a Unicorn* (1972), *Hour of Gold, Hour of Lead* (1973), *The Flower and the Nettle* (1976), *Locked Rooms and Open Doors* (1974), and *War Within and Without* (1980) contain diaries and letters.

LINDSAY, [NICHOLAS] VACHEL (1879–1931), born in Springfield, Ill., attended Hiram College (1897–1900), studied art at Chicago and New York (1900–1905), and decided, after unsuccessful attempts to find employment, to be "a tramp and a beggar." Although he spent his winters in lecturing on art and temperance, much of the time during the following years was devoted to tramping tours of the U.S., on which he bartered verses for food and lodging. His poetic broadsides and leaflets include *The Tree of Laughing Bells* (1905) and *Rhymes To Be Traded for Bread* (1912). In 1912 he began to lecture on "The Gospel of Beauty" and in 1913 he published his first collection, *General William Booth Enters into Heaven and Other Poems,* whose title piece displays the qualities of vivid imagery, vigorous rhythm, and dramatic conception for which Lindsay is best known. The volume also contains such conventional but equally sincere poems as "The Eagle That Is Forgotten," an elegy for the liberal Illinois governor J.P. Altgeld. With the publication of *The Congo and Other Poems* (1914), he was widely recognized as an exponent of the "new poetry," and came to be in great demand as a public reader of his own works. Still preaching the gospel of beauty, he tried to stimulate a popular taste for poetry through a method that he called "the higher vaudeville," in which his recitations were marked by a dramatic use of gesture and chant, emphasizing his strong rhythms and syncopation. This second volume includes "Abraham Lincoln Walks at Midnight," "The Congo," and "The Santa-Fé Trail," all characteristically vivid, imaginative "visions," in which the poet embodies his romantic faith in nature and a life close to the soil, and his fervent patriotism and love for democracy. *The Chinese Nightingale and Other Poems* (1917) marked the peak of his artistic achievement, its title poem and "The Ghost of the Buffaloes" having a subtle beauty of melody and image that he never surpassed, although "In Praise of Johnny Appleseed," commemorating the deeds of his favorite pioneer hero, is one of his most significant pieces. Losing the faculty of self-criticism, he became more prolific but quickly declined in power, and his later poetry is of comparatively little value. Among his later collections are *The Daniel Jazz* (1920); *The Golden Whales of California* (1920); *Collected Poems* (1923, revised 1925); *The Candle in the Cabin* (1926); and *Johnny Appleseed* (1928). His prose works include *Adventures While Preaching the Gospel of Beauty* (1914); *A Handy Guide for Beggars* (1916); *The Golden Book of Springfield* (1920), a mystic Utopia based on his gospel of beauty; and *The Litany of Washington Street* (1929), a book of political essays. His biography (1935) was written by his friend Edgar Lee Masters, and Mark Harris's *City of Discontent* (1952) is an interpretation of his life and his region.

Lippincott's Magazine (1868–1916), Philadelphia literary monthly, was more national in scope than the *Atlantic,* but its contributions were of a similar high caliber. During the 1880s, the magazine was distinguished for the first printing in the U.S. of such English fiction as Wilde's *The Picture of Dorian Gray,* Kipling's *The Light That Failed,* and the first Sherlock Holmes stories. Contributors during its early decades included Frank Stockton, Henry James, Lanier, Simms, Constance F. Woolson, Rebecca H. Davis, and Rose Terry Cooke, and during the 1890s Edgar Saltus, Julian Hawthorne, Gertrude Atherton, P.L. Ford, J.L. Allen, Hearn, Wister, Crane, and Harte. In 1915 the magazine was moved to New York, where its title became *McBride's Magazine.* The following year it was merged with *Scribner's.*

LIPPMANN, WALTER (1889–1974), born in New York, graduated from Harvard (1909, class of 1910), and was associated with *The New Republic* at its inception. In 1917 he resigned to become an assistant to the secretary of war, and to aid in preparing data for the peace conference. After another period with *The New Republic* (1919–21), he became the leading editorial commentator for the New York *World,* then for the *Herald Tribune* (1931–62), the *Washington Post* (1963–67), and *Newsweek* (1963–70). His social philosophy was opposed to any planned society or collectivism, and he placed his faith in a liberalism regulated by the necessities of economic markets, justifying governmental interference only in cases of abuse. *A Preface to Morals* (1929) expounds his thesis that modern society requires realistic analysis and objective virtue for the attainment of individual freedom, rather than loyalty to persons or causes. His other books include *A Preface to Politics* (1913); *Drift and Mastery* (1914); *The Stakes of Diplomacy* (1915); *The Political Scene* (1919); *Public Opinion* (1922); *The Phantom Public* (1925); *The Method of Freedom* (1934); *The Good Society* (1937); *Some Notes on War and Peace* (1940); *U.S. Foreign Policy: Shield of the Republic* (1943); *U.S. War Aims* (1944); *The Cold War* (1947); *Isolation and Alliances* (1952); *The Public Philosophy* (1955); *The Communist World and Ours* (1959); and *The Coming Tests with Russia* (1961). He was awarded special Pulitzer Prize citations in 1958 and 1962.

Literary History of the United States, cooperative "redefinition of our literary past" from the vantage point of the mid-20th century, issued in three volumes (1948) under the editorship of Robert E. Spiller, Willard Thorp, Thomas H. Johnson, and Henry Seidel Canby, with Howard Mumford Jones, Dixon Wecter, and Stanley T. Williams as associates. The first two volumes were written by 55 scholars, including those above, and the third volume, a bibliography, is the work of Thomas Johnson, with a *Bibliography Supplement* (1959) by Richard M. Ludwig, followed by a *Supplement II* (1972).

Literati of New York City, The, critical review by Poe♦ of the Knickerbocker Group♦ and other New York authors, published in *Godey's Lady's Book* (1846). Among the 38 authors are Halleck (the third principal contemporary poet, "a somewhat better position than that to which on absolute grounds he is entitled"); C.P. Cranch ("unusual vivacity of fancy and dexterity of expression . . . one of the least intolerable of the school of Boston transcendentalists"); Caroline Stansbury

Kirkland ("has a province of her own, and in that province has few equals"); Epes Sargent ("one of the most prominent members of a very extensive American family—the men of industry, talent, and tact"); E.A. Duyckinck ("the excessively tasteful"); Anna Mowatt ("She evinces more feeling than ideality"); Lewis G. Clark ("he is noticeable for nothing in the world except for the markedness by which he is noticeable for nothing"); C.F. Hoffman ("a true idealist . . . one sensitively alive to beauty in every development"); Margaret Fuller ("tainted with the affectation of the transcendentalists, but brimful of the poetic sentiment"); and N.P. Willis ("As a poet he is not entitled to as high a rank as he may justly claim for his prose"). Poe's unfavorable comments on T.D. English, whom he satirizes as "Thomas Dunn Brown," provoked a scurrilous reply by English, to which Poe retaliated with a successful libel suit.

Little Eva, a character in *Uncle Tom's Cabin.* ♦

Little Lord Fauntleroy, novel by Frances H. Burnett, ♦ published in 1886 and dramatized by the author in 1888.

The son of an English earl alienates his arrogant old father by marrying an American, who after his death raises their son in New York, calling him Cedric Errol. The boy wears his hair in long curls, converses with grave volubility, and endears himself to everyone by his cheerfulness, generosity, and affection. His special friends are Mr. Hobbs the grocer and Dick the bootblack, whom he leaves regretfully when he goes to England as heir to Dorincourt, following the deaths of his uncles. As Lord Fauntleroy he is indulged by the gouty old earl, who, however, refuses to meet the boy's mother, giving her a house nearby, where the seven-year-old lord visits her daily. Fauntleroy enjoys his new wealth and wins his grandfather's devotion, persuading him to undertake charitable projects and improve his tenants' living conditions. When another American woman appears to claim the estate for her son, the earl is furious but helpless. Dick, in New York, recognizes the woman from a newspaper picture as the former wife of his brother Ben. With Mr. Hobbs the brothers go to England and discredit the woman's false claim. The earl is reconciled with Fauntleroy's mother, and the three live happily at Dorincourt.

Little magazine, name applied to an advance-guard literary journal, primarily concerned with the publication of writers or writing not likely to be acceptable to established journals of larger circulation. *The Yellow Book* (1894–97), founded by Henry Harland, and *The Savoy* (1896), both English magazines that revolted against Victorian rationalism, morality, and emphasis upon science, set the standards that others followed. Their art-for-art's sake credo was imitated by such American magazines as *The Bibelot* (1895–1915), a monthly reprint of prose and poetry from obscure works, edited by T.B. Mosher, and *The Chap Book* ♦ (1894–98), issued from Chicago. *The Lark* ♦ (1895–97), published at San Francisco, was a distant reflection of this school, but had gaiety as its only policy. The little magazine came into particular importance in the U.S. just before and after World War I, as a protest by those who believed artists were being enslaved and repressed by Mammon and Puritanism. *Poetry: A Magazine of Verse* ♦ (1912–) is an eclectic publication, championing new poets of all nations and schools. *The Little Review* ♦ (1914–29), frequently considered the most significant American magazine of the type, had tremendous vitality and never settled into any one pattern. During the postwar period, some magazines, like *The Seven Arts* (1916–17), were concerned with an objective scrutiny of American culture. Others, like *The Frontier* (1920–39), a Northwestern journal, *The Fugitive* ♦ (1922–25), and *The Reviewer* (1921–25) of Virginia, were regional in tendency; and still others, like *Secession* (1922–24), *Broom* (1921–24), *transition* ♦ (1927–50), and *This Quarter* (1925–32), were eclectic in character and were edited from abroad by expatriates. *The Dial* ♦ (1917–29) was in a sense the heir of the previous experimentation, but maintained a more detached, urbane, and cosmopolitan tone. *Hound and Horn* ♦ (1927–34), the outstanding little magazine edited by university students, held policies similar to those of other publications in the movement.

During the Depression after 1929, advance-guard writers turned their attention to social and economic reform, and for a time the significance of little magazines began to disappear. Some of their purposes were taken over by literary quarterlies issued from universities, but many new little magazines continued to appear, some with an international view, like *Paris Review* ♦ or *Botteghe Oscure* (1949–60); some were issued as journals, like *Evergreen Review,* and some published as paperbacks, like *discovery* and *New World Writing.*

The publication of little magazines increased greatly beginning in the 1950s. In 1978 the editors of a book on the subject guessed that at least 1500 such journals were being published in the U.S. They are and have been of the most diverse sorts, championing a great range of aesthetic, critical, social, and cultural views. Some, like *The Floating Bear* (1961–69), were essentially newsletters for rapid communication among authors of experimental literature; others, like *Big Table* (1959–60), were founded to print what was unacceptable to more conventional publications; some, like *The Black Mountain Review*♦ (1954–59), were organs of a special school of literature; some, like Reed Whittemore's *Furioso* (1939–53), Cid Corman's *Origin* (1951–71), and Gilbert Sorrentino's *Neon* (1956–60), reflected the views of a major young writer; some, like *Salmagundi* (1965–) and *Tri-Quarterly* (1958–), are closely related to a university or college; and some, like *Yardbird Reader* (1972–), are dedicated to the writings of ethnic minorities.

Over the 90 years or more that they have flourished, little magazines have printed a good deal of insignificant or bizarre work, but they have justified themselves by providing a medium for all kinds of aesthetic experimentation and innovative and unpopular beliefs. By initial circulation in these magazines the novelties, heresies, and unknown authors of one era have often become accepted and valued in a succeeding period.

Little Men, story for children by Louisa May Alcott. ♦

Little Regiment, The, and Other Episodes of the American Civil War, six short stories by Stephen Crane,♦ published in 1896 and issued in England as *Pictures of War* (1916).

The title story tells of two brothers in the Union army, whose seeming antagonism conceals a deep affection. During a battle, one of them is believed killed, and the other shows signs of bitter grief. When his brother suddenly reappears, they greet each other with a curt "hello" and resume their pose of hostility. "Three Miraculous Soldiers" shows the reactions of an ignorant Southern girl, who is terrified when a Union detachment camps on her mother's farm. She helps three Confederate prisoners to escape, but breaks into hysterical tears over a sentry they have wounded. "A Mystery of Heroism" is concerned with the reckless feat of a private who crosses a field during a violent battle to fetch a pail of drinking water. When he returns,

apparently by miracle, the water is accidentally spilled before any of it can be used. "The Veteran" tells of the heroism of an aged ex-soldier who sacrifices his life to save the animals in a burning barn.

Little Review, The (1914–29), monthly little magazine founded at Chicago by Margaret C. Anderson "as an organ of two interests, art and good talk about art." "Making no compromise with the public taste," the *Review* was best known for its serialization of Joyce's *Ulysses;* Ezra Pound was its foreign editor (1917–19). Such special issues were published as the one devoted to the works of Henry James (Aug. 1918), and in general the magazine tended toward favorable criticism of all extreme modern theories of art, although its aesthetic bias was temporarily interrupted (1916–17) when the editor became interested in social problems and the writings of Emma Goldman. This social concern was abandoned when Miss Anderson "found the tenets of anarchism to be simple and beautiful but quite uninteresting." For a short time, the magazine was published at San Francisco, and later at New York. With Miss Anderson's removal to Paris, it was published there as a quarterly (1924–29), mainly edited by Jane Heap, who had long been associated with it. The *Review* gave space to "23 new systems of art . . . representing 19 countries," and published works by such authors as T.S. Eliot, W.C. Williams, W.B. Yeats, Malcolm Cowley, Ford Madox Ford, Wallace Stevens, Amy Lowell, Ben Hecht, Sherwood Anderson, and Carl Sandburg. Miss Anderson wrote of her editorship in *My Thirty Years' War* (1930).

Little Shepherd of Kingdom Come, The, novel by John Fox,♦ published in 1903 and dramatized by Eugene Walter (1916).

Little Women, novel by Louisa May Alcott,♦ published in 1868–69.

This favorite book for children, based on the author's own youthful experiences, describes the family life of the Marches in a small New England community. Mrs. March is busy, cheerful, and sympathetic; her husband is an improvident army chaplain in the Civil War; and there are four daughters, Meg, Jo, Beth, and Amy. Jo at 15 is ungainly, unconventional, and enterprising, with an ambition to be an author. Meg, a year older, is pretty and wishes to be a lady. Beth is a delicate child of 13 with a taste for music. Amy is a blonde beauty of 12. Their domestic adventures, their attempts to increase the family's small income, their friendship with the neighboring Laurence family, and their later love affairs are the interests of the narrative. Meg marries John Brooke, tutor of Laurie, Mr. Laurence's grandson. Laurie loves Jo, but when she does not respond he goes to Europe to forget her. There he meets and falls in love with Amy, whom he marries. Beth falls ill and dies. Jo becomes a writer of melodramatic fiction, and later marries Dr. Bhaer, a middle-aged professor.

Littlepage Manuscripts, trilogy of novels by Cooper♦ tracing the history of the Littlepage family through three generations in New York state, during the difficulties between the propertied and propertyless classes that ended in the Anti-Rent War.♦ The novels are *Satanstoe,*♦ *The Chainbearer,*♦ and *The Redskins.*♦

Local color, term applied to fiction or verse which emphasizes its setting, being concerned with the character of a district or of an era, as marked by its customs, dialect, costumes, landscape, or other peculiarities that have escaped standardizing cultural influences. The earliest American writing reflects its locale, as all literature must, but the local-color movement came into particular prominence in the U.S. after the Civil War, perhaps as an attempt to recapture the glamour of a past era, or to portray the sections of the reunited county one to the other. Specifically, American influences upon those authors known as local-color writers may be found in Down East humor and in the frontier tradition of tall tales. Other influences include the writings of Irving, the English tradition of Scott, Maria Edgeworth, and Bulwer-Lytton, and the French romantic tradition of *couleur locale* represented by Hugo, Mérimée, and Bernardin de Saint-Pierre. According to Edward Eggleston, another influence was the national and racial bias of the historical works of Taine, which specifically impelled him to a closer observation of his own region. In local-color literature one finds the dual influence of romanticism and realism, since the author frequently looks away from ordinary life to distant lands, strange customs, or exotic scenes, but retains through minute detail a sense of fidelity and accuracy of description. Harte's "The Luck of Roaring Camp"♦ (1868) is usually considered the first local-color story. The most distinguished writing engendered by the movement was in

the form of the short story, whose development was thus deeply affected. Besides Harte, the local-color school produced such prominent authors as Harriet Beecher Stowe, Sara Orne Jewett, Mary W. Freeman, Rose Terry Cooke, and R.E. Robinson in New England; T.N. Page in Virginia; J.C. Harris in Georgia; G.W. Cable and Kate Chopin in Louisiana; Mary N. Murfree and John Fox in Tennessee and Kentucky; John Hay in Illinois; Riley and the Egglestons in Indiana; Clemens in California and on the Mississippi; E.W. Howe, Garland, and Zona Gale in the Middle West; and R.H. Davis, H.C. Bunner, Brander Matthews, and O. Henry in New York City. A broader concept of sectional differences lies behind regionalism.♦

LOCKE, DAVID ROSS (1833–88), born in New York state, became an itinerant printer and journalist mainly in Ohio, where he achieved fame during the Civil War as a humorist under the pseudonym Petroleum V. Nasby. The first Nasby letter appeared in the Findlay *Jeffersonian* (March 21, 1861), of which he was editor. "Petroleum Vesuvius Nasby, late pastor uv the Church uv the New Dispensation, Chaplain to his excellency the President, and p. m. at Confederate x roads, kentucky," was a dissolute, illiterate country preacher, who intended to support the South by his foolish arguments and "advenchers," but ironically made its cause appear ludicrously inept. In his caricature of this stupid and corrupt Copperhead, Locke followed the humorous style of Artemus Ward, using the devices popular among literary comedians of the time: ridiculous spellings, deformed grammar, monstrous logic, puns, malapropisms, incongruous juxtaposition of ideas, and anticlimax. In 1865 he became editor of the Toledo *Blade,* and later its owner, contributing to it his immensely popular letters until his death. Lincoln greatly admired Locke's humor, and even read the latest Nasby letters to his cabinet, as comic relief, before outlining the Emancipation Proclamation. *The Nasby Papers* (1864) was the first of several collections, and Locke also published a political novel, *The Demagogue* (1891), and other writings on politics, especially in favor of liquor prohibition.

Log of a Cowboy, The, semi-autobiographical novel of "the Old Trail Days," by Andy Adams,♦ published in 1903.

LOGAN, JOHN (1923–), Iowa-born poet, after graduation from Coe College and an

M.A. from Iowa University has taught at Notre Dame and the State University of New York, Buffalo. His vigorous poetry, marked by vivid imagery and great variety of technique, often deals with religion. It has been issued in *Cycle for Mother Cabrini* (1955), *Ghosts of the Heart* (1960), *Spring of the Thief* (1963), *The Zig-Zag Walk* (1969), *The Anonymous Lover* (1973), *The Bridge of Change* (1981), and *A Ballet for the Ear* (1983).

Lolita, novel by Nabokov,♦ published in Paris (1955) and in the U.S. (1958).

In the psychopathic ward of a prison while awaiting trial for murder, 37-year-old Humbert Humbert writes out his life story. Though once wed to a woman of about his age, he has long been obsessed by a passion for nymphets: girls between the ages of nine and 14. Coming from Europe to the U.S. on business, he meets and marries the widowed Charlotte Haze only to be near her 12-year-old daughter Lolita. To achieve this he considers murdering Charlotte, but when she is killed by accident he takes Lolita on a cross-country junket, planning to seduce her, only to be seduced by her, for she is no longer a virgin. Lolita escapes from his jealous protection, and he does not learn of her again until she is 17, married, and pregnant. Then she tells him that during her days with him she had loved Clare Quilty, a famous playwright. Even though their affair is long in the past, the infuriated Humbert Humbert murders Quilty and is jailed but dies of a heart attack before his trial.

LONDON, JACK (JOHN GRIFFITH LONDON) (1876–1916), born in San Francisco, is said to have been the illegitimate son of William Henry Chaney (1821–1903), an itinerant astrologer. Reared by a family without fixed occupation or residence, he lived along the Oakland waterfront described in *Martin Eden* and *John Barleycorn,* and attended school only until he finished grammar school at 14. As a boy he bought a sloop and with some cronies raided the oyster beds about the bay, as he later told in *The Cruise of the Dazzler* (1902) and *Tales of the Fish Patrol* (1905). He abandoned this lawless, reckless occupation in 1893, to join a sealing cruise which took him as far as Japan. After a tramping trip through the U.S. and Canada, and a period of education including a semester at the University of California (1896), he returned to the Oakland waterfront with an interest in sociology and the Socialist party, which ap-

pears in several of his later books. In 1897 he joined the gold rush to the Klondike, where he made an unsuccessful attempt at mining, came to know the men who were prototypes of his elemental, hard-living heroes, and continued to read Spencer, Darwin, and Karl Marx. Stricken with scurvy, he returned to Oakland the following year and began to write of his experiences.

His short stories of the Yukon were published in the *Overland Monthly* (1898) and the *Atlantic Monthly* (1899), and in 1900 his first collection, *The Son of the Wolf,* was issued, bringing him national fame for his Kiplingesque portrayal of the brutal, vigorous life of the Far North. He continued to write in this vein, producing an enormous output of stories and novels, and in 1902, with an established reputation, went to London, where he made a close study of slum conditions for his descriptive work *The People of the Abyss* (1903). The remainder of his short but full life was spent under the balmy influence of popularity and success. He reported the Russo-Japanese War for the Hearst papers, made lecture tours, went on sailing voyages to the Caribbean and the South Seas, was a correspondent for *Collier's* in Mexico, and lived on his great patriarchal estate in California. His popularity, journalistic training, and eagerness for money caused him to write too prolifically, but his energy and ability as a storyteller gave even his worst writing a great appeal.

Besides several collections of short stories, including *Love of Life* (1907); *Lost Face* (1910), in which was printed the popular "To Build a Fire"♦; *South Sea Tales* (1911); and *On the Makaloa Mat* (1919), giving a sense of rugged life close to nature, his longer fiction also showed a deep concern with physical energy, the cult of "red blood," and a breed of Nietzschean supermen engaged in violent struggles of various sorts. This includes many novels, the best known of which are *The Call of the Wild*♦ (1903), the story of a dog in the Far North, who escapes from civilization to lead a wolf pack; *The Sea-Wolf*♦ (1904), about the powerful, ruthless captain of a sealing ship; *The Game*♦ (1905), the story of a prizefighter; *Before Adam*♦ (1906), concerned with the life of prehistoric savages; *White Fang*♦ (1906) telling of a wild dog who is tamed; *Martin Eden*♦ (1909), a semi-autobiographical novel about a writer's struggles; *Burning Daylight* (1910), the story of Daylight, a man of tremendous energy who wrests a fortune from the Klondike, then idealistically renounces his hard-won wealth;

Smoke Bellew (1912), about a journalist's strenuous adventures in the Yukon; *John Barleycorn* (1913), an autobiographical memoir intended as propaganda for temperance; and *Jerry of the Islands*♦ (1917), the story of an Irish setter pup in the South Seas.

London also wrote socialistic treatises, such as *War of the Classes* (1905) and *The Human Drift* (1917), as well as novels concerned with socialists and class struggle, of which the most famous are *The Iron Heel*♦ (1908), prophesying a fascist revolution to be followed eventually by an equalitarian golden age, and *The Valley of the Moon*♦ (1913), in which the economic problem is solved by a return to the land.

In spite of his belief in collectivism as an inevitable next step in human evolution, London was most convincing in his depiction of individualistic struggle and primitive violence. The very titles of many of his books, e.g. *The Strength of the Strong* (1911) and *The Absymal Brute* (1913), indicate his preoccupation with the concept of the brute which underlies the social behavior of men and animals. Buck, in *The Call of the Wild,* shows a retrogression, while *White Fang* and *Jerry of the Islands* depict the brute under control or in process of subjugation. Wolf Larsen is a combination of civilized brain with primitive force. In *The Iron Heel,* one of the most impressive scenes shows the people of the abyss fighting with bestial, reckless fury against their oppressors. London worshipped Marx and Nietzsche impartially, grasping what he could of their diametrically opposed theories, and championing now one, now the other, both in his novels and in his own life.

Long Day's Journey into Night, semi-autobiographical play by Eugene O'Neill,♦ written in 1941, posthumously produced and published (1956).

Recently released from an institution as cured of her drug addiction, Mary Tyrone, a handsome, nervous woman, is, in August 1912, once again at her summer home with her husband James, an aging former matinee idol, and their sons, Jamie, at 33 a hard-drinking, cynical Broadway hanger-on, and Edmund, a sickly, morbid intellectual. Mary's appearance and detached conversations soon make clear that she is not cured, and as the men drink heavily to escape reality, she nostalgically revives past dreams of becoming a nun or a concert pianist, and seems an innocent girl again. But she also reveals her addiction began when her miserly husband chose a quack doctor who treated her with morphine after her sickness in giving birth to Edmund. Like his mother, Edmund wants to "be alone . . . in another world . . . where life can hide from itself." Like her too, he shows both love and hate for his family as he confronts his limited future as a consumptive, realizing that his father will send him to the cheapest state sanitarium, since he is expected to die. A similar ambivalence is exhibited by the debauched Jamie, who drunkenly tells Edmund how much he loves him and yet how much he hates him as responsible for their mother's addiction. As James curses the sad spectacle, Mary appears, trailing her wedding gown, utterly immersed in the happier past. Realizing that she is forever lost to them and that their fates are intimately bound with hers, they impassively contemplate their own destruction.

Long Valley, The, 13 short stories by Steinbeck,♦ published in 1938. "The Red Pony" and "Saint Katy the Virgin" had previously appeared in separate editions.

Set in towns and on farms of the Salinas Valley in California, these realistic tales are mainly concerned with the relations of people with growing things, and dramatize the author's frequently mystical concept of animal and vegetable nature. "The Red Pony" presents three episodes in the boyhood of Jody Tiflin, a farm boy whose knowledge of life matures through his loss of a beloved red pony, his meeting with the mysterious *paisano* Gitano, and the death of a mare during the birth of her colt. "The Snake" tells of a woman's morbid obsession with the natural functions of a captive male rattlesnake. "The Leader of the People," which has the same characters as "The Red Pony," is concerned with the pathetic old age of Jody's pioneer grandfather. "Saint Katy the Virgin," in a different mood and style, is an ironic parable of medieval times, telling of the conversion and beatification of a brood sow.

LONGFELLOW, HENRY WADSWORTH (1807–82), descendant of a colonial family, was born at Portland, Me., and educated in private schools and at Bowdoin, where he graduated (1825) as a classmate of Hawthorne. Soon after graduation, he was offered a professorship of modern languages at Bowdoin, on the condition that he prepare himself by studying abroad. Accordingly, he spent the years from 1826 to 1829 in France, Spain, Italy, and Germany. While professor and librarian at Bowdoin (1829–35), he contributed essays and sketches to many magazines, and his teaching was so successful that he was recommended by George Ticknor to be his successor in the Smith professorship of French and Spanish at Harvard. To improve his knowledge of languages, Longfellow went abroad in 1835. His wife, to whom he had been married in 1831, died at this time. In 1836 began his 18 years of teaching at Harvard, during which he became a significant figure in the literary and social life of Cambridge.

His first prose work, *Outre-Mer: A Pilgrimage Beyond the Sea* (1833–34), reminiscent of Irving's *Sketch Book,* was followed by *Hyperion* (1839), a semi-autobiographical romance, interspersed with prose and verse concerned with German romanticism, which had greatly impressed him. *Voices of the Night* (1839), his first book of poetry, contains "Hymn to the Night," "A Psalm of Life,"♦ and other poems foreshadowing his later work. *Ballads and Other Poems* (1841) contains such favorites as "The Village Blacksmith,"♦ "The Wreck of the Hesperus,"♦ "Excelsior,"♦ and "The Skeleton in Armor," and did more to establish his fame than *Poems on Slavery* (1842), an outgrowth of his antislavery interests.

In 1843 he married Frances Appleton, the prototype of the heroine of *Hyperion,* whom he met abroad. Her father, a wealthy cotton-mill proprietor, presented the couple with Craigie House as a wedding present. Longfellow's life now flowed on placidly in the congenial Cambridge society. Besides the three daughters who figure in his poem "The Children's Hour,"♦ two sons were born of this second marriage.

Meanwhile his fame increased with the publication of *The Spanish Student* (1843), a poetic drama; *The Belfry of Bruges and Other Poems*♦ (1845), including "The Bridge,"♦ "The Arrow and the Song,"♦ and "The Belfry of Bruges"; *Evangeline*♦ (1847), his narrative poem on the Acadians; *Kavanagh* (1849), a semi-autobiographical prose tale; *The Seaside and the Fireside* (1849), a volume of poems best known for "The Building of the Ship"♦; *The Golden Legend* (1851), a dramatic poem on medieval Germany; and *Hiawatha*♦ (1855), his celebrated "Indian Edda." In 1854 he resigned his professorship, which he said was "a great hand laid on all the strings of my lyre, stopping their vibration."

His popularity throughout the U.S. and Europe was so great that, on the publication of *The Courtship of Miles Standish*♦ (1858), more than 15,000 copies were sold during the first day in Boston and London. His happiness and the even course of his writing were sharply broken, however, when his wife was burned to death (1861). For a long time his grief stopped his creative work, and it was so persistent that it is implicit in "The Cross of Snow," written 18 years afterward. The *Tales of a Wayside Inn,*♦ including "Paul Revere's Ride,"♦ began to appear in book form in 1863, but they were in large part completed before the death of his wife. For solace he turned to his translation of Dante's *Divine Comedy* (published 1865–67), done with the aid of Lowell and C.E. Norton, who met with him every week in the Dante Society that they formed. He added two lengthy pieces to *The Golden Legend,* which appeared in final form as *Christus* (1872); added to the *Tales of a Wayside Inn;* and wrote many sonnets, including a sequence of six, "Divina Commedia," now considered to be among his most significant work.

During his remaining years, honors were heaped upon him and his home became a shrine for Americans and a point of visit for distinguished foreigners. During a tour of Europe (1868–69), he received degrees from Cambridge and Oxford, and was given a private audience by Queen Victoria. His last poems, including "Morituri Salutamus,"♦ were collected in *The Masque of Pandora* (1875), *Kéramos* (1878), *Ultima Thule* (1880), and *In the Harbor* (1882). After his death, he became the only American to be honored with a bust in the Poet's Corner of Westminster Abbey.

The gentleness, sweetness, and purity for which his poetry was popular during his lifetime were the very qualities that caused a reaction against it after his death. His writings belong to the milder aspects of the romantic movement, and he was strongly influenced by the German romantic lyrists. Throughout his work and his life, he was consistently high-minded but conventional, and untouched by the religious and social struggles that disturbed his contemporaries, with the exception of his interest in antislavery, for which his friendship with Sumner was partly responsible. He exercised a great influence in bringing European culture to the U.S., and likewise did much to popularize American folk themes abroad, where his work was immensely popular and widely translated. In his own time he was universally respected, except by a very few detractors, such as Poe in his article "Longfellow and Other Plagiarists." Even today Poe's criticism cannot be accepted, despite Longfellow's indebtedness to foreign models, e.g. *Hiawatha* to the meter of the Finnish *Kalevala,* and "The Wreck of the Hesperus" to the ballad "Sir Patrick Spens." A later age, with different standards, has also accused him of undue didacticism and excessive symbolism, as in "A Psalm of Life," "Excelsior," "The Village Blacksmith," and "My Lost Youth." ◆ The very simplicity that has made him a children's poet has lessened his mature audience, since, despite his great metrical skill, he is lacking in passion and high imagination, and is too decorous, benign, and sweet. More recent serious scholarly interest is indicated by the editing of his *Letters* (6 vols., 1966–82).

LONGSTREET, Augustus Baldwin (1790–1870), Georgia jurist, educator, and author. He is best known for his *Georgia Scenes, Characters, and Incidents* (1835), humorous realistic sketches of the life of the Old Southwest, which were forerunners of the work of such writers as J.G. Baldwin, G.W. Harris, J.J. Hooper, W.T. Thompson, and Clemens. He was a fervent advocate of nullification, establishing a newspaper and writing several pamphlets for this cause. He served successively as president of Emory College (1839–48), Centenary College (1849), the University of Mississippi (1849–56), and the University of South Carolina (1857–65). *Master William Mitten* (1864) is a semi-autobiographical novel of his youth in Georgia. Later stories and sketches in the vein of his first book were less successful.

Lonigan, Studs, character whose life from a squalid adolescence on Chicago's South Side to his physical and moral disintegration and death in his late twenties is chronicled in the trilogy of novels, *Young Lonigan,* ◆ *The Young Manhood of Studs Lonigan,* ◆ and *Judgment Day,* ◆ by James T. Farrell.

Look Homeward, Angel: *A Story of the Buried Life,* autobiographical novel by Thomas Wolfe◆ published in 1929. A dramatization (1957) by Ketti Frings won a Pulitzer Prize. *Of Time and the River* ◆ is a sequel to the novel.

Eugene Gant grows up in Altamont, Catawba (Asheville, N.C.), the youngest of six children of Oliver Gant, stonecutter and amateur orator, whose demonic passions both fascinate and terrify Eugene, and whose love of craftsmanship and rhetoric dominate the boy's character. Eliza, Oliver's crafty, miserly wife, has frequent quarrels with her husband, and leaves him, while Eugene is yet a child, to operate a boardinghouse. The other children include Steve, lazy, selfish, and corrupt; Daisy, shy and retiring; Helen, her father's favorite, "strung on the same wires"; Ben, quiet and intelligent, who becomes a newspaperman, and whose death is Eugene's most poignant loss; and Luke, exuberant and lovable. Eugene, the "baby" of the family, has a relatively solitary youth, delivering newspapers in the black quarter and becoming acquainted with the town's "characters." He reads and memorizes English classics, attending a private school where he receives a limited but more balanced education. At 16 he enters the state university, where he continues to feel lonely and "different," but by the time of his graduation makes important personal adjustments to the world, editing the literary magazine, having his first sexual encounters and youthful love affairs, and finally breaking with his family to make what he conceives to be a pilgrimage in search of "the lost lane-end into heaven, a stone, a leaf, an unfound door. . . ."

Looking Backward, 2000–1887, Utopian romance by Edward Bellamy,◆ published in 1888. Its immense popularity led to the founding of Bellamy clubs and a Nationalist party. *Equality* (1897), a sequel, is more a tract than a novel.

Conceived as a "fairy tale of social felicity," the book describes a future social and economic order through the narrative of Julian West, a young Bostonian, who enters a hypnotic sleep in 1887 and is revived 113 years later in the changed city. He falls in love with Edith Leete, a descendant of his former fiancée, and through her father, a physician, learns of the scientific and social developments that have taken place. In contrast with the squalor of the slums and the injustices and inequalities of the earlier time, he finds an America in which the business monopolies have evolved to become "The Great Trust," economic chaos having been replaced by a democratic form of state capitalism. Private enterprise has disappeared, each citizen is both an employee and a member of the state, and the collective organization of wealth and industry has eradicated crime, poverty, advertising, warfare, and many diseases. The cultural level of the people has consequently risen, and Dr. Leete ascribes these changes to the spread of social intelligence and social ethics among a good people formerly victimized by an evil system.

LOOS, ANITA (1893–1981), author of *Gentlemen Prefer Blondes* (1925), subtitled the "Illuminating Diary of a Professional Lady," a novel satirizing a pair of naïve, pert sirens of the jazz age. This was followed by a less successful sequel, *But Gentlemen Marry Brunettes* (1928). Later fiction includes *No Mother To Guide Her* (1961), a satire set in Hollywood. Other views of Hollywood are in her memoir *The Talmadge Girls* (1979), about two early-day film stars, and her autobiographical *This Brunette Prefers Work* (1956), *A Girl Like I* (1966), *Kiss Hollywood Good-by* (1974), and *Cast of Thousands* (1977). Her plays include a dramatization of her first book (1926); *Happy Birthday* (1947); *A Mouse Is Born* (1951); and *Gigi* (1952), based on Colette's novel; as well as motion pictures. *Twice Over Lightly* (1972) prints her memoirs and reactions to New York City and those of Helen Hayes.

Lord Weary's Castle, collection of poems by Robert Lowell,♦ published in 1946.

Deriving its title from a folk ballad about Lord Weary's refusal to pay his stonemason Lambkin for building his castle, and Lambkin's murder of the lord's wife and child, the symbolic significance, as John Berryman pointed out in a review, is that the "castle is a house of ingratitude, failure of obligation, crime and punishment." These are among the themes of the volume's lyrics, some of which were revised from Lowell's previous book, *Land of Unlikeness,* some of them related to World War II and others to the author's New England heritage. Major works include "The Quaker Graveyard in Nantucket," an elegy for a cousin, alluding to Melville and Thoreau and treating man's equivocal relations to nature and the theological issues of innocence, corruption, sin, and redemption; "Mr. Edwards and the Spider," drawing with antipathy upon Jonathan Edwards's *Sinners in the Hands of an Angry God;* and "Christmas Eve Under Hooker's Statue," relating the Civil War and World War II, and contrasting childhood innocence and adult materialistic belligerence.

Los Angeles, in southern California, the largest city of the state, has had a tremendous growth in recent years, increasing in population from 102,000 in 1900 to 2,952,511 in 1980. This influx, mainly of native Americans from the Middle West, is due to such diverse causes as the discovery of a great oil field, the rise of Hollywood,♦ and the development of manufacturing and of citrus and other agricultural interests. The site of an Indian village and later of a Spanish pueblo (founded 1781), Los Angeles was captured by the U.S. Army (1846–47), but had a secondary place in California industry and trade until the turn of the century. Situated there or nearby are the Henry E. Huntington Library, the California Institute of Technology, University of California at Los Angeles, Occidental College, and University of Southern California.

Lost generation, name applied to the disillusioned intellectuals and aesthetes of the years following World War I, who rebelled against former ideals and values but could replace them only by despair or a cynical hedonism. The remark of Gertrude Stein, "You are all a lost generation," addressed to Hemingway, was used as a preface to the latter's novel *The Sun Also Rises,* which brilliantly describes an expatriate group typical of the "lost generation." Other expatriate American authors of the period to whom the term is generally applied include Malcolm Cowley, E.E. Cummings, F. Scott Fitzgerald, Archibald MacLeish, and Ezra Pound.

Lost Lady, A, novel by Willa Cather,♦ published in 1923.

Niel Herbert, a boy in the Midwestern town of Sweet Water, tells the story of Marian Forrester, who brings a knowledge of gracious living to the new country as the youthful wife of old Captain Forrester, retired railroad builder and aristocrat of the pioneer generation. Mrs. Forrester's beauty and charm set her apart from her crass, commonplace neighbors, as do her husband's rugged strength, integrity, and love of fine possessions. The captain is devoted to his wife, but her passionate nature causes her to become the secret mistress of his bachelor friend Frank Ellinger. When Forrester loses his fortune by assuming responsibility in the failure of his bank, he suffers a paralytic stroke. His wife nurses him carefully, but after his death she is left in financial straits. Ivy Peters, a pushy businessman of the new generation, acquires her beautiful home and becomes her lover, to the bitter disillusion of Niel, who regards her as "a lost lady," although he never ceases to admire her. She goes West to her childhood home when Peters marries and occupies the Forrester mansion, and for Niel this symbolizes the end of the great era of the pioneers. Years afterward, he learns that she married a wealthy Englishman in South America, and until her death won admiration for her gracefulness, charm, and taste.

Love Song of J. Alfred Prufrock, The, poem by T.S. Eliot,♦ first published in *Poetry* (June 1915) and collected in *Prufrock and Other Observations* (1917). In the form of a dramatic monologue it presents with irony and pathos the musings of an aging young man, uncertain, uneasy, and unable to commit himself to the love he desires or to life at all, a figure representative of frustrations in modern life and of the aridity of a sterile upper-class culture.

LOVECRAFT, H[OWARD] P[HILLIPS] (1890–1937), author of science fiction for popular magazines, whose posthumously collected works include *The Outsider and Others* (1939) and *Beyond the Wall of Sleep* (1943). August Derleth published a critical biography (1945) of him.

LOWELL, AMY [LAWRENCE] (1874–1925), collateral descendant of James Russell Lowell, was born in Brookline, Mass. Her first book, *A Dome of Many-Coloured Glass* (1912), lacks the vivid individuality and technical experimentation that characterize the poetry in *Sword Blades and Poppy Seed* (1914), *Men, Women, and Ghosts* (1916), *Can Grande's Castle* (1918), *Pictures of the Floating World* (1919), and *Legends* (1921).

In 1913 Miss Lowell became identified with the movement of Imagism,♦ and after Ezra Pound abandoned the group she was its dominating force. Her technical experimentation includes not only the modes of the Imagists but also polyphonic prose,♦ a free-verse method of which she and John Gould Fletcher were the leading exponents. Although her work attracted wide attention, it has been criticized as dealing too exclusively with sensual images, particularly visual ones, and as neglecting emotional values. Her distinctive personality informs *A Critical Fable* (1922), a witty *Who's Who* of contemporary poets patterned after *A Fable for Critics*. Her biographical study *John Keats* (1925) has been called an uncritical amassing of materials, although it is distinguished by the zest that marks all her work. Among the most noted of her poems are "Patterns," published in *Men, Women, and Ghosts,* a free-verse dramatic monologue on the clash between desire and convention within the mind of a woman of the 18th century, and "Lilacs," an Imagistic descriptive piece published in *What's O'Clock?* (1925), a volume for which she was posthumously awarded the Pulitzer Prize (1926).

Her other books of verse include *East Wind* (1926) and *Ballads for Sale* (1927), and she wrote two further critical studies, *Six French Poets* (1915) and *Tendencies in Modern American Poetry* (1917). Her correspondence with Florence Ayscough about translations from the Chinese (*Fir-Flower Tablets,* 1921) was published in 1946.

LOWELL, JAMES RUSSELL (1819–91), descendant of a distinguished colonial family, was born at Cambridge, and graduated from Harvard as class poet (1838; LL.B., 1840; M.A., 1841). Finding law not to his liking, he was generally confused about his place in life and went through a morose period from which he was rescued by his future wife, Maria White Lowell. His early poetry, in *A Year's Life* (1841), shows a sharp difference from the *Poems* (1844) published the year of his marriage. Under the influence of his wife, an ardent Abolitionist and liberal, he temporarily submerged his native conservatism and was stimulated to forceful thinking and writing. His first journalistic venture was the short-lived *Pioneer* (1843), but inspired by his wife he became a contributor to and editor of the *National Anti-Slavery Standard* (1848–52) and contributed to the *Pennsylvania Freeman.*

The year 1848 marked his most important writing in his youth, for it included the publication of works that established him as a poet, critic, humorist, and political satirist: *Poems . . . Second Series, A Fable for Critics,♦* the first series of *The Biglow Papers,♦* and *The Vision of Sir Launfal.♦* His prose and poetry continued in these varied categories, and his great facility permitted him to become a competent, if not brilliant, author in all these fields. With the exception of these four books, published in his twenty-ninth year, most of his writing lacks vitality, is too hortatory, depends too much on verbal pranks, ingenious rhymes, and pleasant sounds, and represents the output of a man of taste who was a Bostonian and a Victorian.

His wife died in 1853, and it is significant that until the publication of *Fireside Travels* (1864), a volume of literary essays, he published no books. He entered the academic world in 1855, succeeding Longfellow as Smith Professor of French and Spanish at Harvard, in which capacity he continued his predecessor's task of directing Americans to the literature of Europe, past and present. After a European journey to perfect his linguistic knowledge, he occupied the post and was nominally professor until 1886, although his teaching career really ended in 1876. As a professor he published little poetry and turned to scholarly interests, emphasizing literary criticism and losing contact with the immediate world.

His criticism, contributed to periodicals and later assembled in book form, includes *Among My Books* (1870), *My Study Windows* (1871), a second series of *Among My Books* (1876), *Latest Literary Essays and Addresses* (1891), and *The Old English Dramatists* (1892). Lowell was the first editor of the *Atlantic Monthly* ♦ (1857–61), in this position being a leader among the mid-19th-century authors who are said to have brought a renaissance to New England.

In 1864 he temporarily joined C.E. Norton as editor of *The North American Review,* and here also exerted a powerful influence on public taste and opinion. His *Political Essays* (1888) were gathered from his prose articles in these magazines, and in addition he contributed to the *Atlantic* his second series of *The Biglow Papers* ♦ (1867), trenchantly criticizing England's part in the Civil War and stating the patriotic sentiments of Northerners. His feeling for the Union cause was also expressed in one of his most important poems, "Ode Recited at the Harvard Commemoration" (1865), in honor of the Harvard men who died in the war. *The Cathedral* (1869) is probably the best of his later poems.

As a staunch Republican, he was appointed a presidential elector in 1876, and his firm stand for Hayes was rewarded by his appointment as minister to Spain (1877–80), and Garfield appointed him minister to England (1880–85). As a charming gentleman who had long since reverted to his natural conservatism, he was popularly received in European and English society and helped interpret American ideals to the Old World, both through personal contacts and through more formal addresses, such as *On Democracy* (1884). After the death of his second wife (1885) he gave up public life and returned to his Cambridge home, Elmwood. The works on which his reputation rests most securely were written before he was 30. Most of his books are periodical or lecture collections, and his writings, loosely connected, though brilliant in parts, have a diffused totality.

LOWELL, ROBERT [TRAILL SPENCE, JR.] (1917–77), great-grandson and namesake of the 19th-century poet and novelist and member of the prominent Boston family, was himself reared in Boston, as frankly described in *Life Studies,* and educated at Harvard and at Kenyon College. The year of his graduation (1940) was also marked by his marriage to his first wife, the writer Jean Stafford (he was later married—1949–72—to the novelist Elizabeth Hardwick), and his conversion to Catholicism. During World War II he was refused the status of a conscientious objector and was jailed. His poetry, first published in *Land of Unlikeness* (1944), is marked by themes of rebellion, depiction of corruption and chaos in the modern world, and quest for spiritual values in his adopted faith. A baroque intensity continues in his later poems collected in *Lord Weary's Castle* ♦ (1946, Pulitzer Prize), *The Mills of the Kavanaughs* (1951), and *For the Union Dead* ♦ (1964), as does his great technical skill, but his rich allegory shows a greater sense of acceptance in a more philosophic mood after he became an agnostic. *Life Studies* ♦ (1959) includes frank prose and poetry about his family and himself. Lowell next wrote verse adaptations of foreign poems, collected in *Imitation* (1961), and made a free translation of Racine's play as *Phaedria* (1961). Translations also appeared with original poems in *Near the Ocean* (1967). In 1965 he published *The Old Glory,* three one-act plays based on Melville's "Benito Cereno" and Hawthorne's "My Kinsman, Major Molyneux" and "Endicott and the Red Cross," and in 1969 he issued a prose *Prometheus Bound* derived from Aeschylus. *Notebooks, 1967–68* (1969) contains 274 sonnets on the contemporary scene and Lowell's personal situation in a time of upheaval, those dealing with his wife and daughter being reprinted in *For Lizzie and Harriet* (1973). *History* (1973) also draws upon the poems from his *Notebooks* and adds others that convey the poet's reflections on world events, past and present. *The Dolphins* (1973, Pulitzer Prize) is a cycle of sonnets about Lowell's life in England and New York, his third marriage, and the birth of a son. It was followed by a final collection of poems, *Day by Day* (1977).

LOWELL, ROBERT TRAILL SPENCE (1816–91), elder brother of J.R. Lowell, graduated from Harvard (1833) and for some time was an Episcopal clergyman in Newfoundland, the basis for his novel *The New Priest in Conception Bay* (1858). *Anthony Brade, A Story of a School* (1874) derives from his experiences as headmaster of St. Mark's, and *A Story or Two from an Old Dutch Town* (1878) is set in Schenectady, where he taught at Union College. The best known of his *Poems* (1864) is "The Relief of Lucknow," about the Sepoy rebellion in Lahore (1857).

LOY, MINA (MINA GERTRUDE LOWY) (1882–1966), English-born poet whose contributions to little magazines of the 1920s are collected in *Lunar Baedecker* (1923). She was praised by T.S. Eliot, and called by Yvor Winters a master of free verse "so simplified, so denuded of secondary accent, as to be indistinguishable from prose." Her cool poems of the first volume and some additions were issued as *Lunar Baedeker & Time-Tables* (1958) and with further additions as *The Last Lunar Baedeker* (1982).

Luck of Roaring Camp, The, story by Bret Harte,♦ published in the *Overland Monthly* (1868) and reprinted in *The Luck of Roaring Camp and Other Sketches* (1870). It is often called the first example of local-color fiction.

A child is born to Cherokee Sal, a prostitute in the California gold-mining settlement of Roaring Camp. The mother dies, and the child, christened Thomas Luck, is adopted by the hardened miners, whose spirit is changed to a beautiful though awkward sympathy. The following year, when the river rises, Roaring Camp is engulfed, and Kentuck, one of the miners, is drowned with The Luck in his arms.

LUDLOW, FITZ HUGH (1836–70), born in New York City, graduated from Union College, and the following year won notoriety for his book *The Hasheesh Eater* (1857), based on his own experiences as a drug addict. Among his periodical contributions was a series of descriptive sketches written during a tour of the West (1863) for the *Atlantic Monthly* and later collected as *The Heart of the Continent* (1870); an article on the effects of opium, "What Shall They Do To Be Saved?"; and the short stories collected in *Little Brother and Other Genre-Pictures* (1867).

LUHAN, MABEL DODGE (1879–1962), born at Buffalo, N.Y., severed her ties with her socially prominent family and became a leader of liberal intellectual and aesthetic movements. In Italy (1902–12) and in New York City (1912–18) she established salons to which were attracted Eleonora Duse, Gertrude Stein, Steffens, Isadora Duncan, John Reed, Walter Lippmann, Van Vechten, and Max Eastman. She moved to New Mexico (1918), and there in 1923 married her fourth

husband, Antonio Luhan, a Taos Indian. Her life at Taos is described with painful detail in several books. *Lorenzo in Taos* (1932) is an account of her turbulent intimacy with D.H. Lawrence, while *Winter in Taos* (1935) is a narrative of the region's background. Her autobiography, *Intimate Memories,* comprises four volumes, *Background* (1933), *European Experiences* (1935), *Movers and Shakers* (1936), and *Edge of Taos Desert* (1937).

LUMPKIN, GRACE, proletarian novelist, author of *To Make My Bread* (1932), the story of a North Carolina mill strike, which was dramatized by Albert Bein as *Let Freedom Ring* (1936). Her other novels include *A Sign for Cain* (1935), dealing with Southern sharecroppers, *The Wedding* (1939), and *Full Circle* (1962).

LURIE, ALISON (1926–), Chicago-born novelist, a member of the English department at Cornell, as is her husband. Her fiction, generally marked by quiet satire and dealing with the lives of academics and authors, includes *Love and Friendship* (1962), *The Nowhere City* (1965), *Imaginary Friends* (1967), *Real People* (1969), *The War Between the Tates* (1974), *Only Children* (1979), in which her usual complex relationships of people concentrates on children; and *Foreign Affairs* (1984), about two American professors of English, a man and a woman, on leave in London and experiencing it on very different levels. *The Language of Clothes* (1981) is a nonfictional study of the way people dress.

Lutherans, Protestants who adhere to the teachings of Martin Luther. The views of the Evangelical Church, which stem from his principles, are conservative as compared with those of the Reformed Church, based on Calvinistic doctrines. Luther emphasized the responsibility of the individual conscience to God alone, taught that the Scriptures are the only necessary guide to truth and that baptism is essential for regeneration, and permitted the retention of altars and vestments. A synodical form of church organization has developed, but the unity is one of doctrine rather than of organization, since each church makes its own decisions. The first Lutherans in America came to Manhattan from the Netherlands (1623). Another congregation was established in Delaware by Swedish settlers (1638). Others were attracted by the tolerance of the Quakers in Pennsylvania, but the creation of the first Lutheran synod and its independence from European affiliation resulted from the work of the German-born minister Heinrich Melchior Mühlenberg, who came to America in 1742. In 1980 there were more than eight and a half million Lutherans in the U.S.

Lyceums, popular societies for literary and scientific education. The first "American Lyceum" was founded at Millbury, Mass. (1826), by Josiah Holbrook, and under his leadership nearly 100 branches were established during the next two years, embodying his program of providing educational opportunities for adults, stimulating teacher-training and interest in schools, and founding museums and libraries. Eight years after Holbrook began the work, approximately 3000 lyceums had been founded in towns and cities throughout the U.S. The most notable was the Boston lyceum, with Daniel Webster as president. Among the popular and well-paid lyceum speakers were Emerson, whose essays were often first presented as lyceum lectures, Webster, Thoreau, Holmes, H.W. Beecher, Agassiz, Lowell, Clemens, and Barnum. Reform movements were stimulated by such lecturers as Garrison, Greeley, Lucy Stone, and Elizabeth Stanton. After 1890, Chautauqua♦ societies took the place of the original lyceums, which became centers of popular entertainment.

LYND, ROBERT S[TAUGHTON] (1892–1970), professor of sociology at Columbia, with his wife Helen Merrell Lynd (1896–1982) wrote *Middletown* (1929) and *Middletown in Transition* (1937), comprehensive sociological studies of a small American city (Muncie, Ind.), which she continued in *Update: Middletown Families: Fifty Years of Change and Continuity* (1982). *Middletown,* a television series based on the books, was produced in 1982 by Peter Davis, author of the novel *Hometown* (1982), set in a small Ohio town.

LYNES, [JOSEPH] RUSSELL [JR.] (1910–   ), graduated from Yale (1932), and was managing editor of *Harper's Magazine* (1947–67). His books include *Highbrow, Lowbrow, Middlebrow* (1949), a witty study of cultural levels; *Snobs* (1950), clever definitions; *Guests; or, How To Survive Hospitality* (1951); *The Tastemakers* (1954), an amusing interpretation of shapers of taste; *A Surfeit of Honey* (1957), on current U.S. manners and customs; *Cadwallader* (1959), a light fantasy about a cultivated rat resident at Columbia University; *The Domesticated Americans* (1963), a lively account of the American home of the 19th and 20th centuries; *The Art-Makers of Nineteenth-Century America* (1970), putting art and architecture in its social setting; and *Good Old Modern* (1973), on New York's Museum of Modern Art.

LYTLE, ANDREW NELSON (1902–   ), born in Tennessee, graduated from Vanderbilt, where he was part of the group active with *The Fugitive.*♦ He has taught history at Florida and the University of the South and edited *The Sewanee Review.* His books include *Bedford Forrest* (1931), a biography; *The Long Night* (1936) and *The Velvet Horn* (1957), novels set respectively just before and just after the Civil War; *At the Moon's Inn* (1941), a historical novel about De Soto; and *A Novel, A Novella, and Four Stories* (1958), reprinting *A Name for Evil* (1947), a ghost story about the restoration of a Southern mansion told with symbolic significance. *The Hero with the Private Parts* (1966) collects literary essays, and *A Wake for the Living* (1975) is his family chronicle.

M

Names beginning with "Mc" are placed as though beginning with "Mac."

McALMON, ROBERT (1896–1956), expatriate U.S. author, whose books, published mainly in France, made him a spokesman of the postwar nihilistic pessimists of the "lost generation." His poems in free verse were published in *Explorations* (1921), *The Portrait of a Generation* (1926), *North America, Continent of Conjecture* (1929), and *Not Alone Lost* (1937). *Village: As It Happened Through a Fifteen Year Period* (1924) is a group of impressionistic sketches showing the repressive effect of an American village on its youth, in the manner of Anderson's *Winesburg, Ohio. Being Geniuses Together* (1938) is his autobiography, extended (1968) by Kay Boyle,♦ who interspersed chapters of her own recollections. *McAlmon and the Lost Generation* (1962) is a self-portrait created by Robert E. Knoll from autobiographical fragments.

MacARTHUR, CHARLES (1895–1956), Pennsylvania-born playwright, as a journalist in Chicago was an intimate of its literary group. His plays include *Lulu Belle* (1926), written with his uncle Edward Sheldon♦; *Salvation* (1927), with Sidney Howard; and *The Front Page* (1928), *20th Century* (1932), and *Ladies and Gentlemen* (1939) with Ben Hecht, with whom he also wrote motion pictures. His wife, the actress Helen Hayes (1900–), has starred in Barrie's *What Every Woman Knows,* Housman's *Victoria Regina,* and Anderson's *Mary of Scotland. A Gift of Joy* (1965) is her autobiography.

MACAULEY, ROBIE [MAYHEW] (1919–), born in Michigan, graduated from Kenyon College (1941), to which he returned to become the editor of the *Kenyon Review* (1959–66). His writings include *The Disguises of Love* (1952), a novel about a psychology professor's extramarital affair and its impact upon him, his wife, and his son; *The End of Pity* (1957), stories; and *A Secret History of Time To Come* (1979), about human reversion to barbarism after a global war.

McCARTHY, CORMAC (1933–), novelist born in Rhode Island and educated in Tennessee, whose fiction includes *The Orchard Keeper* (1965), concerning life and a murder in the Great Smoky Mountains; *Outer Dark* (1968), another Gothic tale in a Southern setting, treating the wanderings of a woman searching for the son she had by her brother; *Child of God* (1974), presenting grotesque characters of the Kentucky backwoods; and *Suttree* (1979), about a loner in the violent tenderloin district of Knoxville.

McCARTHY, MARY [THERESE] (1912–), born in Seattle, was orphaned as a child and reared by diverse relatives, as she recalled in *Memories of a Catholic Girlhood* (1957). After graduation from Vassar (1933) she became a drama critic of the *Partisan Review,* and her reviews and articles from 1937 to 1956 were collected in *Sights and Spectacles* (1956). She also taught English briefly at Bard and at Sarah Lawrence College. She was wed to and divorced from Edmund Wilson. In 1984 she was awarded the National Medal for Literature. She has written *Venice Observed* (1956) and *The Stones of Florence* (1959), descriptive profiles of two cities she knows well, and has published literary essays in *On the Contrary* (1961), *The Writing on the Wall* (1970), and *Ideas and the Novel* (1980), but is best known for social commentary and fiction. Her novels are *The Company She Keeps* (1942), a witty portrait of a bohemian, intellectual young woman; *The Oasis* (1949), a brief satirical tale of a Utopia created by some intellectuals on a New England mountain top; *The Groves of Academe* (1952), a satirical portrait of faculty life at a liberal college for women; *A Charmed Life* (1955), set in an artists' colony where life is more destructive than creative; *The Group* (1963), about the misadventures of eight Vassar alumnae of 1933 in the 30 years after their graduation; *Birds of America* (1971), treating strained relations between a mother and son because of their different generations and values; and *Cannibals and Missionaries* (1979), depicting modern terrorism in an airplane hijacking. *Cast a Cold Eye* (1950) collects stories. *Vietnam* (1967), *Hanoi* (1968), and *Medina* (1972) are short books collected in *The Seventeenth Degree* (1974), about the U.S. war in Vietnam. *The Mask of State* (1974) contains portraits of persons involved in the Watergate scandal.

McCaslin family, characters in the fiction of Faulkner,♦ an old Jefferson (Mississippi) family figuring most prominently in the stories in *Go Down, Moses,* particularly "The Bear,"♦ in *Intruder in the Dust,*♦ and in *The Reivers,*♦ although frequently mentioned elsewhere. The McCaslin family perhaps embodies more clearly than any other single genealogy Faulkner's concern with the historical and moral implications of relations between the black and white races. A son of Lancaster McCaslin, Lucius Quintus Carothers ("old Carothers") McCaslin comes to Mississippi in 1813, buys land from the Chickasaw, and builds a plantation house near what is to become Jefferson. He legitimately fathers twin sons, Theophilus and Amodeus, and a daughter, Mary, but also takes a black mistress, his slave Eunice, and sires her daughter Tomasina (Tomey). This daughter dies while herself bearing him a son, Terrel (called Turl or Tomey's Turl), a relationship that leads Eunice to drown herself in despair upon learning of her daughter's incestuous pregnancy. In time Turl marries Tennie Beauchamp, a slave girl, and founds the black Beauchamp family. Theophilus (Uncle Buck) and Amodeus (Uncle Buddy), morally opposed to slavery, free the McCaslin blacks. Buck, long a confirmed bachelor, marries Sophonisba Beauchamp, sister of a neighboring plantation owner, and they have a child, Isaac (later Uncle Ike) McCaslin, who, born in 1867 and orphaned early (see *The Bear*), learns woodcraft and respect for nature from Sam Fathers, the Negro-Chickasaw bought long ago from Ikkemotubbe♦ by old Carothers. When he falls heir to the family estate, Isaac renounces the inheritance on grounds which he debates with McCaslin (Cass) Edmonds, the grandson of Mary McCaslin, who eventually inherits the lands. Having learned that old Carothers left legacies to his illegitimate grandchildren, Isaac tries to deliver the money to Tennie and Turl's surviving children, James Thucydides (Tennie's Jim), Sophonisba (Fonisba), and Lucas Beauchamp. Lucas wins in a showdown with Zachary (Zack) Edmonds, Cass's son and the new owner of the estate, over

the return of Lucas's wife Mollie from the main house, where she has nursed Zack's son Carothers (Roth) Edmonds. Later Lucas again is victorious, this time against a false murder charge. Lucas remains on the place and is the oldest descendant of old Carothers when Roth inherits the lands. Roth has an illegitimate son by a girl who, unbeknownst to him, is a granddaughter of Tennie's Jim, thus echoing his great-great-great-grandfather's original incest. When she appears with the child, Roth asks Isaac, now an old man, to send her away, and Isaac, in anger and despair at McCaslin behavior, laments, "No wonder the ruined woods don't cry for retribution! The people who destroyed it [the land] will accomplish its revenge."

McCLURE, MICHAEL [THOMAS] (1932–), Kansas-born author, long resident in San Francisco, with whose Beat movement♦ he has been associated. His personal and passionate poetry includes *Hymns to St. Geryon* (1959), *For Artaud* (1959), *Dark Brown* (1961), *September Blackberries* (1974), and *Fragments of Perseus* (1983). *Ghost Tantras* (1964) is verse meant for oral presentation, moving toward his dramas, of which the best known is *The Beard* (1967), an erotic conversation between the symbolized figures of Jean Harlow and Billy the Kid, while *Gorf* (1976) is another intense fantasy play. *Freewheelin Frank Secretary of the Angels* (1969) is an account of the Hell's Angels motorcyclists. *The Adept* (1971) is a novel about a cocaine dealer. *Scratching the Beat Surface* (1982) prints essays.

McClure's Magazine (1893–1929), popular monthly, was published and edited by S[amuel] S[idney] McClure (1857–1949), Irish-born publisher who in 1884 established the first newspaper syndicate in the U.S. and went on from that success to found the magazine that bore his name. It was intended to present at a small price the work of the most famous contemporary English and American authors, as well as to report current scientific knowledge and world affairs. It became a leading vehicle in muckraking♦ (1901–12), producing lively articles on complex subjects, and was a spearhead of the reform movement, investigating every aspect of American life. Contributors included O. Henry, F.P. Dunne, Jack London, and W.A. White, and among the leading articles were "The History of the Standard Oil Company," by Ida Tarbell; "The Shame of Minneapolis," by Lincoln Steffens; and "The Right to

Work," by R.S. Baker. Its period of significance passed with the waning of public enthusiasm for reform, and McClure's own success diminished. The work he called *My Autobiography* (1914) was written by Willa Cather.

McCONKEY, JAMES [RODNEY] (1921–), Ohio-born professor of English at Cornell (1956–) and author whose novels include *Crossroads* (1968), subtitled an "autobiographical novel" that in fragmented fictionized sketches presents moments of experience from boyhood on; *A Journey to Sakhalin* (1971), treating violent racial conflict on a campus like Cornell, its title alluding to a Russian concentration camp once visited by Chekhov; and *The Tree House Confessions* (1979), about a 50-year-old man remembering his past while visiting the tree house he once built for his now dead son. *Court of Memory* (1983) contains two series of meditative memoirs, the first published as *Crossroads*.

McCORD, DAVID [THOMPSON WATSON] (1897–), graduated from Harvard (1921) and was long an editor of its *Alumni Bulletin*. The many volumes of his light verse include *Bay Window Ballads* (1935), *On Occasion* (1943), and *Selected Poems* (1957), while familiar essays include *Oddly Enough* (1926), *Stirabout* (1928), and *About Boston* (1948). *One at a Time* (1977) collects five volumes of poems for children.

McCOY, HORACE (1897–1955), born in Tennessee, after service in World War I was for many years the sports editor of a Dallas newspaper but also spent time in Paris among expatriate U.S. writers, to whose little magazines he contributed. In 1931 he became a Hollywood screenwriter. His first novel, *They Shoot Horses, Don't They?* (1935), a first-person narrative of a man awaiting execution for the murder of his marathon dance partner, at her insistence, is a violent tale of sordid experience that won him a reputation, in France even more than in the U.S., as a serious writer in the vein of what was to be called existentialism. His other novels are *No Pockets in a Shroud* (1937), about crime and corruption in a seemingly decent American town; *I Should Have Stayed Home* (1938), about degradation in Hollywood; *Kiss Tomorrow Good-Bye* (1948), about a decent college graduate who seeks out a life of crime and brutality; and *Scalpel* (1952).

McCULLERS, CARSON [SMITH] (1917–67), was born in Georgia, where most of her works are set, although she was long resident in New York City. She immediately achieved great critical prominence with her first novel, *The Heart Is a Lonely Hunter*♦ (1940), in which a deaf-mute in a Southern town loses his only friend, another mute, and turns to others who give him their confidence, such as a lonely, music-loving girl, a black doctor, and a young radical. It was appreciated for its compassionate treatment of individualism and its sensitive style, and also because it was considered a symbolic commentary on fascism. Her second novel, *Reflections in a Golden Eye* (1941), is a shorter work, a macabre story of experiences in an army camp in the South before World War II. *The Member of the Wedding*♦ (1946) with great sensitivity presents the feelings of a 12-year-old girl on the occasion of her brother's impending wedding, and was successfully dramatized by the author in 1950. Her next work was also a play, *The Square Root of Wonderful* (1958), about the maturing of a woman twice married to and twice deserted by the same husband. Her next novel, *Clock Without Hands*♦ (1961), set in a small Georgia town, treats the involvements of some whites and a black boy, thereby illuminating her common theme, the discovery of selfhood. *The Ballad of the Sad Café*♦ (1951) collects stories and novels, the title work being dramatized by Edward Albee (1963), and *The Mortgaged Heart* (1971) collects early stories.

McCUTCHEON, GEORGE BARR (1866–1928), Indiana novelist, author of some 40 works of fiction within 28 years. His *Graustark* (1901) follows the style popularized by Anthony Hope's *Prisoner of Zenda* (1894) and deals with court intrigue in a fictional land, with high-flown romance between American heroes and titled heroines. This was followed by a series of romances dealing with the same mythical principality. His comic fantasy *Brewster's Millions* (1902) was equally popular and was successfully dramatized by Winchell Smith in 1906. He wrote one realistic novel of Midwestern life, *Mary Midthorne* (1911).

MACDONALD, DWIGHT (1906–82), after graduation from Yale and editorial posts on *Fortune* and *Partisan Review* founded his own journal, *Politics* (1944–49), as an organ of philosophical anarchism and pacifism. His later work on the staff of *The New Yorker* and as motion-picture critic for *Esquire* was more sociological than political. His books include *Henry Wallace: The Man and the Myth* (1948); *The Ford Foundation: The Man and the Millions* (1956); *Memoirs of a Revolutionist* (1957), essays in political criticism written over the previous 20 years; *Against the American Grain* (1963), sociocultural essays written from an astringent, minority point of view; *The Ghost of Conspiracy* (1965), a critique of the Warren Commission's report on President Kennedy's assassination; and *Discriminations* (1974), political and literary essays.

MacDONALD, JOHN D[ANN] (1916–), popular writer of mystery novels under his own name and several pseudonyms, some of the works featuring his detective Travis McGee. He has also written several works of science fiction. In addition to 65 novels (1946–80) said to have sold 70,000,000 copies, he has published 500 stories in magazines.

MacDONALD, ROSS, pseudonym of Kenneth Millar (1915–83), California-born novelist, reared in Canada. After graduation from the University of Western Ontario, naval service, and a Ph.D. from the University of Michigan, he published under his own name *The Dark Tunnel* (1944), a spy story set in Hitler's Germany. It was the beginning of a prolific career, best known for his hard-boiled detective novels set in southern California, featuring the private investigator Lew Archer and having as background generational differences in families. These works include *The Galton Case* (1959), *The Goodbye Look* (1964), *The Far Side of the Dollar* (1965), and *The Underground Man* (1971). *Self-Portrait* (1982) collects essays on ideas and experiences.

MacDowell Colony, founded (1907) by the pianist Marian Nevins MacDowell, wife of the composer Edward MacDowell, on their Peterborough, N.H., farm as a retreat for committee-selected authors, painters, musicians, and other artists to work in privacy in the Colony's 42 cabins and studios.

McFEE, WILLIAM [MORLEY PUNSHON] (1881–1966), born in London, was educated in England, and, following the family tradition, became a ship's engineer. His experiences furnished the material for *Letters from an Ocean Tramp* (1908, revised 1921). In 1911 he entered the American merchant marine and established his home in the U.S., although in World War I he served in the British navy. After the war he returned to the U.S. (1922), became an American citizen (1925), and settled at Westport, Conn. His novels include *Aliens* (1914, revised 1918), set in New Jersey, about British ships' officers and their families; *Casuals of the Sea* (1916), concerning a London family and its aimless struggles; *Captain Macedoine's Daughter* (1920), an adventure story with a Mediterranean setting, showing McFee's indebtedness to Joseph Conrad; *Command* (1922), about a ship's officer who is a nonentity until war experiences bring him self-knowledge and authority; *Race* (1924), portraying middle-class London life in the late 19th century; *Pilgrims of Adversity* (1928), an adventure novel set in Central and South America; *North of Suez* (1930), a romantic novel of the Near East; *The Harbourmaster* (1931), an exotic tale set in Salonika and South America; and *No Castle in Spain* (1933), a romance contrasting modern American standards with the traditions of a South American aristocrat. *Harbours of Memory* (1921) and *More Harbours of Memory* (1934) are sketches on travel and life at sea. *In the First Watch* (1946) is an account of McFee's early days on tramp steamers.

M'Fingal, mock epic by John Trumbull,♦ of which the first two cantos were published separately (1775–76) and the complete work in 1782. This burlesque, in four cantos of Hudibrastic couplets, satirizes the events of the year 1775, deals humorously with the leading figures of the Revolution, and presents the character of M'Fingal, a Tory New England squire whose arguments are so inept that he is entirely overwhelmed by Honorius (seemingly John Adams).

McGINLEY, PHYLLIS (1905–78), Oregon-born author of light verse, educated at the universities of Utah and California, resident in New York.

McGUANE, THOMAS [FRANCIS III] (1939–), Michigan-born author whose novels include *The Sporting Club* (1969), a fantastic satire about wealthy sportsmen and their Michigan forest club; *The Bushwhacked Piano* (1971), also marked by black humor in its tale of a young man rebelling against his Establishment background; *Ninety-Two in the Shade* (1973), a much darker story of fishermen guides in Florida; *Panama* (1979), a novelette about a rock musician on the way down; *Nobody's*

Angel (1982), set in Montana's cattle-ranching country, where he has long lived; and *Something To Be Desired* (1984), presenting a Montana rancher torn between love of his wife and a passionate woman who murdered her husband. *An Outside Chance* (1980) collects essays on McGuane's enthusiastic participation in sports. He has also written and directed films.

McGUFFEY, William Holmes (1800–1873), born in Pennsylvania, was educated in rural schools and was thought to be a prodigy because of his remarkable memorization. He graduated from Washington and Jefferson College (1826), taught school in Kentucky, and became professor of languages, philosophy, and philology at Miami University (Oxford, Ohio, 1826–36), president of Cincinnati College (1836–39) and Ohio University (1839–43), and professor at Woodward College, Cincinnati (1843–45), and the University of Virginia (1845–73). While at Miami, he began to compile his *Eclectic Readers,* six schoolbooks (1836–57) that combined literary lessons, obvious moral teachings, and carefully selected extracts from great English writers. Their estimated sales totaled 122,000,000 copies, and their constant use in mid-19th-century schools had a profound effect upon the moral and cultural shaping of the American mind.

McKAY, Claude (1890–1948), black author, emigrated from his native Jamaica to the U.S. (1912). His books include *Songs of Jamaica* (1912) and *Harlem Shadows* (1922), poems; and the virile novels, *Home to Harlem* (1928), the story of a black soldier deserting from the army in France to return to America; *Banjo* (1929), set on the Marseilles waterfront, where McKay worked for a time; and *Banana Bottom* (1933), about a black girl in Jamaica, who is torn between racial traditions and the education she has received in England. *Gingertown* (1932) collects short stories. His novels have sometimes been criticized for emphasizing the primitive and voluptuous aspects of black life dwelt upon by Van Vechten. *A Long Way from Home* (1937) is his autobiography. *Harlem: Negro Metropolis* (1940) is a sociological study.

McKENNEY, Ruth (1911–72), author of *My Sister Eileen* (1938), humorous sketches about the youth of her sister, later married to Nathanael West. This work was dramatized (1941) and made into the musical comedy *Wonderful Town* (1953). Other works on her family include *The McKenneys Carry On* (1940) and *The Loud Red Patrick* (1947). *Industrial Valley* (1939) is nonfiction about labor strife in Akron, and *Jake Home* (1943), a novel sympathetically treating a Communist labor organizer, deals with the Sacco-Vanzetti case.

McKUEN, Rod (1933–   ), popular author of sentimental poems and songs, native and resident of California. His books include *Stanyan Street and Other Sorrows* (1966), *Listen to the Warm* (1967), *Come to Me in Silence* (1973), and *Looking for a Friend* (1980). *Finding My Father* (1976) is a prose account of his quest for his unknown father.

MacLEISH, Archibald (1892–1982), born in Illinois, graduated from Yale (1915), served in World War I, and received his LL.B. from Harvard (1919), after which he practiced law. His poetic career falls into three principal divisions. The first, signalized by his expatriation in Europe (1923–28) and in part the result of his reactions to the war, extends from *Tower of Ivory* (1917) to *The Hamlet of A. MacLeish* (1928). These works, along with *The Happy Marriage* (1924), *The Pot of Earth♦* (1925), *Streets in the Moon* (1926), and *Nobodaddy* (1926), a verse drama, show the influence of Ezra Pound and T.S. Eliot, and are subjective in content. MacLeish's work at this time was a voice of the hopeless individual in a chaotic postwar world.

Upon his return to the Depression-ridden U.S., he showed, from the publication of *New Found Land* (1930) to *Frescoes for Mr. Rockefeller's City* (1933), a new attitude, in which his poetic influences were less obvious and his awareness of a national, social, and cultural heritage more sensitive and pronounced. *New Found Land* contains his poem "You, Andrew Marvell," addressing the 17th-century poet who heard "Time's wingèd chariot hurrying near," and, three centuries before MacLeish, discovered, in the words of the latter, that "the shadow of the night comes on . . ." to bury the struggling heart in final darkness. His main book of this period was *Conquistador* (1932, Pulitzer Prize), an epic of the conquest of Mexico, in which Díaz tells of the battles to win territory named "for the kings that bear no scars" and "the bishops, rich-men, generals, cocks-at-arms." The end of the period was marked by the collection of *Poems, 1924–1933* (1933).

In *Panic* (1935), a verse drama, he turned his attention to immediate social issues of the American scene, while in *Public Speech* (1936) he definitely announced his intention to take his part in collectivist social thought. This dual interest in drama and social ideas was extended in the radio plays in verse, *The Fall of the City* (1937), exposing totalitarian dictatorship as a hollow mockery of leadership, and *Air Raid* (1938), depicting the impersonal cruelty of modern warfare. He chose the medium of these works in accordance with his belief that "the imagination works better through the ear than through the eye." In *America Was Promises* (1939), he restated in poetry his theme of the need for action to save democracy, and *Colloquy for the States* (1943) is another poetic statement of patriotism.

Later poetry includes *Actfive* (1948); *Songs for Eve* (1954), lyrics; and *Collected Poems, 1917–1952* (1952, Pulitzer Prize). He returned to verse drama with *This Music Crept by Me Upon the Waters* (1953); *J.B.* (1958, Pulitzer Prize), treating Job's trials in a modern setting and idiom; *Herakles* (1967), relating aspects of the myth of Hercules to modern man; and *The Great American Fourth of July Parade* (1975), in which Adams and Jefferson comment on the U.S. of the 1970s. MacLeish brought together his poetry from 1917 onward in *New and Collected Poems* (1976). His prose includes *The Irresponsibles* (1940), an attack on American scholars and authors of the time for allegedly failing to take an active stand for democracy; *The American Cause* (1941), asserting the artist's usefulness in a democracy; *A Time To Speak* (1941) and *A Time To Act* (1943), addresses; *The American Story* (1944), radio sketches; and *Poetry and Opinion* (1950), *Poetry and Experience* (1960), *A Continuing Journey* (1968), and *Riders on the Earth* (1978), essays, addresses, memorials, and memoirs. *Scratch* (1971) is a prose dramatization of S.V. Benét's *The Devil and Daniel Webster.* ♦ *His Letters 1907 to 1982* was published in 1983. His many important posts included Librarian of Congress (1939–44), Assistant Secretary of State (1944–45), and Boylston Professor at Harvard (1949–62).

McPHEE, JOHN [ANGUS] (1931–), graduate of Princeton, where he has occasionally taught journalism, became a staff writer for *The New Yorker* in 1965. For its "Profiles" he has written on such diverse people as a professional basketball player from Princeton, the director of the Metropolitan Mu-

seum of Art, championship tennis stars, and a nuclear physicist, all reissued as books. His short books on natural history include *Oranges* (1967), on the botany, history, and industry of the fruit; *The Pine Barrens* (1968), about a wilderness area of New Jersey; *The Survival of the Bark Canoe* (1975); and the more substantial *Coming into the Country* (1977), about Alaska, *Basin and Range* (1981), studying the geology of the Utah-California region, and *La Place de la Concorde Suisse* (1984), about the Swiss army. These works too were first printed in *The New Yorker*.

McPHERSON, JAMES ALAN (1943–), Georgia-born author, after graduation from a local college and degrees from Harvard Law School and Iowa's writing curriculum became a professor of literature at the University of California, Santa Cruz, and then the University of Virginia, and wrote the short stories, mostly set in the South, published in *Hue and Cry* (1969) and *Elbow Room* (1977), the latter collection a Pulitzer Prize winner.

McTeague, novel by Frank Norris, ♦ published in 1899.

McTeague, a strong but stupid San Francisco dentist, marries Trina Sieppe, having met her through Marcus Schouler, her cousin and his friend. Trina wins $5000 in a lottery, and by careful saving, investment, and shrewd deception increases the sum. Schouler, who formerly hoped to marry Trina, feels he has been cheated of this fortune. In revenge he exposes McTeague's lack of either diploma or license, so that, forbidden to practice, he becomes mean and surly. Trina, grown miserly, refuses to let him use her money, and they sink into poverty. Greed, the motive underlying these events, also dominates the two figures of the subplot, Maria Macapa, a mad charwoman, and Zerkow, a Jewish junk dealer; fascinated by her obsession with a set of gold plate, he marries her, becomes insane, kills her, and commits suicide. Meanwhile McTeague has deserted Trina, stealing some of her savings. In an attempt to obtain the remainder, he murders her. Fleeing, he tries to cross Death Valley, where he is apprehended by Schouler. McTeague kills his captor, but before he dies the latter manages to handcuff their wrists together, so that McTeague is doomed to die of thirst, locked to the body of his enemy.

McWILLIAMS, CAREY (1905–80), California attorney and sociologist, whose books include *Ambrose Bierce* (1929), a biography; *Factories in the Field* (1939), a survey of migratory agricultural workers in California; *Ill Fares the Land* (1942), discussing changes in U.S. agriculture, especially the dislocation of workers; *Brothers Under the Skin* (1943), about nonwhite minorities in the U.S.; *Prejudice; Japanese-Americans: Symbols of Racial Intolerance* (1944); *A Mask for Privilege* (1948), about anti-Semitism in the U.S.; *North from Mexico* (1949), on Spanish-speaking people in the U.S.; *Witch Hunt* (1950), about civil rights; and *Southern California Country* (1946) and *California: The Great Exception* (1949), sociological analyses. *The Education of Carey McWilliams* (1979) is a memoir. He was editor of *The Nation* (1955–79).

Madame Butterfly, one-act tragedy (1900) by Belasco♦ and John Luther Long (1851–1927), adapted from a story by Long (1898). It was made into an opera by Puccini (1906).

　　Cho-Cho-San, a Japanese girl, has a liaison with Pinkerton, an American naval lieutenant, which she considers a marriage. For two years, with their infant son, she awaits his return. Then she finds he has married an American girl, and, realizing her status, kills herself.

Maggie: A Girl of the Streets, novel by Stephen Crane,♦ privately issued (1893) under the pseudonym Johnston Smith, but not regularly published until 1896.

　　In a slum district of New York City called Rum Alley, Maggie Johnson and her brother Jimmie are the maltreated and neglected children of a brutal workingman and his dipsomaniac wife. Maggie, attractive though ignorant and ill cared for, somehow preserves an inner core of innocence in her miserable, filthy environment. She finds work as a collar maker in a sweatshop, while Jimmie becomes a truck driver, typically hard-boiled and fight-loving. Their mother, now widowed, is constantly drunk and has acquired a lengthy police record. Maggie falls in love with Jimmie's tough friend Pete, a bartender, who easily seduces her. For a brief time she lives with Pete, having been melodramatically disowned by her mother. Jimmie offers only the questionable assistance of administering a beating to his former friend. Pete abandons Maggie, who becomes a prostitute for a few months. Then, heartbroken and unable to succeed in this uneasy, exacting occupation, she commits suicide. Her mother makes a great display of grief, sends Jimmie to fetch

home the body, and allows herself to be persuaded by her drinking companions to "forgive" her "bad, bad child."

Maggie Verver, heroine of *The Golden Bowl.* ♦

Magnalia Christi Americana, ecclesiastical history of New England by Cotton Mather,♦ published at London in 1702. The work is in seven parts: (1) the settlement of New England; (2) lives of the governors; (3) biographies of 60 famous divines; (4) an account of Harvard College, with the lives of some famous graduates; (5) a history of the Congregational Church in New England; (6) a record of remarkable providences, i.e. events in which God directly revealed His power in the colonies; and (7) a history of various disturbances in the churches, with an appendix on remarkable occurrences in the wars with the Indians (1688–98). The *Magnalia* reprints many of the author's sermons, biographies, and historical narratives, insofar as they could be worked into a rather loose general scheme. The unity of the whole appears in Mather's intention to exalt godliness and celebrate the triumphs of Christ in the New World. It is valuable as a historical source, and the second and third parts indicate Mather's most significant writing to be in the form of biography. The feeling that he was writing a religious epic, buried by the scholarship and digression, is seen in the epic line of the introduction, "I write the wonders of the Christian religion, flying from the depravations of Europe, to the American strand. . . ."

Magnificent Ambersons, The, novel by Tarkington,♦ published in 1918, won a Pulitzer Prize. It is the second part of the trilogy *Growth,* which also includes *The Turmoil* (1915) and *The Midlander* (1923).

Mahican Indians, Algonquian confederacy that originally occupied both banks of the upper Hudson River. Crowded by the white settlements, the Mahicans moved to Pennsylvania and thence with the Delawares to the Ohio region, where they were dispersed. The only Mahicans who have preserved the tribal identity are the Stockbridge Indians. In *The Last of the Mohicans* Cooper confuses Mahicans with Mohegans, ♦ with whom they were closely affiliated.

MAILER, Norman (1923–　), born in New Jersey, reared in Brooklyn, began writing fiction before graduation from Harvard (1943). After serving with the army in the Pacific he wrote *The Naked and the Dead*♦ (1948), a realistic and naturalistic novel of the fates of 13 men in an infantry platoon who survive the invasion of a Japanese-held island. Both a popular and a critical success, it was followed by two novels in which he turned from naturalistic to existential and allegorical views and which were far less well received: *Barbary Shore* (1951), a symbolic treatment of the conflict between leftist and rightist political forces in the U.S., and *The Deer Park* (1955, dramatized 1967), a bitter view of Hollywood as representative of the entire nation, seen through the stories of three men, a film director whose desire to create honest pictures is threatened by the rightist House Committee on Un-American Activities, an air force veteran who can find no significant place in the postwar society, and a pimp who is both ambitious and philosophic in the style of a modern Faust. Mailer next published *Advertisements for Myself* (1959), in which he not only collected fiction but began his authorship of distinguished nonfiction works analyzing aspects of his times, in this one concentrating on himself as author in the postwar setting. It was followed by *The Presidential Papers of Norman Mailer* (1963), whose diverse views include one of Kennedy in the position of President as hero. Mailer returned to fiction with *An American Dream*♦ (1965), a lurid depiction of a disintegrating marriage and a corrupt society, and the coruscating and symbolic *Why Are We in Vietnam?* (1967), in which an obsessed disc jockey in Texas tells of an Alaskan bear hunt made in his youth with his father and a friend, whose quest to prove masculinity and relish the kill is a commentary on America's foray into Vietnam. The investigation of American character in that novel also animated his succeeding nonfiction: *The Armies of the Night*♦ (1968, Pulitzer Prize), treating his experiences and reflections during a pacifist march on the Pentagon (1967); *Miami and the Siege of Chicago* (1968), his view of the current Republican and Democratic presidential conventions; *Of a Fire on the Moon* (1970), analyzing the lunar landings; *The Fight* (1975), his feelings about a world championship boxing match; and *The Executioner's Song* (1979, Pulitzer Prize), a very lengthy so-called true life novel about Gary Gilmore, a convicted murderer, the first person to be executed (1977) in the U.S. for more than a decade. Other nonfictional works are *Canni-*

bals and Christians (1966), mainly essays; *The Idol and the Octopus* (1968), about the contemporary political scene; *The Prisoner of Sex* (1971), a reply to a proponent of women's liberation; *Existential Errands* (1972), miscellaneous recent writings; *Marilyn* (1973), a speculative biography of the film star Marilyn Monroe; *Of Women and Their Elegance* (1980), an "imaginary memoir" of Marilyn Monroe; and *Pieces and Pontifications* (1982), brief writings and interviews from the preceding decade. *Some Honorable Men* (1975) collects his reports on national political conventions; *Genius and Lust* (1976) is an anthology of writings by Henry Miller with Mailer's critical commentary. Mailer returned to the novel with *Ancient Evenings* (1983), a lengthy tale of Egypt of some 3000 years ago, followed by *Tough Guys Don't Dance* (1984), a tough mystery story. Mailer collected his poems in *Death for the Ladies and Other Disasters* (1962) and his stories in *Short Fiction* (1967). *A Transit to Narcissus* (1978) is a facsimile of the typescript of a novel about life in a mental institution that he wrote at the age of 20.

Main Street, novel by Sinclair Lewis,♦ published in 1920 and dramatized in 1921 by Harvey O'Higgins♦ and Harriet Ford.

Carol Milford, a girl of quick intelligence but no particular talent, after graduation from college meets and marries Will Kennicott, a sober, kindly, unimaginative physician of Gopher Prairie, Minn., who tells her that the town needs her abilities. She finds the village to be a smug, intolerant, unimaginatively standardized place, where the people will not accept her efforts to create more sightly homes, organize a dramatic association, and otherwise improve the village life. A few characters stand above the apathy and provinciality of the rest: Vida Sherwin, the repressed and acidulous schoolteacher; Guy Pollock, the learned lawyer who has been entrapped by the "village virus"; and Miles Bjornstam, a laughing, iconoclastic Swedish vagabond. Carol draws away from her husband, falls in love with Erik Valborg, a kindred spirit, and finally goes to Washington to make her own life. When Kennicott comes for her, two years later, she returns with him, for, though she feels no love, she respects him, and being incapable of creating her own life appears not unhappy to return to the familiar, petty Gopher Prairie.

Main-Travelled Roads, short stories by Hamlin Garland,♦ published in 1891. Late examples of the school of local color, these tales deal with farm life in the Middle West. The volume is unified by the author's conception of "The Main-Travelled Road in the West," which "may lead past a bend in the river where the water laughs eternally over its shallows. . . . Mainly it is long and wearyful. . . . Like the main-travelled road of life it is traversed by many classes of people, but the poor and the weary predominate."

Maine Woods, The, autobiographical narrative by Thoreau,♦ posthumously published (1864) as edited by the younger W.E. Channing. It contains three accounts of trips to Maine: "Ktaadn" (*Union Magazine,* 1848), describing an excursion to Mt. Ktaadn in 1846; "Chesuncook" (*Atlantic Monthly,* 1858), about a journey from Bangor to Chesuncook Lake in 1853, with an Indian guide, Joe Aitteon; and "The Allegash and East Branch," concerned with a voyage (1857) with "a relative" and the Indian guide Joe Polis, from Bangor to the St. John's lakes by way of Moosehead and Chesuncook, returning by the East Branch of the Penobscot. During this excursion, Thoreau made an extended study of Polis, "one of the aristocracy" of the Penobscot Indians, a silent, capable hunter and backwoodsman.

Making of Americans, The, novel by Gertrude Stein,♦ written in 1906–8 and published in 1925. It deals with the wanderings and mental development of three generations of her own family, beginning as the history of a family's progress, but becoming the history of "everyone who ever was or is or will be living." The simple language is marked by recurrent phrases and other devices to create the feeling of a prolonged present and a constant "beginning again and again."

MALAMUD, BERNARD (1914–   ), born in Brooklyn of immigrant Russian parents, after graduation from the City College of New York and holding various odd jobs worked for an M.A. at Columbia while teaching night classes in a high school. His first novel, *The Natural* (1952), is a comic treatment of baseball in terms of a mythic view of the American hero. His second novel, *The Assistant*♦ (1957), is more realistic in its depiction of a pathetically unfortunate family of New York Jews and the assistant in their failing grocery store, but its treatment of the main character's search for the good life and his attempt to change himself is as much concerned with moral issues. His next novel, *A New Life* (1961), is both witty

and satirical in its treatment of the life of a Jewish professor of English literature at an Oregon "cow college," but it too presents the theme of a man changing his life. Later novels include *The Fixer*♦ (1967, National Book Award, Pulitzer Prize), the story, based on a Russian case in 1913, of a Jew falsely accused of murder and the resultant attempt to break his spirit and that of all Jews in the country; *Pictures of Fidelman* (1969), about a middle-aged Bronx resident who goes to Italy to be an artist; *The Tenants* (1971), treating conflicts between a white and a black writer, the sole residents of a Lower East Side tenement: *Dubin's Lives* (1979), about a famous author's marriage and love affair; and *God's Grace* (1982), a pseudo-Biblical fable about a man who is the sole human survivor of a nuclear war and begins a new civilization among apes. Malamud's stories, also often wryly treating unhappy experiences of Jews, are collected in *The Magic Barrel* (1958, National Book Award), *Idiots First* (1963), and *Rembrandt's Hat* (1973); 25 of them are reprinted in a selected *Stories* (1983). He has taught English at Oregon State University (1949–61) and at Bennington College (1961–   ).

MALCOLM X (MALCOLM LITTLE) (1925–65), Omaha-born militant black leader, a preacher in the Black Muslim religion until ousted (1963), when he founded a rival church, soon after which he was shot to death. *The Autobiography of Malcolm X* (1964) was told to Alex Haley.♦ *One Day, When I Was Lost* (1972) by James Baldwin is an unfilmed scenario of the *Autobiography.* Two volumes of his speeches have been published (1965, 1968).

MAMET, DAVID [ALAN] (1947–   ), Chicago playwright whose works include *Sexual Perversity in Chicago* and *Duck Variations,* two one-act plays (produced 1974, published 1977), lively comedies, respectively about two young men on the prowl for women and two loquacious old men who can't do much but talk. *American Buffalo* (1977) is a two-act naturalistic play presenting some petty criminals. *A Life in the Theater* (produced 1977, published 1978) is a one-act play depicting a seasoned actor and a young actor on and off stage with symbolic overtones about different ways of life. *Edmond* (1982) is a play about a middle-class New Yorker who leaves wife and home to find his true nature by experiencing life in the city's corrupt and violent underworld; and *Glengarry Glen Ross* (1984) presents tough, crooked real-estate salesmen.

He has also had several other plays produced but not published and wrote the film script for Cain's *The Postman Always Rings Twice.*

Man Against the Sky, The, ode by E.A. Robinson,♦ with a basic pentameter line and varying meters and rhymes, the title piece of a volume published in 1916.

A figure seen on a hilltop, against the sunset sky, symbolizes mankind looming "before the chaos and the glare As if he were the last god going home Unto his last desire." Conjecturing as to the attitude of mind of this solitary figure, the poet reviews the various *raisons d'être* advanced by philosophy, mysticism, common sense, and emotion, but indicates his skeptical view that men "Must each await alone at his own height Another darkness or another light. . . ." Life seems a "blind atomic pilgrimage," to which we are led by "crass chance," yet we have hints of some deeper meaning. This he conceives as "an orient Word that will not be erased," vouchsafed in "incommunicable gleams Too permanent for dreams." Earthbound and narrow-visioned, men gain only "a little wisdom and much pain"; but if they are to continue living they must cling to hope, realizing that "Eternity records Too vast an answer for the time-born words We spell. . . ."

Man That Corrupted Hadleyburg, The, story by Clemens,♦ published under his pseudonym Mark Twain as the title piece of a collection of essays and fiction (1900).

Hadleyburg is proud of its distinction as "the most honest and upright town in all the region round about." A stranger, offended in some way by its people, determines to ruin its reputation. He leaves a sack with bank cashier Edward Richards that he says contains a fortune in coins, and a note announcing that the money is to go to a townsman who once befriended him, and who can be identified by a remark he made, which is written on an enclosed paper. Nineteen of Hadleyburg's leading men receive notes pretending to divulge the remark. Scruples dissolve under this temptation, and even the hitherto honest Richards begins to think he may have made the remark. At a town meeting, 18 of the citizens are exposed to ridicule when the Rev. Mr. Burgess reads the notes setting forth their claims to the remark. Burgess has lost Richard's note, and the cashier becomes a hero. The victims pay an enormous sum to avoid having their names recorded on the lead slugs that prove to be

the sole contents of the sack, and this amount is given to Richards as a reward for his supposed integrity. Conscience destroys the health of the old man and his wife, who in their dying delirium expose their guilt; thus "the town was stripped of the last rag of its ancient glory."

Man with the Blue Guitar, The, title poem of a collection by Wallace Stevens,♦ published in 1937.

Divided into 33 parts, the poem, in four-stress unrhymed couplets, is constructed like variations played on a guitar. Suggested by Picasso's use of a guitar and the color blue, the poem is a statement by Stevens about the relations between reality (often symbolized by green), imagination (symbolized by blue), and understanding or interpretation through art. "Things as they are Are changed upon the blue guitar."

Man with the Golden Arm, The, novel by Nelson Algren,♦ published in 1949.

Francis Majcinek, called Frankie Machine, comes back to Chicago's Polish community from World War II with a Purple Heart and a morphine habit. In the seedy setting of Division Street he is a dealer in a poker parlor, and is known as the "Man with the Golden Arm," because of both his rapid reflexes and his drug addiction. His wife Sophia, called Zosh, has been crippled in an auto accident caused by Frankie's drunken driving and spends her dreary days making him feel guilty. In Molly Novotny, a sweet 20-year-old part-time prostitute, Frankie finds love and solace, but he remains trapped in his marriage and morphine habit. He accidentally breaks the neck of his drug supplier, Nifty Louie Fomorowski, and next gets caught committing a robbery with his friend Solly Saltskin, variously called "The Punk" or "The Sparrow." After serving a brief prison term for the latter offense he returns to his old haunts and to Molly, but when about to be arrested for the killing, he hangs himself just before the police arrive.

Man with the Hoe, The, poem by Edwin Markham. ♦

Man Without a Country, The, story by E.E. Hale,♦ published in the *Atlantic Monthly* (1863), reprinted in pamphlet form (1865), and collected in *If, Yes, and Perhaps* (1868). Written to inspire patriotism during the Civil War, it was suggested by the remark of Vallandigham, a former Ohio congressman, that he did not wish to live in a country that tolerated Lincoln's administration. Although entirely fictitious, the story has a realism reminiscent of Defoe. There was a real Philip Nolan, whose true history forms the basis of Hale's complementary novelette, *Philip Nolan's Friends* (1876). Arthur Guiterman adapted Hale's first story as a libretto for an opera by Damrosch (1937).

On trial with Aaron Burr for conspiracy, Philip Nolan cries out, "Damn the United States. I wish I may never hear of the United States again." The court-martial accordingly condemns him to a life at sea, where he will be denied any news of his country. His spirit is broken when one day he reads the lines from the *Lay of the Last Minstrel,*

> Breathes there a man with soul so dead
> Who never to himself hath said,
> "This is my own, my native land."

Thereafter he is a pathetic figure, desiring to aid the U.S. and showing great bravery in a sea battle during the War of 1812. After 57 years of exile, he dies happily, having learned of his country's increased greatness.

Mandan Indians, northern Plains tribe affiliated with the Arikara, combined bison hunting with agricultural pursuits. La Vérendrye visited the Mandan in 1738, and every later expedition up the Missouri knew them. By 1776 smallpox and attacks by neighboring tribes had reduced them to a single village. In 1870 they settled with other tribes on the Fort Berthold reservation in North Dakota. The Mandan figure in the journals of Lewis and Clark and are the subject of a study and many paintings by George Catlin.

MANFRED, FREDERICK (FREDERICK FEIKEMA) (1912–), Iowa-born author of Frisian ancestry who also called himself Feike Feikema (1944–51). He began his career as a journalist but in his thirties became a prolific novelist of his native region, which he calls Siouxland, the area of the Minnesota and South Dakota border. His energetic and also poetic novels, often primitive in vision and rough in style, include *The Golden Bowl* (1944), about a conflict between two generations of Midwest farmers; *Boy Almighty* (1945), a semi-autobiographical tale of a writer's life as a patient in a Midwest tuberculosis sanitarium; *This Is the Year* (1947), portraying a willful Frisian farmer; *The Chokecherry Tree* (1948), depicting an aspiring boy in conflict with Midwest society; *The Primitive* (1949), *The Brother* (1950), and *The Giant* (1951), gathered in the

trilogy *Wanderlust* (1962), about a farm boy who goes to New York; *Lord Grizzly* (1954), based on the life of the mountain man Hugh Glass; *Morning Red* (1956), treating journalism and politics in a small Minnesota town; *Riders of Judgment* (1957), about cattle wars in Wyoming during the 1890s; *Conquering Horse* (1959), presenting the adolescence of an Indian boy; *Scarlet Plume* (1964), about a white woman captured by the Sioux in 1862; *King of Spades* (1966), in part depicting the gold rush of the 1870s into the Black Hills of South Dakota; *Eden Prairie* (1968), a frank tale of the lives of Midwest rural schoolteachers in the 1920s; *The Manly-Hearted Woman* (1976), about Indian experiences of life and death; *Milk of Wolves* (1976), portraying a stonecutter who becomes a sculptor; *Green Earth* (1977), about a Frisian family of tenant farmers in Iowa at the opening of the 20th century; and *Sons of Adam* (1980), presenting the story of Cain and Abel in the Midwest of the Depression era. *Arrow of Love* (1961) and *Apples of Paradise* (1968) collect stories. *Winter Count* (1966) is a volume of poems. *The Wind Blows Free* (1980) is a memoir of hitchhiking from Iowa to the Rockies in the 1930s.

Manhattan Transfer, novel by John Dos Passos, ♦ published in 1925. It is marked by stylistic innovations, impressionistic descriptive effects, and a naturalistic attempt to depict the complex life of modern New York City. The careers of a dozen or more representative citizens are traced simultaneously, in a succession of brief dramatic episodes.

A country youth, Bud Korpenning, comes to the city to seek work, but after ten years of infrequent employment, and very close to starvation, commits suicide. Joe Harland, the "Wizard of Wall Street," loses fortune and power through excessive drinking and is reduced to common labor and beggary. Gus McNeil, a wealthy contractor, and Joe O'Keefe, a radical union organizer, exhibit the opposite ends of the scale in the building trades. Ellen Thatcher Oglethorpe, with various changes of name, rises from the lower middle class to become a featured actress, at the cost of integrity and happiness. Her first husband, John Oglethorpe, is a homosexual, whom she divorces. She endures the attentions of the impresario Harry Goldweiser, whom she despises. The one man she really loves, Stan Emery, takes to drink, marries another actress, and dies in an apartment-house fire. Ellen marries devoted Jimmy Herf, but even though they have a child and she quits the stage they cannot be happy and are soon divorced. Jimmy, a cousin of Joe Harland, has an unhappy, struggling career in journalism, which he leaves to begin life anew outside the city. These and such other characters as Congo Jake, the bootlegger, James Merivale, the banker and society man, George Baldwin, the unscrupulous lawyer and politician, and Cassandra Wilkins, the absurd aesthete, serve to illustrate the author's pessimistic view of the decadent city and to bind together his portrait of its teeming activity.

Mansion, The, novel by William Faulkner, ♦ published in 1959, the third of a trilogy including *The Hamlet* ♦ and *The Town.* ♦

In 1908 Mink Snopes, a poor sharecropper in Frenchman's Bend, Yoknapatawpha County, Mississippi, kills a rich neighbor in a dispute over a fee charged for pasturing his cow. Sent to prison, in part because his cousin Flem would not help him, Mink is determined to seek revenge. Meanwhile Flem has moved to Jefferson, become wealthy, and gained a respectable position as president of the Sartoris bank but, fearing Mink, concocts a plot to have another relative, Montgomery Ward Snopes, aid Mink to escape from prison in such a way that he will be captured and receive an added sentence. The plot fails, but Mink is reconfirmed in his belief in Old Moster, a personification of vengeance who "jest punishes," as he himself lives for the time when he can kill Flem. Linda Snopes, the daughter of Flem's wife Eula by her lover, is also intent on vengeance against her stepfather since Flem had cheated her of her inheritance and driven her mother to suicide. Linda is aided by her lawyer, Gavin Stevens, who has had a long-standing fight with the rest of the Snopes family. Through Gavin's efforts Mink is pardoned after 38 years of imprisonment. As soon as he is free he goes to Flem's mansion and kills him. Linda helps Mink to escape, as does Gavin, but, utterly spent, Mink "jest lay down" to sleep and to die.

MS. Found in a Bottle, story by Poe, ♦ published in 1833 and reprinted in *Tales of the Grotesque and Arabesque* (1840).

The narrator takes passage on a ship bound from Batavia to the Sunda Islands. During a terrible storm, the entire crew is swept overboard, except for this passenger and a Swedish sailor. The storm continues for several days, when suddenly a huge ship under full sail bears down on them, the narrator alone being saved by being hurled upon the rigging of the strange craft. This is the beginning of his long stay aboard the ship, whose aspect is unlike anything he has known, and whose ghostly sailors neither see nor speak to him. He writes a journal of his experiences, intending to seal it in a bottle and throw it into the sea "at the last moment." It concludes with a description of a fearful driving current and final whirlpool in which the ship is going down.

Maple, narrative poem in blank verse by Robert Frost, ♦ published in *New Hampshire* (1923).

Although others commonly misunderstand it as "Mabel," Maple, the name of a New England girl, given her at birth by her dying mother, guides her life and endows her with a mysterious poetic quality. Her father is unable or unwilling to make clear the intended meaning, and Maple is able to find only partial clues, but the man she marries discerns her kinship with the spirit of the trees, and they share this secret as a motive of their love.

Marble Faun, The, romance by Hawthorne, ♦ published in 1860. It was issued in England as *Transformation.*

Kenyon, an American sculptor, Hilda, a New England girl, and the mysterious Miriam are friends among the art students in Rome. They become acquainted with Donatello, Count of Monte Beni, a handsome Italian who resembles the Faun of Praxiteles, not only physically, but also in his mingling of human and animal qualities, his amoral attitude, and his simple enjoyment of the life of the senses. The dark, passionate Miriam is loved by Donatello, but she is haunted by an unrevealed sin and by the persecution of a mysterious man who dogs her footsteps after an accidental meeting in the Catacombs. Donatello is enraged by this man, and after an encouraging glance from Miriam flings him to his death from the Tarpeian Rock. Thereafter they are linked by their mutual guilt, which they keep secret. Donatello becomes brooding and conscience-stricken, and, though humanized by his suffering, is a broken spirit when he finally gives himself up to justice. Hilda, who saw the crime committed, is also involved in the sin until she forsakes Puritan tradition and pours out her secret at a church confessional. The unhappy Miriam disappears into the shadowy world from which she came, and Hilda and Kenyon are married.

Mardi: And a Voyage Thither, allegorical romance by Melville,♦ published in 1849.

Taji, the hero, and his Norse companion Jarl desert from a whaling ship in southern Pacific waters and meet the brigantine *Parki,* abandoned except for the comic Polynesian husband and wife, Samoa and Annatoo. The four pass pleasant days aboard the *Parki,* until it sinks during a storm and Annatoo is drowned. Adrift in a whaleboat, Taji, Jarl, and Samoa meet a native priest and his ward, the mysterious white maiden Yillah, whom he is taking to be sacrificed. They rescue the maiden and reach Mardi, the realm of transcendental beauty, where Taji and Yillah spend a blissful period in love. When she suddenly vanishes, beauty and delight are also gone, and Taji searches for her through the islands of Mardi. He is accompanied by Media, king of Odo, Mohi (Braidbeard) the historian, Babbalanja the philosopher, and Yoomy the poet; as they travel, they discourse on many topics, and their search brings them to Dominora (Great Britain), Vivenza (the U.S.), and other lands, which are the subjects of Swiftian satire. They also visit Serenia, ruled by Alma (Christ), in whose doctrine of love Babbalanja finds the ultimate in earthly wisdom, but Taji, seeing the doctrine disregarded in practice, remains dissatisfied. At last they reach Flozella-a-Nina, where Queen Hautia has transformed Yillah into one of her dusky handmaidens. Hautia nearly overwhelms Taji by her sensual blandishments, but, leaving his companions, he sets sail alone, pursued by "three fixed spectres," to continue his search "over an endless sea."

Marginalia, brief critical notes published by Poe♦ in various periodicals, including *Graham's Magazine* and the *Southern Literary Messenger,* during the 1840s. These were frequently excerpts from previously published reviews and articles, and dealt with such diverse subjects as "Defoe," "The Drama," "Antigone," "Plagiarism," "Rhetoric," "The Dash," and "Men of Genius."

MARK TWAIN, pseudonym of Samuel L. Clemens.♦ The name, a phrase meaning "two fathoms deep," was employed in making soundings on Mississippi riverboats. According to Clemens's questionable account in *Life on the Mississippi,* the name had been used previously by an older pilot, Isaiah Sellers (1803–64), to sign the pompous articles he contributed to the *New Orleans Picayune.* Clemens claims he burlesqued these in the New Orleans *True Delta* and that the parody so affected Sellers that he never published again. Therefore, Clemens declares, he adopted the name as a form of reparation. In that account he also paid tribute to Sellers as "the patriarch of the craft" of steamboat piloting. Clemens's first-known use of the name occurs in a contribution to the Virginia City *Territorial Enterprise* on February 3, 1863.

MARKFIELD, WALLACE (1926–), Brooklyn-born novelist whose books include *To an Early Grave* (1964), a wry, comic view of New York's Jewish intellectual life; *Teitlebaum's Window* (1970), a story of a boy growing up in Brooklyn during the 1930s; and *You Could Live It If They Let You* (1974), another treatment of New York Jewish experience.

MARKHAM, EDWIN [CHARLES] (1852–1940), Oregon-born poet, lived in California (1857–1901), where he became a schoolteacher. He won widespread popularity for the title poem of *The Man with the Hoe and Other Poems* (1899), inspired by Millet's painting. This blank-verse depiction of a brutalized farmer, "bowed by the weight of centuries . . . The emptiness of ages in his face," is a somewhat rhetorical protest against the degradation of exploited labor. *Lincoln and Other Poems* (1901), in the same vein, was also very popular. His many later volumes are generally mediocre, marked by a lofty and occasionally tumid melody. The character Presley in Norris's *The Octopus*♦ is said to represent Markham.

MARQUAND, J[OHN] P[HILLIPS] (1893–1960), Massachusetts author, born in Wilmington, Del., whose literary career began with popular romances, including *The Unspeakable Gentleman* (1922), *The Black Cargo* (1925), *Warning Hill* (1930), and *Ming Yellow* (1935), and detective stories about Mr. Moto, a Japanese sleuth. His more serious comedies of manners, often observing the struggle between inherited conformity and personal desire, include *The Late George Apley*♦ (1937, Pulitzer Prize), a supposed memoir of Boston Brahmin life; *Wickford Point* (1939), a similar satire of a New England family; *H. M. Pulham, Esquire* (1941), about a New Englander 25 years out of college; *So Little Time* (1943), about a play doctor who regrets an uncreative career; *B. F.'s Daughter* (1946), characterizing an industrialist's daughter who tries to dominate her husband; *Point of No Return* (1949), about a middle-aged banker, no longer able to turn from his path of materialism; *Melville Goodwin, USA* (1951), tracing the stultifying career of an army officer; *Sincerely, Willis Wayde* (1955), an ironic character study of an egocentric tycoon's rise to power; and *Women and Thomas Harrow* (1958), presenting a New Englander, once a successful dramatist, as he remembers his first wife and his happier past. *Lord Timothy Dexter* (1925) is the life of an 18th-century New England eccentric, and *Timothy Dexter Revisited* (1960) adds autobiographical information about Dexter's, and Marquand's, hometown, Newburyport. *Thirty Years* (1954) collects stories and articles, and *Life at Happy Knoll* (1957) assembles sketches in epistolary form about the problems of a country club.

MARQUIS, Don[ALD ROBERT PERRY] (1878–1937), Illinois-born journalist in Atlanta (1902–9) and New York (1909–22), became noted as a humorist through his columns, "The Sun Dial" in the New York *Sun* and "The Lantern" in the New York *Tribune*. His most famous works are *The Old Soak* (1921), which he dramatized successfully in 1922, "a kind of gol-dinged autobiography of what me and Old King Booze done before he went into the grave and took one of my feet with him"; and *archy and mehitabel*♦ (1927) and its sequels, which provided a medium for Marquis's opinions on contemporary life. His mordant satire, in the vein of Mark Twain, also appears in *Hermione and Her Little Group of Serious Thinkers* (1916); *Carter and Other People* (1921), including sketches of black characters and the ironic one-act play "Words and Thoughts"; *The Revolt of the Oyster* (1922), stories; *The Old Soak's History of the World* (1924); *The Almost Perfect State* (1927); *A Variety of People* (1929), stories; *Off the Arm* (1930), a novel set in Paris, Hollywood, and New York; *Chapters for the Orthodox* (1934), stories; and *Master of the Revels* (1934), a four-act comedy set in Tudor times. His books of humorous verse, besides those dealing with archy, include *Noah an' Jonah an' Cap'n John Smith* (1921); *Sonnets to a Red-Haired Lady (by a Gentleman with a Blue Beard) and Famous Love Affairs* (1922); and *Love Sonnets of a Cave Man* (1928). Marquis was less successful with his serious works, including an unfinished autobiographical novel, *Sons of the Puritans* (1939).

Marshes of Glynn, The, poem by Lanier,♦ published anonymously in the anthology *A Masque of Poets* (1878). It is one of six projected "Hymns of the Marshes," of which the poet completed only three others, "Sunrise," "Individuality," and "Marsh-Song—At Sunset." In anapestic measure, it employs shifting accents, initial truncation, and from one to 17 syllables in a line, to achieve a musical cadence. The poem describes the sea marshes of Glynn County, Georgia, where the author is stimulated to a pagan ecstasy:

> Oh, what is abroad in the marsh and the terminal sea?
> 　　Somehow my soul seems suddenly free
> From the weighing of fate and the sad discussion of sin,
> By the length and the breadth and the sweep of the marshes of Glynn.

Martin Chuzzlewit, The Life and Adventures of, novel by Dickens,♦ published in 1844. It was partially an outgrowth of his American tour (1842).

Martin, the grandson of wealthy, misanthropic old Martin Chuzzlewit, is in love with Mary Graham, his granfather's ward. When the old man refuses to allow him to marry Mary and has him dismissed from his position with his cousin, the architect Pecksniff, Martin sails to the U.S. to make his fortune, accompanied by Mark Tapley, his servant. He is defrauded in his work as an architect for the Eden Land Corporation (Cairo, Ill.), loses his money, and nearly dies of a fever. The example of his devoted, cheerful servant, also stricken, teaches him unselfishness. When he returns to England, his grandfather appreciates his newly revealed good qualities, becomes aware of the hypocritical Pecksniff's meanness and treachery, and gives his blessing to the wedding of young Martin and Mary.

Martin Eden, novel by Jack London,♦ published in 1909.

Like the author, the hero is a sailor and laborer whose endurance and intellectual curiosity lead him to educate himself so that he may share what he conceives to be the fine, high-thinking life of the wealthy bourgeoisie. He is inspired by Ruth Morse, a college-trained society girl, to him a symbol of what he considers are the values of her class. He becomes a writer, expressing the view of life to which his reading of Spencer has guided him, but only Russ Brissenden, a socialist poet (said to be based on George Sterling), understands the power and beauty of his work. His fiancée Ruth, like her family and class, "worshipping at the shrine of the established" and financially successful, deserts him, believing him a failure when magazines will not buy his writing, and is outraged by the notoriety attaching to a newspaper's false accusation that he is a socialist. When one of his books makes him wealthy and famous, she attempts to resume their engagement, but his love is killed by recognition that she really admires only his acclaim and financial success. This realization, the suicide of Brissenden, the loss of affiliation with his own class, and the contempt for the values of the class to which he has climbed rob him of his zest for living. He makes a voyage to the South Seas, and, his will to live destroyed, jumps from the ship and drowns.

MARTINEAU, HARRIET (1802–76), English author, wrote popularizations of social, philosophic, and economic subjects, as well as novels and stories for children. In 1834–36 she traveled from New England and New York to the Great Lakes and New Orleans. Returning to England, she published *Society in America* (1837), a study of American economic, political, and social institutions, and *Retrospect of Western Travel* (1838), sketches of her experiences. The latter was entertainingly written and had a popular success, but the former, although sympathizing in general with American principles, was antagonistic toward the South. A typical reply was Simms's *Slavery in America* (1838), which not only attacked Miss Martineau's ideas, but also vilified her character and made sport of her deafness. Although adversely criticized in *Blackwood's,* her book was well received in England and was among the most popular of her 52 volumes. Her *Autobiography* (1877) was edited by her friend Maria W. Chapman.

Mason, PERRY, hero of many detective stories by Erle Stanley Gardner. ♦

Masque of the Red Death, The, story by Poe, ♦ published in *Graham's Magazine* (1842).

In a land devastated by a horrible plague, the "Red Death," Prince Prospero determines to preserve himself and his friends, and removes to a secluded castle, where, with 1000 knights and ladies, he spends several months in extravagantly gay pursuits. At a masquerade in the imperial suite, when the courtiers appear in masks and fantastic costumes, a terrifying corpse-like figure joins them, garbed as the Red Death. Attempting to stab him, the Prince dies; when others seize the apparition, it is discovered to have no tangible body. They realize that this is the Red Death itself, and, as midnight strikes, they die: "and Darkness and Decay and the Red Death held illimitable dominion over all."

Massachuset Indians, tribe or tribes of Algonquian stock, inhabited the New England coast at the arrival of the white colonists, although their power was already on the decline. John Eliot ♦ preached to them, and they joined the Praying Indians. ♦

Massachusetts Bay Company, English chartered company, organized for trading and settlement as a large colonial counterpart to Virginia, with a Puritan flavor. In 1628 it received a new patent, from Gorge's Council for New England, with a grant of land between the Charles and Merrimac rivers, extending indefinitely westward. The royal charter (1629) confirming the patent was given entirely into the hands of the settlers who arrived (1630) at Salem and later at Boston. Self-government was conducted by a governor and General Court, although suffrage was extended only to church members. The Crown's objections to the colony's coining of money, suffrage restrictions, extension of authority over Maine and New Hampshire, refusal to comply with the Navigation Acts, and general independence led to the rescinding of the charter (1684), when the colony joined with that at Plymouth. ♦ The original settlers of the Bay Colony were Puritans, as distinguished from the Plymouth Separatists. The leading governors were John Endecott and John Winthrop, ♦ and the latter kept an important journal on the voyage and the founding. The Company's records have also been published.

Massachusetts Historical Society, founded in 1791 by Jeremy Belknap and other historical scholars, whose gift of books and manuscripts became the nucleus of its present great collection. This, the first organization of its kind in the U.S., began to make available its Americana by publishing volumes of collections, augmented by a series of *Proceedings* and special publications. Among the many notable documents thus published for the first time are Bradford's *History of Plimmoth Plantation* and *The Diary and Letter Books of Samuel Sewall.* Its collections were first published in the *American Apollo* (1792–94), a Federalist weekly newspaper.

Masses, The (1911–53), weekly journal of news and social criticism, founded at New York by Piet Vlag as "an outgrowth of the cooperative side of Socialist activity." Under the editorship of Thomas Seltzer, it pursued no consistent political policy, and stressed literature with a liberal bias, drawing largely upon European fiction by such authors as Sudermann and Bjorkman. In 1912 Max Eastman became editor, assisted by Floyd Dell, John Reed, and others, and the magazine followed a more consistently Socialist policy, until it was suppressed by the government (Dec. 1918). Three months later, the editors founded *The Liberator*, a weekly journal of social criticism with an increasingly radical point of view. In 1922 the staff voted to affiliate the magazine with the Communist party. Suspended in 1924, it was revived in 1926 as the *New Masses* and combined the political views of *The Liberator* and the aesthetics of *The Masses*. In 1948 it merged with another Marxist journal to become the monthly *Masses and Mainstream*.

MASTERS, Edgar Lee (1868?–1950), Kansas-born lawyer in Chicago (1891–1920), was suddenly catapulted into fame with the publication of *Spoon River Anthology* (1915), free-verse epitaphs revealing the secret lives of persons, fictive and historical, buried in a Midwestern cemetery. Masters did not again achieve the directness and simplicity that characterize these poems, although he employed the same method in *The New Spoon River* (1924), a bitter commentary on the vicious urban standards of changing America. *Domesday Book* (1920) and its sequel, *The Fate of the Jury* (1929), are considered to be among the best of his later poetry. His prose books include novels based on his youth; *Children of the Market Place* (1922), a novel about Stephen Douglas; and such biographical studies as *Lincoln, the Man* (1931), bitterly attacking its subject, *Vachel Lindsay* (1935), *Walt Whitman* (1937), and *Mark Twain* (1938), the last presenting Clemens as a frustrated genius. *Across Spoon River* (1936) is an autobiography.

MATHER, Cotton (1663–1728), eldest son of Increase Mather, and grandson of Richard Mather and John Cotton, was so impressed by his heritage that he not only thought of himself as the destined leader of the Mas-

sachusetts church and state, but attempted to recapture the spirit of his forefathers in a time when such a spirit was no longer progressive. He entered Harvard at the age of 12, the youngest student ever admitted, and was justifiably considered a prig by his fellows. After some study of medicine, he prepared for the church, received an M.A. (1681), and assisted his father at the Second Church in Boston, where he was co-minister until 1723, and afterward minister. When his father went to England to plead for the restoration of the Massachusetts charter, Cotton conducted the church and worked at home for the same political ends, writing the manifesto *The Declaration of the Gentlemen, Merchants, and Inhabitants of Boston* (1689). He had now written some dozen works, given evidence of being a great preacher, and been made an overseer of Harvard.

When his father returned with the new charter and the new governor, Phips, Cotton wrote much to defend both, two of his works being *Political Fables* and *Pietas in Patriam* (1697), a life of Phips. The latter began the investigation known as the Salem witchcraft trials,♦ in which Mather became fervently interested. Although he believed that the possessed persons should be treated by fasting and prayer, rather than executed, he affirmed the justice of the verdicts and made no public protest except in his semi-scientific writings. *Memorable Providences, Relating to Witchcrafts and Possessions* (1689) was an early study of a victim whom he took into his home. *The Wonders of the Invisible World* (1693) was a narrative of some of the Salem trials, containing theological observations on the operations of devils. This was answered by Robert Calef, a rationalist opponent of the Mather influence in church and state. Mather was himself as rational as Calef, as may be seen in his scientific interests and writings, recognized by his election to the Royal Society of England (1714), and in his statement of opposition to the methods of the witchcraft trials in his *Magnalia Christi Americana♦* (1702). Nevertheless, his aggressiveness in controversy, arrogant manner, and indication that he felt himself to be the political and religious leader of Massachusetts, all made him the butt of the critics of the Salem trials.

His inability to succeed his father as president of Harvard or to control Governor Joseph Dudley, and his general conservatism in a period of change, made him feel that many of his ambitions were frustrated, even though he remained a great power in the church. His irritable nerves were overtaxed by his indefatigable industry, and he was given to transports of religious feeling, which sometimes seemed self-conscious attempts to prove the existence of a saintly fire within him. On the other hand, he showed himself in harmony with the new age by championing smallpox inoculation, urging tolerance in the ministry in his *Manuductio ad Ministerium* (1726), and propounding ideas looking toward deism in his *Christian Philosopher* (1721). Possessing a library of nearly 2000 volumes, he was probably more widely read than any other American of his time, and he knew seven languages well.

His writing was scholarly, sometimes pedantic, and exhibited a zeal which occasionally led him into specious reasoning. His more than 450 works include histories, biographies, essays, sermons, fables, verses, theological treatises, philosophy, science, medicine, and practical piety. He had a definite theory of style, believing that though a work should be replete with allusions and quotations, richness of content was more important than elegance of expression; and that the chief function of writing being instruction, the more information it conveyed the better its style. Among his important writings are *The Present State of New England* (1690); *Some Few Remarks upon a Scandalous Book . . . by One Robert Calef* (1701); *The Negro Christianized* (1706); *The Good Education of Children* (1708); *Bonifacius* (1710), usually called *Essays To Do Good; Psalterium Americanum* (1718), a translation of the psalms; *An Account . . . of Inoculating the Small-Pox* (1722); *The Angel of Bethesda* (1722), a medical manual; and *Parentator* (1724), a biography of his father. His enormous *Diary* has been published in seven volumes by the Massachusetts Historical Society (1911–12).

MATHER, INCREASE (1639–1723), youngest son of Richard Mather, was reared in the strict Puritan tradition of his father's household, educated at Harvard (1656), and received an M.A. from Trinity College, Dublin (1658). He preached in England at Congregational churches, until the Restoration and the return to Anglicanism forced him to quit England for his native land. He became teacher of the Second Church in Boston (1664), where he worked fervently until his death. His intellectual activities outside of the church may be judged from his publication of some 25 books before 1683, his organization of a society to discuss scientific matters, and

his central position in many types of Massachusetts activities. After having once refused the presidency of Harvard College, by placing his duty to his church before anything else, he was nevertheless appointed acting president in 1685, and the following year took complete charge with the title of Rector. During his presidency to 1701, he encouraged scientific study, while at the same time resisting all efforts to undermine the college's fundamental Congregationalism.

In 1688 he sailed for England, after having been appointed by the Congregational churches to bring a petition in the matter of the abrogated colonial charter. His interviews with James II came to naught when the king was deposed by the Revolution of 1688, but he continued to appeal to William III, and in 1690 was made an official representative of the colonial government. His work was successful, for Governor Andros was replaced by Sir William Phips, and a new charter gave the colonists some of the powers they demanded.

After his return his power waned, since many rebelled against his influence in church and state, were dissatisfied with the charter, and in time opposed the attitude of Phips and himself in the Salem witchcraft trials. ♦ The witchcraft excitement had begun before his return, but, though he avoided the matter for some time, he was accused by Calef and others of responsibility for Phips's actions. Actually, Mather's book *Cases of Conscience Concerning Evil Spirits* (1693) disapproved the emphasis the court put on "spectral evidence," and generally had the attitude that it was better for a guilty witch to escape than for an innocent man to die. His rational point of view may also be seen in his championship of the unpopular cause of inoculation during a smallpox epidemic.

Although he was by no means as bigoted as later popular opinion has claimed, he was firmly convinced of the rectitude of his own ideas, and supported them by his hot temper and tremendous power, in the belief that what he did was for the public good. He was the author of some 130 books, and contributed to more than 65 works by others. His style was simple, strong, and direct, although without brilliance. The works, which sweep the entire circuit of sacred and secular themes of the day, include *Life and Death of That Reverend Man of God, Mr. Richard Mather* (1670); *A Brief History of the War with the Indians* (1676); *An Essay for the Recording of Illustrious Providences* (1684), generally known as *Remarkable Providences;* and many political tracts. *Parentator* (1724), his biography, was written by his son Cotton Mather.

MATHER, Richard (1596–1669), preached in England until 1633, when he was suspended from the ministry for his Puritanism. Stimulated by John Cotton and Thomas Hooker, he emigrated to Massachusetts Bay (1635) and the following year became teacher of the church in Dorchester, where he continued his ministry until his death. He was a prominent preacher and a leader in the development of the church polity. His anonymously published works included *Church-Government and Church-Covenant Discussed* (1643), the earliest complete exposition of the New England theory of the church, and *Apologie of the Churches in New-England for Church Covenant* (1643), arguing for a covenant of members as the basis of the Congregational Church. With John Eliot and Thomas Welde, Mather was an author of the *Bay Psalm Book*♦ (1640). His most important work was the original draft of *A Platform of Church-Discipline* (1649), the celebrated Cambridge Platform, which was the basic statement of New England Congregationalism. He was the author of many other works and was the subject of biographies by his son Increase and his grandson Cotton, being famous as the founder of the "Mather Dynasty" in New England.

MATHEWS, Harry (1930–), New York City-born author, long expatriated in France, whose esoteric, experimental works include short novels concerned with curiously convoluted quests. *The Conversions* (1962) presents a person who can inherit a huge fortune if able to answer three recondite riddles. *Tlooth* (1966), also told by an obscure narrator, is a kind of plotless story of a search for revenge. *The Sinking of the Odradek Stadium* (1975) is an odd epistolary account of a search for treasure. *Selected Declarations of Dependence* (1977) prints a novella and "Proverbs and Paraphrases." *The Ring* (1970), *The Planisphere* (1974), and *Trial Impressions* (1977) collect poems. *Country Cooking* (1981) gathers stories.

MATTHIESSEN, F[rancis] O[tto] (1902–50), graduated from Yale, was a Rhodes Scholar, and received a Ph.D. from Harvard before becoming an instructor at Yale (1927–29) and professor at Harvard (1929–50). An influential teacher, he was liberal in politics, deeply religious, and incisive in literary judgments. His books include *Sarah Orne Jewett*

(1929); *The Achievement of T.S. Eliot* (1935, revised 1947); *American Renaissance*♦ (1941), analyzing "art and expression in the age of Emerson and Whitman"; *Henry James: The Major Phase* (1944); *The James Family* (1947); *The Notebooks of Henry James* (1947), with Kenneth Murdock; *From the Heart of Europe* (1948); *The Oxford Book of American Verse* (1950); and *Theodore Dreiser* (1951).

MATTHIESSEN, Peter (1927–), began his literary career with three short novels, *Race Rock* (1954), *Partisans* (1955), and *Raditzer* (1960), followed by *The Cloud Forest* (1961), recording his observations of primitive people and wild fauna in the wilderness of South America; *Under the Mountain Wall* (1963), dealing with his experience of a savage tribe in New Guinea; *Oomingmark* (1967), concerning an expedition, of which he was a member, to a Bering Sea island, searching for a rare breed of musk ox; *Blue Meridian* (1971), about another expedition, this one for a great white shark; *The Tree Where Man Was Born* (1972), dealing with his trips to East Africa; *The Snow Leopard* (1978, National Book Award), telling of his trek to Tibet in quest of enlightenment; and *Sand Rivers* (1981), about a safari in Tanzania. His travels through the U.S. to observe the spoliation of Indian lands resulted in *Indian Country* (1984). *Sal si Puedes* (1970) is a profile of Cesar Chavez. A novel, *At Play in the Fields of the Lord* (1965), deals with missionaries and other outsiders, who for their own, diverse reasons despoil the culture of an Indian tribe in the Amazon jungle.

Mauberley, see *Hugh Selwyn Mauberley*.

Maud Miller, poetic idyll in four-stress couplets by Whittier,♦ published in 1854 and collected in *The Panorama and Other Poems* (1856). It tells of the brief meeting of a wealthy judge with the rustic maiden Maud Muller, of their momentary thoughts of love, and of the memories of the incident that recur during their years of toil and disappointment.

MAULDIN, Bill (William H. Mauldin) (1921–), New Mexico-born cartoonist, famous for his realistic, bitterly humorous drawings of front-line soldiers in World War II, printed with his complementary text on army life and war in *Up Front* (1945). After the war he extended his subjects in *Back Home* (1946), wrote *A Sort of a Saga* (1949), about his youth, created cartoons of the

Korean War, and became a newspaper cartoonist of current events, collecting his work in such books as *What's Got Your Back Up?* (1961).

Maximus Poems, The, see *Olson, Charles.*

MAXWELL, WILLIAM (1908–), born in Illinois, graduated from the state university and, after an M.A. from Harvard, taught there briefly before trying his hand at a variety of jobs, including editorial work for *The New Yorker.* His novels include *Bright Center of Heaven* (1934); *They Came Like Swallows* (1937), about a woman of character and warmth who helps diverse people and leaves them to find themselves upon her death; *The Folded Leaf* (1945), quietly and tenderly treating the lives of two boys who are friends through school and college; *Time Will Darken It* (1948), about an impossibly idealistic man, set in Illinois in 1912; *The Château* (1961); *The Old Man at the Railroad Crossing* (1966); and *So Long, See You Tomorrow* (1979), about two 13-year-old boys whose friendship is abruptly ended after a murder in their Midwestern town. *Over by the River* (1977) collects stories. *Ancestors* (1971) is a history of the author's forebears and their religious views. *The Writer as Illusionist* (1955) studies fiction.

May-Day, title piece of a volume of poems by Emerson,♦ published in 1867. It is a rhapsodic ode in praise of nature's beauties, in irregular tetrameter verse, alternately rhymed or in couplets. The poet conceives Spring, "Daughter of Heaven and Earth," to be languishing "with sudden passion" on May Day, following the snowbound winter. In a series of vivid images, he evokes the specific beauties of the season and their invigorating effect on all life. In accord with the philosophic doctrines developed in *Nature,* he shows that as lovely Spring complements unlovely Winter, so nature contains a variety of elements, which must be seen in their complex interrelations in order that the whole may be understood.

Mayflower, ship that brought 102 Pilgrims♦ from England to Plymouth Colony.♦ After twice setting sail accompanied by the unseaworthy *Speedwell,* the voyagers abandoned this smaller ship, and left Plymouth, England (Sept. 16, 1620), arriving in the present Provincetown harbor (Nov. 21). A land party went to the present Plymouth (Dec. 21),

followed five days later by the ship. The Mayflower Compact (drafted Nov. 11) was an agreement among the 41 adult males, binding them together in a civil body politic to enact, constitute, and frame laws, ordinances, acts, constitutions, and offices, with reference to the general good of the proposed colony. *Mourt's Relation* contains a journal of the voyage and a record of the compact, as does the *History of Plimmoth Plantation*♦ by Bradford.

Maypole of Merrymount, The, allegorical tale by Hawthorne,♦ published in 1836 and collected in *Twice-Told Tales* (1837). It is based on historical accounts of the Anglican settlement at Merry Mount.♦

Among the revelers about the Maypole at Merrymount are a handsome youth and a beautiful maiden, who, at the height of the festivities, are married by a jolly Anglican priest. At this moment the proceedings are interrupted by a raid of Endecott and his Puritan followers. The latter are dissuaded from punishing the pair when each pleads for the other, and they join the Puritan colony, becoming sober and respectable citizens.

MELTZER, DAVID (1937–), New York-born poet identified with the Beat movement♦ of San Francisco. His poems include *Ragas* (1959), *The Process* (1965), *The Dark Continent* (1967), and *Tens* (1973). He has also written experimental fiction with erotic themes and *We All Have Something To Say to Each Other* (1962), which includes an essay on Kenneth Patchen and four poems.

MELVILLE, HERMAN (1819–91), was born in New York City, a descendant of English and Dutch colonial families in whom he took great pride. His father, a cultivated gentleman, underwent financial reverses, entered bankruptcy, and died when Herman was 12 years old. The boy's mother, left virtually destitute with seven other children, seems from the portrait of Mrs. Glendinning in *Pierre* to have been an imperious, unsympathetic woman. His schooling ended when he was 15, and, after clerking in a New York bank, working in his brother's fur and cap store, farming, and teaching, he shipped as a cabin boy to Liverpool (1839). This voyage, described in *Redburn,* was both romantic and harrowing, and ingrained in him a love for the sea. Upon his return, he again taught school in upstate New York, until he sailed on the whaler *Acushnet* for the South Seas

(Jan. 1841). The 18-month voyage provided a factual basis for his later novel *Moby-Dick.* When he tired of whaling, he jumped ship at the Marquesas (July 1842) with a companion, Richard Tobias Greene, and lived for a month in the islands, as he later described in *Typee* and *Mardi.* He escaped from the savages who were holding him captive in the valley of Typee on an Australian trader, from which he deserted at Papeete (Sept. 1842). In Tahiti he worked for a time as a field laborer, studying the island life that he later depicted in *Omoo.* He left Tahiti on a whaler, and at Honolulu enlisted as an ordinary seaman on the frigate *United States* (Aug. 1843). His life aboard the man-of-war until his discharge at Boston (Oct. 1844) is the basis of *White-Jacket.* Having completed his education in what he later termed the only Harvard and Yale that were open to him, he returned home to begin fashioning novels from his experiences, and to enter literary society in New York and Boston.

His first five books, *Typee*♦ (1846), *Omoo*♦ (1847), *Mardi*♦ (1849), *Redburn*♦ (1849), and *White-Jacket*♦ (1850), won him fame and a wide following. He became a member of the literary circle of the Duyckinck brothers, who opened a new world of literature to him through their great libraries. In 1849 he made a trip to England to arrange for foreign publication, and visited Paris. The following year, with his wife, whom he had married in 1847, he moved to the Massachusetts farm that was his home for the next 13 years. Here he formed a friendship with his neighbor Hawthorne, who became his confidant after he outgrew the Duyckinck set of New York literati. His greatest work, *Moby-Dick*♦ (1851), was dedicated to Hawthorne, and it is worth noting that the tortured novel *Pierre*♦ (1852) was published at the same time as Hawthorne's *Blithedale Romance,* since both deal with idealists who are crushed in their attempts to pursue the ways of heaven upon earth.

Melville's popularity, which began to wane with the publication of *Moby-Dick,* was entirely lost through the confused metaphysics and iconoclasm of *Pierre,* for the public's preference was always for his early exotic romances. Opportunity for revaluation was lost when a fire at his publishers' (1853) destroyed the plates of his books and most of the unsold copies. Hawthorne's removal to Concord deprived him of his last great stimulus, and from this time he drew farther within himself in his tireless search for a key

to the universal mystery. *Israel Potter*♦ (1855), the story of the Revolutionary soldier, was a weak historical romance, but it was followed by Melville's finest achievements in short fiction, *The Piazza Tales*♦ (1856), which includes "Bartleby the Scrivener,"♦ "Benito Cereno,"♦ and "The Encantadas."♦ After *The Confidence Man*♦ (1857), an abortive satire on the commercialism and selfishness of the age, he wrote no further prose except the novelette *Billy Budd,*♦ completed just before his death.

Clarel♦ (1876), a long, involved poem concerned with his search for religious faith, grew out of a tour to the Holy Land (1857). His diary of the trip was published as *Journal Up the Straits* (1935). Melville's other verse includes *Battle-Pieces and Aspects of the War*♦ (1866), *John Marr and Other Sailors*♦ (1888), and *Timoleon* (1891), the last containing poems based on his travels in Greece and Italy. *Clarel, John Marr,* and *Timoleon* were privately financed and published in small editions. About 80 short uncollected poems were first printed in the collected edition of his works (1924).

Melville's great creative period having perished from public neglect and his own inanition, he attempted to eke out a living by lecturing. Failing to receive a desired consulship, after a trip to San Francisco (1860) on a clipper ship commanded by his brother, he moved to New York City (1863), and three years later received a mean appointment as an outdoor customs inspector, in which position he continued for 19 years. His last years were spent in complete obscurity, and his death passed virtually unnoticed. It was not until 1920 that he was rediscovered by literary scholars, and in subsequent years the previous neglect was atoned for by a general enthusiasm. An elaborate collected edition appeared (12 vols., 1922–23), including some work left in manuscript; individual works were frequently reprinted; and some magazine sketches were collected as *The Apple-Tree Table*♦ (1922). Other books published for the first time included *Journal of a Visit to London and the Continent* (1948), *Journal of a Visit to Europe and the Levant* (1955), and *Letters* (1960), including all 271 then known.

A wealth of scholarly research on his life and writings has been made, and recent students have revaluated his long-obscure literary reputation. A scholarly edition of his *Writings,* projected at 15 volumes, began publication in 1968. Since the 1930s he has come to be considered not only an outstanding writer of the sea and a great stylist who mastered both realistic narrative and a rich, rhythmical prose, but also a shrewd social critic and philosopher in his fiction.

Member of the Wedding, The, novel by Carson McCullers,♦ published in 1946 and dramatized by the novelist in 1950.

Frankie Adams, a lonely, sensitive 12-year-old girl, lives in a small Southern town with her widowed father and Berenice Sadie Brown, the warm, understanding, thrice-married black cook. Except for play with Berenice and John Henry West, her bespectacled six-year-old cousin, Frankie is "a member of nothing" until her brother Jarvis and his fiancée, Janice, ask her to be a member of their wedding and she suffers the misapprehension that they will live as a happy threesome. On the day before the wedding, sure that it is her last at home, she makes a farewell tour of the town, meets a drunken soldier who invites her to a tryst, another of her many experiences with problems of love, chance, and selfhood, and she violently resists his advances. The wedding itself becomes another unhappy experience because of her unbudging refusal to get out of the honeymoon car as she hysterically cries "Take me, take me." Sadly determined to escape home and find experience, Frankie runs away, but is found at the café where she had met the soldier and is brought back to her house. Although John Henry dies of meningitis and Berenice leaves for her own new marriage, Frankie, now 13, manages to recover from her painful past in the new happiness of close friendship with a contemporary, Mary Littlejohn, with whom she imaginatively plans a trip around the world.

Memoranda During the War, prose account by Whitman♦ of his Civil War experiences, published in 1875, and reprinted in *Specimen Days and Collect♦* (1882).

Men Without Women, 14 short stories by Hemingway,♦ published in 1927.

"The Undefeated" tells of the futile heroism of Manuel Garcia, a Spanish bullfighter just released from a hospital, who stubbornly refuses to retire, secures an ill-paid "nocturnal" engagement, and gives an adequate performance before an unappreciative audience, but is seriously injured and returned to the hospital. "The Killers" describes the tense atmosphere in a small-town lunchroom when two Chicago gangsters enter to await Ole Andreson, whom they have been paid to murder. He fails to arrive, and they finally

leave. Nick, the waiter, goes to Andreson's room, and finds the victim aware of his impending doom but paralyzed by fear and unwilling to attempt escape. "Fifty Grand" is the story of a champion prizefighter, Jack Brennan, and his bout with the contender Walcott. The middle-aged champion, worried by his responsibilities, cannot train properly, decides he is bound to lose, and bets $50,000 on his own defeat. He fights well for several rounds, until brutally fouled by his opponent. Insisting that this was an accident, he continues with difficulty, then suddenly ends the matter by an obvious foul on Walcott. " 'It's funny how fast you can think when it means that much money,' " he says.

MENCKEN, H[ENRY] L[OUIS] (1880–1956), Baltimore journalist, critic, and essayist, began his career on local newspapers in 1899, becoming editor of the *Evening Herald* (1905–6), and thereafter serving on the staff of the *Evening Sun,* during 1916–17 as war correspondent in Germany. He became literary critic of *The Smart Set♦* in 1908, and was co-editor of this lively periodical with George Jean Nathan (1914–23). His collaboration with Nathan continued during the early years of *The American Mercury,♦* which they founded in 1924 and which Mencken edited until 1933. He is best known for the aggressive iconoclasm of his editorial policies in these magazines, especially during the decade following World War I, when he exhibited a savagely satirical reaction against the blunders and imperfections of democracy and the cultural gaucheries of the American scene. Although this attitude implied doubt of the ultimate effectiveness of American institutions, he was equally vehement in his denunciation of European patronage of this country, and in his advocacy of an indigenous civilization. His critical views were widely influential, especially in his encouragement of such writers as Dreiser, Lewis, Cabell, and Sherwood Anderson, although he aroused much popular antagonism.

His most important work is *The American Language♦* (1919, revised 1921, 1923, 1936; supplementary volumes, 1945 and 1948), a discussion of the English language in the U.S., noting its significant American development. Besides six series of *Prejudices* (1919–27), frankly biased, raucous critical essays championing his literary enthusiasms and attacking mediocrity in America, he wrote introductions and notes for editions of Ibsen, Nietzsche, and others; *A Book of Burlesques* (1916); *A Book of Prefaces*

(1917); *In Defense of Women* (1918); *Notes on Democracy* (1926); *Treatise on the Gods* (1930); *Treatise on Right and Wrong* (1934); *Happy Days, 1880–1892* (1940); *Newspaper Days, 1899–1906* (1941) and *Heathen Days, 1890–1936* (1943), humorous autobiographical sketches; and *Minority Report* (1956), jottings drawn from his notebooks. His *Letters* (1961) prints some correspondence on literary matters only.

Mending Wall, blank-verse poem by Robert Frost, ♦ published in *North of Boston* (1914). Describing the time he and a neighboring farmer spent the day in replacing fallen stones on the wall which divides their land, the poet declares, "Something there is that doesn't love a wall," and expresses his philosophy of tolerance, generosity, and brotherhood in the contrast between his neighbor's dogmatic "Good fences make good neighbours" and his own more considered

> Before I built a wall I'd ask to know
> What I was walling in or walling out.

Mennonites, members of a Protestant sect that originated in Friesland in the 16th century, deriving its name from the Dutch religious reformer Menno Simons (1492–1559). They accept the Bible as their sole rule of faith, wish to restore apostolic Christianity, administer baptism to adult believers only, are ardently pacifistic, and attempt to live apart from other groups. Suffering persecution in Europe, they emigrated to America, first settling in Pennsylvania (1683) and spreading throughout the South and Middle West. Their numbers have greatly increased, although they are divided into several branches. One of these is the Amish, followers of Jacob Amman, who separated from the orthodox body in the 17th century. In 1980 there were *c.*205,000 Mennonites in various churches.

MEREDITH, WILLIAM [MORRIS] (1919–), poet born in New York City, after graduation from Princeton and service as a navy aviator has taught English at Connecticut College. *Love Letter from an Impossible Land* (1944) was in the Yale Series of Younger Poets, and succeeding volumes—*Ships and Other Figures* (1948), *The Open Sea* (1958), *The Wreck of the Thresher* (1964)—use his naval background for themes and show the influence upon him both of Frost and of a metaphysical tradition. *Earth Walk* (1970) gathers these

poems and in new verse reflects upon them. *Hazard, the Painter* (1975) presents poetic reflections upon a fictional painter's life and art; and *The Cheer* (1980) collects recent poems. Meredith translated Apollinaire's *Alcools* (1964).

MERRILL, JAMES [INGRAM] (1926–), born in New York, after graduation from Amherst (1947) began his literary career with *First Poems* (1951), followed by further and increasingly philosophic poetry marked by an elegant and disciplined style in *The Country of a Thousand Years of Peace* (1959), *Water Street* (1962), *Nights and Days* (1966, National Book Award), *The Fire Screen* (1969), *Braving the Elements* (1972), *The Yellow Pages* (1974), and *Divine Comedies* (1976, Pulitzer Prize), including the long narrative "Book of Ephraim." That work, partly a Platonic symposium incorporating fictive and real characters (principally Auden), was continued and elaborated in his next two volumes of verse, *Mirabell* (1978) and *Scripts for the Pageant* (1980). *From the First Nine Poems* (1982) and *The Changing Light at Sandover* (1982) collect his poems. Merrill won a Bollingen Prize in 1973. He has also written prose plays, *The Immortal Husband* (1956) and *The Bait* (1960), and novels, *The Seraglio* (1957), about an aging, much-married businessman's involvements with women, and *The (Diblos) Notebook* (1965), about the attempts of a young American author to transform his experiences on a Greek island into a novel.

Merriwell, FRANK, character in the juvenile stories by W.G. Patten. ♦

Merry Mount, settlement at Mount Wollaston (now Quincy), Mass., founded in 1625 by Captain Wollaston and Thomas Morton (1590?–1647), a British adventurer and Anglican. When the captain withdrew to Virginia with his indentured white servants, Morton took possession of the site, which was renamed Ma-re-Mount. There, according to Bradford, the Anglican settlers established a "schoole of athisme," whose members revived "the beastly practices of the madd Bachanalians." The frolicking of the colonists about a Maypole and their trading of weapons to the Indians caused Myles Standish to be sent to seize Morton, who was transferred to England under arrest (1628). Although the colony was dispersed, several "revelers" lingered on. Morton's *New English Canaan* (1637) presents his version of events, while Bradford and John Winthrop represent the Puritan and Separatist views in their histories. Hawthorne's "The Maypole of Merrymount"♦ (1837) is an allegorical tale, and other literary treatments include Motley's romance *Merrymount* (1849) and the operatic version by Howard Hanson and R.L. Stokes, *Merry Mount* (1934).

MERTON, THOMAS (1915–69), religious writer, an American born in France, reared there, in England, and the U.S., while at Columbia University was converted to Roman Catholicism. In 1941 he became a Trappist at a Kentucky monastery and was later ordained as Father M. Louis. His books include *The Seven Storey Mountain* (1948), autobiography; *The Waters of Siloe* (1949), on the Trappists; *Seeds of Contemplation* (1949), on the spiritual life; *The Ascent to Truth* (1951), *The Sign of Jonas* (1953), *No Man Is an Island* (1955), *The Silent Life* (1957), *Silence in Heaven* (1957), *Thoughts in Solitude* (1958), *The New Man* (1962), *Life and Holiness* (1963), *Seeds of Destruction* (1964), *Conjectures of a Guilty Bystander* (1966), and *Mystics and Zen Masters* (1969), meditations and essays. His poetry includes *A Man in the Divided Sea* (1946), *Figures for an Apocalypse* (1947), and *Cables to the Ace* (1968). Other publications include a *Secular Journal* (1959) and his correspondence with Van Wyck Brooks (1970).

MERWIN, W[ILLIAM] S[TANLEY] (1927–), New York-born poet, after graduation from Princeton (1948) and further study of Romance languages began his career with *A Mask for Janus* (1952), issued in the Yale Series of Younger Poets. This collection has been followed by others, including *The Dancing Bears* (1954), *Green with Beasts* (1956), *The Drunk in the Furnace* (1960), *The Moving Target* (1963), *The Lice* (1967), *The Carriers of Ladders* (1970, Pulitzer Prize), *Writings to an Unfinished Accompaniment* (1973), *The Compass Flower* (1977), in which his poetry has moved from the relatively formal and traditional early work to poems that are intense and existential, and *Opening the Hand* (1983). *The Miner's Pale Children* (1970) and *Houses and Travellers* (1977) collect prose parables. *Darkling Child* (1956), *Favor Island* (1957), and *The Gilded West* (1961) are plays, the first written with Dido Milroy. He has also made translations, including *Poem of the Cid* (1959), *The Satires of Perseus* (1961), and *The Song of Roland*

(1963). *Unframed Originals* (1982) is a volume of recollections.

Message to Garcia, A, essay by Elbert Hubbard,♦ published in 1899. It recounts an incident in the Spanish-American War, when Lieutenant Andrew S. Rowan was sent by McKinley to meet General Calixto Garcia y Inigues, head of the Cuban insurgent forces, in order to ascertain what help was needed by Garcia against the Spanish. Because of the heroic aspects of Rowan's persistence during his difficult journey, and the inspirational moral drawn from it by Hubbard, the essay became tremendously popular.

Metaphysical verse, term applied to writing like that of the 17th-century British poets Donne, Crashaw, Cowley, Herbert, and Vaughan, which conveys a direct emotional apprehension of thought, employing a psychological analysis of love or religion, using the conceit to bring into eccentric and startling juxtaposition the contradictions of life, and usually placing more stress on subtlety of thought than on conventional form. American poets of this sort include Edward Taylor, Emerson, Jones Very, and Emily Dickinson. Many modern poets have been influenced by T.S. Eliot's interest in the 17th-century metaphysicals. They include Aiken, Louise Bogan, Cummings, Horace Gregory, Marianne Moore, MacLeish, Ransom, Wallace Stevens, Taggard, Tate, W.C. Williams, and Elinor Wylie.

Methodism, the doctrines, polity, and worship of those religious organizations developed from the evangelistic teaching of John Wesley (1702–91), his brother Charles, and George Whitefield. ♦ As students at Oxford, they conducted meetings for religious exercises according to such precise rules that they were dubbed Methodists. They accepted the teachings of the Church of England, and, although influenced by the Moravians, intended no more than a revival of personal religion, emphasizing the immediacy of the Holy Spirit. Their zeal led the Anglican churches to be closed to them, but they carried on their evangelistic work in open-air meetings. No legal constitution was adopted until 1784, and it was not until 1791 that they broke from the Church of England to found the Wesleyan Methodist Church, known in America as the Methodist Episcopal Church. There have been many schisms on matters of government and, in America, also on issues raised by the Civil War. The Wesleys visited Georgia in 1735, and Whitefield made many visits, beginning in 1738–39, when he was a leader of the Great Awakening. The beginnings of the organized church are attributed to the preacher Philip Embury, who arrived in 1776. Francis Asbury was sent to America by Wesley in 1771, and became one of the church's first American bishops (1784). The three main branches of the church were united in 1938. In 1980 there were about 12,826,000 Methodists in the U.S.

MICHAELS, LEONARD (1933–), born in New York City, a professor of English at the University of California, Berkeley, is the author of collections of short stories, *Going Places* (1969) and *I Would Have Saved Them If I Could* (1975), and the novel *The Men's Club* (1981), about a rambunctious night out of a gathering of chauvinist males in California.

MICHENER, JAMES A[LBERT] (1907–) New York-born novelist, after graduation from Swarthmore (1929), study at Colorado State College, teaching of social sciences, and work as a book editor, was led into literature by his naval experiences in World War II. His 18 related sketches, *Tales of the South Pacific* (1947, Pulitzer Prize), were adapted by Rodgers and Hammerstein as a musical comedy, *South Pacific* (1949). *The Fires of Spring* (1949) is a more conventional novel, concerning a boy's growth to maturity during the 1920s and the Depression. After *Return to Paradise* (1951), which dealt with the scene of his first work in a mingling of fact and fiction, and *The Voice of Asia* (1951), a study of the contemporary Orient, he wrote the novels *The Bridges at Toko-ri* (1953) and *Sayonara* (1954), using the Korean war as background, the latter emphasizing Japanese and American good relations through its love story. *Hawaii* (1959) is a panoramic novel of the fiftieth state's social history; *Caravans* (1963) is a novel about a romantic American girl in Afghanistan; *The Source* (1965) is a novel about the Holy Land, ancient and modern. *The Drifters* (1971), a contemporary tale, depicting six young people of various nations, all wandering the world in search of their diverse conception of the good life, was followed by further lengthy novels: *Centennial* (1974), presenting life in Colorado from prehistory through 200 years of life, Indian and white, concentrating on the last century; *Chesapeake* (1978), a chronicle of 400 years of life on Maryland's Eastern Shore, some of which was excerpted in *The Watermen* (1979); *The Covenant* (1980), a sweeping historical novel about South Africa from

earliest days to the present; *Space* (1982), about U.S. astronauts involved in a flight to the dark side of the moon; and *Poland* (1983), presenting Polish history. *Texas,* which is self-explanatory, was published in 1985.

The Floating World (1954) is a study of an art form continued in *Japanese Prints* (1959). *The Bridge at Andau* (1957) is a documentary account of the Hungarian revolt against the Communists in 1956. *Report of the County Chairman* (1961) treats his experiences as chairman of the Bucks County, Pennsylvania, Citizens for Kennedy; and other nonfictional writings include *Iberia* (1968), presenting experiences and reflections on Spanish travels; *Presidential Lottery; The Reckless Gamble in Our Electoral System* (1969); *The Quality of Life* (1970); *Kent State; What Happened and Why* (1971), treating the demonstrations on the Ohio university campus that ended with the shooting of four students by the National Guard; and *Sports in America* (1976). With A. Grove Day he wrote *Rascals in Paradise* (1957), sketches of colorful characters in the Pacific.

Middle Border, the prairie region of Minnesota, Wisconsin, Nebraska, and the Dakotas, which was an important agricultural frontier (c.1870–1900) when Scandinavian, Slavic, and Irish immigrants settled there to establish one of the great grain-raising areas of the U.S. Authors who have written of the region and its people during the frontier period include Garland, Rölvaag, Willa Cather, Bess Streeter Aldrich, and Frederick Manfred.

Middle of the Journey, The, novel by Lionel Trilling,♦ published in 1947.

John Laskell, a middle-aged man recuperating from an almost fatal sickness, still feels close to death and attracted by it. He is assisted to life by an affair with Emily Caldwell but plunged into a new crisis when her drunken husband, Duck Caldwell, accidentally kills their young daughter. The event affects Laskell not only emotionally but intellectually as he finds his friends, Professor Croom and his wife, contending that not Duck but social forces are responsible for the tragedy, while another friend, Gifford Maxim, a doctrinaire Christian, argues that Duck, being responsible for his acts, is eternally damned unless saved by God's mercy. Faced by these opposing views, Laskell finally reaches his own view that man is not entirely governed by external forces nor entirely possessed of a free will.

Middletown, see *Lynd, Robert S.*

Midnight Ride of Paul Revere, The, see *Paul Revere's Ride.*

MILES, JOSEPHINE (1911–85), after graduation from the University of California, Los Angeles, and graduate degrees in English from Berkeley, in 1940 joined the faculty of the latter campus. Her concise, disciplined, observant, and often witty poetry appeared in *Lines at Intersection* (1939), *Poems on Several Occasions* (1941), *Local Measures* (1946), *Prefabrications* (1955), *Poems 1930–1960* (1960), *Kinds of Affection* (1967), *Fields of Learning* (1968), *To All Appearances* (1974), *Coming to Terms* (1979), and *Collected Poems* (1983). She wrote scholarly studies of poetic diction in *The Vocabulary of Poetry* (1946), *The Continuity of English Poetic Language* (1951), *Eras and Modes in English Poetry* (1957), *Renaissance, Eighteenth Century and Modern Language in Poetry* (1960), and *Poetry and Change* (1974).

MILLAY, EDNA ST. VINCENT (1892–1950), born in Maine, graduated from Vassar (1917) having already won fame with the publication of "Renascence"♦ (1912), the title poem of her first volume, *Renascence and Other Poems* (1917), which exhibited technical virtuosity, startling freshness, and a hunger for beauty. *A Few Figs from Thistles* (1920) showed that, though the disillusion of the postwar years was crowding in upon her, she was attempting to maintain gaiety with a consciously cynical flippancy. With *Second April* (1921) she revealed a more mature emotional tone, which, like her use of Elizabethan words and tight metrical forms, marked her subsequent volumes. While living in Greenwich Village, she became associated with the Provincetown Players,♦ for whom she wrote *The Princess Marries the Page* (1918, published in 1932), *Aria da Capo* (1919, published 1921), and *Two Slatterns and a King* (1921), all one-act satirical fantasies. *The Lamp and the Bell* (1921), written for a Vassar commencement, is a five-act poetic drama. *The Ballad of the Harp-Weaver* (1923, Pulitzer Prize), later retitled *The Harp-Weaver and Other Poems,* is noted for poems showing a further deepening from her earlier arch attitude to a more disillusioned bitterness. Her mature technical ability, particularly in the sonnet, her lyric gift, and her directness were exhibited in further volumes: *The Buck in the Snow* (1928); *Fatal Interview* (1931), a sonnet cycle in the Elizabethan

manner; *Wine from These Grapes* (1934); *Conversation at Midnight* (1937), a dramatic narrative showing her increasing interest in contemporary social problems; *Huntsman, What Quarry?* (1939); *Make Bright the Arrows* (1940), "poems for a world at war"; and *The Murder of Lidice* (1942), a ballad written for radio. Her *Collected Sonnets* appeared in 1941, *Collected Lyrics* in 1943, and *Collected Poems* in 1956. Other works include *Distressing Dialogues* (1924), a volume of sophisticated prose sketches, written under the pseudonym Nancy Boyd, *The King's Henchman* (1927), the libretto of an opera by Deems Taylor, set in Saxon England, and a translation of Baudelaire's *Flowers of Evil* (1936) with George Dillon. *Mine the Harvest* (1954) posthumously collects 66 poems, and her *Letters* was published in 1952.

MILLER, ARTHUR (1915–), New York author, graduated from the University of Michigan (1938), where he began to write plays. His first, *Man Who Had All the Luck* (1944), treats an auto mechanic whose success in marriage and business is the result of work and care, and was followed by a nondramatic work of reportage, *Situation Normal* (1944), about military life at army bases, and *Focus* (1945), a novel about anti-Semitism. He returned to the drama with *All My Sons* (1947), about a manufacturer whose defective airplane parts cause the death of his son and other aviators in wartime. His most impressive play is *Death of a Salesman*♦ (1949, Pulitzer Prize), fusing realism and symbolism in reviewing the tragic life of a salesman victimized by his own false values and those of modern America. It was followed by *The Crucible* (1953), treating the Salem witch trials of 1692 as a parable for America during the era of McCarthyism, as the play probes into problems of individual conscience and guilt by association. *A View from the Bridge* (1955, Pulitzer Prize) presents two Italian longshoremen illegally in the U.S., and *A Memory of Two Mondays,* another short play included with it in production and publication, presents varied views of workers in a Manhattan warehouse. *The Misfits* (1961), a so-called cinema-novel, that is, fiction based on what the camera can see, is actually the script of a motion picture for his wife Marilyn Monroe, which deals with a beautiful woman in Nevada for a divorce who falls in with three men who herd old horses for slaughter and of her emotional relations with the men and feelings for the animals. *After the Fall* (1964) is a play in two long acts in which the quasi-autobiographical protagonist seeks self-knowledge, a sense of the meaning of his past and its meaning for his future as he reviews his marriages and other major experiences. *Incident at Vichy* (1965), a short play, concerns the treatment of diverse Frenchmen picked up by the Nazis in 1942. *The Price* (1968) is a play contrasting two brothers' views and ways of life as they meet after long separation to dispose of their parents' possessions; and *The American Clock* (1979) depicts an American family caught in the Depression. *I Don't Need You Anymore* (1967) collects nine stories, including "The Misfits"; *The Creation of the World and Other Business* (1972) is a serio-comic treatment of the book of Genesis; *Theater Essays* (1978) includes interviews. With his wife Inge Morath, a photographer, he has created books of text and pictures: *In Russia* (1969), *In the Country* (1977), set in rural Connecticut, and *Chinese Encounters* (1979). *Salesman in Beijing* (1984) is an account of producing his play in China in 1983. He made an adaptation of Ibsen's *An Enemy of the People* (1951).

MILLER, CAROLINE (1903–   ), Georgia novelist whose works include *Lamb in His Bosom* (1933, Pulitzer Prize), about backcountry Georgia life before the Civil War, and *Lebanon* (1944), about a Georgia girl's life on the frontier.

MILLER, HENRY (1891–1980), New York-born author, lived in various parts of the U.S., as an expatriate in Europe (1930–40), and after 1942 in California. His books are essentially autobiographical, expressing with gusto his intense individualism, his love of freedom, his affection for natural responses, his hatred of all that blocks or blunts human impulses, and his enthusiastic search for intellectual and aesthetic adventure. Their energetic lyrical prose merges Rabelaisian dialogue and descriptions with sprawling statements of the author's own emotions, moods, and beliefs. Among his many works the best known is *Tropic of Cancer*♦ (France, 1934; U.S., 1961), an intense personal narrative in fictive form of the emotional and intellectual life of an American expatriate in Paris, marked by its frank treatment of sexual relations and animated by a belief that "more obscene than anything is inertia." A similar autobiographical narrative is *Tropic of Capricorn*♦ (France, 1939; U.S., 1962), treating the adolescence of the author in New York, and a related work is *Black Spring* (France,

1936; U.S., 1963), gathering autobiographical essays and sketches ranging from his Brooklyn boyhood to his Paris experiences. His other writings include *Aller Retour New York* (1935), a letter about a round-trip voyage during his expatriation; *Max and the White Phagocytes* (1938), on one of his unusual friends; *The Cosmological Eye* (1939), fiction and essays; *The Wisdom of the Heart* (1941), a similar collection; *The Colossus of Maroussi* (1941), an unconventional travel account on the spirit of Greece, emphasizing people, not sites, in a search for "a world of light"; *Sunday After the War* (1944), sketches; *The Air-Conditioned Nightmare*♦ (1945) and its sequel, *Remember To Remember* (1947), on his responses to the American scene; *The Smile at the Foot of the Ladder* (1948), a tale; *The Books in My Life* (1952), about the very varied reading that affected him; *Nights of Love and Laughter* (1955), stories; *The Time of the Assassins* (1956), a study of Rimbaud; *Big Sur and the Oranges of Hieronymus Bosch*♦ (1957), treating his life in California; *To Paint Is To Love Again* (1960), containing reproductions of his art; *Stand Still Like a Hummingbird* (1962), essays; *Just Wild About Harry* (1963), a play; and *My Life and Times* (1971), tape-recorded interviews. *The Rosy Crucifixion,* composed of *Sexus* (1949), *Plexus* (1953), and *Nexus* (1960), is a memoir of his youth and life prior to expatriation in a form partly fictive, partly essay-like. *Genius and Lust* (1976) is an anthology of his writings selected by Norman Mailer, who wrote a lengthy introduction to it. Posthumous publications include *Opus Pistorum* (1983), fictive erotic adventures of an American in Paris, and *From Your Capricorn Friend* (1984), short pieces from a Greenwich Village journal. Many volumes of Miller's correspondence have been printed, including *Hamlet* (2 vols., 1939, 1941), philosophic exchanges with Michael Fraenkel; and with Durrell (1963) and with Anaïs Nin (1965). Miller was a major influence on the Beat movement. ♦

MILLER, JOAQUIN, pseudonym of Cincinnatus Hiner (or Heine) Miller (1841?–1913), at first a nickname, as his earliest writing was a defense of the Mexican bandit Joaquin Murietta. His early biography is cloaked in exaggeration; he was born in Liberty, Ind., supposedly went West in a covered wagon, lived in frontier Oregon and with the Indians in northern California, was at various times horse thief, Portland lawyer, pony-express messenger, newspaper editor, and Indian fighter, before turning to the poetry published as *Specimens* (1868) and *Joaquin et al* (1869). He drifted to San Francisco to enter literary society, and to London, where his private printing of *Pacific Poems* (1870) and *Songs of the Sierras* (1871) brought him acclaim from the English, who were fascinated by the discovery of a "frontier poet." Hailed as "the Byron of Oregon," he dramatically attempted to live up to his title. He soon returned to America, where his energetic rhetorical poems continued to appear, although later his bombast, coupled with his imitativeness and metrical weakness, caused him to lose the acclaim he first received. *The Danites in the Sierras* (1877), a Mormon play, was the most popular of his dramas, and besides several novels he wrote the autobiographical *Life Amongst the Modocs* (1873) and *Memorie and Rime* (1884).

MILLER, PERRY [GILBERT EDDY] (1905–63), scholar of American literature, member of the Harvard faculty, best known for his writings on Puritanism and the intellectual history of New England. His books include *Orthodoxy in Massachusetts* (1933), *The New England Mind: The Seventeenth Century* (1939), *The New England Mind: From Colony to Province* (1953), *Jonathan Edwards* (1949), *Roger Williams* (1953), *The Raven and the Whale . . . the Era of Poe and Melville* (1956), and *Errand into the Wilderness* (1956) and *Nature's Nation* (1967), the latter two collecting essays. He also compiled several important anthologies, including *The Puritans* (1938) with T.H. Johnson.

Millerites, religious sect more properly called Second Adventists. These followers of the New York farmer William Miller (1782–1849) believed in the physical second advent of Christ in 1843. After the Day of Judgment failed to arrive that year, the date was set for October 23, 1844. Even after the second disappointment many followers remained faithful, continuing to anticipate a second coming. Another group, the Seventh-Day Adventists, holding to a similar belief, adopted Saturday as the sabbath. In 1980 this body had 571,000 members, and other Adventist sects some 35,000. Edward Eggleston's *The End of the World* and the works of Jane M. Parker♦ are among books dealing with Millerites.

MILLETT, KATE (KATHERINE MURRAY) (1934–), feminist activist, whose doctoral dissertation for Columbia University (1970) was published as *Sexual Politics* (1970), a study of the history and nature of the exploitation of women and the relationships between men and women. She followed this seminal book with two autobiographical works, *Flying* (1974), telling of her marriage to a Japanese sculptor and her love affairs with women, and *Sita* (1977), describing a mental breakdown and a lesbian romance. *The Basement* (1979) is an inquiry into an actual case of sadism: the torture and murder of a teenage girl by a woman who served her as a kind of foster mother. *Going to Iran* (1982) deals with Middle East feminine issues.

MILLHAUSER, STEVEN (1943–), born in New York City, reared in Connecticut, graduated from Columbia (1965) and later studied and taught at Brown. His novels are *Edwin Mullhouse: The Life and Death of an American Writer, 1943–1954 by Jeffrey Cartwright* (1972), a comic Nabokovian biography in great depth of the 11-year life of a precocious novelist by his young chum; and *Portrait of a Romantic* (1977), the memoir by a 29-year-old man of his juvenile, romantic high-school years that were spent with his realistic-minded doppelgänger.

MILOSZ, CZESLAW (1911–), Lithuanian-born poet and man of letters, mainly reared and educated in Poland, in whose diplomatic corps he served (1945–50). He emigrated to the U.S. (1960) and joined the faculty of the University of California, Berkeley. He was naturalized in 1970. His books, written in Polish, in translation include *The Captive Mind* (1953), about the effect of communism on Polish writers; *Native Realm* (1968), an autobiography; *Selected Poems* (1972); *Bells in Winter* (1978), poems; *Visions from San Francisco Bay* (1982), essays; as well as novels and translations into Polish and English. *The Witness of Poetry* (1983) prints lectures at Harvard. He was awarded a Nobel Prize in 1980.

Minister's Black Veil, The, parable by Hawthorne,♦ published in *The Token* (1836) and in *Twice-Told Tales* (1837).

The Rev. Mr. Hooper, a New England Puritan minister, appears one Sunday with his face covered by a black veil. Refusing to explain his action to his terrified congregation, or to his fiancée, who leaves him, he goes through life concealing his face, saying only that the veil is a symbol of the curtain that hides every man's heart and makes him a stranger even to his friend, his lover, and his God.

Minister's Wooing, The, novel by Harriet Beecher Stowe,♦ published in 1859. It is set in Newport, a New England town, shortly after the Revolution. Aaron Burr is a minor character.

Miniver Cheevy, poem in iambic tetrameter quatrains by E.A. Robinson,♦ published in *The Town Down the River* (1910).

This satirical portrait of Miniver, a worldly failure in Tilbury Town, shows him to be unaware of his personal inadequacies, consoling himself with a romantic melancholy that he carries to absurd lengths. "Born too late," he "sighed for what was not," dreaming of "medieval grace" and "the days of old." Thus his life consists of futile yearnings and frustration, to no end except that "Miniver coughed, and called it fate, And kept on drinking."

Minnehaha, character in *Hiawatha.*♦ The name is first mentioned in Mary Eastman's *Life and Legends of the Sioux* (1849), as the Indian name for a waterfall near Minneapolis.

Miss Lonelyhearts, short novel by Nathanael West,♦ published in 1933. A dramatization in two acts by Howard Teichmann was produced and published in 1959.

A nameless middle-aged man, the son of a Baptist minister, unable to find any other job, becomes the writer of a column of advice to the lovelorn for a New York newspaper, and is so troubled himself that he spends much of his time drinking. As Miss Lonelyhearts he is sought out by Fay Doyle, a woman married to a cripple, and ends up going to bed with her. Later he meets Fay's husband Peter, toward whom he feels a sympathetic sense of communion, but Peter, torn between reciprocal love and hatred, plans to shoot him with a gun that he has concealed in a package. Upon embracing Peter, Miss Lonelyhearts jostles the package and is accidentally shot to death.

Miss Ravenel's Conversion from Secession to Loyalty, novel by J.W. De Forest,♦ published in 1867.

At the outbreak of the Civil War, Dr. Ravenel, a scholar who is loyal to the Union, leaves New Orleans for "New Boston" (New Haven, Conn.). With his daughter Lillie, whose sympathies lie with the aristocratic

South, he grows concerned at the entrance into the girl's life of two suitors: Edward Colburne, an intelligent but modest New Boston lawyer; and Lieutenant-Colonel John Carter, a Virginia-born soldier in the Union army, whose dashing manners and aristocratic tendencies match her ideal of Southern manhood. Dr. Ravenel prefers Colburne, an Abolitionist like himself, and fears Carter's reputation for dissipation and lack of scruples. Meanwhile Lillie's conversion has begun, and she has a vital interest in the Northern success when Colburne and Carter participate in the capture of New Orleans. Soon the Ravenels return to their old home, and Carter gives up his life of drink and mistresses to court Lillie and intrigue for promotion. After their marriage, he remains faithful for a time, but during a trip to Washington has a secret affair with her gay young aunt, Mrs. Larue. This ends with the birth of Lillie's son, but Dr. Ravenel, now engaged in the education of freed slaves, learns of Carter's infidelity and informs his daughter, who leaves her husband shortly before he dies as a hero in battle. At the close of the war, Lillie is converted to Abolitionism through her return to New Boston and her marriage to Colburne.

Mission Indians, general term applied to Indians of many tribes, chiefly the Yuma and Shoshone, who were Christianized and gathered into communities by the Spanish Franciscans in southern California (1776–1830s). They were driven out of the missions by the Mexicans, and were neglected by the Americans until after the Civil War, when, largely at the instigation of Helen Hunt Jackson, the government took steps to care for them. Since 1974 they have been located on 31 small reservations in southern California. Mary Austin's *Isidro* and Helen Hunt Jackson's *Ramona* are romantic depictions of the life of the Mission Indians.

Mississippi River, principal river of the U.S., drains the great central basin between the Appalachian and Rocky Mountains. Having its source in northern Minnesota, and flowing through the center of the Prairie and Southern states, the river has for its chief tributaries the Missouri and Ohio rivers. Dominating the economic life of the South and Middle West until the Civil War and the coming of the railroads, the Mississippi was the focus of a distinctive type of American culture during the glamorous period of steamboats and showboats (1811–61), whose most celebrated literary interpreter has been Mark Twain, especially in *Huckleberry Finn* and *Life on the Mississippi,* although other popular treatments, respectively in poetry, the novel, and nonfiction, include John Hay's "Jim Bludso," Edna Ferber's *Show Boat,* and Ben Lucien Burman's *Big River To Cross.* Other writers include those associated with its principal cities, St. Louis♦ and New Orleans.♦ Its earlier history included discovery by De Soto, domination by the French following the explorations by Jolliet, Marquette, La Salle, and Iberville, control by Spain (1763–1800), settlement and exploitation of its valley by the U.S. after the Louisiana Purchase (1803), and the pre-steamboat period of keelboating whose typical folk hero was Mike Fink.♦ By 1860 there were more than 1000 steamboats on the river, helping to tie the Middle West to the South. During the Civil War, the Northern attempts to gain control were finally successful through the siege of Vicksburg and the capture of New Orleans. The river is still of primary importance to U.S. agriculture and trade, as both a constructive and a destructive force; popular conceptions of its power have included the black's personification of "Ol' Man River" and the Indian's of the "Father of Waters."

Mr. Higginbotham's Catastrophe, story by Hawthorne,♦ published in *The Token* (1834) and in *Twice-Told Tales* (1837).

Dominicus Pike, an itinerant tobacco peddler, is informed of the hanging of wealthy old Mr. Higginbotham of Kimballton. He spreads the rumor as he travels, only to have it denied by persons who have seen the old man since his supposed death. Hearing again of the hanging, and being contradicted by Higginbotham's niece, he goes to Kimballton and arrives just in time to save her uncle from actual murder. It is revealed that the murder was planned by three men, two of whom successively lost courage and fled, spreading the rumor. Dominicus is rewarded by becoming Higginbotham's heir, as well as marrying the niece.

Mr. Roberts, novel by Thomas Heggen.♦

Mrs. Wiggs of the Cabbage Patch, story by Alice Hegan Rice,♦ published in 1901 under her maiden name, Alice Caldwell Hegan.

MITCHELL, MARGARET (1900–1949), Georgia author and journalist, from 1926 to 1936 wrote her one book, *Gone with the Wind*♦ (1936, Pulitzer Prize). This long romantic novel of Georgia during the Civil War and Reconstruction, told entirely from the point of view of the middle class in the Old South, won an immediate and unprecedented popularity throughout the U.S. Said to be the fastest-selling novel in the history of American publishing, it had a sales record of 50,000 copies in one day and approximately 1,500,000 during its first year. By May 1941 the sales reached 3,368,000 in the hard-bound editions in the English language, and of the 18 translations made in those first five years, the German was the most popular, selling 500,000 copies. The book's great initial popularity was further enhanced by a lavish motion-picture version first released in 1939.

M'liss, novelette by Bret Harte♦ which in its characterization of a willful young girl and her adventures in the mining country represented an early treatment of life in the gold rush. The earliest version appeared in the *Golden Era* (1860), from which it was expanded for serialization in the same journal (1863) and collection in *The Luck of Roaring Camp and Other Sketches* (1870).

Moby-Dick; or, The Whale, novel by Melville,♦ published in 1851. Within this realistic account of a whaling voyage is set a symbolic account of the conflict between man and his fate. Captain Ahab declares, "All visible objects are but as pasteboard masks," and Melville, holding this thesis, strikes through the surface of his adventurous narrative to formulate concepts of good and evil imbedded as allegory in its events.

The outcast youth Ishmael, feeling "a damp, drizzly November" in his soul, goes to New Bedford, planning to ship on a whaler. There he draws as a roommate Queequeg, a Polynesian prince, and the two become comrades. After Ishmael hears a symbolic sermon by Father Mapple, he and Queequeg go to Nantucket and sign on the *Pequod,* which sails on Christmas Day. The captain, Ahab, is a monomaniac whose one purpose is to capture the fierce, cunning white whale, Moby-Dick, which had torn away his leg during their last encounter. He keeps below deck for some time, but finally declares his purpose and posts a doubloon on the mast as a reward for the man who first sights the white whale. The characters of the sailors are revealed by their reactions. The chief mate, Starbuck, earnest, prudent, and fretful, dislikes it. Stubb, the second mate, is happy-go-lucky and takes perils as they come. Flask, the third mate, is incapable of deep thought and for him killing whales is simply an occupation. Others in the crew include Fedallah and his mysterious Asiatics; the American Indian harpooner, Tashtego; the African, Daggoo; and the black cabin boy, Pip. Through the plot of the voyage, which carries the *Pequod* nearly around the world, runs a comprehensive discussion of the nature of the whale, the history of science and art relating to the animal, and the facts of the whaling industry. Whales are captured during the pursuit, but circumstances seem to conspire against Ahab: storms, lightning, loss of the compass, the drowning of a man, and the insanity of Ahab's favorite, Pip. The white whale is finally sighted, and in the first day's chase he smashes a whaleboat. The second day, another boat is swamped, and the captain's ivory leg is snapped off. On the third day the whale is harpooned, but Ahab, fouled in the line, is pinioned to Moby-Dick, who bears down on the *Pequod*. The ship is sunk and, as the final spars settle in the water, one of the men nails to the mast a sky hawk that pecks at the flag he is placing as a signal. The ship, "like Satan, would not sink to hell till she had dragged a living part of heaven along with her, and helmeted herself with it." Ishmael, the only survivor, is rescued by another whaler, the *Rachel*.

Modern Chivalry, satirical picaresque novel by H.H. Brackenridge. ♦ The first two parts were published in 1792, the third and fourth in 1793 and 1797, a revision in 1805, and a final addition in 1815. The influence of Cervantes is obvious, as is in less degree that of Swift, Fielding, and Samuel Butler, but the work is distinguished as the first extended depiction of backwoods life in American fiction.

Captain John Farrago and his servant, Teague O'Regan, set out from the captain's farm in western Pennsylvania to ride through the country and observe the life and manners of the people. Farrago is an intelligent democrat, part Jeffersonian and part independent, inclining to the ideas of Tom Paine. Teague is a red-headed, long-legged Irish immigrant, part fool and part knave, whose unbounded self-assurance arises from his ignorance. At each stage of their journey they meet some foolish group that admires Teague, and the captain must invent excuses to keep them from bestowing various honors on his servant. Each adventure is followed by a chapter of reflections upon the abuses of democracy. Teague is a universal success,

meets the President, becomes an idol of politicians, beautiful ladies, and scientists, and is finally appointed collector of excise on whiskey, all of his predecessors in this office having been tarred and feathered. Teague receives the same treatment, and is captured as a strange animal by a philosophic society, which sends him to France. There the tar and feathers wear off, and his only article of clothing being in an imperfect state, he is mistaken for a sansculotte and borne off in triumph. In the later addition, the author describes a settlement founded by the captain and his friends, but the lack of the early comedy and satire exposes his plainly didactic purpose of attempting to raise the standards of democracy.

Modern Instance, A, novel by Howells, ♦ published in 1882.

Bartley Hubbard, a clever but unscrupulous Boston journalist, is married to Marcia Gaylord, from whom he becomes alienated because of his shady business practices and his philanderings. Marcia, though still in love with her husband, leaves him, and he sues for divorce. His action is defeated and the divorce granted to Marcia. Hubbard goes to Arizona, where he is killed by a man whose personal affairs he has discussed too frankly in his newspaper. Ben Halleck, who has constantly attended Marcia through her trials, debates with his friend Atherton whether he should forsake the ministry to marry her, but does not come to a decision.

Modoc Indians, tribe of southwest Oregon and northern California. In 1864 the Modoc and the Klamath ceded their territory to the U.S., removing to the Klamath reservation in Oregon. In 1870 a chief known as Captain Jack led a part of the tribe back to the California border, and in the subsequent Modoc War (1872–73) two peace commissioners were killed. After the Indians were overcome and their leaders hanged, the tribe was divided, part being sent to Oklahoma and the rest to the Klamath reservation. Joaquin Miller wrote a colorful but romantically imaginative account supposed to tell of his *Life Amongst the Modocs* (1873).

Mohawk Indians, easternmost tribe of the Iroquois confederacy, located mainly along the Mohawk River, were noted for their ferocity and constant warfare. In the early 17th century, obtaining firearms from Dutch traders, the Mohawk conquered many neighboring tribes, including the Delaware. They were allied with the British in the French and Indian Wars and in the Revolution, after which most of them removed to Canada. The historical Hiawatha was probably a Mohawk, and Joseph Brant♦ was a Mohawk chief. Edmund Wilson's *Apologies to the Iroquois* (1960) treats the modern situation of the tribes in the confederacy.

Mohegan (or MONHEGAN) **Indians,** Algonquian tribe of Connecticut, united with the Pequot under Sassacus, and rebelled against him under the leadership of Uncas. They were allied with the English, and after the death of King Philip (1676) became the only important tribe south of Maine. They finally settled on a reservation near Norwich. Samson Occom♦ was a member of the tribe. In *The Last of the Mohicans,* Cooper confuses Mahicans♦ with Mohegans. The Mohegan figure in *Holdfast Gaines* by Odell Shepard and W.O. Shepard.

Moki Indians, see *Hopi Indians.*

MOMADAY, N[AVARRE] SCOTT (1934–), Oklahoma-born author of Kiowa ancestry whose books include *House Made of Dawn* (1969, Pulitzer Prize), a novel about a young Indian man unable to be at home in either the white or his ancestral society; *The Way to Rainy Mountain* (1969), Kiowa legends told in relation to history and his own youth; *Angle of Geese* (1973) and *The Gourd Dancer* (1976), poems; and *The Names* (1976), a memoir. He was a professor of English as Stanford (1972–81), from which he received a Ph.D. for his critique and edition of the poems of Frederick Goddard Tuckerman, and has more recently been on the faculty of the University of Arizona.

MONROE, HARRIET (1860–1936), Chicago poet and editor, first attained notice with her *Columbian Ode* (1892, published 1893), written in celebration of the World's Columbian Exposition in her native city. With the founding of *Poetry: A Magazine of Verse♦* (1912), she became a leader in the championing of new poetry, and she edited this organ until her death, remaining better known for it than for her several subsequent volumes of minor poetry. Her other works include *Poets and Their Art* (1926, revised 1932), a book of essays, and *A Poet's Life* (1937), her autobiography. The Harriet Monroe Poetry Award established by her will is given, without competition, under the University of Chi-

cago's direction, when sufficient income ($500) is available. Winners include Cummings, Robert Lowell, Marianne Moore, Wallace Stevens, and Yvor Winters.

Monster, The, and Other Stories, seven tales by Stephen Crane,♦ published in 1899.

"The Monster," a novelette set in Whilomville, N.Y., is a bitterly ironic commentary on the cruelty and lack of sympathy of ordinary people for an act of humanity they do not understand. Henry Johnson, a black servant in the home of Dr. Trescott, rescues the physician's young son from a fire. He is terribly disfigured and loses his sanity, so that no home can be found for him in the town. Horrified by the "monster," the townspeople ostracize the doctor and his family because they harbor the man. It finally appears that Trescott has sacrificed his entire happiness for an ethical principle he formerly considered unquestionable. "The Blue Hotel" describes the events that lead to quarrels and a murder at a bar in a small Nebraska town. The victim, a stupid, paranoid Swede, who dies with his eyes fixed on the ironic and symbolic text on a cash register, "This registers the amount of your purchase," is partly responsible for his own death, and his murderer is hardly more responsible than others involved in a sequence of events, although he is sentenced to the penitentiary, because "every sin is the result of a collaboration," and the one who gets the punishment is the one who happens to be at "the apex of a human movement." "His New Mittens" is concerned with the inner reactions of a small boy who runs away from home, and the remaining stories are studies of men in sensational situations or moments of intense excitement.

Mont-Saint-Michel and Chartres, critical work by Henry Adams, ♦ privately printed in 1904, and published in 1913. It is subtitled "A Study of Thirteenth-Century Unity." This interpretation of the dominant attitude of mind from 1150 to 1250 precedes *The Education of Henry Adams♦* in the author's plan to study historical forces by relating two points in time. He chose the 13th century as "the point of history when man held the highest idea of himself as a unit in a unified universe," in order to "measure motion down to his own time" in his autobiography, "a study of Twentieth-Century Multiplicity." In *Mont-Saint-Michel,* he shows philosophy, theology, and the arts to be informed by a spiritual unity, illogical but founded on simple faith and strength of energy. The 16 chapters discuss Norman architecture, giving way to Gothic "flinging its passion against the sky"; the subordinate arts of sculpture and glass; the *Chanson de Roland;* courts of love; the metaphysical system of Aquinas; and the religious mysticism of a period that found its highest symbol in the Virgin, apotheosis of the feminine ideal. Thus there is a unified attitude of mind in men's reaction to the universe, contrasting with the concept of a 20th-century "multiverse" which leads to a philosophy and science of multiple aspects and reactions.

MOODY, WILLIAM VAUGHN (1869–1910), Indiana playwright and poet, graduated from Harvard (1893) and taught English there (1894–95) and at the University of Chicago (1895–99, 1901–7). His first poetic play, *The Masque of Judgment* (1900), deals with the conflict between man and God and the rightful exercise of man's free will, which leads him to rebel. A second verse drama, *The Fire Bringer* (1904), stresses man's duty of rebellion in the story of Prometheus. These works were to have been brought to philosophic completion in a third play dealing with the reconciliation of God and man through the creation of woman, *The Death of Eve* (1912), incomplete at Moody's death. *The Great Divide* (1906), produced and published as *A Sabine Woman* (1906, 1909), contrasts a modern woman—a product of Puritan traditions and inhibitions—and a free individualistic man of the frontier West. Moody's lyric *Poems* (1901) voices a highly spiritual and idealistic belief in the greatness of man's destiny.

MOORE, CLEMENT CLARKE (1779–1863), professor of Biblical learning and author of the poem popularly known as " 'Twas the Night Before Christmas," published anonymously in the *Troy Sentinel* (Dec. 23, 1823), widely copied, and reprinted in the author's *Poems* (1844). The poem's proper title is "A Visit from St. Nicholas."

MOORE, JULIA A. (1847–1920), better known as "The Sweet Singer of Michigan," upon publication of her first book, *The Sweet Singer of Michigan Salutes the Public* (1876), attracted wide attention because her writing was so bad that it seemed to possess almost a touch of genius. Her poems ranged from elegies on deaths caused by yellow fever and choking on roast beef to occasional verse on the Grand Rapids Cricket Club. Her unconsciously childish grammar, and rhymes that went from verse to worse, delighted Clemens, who declared that she had "the touch that makes an intentionally humorous episode pathetic and an intentionally pathetic one funny." Her first book, later retitled *The Sentimental Song Book,* was followed by *A Few Words to the Public with New and Original Poems by Julia A. Moore* (1878). She seems to have thought long before publishing her third book, *Sunshine and Shadow* (1915), a romance of the Revolution.

MOORE, MARIANNE [CRAIG] (1887–1972), born in St. Louis, graduated from Bryn Mawr (1909), and lived mainly in New York City, where she edited *The Dial*♦ (1925–29). She did not publish a book until she was in her mid-thirties, with the issuance of the neutrally titled *Poems* (1921), followed by the more aptly named *Observations* (1924). A long hiatus was followed by *Selected Poems* (1935), which T.S. Eliot in his Introduction declared to be "descriptive rather than lyrical or dramatic." She herself said in the early poem titled "Poetry" that despite "contempt for . . . all this fiddle . . . one discovers in it, after all, a place for the genuine," and the "genuine" she defined as "imaginary gardens with real toads in them." Succeeding collections of poetry appeared in *The Pangolin, and Other Verse* (1936), *What Are Years?* (1941), *Nevertheless* (1944), *Collected Poems* (1951, Pulitzer Prize), *Like a Bulwark* (1956), and *O To Be a Dragon* (1959). In keeping with her conception of the genuine in poetry, these were marked by piquant but precise observation serving as surprising metaphors that often alluded to exotic creatures (e.g. pangolin) based on her knowledge of biology and interest in zoos, as great and enthusiastic as that which she had for her hometown baseball team, the Brooklyn Dodgers. The poems were marked by a disciplined though unconventional use of metrics ("I tend to write in a patterned arrangement, with rhymes . . . to secure an effect of flowing continuity"), and an angular witty, cerebral, ironic attitude. Her so-called *Complete Poems* (1967) gathers all she wished to preserve. Her other works include *The Fables of La Fontaine* (1954), a verse translation; *Predilections* (1955), essays on favorite writers; and *Tell Me, Tell Me* (1966), poems and prose pieces.

MOORE, MERRILL (1903–57), Tennessee poet and a member of the regionalist group that published *The Fugitive*♦ (1922–25). He became a practicing psychiatrist in Boston, who found time for a prodigious body of poetry, all using, with great fluency and flexibility, the sonnet form.

Moravian Church, evangelical Protestant communion that emphasizes Christian unity and personal service, retains a historical episcopacy, and accepts the Scriptures as the sole moral guide. It originated (1457) in Moravia and Bohemia, among the followers of the martyred John Huss, but met severe persecution. The renewed church dates from 1722, when Count Nicolaus Ludwig Zinzendorf (1700–1760) established a refuge in Saxony. The missionary movement began shortly afterward, and Zinzendorf came to America (1741–43), founded a colony at Bethlehem, Pa., and from this and other centers unsuccessfully tried to organize all German sects into the Church of God in Spirit. His biographer, Augustus Gottlieb Spangenberg (1704–92), was also a leader in America after 1735.

Morella, story by Poe,♦ published in 1835 and reprinted in *Tales of the Grotesque and Arabesque* (1840).

Morella, a student of the German mystics, is a woman of extraordinary learning and mental power. Her husband is devoted to her, and acknowledges her intellectual superiority, but she realizes that he does not love her. When she declines in health, he is repelled by her melancholy beauty. She seems resigned, but at last tells him that she is dying and yet shall live, that "her whom in life thou didst abhor, in death thou shalt adore." She dies in childbirth, leaving a daughter who is loved by the lonely father, even though he recognizes her increasing resemblance to his dead wife. He neglects to name the child, but when she is 14 decides to have her baptized. At the font, a perverse impulse causes him to utter the name Morella, at which she falls dead, saying "I am here!" Distracted, the father bears her corpse to the tomb, where he finds no trace of the first Morella.

MORGAN, [GEORGE] FREDERICK (1922–), New York City-born poet, after graduation from Princeton became a founder and the editor of *The Hudson Review.*♦ His first volume, *A Book of Change* (1972), is fre-

quently autobiographical in its quest for values, while *Poems of the Two Worlds* (1977) deals with body and spirit, the mundane and the ideal. Later works are *The Tarot of Cornelius Agrippa* (1978), a prose poem of legendry, and *Death Mother* (1979) and *Northbook* (1982), collections of shorter poems.

MORGAN, LEWIS HENRY (1818–81), called "the Father of American Anthropology," whose *League of the Ho-dé-no-sau-nee, or Iroquois* (1851) is considered the first scientific account of an Indian tribe. His discovery that the kinship system of the Iroquois was similar to that of all American Indians was set forth in *Systems of Consanguinity and Affinity of the Human Family* (1871), an important work on primitive society in general. This led him to propound the doctrine of a common origin and psychic unity of all races, and a theory of social evolution in *Ancient Society; or Researches in the Lines of Human Progress* (1877).

Morgan Library (properly, THE PIERPONT MORGAN LIBRARY), originally the private library of the elder J.P. Morgan, was given to the public by his son. It is housed in an art gallery constructed by McKim, Mead, and White (1905) and an adjoining library building (1920), adjacent to the old Morgan residence in New York City. In addition to an important collection of books and manuscripts, there are significant paintings, drawings, bookbindings, coins, and medals. Among the noteworthy categories in the collection are illuminated manuscripts, incunabula, early liturgical works, and manuscripts or first editions of English and American literature and history. Since its establishment as a public institution (1924), it has been open for research, lectures have been given by prominent scholars, and important exhibitions of its own and of borrowed materials have been arranged.

MORISON, SAMUEL ELIOT (1887–1976), professor of American history at Harvard whose books include *Maritime History of Massachusetts* (1921); *The Oxford History of the United States, 1783–1917* (2 vols., 1927); *Builders of the Bay Colony* (1930); *The Founding of Harvard College* (1935); *Harvard College in the Seventeenth Century* (2 vols., 1936); *Admiral of the Ocean Sea* (1942, Pulitzer Prize), a biography of Columbus; and with H.S. Commager, *The Growth of the American Republic* (2 vols., 1930, periodically revised).

He was the navy's official historian in World War II, and wrote 14 volumes on its many engagements in his *History of U.S. Naval Operations* (1947–60). His study of *John Paul Jones* (1959) earned him another Pulitzer Prize. Even into and beyond his eighth decade he continued his publications with his *Oxford History of the American People* (1965), lives of Commodore Perry (1967), Harrison Gray Otis (1969), a new version of a study issued in 1913, and *Champlain* (1972); and a major work, *The European Discovery of America* (2 vols., 1971, 1974).

Morituri Salutamus, poem in heroic couplets by Longfellow, ♦ written for the fiftieth anniversary of his class at Bowdoin, was collected in *The Masque of Pandora* (1875).

The title derives from the cry of the Roman gladiators, "O Cæsar, we who are about to die salute you!," and in the name of his now aged classmates the poet salutes the familiar scenes, the former teachers, and the young men who are taking the place of his generation, finally addressing his comrades themselves. In an elegiac mood, he recalls the joys and griefs of their long lives, then tells a story, adapted from the *Gesta Romanorum,* of the coming of death, and concludes by urging their continued activity and achievement, while life affords opportunity.

MORRIS, WRIGHT (1910–   ), Nebraska-born author, has set much of his fiction in the Midwest although he attended Pomona College and moved to California in 1961. His numerous finely crafted novels present acute observations of characters, often in an oblique fashion, as they make relations or undergo cleavages with other people. Sometimes these concentrate on one situation diversely affecting the different people involved in it. His novels are *My Uncle Dudley* (1942); *The Man Who Was There* (1945); *The World in the Attic* (1949); *Man and Boy* (1951), a brief but pungent view of a search for a meaningful life, just as another book, *The Works of Love* (1952), treats another basic theme of Morris's, the quest for significant loving relationships; *The Deep Sleep* (1953); *The Huge Season* (1954), a longer book than usual in its revelation of the ethos of the 1920s; *The Field of Vision* (1956, National Book Award), presenting recollections of significant experiences evoked in a group of Americans as they view a bullfight in Mexico; *Love Among the Cannibals* (1957); *Ceremony in Lone Tree* (1960), portraying family members isolated from one another as

they assemble in a Nebraska ghost town to celebrate the ninetieth birthday of one of them; *What a Way To Go* (1962) and *Cause for Wonder* (1963), more broadly comic and with a different setting—Europe—than his other novels; *One Day* (1965), depicting the reactions of diverse Californians to the assassination of President Kennedy; *In Orbit* (1967), concerning the aimless rebellion of a high-school dropout of the time; *Fire Sermon* (1971) and its sequel, *A Life* (1973), further insights into generational relations; *Here Is Einbaum* (1973); *The Fork River Space Project* (1977); and *Plains Song: For Female Voices* (1980), about three generations of lonely Midwestern women. Stories are collected in *Real Losses, Imaginary Gains* (1976). Morris is also a sensitive and sharp-eyed photographer who has created books in which prose and pictures reinforce one another: *The Inhabitants* (1946), *The Home Place* (1948), *God's Country and My People* (1968), *Love Affair* (1972), about Venice, and *Photographs and Words* (1982). *The Territory Ahead* (1958) is a critical study of American literature and the native tradition, further investigated in books of essays: *A Bill of Rites, a Bill of Wrongs, a Bill of Goods* (1968), *About Fiction* (1975), and *Earthly Delights, Unearthly Adornments* (1978). *Will's Boy* (1981) and *Solo: An American Dreamer in Europe* (1983) are memoirs: the first of his youth, the second of his young manhood.

MORRISON, TONI (1931–   ), Ohio-born novelist, originally named Chloe Anthony Wofford, a graduate of Howard University, writes about the problems of black women in the North, like herself. Her novels include *The Bluest Eye* (1970), *Sula* (1973), *Song of Solomon* (1977), and *Tar Baby* (1981). She is also an editor at a New York publishing house.

MOSEL, TAD (GEORGE AULT MOSEL, JR.) (1922–   ), after graduation from Amherst (1947), study at the Yale Drama School, and an M.A. from Columbia began playwriting for television and in 1960 dramatized for the stage James Agee's *A Death in the Family* ♦ under the title *All the Way Home,* a work for which he won a Pulitzer Prize.

MOSS, HOWARD (1922–   ), New York City poet and poetry editor of *The New Yorker* (1948–   ), whose graceful lyrics have been collected in *The Wound and the Weather* (1946), *The Toy Fair* (1954), *A Swimmer in* *the Air* (1957), *A Winter Come, A Summer Gone* (1960), *Finding Them Lost* (1965), *Second Nature* (1968), *Selected Poems* (1971, National Book Award), *Buried City* (1975), *A Swim Off the Rocks* (1976), *Notes from the Castle* (1979), and *Rules of Sleep* (1984). He has also written *The Magic Lantern of Marcel Proust* (1962), *Writing Against Time* (1969), and *Whatever Is Moving* (1981), essays and reviews, and *Instant Lives* (1974), brief biographical sketches of authors, written in parodies of their own styles. *The Folding Green* (1958), *The Oedipus Mah-Jongg Scandal* (1968), and *The Palace at 4 A.M.* (1972) are plays that have been produced.

Mosses from an Old Manse, tales and sketches written by Hawthorne♦ during his residence (1842–46) at the Old Manse in Concord. They were published in two volumes (1846), with an introductory essay, "The Old Manse," followed by 25 short stories and historical sketches. Among them are historical pieces, like "Roger Malvin's Burial"♦; satirical allegories, like "The Celestial Railroad"♦; and allegorical tales of the supernatural, like "Young Goodman Brown,"♦ "Rappaccini's Daughter,"♦ "The Birthmark,"♦ and "The Artist of the Beautiful."♦

Mother Carey's Chickens, story for children by Kate Wiggin.♦

MOTLEY, JOHN LOTHROP (1814–77), descendant of an old and prominent Boston family, after graduation from Harvard (1831) studied law and wrote two novels, *Morton's Hope* (1839), a semi-autobiographical account of an American at a German university, and *Merry Mount* (1849), a romantic novel concerning the colony of Thomas Morton. In 1847 he began his lifelong study of the Netherlands, chosen because he liked the analogy between the United Provinces and the United States, and because it gave him an opportunity to study the triumph of Protestantism in northern Europe and show how it brought freedom where previously there was despotism. The book appeared as *The Rise of the Dutch Republic* (3 vols., 1856) after ten years of preparation. In a picturesque, enthusiastic, and dramatic manner, he presented the political and religious history of the country, although he neglected economic and social matters. He arranged his whole canvas around the two subjects of Protestantism and absolutism, making William of Orange the Protestant hero and Philip II the dark-dyed

autocratic, Catholic scoundrel. The *History of the United Netherlands* (4 vols., 1860, 1867) deals with the period from William's death to the truce of 1609. The period from 1609 to the Thirty Years' War was treated in *The Life and Death of John of Barneveld* (2 vols., 1874).

MOTLEY, WILLARD (1912–65), author of naturalistic novels drawing upon his life in Chicago's slums but little upon his heritage as a black: *Knock on Any Door* (1947), about a boy growing from a juvenile delinquent to a murderer; *We Fished All Night* (1951); and *Let No Man Write My Epitaph* (1958), telling of the search for a decent life by the son of the protagonist of his first novel. *Let Noon Be Fair* (1966) depicts tourist trade corrupting a town in Mexico, the country in which Motley lived from 1951 on. His stories appear in *Soon, One Morning* (1963), and his *Diaries* was published in 1979.

Motor Boys, THE, series of books for boys by Edward Stratemeyer.♦

Mountaineering in the Sierra Nevada, sketches of explorations and experiences in the California mountains, by Clarence King,♦ published in 1872 and revised from the author's notes in 1902. King had been employed in the U.S. Geological Survey since 1863, and the book gives an accurate account of the geology and geography of the Sierra. Its chief importance, however, is based on its vivid narratives of mountain-climbing adventures and of meetings with picturesque and typical characters, such as the chapters on "The Newtys of Pike," concerning a family of emigrants from Pike County; and "Cut-Off Copples's," describing a frontier artist and his rustic romance.

Mountains of California, The, descriptive work of John Muir,♦ published in 1894 and revised in 1911. Describing the geological history and the varieties of flora and fauna of the region, the study is the result of many summers spent by the author in both the Sierra Nevada and the Coast Range and, besides its scientific authority, presents an enthusiastic appreciation of the beauties of the California wilderness.

Mourning Becomes Electra, dramatic trilogy by O'Neill,♦ produced and published in 1931. Based on the ancient Greek legend, its three parts are: (I) *Homecoming;* (II) *The Hunted;* (III) *The Haunted.*

I. At the close of the Civil War, Brigadier-General Ezra Mannon, descendant of a Puritan family, returns to his New England home, where he is awaited by his wife Christine and daughter Lavinia. During his absence and that of her adored soldier son Orin, Christine has had a liaison with the clipper captain Adam Brant, son of Ezra's brother and a family servant, who intended to avenge his mother's disgrace, but instead fell in love with the sensual Christine. Mother and daughter hate each other, for Lavinia is the victim of an inner conflict between her Mannon heritage and the elements of her nature inherited from Christine. Herself in love with Brant, she suspects her mother's relations with him and forces from him the truth. Peter Niles, a childhood friend, loves Lavinia, but she tells him that she hates love and will never marry. When Ezra comes home, it is revealed that he hates his son Orin for possessing Christine's love, which he himself never attained. Pretending to give him medicine, Christine poisons her husband from a box which Brant supplied her, and which Lavinia discovers.

II. Orin returns, to find his father dead and his mother distracted and changed. He resumes an old affair with Hazel, Peter's sister, but Lavinia persuades him to join her revenge plot. They follow Christine to a rendezvous on Brant's ship, and, after she leaves, Orin kills Brant. When Christine learns of this, she commits suicide.

III. Lavinia and Orin go on a long voyage that takes them to the South Sea islands. By the time they return, Orin, harried by guilt and remorse, has grown to resemble his father, while Lavinia, freed of the puritan repressions, has the beauty and amorality of her mother. She wants to marry Peter and now encourages Orin's affair with Hazel, but Orin, preoccupied with writing a confession, breaks with his fiancée, makes an incestuous proposal to Lavinia, and shoots himself. Lavinia makes love to Peter, but he leaves her, repelled by her eagerness. She concludes, "Love isn't permitted to me. The dead are too strong!," and enters the shuttered house, to spend the rest of her life alone with the memory of the Mannon dead.

Mourt's Relation, journal of the voyage of the *Mayflower,* record of its Compact, and description of the earliest days of Plymouth Colony.

Moveable Feast, A, memoir by Hemingway♦ of his life in Paris (1921–26), published in 1964. In brief sketches the work summons up the sense of what Paris meant to him as a writer beginning a career and to other expatriate Americans. It tells how Gertrude Stein came to employ the term "lost generation," of his friendship with and falling out with her, and of Pound, Fitzgerald, and other associates.

MOWATT, ANNA CORA (1819–70), pursued a literary career in New York as a hack writer of widely varied material, until in 1845 her farcical social comedy *Fashion* made her a respected author. This play was followed by a romantic prose and verse drama of the reign of Louis XV, *Armand, the Child of the People* (1847). In 1845 she went on the stage, and achieved great success, which she discussed in her *Autobiography of an Actress* (1854), and which furnished material for her romantic narratives of stage life, *Mimic Life* (1856) and *Twin Roses* (1857). After 1861, she lived abroad, where she wrote romantic novels and historical sketches. Her earlier novels of New York society include *The Fortune Hunter* (1844) and *Evelyn; or, A Heart Unmasked* (1845).

Muckraking movement received its name from Theodore Roosevelt (1906) in his attack upon allegedly biased and sweeping charges of corruption in politics and business. The term originally alluded to a character in *Pilgrim's Progress,* who was so intent upon raking up muck that he could not see a celestial crown held over him. The muckraking movement in the U.S. began in 1902 and in four years had spread throughout the nation. It reached another climax in 1911, but ended as a movement with America's entry into World War I. *The Arena,* a dignified journal of protest, was the precursor of many popular magazines that became the medium for the exposure of unscrupulous methods and motives in private business and in city, state, and national government. *Everybody's, McClure's, The Independent, Collier's,* and the *Cosmopolitan* were the leading periodicals devoted to the movement, and among their principal authors were Ida Tarbell ("History of the Standard Oil Company"), Lincoln Steffens ("The Struggle for Self-Government"), T.W. Lawson ("Frenzied Finance"), R.S. Baker, S.S. McClure, Mark Sullivan, and Samuel Hopkins Adams. A few newspapers, particularly the New York *World* and Kansas City *Star,* aided materially in the campaign, and such books as Sinclair's *The*

Jungle and the novels of D.G. Phillips carried the movement into fiction. An account of its development is given in the *Autobiography* of Steffens.

MUIR, John (1838–1914), naturalist and explorer, was born in Scotland, brought to the U.S. (1849), and educated in chemistry, geology, and botany at the University of Wisconsin. Inspired to further study of these subjects, he made extended journeys throughout the U.S., often on foot. The journal of his trip (1867) from Indiana to the Gulf of Mexico was edited as *A Thousand-Mile Walk to the Gulf* (1916). In 1868 California became his home, and in the following years he studied the glacial formations of the West and the forests of the region, becoming a leader in the forest-conservation movement through his impassioned writings. His books include *The Story of My Boyhood and Youth* (1913); *The Mountains of California* ♦ (1894); *Our National Parks* (1901); *Stickeen* (1909), a sentimental short story about a dog; and *My First Summer in the Sierra* (1911).

MUMFORD, Lewis (1895–   ), socio-cultural critic, whose books include *Sticks and Stones* (1924), which interpreted American life and thought in terms of its architecture. *The Golden Day* (1926) analyzed it in relation to its literature, particularly that of the romantic period. *Herman Melville* (1929) is a critical biography, primarily psychological; *The Brown Decades* (1931) a study of the arts in the U.S. from the close of the Civil War to 1895, seeing that period's development in artistic fields as comparable with the earlier "Golden Day" in literature; four volumes, *Technics and Civilization* (1934), *The Culture of Cities* (1938), *The Condition of Man* (1944), and *The Conduct of Life* (1951), analyze the physical and social composition of cities in the Western world since the 10th century, and plead for a reconstruction of the 20th-century "megalopolis" through regional planning and communal ownership of land. Later works include *The City in History* (1961) and *The Highway and the City* (1963); *The Myth of the Machine* (2 vols., 1967, 1970), *The Urban Prospect* (1968); and autobiography, *Findings and Keepings* (1975), *My Works and Days* (1978), and *Sketches from Life* (1982).

Murder in the Cathedral, verse drama by T.S. Eliot, ♦ produced and published in 1935.

Archbishop Thomas Becket returns in A.D. 1170 to Canterbury from his seven-year exile in France. A women's chorus represents the helpless attitude of the common people toward the schism between church and state, while the ecclesiastical party is represented by Becket's priests, and the royal party by the officers of Henry II. The archbishop, having established relations with the Pope and the king of France, is determined to bring the argument to a crisis, even though he realizes that his life is at stake. Four Tempters show the inner conflict involved in his decision: his youthful love of pleasure, his later ambition for power, the demands of the feudal barons, and the desire for martyrdom. Rejecting all four, he is certain that he must give his life "to the Law of God above the Law of Man," and on Christmas morning delivers a sermon defending this position. Four days later the king's knights arrive, insolent and self-assured, to murder him by royal command, and he refuses to attempt escape. After they stab him to death, the knights address the audience with a pompous, foolish defense of their deed. They withdraw, leaving the stage to the priests, who thank God for having "given us another Saint in Canterbury," and the chorus, which supplicates divine mercy.

Murders in the Rue Morgue, The, story by Poe, ♦ published in 1841 and collected in the *Prose Tales of Edgar A. Poe* (1843). It is his first tale of ratiocination and in it he is considered to have created the genre of the detective story. ♦

The narrator lives in Paris with his friend C. Auguste Dupin, an eccentric genius of extraordinary analytic powers. They read an account of the murders of a Mme L'Espanaye and her daughter Camille in their fourth-story apartment in the Rue Morgue. The police are puzzled by the crime, for its brutal manner indicates that the murderer possessed superhuman strength and agility; his voice, overheard by neighbors, was grotesque and unintelligible; and they can discover no motive. Dupin undertakes to solve the mystery as an exercise in ratiocination. After examing the evidence and visiting the scene of the murders to find new clues, he deduces the fact that the criminal is an ape. An advertisement brings to Dupin's apartment a sailor who confesses that an orangutan, which he brought to Paris to sell, escaped and committed the murders. The police release a former suspect, and the ape is recaptured and sold to the Jardin des Plantes.

MURFREE, Mary Noailles (1850–1922), spent most of her life in her native Tennessee, which she described in local-color fiction published under the pseudonym Charles Egbert Craddock. Her first collection of stories, *In the Tennessee Mountains* (1884), led to the discovery that the popular author was a frail, crippled spinster whose pseudonym was derived from the name of the hero in a very early story. The rhythmical prose and general atmosphere of her tales, and the poetic descriptions of landscape, are romantic, although the careful reproduction of the native dialect and faithful descriptions of specific details give them a realistic appearance. The first volume of stories was followed by more than ten others and a series of Southern historical novels.

Mutiny on the Bounty, first novel in the trilogy about the 18th-century mutiny against Captain Bligh written by James N. Hall♦ and Charles B. Nordhoff.♦

My Ántonia, novel by Willa Cather,♦ published in 1918.

Jim Burden and Ántonia Shimerda arrive as children in pioneer Black Hawk, Neb., he from Virginia and she with her family from Bohemia. With his companion, Jake Marpole, and the frontiersman and hired man Otto Fuchs, Jim lives on his grandparents' prosperous farm; but the Shimerdas are tricked into buying a squalid, undeveloped tract, where the impractical, music-loving father attempts to create a farm, aided by his vulgar, nagging wife, their grown son Ambrosch, the adolescent Ántonia, her young sister Yulka, and the idiot boy Marek. Although the Burdens aid him with food and supplies, Shimerda in homesick despair commits suicide, and Jim's grandfather employs Ambrosch and Ántonia, who later has to work in the fields. After the Burdens move to town, Ántonia becomes a maid in the household of their neighbors. Despite her trying experiences with various employers, including amorous old Wick Cutter, she remains quiet, sincere, and industrious. Jim, after attending the state university and Harvard, learns of Ántonia's elopement with Larry Donovan, a railway conductor who deserts her and her child. She then returns in disgrace to work on her brother's farm. Twenty years later when Jim visits Nebraska, he finds her a stalwart, middle-aged farm wife, married to mild, friendly Anton Cuzak. They have many children, and it is Ántonia's strength that maintains the family, but she still possess the laughter and inner core of pioneer integrity which always distinguished her. "She was a rich mine of life, like the founders of early races."

My Kinsman, Major Molineux, tale by Hawthorne,♦ first published in *The Token* (1832) and collected in *The Snow-Image.* Robert Lowell adapted it as a one-act verse play in *The Old Glory* (1965).

Set in Boston during a period when the colonists were opposing the royal government, the story tells of an 18-year-old country boy, Robin, who comes to town to make his fortune and to seek the aid of his important kinsman, one Major Molineux. He is rebuffed by everyone of whom he inquires, and spends an unhappy "evening of ambiguity and weariness" in his quest. Finally he discovers the Major being hauled through town, tarred and feathered, as all the citizenry laugh at him, and as the contagion seizes Robin his "shout was the loudest there."

My Lost Youth, poem by Longfellow,♦ published in 1855 and collected in *The Courtship of Miles Standish* (1858). In nine-line stanzas, whose meter is reminiscent of ballad measure, the lyric recalls the author's youth in Portland, Me. Each stanza ends with the refrain of a Lapland song: "A boy's will is the wind's will, And the thoughts of youth are long, long thoughts." The title of Frost's collection *A Boy's Will* is derived from this passage.

My Sister Eileen, humorous biography by Ruth McKenney.♦

Mysterious Stranger, The, story by Clemens,♦ posthumously published in 1916. It was edited from various manuscripts by A.B. Paine. A new edition (1969) based on a final manuscript and titled *No. 44, The Mysterious Stranger,* shows that Paine had silently deleted about one-quarter of Mark Twain's text, created a new character (the Astrologer), altered the names of other characters, and conflated three manuscript drafts to create his own version.

The Paine version is set in the medieval Austrian village of Eseldorf, where a mysterious stranger visits young Theodor Fischer and his friends Nikolaus and Seppi. He is discovered to be Satan, and shows his power by building a miniature castle that he peoples with clay creatures, destroying them almost as soon as he brings them to life. He then exerts his power on the villagers, and, when Father Peter is falsely accused of theft by the Astrologer and Father Adolf, he confounds the evil and makes the innocent crazy, since he says earthly happiness is restricted to the mad. Other "kindness" includes the drowning of Nikolaus, who would otherwise live as a cripple. His total indifference to mankind and its conceptions of good and evil shocks the boys' natural moral sense, yet Satan shows that from this moral sense came wars, tortures, and inequalities. Finally he departs, and Theodor realizes that this was a dream, as false as morality, and as illogical as a God who tortured men yet commanded them to worship Him.

The version first published in 1969 is also set in Eseldorf. To it in 1490, not long after the invention of movable type, comes a likable young printer's devil, called only No. 44, who is actually possessed of satanic powers that allow him to master the craft of printing in a few hours. Single-handedly he speedily produces a Bible and magically summons up phantasmagoric people to print innumerable copies. He enjoys playing tricks on the town's magician and on the cruel, hypocritical Father Adolf, while he also travels back and forth in space and time between 19th-century U.S. and medieval Europe. The story of his activities, both diabolical and whimsical, is told by his 17-year-old friend August Feldner, a curious person with a split personality. August's doppelgänger or "Dream-Self," named Emil Schwarz, has powers like those of No. 44 and is caught up in similar adventures and activities. The fanciful tale compounded of burlesque and satire concludes with the revelation of No. 44 to August that "Life itself is only a vision, a dream . . . ," the creation of "a God . . . who mouths morals . . . and has none himself . . . who could make good children as easily as bad, yet preferred to make bad ones."

Mystery of Marie Rogêt, The, detective story by Poe, ♦ published in 1842–43 as a sequel to "The Murders in the Rue Morgue" ♦ and reprinted in *Tales* (1845). The principal details are based on the actual New York murder case of Mary Cecilia Rogers.

Marie Rogêt, a Parisian beauty of uncertain reputation, leaves her mother's home, saying she intends to spend the day with an aunt, but is not seen again. Four days later, her corpse is recovered from the Seine. The Prefect of Police offers a reward to C. Auguste Dupin, scholarly amateur detective, for a solution to the puzzle. One of the girl's admirers, St. Eustache, is proved innocent after his suicide, and by a process of ratiocination Dupin shows that another, Beauvais, cannot be guilty. The newspapers have hinted that the corpse may not be that of Marie, but Dupin refutes this possibility. He sets aside other suggestions, also by logical proof, and decides that the murder must have been committed by a secret lover, who would have thrown the body into the river from a boat, and then cast the boat adrift after reaching shore. Dupin's proposal that the boat be found and examined for clues is followed by the successful solution of the mystery.

N

NABOKOV, VLADIMIR (1899–1977), born in Russia of a patrician family, educated at Trinity College, Cambridge, came to the U.S. (1940) and was naturalized in 1945. He was a professor of Russian literature at Cornell (1948–59) until his own literary success allowed him to retire. His ingenious, witty, stylized, and erudite novels include *Laughter in the Dark* (1938), published in England as *Camera Obscura* (1936), after the original Russian title, about the moral deterioration of a respectable Berliner; *The Real Life of Sebastian Knight* (1941), in which the narrator, a young Russian in Paris, discovers the true nature of his half-brother, an English novelist, by writing his biography; *Bend Sinister* (1947), about a politically uncommitted professor in a totalitarian state who tries to maintain personal integrity; *Pnin* (1957), amusing sketches about the experiences of an exiled Russian professor of entomology at an upstate New York college; *Lolita*♦ (Paris, 1955; U.S., 1958), a farcical and satirical novel of the passion of a middle-aged, sophisticated European émigré for a 12-year-old American "nymphet," and their wanderings across the U.S.; *Invitation to a Beheading*♦ (Russia, 1938; U.S., 1959), a Kafkaesque story of a man sentenced to die for some unknown expression of individuality and his resultant discovery that he has a real soul; *Pale Fire*♦ (1962), a satirical fantasy called a novel, which is a witty, ironic, and complex *tour de force* concerning a poem about an exiled Balkan king in a New England college town and the involved critical commentary on the poem by the king himself; *The Gift* (Russia, 1937; U.S., 1963), a pseudo-autobiography about Russian expatriates in Berlin after World War I; *The Defense* (Germany, 1930; U.S., 1964), about a young Russian master of chess who treats life as another game; *The Eye* (1965), about a Russian émigré living in Berlin; *Despair* (1966), about a man who contrives his own murder; *King, Queen, Knave* (1968), his second novel, originally published in Germany (1928), also the setting for the story of a young man's affair with his married aunt; *Ada or Ardor* (1969), a witty parody whose involved plot, set in a fanciful land, deals with a man's lifelong love for his sister Ada; *Mary* (1970),

the author's first novel (Germany, 1926), about a young Czarist officer exiled in Berlin and his first love affair; *Glory* (1971), the fifth (Paris, 1932) of his nine novels written in Russian, a comic portrait of a Russian émigré's wanderings; *Transparent Things* (1972), a novella about a rootless American's marriage and murder of his wife; and *Look at the Harlequins!* (1974), a novel about an author who very much resembles Nabokov himself. His stories have been gathered in several collections; his light, witty verse appears in *Poems* (1959) and *Poems and Problems* (1971), the latter including also problems in chess, and *The Waltz Invention* (1966) is a play. *Conclusive Evidence* (1951), revised as *Speak, Memory* (1966), gathers autobiographical sketches of life in Imperial Russia. *Strong Opinions* (1973) prints replies to journalists' questions about himself, literature, and public issues. He wrote a study of *Nikolai Gogol* (1944) and made a translation with commentary of *Eugene Onegin* (4 vols., 1964, revised 1977). The correspondence of Edmund Wilson and Nabokov, much of it about his translation of Pushkin, appeared in 1979. Other posthumous publications include *Lectures on Literature* (1980) and *Lectures on Russian Literature* (1981).

Naked and the Dead, The, novel by Norman Mailer,♦ published in 1948.

An American division led by General Cummings invades the Japanese-held island of Anopopei, securing a position in spite of heavy losses. The varied members of Sergeant Croft's reconnaissance platoon are characterized through flashbacks and through their violent language and behavior under the stress of jungle warfare. Despite being undermanned, they withstand a Japanese counterattack, but shoot prisoners and hunt drunkenly among corpses for souvenirs. Personal conflict develops between Cummings, an intellectual who believes that "the morality of the future is a power morality," and Lieutenant Hearn, who is unwilling to fit into the general's "fear ladder," while Private Valsen opposes Croft's brutal implementation of Cummings's military philosophy. For a combination of personal and strategic reasons, the platoon is sent on a dangerous patrol across a mountain range, and returns, deci-mated by casualties, to find the Japanese destroyed and the island taken independently of their efforts.

Naked Lunch, novel by William Burroughs, ♦ published in Paris (1959) and in New York (1962). Based upon the author's notes during a period of deep addiction to drugs, the book's first-person narrator, William Lee, is presented as a "recording instrument" of a surrealistic collage of nightmare fantasies purposefully without any sequential plot. Instead, the spokesman's psychic states, his alienation, and his fight against authority are depicted.

Narragansett Indians, Algonquian tribe, now extinct, which formerly occupied Rhode Is-land and Long Island. They were induced by Roger Williams, whose study of the tribe is contained in his *Key into the Language of America* (1643), to assist the colonists in the Pequot War. During King Philip's War they were suspected of treachery, and in an engagement of 1675, known as the "Swamp Fight," the tribe was virtually annihilated. The Narragansett figure in Cooper's *The Wept of Wish-ton-Wish.*

Narrative of Arthur Gordon Pym, of Nantucket, The, novelette by Poe, ♦ published in 1838. Like "The Journal of Julius Rodman," it is an account of exploration and adventure, heightened by fictional additions, but based on fact. It is extensively paraphrased from Benjamin Morell's *Narrative of Four Voyages to the South Seas and Pacific* (1832) and a manual of seamanship, and owes its origin to a "Report of the Committee on Naval Af-fairs" (1836), concerning the expedition pro-posed by J.N. Reynolds, with whom Poe was acquainted. In the novelette, the fictitious Pym recounts his experiences as a passenger on the *Grampus,* which sailed from Nan-tucket for the South Seas in June 1827. Mutiny, shipwreck, and "horrible sufferings" are followed by a rescue and further sensa-tional adventures in the Antarctic Ocean and on Pacific islands.

NASBY, Petroleum V., pseudonym of D.R. Locke. ♦

NASH, Ogden (1902–71), New York author of light verse, which ranges from acidulous satire and irresponsible good humor to the mildly mad. Nash says that he is indebted to "The Sweet Singer of Michigan," ♦ having

humorously employed the mannerisms of her bad verse: hyperdithyrambic meters, pseudo-poetic inversions, gangling asymmetrical lines, extremely pat or elaborately inexact rhymes, parenthetical dissertations, and un-expected puns. His collections include *Free Wheeling* (1931), *Hard Lines* (1931), *Happy Days* (1933), *The Primrose Path* (1935), *The Bad Parents' Garden of Verse* (1936), *I'm a Stranger Here Myself* (1938), *The Face Is Familiar* (1940), *Many Long Years Ago* (1945), *Versus* (1949), *Family Reunion* (1950), *Parents Keep Out* (1951), *The Private Dining Room* (1953), *You Can't Get There from Here* (1957), and *Everyone But Thee and Me* (1962). As a lyricist he collaborated with Kurt Weill and S.J. Perelman on the musical comedy *One Touch of Venus* (1943).

NAST, Thomas (1840–1902), political carica-turist and illustrator, born in Germany, was brought to the U.S. (1846) and commenced his career as an illustrator at 15. He joined the staff of *Harper's Weekly* (1862) to draw Civil War cartoons that attacked Northern defeat-ists, leading Lincoln to call him "our best recruiting sergeant." He reached the height of his success in the 1870s, with his biting caricatures of the corrupt Tweed Ring. He was the creator of the symbolic Tammany tiger, Republican elephant, and Democratic donkey.

NATHAN, George Jean (1882–1958), born in Indiana, after graduation from Cornell (1904) began his career as a drama critic in New York. In 1908 he became associated with *The Smart Set,* ♦ of which he was co-editor (1914–23) with H.L. Mencken, with whom he then founded *The American Mercury* ♦ (1924), serving as an editor until 1930 and establishing himself as one of the literary arbiters of the period. While Mencken was considered the great satirical realist of the era, Nathan formed his counter-part as a philosophical snob, cynic, and sophisticate, who adopted a pose of detach-ment, following the attitude of his master, Huneker, in holding to standards of art for art's sake. His many books on the contempo-rary theater mainly reprint essays and re-views. Important for their early championing of O'Neill and other talents, these works vary from scathing attacks on sentimentalities to boundless enthusiasms, for Nathan claimed to write "with a pestiferous catholicity of taste that embraces *Medea* and the Follies, Eleanora Duse and Florence Mills." His other books include *The Autobiography of an*

Attitude (1925), epigrammatic self-revelations; *The Avon Flows* (1937), a comedy adapting parts of *Romeo and Juliet, The Taming of the Shrew,* and *Othello* to present the lives of a Romeo and Juliet who do not commit suicide; and *The Bachelor Life* (1941), an apologia.

NATHAN, ROBERT [GRUNTAL] (1894–1984), born in New York, was educated in the U.S. and abroad and is the author of many short novels, noted for their delicate prose and satirical fantasy. These include *Peter Kindred* (1919), the story of a boy's experiences in preparatory school and at Harvard; *Jonah* (1925, published in England as *Son of Amittai*), a witty reconstruction of the Biblical story; *The Bishop's Wife* (1928), about an angel who poses as an archdeacon and falls in love with the bishop's wife; *There Is Another Heaven* (1929), the story of a converted Jew in a Calvinist heaven; *Journey of Tapiola* (1938), travel adventures of a Yorkshire terrier, a canary, and an old gray rat; *Tapiola's Brave Regiment* (1941); *Mr. Whittle and the Morning Star* (1947), about a professor's mystical view of the world's ending; *The Fair* (1964), a whimsical tale of the time of King Arthur; and *The Mallot Diaries* (1965), an ironic view of two anthropology professors living with a Stone Age-culture tribe. Other works include poems and plays.

NATION, CARRY (1846–1911), temperance agitator, after an unhappy youth and irregular schooling during her family's journeying from Kentucky to Texas and Missouri married the intemperate Reverend Gloyd. A second marriage (1877) gave her the name Nation, and following a short period of school teaching she became absorbed in emotional religious activity, convinced that she was divinely appointed to destroy the institution of the saloon. She began her crusade at Medicine Lodge, Kan. (1899), and continued with a spectacular destruction of property in saloons. Her favorite weapon was the hatchet, and she referred to her exploits as "hatchetings" or "hatchetations." Her temperance lectures took her through the U.S. and Europe, and in 1904 she published *The Use and Need of the Life of Carry A. Nation.* Frequently jailed and ridiculed, she gladly suffered martyrdom. Carleton Beals's *Cyclone Carry* (1962) is a lively life.

Nation, The (1865–), New York weekly journal founded "to discuss current affairs . . . to maintain true democratic principles; to work for the equality of 'the laboring class of the South'; . . . the elevation of the Negro; to fix public attention on the importance of public education; . . . criticize books and works of art soundly and impartially." Its first editor (1865–81) was E.L. Godkin; early contributors included C.E. Norton, Howells, the three Jameses, D.C. Gilman, W.C. Brownell, Fiske, Parkman, C.F. Adams, Sumner, and F.W. Taussig. Among the causes for which the magazine worked were civil service and tariff reforms, proportional representation in the legislature, and the ousting of corrupt politicians such as the Tweed Ring. *The Nation* was also rigorous in its criticism of literature and the arts. It was sold to the New York *Evening Post* (1881), of which Godkin became the editor. Under W.P. Garrison (1881–1906), it continued its original policies, although as a subsidiary of the *Post* it lost its prestige. Garrison and later editors, including P.E. More (1909–14), drew on the same distinguished contributors, although adding many new literary figures. In 1918 O.G. Villard became editor and severed the connection with the *Post.* He continued the magazine's liberal stand, opposing the ratification of the Versailles Treaty, sympathetically interpreting the new Russian state, and making the journal a distinguished commentary on international affairs. The literary editors whose views influenced liberal letters included the Van Dorens, John Macy, Ludwig Lewisohn, and J.W. Krutch, and James Agee reviewed films during the 1940s. Villard retired in 1933, selling the magazine in 1935, but it continued its campaign for social justice, although for a time under the editorship of Freda Kirchwey (1933–55) this characteristic was thought to be diminished. Carey McWilliams, who had been associated with the magazine since 1945, was editor, 1955–79. Under him and since his time it continues to be a feisty left-wing commentator on the national and international scene, as well as a review of books and the arts by writers who include James Baldwin, E.L. Doctorow, Studs Terkel, and Kurt Vonnegut.

National Book Awards, founded (1950) by the American Book Publishers Council, American Booksellers Association, and Book Manufacturers Institute, and after 1976 sponsored by the National Book Committee for the year's most distinguished works in the areas of Arts and Letters, Children's Literature, Contemporary Affairs, Fiction, History and Biography, and Poetry. Discontinued in 1979, they were replaced by The American Book Awards of the Association of American Booksellers with numerous categories for hardcover and paperback works, but many authors made strong objection to the criteria of selection. The sponsoring organizations have also awarded an annual National Medal for Literature. ♦

National Book Critics Circle, organization of 300 professional critics and editors, founded (1974) to select the "most distinguished" volumes of fiction, general nonfiction, poetry, and criticism of the preceding year. Each member nominates three books in each category, and the board of directors, which may add selections of its own, votes to elect the winners.

National Institute of Arts and Letters, see *American Academy*.

National Medal for Literature, annual award to honor the achievements of an American's literary career, established by the National Book Committee, a nonprofit educational society founded in 1954, also the sponsor of the National Book Awards. ♦ The sponsors have been The National Institute of Arts and Letters (1975–77), The American Book Awards (1979–83), and the New York Public Library (1978, 1984–). Medalists are Thornton Wilder (1965), Edmund Wilson (1966), Auden (1967), Marianne Moore (1968), Conrad Aiken (1969), R.P. Warren (1970), E.B. White (1971), Lewis Mumford (1972), Nabokov (1973), no awards (1974–75), Tate (1976), Robert Lowell (1977), MacLeish (1978), Welty (1979), Kenneth Burke (1980), John Cheever (1981), no awards (1982–83), Mary McCarthy (1984).

Native Son, novel by Richard Wright, ♦ published in 1940. With Paul Green he dramatized it (1941), and also produced and acted in a film version (1951).

Bigger Thomas, a black boy, reared in the slum world of Chicago, is led by his environment into a life of crime. His patronizing reception by Communist associates of his employer's daughter, combined with other circumstances, throw him into a confused mental state in which he accidentally murders the girl. In the ensuing flight, pursued by a mob, he kills his own sweetheart before he is captured and condemned to death.

Natty Bumppo, see *Leather-Stocking Tales*.

Naturalism, critical term applied to the method of literary composition that aims at a detached, scientific objectivity in the treatment of natural man. It is thus more inclusive and less selective than realism, ♦ and holds to the philosophy of determinism. It conceives of man as controlled by his instincts or his passions, or by his social and economic environment and circumstances. Since in this view man has no free will, the naturalistic writer does not attempt to make moral judgments, and as a determinist he tends toward pessimism. The movement is an outgrowth of 19th-century scientific thought, following in general the biological determinism of Darwin's theory, or the economic determinism of Marx. It stems from French literature, in which Zola emphasizes biological determinism, and Flaubert economic determinism. The Russian novelists also added their influence to the trend. American leaders of the naturalistic movement are considered to include Crane, Norris, Herrick, London, and Frederic, and later such significant figures as Dreiser, Dos Passos, and Farrell.

Nature, essay by Emerson, ♦ published anonymously in 1836 and reprinted in *Nature, Addresses, and Lectures* (1849). Based on his early lectures, this first book expresses the main principles of Transcendentalism. An introduction states that "Our age is retrospective," seeing God and nature at second hand through the ideas and experiences of previous generations, and asks, "Why should not we also enjoy an original relation to the universe?" The eight brief chapters discuss the "lover of nature," the rare poetic person "whose inward and outer senses are still truly adjusted to each other"; the "uses" of nature; the idealist philosophy in relation to nature; evidences of spirit in the material universe; and the potential expansion of human souls and works that will result from a general return to direct, immediate contact with the natural environment. The four uses of nature are (1) "Commodity," or its utilitarian and sensuous contributions to the life of mankind; (2) "Beauty," or the delight in the perception of natural forms, of the high and noble spiritual elements essential to them, and of the intellectual truths inherent in them; (3) "Language," or the symbolic character of natural facts, which convey transcendental meanings to minds prepared for their reception; and (4) "Discipline," or the function of natural environment in educating "both the Understanding and the Reason." In expressing his belief in the mystical "unity of Nature—the unity, in variety,—which meets us everywhere," the author develops his concept of the "Over-Soul" or "Universal Mind." Nature is "to us, the present expositor of the divine mind," which is the spiritual essence everywhere present in, and represented by, material nature, and in which man himself shares.

Nauset Indians, Algonquian tribe formerly living on Cape Cod in Massachusetts. In 1622 they supplied the starving Plymouth colonists with corn and beans. Most of them became Christians, and they remained friendly to the colonists through King Philip's War. They were among those called Praying Indians.

Navajo (or NAVAHO) **Indians,** numerous shepherd tribe now living on a large reservation in the mountains of northern Arizona and New Mexico, and southern Utah. After a long-continued war with the Spanish and American settlers, they were finally subdued by Kit Carson (1863–64) and have since been peaceful and industrious agriculturists, known for the high state of their native culture. They figure in Bandelier's *The Delight Makers,* La Farge's *Laughing Boy,* Cather's *Death Comes for the Archbishop,* and William Eastlake's *Portrait of an Artist with Twenty-Six Horses.*

NEIHARDT, JOHN G[NEISENAU] (1881–1973), born in Illinois, after a varied career including teaching and farming, lived among the Omaha Indians (1901–7), and from his study of this tribe came themes of his poetry and fiction. His five-part epic poem dealing with the Plains Indians and their conquest during the westward movement of the white frontier is published as *The Song of Hugh Glass* (1915), concerned with the legendary episode of 1823, when the frontier trapper was injured, and abandoned at the approach of hostile Indians by his youthful companion, Jim Bridger; *The Song of Three Friends* (1919), telling of the Ashley-Henry expedition of 1822–23; *The Song of the Indian Wars* (1925), recounting the last great struggle for the bison herds of the Plains; *The Song of the Messiah* (1935), telling of the last phase of Indian resistance to the white invasion, when the Indians could only hope that a messianic prophet would arise to deliver them; and *The Song of Jed Smith* (1941). These five works were gathered as *A Cycle of the West* (1949).

Collected Poems (1926) contains rugged lyrics published in earlier volumes, and other books include *The River and I* (1910), an account of a boating trip on the Missouri River; *The Lonesome Trail* (1907) and *Indian Tales, and Others* (1926), short stories about Indians and frontier heroes; *Life's Lure* (1914), a novel of the Black Hills mining camps; *The Splendid Wayfaring* (1920), the story of Jedediah Smith; a play, *Two Mothers* (1921); a volume of essays, *Poetic Values* (1925); and *When the Tree Flowered* (1951) and *Eagle Voice* (1953), fictional accounts based on facts of Sioux life. *All Is But a Beginning* (1972) and *Patterns and Coincidences* (1978) are memoirs of his early years.

NEMEROV, HOWARD (1920–   ), after graduation from Harvard and service as a pilot in World War II became a teacher of English at Bennington, Brandeis, and Washington University, St. Louis. His fiction includes *The Melodramatists* (1949), a satirical portrait of a Boston family's inabilities to find a meaningful way of life; *Federigo, or The Power of Love* (1954), a comedy; *The Homecoming Game* (1957), a satire about a professor failing a star football player, dramatized by Howard Lindsay and Russel Crouse as *Tall Story* (1959); and *A Commodity of Dreams* (1959), stories. His well-wrought poetry has been collected in *Image and the Law* (1947), *Guide to the Ruins* (1950), *The Salt Garden* (1955), *Mirrors and Windows* (1958); *The Next Room of the Dream* (1964), including two verse plays with Biblical themes; *The Blue Swallows* (1967), *Gnomes* (1973), epigrammatic works; *The Western Approaches* (1976); *Collected Poems* (1977); and *Inside the Onion* (1984). His essays appear in *Poetry and Fiction* (1963); *Journal of the Fictive Life* (1966), a psychological inquiry into the creative process; *Reflections on Poetry and Poetics* (1972); and *Figures of Thought* (1978). He was a co-winner of the Bollingen Prize ♦ (1979–80).

NEVINS, ALLAN (1890–1971), after a career in journalism became a professor of American history at Columbia (1931–58) and, upon retirement from teaching, was senior research associate at the Huntington Library. Prior to his academic career he had already made a reputation as a scholar with such books as *The Life of Robert Rogers* (1914), *The Evening Post—A Century of Journalism* (1922), *The Emergence of Modern America* (1927), and *Frémont: The West's Greatest Adventurer* (1928), revised as *Frémont: Path-*

marker of the West (1939). His later books include *Grover Cleveland* (1932, Pulitzer Prize); *Hamilton Fish* (1936, Pulitzer Prize); *John D. Rockefeller* (2 vols., 1940); *This Is England Today* (1941); *America, The Story of a Free People* (1942), with H.S. Commager; *The U.S. in a Chaotic World* (1948); *The New Deal and World Affairs* (1950); *Ordeal of the Union* (2 vols., 1947), on the U.S., 1847–57, and its sequel, *The Emergence of Lincoln* (2 vols., 1950), and, as sequel to these four volumes, another four-volume work under the collective title *The War for the Union,* of which the first were *The Improvised War* (1960) and *The War Becomes Revolution* (1961). With Frank E. Hill he wrote a lengthy work, *Ford* (3 vols., 1954, 1957, 1963), that, as the subtitle of Volume I says, deals with "the times, the man, the company." He also wrote *Herbert H. Lehman and His Era* (1963). *The Gateway to History* (1938) studies methods of historiography.

New Criticism, literary analysis identified mainly with concentration on elements of an isolated literary work (usually a poem) as they illuminate the whole. It concentrates on semantics, meter, imagery, metaphor, and symbol and deals with the work's tone, texture, and tensions to explicate a fused form and content in a piece of writing, rather than dealing with the relation of that piece to an age, a tradition, or an author's whole body of writing. Its views of psychology, of a disrupted moral order, and of organic unity derive from many earlier sources, but its immediate forebears include Pound, I.A. Richards, and T.S. Eliot. Diverse American critics associated with the beliefs and practices of New Criticism to some substantial degree include R.P. Blackmur; Cleanth Brooks; Kenneth Burke; J.C. Ransom, who wrote a book on the subject (1941); Allen Tate; R.P. Warren; and Yvor Winters. However, they differed very much from one another and most did not continue to practice these critical ways so stringently or exclusively as time went on, and the heyday of New Criticism did not outlast the 1950s.

New Directions (1936–), collection of experimental or new prose and poetry founded by James Laughlin IV as an annual, but since 1942 issued sporadically. Its interest in new ideas and forms is akin to that of the publishing house of the same name which issues it. Sections have been devoted to "New Directions in Design" in photography, architecture, and city planning, and issues often emphasize

foreign authors. Contributors have included Kay Boyle, Kenneth Burke, Cummings, Dahlberg, Kerouac, Denise Levertov, Henry Miller, James Purdy, Rexroth, Sorrentino, Wallace Stevens, and W.C. Williams. A *New Directions Reader* (1964) printed works of 58 authors from the first 28 years.

New England, region including the present states of Maine, New Hampshire, Vermont, Massachusetts, Rhode Island, and Connecticut, was named by Captain John Smith in his map of 1616. The harsh climate, rocky soil, and paucity of natural products discouraged colonization, except by the Puritans who sought a new home in which to cultivate their faith, and there early developed a homogeneity emphasized by their intolerance of beliefs at variance from orthodox Calvinism. Accordingly, cooperative action was common in such matters as the public school system, civic rule by town meetings, the organization of the Congregational Church, and the New England Confederation. The resulting early New England mind may be traced through the writings of such divines as the Mathers and Jonathan Edwards, and of such laymen as Bradford, Winthrop, and Sewall. Economic considerations also produced a unity, shipbuilding and fishing being the most characteristic occupations, but the very barrenness of the soil, lack of a staple, and inaccessibility of markets forced the people to develop an ingenuity that flowered in the shrewd, thrifty, independent, and resourceful type known as the Yankee. ♦ Because of its great foreign commerce, which led to the rise of such ports as Boston♦ and Salem, the region was particularly affected by the British Navigation acts, and played an important part in shaping colonial ideas toward the Revolution, producing such leaders as Samuel and John Adams.

After the Revolution the commercial classes became increasingly powerful as the transition to industrialism advanced, calling forth a generally conservative temper that came to be buttressed by a pride of heritage. This attitude, evident in the writings of the Connecticut Wits, may be observed later in the policies of the Cotton Whigs, whose guiding lights were the textile mill owners closely affiliated with the Southern cotton planters. The Brahmin class♦ was therefore long averse to the antislavery movement, but others, with equal pride of heritage and thoughtful of the spirit of Yankee independence, identified themselves passionately with the humanitarian movements of the mid-19th century. Thus Garrison, Whittier, and others agitated for improved conditions of labor in both North and South. Liberalism manifested itself likewise in the growth of Unitarianism, under Channing and Parker, and in the philosophic and literary movement of Transcendentalism, whose school, flourishing at Concord, ♦ included Emerson, Thoreau, Alcott, and Margaret Fuller. True to the cultural tradition that had led to the founding of Harvard as early as 1636, others also maintained the region's distinction as the center of American intellectual activity, and this renaissance of the pre-Civil War years has been termed by such critics as Van Wyck Brooks "the flowering of New England." Among the representative authors of the time may be mentioned Longfellow and Lowell, who show the scholarship and romantic influences of the Cambridge authors; Bryant and Whittier, the love of nature and social liberalism frequently to be observed in New England thought; Holmes, the genteel Brahmin attitude; Hawthorne, the interest in moral problems and in the Puritan past; and Harriet Beecher Stowe, the humanitarianism and later the preoccupation with local color.

The great days of commerce and clipper ships, romantically depicted in such later novels as Hergesheimer's *Java Head*, were now long past, and after the Civil War increasing consciousness of decadence and nostalgia for earlier glories led to a literary Indian summer, represented by such writers of local-color stories as Mary Wilkins Freeman and Sarah Orne Jewett, who were concerned with the decayed grandeur of deserted shipping ports and dwindling farms; T.B. Aldrich, who recalled the glamour of a New England boyhood; and Louisa May Alcott, who presented a cheerful view of Concord in an earlier day; while her contemporary, the recluse Emily Dickinson, distilled both Yankee wit and Transcendentalist mysticism in her gnomic verse. Immigration and a constant rise of *nouveaux riches* altered the character of both upper and lower classes in New England, and the transitional society was described by such novelists as Howells, in *The Rise of Silas Lapham* and other books, and Henry James, who contrasted the nature of New England manners, ranging from those in *The Bostonians* to those in *The Ambassadors,* with views of life elsewhere

The region has drawn increasingly on non-English immigrants for its labor, and the resulting social discord is best symbolized by the Sacco-Vanzetti case, described in Upton Sinclair's *Boston,* which shows the bases of such conflict in 20th-century New England. The earlier homogeneity of culture is thus lost, and the rise of other regions has tended to destroy the leadership of New England in the creative arts, although its schools, including Harvard, Yale, Dartmouth, Williams, Smith, Andover, and Exeter, are still leaders in American education. Among more recent authors, Robinson, Frost, Coffin, and Robert Lowell reveal facets of the original New England spirit in their works, but others have been concerned with the decadence of the tradition, as in O'Neill's *Mourning Becomes Electra*, Santayana's *The Last Puritan,* Marquand's *The Late George Apley,* and Cheever's *The Wapshot Chronicle.*

New England Nun, A, and Other Stories, 24 tales by Mary Wilkins Freeman, ♦ published in 1891. Realistic but frequently sentimental, they are influenced by the local-color movement.

"A New England Nun" tells of Louisa Ellis, whose fiancé spends 14 years in Australia gathering a fortune with which to marry her, but is rejected on his return because she does not wish to disturb the delicate domestic arrangements to which she has become accustomed.

New England Primer, The, Calvinist school book, compiled and published by Benjamin Harris, probably in 1683 and certainly before 1690. In its frequent revisions, it is estimated to have sold more than 5,000,000 copies. Besides the letters of the alphabet, illustrated by crudely rhymed couplets and woodcuts, the book contained simple moral texts based on Old Testament history and wisdom, and the prayer "Now I lay me down to sleep."

New England Renaissance, term sometimes applied to the cultural awakening of the mid-19th century aroused by Unitarianism ♦ and Transcendentalism. ♦

New Englands Trials, autobiographical narrative by Captain John Smith. ♦

New Hampshire, blank-verse poem by Robert Frost, ♦ published in 1923 as the title piece of a volume which won a Pulitzer Prize.

In this familiar monologue, the poet presents a witty defense of his manner of life and philosophic attitude. He describes New Hampshire as "one of the two best states in the Union. Vermont's the other," and as a compact community having "one each of everything as in a show-case." Answering the "glorious bards of Massachusetts" who "taunt the lofty land with little men," he names friends among the New Hampshire people he admires and would not change. "I choose to be a plain New Hampshire farmer," he says, in condemning extremists who demand that he take a radical attitude.

New Harmony, see *Owen, Robert.*

New Home, A,—Who'll Follow? or, Glimpses of Western Life, sketches by Caroline Kirkland,♦ published in 1839 under the pseudonym "Mrs. Mary Clavers, An Actual Settler." These realistic sketches of frontier Michigan during the 1830s describe the log houses, conditions in the towns, the land booms, and the backwoods social standards. Among the characters delineated are a silly romantic girl who marries a clerk, a young blood who embezzles the funds of a wildcat bank, squatters, English upper-class settlers, old-maid gossips, and rampant democrats. The book was reissued as *Our New Home in the West* (1874).

New Republic, The (1914–), weekly journal of opinion and liberal views was founded by Willard D. Straight for editing by Herbert Croly.♦ Croly conceived the purpose of the magazine as being "less to inform or entertain its readers than to start little insurrections in the realm of their convictions." It supported American participation in World War I, and, though it originated the phrase "peace without victory," it broke with Wilson and opposed U.S. ratification of the Treaty of Versailles. It has been consistently distinguished as a liberal organ, and over the years editorial board members have included Walter Lippmann, Stark Young, Malcolm Cowley, Joyce Carol Oates, and Robert Pinsky.

New World Writing (1952–59), eclectic anthology of fiction, drama, essays, and poetry from all the world presenting in paperback book format and to a large public the kinds of writings usually restricted to little magazines or literary quarterlies. Contributors included not only such established authors as Auden, Farrell, Jeffers, Lorca, Schorer, and Dylan Thomas, but newer writers including Algren, James Baldwin, Ionesco, and Kerouac.

New York Public Library, consolidated (1895) from the collections of several previous libraries, including the Astor library founded by J.J. Astor, the scholarly Lenox Library founded by James Lenox, and the English and American literature collection of E.A. Duyckinck. Most of the city's independent libraries were consolidated with the main collection (1901–4). The Library had (1981) 83 publicly supported branches, but the Central Research Library, headquartered at Fifth Avenue and 42nd Street, receives two-thirds of its operating budget from private sources. Its holdings, including the Berg Collection of English and American Literature, contained, as of 1981, over 5,000,000 books and more than 11,500,000 manuscripts.

New York Review of Books, The (1963–), founded during a printers' strike against New York newspapers as a single-issue journal to dramatize the need for a new kind of book review as well as to fill the gap left by the suspension of the book-review sections of *The New York Times* and *Herald Tribune.* Its success led to regular biweekly publication, except for single issues in July and August, that feature lengthy, critical, and informed treatments of a few books, some poetry, and an occasional special article. It is much concerned with sociopolitical matters, national and international, from a liberal point of view. Reviewers include leading U.S. and English critics. Their texts are illustrated by sharp, witty caricatures of authors by the staff artist David Levine, by apposite pictures of animals in human guise from the works of the mid-19th-century French artist Grandeville, and by other exotic or satirical 19th-century illustrations.

New York school, name applied to a group of poets including John Ashbery,♦ Kenneth Koch,♦ Frank O'Hara,♦ and James Schuyler,♦ whose writing, distinguished for visual detail, relates to New York's Abstract Expressionist painters of the 1950s. Several in the group have been art critics or museum curators, and they have collaborated with artists in their publications, as well as among themselves.

New Yorker, The (1925–), weekly humorous magazine, founded and edited by Harold Ross (1892–1951), initially said to be for the "caviar sophisticates" and "not for the old lady in Dubuque." Though more than a half-century old, it retains the special characteristics and quality that it originated: a crisp, satirical style, a warm-hearted concern with humane values, sophisticated amusement at human follies, and urbane attitudes, diversely evident in departments that include "Notes and Comments" and "Talk of the Town," both anonymous, the latter long written by E.B. White. Other distinctive features include "Profiles," sketches not only of persons, but of places and things, occasional "Annals of Crime," contributions from a "Reporter at Large," a frequent "Letter" from its foreign correspondents, and perceptive reviews of films, theater, music, art, and books, whose staff authors or frequent contributors have included Pauline Kael, Wolcott Gibbs, Brendan Gill, Edmund Wilson, and John Updike. Not infrequently it devotes a large part of an issue to a feature article concentrating on a significant social issue (John Hersey's "Hiroshima" occupied an entire issue in 1946), or extends it over several weeks. The body of the journal is composed of stories, poems, and comic drawings. The fiction frequently emphasizes a mood or dwells quietly on a slight but meaningful incident and is said to have an effect on the genre itself or to be "a typical *New Yorker* story," although there cannot be a type since authors have ranged from John O'Hara and S.J. Perelman (long steady contributors) to Donald Barthelme. The poets are just as diverse and have included Ogden Nash and John Ashbery. The drawings often are accompanied by one-line captions, a form the magazine is said to have popularized, but many are without text or jokes. Over the years the various artists have included Charles Addams, Alajalov, Peter Arno, Rea Irvin (whose first-issue cover appears annually on the anniversary of the founding, symbolically depicting a skeptical dandy, Eustace Tilley, and is also indicative of the journal's sense of continuity), Steig, Steinberg, and Thurber. Numerous anthologies have been collected from contributions, and accounts of the magazine by insiders include Thurber's *The Years with Ross* (1959) and Brendan Gill's *Here at The New Yorker* (1975).

Newbery Medal, see *Children's literature in America*.

Newberry Library, private institution in Chicago, founded (1887) with a bequest from Walter Loomis Newberry (1804–68), a local banker. A reference and research collection of rare books and manuscripts concentrating on the humanities, it emphasizes western Europe and America, being particularly famous for its holdings on bibliography, the Renaissance, music, English and American

literature and history, Portugal and Brazil, the trans-Mississippi West, American Indians, and fine printing. The library conducts research and educational programs.

Nez Percé Indians, Northwestern tribe whose name is derived from the custom of wearing nose pendants. First encountered by Lewis and Clark, they were praised in Irving's *Adventures of Captain Bonneville* for their high culture and long-standing friendliness with the whites. After a fraudulent treaty by which the Americans obtained their gold lands, an uprising occurred (1877), led by Chief Joseph.

Nick Carter, name of the hero of many dime novels, also used by many of their authors. John Russell Coryell probably first used it in the 1880s, but more prolific writers produced most of the more than 1000 Nick Carter books.

NICOLAY, JOHN GEORGE (1832–1901), brought to the U.S. in 1838 from his native Germany, grew up in Illinois, where after a journalistic career during his twenties he was appointed Lincoln's private secretary in 1860. His lifelong friend John Hay held a similar position, and the two men, who revered Lincoln, enjoyed an unusual opportunity for intimate study of their hero. From 1875 to 1890 they collaborated on the great biography *Abraham Lincoln: A History* (10 vols., 1890). Nicolay's other works include *The Outbreak of Rebellion* (1881), *A Short Life of Abraham Lincoln* (1902), and the editorship with Hay of Lincoln's writings (12 vols., 1905).

NIEBUHR, REINHOLD (1892–1971), Missouri-born theologian, received his M.A. and B.D. from Yale Divinity School, was a pastor in Detroit's Bethel Evangelical Church (1915–28), where he was concerned with labor union issues before becoming a professor at Union Theological Seminary (1928–60). His neo-orthodox theology, treating the relevance of Christianity to modern man and society, holds that because of original sin man cannot reach Utopia through social reform or revolution, but that social dilemmas can be met in terms of the Christian beliefs and spiritual values contained in the Bible. His views are set forth in *Moral Man and Immoral Society* (1932), *Reflections on the End of an Era* (1934), *Beyond Tragedy* (1937), *Christianity and Power Politics* (1940), *The Nature and Destiny of Man* (2 vols., 1941–43), *The*

Children of Light and the Children of Darkness (1944), *Faith and History* (1949), *The Irony of American History* (1952), *The Self and the Dramas of History* (1955), *Pious and Secular America* (1958), and *Christianity and Power Politics* (1969).

Nigger, The, play by Edward Sheldon,♦ produced in 1909 and published in 1910.

Nigger Heaven, novel by Carl Van Vechten,♦ published in 1926. It is noted for its depiction of the various strata of black society in Harlem.

Night Before Christmas, poem by C.C. Moore.♦

NIMS, J[OHN] F[REDERICK] (1913–), born in Michigan, educated at Notre Dame (A.B., 1937), where he taught English and creative writing (1939–61), a career continued at the University of Illinois and the University of Chicago, and he has also been an editor of *Poetry.* His poems have been collected in *The Iron Pastoral* (1947), *A Fountain in Kentucky* (1950), *Knowledge of the Evening* (1960), *Of Flesh and Bone* (1967), and *The Kiss* (1982), 44 poems on physical, mystical, and symbolic kissing. His translations are the *Poems of St. John of the Cross* (1959) and *Sappho to Valery* (1971).

NIN, ANAÏS (1903–77), French-born author of Spanish-Cuban heritage, brought to the U.S. at the age of 11, lived here intermittently thereafter. Her first book, *D.H. Lawrence, An Unprofessional Study* (1932), was a critical work, but of her later books she has said: "I write as a poet in the framework of prose and appear to claim the rights of a novelist. . . . I intend the greater part of my writing to be received directly through the senses, as one apprehends painting and music." Her fiction includes *The House of Incest* (1936), a treatment of narcissism; *Winter of Artifice* (1939), a psychiatric investigation of the relations between a father and daughter; *Under a Glass Bell* (1944), stories; *This Hunger* (1945), interrelated stories about women who fear human society, and men in particular; *Ladders to Fire* (1946), stories of women who search for their identity; *The Four-Chambered Heart* (1950), a novel about a triangular love conflict; *A Spy in the House of Love* (1954), on a woman's self-questioning about her many transient loves; *Cities of the Interior* (1959), gathering works, including the three preceding ones, into a "continu-

ous novel"; and *Collages* (1964), portraits of characters, real and fictive, in a "novel" set in Los Angeles. *Cities of the Interior* (1965) collects shorter fiction. *Realism and Reality* (1946), *On Writing* (1947), *The Novel of the Future* (1968), *A Woman Speaks* (1975), and *In Favor of the Sensitive Man* (1976) are critical works. *Delta of Venus* (1968) reissues early pornographic work. Her full and frank *Diary* appeared in six volumes (1966–76), and *Linotte* (1978) is a diary kept between the ages of 11 and 17. Henry Miller's letters to her were published in 1965.

1919, novel by Dos Passos published in 1932. It is the second in the trilogy *U.S.A.* (collected 1938), including *The 42nd Parallel*♦ (1930) and *The Big Money*♦ (1936). Interspersed in the narrative are brief biographies of John Reed, Randolph Bourne, Theodore Roosevelt, Paxton Hibben, Wilson, J.P. Morgan, Joe Hill, Wesley Everest, and the Unknown Soldier. (For critical discussion, see *Dos Passos.*)

Joe Williams deserts from the navy and sails on tankers and freighters across the Atlantic, although several times jailed and aboard torpedoed ships. Richard Ellsworth Savage, son of a genteelly poor family, is aided by a politician, who sends him to Harvard. There he is an aesthete until, stirred by the war, he joins an ambulance corps in France and then, through the politician's influence, gets an army commission. His eye ever on the main chance, he gets a post at the Peace Conference with the public relations office of J. Ward Moorehouse. Meanwhile he has an affair with Anne Trent, a confused Texas debutante who is on her way to do relief work in the Near East, but refuses to marry her when she becomes pregnant, for fear of losing his chance to rise with Moorehouse. She gets hysterical, goes on a wild air flight, and is killed when the plane crashes. Ben Compton, a bright young Brooklyn Jew, once a friend of Anne Trent, is active in a strike, becomes a Socialist, is an agitator at a Passaic mill strike, and is jailed. When released, he bums across the U.S., is beaten by police in Seattle because he is an I.W.W. radical, and is sent to prison for his pacifist agitation.

Nobel Prizes, provided by the bequest of Alfred B. Nobel (1833–96), Swedish scientist, have been given annually since 1901 for the most significant contributions in the fields of chemistry, physics, medicine, and literature, and in the cause of peace. Awards are determined by committees at Stockholm and Oslo, and may be given to persons of any nationality. Each prize amounts to approximately $180,000 (1981). American-born recipients in literature are Sinclair Lewis (1930), O'Neill (1936), Pearl Buck (1938), T.S. Eliot (1948), Faulkner (1950), Hemingway (1954), Steinbeck (1962), and Bellow (1976). Recipients have also included two naturalized U.S. citizens who write in other languages: Isaac B. Singer (1978) and Czeslaw Milosz (1980).

Nobody Knows My Name, personal essays by James Baldwin,♦ published in 1961, treating his ten-year expatriation in Europe, his return to Harlem, and his visit to the South during the period of school integration. Baldwin deals with black and white relations in the U.S. and Europe, with the relation of the artist to society, with Richard Wright, Faulkner, and Norman Mailer, and also with his views on the relationships of the sexes.

NORMAN, MARSHA (1947–), Kentucky-born dramatist whose first two-act play, *Getting Out* (1977), about a shattered woman emerging from prison and picking up her life, was followed by *'Night, Mother* (1983, Pulitzer Prize), presenting a young woman about to commit suicide.

NORRIS, FRANK (BENJAMIN FRANKLIN NORRIS) (1870–1902), was born in Chicago, but in 1884 moved to San Francisco with his parents. After a year in a California preparatory school, he was sent to study art in Paris, where he spent his spare time writing medieval romances. While at the University of California (1890–94), he wrote short stories and sketches for student and local publications, as well as a romantic poem in three cantos, *Yvernelle, A Tale of Feudal France* (1892). Under the influence of Zola's fiction, he soon turned from his juvenile romanticism to naturalism and began a novel of lower- and middle-class life in San Francisco, which he later completed as *McTeague♦* (1899). He next spent a year at Harvard, where he wrote more of *McTeague* and parts of *Vandover and the Brute* (1914).

In 1895–96 he was in South Africa, but failed in his project of writing travel sketches because of fighting between the English and Boers, which he reported for *Collier's* and the San Francisco *Chronicle.* He was ordered to leave the country, after being captured by the Boers, and returned to join the staff of *The Wave,* a San Francisco magazine, in which he

serialized *Moran of the* Lady Letty (1898). From his many contributions to this periodical also came the novelette *The Joyous Miracle* (1906) and two collections of short stories, *A Deal in Wheat* (1903) and *The Third Circle* (1909). These works exhibit his divided loyalty to the currently popular romantic realism of Kipling and the naturalistic attitude of Zola. The former influence caused him, like Stephen Crane, to go to Cuba (1898), where he reported the Santiago campaign of the Spanish-American War for *McClure's Magazine.* Upon his return (1899), he was employed by the publishing firm of Doubleday, Page, which that year issued *McTeague♦* and *Blix,* a semi-autobiographical love story. *A Man's Woman* (1900) is a romantic work in the vein of Jack London's novels.

About this time, moved by his growing concern with social and economic forces, Norris conceived the plan of his "Epic of the Wheat," a trilogy to consist of *The Octopus,* a novel dealing with the raising of wheat in California, and the struggle of the ranchers against the railroad; *The Pit,* a tale of speculation in the Chicago wheat exchange; and *The Wolf,* about the consumption of the wheat as bread in a famine-stricken European village. He visited a wheat ranch in California and wrote *The Octopus♦* (1901), which is considered his finest work. Before his sudden death following an appendix operation, he had written *The Pit♦* (1903), which became extremely popular. *The Wolf* was left unwritten.

The Responsibilities of the Novelist (1903), a collection of essays and articles, contains a statement of his artistic credo, in which he says that the novelist "of all men cannot think only of himself or for himself," but must rather sacrifice money, fashion, and popularity for the greater reward of realizing that he has told the truth. The best type of novel, according to Norris, "proves something, draws conclusions from a whole congeries of forces, social tendencies, race impulses, devotes itself not to a study of men but of man." In *McTeague* and *The Octopus,* despite their romantic elements and occasional extravagances, he is considered to have achieved his idealistic purpose and to have presented a vivid, authentic portrayal of contemporary life in California. Other posthumous publications include *Vandover and the Brute,* ♦ printed in 1914 from the uncorrected draft of his second novel; *Frank Norris of The Wave* (1931), a selection of his magazine fiction; and *Works* (10 vols., 1928), containing other previously uncollected articles and stories, with introductions by leading authors, including his brother Charles Norris. His *Letters* were collected in 1956.

North American Phalanx, most scientifically planned of all the American experiments in Fourierism, ♦ was founded at Red Bank, N.J. (1843), by Albert Brisbane, with the advice of Parke Godwin, W.H. Channing, Horace Greeley, and George Ripley. The colony maintained a three-story phalanstery, a grist-mill, and a large orchard, and occupied a considerable area of fertile land. The members, mostly people of culture and refinement, ate their meals together, but each family had separate quarters and each member was allowed to work at the task which best suited him. Careful attention was paid to the education of children. When the mill burned (1854), the association was dissolved.

North American Review, The (1815–1939, 1963–   ), Boston magazine, founded as an outgrowth of *The Monthly Anthology,* was edited by William Tudor, with the assistance of E.T. Channing, R.H. Dana, Sr., and others, as a quarterly literary, critical, and historical review on the order of its English contemporaries, with the purpose of achieving a greater national scope than any previous American magazine. It was nevertheless scholarly and was closely affiliated with Harvard and Boston Unitarianism. Among its early contributions were Bryant's "Thanatopsis" (1817) and "To a Waterfowl" (1818). Edward Everett, Jared Sparks, and J.G. Palfrey, as later editors, continued the magazine's high standards, but were more inclined toward history than belles lettres. The *Review* later became a monthly and included among its editors C.E. Norton, Lowell, Henry Adams, and H.C. Lodge. Among its contributors were Emerson, Irving, Longfellow, Parkman, E.P. Whipple, Motley, Holmes, Howells, Boyesen, Whitman, Clemens, and Henry James. It moved to New York City (1878), where, separated from the Brahmin atmosphere, it plunged into a maelstrom of contemporaneity, becoming concerned with the latest political and social movements. At the turn of the century, it had a diverse list of authors, including Tolstoy, D'Annunzio, Maeterlinck, H.G. Wells, Alan Seeger, Bryan, James Bryce, Clemens, Howells, and Henry James. After World War I, circulation diminished greatly and the magazine became again a quarterly.

It was revived as a quarterly in 1963, published by Cornell College of Iowa, now named the University of Northern Iowa.

North of Boston, poems by Robert Frost. ♦

Northwest, as distinguished from the old Northwest Territory, ♦ is the region including the states of Oregon, Washington, and western Montana and Idaho. Characterized on the Pacific coast by a humid, forested area, and east of the Cascade Mountains by a high arid tableland and great fertile valleys, the region has varied industries, the most prominent being salmon fishing, lumbering, agriculture, and cattle raising. Its central waterway, the Columbia River, was discovered and claimed for the U.S. in 1792, and the Lewis and Clark expedition, as well as the fur-trading activities of John Jacob Astor, further established U.S. interests in the Northwest, later the cause of the Oregon Question, which was not finally settled until 1846. Up to this time, the history of the territory had been that of the fur trade and of pioneer immigration by way of the Oregon Trail, ♦ whose most famous figures were Jedediah Smith and Marcus Whitman. ♦ After 1850 began the marked development of agriculture and industry, with later homesteading encouraged by the railroading accomplishments of Henry Villard and James J. Hill. Washington Irving described the fur trade in *Astoria* ♦; Honoré Morrow's novel *We Must March* tells the story of Marcus Whitman; Emerson Hough's *54–40 or Fight!* and other books are concerned with the Oregon Question; Frank B. Linderman has written of frontier Montana; James Stevens and others have collected the Paul Bunyan stories of the Northwest lumber camps; Oregon in the early 1900s is described in H.L. Davis's *Honey in the Horn;* and modern life in the region is the subject of novels by Archie Binns and Robert Cantwell.

Northwest Passage, novel by Kenneth Roberts. ♦

NORTON, CHARLES ELIOT (1827–1908), is best known as professor of the history of fine art at Harvard (1873–98), although his broad range of scholarship, lofty and catholic taste, and great personal charm extended his influence far beyond the confines of the university. He was a frequent contributor to the *Atlantic Monthly,* co-editor of *The North American Review* (1864–68), a founder and co-editor of *The Nation* (1865), and the author of books as widely varied as a bibliography of Michelangelo and a biography of Kipling, in addition to his Italian scholarship, whose main fruit was a prose translation of the *Divine Comedy* (3 vols., 1891–92).

Notes of a Son and Brother, autobiographical narrative by Henry James,♦ published in 1914. A sequel to *A Small Boy and Others,♦* this volume is concerned with the years from the late 1850s to 1870, and the central figures are again the author, his brother William, and the elder Henry James.

Notes Toward a Supreme Fiction, long poem by Wallace Stevens,♦ published in 1942.

Composed of a prologue, 30 poems divided into three sections ("It Must Be Abstract," "It Must Change," "It Must Give Pleasure"), and an epilogue, each composed of seven stanzas containing three verses in a metric form like iambic pentameter, the poem does not attempt to develop a sequential argument but is composed of meditations concerned with the nature of reality, man's perceptions, and poetic imagination. Reality is always changing; to treat reality requires imagination that may comprehend its variety. The poet in treating reality is concerned with providing a fiction that will please in the way that once a belief in a personal deity gave spiritual joy. In turn such fiction provides a faith by which man, a soldier in wartime, can live and die.

November Boughs, collection of poems and prose by Whitman,♦ published in 1888. Its verse was incorporated in *Leaves of Grass* as "Sands at Seventy," and its prose preface, "A Backward Glance o'er Travel'd Roads,"♦ became the epilogue of *Leaves of Grass* in 1889. The other prose later appeared in the *Complete Writings* (1902).

O Captain! My Captain!, poem by Whitman, ♦ published in *Sequel to Drum-Taps* (1865–66) and in *Leaves of Grass* (1867). Although Whitman thought far less of this elegy on the death of Lincoln than he did of that entitled "When Lilacs Last in the Door Yard Bloom'd," it has attained great popularity because of its relatively regular stanzaic form, rhyme, rhythmic pattern, and refrain. It tells of a ship, representative of the Union, coming safely into port, with "the people all exulting," while the poet sadly walks the deck on which lies his Captain, "fallen cold and dead."

O. HENRY, pseudonym of W.S. Porter. ♦

O Pioneers!, novel by Willa Cather, ♦ published in 1913.

John Bergson, a strong-willed Swedish immigrant, struggles to build a farm on the Nebraska prairie, aided by his wife, their sons Lou and Oscar, and his favorite, the capable, intelligent daughter, Alexandra. At his death, Alexandra assumes responsibility for the farm and the family, since her mother lacks ingenuity or determination, and her older brothers are obstinate and plodding, while her brother Emil is a child of five. She possesses the heroic, creative quality of the passing frontier, and over a period of years her faith in the soil is rewarded by rich harvests. She is not satisfied by her increasing prosperity, however, for after the departure of Carl Linstrum, who seeks a career as an engraver, she lacks companionship in a society of weaker and meaner individuals. Emil is now a grown youth, sensitive and intelligent, for whom Alexandra has great hopes, but he has a secret affair with her friend Marie Shabata, and the two are killed by Marie's jealous husband Frank. Meanwhile Carl has visited the Bergsons on his way to the Klondike, and he and Alexandra find in each other the complementary qualities each needs. When he learns of Emil's death, Carl returns to marry Alexandra, and they plan to share the responsibilities and fulfillments of life on the farm.

OATES, Joyce Carol (1938–), born in Lockport, N.Y., after graduation from Syracuse University and an M.A. from the University of Wisconsin has taught English and creative writing at the University of Windsor (Canada) and Princeton. A prolific writer, whose novels include *With Shuddering Fall* (1964), *A Garden of Earthly Delights* (1967), *Expensive People* (1968), *them* (1969, National Book Award), *Wonderland* (1971), *Do with Me What You Will* (1973), *The Assassins* (1975), *The Childwold* (1976), *The Triumph of the Spider Monkey* (1977), *Son of the Morning* (1978), *Bellefleur* (1980), *A Bloodsmoor Romance* (1982), and *Mysteries of Winterthurn* (1984). These novels are peopled with realistically presented but demonic persons whose attempts to express their own character are frustrated by the grotesque and violent culture of the U.S. (often symbolized by Detroit) and thus lead them into convulsive violence. The savage psychological portrayals of these people caught up in their passions and also victims of forces beyond their control or comprehension are presented as those of dwellers in a dark and destructive society. Her numerous stories have been collected in *By the North Gate* (1963), *Upon the Sweeping Flood* (1966), *The Wheel of Love* (1970), *Marriages and Infidelities* (1972), *The Hungry Ghosts* (1974), *The Goddess and Other Women* (1974), *Where Are You Going, Where Have You Been?* (1974), *The Poisoned Kiss* (1975), *The Seduction* (1975), *Crossing the Border* (1976), *Night-Side* (1977), *A Sentimental Education* (1982), and *Last Days* (1984). She has also written poetry, collected in *Women in Love* (1968), *Anonymous Sins* (1969), *Love and Its Derangements* (1970), *Angel Fire* (1973), *Dreaming America* (1973), *Women Whose Lives Are Food, Men Whose Lives Are Money* (1978), and *Invisible Woman* (1982), and unpublished plays. Her essays and critical writings are gathered in *The Edge of Impossibility* (1971), *The Hostile Sun* (1973), *New Heaven, New Earth* (1974), *Contraries* (1981), and *The Profane Art* (1983).

Objectivist, school of poetry influenced by William Carlos Williams that came to prominence in the 1930s. It sees poetry as process whose form begins with the object dealt with and moves by improvisation through verbal associations inspired by the initial object. Leading Objectivist poets are George Oppen, Charles Reznikoff, and Louis Zukofsky.

Objectivism was also the name given by Ayn Rand♦ to her anti-altruistic theories.

O'BRIEN, FITZ-JAMES (*c.*1828–62), Irishborn journalist and author, came to the U.S. (*c.* 1852), where he was soon a conspicuous figure at Pfaff's Cellar and other New York bohemian rendezvous. His reputation is based on his rococo short stories dealing with psychological subjects reminiscent of Poe. The most notable of these, "The Diamond Lens" (*Atlantic Monthly,* Jan. 1858), tells of the inventor of a powerful microscope, who was enabled to see a sylph-like human being enclosed in a drop of water. After becoming obsessed by this fascinating creature, he went mad when she died.

O'CONNOR, EDWIN (1918–68), born in Rhode Island, after graduation from Notre Dame and service in the Coast Guard during World War II became a radio writer and producer. His books are *The Oracle* (1951), a caricature of a popular radio broadcaster; *The Last Hurrah* (1956), a lively portrayal of a big city boss, a demagogue and a rogue, but withal a warmly human Irish-American, presumably suggested by Boston's longtime mayor James M. Curley; *The Edge of Sadness* (1961, Pulitzer Prize), again set in a city modeled on Boston, portraying with sympathy the rector of a small Catholic parish, himself a reformed drunkard, and other vivid Irish-American characters; and *I Was Dancing* (1964), about an aging vaudeville performer's cunning fight to keep from being sent to a home for old people.

O'CONNOR, FLANNERY (1925–64), Georgia author, whose Gothic novels are *Wise Blood* (1952), about a young religious fanatic who tries to establish a Church Without Christ in his Georgia mountain region; and *The Violent Bear It Away* (1960), a macabre tale set in the backwoods of Georgia and presenting the fanatical mission of a boy intent on baptizing a still younger boy. Her stories, set in the South and also grotesque, are collected in *A Good Man Is Hard to Find* (1955, titled *The Artificial Nigger* in England), *Everything That Rises Must Converge* (1965), and *Complete Stories* (1971). Occasional prose was collected as *Mystery and Manners* (1969) and *The Habit of Being* (1979), and book reviews as *The Presence of Grace* (1983).

Octopus, The: A Story of California, novel by Frank Norris,♦ published in 1901 as the first part of his uncompleted trilogy, "The Epic of the Wheat."

The central theme in this realistic study of California farm life is the growing and harvesting of the wheat. Magnus Derrick operates the great Rancho de los Muertos, near Bonneville in the San Joaquin Valley, and is the leading spokesman for the farmers of the community. His son Harran helps him to manage their tenants and agricultural activities, while another son, Lyman, is a corporation lawyer in San Francisco. Among the neighboring farmers are Broderson, Osterman, and Annixter, all of whom are associated in a struggle to resist the encroachments of the Pacific and Southwestern Railroad, which dominates the state government and gradually extends its monopoly over other industries. The railroad is in complete control of Bonneville, for it subsidizes Genslinger, editor of the town paper, and, through S. Behrman, its unofficial agent, influences prices, interest rates, and all financial transactions. Presley, a poet from the East, stays for a time at Derrick's ranch and learns to sympathize with the cause of the oppressed farmers. He writes a poem about them that is widely popular, but finds it has no effect in the conflict of tremendous issues and resigns himself to being only an observer of the stirring events which follow. The farmers hold much of their land on option from the railroad, which raises the price enormously and puts up the land for public sale. Outraged by the broken promises and unfair tactics of Behrman and the corporation, the farmers form a protective league to protest and influence the state administration in their interests, electing Magnus Derrick their president. The league succeeds in placing Lyman on the state commission to fix rates, but he is bribed by the railroad and betrays his backers. When the railroad causes legal authorities to dispossess the farmers of their land, they revolt and in an armed clash many are killed, including Annixter. The railroad has now won complete domination, and the families of the insurgents are thrown into poverty and suffering. Magnus has been disgraced and ruined and is forced to enter the employment of Behrman, who is later accidentally smothered to death while watching the loading on shipboard of his own dishonestly gained wheat. Presley, indignant over the outrages he has witnessed, visits

Shelgrim, president of the railroad, but instead of the inhumane criminal he had expected finds Shelgrim sentimental and genial, convinced that his actions are dictated by circumstances and economic laws.

Octoroon, The, melodramatic play about slavery by Dion Boucicault,♦ produced in 1859. It was based on *The Quadroon* by Mayne Reid.

Ode Sung at the Occasion of Decorating the Graves of the Confederate Dead, delivered at Charleston (1867), was written by Timrod♦ and published in his *Poems* (1873). In five quatrains of octosyllabic lines, this elegy on "martyrs of the fallen cause." declares that, though no marble column yet honors their defeated valor, the blossom of their fame is blown,

> And somewhere, waiting for its birth,
> The shaft is in the stone.

ODETS, CLIFFORD (1906–63), born in Philadelphia and reared in the Bronx, quit school at 15 to become an actor. After acting with the Theatre Guild, he became a founder of the Group Theatre (1931), and was catapulted to fame by its production of his one-act play *Waiting for Lefty*♦ (1935), dealing with a taxi strike. This success was followed by the production of *Awake and Sing* (1935), about a poor Jewish family in the Bronx whose son becomes a radical to improve society, and the one-act play *Till the Day I Die* (1935), about the struggle of the German Communists at the beginning of the Hitler regime. These plays brought Odets a reputation as the leading proletarian playwright at the time, although he was less concerned with the problems of the worker than with the "fraud" of middle-class civilization, deprived by its economic insecurity of its former status and becoming aware that most of its cherished ideals no longer correspond to realities. Further realistic plays written for the Group are *Paradise Lost* (1935); *Golden Boy* (1937; revised as a musical, 1964), about a young Italian-American violinist whose desire for wealth and fame leads him to become a pugilist, and who dies in an automobile crash, having attempted to find an escape in speed from the loss of his inner security; *Rocket to the Moon* (1938), portraying a Bronx dentist who attempts to find happiness in a belated love affair, but fails because his will has been vitiated by the meanness of his past life; *Night*

Music (1940), the love story of a lower-middle-class couple in New York; and *Clash by Night* (1941), a love "triangle." Later plays, infrequent because of motion-picture work, are *The Big Knife* (1948), about an idealistic actor corrupted by money easily earned from motion pictures; *The Country Girl* (1950), about an alcoholic actor's marriage; and *The Flowering Peach* (1954), a retelling of the Noah tale.

Of Mice and Men, novelette by Steinbeck,♦ published in 1937 and dramatized by the author in 1937.

George Milton and Lennie Small, itinerant farm laborers, come to work on a Salinas Valley ranch in central California. Lennie has tremendous strength but a feeble intellect, and possesses a morbid desire to handle soft objects. George compensates for Lennie's deficiencies by exploiting his strength and cherishing their mutual dream of a small farm of their own. Curley, son of the boss, is an arrogant bully whose bride's promiscuity has already caused quarrels among the farmhands. When jealousy prompts him to pick a fight with Lennie, he emerges with a crushed hand, and his wife begins to admire the unwilling Lennie. She seeks a pretext to be alone with him, and one day in the hayloft tries to arouse his desire. He begins to stroke her hair, and, when she resists, he accidentally breaks her neck. He flees to the river, planning to escape. George and a friend discover the body, and George hurriedly follows, ahead of a mob led by the enraged Curley. Finding Lennie beside a secluded pool, George calms his fears with the frequently repeated description of the farm of their hopes, and shoots him in the head.

Of Thee I Sing, musical comedy, with music by George Gershwin♦ and text by George S. Kaufman,♦ Morrie Ryskind, and Ira Gershwin. Produced in 1931, it was published in 1932 and won a Pulitzer Prize.

Lampooning U.S. politics, the action occurs during a farcical presidential campaign, in street parades, hotel-room sessions, and Madison Square Garden, and, following the election, in White House offices and the Senate chamber. The party nominees are John P. Wintergreen, an energetic romantic hero, for President, and Alexander Throttlebottom, an exceedingly modest and retiring little man, for Vice-President. Seeking a platform issue, "something that everybody is interested in, and that doesn't matter a damn," the party leaders decide that Wintergreen must fall in love and prepare a campaign based on his romance with "the most beautiful girl in America," to be chosen in a contest at Atlantic City. The title is won by Diana Devereaux, a Louisiana belle, but meanwhile Wintergreen has determined to marry Mary Turner, a campaign worker. The ticket is victorious, and John and Mary are simultaneously inaugurated and married by Supreme Court justices. A later complication, caused by Diana's suit for breach of promise, is resolved when Mary regains popular favor by giving birth to twins, and the forgotten Throttlebottom appears to marry Diana.

Of Time and the River: A Legend of Man's Hunger in His Youth, semi-autobiographical novel by Thomas Wolfe,♦ published in 1935 as a sequel to *Look Homeward, Angel.* ♦

Eugene Gant leaves his Southern home for graduate work at Harvard, where the scope of his immense romantic appetite for experience is broadened as he reads voraciously, studies playwriting in the class of Professor Hatcher, and cultivates eccentric acquaintances, including his absurdly erudite uncle, Bascom Pentland. After losing his first bewildered feeling of strangeness, he finds a valued friend in Hatcher's youthful assistant, Francis Starwick, a cultured, fastidious, and affected scholar. During these two years, Eugene tries to bend his creative talent to the exacting dramatic form, and achieves a limited success before he leaves for a brief visit at home, where his father dies after a long and terrible illness. He goes north again, this time to serve as a college instructor of English in New York City, which provides the setting for his tumultuous mystic vision of the modern "manswarm." Companions of this period include Abe Jones, an earnest Jewish student; Joel Pierce, who introduces Eugene to the luxurious life of the Hudson River social set, and whose sister is one of a number of girls who are the objects of Eugene's sudden passions; and bitter, disillusioned Robert Weaver and his mistress, Martha Upshaw. Careful saving makes possible a European tour, during which Eugene meets Starwick, now even more febrile and affected. With Ann and Elinor, two Boston girls, they spend several weeks as tourists in Paris and the provinces. Eugene falls in love with Ann, Elinor with Eugene, and Ann with Starwick, who responds to neither, giving himself up to dissipation during mysterious disappearances. Appalled and disgusted when he dis-

covers that Starwick is a homosexual, Eugene leaves his friends, to tour Europe alone until he is forced by lack of funds to return to the U.S.

O'HARA, Frank (1926–66), poet and art critic whose poetry, published in *A City Winter* (1952), *Meditations in an Emergency* (1957), *Second Avenue* (1960), *Odes* (1960), *Lunch Poems* (1964), and *Selected Poems* (1973, National Book Award), is marked by an extremely autobiographical relation to his New York environment and an immediacy that John Ashbery compared to the painting of Jackson Pollock (about whom O'Hara wrote a book-length catalogue, 1959), for "Like Pollock, O'Hara demonstrates that the act of communication and the finished creation are the same." *Art Chronicles* (1975) collects his criticism; *Standing Still and Walking in New York* (1975) is a gathering of essays and notes, followed by *Early Writing* (1977).

O'HARA, John [Henry] (1905–70), after a journalistic career in his native Pennsylvania and in New York, began to write stories of acid observation on the country-club set, actors, and barroom figures, collected in *The Doctor's Son* (1935), *Files on Parade* (1939), *Pipe Night* (1945), and *Hellbox* (1947). His novels are *Appointment in Samarra* (1934), an ironic, toughly realistic treatment of the fast country-club set of a Pennsylvania city; *Butterfield 8* (1935), based on a New York murder, revealing the sordid and sensational lives of people on the fringe of café society and the underworld; *Hope of Heaven* (1938), about an unhappy love affair between a scenario writer and a bookshop clerk; *A Rage To Live* (1949), treating the tormented life of a woman who could not be faithful to the husband she really loved; *The Farmers Hotel* (1951), a novelette about snowbound people involved in a violent tragedy; *Ten North Frederick* (1955), a character study of a leading Pennsylvania citizen's public and very private life; *A Family Party* (1956), a novella in the form of a speech at a testimonial dinner; *From the Terrace* (1958), following a man through his upper-class life during the first half of the 20th century, treating social as well as personal history; *Ourselves To Know* (1960), about a man who murdered his wife undetected and his life thereafter; *The Big Laugh* (1962), set in Hollywood in the '20s and '30s; *Elizabeth Appleton* (1963), portraying the married life of a society girl and a professor; *The Lockwood Concern* (1965), depicting the dramatic, tangled lives of four generations of an upper-class Pennsylvania family; *The Instrument* (1967), about a Broadway playwright and his manipulation of people; *Lovey Childs* (1970), presenting a wealthy Philadelphia woman's romantic entanglements; and *The Ewings* (1972), treating a Cleveland lawyer's life as illustrative of the era of World War I. *Pal Joey* (1940) presents letters from a nightclub singer, dramatized by O'Hara and others as a musical comedy. *Five Plays* (1961) were all unproduced but one he had fictionized in 1951 as *The Farmers Hotel*. Stories are collected in *Sermons and Soda-Water* (1960), *Assembly* (1961), *The Cape Cod Lighter* (1962), *The Hat on the Bed* (1963), *The Horse Knows the Way* (1964), *And Other Stories* (1968), *The Time Element* (1972), and *Good Samaritan* (1974). *Sweet and Sour* (1954) collects columns on books and authors, and selected *Letters* was issued in 1978.

O'Hara, SCARLETT, character in *Gone with the Wind.* ♦

Oil!, novel by Upton Sinclair, ♦ published in 1927, based on the oil scandals of the Harding administration, especially the Teapot Dome affair.

Ojibway Indians (also OJIBWA or CHIPPEWA), Algonquian hunting tribe of the Great Lakes region. They sided with the French during the French and Indian Wars, and shared in Pontiac's Rebellion. Later most of them were won over to the British side in the War of 1812. One of their chiefs, George Copway, has written about them, and they are the subject of an ethnological study by Schoolcraft. The Ojibway figure in *Hiawatha* as the tribe to which the hero belongs, and they appear in Cooper's *Oak Openings* and Janet Lewis's *The Invasion.*

Okies, name applied to refugees from Oklahoma, Texas, and other Dust Bowl states, who, because of the destruction of their farms by drought and dust storms, in the 1930s emigrated to seek employment elsewhere, mainly in California. Steinbeck's novel *The Grapes of Wrath* is concerned with an Okie family.

Oklahoma!, see *Green Grow the Lilacs.*

Old Corner Bookstore, established in 1828 in Boston on the corner of Washington and School streets, famous under the ownership

of William D. Ticknor and James T. Fields as an adjunct of their publishing firm and as a gathering place of such literati as Emerson, Holmes, Hawthorne, Longfellow, Lowell, and Whittier, so that it was dubbed "Parnassus Corner."

Old Creole Days, seven short stories by G.W. Cable, ♦ published in 1879. Later editions also include the novelette *Madame Delphine,* and all deal with the local color of 19th-century New Orleans.

Old Maid, The, novelette by Edith Wharton, ♦ published in 1924 as one of the series Old New York. Zoë Akins dramatized it (1935).

Old Man and the Sea, The, novelette by Hemingway, ♦ published in 1952.

This parable of man's struggle with the natural world, of his noble courage and endurance, tells of the Cuban fisherman Santiago, who for 84 luckless days has rowed his skiff into the Gulf Stream in quest of marlin. At first accompanied by the boy Manolin, with whom he talked of better days and about the great sport of baseball, he is now alone. Aged and solitary, he goes far out and hooks a great fish that tows his boat all afternoon and night and into the next day as he pits his skill and waning strength against it the way he once did as a wrestler called "El Campéon." As the second night turns to dawn he finally harpoons his catch, lashes it to his small boat, and makes his weary way home. As he sails slowly to port sharks attack his catch and he fights them as best he can with a knife lashed to the tiller gripped in raw hands. When he makes land his marlin is but a skeleton. Proud in defeat, Santiago furls his sail and staggers to his shack, to be found by the boy and other fishermen, who marvel at his catch, while the spent man sleeps and dreams of past experiences.

Old Manse, residence of the Emerson family, at Concord. Hawthorne lived there (1842–46) during the writing of his *Mosses from an Old Manse.*

Old Possum's Book of Practical Cats, by T.S. Eliot, ♦ published in 1939. It collects 15 humorous poems in Edward Lear-like verse, originally written for children Eliot knew. The little volume begins with the significance of "The Naming of Cats" and continues through the presentation of such diverse felines as Growltiger, Mr. Mistoffelees, Gus: The Theatre Cat, Bustopher Jones: The Cat

About Town, Cat Morgan, and Old Deuteronomy, "a cat who has lived many lives in succession. He was famous in proverb and famous in rhyme A long while before Queen Victoria's accession." A very popular musical and dancing show titled *Cats* was adapted from Eliot's book and produced in London (1981) and New York (1982).

Old Southwest, as distinguished from the present Southwest,♦ included the region between the Savannah River and the Mississippi,♦ which constituted the southwestern frontier from colonial times to the early 19th century. The pioneer settlers of this wilderness area, some of whom were called "crackers," created a distinctive folklore, which in turn gave rise to the frontier stories and sketches of T.B. Thorpe, Davy Crockett, G.W. Harris, Joseph Baldwin, J.M. Field, J.J. Hooper, Sol Smith, and A.B. Longstreet, and affected the writings of Mark Twain.

Old Swimmin'-Hole, The, and 'Leven More Poems, first book by James Whitcomb Riley,♦ published in 1883 under the pseudonym "Benj. F. Johnson, of Boone," but having the author's own name in brackets. The poems were originally written for *The Indianapolis Journal,* and include "When the Frost Is on the Punkin." These simple, sentimental poems in the homely Hoosier dialect established Riley's popularity.

OLDSTYLE, JONATHAN, pseudonym of Irving.♦

OLDSTYLE, OLIVER, pseudonym of Paulding.♦

Oldtown Folks, novel by Harriet Beecher Stowe,♦ published in 1869 and dramatized by the author the same year.

Horace Holyoke, who has grown up in Oldtown, Mass., during the post-Revolutionary period, describes the town's typical institutions, its preoccupation with theological discussion, and its leading citizens.

OLIVER, MARY (1935–), Ohio-born poet, whose works include *No Voyage and Other Poems* (1963, enlarged 1965), *The River Styx, Ohio* (1972), *The Night Traveler* (1978), *Twelve Moons* (1979), and *American Primitive* (1983, Pulitzer Prize).

OLMSTED, FREDERICK LAW (1822–1903), landscape architect and conservationist,

noted for his unbiased travel books, *A Journey in the Seaboard Slave States* (1856), *A Journey Through Texas* (1857), and *A Journey in the Back Country* (1860), which were condensed and reissued as *The Cotton Kingdom* (2 vols., 1861). He also wrote *Walks and Talks of an American Farmer in England* (1852). His greatest works in landscape architecture include Central Park and Riverside Park in New York City; the Boston park system; the Capitol grounds at Washington, D.C.; the 1893 World's Fair at Chicago; and the campuses of the University of California and Stanford University. Olmsted was instrumental in making public lands of Niagara Falls and Yosemite, and published works relating to public parks.

OLSEN, TILLIE (1913–), Nebraska-born author, worked as a domestic servant and raised her own four daughters before she found time to write, drawing upon her own experience. Four stories written in the 1950s were collected as *Tell Me a Riddle* (1962). *Yonnondio* (1974) is a novel about life in the 1930s. *Silences* (1978) prints essays and lectures delivered at colleges on writers who have been silenced because of their class or sex. She sympathetically introduced an edition of Rebecca Harding Davis's *Life in the Iron Mills* (1973).

OLSON, CHARLES (1910–70), born in Massachusetts, educated at Harvard, first became known for *Call Me Ishmael* (1947), a rhapsodic study of Melville, including Shakespeare's influence on him, but subsequently became distinguished for his poetry and poetic theory. His ideas, set forth as instructor and Rector of Black Mountain College,♦ greatly influenced Creeley, Duncan, and Levertov, among other students there. His Projective Verse conceived of the poem as an "open field" through which energy moves from its source to the reader, the measure being based on the breath of the speaker-poet. Olson's shorter poems printed in *In Cold Hell, in Thicket* (1953) and *The Distances* (1960) are collected in *The Archaeologist of Morning* (1971). *The Maximus Poems* (1–10, 1953; 11–23, 1956; combined, 1960), *Maximus IV, V, VI* (1968), and *The Maximus Poem* (1975) form a long, organic work in which the persona of Maximus concentrates on the past and present of Olson's hometown, Gloucester. Other works include *The Mayan Letters* (1953), written to Creeley from Mexico about anthropology and views of language; *A Bibliography on America for*

Ed Dorn (1964), succinct commentary on the U.S.; *Human Universe* (1965), essays; *Letters for Origin* (1969), written to Cid Corman♦ about poetry and its publication; *Causal Mythology* (1969), on myth; *Poetry and Truth* (1971), lectures delivered at Beloit; and *The Fiery Hunt* (1978), verse plays. Creeley edited *Selected Writings* (1966).

OLSON, ELDER [JAMES] (1909–   ), Chicago-born poet and critic, professor at the University of Chicago, is known as a leader of its school of neo-Aristotelians, whose critical views were based on the *Poetics* of Aristotle. His poetry, cerebral and formal, appeared in *Thing of Sorrow* (1934), *The Cock of Heaven* (1940), *The Scarecrow Christ* (1954), *Plays and Poems* (1958), *Collected Poems* (1963), and *Olson's Penny Arcade* (1975). *Tragedy and the Theory of Drama* (1961) and *The Theory of Comedy* (1968) are among his critical works.

Omoo, a Narrative of Adventures in the South Seas, fictional account by Melville♦ of his experiences in the Society Islands (1842). It was published in 1847 as a sequel to *Typee.* ♦

At Nukuheva the narrator is taken aboard the short-handed Australian trader *Julia* (actually the *Lucy Ann*). Despite his injured leg, he signs on as a seaman, being assured that he may leave the ship at the next port. He discovers that the ship is in poor condition, and that Captain Guy is ill and untrustworthy, but he admires the mate Jermin and finds a friend in jovial, well-traveled, well-read Dr. Long Ghost. At Papeetee, the consul Wilson orders the *Julia* to sea again, but the unruly crew disobeys, bringing the ship into harbor. Imprisoned for insubordination, the men oppose efforts to force them aboard and at last are deserted when the *Julia* sails with a new crew. They annoy the natives, whose scanty supplies they share, although the old guide "Captain Bob" is friendly. The narrator and the doctor leave Tahiti for Imeeo, where they work for two planters, the Yankee Zeke and the cockney Shorty. Soon tiring of farm labor, they desert the plantation to explore the islands and study the people. Then, leaving Long Ghost in Tahiti, the narrator ships on a whaler, *The Leviathan.*

On Native Grounds, literary study by Alfred Kazin,♦ published in 1942. Subtitled "An Interpretation of Modern American Prose Literature," the work, covering the half century 1890–1940, conceives that "our modern literature in America is at bottom only the experience of our modern life in America" and that this study "is in part an effort at moral history, which is greater than literary history, and is needed to illuminate it."

On the Road, novel by Jack Kerouac,♦ published in 1957.

Sal Paradise (a self-portrait by Kerouac), a struggling author in his mid-twenties, tells of his meeting Dean Moriarty (based on Neal Cassady), a fast-living teenager just out of a New Mexico reform school, whose soul is "wrapped up in a fast car, a coast to reach, and a woman at the end of the road." During the next five years they travel coast to coast, either with each other or to each other. Five trips are described. In the first Sal travels to Denver in July 1947 to be with Dean, whom he finds has left his recent wife Marylou for a woman named Camille. After ten days of wild parties, Sal goes to San Francisco, then Los Angeles, picking up jobs and women before returning to New York to work on his novel. A year and a half later, Dean, back with Marylou, joins Sal in the East to drive to San Francisco. When Dean again deserts his wife for Camille, she and Sal have a brief affair before Sal returns alone to New York. In the spring of 1949 Sal goes to California to find Dean, still living with Camille, who expects her second child, and the two reunited friends leave her to drive to New York, where Dean finds another love, Inez, who bears him a child. Later, Sal, having sold his novel to a publisher, goes with Dean to Mexico, partly so that Dean may divorce Camille. But when Sal falls sick, Dean leaves him, returning to New York and Inez. After a time Sal, settled in New York, and Dean in San Francisco, again with Camille, plan further travels, when Dean goes east and remains there temporarily while Sal goes west again, this time alone.

Once I Pass'd Through a Populous City, poem by Whitman,♦ published in the "Children of Adam"♦ section of *Leaves of Grass* (1860). Although the poem in its original manuscript referred to a man, and Whitman denied that the poem was autobiographical, its declaration that "of all that city I remember only a woman" has led biographers to contend that it refers to a love affair in New Orleans in 1848 which substantially altered Whitman's character.

One Flew Over the Cuckoo's Nest, novel by Ken Kesey,♦ published in 1962. It was dramatized by Dale Wasserman (1974).

Chief Bromden, so named because he is of Indian descent but also because he is the chief sweeper in the psychopathic ward of an Oregon mental hospital, tells how he and the other inmates with whom he has shared confinement for ten years are buoyed by the arrival of Randle Patrick McMurphy. McMurphy, who has gotten himself transferred to the hospital from a prison, where he was serving time for statutory rape of a teenage girl, is a loud, laughing Irishman. He challenges the sadistic control of Head Nurse Ratched, who has browbeaten the frightened men into abject docility. Bit by bit he restores some self-esteem in the men and even stirs the long mute Chief to talk. For fomenting rebellion, and assaulting the Head Nurse, however, he is subjected to repeated shock treatment and a lobotomy that reduces him to blank passivity. As an act of mercy the Chief then smothers McMurphy and escapes into the outer world.

One-Hoss Shay, see *Deacon's Masterpiece.*

Oneida Community, religious society established in central New York state by John Humphrey Noyes (1811–86). The evolution of perfectionist doctrines, coupled with the reading of Fourierist publications, gradually led the group to communism. The original 40 members, grown to some 300, settled on a 900-acre farm, governed themselves democratically, and practiced a system of mutual criticism that took the place of trials and punishments, serving as a cure for both moral delinquencies and physical ailments. The community acquired a reputation for its excellent school system and its profitable manufactures, which included steel traps and silver-plated ware. Among the many books and periodicals published from Oneida and its affiliated communities, the most popular was the weekly *Oneida Circular* (1864–76). Despite the perfectionist doctrine of immediate and total cessation of sin, public opinion was aroused by the community's system of complex marriage, which combined polygamy and polyandry, attempting to propagate children scientifically by pairing the young of one sex with the aged of the other. This was abandoned in 1879, and Noyes soon removed to Canada. When the community was reorganized as a business corporation (1881), its property was valued at $600,000.

O'NEILL, Eugene [Gladstone] (1888–1953), born in New York City, as a child accompanied his father, James O'Neill (1847–1920), a popular romantic actor, on theatrical tours, and later attended a Catholic boarding school and a Connecticut preparatory school. He entered Princeton (1906), but remained there only a year. After secretarial work in New York, he went on a gold prospecting trip to Honduras (1909), but contracted malaria, and returned to the U.S. to be assistant manager of his father's company. Soon tiring of their mediocre vehicle, he shipped as a seaman for Buenos Aires. Employed for a time in Argentina, he then worked his way to South Africa and back on a cattle steamer, and after a period of beachcombing in Buenos Aires returned to New York. His last experience at sea followed, when he worked on ships between New York and Southampton. Next he tried acting during one of his father's tours, and reporting for a Connecticut newspaper, but suffered a physical breakdown and was sent to a sanatorium for six months. He had already written verses, and during this period of enforced rest and reflection turned to the drama as a medium for expressing the view of life he began to develop, based on his life at sea and among outcast and oppressed people in many places.

During the following winter (1913–14), he wrote his first play, *The Web,* seven other one-act plays, and two long plays. He gained further experience as a student in G.P. Baker's 47 Workshop (1914–15), and spent a winter in Greenwich Village. In 1916 he became associated with the Provincetown Players, who during the next three years produced many of his one-act plays, including *Bound East for Cardiff*♦ (1916) and *The Moon of the Caribbees*♦ (1918). This period of practical experiment brought to a climax his years of apprentice work, and he began to win general recognition when three of his plays were printed in *The Smart Set.* With the New York production of *Beyond the Horizon*♦ (1920, Pulitzer Prize), O'Neill was acknowledged as the foremost creative American playwright.

Although he was associated with Robert Edmond Jones in managing the Greenwich Village Theatre (1923–27) and was a director of the Provincetown Players and a founder of the Theatre Guild, which produced his later plays, he became increasingly absorbed in writing, to the exclusion of other interests. He followed *Beyond the Horizon* with further naturalistic studies of tragic frustration set in modern American backgrounds: *Chris Christopherson* (1920), rewritten as *"Anna Christie"*♦ (1921, Pulitzer Prize); *Diff'rent*

(1920); *Gold* (1921); *The Straw* (1921); and *The First Man* (1922). From the same period came his achievements in symbolic expressionism: *The Emperor Jones*♦ (1920) and *"The Hairy Ape"*♦ (1922); but he continued the naturalistic approach in *All God's Chillun Got Wings*♦ (1924), and *Desire Under the Elms*♦ (1924). In the same year he turned to the use of symbolic masks in a Provincetown production of Coleridge's *The Ancient Mariner,* which he adapted and directed.

The romantic and poetic elements of his nature, which had hitherto appeared in details of his plays, dominated *The Fountain* (1925), an affirmation of life and spirit, and "the Eternal Becoming which is Beauty." His next play, *The Great God Brown*♦ (1926), fused symbolism, poetry, and the affirmation of a pagan idealism, in an ironic tragedy of modern materialism; and *Lazarus Laughed* (1927) and *Marco Millions* (1928) similarly attack the contemporary emphasis on acquisition and material standards, in terms of poetic emotion, exotic color, and satirical irony. Always an experimenter in forms, O'Neill attempted in *Strange Interlude*♦ (1928, Pulitzer Prize) to create a dramatic technique using the stream-of-consciousness method, in a nine-act tragedy of frustrated desires. This psychological analysis of motives was followed by a trilogy, *Mourning Becomes Electra*♦ (1931), adapting the Greek theme and preserving the dominant emotions of fear, horror, and a brooding sense of a malignant fate. O'Neill's deep interest in problems of religion in the modern world appears in two plays of this later period: *Dynamo* (1929), in which an electrical dynamo becomes a divine symbol, replacing the old God but destroying its worshippers; and *Days Without End* (1934), in which the hero is irresistibly attracted to Catholicism.

Ah, Wilderness! (1933) is a pleasant New England folk comedy, very different from O'Neill's usual concerns. *The Iceman Cometh*♦ (1946) is a tragedy, realistically set in a Bowery bar, symbolically portraying the loss of illusion and the coming of Death. *Long Day's Journey into Night*♦ (1956), Pulitzer Prize), an autobiographical tragedy written in 1940, and depicting a day in 1912 in the unhappy life of the Tyrone family, was the first of his posthumously produced and published plays. In 1958 came *Hughie,* a one-act character study, and of his projected eleven-play cycle, "A Tale of Possessors Self-Dispossessed," about the effect possessions had on an American family from the colonial era

to the present day, two have been acted and issued: *A Touch of the Poet* (published 1957, produced 1958) and its immediate sequel, *More Stately Mansions* (1964).

O'Neill's works are deeply affected by his wide reading, especially in Greek tragedies, Ibsen, and Strindberg, but it is his own stage experience and his own insight into character that made them so distinguished and earned him a Nobel Prize (1936). His *Poems,* minor works, were collected in 1980.

One's-Self I Sing, poem by Whitman,♦ published as "Inscription" in *Leaves of Grass* (1867) and given its present title in 1871. According to Whitman's plan, the poem is printed first in his book. It celebrates the "simple, separate Person" as a physical, moral, intellectual, emotional, and aesthetic being, but declares that when he sings of himself, he uses the "word *En-masse*" to show that he represents the modern democratic man.

Only Yesterday, informal social history of the U.S. in the 1920s (1931) by Frederick Lewis Allen (1890–1954), a Boston-born journalist.

Onondaga Indians, New York tribe that belonged to the Iroquois Confederacy.♦ The Onondaga aided the British in the French and Indian Wars and in the Revolution. Most of them have since lived in Ontario, although some remain on a New York reservation. They figure in Cooper's *Wyandotté,* and in the Littlepage Manuscripts an Onondaga is one of the heroes.

Open Boat, The, and Other Tales of Adventure, eight short stories by Stephen Crane,♦ published in 1898, mainly "after the Fact" of his own experiences as a reporter and war correspondent.

"The Open Boat" is a realistic account of the thoughts and emotions of four men who escape in a small dinghy from the wrecked steamer *Commodore* off the Florida coast. The captain, the cook, an oiler, and a newspaper correspondent, unable to land because of the dangerous surf, see the beach tantalizingly near, but are forced to spend the night on the sea. Next morning they employ their last strength to swim ashore, and all but the oiler survive. "Death and the Child," reminiscent of *The Red Badge of Courage,* has for its scene a battle of the Greco-Turkish War and is concerned with the psychological reactions of a Greek newspaperman in his first experience of warfare. At first he desires to fight with his countrymen, but as he views the battle more intimately he is overcome by fear and panic, and flees to a nearby mountain, where his self-centered emotion is contrasted with the indifference of an abandoned peasant child. "Flanagan, and His Short Filibustering Adventure" narrates a melodramatic incident of arms smuggling in Cuba before the Spanish-American War. The remaining stories are sardonically realistic adventure tales in Mexico and the Far West. Of these one is "The Bride Comes to Yellow Sky," about a newly married couple, the marshal of Yellow Sky, Tex., and his bride from San Antonio, who arrive on the train in his town at the moment that the local bad man goes on a drunken shooting spree. After a tense meeting, the marshal is spared, not because the bad man was a "student of chivalry; it was merely that in the presence of this foreign condition he was a simple child of the earlier plains."

OPPEN, GEORGE (1908–84), poet reared and resident in California, a protégé of Ezra Pound and a leader of the Objectivist♦ school, whose terse poems appear in *Discrete Series* (1934), *The Materials* (1962), *This in Which* (1965), *Of Being Numerous* (1968, Pulitzer Prize), *Seascape* (1973), *Collected Poems* (1975), and *Primitive* (1978).

Opposing Self, The, work by Lionel Trilling,♦ published in 1955, collects nine discrete essays in criticism, mostly written as introductions to books from the previous 150 years and therefore said to be concerned with the idea of the self and its relation to modern culture. The works include *Little Dorrit, Anna Karenina, The Bostonians,* and *Mansfield Park,* to which are added considerations of Keats, Howells, Wordsworth, Orwell, and Flaubert.

Oregon Trail, The, autobiographical narrative by Parkman,♦ serialized in *The Knickerbocker Magazine* (1847) and issued in book form as *The California and Oregon Trail* (1849). The original title was resumed in later editions.

This account of the author's trip over the eastern part of the Oregon Trail, with his cousin, Quincy Adams Shaw (April–Aug. 1846), tells of their travels from St. Louis by steamboat and horseback to Fort Laramie, Wy., in company with guides and occasional other travelers. They encounter typical adventures in storms, buffalo hunts, and meet-

ings with Indians, soldiers, sportsmen, and emigrants. At Fort Laramie, then a trading post, they find an encampment of Sioux and learn of a war party that is being sent against the Snake Indians. Attempting to join this party, they meet difficulties, and Parkman goes on alone with a guide, promising to rejoin Shaw later. After a dangerous mountain journey, he finds the Sioux band and lives with them for several weeks, sharing their food and shelter and taking part in buffalo hunts and ceremonials, although he sees no battles. Parkman was in ill health, and only managed by strenuous and painful activity to keep the respect of his untrustworthy hosts. After gaining much information and insight into Indian character, which influenced his writings and made this a classic description of Indian life, Parkman rejoined Shaw, and returned east.

Osage Indians, war-like Plains tribe♦ related to the Sioux, were encountered (1673) on the Osage River in Missouri. Besides waging war on many tribes, they were allied with the French in the French and Indian Wars. Irving describes the Osage enthusiastically in *A Tour on the Prairies,* and their descendants, who have become wealthy through the discovery of oil on their Oklahoma lands, figure in Edna Ferber's *Cimarron.* John Joseph Matthews, an Osage, wrote *Wah'kon-tah: The Osage and the White Man's Road* (1932).

Other Voices, Other Rooms, novel by Truman Capote,♦ published in 1948.
Joel Knox, an unloved 13-year-old boy, quests to find his real nature as he matures on a Louisiana plantation and its surroundings, where through reality and dream he loses his innocence and finds his homosexual identity.

Ottawa Indians, tribe originally located on the Ottawa River in Canada, were first noted by Champlain (1615). They were allied with the French and Hurons, and consequently opposed the Iroquois. The latter forced them to flee to the Great Lakes region, and their later wanderings took them throughout the central U.S. Pontiac was an Ottawa chieftain. The tribe figures in Rogers's *Ponteach* and in Doddridge's *Logan.*

Our Old Home, sketches by Hawthorne,♦ published in 1863, describing his observations and experiences during his residence in England.

Our Town, play by Thornton Wilder,♦ produced and published in 1938, when it won a Pulitzer Prize.

The intimate history of a typical American town, Grover's Corners, N.H., is sketched during the years 1901–13. On a bare, uncurtained stage, set with a few chairs and tables, the activities of the townspeople are enacted under the visible direction of the friendly Stage Manager, who addresses the audience, describing the characters and commenting on the action, in what the author calls a "hangover from a novelist technique." Professor Willard and Editor Webb describe the scientific and social backgrounds, and other incidental figures are Joe Crowell, the newsboy; Howie Newsome, the milkman; Simon Stimson, a frustrated creative artist, the town organist and drunkard; Constable Warren; Mr. Morgan, the druggist; Mrs. Soames, the gossip; and Joe Stoddard, the undertaker. Interest is centered in the families of Editor Webb and Dr. Gibbs. The first act, "Daily Life," shows the common occupations of cooking, gardening, school, baseball, the church choir, and domestic concerns. The second act, "Love and Marriage," deals with the courtship and wedding of George Gibbs and Emily Webb. "Death," the third act, presents the funeral of Emily, who has died in childbirth. The buried dead become articulate, expressing the quiet and patience resulting from a view of the world outside of time, and their knowledge of "something way down deep that's eternal about every human being." Finally aware of the mysterious beauty and terror of life, they embody the author's aim "to present illustrations of harmony and of law . . . affirmations about mankind and his ends."

Out of the Cradle Endlessly Rocking, poem by Whitman,♦ published as "A Word Out of the Sea" in *Leaves of Grass* (1860) and given its present title in 1871.

At night, a boy steals out from his Long Island farm home to listen to the calls of a pair of mockingbirds by the sea. One night the female is gone, and her mate, from the nest to which she will never return, issues his plaintive call. The solitary singer becomes a symbol of the poet's daemon, and his mysterious aria is interpreted by the whispering current of the sea as "Death." The sea, symbol of the spiritual world, thus shows the boy that physical love is spiritualized through death for poetic creation, and the poet says, "my own songs awaked from that hour."

Outcasts of Poker Flat, The, story by Bret Harte,♦ published in 1869 and reprinted in *The Luck of Roaring Camp and Other Sketches* (1870). It is a leading example of local-color fiction.

This study of moral contrasts tells of the exile from Poker Flat, a California mining camp of 1850, of the gambler John Oakhurst, two prostitutes known as "the Duchess" and "Mother Shipton," and a drunken sluice-robber, "Uncle Billy." This group is joined by "The Innocent," Tom Simson, and the young girl Piney, who are eloping. When all are trapped by the snow, Mother Shipton starves to save her rations for Piney, Oakhurst gives the one chance of safety to Tom by killing himself, and the Duchess pillows her head on Piney's breast as the two die together.

Outsider, The, novel by Richard Wright,♦ published in 1953.

Cross Damon, a black man who works in the Chicago post office, is caught in a subway accident but escapes without serious injury, though because of a mistaken identity his death is announced. He decides to take advantage of this error to start life anew and thus free himself of his entanglements with women and debts. He goes to New York to live under an assumed name and before long becomes enmeshed in the Communist party. By it he is used as a murderer, until he is himself killed by a Party member.

Overland Monthly (1868–75, 1883–1935), California regional magazine, published from San Francisco, during its first two and a half years was edited by Bret Harte, who contributed "The Luck of Roaring Camp," "Plain Language from Truthful James," and other works that made both author and magazine famous. In its early years, the *Overland* published writings by such authors as C.W. Stoddard, Ina Coolbrith, E.R. Sill, and Prentice Mulford. It was less significant when revived, and rested so obviously on its former reputation that Bierce dubbed it "the warmed-Overland Monthly." For a time it attracted such authors as Gertrude Atherton, Jack London, Edwin Markham, J.G. Neilhardt, Frank Norris, and George Sterling, but it finally died of inanition.

Over-Soul, The, essay by Emerson,♦ published in *Essays, First Series* (1841). The Over-Soul is "that great nature in which we rest . . . that Unity within which every man's particular being is contained and made one with all other." This Platonic concept, first stated in Emerson's early lectures and in such works as *Nature* and the "Divinity School Address," is here developed as a basic principle in the thought of Transcendentalism.

"We live in succession, in division, in parts, in particles. Meantime within man is the soul of the whole." Perceptible only through intuition and not to be communicated through words, this divine spirit is the source of all moral and intellectual growth, for "the heart, which abandons itself to the Supreme Mind, finds itself related to all its works and will travel a royal road to particular knowledge and powers." The revelations of truth received by various original thinkers and teachers proceed from "an influx of the Divine mind" into their minds. "The nature of these revelations is always the same: they are perceptions of the absolute law." What we call genius is simply the true insight derived from an influx of this "same Omniscience . . . into the intellect." This universal and benign omnipresence is neither "our god of tradition" nor "our god of rhetoric," but a God known to men only in moments of mystic enthusiasm, whose visitation leaves them altered, self-reliant, and purified of petty aims. The man who has received intimations of the "Highest Law" in this fashion "will weave no longer a spotted life of shreds and patches, but he will live with a divine unity."

OWEN, ROBERT (1771–1858), "the father of English socialism," at an early age made a commercial success of his cotton mills at New Lanark, Scotland, and then aided workers by instituting economic, moral, and educational reforms. In *A New View of Society* (1813), he set forth his view that to create a good man one must surround him with the proper physical, moral, and social influences. To test his theories he came to America (1824) and founded New Harmony (1825), a socialized, agricultural community whose settlers (about 1000) were impractical idealists, who as a result formed seven different constitutions and underwent ten group secessions before formal dissolution in 1828.

ROBERT DALE OWEN (1801–77), his son, emigrated to the U.S. in 1825, and was active in the New Harmony community and with Frances Wright♦ in the Nashoba Community, as well as in other reform associations.

Ox-Bow Incident, The, novel by Walter Van T. Clark,♦ published in 1940.

A trailhand, Art Croft, in 1885 tells the story of cattle rustlers who murdered a rancher and stole his stock near the Nevada mountain town of Bridger's Wells. A posse is formed to find and lynch the culprits, although the storekeeper Arthur Davies, the sanctimonious Reverend Osgood, and pompous Judge Tyler argue weakly for a fair trial. They are quickly overwhelmed by the old Confederate major Willard Tetley, a prominent rancher, the tough stage driver Bill Winder, the town drunk Monty Smith, and others who ride out and in a small valley with an ox-bow-shaped river find the Mexican Juan Martinez, the senile Alva Hardwick, and a young rancher, Donald Martin, with cattle which they cannot prove they own. Despite Martin's convincing statement about his innocence, the three are hanged, Martin in a bungled way by Tetley's son Gerald, who is forced to the act by the Major. Upon returning to town the posse finds that the three men were innocent. Gerald hangs himself in his father's barn, the elder Tetley kills himself with his old cavalry sword, and Davies, filled with self-pity as much as with remorse, takes up a collection for Martin's widow and children.

Oz, mythical land that is the setting for 14 novels for children by L. Frank Baum,♦ beginning with *The Wonderful Wizard of Oz* (1900). This fanciful region, traversed by a long yellow brick road, is accidentally discovered by Dorothy, a little girl from Kansas, when she and her dog Toto are blown off to it by a cyclone. In this delightful region of surprising adventures dwell such odd characters as a good-hearted Cowardly Lion, a friendly Tin Woodman, and an animate Scarecrow, all basically pleasant and joyful, presided over by a kindly, eccentric Wizard. Although there are threats from external forces, like the Wicked Witch of the West, all turns out happily in Oz.

Baum created a muscial extravaganza for the stage (1901), the first of many adaptations that have included a Technicolor musical film featuring Judy Garland (1939) and a Broadway musical, *The Wiz* (1975), with a black cast and using a modern urban setting.

P

PAGE, THOMAS NELSON (1853–1922), Virginia author distinguished as a leader of the local-color movement. His first short story appeared in 1884, and in 1893 he forsook his legal career to become a professional writer. His first volume of stories, *In Ole Virginia* (1887), depicts romantic aspects of his region before and during the Civil War. Frequently employing Negro dialect, his stories are generally concerned sentimentally with the aristocratic Old South, as in such collections as *Elsket and Other Stories* (1891), *The Burial of the Guns* (1894), and *Bred in the Bone* (1904). Page's novels, dealing with the same background, include *On Newfound River* (1891), the story of a Virginia feud in the period before the Civil War; *The Old Gentleman of the Black Stock* (1897), a romantic tale of an old man who reunites a quarreling pair of young lovers; *Red Rock* (1898), telling of the oppressive military rule of the South during Reconstruction; *Gordon Keith* (1903), contrasting a well-born Southerner with a Northern *nouveau riche; John Marvel, Assistant* (1909), presenting a typical Southerner against the background of contemporary Chicago. His essays and social studies, linked to his fiction in theme and tone, include *The Old South* (1892); *Social Life in Old Virginia* (1897); and *The Old Dominion* (1908). He also wrote semi-historical works and eulogistic biographies, such as *Robert E. Lee, Man and Soldier* (1911), and a volume of dialect verse, *Befo' de War* (1888). His literary career ended when he became U.S. ambassador to Italy (1913–19).

PAGE, WALTER HINES (1855–1918), born in North Carolina, began his journalistic career in 1880, reported on the South for the New York *World* (1881–83), edited the Raleigh *State Chronicle* (1883–85), *The Forum* (1890–95), the *Atlantic Monthly* (1896–99), and the *World's Work* (1900–1913). The prestige thus acquired caused his appointment as ambassador to Great Britain (1913–18), in which position he helped Anglo-American relations, sympathizing strongly with Great Britain even while the U.S. was attempting to maintain neutrality in World War I. His *Life and Letters* (3 vols., 1922–25, Pulitzer Prize) was the work of Burton J. Hendrick.

PAINE, ALBERT BIGELOW (1861–1937), editor, dramatist, biographer, and author of several novels, is best known for his authorized three-volume biography of Mark Twain (1912) and for his editorship of Twain's letters (1917). The title of one of Paine's plays, *The Great White Way* (1901), gave a familiar nickname to New York City's theatrical district.

PAINE, THOMAS (1737–1809), born in England, was the son of a corset maker, to whose trade he was apprenticed when his schooling ended at the age of 13. His unsettled life to 1774 included residence in various towns, two brief unhappy marriages, and such occupations as schoolteacher, tobacconist, grocer, and exciseman. He was twice dismissed from the last post, and was forced into bankruptcy after the publication of *The Case of the Officers of Excise* (1772), a plea to Parliament for higher wages. While lobbying for the excisemen, he met Franklin, who was impressed by his learning and interests and helped him to start anew in America.

Arriving at Philadelphia (1774), Paine achieved wide fame with the publication of *Common Sense♦* (1776), which urged an immediate declaration of independence at a time when others were debating only matters of reform. While serving as a soldier in the Continental army, he continued his political journalism in *The American Crisis♦* (Dec. 1776–April 1783), a series of 16 pamphlets in support of the Revolutionary War. He was rewarded by an appointment (1777–79) as secretary to the congressional committee on foreign affairs, but was forced to resign, after he charged corruption in the negotiations of Silas Deane with France and implied that the French, while still at peace with England, had aided the colonies. The plea for a strong federal union that he had made in *Common Sense* was reiterated in *Public Good* (1780), opposing Virginia's claims to western land.

After an appointment as clerk of the Pennsylvania Assembly and a trip to France (1781) for money and stores, he retired to the farm at New Rochelle that New York presented to him. *Dissertations on Government . . .* (1786), a blast against paper money inflation, was his only political work during this period, when he was engaged in perfecting his invention of an iron bridge. He went to France and England (1787), had his bridge constructed in the latter country, and traveled between Paris and London in the cause of a world revolution.

The Rights of Man ♦ (1791–92), a defense of the French Revolution against the attacks of Edmund Burke, urged the English to create a republic. Having fled to France, he was not directly affected by his English trial for treason and sentence of banishment (1792). He was made a French citizen by the Assembly (1792) and was elected to the Convention, where he allied himself with the moderate republicans, who lost power during the Terror (1793). His citizenship was thereupon revoked, and, although he was outlawed by England, he was arrested by France as an enemy Englishman. In jail (Dec. 1793–Nov. 1794), he wrote *The Age of Reason* ♦ (1794–95), his great deistic work.

At this time he considered himself the victim of a plot contrived by his conservative enemy, the American minister Gouverneur Morris, but it appears that Morris deliberately left him in jail because he was unnoticed there and might be sentenced to death if his case were reopened. Released at the request of Morris's successor, Monroe, Paine returned to the Convention (1795) after the passing of the Terror. Although he did not return to the U.S. until 1802, he played a vicarious part in American politics through his *Letter to George Washington* (1796), accusing the President and Morris of plotting against him, and, through Jefferson's championing of *The Rights of Man,* causing a bitter partisan dispute with J.Q. Adams, who attacked both Paine and Jefferson.

Paine's last years in the U.S. were marked by poverty, ill health, and ostracism. Malevolent persons of all parties, who feared his radical free-thinking, accused him of drunkenness, cowardice, adultery, and atheism. He was buried on his New Rochelle farm when consecrated ground was refused, and in 1819 William Cobbett removed the remains to England, with the intention of erecting a monument to Paine. This was never accomplished, and after Cobbett's death the bones of Paine were lost.

Painted Veils, novel by Huneker, ♦ published in 1920.

Set among the bohemian society of New York artists, critics, and dilettantes, this impressionistic narrative exhibits the author's love of the exotic and the voluptuous, his acceptance of the decorative aspects of Oriental mysticism, and his intimate knowledge of art and artists in his time.

Pale Fire, novel by Nabokov, ♦ published in 1962.

An unfinished poem of 999 lines of heroic couplets, titled "Pale Fire," by John Shade is the subject of an inept but lengthy exegesis of 160 pages by Charles Kinbote. Although ostensibly a literary scholar, Kinbote admits he is actually Charles Xavier, last king of Zembla (1936–58), overthrown in a revolution. One of the revolutionary leaders, Gradus, has pursued the monarch to New Wye, Appalachia, in the U.S., where as Kinbote he is teaching at Wordsmith College. There Kinbote has made friends with the poet John Shade in the hope of persuading him to write an epic immortalizing Zembla and its last monarch. However, Gradus accidentally kills Shade while trying to assassinate the ex-king. Charles makes off with the manuscript of the unfinished poem that he persuades himself is a cryptic version of the desired epic, and therefore in editing the work for publication he creates the very elaborate commentary that forms the body of the novel.

Pale Horse, Pale Rider, volume of short stories by Katherine Anne Porter. ♦

PALEY, GRACE (1922–), born in New York City, a member of the Sarah Lawrence faculty, whose stories have been collected in *The Little Disturbances of Man* (1959) and *Enormous Changes at the Last Minute* (1974).

Paris Review, The (1953–), quarterly journal of poetry, fiction, art and literary criticism and commentary, edited from Paris and New York. It emphasizes the contemporary but its tastes are quite catholic as indicated by its contributors, who include Malcolm Cowley, Jack Kerouac, Philip Roth, W.D. Snodgrass, William Styron, and Joyce Carol Oates. It has featured a notable series of interviews with a variety of authors, including Eliot, Frost, Hemingway, Huxley, Voznesensky, and Joan Didion, some gathered in collections, beginning with *Writers at Work* (1958), that reached a sixth volume in 1984. One of the founders, William Styron, edited a collection of its *Best Short Stories* (1959) from the early years.

PARKER, DOROTHY [ROTHSCHILD] (1893–1967), after a career as a dramatic and literary critic in her native New York City, during which she achieved an almost legendary reputation for her malicious and sardonic *bons mots*, published her first book of poetry, *Enough Rope* (1926). This and the two volumes which followed, *Sunset Gun* (1928) and *Death and Taxes* (1931), all collected in *Not So Deep as a Well* (1936), are works of light, satirical verse, characterized by brilliant concision, flippant cynicism, and caustic variations on certain dominant themes, such as frustrated love and cheated idealism in modern living. Her short stories and sketches, published in *Laments for the Living* (1930) and *After Such Pleasures* (1933), and collected in *Here Lies* (1939), possess the same wry quality and polished technique that are found in her poems. She was a newspaper correspondent in Spain during that country's civil war, and later wrote motion-picture scenarios in collaboration with her husband, Alan Campbell, and with Arnaud d'Usseau wrote a two-act play, *Ladies of the Corridor* (1953), about the lonely lives of wealthy widows in a New York hotel.

PARKER, THEODORE (1810–60), a Unitarian clergyman in a Boston suburb (1837) who believed in the direct intuition of an Absolute Being, and, in agreement with such liberal thinkers as Channing, Emerson, Alcott, Ripley, and Wendell Phillips, developed his intuitive religious beliefs into a system, expressed in *The . . . Question Between Mr. Andrews Norton and His Alumni . . .* (1839), written under the pseudonym Levi Blodgett, and a sermon on "The Transient and Permanent in Christianity" (1841). Having become a Transcendentalist, he was ostracized by the orthodox Unitarian circles, and only enabled to deliver the lectures printed as *A Discourse of Matters Pertaining to Religion* (1842) when laymen invited him to Boston. When he was finally installed as minister of a new Congregational Society of Boston, he devoted his pulpit not only to religious education but to the discussion of problems of war, slavery, temperance, women's rights, and other reforms, in the belief that social wrongs would be cured when men attained consciousness of the infinite perfection of God. Outside the church, he made passionate speeches against slavery, aided New England emigrants to Kansas in the struggle that followed the passage of the Kansas-Nebraska bill, abetted John Brown, was active in attempts to rescue fugitive slaves, and wrote such works as his *Letters . . . Touching the Matter of Slavery* (1848).

PARKMAN, FRANCIS (1823–93), member of a prominent Boston family, graduated from Harvard (1844). In 1846 he set out from St. Louis on a journey to Wyoming, with the dual purpose of studying Indian life and improving his frail health. He observed frontiersmen and Indians at first hand, and gained valuable information, but his strenuous exercise led to a complete breakdown rather than recovery. Incapable of writing, he dictated to his cousin and companion, Quincy A. Shaw, his account of the journey, which he titled *The Oregon Trail*♦ (1849).

Although he was frequently unable to compose more than six lines a day, had to hire others to read and write for him, and employed a special instrument enabling him to write without looking at his manuscript, he nevertheless began in 1848 his *History of the Conspiracy of Pontiac* (1851), the first of a long series of histories of the French and English struggle for colonial America. His only novel is the semi-autobiographical *Vassall Morton* (1856). A new nervous crisis caused him to seek cures in European travel (1858–59) and in an interest in horticulture, which resulted in *The Book of Roses* (1866) and his later appointment as Harvard professor of horticulture (1871).

By sheer will power, he forced himself to return to his historical project. The series concerning the conflict for domination in the New World includes seven separate works: *Pioneers of France in the New World* (1865), concerned with the struggle between French Huguenots and Spanish Catholics for Florida, and the history of Champlain; *The Jesuits in North America in the Seventeenth Century* (1867), telling of the struggle to Christianize the Indians, and the Iroquois victory over the converted tribes (c.1670); *La Salle and the Discovery of the Great West* (1869), originally published as *The Discovery of the Great West*, dealing with La Salle's attempts to colonize the Mississippi Valley; *The Old Regime in Canada* (1874), showing the French feudal dominion of Acadia, the problems of the missionaries, and the faults of autocratic rule; *Count Frontenac and New France Under Louis XIV* (1877), depicting Frontenac as the hero who alone attempted to maintain France's untenable position; *Montcalm and Wolfe* (1884), dealing with the Seven Years' War in America, and the dramatic conclusion of French influence with the defeat of Montcalm on the Plains of Abraham; and *A Half-Century of Conflict* (1892), concerned with border warfare and the siege of Louisburg in the years 1700–1741, between Frontenac's government and the final downfall of France's colonial empire. The series was written in historical sequence, except for the last two works, and the *History of the Conspiracy of Pontiac,* which describes events following those of *Montcalm and Wolfe.*

Parkman depicted history in terms of the two forces of progress and reaction, represented respectively by England and France. He saw the former as ordered democracy, the latter as dictated military despotism, but, placing his faith in neither, admitted in *The Old Regime* what was everywhere implicit: "My political faith lies between two vicious extremes, democracy and absolute authority. . . . I do not object to a good constitutional monarchy, but prefer a conservative republic. . . ." As he was a believer in a middle-of-the-road policy for government, likewise in his approach to history he combined Scott's romantic attitude with the scientific method of German scholarship, to create work both accurate as history and important as literature. His previously lost *Journals* were printed in 1948 and his *Letters* in 1960.

PARRINGTON, VERNON L[OUIS] (1871–1929), scholar of American literature, professor at the University of Washington (1908–29), whose books include *The Connecticut Wits* (1926), *Sinclair Lewis, Our Own Diogenes* (1927), and *Main Currents in American Thought* (3 vols., 1927–30). The last work, of which the third volume was left incomplete, is a historical examination of American ideas and their primary expression in literature, written from the point of view of a Jeffersonian liberal. The first two volumes were awarded a Pulitzer Prize (1928) and the entire work influenced others to reevaluate American literature, following him in an economic interpretation of literary movements.

Partisan, The, first of the Revolutionary Romances by Simms, ◆ published in 1835. Set in South Carolina, it covers the period between the capture of Charleston and the American defeat at Camden.

Partisan Review (1934–), quarterly magazine, originally a partisan of the Communist party, but independent since 1938. Its fight for intellectual freedom has opposed regimentation, whether fascist or communist, but in later years it has been less concerned with specific social or political issues and more with sociocultural subjects and literary and art criticism. It is also noted for its fiction and poetry.

Editors have included Philip Rahv (1934–69) and Delmore Schwartz (1943–55). Contributors have included Auden, Barzun, Bellow, I. Howe, Jarrell, Kazin, Levertov, Robert Lowell, Dwight Macdonald, MacLeish, Mailer, Oates, Roethke, Roth, Sontag, Sorrentino, Tate, Trilling, W.C. Williams, and Edmund Wilson. In earlier years the journal was a monthly for a time and long a bimonthly (until 1955). William Phillips, a founder, sole editor (1970–), and author of *A Partisan View* (1983), a memoir of literary life, co-edited three anthologies drawn from the journal.

Passage to India, poem by Whitman, ◆ the title piece of a pamphlet (1871), was incorporated in *Leaves of Grass* 1876.

Ostensibly celebrating the completion of the Suez Canal and the transcontinental railroad (1869), and such other links as the Atlantic cable (1866), which would effect "the marriage of continents," the poem asserts that it is not only the "facts of modern science," but also the "myths and fables of eld . . . The deep diving bibles and legends," which will unify the world. The welding process must be carried on "not for trade or transportation only, But in God's name, and for thy sake, O soul." The long history of mankind, from Oriental antiquity to the present culture of the West, is now to be crowned in America, when "the Poet, worthy that name; The true Son of God shall come, singing his songs." The new nation shall combine the physical and intellectual vigor of the West with the spirituality and mystical wisdom of the East. The voyages of the former explorers symbolize the search for God, which is to be completed by the passage of the soul to "more than India," through the poet who will restore the divine trinity of God (the universal), Nature (the particular), and Man (the individual).

Passionate Pilgrim, A, story by Henry James, ◆ published in 1871 and collected in *A Passionate Pilgrim and Other Tales* (1875).

Clement Searle, a middle-aged American widower, comes to England to prosecute his claim to a rich estate. Although a melancholy invalid, he is enthusiastic concerning his pilgrimage to the mother country, which has been his lifelong dream, and he shares his new experiences with the narrator, an impressionable American tourist. Penniless, and feeling the approach of death, Searle determines to enjoy to the full his last days. With the narrator, he visits the Searle estate, is received by its furiously conservative and selfish proprietor, and falls in love with his gentle sister. The brother drives his visitors away, and the shock further weakens Searle, who that night believes he sees a traditional family specter. With his companion, he goes to Oxford, still the "passionate pilgrim," but after a few days becomes weaker and dies. On his deathbed he asks for Miss Searle, who is summoned. She appears in mourning, since her brother has been accidentally killed, leaving her "free . . . with what use for freedom?"

PATCHEN, KENNETH (1911–72), born in Ohio and educated at the University of Wisconsin (1929–30), lived in New York and later in California. His poetry, marked by religious symbols and intricate figures recalling the metaphysicals, is also free in structure and associations. Collections include *Before the Brave* (1936), *First Will and Testament* (1939), *Sleepers Awake* (1946), *Selected Poems* (1946, enlarged 1958), *Red Wine & Yellow Hair* (1949), and *Collected Poems* (1969). Many of his works are illustrated with his own abstract, expressionistic art. His prose includes *The Journal of Albion Moonlight* (1941), a stream-of-consciousness account; *The Memoirs of a Shy Pornographer* (1945), a satirical novel; and *See You in the Morning* (1948), a love story about a dying man.

Paterson, long poem by William Carlos Williams, ♦ divided into five Books published in 1946, 1948, 1949, 1951, and 1958. Fragments of the incomplete Book Six were published posthumously (1963) as an appendix to the collection of the first five parts.

Written in the "variable foot" of Williams's free verse, the work incorporates prose passages from historical documents, newspaper accounts, geological surveys, literary texts, and personal letters ranging from one by an anonymous semi-literate black man to those by Edward Dahlberg, Alan Ginsberg, and Ezra Pound, all reinforcing the poem's themes.

The Author's Note declares: "a man in himself is a city, beginning, seeking, achieving and concluding his life in ways which the various aspects of a city may embody—if imaginatively conceived—any city, all the details of which may be made to voice his most intimate convictions."

Using the city of Paterson on the Passaic River near his hometown of Rutherford, N.J., as subject so as to bring forth the universal from a local setting ("there are no

ideas but in things"), the poem presents local history and the natural scene (particularly the Falls and Garrett Mountain) as well as the consciousness of a gigantic, mythic man (Paterson) and of the author, poet and doctor. Book One ("The Delineaments of the Giants") mythologizes "the elemental character of the place": the city (a masculine force), the landscape (a feminine principle), and the vital, unifying river. Book Two ("Sunday in the Park"), concerned with "modern replicas," meditates on failures in communication through language, religion, economics, and sex, but suggests redemption through art, imagination, and memory. Book Three ("The Library") moves from the previous section's "confused uproar" of the Falls to find that "books will give rest sometimes," a sanctuary for "dead men's dreams," but the past represents only desolation, destruction, and death, and "I must find my meaning and lay it, white, beside the sliding water." Book Four ("The Run to the Sea") treats the polluted river below the Falls in terms of human corruption by modern civilization, while recognizing innovations in science, economics, and language, but finally the identity of the river is lost in the sea, although the individual man (Paterson) survives and strides inland to begin again. Book Five (untitled but dedicated to Toulouse-Lautrec) is like a separate work, an oblique commentary on the poem by an aged poet from a point of view more international and universal than local.

Pathfinder, The; or, The Inland Sea, romance by Cooper, ♦ published in 1840 as the third in plot sequence of the Leather-Stocking Tales. ♦

In 1759, Mabel Dunham is on her way to join her father at the British fort at Oswego, Lake Ontario, accompanied by her uncle, Charles Cap; Arrowhead, a Tuscarora Indian; his wife, Dew-in-June; Pathfinder, the scout aged about 40; the Mohican chief Chingachgook; and Jasper Western, a young sailor called Eau-douce by the French. Arrowhead and his wife disappear during skirmishes with the Iroquois, but the others reach Oswego. Then Dunham, Cap, Pathfinder, Mabel, and Lieutenant Muir, who wants to marry her, sail on Jasper's *Scud* to relieve a post in the Thousand Islands. Jasper's loyalty is suspected and he is returned to Oswego. While Dunham and his men are off destroying French supply boats, the rest are warned by Dew-in-June of an Iroquois attack to be led by Arrowhead. Cap and Muir are seized,

Dunham is badly wounded, and Mabel, who defends the blockhouse, promises to wed Pathfinder if he protects her father. After Jasper and Chingachgook rout the Iroquois, Jasper is arrested by Muir as a traitor. Muir is proved the only guilty one and is killed by Arrowhead. Dunham dies, hoping Mabel and Pathfinder will marry, but Jasper has won Mabel's love.

Patriotic Gore, Studies in the Literature of the American Civil War, by Edmund Wilson,♦ published in 1962.

Under a title derived from James Ryder Randall's "Maryland, My Maryland," the work in 16 essays ranges discursively over writings related to the war, including those of soldiers North and South (Grant and Sherman, Mosby and Lee), Confederate women diarists (Sarah Morgan and Mary Chesnut), statesmen North and South (Lincoln, Stephens), and writers of fiction North and South (Bierce and De Forest, Tourgée, Cable, and Page), among other subjects for reflection on literary expression associated with the war.

PATTEN, WILLIAM GILBERT (1866–1945), under the pseudonym Burt L. Standish wrote dime novels and several series of juvenile stories about college life and amateur sports. The best-known series deals with Frank Merriwell, a wholesome college athlete. The series began in 1896, included more than 200 novels, and sold over 25,000,000 copies.

PAUL, ELLIOT [HAROLD] (1891–1958), Massachusetts-born author, served in World War I and became an expatriate while working as literary editor of American newspapers in Europe and later as founder and editor with Eugene Jolas of the little magazine *transition.* His writings include *The Life and Death of a Spanish Town* (1937) which contrasts the idyllic life in the Balearic Islands with havoc wrought by the Spanish Civil War, and another narrative, *The Last Time I Saw Paris* (1942), which intimately reveals the life of Parisians and expatriates.

Paul Revere's Ride, narrative poem by Longfellow,♦ published in 1861 and included as the landlord's tale in his *Tales of a Wayside Inn♦* (1863). In galloping anapestic tetrameter, this literary ballad tells of "the midnight ride of Paul Revere" from Charlestown to Lexington and Concord, to warn the inhabitants of the approach of British troops at the outbreak of the Revolution. Apparently based on Revere's account, the poem, which crystallized an American legend, is very inaccurate, since Revere never waited for signals from lanterns, and it was "a young Dr. Prescott" who carried the news to Concord, while Revere went to Lexington.

PAULDING, JAMES KIRKE (1778–1860), born in New York state, was reared at Tarrytown, where he became intimate with Washington Irving, whose brother William had married Paulding's sister. He was a member of their informal literary group, the "Nine Worthies of Cockloft Hall," and with them collaborated on *Salmagundi♦* (1807–8), of which he published a second series alone (1819–20).

Stimulated by this venture and Irving's *History of New York,* Paulding wrote *The Diverting History of John Bull and Brother Jonathan* (1812), a comic account of the settlement, growth, and revolt of the American colonies. His flair for satire and opposition to the romanticism of Scott led him to write *The Lay of the Scottish Fiddle* (1813), while he defended his own conception of a hero as an oppressed individual who finds freedom on the frontier in the long poem *The Backwoodsman* (1818). His admiration for homespun American qualities and dislike of Tory England led him to answer British critics in a series of books employing both realistic descriptions of the U.S. and burlesques of the English.

He next wrote realistic tales, some published in *Tales of the Good Woman* (1829) and *The Book of St. Nicholas* (1836), which continue to show his dislike of the English, attacking their current literary styles, as represented in Byron and Scott. His novels also continue this realism and satire of false romanticism, in the treatment of historical subjects. *Koningsmarke, the Long Finne* (1823) is concerned with the early Swedish settlement on the Delaware; *The Dutchman's Fireside* (1831) deals with life in upper New York during the French and Indian War; *Westward Ho!* (1832) tells of a Virginia family pioneering in Kentucky; and *The Puritan and His Daughter* (1849) treats 17th-century life in Virginia and New England, condemning the mutual intolerance of Puritans and Cavaliers.

Paumanok, Indian name of Long Island, N.Y., which is separated from Manhattan by the East River and runs almost parallel to the shore of Connecticut. The aboriginal name is frequently used in the works of Whitman, who was born on the island, notably in "Starting from Paumanok."♦

Pawnee (or PANI) **Indians,** four bison-hunting Plains tribes, formerly living in Nebraska and Kansas, on the Platte and Republican rivers, whose descendants reside in Oklahoma. They had highly developed tribal and ceremonial systems and a rich mythology. Their folk tales were collected by Grinnell (1893) and a scholarly *Mythology* was published by G.A. Dorsey (1906). The Pawnee figure in Irving's *Tour on the Prairies,* Cooper's *The Prairie,* and Custis's *The Pawnee Chief.*

PEABODY, ELIZABETH PALMER (1804–94), sister-in-law of Hawthorne and Horace Mann, was like them interested in social reform and education. Her Boston home was the scene of the famous conversational classes of Margaret Fuller (1839–44), and her bookshop was a favorite meeting place of the Transcendental Club. She opened the first kindergarten (1860) in the U.S., and her association with Alcott in his Temple School is described in *Record of a School* (1835). *A Last Evening with Allston* (1886) contains further reminiscences of her life, and reprints some of her essays from *The Dial.* She is said to be the prototype of Miss Birdseye in James's *The Bostonians.*

Pearl of Orr's Island, The, novel by Harriet Beecher Stowe,♦ published in 1862. It is a tale of romance and the lives of local characters on Orr's Island, a fishing community on the Maine coast.

Peck's Bad Boy and His Pa, humorous sketches by George W. Peck (1840–1916), telling about practical jokes played by a mischievous boy on his father. They were collected from the author's Wisconsin newspaper in *Peck's Bad Boy and His Pa* (1883) and later volumes.

Pecos Bill, giant folk hero of Southwestern tales, whose cowboy exploits resemble those of Paul Bunyan and Tony Beaver in the logging camps.

Peder Victorious, novel by Rölvaag,♦ published in Norway (1928) and in translation in the U.S. (1929), the second volume of a trilogy that includes *Giants in the Earth♦* and *Their Fathers' God.♦*

PEIRCE, CHARLES SANDERS (1839–1914), a member of the U.S. Coast Survey, who made

philosophy his avocation, and, except for rare academic appointments, pursued his work single-handed. He was a founder of the school of pragmatism, but, since his principles were more in accord with the separately developed idealism of Josiah Royce than with those popularized by his friend William James, he coined for his beliefs the term "pragmaticism," which he said was "ugly enough to be safe from kidnappers." His extreme precision, highly technical vocabulary, and lack of full explanation for those who were not on his philosophic plane made him a philosopher's philosopher rather than a teacher, and publishers were unwilling to print his works, which were only published posthumously.

PENN, WILLIAM (1644–1718), English Quaker, in 1668 published a tract attacking the doctrine of the Trinity, *The Sandy Foundation Shaken,* for which he was imprisoned in the Tower of London, where he wrote *No Cross, No Crown* (1669), a defense of his faith, and another pamphlet in his own defense. He established American colonies where Quakers♦ might be free from persecution, and in 1681 secured the charter for Pennsylvania, named in honor of his father by Charles II. In America (1682–84), he personally organized the colony, framed its liberal government guaranteeing fundamental democratic liberties, and made equitable treaties with the Indians. After the accession of William and Mary (1688), he continued on friendly terms with James II, and being accused of treason temporarily lost his colony (1692–94). During this troublous time, he wrote his maxims of faith and life contained in *Some Fruits of Solitude* (1693) and *Essay Towards the Present and Future Peace of Europe* (1693), a plan for a general European confederation for arbitration of disputes. A similar idea was applied to a plan (1697) for the union of all the American colonies. After Pennsylvania was returned to him, he revisited it (1699) and revised its charter (1701) toward further democracy. In the same year, he left it for the last time.

Penrod, novel by Tarkington,♦ published in 1914. *Penrod and Sam* (1916) and *Penrod Jashber* (1929) are sequels.

This humorous narrative tells of the typical adventures of a 12-year-old American boy, Penrod Schofield, reared according to middle-class standards in a small Midwestern city. With his mongrel dog, Duke, and such intimates of his own age as Sam Williams and the black brothers Herman and Verman, Penrod is involed in characteristic frays and scrapes, and exhibits a healthy attitude toward the tyranny of parents and teachers, sometimes tolerating them but generally engaging in active warfare and subterfuge.

People, Yes, The, free-verse poem by Sandburg, ◆ published in 1936.

The authentic American rhythms and idioms of the verse embody native legends, folk tales, proverbs, and slang, and employ the daily speech of the people to show their many-sided observations and experiences, their amusements and sufferings, and the values inherent in their lives. Capitalism's tyranny and social injustices are indicated, and a hope for revolution appears in many passages. In substance, the poem is an affirmation of faith in the enduring though blundering progress of the common American people toward justice and a free society.

Pequod, whaling ship which is the scene of *Moby-Dick.* ◆

Pequot Indians, Algonquian tribe originally united with the Mohegans, ◆ which moved south to the Connecticut Valley and there dominated neighboring tribes. The war-like spirit of the Pequot under Sassacus led to one of the most serious of the New England Indian wars (1637), after which members of the tribe were dispersed among other groups. The best account of the Pequot War is that of the English commander John Mason in his *Brief History of the Pequot War,* edited by Thomas Prince (1736). Another officer, John Underhill, described the war in his *News from America* (1638), as did the Rev. Philip Vincent in *A True Relation of the Late Battell Fought in New England* (1638).

PERCY, WALKER (1916–), Alabama-born author, after graduation from the University of North Carolina and an M.D. from Columbia gave up medicine because of ill health and began a literary career. His first novel, *The Moviegoer* (1961, National Book Award), deals with an alienated young stockbroker of New Orleans, addicted to the movies, who during Mardi Gras finally finds his own involvement in life through a compassionate relationship with a woman who has suffered a personal tragedy. *The Last Gentleman* (1966) presents another existential character, a courtly young Southerner resident in New York, where he suffers amnesia but finally returns to his own region in quest of himself.

Love in the Ruins (1971) is a fanciful satire about Dr. Thomas More, a scientist and "bad Catholic" who attempts to redeem the mechanistic culture of the U.S. *Lancelot* (1977) is a more melodramatic and moralistic story about a New Orleans man's murder of his wife's lover. *The Second Coming* (1980) reintroduces the protagonist of *The Last Gentleman,* now a rich, lonely widower of 50, restored to hope by affection for a troubled young girl. *The Message in the Bottle* (1975) contains essays on the philosophy of language, and *Lost in the Cosmos: The Last Self-Help Book* (1983) contains essays and other non-fiction. The orphaned author was reared by an older cousin, William Alexander Percy (1885–1942), a Mississippi poet, whose *Lanterns on the Levee* (1941) is a lyrical autobiography of a Southern gentleman.

PERELMAN, S[IDNEY] J[OSEPH] (1904–79), born in Brooklyn, after education at Brown University became a writer for *Judge* and for 45 years was a contributor to *The New Yorker* of short humorous and satirical pieces, often in the form of brief, fantastic dramas which, with a surrealistic style and a Joycean use of words, lampoon the world of advertising, motion pictures, popular fiction, and other vacuities. His writings have been collected in many books, including *Dawn Ginsbergh's Revenge* (1929), *Parlor, Bedlam and Bath* (1930), *Strictly from Hunger* (1937), *Look Who's Talking* (1940), *The Dream Department* (1943), *Keep It Crisp* (1946), *Westward Ha!* (1948), *Listen to the Mocking Bird* (1949), *The Ill-Tempered Clavichord* (1953), *The Road to Miltown; or, Under the Spreading Atrophy* (1957), *The Rising Gorge* (1961), *Chicken Inspector No. 23* (1966), *Baby, It's Cold Inside* (1970), *Vinegar Puss* (1975), and *Eastward Ha!* (1977), a travel account. His comic plays include *One Touch of Venus* (1943) with Ogden Nash and *The Beauty Part* (1963). *The Last Laugh* (1981) posthumously collects an unfinished autobiography and comic sketches.

Perfectionism, radical religious doctrine, assuming the immediate and total cessation of sin, advanced by J.H. Noyes, was the leading principle of his Oneida Community. ◆ Perfectionism was a manifestation of the mid-19th-century enthusiasm for liberal social and religious beliefs that particularly affected New England, and was allied in temperament to the spirit that created Millerism, Shaker communities, Come-outers, and even Transcendentalism. Noyes's religious Utopianism held that a church on earth was rising to meet the approaching kingdom in heaven, and that the element of connection was direct communion with God, which leads to perfect holiness or complete salvation from sin.

PETERKIN, JULIA [MOOD] (1880–1961), novelist of South Carolina, known for her sympathetic depiction of the region's Gullah blacks, whom she understood through long association with them as the wife of a plantation manager. The poignant characterizations of the daily lives and folklore of these tragic, isolated laborers are presented in the novels *Black April* (1927), *Scarlet Sister Mary* (1928, Pulitzer Prize), and *Bright Skin* (1932); a collection of sketches, *Green Thursday* (1924); and a descriptive narrative accompanying a book of photographs, *Roll, Jordan, Roll* (1933).

Peterkin Papers, The, stories for children by Lucretia Hale (1820–1900).

Petrified Forest, The, play by Robert Sherwood,♦ produced in 1934 and published in 1935. Set in the Black Mesa Bar-B-Q, a gasoline station and lunch room in the Arizona desert, it melodramatically brings together representatives of a decadent civilization, in which Nature is "taking the world away from the intellectuals and giving it back to the apes."

PETRY, ANN (1911–   ), born in and still a resident of Old Saybrook, Conn., after graduation from the state university and work in the family drugstore published *The Street* (1946), a novel in the Richard Wright tradition, about blacks trapped in the ghetto life of Harlem. It was followed by *Country Life* (1947), a novel depicting class conflict in a setting like her hometown, and *The Narrows* (1953), which combines previous themes in its concern with black people like herself in a New England community but dramatically presents the romance of a talented black boy and a patrician white girl. Short stories are collected in *Miss Muriel* (1971), and books for children include *The Drugstore Cat* (1949), *Harriet Tubman* (1955), and *Tituba of Salem Village* (1964).

PHILLIPS, DAVID GRAHAM (1867–1911), born in Indiana, began his journalistic career in Cincinnati (1887) and moved to New York (1890), where he worked on the *Sun* and *World.* In 1902 he began to write muckraking magazine articles and fiction concerned with contemporary social problems. During the few years of creative work that followed, he wrote 23 novels, a play, and a book of essays. The novels, which show his training as a reporter as well as his muckraking zeal against fraud and oppression, include *The Cost* (1904) and *The Deluge* (1905), both exposing Wall Street manipulation; *The Plum Tree* (1905), about the operations of a political boss; *Light-Fingered Gentry* (1907), a fictional treatment of recent insurance scandals; and *The Fashionable Adventures of Joshua Craig* (1909), *The Conflict* (1911), and *George Helm* (1912), depicting respectively national, municipal, and state corruption. The remainder of his works deal with the contemporary interest in the "new woman." Phillips's greatest novel, *Susan Lenox; Her Fall and Rise*♦ (1917), combines his previous themes in a muckraking exposé of Cincinnati slum life and New York political corruption, which serve as a background for the life of a country girl who reaches success through prostitution. The promise that Phillips showed in this work, published posthumously, was cut short when he was murdered by a lunatic.

PHILLIPS, WENDELL (1811–84), born in Boston, after graduation from Harvard (1831) and admission to the bar became a prominent Boston Abolitionist and supporter of Garrison. He was an active lyceum lecturer for this and other causes, and was a contributor to *The Liberator* and *National Anti-Slavery Standard.* His *Speeches, Lectures, and Letters* were collected in 1863 and 1891.

Philo Vance, hero of detective novels by W.H. Wright.♦

Philosophy of Composition, The, critical essay by Poe,♦ published in *Graham's Magazine* (1846). It purports to describe the author's usual procedure in composing poetry and is mainly devoted to an analysis of "The Raven" as an example of this procedure. Among the famous dicta announced in the essay are: "If any literary work is too long to be read at one sitting, we must be content to dispense with the immensely important effect derivable from unity of impression. . . . What we term a long poem is, in fact, merely a succession of brief ones"; "Beauty is the sole legitimate province of the poem"; "Beauty . . . in its supreme development, invariably excites the sensitive soul to tears. Melancholy is thus the most legitimate of all poetical tones"; "The death of a beautiful woman is, unquestionably, the most poetical topic in the world." Poe further discusses his principles of versification, use of a refrain, diction, and imagery, and the primary importance of the climax ("The Raven," stanza 16), which was written first so that every effect in the poem should lead in its direction.

Piazza Tales, The, sketches by Melville,♦ collected in 1856. They are "The Piazza,"♦ about the author's farmhouse, Arrowhead, in Pittsfield, Mass.; "Bartleby the Scrivener"♦; "The Encantadas"♦; "Benito Cereno"♦; "The Lightning-Rod Man"; and "The Bell-Tower."

Pierre; or, The Ambiguities, novel by Melville,♦ published in 1852. It is considered to be semi-autobiographical.

Pierre Glendinning, only son of an affluent and haughty widow, is engaged to Lucy Tartan, daughter of another prominent family in upstate New York. He accidentally meets Isabel, discovers that she is his illegitimate half-sister, and feels that it is his duty to protect her in opposition to his proud mother. To acknowledge Isabel as his sister would disgrace his father's memory, so Pierre pretends to marry her. They seek refuge in New York, and Pierre, poor and without friends, turns to writing a book that no publisher will issue. Lucy, still in love with Pierre, follows him to New York. Threatened by her brother and his own cousin, Pierre kills the latter. Both Lucy and Mrs. Glendinning die of grief, and Pierre and Isabel, now in love with each other, commit suicide in his prison cell. In grappling with the ambiguities of good and evil, Pierre has followed the "chronometrical" standards of ideal Christian conduct, instead of the "horological" standards of contemporary society. He is accordingly undone by his ideals, and becomes "the fool of Truth, the fool of Virtue, the fool of Fate."

Pike, character type in American humor, a genus of Western immigrant during the pioneering period of the mid-19th century. The Pike characters were traditionally natives of Pike County, although this locality was variously assigned to Missouri, Arkansas, southern Illinois, northern Texas, or generally to the frontier area. A man from Pike County was usually depicted as an ignorant, suspicious backwoodsman, good-natured as the butt of frequent jokes, but savagely acquisitive. His exaggerated, droll speech was characterized by an expressive, imaginative dia-

lect. In Bayard Taylor's *At Home and Abroad* (1860), he is described as:

> the Anglo Saxon relapsed into semi-barbarism. He is long, lathy, and sallow; he expectorates vehemently; he takes naturally to whisky; he has the "shakes" his life long at home, though he generally manages to get rid of them in California; he has little respect for the rights of others; he distrusts men in "store clothes," but venerates the memory of Andrew Jackson.

The Pike as a specific character was launched in the works of George Derby, but it was not until 1871 that he became generally known to the reading public, through Harte's *East and West Poems* and Hay's *Pike County Ballads.*

Pilgrims, name applied to the persons who came to Massachusetts on the *Mayflower* (1620), or by extension to all the early settlers of Plymouth Colony. Unlike the Puritans, the Pilgrims were Separatists, opposing the episcopal jurisdiction, rites, and discipline of the Church of England. They originated (*c.*1606) at Scrooby, England, whence they emigrated to Amsterdam (1608), and then to Leiden. Almost half of this group came to Plymouth on the *Mayflower.* These 41 believers, including William Bradford, William Brewster, and Edward Winslow, were called Saints; others, including Myles Standish, were called Strangers.

Pilot, The, romance by Cooper,♦ published in 1823. The unnamed hero is supposed to represent John Paul Jones.

During the Revolutionary War, the American schooner *Ariel* and an unnamed frigate, captained by a mysterious Pilot, appear off the coast of England near the residence of Colonel Howard, an expatriated South Carolina Loyalist. The mission of the Americans is to capture prominent Englishmen, in order to force a modification of British impressment, and they decide to raid the guarded Howard residence. In the attempt, the Pilot and others are captured, but make their escape despite the precautions of villainous Christopher Dillon, a suitor of one of Col. Howard's nieces who are also loved by Lieutenants Griffiths and Barnstable, officers aboard the *Ariel.* Long Tom Coffin, a daring old salt, is sent with the captured Dillon, who tries unsuccessfully to escape before the *Ariel* is wrecked in a storm. Meanwhile the Howards have been captured, and in a fierce battle with British warships, the frigate escapes through the shoal waters. Colonel Howard has been wounded, but before he dies he surrenders to the inevitability of American victory in the war, and permits the marriage of his nieces with the officers. The Pilot goes to Holland, while his ship sails for America.

PINSKY, ROBERT (1940–), New Jersey-born poet, after graduation from Rutgers and a Ph.D. from Stanford became a professor of English at Wellesley and the University of California, Berkeley (1980–). His collections include *Sadness and Happiness* (1975), *An Explanation of America* (1979), and *History of My Heart* (1984). Critical works include *Landor's Poetry* (1968) and *The Situation of Poetry* (1977).

Pioneers, The; or, The Sources of the Susquehanna, romance by Cooper,♦ published in 1823. It is the fourth in plot sequence of the Leather-Stocking Tales. ♦

During the decade after the Revolutionary War, Judge Marmaduke Temple, a retired Quaker merchant, is the leading landowner of Otsego County on the New York frontier, having acquired the estate of the Loyalist father of his friend Edward Effingham. While hunting deer he accidentally shoots Oliver Edwards, young companion of Natty Bumppo (Leather-Stocking), a veteran frontiersman. The judge and his daughter Elizabeth befriend the young man, who becomes their overseer, although persisting in his mysterious association with Bumppo and old chief Chingachgook (John Mohegan), who is rumored to be his father. Elizabeth and her friend Louisa Grant, the rector's daughter, disdain the company of the supposed half-breed. After Bumppo is released from jail, following his arrest for shooting deer out of season, Elizabeth visits him and is trapped by a forest fire. She is saved by Edwards, but Chingachgook dies after his rescue by Bumppo. Elizabeth and Edwards now admit their love, and his identity is made known when a searching party discovers demented old Major Effingham, and it is revealed that Edwards is his grandson, that Bumppo had been an employee of his family, and that Chingachgook had adopted them into his tribe. The young couple is betrothed and given half of the judge's estate.

Pioneers! O Pioneers!, poem by Whitman,♦ published in *Drum-Taps* (1865) and in the "annex" to *Leaves of Grass* (1867).

In 26 quatrains, each ending with the refrain that gives the poem its title, Whitman celebrates the frontier spirit with a paean of praise concerning the unique American qualities of optimism, self-reliance, equality, and revolt against the European past.

Pit, The: A Story of Chicago, novel by Frank Norris,♦ posthumously published in 1903 as the second part of his "Epic of the Wheat."

Laura Dearborn comes to Chicago from Massachusetts to live with her Aunt Wess' and her younger sister Page. She soon attracts three suitors: Sheldon Corthell, wealthy artist and dilettante; Landry Court, a young stockbroker who later marries Page; and Curtis Jadwin, a powerful, virile capitalist, who is lonely despite his wealth and position. She is won by Jadwin's honesty and simplicity, although she does not respond fully to his possessive affection. He succumbs to the lure of the Board of Trade and becomes a leading speculator, by a combination of boldness and luck gaining a corner on the wheat market. His preoccupation with business affairs causes him to neglect Laura, who drifts into an affair with Corthell, returned from a long absence in Europe. Natural laws defeat Jadwin's speculative coup, when his monopoly is broken by an unforeseen production of wheat in the West. His financial ruin is accompanied by a physical breakdown, and Laura, who has been about to elope with Corthell, nurses her husband to health, coming to realize the bond between them. Although they lose their mansion and rich possessions, they face a future of hard work and simple living in the West with renewed hope and enthusiasm.

Pit and the Pendulum, The, tale by Poe,♦ published in *The Gift* (1843).

A prisoner of the Spanish Inquisition at Toledo describes his horrible tortures. Sick from long suffering, he faints when the death sentence is pronounced; upon recovering consciousness, he finds himself on the stone floor of a dark dungeon. Exploring the cell, he is saved from plunging into a deep pit when he accidentally trips and falls. He sleeps, and awakes to discover that he is now strapped to a wooden framework, while a great pendulum swings slowly back and forth overhead, its end being a steel crescent sharpened to a razor edge. The menacing blade gradually descends, and rats swarm about his highly seasoned food and over his body. As the pendulum reaches him, the rats gnaw his bonds, from which he frees himself to find the cells' metal walls are heated and are slowly closing in. Just as he gives way to an agony of terror, the city is captured by

French soldiers, and the hand of General Lasalle stays him from tumbling into the pit.

Plain Language from Truthful James, comic ballad by Bret Harte,♦ published in the *Overland Monthly* (Sept. 1870). This narrative of a euchre game, in which Truthful James and his friend Bill Nye intend to cheat the Chinese gambler Ah Sin but are themselves deceived by the "ways that are dark" of their wily opponent, soon had a popular vogue throughout the country, was frequently quoted, and was pirated in broadside and pamphlet editions as *The Heathen Chinee.*

Plains Indians, general term applied to the many tribes that lived in the Plains and Prairie regions. Their more or less homogeneous culture was based economically on the hunting of bison, although some of the eastern tribes also grew maize. Principally nomadic, they used dogs and later horses for transportation, and were noted for their vigorous and constant warfare and for their mystical pursuit of visions and supernatural power. The popular conception of the heroic Indian brave—tall, muscular, and dignified, with braided hair, costume of skins, and feathered headdress, living in tepees and skilled in horsemanship—derives from contact with the Plains tribes. Among the most prominent of these were the Sioux,♦ Comanche,♦ Cheyenne,♦ Pawnee,♦ Blackfoot,♦ Osage,♦ and Mandan.♦ The Plains Indians figure in the writings of Cooper, Neihardt, Garland, Parkman, and Lewis and Clark, in Longfellow's *Hiawatha* and novels and nonfiction by Mari Sandoz, as well as in the more scientific descriptions by Schoolcraft, Catlin, Grinnell, Dorsey, and Wissler.

Plains region, country sloping gradually from the Rocky Mountains eastward to the Prairie region,♦ includes Nebraska, Kansas, Oklahoma, and Texas, as well as the eastern parts of Montana, Wyoming, Colorado, and New Mexico, and the western parts of North and South Dakota. The region is marked by broad, level river valleys and rolling plains, which were the habitat of great herds of bison and the Plains Indians♦ who hunted them. Later the plains were devoted to cattle raising, but during most of the 20th century they have been planted in wheat and other crops. This change, involving the removal of grass and consequent erosion of the topsoil, resulted in dust storms and drought, especially in the 1930s, and caused the region to

be called the Dust Bowl. Oklahoma and Texas in particular were disastrously affected, causing a great migration of refugees, popularly and invidiously called "Okies," to other regions, notably California. Parkman's *Oregon Trail* is the most famous narrative of the Indians and white pioneers on the plains; Andy Adams has written of the cattle industry; the plays of Lynn Riggs deal with the transitional Indian Territory; Edna Ferber's *Cimarron* tells of the Oklahoma land rush and its aftermath; E.W. Howe and William Allen White, both Kansas editors, wrote stories of local life; Willa Cather describes the life of the region in many novels; Mari Sandoz treats Nebraska, past and present, in novels and nonfiction, as does Wright Morris; and Steinbeck's *Grapes of Wrath* tells of the migrants from the Dust Bowl.

PLATH, SYLVIA (1932–63), born in Massachusetts, attended Smith College on a scholarship endowed by Olive Higgins Prouty,♦ who later befriended her and appeared in her fiction. She suffered a nervous breakdown (1953) but returned to Smith to graduate (1955). These experiences formed the basis of her moving novel *The Bell Jar♦* (1963), published under the pseudonym Victoria Lewis. A scholarship took her to England, where she married the British poet Ted Hughes. They lived briefly in the U.S., while she taught at Smith, but after returning to England and seemingly settling down with family and as an author, she suddenly took her life. Her intense, candid, and personal poems were published in the U.S. as *The Colossus* (1962), *Ariel* (1966), *Crossing the Water* (1971), and *Winter Trees* (1972). *Johnny Panic and the Bible of Dreams* (1977) collects various prose writings. *Letters Home* (1975) is a selection of correspondence. Her *Journals* was published in 1982. Her *Collected Poems* (1981) was awarded a Pulitzer Prize.

Play It as It Lays, novel by Joan Didion,♦ published in 1970.

Maria Wyeth, a 31-year-old former motion-picture actress, separated from her husband Carter, a film director, and the mother of Kate, a retarded, institutionalized child, reaches a degree of nihilism so intense that day after day she leaves her Beverly Hills house to drive aimlessly on the freeways of southern California. When she discovers that she is pregnant by Carter, who persuades her to have an abortion, her depression is deepened and she gives herself to meaningless, frenetic sex. She has a nervous breakdown, and in the institution to which she is sent for cure she dreams of a time when she and Kate can be together in a happy home, but she is determined that whatever happens she will not resort to suicide but live instead with the knowledge of "what nothing means and keep on playing."

Plimmoth Plantation, History of, was begun by William Bradford,♦ about ten years after the landing of the Pilgrims. Book I was completed within a year or two, Book II written between 1646 and 1650, and the list of *Mayflower* passengers added in 1651. The manuscript, probably not intended for publication, came at Bradford's death into the hands of his nephew, Nathaniel Morton, who drew on it heavily for *New Englands Memoriall* (1669), and it was similarly used by a later owner, Thomas Prince, for his *Chronological History of New England* (1736), as well as by Thomas Hutchinson as a source of his *History of the Colony of Massachusetts Bay* (1764, '67). During the Revolution the manuscript disappeared. Discovered in the library of the Bishop of London (1855), it was returned to the Commonwealth of Massachusetts. The entire work was first published in 1856, although Book I had been printed from the Plymouth church records (1841). In presenting his narrative, Bradford endeavors to go to "the very root and rise of the same," and the opening book sketches the origin of the Separatist movement, the flight from England to Holland, the settlement at Leiden, the plans for the settlement in New England, and the *Mayflower* voyage. The second book, which includes the major part of the history, is in the form of annals from 1620 to 1646, and describes every aspect of the life of the Pilgrims. Besides being a primary historical source, the work has artistic value because of its dignified, sonorous style, deriving from the Geneva Bible. The narrative is naturally grave, but it has vigorous qualities and an occasional strain of pithy sarcasm.

Plymouth Colony, settlement founded on the Massachusetts coast (1620) by the Pilgrims,♦ who arrived on the *Mayflower.* They obtained their charter from the Council for New England. John Carver was the first governor, and the Mayflower Compact remained the basis of government until 1691. This group was independent of the Puritan colony of Massachusetts Bay until the merger in 1684. William Bradford was the most notable early governor of the Plymouth Colony. Among the sources of the colony's early history are *Mourt's Relation,* Bradford's *History of Plimmoth Plantation,* Winslow's *Good News from New England,* and Winthrop's *Journal.*

POCAHONTAS (*c.*1595–1617), daughter of Indian chief Powhatan, was really named Matoaka. Her popular name means "sportive." The fame of Pocahontas is largely based on the story in Book III, Chapter 2, of John Smith's *Generall Historie* (1624), which is considered apocryphal. In 1608, according to Smith,♦ when Powhatan was about "to beate out his brains, Pocahontas the Kings dearest daughter, when no intreaty could prevaile, got his head in her armes, and laid her owne upon his to save him from death." The story has been frequently studied by historians and repeated in literature. The first treatment in the latter form was John Davis's novel *The First Settlers of Virginia* (1805), and later examples include J.N. Barker's *The Indian Princess,* G.W.P. Custis's *Pocahontas,* and Robert Dale Owen's *Pocahontas,* all dramas; and Seba Smith's metrical romance *Powhatan.* Hart Crane treats Pocahontas as a mythic and symbolic figure in *The Bridge,* as, in a manner closer to history, does Louis Simpson in *At the End of the Open Road.* In 1613 she was held as hostage for English prisoners, and in Jamestown became converted to Christianity and married John Rolfe. She went to England with him (1616), and died there. Their descendants include many prominent Virginia families. Her name has been spelled Pokahontas, as in J.E. Cooke's novel *My Lady Pokahontas.*

PODHORETZ, Norman (1930–   ), Brooklyn-born literary critic, as a student at Columbia was influenced by Lionel Trilling, at Clare College, Cambridge, by Leavis. His sociocultural essays are collected in *Doings and Undoings: The Fifties and After in American Writing* (1964). *Making It* (1967) is a witty, self-deprecatory revelation of the writer's successful efforts to succeed in New York intellectual society. *Breaking Ranks* (1979) is an equally candid memoir of recent political issues and his turn toward the right. *Why We Were in Vietnam* (1982) supports the purposes of the U.S. intervention and attacks the New Left's views. He became editor of *Commentary* in 1960 and moved it to his conservative views.

POE, Edgar Allan (1809–49), son of itinerant actors, was born in Boston. His father died the following year, and may have deserted his wife before that time, for she continued to support herself, taking the child with her from place to place until her death at Richmond, Va. (1811), when she left penniless Edgar and two other children: William Henry Leonard Poe (1808–31), who became a poet and may have collaborated with his brother; and Rosalie Poe (1810–74). Edgar was taken into the home of a Richmond merchant, John Allan. Although never legally adopted, for a long while he used his foster father's name, employing it as a middle name after 1824. He went to England (1815–20) with the Allans, and there attended school, as described in the semi-autobiographical story "William Wilson." ♦ After their return to Richmond, Mr. Allan, who had inherited a great fortune, was neither faithful to his wife nor sympathetic with his stepson, whose favoring of Mrs. Allan caused him to counter with remarks besmirching the character of Edgar and hinting at the possible illegitimacy of Rosalie. The relationship was further strained during Poe's attendance at the University of Virginia (1826), when Allan would give him no money, and he resorted unsuccessfully to gambling.

Allan insisted on Poe's preparation for a legal career, and after a violent quarrel the youth went to Boston, where he published *Tamerlane* ♦ (1827), issued anonymously at his own expense, which found no public. Under an assumed name and an incorrect age, he entered the U.S. army (1827) and was sent to Sullivan's Island, South Carolina, the setting for his later stories "The Gold-Bug" ♦ and "The Balloon Hoax." ♦ Mrs. Allan's deathbed plea caused a cool reconciliation with Allan, who aided Poe in obtaining an appointment to West Point and sent him a small sum to live on meanwhile in Baltimore, where he stayed with his brother and his aunt, Mrs. Maria Clemm, while arranging for the publication of *Al Aaraaf* ♦ (1829), which contained the sonnet "To Science" ♦ and "Tamerlane." Admitted to West Point (1830), he soon set about by gross neglect of duty to get himself dismissed (1831), since his reason for attendance, the desire to reinstate himself with Allan, had already been lost.

During a short stay in New York, he published *Poems by Edgar A. Poe* (1831), containing early versions of "Israfel," ♦ "To Helen," ♦ and "The City in the Sea," and then went to live with Mrs. Clemm in Baltimore (1831–35), where he began to publish stories in magazines. He first attracted attention with "MS. Found in a Bottle," ♦ which won a contest and brought him to the attention of J.P. Kennedy, who got him an editorial position on the *Southern Literary Messenger,* although he was discharged because of his drinking. At Baltimore he obtained a license (1835) to marry his cousin, Mrs. Clemm's daughter Virginia, aged 13, and may have married her before the public ceremony (1836). Reemployed by the *Messenger,* he moved with Mrs. Clemm and Virginia to Richmond, where, before he was finally discharged (1837), he had published the unfinished tragedy *Politian,* ♦ 83 reviews, 6 poems, 4 essays, and 3 short stories, and greatly increased the magazine's circulation.

He moved his family to New York (1837–38), where he did hackwork and published *The Narrative of Arthur Gordon Pym,* ♦ then going to Philadelphia, where as co-editor of *Burton's Gentleman's Magazine* (1839–40) he contributed "The Fall of the House of Usher," ♦ containing the previously published "Haunted Palace" ♦; "William Wilson" ♦; "The Journal of Julius Rodman" ♦; "Morella" ♦; and other works; and published *Tales of the Grotesque and Arabesque* ♦ (1840), his first collection, which included "Berenice" ♦; "Ligeia," ♦ containing "The Conqueror Worm" ♦; "The Assignation" ♦; "The Unparalleled Adventure of One Hans Pfaall" ♦; and other stories. Leaving Burton, he made plans for his own magazine, which led to an acquaintance with T.H. Chivers, ♦ whose similar poetry caused attacks and counterattacks of plagiarism after Poe's death. Poe was literary editor of *Graham's Magazine* (1841–42), to which he contributed "The Murders in the Rue Morgue," ♦ "A Descent into the Maelström," ♦ "The Masque of the Red Death," ♦ and other works, including some acute criticism which heightened his reputation. To the same magazine he later contributed "The Imp of the Perverse" ♦ (1845) and "The Philosophy of Composition" ♦ (1846). He came to know Rufus Wilmot Griswold, who followed him as editor and bitterly attacked him after his death.

In 1842–43 he published "The Mystery of Marie Rogêt" ♦ in a New York magazine, and won a prize in a Philadelphia newspaper for "The Gold-Bug," but even this did not help him, since he had wasted opportunities for further publication in Philadelphia. In New York (1844), he wrote "The Raven," ♦ became associated with the *New-York Mirror,* and as literary critic (1844–45) conducted his war there with Longfellow, whom he accused of plagiarism. These attacks he continued after becoming proprietor of the *Broad-*

way *Journal*♦ (1845), where he also printed "The Pit and the Pendulum,"♦ "Eleonora,"♦ and "The Premature Burial," and reprinted "The Tell-Tale Heart"♦ and other works. His eighth book, *Tales* (1845), reprinted previous works selected by E.A. Duyckinck, and included "The Black Cat"♦ and "The Purloined Letter."♦ *The Raven and Other Poems* appeared the same year. Next associated with *Godey's Lady's Book,* Poe published "The Cask of Amontillado"♦ and his critical articles on "The Literati of New York City,"♦ whose harsh criticism of Thomas Dunn English prompted an answer, to which Poe replied with a successful libel suit.

Lacking regular employment, he with his wife and Mrs. Clemm nearly starved in their Fordham home, and Virginia died of tuberculosis during the winter. Although he published "Ulalume"♦ and "The Domain of Arnheim,"♦ and was at work on "The Bells"♦ and *Eureka,* ♦ he was now more than ever in a thoroughly abnormal condition of body and mind, for which he attempted to find solace in the company of a Mrs. Shew, the poet Sarah Whitman, and the Mrs. Richmond addressed in "To Annie." Torn between the love of the latter two, he attempted suicide. His erratic mind, depressed in personal affairs, nevertheless showed extreme exaltation in the lecture *Eureka,* in which he attempted to establish an all-embracing theory of cosmogony. Upon his return to Richmond (1849), where he wrote "Annabel Lee,"♦ he made a vigorous attempt to end his addiction to liquor, and became engaged to Mrs. Shelton, a former neighbor of the Allans, with whom he had had an early affair. On his way north to bring Mrs. Clemm to the wedding, he stopped in Baltimore, where five days afterward he was discovered in a delirious condition near a saloon that had been used for a voting place. It has been supposed that he was captured in a drunken condition by a political gang, which used him for the then common practice of repeating votes. Four days later he died, and was buried in Baltimore beside his wife.

There have been strongly divergent evaluations of Poe's literary significance, from Emerson's dismissal of him as "the jingle man" and Lowell's "three-fifths genius and two-fifths sheer fudge" to Yeats's declaration, "always and for all lands a great lyric poet." The difference of opinion is at heart directed at his criticism, for the poetry consistently exemplifies the theories set forth in "The Philosophy of Composition,"♦ "The Rationale of Verse,"♦ and "The Poetic Principle,"♦ in which he indicated his conception of poetic unity to be one of mood or emotion, and especially emphasized the beauty of melancholy. This romantic attitude has led to the criticism that his poetry is no more than a sustained tone, entirely dominated by its atmosphere. His reputation is also grounded on his use of the short story, which he preferred to the novel on the same basis that he preferred the short poem to the long. The stories may be said to fall into two categories, those of horror, set in a crepuscular world, and those of ratiocination, which set the standard for the modern detective story and conform to the critical theories expounded in *Eureka.* Although Poe was strongly influenced by many authors—e.g. Tennyson in his poetry, Coleridge in his criticism, and Charles Brockden Brown in his fiction—he himself proved a source of influence on such Americans as Bierce and Hart Crane, and such Englishmen as Rossetti, Swinburne, Dowson, and Stevenson, besides having a profound effect on the French Symbolists.

Poetic Principle, *The,* lecture by Poe,♦ delivered in various cities (1848–49) and posthumously published in *The Union Magazine* (1850). Partly an elocutionary vehicle, it contains short poems by Willis, Longfellow, Bryant, Shelley, Thomas Moore, Hood, Byron, and Tennyson.

Developing the theories already stated in "The Philosophy of Composition"♦ and other places, Poe declares that "a long poem does not exist. . . . A poem deserves its title only inasmuch as it excites, by elevating the soul. . . . That degree of excitement . . . cannot be sustained throughout a composition of any great length." This is true because of "that vital requisite in all works of Art, Unity," and the "absolute effect of even the best epic under the sun is a nullity." He proceeds to "the heresy of the Didactic": "there neither exists nor *can* exist any work more thoroughly dignified, more supremely noble than [the] poem which is a poem and nothing more—[the] poem written solely for the poem's sake." The proper mood for teaching a truth is completely opposed to the poetic mood. Poetry arises in the passionate reaching out "to apprehend the supernal Loveliness," to attain a vision, however brief, of the ideal beauty which is usually beyond our ken. "I would define, in brief, the Poetry of words as *The Rhythmical Creation of Beauty*. Its sole arbiter is Taste." Love, "the purest and truest of all poetical themes," is the highest variety of beauty, and beauty is "the province of the poem. . . . The incitements of Passion, or the precepts of Duty, or even the lessons of Truth, may . . . be introduced . . . but the true artist will always contribute to tone them down in proper subjection to . . . Beauty."

Poetry: A Magazine of Verse (1912–), founded at Chicago by Harriet Monroe♦ and edited by her until 1936. Later editors have included Karl Shapiro (1950–55). Long the major journal exclusively devoted to poetry, and the precursor of many other little magazines, *Poetry* has had an extremely stimulating influence on American literature. Without confining itself to any school or type, it has published the work of such diverse authors as Sandburg, Amy Lowell, T.S. Eliot, Frost, H.D., Ezra Pound (for a time an editor), Vachel Lindsay, and Hart Crane, and in many cases first brought them to public attention.

Pollyanna, character in the juvenile novels of Eleanor Porter.♦

Polyphonic prose, free-verse form that employs a succession of varied rhythms and all the devices of poetry, but is printed as prose and follows a mood rather than a strict metrical pattern. French in origin, it was frequently used by Amy Lowell and John Gould Fletcher.

Ponteach, or, The Savages of America, blank-verse play by Robert Rogers,♦ published in 1766. It was the first tragedy to be written about the Indians.

Poor Richard's Almanack, written and published by Franklin♦ at Philadelphia (1733–58), is the most famous of American almanacs,♦ although it followed the pattern previously established in the colonies and in England. *Poor Richard's* undoubtedly derives from *Poor Robin's,* the English almanac which began publication in 1663, and the name Richard Saunders, with which Franklin signed his prefaces, is the same as that of the English editor of *Apollo Anglicanus.* Franklin likewise owed other debts to predecessors, particularly to his Pennsylvania contemporary, Titan Leeds, on whom he played a hoax that resembles Swift's humorous prognostication of the death of a rival almanac maker. To the almanac Franklin introduced characters on whom he draped his humor and homely wisdom, and the figures Richard and Bridget

Saunders became popular in the contemporary American mind. Many of the shrewd maxims and proverbs that Franklin wrote and collected were brought together in *Father Abraham's Speech,* the harangue of a wise old man to the people attending an auction, and were published in the almanac of 1758. They were separately published under that title the following year, but many later reprints appeared with a title that was not Franklin's: *The Way to Wealth.* The title was not inappropriate, for the gathering of apothegms included only those that inculcated virtue and frugality, and not the many other witty and cynical observations. The almanacs from 1748 on were called *Poor Richard Improved,* and probably did not contain any writing by Franklin, who sold the almanac (1758), although it continued to be published until 1796.

Poor White, novel by Sherwood Anderson,♦ published in 1920.

It depicts the moral degradation of an Ohio farming community as it develops into a strife-torn industrial town and its effect upon the local populace, particularly the shy inventor Hugh McVey.

Porgy, novel by Dubose Heyward,♦ published in 1925. The dramatization by the author and his wife Dorothy was awarded a Pulitzer Prize. Gershwin's *Porgy and Bess* (1935) is an opera based on the story.

In the black tenement section of the Charleston waterfront, known as Catfish Row, Porgy is a crippled beggar, celebrated for his luck with dice. He gambles regularly with the black men Robbins and Crown, until Crown kills Robbins in a quarrel and escapes to a thicket outside the town. Porgy denies knowledge of the crime, but old Peter, another denizen of the tenement, is imprisoned as a witness. Thus losing the friend who has helped him to move about, Porgy buys a goat cart, and continues to beg. Bess, formerly "Crown's Bess," becomes his mistress, and for a time they live happily together, until she returns to her addiction to narcotics and discovers Crown's hiding place. Porgy is forced to stab Crown, to protect Bess from his influence. He is not suspected of the murder, but is wanted as a witness, and is jailed when he tries to escape. After his release, he resumes his life in Catfish Row, but Bess, who has lost hope of his return, has left with a group of river workers for the cotton plantations.

PORTER, Eleanor Hodgman (1868–1920), author of juvenile novels, best known for her character Pollyanna, the "glad child." Her works include *Cross Currents* (1907); *Miss Billy* (1911); *Pollyanna* (1913); and *Pollyanna Grows Up* (1915).

PORTER, Gene Stratton, see *Stratton-Porter.*

PORTER, Katherine Anne (1890–1980), born in Texas of a family with a long Southern heritage, was educated in convent and private schools. She later traveled widely, and the settings for her fiction, in addition to her native state, include Mexico, where she lived for some time, and Germany, where she resided more briefly. France, where she lived during her first marriage, presumably did not affect her literary career, except that she translated an old *French Song-Book* (1933). Her early stories, published as *Flowering Judas ♦* (1930), immediately won her a critical reputation as a pure stylist who handled complex subjects with economy while penetrating the psychology of characters with great subtlety. *Hacienda* (1934) and *Noon Wine* (1937) are stories of intense emotions, the former being set in Mexico and concerned with the making of a film by the Soviet cinema director Eisenstein, the latter set on a Texas farm and dealing with a homicidal maniac. *Pale Horse, Pale Rider* (1939) incorporates *Noon Wine* with two other long stories, "Old Mortality" and the title piece, about a girl's love for a soldier who dies in an epidemic during World War I. Stories were also gathered in *The Leaning Tower* (1944) and *Collected Stories* (1965). *The Days Before* (1952) collects personal essays, articles, and book reviews. In 1962 appeared the long awaited novel *Ship of Fools,* a moral allegory about the voyage of life and, according to the author, the way in which "evil is always done with the collusion of good," treated by means of presenting a variety of people—most of them Germans on the eve of Hitler's accession—as they travel on the *Vera,* a passenger freighter, from Mexico to Germany during 27 days of 1931. Her life work as a creator of stories was recognized by both a National Book Award and a Pulitzer Prize in 1966. In 1977 she published a brief memoir, *The Never-Ending Wrong,* about her protests during the Sacco-Vanzetti case.

PORTER, William Sydney (1862–1910), best known by his pseudonym O. Henry, was born in North Carolina, where after a brief schooling he worked in a drugstore. In 1882 he went to Texas to seek his fortune, and after trying his hand at various types of work, including a position as teller in an Austin bank (1891–94), founded a humorous weekly, *The Rolling Stone* (1894–95), and wrote for a Houston paper (1895–96) a daily column whose main staple was humorous anecdotes. In 1896 he was indicted for alleged embezzlement of funds at the bank for which he had worked. Since the bank was loosely run and his loss of a small sum was a case of technical mismanagement rather than crime, he might have been acquitted had he not fled to Honduras, from which he returned to Austin when his wife was on her deathbed. During his three-year imprisonment, he began to write short stories based on the life he knew in Texas, Honduras, and elsewhere, and it was the penitentiary ordeal that changed him from a newspaper columnist to a mature author.

After his release he went to New York (1902) to continue his literary career, and remained there for the rest of his life, making the city the scene of much of his fiction. As a contributor to magazines he became immensely popular, turning out stories at the rate of one a week. *Cabbages and Kings* (1904), his first book, is a series of stories of revolution and adventure in Latin America, integrated by a loose general plot and a single group of characters into the form of a novel. His later collections of stories followed each other with great rapidity: *The Four Million* (1906); *Heart of the West* (1907); *The Trimmed Lamp* (1907); *The Gentle Grafter* (1908); *The Voice of the City* (1908); *Options* (1909); *Roads of Destiny* (1909); *Whirligigs* (1910); and *Strictly Business* (1910). He had written so prolifically that after his death posthumous collections continued to appear, including *Sixes and Sevens* (1911), *Rolling Stones* (1913), *Waifs and Strays* (1917), and *Postscripts* (1923). "A Retrieved Reformation," his story of a reformed burglar, was the basis of Paul Armstrong's popular play *Alias Jimmy Valentine* (1909).

Although his stories are set in many parts of the U.S., as well as in Central and South America, Porter is best known for his observations on the diverse lives of everyday New Yorkers, "the four million" neglected by other writers. He had a fine gift of humor and was adept at the ingenious depiction of ironic circumstances, in plots frequently dependent upon coincidence. A master in presenting vignettes of the whirligig of fortune, he saw life always in episodic form and was incapable of longer unified work or any philosophic generalization of his fatalistic outlook. His characters, plain, simple people, and his plots, depending often on the surprise ending, have little diversification, but he was skilled at ringing the changes on a few themes. "The Gift of the Magi" and "The Furnished Room," in *The Four Million,* ♦ are among the best known of the tales that illustrate his technique of ironic coincidence and the surprise ending. *O. Henry Encore* (1939) is a collection of stories and illustrations recovered from his early contributions to the Houston *Post.*

Portnoy's Complaint, novel by Philip Roth, ♦ published in 1969.

Told as if to a psychiatrist, Dr. Spielvogel, the story is the autobiography of Alexander Portnoy of Newark, N.J., the bright but driven son of Sophie, a quintessential "Jewish mother" type, given to playing Mah-Jongg, worrying about warm clothes, fatty foods, money, and manners, and her passive husband Jack, a life insurance salesman. The price Portnoy pays for his mother's domination and his accomplishments at school is his compulsive masturbation, carried on in all ways and all places. As he matures, with achievements at Columbia Law School and as a lawyer for a congressional committee, he graduates also to more mature but equally compulsive sexual activity with a variety of Gentile girls, though with a final Oedipal irony, during a visit to Israel, he becomes impotent when attempting to have sex with the forceful Jewish women he meets there.

Portrait of a Lady, The, novel by Henry James, ♦ published in 1881.

Mrs. Touchett, estranged wife of an expatriated American banker, brings to England her penniless niece, Isabel Archer, in her early twenties, intelligent and beautiful, who immediately attracts old Mr. Touchett, his invalid son Ralph, and their wealthy neighbor, Lord Warburton. The nobleman proposes marriage, but Isabel refuses him, and her courage and independence win the admiration of the Touchetts. Casper Goodwood, a sincere, persistent suitor, comes from America to renew his proposal, but Isabel tells him that her personal independence is her most valued possession and that she must have two years before giving him her answer. Ralph is also in love with her, but realizes that they cannot marry and arranges for her financial security by persuading his father to make her his heir. At the old man's death, Isabel

becomes wealthy and goes to Florence with Mrs. Touchett. There Madame Merle, a gracious expatriate, introduces her to Gilbert Osmond, an American dilettante and widower. Incapable of perceiving that he desires her fortune, Isabel is won by Osmond's taste and intellectual detachment, despite the protests of Casper and her other friends. During the following years, she becomes aware of her husband's shallow aestheticism and lack of moral depth, but decides against a separation because of her pride, determination to fulfill her obligations, and sympathy for Pansy, Osmond's frail young daughter. Warburton, who still loves her, becomes a constant visitor and seeks to marry Pansy. Madame Merle is active in this new matchmaking, and she and Osmond urge Isabel to use her influence with Warburton, but Isabel withdraws when Pansy shows that she does not desire the marriage. This widens the breach between Isabel and her husband, who accuses her of an affair with Warburton. Summoned to England, where Ralph is dying, Isabel feels that she may never return to Italy, especially when she learns that Pansy's mother is Madame Merle. After comforting Ralph on his deathbed, she is joined by Casper, for whom she finally admits her affection. Conscience and her duty to Pansy dominate her desires, however, and she dismisses Casper and returns to her unhappy home.

POST, EMILY (1873–1960), author of *Etiquette* (1922, frequently revised), a very popular and widely accepted guide to good behavior and social proprieties.

Postman Always Rings Twice, The, novel by James M. Cain. ♦

Potawatami Indians, Algonquian tribe affiliated with the Ojibway and Ottawa. They aided the French in the French and Indian Wars, joined in Pontiac's Rebellion, and were on the side of the British during the Revolution and the War of 1812. They figure in Cooper's *Oak Openings.*

POUND, EZRA [WESTON LOOMIS] (1885–1972), Idaho-born poet and critic, reared in Pennsylvania, attended the University of Pennsylvania and Hamilton College, and taught briefly at Wabash College, until dismissed because of his impatience with academic ways, despite his scholarly ability. He went to Italy (1908), where his first book, *A Lume Spento* (1908), was published. He later lived in London (1908–20), in Paris (1920–24), and until the end of World War II at Rapallo, Italy.

In 1909 he published two volumes of verse, *Personae* and *Exultations* (poems from both reprinted as *Personae,* 1926), whose intensity and disciplined metrical experimentation attracted attention, as did his knowledge of medieval literature, Provençal singers, and troubadour ballads. *Provença* (1910), *Canzoni* (1911), and *Ripostes* (1912) extended the paths he had marked for himself, but also indicated his tendency to allow esoteric lore to become an unduly important part of his poetry. This trend continues in his translation of *The Sonnets and Ballate of Guido Cavalcanti* (1912); *Cathay* (1915), translations from the Chinese, based on notes of an American Orientalist, Ernest Fenollosa; *Umbra* (1920); translations and selections from some of his earlier poems; and *Hugh Selwyn Mauberley* ♦ (1920).

He began to scatter his interests and became a leader of the Imagists, ♦ and sponsored diverse authors in the anthologies and little magazines that he helped edit. He established the importance of such journals as *Poetry* and *The Little Review,* and wrote much about his successive enthusiasms, later generally acknowledged as significant. Those he championed include T.S. Eliot, James Joyce, Tagore, the musician George Antheil, and the sculptor Gaudier-Brzeska.

Lustra (1916), including earlier work, was followed by *Quia Pauper Amavi* (1919), containing the first three cantos of a lengthy work, with a flexible, conversation-like structure. His later poetry was almost entirely devoted to these *Cantos,* ♦ finally collected in 1970. They are so filled with esoteric lore and recondite theories that they often seem pedantic and confusing, yet they have had a tremendous influence on modern poetry, and works that are indebted to them include *The Waste Land, The Bridge,* and *Conquistador.*

Pound's prose includes *The Spirit of Romance* (1910); *Certain Noble Plays of Japan* (1916) and *Noh—or, Accomplishment* (1916), edited from the notes of Fenollosa, whose literary executor he was; *Gaudier-Brzeska* (1916), a biography; *Pavannes and Divisions* (1918); *Instigations* (1920); *Indiscretions* (1923); *Antheil and the Treatise on Harmony* (1924); *ABC of Economics* (1933); *ABC of Reading* (1934); *Make It New* (1934); *Jefferson and/or Mussolini* (1935); *Polite Essays* (1937); *Guide to Kulchur* (1938, revised 1952); *Patria Mia* (1950), an essay written in 1912; *Money Pamphlets by Pound* (1950–52);

The Literary Essays (1954), collected with an introduction by T.S. Eliot; *Pavannes and Divagations* (1958); and *Impact, Essays on Ignorance and the Decline of American Civilization* (1960), a compilation on politics, economics, and literature. His *Letters, 1907–41* was published in 1950. Later translations include *Confucius: The Unwobbling Pivot and the Great Digest* (1947); *Confucian Analects* (1951); *The Classic Anthology* (1954), Chinese poems; and *The Women of Trachis* (1956), a version of Sophocles' play.

Pound, who termed himself a "Jeffersonian Republican," professed to find "the heritage of Jefferson" in Mussolini's Italy, and prior to World War II espoused political views that included opposition to capitalism, the Jews, and the English, and support of the principle of censorship. During the war he broadcast Fascist propaganda over the Rome radio, and was afterward returned to the U.S. to face trial for treason. Adjudged to be of unsound mind, he was committed (1946–58) to a sanitarium instead of being tried. When the indictment was finally withdrawn he was released, and he returned to Italy.

POWELL, JOHN WESLEY (1834–1902), reared in Illinois, after service in the Civil War, in which he rose to be a major but lost his right arm, he taught geology and led expeditions, the most notable being one which by boats explored, mapped, and obtained geologic data on the Green and Colorado rivers (1869). This and a second trip (1872) are reported in *Exploration of the Colorado River of the West and Its Tributaries* (1875), revised as *Canyons of the Colorado* (1895), a scientific but colorful book. After more geographic and geologic work, he entered the U.S. Geological and Geographical Survey (1875) and wrote a precise, sociologically realistic *Report on the Lands of the Arid Region of the U.S.* (1878). Under his administration (1881–94), the greatly expanded Survey issued many detailed maps and surveys clarifying Western topography, geology, irrigation, and ethnology. His scientific standards, concepts of government planning, and organization of bureaus helped shape U.S. reclamation and conservation policies. His "second opening of the west" is the subject of Wallace Stegner's *Beyond the Hundredth Meridian* (1954).

Power of Sympathy, The; or, The Triumph of Nature, anonymously published in 1789, is called "the first American novel." Although now known to be by William Hill Brown, ♦ it was long attributed to another author, Sarah

Wentworth Morton, because it deals partly with events in her life.

POWERS, J[AMES] F[ARL] (1917–), born and educated in Illinois, first achieved a reputation with his stories of the various lives of the Catholic clergy of the Midwest in *Prince of Darkness* (1947) and *The Presence of Grace* (1956). *Morte d'Urban* (1962), which won a National Book Award, is a novel about the life of Father Urban, a worldly but dedicated worker for his order in modern America. Later stories, many also about priests, and a short play appear in *Look How the Fish Live* (1975).

Powhatan Indians, confederacy of Algonquian tribes in Virginia and Maryland, were visited by some of the earliest explorers and are noted for their relations with the settlement at Jamestown (1607). Hostilities provoked by the exactions of the colonists ended when Pocahontas,♦ daughter of the chief known as Powhatan, married the English settler John Rolfe. After Powhatan's death (1618), a successor, Opechancanough, led a general uprising that resulted in the destruction of every white settlement except those around Jamestown. The ensuing war of extermination lasted 14 years (1622–36). Another serious uprising was led by the same chief in 1641. After his capture and execution, the confederacy was broken up and its tribes declined.

Pragmatism: A New Name for Some Old Ways of Thinking, lectures by William James♦ delivered at the Lowell Institute and at Columbia (1906–7), and published in 1907. *The Meaning of Truth* is a sequel.

Asserting the inadequacy of both rationalism and empiricism in "the present dilemma in philosophy," James proposes pragmatism as "a mediating system."

> A pragmatist . . . turns away from abstraction and insufficiency, from verbal solutions, from bad *a priori* reasons, from fixed principles, closed systems, and pretended absolutes and origins. He turns towards concreteness and adequacy, towards facts, towards action and towards power.

James applies pragmatism to such metaphysical problems as those of substance, personal identity, materialism, design, and "freewill." He opposes the dogmatism of absolute monism and states his own pluralistic belief. Finally he discusses pragmatism in relation to religious questions, and contends that here too it mediates between extreme views.

Prairie, The, romance by Cooper,♦ published in 1827. It is the fifth in plot sequence of the Leather-Stocking Tales.♦

Natty Bumppo, though nearly 90 in 1804, is still competent as a frontiersman and trapper on the Western plains, clinging to his faithful hound Hector and his rifle Killdeer. He encounters an emigrant train led by surly Ishmael Bush and his rascally brother-in-law Abiram White, in whose party are also the naturalist Dr. Obed Battins; a woman captive concealed in a covered wagon; her attendant, Ellen Wade; and the bee-hunter Paul Hover, who is in love with Ellen. The old trapper barely averts an Indian raid on the train, which he then guides to a safe camp. He is joined by a young soldier, Duncan Uncas Middleton, whom he is overjoyed to recognize as a descendant of an old friend, Duncan Heyward (see *Last of the Mohicans*). Middleton, on an army mission, is also seeking his betrothed, Doña Inez de Certavallos, who has been kidnapped for ransom. Discovering that she is Ishmael's captive, he rescues her with the aid of the trapper. With Paul and Ellen, they leave the emigrants, only to be captured by the Sioux. Escaping, they are endangered successively by a prairie fire and a buffalo stampede, but saved by the skill of Bumppo. Recaptured by the Sioux, they are rescued by a successful Pawnee attack, but during the confusion Ishmael captures them. He accuses Bumppo of the murder of one of his men, but Abiram is found to be guilty. After his friends find safety with Middleton's soldiers, Bumppo finally yields to the weakness of his years, and dies quietly, surrounded by his Pawnee and white friends.

Prairie region, the level, unforested farming area, formerly grassland, that stretches westward from the Ohio River to the Plains region.♦ The Prairie states include Ohio, Indiana, Illinois, and Iowa, as well as eastern North and South Dakota, northern Missouri, and southern Wisconsin, Minnesota, and Michigan, encompassing much of the Midwest. The Mississippi River♦ flows through the center of the region, originally the Northwest Territory,♦ whose culture has come to be considered distinctively American, with Abraham Lincoln as its typical hero. Since the pioneering period of the late 18th and early 19th century, described by James Fenimore Cooper and others, the Prairie states have become the nation's food-producing center, with a large, stable farming population, and with great cities like Chicago as points of distribution. Representative authors include Edward Eggleston, Booth Tarkington, James Whitcomb Riley, and other Hoosiers; Wisconsin writers such as Hamlin Garland, Zona Gale, and Glenway Wescott; O.E. Rölvaag, who wrote of Norwegian and Irish immigrants in the Dakotas; and many whose careers are in some way associated with the Chicago school, including Dreiser, Herrick, E.L. Masters, Sandburg, Lindsay, Sinclair Lewis, Sherwood Anderson, and Hemingway. The paintings of Grant Wood are expressive of the life of rural Iowa; Louis Sullivan and J.W. Root were the first of the Chicago school in architecture that has influenced urban construction by introducing the skyscraper; and Frank Lloyd Wright's "Prairie style" of domestic architecture was designed to be appropriate to the Midwestern landscape.

Praying Indians, name applied to the New England tribes, including the Nauset and Massachuset, which were early converted to Christianity. They remained friendly with the colonists during King Philip's War, and were led for a time by Daniel Gookin. Among the missionaries to these Indians was John Eliot. ♦

Presbyterianism, system of church polity, occupying a middle position between episcopacy and congregationalism. Its organization is administered by representative courts, composed of clerical and lay presbyters of equal status, divided, according to their functions, into ministers and ruling elders. Such polity may be found throughout the history of the Christian church, but its modern movement is primarily attributed to the doctrine of Calvin. In its simple form of worship, the Bible is considered the sole rule of faith and conduct, the two sacraments being baptism and the Lord's Supper. Presbyterianism was first introduced in America by French Huguenot followers of Jean Ribaut, who settled in South Carolina (1562) and by followers of Laudonnière, who settled in Florida (1564). Groups of Presbyterians settled in most of the English colonies during the 17th century, many of them coming from Scotland. They flourished particularly in New England, whose churches have been described as representing "a Congregationalized Presbyterianism." The first organization of the various churches was accomplished by Francis Makemie in the late 17th century. During the Great Awakening, a split occurred between the evangelical New Side and the conservative Old Side, the former group,

under the direction of the Tennents, being responsible for the founding of Princeton University. Presbyterians were particularly strong on the frontier, where under a Plan of Union with Congregationalists they frequently presided over mixed congregations. There have been various schisms, most of them temporary.

PRESCOTT, WILLIAM HICKLING (1796–1859), member of a prominent Massachusetts family, was born at Salem and educated at Harvard (A.B., 1814; M.A., 1817), where the course of his life was changed when, during boyish play, he was hit in the eye by a hard crust of bread. Although blinded in one eye and virtually incapable of using the other, he determined upon a literary career. He went to Europe (1815–17) to convalesce and get background for historical writing. His first works in his chosen field of Spanish history were articles and reviews, which, with other essays and a short "Life of Charles Brockden Brown," were collected in *Biographical and Critical Miscellanies* (1845). Three years of preparation preceded the writing of the first chapter of the *History of . . . Ferdinand and Isabella,* begun in 1829 and published in three volumes (1838). The reception of this accurate but picturesque history encouraged him to write his *History of the Conquest of Mexico* (3 vols., 1843), upon which he began research in 1839. This work, in an almost neglected field, has come to be considered his greatest triumph, not only because of his historical accuracy, but because of its epic sweep, which, following in the vein of Scott, arranged itself around the two heroic figures of Cortés and Montezuma to create a dramatic tragedy. The only criticism of the *Conquest of Mexico,* leveled also at Prescott's other writings, is that he was so concerned with the large panorama that he tended to neglect social and economic problems, and based his structure on documented romance rather than a philosophy of history. *History of the Conquest of Peru* (2 vols., 1847) is a shorter companion piece, utilizing the same method of a dramatic, large-scale canvas, with the figure of Pizarro as its center. It is considered to be less unified and less valuable, however, because of its less comprehensive survey of the background of the civilization. After a trip abroad (1850), during which his English reputation was signalized by an Oxford degree and a reception by the queen, Prescott returned to write *History of the Reign of Philip the Second,* begun in 1849 and hastened by his realization that, with his failing sight, he might never cover the extensive materials. Planned to include four volumes, the work included only three by the time of his death (the first two in 1855, the last in 1858). His work on this book was interrupted by his preparation of an appendix to *The History of the Reign of the Emperor Charles the Fifth* (1857) by William Robertson, who, with Scott, was his master.

Presidential Medal of Freedom, initially (1945–63) to honor service in national security, since 1963 has been given upon occasion as the nation's highest civilian award for contributions to the national interest and security, aid to world peace, or public and private endeavors beneficial to the U.S. Many winners have written books, but those with specifically literary careers are Thornton Wilder and Edmund Wilson (1963); J. Frank Dobie, T.S. Eliot, Samuel Eliot Morison, Lewis Mumford, Sandburg, and Steinbeck (1964); Ralph Ellison (1969); Bruce Catton, Ariel and Will Durant, MacLeish, and Michener (1977); Rachel Carson (posthumous), R.P. Warren, Eudora Welty, Tennessee Williams (1980); Eric Hoffer (1983), Clare Booth Luce (1983), Dumas Malone (1983).

PRICE, REYNOLDS (1933–), North Carolina-born author, graduated from Duke and has taught there, after a Rhodes scholarship to Oxford. His fiction, set in his native state, includes *A Long and Happy Life* (1962) and *A Generous Man* (1963), both concerning a small-town North Carolina family, reissued in *Mustian* (1983); *Love and Work* (1968), about a young teacher-novelist's problems with marriage and writing; *The Surface of the Earth* (1975), presenting the saga of rural Virginia and North Carolina families during the first 40 years of this century, continued in *The Source of Light* (1981), concentrating on a grandson studying at Oxford in the 1960s until called back to his ancestral home. *The Names and Faces of Heroes* (1963) and *Permanent Errors* (1970) print stories. *Things Themselves* (1972) collects personal and critical essays. *A Palpable God* (1978) is an essay on and a translation of Biblical stories. *Early Dark* (1977) dramatizes his first novel. *Vital Provisions* (1982) is a volume of poems.

Prince and the Pauper, The, novel by Clemens,♦ published in 1882 under his pseudonym Mark Twain. Designed to be a children's book, it shows an essentially adult point of view in its attack on the social evils of Tudor England.

Prince Edward (later Edward VI) discovers Tom Canty, a pauper boy, to be his exact twin in appearance. When they exchange clothes, the prince is by error driven from the court, and the pauper is forced to act the part of royalty. Edward finds Tom's family, is mistreated, and runs away with Sir Miles Hendon, a disinherited knight, who takes pity on him, thinking his assertions of royal birth a sign of madness. In their wanderings, the prince sees the cruelty of church and court toward the poor, and learns the sufferings of his people through such dramatic incidents as the burning of two women whose only crime is that of being Baptists. Tom meanwhile is also thought unbalanced because of his peculiar behavior; becoming accustomed to his situation, however, he attempts to act the part of the real prince. On the morning of his coronation, Edward gets to Westminster Abbey and proves his identity by revealing the hiding place of the Great Seal, which Tom did not recognize after having taken it to crack some nuts. During his brief reign, Edward tempers the harshness of the law with a sense of justice, learned during his contact with the common people.

Princess Casamassima, The, novel by Henry James,♦ published in 1886. The Princess also appears in *Roderick Hudson.*♦

Hyacinth Robinson, an illegitimate orphan, is raised by the quiet spinster Miss Pynsent in lower-class London, where he is influenced by the anarchist musician Anastasius Vetch and the French Communist bookbinder M. Pupin, who teaches him his trade. The youth's sympathy for the downtrodden is further stimulated by the realistic revolutionary Paul Muniment, who leads him to pledge his life to the cause. He also meets the Princess Casmassima, who is separated from her wealthy Italian husband, and in her Hyacinth encounters for the first time a spirit like his own, combining an artistic and aristocratic temperament with a profound, restless sympathy for the oppressed. After Miss Pynsent's death, he uses her small legacy to travel in Europe, where he discovers values whose existence he has never suspected, and returns realizing that revolution cannot effect his personal salvation. He is determined, however, to devote himself to the cause, and is soon called upon by Muniment to assassinate a certain duke. The Princess, partly to save Hyacinth, partly to associate herself more closely with the revolutionaries, sets herself to fascinate Muniment, who nevertheless refuses to interfere.

Hyacinth is in despair, believing that the two have abandoned him. Finally the Princess offers herself as a substitute in the assassination, and goes to inform Hyacinth. On arriving at his rooms, she finds that he has committed suicide.

Professor's House, The, novel by Willa Cather,♦ published in 1925.

Godfrey St. Peter, professor at a Midwestern university, on reaching middle age completes his great work on the Spanish adventurers in America. He is now well-to-do, but does not desire material comfort, and, when he and his pleasure-loving wife Lillian move to a beautiful new home, he keeps the homely old house whose garret study he has long shared as a workroom with the German seamstress Augusta. His daughters have grown away from him since their marriages, Rosamond to Louie Marsellus, a lavish, enterprising Jew, and Kathleen to Scott McGregor, a journalist who suppresses his artistic leanings to write "glad" pieces for a living. Marsellus is rich, having marketed a gas patent bequeathed to his wife by her former fiancé, Tom Outland, the professor's favorite student, who died in World War I. The story of Outland's exploration, with his companion Roddy Blake, of an ancient New Mexican cliff city, is recalled by the professor. Marsellus's patronizing attitude toward the dead Outland alienates the professor, but his generosity and love of beauty strike a sympathetic chord in Lillian, who tours Europe with him and Rosamond. During a lonely summer, the professor loses interest in life, and when gas from a faulty stove fills his study one night, he is about to let it suffocate him when he is saved by Augusta. This crisis, and his appreciation of the quiet patience of the old seamstress, reconcile him to continued existence, which he faces with a certain apathy but "at least . . . the ground under his feet."

Progress and Poverty, economic treatise by Henry George,♦ published in 1879.

Attempting to discover why individual poverty increases while the nation is becoming more prosperous, George indicates a solution in the fact that private property in land confines interest and wages to marginal gains, while landlords, who are nonproducers, reap the benefits of social advance. Therefore labor and capital should be freed of this incubus, so that the community-created value may be returned to the community. George advocates for this purpose a "Single Tax," amounting to the whole or almost the whole of economic rent. This would permit the abolition of all other taxation, leaving production unpenalized, and improve the conditions of both capital and labor.

Progress of Dulness, The, satirical poem in octosyllabic couplets by John Trumbull,♦ published in three parts (1772–73).

The first part of this satire on contemporary education tells of the difficulties at college of Tom Brainless, who learns how to manage without studying and achieves a diploma that crowns him as learned. As a conservative, he is welcomed into the ministry, and becomes a pontifical fool. The second part deals with Dick Harebrain, a wealthy fop, who, though he learns nothing solid at college, manages to pick up cheap infidelity secondhand from Hume and Voltaire, and finally, running the course of coxcombery and dissipation, ends in jail, racked by disease. The third part recounts the adventures of Miss Harriet Simper, who, lacking any sensible education, becomes a coquette, modeling her life on romantic novels. After jilting her other admirers, she falls victim to Harebrain, and when discarded by that beau finally settles down to dullness by marrying Tom Brainless.

Progress to the Mines, A, journal written during 1732 by William Byrd,♦ was found among his Westover Manuscripts, from which it was published in 1841. A brief account of his least arduous journey, it is told in the witty and observant manner of all his charming memoranda, and includes comments on London literary gossip and Gay's *The Beggar's Opera,* typical of this Virginian's influence by English authors of the time.

PROKOSCH, FREDERIC (1908–), Wisconsin-born author, whose wide-ranging interests and extensive travels are suggested by the subjects and settings of his novels, which include *The Asiatics* (1935), about an American who travels across Asia; *The Seven Who Fled* (1937), concerned with demoralized Russian exiles, the torments of their flight, and their conclusion that the only victory is that of having lost with "dignity of heart . . . and nobility of spirit"; *Night of the Poor* (1939), a tale of a boy's impressions as he drifts from Wisconsin to Texas; *The Skies of Europe* (1941), a panorama of Europe on the eve of World War II; *The Conspirators*

(1943), a novel of spies and refugees in wartime Lisbon; *Age of Thunder* (1945), a tale in poetic prose about *maquisards; The Idols of the Cave* (1946), about postwar decadence; *Storm and Echo* (1948), about men's search for themselves as they travel in darkest Africa; *A Tale for Midnight* (1955), a fictional account of Beatrice Cenci; *A Ballad of Love* (1960); *The Seven Sisters* (1963); *The Dark Dancer* (1964), about the Indian prince who built the Taj Mahal; *The Wreck of the Cassandra* (1966), dealing with people shipwrecked on a desert isle; *The Missolonghi Manuscript* (1968), a fictive autobiography of Byron; and *America, My Wilderness* (1972), about a foundling black's wanderings through and affection for America. Prokosch's poems, including *The Assassins* (1936), *The Carnival* (1938), and *Death at Sea* (1940), are romantic and individualistic. *Voices* (1983) prints vignettes of famous people Prokosch knew.

Proletarian literature, name applied to the school of writing that contends that experience is primarily conditioned by the social, economic, and political environment and that the author is able to understand this environment by Marxist theory, which explains the dialectical relation of class cultures to the prevailing economic and social structure. During the Depression, when they flourished, proletarian writers contended that it was life itself, not the Communist party, that forced them to be interested in such phenomena as strikes, agricultural and industrial conditions, and persecution and oppression of racial minorities and the working class. During the 1920s and '30s Dos Passos, Farrell, and Steinbeck were among the leading writers who sympathized with the broader concepts of proletarian literature, but they refused to be confined by what they viewed as dogmatic restrictions. During the Depression other authors who moved to the far left in their social views and were avowedly or apparently in major accord with the tenets of proletarian literature included the novelists Robert Cantwell, Jack Conroy, Waldo Frank, Albert Halper, Josephine Herbst, and Grace Lumpkin, the dramatists John Howard Lawson, Clifford Odets, and Irwin Shaw, and the critics V.F. Calverton, Joseph Freeman, Michael Gold, and Granville Hicks. *The Masses* and its successor, the *New Masses,* were the leading proletarian journals.

Protestant Episcopal Church, the U.S. institution of the Anglican Communion, directly descended from the established Church of England. The creeds are the Apostles' and the Nicene, and the standards of doctrine are the Thirty-Nine Articles and the Book of Common Prayer. Church of England services were first regularly held in America at Jamestown (1607), and the Church flourished in the Southern colonies, particularly in Virginia and Maryland. In New England the Puritans forbade Anglican services, and it was not until the revocation of the Massachusetts colonial charter (1686) that Church of England clergymen were appointed to this region, leading to the establishment three years later of King's Chapel, Boston. In the same year, Trinity Church was consecrated in New York City. The earliest educational institution founded by the Church was William and Mary (1693). King's College (Columbia University) was founded in 1754; and other Episcopalian-founded institutions include Kenyon College, Ohio; Trinity College, Connecticut; the University of the South, Tennessee; and Hobart College, New York. During the Revolution the Church was severely torn, many of its clergy being Loyalists who returned to England. The majority of the laity were patriots, however, and these included Washington and two-thirds of the signers of the Declaration of Independence. In 1784 Samuel Seabury was consecrated the first bishop of the Church in America, which began its separate existence as an American ecclesiastical body with its own episcopate in 1789.

Provincetown Players, THE, little-theater group of authors, actors, and artists, first drawn together at Provincetown, Mass. (1915). Their association continued, with changes of place and personnel, until *c.*1929. The first plays were produced under the direction of George Cram Cook in a remodeled fishing smack, The Wharf Theatre. One-act plays continued to be produced at Greenwich Village, in The Playwright's Theatre, and later the expanded organization presented three-act plays in this and the Greenwich Village Theatre. By 1925 the Provincetown productions had included 93 new plays by 47 playwrights, greatly influencing the standards of American drama. Among these plays were all the works of Eugene O'Neill up to that date; Edna St. Vincent Millay's *The Princess Marries the Page* and *Aria da Capo;* Sherwood Anderson's *The Triumph of the Egg.* Later plays included Paul Green's *In Abraham's Bosom* and E.E. Cummings's *him* (1928).

Prufrock and Other Observations, a small collection of poems by T.S. Eliot,♦ published in 1917, whose title piece is "The Love Song of J. Alfred Prufrock."♦

Prynne, HESTER, heroine of *The Scarlet Letter.* ♦

Psalm of Life, A, poem by Longfellow,♦ published in *Voices of the Night* (1839). In nine quatrains of alternately rhymed trochaic tetrameters, this popular didactic piece stresses the importance of a full and sincere activity in making the most of life's brief span, rather than succumbing to moods of vain regret or dejection.

Pudd'nhead Wilson, The Tragedy of, novel by Clemens,♦ published in 1894 under the pseudonym Mark Twain. It was dramatized by Frank Mayo (1895).

On the Mississippi during the 1830s, at Dawson's Landing, Mo., lives Percy Driscoll, a prosperous slave owner. On the day his son Tom is born, his nearly white slave Roxy gives birth to a son, Chambers, whose father is a Virginia gentleman. Since Tom's mother dies when he is only a week old, he is raised by Roxy along with Chambers, whose twin he is in appearance. Roxy, fearful that her son may some day be sold down the river, changes the two children, and upon the death of Percy, his brother Judge Driscoll adopts Chambers, believing him to be Tom. The boy grows up a coward, a snob, and a gambler. Even though Roxy tells him that she is his mother, he sells her to pay his gambling debts. On escaping, she blackmails him. To obtain money he robs the judge and murders him with a knife stolen from Luigi, one of a pair of Italian twins with whom the judge once fought a duel. The evidence is against the twins, who are defended by David Wilson, an unsuccessful lawyer, whose "tragedy" consists in the ridicule that has resulted from his eccentric originality and iconoclasm; his humor and his interest in palmistry and fingerprints cause the people of Dawson's Landing to call him "Pudd'nhead." Wilson feels secure in his case for the twins, since the fingerprints on the knife are not those of the accused. One day he acquires the fingerprints of the spurious Tom, and with this evidence is able to vindicate his methods, and to win at last the admiration of his fellow townsmen, by saving the twins and convicting Chambers, who is sold down the river while the real Tom is restored to his rightful position.

Pulitzer Prizes in Journalism and Letters, created as a result of Joseph Pulitzer's bequest of $2,000,000 to found the Columbia University School of Journalism, with the income from $500,000 of that sum to be devoted to annual prizes "for the encouragement of public service, public morals, American literature, and the advancement of education." Pulitzer's will established four categories of American literature: novel, play, U.S. history, and American biography. The will empowered an Advisory Board, which was retitled the Pulitzer Prize Board (1979), to alter these categories or to create new ones. Its annually appointed juries for each of the categories make their nominations to the Advisory Board, which may accept or reject them or even substitute its own choices. The Advisory Board (until 1950 associated with the School of Journalism) passes its nominations to the Board of Trustees of Columbia University (in 1975 the Trustees delegated their power to the University president), which can accept or reject nominations but cannot make substitutions. The Advisory Board has the power to withhold awards if nominees do not meet its unpublished criteria. Prizes for novels, plays, U.S. history, and American biography were established in 1917, but that year no works were judged acceptable in the first two categories. Prizes for poetry were first established for the year 1922, but Columbia University gave its approval to prizes granted in 1918 and 1919 by the Poetry Society of America. With the powers granted to it, the Advisory Board in 1947 redefined the award for novels to "fiction in book form" so that it might select for the award of 1948 a work comprised of short stories. In 1962 it created a new category: general nonfiction. The dollar value of the prizes has varied over the years but has been $1000 since 1968.

Pulp magazine, name applied to a periodical printed on coarse wood pulp paper and containing short stories, novelettes, and serials usually of violent and exotic adventure. This type of magazine carries on the tradition of the dime novel, combining melodrama and conventional romance based on innocent morality. Produced by hack writers, the fiction is based on a few accepted formulas, which have been described as "making all heroines very young girls, presenting the West purely as a cowboys' Valhalla, and bringing all criminals—except those of the Robin Hood type—to summary and violent justice." The pulp magazines generally specialize in a single variety of fiction, e.g. crime detection and the chase of criminals; "Western" adventure; "horror"; pseudo-erotic or saccharine "love"; and pseudo-scientific "amazing" stories. Always the basis of the tale is sensational situation rather than plot, and development of character is frowned upon, for, as a critic has termed it, pulp-magazine publishing is "the business of purveying predigested daydreams to people who cannot dream for themselves." Many journals of this sort have been superseded by series of paperback books devoted to analogous themes and subjects.

PURCHAS, SAMUEL (1575?–1626), English clergyman, whose best-known religious writing is *Purchas his Pilgrim. Microcosmus, or the histories of Man* (1619). He is famous for carrying on the work of Hakluyt, although his editions of contemporary travel narratives are considered inferior in style and scholarship to those of his predecessor. In 1613 he published his first collection, *Purchas his Pilgrimage; or, Relations of the World and the Religions observed in all Ages and places discovered, from the Creation unto this Present.* The final revision of this work (1626) constitutes a supplementary volume to his comprehensive extension of Hakluyt's collection, *Hakluytus Posthumus, or Purchas his Pilgrimes, contayning a History of the World in Sea Voyages and Lande Travells, by Englishmen and others* (4 vols., 1625). The first half of this enthusiastic work is devoted to travels in the Old World and the Far East, while the second half contains narratives of voyages to America.

PURDY, JAMES (1923–   ), Ohio-born author of *Malcolm* (1959), a bizarre, comic novel of the picaresque, presenting the strange experiences of a 15-year-old boy as in his search for his lost father he wanders through a world of depravity. It was dramatized (1965) by Albee. *The Nephew* (1960), his second novel, tells of the revelations following the death in war of the nephew of a doting spinster, a retired schoolteacher, in a small Midwest town, who decides to write a memorial booklet. She thereby learns more than she wants to about him and about life as she discovers he was a homosexual. *Cabot Wright Begins* (1964), a satirical novel on the American scene, presents a compulsive but mild-mannered rapist who is himself "raped" by editors and publishers wanting to create a best seller out of his experiences. *Eustace Chisholm and the Works* (1967) treats loving relations as well as destructive encounters

between homosexuals. *I Am Elijah Thrush* (1972) presents a story of even more complex relations among men of different ages, backgrounds, and natures. *In a Shallow Grave* (1975) is about a hideously disfigured veteran trying to return to his childhood sweetheart, a different instance of alienation. *Sleepers in Moon-Crowned Valleys* is a trilogy composed of *Jeremy's Version* (1970), *The House of the Solitary Maggot* (1974), and *Mourners Below* (1981), about the strained, bizarre relations of a Midwest family. *Narrow Rooms* (1978) is a novel about homosexual passions, and *On Glory's Course* (1984) treats the lives and often odd loves of a town of Midwesterners in the 1930s. *The Color of Darkness* (1957) collects stories and a novella, which Purdy and a collaborator adapted for the stage (1963). *Children Is All* (1962) also collects stories and two plays, and further plays appear in *A Day After the Fair* (1977) along with poems. *The Running Sun* (1971) and *Sunshine Is an Only Child* (1973) are volumes of poetry.

Puritanism, attitude of a party within the Established Church of England, which, under Elizabeth I and the Stuarts, desired a more thoroughgoing reformation of the Church in the direction of continental Protestantism. At first the Puritans wished only to eliminate certain ceremonial vestments and rituals, and, having no doctrinal quarrel, they were not Separatists,♦ but definitely believed in a state church. As the conflict grew that led to the Revolution of 1640–60, there arose many political Puritans, whose main interest was in the establishment of parliamentary authority as opposed to the regal theory of divine right. The Puritan movement was at its height when it found an outlet in American colonization, and, though the Pilgrims♦ were Separatists, the later colonists were primarily Puritans who came from the English middle class. The Puritans' doctrine, as expressed in the Cambridge Platform (1646), had the theology of Calvinism♦ and the church polity of Congregationalism.♦ The word Puritan is used to refer either to this theology or to this polity. Later the word has been used to denote a strictness in morality that verges on intolerance, and refers to a supposed parallel with the moral severity of the early New England settlers.

Purloined Letter, The, detective story by Poe,♦ published in his *Tales* (1845).
The prefect of the Paris police visits C. Auguste Dupin, scholarly amateur detective,

for advice on a baffling case concerning a cabinet minister who has gained power over, and consequently practiced blackmail upon, a royal lady from whom he has stolen a letter that she cannot have made public. After several months of elaborate search, the prefect concludes that the letter is not on the minister's person or premises. Dupin soon finds the letter, explaining later that the police seek only obscure hiding places such as would be avoided by the acute minister. Dupin, therefore, visited him openly, looked in the most obvious places, and found the letter, turned inside out and disguised in an exposed card rack. Diverting the minister the next day by means of an arranged street disturbance, he substituted a facsimile and took the purloined letter with him.

PYNCHON, Thomas (1937–), novelist, born on Long Island, N.Y., after service in the navy, graduation from Cornell (1958), work as a technical writer for Boeing Aircraft in Seattle, and a year in Mexico, published his first novel, *V.,* ♦ in 1963. A richly complex work, philosophically influenced by *The Education of Henry Adams* and Wittgenstein, it deals with two major figures in its plot. One is Benny Profane, a constant failure, who drifts through life in such enterprises as hunting alligators in New York's sewers and is associated with his friends, the Whole Sick Crew. Another major figure, the cultivated Herbert Stencil, is more purposeful as he searches the world for V., the mysterious female spy and anarchist, who is by turns Venus, Virgin, and Void. Pynchon's second novel, *The Crying of*

Lot 49 ♦ (1966), is a shorter fable but marked by the same characteristics. Pynchon's plots are mystery stories combined with science fiction, but the novels' larger metaphors present in baroque fashion motifs not only of quest but of entropy, showing a closed world losing energy as time decays toward timelessness, and order disintegrates into alienation or chaos. Filled with endless esoteric references (including the parodying of other authors' styles) that range from high culture to trivial events, and marked by humor of wild comedy, the mock-heroic, and satire, the novels present the reader with a huge array of clues but no clear direction in their purposeful ambiguity. In his second novel the main figure is Oedipa Maas, a California woman whose legacy from a friend requires her to discover the true nature of her inheritance by following clues to a cabalistic social system known to many dispossessed Americans but hidden from people who live within conventional society. Pynchon's very long third novel, *Gravity's Rainbow* ♦ (1973, National Book Award), set in the closing years of World War II, is a story of plots and counterplots involving a Nazi Lieutenant Weissmann (once V.'s lover, for Pynchon's novels have echoes), disguised as Captain Blicero, and the American sleuth, Lieutenant Tyrone Slothrop, while V-2 rockets fall on London. Like all Pynchon's works, the mood moves from black humor to lyricism, and the dream-like fantasy is marked by labyrinthine interconnections until the reader is uncertain about what is "real" and what ·is imagined. Stories written between 1958 and 1964 are collected in *Slow Learner* (1984).

Q

Quakers, the religious body properly called the Society of Friends. They originally called themselves Children of Truth, Children of Light, or Friends of Truth, and received their sobriquet either because of association with highly emotional states manifested physically or because their leader once commanded a judge to "tremble at the word of the Lord." The Society of Friends arose in England under the guidance of George Fox (1624–91), who after 1647 preached a simple personal religion, as opposed to formal worship and ceremonial. Their fundamental doctrines do not differ greatly from those of other Christian bodies, but they avoid rigid creeds, making their belief less a system than an attitude of mind. They believe that the same spirit that gave forth the Scriptures still guides men to a right understanding of them, and therefore they refuse set forms of worship and have no trained leaders. Because they declined to support the Established Church, resisted the taking of oaths, and were pacifistic, they were continually persecuted in England until the Toleration Act (1689). In America, to which they came in the 1650s, they were likewise persecuted by the Puritans because of their opposition to theocracy. They flourished nevertheless, and in 1681 the colony of Pennsylvania was granted to their leader, William Penn. They became widely known for their humanitarianism, both in their relations with the Indians and in their opposition to slavery of blacks. This attitude may be seen in the writings of John Woolman, while such Quakers as Whittier and Lucretia Mott were prominent among 19th-century Abolitionists. Although for conscience's sake most Quakers refused to participate in the Revolutionary War, some of them, called Free Quakers, took up arms. In 1827 Elias Hicks pressed the doctrine of the "inward light" to its extreme, and split the Society of Friends into two parts, the Hicksites and the orthodox group. Another schism occurred (1845), with the Wilburites following John Wilbur in returning to what they considered the original principles of the movement. Various groups, holding to common fundamental beliefs, had over 130,000 members in 1980.

QUEEN, Ellery, pseudonym of Frederic Dannay (1905–82) and Manfred Lee (1905–71), under which they wrote many detective novels, beginning with *The Roman Hat Mystery* (1929). They also collaborated on an anthology of detective stories, *A Challenge to the Reader* (1938), and editorship of *Ellery Queen's Mystery Magazine* (1941–).

Queequeg, character in *Moby-Dick.* ♦

R

Rabbit, Run, novel by John Updike,♦ published in 1960. The first in a series of three, it presents 26-year-old Harry Angstrom, whose nickname, Rabbit, comes from his glorious days as a high-school basketball champion in the small town of Brewer, Pa. Now, frustrated by the responsibilities of marriage to Janice (pregnant and an alcoholic) and fatherhood to three-year-old Nelson, and by an inconsequential job demonstrating the MagiPeel kitchen implement, he decides to run away. His former athletic coach, Tothero, bucks him up and introduces him to an appealing young woman, Ruth, who becomes pregnant by him. With tragic irony, his legitimate child is born but soon accidentally drowns when his drunken wife is bathing her.

Rabbit, Redux (1971) depicts the Angstrom household just ten years later, long after Harry's return to a marriage that is still a shambles. He gets no stability from his father-in-law's successful place in the town's middle-class society as owner of an automobile sales agency. On the contrary, a suave Greek salesman for Springer Motors, Charlie Stavros, temporarily woos Janice away from Rabbit. Caught up in the social turmoil of the 1960s, he befriends two radicals, a young man and woman, and the latter is accidentally killed by neighbors who are infuriated by the young people's way of life.

Rabbit Is Rich (1981) treats the Angstroms still another decade later. Rabbit and Janice have now inherited a half interest in his late father-in-law's business and, having found a kind of place in society, he is a member of the local country club. He is resigned to good relations with Stavros, and he sees Ruth to determine if a chance acquaintance is their daughter. Rabbit finds that the girl is not his daughter, but he does become involved in paternal problems with his son Nelson, now in college, who has gotten his girl friend pregnant.

RABE, DAVID [WILLIAM] (1940–), Iowa-born dramatist, after army service in Vietnam and teaching at Villanova University began his career as playwright with *The Basic Training of Pavlo Hummel* (1971) and *Sticks and Bones* (1971), both published in 1973, both treating the effect of the Vietnam War

on people, the latter presenting a blinded soldier returning to his commonplace family and ironically being the only one capable of seeing. *The Orphan* (1973), also with a Vietnam background, relates the mythology of the *Oresteia* to modern cruelty. *In the Boom Boom Room* (produced 1973, published 1975) presents the sleazy life of a tawdry woman. *Streamers* (produced 1976, published 1977) is a violent depiction of homosexuality and murders in an army camp. *Hurlyburly* (1984) presents men floundering through banal, meaningless lives.

Ragtime, novel by E.L. Doctorow.♦

RAHV, PHILIP (1908–73), Ukrainian-born literary critic, came to the U.S. in 1922 and within a decade became an important figure in its culture as co-founder and editor of *Partisan Review.*♦ His essays are collected in *Image and Idea* (1949), including the seminal "Paleface and Redskin," on the dichotomy between experience and consciousness in American writers; *The Myth and the Powerhouse* (1965); and *Literature and the Sixth Sense* (1969). *Essays on Literature and Politics* (1978) is a posthumous collection. Beginning in 1957 he was a member of the Brandeis faculty.

Ramona, novel by Helen Hunt Jackson,♦ published in 1884.

A romantic story set in mid-19th-century California, it tells of the love between Ramona Ortegna, a half-Indian and half-Scotch girl adopted by a haughty Spanish landowner, and Alessandro, a full-blooded Indian, and how they, and Mexicans in general, are harried by the avaricious hordes of Americans who have conquered the region.

RAND, AYN (1905–82), Russian-born novelist, graduated from the University of Leningrad, came to the U.S. (1926), where she was naturalized. Her first writing was a mystery play, *The Night of January 16th* (1935), but later works shows her deep concern with the theme of extreme individualism. Her first novel, *We, the Living* (1936), depicts young Russian individualists trapped and destroyed by totalitarian dictatorship. *Anthem* (England, 1938; U.S., 1946) is a short novel about a heroic dissenter in a future mono-lithic and collectivized state. *The Fountain-head*♦ (1943) is a long biographical novel praising the independence of an architect ostensibly modeled on Frank Lloyd Wright. *Atlas Shrugged* (1957) treats the value of a superior concept of individualism related to people who plan a new society based on the oath "I will never live for the sake of another man, nor ask any other man to live for mine." *For the New Intellectual* (1961) collects the philosophic passages of these four novels to present her theory of Objectivism, which is antiromantic and antialtruistic in its fervent appeal to a code of "rational self-interest." *The Romantic Manifesto* (1969) is her "phi-losophy of literature."

RANSOM, John Crowe (1888–1974), Ten-nessee poet, was educated in his native state and as a Rhodes Scholar at Oxford (1913). He was a member of the English department of Vanderbilt University (1914–37) and early became a leader of the Agrarians♦ and an editor of *The Fugitive.* ♦ In 1937 he joined the faculty of Kenyon College, where he re-mained until retiring in 1958. He founded and edited the *Kenyon Review,* ♦ placing stress on the New Criticism more than on the regional-ism that he formerly emphasized. His first verse, *Poems About God* (1919), although not sufficiently valued by him for selection in later volumes, was already marked by the irony that is more accomplished in *Chills and Fever* (1924). *Grace After Meat* (1924) is an English selection from these two books, which was followed by *Two Gentlemen in Bonds* (1927). His balanced judgment of opposites and his portraits of people in his elegies are distinguished by a witty and oblique style. His *Selected Poems* (1945) was issued in revised, enlarged editions (1963, 1969). His criticism appears in *God Without Thunder: An Unorthodox Defense of Ortho-doxy* (1930), an attack on science as destruc-tive of the old mystery of God, a theme to which he returned in *The World's Body* (1938), on the failure of science to achieve the body that is in poetry; and he gathered later essays in *Beating the Bushes* (1972). *Selected Essays* was published in 1984. He contributed to the Agrarian anthology *I'll Take My Stand*♦ (1930), and later analyzed contemporaries and called for an ontological critic in *The New Criticism* (1941).

Rappaccini's Daughter, allegorical tale by Hawthorne,♦ published in 1844 and re-printed in *Mosses from an Old Manse* (1846).

Giovanni Guasconti comes to study at the University of Padua and lodges next door to the house of Giacomo Rappaccini, a doctor. In the latter's garden he sees and falls in love with Rappaccini's daughter Beatrice, whose beauty strangely resembles that of her father's poisonous flowers. Pietro Baglioni, a friendly professor, warns Giovanni that Rap-paccini's love of science has led him beyond moral or humane considerations, and that the girl's nature seems a product of his sinister art, but the young man is undeterred. Under the scientific regard of her father, the affec-tion of the two grows deeper, and Giovanni himself becomes tainted by the poisonous breath of the garden. Then he gives Beatrice a potion that Baglioni has supplied him as an antidote to all poisons. She drinks it, but "as poison had been life, so the powerful antidote was death; and thus the poor victim of man's ingenuity and of thwarted nature . . . per-ished there, at the feet of her father and Giovanni."

Rationale of Verse, The, essay by Poe,♦ published as "Notes on English Verse" in *The Pioneer* (1843), and in its final form under the present title in the *Southern Liter-ary Messenger* (1848). It is the most complete expression of Poe's theories of poetic tech-nique, although critics, indicating its inconsist-encies, assert that he did not follow his own dicta.

Refuting the notion that prosody is con-cerned with the regular "alternation of long and short syllables," Poe establishes a distinc-tion between "natural" and "unnatural" met-rical units. "The *natural* long syllables are those encumbered . . . with [difficult] conso-nants. . . . *Accented* syllables are of course always long, but, where *un*encumbered with consonants, must be classed among the *un*-naturally long." He upholds a "principle of equality," according to which each verse foot must be pronounced in the same time as every other foot in the line, regardless of the number of its syllables. This applies only to single lines, although to be effective a stanza should contain lines arranged in strict pat-tern; and rhyme, alliteration, and the use of refrains should be governed by the same rule. Since duration is the standard by which this "equality" is to be judged, there should be no "blending" or substitution of one metrical foot for another. Contractions or elisions should be avoided, although additional un-stressed syllables may be used if they can be pronounced rapidly. The "cæsura" (in this usage, a "variable foot" occurring at the end or middle of a line, and consisting of one long syllable) is discussed as being one of the most important of metrical feet. The essay concludes with a passage, especially referring to Longfellow's poems, which denies the possibility of the successful use of Greek hexameters in English, because of the "natural" pronunciation peculiar to English words.

Raven, The, poem by Poe,♦ the title piece of a volume (1845), was several times revised in later publications. To Poe's account of writing it, in "The Philosophy of Composition,"♦ must be added the influence upon the meter of Mrs. Browning's "Lady Geraldine's Courtship" and Chivers's "Isadore." The poem consists of 18 six-line stanzas, the first five lines of each being in trochaic octameter, and the sixth line trochaic tetrameter. The rhythm is varied by frequent syncopation, caused by effects of double rhyme and alliteration. The rhyme pattern is *abcbbb,* in which the *b* rhymes are based on the constant refrain "Nevermore," a word that merged Poe's favorite theme of grief occasioned by the death of a beautiful woman (in this case "Lenore"), the distinctive theme of despair at the denial of personal immortality, and the sonorous sound of the *o* and *r* in the refrain itself.

A weary student is visited in his room, one stormy midnight, by a raven who can speak the single word "Nevermore." Tortured by grief over the loss of his beloved, the student questions the bird concerning the possibility of meeting her in another world. He is driven to wilder demands by the repetition of the fatal word, until the raven becomes an irremovable symbol of his dark doubts and frustrated longing.

RAWLINGS, MARJORIE KINNAN (1896–1953), born in Washington, D.C., graduated from the University of Wisconsin (1918), became a journalist, and in 1928 "deliberately cut her civilized ties . . . and migrated to the firmly intrenched outpost of the vanishing frontier," the hummock country of Florida that forms the setting of her fiction. *Cross Creek* (1942) is a humorous account of her adoption of Florida as a home and a source of literary material. She published her first novelette, *Jacob's Ladder,* and stories of the region's poor-white farmers, hunters, trappers, fishermen, and moonshiners in *When the Whippoorwill* (1940). She further depicted this region in her novels *South Moon Under* (1933), *Golden Apples* (1935), and *The Yearling* (1938, Pulitzer Prize),

about a boy's love for his pet fawn, which his father is forced to kill when it ruins his meager crops. Her *Selected Letters* was published in 1982.

Realism, term applied to literary composition that aims at an interpretation of the actualities of any aspect of life, free from subjective prejudice, idealism, or romantic color. It is opposed to the concern with the unusual which forms the basis of romance, but it does not proceed, as does naturalism,♦ to the philosophy of determinism and a completely amoral attitude. Although the novel has generally been considered the form best suited to the artistic treatment of reality, realism is not limited to any one form. As an attitude of the writer toward his materials, it is relative, and no chronological point may be indicated as the beginning of realism, but the 19th century is considered to mark its origin as a literary movement. The example of science, the influence of rational philosophy, the use of documentation in historical study, as well as the reaction against attenuated romanticism, all had their effect in creating the dominance of realism at this time. Although influenced by English and foreign authors, to a great extent the American transition from romance to realism in fiction was indigenous, but it occurred gradually. Frontier literature, frequently realistic in its observation of detail, merged in the general stream of influence through the work of such authors as Clemens, while the all-inclusive zest for experience displayed in Whitman's descriptive poems is another primary source of modern realism. A realistic attitude toward their materials may be noted in the stories of Harriet Beecher Stowe, De Forest, and Rebecca H. Davis, but the first concerted movement was probably that excited by the interest in local color.♦ Although such writers as Harte, Sarah Orne Jewett, Cable, and F.H. Smith were frequently romantic in stressing eccentric manners, they were realistic in attending to minute details, and to some extent in their treatment of character. The tendencies of these writers were carried further by such novelists as Joseph Kirkland, Edward Eggleston, Hamlin Garland, and E.W. Howe. Although far less concerned with homely setting or themes, Howells, Henry James, and later Edith Wharton were also realistic in their depiction of certain special social environments, extending realism into the comedy of manners and into psychological perception of character. Somewhat later novelists such as H.B. Fuller, Upton Sinclair, and Ernest Poole, although often sentimental, were concerned with exposing the social evils that thwarted the happiness of their characters, and thereby used realism for humanitarian protest of a sort that later became much more determined as used by writers of proletarian literature. Although there have been substantial shifts of sensibility in 20th-century American literature, as for example to a new concern with the novel as romance, realism has continued to be a major mode of expression.

Realms of Being, The, general title of a series of philosophical works by Santayana,♦ to which *Scepticism and Animal Faith* (1923) serves as an introduction, while *The Realm of Essence* (1927), *The Realm of Matter* (1930), *The Realm of Truth* (1937), and *The Realm of Spirit* (1940) form the body. In these books, Santayana modifies and supplements his philosophy as expressed in *The Life of Reason* (1905–6).

Rebecca of Sunnybrook Farm, novel by Kate Douglas Wiggin,♦ published in 1903.

RECHY, JOHN [FRANCISCO] (1934–), born in Texas, served in the army in Germany, is a novelist of the underground life of sex and drugs, mainly of homosexuals, presented with candid directness in *City of Night* (1963), *Numbers* (1967), *This Day's Death* (1970), *The Vampires* (1971), *The Fourth Angel* (1973), and *Rushes* (1979). *The Sexual Outlaw* (1978) is a documentary account of men engaged in promiscuous, anonymous sex in public places.

Red Badge of Courage, The: An Episode of the American Civil War, novel by Stephen Crane,♦ published in 1895. The original manuscript, containing 5000 words (about 10 per cent of the entirety) deleted by the original publisher, was printed for the first time in 1982. This psychological study of a soldier's reactions to warfare was written before Crane had ever seen a battle. His knowledge was at least partly derived from a popular anthology, *Battles and Leaders of the Civil War*. The unnamed battle of the novel has been identified as that at Chancellorsville.

Henry Fleming, generally called simply "the youth" or "he," is an ordinary, inexperienced soldier, "an unknown quantity," torn between a "little panic-fear" and "visions of broken-bladed glory" as he faces his first battle. He begins with the state of mind of the raw recruit who is anxious to get into battle so that he may show his patriotism and prove himself a hero. He swaggers to keep up his spirits during the delay that precedes his suddenly being thrust into the slaughter. Then he is overcome by unthinking fear and runs from the field. He is ashamed when he joins the wounded, for he has not earned their "red badge of courage," and then he becomes enraged when he witnesses the horrid dance of death of his terribly maimed friend, Jim Conklin. Later, by chance, he gets a minor head wound in a confused struggle with one of the retreating infantrymen of his own army. The next day, when his pretense is accepted that the wound is the result of enemy gunfire, he suddenly begins to fight frantically, and then automatically seizes the regiment's colors in the charge that reestablishes its reputation. He moves through this sultry nightmare with unconscious heroism, and emerges steady, quiet, and truly courageous.

Red Pony, The, story by Steinbeck, reprinted in *The Long Valley.* ♦

Redburn: His First Voyage, novel by Melville,♦ published in 1849 and based on his own experiences during his first voyage (1837).

Wellingborough Redburn, son of an impoverished middle-class New York family, ships as a "boy" on the *Highlander*, bound for Liverpool. Captain Riga treats him with ironic kindness until the ship sails, after which he withdraws to his solitary cabin, placing his mate in command. Clumsy and inexperienced, Redburn receives only contempt from the sailors. During six weeks in Liverpool, he explores the city, aided by his guidebook, and sees especially the lack of democracy and the vicious living conditions of the poor. He becomes friendly with Harry Bolton, a spendthrift young aristocrat, who takes him on a riotous trip to London, shocking the boy by his excesses and reckless actions. The return voyage, on which Harry is also a sailor, is full of tragic incidents, for the steerage passengers nearly starve, an epidemic of cholera kills many, and the crew is maltreated. In New York, Captain Riga refuses to pay Redburn and Harry, and the friends part, the boy going to his home and the Englishman signing for a whaling voyage, during which he is killed.

REED, Ishmael [Scott] (1938–　), Chatta-
nooga-born black author, long resident in
Berkeley, Cal. His experimental novels of
preposterous plots marked by fantasy, sometimes surrealistic, sometimes caricatured and
satiric, include *The Free-Lance Pallbearers*
(1967), depicting violence and corruption in a
fictive land; *Yellow Back Radio Broke Down*
(1969), presenting the fantastic adventures of
a black cowboy; *Mumbo Jumbo* (1972), a
freewheeling tale about black-white relations
over the ages; *The Last Days of Louisiana Red*
(1974), a bizarre tale of blacks and whites set
in Berkeley during the 1960s; and *Flight to
Canada* (1976), fusing 19th- and 20th-century
characters and situations in a surrealistic
presentation of American slavery. *The Terrible Twos* (1982) is a bitter, satirical fantasy of
political and social corruption in the U.S. of
today and the future. His poetry is collected in
*Catechism of the Neo-American HooDoo
Church* (1970), *Conjure* (1972), *Chattanooga*
(1973), and *Secretary to the Spirits* (1978).
Shrovetide in Old New Orleans (1978) and
God Made Alaska for the Indians (1982)
contain brief prose pieces.

REED, John (1887–1920), born of wealthy
parents in Portland, Ore., graduated from
Harvard (1910), then traveled in Europe.
Aided by Lincoln Steffens, he obtained
employment with *The American Magazine,*
but he submitted his most sincere work to
The Masses. His report of the Paterson silk
mills strike won him recognition, and in 1913
he was sent by the New York *World* to cover
the Mexican revolt of Villa. During the same
year he reported the miners' strike at Ludlow, Colo., for the *Metropolitan Magazine*
and wrote his impressions of Villa and others
in *Insurgent Mexico* (1914). As a war correspondent for the *Metropolitan,* as well as for
The Masses and *The Seven Arts,* he wrote
the articles republished in *The War in
Eastern Europe* (1916). Already sympathetic
with the cause of the Russian Revolution,
Reed became friendly with the Bolshevik
leaders and, after reporting their coup
(1917), returned to America to be active in
the organization of the first Communist
party of the U.S. Difficulties encountered in
this enterprise sent him back to Russia,
where he died and was accorded the honor
of burial in the Kremlin. His eyewitness
story of the Russian Revolution is contained
in *Red Russia* (1919) and his most important
work, *Ten Days That Shook the World*
(1919), a graphic and sympathetic reportorial account of the Russian revolution, officially approved by the Soviets, and for which
Lenin wrote an introduction to a later
edition.

REESE, Lizette Woodworth (1856–1935),
Baltimore poet and schoolteacher, whose
poetry is distinguished for its concision,
intense emotion, and simple personal interpretation of pastoral subjects. The direct and
rather crisp quality of the lyrics in her early
books, *A Branch of May* (1887), *A Handful
of Lavender* (1891), and *A Quiet Road*
(1896), marks a great advance over the
Victorian sentimental treatment of nature,
and she maintained her high standards in
later collections: *A Wayside Lute* (1909),
containing her best-known poem, "Tears," in
which she prays for clear vision with which to
"see aright How each hath back what once he
stayed to weep."

Reformed Church in America, founded in
colonial times by Protestant settlers from the
Netherlands, is Calvinistic in faith and presbyterian in government. Until the English
conquest in 1664, it was the established
church of New Netherland. In 1771 it became
independent of the mother church. For a long
time it was a strong denomination in New
York and New Jersey, moving toward the
Middle West in the mid-19th century. Among
the educational institutions it has sponsored
is Rutgers University.

Reformed Church in the United States, established in America in the early 18th
century by German, Swiss, and French
settlers, was known officially until 1869 as
the German Reformed Church. Its origin
stems from the works of Zwingli, Calvin,
and Melanchthon, and the Heidelberg Catechism of 1563 is still its standard for
Scriptural instruction. In 1793 it declared
itself independent of the Classis of Amsterdam, and at later dates it has been allied
with other reformed churches in America.

Regionalism, term applied to literature which
emphasizes a special geographical setting and
concentrates upon the history, manners, and
folkways of the area as these help to shape
the lives or behavior of the characters. It
generally differs from local color♦ in that it
lays less stress upon quaint oddities of dialect,
mannerisms, and costume and more on basic
philosophical or sociological distinctions,
which the writer often views as though he
were a cultural anthropologist. One major
form of regionalism flourished in the South,

particularly among the Agrarians of the 1920s and '30s. Its adherents contended that their ideas were based on a creative, scientific approach to the cultural, geographic, and economic differences of particular sections of the U.S. This detached view necessitated scholarly antiquarianism in studying the relation of folklore to literature, and led away from realism toward a critical interpretation of historical backgrounds. Allen Tate, one of its proponents, declared, "Only a return to the provinces, to the small self-contained centres of life, will put the all-destroying abstraction America safely to rest." Tate collaborated with J.C. Ransom, Donald Davidson, and R.P. Warren in publishing *The Fugitive* (1922–25) and the symposia *I'll Take My Stand* (1930), *Culture in the South* (1934), and *Who Owns America?* (1936). These works assert that as people adapt their lives to the geography of a region and create an economic system that gradually becomes natural, this pattern in turn becomes aesthetic. Their program was intended to combat the Northern drive toward industrializing the South, which would have made for eclecticism and standardization; to champion an agrarian economy; and, as Davidson said, to "speak for the South as a living historic entity which is separate from America though bound to it."

REID, [THOMAS] MAYNE (1818–83), Irish-born novelist, came to the U.S. (1840), where he had a varied career as journalist, storekeeper, overseer of slaves, schoolmaster, captain in the Mexican War, actor, dramatist, Indian fighter, and frontier hunter. He returned to England (1850) and was in America again only from 1867 to 1870, but during his years in the U.S. he knew not only the East but also the South, the prairies, and the Western frontier. He wrote a long series of romances, whose exciting adventures endeared him to millions of boys, and whose descriptions of the Southern and Western U.S. made him a prominent foreign follower of Cooper in depicting pioneer customs and the life of the Indians.

Reivers, The, novel by Faulkner,♦ published in 1962 and awarded a Pulitzer Prize.

Told to his grandson as "A Reminiscence," Lucius Priest's monologue recalls his adventures in 1905 as an 11-year-old, when he, the gigantic but childish part-Indian Boon Hogganbeck, and a black family servant, Ned William McCaslin, become reivers (stealthy plunderers) of the automobile of his grand-

father, the senior banker of Jefferson, Miss. Driving 80 miles to Memphis, they stay at Miss Reba's brothel, where Boon falls in love with one of the girls, Everbe Corinthia, whom he later weds, while Ned, believing the grandfather would prefer a racehorse, trades the car for a poor mount. After various machinations the horse is successfully jockeyed by Lucius in a race that wins back the car and delights his grandfather, only to lead to another race in which both horse and a $500 bet of the grandfather are lost, although the grandfather counts the experience worthwhile.

REMINGTON, FREDERIC [SACKRIDER] (1861–1909), sculptor, illustrator, and painter, chose for his different media the subjects of soldiers, Indians, and cowboys, frequently in lively action. His bronze statuettes and frequently reproduced canvases are of more historical than artistic value. In addition to being a popular magazine illustrator, he was the author of several books displaying the same temper as his graphic art. These include *Pony Tracks* (1895), *Crooked Trails* (1898), and *The Way of an Indian* (1906). *My Dear Wister* (1972) collects his correspondence with Owen Wister.

Renascence, poem in octosyllabic couplets by Edna St. Vincent Millay,♦ published in 1912 and collected in *Renascence and Other Poems* (1917).

With an air of casual simplicity, the poet tells how "Infinity came down and settled over me . . . I saw and heard, and knew at last the How and Why of all things. . . ." For this omniscience she pays in "infinite remorse," feeling as her own all the sin, regret, and agony of mankind. "Close-sepulchred" thus, she cries to God for new birth, and, upon casting off her self-centered belief and discovering again "Thy radiant identity," is granted the return of her own life to enjoy the freshness and beauty of the world.

Representative Men, seven essays by Emerson,♦ published in 1850. Probably suggested by Carlyle's *Heroes and Hero-Worship,* they were originally lectures delivered in Boston (1845–46), and in Manchester and London (1847).

The six representative men are Plato, the philosopher; Swedenborg, the mystic; Montaigne, the skeptic; Shakespeare, the poet; Napoleon, the man of the world; and Goethe, the writer. In the first lecture, "On the Uses of Great Men," Emerson contends that humanity, being pervaded by the spirit of the

Deity, is not made up of a number of individuals. A great man is one who represents more of this divine essence than his fellows, and thus enables mankind to appreciate its own possibilities.

Requiem for a Nun, novel by Faulkner,♦ partly in dramatic form, published in 1951 as a sequel to *Sanctuary* (1931).

REXROTH, KENNETH (1905–82), Indiana-born poet and critic, resident in San Francisco after 1927, where he was associated in different eras with radical social views, Objectivist poetry, and the Beat movement. His collections of poems include *In What Hour* (1940), *The Phoenix and the Tortoise* (1944), *The Signature of All Things* (1949), *In Defence of the Earth* (1956), *Natural Numbers* (1963), *Shorter Poems* (1966), *Longer Poems* (1968), and *New Poems* (1974). He also wrote verse plays, *Beyond the Mountains* (1951), a verse travel journal, *The Dragon and the Unicorn* (1952), and many adaptations or translations from the French, Chinese, and Japanese. His essays appeared in many volumes, including *Bird in the Bush* (1959), *Assays* (1961), *The Alternative Society* (1971), *With Eye and Ear* (1971), and *The Elastic Retort* (1974). His orphaned youth and experiences to the age of 21 appear in *An Autobiographical Novel* (1966), and a brief treatment of later years appears in *Excerpts from a Life* (1981). His anti-Establishment beliefs are treated in a survey, *Communalism* (1975), and his dedication to great literature of the past is seen in his *Classics Revisited* (1969).

REZNIKOFF, CHARLES (1894–1976), poet of the Objectivist♦ school, so little known during his lifetime in New York that he published many of his works himself. Marked by a deep dedication to a Jewish tradition and by his talent for imagistic lyrics, his poems include *Inscriptions* (1959) and *By the Waters of Manhattan* (1962). *Testimony: The United States 1885–1915* (1965) is the initial part (to 1890) of a projected four-volume recitative narrating diverse aspects of U.S. history. *Holocaust* (1975) prints poems based on testimony at the Nuremberg trials. *By the Well of Living and Seeing* (1974) is a selection of poems since 1918 made by Seamus Cooney (1933–   ), an Irish-born professor of English in the U.S. who is also editing Reznikoff's complete poems. *Family Chronicle* (1969) is a prose account of New York City ghetto life.

RHODES, EUGENE MANLOVE (1869–1934), Nebraska-born author, lived as a boy and into his late thirties mostly in New Mexico, where he was both cowboy and writer, and, after a long residence in New York (1906–26), returned late in life to New Mexico and California. He wrote a great many stories for *The Saturday Evening Post* and other popular journals, sometimes revising and expanding these, so that his novel *Bransford in Arcadia* (1914), variously retitled in reprints, was an outgrowth of "The Little Eohippus," and *West Is West* (1917) fused several stories. The others of his ten novels, mainly about ranch and range life in the Southwest, were not only widely read but were praised for their interpretations of cowboy life and their descriptions of its scene.

RHODES, JAMES FORD (1848–1927), historian principally famous for his *History of the United States from the Compromise of 1850* (7 vols., 1893–1906), which covered the years 1850–77 as a clash between civilizations based on opposed abstract ideas. Other works are *History of the Civil War* (1917, Pulitzer Prize) and *History of the United States from Hayes to McKinley* (1919).

Rhodora, The: On Being Asked, Whence Is the Flower?, poem in iambic pentameter couplets by Emerson,♦ written in 1834 and first published in *The Western Messenger* (1839). It is collected in *Poems* (1847). Apropos of the beautiful New England flower, the poet condemns the questioning of the divine creative power: ". . . if eyes were made for seeing, Then Beauty is its own excuse for being."

RICE, ELMER (ELMER REIZENSTEIN) (1892–1967), New York dramatist, producer, and novelist, graduated from the New York Law School (1912), but soon abandoned this profession for writing. His first play, *On Trial* (1914), was a murder mystery employing the technique of the motion-picture "cutback" to present scenes that are described by the trial witnesses. His works for the Morningside Players, a little-theater group, were published in *Morningside Plays* (1917). In 1923 he obtained his second success with *The Adding Machine*, a satirical, expressionistic fantasy. His interest in the social aspects of life is further exhibited in the realistic play *Street Scene* (1929, Pulitzer Prize); *We, the People* (1933); *Judgment Day* (1934), dealing with the ideologies involved in the trials for the burning of the Reichstag building; *Between Two*

Worlds (1934); *American Landscape* (1938); *Two on an Island* (1940); *Flight to the West* (1941); and *A New Life* (1943). His other plays, mainly farces and melodramas, include *Wake Up, Jonathan* (1921), with Hatcher Hughes; *Cock Robin* (1928), with Philip Barry; *Close Harmony* (1929), with Dorothy Parker; *The Subway* (1929); *See Naples and Die* (1929); *The Left Bank* (1931); *Counsellor-at-Law* (1931); *Black Sheep* (1932); and *Dream Girl* (1945). His novels include *A Voyage to Purilia* (1930); *Imperial City* (1937), on New York; and *The Show Must Go On* (1949). *The Living Theatre* (1959) collects essays, originally lectures, on the theater as a social institution. *Minority Report* (1963) is an autobiography from his beginnings as a lawyer through his theatrical career, which included regional directorship of the New York Federal Theatre Project and helping to found the Playwright's Producing Company and to direct some of its plays.

RICH, ADRIENNE [CECILE] (1931–), Baltimore-born writer, whose first volume of poems, *A Change of World* (1951), was published in the Yale Series of Younger Poets the year she was graduated from Radcliffe. Succeeding collections were *The Diamond Cutters* (1955), *Snapshots of a Daughter-in-Law* (1963), *Necessities of Life* (1966), *Selected Poems* (1967), and *The Fact of a Doorframe* (1984). With *Leaflets* (1969), *The Will To Change* (1971), *Diving into the Wreck* (1973), *Poems Selected and New* (1975), *The Dream of a Common Language* (1978), and *A Wild Patience Has Taken Me This Far* (1981) her commitment to radical politics and to the cause of women was manifested. *Of Woman Born* (1976) is a study of motherhood as a social institution.

Richard Cory, poem by Robinson. ♦

Richard Hurdis; or, The Avenger of Blood, romance by Simms, ♦ published in 1838 as one of his series of Border Romances. ♦ Like its sequel, *Border Beagles,* it is based on the activities of the Southwest bandit Murrell.

RICHARDSON, JACK [CARTER] (1935–), New York City-born dramatist, graduate of Columbia, whose plays include *The Prodigal* (1960), a version of the Orestes-Agamemnon tale as a tragi-comic conflict between idealism and society's demands; *Gallows Humor* (1961), a two-part play contrasting a condemned man's acceptance of his execution

and the hangman's loathing of his life; *Lorenzo* (1963), set in renaissance Italy; *Xmas in Las Vegas* (1965); and *As Happy as Kings* (1968). *The Prison Life of Harris Fillmore* (1963) is a novel about a banker who prefers jail to freedom. *Memoir of a Gambler* (1980) is a memoir of the author's addiction to gaming.

RICHTER, CONRAD [MICHAEL] (1890–1968), Pennsylvania-born author, later long resident in New Mexico before returning to his native state. His novels include the trilogy *The Trees* (1940), about a rough, 18th-century pioneering family in Ohio, *The Fields* (1946), concerning the family and the region during the Civil War era, and *The Town* (1950, Pulitzer Prize), on the later family, its pioneer spirit urbanized, torn between idealism and realism. His other novels include *The Sea of Grass* (1937), about an Eastern woman's life in the Southwest; *Tacey Cromwell* (1942), about a prostitute in early 20th-century Arizona; *The Light in the Forest* (1953), about a white boy captured by Delaware Indians, rescued, and then nostalgic for their way of life; *The Waters of Kronos* (1960), a novella of mysticism in which a man in old age returns as a stranger to his Pennsylvania hometown to see himself as a youth; and *A Simple Honorable Man* (1962), treating the noble character of the father of the hero of *The Waters of Kronos.*

RIDING, LAURA (LAURA REICHENTHAL) (1901–), born in New York City, was long expatriated in Mallorca and England before returning to the U.S. (1959) to live in Florida. Her early writings include *Contemporaries and Snobs* (1928) and other critical works, as well as *A Survey of Modernist Poetry* (1927), one of several collaborations with Robert Graves. Her fiction includes *A Trojan Ending* (1937), about the Trojan War; *Lives of Wives* (1939), considering Cyrus, Aristotle, Caesar, and other pre-Christian figures as husbands; and *Progress of Stories* (1935), a series of 17 stories, progressively "of Lives . . . of Ideas . . . and Nearly True," and an essay on storytelling. An enlarged edition appeared in 1982. Her early poetry is gathered in *Collected Poems* (1938). After a long silence she published *Selected Poems* (England, 1970; U.S., 1973) and *The Telling* (1975), a philosophic essay. She was married (1941–69) to Schuyler B. Jackson and has sometimes published as Laura (Riding) Jackson.

Rights of Man, The, political tract by Thomas Paine,♦ published at London (2 parts, 1791–92). A defense of the French Revolution against the attacks of Burke, it resulted in a British law against seditious publications and in Paine's flight to France to escape prosecution.

The argument is based on the principle that sovereignty inheres in the will of the present majority, as a continuous compact reaffirmed by each generation. Men left the state of nature because moral virtue was insufficient to rule them, and the end of government is the freedom and security of the individual. In civil communities, civil rights rest on the natural rights inherited from the original condition of mankind. These natural rights include the maximum of freedom of action and thought that is compatible with the natural rights of others. Civil authority should interfere with the natural freedom of individuals only in so far as is required to ensure and protect the security and happiness of the majority of the people.

RIIS, JACOB AUGUST (1849–1914), Danish-born reformer, journalist, and author, came to New York City (1870), where his own experiences in the slums and his observations as a police reporter on New York papers led him to declare war on tenement conditions, child labor, and other abuses of lower-class urban life. His lone fight was aided later by Theodore Roosevelt, who, as head of the city police board, as New York governor, and as U.S. President, gave him great support. Among Riis's books describing his work were *How the Other Half Lives* (1890); *The Children of the Poor* (1892); *Out of Mulberry Street* (1898); and *The Battle with the Slum* (1902). *The Making of an American* (1901) is an autobiography.

RILEY, JAMES WHITCOMB (1849–1916), Indiana poet, contributed to the *Indianapolis Journal* (1877–85) a series of genial poems in rustic dialect, ostensibly written by "Benj. F. Johnson, of Boone." The series, which included "When the Frost Is on the Punkin," was published in *The Old Swimmin'-Hole and 'Leven More Poems* (1883). This was the first of a number of books marked by the frequent use of Hoosier dialect, a simple sentimentality, a quaint whimsical kindliness, and cheerful philosophy, blended with a frequently obtrusive pathos. The most popular of the poems were "Little Orphant Annie," "The Old Man and Jim," "Knee-Deep in June," and "The Raggedy Man."

RINEHART, MARY ROBERTS (1876–1958), born in Pittsburgh, established herself as a leading author of mystery stories with her first books, *The Circular Staircase* (1908) and *The Man in Lower Ten* (1909). The former was dramatized with Avery Hopwood as *The Bat* (1920). She continued to write popular stories of horror and crime detection, as well as several plays and a series of humorous novels whose heroine is the eccentric old maid "Tish." *My Story* (1931, revised 1948) is her autobiography.

Rip Van Winkle, tale by Irving,♦ published in *The Sketch Book*♦ (1819–20). Joseph Jefferson is famous for his acting of the title role in a dramatic version, which he made with Boucicault in 1865.

Rip, an indolent, good-natured Dutch-American, lives with his shrewish wife in a village on the Hudson during the years before the Revolution. One day, while hunting in the Catskills with his dog Wolf, he meets a dwarf-like stranger dressed in the ancient Dutch fashion. He helps him to carry a keg, and with him joins a party silently engaged in a game of ninepins. After drinking of the liquor they furnish, he falls into a sleep which lasts 20 years, during which the Revolutionary War takes place. He awakes as an old man, returns to his altered village, is greeted by his old dog, who dies of the excitement, and finds that his wife has long been dead. Rip and his associates are almost forgotten, but he goes to live with his daughter, now grown and the mother of a family, and soon wins new friends by his generosity and cheerfulness.

Rise of American Civilization, The, history by Charles A. Beard♦ and Mary R. Beard.♦

Rise of Silas Lapham, The, novel by Howells,♦ published in 1885.

Colonel Silas Lapham, a typical self-made businessman, has risen from a Vermont farm to wealth and prominence as a paint manufacturer. He establishes his family in Boston, where he begins to build a mansion, and urges his wife, Persis, and their daughters, Penelope and Irene, to enter Brahmin society, for which their wealth would seem to qualify them. Tom Corey and Penelope, the older and more intelligent sister, are in love, but he belongs to the social group to which the Laphams cannot attain, and there is a misunderstanding when Irene, immature and impulsive, believes that Tom returns her love for him. Penelope refuses his proposal, and, at the Coreys' dinner party, which Penelope does not attend, Silas gets drunk and reveals himself as a brash and sturdy *nouveau riche*. He has meanwhile been speculating unsuccessfully and faces bankruptcy. His only hope is the sale of a milling property to an English syndicate, and his former partner, Rogers, presses him to this action, although both know that this will result in disaster to the syndicate. When Lapham's fair play and integrity cause him to refuse the opportunity, he is ruined and returns to Vermont. Although he has fallen in the social scale, he has risen morally. Tom and Penelope are married and go to Mexico to escape the unhappy background of social distinctions between their families.

Rise of the Dutch Republic, The, history by J.L. Motley. ♦

Road Not Taken, The, poem in iambic tetrameter by Robert Frost,♦ published in *Mountain Interval* (1916).
    The poet tells how the course of his life was determined when he came upon two roads that diverged in a wood. Forced to choose, he "took the one less traveled by, And that has made all the difference."

Road to Xanadu, The, a critical study (1927) by John Livingston Lowes (1867–1945), analyzing Coleridge's creative imagination. ♦

Roan Stallion, allegorical narrative in free verse by Jeffers,♦ published in *Roan Stallion, Tamar, and Other Poems* (1925).
    California, a young half-breed woman, is married to Johnny, a farmer of the California mountains. Although she is devoted to her daughter Christine, she loathes her sordid life with her brutal and obscene husband, and longs for a passionate emotional experience, which even her Catholic faith fails to give her. Then her husband brings home a beautiful roan stallion, who arouses in California's primitive mind a feeling of love and adoration, partly sexual, partly religious. After a wild ride in the night, which she imagines to be a sexual encounter, she returns to the drunkenly amorous Johnny, from whose advances she escapes in disgust. She runs to the corral, where he follows, and California helps the stallion to kill her husband, by shooting a dog who interferes. After Johnny has been trampled to death, she is "moved by some obscure human fidelity" to shoot the stallion, and then turns to her daughter "the mask of a woman who has killed God."

ROBBINS, Tom (1936–   ), North Carolina-born author of bizarre fiction very popular in paperback. *Another Roadside Attraction* (1971) is set at the hot dog stand north of Seattle (the author's home area) owned by John and Amanda Ziller, whose friend Plucky Purcell chances on the mummified body of Christ, which he delivers to them as an adornment for their place of business. His next novel, *Even Cowgirls Get the Blues* (1976), almost equally fantastic, is a picaresque tale of a hitchhiking girl with vastly oversized thumbs who ends up at a wild health ranch for cowgirls. *Still Life with Woodpecker* (1980) deals with the daughter of a foreign king exiled in Seattle who has a love affair with a rebellious young American who believes in remaking the world with dynamite and drugs and from whom she learns how to decipher cabalistic messages, of which the most meaningful is found in the pictures and text of a pack of Camel cigarettes. Robbins's eccentric themes, somewhat in the vein of Vonnegut, Brautigan, and Pynchon, are treated in a style marked by whimsical similes and wild wisecracks.

ROBERTS, Elizabeth Madox (1881–1941), born in the Kentucky farming region, which she described in her fiction, graduated from the University of Chicago (1921). Her first publications were volumes of verse, *In the Great Steep's Garden* (1915) and *Under the Tree* (1922, enlarged 1930), and her later poetry is collected in *Song in the Meadow* (1940), containing lyrics and verse legends. *The Time of Man* (1926), her first novel, set in the Kentucky countryside, deals with poor whites possessed by the restless pioneer urge. *My Heart and My Flesh* (1927), another novel with a pastoral background, is the tragic story of a woman driven to the verge of madness. The author's scrupulous and effective recreation of folk customs and speech distinguishes her further fiction, which includes *Jingling in the Wind* (1928), a satirical fantasy whose chief character is a rainmaker on his way to a professional convention; *The Great Meadow* (1930), a historical novel, depicting the beauty and terror of pioneer life in Kentucky; *A Buried Treasure* (1931), a humorous narrative about a farmer and his wife who discover a pot of gold; *The Haunted Mirror* (1932), short stories of Kentucky mountain folk; *He Sent Forth a Raven* (1935), a novel concerned with the relation of farmers to the soil they till; *Black Is My Truelove's Hair* (1938), the story of a village girl and the two love affairs that shape her life; and *Not by Strange Gods* (1941), stories mainly about Kentucky women.

ROBERTS, Kenneth [Lewis] (1885–1957), Maine author known for his historical novels, including *Arundel* (1930), the story of Benedict Arnold's expedition against Quebec, and its sequels, *Rabble in Arms* (1933) and *Captain Caution* (1934); *Northwest Passage* (1937), about Robert Rogers's campaigns against the Indians and his search for a Northwest Passage; and *Oliver Wiswell* (1940), presenting the American Revolution as seen by a colonial soldier and historian loyal to England.

Robert's Rules of Order, manual of parliamentary procedure (1876, revised 1915, 1943), by General Henry Martyn Robert (1837–1923), a military engineer.

ROBINSON, Edwin Arlington (1869–1935), was reared in Gardiner, Me., the prototype of his Tilbury Town, and after studying at Harvard (1891–93) was employed in New York City. His first volume of poems, *The Torrent and the Night Before* (1896), was privately printed. In these early poems, strongly influenced by his reading of Hardy, he presents the first of his spare, incisive portraits of the people of his Tilbury Town,♦ marked by a dry New England manner that proved cryptic to his few readers. One reviewer stated that "The world is not beautiful to him, but a prison house," to which Robinson later replied: "The world is not a 'prison-house,' but a kind of spiritual kindergarten where bewildered infants are trying to spell God with the wrong blocks." Some of the poems of this book were reprinted, with additions, in *The Children of the Night* (1897), containing the "Credo" in which the poet recognizes that there is "not a glimmer" for one who "welcomes when he fears, the black and awful chaos of the night"; but states that he feels "the coming glory of the Light" through an intuition of a spiritual guidance that transcends the life of the senses. Many of the other poems are psychological portraits, similar in form to those of Browning, including such character studies as those of the wealthy and wise Richard Cory, who committed suicide for lack of a positive reason for being; Cliff Klingenhagen, with his mysterious ironic philosophy of life; the spiteful miser Aaron Stark; Luke Havergal, the bereaved lover; and romantic old John Evereldown.

The Children of the Night impressed Theodore Roosevelt, and, upon the publication of *Captain Craig* (1902), the President helped Robinson escape from work as inspector of subway construction to a clerkship in the New York Custom House (1905–10). *The Town Down the River* (1910) contains "Miniver Cheevy"♦ and other portraits. After this date, Robinson was able to give his entire time to poetry, much of which he wrote during his annual summer residence at the MacDowell Colony in New Hampshire.

"The Man Against the Sky"♦ is the title piece of a collection of poems (1916) setting forth the author's philosophy of life with striking symbolic power. Other poems in the volume include "Flammonde,"♦ "Cassandra,"♦ and the Shakespearean study "Ben Jonson Entertains a Man from Stratford." With *Merlin* (1917) he began the Arthurian trilogy completed by *Lancelot* (1920) and *Tristram* (1927, Pulitzer Prize), in which he studied the characters as individuals who act according to their particular passions, independently of supernatural powers. *The Three Taverns* (1920) contains poems further illustrating this attitude, and a volume of *Collected Poems* the next year won a Pulitzer Prize.

Robinson's steady production of verse continued with *Roman Bartholow* (1923), a dramatic narrative presenting a subtle psychological analysis of a sick soul; *The Man Who Died Twice* (1924, Pulitzer Prize), the tragic story of a man's dissipation of his artistic genius; "Dionysus in Doubt," the title poem in a collection (1925), and "Demos and Dionysus" criticize the standardization and materialism of equalitarian society, which the poet found inimical to "romance and love and art" and to the development in a transcendental fashion of the individual "self and soul"; *Cavender's House* (1929), a blank-verse dialogue between Cavender and the ghost of the wife he murdered for a supposed infidelity; *The Glory of the Nightingales* (1930), a verse narrative concerned with the rivalry between two friends for the love of a woman, and their later reconciliation; *Matthias at the Door* (1931), in which the chief figure, through bitter disillusion, loses his egocentric complacency and learns to understand others; *Nicodemus* (1932), adding ten poems to the body of his work, including four on Biblical themes; *Talifer* (1933), a narrative of modern life, which shows the poet in a novel mood of optimistic cheer; *Amaranth* (1934), a somber narrative concerned with a group of frustrated artists; and *King Jasper* (1935), a poetic narrative that constitutes a final statement of Robinson's sense of the tragedy of human life in a chaotic world, and of his unfaltering mystic faith in a "glimmer" of light beyond. He collected his *Sonnets, 1889–1927* (1928), and a selection from his letters was published in 1940.

As an heir of the New England traditions of Puritanism and Transcendentalism, with their emphasis upon the individual, Robinson has been termed a sober Transcendentalist who dealt primarily with the ethical conflicts within the individual and measured the value of the isolated person by his truth to himself. With the reserve typical of the New Englander, he most frequently employed the objective form of dramatic monologue, and, with the traditionalism inherent in his background, confined his experimentation to the use of common speech rhythms, rather than to the creation of new stanzaic forms. His quality of mind is organically expressed by his style, which itself quietly fuses tradition with originality, and romance with realism.

Rocked in the Cradle of the Deep, poem by Emma Willard. ♦

Roderick Hudson, novel by Henry James, ♦ published in 1876. The character Christina also appears in *The Princess Casamassima.* ♦

Rowland Mallet, a wealthy connoisseur, struck by the genius of the amateur sculptor Roderick Hudson, takes the youth abroad to develop his art. Among their friends in Rome are Gloriani, a brilliant French sculptor; Sam Singleton, a modest American painter; Augusta Blanchard, an undistinguished American art student; and shrewd, benevolent old Madame Grandoni. Gloriani predicts that Roderick will "fizzle out," but this does not disturb the confident youth, who studies enthusiastically and produces several fine statues in the intervals between "sterile moods." He depends much on the stimulation of others and is considerably altered after meeting Christina Light, fascinating daughter of an expatriated American widow. He loses interest in sculpture, and Rowland summons from New England Roderick's mother and his fiancée, Mary Garland, who has also attracted Rowland. Roderick's fine bust of his mother is his last important work, for Christina, bowing to her mother's ambitious urging, marries the rich Prince Casamassima. The youth cannot overcome his infatuation, and after a time goes with his friends to Switzerland, where they meet Christina and her husband. With a sudden return of ardor, Roderick attempts to follow

her, and for this purpose even attempts to borrow from Mary, at which Rowland angrily condemns him as an ungrateful egotist. Roderick walks off into the mountains, where he is caught in a thunderstorm. When his body is discovered, it is uncertain whether he fell or jumped from a cliff.

ROETHKE, THEODORE (1908–63), born in Michigan, graduated from its state university and after further study at Harvard began a career of teaching English at various universities, from 1947 at the University of Washington. His career as a poet began with *Open House* (1941), brief, intense lyrics already marked by the plant imagery of growth and decay that pervades all his poetry. *The Lost Son* (1948) lyrically presents psychic and physical biographical experiences of the maturing boy and man. *Praise to the End!* (1951) continues in a more mystic, visionary strain, showing an affinity to Yeats. *The Waking* (1953, Pulitzer Prize) and *Words for the Wind* (1958, Bollingen Prize) collect early and late work, showing great variety and great sensitivity. *I Am! Says the Lamb* (1961) is light verse but in the vein of Blake, and *The Far Field* (1964) is a posthumous gathering, whose final section was printed in a limited education as *Sequence, Sometimes Metaphysical* (1964). *On the Poet and His Craft* (1965) contains essays and lectures, and his *Selected Letters* appeared in 1968. *Straw for the Fire* (1972) comes from his notebooks.

Roger Malvin's Burial, story by Hawthorne, ♦ published in *The Token* (1832) and in *Mosses from an Old Manse* (1846).

Two wounded survivors of a foray against Indians, led by John Lovewell, make their escape through the Maine woods. Roger Malvin, an old man mortally injured, urges his young companion, Reuben Bourne, to desert him and seek safety. Reuben protests, but is finally persuaded and promises to send help. He makes his way home, but cannot bring himself to tell Dorcas Malvin of the circumstances in which he left her father. He claims to have buried him in the forest, is hailed as a hero, and soon marries Dorcas. Their life is not happy, for his conscience disturbs him, and when their son Cyrus is 15, they leave the settlement to seek a new home in the wilderness. One evening Reuben accidentally shoots his son while hunting, and is horrified to discover the boy's body at the same spot where he left Malvin, years before. Dorcas discovers her son's death, and falls unconscious. The upper branch of an oak, where Reuben hung a bloody handkerchief as a signal, has withered and now crumbles and drops, while Reuben prays, feeling that at last his crime is expiated and the curse lifted.

ROLFE, JOHN (1585–1622), English-born colonist, came to Virginia (1609), where he was a leading cultivator of tobacco, and instrumental in making it Virginia's staple commodity. He fell in love with Pocahontas, ♦ daughter of a leading Indian chief, and his marriage to her (1614) ensured peace with the Indians for several years. While on a voyage to England his wife died (1617), and he returned to become a colonial official. In 1622 the Indians destroyed his home, and he seems to have died at their hands. He wrote a description of Virginia for the king, first printed in the *Southern Literary Messenger* (June 1839), and is a figure in J.E. Cooke's novel *My Lady Pokahontas* (1885) and other fiction about his wife.

RÖLVAAG, O[LE] E[DVART] (1876–1931), born in Norway, came to the U.S. in 1896, and attended St. Olaf College, Minnesota, at which he became a professor of Norwegian (1907–31). His *Letters from America* (1912), like all his works, was written in his native language. This book purported to be a collection of correspondence from a young Norwegian in America to his family at home, and was a semi-autobiographical account of the gradual adjustment of an immigrant to the U.S. Rölvaag's greatest works were *Giants in the Earth* (1927), *Peder Victorious* (1929), and *Their Fathers' God* (1931), a trilogy of epic power, realistically depicting the life of the Norwegian immigrants on the northwestern frontier of the U.S., and the psychological effect of the stern pioneer life upon the people whose titanic labors are a constant struggle against the impersonal forces of nature.

Roman Catholic Church in America had its beginnings in the legendary connection between the Norse discoveries of the New World and the medieval church in Greenland. Its modern history began with the colonization by Spain and France. Permanent dioceses were established in Santo Domingo, Haiti, and Puerto Rico (1511), and the see of Cuba ruled the mainland churches (1522–45). The first parish within the boundaries of the present U.S. was established at St. Augustine, Fla. (1565). During the ensuing centuries, much missionary work was done by the Capuchins, Jesuits, ♦ and Franciscans. In the

American territories outside the present U.S., colonization and proselyting have resulted in the dominance of the Catholic faith. In the English colonies, Catholicism was generally attacked, except in Maryland, which was founded by the Catholic Calvert family, and in Rhode Island and Pennsylvania, where there was religious toleration. John Carroll became the first Catholic bishop in the U.S. (1789), when there were approximately 30,000 Catholics in the country. The increase to *c.*49,000,000 by 1980, in large part owing to immigration from Ireland, Germany, and Italy, occasioned in the 19th century much antagonism in this predominantly Protestant country. Although this feeling was chiefly temporary or local, it resulted in such politico-religious movements as the Know-Nothings. Widespread contributions to American culture result not only from the Church's many schools, colleges, and periodical publications but also from the various activities of its members.

Romance, generic name applied to prose fiction that is conceived in terms of the fanciful and idealistic, rather than in terms of observation and faithful description of fact. In his preface to *The House of the Seven Gables,* Hawthorne states that a novel "is presumed to aim at a very minute fidelity, not merely to the possible, but to the probable and ordinary course of man's experience." A romance, on the other hand, while it must keep to "the truth of the human heart—has fairly a right to present that truth under circumstances . . . of the writer's own choosing or creation . . . he may so manage its atmospherical medium as to bring out or mellow the lights and deepen and enrich the shadows of the picture."

Romanticism, term that is associated with imagination and boundlessness, and in critical usage is contrasted with classicism, which is commonly associated with reason and restriction. A romantic attitude may be detected in literature of any period, but as a historical movement it arose in the 18th and 19th centuries in reaction to more rational literary, philosophic, artistic, religious, and economic standards. Since it gathered force gradually in its various manifestations, it does not lend itself to the limitations of a concise summary. The most profound and comprehensive ideal of romanticism is the vision of a greater personal freedom for the individual. Its origins may be traced to the economic rise of the middle class, struggling to free itself from feudal and monarchial restrictions; to the individualism of the Renaissance; to the Reformation, which was based on the belief in an immediate relationship between man and God; to scientific deism, which emphasized the deity's benevolence; to the psychology of Locke, Hartley, and others, who contended that minds are formed by environmental conditions, thus seeming to indicate that all men are created equal and may be improved by environmental changes; to the optimistic humanitarianism of Shaftesbury; and to the writings of Rousseau, who contended that man is naturally good, institutions alone having made him wicked. In American literature, such general influences were strengthened by the great English and French romantic authors, the "storm and stress" writers of Germany, and the idealistic philosophy of Kant. To these were added many indigenous forces: a realized political democracy; the individualism, buoyancy, and optimism of the frontier; the idealism latent in Calvinism, as expressed by Jonathan Edwards and others; intimacy with the wilderness; a predominantly agrarian background; and recognition of the heroism of early Americans.

The romantic movement in America, as elsewhere, left its impress not only on the arts, but also in the more practical spheres of action, as in revolutionary activities for political freedom and individual rights; humanitarian reform (Abolitionism and feminism); liberal religious movements (Unitarianism and Universalism); labor reform (Knights of Labor); and economic experiments in communal living (Brook Farm and New Harmony). The most clearly defined romantic literary movement in the U.S was Transcendentalism,♦ centered at Concord (c.1836–60). Characteristics of the romantic movement exemplified in American literature are sentimentalism (*The Sketch Book*); primitivism and the cult of the "noble savage" (*Hiawatha*); political liberalism (Jefferson, Paine, Barlow); the celebration of natural beauty and the simple life (Cooper, Emerson, Thoreau); introspection (Poe, Thoreau); idealization of the common man, uncorrupted by civilization (Whittier, Cooper); interest in the picturesque past (Irving, Hawthorne); interest in remote places (Melville, Bayard Taylor); medievalism (Longfellow); antiquarianism leading to the revival of the popular ballad (Longfellow, Whittier); the Gothic romance (Brown); concern with a crepuscular world of mystery (Poe, Chivers); individualism (Emerson, Thoreau, Whit-

man); technical innovation (Whitman's prosody); humanitarianism (*The Biglow Papers, Uncle Tom's Cabin*); morbid melancholy (Poe); native legendry (*Evangeline*); and the historical romance (Simms, Cooper).

These characteristics also appear in other arts. The interests that created the Gothic romance♦ also created the Gothic Revival, an architectural movement based on medieval styles, whose design carried the eye above the actual form and conjured up imaginative associations. In painting, romanticism effected the change from the severe portraiture of the 18th century to the work of the Hudson River school, which emphasized the charm and grandeur of the American landscape.

After the original impulse of the movement declined, its forces continued as fashions down to the turn of the century. Although the local-color movement♦ fostered the rise of realism, it also perpetuated the romanticist's interest in strange places and unusual customs. Sentimentalism appeared in the stories of Bret Harte, and exoticism in those of Cable and Hearn. Even such predominantly realistic authors as Clemens veered from vivid depiction of contemporary scenes to historical romancing and idyllic representations of youth. Lesser novelists like Lew Wallace and F.M. Crawford purveyed romantic ideas to the masses. Aldrich, Boker, Taylor, Stoddard, Stedman, and Gilder tended to imitate earlier romantic poets, and, lacking originality, so relied on attenuated romantic conventions that they came to represent the last stand for the genteel elements in the movement. While the genteel tradition found many revolutionary opponents in the advocates of realism♦ and naturalism,♦ both tradition and iconoclasm were products of the romantic movement. New forces were coupled with the old, as for instance when romanticism felt the impact of Freudian psychology, as seen in works by innumerable American authors from the 1920s on.

ROOSEVELT, THEODORE (1858–1919), born in New York City of a distinguished family, graduated from Harvard (1880). After writing a history of *The Naval Operations of the War Between Great Britain and the United States—1812–1815* (1882), he entered politics, serving in the state legislature (1882–84), where he led the Republican "insurgents" against Blaine. He retired to his ranch in Dakota Territory after Blaine's nomination, wrote books on his life in the West and biographies of Thomas Hart Benton (1886) and Gouverneur Morris (1888), and began *The Winning of the West,* before returning to politics (1886) and serving as assistant secretary of the navy (1896–98), retiring to help organize the Rough Riders, in whose Spanish-American War exploits he became the popular hero. His newly won reputation brought him the governorship of New York (1898–1900), but his reforms alienated conservatives, who "shelved" him in the vice-presidency (1900–09), only to have him become President (1901) upon McKinley's assassination.

In addition to his early books, he used authorship to promote his beliefs and tell of his adventures in and out of politics. *The Winning of the West* (4 vols., 1889–96) is considered his most significant work, and others include *American Ideals and Other Essays* (1897); *The Rough Riders* (1899); *The Strenuous Life* (1900), concerned with personal conflicts resulting from his philosophy of life; *African Game Trails* (1910), an account of his hunting expeditions; *African and European Addresses* (1910), a discussion of colonial problems; *The New Nationalism* (1910), a statement of beliefs embodied in his Bull Moose party; *History as Literature, and Other Essays* (1913), on the theory of history illustrated in *The Winning of the West; Theodore Roosevelt: An Autobiography* (1913); *Through the Brazilian Wilderness* (1914), an account of an exploration; and *America and the World War* (1915), *Fear God and Take Your Own Part* (1916), and *The Great Adventure* (1918), views on World War I.

Roots, account by Alex Haley♦ of the successful search for his antecedents, imported to America in slavery from Gambia. Published in 1976, it won a Pulitzer Prize and when dramatized for television inspired a very large audience to an interest in black history and in genealogy.

ROSENFELD, MORRIS (1862–1923), born in Russian Poland, came to the U.S. in 1886, where he eked out an existence in New York City sweatshops. His Yiddish poems, plaintively singing the woes of the workers or satirizing social injustices, attracted the attention of Leo Wiener of Harvard, who translated his work as *Songs from the Ghetto* (1898). This, and later works on similar subjects and on the problems of his fellow Jews, brought Rosenfeld wide notice. His verses are among the earliest Yiddish literature in America.

ROSS, LEONARD Q., pseudonym of Leo Rosten. ♦

ROSTEN, LEO [CALVIN] (1908–   ), political scientist, teacher, and humorist, born in Poland, was brought to the U.S. as an infant, and later educated at the University of Chicago (A.B., 1930; Ph.D., 1937). He is the author of *The Washington Correspondents* (1937), a study of the function, techniques, and personnel of the capital's journalists, and of *Hollywood: The Movie Colony, The Movie Makers* (1941), a similar sociological study of the film center. Under his pseudonym Leonard Q. Ross he has written popular fiction: *The Education of H*Y*M*A*N   K*A*P*L*A*N** (1937), humorous sketches of a New York evening school for adults and its immigrant students' unorthodox approach to the English language, and *The Return of H*Y*M*A*N K*A*P*L*A*N* (1959) and *O K*A*P*L*A*N! My K*A*P*L*A*N!* (1976), sequels. Under his own name he has published *Captain Newman, M.D.* (1961), a witty but serious novel about an army psychiatrist; *The Many Worlds of L*E*O R*O*S*-T*E*N* (1964), a collection of 30 years of writing; *A Most Private Intrigue* (1967), a spy story; *The Joys of Yiddish* (1968); *The 3:10 to Anywhere* (1976), reminiscences of travel; and *Passions and Prejudices* (1978), essays.

ROTH, PHILIP (1933–   ), New Jersey-born author, after graduation from Bucknell and an M.A. from the University of Chicago taught English there and creative writing at Iowa and Princeton. His first book, for which he won a National Book Award, was *Goodbye, Columbus* (1959), whose title novella and five short stories present witty, ironic, and perceptive depictions of Jewish life in the U.S. in a flip, personal style. *Letting Go* (1962), his first novel, employs something of the same vein less successfully in treating the lives of young Jewish intellectuals at the University of Chicago, in New York, and elsewhere. His succeeding fiction is *When She Was Good* (1967), a removal from his basic subject and territory in treating a Midwestern Protestant housewife who is destructively dedicated to reforming first her father, then her husband; *Portnoy's Complaint*♦ (1969), a wildly comic depiction of his middle-class New York Jewish world in the portrait of Alexander Portnoy, whose possessive mother makes him so guiltily insecure that he can seek relief only in elaborate masturbation and sex with forbidden Gentile girls; *Our*

Gang (1971), a broad satire of President Trick E. Dixon; *The Breast* (1972), a novella about a male professor of literature who suffers a Kafka-like transformation into a gigantic breast; *The Great American Novel* (1973), at once a burlesque and an allegory, its telling of the downfall of a great baseball team serving as a satirical parallel to contemporary American political and social events; *My Life as a Man* (1974), depicting the personal and literary frustrations of an author, partly through two of his short stories; and *The Professor of Desire* (1977), a novel about the romances of the Jewish professor who was the subject of *The Breast*. *The Ghost Writer* (1979) is a brief but intricate tale about a young writer who, when accused of travestying his fellow Jews, seeks counsel from a respected older Jewish author and finds this distinguished figure ambiguously involved with a girl whom the young writer fantasizes to be Anne Frank. *Zuckerman Unbound* (1981) is a sequel about the young writer years later as a major American author and his poignant personal life; *The Anatomy Lesson* (1983) is a third portrayal of Zuckerman, aged 40 and having lost "his health, his hair, and his subject;" and *Zuckerman Bound* (1985) prints the trilogy and an epilog. The psychosomatically sick author caught in a writer's block and castigated by an academic critic as the writer of trivial, scurrilous, and anti-Semitic fiction yearns for a new career as a doctor. *Reading Myself* (1975) collects interviews, essays, and articles.

Roughing It, autobiographical narrative by Clemens,♦ published in 1872 under his pseudonym Mark Twain. He records a journey from St. Louis across the plains to Nevada, a visit to the Mormons, and life and adventures in Virginia City, San Francisco, and the Sandwich Islands. The book is based on Clemens's own experiences during the 1860s, but facts are left far behind in his creation of a picture of the frontier spirit and its lusty humor. The entire work is unified by the character of the author and the ways in which his experiences changed him into a representative of the Far West, but seemingly little attempt is made to integrate the tall tales, vivid descriptions, narratives of adventure, and character sketches, except in so far as all of them constitute a vigorous, many-sided portrait of the Western frontier.

Rover Boys, series of books for boys by Edward Stratemeyer. ♦

ROWLANDSON, MARY [WHITE] (*c.*1635–*c.*1678), daughter of John White, an early settler and wealthy proprietor of Lancaster, Mass., in 1656 married Joseph Rowlandson, a Congregational minister. During King Philip's War, when the Narragansett attacked Lancaster (Feb. 10, 1676), she was abducted by the Indians, who held her for 11 weeks and five days, until she was ransomed. Her account of this captivity was published in Cambridge (1682) as *The Sovereignty & Goodness of God, Together with the Faithfulness of His Promises Displayed; Being a Narrative of the Captivity and Restauration of Mrs. Mary Rowlandson.* This was the second edition; the first edition, which has not been found, was apparently published earlier in the same year. The book is one of the most popular examples of 17th-century American prose and has been reprinted and reedited approximately 30 times. In pure, idiomatic, sinewy English, Mrs. Rowlandson shows the dangers in which the settlers lived, their contempt for the Indians, their devout dependence upon the Bible for support, and their actual treatment during such enforced captivities.

ROWSON, SUSANNA [HASWELL] (*c.*1762–1824), English-born author, accompanied her father, a naval lieutenant, to his station in Massachusetts. The family returned to England in 1777, where she published several novels, including *Charlotte Temple*♦ (1791), a sentimental didactic romance, which was extremely popular in the U.S., where it is mainly set. She came to the U.S. (1793), where she appeared on the stage, and wrote a topical comic opera, *Slaves in Algiers* (1794); *The Volunteers* (1795), a musical farce; *The Female Patriot* (1795), adapted from Massinger's *The Bondsman; Americans in England* (1796), a social comedy revised as *The Columbian Daughter* (1800); *Reuben and Rachel; or, Tales of Old Times* (1798), a historical novel tracing the lives of some descendants of Columbus; *Miscellaneous Poems* (1804); *Sarah; or, The Exemplary Wife* (1813), a semi-autobiographical novel; and the posthumously published *Charlotte's Daughter; or, The Three Orphans* (1828), a sequel to *Charlotte Temple*, usually known as *Lucy Temple.*

ROYCE, JOSIAH (1855–1916), born in California, graduated from the state university (1875), and had a deep feeling for his native background, exhibited in *California . . . A Study of American Character* (1886) and his only novel, *The Feud of Oakfield Creek* (1887), treating the same conflict that is central to Frank Norris's *The Octopus.* He was brought to Harvard (1882) by William James, with whom he remained friendly, though they split on philosophic ideas. *The Religious Aspect of Philosophy* (1885) postulates a goodness at the heart of things that "satisfies the highest moral needs," and proceeds to prove that there is an absolute or universal knower affirming judgments and experiencing objects transcending man's limitations. *The Conception of God* (1897) sustains the autonomy of the individual by contending that the absolute Will is distributed among human beings for independent use. *The Philosophy of Loyalty* (1908) contends that individual salvation lies in loyalty to a cause, supplemented by "loyalty to loyalty." Among his many other works, the most popular was *The Spirit of Modern Philosophy* (1892), which brilliantly examines the whole field, with particular attention to such German idealists as Fichte, to whom his beliefs were indebted.

Ruggles of Red Gap, novel by H.L. Wilson. ♦

RUKEYSER, MURIEL (1913–80), New York poet, whose poems in *Theory of Flight* (1935), *U.S. 1* (1938), *A Turning Wind* (1939), *Wake Island* (1942), *Beast in View* (1944), *The Green Wave* (1948), *Orpheus* (1949), *Body of Waking* (1958), *Waterlily Fire* (1962), *The Speed of Darkness* (1968), *Breaking Open* (1973), *The Gates* (1976), and *Collected Poems* (1979) are marked by elliptical, metaphysical style and intense feeling concerned with the solution of individual problems through social justice, also seen in her long poem, *The Soul and Body of John Brown* (1940). Her other books include *Willard Gibbs: American Genius* (1942), a prose study; *One Life* (1957), an interpretation of Wendell Willkie in prose and verse; *The Life of Poetry* (1949); translations of the *Selected Poems of Octavio Paz* (1963); *The Orgy* (1965), evoking the rites of Ireland's Puck Fair; and *The Traces of Thomas Hariot* (1971), a study of the English scientist and his influence.

Rules by Which a Great Empire May Be Reduced to a Small One, satirical essay by Franklin, ♦ published in the *Public Advertiser* (London, Sept. 1773).

In this popular hoax, Franklin ironically assumes that the minister to whom his rules are addressed wishes to reduce the extensive dominions that he must govern. The rules that he offers as solutions of this problem contain actual grievances of the American colonies against the mother country, e.g. don't send wise or good governors, don't hesitate to impose heavy taxes, don't fail to perplex colonial commerce with infinite regulations, don't notice petitions, don't treat the colonists except as though they were about to revolt. He blandly affirms that close adherence to such rules will assuredly have the desired result of losing the colonies.

RUNYON, [ALFRED] DAMON (1884–1946), journalist and sports columnist, also known for his short stories of the underworld, professional athletes, Broadway hangers-on, and other American types, distinguished for their use and invention of slang. These were collected in such volumes as *Guys and Dolls* (1932), which inspired the musical comedy of the same title (1950) by Abe Burrows and others, *Take It Easy* (1938), *My Wife Ethel* (1940), *Runyon à la Carte* (1944), *In Our Town* (1946), and *Short Takes* (1946). With Howard Lindsay he wrote the farce *A Slight Case of Murder* (1935).

RYNNING, OLE (1809–38), leader of Norwegian colonists, came to Illinois (1837), where before his untimely death he wrote the book published in Norway (1838) and later translated as *A True Account of America for the Information and Help of Peasant and Commoner.* This work, comprehensively surveying American climate, soil, government, language, religious toleration, and opportunities for immigration, was known among Norwegian peasants as the "America Book," and was instrumental in encouraging the great Norwegian migration.

S

Sacred Fount, The, novelette by Henry James,♦ published in 1901.

The narrator, whose temperament and interests resemble those of the author, is a guest at an English weekend party, where his excessively refined curiosity becomes absorbed in studying Guy and Grace Brissenden, the husband not yet 30, and the wife in her middle forties, who after a few years of marriage seem to have exchanged physical and mental ages. He derives from their case a "law" that, in such uneven matches, the older partner always draws energy, youth, and wit from the "sacred fount" of the other's personality, which becomes correspondingly depleted. Then he attempts to apply his law to another guest, Gilbert Long, who seems to have exchanged his character of a stupid though handsome young man for that of a witty and understanding man of the world. The narrator's prying mind seeks to discover the mistress who must have given Long this new power. Rejecting the bright, superficial Lady John, he settles on Mrs. May Server, an attractive woman who is obviously attempting to conceal a profound emotional disturbance and weakness. He even believes that he observes a realignment of the couples, resulting from the mutual weakness and defeat of Brissenden and Mrs. Server, and the common vigor and strength of will of Long and "poor Briss's" wife. His whole structure of hypothesis is overthrown, however, when Mrs. Brissenden says he is "crazy" and repudiates his hinted accusations as "houses of cards," though it is never certain whether his rout is caused by lies on her part or by his own unduly fanciful conjectures.

Sacred Wood, The, essays by T.S. Eliot. ♦

St. Nicholas (1873–1940), monthly magazine for children, was long distinguished for the high quality of its fiction, and its realization that a children's magazine should not "be a milk-and-water variety of the periodical for adults," or a place for "sermonizing" or "wearisome spinning out of facts." In addition to Mary Mapes Dodge, the editor (1873–1905), contributors included Rebecca Harding Davis, D.G. Mitchell, Trowbridge, Louisa May Alcott, Frank Stockton, Frances Hodgson Burnett, C.E. Carryl, Edward Eggleston, Mayne Reid, T.N. Page, Clemens, Howard Pyle, Stevenson, Henty, Kipling, Cable, Howells, Burroughs, Harte, A.B. Paine, Palmer Cox, and Gelett Burgess. At the turn of the century, when the regular contributions seemed to be less significant, the magazine established a department of contributions from its juvenile readers. Among the authors who thus received their first publication were E.B. White, Edna St. Vincent Millay, Faulkner, F. Scott Fitzgerald, Lardner, the Benéts, Robert Benchley, Elinor Wylie, Edmund Wilson, and Babette Deutsch. After 1930 it changed owners and policies several times, finally becoming a picture magazine for very young children, under the control of the Woolworth Stores (1939).

Salem witchcraft trials occurred at Salem, Mass., the result of a belief in witchcraft assignable not to Puritanism, but to the temper of the times as evidenced also in England and on the Continent. Before 1688 four persons had been hanged for witchcraft near Boston, but the principal outbreak of persecution took place in 1692, when an epidemic disease resembling epilepsy spread through Danvers (part of Salem). Discouraged by the inability of physicians to control this disease, and encouraged by sermons from such clergymen as Cotton Mather, ♦ the belief was soon widespread that evil spirits in the form of witches were able to afflict the people at large. Increase Mather is frequently held responsible for fomenting the trials, although his *Cases of Conscience Concerning Evil Spirits* (1693) showed a rational attitude in disapproving "spectral evidence." During the prevalence of the delusion, in the spring and summer of 1692, 19 persons were hanged; one, Giles Corey, was pressed to death; 55 were frightened or tortured into confessions of guilt; 150 were imprisoned; and more than 200 were named as deserving arrest. Learned and distinguished men promoted the delusion by acquiescing in the proceedings of the court instituted by the governor, Sir William Phips. When the governor's wife, some near relatives of Cotton

Mather, and the sons of ex-Governor Bradstreet became objects of suspicion, the spell began to break. Many of the accusers published solemn recantations, and Samuel Sewall was among those who did public penance, he for his part as a member of the Special Court of Oyer and Terminer.

A Brief and True Narrative of Witchcraft at Salem Village (1692) was written by Deodat Lawson; Cotton Mather's affirmations are to be found in *The Wonders of the Invisible World* (1693) and *A Brand Pluck'd Out of the Burning* (1693), to which Robert Calef replied in *More Wonders of the Invisible World* (1700). Mather in turn replied in *Some Few Remarks Upon a Scandalous Book . . . by One Robert Calef* (1701). A 20th-century edition of the *Narratives of the Witchcraft Cases* (1914) was edited by G.L. Burr. Novels about Salem's witchcraft cases include John Neal's *Rachel Dyer,* Paulding's *The Puritan and His Daughter,* De Forest's "Witching Times," and Esther Forbes's *A Mirror for Witches;* poems include Longfellow's *New England Tragedies;* and plays include J.N. Barker's *Superstition,* Cornelius Mathews's *Witchcraft,* Mary W. Freeman's *Giles Corey, Yeoman,* and Arthur Miller's *The Crucible.*

SALINGER, J[EROME] D[AVID] (1919–), New York-born writer, resident in New Hampshire, began to publish stories in the early 1940s; and after service as an infantry sergeant in Europe during World War II he wrote more stories, but has not chosen to collect them from *Collier's, The Saturday Evening Post, Story,* and other journals. His first book was *The Catcher in the Rye♦* (1951), about an unhappy teenage boy, Holden Caulfield, who runs away from his boarding school as part of his disgust with "phoniness," and who because of his feelings and the idiom in which he communicated them became, particularly for a generation of high-school and college students, a symbol of purity and sensitivity. In *Nine Stories* (1953), printing stories written beginning in 1948, including "A Perfect Day for Bananafish," Salinger introduced his chronicle of an eccentric, warm-hearted family named Glass, continued in his next books of stories. *Franny and Zooey* (1961) presents two members of the Glass family, sister and brother, in two long stories. Franny, a college senior, visits her boyfriend on a football weekend which is made desperately unhappy because she is dissatisfied with him, herself, and life. Zooey, her older brother, a television actor, tries to ease her feelings after this weekend, and

his sensitive aid is first described by their still older brother, Buddy, whom the author calls his "alter ego." *Raise High the Roof-Beam, Carpenters* and *Seymour: An Introduction* (1963), a single volume, reprints stories from *The New Yorker* (1955, 1959), in which Buddy Glass tells, first, of his return to New York during the war to attend his brother Seymour's wedding and of Seymour's jilting of the bride and then of their later elopement; and, second, after Seymour's suicide, of Buddy's own brooding, to the point of breakdown, upon Seymour's virtues, human and literary. In the early 1960s Salinger retired to his rural home, withdrew from the literary scene, and has not published since "Hapworth 16, 1924," a story about Seymour aged seven, in *The New Yorker* (June 19, 1965).

Salmagundi; or, the Whim-Whams and Opinions of Launcelot Langstaff, Esq. and Others, satirical essays and poems, published in 20 periodical pamphlets (Jan. 24, 1807–Jan. 25, 1808), by Washington♦ and William Irving and J.K. Paulding,♦ who used such pseudonyms as Anthony Evergreen, Jeremy Cockloft the Younger, Will Wizard, and Pindar Cockloft, Esq. The work was collected in book form (1808).

Modeled on the *Spectator,* these whimsical pieces travesty contemporary New York's tastes, society, and politics, showing the authors' aristocratic Federalism. The "letters" of the visiting Mustapha-Rub-a-Dub Keli Khan to Asem Haachem satirically describe "mobocratic" and "logocratic" Jeffersonian democracy, while other essays and poems deal in a humorous, pseudo-learned style with such various topics as fashions in women's clothing, the vulgarity of *parvenus,* theatrical and musical criticism, style in literature, and caricatures of celebrities. A second series of *Salmagundi* papers was written by Paulding alone (May 1819–Sept. 1820).

Salut au Monde, poem by Whitman,♦ published as "Poem and Salutation" in *Leaves of Grass* (1856) and given its present title in 1867.

In the form of a colloquy, the poem opens with the demand, "O take my hand, Walt Whitman!" and the question, "What widens within you, Walt Whitman?" This is answered by long catalogues of what the poet sees and hears throughout the world, and the statement,

My spirit has passed in compassion and determination around the whole earth; I have look'd for equals and lovers, and found them ready for me in all lands; I think some divine rapport has equalized me with them.

Sam Spade, detective in novels by Dashiell Hammett. ♦

Sanctuary, novel by Faulkner, ♦ published in 1931. The original text, in which Horace Benbow is the central character, was published in 1981. *Requiem for a Nun* (1951) is a sequel.

Temple Drake, an 18-year-old Mississippi college girl, goes to a petting party with a drunken escort, Gowan Stevens (see *Gavin Stevens*), who wrecks his car on a lonely road. They walk to a nearby house, which is a bootleggers' hideout, inhabited by a number of vicious criminals of whom the chief is the killer Popeye, emasculated and of subnormal intellect as the result of a childhood accident. Temple's cowardly escort escapes after a severe beating, but the girl, whose virginity makes her the object of several attacks, is finally raped by Popeye, who incidentally murders one of his men. He then places her in the Memphis brothel of Miss Reba, who is at first pleased to have the custom of this influential man, then horrified by his degenerate conduct. Goodwin, one of the bootleggers, is arrested for the murder that Popeye committed and is defended by a member of the distinguished Benbow family ♦ of Jefferson, Horace Benbow, a lawyer who wishes to redeem his conventional career by serving justice in this unpopular case. He learns of Popeye's guilt and of the plight of Temple, whom he persuades to testify. The girl's mind is already unbalanced, and her testimony only increases the unreasoning vindictiveness of the jurors, who convict Goodwin. The latter is brutally lynched; Benbow manages to escape with his life; Temple is taken by her broken father to live in Paris; and Popeye, who has escaped to Alabama, is apprehended and hanged for another murder, which he did not commit.

SANDBURG, CARL [AUGUST] (1878–1967), born in Galesburg, Ill., of a Swedish immigrant family, after irregular schooling, and a youth spent as an itinerant laborer throughout the Middle West, went to Puerto Rico as a soldier in the Spanish-American War. On his return he worked his way through Lombard College in Galesburg, and after leaving (1902) became an advertising writer, journalist, and organizer for the Social Democratic party in Wisconsin. He was secretary to the socialist mayor of Milwaukee (1910–12).

His earliest poems were privately printed in a small pamphlet (1904), but he was unknown as a poet until 1914, when *Poetry* published a number of his short pieces, including "Chicago," ♦ whose colloquialism and vigorous free verse stimulated a critical controversy and established him as the leading figure in the Chicago group of authors that was then beginning to flourish. *Chicago Poems* (1916), besides its title piece, contained such vivid impressionistic poems as "Fog," "Grass," and "Nocturne in a Deserted Brickyard," and verses defining the poet's liberal social position, such as "I Am the People, the Mob," and "To a Contemporary Bunk Shooter." These simple, powerful utterances depicted the crude, vital American that the author knew at first hand, and that Whitman had taught him to recognize as symbolic of a free, untrammeled, democratic promised life.

His sensitive appreciation of the beauty of ordinary people and commonplace things, in which he accepted the rude and savage ("Galoots") as well as the delicate and lovely ("Smoke Rose Gold"), was expressed with a firmer touch and greater power in the succeeding collections, *Cornhuskers* (1918; special Pulitzer award, 1919), *Smoke and Steel* (1920), *Slabs of the Sunburnt West* (1922), and *Good Morning, America* (1928). These volumes included such characteristic poems as "Cool Tombs," ♦ "Smoke and Steel," "Broken-Face Gargoyles," "Prairie," "Good Morning, America," "Prayers of Steel," "Four Preludes on Playthings of the Wind," "Clean Curtains," and "Losers," all of which display a combination of precise realism, born of personal experience, with playful fantasy and love of color. *The People, Yes* ♦ (1936) is a panoramic depiction in verse of America and the American spirit as expressed in folklore and folk history, which sums up Sandburg's profound social sympathies and his faith in the future of the working classes. His *Complete Poems* (1950) was awarded a Pulitzer Prize. *Harvest Poems, 1910–1960* (1960), *Wind Song* (1960), *Honey and Salt* (1963), and *Complete Poems* (1970) collect late poems.

Throughout his work there is a constant, and frequently successful, attempt to capture the distinctive flavor of the American idiom and way of thought, particularly of his native Middle West. This interest led also to his compilation of ballads and folk songs in *The*

American Songbag (1927), and strongly influenced his original books for children, *Rootabaga Stories* (1922), *Rootabaga Pigeons* (1923), and *Potato Face* (1930). Besides his poetry and journalism, he devoted much time and careful research to his monumental biography of Lincoln, *Abraham Lincoln: The Prairie Years* (2 vols., 1926) and *Abraham Lincoln: The War Years* (4 vols., 1939, Pulitzer Prize), both abridged by the author in one volume (1954), and from which he selected a "profile" of the Civil War years titled *Storm Over the Land* (1942). His other prose includes *The Chicago Race Riots* (1919); *Steichen the Photographer* (1929); whose subject was the author's brother-in-law; *Mary Lincoln, Wife and Widow* (1932), written with Paul M. Angle; *Home Front Memo* (1943), a collection of wartime writings in verse and prose; *Remembrance Rock* (1948), a large, loose, poetic novel tracing an American family from its 17th-century English origins to World War II as it develops the theme of the American Dream; and *Always the Young Strangers* (1953), a memoir about his youth, from which he excerpted for children a section titled *Prairie-Town Boy* (1955). His *Letters* was published in 1968.

SANTAYANA, GEORGE (1863–1952), born in Spain, was christened Jorge Ruiz de Santayana y Borrais, but always used the English form of his name after he was brought to the U.S. (1872). Reared in Boston, he graduated from Harvard (1886), and after study in Germany and England received his Ph.D. from Harvard (1889). From that year until 1912 he was professor of philosophy at that university. After 1914 he made his home in Europe, first in France and England, and thereafter in Italy.

He is known as both a philosopher and a man of letters, having begun his literary career with *Sonnets and Other Verses* (1894); *The Sense of Beauty* (1896), a treatise on aesthetics; *Lucifer: A Theological Tragedy* (1899, revised 1924), a play in verse; *Interpretations of Poetry and Religion* (1900); and another book of poems, *A Hermit of Carmel* (1901). He collected his *Poems* in 1923, but after the turn of the century the body of his work was philosophical, having literary significance because of his rich style, whose cadence, reminiscent of Pater, is illumined by lucid, pithy statements of philosophical problems. His outstanding early work is *The Life of Reason* (5 vols., 1905–6), a study of reason in common sense, society, religion, art, and science, in which he finds matter to be the only reality,

and the source of the myths, institutions, and definitions that men use to describe or express that reality. With *Scepticism and Animal Faith* (1923), he introduced a new philosophy to modify and supplement this concept. This books serves as a prologue to the series entitled *The Realms of Being*. In these works he found knowledge to be faith in the unknowable, symbolized by essences. He contended that, though logical analysis may lead to complete skepticism concerning the existence of anything, animal faith continues to believe in a world whose material events have aroused intuitive essences, which are signs of the environment in which all animals live and suffer. Santayana's other works include *Three Philosophical Poets* (1910), studies of Lucretius, Dante, and Goethe; *Character and Opinion in the United States* (1920), concerned with the conflict of materialism and idealism in American life; and *The Genteel Tradition at Bay*◆ (1931), analyzing the adulteration and formalization of Calvinism and Transcendentalism. *The Last Puritan*◆ (1935) is a novel set in America during the period of the waning strength of Calvinism, in which the contrasting characters, one a Puritan, the other a hedonist, represent "potentialities which from my earliest youth I felt in myself . . ."; through such concrete externalizations Santayana gave fictional form to his argumentative philosophy.

Sapphira and the Slave Girl, novel by Willa Cather,◆ published in 1940.

SAROYAN, WILLIAM (1908–81), California author, whose short stories are marked by an impressionistic, rhapsodic manner, and a sentimental exaltation of characters ranging from Armenian-American workers like himself to middle-class businessmen, all somehow optimistically associated with the glory of an American dream. His impetuous and undiscriminating love for all sorts of people and situations, his very common fictionalizing of personal experience, and his ability to use what he calls the "jump-in-the-river-and-start-to-swim-immediately" type of writing allowed him to produce a steady flow of short fiction, published in *The Daring Young Man on the Flying Trapeze* (1934); *Inhale and Exhale* (1936); *Three Times Three* (1936); *Little Children* (1937); *A Native American* (1938); *The Trouble with Tigers* (1938); *Love, Here Is My Hat* (1938); *Peace, It's Wonderful* (1939); *My Name Is Aram* (1940), about the exuberant experiences of some Armenian children in California; *Fables* (1941); *Dear Baby* (1944); *The Whole Voyald* (1956); and *I*

Used To Believe I Had Forever, Now I'm Not So Sure (1967), composed of stories, essays, and poems.

His novels include *The Human Comedy* (1943), set in California and mainly about children; *The Adventures of Wesley Jackson* (1946), a loosely knit, whimsical account of a Saroyanesque army private's war experiences, incorporated in *The Twin Adventures* (1950) with "The Adventures of William Saroyan," an "hour-to-hour chronicle of a writer at work on the writing of a novel"; *Rock Wagram* (1951); *Mama, I Love You* (1956), about a nine-year-old girl's fantastic theatrical life with her mother; *Papa, You're Crazy* (1957); *Boys and Girls Together* (1963), a novella about a young writer and his wife; and *One Day in the Afternoon of the World* (1964), a bittersweet picture of an aging author.

His many plays are also written in his own characteristic loose style and set forth views like those of his fiction. *My Heart's in the Highlands* (1939) is an amorphous short play illustrating the idea that worldly success means nothing and that only aspiration counts. *The Time of Your Life* (1939), awarded a Pulitzer Prize that Saroyan refused, is a full-length play about people at a San Francisco waterfront bar, whose basic virtue is revealed when a wealthy drunk gives them money to pursue their hopes and dreams. Other plays include *Love's Old Sweet Song* (1941), a farce comedy; *The Beautiful People* (1941), with a theme like that of *The Time of Your Life*, and included with *Sweeney in the Trees* and *Across the Board on Tomorrow Morning* in *Three Plays* (1941); *Razzle-Dazzle* (1942), short plays; *Get Away Old Man* (1944), about a young writer in Hollywood; *Jim Dandy, Fat Man in a Famine* (1947), symbolizing Saroyan's conception of brotherly love; *Don't Go Away Mad* (1949); and *The Cave Dwellers* (1958), a fantasy set in New York.

The Bicycle Rider in Beverly Hills (1952) is an autobiographical work, and he wrote more in this vein and less fiction as he grew older, but his recollections are also very creative. They include *Here Comes, There Goes, You Know Who* (1962); *Not Dying* (1963); *Short Drive, Sweet Chariot* (1966), musings and a conversation while driving across the U.S.; *Days of Life and Death and Escape to the Moon* (1970); *Places Where I've Done Time* (1972); *Sons Come and Go, Mothers Hang In Forever* (1976); *Chance Meetings* (1978); and *Obituaries* (1979), digressive recollections of deceased celebrities with reflections on death and life.

SARTON, [ELEANOR] MAY (1912–), born in Belgium, brought to Massachusetts at age four when her father became a professor at Harvard; she, like her parents, became a U.S. citizen. Her first book, *Encounter in April* (1937), collected lyrics; later volumes of poetry include *Inner Landscape* (1939), *The Lion and the Rose* (1948), *The Land of Silence* (1953), *In Time Like Air* (1957), *Cloud, Stone, Sun, Vine* (1961), *A Private Mythology* (1965), and *Collected Poems* (1974). Her novels include *The Single Hound* (1938), about a young English poet solaced by an elderly Belgian woman and by her poetry; *The Bridge of Years* (1946), dealing with Belgian life between the world wars; *Shadow of a Man* (1950); *A Shower of Summer Days* (1952); *Faithful Are the Wounds* (1955), about the life and suicide of a distinguished Harvard professor, dedicated to literature and to social and political movements on the left; *The Birth of a Grandfather* (1957), about an old New England family; *The Small Room* (1961), set at a New England women's college; *Mrs. Stevens Hears the Mermaids Singing* (1965), about the nature of artistic creativity; *Crucial Conversations* (1975), depicting the breakup of a marriage through conversations of related persons; *As We Are Now* (1973), presenting the diary of a retired schoolteacher coping with life in an old people's home; *A Reckoning* (1978), depicting the recollections of a woman dying of cancer; and *Anger* (1982), about an unhappy marriage. She taught at Harvard and Wellesley, has written a play, *The Underground River* (1947), and in *I Knew a Phoenix* (1959) has created what she subtitles "sketches for an autobiography," continued in *A Plant Dreaming Deep* (1968) and *A World of Light* (1976). *Journal of a Solitude* (1973) records reflections during one year, as do *Recovering* (1980) and *At Seventy* (1984).

Sartoris, novel by Faulkner,♦ published in 1929 with editorial cuts. *Flags in the Dust* (1973) is the full text.

Bayard Sartoris comes home to Jefferson, Miss., from combat as an aviator in World War I, in which his twin brother John, also a flyer, has been killed. His grandfather, old Bayard, head of the Sartoris banking interests, and Miss Jenny, old Bayard's aunt, and others, including prewar associates and black tenants, frame young Bayard's attempted reentry into normal life, along with a complex family background of feudal tradition, stubborn pride, and a certain "glamorous fatality" bound up in the family names them-selves. The names recall old Bayard's father, John, the founder of the Sartoris house in Mississippi, and his brother, another Bayard, killed in the Civil War, as well as young John, who all exist as active presences and influences, "palpable ghosts." Desolated by his twin's death, and the deaths of his wife Caroline and their infant son, Bayard rides, drives, drinks, and hunts with cold reckless-ness, alone in the "bleak and barren world" of his despair, deliberately courting death. He marries Narcissa, of the prominent Ben-bow family,♦ to whom Byron Snopes, a bookkeeper at the bank, has been sending anonymous letters of crazed lust, and whose brother Horace, like Bayard, has returned from the war obsessed with a poetic image of "the meaning of peace." But neither Nar-cissa's love nor their expected child, nor even his guilt over old Bayard's death from heart failure during a wild auto ride, can alter his despair. He leaves home, wanders in South America and the U.S., and is killed testing a new kind of aircraft he seems to know is unsafe. On the day he dies his son is born and named Benbow Sartoris, Narcissa's gesture away from the Sartoris nomenclature, the "dusk" of names "peopled with ghosts of glamorous and old disastrous things."

Sartoris family, characters in Faulkner's fic-tion, figuring most importantly in *Sartoris*♦ and *The Unvanquished.*♦ The founder of the Jefferson, Yoknapatawpha County, family, Colonel John, arrives soon after the town's establishment and becomes the commander of its first regiment in the Civil War. First married to Rosa Millard's daughter, by whom he has all his children, he later weds Drusilla Hawk, who rode with his regiment after her fiancé was killed. A man of violence, Colonel John kills two men for trying to permit black people to vote and goads his partner Ben Redmond (or Redlaw) until he is shot by him. His widowed sister Virginia (Aunt Jenny) bears this death with resignation, as she had the death in war of her other brother, Bayard. Colonel John's son Bayard (later called "old Bayard") as a boy worships his father, whose violence he emulates by killing Grumbly, a Southern renegade who had murdered Bayard's grandmother Rosa. Later he cools temperamentally and leaves his father's death unavenged, and in course of time he becomes the old aristocrat trying to withstand change and the coming of the Snopeses. His son John has twins, Bayard (young Bayard) and John, who both join the

RAF in World War I, John dying in combat and Bayard returning home, feeling morbidly guilty over his brother's death and the deaths of his wife Caroline and their infant son. Bayard marries Narcissa Benbow, becomes increasingly restless, causes old Bayard's death of heart failure in a wild auto ride, and, cut off from associations, abandons Narcissa and is killed testing an aircraft he suspects to be a deathtrap. On the day he dies his son is born and named by his mother Benbow Sartoris as if to break the spell of violence associated with Sartoris names. Benbow ap-pears as a ten-year-old in *Sanctuary,* is one of the county's best shots at 17 in *The Mansion,* and is an officer in World War II in *Knight's Gambit.*

Saturday Club, THE, dinner club founded at Boston for informal literary discussion (1855). The organization was foreshadowed by the Symposia of Emerson and Alcott (*c.*1836–44), but credit for bringing the group together is given to Horatio Wood-man, a lawyer and publishing agent. At first there were really two clubs, both nameless. The one was purely social; the other, some-times later called the Magazine Club or the Atlantic Club, was concerned with promoting a literary journal. After the founding of the *Atlantic Monthly* (1857), this group held banquets for the contributors. By 1857 the Saturday Club was named, and its member-ship included Emerson, Lowell, Longfellow, Dana, Holmes, Prescott, Whittier, C.E. Nor-ton, Parkman, Howells, Henry James, and other notable figures in New England litera-ture. A history down to 1920 was written by E.W. Emerson and M.A. DeW. Howe (2 vols., 1918, 1927).

Saturday Evening Post, The (1821–1969, 1971–), Philadelphia weekly, whose first issue appeared August 18, 1821, although beginning in 1897 the cover page has carried the statement that it was founded by Franklin in 1728. Its only connection with Franklin is that it was originally issued from an office at one time occupied by his *Pennsylvania Ga-zette,* one of whose later publishers founded the *Post.* Its original purpose was to furnish light Sunday reading for Philadelphians, and its contributors included Cooper, Poe, N.P. Willis, and Harriet Beecher Stowe. Its mod-ern period did not come until it was pur-chased by Cyrus H.K. Curtis (1897). It was edited by George Horace Lorimer from 1899 to 1936. He increased its circulation from

1800 to 3,000,000 copies weekly by making it a popular magazine for the average American, and publishing stories with mass appeal. He also emphasized advertising, to which about 60 percent of the *c.*125 pages were devoted. A *Treasury* of selections appeared in 1954. Changing managements tinkered with design, editorial policy, and frequency of issue to offset loss of advertising revenue in the 1960s, but in 1969 the *Post* succumbed. It was revived as a quarterly in 1971.

Sauk (or SAC) **Indians,** Algonquian tribe related to the Fox Indians of the Great Lakes region, inhabited the Rock River country of Illinois, and the adjacent region in Wisconsin, Iowa, and Missouri. They were united with the Fox after 1730, aided the British in the War of 1812, and in 1832 participated in the Black Hawk War. They figure in historical studies of these battles, Jonathan Carver's *Travels,* W.J. Snelling's *Tales of the Northwest,* and fiction by August Derleth.

Scarlet Letter, The, romance by Hawthorne,♦ published in 1850. Based on a theme that appears in "Endicott and the Red Cross," this somber romance of conscience and the tragic consequences of concealed guilt is set in Puritan Boston during the mid-17th century. An introductory essay describes the author's experiences as an official of the Salem Custom House and his supposed discovery of a scarlet cloth letter and documents relating the story of Hester.

An aged English scholar sends his young wife, Hester Prynne, to establish their home in Boston. When he arrives two years later, he finds Hester in the pillory with her illegitimate child in her arms. She refuses to name her lover and is sentenced to wear a scarlet A, signifying Adulteress, as a token of her sin. The husband conceals his identity, assumes the name Roger Chillingworth, and in the guise of a doctor seeks to discover her paramour. Hester, a woman of strong independent nature, in her ostracism becomes sympathetic with other unfortunates, and her works of mercy gradually win her the respect of her neighbors. Chillingworth meanwhile discovers that the Rev. Arthur Dimmesdale, a revered, seemingly saintly young minister, is the father of Hester's beautiful, mischievous child, Pearl. Dimmesdale has struggled for years with his burden of hidden guilt, but, though he does secret penance, pride prevents him from confessing publicly, and he continues to be tortured by his conscience. Chillingworth's life is ruined by his preoccupation with his cruel search, and he becomes a morally degraded monomaniac. Hester wishes her lover to flee with her to Europe, but he refuses the plan as a temptation from the Evil One, and makes a public confession on the pillory in which Hester had once been placed. He dies there in her arms, a man broken by his concealed guilt, but Hester lives on, triumphant over her sin because she openly confessed it, to devote herself to ensuring a happy life in Europe for Pearl and helping others in misfortune.

Scarlet Sister Mary, novel by Julia Peterkin,♦ published in 1928, awarded a Pulitzer Prize, and dramatized in 1930.

SCHLESINGER, ARTHUR [MEIER], JR. (1917–), son of Arthur Meier Schlesinger (1888–1965) and like his father a professor of history at Harvard (1946–61), is the author of *Orestes A. Brownson* (1939) and *The Age of Jackson* (1945, Pulitzer Prize), in which the struggle of Jacksonian Democracy is shown to be not against Hamiltonian conservatism but against the traditional antistatism of the Jeffersonians. His *Age of Roosevelt* includes *The Crisis of the Old Order* (1957), *The Coming of the New Deal* (1959), and *The Politics of Upheaval* (1960). *The Politics of Hope* (1962) contains essays. He served as a special assistant to President Kennedy, about whose administration he wrote *A Thousand Days* (1965, Pulitzer Prize, National Book Award). *The Bitter Heritage* (1967) treats the effects of American involvement in Vietnam, and *The Crisis of Confidence* (1969) gathers essays on the U.S. in the 1960s. *The Imperial Presidency* (1973) traces the growth of presidential power. *Robert F. Kennedy and His Times* (1978, National Book Award) treats another member of the family to which he has been close.

SCHORER, MARK (1908–77), born in Wisconsin, received his A.B. and Ph.D. from the University of Wisconsin, and while still a graduate student published his first novel, *A House Too Old* (1935), set in his native state. His career then continued to include achievements in both scholarship and fiction. He was a professor of English at the University of California, Berkeley (1945–73). His later novels are *The Hermit Place* (1941) and *The Wars of Love* (1954), and his sensitive stories, many first printed in *The New Yorker,* appear in *The State of Mind* (1947). His major scholarly works are *William Blake: The Poli-*

tics of Vision (1946) and *Sinclair Lewis: An American Life* (1961), a monumental biography. His essays are collected as *The World We Imagine* (1968). *Pieces of Life* (1977) contains autobiographical sketches and short stories.

SCHULBERG, BUDD [WILSON] (1914–), New York-born novelist, reared in Hollywood, which he satirized in *What Makes Sammy Run?* (1941), about a dynamic but vicious opportunist. His other novels are *The Harder They Fall* (1947), about crookedness in prizefighting; *The Disenchanted* (1950), about the last year of an author modeled on F. Scott Fitzgerald, and partly set at Dartmouth, from which Schulberg was graduated in 1936; *Sanctuary V* (1969), about the president of a Latin American nation seeking sanctuary from revolutionaries; and *Everything That Moves* (1980), about a labor union leader's entanglement with gangsters. *Waterfront* (1955) is a fictive version of his film scenario *On the Waterfront*. *Some Faces in the Crowd* (1950) collects stories. He collaborated on a musical version of *What Makes Sammy Run?* (1964) and dramatized *The Disenchanted* (1958). He has also written nonfictional works. *Moving Pictures: Memories of a Hollywood Prince* (1981) is autobiographical.

SCHURZ, CARL (1829–1906), born in Germany, participated in the unsuccessful revolutionary movement (1848–49), and emigrated to the U.S. (1852), where he became prominent in the Republican party and was active in antislavery work. His other services in behalf of Lincoln brought him an appointment as minister to Spain (1861–62), from which he resigned to become a brigadier general. Although his division was accused of cowardice, a court of inquiry found the charges unwarranted and commended him for his actions. After the war he was Washington correspondent of the New York *Tribune,* and edited a Detroit paper and a German daily published in St. Louis, He left journalism to become a senator from Missouri (1869–75), in which capacity he opposed political corruption and jingoism. Hayes appointed him secretary of the interior (1877–81), in which office he was noted for his installation of a merit promotion system, humanitarian treatment of the Indians, and interest in the conservation of natural resources. With E.L. Godkin and Horace White, he became editor of the New York *Evening Post,* ♦ which they made famous for its liberal independence. After differing on editorial policies, he resigned to write for *Harper's Weekly* (1892–98), which he left when he refused to support the policy favoring war with Spain. His later years were devoted to writing and speaking on domestic and foreign matters. In addition to his *Life of Henry Clay* (1887) he left for publication *Reminiscences* (3 vols., 1907–8) and *Speeches, Correspondence, and Political Papers* (6 vols., 1913).

SCHUYLER, JAMES [MARCUS] (1923–) Chicago-born author associated with the New York school of poets, including Ashbery, Kenneth Koch, and Frank O'Hara,♦ is on the staff of the Museum of Modern Art. His first poems, *Salute* (1960), part of a series to which the other members of the school also contributed, showed their close relation to painting by being issued with prints that are not intended to be illustrative but are just as important as the texts. Later poems, generally underplayed and quietly observant of particulars, pastoral and urban, appear in *May 24th or So* (1966), *Freely Espousing* (1969), *The Crystal Lithium* (1972), *Hymn to Life* (1974), and *The Morning of the Poet* (1980, Pulitzer Prize). He has also written experimental plays and has collected prose and poetry in *The Home Book* (1977). *Alfred and Guinevere* (1958) is a short novel about the summer holiday of a boy and his sister; *A Nest of Ninnies* (1969) is a novel written with Ashbery that comically travesties the lives of suburbanites; and *What's for Dinner?* (1979) is an amusing but serious novel about middle-class suburbanites, some "normal," others institutionalized as mentally troubled.

SCHWARTZ, DELMORE (1913–66), Brooklyn-born poet, critic, and teacher, graduated from New York University (1935), and was an editor of *Partisan Review* (1943–55). His books include *In Dreams Begin Responsibilities* (1938), poems; a translation of Rimbaud's *A Season in Hell* (1939); *Shenandoah* (1941), a verse play; *Genesis* (1943), a tale in prose and poetry about the identity of an American Jew; *Vaudeville for a Princess* (1950), poems; *Summer Knowledge* (1959, Bollingen Prize), collecting the poems in his first volume, selecting some from other early books, and adding new works; and collections of stories, *The World Is a Wedding* (1948) and *Successful Love* (1961). His *Last and Lost Poems* was published in 1979 and selected *Letters* in 1984. He was the model for Von Humboldt Fleisher in Saul Bellow's *Humboldt's Gift.* ♦

Science fiction, stories of fantasy dealing with the unknown in scientifically conceivable terms of reference. They use imaginary inventions and discoveries; settings that include the earth's interior, other planets, and the atom; and time in the remote future, the prehistoric past, and a new dimension. They sometimes resemble Utopian fiction, but their direct ancestors include Mary Shelley's *Frankenstein* and works by Poe, Verne, Fitz-James O'Brien, and H.G. Wells. Although Utopias and satires occasionally use some of the materials or techniques of science fiction and although Mark Twain's *A Connecticut Yankee in King Arthur's Court* used a favorite theme of traveling through time, their emphasis is not on pseudo-science and the creation of a sense of wonder. The vogue for science fiction became particularly evident around the turn into the 20th century, perhaps because people felt they were moving into a new era and because they were much impressed by the many recent inventions. The genre was given further impetus by the founding of *Amazing Stories* (1926) by Hugo Gernsback (1884–1967), an émigré from Luxembourg, who is commemorated by annual (since 1953) Hugo awards, and by the founding (1937) of another magazine, *Astounding,* by John W. Campbell, the "discoverer" of Asimov and Heinlein. The awe-inspiring scientific inventions of World War II and the subsequent era of manned travel into outer space made science fiction both more interesting and more acceptable to many readers. Postwar science fiction placed more emphasis on accuracy and less on weird adventures and also became more concerned with sociopolitical ideas; it also moved out of magazine publication to the greater solidity of books, both paperback and hardbound.

SCOTT, EVELYN (1893–1963), born in Tennessee, was reared in New Orleans, and at the age of 20, in revolt against contemporary U.S. standards, became an expatriate in Brazil, which she describes in her autobiographical narrative *Escapade* (1923). Returning to the U.S., she published her first work, *Precipitations* (1920), a book of poetry, and a play, *Love* (1920). Her first two novels, *The Narrow House* (1921) and *Narcissus* (1922), attack middle-class morality and aims. *The Wave* (1929), her first popular novel, deals with the Civil War. After another volume of poetry, *The Winter Alone* (1930), she returned to serious fiction in *A Calendar of Sin* (1931), chronicling the life of five generations of one family; *Eva Gay* (1933), studies of a

woman and her lovers; *Breathe Upon These Slain* (1934), reconstructing the lives of people whom the narrator knows only through their photographs and the furniture that she finds in her rented house; *Bread and a Sword* (1937), the story of the struggles of an author for life in the modern economic order; and *The Shadow of the Hawk* (1941), about a boy who grows up knowing his father had been executed for a murder he did not commit. *Background in Tennessee* (1937) is an autobiographical account of the author's youth.

Scribner's Magazine (1887–1939), literary monthly, founded by the younger Charles Scribner (1854–1930), after his father sold *Scribner's Monthly.* It immediately won distinction as a dignified literary journal for educated readers. Contributors included Stevenson, Henry and William James, Harte, Kipling, Cable, Edith Wharton, Meredith, Stephen Crane, and Huneker, and among the illustrators were Stanford White, Howard Pyle, A.B. Frost, and Frederic Remington. Through the years the magazine maintained its high standards, ever open to new authors, and was the first important magazine to publish the fiction of Hemingway and Wolfe. Loss of circulation resulted in its purchase by a new editor (1936), who attempted to popularize it by meeting a lower level of public taste.

Scribner's Monthly (1870–81), literary journal founded by the elder Charles Scribner (1821–71), with J.G. Holland as editor. It was notable for its many departments; for its serials, including the editor's *Sevenoaks,* Hale's *Philip Nolan's Friends,* Stockton's *Rudder Grange,* Harte's *Gabriel Conroy,* Eggleston's *Roxy,* and Cable's *The Grandissimes;* for its short stories by Julian Hawthorne, Constance F. Woolson, and Helen Hunt Jackson; for its essays by C.D. Warner, Burroughs, Muir, Stedman, and W.C. Brownell; and for its poems by R.H. Stoddard, Emma Lazarus, Hayne, Lanier, Irwin Russell, and Joaquin Miller. The magazine was also distinguished for its engravings and typography. Its policies were continued after 1881 in *The Century Illustrated Monthly Magazine.* ♦

Sea-Wolf, *The,* novel by Jack London, ♦ published in 1904.

Humphrey Van Weyden, a dilettante literary critic, is picked up by the sealing schooner *Ghost* when the ferry boat on which he is traveling across San Francisco Bay collides with a tramp steamer. The captain of the *Ghost,* Wolf Larsen, is a man of tremendous physical power who is utterly ruthless. When the *Ghost,* on the sealing grounds off Japan, saves some refugees from an ocean disaster, a struggle commences between the hyper-civilized, moral Van Weyden and the primitive, individualistic Larsen over the poet Maude Brewster. Miss Brewster and Van Weyden escape to a deserted island to which the *Ghost,* dismasted and near sinking, is later driven. Larsen, deserted by his crew, is aboard, but, blinded by cerebral cancer, is doomed to slow paralysis. Van Weyden and Miss Brewster manage to rehabilitate the vessel and sail back to civilization, but Larsen dies, indomitably pagan.

SEAGER, ALLEN (1906–68), born in Michigan and educated at the University of Michigan, where he taught, and at Oxford, wrote *Equinox* (1943), *The Inheritance* (1948), *Amos Berry* (1953), *Hilda Manning* (1956), and *Death of Anger* (1960), novels of characters involved in violence, and *The Old Man of the Mountain* (1950), stories. *A Frieze of Girls* (1964) is an amusing autobiography, subtitled *Memoirs as Fiction,* about his youth in the U.S. and England. *The Glass House* (1968) is a life of Roethke.

SEAMAN, ELIZABETH COCHRANE (1867–1922), journalist who used the pseudonym Nelly Bly, adopted from a song by Stephen Foster. Sponsored by the *New York World,* she made a tour of the world in 72 days, 6 hours, and 11 minutes (1889), which brought her international notice and furnished material for *Nelly Bly's Book: Around the World in Seventy-Two Days* (1890).

Secret Life of Walter Mitty, The, short story by James Thurber,♦ published in *The New Yorker* (1939) and collected in *My World—and Welcome to It* (1942).

Henpecked Walter Mitty daydreams as he drives his wife downtown, attends to errands she requires, and waits while she has her hair done, envisioning himself as the beloved commander who gets his men through the worst storm in 20 years of navy flying; as the brilliant surgeon who saves the life of a millionaire banker; as the world's greatest pistol shot testifying in a murder case and refusing to be bullied by a nasty district attorney; as the British bombardier preparing to attack a German ammunition dump on a

dangerous solo flight; and then, as his wife momentarily leaves him waiting outside a drugstore, he snaps away his cigarette, disdains a blindfold, and faces "the firing squad; erect and motionless, proud and disdainful, Walter Mitty the Undefeated, inscrutable to the last."

SEDGWICK, CATHARINE MARIA (1789–1867), Massachusetts author of fiction depicting the simple domestic virtues of the American home, which she considered the safeguard of the Republic. *A New-England Tale* (1822) and *Redwood* (1824) are conventional romantic novels, illustrating their author's moral belief, and valuable for their realistic depiction of social customs in early 19th-century New England. *Hope Leslie; or, Early Times in the Massachusetts* (1827) tells of the romantic adventures which befall colonial settlers, through Indian captivities and massacres. *Clarence; or, A Tale of Our Own Times* (1830), set in and around New York City, contrasts the lives of a sensible and an adventurous girl, and *The Linwoods; or, "Sixty Years Since" in America* (1835) presents the social life of New York City during the last two years of the Revolution. *Married or Single?* (1857), her last novel, was again a story of society and a contrast of different types of women, with the ostensible purpose of showing the valuable activities in which an unmarried woman might engage.

SEEGER, ALAN (1888–1916), New York–born poet, graduated from Harvard (1910), went to Paris (1913), and at the beginning of World War I enlisted in the French Foreign Legion. He was killed at Belloy-en-Santerre, in the Battle of the Somme. "I Have a Rendezvous with Death" (*North American Review,* Oct. 1916) is the most famous of his war poems, which were collected in *Poems* (1916). His *Letters and Diary* was published in 1917.

SELBY, HUBERT (1928–   ), Brooklyn-born novelist whose fiction, set in his native area, is *Last Exit to Brooklyn* (1964), a vivid view of corruption and violence in contemporary urban life; *The Room* (1971), depicting the sadistic and sexual fantasies of a jailed prisoner; *The Demon* (1976), presenting a young businessman's "dark consciousness" and sexual impulses; and *Requiem for a Dream* (1978), about heroin addicts and others frustrated in their dreams.

Self-Reliance, essay by Emerson,♦ published in *Essays, First Series* (1841).

"Trust thyself," a central doctrine in the author's ethical thought, is the theme developed here. "Envy is ignorance . . . imitation is suicide"; a man "must take himself for better, for worse, as his portion." "Society everywhere is in conspiracy against the manhood of every one of its members. . . . Whoso would be a man must be a nonconformist." The two terrors that discourage originality and creative living are fear of public opinion and undue reverence for one's own consistency. The great figures of history have not cared for the opinions of their contemporaries; "to be great is to be misunderstood"; and if a man honestly expresses his nature he will be largely consistent. Deference to authority, to institutions, or to tradition is disobedience to the inner law that each of us must follow in order to do justice to himself and to society. We must speak the truth, and truth, revealed intuitively, cannot be achieved except through the development and expression of one's individual nature. "Nothing is at last sacred but the integrity of your own mind."

Sellers, COLONEL BERIAH, character in *The Gilded Age.*♦ In the dramatization he was called Colonel Mulberry Sellers, and under the latter name reappears in *The American Claimant.*♦

Seminole Indians, Florida tribe composed mainly of refugees from the Creeks,♦ with a large element of black ex-slaves. Still under Spanish rule, they were hostile to the U.S. in the War of 1812. In the first Seminole War (1817–18) they were subdued by Andrew Jackson, after which Spain ceded Florida to the U.S. The attempt to remove the tribe beyond the Mississippi provoked a second Seminole War (1835–42), which, at a cost of 1500 American lives and $20,000,000, resulted in the removal of most of the Seminoles and the death of their leader Osceola. The present Seminoles live in Oklahoma and southern Florida. Kirk Munroe's *The Flamingo Feather* (1887) is a romance about the tribe in the 16th century.

SENDAK, MAURICE [BERNARD] (1928–), Brooklyn-born illustrator and author, known for his playfully grotesque stories and drawings for children. His fantasies, comic but touched with eerie imagination, feature impish menacing creatures of strange scale, some dwarf-like, some depicting babies or small animals of gigantic size. His prolific publications include *The Sign on Rosie's Door* (1960), which led to a television show and a musical play; *Where the Wild Things Are* (1963, Caldecott Medal), *In the Night Kitchen* (1970), and *Outside Over There* (1981), a trilogy; *Zlateh the Goat* (1966); and *Higglety Pigglety Pop, or There Must Be More to Life* (1967).

Seneca Indians, tribe of the Iroquois Confederacy.♦ They were allied with Pontiac, aided the British during the Revolution, and largely supported the American side in the War of 1812. They now live mainly on several reservations in New York state. They are celebrated in poems by William H.C. Hosmer,♦ and Edmund Wilson's *Apologies to the Iroquois* (1960) tells of the modern status of the tribes in the Confederacy.

Separatists, name applied to those who split from the Established Church of England in the 17th century, organizing independent congregations. They had much in common with the Puritan party within the State Church, but went beyond them in desiring not merely a purification in ceremonial but also complete independence. Frequently they had no stated ministry, emphasizing only the bare letter of Scripture, believing in voluntary church membership, and a relatively democratic organization within the local church. The Pilgrims♦ were Separatists, but most of the other New England settlers, such as those of the Massachusetts Bay Colony, were Puritans. In America the two groups tended to merge, but extreme Separatists, such as Roger Williams and Anne Hutchinson, were persecuted. Certain ministers, such as Thomas Hooker and John Wise, opposed the dominant oligarchy of New England ministers on essentially Separatist principles.

Septimius Felton; or, The Elixir of Life, unfinished romance by Hawthorne,♦ posthumously published in 1872.

During the Revolutionary War, Septimius Felton, a scholar who seeks a method of attaining earthly immortality, kills a British officer who has insulted his fiancée, Rose Garfield. On the hill top where he has buried the officer, he meets Sybil Dacy, a strange, unearthly creature, who is looking for a flower she expects to grow from the grave, and they become close friends. Before he died, the officer gave Septimius an old manuscript, containing the formula for an elixir of life, requiring the juice of the flower Sybil seeks. A Dr. Portsoaken, her uncle, visits Septimius and reveals that the scholar may be the heir to a British estate. Robert Hagburn, an American soldier and friend of Septimius, becomes engaged to Rose, after it is discovered that she is the scholar's half-sister. At the wedding of Robert and Rose, Sybil discloses to Septimius, who is about to drink the potion he has finally concocted, that the officer he killed was her lover, and that she has intended to seek revenge, but now loves Septimius. She drinks part of the potion, throws away the rest, and dies. Septimius disappears, and is believed to have gone to claim his English estate.

Servant to Servants, A, blank-verse dramatic monologue by Robert Frost,♦ published in *North of Boston* (1914).

A lonely, overworked New England farm wife talks with a visiting naturalist, and through her eager conversation reveals the tragic story of her life. Reared in a loveless family, in which her mother's life had been embittered by the necessity of caring for an obscenely mad brother-in-law, she herself had been influenced for a time by the inherited strain of insanity, and welcomed the opportunity to marry Len, the unfeeling husband who neglects her for his many business enterprises. Though she craves personal freedom, love, and the touch of beauty, she is burdened by innumerable menial tasks, including the feeding of the brutal farmhands, whose "servant" she has become.

SETON, ANYA (1916–   ), daughter of Ernest Thompson Seton, whose popular fiction includes the historical romances *My Theodosia* (1941), about Aaron Burr's daughter; *Katherine* (1954), about John of Gaunt's wife; and *The Winthrop Woman* (1958), set in Massachusetts Bay Colony. *Dragonwyck* (1944) and *The Turquoise* (1946) are romantic novels set in 19th-century America. Later novels are *Devil Water* (1962), set in England and Virginia of the 18th century; *Avalon* (1965), which deals with King Arthur's era and his descendants; and *Green Darkness* (1973).

Seven Arts, The (Nov. 1916–Oct. 1917), monthly little magazine intended to foster native talents and points of view and encourage freer expression than could be countenanced in the more conservative quality magazines. Its editors included James Oppenheim, Waldo Frank, and Van Wyck Brooks, and among its contributors were Anderson, Amy Lowell, Frost, John Reed, Dos Passos, R.S. Bourne, Vachel Lindsay, Dreiser, Spingarn, W.H. Wright, and Mencken. The magazine's pacifism caused its subsidy to be withdrawn, and its financial failure.

SEWALL, SAMUEL (1652–1730), born in England of a family that had previously resided in the colonies, was brought at the age of nine to Boston, with which his later life is identified. After graduation from Harvard (1671), he was for a long time a tutor at the college, but in 1679 began his long political career, including such early offices as manager of the colony's printing press, deputy to the general court, and member of the Council (1684–86). While in England on business (1688–89), he aided Increase Mather in appealing to William III to recover the abrogated Massachusetts charter. Upon his return he resumed his position on the Council, and was a councilor of the new charter (1691–1725).

In 1692 he was appointed by Governor Phips as a special commissioner in the Salem witchcraft trials, in which he later regretted having participated, and in 1697, on a fast day set aside for repentance concerning errors in the trials, he was the only judge publicly to recant by standing in the Old South Church while the clergyman read his confession of error and guilt. After holding several judicial posts, he became chief justice of the superior court of judicature (1718–28), and despite his lack of legal training was considered a good and rather liberal jurist.

His various pamphlets give evidence of the many different matters in which he was interested. *The Revolution in New England Justified* (1691), written with Edward Rawson, is a loquacious but logical justification of the New Englanders who deposed Andros and resumed charter government in 1689. *Phænomena quædam apocalyptica . . .* (1697) is a prediction that New England will be the eventual seat of the New Jerusalem. *The Selling of Joseph*♦ (1700) is an early antislavery appeal, and other works include *A Memorial Relating to the Kennebeck Indians* (1721), an early argument for humane treatment of the Indians. "Talitha Cumi" is an essay, not published until 1873, which argues against those who deny the resurrection of women.

Both as man and as author, Sewall is best remembered for the *Diary,* which was published by the Massachusetts Historical Society (3 vols., 1878–82), and which covers the period from 1674 to 1729, with a gap between

1677 and 1685, in an intimate and minute manner. Because he not only relates in detail the homely activities of Boston but also gives an honest revelation of his own character, he has been compared with his British contemporary, Samuel Pepys. He reveals, evidently unconsciously, the twilight of the Puritan tradition and the rise of the New England Yankee period, which transition he himself represented in his religious orthodoxy, tempered by an emphasis upon mercantilism in his capacity as a merchant. His practical Yankee bent made him less concerned with ideas and more with daily happenings. The thought in Cotton Mather's *Diary* thus receives a complementary balance for the student of the period in the journal of Sewall, which recounts such incidents as his unsuccessful wooing of Madam Winthrop with gifts of gingerbread, sermons, and a shilling and a half's worth of sugar almonds, and their disputes over the marriage settlement and whether he should wear a wig and keep a coach.

Sewanee Review (1892–), literary quarterly published by the University of the South, Sewanee, Tenn.; founded by William Peterfield Trent (1862–1932) while he was a professor of English there (1888–1900). It is now the oldest critical and literary quarterly in the U.S. and, though academic in outlook, is not a university organ. Its contributors are mainly Southerners, and it devotes much attention to the reinterpretation of the role of the South in U.S. culture. Beginning with Allen Tate's editorship (1944–46) it has laid more emphasis on modern literature. Andrew Lytle was the editor (1961–73).

SEXTON, ANNE (1928–74), poet who lived in her native Massachusetts and traced her ancestry to *Mayflower* Pilgrims, but whose writing is concerned not with heritage or region but very frankly with her firsthand experience. Her first book, *To Bedlam and Part Way Back* (1960), was the outcome of a nervous breakdown. The poems in *All My Pretty Ones* (1962) are equally revealing. The same characteristics are evident also in the lyrics of *Live or Die* (1966, Pulitzer Prize) and *Love Poems* (1969). Her dark, bitter views of life are evident in *Transformations* (1971), retellings of the Grimms' fairy tales; *The Book of Folly* (1972), poems and prose parables; and *The Death Notebooks* (1974), which were followed by the poems in *The Awful Rowing Toward God* (1975), published after her suicide. *45 Mercy Street*

(1976), *Words for Dr. Y* (1978), and *The Complete Poems* (1981) are posthumous collections of poems. A *Self-Portrait in Letters* appeared in 1977.

SHAARA, MICHAEL [JOSEPH, JR.] (1929–), New Jersey-born author, after graduation from Rutgers and service as a paratrooper was a professor of English at Florida State University (1961–73). His novels are *The Broken Place* (1968), about a soldier who is a boxer, *The Killer Angels* (1974, Pulitzer Prize), which presents the Battle of Gettysburg as seen by Southern officers, and *The Herald* (1981), about a world depopulated by a death ray. *Soldier Boy* (1982) collects stories.

Shadows on the Rock, novel by Willa Cather,♦ published in 1931.

Life in early 17th-century Quebec is depicted on this "rock" in the St. Lawrence, between visits by ships from France. Against a background of such figures as the Intendant, Frontenac, the rival bishops—generous, self-sacrificing old Bishop Laval and extravagant, haughty young Monseigneur de Saint-Vallier—and Mother Juschereau and her nuns are placed the stories of humble citizens. Euclide Auclair, "the philosopher apothecary," has followed Frontenac from France, and after his wife's death lives with his daughter Cécile, cherishing memories of Europe. Cécile and her father befriend Jacques, son of a sailor and a woman of the town, 'Toinette Gaux. Among their friends are Bishop Laval; Noël Pommier, the cobbler; Father Hector Saint Cyr, the missionary; Antoine Frichette, the trapper; and Pierre Charron, *coureur de bois* and fur trader, a romantic figure driven to his lonely occupation by a love affair with a girl who chose to become a religious recluse. The apothecary is despondent at the death of Frontenac, and when Charron comes to cheer his friend, he discovers that he loves Cécile. They marry, and Jacques becomes a sailor, while Auclair, no longer caring to return to France, spends his last years on "the rock."

SHANGE, NTOZAKE (1948–), New Jersey-born author, graduated from Barnard (1970), in 1971 changed her original name, Paulette Williams, which she called a slave name because the first one derived from a man and the second from an irrelevant Anglo-Saxon culture, to a Zulu combination meaning "she who comes with her own things" and "she who walks like a lion." Her first successful work was *For Colored Girls Who Have Considered Suicide/When the Rainbow Is Enuf* (1975), which she called a "choreo-poem," a stage production loosely combining poetry, dance, and music in evoking experiences of black women. It was followed by "A Photograph: A Study of Cruelty" (1977), an unpublished musical poem/play, and "Where the Mississippi Meets the Amazon" (1977), a collaborative work in the same vein. *Sassafras* (1976) is a novel, *Natural Disasters and Other Festive Occasions* (1977), poems and prose, *Nappy Edges* (1978), poems, and *See No Evil* (1984), brief writings.

SHAPIRO, KARL [JAY] (1913–), Baltimore-born author whose first volume of *Poems* (1935) was followed by *Person, Place and Thing* and *The Place of Love,* both issued in 1942. He came to major prominence with *V-Letter and Other Poems* (1944, Pulitzer Prize), written while he was a soldier in the South Pacific. Later volumes of his pungent poetry include *Essay on Rime* (1945), a critique in verse of modern poetry; *Trial of a Poet* (1947); *Poems 1940–1953* (1953); *Poems of a Jew* (1958), on coming to terms with his heritage; *Adult Bookstore* (1976); and *Collected Poems* (1978). He has written a novel, *Edsel* (1971), about an aging poet-professor at a Midwestern state university, and literary studies, including *Beyond Criticism* (1953), essays on poetry; *In Defense of Ignorance* (1960), polemical lectures and essays praising Whitman and D.H. Lawrence and attacking highly intellectual writers; *Prose Keys to Modern Poetry* (1962); *The Bourgeois Poet* (1964), a poetic treatment of the poet's relation to other men and of men to society; *To Abolish Children* (1968), essays and fiction; and *The Poetry Wreck* (1975), essays. He edited *Poetry* (1950–55) and *Prairie Schooner* (1956–66) and has taught at the University of Nebraska (1956–66) and the University of California, Davis (1968–).

SHAW, HENRY WHEELER (1818–85), Massachusetts-born humorist, better known under his pseudonym Josh Billings. Until the age of 45, when he began his literary career by writing for small newspapers, he attempted a variety of occupations, including Western exploration, farming, commanding a riverboat, selling real estate, and auctioneering. His writings soon attracted the attention of C.F. Browne, who arranged for the publication of his first book, *Josh Billings, His Sayings* (1865). Thereafter he became a successful cracker-barrel philosopher, em-

ploying the devices popular among the literary comedians of the time: ridiculous spellings, deformed grammar, monstrous logic, puns, malapropisms, incongruous juxtapositions of idea, and anticlimax. Both in his lectures and in his books, he showed his gift for aphorism rather than sustained storytelling or characterization. From 1869 to 1880 he issued annual *Allminax,* and his other works include *Josh Billings on Ice, and Other Things* (1868); *Josh Billings' Trump Kards* (1877); *Old Probability: Perhaps Rain—Perhaps Not* (1879); and *Josh Billings Struggling with Things* (1881).

SHAW, IRWIN (1913–84), Brooklyn-born writer whose works are marked by dramatic intensity and social awareness. His novels are *The Young Lions* (1948), tracing the fortunes of two American soldiers, one a Jew, the other a Gentile, and of the Nazi who kills the first and is killed by the second; *The Troubled Air* (1951), about radio actors harried by flimsy charges of Communist sympathies; *Lucy Crown* (1956), about a middle-aged woman's romance; *Two Weeks in Another Town* (1960); *Voices of a Summer Day* (1965), a middle-aged man's bittersweet memories; *Rich Man, Poor Man* (1970), the stories of two brothers and their sister set against the world scene from the 1940s to 1970; *Evening in Byzantium* (1973), portraying an aging Hollywood producer; *Nightwork* (1975), a lively depiction of a sophisticated international confidence man; *Beggarman, Thief* (1977), a melodramatic sequel to *Rich Man, Poor Man; The Top of the Hill* (1979), about a successful businessman trying to find himself; *Bread Upon the Waters* (1981); and *Acceptable Losses* (1982). *Sailor Off the Bremen* (1939), *Welcome to the City* (1941), *Act of Faith* (1946), *Mixed Faith* (1950), *Tip on a Dead Jockey* (1957), *Love on a Dark Street* (1965), *God Was Here But He Left Early* (1973), and *Five Decades* (1978) collect stories. He wrote several plays before he became known as a novelist.

Shawnee Indians, Algonquian tribe related to the Sauk, Fox, and Kickapoo, migrated from the Cumberland and Savannah rivers to Pennsylvania and Ohio in the 17th century. Their principal opposition to the whites occurred in the rebellion led by Tecumseh. ◆ They now live in Oklahoma. The Shawnee figure in R.M. Bird's *Nick of the Woods* and other works concerned with Tecumseh, and an 18th-century white boy reared by Shawnees in New York colony is the hero of a trilogy by Hervey Allen, *The City in the Dawn.*

SHEED, WILFRID [JOHN JOSEPH] (1930–), English-born, Oxford-educated author, came to the U.S. (1947), has long been a resident of New York City. His humorous satirical novels include *A Middle Class Education* (1961), about a student at Oxford who comes on a scholarship to the U.S.; *The Hack* (1963), presenting a writer of inspirational verse and fiction for American Catholic journals; *Square's Progress* (1965), depicting an easygoing middle-class American who becomes a hippie; *Office Politics* (1966); *The Blacking Factory and Pennsylvania Gothic* (1968), a short novel and a long story; *Max Jamison* (1970), characterizing a journalistic drama critic; *People Will Always Be Kind* (1973), about an Irish-American's rise in politics; and *Transatlantic Blues* (1978), tracing an American at Oxford who goes on to become a television personality. Other writings include *The Morning After* (1971) and *The Good Word and Other Words* (1979), essays; *Three Mobs: Labor, Church and Mafia* (1974); and *Muhammad Ali* (1975) and *Clare Boothe Luce* (1982), biographies.

SHELDON, CHARLES M[ONROE] (1857–1946), born in New York, attended Brown University and Andover Theological Seminary, and became pastor of the Central Congregational Church of Topeka, Kan., which he left in 1919 to edit *The Christian Herald.* His novel *In His Steps* (1896), a story of a minister following the example of Jesus, was an extraordinary success, being translated into 23 languages and selling millions of copies.

SHELDON, EDWARD [BREWSTER] (1886–1946), born in Chicago, graduated from Harvard (1907), where he studied under G.P. Baker. His first play, *Salvation Nell* (1908), is the story of a reformed saloon girl. After two dramas on American politics, *The Nigger* (1909) and *The Boss* (1911), he wrote *The Princess Zim-Zim* (1911), a romantic play laid in Coney Island. His other plays include *Egypt* (1912), melodrama; *The High Road* (1912), a study of a woman who rises from farm life to make her husband a presidential candidate; *Romance* (1913), concerned with an old man's memories of a love affair; *The Song of Songs* (1914), an adaptation with an American setting of a novel by Sudermann; *The Garden of Paradise* (1914), a poetic fantasy based on Andersen's "The Little Mermaid"; *Bewitched* (1924), a romantic play, written with Sidney

Howard; *Lulu Belle* (1926), a study of a black prostitute, written with his nephew, Charles MacArthur; and *Jenny* (1929) and *Dishonored Lady* (1930), written with Margaret Ayer Barnes. *Ned and Jack* is a play (1981) about Sheldon and John Barrymore, written by Sheldon Rosen.

Sheltered Life, The, novel by Ellen Glasgow,♦ published in 1932.

SHEPARD, SAM (SAMUEL SHEPARD ROGERS, JR.) (1943–), Illinois-born playwright, reared and resident in California. His first works were short plays, beginning with *Cowboys* and *The Rock Garden* (1964), presented off-Broadway. *La Turista* (1967) was his first long play. Other productions followed rapidly from his prolific writing, which includes *The Tooth of Crime* (1972), a fantasy about rock-and-roll pop singers that is a commentary on contemporary American social values, and *The Starving Class* (1978), depicting a lower-middle-class family symbolic of social chaos in the U.S. *Buried Child* (1978, Pulitzer Prize) deals with an even more macabre disintegrating family in Illinois. *True West* (1979) is a tragi-comic study of a modern Cain and Abel situation in California. His plays are marked by an improvisational feeling because of their great variety in moving from the surreal to the realistic in treating people and situations ranging from the mythic to the abstract. He also wrote the screenplay of Antonioni's *Zabriskie Point* (1965). In addition to his plays he has published *Hawk Moon* (1972), short stories, and *Motel Chronicles* (1982), pieces of his notebooks.

SHEPARD, THOMAS (1605–49), educated at Cambridge, became a preacher in England until banned for his puritanism, when he went to New England (1635). There he became pastor of the church at Cambridge and was one of the leaders in New England religious and intellectual life. He was instrumental in the founding of Harvard, was one of the leaders of the synod (1637) that condemned Anne Hutchinson and the Antinomians, was prominent in the conversion of the Indians, and helped draft the Cambridge Platform. He was a tireless worker, and in his preaching and writing was an outstanding though typical representative of the New England Calvinists. His most popular work, *The Sincere Convert* (1641), was frequently reprinted, and was translated into the Indian language by John Eliot (1689). In it he preaches a gospel of love and infinite compassion, indicating that anyone might be saved if he would open his heart to God.

SHERWOOD, ROBERT [EMMET] (1896–1955), New York dramatist. His first play was *The Road to Rome* (1927), a comedy concerning Hannibal's march on Rome and his decision to turn from his goal, which served as a plea against war, followed by *Waterloo Bridge* (1930), set in London during World War I, concerned with a chorus girl turned prostitute, who, in order to preserve the chivalric ideals of a doughboy, refuses to give herself to him. Other plays include *The Petrified Forest* (1935), a melodrama about frustrated lives during a period of social change; *Idiot's Delight* (1936, Pulitzer Prize), a dramatic setting of a plea for world peace; *Abe Lincoln in Illinois* (1938, Pulitzer Prize), concerned with Lincoln's early years and his preparation for his lifework; and *There Shall Be No Night* (1940, Pulitzer Prize), dealing with the Russian attack on Finland and its consequences in altering the attitude of a liberal Finnish scientist. *Roosevelt and Hopkins* (1948, Pulitzer Prize) is "an intimate biography," deriving in part from his association with the president as a speech writer.

Ship of Fools, novel by Katherine Anne Porter. ♦

Shirley Letters, The, see *Clappe, Louise A.K.S.*

Shock of Recognition, The, anthology with critical commentary by Edmund Wilson, ♦ subtitled "The Development of Literature in the United States Recorded by the Men Who Made It," and collecting articles about American authors by their literary contemporaries from 1845 to the publication date of 1943.

SHOLOM ALEICHEM, pen name of Solomon Rabinowitz (1859–1916), meaning "Peace be with you" in Hebrew. Ukrainian-born, a popular and influential journalist, and a leading figure of Yiddish literature for his stories and plays, Sholom Aleichem left Russia because of pogroms. He lived in New York City (Oct. 1906–June 1907), contributing some of his bittersweet tales of Jewish village life to Lower East Side journals and having two of his plays produced there. However, he did not have financial success so he returned to Europe for a reading tour. Experience in the U.S. contributed to his

long series of stories, including *The Adventures of Mottel, the Cantor's Son* (1953), about a boy sometimes called a Jewish Tom Sawyer, just as their author was said to be a Yiddish Mark Twain. When World War I broke out in Europe, Sholom Aleichem returned to New York for the last two years of his life, during which he worked on his incomplete autobiographical fiction. This includes, in posthumous English translation, *The Old Country* (1946), *Tevye's Daughters* (1949), and *The Great Fair* (1955). He was buried in Brooklyn. The success, popular and critical, of Jewish writers in the U.S. during the 1950s and later brought attention to Sholom Aleichem, particularly when the musical play *Fiddler on the Roof* (1964), based on some of his sketches, had 3242 performances in the U.S., making it in its time the longest-running musical production on Broadway.

Short Happy Life of Francis Macomber, The, short story by Ernest Hemingway, ♦ published in *Cosmopolitan* (Sept. 1936) and collected in *The Fifth Column and the First Forty-Nine Stories* (1938).

An American couple on a safari in Kenya, the Macombers have long given the impression of a glamorous and comparatively happy marriage, although the basis for their union is that "Margot was too beautiful for Macomber to divorce her and Macomber had too much money for Margot ever to leave him." The marriage comes to a new straining point when in cowardice he runs from a wounded lion that he has shot badly, and she, in disgust, gives herself that night to the professional hunter and guide, the sturdy Englishman Robert Wilson. The next day, in a surge of excitement, Macomber discovers self-confidence and happiness as he shoots three wild buffalo, but Margot is suddenly made insecure as she sees him at last a man who will dominate their marriage. Forced to go into the hiding place of one of the animals he has only wounded to administer the *coup de grâce,* Macomber seems about to be gored by the buffalo when from the car Mrs. Macomber shoots at the beast and kills her husband instead, after which Wilson says wryly, "Of course it's an accident. I know that."

Shoshone Indians, primitive Northwestern tribe, sometimes erroneously called Snake Indians, which gave its name to a great linguistic family of various cultures, scattered through Montana, Wyoming, New Mexico,

Texas, Oregon, and California. The Shoshonean tribes include the Comanche, Ute, Paiute, Hopi, Bannock, and Mission Indians. The Shoshone figure in books by Joaquin Miller, the Mission Indians in Helen Hunt Jackson's *Ramona* and Mary Austin's *Isidro,* and the Paiute in Mrs. Austin's *The Land of Little Rain.*

Siege of London, The, novelette by Henry James, ♦ the title story of a volume published in 1883.

Nancy Headway, several times married and divorced and now a wealthy widow, leaves the Western U.S. to exert her fascination in Europe, the constant goal of her vulgar ambition. Notorious throughout the West, she is snubbed in New York, and her dearest hope is to annoy her detractors by a social success in Paris and London. She attracts Sir Arthur Demesne, a weak, cautious, but romantically inclined English Tory, who follows her about without being able to decide to marry her. She meets a former Western acquaintance, Mr. Littlemore, who introduces her to his friend Waterville, an undersecretary of the U.S. ministry in London. Through these two she tries to establish contacts in British society, and finally, though she arouses the enmity of Sir Arthur's careful mother, she becomes popular because of her naïveté and fresh humor. Lady Demesne appeals to Littlemore and Waterville to disclose their knowledge of Mrs. Headway's past, but, though she wrests from Littlemore the admission that Nancy is "not respectable," the young woman triumphs, marrying her baronet and continuing to be a novel and slightly scandalous social celebrity.

SIGOURNEY, Lydia Huntley (1791–1865), Connecticut poetaster whose sentimental and pious verses were enormously popular, winning her the title "the Mrs. Hemans of America." Her lugubrious preoccupation with death caused her to look at every sick child as a potential angel, and she so consistently wrote melancholy verses on the decease of any prominent person that an elegy from her pen seemed as natural a sequence to death as interment. She wrote some 60 books, ranging from *Moral Pieces in Prose and Verse* (1815) to an autobiography, *Letters of Life* (1866). In addition to editing religious and juvenile publications, she was also a pioneer in the cause of higher education for women.

Silver Cord, The, play by Sidney Howard, ♦ produced in 1926 and published in 1927. It depicts a pathologically possessive mother who causes one son to break his engagement and the other one to escape only finally with his wife's aid.

Silverado Squatters, The, autobiographical narrative by Stevenson, ♦ published in 1883. Written after the author's return to Europe (1882), it describes his trip, with his bride and his stepson Sam (Lloyd Osbourne), from San Francisco through the Napa Valley to Calistoga, and their sojourn (June–July 1880) in a shanty at the deserted mining town of Silverado, on Mt. St. Helena in central California. The book is notable for its character sketches of the Hansons, who were the Stevensons' only neighbors at Silverado; Mr. Kelmar, the shrewd, good-natured Jewish merchant who directed them there; and other people of the countryside; as well as for realistic descriptions of the picturesque scene of their mountain idyll.

SIMMS, William Gilmore (1806–70), Charleston author, began his literary career by writing romantic verse in the vein of Byron, who strongly influenced the local literary standards that Simms earnestly tried to meet. He made his reputation with romances of the frontier and South Carolina history. *Guy Rivers* (1834) deals with the life of Georgia desperadoes. *The Yemassee* (1835) is a story of Indian warfare in his own state, and *The Partisan* (1835), also set there, is a romance of the Revolution. Thus, within two years, Simms had begun writing on the three different subjects for which he is noted.

In the vein of *Guy Rivers* followed the series known as the Border Romances, concerned with colonial and 19th-century life in the South, which includes *Richard Hurdis* (1838), *Border Beagles* (1840), *Beauchampe* (1842), *Helen Halsey* (1845), and *Charlemont* (1856). Generally included with the Border Romances are *The Yemassee* and his other depictions of Indians, *The Wigwam and the Cabin* (1845–46) and *The Cassique of Kiawah* (1859).

The Partisan was the first of a series known as the Revolutionary Romances, dealing with life in the South during the Revolution and centering on the activities of Marion, Greene, and other generals. Among these books are *Mellichampe* (1836); *The Kinsmen* (1841), revised as *The Scout* (1854); *Katharine Walton* (1851); *The Sword and the Distaff*

(1853), revised as *Woodcraft* (1854); *The Forayers* (1855); and *Eutaw* (1856).

Simms, who was tremendously proud of South Carolina, and particularly of genteel, conservative Charleston, was, as the son of a poor storekeeper, snubbed by the social oligarchy, and yet remained loyal to the local taboos, expressing his local patriotism by editing *The Southern Quarterly Review* (1856–57) and writing a *History* (1840) and a *Geography* (1843) of the state.

Because of his two great topics, the frontier and the Revolution, Simms is invariably called a Southern Cooper, and he does resemble the New York novelist in his themes, fluent romantic style, use of stock figures, and melodramatic plots, though he fails to attain the poetic quality of Cooper's depictions of nature, and did not create a character comparable to Natty Bumppo, or a series comparable to the Leather-Stocking Tales.

Simon Legree, villain in *Uncle Tom's Cabin.* ♦

Simple, name given to the titular character, properly Jesse B. Semple, in several works by Langston Hughes.♦ A black resident of Harlem, Simple is a seemingly naïve or stupid man but actually smart in the vein of the shrewd cracker-barrel homespun figure. The satirical sketches in which he surveys contemporary issues were published in newspapers and are collected in *Simple Speaks His Mind* (1950), *Simple Takes a Wife* (1953), *Simple Stakes a Claim* (1957), *The Best of Simple* (1961), and *Simple's Uncle Sam* (1965). *Simply Heavenly* (1963) is a musical play by Hughes adapting some of these stories.

Simple Cobler of Aggawam, The, satirical work by Nathaniel Ward,♦ published under the pseudonym Theodore de la Guard (London, 1647), Theodore being the Greek equivalent of the Hebrew Nathaniel, and de la Guard a free French rendering of Ward. Aggawam was the original name of Ipswich, Mass., and the sobriquet "simple cobler" is explained in the subtitle: "Willing to help 'mend his Native Country, lamentably tattered, both in the upper-Leather and sole, with all the honest stitches he can take." The book is a partisan denunciation of undue tolerance in England and New England of the strife between Parliament and Charles I and of the frivolity of women and foppish fashions of men. In the style of a belated euphuist, Ward grumbles sincerely but wittily concern-

ing all his particular dislikes. His manner recalls the Elizabethan pamphleteers, such as Nashe, Harvey, and Greene.

SIMPSON, Louis [Aston Marantz] (1923–), born in Jamaica, received his B.S. from Columbia (1948) after service in an airborne division in World War II. He received his Ph.D. from Columbia and has taught at the University of California, Berkeley (1959–67), and the State University of New York, Stony Brook (1967–). His poetry, marked by vivid imagination and fine craftsmanship, has been published in *The Arrivistes* (1949); *Good News of Death* (1955); *A Dream of Governors* (1959), including the long narrative poem "The Runner," set in the invasion of Europe in World War II; *At the End of the Open Road* (1963, Pulitzer Prize), including the long poem "The Marriage of Pocahontas," developing history into myth; *Selected Poems* (1965); *Adventures of the Letter I* (1971); *Searching for the Ox* (1976); *Caviare at the Funeral* (1980), *People Live Here* (1983), selected poems since 1949, and *The Best Hour of the Night* (1984). He has also written a novel, *Riverside Drive* (1962), about a young man from Jamaica, his experiences in New York and the army, and his private life; an autobiography, *North of Jamaica* (1972); and critical works, *James Hogg* (1962), *Three on a Tower* (1975), about Pound, Eliot, and W.C. Williams, *A Revolution in Taste* (1979), about Dylan Thomas, Allen Ginsberg, Sylvia Plath, and Robert Lowell, poets who "created art out of the confusion of their lives," and *A Company of Poets* (1981), essays, reviews, talks, and autobiography.

SINCLAIR, Upton [Beall] (1878–1968), born in Baltimore of a prominent but impoverished family, began writing dime novels at the age of 15 in order to pay his way through the College of the City of New York. While doing graduate work at Columbia, he wrote six novels. The tone of these early works was suggested by Sinclair himself, who said that Jesus, Hamlet, and Shelley shaped his thought, and that he was disillusioned when the world did not meet him with the love and trust with which he approached it. In his novel *The Jungle* (1906) he exposed corruption in Chicago's meat-packing industry and the city's politics as well as making clear his belief in socialism. Earnings from this widely read book were invested in a cooperative colony and, after his move to California (1915), in politics, culminating in a campaign that almost elected him the state's governor.

Sinclair was a prolific writer, having published from 1901 to 1940 more than 100 works, ranging from pamphlets, social studies, boys' books, and studies in health, religion, and telepathy to novels, short stories, and plays. The most important of these include *The Metropolis* (1908), describing the morals of a society created by great fortunes; *King Coal* (1917), a novel castigating Colorado's coal-mining industry; *The Profits of Religion* (1918), contending that organized religion is a capitalist tool in teaching the poor that God has allotted them their positions; *Jimmie Higgins* (1919), a pacifist novel; *The Brass Check* (1919), a tract on corruption in contemporary U.S. journalism; *100%, the Story of a Patriot* (1920); *They Call Me Carpenter* (1922), a rich man's dream of a meeting with Christ; *The Goose-Step* (1923), a study of higher education in the U.S.; *The Goslings* (1924), about American schools; *Oil!* (1927), a novel based on scandals during the Harding administration; *Boston* (1928), treating the Sacco and Vanzetti case; *The Wet Parade* (1931), a fictive plea for prohibition of liquor; and *American Outpost* (1932), an autobiography.

World's End (1940) is the first of a series of eleven novels in which Lanny Budd, illegitimate son of a munitions manufacturer and a famous beauty, travels throughout the world, meets famous people, and is a figure in international intrigues and political maneuvers from 1913 to the 1940s. One of these, *Dragon's Teeth* (1942), won a Pulitzer Prize.

SINGER, ISAAC BASHEVIS (1904–), Polish-born author of Yiddish fiction, descendant of rabbis, like his elder brother, Israel Joshua Singer (1893–1944), author of *The Brothers Ashkenazi* (1936), a novel about Polish Jews, turned from a rabbinical background to a career as a writer. In 1935 he followed his brother to New York City, where he became a journalist, writing in Yiddish for the *Jewish Daily Forward,* in which he has also published most of his fiction. His work deals mostly with the exotic heritage of Polish Jews, their traditional faith and folkways, their daily village life, their mysticism, their colorful personal relationships, their religious fanaticism, and their sexuality. His first major work, *Satan in Goray* (Yiddish, 1935; English, 1955) treats the aftermath of a 17th-century Polish pogrom, when the remaining Jews turned to a messianic sect with mystic and erotic beliefs. The first of his books to appear in English (and all dates

following refer to first publications in English) was *The Family Moskat* (1950), realistically presenting the degeneration of a Jewish family in Warsaw from the turn of the 20th century to World War II. This was followed by *The Magician of Lublin* (1960) and *The Slave* (1962), portrayals of diverse aspects of Jewish character in Poland. *The Manor* (1967) and *The Estate* (1969), its sequel, chronicle the lives of Polish Jews during the latter half of the 19th century. *Enemies* (1970) is his first novel set in the U.S., about a Polish Jew who, out of gratitude, marries the girl who helped him escape the Nazis after he believes his wife is dead, takes a mistress whom he bigamously weds when she becomes pregnant, and then discovers that his first wife has also escaped from Poland to New York. In *Shosha* (1978) Singer returned to treat the ghetto life of Poland before World War II. *The Penitent* (1983) is a lesser and a less compassionate novel.

His stories are generally even more esteemed than his longer fiction, portraying more pungently the lives of curious characters in their ghetto settings in situations marked by fantasy and humor. His collections include *Gimpel the Fool* (1957), whose title tale was translated by Saul Bellow, about an innocent man gulled by his shrewish wife and all the world; *The Spinoza of Market Street* (1961); *Short Friday* (1964); *Zlateh the Goat* (1966); *The Séance* (1968); *A Friend of Kafka* (1970); *A Crown of Feathers* (1973); and *Passions* (1978). *Collected Stories* (1982) contains 47 of these tales.

Singer has also written books for children, including *When Shlemihl Went to Warsaw* (1968), folk tales, and *A Day of Pleasure* (1970), reminiscences of his own childhood. His memoirs include *In My Father's Court* (1966), an adult version of *A Day of Pleasure; A Little Boy in Search of God* (1976); *A Young Man in Search of Love* (1978); *Lost in America* (1981); and *Love and Exile* (1984). In 1978 he was awarded a Nobel Prize.

Single Hound, The, 146 brief poems by Emily Dickinson,♦ posthumously edited and published by her niece, Martha Dickinson Bianchi (1914). The selection consists largely of verses sent with flowers or messages to "Sister Sue," Emily's sister-in-law and next-door neighbor, Susan Gilbert Dickinson. Besides several poems expressing her warm feelings of friendship for her sister-in-law, there is a lyric on the death of Elizabeth Barrett Browning. The title of the volume is derived from the first poem:

Adventure most unto itself
The Soul condemned to be;
Attended by a Single Hound—
Its own Identity.

Many of the verses are metaphysical or religious meditations, concerned with ecstatic personal concepts of the Deity and natural phenomena. Others combine fantasy with a transcendental attitude toward Biblical subjects, birds, flowers, the seasons, and the constellations, all in her delicate, elliptical, metaphoric manner.

Sinners in the Hands of an Angry God, sermon by Jonathan Edwards,♦ delivered in 1741 at Enfield, Mass., and published the same year. This fervid, imprecatory sermon was his most famous single contribution to the exposition of God's vindictive justice and man's natural corruption, and its vivid presentation had a strong effect in connection with the Great Awakening.

Sioux (or DAKOTA) **Indians,** confederation of tribes that occupied territory in the present states of Wisconsin, Minnesota, and the Dakotas, and smaller sections in Virginia and the Carolinas. The Siouan linguistic family was the most numerous among the Plains Indians, and included the Assiniboin, Mandan, Hidatsa, Crow, Omaha, Osage, and other tribes. The Sioux proper were friendly with the English, aiding them in the Revolution and the War of 1812. After several unsuccessful treaties, they rose under Little Crow (1862) and massacred more than 800 Minnesota settlers. In a subsequent revolt, when prospectors overran their Dakota reservation, the Sioux were led by such chiefs as Sitting Bull and Crazy Horse against Custer, whose forces they annihilated. They were quelled in 1891. In Cooper's *The Prairie,* the Sioux figure as the "Ishmaelites of the American deserts," and they appear in Neihardt's *Song of the Indian Wars,* Garland's *The Captain of the Gray Horse Troop,* and Longfellow's *The Song of Hiawatha.* Nonfictional descriptions are to be found in Parkman's *The Oregon Trail,* W.J. Snelling's *Tales of the Northwest,* and Mari Sandoz's *Crazy Horse* and *These Were the Sioux.* Charles A. Eastman's works are concerned with the Indians.

Sister Carrie, novel by Dreiser.♦ The first edition was printed in 1900 but is said to have been withheld from circulation by the pub-

lisher because of its supposed immorality. It was reissued in 1907.

Carrie Meeber, penniless and "full of the illusions of ignorance and youth," leaves her rural home to seek work in Chicago, and becomes acquainted with Charles Drouet, a salesman who impresses her by his worldliness and affluence. In Chicago she lives with her sister and brother-in-law, and works for a time at jobs that pay little and oppress her imaginative spirit. After a period of unemployment and loneliness, she allows Drouet to establish her as his mistress, and finds temporary happiness with him. She becomes aware of his inferiority, however, and during his absences falls under the influence of his friend George Hurstwood, middle-aged, married, and comparatively intelligent and cultured, who is the manager of a celebrated bar. They finally elope, first to Montreal and then to New York, where he opens a saloon, and they live together for more than three years. Carrie grows in intellectual and emotional stature, while Hurstwood, away from the atmosphere of success on which his life has been based, steadily declines. When they are impoverished, their relations become strained, until Carrie goes on the stage and begins to support Hurstwood, rising from the chorus to minor acting parts. At last she deserts him, feeling that he is too great a burden, since he has not tried to obtain work except for a brief time as a strikebreaker during a trolley strike. Carrie becomes a star of musical comedies, but in spite of her success she is lonely and dissatisfied. Without her knowledge, Hurstwood sinks lower and lower, and after becoming a beggar commits suicide.

1601, Conversation, *As It Was by the Social Fireside, in the Time of the Tudors,* sketch written by Clemens,♦ under his pseudonym Mark Twain, in 1876 and purporting to transcribe a ribald conversation of Queen Elizabeth, Raleigh, Bacon, Shakespeare, and others on the subjects of flatulency and sexual relations. First privately printed in 1880, the work has often been reprinted.

Sketch Book, The, familiar essays and tales by Irving,♦ written under the pseudonym Geoffrey Crayon, Gent., published serially in the U.S. (1819–20) and in book form in England (1820). Its genial humor and graceful style made it successful both in the U.S. and abroad, where American authors were not yet recognized. Most of the sketches concern his observations as an American visitor in England (e.g. "Westminster Abbey," "The Christmas Dinner," "Stratford-on-Avon," "John Bull," and "The Stage-Coach"), but six chapters deal with American scenes. Of these "Rip Van Winkle"♦ and "The Legend of Sleepy Hollow"♦ are adaptations of German folk tales to the New York backgrounds of Diedrich Knickerbocker; "English Writers of America" opposes the criticisms of the U.S. by British tourists; "Traits of Indian Character" is a romantic defense of the American tribes; "Philip of Pokanoket" is an account of King Philip; and "The Angler" is a whimsical self-exposure of the author as preferring to read Izaak Walton rather than pursue the art of angling in person.

Skin of Our Teeth, The, comedy by Thornton Wilder,♦ produced and published in 1942, winning a Pulitzer Prize. The unconventional use of theatrical devices, such as asides and interruptions, increases the audience's feeling of participation.

George Antrobus, his wife, and his son and daughter represent humanity—the parents are Adam and Eve, and their son Henry is Cain—engaged in the struggle to survive. Their home in Excelsior, N.J., is threatened first by a creeping wall of ice, and later by a long war. Each time they barely escape annihilation, but George, inventor of the alphabet and the wheel, maintains the continuity of learning and culture. Lily Sabina, their maid, the eternal Lilith, nearly succeeds in winning George away from his wife on the Atlantic City boardwalk during a convention of which George is elected president. Constructive attitudes prevail after the war, in which Henry is the enemy. Having reassembled his family, George feels the "most important thing of all: The desire to begin again to start building," and seeks his books to guide him in his struggle.

Slaughterhouse-Five; or The Children's Crusade. A Duty-Dance with Death, novel by Vonnegut,♦ published in 1969.

In telegraphic style and brief impressionistic scenes out of chronological sequence the work tells of the life and death of Billy Pilgrim, once an optometrist in Ilium, N.Y., later a "spastic in time" because he has been chosen by the inhabitants of Tralfamadore, a planet millions of light-years away, to inhabit their zoo. As a result he is freed from time and place, living in present, past, and future, now on earth, now in a distant galaxy. In the U.S. he comes to be considered crazy by everybody except a few eccentrics like the

philanthropist Eliot Rosewater (of Vonnegut's novel *God Bless You, Mr. Rosewater*) and the misanthropic science-fiction writer Kilgore Trout (also a figure in Vonnegut's other writings). In Germany, where he is held as a prisoner of war during World War II, he sees how mad most of humanity is. Forced to work in an underground slaughterhouse in Dresden, he becomes a witness of the terrible firebombing of the city that kills 135,000 people, the greatest single killing of human beings and a dreadful example of the tragic absurdity of mankind.

Sleepy Hollow, see *Sunnyside* and *Legend of Sleepy Hollow.*

Slouching Towards Bethlehem, collection of essays by Joan Didion,♦ published in 1968. The title derives from a poem by Yeats that includes the line "Things fall apart; the center cannot hold." The pieces, reprinted from journals, fall into three groups: "Life Styles in the Golden Land," on California; "Personals," about herself; and "Seven Places of the Mind," about places significant in her experiences.

Small Boy and Others, A, autobiographical narrative by Henry James,♦ published in 1913. Originally intending "to place together some particulars of the early life of William James and present him in his setting," the author found, he says, that "To knock at the door of the past was . . . to see it open to me quite wide—to see the world within begin to 'compose' . . . round the primary figure, see it people itself vividly and insistently." This account, consequently, is a richly detailed narrative, vivacious and revealing, of the boyhood experiences of the celebrated brothers, their family circle, and the cosmopolitan background that formed their minds, from the period of James's earliest recollections to the year 1859. The narrative is continued in *Notes of a Son and Brother*♦ (1914).

Smart Set, The (1890–1930), monthly magazine, grew beyond its original purpose of chronicling New York society; under the editorship of Willard Huntington Wright (1913–14), its primary purpose was "to provide lively entertainment for minds that are not primitive." Although the circulation was far greater than that of the average little magazine, its gaiety, vitality, and aesthetic credo were akin to the traits of this type of publication. Wright attracted new and stimulating American authors, and was also the first American editor to publish periodical contributions by such authors as George Moore, D.H. Lawrence, Joyce, D'Annunzio, and Ford Madox Ford. In 1914 Mencken and Nathan assumed joint editorship, and, although their policy was somewhat less stirring during the World War, after 1918 they continued Wright's vigorous policy, beginning such satirical departments as that of "Americana," which baited what they called the "booboisie." They also published the early writings of Eugene O'Neill, F. Scott Fitzgerald, J.W. Krutch, and Lewis Mumford. When the magazine was purchased by Hearst (1924), new editors and a more conventional policy were introduced.

SMITH, CHARLES HENRY (1826–1903), Southern humorist known by his pseudonym Bill Arp, practiced law, and, loyal to the Confederacy, "joined the army and succeeded in killing about as many of them as they of me." His humorous writing was begun during the first year of the war, when he contributed to a newspaper of his native Georgia letters addressed to "Mr. Abe Linkhorn," signed "Bill Arp," which satirized the North by sympathizing with the Yankees in a deliberately inept manner. This device, used by D.R. Locke for the North, won Smith great popularity, causing him to devote most of the remainder of his life to writing. Although he retained the character of Bill Arp, he transformed him into a shrewd, cracker-barrel philosopher, and by 1866 dropped the device of comic misspelling to depend upon direct satire and homespun philosophy in his comments on woman suffrage, income tax, Reconstruction, rights for blacks, etc. Upon occasion he employed the dialect of the Georgia "cracker" and the Negro, in which he is supposed to have influenced Joel Chandler Harris. His works include *Bill Arp, So-Called* (1866), *Bill Arp's Letters* (1868), *Bill Arp's Peace Papers* (1873), *Bill Arp's Scrap Book* (1884), and *Bill Arp: From the Uncivil War to Date* (1903).

SMITH, FRANCIS HOPKINSON (1838–1915), great-grandson of Francis Hopkinson, was born in Baltimore and became an engineer, with painting as an avocation. At the age of 50 he turned to literature, and became widely known following the publication of *Colonel Carter of Cartersville* (1891), a novelette in the local-color manner, portraying a Southern gentleman down on his luck.

SMITH, JOHN (1580–1631), English explorer and adverturer, left home at the age of about 16 to begin life as a soldier of fortune, in the Low Countries and elsewhere on the Continent. In 1602 he served with the Austrian forces against the Turks, on the Hungarian and Transylvanian border. The only sources of information for his life during these years are Smith's *The True Travels* and a lost Italian source mentioned by Purchas, so that his veracity has frequently been questioned.

Although only 26 when the Virginia Company received its patent, he energetically participated in the promotion and organization of the enterprise, and set sail with the early colonists, who disembarked at Jamestown (1607). He was active in exploration and in procuring food from the hostile Indians for the famished colony. On one of his expeditions, he was supposedly captured and condemned to death by the chief Powhatan, and dramatically rescued by the intercession of Pocahontas. This story, which Smith told in varying versions in different books, has sometimes been considered apocryphal.

Back in the colony in January 1608, he again faced death at the hands of his political rivals, being charged with having lost two of his men. In the midst of wrangling about authority, he was dangerously burned by a gunpowder explosion, and forced to leave for England (Oct. 1609), where the charges were dropped, though he was refused further employment by the Virginia Company.

Still interested in exploration, he was next employed by some London merchants to explore the region that he named New England, and to find gold mines and kill whales for them. Because he brought back fish and furs instead of fulfilling their fantastic desires, for which he showed contempt, he received only the empty title of Admiral of New England. He made two unsuccessful attempts to reach New England, once being captured by pirates. He next tried to interest the Puritans in his guiding them to New England, but they loftily replied that, though his books and maps were valuable to them, he himself was not a desirable person.

He then settled in London to continue his writings on his own life and in furtherance of colonization in the New World. His books include *A True Relation of such occurrences and accidents of noate as hath hapned in Virginia since the first planting of that Collony* (1608), a pamphlet giving the earliest firsthand account of the settlement, but not mentioning his rescue by Pocahontas; *A Map of Virginia with a Description of the Country*

(1612), continuing the account of his governorship; *A Description of New England: or the Observations and Discoveries of Captain John Smith* . . . (1616); and *The Generall Historie of Virginia, New England, and the Summer Isles* (1624), a lengthy and more magniloquent reworking of his earlier writings, containing an extended account of the Pocahontas story.

SMITH, LILLIAN [EUGENIA] (1897–1966), Florida-born social worker in Georgia, whose treatment of Southern problems in novels appears in the love story of a mulatto girl in *Strange Fruit* (1944), which she dramatized (1945), and *One Hour* (1960), about the response of a Southern town to the hysterical accusation of immorality that a young girl makes against an older man.

SMITH, [LLOYD] LOGAN PEARSALL (1865–1946), New Jersey-born essayist reared in Philadelphia, educated at Haverford, Harvard, and Oxford, resided in England and on the Continent after 1888. His books of aphorisms and essays include *Trivia* (1902), *More Trivia* (1921), *Afterthoughts* (1931), the collection *All Trivia* (1933, revised 1945), and *Reperusals and Re-collections* (1936). He also published *The Youth of Parnassus* (1895), short stories; two slight collections of poetry, *Sonnets* (1908) and *Songs and Sonnets* (1909); various pamphlets on English vocabulary; *On Reading Shakespeare* (1933); a biography of Sir Henry Wotton (1907); and editions of authors as various as Donne and Santayana. *Milton and His Modern Critics* (1941) is a defense of Milton and an attack on T.S. Eliot and Ezra Pound. His autobiography, *Unforgotten Years* (1938), describes his Quaker boyhood, his acquaintance with Whitman, his activities as a bibliophile, and his experiences as an expatriate.

SMITH, SEBA (1792–1868), born in Maine, graduated from Bowdoin (1818), founded the daily *Portland Courier* (1829), and achieved fame when he began to publish in his newspaper (1830) a series of letters from "Major Jack Downing," a Down East Yankee, whose comic rustic speech and homespun sagacity made him an outstanding character in the development of American humor. Although Smith created the character as a Yankee peddler, he soon had him turn his attention to local politics, and then, as the letters began to be printed in other newspapers and Downing began to capture the popular imagination, he made him into a confidant of Andrew Jackson, so that he might shrewdly satirize Jacksonian Democracy and matters of contemporary politics.

This use of his character and Smith's freedom from party politics made him the inaugurator of the American tradition of commenting on current events with great shrewdness cloaked under a guise of simplicity, and gave to the country a line of homespun political philosophers that has included Hosea Biglow, Mr. Dooley, and Will Rogers. In his own day, Smith found so many imitators, some of whom used Downing's own name, that Downing said he knew himself only by a scar on his left arm. His most important work is *The Life and Writings of Major Jack Downing of Downingville* (1833).

SMITH, THORNE (1892–1934), humorist whose first book, *Biltmore Oswald: The Diary of a Hapless Recruit* (1918), based on his experiences in the navy during World War I, was enormously popular at the time. With *Topper* (1926) he established the vein of ribald fantasy for which he is best known. This novel deals with two capricious ghosts, whose ectoplasmic reappearances and whimsically insane actions disturb the staid life of the inhibited banker Cosmo Topper.

SMITH, WILLIAM JAY (1918–   ), Louisiana-born poet whose education came from Washington University, St. Louis, a Rhodes Scholarship, and graduate study in Florence and whose later affiliations include service in the navy, membership in the Vermont House of Representatives, and teaching at Williams and at Hollins College (1965–   ). He is married to the poet Barbara Howes. ♦ His poetry is as various as his career, as may be seen in *Poems* (1947); *Celebration at Dark* (1950), lyrics of diverse styles and moods; *The Tin Can* (1966), long poems and translations of Voznesensky; *Mr. Smith* (1968), light and nonsense verse for children; *Poems from Italy* (1972), translations; *Venice in the Fog* (1975); *The Telephone* (1978), a verse adaptation of a Russian children's story; *The Traveler's Tree* (1980), new and selected poems; and *A Green Place: Modern Poems* (1982). *The Spectra Hoax* (1961), dealing in part with the parodies of Witter Bynner♦ and A.D. Ficke, and *The Streaks of the Tulip* (1972) are critical works. *Army Brat* (1980) is a memoir of his youth.

Snake Indians, name loosely applied to the Shoshone and related tribes. It is now used by scholars to refer to certain Oregon tribes. Beginning with the *Journals* of Lewis and Clark, the Snake Indians often figure in accounts of overland crossings.

SNODGRASS, W[ILLIAM] D[EWITT] (1926–), born in Pennsylvania, educated at the University of Iowa (B.A., 1949), where he also did graduate work, has taught English and speech at Syracuse (1968–). He is known for the fine craftsmanship and deep feeling of his first collection of poems, *Heart's Needle* (1959, Pulitzer Prize), whose title work, about a father's love for a daughter he can see only infrequently, is perhaps autobiographical but has universality in its theme of separation. Later works, also marked by formal technique and personal revelation, include *After Experience* (1968), incorporating translations of Rilke; *Gallows Songs of Christian Morgenstern* (1967); *The Führer Bunker* (1977), poems on the end of the Third Reich in the voices of major Nazis; and *If Birds Build with Your Hair* (1982), modern pastorals. *Six Troubadour Songs* (1977) prints translations. *In Radical Pursuit* (1975) collects essays and lectures on poetry.

Snopes family, characters in Faulkner's fiction, figuring most prominently in the trilogy, *The Hamlet,* ♦ *The Town,* ♦ and *The Mansion,* ♦ but appearing also in *The Unvanquished, Sartoris,* and *As I Lay Dying.* Their origins obscure, they are "just Snopeses, like colonies of rats or termites are just rats and termites." They emerge from the Yoknapatawpha country, entrench themselves in Frenchman's Bend and later in the county seat, Jefferson, and finally replace, largely in the person of Flem Snopes, the old order as represented by the Sartoris♦ and Compson♦ families. Abner (Ab) Snopes, who settles as a sharecropper on Will Varner's land in Frenchman's Bend in the 1890s, a bitter man with a reputation for sharp horse trading and barn burning, is the most successful family member of his generation. His son Flem continues his father's rapacity and corruption, surpassing his cousins: Mink, who is imprisoned for murder; Ike, an idiot who falls in love with a cow; Wesley, tarred and feathered for his relations with a young girl; I.O., a bigamist; Launcelot (Lump), who sells tickets to view Ike's perverted relations with the cow; and Eckrum (Eck), atypically honest, but who blows himself to bits in an explosion. Flem is also more successful in his rapacious progress toward power and seeming respectability than is the next generation, which includes Wesley's son Byron, who absconds with a little money from a bank, marries an Apache squaw, and "mails" their four children back to Flem; I.O.'s sons, including Montgomery Ward, who makes money from pornographic pictures and bootlegging, the twins Bilbo and Vardaman, and Clarence, a venal state senator; and Eckrum's sons, Admiral Dewey and Wallstreet Panic, the latter as honest and therefore as unlike a Snopes as his father. Although Flem succeeds beyond any other Snopes, becoming president of the Sartoris bank, the owner of the De Spain mansion, and the possessor of wealth, it is Linda, his wife's daughter by another man, a Snopes in name only, who brings him down to death. In revenge for his treatment of her, which included obtaining her inheritance and driving her mother, Eula Varner Snopes, to suicide, Linda persuades Gavin Stevens to obtain a pardon for Mink. Suffering from the hardships of 38 years in prison, attributing his long sentence to Flem's initial failure to help him, and knowing that it was extended by a plot which Flem engineered, Mink comes to Flem's home and shoots him dead.

Snow-Image, The, and Other Twice-Told Tales, 17 short stories by Hawthorne,♦ published in 1851. The volume includes historical sketches, tales of the supernatural, and such allegorical stories as "Ethan Brand," ♦ "My Kinsman, Major Molyneux," ♦ and "The Great Stone Face." ♦

"The Snow-Image: A Childish Miracle" is an allegory in which Peony and Violet Lindsey, gay, fanciful children, build an image of snow, encouraged by their mother, who tells them it will be their snow-sister and playfellow. In their enthusiasm they are hardly surprised when the image comes to life as a beautiful child in a flimsy white dress, who plays with them in the garden. When the children's father, a matter-of-fact merchant, comes home, he disregards their remonstrances and takes the snow-child into the house, intending to clothe her, feed her, and take her to her own home. But the child vanishes, and only a pool of water remains before the stove. The author concludes that "should some phenomenon of nature or providence transcend" the system of men of Lindsey's stamp, "they will not recognize it, even if it come to pass under their very noses. What has been established as an element of good to one being may prove absolute mischief to another."

Snow White, novel by Donald Barthelme. ♦

Snow-Bound: A Winter Idyl, poem by Whittier, ♦ published in 1866. It is mainly in iambic tetrameter couplets, although the verse is sometimes varied by alternating rhymes.

The poet recalls the years of his boyhood, when a sudden snowstorm would transform his Quaker father's Massachusetts farm and its usual routine into an enchanted white realm of adventure. The family gathered during the evening before the fireplace, where his father told of his early experiences in the Canadian woods and the New England farms and fisheries, and his mother read from Quaker religious books, or described family adventures during Indian raids. An uncle, "innocent of books," offered tales of hunting and fishing, and an aunt shared memories of her girlhood, while other participants in the quiet festivities were the poet's brother and sisters, the merry schoolmaster, and a guest, the religious enthusiast Harriet Livermore. Later, after all retired, they lay awake listening to the unaccustomed sounds of the storm. In the morning, the snow-blanketed world outside appeared quiet and strange, but soon there was a bustle of visits and domestic activity, although the little community might remain isolated for weeks. After the poet has given these minute Flemish pictures of his own childhood, he realizes that the "Angel of the backward look" must clasp the book of the past, and recognizes that he must attend to the duties of later years. Yet haply, as life slopes down to death, he may pause in some lull of life, realize "the grateful sense of sweetness near," stretch forth the hands of memory "and, pausing, take with forehead bare the benediction of the air."

Snows of Kilimanjaro, The, story by Hemingway, ♦ published in *Esquire* (Aug. 1936) and collected in *The Fifth Column and the First Forty-Nine Stories* (1938).

Dying with "a great tiredness and anger" of blood poisoning from his gangrenous leg, the novelist Harry lies in camp on his African safari, accompanied by his wife and native attendants, waiting for a rescue plane that he knows will arrive too late, and remembers experiences that were to have served as subjects of stories when he knew enough to write them well. But he realizes too that he has destroyed his talent by sloth, by enjoyments such as the marriage with his rich wife could bring, and that he hates himself as he

vents his cruelty on her. As he knows he will die that night, he tries to write, but vividly he feels and sees and smells death as he drops off, dreaming that the plane has come and taken him not to a hospital but to the very top of Kilimanjaro, said to be the highest mountain in Africa, where, according to the story's epigraph, close to the summit that is called the House of God "there is the dried and frozen carcass of a leopard. No one has explained what the leopard was seeking at that altitude."

SNYDER, GARY [SHERMAN] (1930–   ), San Francisco-born poet, after graduation from Reed College, work in the Forest Service, and study of Oriental languages at the University of California, Berkeley, participated in the local poetic renaissance that featured the Beat movement. ♦ He was later a tanker seaman and lived in Japan to take formal Zen training until he settled on a northern California farm. He has said of himself, "I hold the most archaic values . . . the fertility of the soul, the magic of animals, the power-vision in solitude, . . . the common work of the tribe" in his sacramental view of man's relation to the universe. His poems appear in *Riprap* (1959), based on his experiences in the forest service and as a tanker seaman; *Myths and Texts* (1960), a series unified by the themes of the failure of Western culture and the contrasting values of Buddhism and American Indian primitivism (enlarged in 1965 with "Cold Mountain Poems," translations from the Chinese); *Six Sections from Mountains and Rivers Without End* (1965, expanded 1970), part of an ongoing long work treating journeys, literal and metaphoric; *A Range of Poems* (1966), a selection of previous publications with additions; *The Back Country* (1968), on early experiences in the Far West, Japan, and India and his return to the U.S.; *Regarding Wave* (1970), poems both philosophic in his dedication to Buddhism and personal in telling of his love for his Japanese wife; *Manzanita* (1972), a limited edition forming part of *Turtle Island* (1974, Pulitzer Prize), poetry and prose setting forth his views of humanity, nature, and religion; and *Axe Handles* (1984). *Earth House Hold* (1969) collects essays and journal jottings on poetry, primitivism, communal life, and ecology, *The Old Ways* (1977) is a small, lesser collection of essays, and *The Real Work* (1982) gathers interviews and talks. Snyder figures as Japhy Ryder in Kerouac's *The Dharma Bums.*

Society and Solitude, essays by Emerson, ♦ based on lectures delivered as early as 1858, revised and published in 1870. The subjects are "Society and Solitude," "Civilization," "Art," "Eloquence," "Domestic Life," "Farming," "Works and Days," "Books," "Clubs," "Courage," "Success," and "Old Age."

The title piece is concerned with the individual's problem of social conduct. For those who have originality and a sense of personal integrity, the necessity for solitude is deeply felt and "organic." Constant social friction is wearing and difficult, and one naturally seeks to be alone. "But this banishment to the rocks and echoes . . . is so against nature, such a half-view, that it must be corrected by a common sense and experience." A man can live significantly only through contact with his fellows; sympathy and cooperation make possible the advancement of common causes; "the benefits of affection are immense"; and, moreover, "society cannot do without cultivated men." On the other hand, "the people are to be taken in very small doses." Overmuch company is degrading, since "men cannot afford to live together on their merits, and they adjust themselves by their demerits." The remedy is to strike a balance between social and solitary ways of living, "and a sound mind will derive its principles from insight, with ever a purer ascent to the sufficient and absolute right, and will accept society as the natural element in which they are to be applied."

Soldiers' Pay, novel by Faulkner, ♦ published in 1926.

Lieutenant Donald Mahon, an American in the British air force during World War I, is discharged from the hospital where he has been treated for a critical head wound, and makes his way home to Georgia. The wound leaves a horrible scar, and causes loss of memory and later blindness. On the train from New York he is aided by Joe Gilligan, an awkward, friendly, footloose ex-soldier, and Margaret Powers, an attractive young widow whose husband was killed in the war. Margaret, strangely attracted to the dying, subhuman Donald, decides to go home with him, as does Gilligan, who is in love with her. Their reception in the Georgia town reveals the character of the fickle people: Donald's father, an Episcopal minister whose optimism and idealism prevent his recognition of his son's tragedy, until the accumulation of ugly facts destroys his faith; Donald's pathetic, homely cousin, Emmy, whom he had loved;

his fiancée, Cecily Saunders, a selfish girl now in love with another man but afraid of her conventional parents and public opinion; and George Farr, Cecily's lover, who considers nothing but his own desire. Sentiment in town soon turns against Donald because of his fearful appearance and his suspected liaison with Margaret, who remains to nurse him. As months pass, Cecily elopes with George, and Gilligan good-naturedly stays on, despite Margaret's rejection of his proposals and her eventual marriage to Donald. The suffering aviator finally dies, and Margaret leaves, once more refusing Gilligan, who remains for a time with the elder Mahon. The latter is a changed man as the result of his ordeal: "Who knows; perhaps when we die we may not be required to go anywhere nor do anything at all. That would be heaven."

Son of the Wolf, The, nine short stories by Jack London, ♦ published in 1900. These tales of white men in the Klondike and Yukon have their tone set in the title story, in which the daughter of an Indian chief is captured by her white lover, Scruff Mackenzie, despite the racial antipathy of her native suitors.

Song of Myself, poem by Whitman, ♦ the untitled introduction to the first edition of *Leaves of Grass* (1855), later called "A Poem of Walt Whitman, An American" and "Walt Whitman," and given its present title in 1881.

Declaring "I celebrate myself . . . Walt Whitman, a kosmos," the poet sets forth two principal beliefs: the first, a theory of universality ("of every hue and caste am I, of every rank and religion"), is illustrated by lengthy catalogues of people and things; the second is that all things are equal in value ("I am the poet of the Body and . . . of the Soul . . . not the poet of goodness only, . . . of wickedness also. . . . I believe a leaf of grass is no less than the journey-work of the stars."). This equalitarian doctrine is based both on the theory of evolution and on a pantheistic belief; at one time Whitman is a mystic, and at another he proclaims, "Hurrah for positive science!," while yet admitting that facts serve only to give entrance to "an area of my dwelling." This inconsistency, however, he confesses and accepts: "Do I contradict myself? Very well then, I contradict myself; (I am large, I contain multitudes.)" and at the end he reiterates his mystical pantheism ("I bequeath myself to the dirt, to grow from the grass I love, If you want me again look for me under your boot-soles . . .").

Song of the Broad-Axe, poem by Whitman, ♦ published in *Leaves of Grass* (1856) as "Broad-Axe Poem," and given its present title in 1867.

The "weapon, shapely, naked, wan," is traced from the extraction of the rough ore from the earth to its shaping for the utilitarian purposes to which it has been put in different periods of history. The use of the axe by American pioneers, firemen, shipbuilders, carpenters, and butchers is contrasted with its use in foreign countries at earlier periods by sacrificial priests, warriors, and executioners. Thus it becomes symbolic of the freedom of democracy, contrasted with the restrictions of autocratic rule.

Song of the Chattahoochee, The, poem by Lanier, ♦ published in 1883 and reprinted in *Poems* (1884). Mainly in iambics, with a variation of meters to produce musical sounds, the poem is an onomatopoeic expression of the river's flow "to be mixed with the main," obeying "the voices of Duty" to turn the mills and water the fields during its course.

Song of the Lark, The, novel by Willa Cather, ♦ published in 1915.

Thea Kronborg, daughter of a Swedish minister in Colorado, during her growth to adolescence develops an obsessive interest in music. Her ability on the piano is encouraged by her eccentric German music teacher, Professor Wunsch, and by Dr. Howard Archie, a kindly, educated physician whose unfortunate marriage taints his life. Set apart from the townspeople by her talents and ardent nature, she prefers such friends as "Spanish Johnny" Tellamantez and the railroad worker Ray Kennedy, who falls in love with her but dies in a train wreck, leaving her his insurance. With this sum she goes to Chicago, at 17, to study with the pianist Andor Harsanyi, who finds in her the same innate taste and artistic integrity that mark his own character. When he discovers that she is earning her way by singing in a church choir, he listens to her voice, and finds it has great possibilities. He sends her to study voice with Madison Bowers, whose chill, selfish attitude repels her, but through him she meets the wealthy young brewer Fred Ottenburg, who introduces her to such socially prominent friends and art patrons as the Nathanmeyers. After she becomes ill and discouraged, despite her progress, Ottenburg invites her to his father's Arizona ranch. They fall in love, and travel together in

Mexico, but separate because Fred, already married, is unable to obtain a divorce. Dr. Archie advances her the money necessary for study in Europe, and after ten years she becomes a great Wagnerian soprano of the Metropolitan Opera. Although she later marries Ottenburg after his wife's death, her life is expressed and bound up in her career, in which she finds not happiness but the fulfillment of the driving artistic impulse that has always ruled her.

SONTAG, SUSAN (1933–), best known for her essays collected in *Against Interpretation* (1966), arguing that the proper response to creative works is sensory or emotive, not intellectual; *Trip to Hanoi* (1968), about her view of North Vietnam during the U.S. war against it; *Styles of Radical Will* (1969), on different ways of changing consciousness, as through drugs, for aesthetic purposes; *On Photography* (1977), about the social and cultural roles of photography; *Illness as Metaphor* (1978), concerning psychlogical relations to physical ailments; and *Under the Sign of Saturn* (1980). She has also written novels, *The Benefactor* (1963) and *Death Kit* (1967), and stories, *I, etcetera* (1978), as well as film scripts.

Sophie's Choice, novel by William Styron, ♦ published in 1979.

Narrated by the author's autobiographical persona, Stingo, a young would-be novelist from Tidewater Virginia, it tells of his experiences in New York City, where he was first a publisher's reader, then a resident of the Bronx, able to be jobless and to concentrate on the creation of his first novel thanks to a small legacy of money deriving directly from the sale, generations before, of a family slave. In his boardinghouse Stingo becomes the devoted friend of Nathan Landau, a slightly older, brilliant but drug-deranged manic-depressive Jewish intellectual, and his beloved Sophie Zawistowska, an émigré Polish Catholic beauty, with whom he has a tortured relationship marked by frenzied sex. The account of her frightful experiences during World War II as told to Stingo make him recognize "a sinister zone of likeness between Poland and the American South," thus creating another dimension for the novel and its narrator. Her father, a professor of law, and her husband had been killed by the Nazis, and she and her children had been imprisoned in the concentration death camp of Auschwitz. From it she had escaped, first by becoming the secretary of its commandant, Rudolf Höss, then by appealing to him by diverse means, including a pamphlet written years before by her anti-Semitic father. Although thus saved from death, she suffers her own perdition in the years of life left to her.

SORENSEN, Virginia (1912–   ), Utah-born novelist, many of whose works, including *A Little Lower Than the Angels* (1942), *On This Star* (1946), *The Evening and the Morning* (1949), *Many Heavens* (1954), and *Kingdom Come* (1960), deal sympathetically and knowingly with Mormon life. She has also written books for children and *Where Nothing Is Long Ago* (1963), recollections of her childhood as a Mormon. She lives in Morocco with her husband, Alec Waugh.

SORRENTINO, Gilbert (1929–   ), Brooklyn-born poet and experimental novelist. His first novel, *The Sky Changes* (1966), is a parody telling of an unhappily married couple driving across the U.S. on a "second honeymoon" that ends when she leaves him. It was followed by *Steelwork* (1970), depicting Brooklyn from the 1930s through World War II; *Imaginary Qualities of Actual Things* (1971), like its predecessor a work of fiction without plot, but a bitter satire on New York literati; *Mulligan Stew* (1979), a comic novel about a novelist; *Flawless Play Restored* (1975), a segment in the form of a drama from that novel; *Aberration of Starlight* (1980), a quasi-autobiographical story of life in a New Jersey boardinghouse, seen from four points of view; *Crystal Vision* (1981), an early but previously unpublished comic novel; and *Blue Pastoral* (1983). *The Darkness Surrounds Us* (1960), *Black and White* (1964), *The Perfect Fiction* (1968), *Corrosive Sublimate* (1971), *The Orangery* (1978), and *Selected Poems* (1981) collect poems that belong to the school of Pound, Williams, and Creeley. *Splendide-Hotel* (1973) is a novella-like essay about the role of the poet. *Something Said* (1984) collects essays and reviews. He also edited the little magazine *Neon* (1956–60), which featured the Beat authors.

Sot-Weed Factor, The, novel by John Barth ♦; published in 1960 and in a revised version in 1966.

In a lusty picaresque tale that satirizes conventional historical fiction, the novel creates a fictive biography of Ebenezer Cook, the 18th-century Maryland author of satirical verse about tobacco, endowing him with a twin sister, Anna. After failing in his studies at Cambridge, though abetted by a tutor, Henry Burlingame, Ebenezer is ordered by his father to manage the family tobacco plantation in Maryland. There he spends most of his time writing poetry and protecting his virginity, both of which are under constant assault. Finally he achieves fame as a writer while simultaneously losing his poetic inspiration and his virginity.

Souls of Black Folk, The, collection of essays and sketches by W.E.B. DuBois, published in 1903. The 15 pieces in the book include sociological studies of sharecroppers and small farmers, sensitive interpretation of music related to black religious services, a historical study of the Freedmen's Bureau, and a searching consideration of Booker T. Washington, praising some of his activities but going beyond him in calling for higher education for blacks and for more militant action.

Sound and the Fury, The, novel by Faulkner, ♦ published in 1929. The story is told in four parts, through the stream of consciousness of three characters (the sons of the Compson family, ♦ Benjy, Quentin, and Jason), and finally in an objective account.

The Compson family, formerly genteel Southern patricians, now lead a degenerate, perverted life on their shrunken plantation near Jefferson, Miss. The disintegration of the family, which clings to outworn aristocratic conventions, is counterpointed by the strength of the black servants, who include old Dilsey and her son Luster. The latter tends the idiot Benjy Compson, who is 33 and incapable of speech or any but the simplest actions. Through his broken thoughts, which revert to his childhood at every chance stimulation of his acute senses, is disclosed the tragedy of his drunken father; his proud, sniveling, hypochondriac mother; his weak-minded Uncle Maury; his sister Candace (Caddy), whom he adores because she is kind to him; his mean, dishonest brother Jason; and his sensitive brother Quentin, a promising student at Harvard, who goes mad, obsessed by love of Caddy, and, shamed by her seduction, commits suicide. When Caddy is forced to marry and leave home, Benjy is desolate, but he plays like a child with her illegitimate daughter, until she grows up, gives evidence of her mother's nymphomaniac strain, runs away with a tent-show performer, and steals a sum of money from Jason.

South Atlantic Quarterly (1902–), founded at Trinity College (since 1924, Duke University) at Durham, N.C., by John S. Bassett, a professor of history, primarily as a sober but generally liberal medium for discussion of Southern history, economics, education, and culture in a broad perspective. The policy continued after Bassett's editorship ended (1905), as may be seen in W.B. Hamilton's history and anthology, *Fifty Years of the South Atlantic Quarterly* (1952). A few special issues (e.g. on 18th-century literature, the Renaissance, and Soviet foreign policy) have served as festschrifts for university professors.

Southern Literary Messenger (1834–64, 1939–44), magazine founded at Richmond by Thomas W. White, whose first nine numbers were edited by James E. Heath. Poe's first contribution was "Berenice" (March 1835), and in December of that year he became the editor, at a salary of $15 per week. He published 83 reviews, 6 poems, 4 essays, and 3 stories, and increased the magazine's subscription list from 500 to more than 3500. His "tomahawk" method of criticism made the *Messenger* famous, and led to literary feuds with such authors as those of the Knickerbocker Group. ♦ His persistent drinking led to his loss of the editorship (Jan. 1837). White then became editor, with aid from others, until his death (1843), after which Benjamin B. Minor became publisher and editor. Although Poe wrote two unimportant articles, and other former contributors continued, the magazine declined in literary significance, and gave great attention to military and naval affairs. Under J.R. Thompson (1847–60), G.W. Bagby (1860–64), and Frank H. Alfriend (1864), it dwindled to death. *The Contributors and Contributions to the Southern Literary Messenger* was published in 1936, and the magazine was revived (1939–44).

Southern Review (1935–42, 1965–) published quarterly at Baton Rouge, La. Although issued by the Louisiana State University Press, it was not a university organ, but was primarily a regional review. Its editors included R.P. Warren, and it printed contributions from J.P. Bishop, Kenneth Burke, Herbert Agar, Katherine Anne Porter, J.C. Ransom, and Allen Tate. It was revived with similar policies under new editors in 1965.

SOUTHWORTH, E[mma] D[orothy] E[liza] N[evitte] (1819–99), popular feminine novelist of the domestic-sentimental school, lived most of her life in Washington, D.C. Her *Retribution* (1849) was followed by some 60 similar romances with melodramatic plots, originally written as magazine serials, and usually set in the South. Among the most popular works were *The Curse of Clifton* (1852), *The Missing Bride* (1855), *The Hidden Hand* (1859), *The Fatal Marriage* (1869), *The Maiden Widow* (1870), and *Self-Raised* (1876).

Specimen Days and Collect, autobiographical narrative by Whitman, ♦ published in 1882. It incorporates *Memoranda During the War* (1875).

The first part contains the author's reminiscences of his early life and the fascinating panorama of New York. This is followed by journal jottings and memoranda of the Civil War, both on the front and in Washington hospitals. The last part of the book deals with his observations of nature and his own sensations, and incorporates travel sketches of his excursions to the West, Canada, and Boston, with literary criticism of the authors he met and others who interested him, such as Carlyle.

SPENCER, Elizabeth (1921–), Mississippi-born novelist, resident for some time in Italy. Since 1958 she and her husband have lived in Canada. Her first novels, *Fire in the Morning* (1948), *This Crooked Way* (1952), and *The Voice at the Back Door* (1956), are set in her native state and in various ways contrast established and new modes of life in the Old South. Her next novels, *The Light in the Piazza* (1960) and *Knights and Dragons* (1965), both set in Italy, are very brief works sensitively dealing with Americans in Italy. Like her earlier fiction they are distinguished by fine craftsmanship and intense plots that reveal the essential natures of the characters. *The Snare* (1972) is a longer, more complex novel set in the underworld of New Orleans, and the setting of *The Road to Lagoa Santa* (1984), the hurricane-wrecked Mississippi Gulf Coast, is symbolic of its characters' lives. *Ship Island* (1968) collects stories, as does *The Stories of Elizabeth Spencer* (1981). *Marilee* (1981) contains three stories about the growing up of a girl in the deep South.

SPEYER, Leonora (1872–1956), New York poet whose lyrics in *A Canopic Jar* (1921) promised the command of form and intense personal idiom that were fulfilled in *Fiddler's Farewell* (1926, Pulitzer Prize), especially noted for its wit and understanding of feminine character. The poems in *Naked Heel* (1931) have been criticized as emotionally "thin" and excessively formal. *Slow Wall* (1939) appeared in an enlarged edition in 1946.

Sphinx, The, poem by Emerson,♦ first published in *The Dial* (1841) and collected in his *Poems* (1847).

In 17 stanzas of two quatrains with irregular two- and three-stress lines, it tells of a poet meeting the Sphinx and solving the riddle of the all-inclusive divine spirit: "Who telleth one of my meanings, Is master of all I am." Emerson paraphrased the poem in his notebook (1859): "The perception of identity unites all things and explains one by another. . . . But if the mind live only in particulars . . . then the world addresses to this mind a question it cannot answer."

SPILLANE, MICKEY [FRANK MORRISON] (1918–   ), author of tough detective stories, emphasizing sadism more than mystery. His enormously popular books include *I, The Jury* (1947), *My Gun Is Quick* (1950), *The Big Kill* (1951), and many others published during the 1960s.

Spirit of the Times (1831–61), New York journal, a racy "Chronicle of the Turf, Agriculture, Field Sports, Literature, and the Stage" at one time probably had a circulation over 40,000, and was the medium for many "original contributions" from subscribers in every section of the country, but particularly in the Old Southwest. These contributions were distinctly masculine tales based on oral humor of the frontier. Some of the Sut Lovingood sketches were first published here, and other contributions included T.B. Thorpe's "The Big Bear of Arkansas" and work by J.J. Hooper, W.T. Thompson, Sol Smith, and J.M. Field.

Spiritual, religious folk song of blacks, perhaps stemming from the camp-meeting songs and spirituals of the white evangelistic sects, and characterized by melancholy, pathos, and naïve faith. It frequently consists of stanzas in which a single line is repeated several times with a line of refrain which unites the whole. The songs are essentially folk creations, often the result of mass extemporizing, lending themselves to many variations. Among the more famous are "Golden Slippers"; "Roll, Jordan, Roll"; and "Swing Low, Sweet Chariot."

SPOFFORD, HARRIET [ELIZABETH] PRESCOTT (1835–1921), New England author best known for her numerous romantic short stories. Her first novel, *Sir Rohan's Ghost* (1860), in the tradition of Poe and the Gothic romance, is the story of a man who tries to kill his mistress and is later plagued by her daughter, with whom he falls in love. *Azarian: An Episode* (1864) is a poetic tale concerning Constant Azarian, an artistic Bostonian who is too self-centered to appreciate the devotion of idealistic Ruth Yetton. *The Amber Gods and Other Stories* (1863) was the first of Mrs. Spofford's many collections of romantic tales. After her marriage (1865) she lived much of the time in Washington, D.C., and her interest in the local color of this city is shown in *Old Washington* (1906). She wrote many volumes of poetry, including *In Titian's Garden* (1903).

Spoils of Poynton, The, novel by Henry James,♦ published in 1897.

Old Mrs. Gereth and young Fleda Vetch, while visiting the English country place of the vulgar Brigstocks, find a bond of sympathy in their dislike of their hosts' bad taste. Mrs. Gereth, who has been seeking a desirable wife for her undistinguished son Owen, invites Fleda to visit her at her house at Poynton, in which she takes great pride. There she has assembled a magnificent collection of furniture and objects of art, and Fleda is moved to tears by its splendor. In that setting Fleda falls in love with Owen, but he has decided to marry Mona Brigstock, whom he brings to visit Poynton, his property under his father's will. The antipathy of Mona and Mrs. Gereth flares up at once, and Owen, realizing that his mother must vacate the house, asks Fleda's aid in persuading her to leave. Mrs. Gereth takes revenge by removing her greatest treasures from Poynton, and Mona threatens to break with Owen unless they are returned. He has meanwhile fallen in love with Fleda, who urges his mother to send the "spoils" back to Poynton. When Owen comes to Fleda's shabby home and asks her to marry him, she tells him that he must first break with Mona. The next news received by Mrs. Gereth and Fleda is that of his sudden marriage to Mona. After a time Fleda receives a letter from Owen, asking her to take from the house whatever object she values most. On arriving at Poynton, she finds the place in ruins as the result of an accidental fire. Its treasures, which have twisted so many lives, have been entirely destroyed.

Spontaneous Me, poem by Whitman,♦ published in *Leaves of Grass* (1856) as "Bunch Poem," included in "Children of Adam" (1860), and given its present title in 1867. It illustrates the author's pantheism and his amorous hyper-sensitivity by a catalogue of vital experiences—"the real poems, (what we call poems being merely pictures)."

Spoon River Anthology, free-verse poems of Edgar Lee Masters. ♦

Spy, The: A Tale of the Neutral Ground, romance by Cooper, ♦ published in 1821, and dramatized by C.P. Clinch (1822).

Harvey Birch, supposed to be a Loyalist spy but secretly in the intelligence service of General Washington, operates in the "neutral ground" of his native Westchester County, New York, and aids his neighbors, Henry Wharton, a Loyalist who pretends to be neutral, his daughters Sarah and Frances, and a son, Captain Henry Wharton of the British army. In 1780, Washington, in his accustomed disguise as Mr. Harper, is sheltered at the Wharton home, where he is impressed by the rebel sympathies of Frances. To repay the family's hospitality, Birch warns Captain Henry of his impending capture, but the young man, refusing to leave, is taken by a rebel force under Captain Jack Lawton. Frances appeals to her fiancé, the patriot Major Peyton Dunwoodie, but meanwhile Captain Henry escapes during a battle, only to be recaptured with Colonel Wellemere, Sarah's British admirer. Birch is almost captured by Lawton, who mistakes him for a spy, but in their struggle he spares Lawton's life, a good deed repaid by Lawton when Birch is later turned over to him by the "Skinners," a band of marauding patriots. The wedding of Wellemere and Sarah is interrupted by Birch, who reveals that Wellemere is already married, and the Englishman escapes during a raid by the marauders, who destroy the Wharton home. Captain Henry is sentenced to be executed as a spy, but Birch helps him escape, and Frances, seeking them, goes to Birch's mountain retreat, where she finds "Mr. Harper" and persuades him to end the pursuit of her brother. Birch takes Captain Henry to a British ship, Frances and Dunwoodie are married, Lawton is killed in battle, and Birch, ending his service to Washington, refuses rewards, preferring to remain an itinerant peddler.

STAFFORD, JEAN (1915–79), California-born novelist reared in Colorado, after graduation from the University of Colorado and further study there and in Germany began the writing of fiction noted for sensitive interpretations of adult isolation and the problems of adolescence. *Boston Adventure* (1944) presents the character of a foreign girl working as secretary to a wealthy Boston spinster; her second novel, *The Mountain Lion* (1947), depicts the unhappy youth of a brother and sister and their escape on a Colorado ranch. Later novels include *The Catherine Wheel* (1952) and *A Winter's Tale* (1954). *Children Are Bored on Sunday* (1953) and *Bad Characters* (1964) collect stories, definitively assembled in *Collected Stories* (1969, Pulitzer Prize). Her only work of nonfiction was *A Mother in History* (1966), about Lee Harvey Oswald's mother. She was married to Robert Lowell (1940–48) and A.J. Leibling (1959–63).

STAFFORD, WILLIAM [EDGAR] (1914–), Kansas-born poet and professor at Lewis and Clark College (Portland, Ore.) since 1948. His poems, mostly short lyrics, have been published in *Down in My Heart* (1947), *West of Your City* (1960), *Traveling Through the Dark* (1962, National Book Award), *The Rescued Year* (1966), recalling his rural youth, *Allegiances* (1970), *Someday, Maybe* (1973), *Stories That Could Be True* (1977), *The Quiet of the Land* (1982), and *A Glass Face in the Rain* (1982). *Segues* (1984) is a correspondence carried on in poetry with Marvin Bell, each man the author of 22 poems. His critical writing appears in a work on Brother Antoninus♦ (1967) and *Friends to This Ground* (1968). *Writing the Australian Crawl* (1978) collects articles and interviews on his poetry and that of others.

STANDISH, MYLES (or MILES) (c.1584–1656), engaged by the Pilgrims to sail with them on the *Mayflower* (1620) as a military leader. His measures of defense and diplomatic ability in handling his soldiers soon made him more than an employee, and he may have become a member of their church. Among his important actions was the dispersal of the settlement of Thomas Morton, by whom, in the *New English Canaan,* he was called "Captain Shrimp, a quondam drummer." There is no historical basis for Longfellow's "The Courtship of Miles Standish," ♦ for Standish was twice married. He also figures in Jane G. Austin's *Standish of Standish* and Motley's *Merry Mount.*

STANTON, Elizabeth Cady (1815–1902), began her long career for woman's rights at the convention dedicated to this subject in her hometown of Seneca Falls, N.Y., in 1848. Soon thereafter she became the lifelong collaborator with Susan B. Anthony♦ in working for woman suffrage, as well as for temperance laws and the abolition of slavery. While the plain Miss Anthony was a talented organizer, the warm, attractive Mrs. Stanton was more effective as a public speaker and a vigorous journalist. Together they published the journal *Revolution* (1868–69) and compiled and edited the three volumes of the monumental *History of Woman Suffrage* (1881–86). Mrs. Stanton alone created *The Woman's Bible* (2 vols., 1895, 1898), interpreting from her point of view all references to women in the Bible. Her last major work was her autobiography, *Eighty Years and More* (1898).

"Star-Spangled Banner, The," song by Francis Scott Key,♦ became the U.S. national anthem by act of Congress (1931), although it had long been popularly considered the anthem and had been officially used by the army and navy since the Spanish-American War. Key, on a legal mission, was detained by the British and forced to view the bombardment of Fort McHenry, near Baltimore, during the night of September 13–14, 1814. The sight of the flag still flying inspired his verses, set to the music of "Anacreon in Heaven" by the Englishman John Stafford Smith (1750–1836), the anthem of the Anacreontic Societies, clubs of musical amateurs. Key's song was published as "Defence of Fort M'Henry" in *Baltimore Patriot* (Sept. 20, 1814), perhaps preceded by a broadside. It was collected in Key's *Poems* (1857).

Star-Splitter, The, blank-verse narrative by Robert Frost,♦ published in *New Hampshire* (1923).

Brad McLaughlin's "life-long curiosity About our place among the infinities" culminates in his burning his house down for the insurance, to buy a telescope. He earns a living as a railroad ticket agent and uses his leisure "for star-gazing" through his glass, "the Star-splitter." Brad and his friend, the poet, often spend their nights in this activity, but though it provides material for "some of the best things we ever said," they remain in ignorance of the real nature of the universe: "We've looked and looked, but after all where are we?"

STARBUCK, George [Edwin] (1931–), Ohio-born poet, has been on the faculty of the University of Iowa and of Boston University, whose works include *Bone Thoughts* (1960), *White Paper* (1966), *Elegy in a Country Church Yard* (1975), *Desperate Measures* (1977), and *The Argot Merchant Disaster* (1982).

Starting from Paumanok, poem by Whitman first published in *Leaves of Grass* in 1860 as "Proto-Leaf," revised and given its present title in 1867, and further revised in 1881. Beginning with reference to his birth on Paumanok, the Indian name of Long Island, in 19 sections the poem treats such major themes as the subject matter with which the author will deal in all his writing, the New World and the United States, comradeship, love, individualism, equality, liberty, and the soul.

STEEGMULLER, Francis (1906–), author of literary and biographical studies, including *Flaubert and Madame Bovary* (1939), *Maupassant: A Lion in the Path* (1949), *The Two Lives of James Jackson Jarves* (1951), *Apollinaire, Poet Among the Painters* (1963), and *Cocteau* (1970).

STEFFENS, [Joseph] Lincoln (1866–1936), born in San Francisco, graduated from the University of California (1889), studied abroad, and entered New York journalism (1892). He is best known for his leadership of the muckraking movement.♦ As managing editor of *McClure's Magazine* (1902–6) and associate editor of *American Magazine* and *Everybody's* (1906–11), he was a contributor to the journalistic exposé of business and government corruption. His articles are collected in *The Shame of the Cities* (1904), *The Struggle for Self-Government* (1906), and *Upbuilders* (1909). His *Autobiography* (1931) tells the story of his gradual evolution of a theory of government and his transition from sensational reporting to the belief in a fundamental relation between the various forms of corruption he had discovered. It also contains an account of modern liberal and radical movements, with which he was affiliated during much of his life. *Lincoln Steffens Speaking* (1936) is a posthumous collection of articles written during his later years, and his *Letters* were collected in 1938.

STEGNER, Wallace [Earle] (1909–), Iowa-born author, graduated from the University of Utah and is a professor at Stanford. His novels are *Remembering Laughter* (1937), set in Iowa; *On a Darkling Plain* (1940), about a Canadian veteran seeking solitude on the prairie; *Fire and Ice* (1941), about a college student temporarily joining the Communist party; *The Big Rock Candy Mountain* (1943), about a Far Westerner who moves his family from one home to another in a futile search for fortune; *Second Growth* (1947), contrasting the lives of visitors and villagers in New Hampshire; *The Preacher and the Slave* (1950), about Joe Hill of the I.W.W.; *A Shooting Star* (1961), presenting ways of life among established, wealthy northern Californians; *All the Little Live Things* (1967), contrasting ways of life of a cultivated older man and a young hippie; *Angle of Repose* (1971), a fictional rendering of the life of Mary Hallock Foote that won a Pulitzer Prize and was adapted as an opera by Oakley Hall and Andrew Imbrie (1976); *The Spectator Bird* (1976, National Book Award), in which the older man of *All the Little Live Things* recalls a romantic interlude of his youth; and *Recapitulation* (1979), presenting a retired U.S. ambassador's unsettling return to Utah, where he was reared. *The Women on the Wall* (1950) and *The City of the Living* (1956) collect stories. His nonfiction includes *Mormon Country* (1942), presenting the local scene and its folkways; *One Nation* (1945), depicting U.S. minorities; *Beyond the Hundredth Meridian* (1954), about John Wesley Powell's explorations of the western U.S.; *This Is Dinosaur* (1955), a conservationist plea for a Utah and Colorado national monument; *Wolf Willow* (1962), a warmly understanding personal and public history and recollection of the "last plains frontier" where Montana and Saskatchewan meet, the area where the author's youth was spent; *The Gathering of Zion* (1964), about the Mormon trek and trail to Utah; *The Sound of Mountain Water* (1969), diverse considerations of the West; *The Uneasy Chair* (1974), a life of Bernard De Voto, whose *Letters* (1975) Stegner edited; and *One Way To Spell Man* (1982), essays.

STEIN, Gertrude (1874–1946), born in Pennsylvania, was educated abroad, at California schools, and graduated from Radcliffe (1897). She was stimulated at college by William James, and her psychological experiments led her to study the anatomy of the brain at Johns Hopkins. Tiring of scientific work, she went abroad (1902), where she lived until her death, her *salon* in France

attracting prominent writers as well as painters, particularly Matisse, Picasso, and Juan Gris, whose works she collected. Her early fiction, including *Three Lives* (1909), stories of two servant girls and an unhappy black woman, *The Making of Americans*♦ (1925), and *A Long Gay Book* (1932), shows a breakdown of traditional plot structure and discursive writing, and dependence upon intuitive means of expressing the actual present.

Her later writings include *Tender Buttons* (1914), poetry without conventional logic or grammar, intended to express the qualities of objects; *Geography and Plays* (1922); *Composition as Explanation* (1926), lectures given at Oxford and Cambridge; *Lucy Church Amiably* (1930), a novel; *How To Write* (1931), a book of examples; *The Autobiography of Alice B. Toklas* (1933), her own autobiography, composed as though by her secretary and friend Alice B. Toklas♦; *Four Saints in Three Acts* (1934), an opera with music by Virgil Thomson; *Portraits and Prayers* (1934); *Narration* (1935), four critical lectures delivered at the University of Chicago; *The Geographical History of America* (1936), a formless work illustrating her literary theories; *Everybody's Autobiography* (1937), an account of her American lecture tour; *Picasso* (1938); *The World Is Round* (1939), a book for children; *Paris France* (1940), a sympathetic study of the French way of life; *Ida* (1941), a "novel"; *Wars I Have Seen* (1945) and *Yes Is For a Very Young Man*♦ (1946), about life in France during World War II, respectively in a personal account and a play; and *Brewsie and Willie* (1946), about lives of American soldiers in France during World War II.

Her *Lectures in America* (1935) explains her philosophy of composition, which is partly indebted to the aesthetic theories of William James and Bergson's concept of time. She contends that it is the "business of art" to live in "the complete actual present," and in describing her technique she compares it with that of the cinema. No two frames of a motion picture are exactly alike, yet the sequence presents to the eye a flowing continuity. Similarly, Miss Stein, by the use of partly repetitive statements, each making a limited advance in the theme, presents an uninterrupted series of instantaneous visions, so that one grasps a living moment in precise, ordered forms. This "moment to moment emphasis in what is happening" appears particularly in her early "portraits," and in *Three Lives* and *The Making of Americans*. Another of her concerns was "to tell what each one is without telling stories . . . so that the essence of what happened would be . . . the essence of the portraits." She was also interested in "the relation between color and sound."

In order to convey her concept of movement in the motion-picture manner, she set up a rhythmic pattern and placed her emphasis upon the verb. Nouns being names, she felt that "things once they are named the name does not go on doing anything to them and so why write in nouns." She felt that most punctuation is "an unnecessary name of something." "It is evident that when you ask a question you ask a question . . . and so why add to it the question mark." Other punctuation also interfered with the need for capturing motion: "If writing should go on what had colons and semi-colons to do with it." In her poetry she holds a different theory about language; for, though naming, or noun-using, does not carry prose forward, "you can love a name and if you love a name then saying that name any number of times only makes you love it more . . ." and poetry is "really loving the name of anything." Thus, for her, poetry is a method of dealing "with everything that was not movement in space."

Her practice of these theories influenced other authors. Sherwood Anderson felt that she revivified language and was stimulated by her method of repetition with minute variations, as was Hemingway, both in the rhythms of his prose and in his way of conveying emotions as immediate experience. Yale, which inherited her manuscripts, in 1951 began printing all unpublished works, initially edited by Van Vechten.

STEINBECK, John [Ernst] (1902–68), California novelist, attended Stanford University (1919–20, 1922–23, 1924–25), and worked at odd jobs, beginning his literary career with *Cup of Gold* (1929), a romantic novel based on the career of Sir Henry Morgan, the buccaneer. This was followed by *The Pastures of Heaven* (1932), a collection of short stories portraying the people of a farm community in a California valley. His second novel, *To a God Unknown* (1933), tells of a California farmer whose pagan religion of fertility becomes a mystical obsession, and after a season of drought leads to his suicide as a sacrifice on the sylvan altar at which he has worshiped.

Tortilla Flat ♦ (1935) won Steinbeck popular attention for the first time, with its sympathetically humorous depiction of the lives of Monterey *paisanos. In Dubious*

Battle ♦ (1936), the story of a strike of migratory fruit pickers, was the first of his novels concerned with the conditions of this class, which continued to hold his interest. In *Of Mice and Men* ♦ (1937), the story of two itinerant farmhands represents the tragedy of a class that yearns for a home, of which it is perpetually deprived. After dramatizing this work with great success (1937), Steinbeck published a volume of short stories, *The Long Valley* ♦ (1938), containing the previously published *Saint Katy the Virgin* (1936) and *The Red Pony* (1937), published separately with additional material in 1945. His concern with the problems of the landless farm laborer received greatest emphasis in *The Grapes of Wrath* ♦ (1939, Pulitzer Prize), a saga of a refugee family from the Dust Bowl, its migration to California, and the struggle to find work under an almost feudal system of agricultural exploitation.

In the 1940s Steinbeck wrote very various works. They include *The Forgotten Village* (1941), the script of a film depicting Mexican village life; *Sea of Cortez* (1941), written with his friend Edward F. Ricketts, a marine biologist, presenting a journal of their travels and marine research in the Gulf of California and containing Steinbeck's reflections on life; and *The Pearl* (1948), a short parable about a Mexican fisherman who finds a great pearl that brings evil to his family. This decade was also one of war writings: *Bombs Away: The Story of a Bomber Team* (1942); his dispatches of 1943 gathered in *Once There Was a War* (1958); and *A Russian Journal* (1948). Out of the same background came *The Moon Is Down* (1942), a novelette he dramatized (1942), about Norwegian resistance to the German occupation.

He returned to the setting and mood of *Tortilla Flat* in *Cannery Row* ♦ (1945), a whimsical tale of idlers in Monterey and their relations with a sympathetic biologist. These people and this place appear again in *Sweet Thursday* (1954). *The Wayward Bus* (1947) is a novel presenting a microcosm of frustrations in contemporary America through the stresses on a group of people stranded on a bus in rural California. *Burning Bright* (1950) in novelette form is a symbolic morality play about a man whose sterility forces him to accept another's child as his own. *East of Eden* ♦ (1952), his first major novel after *The Grapes of Wrath,* is a long family saga from the Civil War to World War I, partly set in the Salinas Valley, using the theme of Cain and Abel in a story both symbolic and realistic of man's struggle between good and evil. After a brief and minor novel, *The Short Reign of Pippin IV* (1957), a lighthearted comedy about a 20th-century French king, Steinbeck returned to full-bodied and serious fiction with *The Winter of Our Discontent* (1961), treating the moral collapse of a descendant of an old New England family, a man of high integrity, under the pressures of the mid-20th century.

Steinbeck's fiction combines realism and romance, but not always harmoniously. His settings are often rural areas, where people live most happily when close to nature, but where malevolent forces, such as drought or labor and market conditions or human greed, destroy this vital relationship. In dealing with the consequent problems Steinbeck's approach is sometimes lyric and mystical, sometimes realistic and sociological. Although he suffered a long period of adverse criticism, particularly in the United States, he remained popular and esteemed in Europe, and in the year when he published his account of a tour of 40 states, accompanied by his poodle, as *Travels with Charley in Search of America* (1962), he became the seventh American-born author to win a Nobel Prize.

His posthumously published works include *The Acts of King Arthur and His Noble Knights* (1976), a retelling of the tales. Correspondence appears in *Journals of a Novel: The East of Eden Letters* (1969), *Steinbeck: A Life in Letters* (1975), and *Letters to Elizabeth* (1978).

STERLING, GEORGE (1869–1926), born in New York, was educated under Father Tabb in Maryland, went to California, and was thereafter identified with the state as a noted author and bohemian. He fell under the influence of Bierce, "the Great Cham" of literature on the West Coast, and consistently submitted his poetry to his master for criticism. Although later he recognized the significance of modern poets, as evidenced in his *Robinson Jeffers, the Man and the Artist* (1926), his own verse harked back to what he had been taught by Bierce, and, with its emphasis upon exotic romanticism and rhythmical regularity, looked backward rather than forward and failed to appeal to Eastern critics. He was best known for his sonnets, influenced by Keats, his simple musical lyrics, and his lush, grandiose longer poems. His most important books, whose titles reveal his characteristic attitude, include *The Testimony of the Suns* (1903), *A Wine of Wizardry* (1909), and *The House of Orchids* (1911). Among his later books are *Thirty-Five Son-*

nets (1917) and *Selected Poems* (1923). He committed suicide in 1926. He is said to be the prototype of Brissenden in London's *Martin Eden.*

STERN, RICHARD G[USTAVE] (1928–   ), born in New York City, a professor of English at the University of Chicago, whose novels include *Golk* (1960), a satire on television production; *Europe; or Up and Down with Baggish and Schreiber* (1961), about U.S. civil service men in postwar Germany; *In Any Case* (1963), treating a father's fight to clear his dead son of a charge of treason while being essentially treasonable to him; *Stitch* (1965), depicting an aged, expatriate American sculptor modeled on Ezra Pound; *Other Men's Daughters* (1973), the story of a middle-aged Harvard professor who falls in love with a young student; and *Natural Shocks* (1978), treating a journalist having to cope with the subject of death. Stories are collected in *Teeth, Dying, and Other Matters* (1964), *1968: A Short Novel* (1970), and *Packages* (1980). Essays appear in *The Books in Fred Hampton's Apartment* (1973). *The Invention of the Real* (1982) collects essays, poems, and short prose pieces.

Stevens, GAVIN, character in Faulkner's Yoknapatawpha saga, first appears as a Harvard graduate and young district attorney in *Light in August.* As Uncle Gavin, a county attorney in *Intruder in the Dust,* ♦ he is persuaded by his nephew Chick Mallison to defend Lucas Beauchamp against the murder charge of which he is innocent. Gavin solves various crimes in *Knight's Gambit,* and in *Requiem for a Nun* he defends Nancy Mannigoe and takes Temple Drake to confess to the governor. In *The Town* he fights the rising power of the Snopeses while falling in love with Eula Varner Snopes, who tries to have him wed her daughter Linda. In *The Mansion* he continues his idealistic and "meddlesome" ways but he marries Melisandre Backus Harris, a widow.

GOWAN STEVENS, Gavin's nephew, in *Sanctuary* is the man whose drunken actions lead to Temple Drake being seized by bootleggers. In *Requiem for a Nun* he has atoned by marrying Temple. In *The Town* Gowan is called Gavin's cousin and is the source of much of the novel's lore.

STEVENS, WALLACE (1879–1955), Pennsylvania-born poet, educated at Harvard (1897–1900) and at New York University Law School, made his business career as an executive of an insurance firm in Hartford, Conn. The few early poems he chose to save appear among later work in *Harmonium*♦ (1923), published when he was almost 44, but most of his poetry was written after he was fifty, although its gaiety, vitality, and exotic imagination give no sense that it is the work of a man of such age and with a full-time business. His earliest poems have the finish, the elegant wit, the bizarre images, the lush figures, and the recondite diction that characterize all his work.

His poems range from descriptive and dramatic lyrics to meditative and discursive discourse, but all show a deep engagement in experience and in art. His musical verse, rich in tropic imagery but precise and intense in statement, is marked by concern with means of knowledge, with the contrast between reality and appearance, and the emphasis upon imagination as giving an aesthetic insight and order to life. These ideas are treated in "Sunday Morning,"♦ "Thirteen Ways of Looking At a Blackbird,"♦ "The Emperor of Ice Cream,"♦ and "Anecdote of the Jar,"♦ among other poems in *Harmonium. The Man with the Blue Guitar*♦ (1937) and *Notes Toward a Supreme Fiction*♦ (1942) are longer works that develop the ideas and techniques of the early poems at greater length.

Other collections of poems include an altered, enlarged edition of *Harmonium* (1931), *Ideas of Order* (1935), *Owl's Clover* (1936), *Parts of a World* (1942), *Transport to Summer* (1947), *The Auroras of Autumn* (1950), and *Collected Poems* (1954). *Opus Posthumous* (1957) collects plays, essays, some poems, including the full version of *Owl's Clover,* and epigrams. *The Palm at the End of the Mind* (1971) prints a selection of poems and the play "Bowl, Cat and Broomstick," complete in a book for the first time. Throughout this substantial body of work Stevens's philosophical views remain constant, as does the belief that

> The poem is the cry of its occasion
> Part of the res itself and not about it.

The Necessary Angel (1951) collects seven essays "on Reality and the Imagination." A collection of Stevens's *Letters* (1966) was selected and edited by his daughter Holly Stevens.

STEVENSON, ROBERT LOUIS (1850–94), Scottish novelist, essayist, poet, and traveler, in 1880 married an American, Fanny Van de Grift Osbourne, whom he had followed from

Europe to California. His residence in California and his travels to it are described in *The Silverado Squatters*♦ (1883), *The Amateur Emigrant* (1894), and *Across the Plains* (1894). In 1887–88 he returned to the U.S., living for several months at Saranac Lake, writing essays for *Scribner's Magazine* and, with his stepson Lloyd Osbourne, a farcical story, *The Wrong Box* (1888). In 1888, financed by the publisher S.S. McClure, he went to Samoa and the South Seas, where his writing included a vindication of Father Damien; and, with Osbourne, *The Wrecker* (1892), partly set in San Francisco, in which Pinkerton is modeled on McClure, and *The Ebb-Tide* (1894), set in the South Seas.

STEWART, GEORGE R[IPPEY] (1895–1980), a professor of English at the University of California, Berkeley (1923–62). His nonfiction includes *Bret Harte* (1931); *Ordeal by Hunger* (1936), about the Donner Party; *John Phoenix, Esquire* (1937), a life of George H. Derby; *Names on the Land* (1945, extended 1957), a historical account of place-naming in the U.S.; *U.S. 40* (1953), pictures and text on the transcontinental highway; *American Ways of Life* (1954); *N.A. 1* (2 vols., 1956), about the highway from Alaska to Costa Rica; *Pickett's Charge* (1959), a vivid history of the final attack at Gettysburg; and *The California Trail* (1962), a study of the main overland route to California in the 1840s and '50s. Stewart's novels are *East of the Giants* (1938), set in pre-gold-rush California; *Doctor's Oral* (1939), about a Ph.D. examination; *Storm* (1941), whose main "character" is a low-pressure area that occasions dramatic events as it bursts over California and sweeps the continent; *Fire* (1948), a similar treatment of a forest fire; *Man: An Autobiography* (1946), the story of mankind; *Earth Abides* (1949), about life after a disaster has killed all but a few people; *Sheep Rock* (1951), the ages-long history of a Nevada site; and *The Years of the City* (1955), the life cycle of a Greek city.

STICKNEY, [JOSEPH] TRUMBULL (1874–1904), New England poet, was known during his lifetime only as a classical student, despite the publication of his *Dramatic Verses* (1902). When his *Poems* was published by William Vaughn Moody and others (1905), it was discovered that he was a representative poet of his period.

STOCKTON, FRANK R. (FRANCIS RICHARD STOCKTON) (1834–1902), Philadelphia novel-

ist and short-story writer, was first known as
an author of children's stories, some of which
were contributed to *St. Nicholas,* ♦ of which
he was an editor (1873–81). After the publication of his whimsically fantastic novel *Rudder
Grange* (1879), he began to write for adults,
although continuing the same use of absurd
situations that had made his juvenile tales
popular. Among his later works are the
volume of short stories (1884) whose title
piece was the sensationally popular "The
Lady or the Tiger?" ♦ and the amusing novel
*The Casting Away of Mrs. Lecks and Mrs.
Aleshine* (1886), and its sequel *The Dusantes*
(1888).

STODDARD, Charles Warren (1843–
1909), California author, whose *Poems*
(1867), edited by Bret Harte, preceded his
wide travels that furnished material for his
more famous works: *South-Sea Idyls* (1873),
A Cruise Under the Crescent (1898), and *The
Lepers of Molokai* (1885), first calling public
attention to Father Damien and probably
prompting his friend Stevenson to write his
famous defense of the missionary.

STOCKTON, Elizabeth Drew [Barstow]
(1823–1902), collaborated on minor works
with her husband Richard Henry Stoddard
and wrote *The Morgesons* (1862), *Two Men*
(1865), and *Temple House* (1867), realistic
novels set in her native Massachusetts. Although praised by Hawthorne, these were
considered too grim for the average reader
because of their truthful use of local color,
anticipating Sarah Orne Jewett and Mary W.
Freeman. Her *Poems* (1895) display poor
technique, but have an intense, sometimes
morbid, quality of personal revelation.

STODDARD, Richard Henry (1825–1903),
born in Massachusetts, was reared in squalid
surroundings there and in New York City,
and educated himself while working as an
iron molder. He published a volume of
romantic *Poems* (1852), and through Hawthorne's aid obtained a position as inspector
of customs in New York (1853–70). After
occupying other political posts, he became
the literary editor of the New York *Mail and
Express* (1880–1903). His poetry, published
in such volumes as *Songs of Summer* (1857),
Abraham Lincoln: An Horatian Ode (1865),
Poems (1880), and *The Lion's Cub, and
Other Poems* (1890), was greatly admired in
his day, but has come to be considered
artificial, sentimental, and lacking in force,
despite his gifts of melody and imagery. After

1870 Stoddard and his wife held a salon that
was considered a center of New York literary
life, and included not only such prominent
contemporaries as Bayard Taylor and E.C.
Stedman, but lesser-known figures like Melville, whom he befriended.

STONE, Irving (1903–), California author
of widely popular fictionized biographies that
include *Lust for Life* (1934), on van Gogh;
Sailor on Horseback (1938), on Jack London;
Immortal Wife (1944), on Jessie Benton
Frémont; *Adversary in the House* (1947), on
Debs; *The President's Lady* (1951), on Ra-
chel Jackson; *Love Is Eternal* (1954), on
Mary Todd Lincoln; *The Agony and the
Ecstasy* (1961), on Michelangelo; *Passions of
the Mind* (1971), on Freud; *The Greek
Treasure* (1975), on Schliemann; and *The
Origin* (1980), on Darwin.

STONE, Robert [Anthony] (1937–),
Brooklyn-born novelist, after service in the
navy (1955–58) studied a year at New York
University and another at Stanford before beginning to write. His works are *A Hall of Mirrors* (1967), a dark, intense story set in New
Orleans during Mardi Gras, which is seen as a
shocking nightmare; *Dog Soldiers* (1974, National Book Award), another view of a corrupt world, this one of drug dealing from Vietnam to California; and *A Flag for Sunrise*
(1982), a dramatic tale with political and
philosophic views of a Latin American country undergoing revolution in the post-Vietnam
era.

Stopping by Woods on a Snowy Evening, lyric
poem in iambic tetrameter quatrains by
Robert Frost, ♦ published in *New Hampshire*
(1923). The poet stops his horse in the winter
twilight to observe the beauty of the forest
scene, and then is moved to continue his
journey:

> The woods are lovely, dark and deep.
> But I have promises to keep,
> And miles to go before I sleep. . . .

STOWE, Harriet [Elizabeth] Beecher
(1811–96), daughter of Lyman Beecher
(1775–1863), a fiery Presbyterian minister,
and sister of Henry Ward Beecher (1813–87),
a popular Congregational minister and lecturer, was reared in Connecticut under the
Calvinist tutelage of her father. Her youth
was one of morbid introspection, tempered
partly by the liberal beliefs of her uncle,
Samuel Foote, and the reading of such

romantic fiction as that of Scott, which influenced her own later work. In 1832 she moved with her family to Cincinnati, where she taught at a girls' school, and began to write sketches of New England life. In 1836 she married Calvin Ellis Stowe (1802–86), who was then a professor in her father's theological seminary. She observed the life of slaves during a visit to Kentucky, was influenced by the antislavery sentiment prevailing at her father's school, and stored impressions that she used later in fiction.

Upon moving to Maine (1850), she was stirred more than ever by antislavery discussion and availed herself of leisure time to write *Uncle Tom's Cabin*♦ (1852), which brought her nationwide prominence. Although she was not an Abolitionist, her supporters were, and to defend herself from attacks on the accuracy of her book she wrote *A Key to Uncle Tom's Cabin* (1853), a compilation of facts drawn from laws, court records, newspapers, and private letters. At the height of her fame, she made a trip to England (1853), where she was enthusiastically received, and of which she wrote in *Sunny Memories of Foreign Lands* (1854). To further the antislavery cause, she wrote her second novel, *Dred: A Tale of the Great Dismal Swamp* (1856), which showed the demoralizing influence of slavery upon the whites.

After another trip abroad, during which she was honored by Queen Victoria, Mrs. Stowe returned to begin the writing of a series of books set in New England and having fiction rather than propaganda for their purpose. *The Minister's Wooing* (1859) was a romance partly based on her sister's life, and contained an attack on the injustices of Calvinism, a religion that she eventually deserted. *The Pearl of Orr's Island* (1862) was another novel using New England local color, as was also *Oldtown Folks* (1869). In 1869 she again went abroad and met Lady Byron, from whom she obtained the information she published in *Lady Byron Vindicated* (1870). Her charge that Byron had had incestuous relations with his sister caused her to be accused of scandal mongering, and turned a great part of the English public against her.

She returned to New England themes in *Sam Lawson's Oldtown Fireside Stories* (1872), and in *Poganuc People* (1878) she wrote a novel closely based on her own childhood. *Agnes of Sorrento* (1862) is a historical novel set in Italy; *Pink and White Tyranny* (1871), a social satire; and *My Wife*

and I (1871), a fictional essay defending woman's right to a career, which had as its sequel *We and Our Neighbors* (1875). Her *Religious Poems* was published in 1867, and some of her many lesser works were issued under the pseudonym Christopher Crowfield. After the Civil War, Mrs. Stowe lived mainly in Florida, and she described her quiet life there in *Palmetto-Leaves* (1873).

STRAND, MARK (1934–), Canadian-born poet, educated in the U.S., has taught at various universities. His poems of alienation, treating darkness and doubleness in man, are minimalist in style and affected by surrealism. His lyrics appear in *Sleeping with One Eye Open* (1964), *Reasons for Moving* (1968), *Darker* (1970), *The Story of Our Lives* (1973), *Another Republic* (1976), *The Monument* (1978), *The Late Hour* (1978), *Selected Poems* (1980), and *The Planet of Lost Things* (1981).

Strange Fruit, novel by Lillian Smith,♦ published in 1944.

Strange Interlude, drama in two parts and nine acts by O'Neill,♦ produced and published in 1928 and awarded a Pulitzer Prize. Its stream-of-consciousness technique uses asides to reveal the inner thoughts of the characters, often in ironic contrast with their speech.

Nina Leeds is the daughter of a New England professor, who, in his anxiety to keep her with him, persuaded her fiancé, Gordon Shaw, not to marry her before he went to France in the World War. Gordon was killed, and Nina despises herself because she did not give herself to him, and hates her father. She grows neurotic, and as a nurse in a soldiers' hospital offers herself indiscriminately to the men in sacrifice to her dead lover. After her father dies, she feels a filial affection for Charles Marsden, a novelist secretly in love with her but excessively attached to his mother. On his advice and that of Dr. Edmund Darrell, another admirer, who represses his love for her in the interests of his scientific career, she marries Sam Evans, ineffectual and adoring, for whom she cares little. When Nina discovers happily that she is pregnant, Sam's mother reveals to her a strain of insanity in his family, and as a result Nina has an abortion. Hiding this from her husband, she has a child by Dr. Darrell, whom she comes to love. Sam, believing the child to be his, is inspired by his supposed fatherhood to confidence and success in his business career. Marsden suspects the relations of Darrell and Nina, but they are not disclosed, since Nina refuses Darrell's request that she divorce Sam and marry him, and they do not meet again for 11 years. Then the boy, Gordon, prefers Sam to his real father and grows away from the influence of his passionate mother. Nina has lost both Darrell and her son, and Sam's sudden death prevents her from disillusioning him about Gordon. After the funeral, she is unable to destroy her son's love for Madeline Arnold, and the two go off to be married. Nina is left with the quiet affection of Marsden, whom she marries, and the bitter conclusion that "our lives are merely strange dark interludes in the electrical display of God the Father."

STRATEMEYER, EDWARD (1863–1930), author of several series of fiction for boys and girls, often under a variety of pen names. His most popular series includes 20 volumes of the Rover Boys (1899–1916) under the pseudonym Arthur M. Winfield, tales of preparatory school and college life, continued with ten volumes (1917–26) on the original boys' sons, and 40 volumes of works about the inventive Tom Swift (1910ff.). Other popular series include those about the peripatetic Motor Boys (1906ff.) and those for girls concerning the Bobbsey Twins, written under the name Laura Lee Hope. The Stratemeyer Syndicate (established 1914) produced books that Stratemeyer himself outlined and edited. All told, he is supposed to have written at least 150 full-length, hardbound novels.

HARRIET STRATEMEYER ADAMS (1894–1982), his daughter, continued all his series after her father's death, and expanded considerably on her father's three volumes about Nancy Drew, a girl detective whose exploits were described in works attributed to Carolyn Keene. Mrs. Adams was the major author of the Hardy Boys series, begun in 1927 by the Syndicate.

STRATTON-PORTER, GENE[VA] (1863–1924), Indiana author of books for girls, including sentimental novels and nature studies illustrated by her own drawings. Her most popular are *Freckles* (1904), about an Indiana waif who believes himself to be an orphan but is eventually reclaimed by his wealthy father; *A Girl of the Limberlost* (1909), the story of the companion of Freckles, Eleanora, who hunts the swamps for moths, which she sells to get money for an education; and *The Harvester* (1911), about a naturalist who resembles Thoreau. The au-

thor was known in private life as Mrs. Porter but signed her books by hyphenating her maiden and married names.

Stream of consciousness, a development of realism,♦ influenced by modern psychological knowledge, is a method of the contemporary novel used to depict the mental and emotional reactions of characters to external events, rather than the events themselves. As opposed to the usages of conventional plot structure, description, and characterization, the action is presented in terms of images and attitudes within the mind of one or more figures, often to get at the psychic nature of the characters at a level distinct from that of their expression of ordered, verbalized thought. The term was coined by William James in *The Principles of Psychology* (1890) for psychologists but has long been applied to literature along with Edouard Dujardin's term, "interior monologue." Poe, especially in such a story as "The Tell-Tale Heart," and Melville and Henry James are considered to be among the American predecessors of the technique, even if Poe and James did not specifically practice it. Dujardin's *Les Lauriers sont coupés* (1887) and Joyce's *Ulysses* (1922) are considered the real forerunners and influences. After the impact of Joyce's work, the technique became pervasive, and American novelists who have used it include Conrad Aiken, Sherwood Anderson, Dos Passos, James T. Farrell, Faulkner, Hemingway, Robert Penn Warren, Eudora Welty, W.C. Williams, and Thomas Wolfe. In *Strange Interlude,* O'Neill transferred this approach to the theater by the use of soliloquies and asides.

Streetcar Named Desire, A, play by Tennessee Williams,♦ produced and published in 1947 and awarded a Pulitzer Prize.

Blanche DuBois, visiting the New Orleans home of her sister Stella and brother-in-law Stanley Kowalski, is horrified by the contrast between their squalid surroundings and her idealization of life at Belle Reve, the family estate now lost through bankruptcy. She reacts against Stanley's crude humor and animal maleness, while he resents her affected refinement and intrusion on his sensual privacy with his wife. At Stanley's poker party, Blanche meets Mitch and, sensing that he is lonely like herself and "superior to the others," she begins to think of marriage to him as a refuge from the past, which she has already sought in liquor and self-delusions about her age, beauty, and former admirers.

Blanche contends that Stella's marriage and unborn child are products of lust, as aimless as the "street-car named Desire" shuttling through the narrow streets, and urges her not to "hang back with the brutes." In retaliation Stanley tells Mitch that Blanche lost her schoolteaching job because of an affair with a student and that she has become a nymphomaniac in quest of love to compensate for the loss of her homosexual husband by suicide. Mitch accordingly makes the kind of advances that he now thinks suitable, and although Blanche refuses him hysterically she is violently raped by Stanley in angry lust. Upon her return from the hospital with her baby, Stella is told the story by Blanche, but believing it an example of her fantasies, she has her committed to a mental institution. Blanche leaves with the doctor, saying, "Whoever you are—I have always depended on the kindness of strangers."

Strenuous Life, The, essays by Theodore Roosevelt. ♦

STUART, JESSE [HILTON] (1907–84), Kentucky author of regional literature. His works on his native state include poems: *Man with a Bull-Tongue Plow* (1934), 700 sonnets; *Album of Destiny* (1944); *Kentucky Is My Land* (1952); and *Hold April* (1962); and collections of stories, including *Head o' W-Hollow* (1936), *Men of the Mountains* (1941), *Tales from the Plum Grove Hills* (1946), *Plowshare in Heaven* (1958), and *Save Every Lamb* (1964). His novels, also set in Kentucky, include *Trees of Heaven* (1940), about a farm couple and their son's love for the daughter of poor-white squatters; *Mongrel Mettle* (1944), a satirical story of a dog; *Taps for Private Tussie* (1943), about a mountain family's partly humorous adventures in spending insurance money paid after the supposed death of a son in the army; *Foretaste of Glory* (1946); and *Hie to the Hunters* (1950). *Beyond Dark Hills* (1938); *The Thread That Runs So True* (1949); *Year of My Rebirth* (1956), about his recovery from a heart attack, are autobiographies. Other personal works include *God's Oddling* (1960), tales about his father and his own youth; *To Teach, To Love* (1970), reminiscences of his teachers and his teaching; *The Seasons* (1976), a poetic autobiography; and *If I Were Seventeen Again* (1980). *Lost Sandstones and Lonely Skies* (1979) collects essays.

STUART, RUTH [MCENERY] (1849–1917), Louisiana author of local-color stories, which depict the characters of the South in postbellum times. Her sentimentality, optimism, and ability at dialect won her a wide popularity. Her collections include *A Golden Wedding and Other Tales* (1893), *In Simpkinsville: Character Tales* (1897), treating backcountry hill people of Arkansas; *Napoleon Jackson: The Gentleman of the Plush Rocker* (1902), about black people; and *Aunt Amity's Silver Wedding, and Other Stories* (1909). *Sonny* (1896) is a long story, told in monologues, about the poor whites of Arkansas.

Studs Lonigan, hero of a fictional trilogy by James T. Farrell, ♦ which includes *Young Lonigan, ♦ The Young Manhood of Studs Lonigan, ♦* and *Judgment Day.*

STYRON, WILLIAM [CLARK] (1925–), born in Newport News, Va., served in the marine corps before his graduation from Duke (1947). His first novel, which won great critical praise, was *Lie Down in Darkness* ♦ (1951), revealing the tragic life and suicide of a girl whose rich Virginia family was unable to provide her or themselves love, understanding, and security. *The Long March* (1953) is a short novel about a forced training march of marines that results in the death of eight men. *Set This House on Fire* (1960) presents the hectic, finally violent, lives of some drifting, decadent American expatriates in Italy, exploring the mysteries of their complex relations. Styron's next novel, *The Confessions of Nat Turner* ♦ (1967), won him his greatest critical acclaim (including a Pulitzer Prize) while stirring strong protests, mainly from black critics, of the way in which he conceived the protagonist and his followers in the fictive first-person rendering of the historical Nat Turner, leader of a slave rebellion in Virginia during 1831. Thirteen years passed before Styron published another novel, *Sophie's Choice* ♦ (1979), which had comparably great sales and critical approval and denunciation, as he this time dealt with another subject alien to his background: experiences in a Nazi concentration death camp. *In the Clap Shack* (1972) is a comic play set in a venereal disease ward of the World War II navy. *This Quiet Dust* (1982) collects essays, reviews, and reminiscences.

Such Counsels You Gave to Me, free-verse narrative by Jeffers, ♦ the title poem of a volume published in 1937. It is based on the old Scottish ballad "Edward, Edward."

Howard Howren, eager for knowledge and success, has worked his way through high school and a year of college, unaided by his brutal, stupid father. Ill and overworked, he fears a nervous collapse, and returns to the family farm on the California coast, carrying a phial of poison with which to kill himself if his demand for financial aid is refused. His neurotic mother suspects his purpose, and, after his father laughs at his request, she persuades her son that it is better to live, even though he must work on the farm. At the same time she reveals her hatred and fear of her husband, of whose death she says she has been dreaming. A few months later, during an emotional crisis, Howard poisons his father. His mother then reveals her incestuous passion for him, and he realizes that his ambition and inner conflict have arisen from an unnatural love for her. He refuses to possess her, however, and she becomes insane. He acknowledges to himself that his crime developed inevitably from "divided desire and the split will," but decides that, rather than "escape easily" by suicide, he must undergo the ordeal of trial and execution. "There are certain duties," he tells himself, "Even for . . . what did you say? . . . modern man."

SUCKOW, RUTH (1892–1960), Iowa author, whose first novel, *Country People* (1924), is a strongly realistic study of three generations in a German-American family, the Kaetterhenrys, from their settlement in Iowa (1850) to their contemporary wealth and consequent loss of their original culture. *The Odyssey of a Nice Girl* (1925) tells of a young Iowa girl's struggle against the repressions of her family and the surrounding culture, and her eventual escape through marriage. Her subsequent fiction on the life of the region includes *Iowa Interiors* (1926), a collection of short stories published in England as *People and Houses* (1927); *The Bonney Family* (1928), a novel about a minister's household in the mean, unimaginative surroundings of a small Iowa town; *Cora* (1929), relating the Americanization of a German immigrant girl and her family; *The Kramer Girls* (1930), a novel; *Children and Older People* (1931), short stories; *The Folks* (1934), about the good but dull middle-class Fergusons; *New Hope* (1942), about a small-town minister; and *The John Wood Case* (1959), about the effects on others of an embezzlement by a respected citizen. *Carry-Over* (1936) collects *Country People, The Bonney Family,* and stories. *Some Others and Myself* (1952) includes stories and memoirs.

SUKENICK, RONALD (1932–   ), Brooklyn-born author, educated at Cornell and Brandeis, directed the creative writing program at the University of Colorado. His books include *Up* (1968), a satirical novel compounded of autobiography and fantasy in telling of a young man's maturing and his attempts to write a first novel; *Out* (1973), a novel about disaffected young New Yorkers of the 1960s trying to find a better life in southern California; *98.6* (1975), about life on an isolated Far Western commune; *The Death of the Novel* (1969), stories; and a study of Wallace Stevens (1967). The style and structure of his fiction is radically innovative.

Sun Also Rises, The, novel by Hemingway,♦ published in 1926. The title is derived from a pessimistic passage in Ecclesiastes, expressing a cynical disillusion in keeping with the postwar attitude. The English title of the work is *Fiesta*.

Brett, Lady Ashley, "as charming when she is drunk as when she is sober," is traveling on the Continent, waiting for a divorce in order to marry Michael Campbell. Among her other satellites are Jake Barnes, an American newspaper correspondent; his friend Bill Gorton; Robert Cohn, an American Jewish novelist; and an eccentric Greek count. Cohn is weary of his mistress, Frances Clyne, and falls in love with Brett, although neither she nor his other acquaintances feel any real affection for him. The group leave Paris for an excursion in Spain, where they visit the fiesta at Pamplona. They are enthusiastic fans of the bullfights, finding in the ritualistic spectacle a mysterious beauty of precision. Brett and Jake are in love, but unhappily, because a wartime injury has emasculated him. She falls in love with a young bullfighter, Pedro Romero, with whom she elopes; and Cohn departs, expressing his anger by beating Jake, Michael, and Romero. When Romero wants to marry her, Brett decides to return to Michael, who is one of her own kind. She tells Jake, "we could have had such a damned good time together," and he concludes, "Yes. Isn't it pretty to think so?"

Sunday Morning, poem by Wallace Stevens,♦ written in 1915 and published in *Harmonium*♦ in 1923.

In eight 15-line stanzas of blank verse is presented, in the manner of a dialogue, a consideration of the end of life in two senses: its purpose and its conclusion. The issues are raised by an elegant, emancipated modern woman on her tropical patio rather than in church as she meditates upon secular and religious conceptions of reality, death, and the pleasures and beauties of this world as against those of heaven.

Sunnyside, country estate of Irving♦ on the Hudson River near Tarrytown, N.Y. He lived there (1836–42, 1846–59), receiving the visits of other men of letters and writing such works as *Astoria, The Crayon Miscellany, Wolfert's Roost,* and *The Life of George Washington.* The region about Sunnyside is described by Irving in many places, notably in "Sleepy Hollow" (in *Wolfert's Roost*) and "The Legend of Sleepy Hollow."

Susan Lenox: Her Fall and Rise, novel by D.G. Phillips,♦ written in 1908 and posthumously published (2 vols., 1917).

Sut Lovingood. Yarns Spun by a "Nat'ral Born Durn'd Fool," 24 sketches by G.W. Harris,♦ contributed to the *Spirit of the Times* and Tennessee newspapers, collected in 1867. Previously uncollected sketches appear in *The Lovingood Papers* (2 vols., 1962–63).

Sut is a lanky, uncouth Tennessee mountaineer, who loves two things—corn whiskey and a joke. Hence come his humorous adventures in breaking up a black funeral, a wedding party, and a quilting, and being blown up by Seidlitz powders. His vivid, earthy dialect and tall tales come close to the true oral humor of the Southwestern frontier, and he foreshadows Huckleberry Finn, whose adventures have been called parlor versions of Sut's crude pranks.

Sutpen, Thomas, and his family, white and black, are characters in the Yoknapatawpha saga of Faulkner and the subject of *Absalom, Absalom!*♦ They are also mentioned in other novels as one of the region's old families. In *The Unvanquished* Thomas Sutpen is described as second-in-command to John Sartoris but elected by the Jefferson regiment to succeed him and therefore to have the title of Colonel.

SWADOS, Harvey (1920–72), born in Buffalo, educated at the University of Michigan, was author of the novels *Out Went the Candle* (1955), a study of modern America, treating an opportunistic self-made businessman who alienates his children by trying to mold them; *False Coin* (1959), dealing with the problem of the artist trying to preserve integrity in a commercial society; *The Will* (1963), about three very different brothers trying to get

their own way as they struggle over an inheritance; *Standing Fast* (1970), recounting the experiences of a small group of dedicated Marxists; and *Celebration* (1975), depicting the relationship of a 90-year-old progressive educator and his radical grandson. *On the Line* (1957) collects stories about men on an auto assembly line; and other stories appear in *Nights in the Gardens of Brooklyn* (1961) and *A Story for Teddy* (1965). *A Radical's America* (1962) collects essays surveying America from a socialist point of view.

Swallow Barn; or, A Sojourn in the Old Dominion, 49 interrelated sketches by J.P. Kennedy,♦ published in 1832 and revised in 1851. In an Addisonian style, and undoubtedly under the influence of Irving, the work is a sketchbook of country life in Virginia during the first quarter of the 19th century. The slender thread of story, concerned with a friendly litigation between neighbors, which terminates in a love affair, has as a background a charming picture of Virginian life and local types, including the old Southern gentleman, the eccentric, oracular country lawyer, and the lovely young Southern girl.

Swedenborgianism, religious system incorporated in the Church of the New Jerusalem, based on the beliefs of the Swedish theologian Emmanuel Swedenborg (1688–1772). He contended that the inner meaning of the Bible is made clear through understanding that each natural object is the expression of a spiritual cause. He taught that there is one God, and that the Trinity is a division of essences, not of persons. The Father is the divine essence of love, the Son the divine Wisdom or Word to accomplish the redemption of mankind, and the Holy Spirit the divine proceeding by which life and love flow forth in act. The death and resurrection of Jesus symbolize the fate of man, who, if he has worked with the spirit of Jesus in love and obedience, will put aside his material body to pass from this probationary world to assume a spiritual body, becoming subject to a process of infinite perfectibility. The Church of the New Jerusalem held its first meeting in London (1788), although its teachings were known previously and had reached America in 1785. The formal organization was begun in America (1792), and has been strongest in Boston, Philadelphia, and Baltimore. One of its leaders was Sampson Reed, whose writings influenced Emerson, and the philosophy of Transcendentalism is indebted to Swedenborgianism for its prophetic optimism and doctrine of correspondence. The elder Henry James♦ was also strongly impressed by these doctrines.

Sweeney, symbolic character in the poetry of T.S. Eliot,♦ representing the vulgar but vital force of life, particularly in modern man. He is introduced in "Mr. Eliot's Sunday Morning Service" (1918) as a contrast to the febrile presbyters. In "Sweeney Among the Nightingales" (1918) this ape-like man is ironically contrasted to Agamemnon, and in "Sweeney Erect" (1919) the sordid figure is further juxtaposed with great persons and ideas of cultural history. He appears incidentally in *The Waste Land* (1922) as a symbol of lust. *Sweeney Agonistes* (originally published in parts, 1926–27; combined, 1932) presents a different concept of Sweeney, who had formerly been associated with the slain Agamemnon, but who in this play becomes analogous to the slayer Orestes.

SWENSON, MAY (1927–   ), born and reared in Utah of Swedish parents who were Mormons. Her poems, oracular, imagistic, and marked by experimentalism in technique and typography of shaped forms, appear in *Another Animal* (1954), *A Cage of Spines* (1958), *To Mix with Time* (1963), *Half Sun Half Sleep* (1967), *Iconographs* (1970), and *New and Selected Things Taking Place* (1979). *Poems To Solve* (1966) and *More Poems To Solve* (1971) are riddles for children. *Windows and Stones* (1972) is a translation of a Swedish poet. She was a co-winner of the Bollingen Prize♦ (1979–80).

Swift, TOM, hero of books for boys by Edward Stratemeyer.♦

Symphony, *The,* poem by Lanier,♦ published in 1875 and collected in his *Poems* (1884). Employing a rich, complex versification to give an onomatopoetic expression to the different instruments in an orchestra, Lanier personifies each of them to discuss social questions of the time, particularly the inhumanities of trade and industrialism, and to set forth a philosophy of aesthetics, ending "Music is Love in search of a word."

T

TABB, JOHN B[ANISTER] (1845–1909), Virginia-born poet, served as a Confederate blockade runner in the Civil War, and taught school in Baltimore. He was converted to Catholicism, and after ordination as a priest taught at St. Charles's College, near Baltimore (1884–1909), where George Sterling was one of his students. Tabb began early to write poetry but first attained fame when he published his *Poems* (1894). Later books included *Lyrics* (1897), *Later Lyrics* (1902), and *The Rosary in Rhyme* (1904). His brief, classically modeled poems, generally in the form of quatrains or musical lyrics, are marked by religious intensity and a cryptic, epigrammatic manner. His occasional humor, based on conceits, has caused his poetry to be compared both to that of his contemporary, Emily Dickinson, and to the work of the 17th-century English metaphysical poets.

Tablets, essays by Bronson Alcott,♦ published in 1868. The book is divided into two parts, the first "Practical," containing discussions on "The Garden," "Books," "Counsels," "Friendship," and other subjects in a manner somewhat reminiscent of Montaigne; the second "Speculative," dealing with "Instrumentalities," "Mind," "Genesis," and "Metamorphoses," in a more transcendental vein. The philosophic ideas in both sections are interspersed by original poems, which supplement the prose and frequently carry it beyond the logical development onto a more spiritual plane.

TAGGARD, GENEVIEVE (1894–1948), born in Washington, reared in Hawaii, graduated from the University of California (1919). Her volumes of poetry include *Words for the Chisel* (1926), *Remembering Vaughan in New England* (1933), *Calling Western Union* (1936), *Long View* (1942), and *Slow Music* (1946). She also wrote a study of Emily Dickinson and compiled anthologies of metaphysical poetry and of radical modern verse. She taught English at Mount Holyoke (1929–31) and Sarah Lawrence (1935–48).

Tales of a Traveller, 32 stories and sketches by Irving,♦ published in 1824.

Tales of a Wayside Inn, series of narrative poems by Longfellow,♦ published in three parts (1863, 1872, and 1874) and collected in 1886. The concept of a succession of tales by a group of congenial acquaintances was obviously derived from Chaucer, Boccaccio, and other authors. The setting is at a real inn near Boston, and the characters are based on Longfellow's friends. The musician is Ole Bull; the Spanish Jew, Israel Edrehi; the poet, T.W. Parsons; the theologian, Professor Daniel Treadwell; the student, Henry Ware Wales, a young Harvard scholar; the Sicilian, Luigi Monti; and the landlord, Lyman Howe, actual keeper of the inn at Sudbury. Of the 21 stories, only three deal directly with American themes.

Part First opens with the description of the inn and the members of the group. The first tale is "Paul Revere's Ride,"♦ told by the landlord. The second is the student's tale, "The Falcon of Ser Federigo," derived from Boccaccio and telling of a knight who kills his beloved falcon to furnish a breakfast for his lady. The Jew tells "The Legend of Rabbi Ben Levi," a tale from the Talmud, and the Sicilian relates the story of "King Robert of Sicily," whose exalted spirit is broken when an angel in disguise takes his place on the throne and he is forced to serve as the jester until his arrogance disappears. The musician's tale, "The Saga of King Olaf," is derived from Snorre Sturleson's account of the king who championed Christianity among his heathen countrymen. The theologian's tale, "Torquemada," tells of a father who denounces his daughters for some doctrinal heresy during the Inquisition. The poet's tale, "The Birds of Killingworth," concerns Connecticut farmers who killed the small birds that destroyed their crops, and the way in which the birds were avenged by a plague of caterpillars who made the lands a desert.

In Parts Second and Third, each of the friends relates two further narratives, most of them based on European legends, although "Elizabeth," the theologian's tale in Part Third, is a love story set in rural Pennsylvania among Quakers.

Tales of Soldiers and Civilians, 19 stories by Ambrose Bierce,♦ published in 1891 and retitled *In the Midst of Life* (1892, revised 1898).

These grim, vivid stories, reminiscent of Poe's tales of horror, are marked by an ingenious use of the surprise ending and a realistic study of tense emotional states. Among the tales of soldiers, dealing with Civil War scenes, are "A Horseman in the Sky," telling of a soldier in the Union army, who, stationed as a picket near his Southern mountain home, encounters his father, a Confederate cavalry officer, and is forced to shoot, plunging him over a steep cliff to his death; "An Occurrence at Owl Creek Bridge," which is concerned with the illusory thoughts of a Southern planter who is being hanged by Union soldiers, depicting his mind in the interval between the tightening of the rope and the breaking of his neck, during which he imagines that he has escaped; and "Chickamauga," a lurid account of a deaf-mute child amid the horrors of a bloody battle that destroys his home and family. The tales of civilians also deal with sensational effects of mystery and terror, as in "The Middle Toe of the Right Foot," the story of the ghostly return of a wife to terrify the husband who murdered her, causing his death in a duel.

Tales of the Grotesque and Arabesque, first collection of stories by Poe,♦ published in two volumes in December 1839, dated 1840. The title was suggested by an essay of Sir Walter Scott, and the collection included 25 stories, among them "MS. Found in a Bottle,"♦ "The Assignation,"♦ "Berenice,"♦ "Morella,"♦ "Ligeia,"♦ "The Fall of the House of Usher,"♦ "William Wilson,"♦ and "The Unparalleled Adventure of One Hans Pfaall."♦

Talifer, blank-verse narrative by E.A. Robinson,♦ published in 1933.

Tall tale, term applied to the type of frontier anecdote characterized by exaggeration or violent understatement, with realistic details of character or local customs that work toward a cumulative effect of the grotesque, romantic, or humorous. Tall tales depend for their humor partly upon the incongruity between the realism in which the scene and narrator are portrayed and the fantastically comic world of the enclosed narrative. Frontier storytellers created the oral tradition of the tall tale, and folk legends and myths were developed through this medium, especially about such heroes as Paul Bunyan,♦ Mike Fink,♦ and Davy Crockett.♦ Later, the anecdotes began to be printed, and the tall tale became a distinct literary genre, which delightfully pictures the social life of the frontier. These mock oral tales were frequently published in almanacs and in such newspapers as the *Spirit of the Times,*♦ and were of a length dictated by the necessities of such publication. They were not only the creation of the frontier journalist, but the occasional amusement of lawyers, merchants, doctors, soldiers, actors, travelers, and gamblers who turned amateur writer. Among the most famous literary examples are Longstreet's *Georgia Scenes,* Hooper's *Simon Suggs,* Thompson's *Major Jones,* Harris's *Sut Lovingood,* Baldwin's *Flush Times of Alabama and Mississippi,* Thorpe's "Big Bear of Arkansas," and many passages in the works of Clemens.

Tamar and Other Poems, collection by Jeffers,♦ published in 1924. The volume contains "The Tower Beyond Tragedy,"♦ "Night," "Shine, Perishing Republic," and "The Coast Range Christ." The title piece is a free-verse narrative, suggested by a passage in II Samuel 13.

An incestuous strain in the Cauldwell family, farmers on the California coast, begins with the passion of David and his sister Helen. Helen dies, but a generation later David's son and daughter by his wife, Lee and Tamar, break the same moral law, and Tamar becomes pregnant. She has desired "a love sterile and sacred as the stars," and now, terrified, attempts to conceal her sin by taking Will Andrews, a former suitor, as her lover. David's sister Stella becomes a psychic medium for the restless spirit of the dead Helen, impelling Tamar to further crime, for Tamar is jealous of Lee, who is about to leave for France to serve in the World War, and stirs her father to lust. In a paroxysm of contempt and desire, she brings Lee, Will, and David together in her bedroom, and by a fabric of lies sets them to fighting. During this violent encounter, an idiot aunt, Jinny, sets fire to the house, which is destroyed with all its occupants. This dramatic tale, of "passions turned inward, incestuous desires, and a fighting against ghosts," embodies the poet's allegorical warning to humanity against its growing introversion of values. Ending with desolation after a holocaust, it serves to demonstrate his vision of a culminating disaster, to be desired rather than feared, which threatens mankind because of its foolish and perverse attempt at self-deification.

Tamerlane and Other Poems, first collection by Poe,♦ anonymously published in Boston (1827). The title piece is a narrative poem, revised in later editions, which shows the strong influence of Byron and purports to be the dying confession of the Asiatic conqueror to a strange friar, mainly concerned with memories of a passionate love.

Tanglewood Tales, see *Wonder-Book.*

TARKINGTON, [NEWTON] BOOTH (1869–1946), Indiana novelist, first won popularity with his *Monsieur Beaucaire* (1900), the adventures in 18th-century England of the Duke of Orleans, who, disguised as a barber, has an affair with Lady Mary Carlisle from which he emerges a hero and she a cheat. Tarkington had already published *The Gentleman from Indiana* (1899), concerned with the crusade of a country editor against political corruption, and he now wrote a series of novels of life in the Middle West, of which two won Pulitzer Prizes: *The Magnificent Ambersons* (1918), the chronicle of three generations of a leading Indiana family and their decline during a period of transition, and *Alice Adams* (1921), a study of a commonplace girl whose illusions are destroyed when a love affair with a man above her in social rank is ended by his acquaintance with her mediocre family. *Growth* (1927) is the title given to his trilogy of Midwestern city life: *The Turmoil* (1915), *The Magnificent Ambersons,* and *The Midlander* (1923). Tarkington is also noted for his books about boys and adolescents, of which the most famous are *Penrod* (1914), its sequels *Penrod and Sam* (1916) and *Penrod Jashber* (1929), and *Seventeen* (1916), about "Silly Billy" Baxter's puppy-love romance. His many plays include dramatizations of *Monsieur Beaucaire* (1901) and *Clarence* (1919) and several comedies with Harry Leon Wilson and Julian Street.

Tarzan, hero of juvenile adventure stories by Edgar Rice Burroughs. ♦

TATE, [JOHN ORLEY] ALLEN (1899–1979), Tennessee author, began his career as an editor of *The Fugitive*♦ (1922) and also showed interest in regionalism through his contributions to the symposium *I'll Take My Stand*♦ (1930), and his interpretive biographies of Stonewall Jackson (1928) and Jefferson Davis (1929). He is best known for his poems, published in *Mr. Pope and Other Poems* (1928), *Three Poems* (1930), *Poems, 1928–1931* (1932), *The Mediterranean and*

Other Poems (1936), *Selected Poems* (1937), *Winter Sea* (1944), *Poems, 1922–1947* (1948), *The Swimmers* (1971), and *Collected Poems* (1977).

His metaphysical poetry is distinguished by a neoclassical polish and satire, achieving sharp contrasts through use of archaisms verging on the baroque. He described his technique as "gradually circling round the subject, threatening it and filling it with suspense, and finally accomplishing its demise without ever quite using the ultimate violence upon it."

His criticism has been published as *Reactionary Essays on Poetry and Ideas* (1936); *Reason in Madness* (1941); *On the Limits of Poetry* (1948), including essays from the preceding volumes; *The Hovering Fly* (1949), literary essays; *The Forlorn Demon* (1953), "didactic and critical essays"; *Collected Essays* (1959); *Essays of Four Decades* (1969); and *Memoirs and Opinions* (1975). *The Fathers* (1938) is a novel set in pre-Civil War Virginia. With his former wife, Caroline Gordon, he wrote the text *The House of Fiction* (1950). Tate edited the *Sewanee Review* (1944–46) and taught at the University of Minnesota (1951–68).

TATE, JAMES [VINCENT] (1943–   ), poet born in Kansas City, a member of the English department at the University of Massachusetts (1971–   ), came to prominence aged only 23 when his *The Lost Pilot* (1967) won the award of the Yale Series of Younger Poets. He was praised by Robert Lowell for his "low-keyed, offhand style," counterpointing "feelings of estrangement, anger, and self-abasing humor," and noted too for his wit. Later lyrics have been collected in *The Oblivion Ha-Ha* (1970), *Absences* (1972), *Viper Jazz* (1976), *Riven Doggeries* (1979), *Constant Defender* (1983), and other publications.

TAYLOR, [JAMES] BAYARD (1825–78), born in Pennsylvania of a Quaker family, early showed a poetic gift and desire to escape from his quiet surroundings. After the publication of his romantic verse, *Ximena* (1844), he went to England and the Continent, writing letters for the *New-York Tribune* and collecting material for *Views A-foot* (1846). The *Tribune,* delighted by his charming exoticism, made him manager of its literary section and sent him to California during the gold rush. After a year, he returned to publish *Eldorado* (2 vols., 1850), which augmented his popularity as an adventurous hero.

The following year, he departed for travels in Egypt, Abyssinia, Turkey, India, and China, and joined the Pacific squadron of Commodore Perry. Upon his return to New York (1853), he published in quick succession *A Journey to Central Africa* (1854), *The Lands of the Saracen* (1855), and *A Visit to India, China, and Japan, in the Year 1853* (1855), and was in steady demand as a lyceum lecturer. His prose accounts were supplemented by *Rhymes of Travel, Ballads and Poems* (1849), *A Book of Romances, Lyrics, and Songs* (1852), *Poems of the Orient* (1855), and other verse. From 1863 to 1870 he wrote novels, in which for the first time he considered the U.S., including *The Story of Kennett* (1866), a character study set in his native town of Kennett Square during the 18th century. Taylor's last years were devoted to a translation of Goethe's *Faust,* in the original meters (2 vols., 1870–71), which brought him a nonresident professorship of German at Cornell (1870–77) and the ministry to Germany (1878). This has come to be considered his most lasting work, even though the poetry itself rarely rises above the mediocrity that stamps all Taylor's sonorous but shallow verse, and which won him the somewhat hollow title of "laureate of the Gilded Age."

TAYLOR, EDWARD (*c.*1644–1729), English-born poet, emigrated to Boston (1668) and after graduation from Harvard (1671) became the pastor and physician of the Massachusetts frontier town Westfield, where he remained until his death. Not until 1937, when some of his poems were first published from manuscript, was he discovered to be an author of importance. His work as a Puritan sacred poet has been hailed as the finest 17th-century American verse. He is in the direct line of the English devotional metaphysical poets, such as Herbert, Crashaw, and Quarles, and his writings, though considered less important than those of his masters, are matched by none of his colonial contemporaries. His grandson, Ezra Stiles, in accordance with the request that none of his "poetical works" should be published, kept them in manuscript. Not until 1939 was the volume *Poetical Works,* edited by Thomas H. Johnson, published from the papers at Yale, followed by a more comprehensive edition of *Poems* in 1960. Fourteen related sermons, delivered 1701–3, and preparatory meditations in verse were first edited as *Christogra-*

phia (1962). Diverse *Unpublished Writings* were collected in three volumes (1981).

TAYLOR, PETER [HILLSMAN] (1917–), born in Tennessee. His stories, which sensitively depict characters and situations of contemporary middle-class life in the South, appear in *A Long Fourth* (1948), *The Widows of Thornton* (1954), *Happy Families Are All Alike* (1959), *Miss Leonora When Last Seen* (1963), *Collected Stories* (1969), and *In the Miro District* (1977). *A Woman of Means* (1950) is a short novel, and *Tennessee Day in St. Louis* (1956), *A Stand in the Mountains* (1968), and *Presences* (1973) are plays. He has taught English and creative writing at the University of North Carolina (1946–67) and the University of Virginia (1967–).

TAYLOR, ROBERT LEWIS (1912–), the author of books on W.C. Fields, Churchill, and Carry Nation, has collected his numerous profiles from *The New Yorker,* and written several rollicking picaresque novels, including *The Travels of Jamie McPheeters* (1958, Pulitzer Prize), about a teenage boy en route to California in the gold rush, *A Journey to Matecumbe* (1961), and *Two Roads to Guadalupé* (1964).

TEASDALE, SARA (1884–1933), lyric poet born in Missouri, made her home in New York, and became known for her unaffected quatrains, which, almost bare of imagery and sparing in metaphor, attempt the articulation of a mood, rather than the quest of universals. Her works include *Sonnets to Duse and Other Poems* (1907), *Helen of Troy* (1911), *Rivers to the Sea* (1915), *Love Songs* (1917, special Pulitzer award), *Flame and Shadow* (1920), *Dark of the Moon* (1926), *Strange Victory* (1933), and *Collected Poems* (1937).

Telling the Bees, poem by Whittier, ♦ in an approximation of ballad meter, published in 1858 and collected in *Home Ballads* (1860). A young man passes the farm of his beloved, where he sees the hired girl observing the old New England custom of dressing the hives in mourning and informing the bees of a death. He thinks his Mary's grandfather has died, but is stunned to hear the chore girl tell the bees, "Mistress Mary is dead and gone!"

Tell-Tale Heart, The, story by Poe, ♦ published in *The Pioneer* (1843). It has been considered the most influential of Poe's stories in the later development of stream-of-consciousness fiction.

A victim of a nervous disease is overcome by homicidal mania and murders an innocent old man in whose home he lives. He confuses the ticking of the old man's watch with an excited heartbeat, and although he dismembers the body he neglects to remove the watch when he buries the pieces beneath the floor. The old man's dying shriek has been overheard, and three police officers come to investigate. They discover nothing, and the murderer claims that the old man is absent in the country, but when they remain to question him he hears a loud rhythmic sound that he believes to be the beating of the buried heart. This so distracts his diseased mind that he suspects the officers know the truth and are merely trying his patience, and in an insane fit he confesses his crime.

Temple, family name of characters in the Leather-Stocking Tales♦ and other novels of Cooper.

Temple Drake, character in Faulkner's *Sanctuary*♦ and its sequel, *Requiem for a Nun.*

Ten Days That Shook the World, history by John Reed,♦ published in 1919. A dramatization by Robert E. Lee was produced in 1973.

Ten Nights in a Barroom and What I Saw There, melodramatic story by T.S. Arthur,♦ published in 1854. It became a favorite text for temperance lecturers, and was popular in the dramatic version by William W. Pratt (1858). A temperance song by Henry Clay Work, "Come Home, Father," which begins:

Father, dear father, come home with me now,
The clock in the belfry strikes one

was introduced into the play about 1864.

A traveler, who visits the town of Cedarville from time to time during a period of ten years, notes the changing fortunes of the citizens, and places the responsibility on the evil influences of Simon Slade's saloon, the "Sickle and Sheaf." The landlord rises to affluence but then gradually sinks into poverty and degradation, and among the gruesome events that are described are Slade's accidental murder of little Mary, the daughter of Joe Morgan the drunkard, who comes to fetch her father home from the saloon and is hit by a glass which is thrown at him in a brawl; the disastrous gambling experiences of Willy Hammond with the cheating Harvey Green, who murders him; the insanity of Mrs. Slade, resulting from her son's rowdyism; and finally

the son's murder of his father. Following this last outrage, the townspeople hold a mass meeting, decree a prohibition on the sale of liquor, destroy the saloon's stock, and disperse with new hope for the town's future.

Tender Is the Night, novel by F. Scott Fitzgerald,♦ published in 1934. Early versions date back to 1925, and the one first published began with Rosemary's arrival in the Diver circle; but in the last two years of his life Fitzgerald reorganized the story into chronological order in a version first issued, with Malcolm Cowley's commentary, in 1948.

Dick Diver, a young American psychiatrist completing his training in Zurich at the end of World War I, becomes interested in the case of Nicole Warren, a beautiful American girl with acute schizophrenia resulting from an incestuous relation with her father. As she recovers, she falls in love with Dick and comes to rely on him for stability and identity in what is for her a new and uncertain world. He returns her love, but also allows himself to acknowledge, if not to accept, a suggestion from her wealthy family, represented by her sister Baby, that he remain married with her in order to care for her. Thus, in their marriage, the psychiatrist is involved, and to a degree confused, with the lover and the companion, and "her problem was one they had together for good now." Dick ceases "temporarily" to practice, though continuing to work on a new book. They have two children, and settle into a life of leisure on the Riviera with a circle of friends including Abe North, an alcoholic composer, and Tommy Barban, a French soldier of fortune in love with Nicole. Dick's effortless charm, which lets people feel at ease, makes him an ideal host, but although he is loved and admired, he is spending emotional resources which are not being replenished. Rosemary Hoyt, a naïve American movie actress who joins the group, falls in love with Dick and, attending a party at the Divers' villa, sees their life as magnificent, tasteful, and free, but she is "unaware of its complexity and lack of innocence." Out of touch with his work, his marriage and his very love for Nicole increasingly defined in terms of her illness, Dick becomes infatuated with Rosemary. He begins to drink more; his easy confidence begins to wear thin; and though in moments of crisis and relapse Nicole appeals to him, both her confidence in him and her dependence on him are gradually undermined. The same "transference" that partially drew her to him at the outset now draws his psychological strength toward her. Abe, long recognized by Dick as a hopeless case, fails in an effort to go back to America and to work, and is beaten to death in a Paris bar. Dick himself is involved in a brawl in Rome, and Baby, who extricates him, thus gains a "moral superiority" as well as a financial one over him. He is without illusions, having "managed to keep alive the low painful fire of intelligence," but he has lost himself through the intricacies of his relation to Nicole and his habitual desire to please her. Tommy, who loves Nicole but does not try to understand her, becomes her lover, and after they confront Dick for a divorce, he returns to America to sink into final obscurity.

Tennessee's Partner, tale by Bret Harte,♦ published in the *Overland Monthly* (1869) and in *The Luck of Roaring Camp and Other Sketches* (1870).

Tennessee, "known to be a gambler . . . suspected to be a thief," works a mining claim at Sandy Bar, Cal., with his unnamed "Partner." Although Tennessee once eloped with his Partner's wife, returning after she deserted him too, the Partner remains his affectionate friend. One day Tennessee is captured as a highway robber, and during an impromptu trial his Partner innocently offers his entire "stake" in return for Tennessee's life. This strengthens the determination of the "court" to punish the thief, and he is hanged from a nearby tree. Tennessee's Partner arrives with a donkey cart to claim the body of "the diseased," and the crowd joins him in a rude but tender funeral ceremony. After this loss, the Partner declines in health. When he dies the following spring, he imagines that he sees his friend coming to welcome him.

Tenth Muse, The, see *Bradstreet, Anne.*

TERHUNE, MARY VIRGINIA (1830–1922), popular romantic novelist, whose 26 novels, mostly concerned with the South before or during the Civil War, marked by a strongly moral manner, include *Alone* (1854), *Sunnybank* (1866), and *A Gallant Fight* (1888). She wrote under the pseudonym Marion Harland, and was also well known for her travel books, biographical studies, and works on household management.

TERKEL, STUDS [LOUIS] (1912–), Chicago radio and television interviewer, whose books are *Giants of Jazz* (1957), brief biographies of 12 musicians; *Division Street: America* (1966), transcriptions of his conversations with 70 very diverse persons of the Chicago area presenting a cross section of people and their concerns; *Hard Times* (1970), comparable conversations to create "an Oral History of the Great Depression"; *Working* (1974), further interviews; *Talking to Myself* (1977), "a memoir of my times"; *American Dreams: Lost and Found* (1980), interviews with plain people, which tell their autobiographies; and *The Good War* (1984), using the same techniques to document World War II. He also wrote a play, *Amazing Grace* (1959).

THACKERAY, WILLIAM MAKEPEACE (1811–63), English novelist, twice visited the U.S. (Nov. 1852–April 1853; Oct. 1855–April 1856), delivering lectures on English literature and history. Prior to his first trip he had published *Henry Esmond,* the conclusion of which deals with colonial Virginia. Its sequel, *The Virginians,* was the result of research begun during the second visit, when he outlined the idea to J.E. Cooke and received suggestions from J.P. Kennedy.

Thanatopsis, blank-verse poem by Bryant,♦ written when he was 16 years old, after reading Blair's *Grave,* Cowper's *Task,* and various poems by Southey and Henry Kirke White. The early version of "Thanatopsis," whose Greek title means "view of death," was published in *The North American Review* (1817). It lacked the first 17 lines and the last 15 of the present work, which was first collected in the author's *Poems* (1821). These passages materially altered the philosophic significance of the poem, in which Nature, rather than the author's "better genius," now discusses death. Nature speaks a varied language to man, the poet observes; when "thoughts of the last bitter hour" come, it teaches that earth claims all it has nourished. Man must therefore learn to conduct his life in such a way that he need have no fear when his summons comes to join the "innumerable caravan."

THAXTER, CELIA [LAIGHTON] (1835–94), was the daughter of a lighthouse keeper on the Isles of Shoals, off the New Hampshire coast, where she spent most of her life. Her depiction of the various moods of the sea form the subject matter of her *Poems* (1872), *Drift-Weed* (1879), *Idyls and Pastorals* (1886), and other volumes. Her prose sketches devoted to the same subjects appear in *Among the Isles of Shoals* (1873) and *An Island Garden* (1894). She was as well known for her personality as for her poetry, and visitors at the hotel conducted by her family included Thoreau, Lowell, Whittier, and other authors and artists.

Their Fathers' God, novel by Rölvaag,♦ published in Norway (1931) and in translation in the U.S. the same year. It is the concluding volume of a trilogy which includes *Giants in the Earth*♦ and *Peder Victorious.* ♦

Theory of the Leisure Class, The, economic treatise by Thorstein Veblen, published in 1899. The book enjoyed a popular vogue and profoundly influenced economic thought, but provoked controversial replies, of which the most sensational was Mencken's "Professor Veblen" in *Prejudices* (1919).

There Was a Child Went Forth, poem by Whitman,♦ published without title in *Leaves of Grass* (1855), as "Poem of the Child That Went Forth, and Always Goes Forth, Forever and Forever" (1860), and under its present title in 1871.

This short poem states in simple terms Whitman's concept of man's identification with nature and the persons who surround him, and declares that those objects and people that he looked upon "became part of that child who went forth every day and who now goes, and will always go forth, every day."

THEROUX, PAUL [EDWARD] (1941–), Massachusetts-born author, resident abroad (1963–72) as a teacher of English in Italy, Malawi, Uganda, and Singapore, began his prolific literary career with *Waldo* (1966), a comic, surreal novel about eccentric individuals encountered by the title character as he travels after leaving a school for delinquent boys. Later novels include *Fong and the Indians* (1968), a satiric view of preposterous residents of a new East African country: natives, Chinese, and Americans; *Girls at Play* (1969), depicting in crueler fashion Afro-Indian, American, and English women schoolteachers in Kenya; *Jungle Lovers* (1971), set in Malawi and presenting a New England insurance salesman married to a native; *Saint Jack* (1973), treating people of diverse nations and natures drifting through life in Singapore; *The Black House* (1974), about an anthropologist returning from Africa to his native England and finding it stranger than the land he has been studying; *The Family Arsenal* (1976), dealing with professional terrorists in the seamy underworld of London; *Picture Palace* (1977), a

fictive biography of a famous, aging woman photographer; and *The Mosquito Coast* (1982), about a Yankee engineer who seeks a new life in Honduras. Theroux has also written a book on the West Indian novelist V.S. Naipaul (1972), short stories collected in *Sinning with Annie* (1972) and *World's End* (1980), and *The Consul's File* (1977), tales for children. He also wrote two accounts of traveling by train, through Asia in *The Great Railway Bazaar* (1975) and through the Americas in *The Old Patagonian Express* (1979), as well as *The Kingdom by the Sea* (1983), telling of travels around the English coastline.

Thirteen Ways of Looking at a Blackbird, poem by Wallace Stevens,♦ composed in 1917 and published in *Harmonium*♦ (1923).

The work is composed of 13 brief but suggestive imagistic statements, in each of which a blackbird is the point of reference. Although the blackbird is central to the context of each verse, the bird does not possess a constant symbolic meaning. It is considered in more general philosophic terms that relate the 13 views to issues concerning reality and the imagination, but these are not presented in an orderly or sequential relationship.

This Side of Paradise, novel by F. Scott Fitzgerald,♦ published in 1920.

Amory Blaine, after a pampered childhood with his wealthy, affected mother, Beatrice, attends preparatory school, where his indolence and aristocratic pose set him apart, until after an unhappy year he is accepted as a brilliant though eccentric athlete and leader. Although he is never religious, he has an affectionate father-and-son relation with his mother's friend Monsignor Darcy, a hedonist converted to Catholicism. He goes to Princeton, and there becomes a "literary bird," writing for the *Princetonian*, joining the Triangle Club, and discovering the English *fin de siècle* poets. Among his companions are Alec Connage, an unoriginal youth, and Tom D'Invilliers, whose radicalism and poetry they try to reform. Amory has a romance with a childhood friend, Isabelle; is involved in a student revolt led by Burne Holiday, an earnest radical who becomes a pacifist during the World War; nearly falls in love with his widowed cousin Clara, a beautiful "St. Cecilia" who has "never been in love"; and goes to France as a lieutenant. On his return he finds Beatrice dead and his wealth diminished, and he becomes an advertising writer.

He has a passionate affair with Alec's debutante sister Rosaline—his one unselfish emotional experience—but she marries another man because she believes she cannot be happy without wealth. Amory drowns his disillusion in drink, but on a visit to Maryland meets Eleanor, a vivid, nervous personality even more egocentric than himself. They love for a few "bitter-sweet" weeks, and Amory continues his search for inner peace. He is penniless, and seeks employment. After Darcy's death, Amory realizes that his own unselfishness is the "the most living part" of himself, and considers his total experience at 24: " 'I know myself,' he cried, 'but that is all.' "

THOMAS, ISAIAH (1749–1831), printer, editor, and publisher of Worcester, Mass., was the leading publisher of his day, the quality of his work causing Franklin to call him "the Baskerville of America." He issued *A Specimen* of his types (1785), which gives important evidence concerning early American printing. His *History of Printing in America* (2 vols., 1810) is the most significant early work on the subject. He founded the American Antiquarian Society (1812).

THOREAU, HENRY DAVID (1817–62), born in Concord of a family whose French, Scottish, Quaker, and Puritan stock helps to account for his temper of mind. Just as his heritage was mixed, so his philosophy of life combined diverse strains, and he called himself "a mystic, a transcendentalist, and a natural philosopher to boot." At heart, he was predominantly individualistic, and his great interest was "to observe what transpires, not in the street, but in the mind and heart of me!" Although his reading carried him far afield, he could truthfully say "I have travelled a good deal in Concord." In addition to his natural education in the woods near Concord, and the ordinary preparatory schooling, he graduated from Harvard (1837), where he was primarily influenced by Edward Tyrrell Channing's teaching of composition, and the knowledge of Greek and the metaphysical poets that he derived from Jones Very. His temporary residence in the home of Orestes Brownson, from whom he learned German, was also influential. Above all he fell under the sway of Emerson, and it has been frequently said that he was the answer to Emerson's plea for an "American Scholar."

After graduation he taught school in his native town, for a time in collaboration with his brother John, following the principles of Bronson Alcott. With his brother he also made a trip on the Concord and Merrimack rivers (1839), of which he wrote during his residence at Walden in *A Week on the Concord and Merrimack Rivers*♦ (1849). After closing his school, he lived with Emerson (1841–43), serving him as a general handyman, although their relation was also one of master and disciple. At this time he became an intimate of the members of the Transcendental Club♦ and a contributor to *The Dial* and other magazines. During 1843 he was a tutor in the Staten Island home of William Emerson, where he made the acquaintance of Horace Greeley, Lucretia Mott, and the elder Henry James.

After his return to Concord, Thoreau built himself a hut at nearby Walden Pond, where he lived from July 4, 1845, to September 6, 1847, a period of which he wrote in his most famous book, *Walden*♦ (1854). While other Transcendentalists sought a retreat at Brook Farm, Thoreau, ever an individualist, having no use for cooperative plans, found his solution at Walden. He wanted to get back to the naked simplicity of life, where he might "subdue and cultivate a few cubic feet of flesh," chew the cud of his thoughts, and get to the very core of the universe, by living deep and sucking out all the "marrow of life." His desire was "so to love wisdom as to live according to its dictates, a life of simplicity, independence, magnanimity, and trust . . . to solve some of the problems of life, not only theoretically, but practically." He wanted neither to be interfered with nor to interfere with others, and he declared, "I would not have anyone adopt my mode of living, each should find out his own way, not his neighbor's or his parents'."

His residence at the Pond was interrupted by a day's imprisonment for refusal to pay a poll tax to a government that supported the Mexican War, a war he considered merely a land-grabbing scheme of the Southern slaveholders. This action was in accord with his belief in passive resistance, a means of protest he explained in his essay "Civil Disobedience"♦ (1849). It was a means of accentuating his belief, expressed in *Walden,* that each man should save himself and all would be saved. He not only believed with Jefferson that that government is best which governs least, but he also contended that "they are the lovers of law and order who observe the law when the government breaks it." His belief in the individual and in a moral law superior to statutes and constitutions was also expressed in "Life Without Principle" ♦ (1863).

After he left Walden Pond, he lived for a year in Emerson's home while the essayist was abroad and formed his close friendship with the younger William Ellery Channing, who in writing the first biography of Thoreau aptly called him "the poet-naturalist." His observations of nature were distinguished not merely by his scientific knowledge, which was occasionally erroneous, but by his all-inclusive love of life, expressed now in an earthy manner with a Yankee twang, now with a sweet, pure English, having, as Lowell said, "an antique purity like wine grown colorless with age." Though he enjoyed the scientific view of nature, he was also a Transcendentalist, ♦ defining his attitude when he said he wanted more the wideness of heaven than the limit of the microscope. His statement that he liked "better the surliness with which the wood chopper speaks of his woods, handling them as indifferently as his axe, than the mealy-mouthed enthusiasm of the lover of nature" shows him as an observer who wanted his answers concerning nature not only in facts but in terms of faith.

He made several brief trips (1849–53), which supplied the material for his posthumously published books *Excursions* ♦ (1863), *The Maine Woods* ♦ (1864), *Cape Cod* ♦ (1865), and *A Yankee in Canada* ♦ (1866). Meanwhile he continued his outwardly parochial life in Concord, where he wrote his journals, containing some two million words, the basis of all his books. During these years he became increasingly involved in the anti-slavery movement and delivered such speeches as "Slavery in Massachusetts" (1854). He was profoundly stirred by his meeting with John Brown at Emerson's home (1857) and praised Brown's actions at Harpers Ferry, for here was a man who was carrying out the principles that he himself championed. He eulogized him in three lectures, "A Plea for Captain John Brown" (1859), "The Last Days of John Brown" (1860), and "After the Death of John Brown" (1860).

During his last years, Thoreau made further trips to Cape Cod and Maine, and to New York City, where he met Whitman, but he was a victim of tuberculosis, which gradually weakened him and finally caused his death. He worked indefatigably, in spite of this handicap, on a long, unpublished ethnological study of the Indians and continued to make scientific observations and to carry on his own way of life both privately and as a lyceum lecturer. An invalid, he made an attempt to recapture health by journeying to the Great Lakes and the Mississippi (1861), but returned home, knowing that he was shortly to die, to engage in a last attempt to edit his journals for publication. He published two books and a few articles and speeches during his lifetime, but it was not until after his death that selections from his journals were edited by his friend Harrison G.O. Blake as *Early Spring in Massachusetts* (1881), *Summer* (1884), *Winter* (1888), and *Autumn* (1892). The complete *Journal* was issued (14 vols.) in 1906 and the text of a lost journal (1840–41) was edited by Perry Miller as *Consciousness in Concord* (1958). Other miscellaneous work was published in his collected *Writings* (20 vols., 1906), and Emerson's edition of the *Letters* (1865) was enlarged (1894) and further amplified and edited as *Correspondence* (1958). His *Poems of Nature* appeared in 1895 and Carl Bode edited the *Collected Poems* in 1943. A scholarly edition of his *Writings* began publication in 1971.

Three Lives, stories by Gertrude Stein, ♦ published in 1909.

These unconventional character portraits, the author's first published fiction, exhibit her typical experimental attitude toward style and subject matter, and her attempt to reach an intuitive expression of consciousness and emotions. "The Good Anna" tells of Anna Federner, a sober, faithful housekeeper "of solid lower middle-class south german stock," who comes to the American city of Bridgepoint, and works successively for Miss Mary Wadsmith, "a large, fair, helpless woman," whose nephew and niece she helps to raise; Dr. Shonjen, a friendly physician; and Miss Mathilda, who goes to Europe and leaves Anna her house. She takes in boarders, but loses money by her simple generosity, and dies as a result of overwork. "The Gentle Lena" is concerned with a German girl who works as a maid in Bridgepoint, is married by her aunt to a stupid German tailor, apathetically endures her miserable life, and dies at the birth of her fourth child. The long story, "Melanctha," tells of the "subtle, intelligent, attractive, half white girl" Melanctha Herbert, who grows up in a Southern town, unloved by her brutal black father and weak mulatto mother. She has an unhappy love affair with the mulatto Dr. Jeff Campbell, who never returns her passionate affection. After she breaks with Jeff, she is engaged to a black gambler, Jem

Richards, but, after he deserts her, she contracts consumption and dies.

Three Soldiers, novel by John Dos Passos,♦ published in 1921.

Threnody, elegiac poem by Emerson,♦ published in *Poems* (1847). Arranged in alternately rhymed couplets of irregular four-stress lines, the work is a lyric expression of the poet's sorrow at the death of his five-year-old son Waldo. Following a passage of deep grief and lamentation, he concludes by finding consolation in the Platonic theory of an eternal changeless divinity into which all transitory appearances are finally resolved:

> House and tenant go to ground,
> Lost in God, in Godhead found.

THURBER, JAMES [GROVER] (1894–1961), Ohio-born humorous writer and artist, in 1927 began his lifelong association with *The New Yorker,* in which most of his work first appeared. Of the journal and its editor, Harold Ross, he wrote a personal history, *The Years with Ross* (1959). His essays, sketches, fables, stories, parables, and reminiscences, illustrated by his distinctive and fluid drawings, include *Is Sex Necessary?* (1929), written with E.B. White, satirizing pseudo-scientific sex manuals; *The Owl in the Attic and Other Perplexities* (1931); *The Seal in the Bedroom & Other Predicaments* (1932); *My Life and Hard Times* (1933), amusing recollections; *The Middle-Aged Man on the Flying Trapeze* (1935); *Let Your Mind Alone!* (1937), satirizing inspirational books and popularizations of psychology; *The Last Flower* (1939), an ironic parable of modern war; *Fables for Our Time, and Famous Poems Illustrated* (1940); *My World—and Welcome to It* (1942), essays, sketches, and stories, including the well-known tale "The Secret Life of Walter Mitty"♦; *Thurber's Men, Women, and Dogs* (1943), drawings; *The Thurber Carnival* (1945); *The Beast in Me and Other Animals* (1948); *Thurber Country* (1953); *Further Fables for Our Time* (1956); *Alarms and Diversions* (1957); *Lanterns & Lances* (1961), essays that are final examples of light and shafts cast by the author; and *Credos and Curios* (1962), a posthumous collection of stories and sketches. *Many Moons* (1943), *The Great Quillow* (1944), *The White Deer* (1945), *The 13 Clocks* (1950), and *The Wonderful O* (1957) are fantasies for children. With Elliott Nugent he wrote *The Male Animal* (1940), a comedy dealing with the rivalry between an

English professor and an ex-football player for the love of the professor's wife.

Thurber's humorous prose and drawings are never raucous, for, as he said, "the little wheels of their invention are set in motion by the damp hand of melancholy," in keeping with his view that "humor is a kind of emotional chaos told about calmly and quietly in retrospect." His fantastic people and animals move with sad persistence through incredible upsets, and are all misshapen and repressed, products of a malignant fate which they stoically survive or combat. Across the puzzling scene that is surveyed by resigned dogs move predatory women at war with docile men who, caught by life's conventions, quietly dream of escape and deeds of derring-do.

Thurso's Landing, free-verse narrative by Jeffers,♦ the title poem of a volume published in 1932.

This tale of suffering, violence, and desperate courage on a California coast farm is principally concerned with stubborn, powerful Reave Thurso, his wife Helen, and his brother Mark, who has been crippled in the World War and loves and sympathizes with his lonely sister-in-law, as her unfeeling husband cannot. Grim old Mrs. Thurso hates Helen, realizing the younger woman's passionate, sensual nature and her dissatisfaction with the limited life of the Landing, but is powerless to prevent Reave from bringing her home again after she elopes with his friend Rick Armstrong. When Reave takes a girl servant as his mistress, Helen is wildly jealous, but he is soon crippled and made impotent when a cable snaps while he is felling trees. A struggle of wills ensues between husband and wife, he clinging grimly to his useless life, and she wishing him dead but admiring his immense courage. Mark goes mad because of his lust for Helen and visions of his father's ghost, and hangs himself, after which Helen kills Reave and commits suicide. Old Mrs. Thurso, who says of Helen that she "had a wasteful gallant spirit," calls herself "the last And worst of four: and at last the unhappiest: but that's nothing."

TICKNOR, WILLIAM DAVIS (1810–64), Boston publisher, in 1832 founded the firm known after 1854 as Ticknor and Fields, which published the works of his friends Longfellow, Holmes, Lowell, Emerson, Thoreau, Hawthorne, and many of their distinguished contemporaries. The firm published the *Atlantic Monthly* (1859ff.) and *The North American Review* (1854–64), and owned the Old Corner Bookstore. ♦

Tilbury Town, fictitious setting of many poems by Edwin Arlington Robinson, ♦ a place of conventional and materialistic values, presumably modeled on his hometown, Gardiner, Me. In it dwell such characters as Miniver Cheevy, ♦ Flammonde, ♦ Annandale, Richard Cory, John Evereldown, Mr. Flood, and Luke Havergal, whose characterizations and soliloquies reveal their conflicts with the prevailing town mores. Sixty-three of the poems were gathered as *Tilbury Town* (1953) by Lawrance Thompson.

Time of Your Life, The, play by William Saroyan. ♦

Timoleon, poems by Melville, ♦ privately printed in 1891. Besides the title piece, the volume contains some 40 other light poems inspired by the author's travels in Greece and Italy (1857), as well as the unique and contrasting "After the Pleasure Party," which is concerned with "the sexual feud that clogs the aspiring life" and a bitter arraignment of the fate that makes "selfhood" seem "incomplete" and yet seldom allows the mating of "matching halves."

TIMROD, HENRY (1828–67), born in Charleston, was educated at Franklin College (the present University of Georgia). During his brief life he published only one volume of *Poems* (1860), delicate treatments of nature showing his training in the classics. The tuberculosis from which he later died made him unfit for military service in the Civil War, and he unsuccessfully attempted to eke out a living by editing a Columbia newspaper and writing poetry. These sad last years he summed up when he wrote to his friend Paul Hamilton Hayne, "You ask me to tell you my story for the last year. . . . I can embody it all in a few words: beggary, starvation, death, bitter grief, utter want of hope!" Nevertheless, his trials stirred him to write his greatest poetry, which, no longer showing the dependence of his earlier work, included such poems as "Ethnogenesis," ♦ "The Cotton Boll," ♦ and "Ode" ♦ on the graves of the Confederate dead, whose passionate emotion is the more effective because of the cool, severe utterance. After his death, Hayne collected his *Poems* (1873), with a sympathetic introduction. Later publications include *Katie* (1884), a long love lyric addressed

to his wife, and *Complete Poems* (1899). He is called "the laureate of the Confederacy."

Titan, The, novel by Dreiser, ♦ published in 1914 as a sequel to *The Financier* ♦ and based on the career of C.T. Yerkes, a flamboyant financier of Philadelphia, Chicago, and London.

Frank Cowperwood, having married his mistress Aileen Butler, establishes a home in Chicago. Their history becomes known, and they fail to make their desired entry into society, but Cowperwood's business affairs prosper. After successful speculations in the grain exchange and in stocks, he effects a great merger of the growing city's public utilities, and acquires a tremendous fortune, as well as political power and prestige, through his streetcar business, his gift of an observatory to a university, and his fine collection of paintings acquired during trips to Europe. Meanwhile he is dissatisfied with Aileen and pursues other women, arousing her bitter resentment. Once she physically attacks a current mistress, but even this cannot restore her control of him, and she becomes increasingly coarse and dissipated, taking several lovers herself. When he establishes a palatial residence in New York City, Cowperwood discovers his "ideal" in Berenice Fleming, the beautiful, sensitive, and innocent daughter of a former brothel keeper. Although he is twice her age, he succeeds in winning the girl's love, and she accompanies him to Europe after he is finally ousted by his Chicago competitors.

To a Waterfowl, lyric poem by Bryant, ♦ written in 1815, published in 1818, and collected in *Poems* (1821). Called by Matthew Arnold "the most perfect brief poem in the language," it is arranged in alternately rhymed quatrains, and expresses the poet's grateful vision, at the close of a day of self-doubt and despair, of a solitary bird on the horizon, and his sense of the protective guidance of everything in nature by a divine Power, who "In the long way that I must tread alone, Will lead my steps aright."

To Build a Fire, short story by Jack London, ♦ first published in *The Century* (Aug. 1908) and collected in *Lost Face* (1910).

A *chechaquo,* as newcomers to the Arctic are called, travels on a little-used route off the main Yukon trail one sunless winter day of "tremendous cold" at 75 degrees below zero. His every action has to be careful, but nevertheless he accidentally steps into a spring hidden under the snow and so immediately has to dry his boots and feet. The fire he builds is put out by snow that falls from a bough and his hands and feet begin to freeze. With the heels of his frozen hands he awkwardly grasps and lights his matches but burns himself and the fire fails to catch the twigs and grasses painfully scraped together. To save himself he decides to kill his husky dog and to bury his hands in the warm body until the numbness might go out of them, but he cannot hold his knife, and the frightened dog evades him. In desperation he runs to restore circulation, but he flounders, lies down, and drowses off to death.

To Earthward, lyric poem in three- and two-stress iambic meter, by Robert Frost,♦ published in *New Hampshire* (1923). The poet contrasts the sweet joys of youthful experience ("The petal of the rose It was that stung") with the bitter passions of maturity ("Now no joy but lacks salt That is not dashed with pain And weariness and fault . . .").

To Have and Have Not, novel by Hemingway,♦ published in 1937.

Harry Morgan, a tough "conch," as natives of Key West, Fla., call themselves, has devoted his life to the single-minded effort to keep himself, his wife, and his children on the upper fringe of the "have-nots." He hires out his powerboat to wealthy men for fishing trips, but, when the Depression destroys this source of income and a rich tourist welshes on payment for lost fishing tackle, he is obliged to turn to illegal activities. He contracts to smuggle Chinese from Cuba into the U.S., but, taking their money, murders their leader and abandons the others. While smuggling illegal liquor, he is captured in a gun battle by federal officers, loses an arm, and has his boat confiscated. In a last desperate attempt to obtain money, he aids in the escape of four bank robbers, although realizing that unless he kills them, they will kill him. This he does, but they wound him fatally. Picked up by the Coast Guard and accused of being a member of the gang, he stammers, " 'A man . . . ain't got no hasn't got any can't really isn't any way out. . . . One man alone ain't got . . . no chance.' He shut his eyes. It had taken him a long time to get it out and it had taken him all his life to learn it."

To Science, sonnet by Poe,♦ published as a prologue to "Al Aaraaf"♦ in *Al Aaraaf, Tamerlane, and Minor Poems* (1829). The

poet apostrophizes Science as one whose peering eyes alter all things, as a destroyer of beauty, preying upon the heart of its lover, and as a "Vulture, whose wings are dull realities." Poe developed the theme of the conflict of scientific thought and poetic feeling in his prose, but later, as in *Eureka,* considered that the beauty of poetry depended on its representing a scientific concept of an ordered universe.

To the Finland Station, work by Edmund Wilson,♦ published in 1940 and subtitled "A Study in the Writing and Acting of History."

The study treats European ideas of socialism and revolution from their intellectual rise with Michelet through the activities of Saint-Simon, Fourier, and Robert Owen to anarchistic deviation by Bakunin, their dwindling in Renan, Taine, and Anatole France, then to the heights of theory in Marx and Engels, and finally to the actions and ideas of Trotsky and Lenin, who both wrote and made history. They are all treated in terms of character studies as well as elements of intellectual history.

To the Fringed Gentian, poem by Bryant,♦ published in *Poems* (1832). In iambic tetrameter quatrains, it depicts the blossom, "colored with heaven's own blue," which blooms late in autumn after other flowers are gone, and expresses the poet's wish that, as death approaches, "Hope, blossoming within my heart, May look to heaven as I depart."

Tobacco Road, novel by Erskine Caldwell,♦ published in 1932. The sensational dramatization by Jack Kirkland (1933) had a continuous run of 3182 Broadway performances.

TOCQUEVILLE, ALEXIS, Comte de (1805–59), French liberal politician and writer, at the request of his government came to the U.S. (May 1831–Feb. 1832), to report on the penitentiary system and its possible application in France. His general observations of American society during this period resulted in *De la démocratie en Amérique* (2 vols., 1835; 2 supplementary vols., 1840; first American edition, 1838). The work deals with the social conditions in the U.S. and the governmental and administrative systems. The advantages and disadvantages of democracies are treated according to their influences on American intellect, feelings, manners, and politics. Generally impartial, the study has taken its place as the earliest important analysis of its subject. In his survey of American literature, Tocqueville finds a retardation attributable to the disrepute in which art and letters were held by early settlers, as well as to lack of leisure and easily accessible English writings. Since there was a large, heterogeneous potential reading public, he expected that a literature would be created that would be free from conventional rules, vehement and bold, lacking in profundity, of great variety, quickly read, easily understood, and obsessed with a magnificent image of patriotic exaltation. He thought that equalitarianism would give poets an instinctive distaste for the ancient, make the use of demigods or heroes impossible, and leave as the only subject man himself, his passions, doubts, propensities, and wretchedness, standing in the presence of nature and God.

TODD, MABEL LOOMIS (1856–1932), Massachusetts author, wife of David Peck Todd, professor of astronomy at Amherst, came to know Emily Dickinson, and, with T.W. Higginson, edited two series of her friend's *Poems* (1890–91). She alone edited a third series (1896) and the *Letters of Emily Dickinson* (2 vols., 1894). Her own books include popular works on science, a novel, and *A Cycle of Sonnets* (1896). She had a long love affair with Emily Dickinson's brother Austin. Many of their letters were published (1983).

TOKLAS, ALICE B[ABETTE] (1877–1967), San Francisco-born friend, constant companion, and secretary of Gertrude Stein♦ from 1907 on. Gertrude Stein made her the ostensible author of *The Autobiography of Alice B. Toklas* (1933), which she declared was written "as simply as Defoe did the autobiography of Robinson Crusoe," although it was her own life story. Miss Toklas finally spoke out herself in a brief memoir, *What Is Remembered* (1963), and she also wrote *The Alice B. Toklas Cook Book* (1954), recipes and reminiscences; and *Aromas and Flavors of Past and Present* (1958), a French cookbook. *Staying On Alone* (1973) collects letters written after Gertrude Stein's death.

TOLSON, MELVIN B[EAUNORUS] (1900–1966), Missouri-born black poet, after graduation from Lincoln University (Pennsylvania) taught at Langston University (Missouri), of whose town he was also the mayor. His works appear as *Rendezvous with America* (1944); *Libretto for the Republic of Liberia* (1953), written for the nation's centennial; and *Harlem Gallery; Book 1, The Curator* (1965), the beginning of a projected, uncompleted epic on blacks in America. He also wrote plays, *Black No More* (1952) and *The Fire in the Flint* (1952), adaptations of others' narratives; and *Black Boy* (1963).

Tom Sawyer, The Adventures of, novel by Clemens,♦ published in 1876 under his pseudonym Mark Twain. Its classic sequel, *Huckleberry Finn,*♦ was followed by the relatively unimportant *Tom Sawyer Abroad*♦ and *Tom Sawyer, Detective.*♦

In the drowsy Mississippi River town of St. Petersburg, Mo., Tom Sawyer, imaginative and mischievous, and his priggish brother Sid live with their simple, kind-hearted Aunt Polly. Sid "peaches" on Tom for playing hooky, and Tom is punished by being made to whitewash a fence, but ingeniously leads his friends to do this job for him by pretending it is a privilege. When his sweetheart, Becky Thatcher, is angered because Tom reveals that he has previously been in love, he forsakes a temporary effort at virtue, plays hooky, and decides to become a pirate or a Robin Hood. With his boon companion, Huck Finn, a good-natured, irresponsible river rat, Tom goes to a graveyard at midnight to swing a dead cat, an act advised by Huck as a cure for warts. They watch Injun Joe, a half-breed criminal, stab the town doctor to death and place the knife in the hands of drunken Muff Potter. After being further scolded by Aunt Polly, and further spurned by Becky, Tom, with Huck and Joe Harper, another good friend, hides on nearby Jackson's Island. Their friends believe them drowned, but their funeral service is interrupted by the discovery of the "corpses," who are listening from the church gallery. Tom returns to school, is reconciled with Becky and his aunt, and becomes a hero at the trial of Muff Potter, when he reveals Injun Joe's guilt. Tom and Becky attend a school picnic, and are lost for several days in a cave, where Tom spies Injun Joe. Later the half-breed is found dead, and his treasure is divided between Tom and Huck, after which the latter is adopted by the Widow Douglas. His only consolation, since he has surrendered his state of unwashed happiness, lies in Tom's promise to admit him to his robber gang on the strength of his social standing.

Tom Sawyer Abroad, short novel by Clemens,♦ published in 1894 under his pseudonym Mark Twain.

As a sequel to "all them adventures" in the book bearing his name, Huck Finn tells of further exploits with Tom Sawyer and Jim, the former slave, in a story that concerns a balloon voyage to the Sahara and Near East, involving a mid-Atlantic storm, encounters with Bedouins and wild lions, and a final takeoff for the return home from Mt. Sinai. Tom's romancing and knowledge, Huck's common sense, and Jim's superstitions are revealed by various incidents.

Tom Sawyer, Detective, story by Clemens,♦ published in 1896 under his pseudonym Mark Twain.

As a final sequel to previous adventures, Huck Finn tells of the remarkable way in which Tom Sawyer solves an intricate mystery involving a diamond robbery and a false accusation of murder made against his Uncle Silas, as well as a case of mistaken identity between a real and a supposed corpse.

Tom Swift, hero of a series of books for boys by Edward Stratemeyer.♦

TOOLE, JOHN KENNEDY (1937–69), born in New Orleans, educated at Tulane and at Columbia University (M.A.), served in the army and taught at colleges, but, depressed at his inability to find a publisher for his novel, *A Confederacy of Dunces,* committed suicide. His mother urged it on Walker Percy, who convinced a university press to print it (1980). It was soon recognized as a great comic and satirical view of the contemporary U.S., set in the raffish French Quarter of New Orleans. It won a Pulitzer Prize.

TOOMER, JEAN (1894–1967), black author, born in Washington, D.C., after graduation from New York University (1918) wrote *Cane*♦ (1923), a miscellany of stories, verses, and a drama concerned with the emotional life of black people. His other books are *Essentials* (1931), aphorisms, and *Portage Potential* (1932). *The Wayward and the Seeking* (1980) is a selection from his writings.

Topper, novel by Thorne Smith.♦

Topsy, character in *Uncle Tom's Cabin.*♦

Tortilla Flat, novel by Steinbeck,♦ published in 1935 and dramatized by Jack Kirkland in 1937.

In the uphill district above Monterey, Cal., live *paisanos,* colored like "a well-browned meerschaum pipe" and combining "Spanish, Indian, Mexican and assorted Caucasian bloods," a feckless, innocently amoral group of men and women. Among them is Danny,

the chance owner of two houses, one of which he rents to his friend Pilon for $15, which is never paid, and to their drinking companion Pablo. The three of them pilfer from their neighbors, drink gallons of wine from the saloon of the formidable Torrelli, and pursue amours with such gallant ladies as Sweets Ramirez, Tia Ignacio, Mrs. Morales, and the incredibly promiscuous Cornelia Ruiz. The circle of "Danny's friends" also includes Big Joe Portagee, Jesus Maria Corcoran, and the half-witted Pirate, always accompanied by five dogs. This "Round Table" of friends, whose primitive love of pleasure is balanced by a superstitious love of the Church, comes to an end when an unusually uproarious party leads to Danny's death and the burning of his house.

Tour on the Prairies, A, autobiographical narrative by Irving,♦ published as the first volume of *The Crayon Miscellany* (1835). The narrative describes the author's adventures in the Indian territories of the Midwestern frontier, during a journey (Oct.–Nov. 1832) in which he was accompanied by Charles J. Latrobe, a British traveler; Count de Pourtalès, a Swiss youth; Henry L. Ellsworth, a government commissioner; and "a little swarthy, meagre, wiry French creole, named Antoine, but familiarly dubbed Tonish: a kind of Gil Blas of the frontier." From Fort Gibson, in the present Oklahoma, Irving and his companions traveled westward, living among the frontiersmen and in camps and buffalo-hunting grounds of the Pawnee, Osage, and Creek tribes. Irving was particularly interested in gathering examples of folklore, and the *Tour* recounts such legends as that of the Pacing Mustang. The descriptions of Western life are presented in Irving's characteristically softened and romanticized manner, and when compared with Ellsworth's manuscript account show many omissions and alterations of fact.

TOURGÉE, ALBION W[INEGAR] (1838–1905), born in Ohio, was for two years a student at the University of Rochester, but left to become a Union officer in the Civil War, in which he was seriously wounded. In 1865 he moved his family to North Carolina, where he practiced law and entered politics as a carpetbagger. His venomous political stand and obviously biased attitude as a judge made him unpopular with his fellow citizens, but he became wealthy through corrupt administration of the courts. He founded and edited journals primarily devoted to a radical Reconstruction policy, and wrote several novels setting forth his political beliefs and depicting the South during Reconstruction. After 1878 he made his home in New York, and his only political affiliation was an appointment as consul at Bordeaux (1897). His fiction, which is romantic in plot but realistic in its presentation of the contemporary scene, includes *'Toinette* (1874), republished as *A Royal Gentleman* (1881), a story of the antebellum and Civil War South; *Figs and Thistles* (1879), set in Ohio and the South during the Civil War, and said to be a fictional account of the political career of Garfield, though others claim it to be semi-autobiographical; *A Fool's Errand* (1879), a story of Reconstruction, definitely based on the author's own life and considered his best work; *Bricks Without Straw* (1880), concerned with blacks and whites in North Carolina during the turbulent postwar period; *John Eax and Mamelon* (1882) and *Hot Plowshares* (1883), also dealing with this period; and *Pactolus Prime* (1890), set in Washington and telling of a black who brings up his own light-complexioned child as a white. He published and edited *The Continent* (1882–84), a weekly literary magazine that serialized his own work and was flavored by his strong Republican attitude, defense of the blacks, and antipathy to the Ku Klux Klan.

Tower Beyond Tragedy, The, free-verse drama by Jeffers,♦ published in *Tamar and Other Poems* (1924).

In this original treatment of the Electra theme, Jeffers represents the homecoming of Agamemnon to Mycenæ; his murder by his queen Clytemnestra and her lover Ægisthus; the entry of Agamemnon's spirit into the body of the captive Trojan princess, Cassandra, to prophesy the retribution at the hands of Orestes; and the escape of the child Orestes with his sister Electra. When Orestes reaches manhood, he and Electra, determined to accomplish their filial obligation, return to Mycenæ, where Clytemnestra and Ægisthus have established their rule. With the assistance of Cassandra, who has served as the queen's slave, they arouse the palace, and Orestes kills both his mother and her consort. The people choose their returned prince to be king, but the horror of matricide drives him temporarily insane, and he spends a night in the hills. The following morning he reappears, announcing to Electra his return to sanity, despite a dream vision in which he possessed her, "entered the fountain," as he had, in a different sense, by killing his

mother. Electra tries to persuade him to remain as ruler, even offering, with some eagerness, to accept him as her lover. The youth declines, asserting that his crime and the consequent derangement have left him with a new wisdom, which impels him to lead a wandering life away from the city. Lying on the hillside at night, he came to realize that men have gone mad by a sort of racial introversion. He himself has discovered peace by a pantheistic identification of himself with all nature. He has attained "the pure flame and the white," having "fallen in love outward." With this phrase, the key to the author's philosophic pantheism, Orestes dismisses Electra's plea, and departs to pass his life in exile from humanity, having

> . . . climbed the tower beyond time,
> consciously,
> and cast humanity, entered the earlier
> fountain.

Town, The, novel by William Faulkner,♦ published in 1957, the second of a trilogy including *The Hamlet*♦ and *The Mansion.*♦

Having come from Frenchman's Bend to Jefferson, Yoknapatawpha County, Mississippi, with his wife Eula Varner Snopes and Linda, her daughter by a former lover, Flem Snopes gradually entrenches himself in the town's economic life, moving through a succession of jobs up to a vice-presidency of the Sartoris bank. In his wake come his cousins and their offspring like "rats or termites" to infest the town. Himself impotent and his marriage but a means of furthering his ambition and greed, Flem feigns ignorance of Eula's affair with Manfred de Spain, the mayor and bank president, biding his time until his knowledge can be turned to most advantage. He first wins the confidence of Linda so that he can secure for himself her future inheritance of bank stock and then by exposing Eula's liaison he forces De Spain to sell him bank stock and hand over the bank presidency. Eula asks the idealistic attorney Gavin Stevens to marry Linda and then kills herself. Stevens sees to it that Linda finds new surroundings; De Spain leaves Jefferson too and Flem moves into the De Spain mansion, ridding himself of other Snopeses who threaten his "respectability."

Track of the Cat, The, novel by Walter Van Tilburg Clark,♦ published in 1949.

Tragic Muse, The, novel by Henry James,♦ published in 1890.

To Paris from London comes widowed Lady Agnes Dormer, who wishes to "settle" the lives of her children: Nick, whom she desires to turn from painting to politics; Grace, a conventional girl for whom she seeks a successful marriage; and young Biddy (Bridget), who shares Nick's artistic interests, and whom she also wishes to be married. Among their acquaintances are the aesthete Gabriel Nash, who encourages Nick to paint; Peter Sherringham, a cousin in the diplomatic service, whose avocation is theatergoing; Miriam Rooth, a bold, talented girl, whose genteelly poor mother fosters her ambition to be an actress and uses Peter to obtain an introduction to the great Mme Carré, who trains the girl; and Julia Dallow, Peter's widowed sister, who loves Nick and employs her fortune to back him in a parliamentary election, which causes the family's return to England. To please his mother, Nick proposes to Julia after his election, and for a time concentrates on his political career. He drifts back to painting, however, and one day, when Miriam is posing for a portrait, Julia pays him a visit, after which she breaks their engagement. Nick resigns his seat in Parliament and devotes himself to portraiture. Although Biddy is obviously in love with Peter, the latter has become infatuated with Miriam, who develops into a fine and famous London actress. She refuses Peter, marries her leading man, Basil Dashwood, and causes Peter to pass through a period of despair, from which he emerges to fall in love with Biddy, whom he marries and takes to America. Nick has achieved a modest success as a portraitist, and the unhappy Julia, who has abandoned her political ambitions, invites him to paint her. It seems, to the immense relief of Lady Agnes, that the two may yet marry.

Trail of the Lonesome Pine, The, novel by John Fox,♦ published in 1908 and dramatized by Eugene Walter (1912).

Tramp Abroad, A, travel narrative by Clemens,♦ published in 1880 under his pseudonym Mark Twain. It is a record of his European tour (1878) with Joseph H. Twichell, whom he calls "Harris," and describes their adventures in Germany, Italy, and Switzerland, chiefly during a walking trip through the Black Forest and the Alps. Besides the serious, journalistic account of European natural beauties, society, folklore, and history, including enthusiastic descriptions of Alpine scenery that do not fail to praise comparable regions of the U.S.,

there are passages ranging from crude farce to tall tales and typical satire. Thus a retelling of Whymper's conquest of the Matterhorn is complemented by the author's "ascent of Mont Blanc by telescope," and a description of ravens in the Black Forest prompts him to recount "Baker's Blue-Jay Yarn," concerned with the sense of humor of California jays. Characteristic humor also appears in Clemens's inept drawings, purportedly the work of an art student, and the satirical passages on subjects alien to the average American, such as "the awful German language," Wagnerian opera, and "The Great French Duel."

Transcendental Club, name applied by outsiders to the New England intellectuals who met occasionally and informally, during the seven or eight years following 1836, at Emerson's home in Concord and elsewhere, to discuss philosophy, theology, and literature. The members called themselves the Symposium, or the Hedge Club, the latter name being due to the fact that meetings were frequently called when Dr. F.H. Hedge made a trip from his Bangor home to Boston. The assemblage, which assumed the nature of an open forum, included Emerson, Alcott, J.F. Clarke, the younger W.E. Channing, Parker, Margaret Fuller, Ripley, Brownson, Elizabeth Peabody, Thoreau, Hawthorne, Jones Very, C.P. Cranch, Charles Follen, W.H. Channing, Convers Francis, and others. The Brook Farm enterprise was only remotely connected with the Club, whereas *The Dial*♦ was more intimately associated with the group, who led the movement called Transcendentalism.♦

Transcendentalism, a philosophic and literary movement that flourished in New England, particularly at Concord (*c.*1836–60), as a reaction against 18th-century rationalism, the skeptical philosophy of Locke, and the confining religious orthodoxy of New England Calvinism. This romantic, idealistic, mystical, and individualistic belief was more a cast of thought than a systematic philosophy. It was eclectic in nature and had many sources. Its qualities may be discerned in Jonathan Edwards's belief in "a Divine and Supernatural Light, immediately imparted to the soul by the spirit of God," and the idealism of Channing, whose Unitarianism was a religious predecessor of this belief in an indwelling God and intuitive thought. It was also a manifestation of the general humanitarian trend of 19th-century thought. The name, as well as many of the ideas, was derived from Kant's *Critique of Practical Reason* (1788), in which he declares: "I call all knowledge *transcendental* which is concerned, not with objects, but with our mode of knowing objects so far as this is possible *a priori.*" From other German philosophers, such as Jacobi, Fichte, Schleiermacher, Schelling, and Herder, it received impulses toward mysticism and toward practical action as an expression of the will. Through Goethe, Richter, Novalis, and other literary figures, the philosophy was more easily communicated to American authors, and, at second remove, the doctrines of German transcendentalism were reflected in the poetry and criticism of such English authors as Coleridge, Carlyle, and Wordsworth. In addition, the New England Transcendentalist belief was shaped by the ideas of Plato, Plotinus, and such English neo-Platonists as Cudworth and More, as well as by certain aspects of the teachings of Confucius, the Mohammedan Sufis, the writers of the Upanishads and the *Bhagavad-Gita,* the Buddhists, the eclectic idealist Victor Cousin, the Hebrew and Greek scriptural authors, Thomas à Kempis, Pascal, and Swedenborg.

Although the very spirit of Transcendentalism permitted contradiction, and its eclectic sources made for diverse concepts, in its larger outlines the belief had as its fundamental base a monism holding to the unity of the world and God and the immanence of God in the world. Because of this indwelling of divinity, everything in the world is a microcosm containing within itself all the laws and meaning of existence. Likewise, the soul of each individual is identical with the soul of the world, and latently contains all that the world contains. Man may fulfill his divine potentialities either through a rapt mystical state, in which the divine is infused into the human, or through coming into contact with the truth, beauty, and goodness embodied in nature and originating in the Over-Soul. Thus occurs the doctrine of correspondence between the tangible world and the human mind, and the identity of moral and physical laws. Through belief in the divine authority of the soul's intuitions and impulses, based on this identification of the individual soul with God, there developed the doctrine of self-reliance and individualism, the disregard of external authority, tradition, and logical demonstration, and the absolute optimism of the movement.

These primary beliefs varied greatly as they were interpreted in the writings of different authors, although the most impor-

tant literary expression of transcendental thought is considered to lie in Thoreau's *Walden*♦ and in such works of Emerson as *Nature,* ♦ *The American Scholar,* ♦ the Divinity School Address, ♦ "The Over-Soul," ♦ "Self-Reliance," ♦ and "Compensation." ♦ Other members of the informal Transcendental Club♦ whose prose and poetry express similar ideas, included Alcott, Margaret Fuller, the younger W.E. Channing, Ripley, Jones Very, C.P. Cranch, J.F. Clarke, Theodore Parker, Brownson, Elizabeth Peabody, and W.H. Channing. Since there was no formal association, many writers of the time, such as Hawthorne and Julia Ward Howe, were on the fringe of the steadfast believers, and in one way or another the beliefs affected many not usually associated with the movement, including Lowell, Longfellow, Bryant, Whittier, Melville, and Whitman. So far as the movement had a central voice, *The Dial*♦ (1840–44) may be considered its organ, and, although it necessarily remained on an idealistic plane, it was instrumental in the formation of such social experiments as Brook Farm♦ and Fruitlands. ♦

transition (1927–38), monthly little magazine founded in Paris as "an international magazine for creative experiment." Its editors, Eugene Jolas and Elliot Paul, believed that the literary imagination of the time was too photographic and that the study of the irrational was an *a priori* condition for giving the imagination a new dimension. They therefore explored "a nightworld hitherto neglected" and tried to liberate conventional language, using new words and new grammar to evoke such states of mind as dream, hallucination, and half-sleep. Joyce's "Work in Progress" (*Finnegans Wake*), which attempted, according to the editor, "to give a time-and-spaceless panorama of the nocturnal world," was one of their leading documents. Other contributors included Gertrude Stein, Hemingway, Hart Crane, and W.C. Williams, and the magazine published translations of foreign authors. In the summer of 1928 it became a quarterly, and it was temporarily discontinued (1930–32) when "it threatened to become a mercantile success."

Traveler from Altruria, A, novel by Howells, ♦ published in 1894. *Through the Eye of the Needle*♦ is a sequel.

Mr. Homos, a visitor from the Utopian republic Altruria, founded on principles of altruism, comes to spend his vacation at a fashionable American summer resort. In a series of discussions with Mr. Twelvemough, a popular novelist, and other wealthy Americans, he applies his naïve Christian socialism to modern society. Mrs. Makely, a bourgeois intellectual, arranges for Homos to lecture on Altrurian conditions, and, though his point of view is antithetical to that of most of the hotel guests, he is loudly cheered by the impoverished farmers of the neighborhood. The local minister looks upon Altruria as heaven on earth, a manufacturer's faith in the profit system is shaken, Professor Lumen, avoiding principles, damns the republic as a rehash of famous Utopias, and Mrs. Makely is entirely unmoved by the results of her stimulating evening. The economy of Altruria, as outlined by Homos, requires all citizens to work three hours a day at manual tasks, in return for food and other goods from government sources. In this thoroughly equalitarian state, property is communally owned, most modern machinery is outlawed, family life is subordinated to civic life, and fashions in everything from dress to architecture are under the supervision of aesthetic commissioners.

TRAVEN, B., pseudonym of a mysterious author whose full name is believed to be Berick Traven Torsvan. He is said to have been born in Chicago in 1890 of Swedish parents, but it has also been said that he was a German named Ret Marut or used that name during residence in Germany. He seems to have been active in the I.W.W. in the U.S., to have been in Germany during World War I, and to have lived in Mexico from the 1920s or '30s to his death in 1969. His novels include *The Death Ship* (Germany, 1926; U.S., 1934), about a New Orleans sailor stranded in Antwerp, shunted around Europe, and finally hired on a ship which the owners plan to sink for insurance money; *The Treasure of the Sierra Madre* (Germany, 1927; U.S., 1935), analyzing the psychology of greed in telling of three Americans searching for a lost gold mine in Mexican mountains; *The Bridge and the Jungle* (Germany, 1929; U.S., 1938), in which an explorer in a Central American jungle becomes involved in the drowning of a boy; and *The Rebellion of the Hanged* (Germany, 1936; U.S., 1952), treating the exploitation of Indian lumber camp workers in Mexico during the 1910 revolt against Diaz. Other novels were published in Germany and England, and shorter fiction is collected in the U.S. as *Stories by the*

Man Nobody Knows (1961) and *The Night Visitor* (1973).

TRILLIN, CALVIN (1935–), Kansas City-born journalist, after graduation from Yale was a reporter for *Time* and then a staff writer for *The New Yorker*. His nonfictional works include *An Education in Georgia* (1964), about the first blacks to be admitted to a public university in Georgia; *U.S. Journal* (1971), vignettes of life in varied parts of the nation; *American Fried* (1974), on good food in the U.S.; *Alice, Let's Eat* (1978) and *Third Helpings* (1983), further adventures of a happy eater; *Uncivil Liberties* (1982), witty essays; and *Killings* (1984), about sudden deaths, mainly murders. His fiction includes *Barnett Frummer Is an Unbloomed Flower* (1969), humorous stories; *Runestruck* (1977), a funny tale of a New England town thought to be a Viking landing place; and *Floater* (1980), a comic treatment of work on a weekly news magazine.

TRILLING, DIANA (1905–), essayist on literary, social, and political subjects, whose books include *Claremont Essays* (1964), *We Must March My Darlings* (1977), *Reviewing the Forties* (1978), and *Mrs. Harris* (1981), a study of an elegant lady condemned for murdering her lover.

TRILLING, LIONEL (1905–75), professor of English at Columbia, also affiliated with the Kenyon School of English, *The Kenyon Review,* and the *Partisan Review.* He wrote the studies *Matthew Arnold* (1939) and *E.M. Forster* (1943), and his other critical writings include *The Liberal Imagination♦* (1950) and *The Opposing Self♦* (1955), essays; *Freud and the Crisis of Our Culture* (1956), lectures; *A Gathering of Fugitives* (1956), brief essays; *The Life and Work of Sigmund Freud* (1962); *Beyond Culture* (1965), essays; *Sincerity and Authenticity* (1972); and *Mind in the Modern World* (1973). *The Middle of the Journey♦* (1947) is a novel of the moral and political climate of the 1930s and '40s. Posthumous publications include his *Collected Works* (12 vols., 1978–80) and *Speaking of Literature and Society* (1980), previously uncollected critical writings. Diana Trilling was his wife.

Trivia, volume of aphorisms and essays written by Logan Pearsall Smith. ♦

TROLLOPE, FRANCES (1780–1863), English author, resided in the U.S. (1827–30), during which time her husband operated a fancy-goods bazaar in Cincinnati. The business failed, but Mrs. Trollope's book *Domestic Manners of the Americans* (1832) attained notoriety. Although she admitted that the material status of Americans was superior to that of Europeans, she remarked on the tendency of democracy to lower the level of intellectual attainment, attacked slavery, was offended by revivals, disliked the affected delicacy of American women, and criticized the general boastfulness and sharp practices in business. The work caused a sensation and prompted many replies both in magazines and in books. Mrs. Trollope wrote other travel books and novels, of which four deal with America: *The Refugee in America* (1832); *Jonathan Jefferson Whitlaw* (1836), attacking black slavery; *The Barnabys in America* (1843); and *The Old World and the New* (1849). Her sons, the novelist Anthony Trollope (1815–82) and Thomas Adolphus Trollope (1810–92), both wrote studies of American institutions. The several trips that Anthony made to America resulted in *North America* (1862) and some letters in the Liverpool *Weekly Mercury* (1875), of which one was reprinted as *A Letter from Anthony Trollope Describing A Visit to California* (1946).

Tropic of Cancer, novel in the form of a personal narrative by Henry Miller,♦ first published in Paris in 1934 but censored in the U.S., where it was not printed until 1961.

In a first-person monologue that is heavily anecdotal and quasi-philosophic, it tells of the life of an expatriate American author in Paris during the 1920s and '30s. By turns angry and humorous, it presents very frankly the doings of an impoverished artist, including his sexual experiences, which are good when animated by love and when not are viewed as being as vulgar as the ultimate obscenity of inertia.

Tropic of Capricorn, novel in the form of a personal narrative by Henry Miller,♦ first published in Paris in 1939 but because of censorship not printed in the U.S. until 1962.

In a form like that of *Tropic of Cancer*♦ the autobiographical account describes the writer's boyhood in Brooklyn, his quest to discover himself by sexual experiences and by other means, and his fury at the faults he finds in many of the values and ways of life in the U.S.

TRUMBULL, JOHN (1750–1831), member of the Connecticut Wits,♦ graduated from Yale

(1767), where with Timothy Dwight and David Humphreys he attempted to liberalize the course of studies and create an interest in modern literature. His valedictory oration, *An Essay on the Uses and Advantages of the Fine Arts,* attacks subservience to neoclassical rules, but its concluding verses, "Prospect of the Future Glory of America," are perfect examples of neoclassical versification. After receiving his master's degree (1770), and while tutoring at the college, he wrote *The Progress of Dulness*♦ (1772–73), a satire on college education. Removing to Boston (1773), he studied law in the office of John Adams, and was stimulated by him to interest himself in the patriotic movement and write his bombastic poem *An Elegy on the Times* (1774). While practicing law at New Haven and Hartford (1774–1825), he was drawn into the poetic circle of the Wits and into politics. Although he aligned himself on the side of the revolutionaries, he was cautious and moderate, as indicated in his literary contributions to the cause. He was a thinker rather than a man of action. At the instigation of "some leading members of the first Congress," he wrote the mock epic *M'Fingal*♦ (1782), satirizing the stupidity of the British. Later, he joined the conservative Federalists, cooperating with them in *The Anarchiad,* satirizing democratic liberalism.

TUCHMAN, BARBARA W[ERTHEIM] (1912–   ), New York-born journalist and historian, author under her maiden name of *The Lost British Policy* (1938); *Bible and Sword* (1956); and *The Zimmerman Telegram* (1958), about the German foreign minister's cable in World War I proposing that Mexico attack the U.S. and regain Southwestern territory. Under her married name she wrote *The Guns of August* (1962, Pulitzer Prize), on the battles during the first month of World War I; *The Proud Tower* (1965), on the 24 years preceding that month; *Stilwell and the American Experience in China, 1911–45* (1972, Pulitzer Prize); *Notes from China* (1972); *A Distant Mirror* (1978), on Europe in the 14th century; and *The March of Folly* (1984), treating human inanity throughout history. *Practicing History* (1981) collects essays.

TUCKERMAN, FREDERICK GODDARD (1821–73), member of a distinguished Massachusetts family, was little known during his lifetime because, after graduation from Harvard and a short period of legal practice, he lived as a recluse and issued only one volume of *Poems* (1860), for which he is now highly regarded. This privately printed collection was reissued in 1864 and 1869, and *Complete Poems* (1965) was edited from manuscripts. The modern discovery of Tuckerman was effected by Witter Bynner, who republished the best of his *Poems,* together with three hitherto unpublished sonnet sequences, as *Sonnets* (1931). In a highly eulogistic introduction Bynner calls these works among "the noblest in the language" for their expression of grief, their imagery, and their radical use of a conventional form. Yvor Winters contends that "in the description of natural detail . . . he surpasses the British romantics except, perhaps, for an occasional line or short passage in Wordsworth." Winters lays particular stress on a late poem, "The Cricket" (first published in an imperfect text, 1950), an ode sensitively evoking the insect and treating the theme of differences and relations between the human and natural worlds.

Turn of the Screw, The, story by Henry James, ♦ published in 1898. The ambiguities of the tale have led to a large body of interpretations, particularly Freudian and anti-Freudian analyses, of which the best known is Edmund Wilson's in *The Triple Thinkers,* itself twice revised. The story was dramatized by William Archibald as *The Innocents* (1950) and Benjamin Britten created an operatic version under the original title in 1954.

This mysterious tale of ghastly apparitions is recounted from the diary of a neurotic spinster who in her youth was a governess on a lonely British estate. Her unusually beautiful and precocious pupils, the children Miles and Flora, are subjected, she believes, respectively to the evil influence of two ghosts: Peter Quint, once a valet on the estate, and Miss Jessel, their former governess. The frustrated new governess, infatuated by the children and particularly by the boy, pits her will against that of the ghosts, for these specters, she believes, morally dominate the children and have an evil relationship with them. She justifies her belief by winning the housekeeper to her cause, although this kindly, simple woman never sees the apparitions. Fearing to report the untoward events to her employer, the children's uncle, for whom she entertains an unrealized and thwarted passion, the governess attempts to exorcise the malicious influences by directly challenging Flora, whose resultant fear is so great she cannot again face the governess. A

similarly impassioned attack on Miles results in his death in the arms of the governess, who thought she was saving his life from a demon.

TURNER, Frederick Jackson (1861–1932), historian noted for his essay "The Significance of the Frontier in American History" (printed 1894), which inaugurated a new interpretation of the West. He wrote little, and when he published *The Frontier in American History* (1920) there were only a dozen short essays that he cared to reprint along with his original paper on the frontier. *The Significance of Sections in American History* (1932) was a posthumous recipient of a Pulitzer Prize. (For a brief survey of his theory, see *Frontier.*)

Tuscarora Indians, tribe related to the Iroquois, which was driven by white settlers from its original home in North Carolina to take refuge with the Iroquois Confederacy, which then became the Six Nations. Because they remained friendly with the Americans in the Revolution, they were attacked and dispersed by the British. The Tuscarora chief Wyandotté is the central figure in Cooper's novel of that name, and Edmund Wilson's *Apologies to the Iroquois* (1960) tells of the 20th-century situation of the tribes in the Confederacy.

TWAIN, Mark, see *Mark Twain.*

'Twas the Night Before Christmas, poem by C.C. Moore. ♦

Twice-Told Tales, 39 stories by Hawthorne, ♦ printed in *The Token,* collected (1837) and enlarged (1842). Among the tales, many of them marked by the author's interest in the supernatural, are sketches of New England history, like "The Grey Champion," ♦ "Endicott and the Red Cross," ♦ "The Maypole of Merrymount," ♦ and the four "Legends of the Province House," which include "Howe's Masquerade" ♦ and "Lady Eleanor's Mantle"♦; stories of incident, like "Mr. Higginbotham's Catastrophe"♦; and moral allegories, like "The Minister's Black Veil," ♦ "Dr. Heidegger's Experiment," ♦ and "The Ambitious Guest." ♦

Two Look at Two, blank-verse poem by Robert Frost, ♦ published in *New Hampshire* (1923).

A pair of lovers climb a wooded mountain, and at the approach of night prepare to turn back but are halted on seeing a doe staring at them across a fence. The spell broken when she calmly walks off, they are about to go on again, but are stopped a second time by the appearance in the same place of "an antlered buck of lusty nostril" who "viewed them quizzically with jerks of head." After a moment he too disappears, but the lovers stand spellbound,

> As if the earth in one unlooked-for favor
> Had made them certain earth returned their love.

Two Rivulets, discursive work by Whitman, ♦ the second volume of a collected edition (1876) whose first volume was *Leaves of Grass.* The title suggests not only the blending of prose and verse, but also the combination of thoughts on American politics and literature with realistic and imaginative speculations on death and immortality. *Two Rivulets* incorporates *Democratic Vistas* ♦ (1871) and *Memoranda During the War* (1875) as prose, and its poetry includes the previous pamphlets *As a Strong Bird on Pinions Free* (1872) and *Passage to India* ♦ (1871), a group of "Centennial Songs," and other fugitive writings.

Two Years Before the Mast, personal narrative of life at sea by R.H. Dana, Jr., ♦ published anonymously in 1840. It is written in the form of an extended diary, based on a journal that the author kept during his voyage, for the purpose of presenting "the life of a common sailor at sea as it really is,—the light and the dark together." A concluding chapter furnishes a general statement of conditions prevailing on merchant ships at the time, and suggests measures to diminish the hardships of the sailors' daily lives.

The narrative begins with Dana's abrupt change from the life of a Harvard undergraduate to that of an ordinary seaman, sailing on the brig *Pilgrim* (Aug. 14, 1834) for a voyage from Boston around Cape Horn to California. In a clear-sighted, hardheaded, and self-controlled manner, he describes the 150-day voyage, with all its petty details and routine, as well as the sailors' off-hour occupations and conversation. One of the most dramatic events is the flogging of two of his shipmates, and his vow "to redress the grievances and sufferings of that class of beings with whom my lot had so long been cast." During his residence on the California coast (Jan. 13, 1835–May 8, 1836), he describes with similar detailed realism his life on shore, curing hides and gathering them at such ports as Santa Barbara, San Diego,

Monterey, and San Francisco. There are also character portraits of such persons as Hope, a Kanaka "noble savage" who blindly adored Dana; his young shipmate, self-educated Tom Harris; the older high-tempered sailor, John the Swede; and the cruel Captain Thompson, who could gladly knock a sailor down with a handspike. Although designed to be purely objective, the narrative also reveals the author as torn between antagonistic points of view, and during the return trip on the ship *Alert* (May 8–Sept. 20, 1836) and the stormy rounding of Cape Horn, he tells of his intense desire to return to his original milieu and his eventual discovery that when the hardships and the realities of the voyage were finished, it assumed the character of a symbol of liberation, so that "the emotions which I had so long anticipated feeling I did not find, and in their place was a state of very nearly entire apathy." To later editions was added the chapter "Twenty-Four Years After," describing Dana's nostalgic return to California in 1859.

TYLER, ANNE (1941–), novelist born in Minneapolis, educated at Duke University (B.A., 1961), lives in Baltimore, the scene of some of her fiction, which also is often set in small Southern towns. Her first novels—*If Morning Ever Comes* (1965), *The Tin Can Tree* (1966), and *A Slipping Down Life* (1970)—published before she was 30, deal with families and the separations they suffer through deaths and through the unhappy isolation of one member from another. These themes are also presented in later novels: *The Clock Winder* (1973), *Celestial Navigation* (1975), *Searching for Caleb* (1976), *Earthly Possessions* (1977), *Morgan's Passing* (1980), and *Dinner at the Homesick Restaurant* (1982), the last telling of the long, often unhappy life of a deserted wife who is a possessive and domineering mother.

TYLER, ROYALL (1757–1826), born in Boston, after graduation from Harvard (1776) practiced law and helped to suppress Shays's Rebellion. While on a visit to New York City, he saw a production of *The School for Scandal,* and within three weeks wrote *The Contrast* ♦ (1787), a social comedy contrasting homespun American dignity with the alien foppery of the British, the second play and the first comedy to be written by an American. Tyler wrote other plays, lost and unpublished, a picaresque novel *The Algerine Captive* (1797), and *Yankey in London* (1809), a series of letters supposedly written by an American resident in England. Previously uncollected *Verse* and *Prose* appeared respectively in 1968 and 1972.

Typee, fictional narrative by Melville,♦ published in 1846. It is based on the author's experiences when he deserted the whaler *Acushnet* (1842).

Tom and Toby desert their whaling ship because the poor food, hard work, and tyranny of the captain have become unbearable. They take refuge with the peaceful Typee savages on a Marquesas island. When Tom falls sick, Toby seeks aid and through misadventure is shipped aboard a vessel bound for the U.S. Left alone with the Typees, Tom makes sharp observation of the social, religious, and moral standards of the natives. Tom enjoys the idyllic life with Fayaway, a native belle, and is aroused from his pleasant captivity of three months only when the tribe insists he be tattooed and when he fears the cannibals may turn from eating Happars to eating white men. He finally escapes on an Australian trading vessel. A second edition (1846) containing some deletions and revisions prints a sequel telling the story of Toby's safe return.

U

U.S.A., trilogy by Dos Passos,♦ which includes the novels *The 42nd Parallel,*♦ *1919,*♦ and *The Big Money.*♦

Ulalume, poem by Poe,♦ published in the *American Whig Review* (Dec. 1847). This lyrical poem, called by Poe a ballad, expresses the writer's grief over the death of his beloved "Ulalume," and in its first magazine publication had ten stanzas ranging from the nine lines of the first stanza to the 13 of the penultimate, which in later publications became the final stanza. The meter is anapestic trimeter. It tells of the lover's unwitting return to the tomb where he had buried his Ulalume:

> It was hard by the dim lake of Auber
> In the misty mid region of Weir—
> It was down by the dank tarn of Auber,
> In the ghoul-haunted woodland of Weir.

Uncle Remus: His Songs and His Sayings, verses and tales based on black folklore, by Joel Chandler Harris,♦ published in periodicals and collected in 1881.

Uncle Tom's Cabin, or, Life Among the Lowly, novel by Harriet Beecher Stowe,♦ published serially in the *National Era* (1851–52) and in book form in 1852. During its first year after publication, more than 300,000 copies were sold, and it became the most popular American novel, having a powerful antislavery influence. Attacks upon its truth caused Mrs. Stowe to publish *A Key to Uncle Tom's Cabin* (1853), defending the accuracy of its facts. The story was frequently translated and republished and was successfully dramatized by George Aiken♦ (1852), without Mrs. Stowe's consent.

Uncle Tom is a noble, high-minded, devoutly Christian black slave in the kindly Shelby family. The Shelbys, in financial difficulties, are about to sell their slaves, and the mulatto girl Eliza and her child escape across the frozen Ohio River, but Tom remains because he does not wish to embarrass his master. Separated from his wife and children, he is sold to a slave trader, and young George Shelby promises some day to redeem him. On the voyage down the Mississippi, Tom saves the life of little Eva, the daughter of St. Clare, who in gratitude purchases him as a servant for his New Orleans home. Tom is happy for two years with the easygoing St. Clare, the angelic little Eva, and her mischievous companion, the black child Topsy, who, when questioned about her family, says: "Never was born, never had no father, nor mother, nor nothin' . . . I 'spect I growed." Eva's delicate constitution fails, and she soon dies. St. Clare is accidentally killed, and Tom is sold at auction to Simon Legree, a brutal, drunken, degenerate planter. The slave's courage and religious fortitude impress his criminal master, who becomes desperately fear-ridden. Cassie and Emmaline, two female slaves, take advantage of his state of mind and pretend to escape. When Tom refuses to reveal their hiding place, Legree is furious, and has him flogged to death. George Shelby arrives as Tom is dying, and vows to devote himself to the cause of abolition.

Unitarianism, religious doctrine of the single personality of God, as contrasted with the Trinitarian concept. The name does not fully indicate the significance of the Unitarian movement, which lies in its liberal rationalism and its opposition to the doctrines of inherited guilt, loss of free will, eternal punishment, and vicarious atonement. Modern Unitarianism traces its origin to the Reformation, and its history in England and America began in the 17th and 18th centuries. More a cast of thought than a systematic theology, the movement in America was at first a reaction against the confining orthodoxy of New England Calvinism, and was to a large extent the result of liberal scientific thought. It was first evidenced in the rationalistic teachings of such divines as Jonathan Mayhew. Independently, the Anglicans of King's Chapel, Boston, adopted a liturgy eliminating the doctrine of the Trinity (1785) and so became America's first Unitarian church. Congregational churches in Salem were influenced by English Unitarians, of whom the most prominent, Joseph Priestley, emigrated to organize Unitarian churches in the U.S. (1794). Henry Ware was instrumental in promulgating Unitarian ideas as the first nonorthodox professor of divinity at

Harvard (1805–40) and as founder of the college's Divinity School (1819). William Ellery Channing, whose sermon at the ordination of Jared Sparks (1819) indicated a clear break with orthodox Calvinism, was looked upon as the great apostle of Unitarianism. The thought at this time was an attempt to combine rationalism with a modified supernaturalism, and was devoted to practical Christianity and humanitarianism. From about 1835, it was strongly influenced by German idealistic philosophy in both its mystical and its rationalistic aspects, and Theodore Parker, George Ripley, and J.F. Clarke were its great exponents. As a stimulating force in the intellectual life of New England, it did much to prepare the way for Transcendentalism, whose leaders included former Unitarian ministers. Since 1885 Unitarianism has been increasingly rational, employing independent judgment, common sense, and the scientific method. The Church in 1981 had some 170,000 members, including followers of Universalism. ♦

Unparalleled Adventure of One Hans Pfaall, The, story by Poe, ♦ published in the *Southern Literary Messenger* (June 1835) and collected in *Tales of the Grotesque and Arabesque* (1840).

Five years after the disappearance of Hans Pfaall from Rotterdam a balloon of odd shape and structure came over the city and from it a strange little person dropped a letter describing in pseudo-scientific detail Pfaall's own balloon ascension to the moon on a 19-day voyage that began on April 1 of an unnamed year. In a concluding Note the author declares the "sketchy trifle" is a hoax and links it to the Moon Hoax of Richard A. Locke.

Unvanquished, The, novel by Faulkner, ♦ published in 1938. The first six of the seven chapters were originally published as short stories, all but one in *The Saturday Evening Post.*

Young Bayard Sartoris ♦ from his teens to his young manhood tells about his own experiences as well as the exploits of his father, Colonel John Sartoris, and other members of his clan during the Civil War and the resultant era of the collapse of the old Southern order.

Up from Slavery, autobiography of Booker T. Washington, ♦ published in 1901. Developed from a series of articles in *The Outlook,* it tells of his childhood in slavery on a Virginia plantation, of his struggle for education, his schooling at Hampton Institute, and his presidency of Tuskegee Institute in Alabama. The work concludes with an account of travels, speeches, meetings with leaders including Theodore Roosevelt in the White House, and testimonials to his beliefs and accomplishments. The work has a didactic tone as it sets forth the author's views on the social separation of the races, his faith in education, largely vocational for blacks, and his belief in honesty, industry, frugality, and self-discipline.

UPDIKE, JOHN [HOYER] (1932–), Pennsylvania-born novelist and poet, after graduation from Harvard (1954) worked for *The New Yorker* (1955–57), before publishing his first novel, *The Poorhouse Fair* (1959), a short work about the revolt of a poorhouse's aged inhabitants against a sociologically oriented director, a seeming parable about individuals' antipathy to the welfare state. *Rabbit, Run* ♦ (1960), a full-length novel, treats an unstable, immature young man who, still hankering for the glamour and applause of his days as a high-school athlete, deserts his wife and child. *Rabbit Redux* (1971) is a sequel whose protagonist, age 36, is now seen with his life having crumbled around him. In a later sequel, *Rabbit Is Rich* (1981, Pulitzer Prize), the major character is middle-aged and well-to-do. *The Centaur* ♦ (1963) combines realism with mythology in presenting three days important in the lives of a teenager and his father, a high-school science teacher, who, like other characters, are also presented as figures of Greek mythology, respectively Prometheus and Chiron, the centaur who was a teacher of heroes. *Of the Farm* (1965) presents tensions between a man's mother and his second wife. Updike's fiction had all been set in or near his small hometown in Pennsylvania, but his next novel, *Couples* ♦ (1968), like many succeeding works, takes place in Tarbox, which is similar to Ipswich, Mass., to which he moved in 1957. It depicts the town's stylish set of young marrieds in their almost religious observance of modern morality with its easy-going sexual pairings. *Bech: A Book* ♦ (1970) takes a new subject in portraying a successful Jewish novelist in a quest for approbation; *Bech Is Back* (1982) is a sequel. *A Month of Sundays* (1975) portrays a clergyman's sexual adventures during a month's enforced stay in a rest home. *Marry Me* (1976) tells of two couples' affairs when they exchange mates. *The Coup* (1979) is a semi-comic view of the head of state of a barren African nation. *Buchanan Dying* (1974) is a play about the onetime President. *The Witches of Eastwick* (1984) concerns three mischievous suburban divorcées and the curse they put on Eastwick, Rhode Island. Stories are collected in many volumes, including *The Same Door* (1959), *Pigeon Feathers* (1962), *The Music School* (1966), *Museums and Women* (1972), *Too Far To Go* (1979), and *Problems* (1979). Updike is known as a brilliant stylist in his fiction, but he has also written many poems, generally light, collected in *The Carpentered Hen and Other Tame Creatures* (1958), *Telephone Poles* (1963), *Midpoint* (1969), *Seventy Poems* (1972), and *Tossing and Turning* (1977). *Picked Up Pieces* (1975) and *Hugging the Shore* (1983) contain book reviews, interviews, and essays.

URIS, Leon (1924–), Baltimore-born author of very popular novels that include *Battle Cry* (1953), about the U.S. Marines in World War II, with whom he served as a private (1942–46); *The Angry Hills* (1955), treating the Palestine Brigade's service in Greece; *Exodus* (1958), the tale of the creation of Israel; *Mila 18* (1961), about the revolt of the Warsaw ghetto against the Nazis; *Armageddon* (1964), set in Berlin after World War II; *Topaz* (1967), a romantic story of Soviet espionage in France; *QBVII,* about the trial of an American novelist in Queen's Bench 7 for libeling a Polish surgeon by contending he performed experimental sterilizations of Jews in a concentration camp; *Trinity* (1976), concerning conflicts in Northern Ireland from 1840 to 1916 among Catholics, Protestants, and British gentry; and *The Haj* (1984), treating modern Palestinians in relation to other Arabs and Israel. *Ireland: A Terrible Beauty* (1975) is a portrait of contemporary Ireland in text and photos created with his wife Jill.

Ushant, autobiography of Conrad Aiken. ♦

V., novel by Thomas Pynchon,♦ published in 1963.

Benny Profane, a schlemiel as sailor and human being, recently discharged from the U.S.S. *Scaffold,* after wandering around the East Coast of the U.S. looking for a way of life, joins Zeitzuss's Alligator Patrol, a quasi-military organization whose business is to hunt through the sewers of New York City for the blind, albino alligators that roam there, having been flushed down toilets when they grew too large to be children's pets. Also traveling through this underground world but in a purposeful way is Herbert Stencil, trying to trace the secret of a 19th-century manuscript dealing with one V., a mysterious woman involved in anarchic plots and international spying. By turns she is associated with Victoria Wren, an expatriate British aristocrat and "self-proclaimed citizen of the world," with Vera Meroving, a German woman possessed of an artificial eye in which is implanted a clock, and with other esoteric figures to be conceived variously as Venus, Virgin, and Void. The quest for V. involves Stencil in investigations of remote and exotic regions and curious historical lore as well as encounters with many odd characters, including Benny Profane, whose path he crosses more than once. The ceaseless pursuit of his mysterious woman takes Stencil, as it took his father before him, through a maze of complex puzzles whose relationships are both labyrinthine and phantasmagoric.

Valentine, *Alias Jimmy,* see *Porter, W.S.*

Valley of the Moon, The, novel by Jack London,♦ published in 1913.

Saxon Brown, a young girl who works in a laundry at Oakland, Cal., falls in love with Billy Roberts, a teamster and ex-prizefighter, who is also attempting to maintain himself in the industrial society of the town. Not long after their marriage, the teamsters' union goes on strike, and Billy, an ardent advocate of the strike, becomes poverty-stricken. Saxon's baby is born dead when she witnesses a horrible fight between police and strikers, in which Billy's best friend is killed. Brutalized by his ensuing economic struggle, Billy is jailed for assault. Upon his release, he and Saxon leave the town and the unsuccessful strike, determining to find a homestead. At Carmel they are befriended by various bohemians, on whose advice they go to the "Valley of the Moon," in Sonoma County, where they find peace and economic stability, and await the birth of another child.

VAN DOREN, CARL [CLINTON] (1885–1950), professor at Columbia (1911–34), and literary editor of *The Nation* (1919–22) and *The Century* (1922–25), whose critical works include *The American Novel* (1921, revised 1940), *Contemporary American Novelists, 1900–1920* (1922), *James Branch Cabell* (1925), *Swift* (1930), *Sinclair Lewis* (1933). He was managing editor of the *Cambridge History of American Literature* (4 vols., 1917–20). Studies of American history include *Benjamin Franklin* (1938, Pulitzer Prize), a biography.

VAN DOREN, MARK [ALBERT] (1894–1972), brother of Carl Van Doren, was also a professor of English at Columbia (1920–59) and literary editor of *The Nation* (1924–28). He wrote critical studies of Thoreau (1916), Dryden (1920), Shakespeare (1939), and Hawthorne (1949). Major criticism is collected in *Private Reader* (1942), *The Happy Critic* (1961), and other volumes; and he published his views in *Liberal Education* (1942) and studied ten great poems in *The Noble Voice* (1946). His novels include *The Transients* (1935) and *Windless Cabins* (1940), the latter a study of a youth haunted by fear after inadvertently killing an evil man. *Nobody Say a Word* (1953) and *Home with Hazel* (1957) are among the sources of *Collected Stories* (1962). His poetry includes *Spring Thunder* (1924), bucolic verse; *Jonathan Gentry* (1931), a narrative; *Collected Poems* (1939, Pulitzer Prize); *The Mayfield Deer* (1941), retelling a frontier legend; *Our Lady Peace* (1942) and *The Seven Sleepers* (1944), war poems; *The Country New Year* (1946), lyrics on rural life; *New Poems* (1948); *Morning Worship* (1960); *Collected and New Poems* (1963); and *Good Morning* (1973). *The Last Days of Lincoln* (1959) is a play. He wrote an *Autobiography* (1958), and his wife Dorothy wrote *The Professor and I* (1958).

Vandover and the Brute, novel by Frank Norris,♦ written in 1894–95 and posthumously published from an unfinished manuscript in 1914.

Vandover, a young artist and dilettante of San Francisco, has always considered his natural passions as an expression of his baser side, but after graduating from Harvard he drifts into dissipation, and his prudishness is overcome. The respectable factors of his life—social position, fortune, fiancée, and art—are lost to him, and his brutal desires manifest themselves in vice, idleness, and self-indulgence. To amuse his friends, he has sometimes imitated a wolf, but now as his character weakens the "wolf" becomes identified with the "brute" he feels within him. Years pass, and he squanders all he owns by gambling and extravagance, sinking to the lowest plane of society and squalid living. Finally, broken in body and spirit, he is reduced to earning a bare subsistence by cleaning tenement cottages.

VAN DRUTEN, JOHN [WILLIAM] (1901–57), English-born playwright and novelist, came to the U.S. in 1925 with his first play, *Young Woodley,* after it had been banned from production in England. He later rewrote the play as a novel (1929) with the same title. He became a U.S. citizen in 1944. His later plays include *The Voice of the Turtle* (1943), a bittersweet romantic comedy; *I Remember Mama* (1944), based on autobiographical sketches of San Francisco life by Kathryn Forbes; *Bell, Book, and Candle* (1950), a light comedy about modern witchcraft; and *I Am a Camera* (1951; published, 1952), based on Christopher Isherwood's sketches of Berlin life, *Goodbye to Berlin.*

Vanity Fair (1868–1936) was issued in New York with various subtitles. Its purpose was "a weekly show of political, social, literary, and financial wares." It was edited for a time by Frank Harris. In 1913 it was purchased by Condé Nast, and until it was absorbed by *Vogue* (1936), a women's fashion magazine, it was edited as a sophisticated review of contemporary literature, art, and society. It was revived in 1983.

VAN VECHTEN, CARL (1880–1964), born in Iowa, graduated from the University of Chicago (1903), and became assistant music critic for the *New York Times* and dramatic critic for the New York *Press.* His critical articles are collected in several books, and the leading contents of these are preserved in two later selections, *Red* (1925) and *Excavations* (1926). With wit, urbanity, watered aesthetics, and an agile pen, Van Vechten described the manners and mannerisms of his era's decadent elegance in several novels: *Peter Whiffle* (1922), *The Blind Bow-Boy* (1923), and *Firecrackers* (1925), dealing with the sophisticated artistic set of New York; *Spider Boy* (1928), a satirical extravaganza on Hollywood; and *Parties* (1930), dealing with a group of sophisticated New York idlers. *The Tattooed Countess* (1924) is a novel set in the Iowa of the author's youth, and *Nigger Heaven* (1926) is a sympathetic, realistic treatment of Harlem life, which did much to stimulate the interest of sophisticates in black culture. After *Sacred and Profane Memories* (1932) he forsook writing for photography. He was editor of Gertrude Stein's posthumously published books.

Varieties of Religious Experience, The, psychological study by William James,♦ published in 1902, originally delivered in two courses of lectures at the University of Edinburgh (1901–2).

This "description of man's religious constitution" is written from the point of view of a psychologist, and based on the principle that "All states of mind are neurally conditioned" and that "Their significance must be tested not by their origin but by the value of their fruits." Asserting that institutional religion is "an external art" of "ritual acts," the author limits his study to personal religion, in which "the inner dispositions of man himself . . . form the center of interest, his conscience, his deserts, his helplessness, his incompleteness." He offers an "arbitrary" definition of religion: "the feelings, acts, and experiences of individual men in their solitude, so far as they apprehend themselves to stand in religion to whatever they may consider the divine." Pointing out that it is thus a "way of accepting the universe," and is of great value "from the biological point of view," he proceeds to the consideration, profusely documented by individual case histories, of such phenomena as "the religion of healthy-mindedness," "the sick soul," "the divided self, and the process of its unification," conversion, and saintliness. The study concludes with a discussion of values in the religious life, mysticism, and religious philosophy, as well as a definition of the author's own position as a refined "piecemeal super-naturalism" and philosophic pluralism.

Varner, WILL, character in Faulkner's *The Hamlet,* ♦ *The Town,* ♦ and *The Mansion,* ♦ who has economic control of Frenchman's Bend.

Vein of Iron, novel by Ellen Glasgow, ♦ published in 1935.

VERY, JONES (1813–80), born in Salem, Mass., graduated from Harvard (1836) and was a tutor of Greek while studying at the Divinity School. During this period he turned from his previous mild Unitarianism under the influence of a spiritual exaltation in which he had poetic visions of the Holy Ghost. He claimed that his religious sonnets were communicated to him in these visions. Although Emerson appreciated his poetry and prose and arranged for him to speak at Concord, the Harvard faculty questioned his sanity, and he allowed himself to be committed to an asylum for the insane. He continued to write, however, and some of his verse was published in *The Western Messenger,* through the influence of J.F. Clarke, who in answer to critics declared that, instead of monomania, Very had "monosania." Emerson, who also thought him "profoundly sane," helped in the selection of his *Essays and Poems* (1839), Very's only book published during his lifetime. He was a friend of the Transcendentalists, but his poems show that he was a mystic, whose belief in the absolute surrender of the will to God made his theological and spiritual affiliations closer to those of the early Puritans and Quakers. His poems of religious experience rightly caused him to be compared with George Herbert and other 17th-century metaphysical poets. His essays in literary criticism, such as "Epic Poetry," "Hamlet," and "Shakespeare," also reveal his mystic approach. After a brief time (1838) in the asylum, Very, without a degree in divinity, held temporary pastorates in Maine and Massachusetts, but, being too shy to preach well, retired to live as a recluse under the care of his sister Lydia (1823–1901), who wrote more conventional nature poetry. Two posthumous editions of his works were published, *Poems* (1883) and *Poems and Essays* (1886), "a complete" edition containing some 600 poems, edited by J.F. Clarke.

VIDAL, GORE (1925–), after army service in World War II published his first novel, *Williwaw* (1946), about the reactions of pas-sengers on a freighter caught in an Aleutian storm. Later novels include *In a Yellow Wood* (1947), characterizing a nonconforming army veteran; *The City and the Pillar* (1948, revised 1965), a sympathetic portrait of a young man isolated from most people because he is a homosexual; *The Season of Comfort* (1949), about a boy's conflict with his mother; *A Search for the King* (1950), about a troubadour's affection for his king, Richard the Lion-Hearted; *Dark Green, Bright Red* (1950), about a U.S. army officer in a Latin-American revolution; *The Judgment of Paris* (1952, revised 1965), a modern version of the Trojan tale applied to an American who finds himself during European travel; *Messiah* (1954, revised 1965), on a modern Madison Avenue messiah; *Julian* (1964), about the 4th-century Roman emperor who renounced Christianity; *Washington, D.C.* (1967), treating politics in the F.D.R. and Truman years; *Myra Breckenridge* (1968), a satire about the lurid adventures of a transsexual, and *Myron* (1974), a sequel, set in Hollywood; *Two Sisters* (1970), counterpointing the 4th-century Roman empire and modern life; *Burr* (1973), a favorable fictive view of Aaron Burr; *1876* (1976), a story of American society a century earlier; *Kalki* (1978), a satire on feminism in the post-Vietnam War world; *Creation* (1981), set in the 5th-century world of Darius, Xerxes, and Confucius; *Duluth* (1983), set in the late 20th-century U.S.; and *Lincoln* (1984), another historical novel. Among his television plays, *Visit to a Small Planet* (1956) was rewritten for a Broadway production (1957). This satire drawing upon science fiction was followed by another legitimate drama, *The Best Man* (1960), on politics. *A Thirsty Evil* (1956) collects stories, and *Rocking the Boat* (1962), *Reflections on a Sinking Ship* (1969), incorporating two essays explaining his revision of earlier works on the grounds that "what's worth keeping should be made as good as possible," *Homage to Daniel Shays* (1973), *Matters of Fact and of Fiction* (1977), and *The Second American Revolution* (1982) collect essays.

VIERECK, PETER (1916–), professor of history at Mount Holyoke College (1948–), author of *Metapolitics—From the Romantics to Hitler* (1941), *Conservatism Revisited—The Revolt Against Revolt—1815–1949* (1949), *Shame and Glory of the Intellectuals* (1953), *Dream and Responsibility: The Tension Between Poetry and Society* (1953), *The Unadjusted Man: A New Hero for Americans*

(1956), *Conservatism from John Adams to Churchill* (1956), *Metapolitics, the Roots of the Nazi Mind* (1961), and *Conservatism Revisited* and *The New Conservatism—What Went Wrong?* (two works combined and revised 1962). His lyric poems include *Terror and Decorum* (1948, Pulitzer Prize), *Strike Through the Mask!* (1950), *The First Morning* (1952), *The Persimmon Tree* (1956), and *New and Selected Poems* (1967). *The Tree Witch* (1961) is a verse drama.

Village Blacksmith, The, eight-stanza poem in ballad measure by Longfellow,♦ published in *Ballads and Other Poems* (1841). The smith is described at work, with the children stopping on the way from school to watch his flaming forge and roaring bellows, his mighty arms and hands, and his brow "wet with honest sweat." At church, his daughter's voice in the choir reminds him of "her mother's voice, Singing in Paradise!" In the last stanza, the poet makes of him a symbol of the proper conduct of life. The poem was suggested by a smithy under a spreading chestnut tree, near the poet's house in Cambridge.

Virginia Quarterly Review, The (1925–), journal of liberal opinion on social and economic affairs, which also publishes fiction, poetry, and literary criticism. Although issued at the University of Virginia, the review is neither an academic organ nor sectional in point of view. In addition to foreign authors, its contributors have included Allen Tate, Robert Frost, Sherwood Anderson, Thomas Wolfe, Conrad Aiken, T.S. Eliot, C.A. Beard, E.A. Robinson, Elizabeth Madox Roberts, John Berryman, and Julian Green.

Virginian, The: A Horseman of the Plains, romantic novel by Owen Wister,♦ published in 1902 as a companion piece to his *Lin McLean* (1898).

This tale of the cowpunchers of the Wyoming cattle country during the exciting 1870s and '80s is chiefly concerned with the adventures of a handsome, heroic figure known only as "the Virginian," his chivalry and daring, and his successful wooing of Molly Wood, a pretty schoolteacher from Vermont. The celebrated phrase, "When you call me that, *smile!,*" is one of the many colloquial expressions with which the book is peppered.

Virginians, The; A Tale of the Last Century, romance by Thackeray,♦ published in England (2 vols., 1858–59), in the U.S. in 1859.

Thackeray conceived the idea and began his research during a visit to the U.S (1855–56) and received information and suggestions from J.P. Kennedy, who accompanied him on a tour of Virginia. The work is a sequel to *Henry Esmond.*

Vision of Columbus, The, see *Columbiad.*

Vision of Sir Launfal, The, verse parable by Lowell,♦ published in 1848. The work is in two parts, each with a prelude, and the basic meter is iambic tetrameter. The plot is derived from legends of the Holy Grail in Malory, and perhaps influenced by Tennyson.

Beginning with a joyous paean to summer's beauty ("And what is so rare as a day in June?"), the poet tells of Sir Launfal's decision to search for the Grail. He orders his armor prepared, and, sleeping, dreams that he has started on his journey. As he rides out, he encounters a begging leper, and, displeased at this "one blot on the summer morn," out of a sense of duty scornfully tosses a piece of gold, which the leper leaves where it falls. After the passage of many years, Sir Launfal returns at Christmas to his winterbound castle, "an old, bent man, worn out and frail." His search has been fruitless, "but deep in his soul the sign he wore, The badge of the suffering and the poor." Again he meets the leper, beholding in him now the image of Christ, for whose sake he shares with him his crust of bread. The musing knight sees the leper glorified before him as Christ himself, who tells Sir Launfal the Grail is the wooden cup of charity from which they have drunk from the brook, and "Who bestows himself with his alms feeds three,— Himself, his hungering neighbor, and Me." Sir Launfal awakes from this dream vision, and abandons preparations for the journey. ("He must be fenced with stronger mail Who would seek and find the Holy Grail.") The lesson learned, he turns philanthropist, and alters his feudal rule so that "there's no poor man in the North Countree But is lord of the earldom as much as he."

Visit from St. Nicholas, A, poem by C.C. Moore.♦

Voices of the Night, first collection of poems by Longfellow,♦ published in 1839. It contains such famous works as "Hymn to the Night,"♦ "A Psalm of Life,"♦ and "The Beleaguered City."

Voluntaries, poem by Emerson,♦ published in the *Atlantic Monthly* (1863) to commemorate the death in battle of Colonel Robert G. Shaw, leader of a regiment of black soldiers in the Civil War. It was collected in *May-Day* (1867). In five stanzas of alternately rhymed, irregular four-stress lines, it celebrates the heroism of those who sacrifice their lives in the cause of freedom:

> So nigh is grandeur to our dust,
> So near is God to man,
> When duty whispers low, *Thou must,*
> The youth replies, *I can.*

VONNEGUT, KURT, JR. (1922–), born in Indianapolis, studied biochemistry at Cornell before being drafted into the infantry in World War II. Captured by the Germans, he was housed in the underground meat locker of a slaughterhouse in Dresden when that city was annihilated by U.S. and British bombs. He emerged to find "135,000 Hansels and Gretels had been baked like gingerbread men." After the war Vonnegut studied anthropology at the University of Chicago and worked in public relations for General Electric. His first novel, *Player Piano* (1952), satirizes the tyrannies of automation observed at G.E. and his second, *The Sirens of Titan* (1959), uses the mode of science fiction. *Mother Night* (1961) presents an American spy in Germany during World War II who transmits secret messages via open pro-Nazi, anti-Semitic radio talks; its moral, Vonnegut declared, was that "We are what we pretend to be, so we must be careful about what we pretend to be." *Cat's Cradle♦* (1963), like his other novels, uses science fiction concepts for quietly satirical consideration of mankind and its need for sympathy and compassion, proposing that we live by "foma," lies that make for human happiness. *God Bless You, Mr. Rosewater♦* (1965), in a similar vein, is also marked by freedom of form and by fanciful black humor in presenting the duplicity and absurdity of modern life, and its lack of generosity and gentleness. *Slaughterhouse-Five; or The Children's Crusade♦* (1969), inspired by his Dresden experience, also uses the vein of surrealism and science fiction, and is marked by the dark comedy, philosophic meditation, and brief, impressionistic scenes of the sort that characterized *Cat's Cradle. Breakfast of Champions; or, Goodbye Blue Monday!* (1973) is a lesser, though popular, novel that in chronicling the fantastic adventures of several Americans makes nihilistic comment upon contemporary society. *Slapstick; or, Lonesome No More!* (1976), also a slighter novel, as a broad comedy treats the problem of loneliness. *Jailbird* (1979) is a more straightforward novel portraying the fanciful life of a fictitious participant in the Watergate conspiracy as it satirizes American politics. *Deadeye Dick* (1982) deals with the accidental explosion of a neutron bomb in Ohio. *Welcome to the Monkey House* (1968) collects stories and essays, and *Wampeters, Foma and Granfalloons* (1974) is a volume of essays, reviews, and speeches, whose title employs words used in *Cat's Cradle. Palm Sunday* (1981) is a similar collection. *Happy Birthday, Wanda June* (1970) is a play that satirically presents the afterlife (on earth and in heaven) of two American military heroes who dropped the atomic bomb on Nagasaki, and *Between Time and Timbuktu* (1973) is a television script drawing upon *Cat's Cradle* and *The Sirens of Titan.*

Waiting for Lefty, short play by Clifford Odets,♦ produced by the Group Theatre in 1935 and published the same year. Members of the taxicab drivers' union meet to decide whether or not to strike, and while they await the arrival of the popular committeeman Lefty Costello, they are addressed by the capitalist agent Harry Fatt, who attempts to discourage the plan. Six blackout scenes show the causes of the strike in terms of injustice, corrupt practices, and personal tragedy. When a messenger arrives to report the murder of Lefty, a labor leader arouses the men's fighting spirit and they go on strike.

WAGONER, DAVID [RUSSELL] (1926–), born in Ohio, a professor at the University of Washington since 1954, is best known as a poet of quiet and accomplished lyric power, often writing of the Northwestern scene. His poems are collected in *Dry Sun, Dry Wind* (1953), *A Place to Stand* (1958), *The Nesting Ground* (1963), *Staying Alive* (1966), *New and Selected Poems* (1969), *Working Against Time* (1970), *Riverbed* (1972), *Sleeping in the Woods* (1974), *Collected Poems* (1976), *In Broken Country* (1979), and *Landfall* (1981). He has also written numerous novels, some serious fables set in the present day, others lighthearted tales of amusing adventures in the 19th-century U.S. They are *The Man in the Middle* (1954), *Money Money Money* (1955), *Rock* (1958), *The Escape Artist* (1965), *Baby, Come On Inside* (1968), *Where Is My Wandering Boy Tonight?* (1970), *The Road to Many a Wonder* (1974), *Tracker* (1975), *Whole Hog* (1976), *The Hanging Garden* (1980), and *First Light* (1983). He has written a volume of poems derived from the legendry of Northwest Indians, *Who Shall Be the Sun?* (1978), and edited as *Straw for the Fire* (1972) the notebooks of Theodore Roethke, who was a great influence upon him.

WAKOWSKI, DIANE (1937–), California-born poet who began to publish books soon after graduation from the University of California, Berkeley (1960). Her very personal, intense poems appear in *Coins and Coffins* (1961), *Discrepancies and Apparitions* (1966), *The George Washington Poems* (1967), *Inside the Blood Factory* (1968),

Motorcycle Betrayal Poems (1971), *Virtuoso Literature for Two and Four Hands* (1976), *Waiting for the King of Spain* (1977), *The Man Who Shook Hands* (1978), and *Cap of Darkness* (1980).

Walam Olum, tribal chronicle of the Leni-Lenape, or Delaware Indians, divided into five books of 183 short verses that relate the story of the tribe from creation through its migration to North America and to its meeting with white men.

Walden, *or Life in the Woods,* narrative by Thoreau,♦ published in 1854. Between the end of March 1845 and July 4, when he began occupation, the author constructed a cabin on the shore of Walden Pond, near Concord. There he lived alone until September 1847, supplying his needs by his own labor and developing and testing his transcendental philosophy of individualism, self-reliance, and material economy for the sake of spiritual wealth. He sought to reduce his physical needs to a minimum, in order to free himself for study, thought, and observation of nature and himself; therefore his cabin was a simple room and he wore the cheapest essential clothing and restricted his diet to what he found growing wild and the beans and vegetables he himself raised. When not engaged in domestic and agricultural labors, or in fishing, swimming, and rowing, Thoreau devoted himself enthusiastically to careful observation and recording of the flora and fauna of the locality, to writing his voluminous journals, and to reading ancient and modern poetry and philosophy. His thought about this experience was developed in the journals over a period of years, and the result is *Walden,* a series of 18 essays describing Thoreau's idealistic creed as affected by and expressed in his life at the Pond. The chapter on "Economy" asserts that the only standard of value is in vital experience, and that the complexities of civilization stand in the way of significant living. To escape the demands of society and to realize the best powers of mind and body, Thoreau decides for an ascetic withdrawal from organized society, since in his desire "to live deep and suck out all the marrow of life," he found that the essential necessity was to "simplify, simplify." Among the matters described in subsequent chapters are the practical operation of this economy; Thoreau's intimacy with such different neighbors as the moles in his cellar, an educated Canadian woodcutter, and the pickerel in Walden Pond; his temporary imprisonment for refusing to pay a poll tax because he would not support a state that returned fugitive slaves to the South; the music of the wind in the telegraph wires, and the distant railroad whistle; the varied seasonal aspects of the woods; and the joys of outdoor labor and solitary study. From this many-sided discussion, expressed in an agile, compact, lucid, and often poetic style, emerges Thoreau's philosophy of individualism brought almost to the point of anarchy, and his idealistic exaltation of arts and ideas balanced by a vital appreciation of the life of the senses.

WALKER, ALICE (1944–), Georgia-born author of fiction and poetry about black people, after graduation from Sarah Lawrence (1965) taught at Wellesley and Yale and has been an editor of *Ms.* Her novels include *The Third Life of Grange Copeland* (1970), depicting violence among three generations of men in a black sharecropping family; *Meridian* (1976), about a black woman torn between the revolutionary civil rights movement of the 1960s in the North and her affection for the unsophisticated blacks of the South; and *The Color Purple* (1982), treating two devoted sisters, black women, one of whom leaves the U.S. to live in Africa. Her poems include *Once* (1968), dealing with both the civil rights movement and her experiences of living in Africa; *Revolutionary Petunias* (1973), autobiographical works about a Georgia childhood, black militancy in the North, and love poems; and *"Good Night, Willie Lee, I'll See You in the Morning"* (1979). She has also written short stories about black women, collected in *In Love and Trouble* (1973) and *You Can't Keep a Good Woman Down* (1981), a biography of Langston Hughes (1973), edited an anthology of the writings of Zora Neale Hurston (1979), and collected articles, reviews, and other pieces related to women in *In Search of Our Mothers' Gardens* (1984), and poems in *Horses Make a Landscape Look More Beautiful* (1984).

WALLACE, LEW[IS] (1827–1905), Indiana author, whose early career included military service in the Mexican War and in the Civil

War, in which he rose to the rank of major general and was instrumental in defending Washington from capture by the Confederate army. After a residence in Mexico, where he interested himself in the attempt of Juárez to gain power, he returned to his native state to practice law and complete his novel *The Fair God* (1873), a story of the Spanish conquest of Mexico. The success of this romance caused him to write *Ben-Hur* (1880), a romantic depiction of the late Roman empire and the rise of Christianity, which is said to have sold 2,000,000 copies, besides being translated into many foreign languages. He followed this with a narrative, *The Boyhood of Christ* (1888). After having served as territorial governor of New Mexico (1878–81), he became minister to Turkey (1881–85), and his interest in that country inspired him to write *The Prince of India* (1893), a turgid novel based on the story of the Wandering Jew. *Lew Wallace: An Autobiography* (1906) was completed by his wife Susan Arnold Wallace (1830–1907), an author in her own right.

WALLANT, EDWARD LEWIS (1926–62), author and graphic artist whose novels *The Human Season* (1960), *The Pawnbroker* (1961), *The Tenants of Moonbloom* (1963), and *The Children at the Gate* (1964) present Jewish characters, lonely and anguished, but sometimes possessed of a warm sense of humanity.

Wampanoag Indians, Algonquian tribe of Massachusetts, the first to be encountered by the Pilgrims. Under Massasoit they were friendly with the whites, but his son King Philip precipitated a war (1675) that ended disastrously, the Indians being nearly exterminated. They figure in J.A. Stone's *Metamora* and in the many accounts of King Philip.

Wapshot Chronicle, The, novel by John Cheever,♦ published in 1957.

The quaint, rather run-down old fishing town of St. Botolphs, Mass., is the home of the eccentric Wapshot family. Its senior members are the cousins Leander and Honora. In his old age Leander operates a decrepit ferryboat to a nearby island tourist park (until his second wife, Sarah, renovates it as "The Only Floating Gift Shoppe in New England"), and keeps a laconic journal with reminiscences about his raffish life, until one day he swims out from shore, never to return. The diminutive Honora, possessed of a leonine face, feuds with Leander, whose house and boat she owns, but is fond of his sons, Moses and Coverly. In time both young men leave home to seek their fortunes. Moses, in picaresque style, gets a fine post in a secret government agency until ousted as a security risk because of his liaison with a woman of erratic behavior. He then obtains an executive position in New York City and becomes the second husband of Melissa, the ward of his quirky relative, the misanthropic Justina Wapshot Molesworth Scaddon. Coverly follows a simpler path as the husband of Betsy, an initially pleasant young woman from Georgia, but their marriage also appears unpromising as she is left friendless during their life on a Midwestern military base where he has found a job.

The Wapshot Scandal, a sequel, published in 1964, continues the family saga after the deaths of Leander and Sarah. Honora, who has grown more eccentric over the years, throws all her mail unopened into the fireplace and so has never paid income taxes. When approached by a government agent, she flees to Italy but is relieved to be extradited home. In time she drinks and starves herself to death. Meanwhile Coverly and Betsy continue in their unhappy marriage, while Moses and Melissa drift into even greater instability and inconstancy. Melissa takes a young grocery boy as lover and in a fantastic sequence of events they go to live together in Italy. Moses finds what comfort he can in alcohol and copulation with the widow Willston of St. Botolphs for, like his brother, he has drifted back to their ancestral hometown.

WARD, ARTEMUS, pseudonym of C.F. Browne. ♦

WARD, ELIZABETH STUART PHELPS (1844–1911), Massachusetts author of a fervently emotional novel *The Gates Ajar* (1868), which is less a novel than a series of conversations by fictional characters concerning the beauties of Heaven. The immense popularity of this work, which seems to have brought solace to innumerable women, was continued in other fictional discussions of the future life: *Beyond the Gates* (1883), recounting the dream of a woman who thinks she dies and goes to Heaven; *The Gates Between* (1887), telling the afterlife adventures of an agnostic doctor; and *Within the Gates* (1901), a reworking of the latter novel. *Hedged In* (1870), a novel having as its theme the hypocrisy of society in its treatment of women who transgress against

conventional moral standards, was followed by other pleas for social justice for women. These are *The Silent Partner* (1871), a story of New England mill girls; *The Story of Avis* (1877), concerned with a woman's attempt to have a career as a painter; and *Dr. Zay* (1882), an account of a woman physician. *The Madonna of the Tubs* (1886) and *Jack, the Fisherman* (1887) are novelettes, more realistic in their presentation of the lives of Gloucester fishermen. *A Singular Life* (1894) parallels the life of Christ in that of a young New England minister whose sincerity causes him to be rejected by the orthodox church.

WARD, NATHANIEL (*c.*1578–1652), English-born Congregational clergyman, emigrated to Massachusetts (1634), where he served as minister (1634–36) at Aggawam (now Ipswich). Upon retiring from the ministry, he formulated the colony's first code of laws, "The Body of Liberties" (1641), which is considered fundamental in American constitutional history. His best-known work, *The Simple Cobler of Aggawam* ♦ (1647), is a crotchety and amusing satirical blast against religious toleration and other matters of annoyance to him. Ward also wrote commendatory verse prefixed to the poems of Anne Bradstreet, and published some poetry in his own book. He returned to England as a clergyman (1647) and several later political and ecclesiastical tracts have been attributed to him.

WARNER, CHARLES DUDLEY (1829–1900), was born in Massachusetts, reared in western New York, and graduated from Hamilton College (1851). Determining upon a literary and journalistic career, he made his home in Hartford, Conn., and after 1861 was editor of the *Courant,* although frequently occupied in other matters. His first mature book, *My Summer in a Garden* (1870), a series of essays about his farm, possessed the quiet humor and mellow grace of Irving, which also characterized his later essays, ranging from recollections of his childhood to literary criticism and travel sketches.

His first novel, written with his friend Clemens, was *The Gilded Age* ♦ (1873). The original idea has been attributed to Warner, and the character Philip Sterling is considered partly autobiographical, but the book's realism is more attributable to Clemens. Possibly prompted by this investigation of the shoddy Reconstruction era of big finance, Warner forsook the easy, rather shallow character of his essays to write his trilogy of novels on the creation, immoral use, and dissipation of a great fortune: *A Little Journey in the World* (1889), *The Golden House* (1894), and *That Fortune* (1899).

WARNER, SUSAN BOGERT (1819–85), New York author of juvenile novels, distinguished by sentimental piety, who wrote under the pseudonym Elizabeth Wetherell. *The Wide, Wide World* (3 vols., 1850) recounts the moral development of a young orphan, as does *Queechy* (1852), another popular work.

WARREN, MERCY OTIS (1728–1814), sister of James Otis, wife of James Warren (1726–1808), president of the Provincial Congress of Massachusetts, was herself at the center of Revolutionary politics and a frequent correspondent with the leaders. Her political satires in dramatic form, *The Adulateur* (1773) and *The Group* (1775), attack Governor Hutchinson and other Loyalists. Probably neither play was performed, and both are conversations rather than dramas. Her *History of the Rise, Progress, and Termination of the American Revolution* (3 vols., 1805) is a lively and astute work, important as a contemporary record. Her *Poems Dramatic and Miscellaneous* (1790) contains two verse tragedies, "The Sack of Rome" and "The Ladies of Castile."

WARREN, ROBERT PENN (1905–), born in Kentucky, by heritage has deep associations with the issues and traditions of the South, early indicated by his affiliation with the regionalist group that published *The Fugitive♦* while he was a student at Vanderbilt University (B.A., 1925). After receiving an M.A. at the University of California (1927) and further study at Yale and as a Rhodes Scholar at Oxford, Warren, while establishing himself as an author, began an academic career that has included posts as a professor at Louisiana State University (1934–42), Minnesota (1942–50), and Yale (1950–73). The range and variety of his talents as well as a continuing concern with his regional background are evident in his early works: *John Brown: The Making of a Martyr* (1929), a biographical study; *Thirty-Six Poems* (1935); and *Night Rider* (1939), a novel treating moral issues relating to the fight between tobacco growers and manufacturers in Kentucky at the opening of the 20th century. At this time he was also a founder and editor of *The Southern Review* (1935–42).

His second novel was *At Heaven's Gate* (1943), depicting an unscrupulous financier who, though he controls his Southern state, loses his daughter, who commits suicide; followed by *All the King's Men♦* (1946, Pulitzer Prize), treating a corrupt Southern governor like Huey Long but having a moral significance extending far beyond its topical subject; *World Enough and Time* (1950), a version of the notorious Kentucky Tragedy; *Band of Angels♦* (1955), a lush, full-bodied Civil War story about a Kentucky plantation owner's daughter sold into slavery whose fight becomes an inquiry into the nature of freedom and the quest for individual identity; *The Cave* (1959), a labyrinthine study of the way in which diverse people, affected by the plight of a young Tennessee hillbilly immured in a cave, reveal in thought and action their basic natures; *Wilderness* (1961), the portrait of a Bavarian Jew who comes to the U.S. to fight for freedom with the Union army; *Flood* (1964), presenting people in a small western Tennessee town that is to be obliterated by the building of a dam and who are thereby forced to face their essential natures; *Meet Me in the Green Glen* (1971), about the tragic romance of a young Italian-American and a middle-aged farm wife of western Tennessee; and *A Place To Come To* (1977), the reminiscences of a 60-year-old classics scholar from his youth in Alabama. *The Circus in the Attic* (1947) collects stories.

Warren's poetry, first marked by metaphysical influences but later simpler, more regional, and more narrative in character, is published in *Eleven Poems on the Same Theme* (1942); *Selected Poems, 1923–1943* (1944); *Brother to Dragons* (1953, revised 1979), a "tale in verse and voices" of the lurid early-19th-century Kentucky frontier murder of a black by nephews of Jefferson, and also an inquiry into the nature of evil and the quest of the individual for order; *Promises* (1957, Pulitzer Prize); *You, Emperors, and Others* (1960); *Incarnations* (1968); *Audubon: A Vision* (1969); *Or Else-Poem* (1975); *Now and Then* (1978); *Being Here* (1980); *Rumor Verified* (1981); and *Chief Joseph of the Nez Percé* (1983). Two brief nonfictional works are *Segregation: The Inner Conflict in the South* (1956) and *The Legacy of the Civil War* (1961), on the ways the war shaped American society and sensibilities. *Who Speaks for the Negro?* (1965) treats problems of integration, in large part through interviews with black leaders.

Warren's literary essays associate him with the New Criticism,♦ as do several works, written with Cleanth Brooks, that served as influential college texts, including *Understanding Poetry* (1938) and *Understanding Fiction* (1943). His other critical writings include *Homage to Theodore Dreiser* (1971), *John Greenleaf Whittier* (1971), and *Democracy and Poetry* (1975). He is married to Eleanor Clark. ♦

WASHINGTON, BOOKER T[ALIAFERRO] (1856–1915), son of a black slave and a white man, was born into slavery on a Virginia plantation. Freed, he taught himself to read from Webster's "Blue-back spelling book," adopted his inspirational surname, and walked most of the 500 miles to attend Hampton Institute (Virginia) for vocational training. Ten years later, aged 25, he was selected to head Tuskegee Institute ♦ (Alabama), a normal school for blacks. He developed it beyond a school for industrial training into a college with nearly 200 faculty members offering instruction in professions as well as in trades. His leadership in education as well as his talents as a public speaker made him the outstanding black man of his time and a spokesman for his people, although many persons considered his approval of the separation of the races, lack of emphasis on political rights, and stress on industrial training inhibiting to the progress of his people. His books include *Up from Slavery* ♦ (1901), an autobiography; *The Future of the American Negro* (1899); *Working with the Hands* (1904); and *The Story of the Negro* (1909). His *Papers* (1972–) are being published in a 13-volume set.

Washington Square, novel by Henry James, ♦ published in 1881.

As Catherine Sloper grows up in her father's New York house in Washington Square, she realizes that he has been embittered by the early loss of his wife and son, and that her own plainness and lack of wit further disappoint him. At 20, Catherine's one advantage is her prospect of inheriting a fortune, and this attracts a suitor, Morris Townsend. The girl is overjoyed, but Dr. Sloper investigates Townsend's status and finds him penniless. When Catherine dutifully tells her father that she has accepted Townsend's proposal, the doctor refuses his consent, stating that if she marries she will forfeit her inheritance. She is deeply hurt, and after her father forbids Townsend's visits she continues to meet him secretly, finally promising to marry him when he is ready, for she does not realize that what he is waiting

for is a change in Dr. Sloper's attitude. Exasperated at his daughter's obstinacy, the doctor takes her to Europe for a year, but this only strengthens her feeling for Townsend. At length, however, she realizes the reason for his interest, and, assuming a stolid calm, informs her father that she has broken the engagement. She refuses to see Townsend again, although later she declines her father's dying request that she vow never to marry Townsend, and he consequently reduces his bequest to her. After a time, Townsend proposes again, abetted by Catherine's aunt, Mrs. Penniman, who had encouraged his suit before, but the disillusioned girl refuses him. She feels that emotion and affection are now past in her life, and remains with the integrity of her sentiment and her position as "maiden-aunt to the younger portion of society."

Waste Land, The, poem on the theme of the sterility and chaos of the contemporary world by T.S. Eliot, ♦ published in 1922. This most widely known expression of the despair of the postwar era has as a structural framework the symbolism of certain fertility myths that reputedly formed the pagan origins of the Christian Grail legend.

The Waste Land itself is a desolate and sterile country ruled by an impotent king, and the poem is divided into five parts: "The Burial of the Dead," representing the rebirth of the land after the barren winter; "The Game of Chess," a contrast between the splendor of the past and the squalor of modern life; "The Fire Sermon," vignettes of the sordidness of modern life; "Death by Water," the vision of a drowned Phoenician sailor who at least dies by water, not thirst; and "What the Thunder Said," representing the decay of modern Europe through symbols of the Grail legend. The poem concludes with quotations from the Upanishads, its last word, three times repeated, being "Shantih," meaning "the peace which passeth understanding." In the 433 lines of the poem are included quotations from, allusions to, or imitations of some 35 different writers, as well as several popular songs and passages in six foreign languages, including Sanskrit. The original poem was far longer than the published text, which was severely pruned and edited by Ezra Pound, to whom the work is dedicated. The original version with Pound's annotations was published in 1971.

WATTS, ALAN (1915–73), English-born leader of the Zen Buddhist movement in U.S., where he lived after 1938 and where he was naturalized in 1943. For a time an Episcopal minister and university chaplain and teacher, he became more widely known as a lecturer on Oriental philosophy, an experimenter with mind-altering drugs, described in *The Joyous Cosmology* (1962), and associate of the Beat movement. ◆ His books include *The Spirit of Zen* (1936), *Behold the Spirit* (1947), *The Way of Zen* (1957), *Beat Zen, Square Zen and Zen* (1967), *Beyond Theology* (1973), and *In My Own Way* (1973), an autobiography.

Way to Wealth, The, see *Poor Richard's Almanack.*

Wayside Inn, located near the village of Sudbury, about 20 miles from Cambridge, Mass., is also known as the Red-Horse Inn (founded 1686). It was originally the country house of an English family named Howe, who later kept it as a public place. It is famous as the scene of *Tales of a Wayside Inn.* ◆ In 1923 Henry Ford made it a Longfellow shrine and colonial museum; it was partially burned (1955) and has been restored.

Weary Blues, The, first collection of poetry by Langston Hughes. ◆

WEAVER, JOHN V[AN] A[LSTYN] (1893–1938), North Carolina-born author, whose poems, using American slang to depict shopgirls, salesmen, and other urban types in a toughly sentimental style, appear in *In American* (1921), *Finders* (1923), *More "In American"* (1925), *Trial Balance* (1931), and other books. He also wrote novels and scenarios, and of his plays the best known, written with George Abbott, is *Love 'Em and Leave 'Em* (1926).

Web and the Rock, The, novel by Thomas Wolfe, ◆ posthumously published in 1939. *You Can't Go Home Again* ◆ is a sequel. Both are clearly autobiographical.

George Webber, born in 1900 in Libya Hill, a small city in the state of Old Catawba (North Carolina), grows up torn between the Southern values of his mother's family and the more dynamic ways of his father, who came from Pennsylvania and who deserted his family when George was a boy. When his father dies, George receives a small inheritance that allows him to attend a local Baptist college, where his friends include Jim Randolph, a football star, and Gerald Alsop, an intellectual aesthete. In time all seek a larger

life in New York City, but Jim goes on to South America, looking for the excitement and adulation he had known in college, and Alsop grows more and more precious and reactionary. George has an affair with Esther Jack, an older, married woman, a sophisticated member of theatrical and literary society. Although she helps him by trying to get his lengthy novel published, their relations are tempestuous and he storms off to Europe. There he is torn between the desires of his Mind and his Body, as he puts it, as well as between the inspiration of foreign lands and recollections of youth, and the recognition that "you can't go home again."

WEBSTER, JEAN (1876–1916), New York author of juvenile novels, whose best-known works are *Daddy-Long-Legs* (1912), a sentimental, humorous story of orphanage life, and the Patty series about a young college girl. The prototype of the heroine of both the novel and the series is said to have been her friend Adelaide Cropsey, whose *Verse* she edited (1915).

WEBSTER, NOAH (1758–1843), Connecticut lexicographer and philologist, after graduation from Yale (1778) began his career with the publication of *A Grammatical Institute of the English Language* (1783–85). The first part of this work became his famous *Spelling Book,* which was designed to meet American needs and long played a fundamental part in American education by its aid in standardizing spellings that differed from the English. It was so widely used that by 1890 this work, with its various revisions, had sold more than 60,000,000 copies. His attempts to obtain a copyright for his book led Webster into politics as a zealous Federalist, for his need to obtain the proper legislation in 13 states caused him to champion a strong central government that could control matters of this sort. His ideas on a federal union were set forth in *Sketches of American Policy* (1785). He also wrote graceful essays, works on economics, science, and medicine, edited the *Journal* of John Winthrop (1790), and, prompted by Franklin, wrote *Dissertations on the English Language* (1789), with radical views on reformed spelling, although his other orthographical works were on the whole traditional. His *Compendious Dictionary of the English Language* (1806) was a forerunner of his scholarly work, *An American Dictionary of the English Language* (2 vols., 1828). At the time of its publication, there raged a "War of the Dictionaries" with the rival lexicographer Joseph Worcester, ♦ but Webster's work, adding some 5000 words not before included in English dictionaries, making use of Americanisms, and basing its definitions on the usage of American as well as English writers, soon became the recognized authority. In 1840 Webster revised his work to include 70,000 words instead of the original 38,000, and it has remained a recognized American authority in the many revisions made since his death.

WECHSBERG, JOSEPH (1907–1983), Czechoslovakian-born journalist and novelist, came to the U.S. in 1938 and was naturalized in 1944. His writings include *Looking for a Bluebird* (1945) and *Sweet and Sour* (1948), witty sketches, many first published in *The New Yorker,* of his life as a musician in Europe and his travels; *Homecoming* (1946), describing his return as a U.S. soldier to his old home of Prague; *Avalanche!* (1958), an account of a disastrous Austrian landslide; and *Blue Trout and Black Truffles* (1953), on fine cuisine, one of his subjects, along with music, wine, and travel, in *The Best Things of Life* (1964).

Week on the Concord and Merrimack Rivers, A, autobiographical narrative by Thoreau, ♦ published in 1849. It was written, mainly during the period described in *Walden,* from earlier journal entries, poems, and essays. The narrative describes seven days in a small boat during a trip (Aug. 31–Sept. 13, 1839) which the author made with his brother John to the White Mountains in New Hampshire. From the description of the homemade dory, which was "painted green below, with a border of blue, with reference to the two elements in which it was to spend its existence," to the account of New Hampshire people, the book maintains a certain air of romantic adventure, but the travel narrative is subordinated to learned digressions into history, religion, and philosophy; poetry; discussions of literary classics; and such Emersonian essays as the one on friendship. Some of the passages have been frequently quoted, for Thoreau's style was already fully developed, and was said by Lowell to have "an antique purity." During the author's lifetime, the book was not popular. Later editors, like H.S. Canby, have given it a more compact form by eliminating "indoor additions."

WEEMS, MASON LOCKE (1759–1825), Episcopal clergyman, temporarily at Pohick Church, Mount Vernon parish, where Washington is supposed to have been one of his parishioners. For more than 30 years he was also an author and peddler of chapbooks, and a book agent, mainly for Mathew Carey, contending that the selling of "good books" was a field for God's work. Among his short biographies the best known is *The Life and Memorable Actions of George Washington* (*c.*1800), which first gives the story of the cherry-tree episode in the so-called Fifth Edition of 1806 and is responsible for much of the Washington myth. He also wrote lives of Francis Marion (1809), Franklin (1815), and Penn (1822), and moral tracts, ranging from *Hymen's Recruiting Sergeant* (*c.*1799), a plea for brotherly love, to *God's Revenge Against Adultery* (1815).

WEIDMAN, JEROME (1913–), New York author, known for his frank, unpleasant portraits of Jewish characters, whose novels include *I Can Get It For You Wholesale* (1937) and its sequel, *What's in It for Me?* (1938), about an unscrupulous New Yorker's dress-manufacturing business. Weidman's plays include *Fiorello!* (1960, Pulitzer Prize), a collaboration with George Abbott; *Tenderloin* (1961); and a dramatization of *I Can Get It for You Wholesale* (1962).

WELD, THEODORE DWIGHT (1803–95), Massachusetts reformer, was a disciple of Charles Stuart and himself the earliest and most influential of American Abolitionists. His speeches and campaigning in New York, Ohio, the Southern states, and elsewhere were largely responsible for consolidating antislavery feeling and for converting such later leaders as J.G. Birney, E.M. Stanton, Lyman Beecher, and the Grimké sisters. Harriet Beecher Stowe attributed the inspiration for *Uncle Tom's Cabin* to the tract *American Slavery as It Is* (1839), compiled by him and his wife Angelina Grimké. ♦

WELTY, EUDORA (1909–), Mississippi author, whose books include *A Curtain of Green* (1941), *The Wide Net* (1943), *The Golden Apples* (1949), *The Bride of the Innisfallen* (1955), and *Moon Lake* (1980), stories set mainly in her region and depicting characters, often grotesque, who fail to know themselves or their neighbors; and *The Shoe Bird* (1964), tales for children. Her longer works include *The Robber Bridegroom* (1942), a novelette combining fairy tale and ballad form, telling of the wooing of Rosamond, the daughter of a Mississippi planter, by a bandit chief; *Delta*

Wedding (1946), a novel subtly revealing the sensibilities of a modern plantation family; *The Ponder Heart* (1954), a comic fantasy of small-town Mississippi life, dramatized (1957) by Jerome Chodorov and Joseph Fields; *Losing Battles* (1970), depicting a family of Mississippians trying to preserve their way of life in the 1930s; and *The Optimist's Daughter* (1972, Pulitzer Prize), treating conflicts between the daughter and the second wife of a New Orleans judge. *One Time, One Place* (1971) collects snapshots of Mississippi taken just after the author returned home following graduation from the University of Wisconsin (1929). *The Eye of the Story* (1978) collects essays and reviews. *One Writer's Beginnings* (1984) prints her autobiographical Charles Eliot Norton lectures at Harvard. *The Robber Bridegroom* was made into a musical (1975) by Alfred Uhry and Robert Waldman.

WESCOTT, GLENWAY (1901–), Wisconsin author, known for his writings about his native region, although he has lived mainly abroad. After publishing *The Bitterns* (1920), poems, he wrote *The Apple of the Eye* (1924), a novel of the frontier West about a boy torn between the crabbed orthodoxy of his aunt, a typical pioneer woman, and the pagan acceptance of the beauty of life taught him by a friend. After *Natives of Rock* (1925), a volume of poems, and *Like a Lover* (1926), short stories, he wrote his best-known work, *The Grandmothers* (1927), published in England as *A Family Portrait.* This is the story of a pioneer Midwestern family told through the imagination of a youth, Alwyn Tower, who, having escaped to Europe from his uncongenial background, nostalgically turns the pages of a photograph album and from the faces of his ancestors reconstructs their sad, frustrated lives. *Good-Bye, Wisconsin* (1928) is a collection of short stories presenting the same dour interpretation of the Midwest. Wescott's other books include *The Babe's Bed* (1930), an allegorical story about a young man who returns to his Midwestern home to ponder on the future of a newly born child; *Fear and Trembling* (1932), a book of essays on political and social problems of central Europe based on a firsthand view; and *A Calendar of Saints for Unbelievers* (1932), marked by mysticism and agnosticism. *The Pilgrim Hawk* (1940), his first work of fiction in ten years, is set in a Paris suburb during the 1920s and concerns three couples, linked by three different kinds of love. *Apartment in Athens* (1945) is a novel about a Nazi officer quartered with a Greek family, and a series of events that ends with the mother planning for her children to take part in the underground resistance. *Images of Truth* (1962) is a collection of essays about literary friends, subtitled "Remembrances and Criticism."

WEST, JESSAMYN (1907–84), Indiana-born author, graduate of Whittier College, was long resident in California. Her first work, *The Friendly Persuasion* (1945), gives a sense of her heritage through its tender, fictive sketches of mid-19th-century Quaker life in Indiana. Her next work, *The Witch Diggers* (1951), also set in her native state, is a symbolic novel about life on a poor farm in the 1890s and of the experiences of the superintendent's family and some inmates who dig for Truth. Other fiction includes *Cress Delahanty* (1953), charming sketches of the life of an adolescent California girl on a ranch and in town. *South of the Angels* (1960) is a large and panoramic novel about settlers on a vast real-estate development near Los Angeles at the opening of the 20th century; *A Matter of Time* (1966) is a semi-autobiographical tale of a woman attending to her "young-middle-aged" sister dying of cancer; *Leafy Rivers* (1967), set on the 19th-century Ohio frontier, is a story of a young woman growing to maturity during the early years of her marriage; *Except for Me and Thee* (1969) is in spirit and subject a companion piece to *The Friendly Persuasion; The Massacre at Fall Creek* (1975), also set on the Indiana frontier, is a depiction of the trial of whites who murdered Indians; and *The Life I Really Lived* (1979) is about the complex loving relations and affairs of a Midwestern woman transplanted to California. Stories are collected in *Love, Death, and the Ladies' Drill Team* (1959) and *Crimson Ramblers of the World, Farewell* (1970). *Love Is Not What You Think* (1959) is an essay; *To See the Dream* (1957) treats her experiences with the filming of her first book; and *A Mirror for the Sky* (1948) is a libretto for an opera about Audubon. Autobiographies are *Hide and Seek* (1973), from childhood to young womanhood; and *The Woman Said Yes* (1976), about her own sickness, tuberculosis, and the sickness and suicide of her sister, which she had fictionalized in *A Matter of Time. The Secret Look* (1974) collects poems. *Double Discovery* (1980) prints her European travel diary of 1929.

WEST, NATHANAEL (1903–40), pseudonym of Nathan Wallenstein Weinstein, New York author who, after graduation from Brown

University (1924) and two years in Paris, returned to his native city to begin writing his bitter, macabre fiction, which attracted little notice in his time but great recognition from critics after his death. His first works were *The Dream Life of Balso Snell* (1931), a scatological fantasy dwelling on human corruption; *Miss Lonelyhearts♦* (1933), a sad and bitter satire of a newspaperman enmeshed in the lives of the writers to his lovelorn column; and *A Cool Million* (1934), a fantastic travesty and savage attack on the Horatio Alger theme. Script writing in Hollywood gave West a sense of that community and business that led to his most significant novel, *The Day of the Locust♦* (1939), a grotesque depiction in surrealist style of the sham of the city and the pathological misfits who inhabit it. West, who was S.J. Perelman's brother-in-law, was married to Eileen McKenney, the heroine of Ruth McKenney's *My Sister Eileen.*

WEXLEY, JOHN (1907–   ), New York dramatist, whose plays include *The Last Mile* (1930), dealing with the last days of a condemned prisoner; *Steel* (1931); *They Shall Not Die* (1934), concerned with the Scottsboro case; and *Running Dogs* (1938), dealing with the struggle between Chinese conservatives and Communists prior to the Japanese invasion. *The Judgment of Julius and Ethel Rosenberg* (1955) is a work of nonfiction.

WHALEN, PHILIP (1923–   ), Oregon-born poet, associated with the Beat movement,♦ later resident for some time in Japan. His poetry, some of which has its layout and typography designed to reinforce the text, has appeared in *Self-Portrait from Another Direction* (1959), *Memoirs of an Inter-Glacial Age* (1960), *Like I Say* (1960), *Monday in the Evening* (1964), *Every Day* (1965), *Highgrade* (1966), *On Bear's Head* (1969), *The Kindness of Strangers* (1976), and *Enough Said* (1980). *You Didn't Even Try* (1966) is a novel.

WHARTON, EDITH [NEWBOLD JONES] (1862–1937), member of a distinguished New York family, was privately educated in the U.S. and abroad. Her short stories, *The Greater Inclination* (1899), were followed by *The Touchstone* (1900), published in England as *A Gift from the Grave* (1900), which showed the influence of Henry James both in its form as a novelette and in its occupation with ethical values. It is concerned with a man torn

between his desire to obtain money to marry the woman he loves and his reluctance to sell the love letters written to him by a celebrated woman. *The Valley of Decision* (1902), her first long novel, is notable for its depiction of an 18th-century Italian aristocrat of liberal sympathies. After another novelette, *Sanctuary* (1903), she wrote *The House of Mirth♦* (1905), the story of a New York girl whose attempts to make a brilliant marriage lead to ostracism because she breaks conventional standards. As in Henry James, her study of the effects of false values here rises above the level of the novel of manners to become tragedy.

In 1907 Mrs. Wharton moved to France, which she made the scene of her novelette *Madame de Treymes* (1907), contrasting French and American concepts of honor. Her next novel, *The Fruit of the Tree* (1907), set with a background of a great American woolen mill, is concerned with the inner conflict of a business executive between the demands of his work and those of the two women he loves. *Ethan Frome♦* (1911), a sharply etched novelette concerning simple New England people, is considered her greatest tragic story, and shows a marked departure from the ironic contemplation of aristocratic mores and highly complex characters. Yet, as in *The House of Mirth,* the central problem is that of the barriers imposed by local conventions upon an individual whose happiness depends on rising above them. From the fine simplicity of this work the author returned to complex treatments of moral and social conflicts in *The Reef* (1912) and *The Custom of the Country* (1913), stories of Americans in France. The latter is an international novel of manners, contrasting the background of an American social climber with the standards of her third husband, a French patrician. *Summer* (1917) again employs the direct realism of *Ethan Frome,* in the study of a New England girl who returns to live with a degenerate group of outlaws in order to escape the mean life of the village to which she has been taken.

During World War I, Mrs. Wharton not only gave her energy to relief work, as described in *Fighting France, from Dunkerque to Belfort* (1915), but also made the events of the time the subject of her fiction in *The Marne* (1918) and *A Son at the Front* (1923). *The Age of Innocence♦* (1920, Pulitzer Prize), considered her most skillfully constructed work, shows the obvious influence of James in the unified view of the action as revealed through the consciousness of one character, and in the ironic handling of Victorian social standards in New York high society. After an international novel of manners, *The Glimpses of the Moon* (1922), the author returned to the American scene in *Old New York* (1924), four novelettes, *False Dawn, The Old Maid, The Spark,* and *New Year's Day,* depicting the decades from the 1840s through the 1870s. Her next three novels deal with the relations of parents and children; they are *The Mother's Recompense* (1925), *Twilight Sleep* (1927), and *The Children* (1928). *Hudson River Bracketed* (1929) is a contrast of the culture of the Middle West with that of settled New York society, and its sequel, *The Gods Arrive* (1932), carries the contrast of morals and social conventions to England and the Continent.

Although she wrote two volumes of poetry, *Artemis to Actæon* (1909) and *Twelve Poems* (1926), Mrs. Wharton's main form outside the novel was the short story. Her stories are collected in *Crucial Instances* (1901); *The Descent of Man* (1904); *The Hermit and the Wild Woman* (1908); *Tales of Men and Ghosts* (1910), cerebral ghost stories in the James manner, in which the ghosts are projections of men's mental obsessions; *Xingu and Other Stories* ♦ (1916), which in brief form uses her major themes—the brittle standards of high society, the supernatural, the background of the World War, the historical study, the stunted middle-class lives in 19th-century New York; *Here and Beyond* (1926); *Certain People* (1930); *Human Nature* (1933); *The World Over* (1936); and *Ghosts* (1937).

The Writing of Fiction (1925) shows her artistic credo to be that of James, who felt, she says, "every great novel must first of all be based on a profound sense of moral values, and then constructed with a classical unity and economy of means." She insists that the author must "bear in mind at each step that his business is not to ask what the situation would be likely to make of his characters, but what his characters, being what they are, would make of the situation. . . ." In addition to travel books, such as *Italian Backgrounds* (1905), *A Motor-Flight Through France* (1908), and *In Morocco* (1920), she wrote an autobiography, *A Backward Glance* (1934). She left an unfinished novel, *The Buccaneers* (1938), concerned with the attempt of socially unsuccessful American girls to enter English society.

What Is Man?, essay by Clemens ♦ based on his paper, "What is Happiness?," delivered before the Monday Evening Club of Hartford

(Feb. 1883), rewritten (1898), privately published without the author's name (1906), and posthumously collected in *What Is Man? and Other Essays* (1917).

In this Platonic dialogue between a Young Man and a disillusioned Old Man, the mouthpiece of the author's pessimistic view of mankind, the Old Man considers human beings to be merely mechanisms, lacking free will, motivated selfishly by a need for self-approval, and completely the products of their environment. In an "Admonition to the Human Race," he pleads for the raising of ideals of conduct to a point where the individual's satisfaction will coincide with the best interests of the community.

What Maisie Knew, novel by Henry James, ♦ published in 1897.

Beale and Ida Farange, an idle, spendthrift English couple, are divorced when their daughter Maisie is six. Each sues for custody of the unwanted child, and the court arranges that she shall live with them alternately for six-month periods. This serves their purpose of spite, and they earnestly indoctrinate Maisie with hateful notions of each other. First she stays with Beale, and then with her mother and a governess, attractive Miss Overmore. The governess is apparently strongly attached to her pupil, but quarrels with Ida, who discharges her in favor of Mrs. Wix, an untidy, incompetent old woman whose sentimentality and motherliness win Maisie's confidence. The child, precociously acute, has become aware of her position and knows the wisdom of silence, which is misunderstood as a symptom of stupidity. At Beale's again, she finds Miss Overmore as governess, but the young woman now neglects Maisie to busy herself in the affairs of Beale. Mrs. Wix announces the engagement of Ida to Sir Claude, with whom she says Maisie is to stay, but Miss Overmore retorts by telling of her own marriage to Beale. Maisie is now an encumbrance, and when Ida tires of Sir Claude and has a succession of lovers, he in turn falls in love with "Mrs. Beale." Mrs. Wix appeals to him to leave the "bad women" and devote himself to Maisie. The appeal is futile, though Sir Claude goes to France with Maisie, after she refuses to accompany Beale to America with his latest consort. Mrs. Wix joins them in France, informing Sir Claude that "Mrs. Beale" is now free, which causes him to hurry back to England. When he returns, he askes Maisie to give up Mrs. Wix, whom "Mrs. Beale" hates, and come to live with them. The child replies that she will give up Mrs. Wix if he will give up "Mrs. Beale." He loves Maisie, but cannot do this, and Maisie and Mrs. Wix return to England, their income assured by Sir Claude. Still a "little girl," Maisie is far beyond her years in "what she knows," for in her strange situation, aided by her sharp vision and the constant moralizing of Mrs. Wix, she has come to understand "everything."

What Makes Sammy Run?, novel by Budd Schulberg. ♦

What Price Glory?, play by Maxwell Anderson♦ and Laurence Stallings, produced in 1924 and published in 1926.

WHEATLEY, PHILLIS (1753?–84), as a black child from Africa was purchased into slavery by a Boston merchant, John Wheatley, who with his wife treated the girl almost as a daughter and encouraged her education and poetic talent. In 1773 they even sent her to England, accompanied by their son, and there, as previously in the colonies, her deportment, intelligence, and poetry were appreciated. Her *Poems on Various Subjects, Religious and Moral* was published in London (1773) with a foreword by various distinguished Massachusetts men testifying that she indeed had the powers to write the poems signed by her, although Jefferson elsewhere declared her verse was beneath the dignity of criticism. It was conventional in the neoclassical mode of the time and concentrated on the matters cited in the book's subtitle.

WHEELOCK, JOHN HALL (1886–1978), New York poet, while at Harvard wrote, with Van Wyck Brooks, *Verses by Two Undergraduates* (1905). His next works, *The Human Fantasy* (1911) and *The Belovéd Adventure* (1912), are exuberant, athletic lyrics indicating the influence of Whitman and Henley. His later verse shows a change to philosophic poetry, tinged by ethereal mysticism, though still possessed of the same rhetorical qualities. A collection, *Poems, 1911–1936* (1936), was followed by *Poems Old and New* (1956). Later works include *The Gardener* (1961, Bollingen Prize).

When Knighthood Was in Flower, novel by Charles Major. ♦

When Lilacs Last in the Dooryard Bloom'd, elegy on the death of Lincoln by Whitman, ♦

first published in *Sequel to Drum-Taps* (1865–66) and incorporated in *Leaves of Grass* (1867).

The poet, lamenting the death of his hero, brings a sprig of lilac for the "coffin that slowly passes . . ." and perfumes "the grave of him I love" with "the breath of my chant" and "sea-winds, blown from east and west." Held by the lilac and the drooping star in the west, representative of Lincoln the man, the poet cannot answer the "song of the bleeding throat" of the "shy and hidden" thrush until he finds consolation in the thought of immortality announced in the carol of death sung by the gray-brown bird. Hearing it "joyously sing the dead, . . . Laved in the flood of thy bliss, O death," the poet sees a vision of the late war, whose dead are at rest, and whose living alone suffer. Finally the song of the thrush arouses an echo in the poet's soul, and

Lilac and star and bird twined with the chant of my soul,
There in the fragrant pines and the cedars dusk and dim.

Whilomville Stories, 13 tales by Stephen Crane, ♦ published in 1900. Except for "The Knife," concerned with the humorous tribulations of two black men in the town of Whilomville, when both try to steal the same watermelon, the stories deal with typical childhood incidents among boys and girls of this small New York town.

WHITCHER, FRANCES MIRIAM (1814–52), New York author of a popular series of humorous sketches in colloquial dialect. These sketches of Yankee characters contain the first American female comic figures to be portrayed at length, and with good-natured satire depicted typical feminine foibles of the time. After publication in *Godey's Lady's Book* and other magazines, they were collected in *The Widow Bedott Papers* (1856) and *Widow Spriggins, Mary Elmer, and Other Sketches* (1867). In 1879 Petroleum V. Nasby dramatized the Widow Bedott sketches, preserving much of the original dialogue.

WHITE, E[LWYN] B[ROOKS] (1899–1985), humorist and witty critical commentator on contemporary culture, was born in Mt. Vernon, N.Y., and educated at Cornell (A.B., 1921). After newspaper work he became a contributing editor of *The New Yorker*, primarily responsible for "The Talk of the Town" column, from which some of his books were drawn. From 1938 to 1943 he wrote the "One Man's Meat" department for *Harper's*. His books include *The Lady Is Cold* (1929) and *The Fox of Peapack* (1938), poems; *Alice Through the Cellophane* (1933), witty criticism of modern trends; *Every Day Is Saturday* (1934), collecting *New Yorker* editorial essays; *Quo Vadimus? or, The Case for the Bicycle* (1939), stories and sketches about complexities of urban and suburban life; *One Man's Meat* (1942, enlarged 1944), essays on conflicts in life and his solution of rural family living; *The Wild Flag* (1946), reprinting *New Yorker* editorials on world government; *Here Is New York* (1949), an impression of the city; *The Second Tree from the Corner* (1954), essays and poems; and *The Points of My Compass* (1962), further essays. *Stuart Little* (1945), a fantasy about a mouse in a human family, and *Charlotte's Web* (1952), about a girl's pets, a pig and a spider, are children's books also appreciated by adults. With Thurber he wrote the satire *Is Sex Necessary?* (1929), and with his wife Katharine he edited *A Subtreasury of American Humor* (1941). A brilliant stylist himself, he revised *The Elements of Style* (1959), a manual by William Strunk, Jr. White's *Letters* were published in 1976, and selected *Poems and Sketches* were collected in 1981.

White Album, The, collection of essays by Joan Didion,♦ published in 1979. Opening with a partly autobiographical section that also provides background on persons and situations about which she wrote in the 1960s, it continues with a section of vignettes on California life, followed by one on women, and another on places the author has visited, concluding with "On the Morning After the Sixties." The title derives from an album of recordings by the Beatles; the title of one song, "Helter Skelter," was written in blood by the murderers in the La Bianca-Tate massacre, a subject symbolically cited in the book.

White Buildings, first collection of poems by Hart Crane.♦

White Fang, novel by Jack London,♦ published in 1906 as a complement to *The Call of the Wild.*♦

White Fang, offspring of an Indian wolf-dog and a wolf, is sold by his Indian owner to Beauty Smith, a white man who torments him to make him even more savage, in order that he may win in professional dogfights. He is rescued by a mining engineer, Weedon Scott,

who subdues his ferocity by kindness. His master takes White Fang from his home in the Yukon to California, where the process of domestication is completed. There he is severely wounded while saving the Scott home from an attack by an escaped convict.

White-Jacket; or, The World in a Man-of-War, semi-autobiographical novel by Melville,♦ based on his service on the man-of-war *United States* (Aug. 1843–Oct. 1844), published in 1850.

The narrator, a young seaman nearing the end of a three-year cruise on the U.S. frigate *Neversink,* is nicknamed "White-Jacket" after he buys a white pea jacket in Callao, Peru. On the voyage around Cape Horn and up the Atlantic coast, it protects him in rough weather, distinguishes him among the crew, and nearly causes his death when it wraps about his head in a storm, so that he falls from a yardarm into the sea. There are few other catastrophes, for the interest of the tale derives not from plot but from character and observed detail. The most striking characters include Jack Chase, "our noble first captain of the top," handsome, cultured, "incomparable" young officer who wins the love and admiration of White-Jacket and all the crew; Captain Claret, "a large, portly man, a Harry the Eighth afloat, bluff and hearty"; Mr. Pert, the youthful midshipman; and Surgeon Cuticle, whose indifference to suffering and human values is shown in his unnecessary amputation of the leg of a seaman, which results in the patient's death. During the long voyage from Peru to Virginia, these officers and the diverse crew are depicted in their daily activities, including scenes of ferocious punishment for minor misdeeds, and other malpractices; and the author discusses other evils inherent in the autocratic system, the inhumane regimentation, and the degrading effects of the prevailing living conditions, partly counteracted by the exuberant joys of sea life.

WHITEFIELD, GEORGE (1714–70), English evangelist, while at Oxford (1735) came under the influence of John and Charles Wesley, the founders of Methodism.♦ His histrionic ability, zeal, and belief in himself as a divinely inspired teacher made him the leader of the Methodists after the departure of the Wesleys for Georgia, to which he also went (May-Sept. 1738). He returned to America (1739) and was instrumental in promoting the Great Awakening.♦ Suspended from his ecclesiastical office for his irregular doctrine and actions, he nevertheless attracted such diverse adherents as the Tennents and Jonathan Edwards, and even won the financial support of Franklin. In England (1741–44) Whitefield continued his inflexible but emotional way, even breaking with the Wesleys and becoming a leader of the Calvinistic Methodists, although on his next trip to America (1744–48) many Congregationalists turned against him, the fervor of the Great Awakening having waned. He made several later visits to America, continuing to be famous for his dynamic preaching, since the manner more than the matter attracted his large audiences, and his many sermons, pamphlets, and letters, though widely read, were less effective. A selection of his *Works* was published (6 vols., 1771–72).

WHITMAN, ALBERY ALLSON (1851–1901), black poet and clergyman, whose poems *Not a Man and Yet a Man* (1877), *The Rape of Florida* (1884), reprinted as *Twasinta's Seminoles* (1885), and *An Idyl of the South* (1901) are narratives dealing with blacks and Indians.

WHITMAN, WALT[ER] (1819–92), was born on Long Island, of English, Dutch, and Welsh stock. His family lived in Brooklyn (*c.*1823–33), where Walt was educated, and he later served as printer's devil, journeyman compositor, and itinerant schoolteacher, besides editing the *Long Islander* (1838–39). Meanwhile he was reading the Bible, Shakespeare, Ossian, Scott, Homer, and something of the Greek and Hindu poets, the Nibelungenlied, and Dante, all of which, either in rhythm or thought, influenced his later writing. He entered politics as a Democrat, and after 1841 was actively associated with at least ten newspapers and magazines in New York and Brooklyn. Such poems as he published were conventional and mediocre, and to the *Democratic Review* (1841–45) he contributed many thin, sentimental, melancholy stories. These early writings were gathered in *The Uncollected Poetry and Prose of Walt Whitman* (2 vols., 1921) and *The Half-Breed and Other Stories* (1927). At this time he also wrote a temperance tract, *Franklin Evans; or, The Inebriate: A Tale of the Times* (1842). He became editor of *The Brooklyn Eagle* (1846), a Democratic party paper in which he denounced the "mad fanaticism" of the Abolitionists, but so obviously favored the Free-Soil party that he was discharged (1848). His writings for this paper have been

collected as *The Gathering of the Forces* (2 vols., 1920).

In February 1848 he went to New Orleans with his brother Jeff, who with George was the most intimate with him among his nine brothers and sisters. He was an editor of the New Orleans *Crescent* for three months, during which many biographers have contended he had a love affair with an octoroon, which was the chief force in altering his character. Such assertions are primarily based on interpretations of "Once I Pass'd Through a Populous City," ♦ which is probably more literary than biographical. Whitman's later statement to J.A. Symonds and others that he was the father of illegitimate children is probably one of the legends with which he liked to endow himself.

Returning to Brooklyn, he came by way of St. Louis, Chicago, and upstate New York, for the first time seeing something of the frontier that so strongly affected his philosophy, as in such poems as "Pioneers! O Pioneers!" ♦ and "The Song of the Broad Axe." ♦ He edited various papers, including the Brooklyn *Times,* from which his contributions have been collected in *I Sit and Look Out* (1932). Meanwhile, as before, he was acquainted with the varying aspects of the metropolis, listening to the oratory of the time, becoming intimate with omnibus drivers and ferryboat pilots, joining the crowds at bathing beaches, and hearing Shakespeare and Italian opera, all of which had an effect on the themes and manner of his poetry. Although he had earlier affected the mien of a dandy, he now dressed as a "rough," and his actions and ideas were leading toward the climax of 1855. Just as it has been supposed that he underwent a transformation in New Orleans, it is thought that he passed through some mystical experience at this time. It is probably more realistic to suppose that *Leaves of Grass* grew out of a slow and conscious effort to employ his experiences and his own maturity. Although he consistently celebrated himself as an average man, he was probably feeling his unique qualities more definitely than ever. Divided between faith in democratic equality and belief in the individual rebel against society's restrictions, he combined the figure of the average man and the superman in his conception of himself. He certainly differed in the hypersensitivity that made him as zealous in pursuing emotional freedom through love as he had been in pursuing social freedom through democracy. He differed also in his frequent, forceful declarations of his democratic love for man, and he has been considered a homosexual.

Such abnormal sensitivity and extreme sensuousness appear to be primary forces in his poetry. Other influences included Goethe's autobiography, which showed him a man surveying the universe in terms of himself; Hegel's philosophy, which supplied the idea of a cosmic consciousness evolving through conflict and contradiction toward a definite objective; and Carlyle's *Heroes and Hero Worship,* which suggested that a superior individual is a power above man-made laws. Above all literary influences was that of the Transcendentalists, particularly Emerson, from whom he learned that the individual was not merely an eccentric but an impersonal seer at one with Nature, perceiving what is permanent in flux and revealing its development. He was affected by the typical interest of his period in science, although he considered it cold and intellectual as compared with faith in a divine purpose. He was also concerned with such pseudosciences as phrenology, adopting its specialized terms for his poetry, though his unique use of words comes from sources as widely separated as George Sand and the American Indian.

The first 12 poems written under these many influences were collected, with a critical preface, as *Leaves of Grass* ♦ (1855). Although Whitman uncritically accepted many divergent philosophies and seems at first to have been unconscious of any unifying purpose in *Leaves,* he eventually worked out the belief that it was to show how man might achieve for himself the greatest possible freedom within the limits of natural law, for the mind and body through democracy, for the heart through love, and for the soul through religion. Although his ideas of prosody were also refined later, he already illustrated his belief in a simple style devoid of the ordinary usages of rhyme, meter, or ornament, and distinguished by a natural organic growth, with each part in proportion with the whole. He himself compared his poetry with the "liquid, billowy waves," and some of its most distinctive features are the use of repetition, parallelism, rhetorical mannerisms, and the employment of the phrase instead of the foot as a unit of rhythm, to create forms later called free verse.

Except for his own anonymous and enthusiastic reviews, *Leaves* received comparatively little attention, though Emerson wrote a letter of high praise. Whitman published an enlarged second edition (1856), and during the following years, continuing his writing, became prominent among the bohemian frequenters of Pfaff's Cellar in New York City. The 1860 edition of *Leaves of Grass* for the first time found a regular publisher, and was greatly enlarged, containing two new sections, "Children of Adam" ♦ and "Calamus." ♦

The poet was not intimately affected by the Civil War until late in 1862, when he went to Virginia to see his wounded brother George, and then to Washington to become an unofficial nurse to Northern and Southern soldiers in the army hospitals. He left a record of this period in his prose *Memoranda During the War* (1875), reprinted in *Specimen Days and Collect* ♦ (1882), and in the poems published in *Drum-Taps* ♦ (1865) and *Sequel to Drum-Taps* (1865–66), containing his dirges for Lincoln, "When Lilacs Last in the Dooryard Bloom'd" ♦ and "O Captain! My Captain!" ♦ Nominally a Republican at this time, he became a clerk in the Indian Bureau of the Department of the Interior, but was shortly dismissed by the Secretary, on the ground that *Leaves of Grass* was an immoral book. Whitman was defended by his friends, William O'Connor, who wrote *The Good Gray Poet* (1866), and John Burroughs, who with Whitman's assistance published *Notes on Walt Whitman as Poet and Person* (1867). During these years, Whitman issued two new editions of *Leaves of Grass* (1867, 1871); *Democratic Vistas* ♦ (1871), a prose work; and *Passage to India* ♦ (1871), embodying the concept of the regeneration of the human race through uniting the spiritual wisdom of the East with the materialism of the West.

His Washington residence ended (1873) when he suffered a paralytic stroke, possibly induced by an infection during his hospital work. From this time his writing shows a change of thought. His realistic style becomes one of indirection and suggestion, his materialistic pantheism a more spiritualized idealism, his political views change from individualism to nationalism, and even internationalism, and in general he is less interested in freedom than in regulation. During his last 19 years he lived at Camden, N.J., continuing to revise *Leaves of Grass* and to publish new editions. *Two Rivulets* ♦ (1876) incorporated *Democratic Vistas* and some new poems. His newspaper poems were collected as *November Boughs* (1888), incorporated in the *Leaves* (1889), and contain the preface "A Backward Glance o'er Travel'd Roads." ♦ *Good-Bye, My Fancy* (1891) is a final collection of poems and prose.

Although not previously neglected, he was

particularly in the public eye during the 1870s, when such English writers as William Rossetti, Swinburne, Symonds, Anne Gilchrist, and Stevenson contended that Americans did not fully appreciate him. He also had a circle of immediate disciples, including the Canadian physician Richard M. Bucke, whose official biography (1883) was partly written by Whitman, and Horace Traubel, an enthusiastic young Boswell who preserved every scrap of the poet's conversation in his book *With Walt Whitman in Camden* (3 vols., 1906–14; 3 vols., 1953, 1963, 1982).

During the final years, the poet mellowed, and was content to live quietly at Camden, except for a brief trip to Colorado (1879) for his health, to Canada (1880) to visit Dr. Bucke, and to Boston (1881), where he visited Emerson, for whom he still felt a strong sympathy, although he had long since set himself up as an original genius owing no debt to his onetime master. His executors published a standard edition of his *Complete Writings* (10 vols., 1902), but a scholarly edition of *The Collected Writings of Walt Whitman,* begun in 1961 and projected for 18 volumes, is more complete, including correspondence and all minor writing.

WHITTEMORE, [EDWARD] REED [II] (1919–), after graduation from Yale (1941) and service in the air force during World War II began his academic career as a professor of English at Carleton College in Minnesota (1947–67) and his literary career as a poet whose lyrics, often witty and light, appear in *Heroes and Heroines* (1946); *An American Takes a Walk* (1956); *The Self-Made Man* (1959); *The Boy from Iowa: Poems and Essays* (1962); *The Fascination of the Abomination* (1963), a collection of poems, stories, and essays; *Poems, New and Selected* (1967); *From Zero to the Absolute* (1967); *50 Poems 50* (1970); *The Mother's Breast and the Father's House* (1974); and *The Feel of Rock* (1982). *William Carlos Williams* (1975) is a critical biography, and *The Poet as Journalist* (1976) collects essays and reviews from *The New Republic.* He was co-editor of the little magazine *Furioso* (1939–53). In 1968 he became a professor at the University of Maryland.

WHITTIER, JOHN GREENLEAF (1807–92), Massachusetts poet, born of Quaker stock, had little formal education but found his most important intellectual influences in his religion and in the books he read as a boy, especially Burns, whose poetry led him to see the romance underlying the everyday rural life of New England. His earliest poems were published in Garrison's newspaper, and similar country journals, and through the aid of Garrison he was given an editorial position on a Boston paper (1829), soon followed by similar work on country newspapers. His first book, *Legends of New-England in Prose and Verse* (1831), shows his interest in local historical themes, as does his pamphlet *Moll Pitcher* (1832), on Molly Pitcher, and *Mogg Megone* (1836), a narrative of Indian life in colonial times.

Through the influence of Garrison and his own Quaker conscience, Whittier was now deflected from his original purpose of interpreting the American background to ally his writing with activities in the cause of social justice. As he says, he "left the Muses' haunt to turn the crank of an opinion mill" (*c.*1833–59), becoming an ardent Abolitionist. He was elected to the Massachusetts legislature (1835), spoke at antislavery meetings, edited *The Pennsylvania Freeman* (1838–40) of Benjamin Lundy, and wrote tracts and the verse collected in *Poems Written During the Progress of the Abolition Question* (1838). Disliking the methods of Garrison, Whittier became a founder of the Liberty party, for which he also edited newspapers. He published *Lays of My Home and Other Poems* (1843), and his antislavery verse was collected in *Voices of Freedom* (1846), which included "Massachusetts to Virginia."

As an editor of the *National Era* (1847–60), he contributed to this paper most of the poems and articles which he wrote, and though he continued his antislavery work he had not forgotten his earlier interests, as may be seen in *Leaves from Margaret Smith's Journal in the Province of Massachusetts Bay, 1678–79* (1849). This, his only long work of fiction, is based on records of the period of the Salem witchcraft trials, and is a semi-fictional romance uncovering the mind of Puritan New England in the manner of Hawthorne, steering a middle course between vilification and praise. Other prose works collected from this paper were *Old Portraits and Modern Sketches* (1850) and *Literary Recreations and Miscellanies* (1854). That his humanitarian interests were still predominant may be seen in "Proem" in his first collected *Poems* (1849), in which he says that though he cannot equal "the old melodious lays" of Spenser and Sidney, he can atone for his artistic limitations by "a hate of tyranny intense" and a sympathy for his "brother's pain and sorrow." This creed can be seen in his *Songs of Labor* (1850).

Whittier continued also to write on anti-slavery matters during the eventful years prior to and during the Civil War, on subjects ranging from the Kansas-Nebraska bill and Webster's defection in "Ichabod" to the 13th Amendment in "Laus Deo!" (1865). Meanwhile his reputation as a pure poet of the countryside was increased with *The Chapel of the Hermits* (1853); *The Panorama and Other Poems* (1856), containing "Maud Muller"♦ and "The Barefoot Boy"♦; and *Home Ballads, Poems and Lyrics* (1860), containing "Skipper Ireson's Ride" and "Telling the Bees."♦ Another volume of verse, dealing with contemporary matters, was published as *In War Time and Other Poems* (1864), which included "Barbara Frietchie."♦

After the Civil War, Whittier returned to his poetic interest in the New England scene to write his winter idyll *Snow-Bound*♦ (1866), which is considered his greatest work. This was followed by *The Tent on the Beach* (1867), a cycle of verse narratives in the manner of Longfellow's *Tales of a Wayside Inn*, but also containing his poem "The Eternal Goodness," which praises the "pitying love" of God and sets forth the poet's "fixed trust" in "His goodness and His love." Other volumes of this period, showing his recaptured interest in rural life and colonial history, include *Among the Hills* (1869), *Miriam and Other Poems* (1871), *Hazel-Blossoms* (1875), *The Vision of Echard* (1878), *St. Gregory's Guest* (1886), and *At Sundown* (1890). Many of his poems have been set to music as hymns. In addition, he edited or contributed introductions to many other people's works, of which the best known is his sympathetic edition of Woolman's *Journal* (1871). Whittier's *Letters* was published in three volumes (1975).

Whittier's work, which falls roughly into three periods, has been variously estimated at different times. The poems written up to 1833, in which he is a romantic follower of Burns, are youthful works that he himself attempted to suppress. The poems from 1833 to 1859 present him as a militant Quaker, with liberal political and humanitarian beliefs, and have been most appreciated in recent years. The poems from 1859 to his death show him both as a poet of nature and of homely incidents, rising to his loftiest in *Snow-Bound,* and as a thinker assured of a comprehensive religious faith that led him to become devoted to religious tolerance, humanism, and democratic justice. Whittier has consistently been praised for his ballads and such long narratives as *Snow-Bound.* Many of his poems suffer from either sentimentality or lack of technical ability, and even his best works are not altogether free from faults. Much of his poetry, which is still widely read for its simple sentiment or moral beauty, is marred by flaccidity, diffuseness, undue affection for preaching, and lack of discipline. He properly estimated one of his technical faults by saying he wrote "good Yankee rhymes, but out of New England they would be cashiered." Both his virtues and his vices probably derive from the fact that he was a man of conscience rather than of intellect, and lacked the power to discriminate between his poems of force and spontaneity and his inferior verse.

Who's Afraid of Virginia Woolf?, play by Edward Albee,♦ produced in 1962.

Martha, the middle-aged daughter of the president of a small New England college, and her husband George, an unsuccessful professor in its History Department, entertain a new faculty member, Nick, and his wife Honey in an evening of drunken antagonism, much of it devoted to Martha's game "Humiliate the Host." George and Martha's elliptical references to their 21-year-old son and other revelations lead Nick to confide that he married Honey only because she said she was pregnant. As the evening goes on, Honey gets sick, George wanders off, and Nick tries to sleep with Martha but is impotent. Through all the wild affairs it becomes clear that the older couple invented the story that they have a child and the younger couple's marriage is also sterile because Honey fears childbirth. The entire night is an intense exposure of sadism and masochism, aggression and fearfulness, expressed in an orgy of emotions.

WIDDEMER, MARGARET (1884–1978), Pennsylvania poet whose first book, *The Factories with Other Lyrics* (1915), contains poems passionately championing the rights of oppressed workers. *Old Road to Paradise* (1918, special Pulitzer award) contains softer and more sentimental verse, as does *Ballads and Lyrics* (1925). *The Singing Wood* (1926) is a verse play, and *A Tree with a Bird in It* (1923) is a volume of satirical verse. *The Dark Cavalier* (1958) collects her poems. Miss Widdemer's works also include many novels, on both contemporary issues and historical subjects, and short stories. Her memoirs appear as *Golden Friends I Had* (1964).

Wieland; or, The Transformation, epistolary Gothic romance by C.B. Brown,♦ published in 1798.

The elder Wieland, a German mystic, emigrates to Pennsylvania, erects a mysterious temple on his estate, and dies there one night by spontaneous combustion. His wife dies soon afterward, and their children, Clara and the younger Wieland, depend for friendship on Catharine Pleyel. Wieland marries Catharine, and Clara falls in love with Henry Pleyel, who is engaged to a woman in Germany. Into their happy circle enters a mysterious vagabond, Carwin (see *Memoirs of Carwin*), and at the same time comes the first of a series of warnings from unearthly voices. Henry falls in love with Clara after one of these disembodied voices announces the death of his German fiancée. When circumstances force him to believe that Clara and Carwin have had an affair, Pleyel deserts her, discovers his former fiancée to be alive, and marries her. Wieland, inheriting his father's fanaticism, is driven mad by the voices, and murders his wife and children. Carwin then confesses to Clara that a "mischievous daemon" led him to test the family courage, producing the mysterious voices by ventriloquism. Wieland, escaping from an asylum, is about to murder his sister when Carwin for the last time uses ventriloquism to command Wieland to desist. The unhappy madman commits suicide, Carwin departs to a remote district of Pennsylvania, and Clara marries Pleyel after the death of his first wife.

WIENERS, JOHN (1934–), Boston-born poet, attended Black Mountain College, where he was influenced by Olson and Robert Duncan, and of which he wrote *A Memory* (1969). In San Francisco (1957–60) during the period of the Beat movement,♦ he came to prominence with his locally issued *The Hotel Wentley Poems* (1958), eight poems related to experiences of that year, presenting with deep emotion a world of outcasts, particularly dope addicts and homosexuals. In addition to many broadsides and leaflets, he has published *Nerves* (1970) and *Selected Poems* (1971). His plays, including *Jive Shoelaces and Anklesox* (1967), have been produced in little theaters.

WIGGIN, KATE DOUGLAS (1856–1923), born in Philadelphia, studied under Emma Marwedel, and moved to San Francisco to conduct one of the first kindergartens in the U.S. (1878–84). She wrote novels for adults, and an autobiography, *My Garden of Memory*

(1923), but is best known as a successful author of children's books. The most famous of these are *The Birds' Christmas Carol* (1887), telling of the life and death of an ethereal child, Carol Bird; *Rebecca of Sunnybrook Farm* (1903), about a lovable, precocious little girl; and *Mother Carey's Chickens* (1911), dramatized with Rachel Crothers (1917), the story of a kindly widow and her many children.

WIGGLESWORTH, MICHAEL (1631–1705), brought from England as a child (1638), graduated from Harvard (1651) and during most of his life served as minister of the Congregational church at Malden, Mass. After 1663 he also practiced medicine. He is remembered for his long theological poem in ballad meter *The Day of Doom*♦ (1662).

WILBUR, RICHARD [PURDY] (1921–), after graduation from Amherst (1942) and an M.A. from Harvard (1947) began his teaching career at Harvard (1950–54), continued as a professor at Wesleyan (1955–), and commenced his career as a poet with the mature and polished lyrics of *The Beautiful Changes* (1947). His cultivated and formal poetry, although influenced by the French Symbolists, Marianne Moore, and Wallace Stevens, among others, is highly original in the classic, urbane, often witty, and always intellectual works collected in *Ceremony* (1950), *A Bestiary* (1955), *Things of This World* (1956), *Poems* (1957, Pulitzer Prize), *Advice to a Prophet* (1961), *Walking to Sleep* (1969), *The Mind-Reader* (1976), and *Seven Poems* (1981). *Responses* (1976) collects essays on poetry and other literary subjects. He translated Molière's *Misanthrope* (1955), *Tartuffe* (1963), and *The Learned Ladies* (1978) into English verse, and collaborated with Lillian Hellman on the comic opera *Candide* (1957), based on Voltaire's work, for which he also wrote the lyrics. He turned to French tragedy in a verse translation of Racine's *Andromache* (1982). He has also published *The Whale and Other Uncollected Translations* (1983) and written *Opposites* (1973) and other poems for children.

WILCOX, ELLA WHEELER (1850–1919), Wisconsin poetaster, whose first book, *Drops of Water* (1872), a collection of temperance verse, was followed by nearly 40 volumes of romantic, unctuous verse, distinguished by a sentimental approach to spiritualistic, metaphysical, and pseudo-erotic subjects. Her popular reputation was ensured when *Poems* *of Passion* (1883) was rejected for "immorality." Her platitudes also found expression in many short stories, sketches, and novels. *The Story of a Literary Career* (1905) and *The Worlds and I* (1918) are autobiographical works. Her most famous lines are from her poem "Solitude":

> Laugh, and the world laughs with you;
>> weep, and you weep alone

WILDER, LAURA INGALLS (1867–1957), author of popular children's books about life in her native frontier Wisconsin, including *Little House in the Big Woods* (1932) and *Little House on the Prairie* (1935).

WILDER, THORNTON [NIVEN] (1897–1975), born in Wisconsin, was reared in China and the U.S., and after graduation from Yale (1920) became a teacher at the Lawrenceville School (1921–28) and a professor of English at the University of Chicago (1930–36). His first book, *The Cabala* (1926), is a gracefully written and deftly ironic novel, concerning the sophisticated but decaying Italian nobility of the post-World War II period. After producing *The Trumpet Shall Sound* (1926) at a little theater, he suddenly achieved wide popularity with *The Bridge of San Luis Rey*♦ (1927, Pulitzer Prize), a delicately ironic study of the way Providence has directed disparate lives to one end. His next novels are *The Woman of Andros* (1930), an urbane treatment of human relations and ethical values in its story of a Greek concubine, based on Terence's Latin comedy *Andrea; Heaven's My Destination* (1935), an amused, ironic portrait of an evangelically religious American salesman; and *The Ides of March* (1948), divergent views of Caesar's last months seen through letters and documents.

Having published collections of one-act plays, *The Angel That Troubled the Waters* (1928) and *The Long Christmas Dinner* (1931), and made adaptations, Wilder came to his full development as a playwright with *Our Town*♦ (1938, Pulitzer Prize), depicting the qualities of small-town New England life. Later plays include *The Merchant of Yonkers* (1938), a comedy revised as *The Matchmaker* (1954), and by others made into the musical comedy *Hello, Dolly!* (1963); *The Skin of Our Teeth*♦ (1942, Pulitzer Prize), said to have been inspired by Joyce's *Finnegans Wake; A Life in the Sun* (London, 1955), based on Euripides' *Alcestis* and produced in dramatic (1960) and operatic (1962) versions as *The Alcestiad* in German and finally

published in its English text in the U.S in 1977; and *Plays for Bleecker Street* (1962), three unpublished one-act plays, part of a projected 14-play cycle on the Seven Ages of Man and the Seven Deadly Sins.

Wilder returned to the novel with *The Eighth Day* (1967, National Book Award), a chronicle of two early 20th-century Midwestern families and their involvement in a murder case raising serious questions about human nature; and *Theophilus North* (1973), portraying the good deeds of the title character, a tutor in Newport, R.I., during the 1920s, whose various saintly actions are presented in closely related short stories, by turns comic, sentimental, serious, and optimistic. Wilder's essays were posthumously collected as *American Characteristics* (1979). He was the first person to be awarded a National Medal for Literature (1965).

WILKINS, MARY E., see *Freeman, Mary Wilkins.*

Will To Believe, The, and Other Essays in Popular Philosophy, ten essays by William James♦ collected with a preface in 1896. The ideas of the title piece are amplified in such essays as "Is Life Worth Living?," "The Sentiment of Rationality," "Reflex Action and Theism," and "The Dilemma of Determinism," while other essays treat other ethical and moral problems.

WILLARD, EMMA [HART] (1787–1870), pioneer in women's education, at Middlebury, Vt. (1814), opened her Female Seminary to teach such subjects as mathematics, philosophy, history, and the sciences, which had been previously closed to women. Her *Address . . . Proposing a Plan for Improving Female Education* (1819), sent to Governor Clinton of New York, attracted attention that led to her founding another seminary in Troy (1821), which offered the equivalent of a college education for women, 16 years before Mount Holyoke, the first women's college, was founded. In addition to works on female education and texts for her school, she published a volume of mediocre verse, *The Fulfillment of a Promise* (1831), still remembered for "Rocked in the Cradle of the Deep," which became extremely popular in its musical setting by the English composer Joseph P. Knight.

WILLARD, JOSIAH FLINT (1869–1907), tired of settled life as an Illinois college student and took to the road as a vagrant, although other experiences included study of political science at the University of Berlin, life in literary London as a friend of Arthur Symons, laboring on Tolstoy's Russian estate, and work for a railroad that needed advice on eliminating tramps. From these experiences came his books written under the pseudonym Josiah Flynt: *Tramping with Tramps* (1899); *Notes of an Itinerant Policeman* (1900); *The World of Graft* (1901); a novel, *The Little Brother: A Story of Tramp Life* (1902); and an autobiography, *My Life* (1908).

William Wilson, story by Poe,♦ published in 1839 and collected in *Tales of the Grotesque and Arabesque* (1840). The description of school life in England is partly autobiographical.

The central figure is a willful, passionate youth, who at Dr. Bransby's boarding school leads all his companions except one, a boy of his own age and appearance who bears the same name of William Wilson. This double maintains an easy superiority, which frightens Wilson, and haunts him by constant patronage and protection, noticed only by Wilson himself, whose sense of persecution increases until he flees from the school. He goes to Eton and Oxford, and then travels about Europe, following a career of extravagant indulgence, and becoming degenerate and vicious. At critical times his double invariably appears to warn him or destroy his power over others. Finally at Rome, when the double appears to prevent his planned seduction of the Duchess Di Broglio, Wilson is infuriated, engages the other in a sword fight, and murders him. As the double lies dying, he tells Wilson: "You have conquered . . . Yet henceforward art thou also dead. . . . In me didst thou exist— and, in my death, see by this image, which is thine own, how utterly thou hast murdered thyself."

WILLIAMS, JOHN A[LFRED] (1925–   ), Mississippi-born author, reared in Syracuse, N.Y., from whose university he graduated after naval service in World War II. His novels include *The Angry Ones* (1960), a bitter book about Greenwich Village and the world of black musicians; *Night Song* (1961); *Sissie* (1963), presenting the sad life of an old black woman; *The Man Who Cried I Am* (1967), the autobiographical recollections of a dying black author in the U.S. and Europe; *Sons of Darkness, Sons of Light* (1969), depicting racial conflict in New York City; *Captain Blackman* (1972), about a black soldier wounded in the Vietnam War and the

similarity of his experiences to those of blacks in earlier wars; *Mothersill and the Foxes* (1975); *The Junior Bachelor Society* (1976); and *!Click Song* (1982) about the vicissitudes of a black novelist. His other writing include poems; a biography of Martin Luther King, Jr., *The King God Didn't Save* (1970); and *This Is My Country Too* (1965), about his experiences as a black man traveling in the U.S.

WILLIAMS, ROGER (*c.*1603–83), born in London, early became the protégé of the great lawyer Sir Edward Coke, and was educated at Cambridge and destined for the law. After receiving his B.A. (1627), he determined to become a minister, and by 1629 had taken orders in the Anglican Church. He became increasingly influenced by the Puritans, though he soon went beyond their beliefs. Arriving in Massachusetts (1631), he refused a call from a Boston church because it was not Separatist and after a brief period at the more liberal Plymouth he went to Salem as a minister, holding democratic views of church government even beyond those of Separatists.

He became anathema to the Massachusetts theocracy because of his "leveler" principles, based on the ideals of the New Testament and representing the incarnation of Protestant individualism, as well as for his political views, which caused him to attack the royal charter as an imperialistic expropriation of Indian rights. His extremely democratic church at Salem so disturbed the hegemony that the General Court banished him (1635), and, "sorely tossed for one fourteen weeks, in a bitter winter season, not knowing what bread or bed did mean," he made his way to Rhode Island to found its earliest settlement at Providence (1636). Carrying out his democratic principles, he entered upon his apostolic labors among the Indians, living with them "in their filthy smoky holes . . . to gain their tongue," which efforts resulted in *A Key into the Language of America* (1643).

Meanwhile he became a Baptist for a few months (1639), then a Seeker, believing in the fundamentals of Christianity but in no creed, and espousing a mysticism that held to an indwelling God of love. His colony of those who had followed him from Salem was based on the compact theory which held that government is a man-made institution resting on the consent and equality of its subjects: church and state were separate, family heads had a voice in government, and all shared equally in a land association.

Challenging the views of the Massachusetts

hierarchy, particularly of John Cotton,♦ and pleading for complete religious and political liberty, he published his most celebrated work, *The Bloudy Tenent of Persecution*♦ (1644) and a sequel (1652).

Williams became president of his colony (1654) and obtained a new charter (1663). Illustrating his belief in complete toleration, he admitted both Jews and Quakers, but nevertheless soon found himself involved in a dispute with the latter group. With great vituperation he attacked the followers of the English Quaker, Fox (1672), and published *George Fox Digg'd out of his Burrowes* (1676). Although this and other controversies embittered his last years, as did the necessity to take part with the other colonies in King Philip's War (1675–76) against the Indians, whom he had so long befriended, he continued to the end of his life to be a democratic leader, in both religious and temporal affairs.

WILLIAMS, Tennessee (Thomas Lanier Williams) (1911–83), born in Mississippi and reared there and in St. Louis, began his career as a dramatist with *American Blues* (1939, published 1948), one-act plays, and *Battle of Angels* (1940, published 1945), revised as *Orpheus Descending* (1957). He first achieved success with *The Glass Menagerie*♦ (1944), a play of sentiment and pathos about a frustrated mother, who is a victim of fantasies, and her withdrawn daughter. It not only is his most tender story but also is rather autobiographical.

After publishing a collection of 11 one-act plays, *27 Wagons Full of Cotton* (1946), he adapted, with Donald Windham, a D.H. Lawrence story as *You Touched Me!* (1947), and then wrote his next important play, *A Streetcar Named Desire*♦ (1947), set in a New Orleans slum and bringing into violent contrast a neurotic woman's dreamworld and the animalistic realism of her brother-in-law. *Summer and Smoke* (1948), another study of sexual maladjustment, revised as *The Eccentricities of a Nightingale* (1964), was followed by a comedy of sex, *The Rose Tattoo* (1950), set in a Gulf Coast town and treating a perfervid Sicilian woman's eager quest for love. In *I Rise in Flame, Cried the Phoenix* (1951) he further revealed the influence of D.H. Lawrence, about whose death the play revolves. This was followed by *Camino Real* (1953) and *Cat on a Hot Tin Roof*♦ (1955, Pulitzer Prize), depicting bitter, abnormal family tensions in a struggle for control of a plantation.

These plays reveal the darkest side of life in Gothic situations and settings, but Williams's characters live by experiencing a full emotional involvement in life rather than shrinking from or denying it, despite the terrible violence they encounter. In his depiction of horror he went on to create other treatments of evil in *Suddenly Last Summer* (1958), produced with *Something Unspoken* (1958) as *Garden District,* and telling of the egocentric, sadistic, homosexual son of a doting mother, who is killed and eaten by cannibal natives on a savage island; *Sweet Bird of Youth* (1959), about an aging movie star whose kept young man is castrated by the father of the girl he deserted; *Triple Play* (1959); *Period of Adjustment* (1960), a "serious comedy"; and *The Night of the Iguana* (1962), adapted from an earlier short story, presenting diverse characters in a mean Mexican hotel who, like its chained iguana, are balked and imprisoned.

Later plays include *Slapstick Tragedy* (1965), composed of two short works, *The Mutilated* and *The Gnaidige Fräulein; Kingdom of Earth* (1968), acted in abbreviated form as *The Seven Descents of Myrtle,* presenting relations among a dying transvestite, his sluttish bride, and his brother; *In the Bar of a Tokyo Hotel* (1969), a bitter characterization of a painter; *Small Craft Warnings* (1972), portraying a group of "castoffs" gathered at a California coastside bar; and *Outcry* (1973), a slightly altered version of *The Two-Character Play* (1969), presenting two actors, a brother and sister, deserted by their company and trying to sort out the relations between life and art.

Nondramatic works include *The Roman Spring of Mrs. Stone* (1950), a novelette about an aging actress and her sordid last affair with a gigolo; *One Arm* (1948, revised 1954), *Hard Candy* (1954), and *Eight Mortal Ladies Possessed* (1974), stories; *The Knightly Quest* (1966), a Gothic science fiction novella and four stories; *Moise and the World of Reason* (1975), a novel about a homosexual writer recalling his childhood and his search for love; *In the Winter of Cities* (1956) and *Androgyne, Mon Amour* (1977), collections of poems; and *Memoirs* (1975), reminiscences and discussion of the creation of his plays. Williams's letters to Donald Windham were published by the recipient in 1977. *Baby Doll* (1956) is a film script Williams created from two of his one-act plays.

WILLIAMS, William Carlos (1883–1963), born in Rutherford, N.J., his lifelong home, where he practiced medicine as a pediatrician. While studying at the University of Pennsylvania Medical School he became a friend of Pound and of H.D. and shared their subscription to the tenets of Imagism,♦ as is evident in his first books, *Poems* (1909) and *The Tempers* (1913), and, to some extent, in all the writing of his long career. However, the limited nature of Imagism was extended in *Al Que Quiere!* (1917), the prose poems of *Kora in Hell* (1920), *Sour Grapes* (1921), and *Spring and All* (1922) to Expressionism,♦ characterized by a clean stripping of poetry to essentials, by a holding of emotion at arm's length, and by vivid observations, restricted almost entirely to sensory experience. Williams declared that his poetry belonged to the school of Objectivism,♦ whose publications, like his *Collected Poems, 1921–1931* (1934), were issued from the short-lived Objectivist Press. In its defense, Williams said: "Imagism . . . though it had been useful in ridding the field of verbiage, had no formal necessity implicit in it" and so "it had dribbled off into so-called 'free verse' . . . but, we argued, the poem . . . is an object . . . that in itself formally presents its case and its meaning by the very form it assumes . . . this was what we wished to imply by Objectivism."

In this vein his poetry was continued in *An Early Martyr* (1935), *Adam & Eve & The City* (1936), *The Complete Collected Poems . . . 1906–1938* (1938), *The Broken Span* (1941), *The Wedge* (1944), *The Desert Music* (1954), *Journey to Love* (1955), and *Pictures from Brueghel* (1963, Pulitzer Prize). Marked by vernacular American speech and direct observation, his poetry has the character, he declared, that one finds "as a physician works upon a patient, upon the thing before him, in the particular to discover the universal." *Paterson*♦ (5 vols., 1946–58) is a long, structureless poem, including much quoted prose, relating to the history, formal and informal, the surroundings, and the appearance of a New Jersey city and about one human figure, partly autobiographical, partly mythic.

His prose includes *The Great American Novel* (1923), impressionistic essays; *In the American Grain*♦ (1925), more impressionistic essays, on discoverers of the New World from Eric the Red to Lincoln, bodying forth American values; and *Selected Essays* (1954). He wrote plays collected in *Many Loves* (1961); stories collected in *The Knife of the Times* (1932), *Life Along the Passaic River* (1938), *Make Light of It* (1950), and *The Farmers' Daughters* (1961); and four novels:

A Voyage to Pagany (1928), autobiographical fiction about a small-town American doctor in Europe; and a trilogy, *White Mule* (1937), about immigrants adjusting to the U.S.; *In the Money* (1940), continuing the chronicle of a middle-class family and its young children; and *The Build-Up* (1952), carrying the story along in its New Jersey setting from 1900 to World War I. He published an *Autobiography* (1951), *Selected Letters* (1957), and *Yes, Mrs. Williams* (1960), a memoir of his mother.

WILLIAMSON, THAMES [ROSS] (1894–   ), Idaho-born author, ran away from home at 14 and became successively a tramp, circus hand, sailor, sheepherder, reporter, and prison officer. After graduation from the University of Iowa (1917) and study at Harvard, he taught for a time at Simmons and Smith, and wrote textbooks on economics and sociology. Besides writing stories for children, often under pseudonyms, he is the author of novels, which include *Run, Sheep, Run* (1925), dealing with a California sheepherder; *Stride of Man* (1928), about an Oregon pioneer and inventor; *Hunky* (1929), a psychological study of a Polish-American workingman; *The Earth Told Me* (1930), concerned with the lives of Eskimos; *In Krusack's House* (1931), a sequel to *Hunky; The Woods Colt* (1933), the story of an illegitimate Ozark Mountain boy; *D Is for Dutch* (1934), about the superstitions of a Pennsylvania Dutch farmer.

WILLINGHAM, CALDER [BAYNARD, JR.] (1922–   ), Georgia-born novelist whose works include *End as a Man* (1947), a satirical view of a Southern military academy like the one the author attended; *Geraldine Bradshaw* (1950) and *Reach to the Stars* (1951), both views of life as seen by hotel bellboys; *Natural Child* (1952); *To Eat a Peach* (1955); *Eternal Fire* (1963); *Providence Island* (1969); *Rambling Rose* (1972); and *The Big Nickel* (1975). He adapted his first novel as a play (1953), and he has written several successful film scenarios. *The Gates of Hell* (1951) collects stories.

WILLIS, N[ATHANIEL] P[ARKER] (1806–67), born in Maine and reared in Boston, while at Yale published blank-verse paraphrases of Biblical themes, for which he was hailed as a leading U.S. poet. His collection of verse *Sketches* was published the year of his graduation (1827). He founded the *American Monthly Magazine* (1829–31), a literary journal in which he published some of his best stories and sketches, later frequently reprinted. Although the magazine lasted only two years, and Willis was less than 25, he was established as the most worldly and fluent of American editors. His representation of himself as an aesthete led Holmes to say "He was something between a remembrance of Count D'Orsay and an anticipation of Oscar Wilde." As a sort of foreign correspondent on social affairs for the *New-York Mirror,* he traveled on the Continent, in England, and through Turkey and the Middle East (1832–36), writing letters collected in *Pencillings by the Way* (3 vols., London, 1835; Philadelphia, 1836; complete edition, New York, 1844) and *Loiterings of Travel* (3 vols., 1840). Returning to the U.S., he wrote romantic tragedies, *Bianca Visconti* (1837) and *Tortesa the Usurer* (1839); American sketches, collected in *A l'Abri; or, The Tent Pitch'd* (1839) and *American Scenery* (2 vols., 1840); *Dashes at Life with a Free Pencil* (1845), short stories whose surprise endings foreshadow those of O. Henry; his only novel, *Paul Fane* (1857), the story of a young painter adored by women as a celebrity but disdained as a social inferior.

WILLIS, Sara Payson (1811–72), sister of N.P. Willis, was a popular author under the pseudonym Fanny Fern. Her first book, *Fern Leaves from Fanny's Portfolio* (1853), became popular for its sharp, playful sketches. This was followed by several similar works, continuing her style of feminine wit plus bloodcurdling melodrama and touchingly tender tales. Her brother's reputation as a rake so infuriated her that she wrote *Ruth Hall* (1855), a scurrilous fictional satire. For many years she was a columnist for the *New York Ledger.* She married James Parton in 1856.

WILSON, Edmund (1895–1972), born in New Jersey, graduated from Princeton (1916), after service abroad during World War I began the writing career that made him a leading man of letters in various genres, best known as a literary critic. He long held several journalistic posts, including managing editor of *Vanity Fair* (1920–21), associate editor of *The New Republic* (1926–31), and book reviewer for *The New Yorker* (1944–48), but he always kept himself independent of organizations in pursuing the varied interests that led to his many diverse books.

His works of nonfiction begin with *Axel's Castle*♦ (1931), a study of Symbolist litera-

ture, and during the succeeding 16 years include *The American Jitters: A Year of the Slump* (1932) and *Travels in Two Democracies* (1936), social reporting from a Marxist point of view, the latter concerning Russia and the U.S., combined in *The American Earthquake* (1958); *The Triple Thinkers* (1938, revised and enlarged 1948) and *The Wound and the Bow* (1941), essays on literature ranging from analyses of particular authors—Hemingway, James, Edith Wharton—to Freudian literary theory and the relationship of Marxism and historical interpretation to literature; *To The Finland Station*♦ (1940), tracing European revolutionary traditions from Michelet to Lenin to Trotsky; *The Boys in the Back Room* (1941), notes on modern California authors; *The Shock of Recognition* (1943), an anthology of American writers' critical views of one another, from the mid-19th century on; and *Europe Without Baedeker* (1947, revised 1966), travel sketches. From his journal publications during these years he collected *Classics and Commercials* (1950), articles and reviews about the 1940s; *The Shores of Light* (1952), a comparable anthology of his writings of the 1920s and 1930s; and *The Bit Between My Teeth* (1965), a similar literary chronicle of the 1950s and '60s. During the 1950s and 1960s he published *The Scrolls from the Dead Sea* (1955), revised and extended on new findings as *The Dead Sea Scrolls, 1947–1969* (1969); *Red, Black, Blond and Olive* (1956), studies in four civilizations: Zuñi, Haitian, Russian, and Israeli; *A Piece of My Mind* (1956), "reflections at sixty" in the form of essays on diverse and important topics; *Apologies to the Iroquois* (1960), on the history and present status of the Indian Confederacy; *Patriotic Gore*♦ (1962), substantial "studies in the literature of the American Civil War"; *The Cold War and the Income Tax* (1963), on his difficulties with, and objections to, federal taxation; and *O Canada* (1965), on Canadian culture. In the last year of his life and following his death there appeared *A Window on Russia* (1972), essays on Russian literature and language; *The Devils and Canon Barham* (1973), literary essays; and *The Twenties* (1975), from his notebooks of the time, a compilation completed by Leon Edel.

Wilson published his verse in *The Undertaker's Garland* (1922), a collaboration with John Peale Bishop; *Poets, Farewell!* (1929); *Note-Books of Night* (1942), which, like the others, contains some prose; and *Night Thoughts* (1961), collecting from the two previous books. Wilson's fiction is printed in *I Thought of Daisy* (1929, revised 1967), a novel about bohemian literary New York, and *Memoirs of Hecate County* (1946), stories about the lives of wealthy New York suburban intelligentsia. His plays are *Discordant Encounters* (1926), dialogues and short dramas; *This Room and This Gin and These Sandwiches* (1937), three "experimental" plays; *The Little Blue Light* (1950); *Five Plays* (1954), adding one work to the two previous books; and *The Duke of Palermo* (1969).

A Prelude (1967) draws on journals (1908–19) to portray his early life; *Upstate* (1971) contains recollections (1950–70) of his life in the family house of northern New York, where he summered. Correspondence is gathered in *Letters on Literature and Politics* (1977) and *The Nabokov-Wilson Letters* (1979).

WILSON, HARRY LEON (1867–1939), was an editor of the humorous weekly *Puck* (1896–1902), after which he began writing fiction. His novels include *The Spenders* (1902), contrasting a pioneer of the Far West and his grandchildren, effete Easterners; *The Lions of the Lord* (1903), on the great Mormon trek to Utah under Brigham Young; *Bunker Bean* (1913), about a timorous man who suddenly asserts himself; *Ruggles of Red Gap* (1915), the story of a British valet employed in a Far Western cattle town; and *Merton of the Movies* (1922), about a movie-struck clerk who achieves success because he unconsciously burlesques serious roles. *Merton* was dramatized (1922) by Marc Connelly and George S. Kaufman, and Wilson collaborated with Tarkington in writing *The Man from Home* (1907) and other plays. After 1912 Wilson, who was born in Illinois, lived in Carmel, Cal.

WILSON, LANFORD (1937–), Missouri-born playwright, reared by his mother in the Ozarks and then in the Midwest until, as a teenager, he went to southern California to be with his long-divorced father. Wilson's dramatic career began at Caffe Cino, a small off-off-Broadway coffeehouse in Greenwich Village. His one-act plays produced there include *So Long at the Fair* (1963); *Home Free* (1964), about the incestuous love of a brother and sister; and *The Madness of Lady Bright* (1964), presenting a pathetic, aging, flamboyant homosexual. These were followed by a

move to off-Broadway with the full-length plays *Balm in Gilead* (1964), a view of life in an all-night New York diner; and *The Rimers of Eldritch* (1965), depicting blighted lives in a Midwestern ghost town. *This Is the Rill Speaking* (1965) is a happier nostalgic view of life in an Ozarks village.

Wilson's plays moved to Broadway and other major producing centers with *The Gingham Dog* (1968), treating the breakup of the marriage of a liberal white architect and his young black wife; *Lemon Sky* (1970), about a young boy leaving his divorced mother to live in California with his father and finding that no better as he is falsely accused of homosexuality; and *Serenading Louie* (1970), presenting the deteriorating lives of two couples, which had seemed so bright in college days.

Wilson joined the Circle Theatre Company (founded 1969), a small upper Broadway team of actors, playwrights, and designers, for which he wrote one-act plays and longer works. *The Hot l Baltimore* (1973), set in a derelict hotel whose sign has even lost a letter, is peopled in its last days by pathetic outcasts who still live on wistful hopes. *The Mound Builders* (1975) contrasts views of the earth, and thus metaphorically of life, by archaeologists digging an ancient Indian site in the Midwest and the realtor who hopes to develop it. *Fifth of July* (1978) views the disintegration of radicals and flower children of the 1960s as they live into a new decade. The parents of some of these characters are presented in *Talley's Folly* (1979, Pulitzer Prize), treating the romance of an unlikely couple, a shy Missouri village girl and an older, Jewish accountant from a big city. *A Tale Told* (1981) is a third view of the Talley family, set in 1944 at the same time as the preceding play's depiction of the romance between Matt Friedman and Sally Talley. *Angels Fall* (1982) brings together at an isolated mission in New Mexico a disparate group of people stranded because of an accident at a nearby uranium mine. They are a jolly priest, an insecure New England college professor of art history and his wife, the widow of a local painter and her lover, a professional tennis player, and an educated Indian of the region, and all reveal themselves through their plotless relationships. Wilson has also written an adaptation for the screen (1970) of Tennessee Williams's story "One Arm"; a television play, *The Migrants* (1974), with him; and the libretto for an operatic version (1971) of his *Summer and Smoke*.

WILSON, [THOMAS] WOODROW (1856–1924), after a career as a professor of political science at Princeton and its president (1902–10) was elected as a Democrat to the governorship of New Jersey (1910–12) and then to the presidency of the U.S. (1913–21). His first term was notable for his liberal domestic reforms and his second for the nation's participation in World War I, which he hoped would make the world "safe for democracy." At the war's end he proposed a peace treaty of "open covenants openly arrived at" with liberal principles and the creation of a League of Nations. His plans were frustrated though he won a Nobel Peace Prize. His many books include *The State: Elements of Historical and Practical Politics* (1889, revised 1898, 1918), *An Old Master and Other Political Essays* (1893), *Mere Literature and Other Essays* (1896), *A History of the American People* (5 vols., 1902), *Constitutional Government in the United States* (1908), *The New Freedom* (1913), *Division and Reunion 1829–1889* (1893), and *Robert E. Lee* (1924). A 40-volume edition of his *Papers* was begun in 1966.

Winesburg, Ohio, 23 stories by Sherwood Anderson,♦ published in 1919. The preface, "The Book of the Grotesque," explains the author's unifying conception of his characters: "It was the truths that made the people grotesques. . . . The moment one of the people took one of the truths to himself, called it his truth, and tried to live his life by it, he became a grotesque and the truth he embraced became a falsehood." In a simple and intense style these psychological portraits of the sensitive and imaginative of Winesburg's population are seen through the eyes of a young reporter, George Willard.

"Hands" is the story of Wing Biddlebaum, who has an innocent passion for caressing living things and is driven from the town because of this misunderstood eccentricity. "Queer" tells of Elmer Cowley, who has grown up on a farm, and is lonely and frustrated in Winesburg, until, obsessed by the idea that he is considered "queer," he runs away to begin life anew. "Godliness" is a long tale concerned with Jesse Bentley, who prays for a David to help him despoil his Philistine neighbors of their farms and is himself nearly slain by a stone from the sling of the young David, his grandson. "The Strength of God" tells of the religious Rev. Curtis Hartman, who is obsessed with sexual desire until his "cure" after an intense inner struggle, in which he believes that "God has

manifested himself to me in the body of a woman."

Wings of the Dove, The, novel by Henry James,♦ published in 1902. The novel formed the basis for an opera of this title (1961) by Douglas Moore.

Kate Croy, daughter of an impoverished English social adventurer, is in love with Merton Densher, a London journalist, and they become secretly engaged, although she will not marry him while he is without wealth. While Densher is in America on business, Kate's shrewd, worldly aunt Mrs. Lowder has as guests the Americans Mrs. Stringham and her wealthy protégée, Milly Theale. The latter, an unselfish, poetically lovely girl suffering from a mysterious illness, confides in Kate, who in turn tells everything of herself except her affair with Densher, who has previously been acquainted with Milly, deeply attracting her by his charm and honesty. Sir Luke Strett, a celebrated surgeon, reveals to Mrs. Stringham that Milly's only possibility of postponing her approaching death is to be as happy and cheerful as possible. Kate, learning of this, devises a scheme that she thinks will solve the problems of all. Densher returns to London, and Kate encourages Milly's interest in him, believing that her marriage to the journalist will contribute to her happiness, while, following the girl's imminent death, Densher will inherit her fortune and be able to marry Kate. She simply tells him to be kind to Milly, and, carried away by his love and faith in her ability to manage affairs, he obeys. Milly, who thinks that Densher has been rejected by Kate, is ecstatically happy for a time. In the autumn they all meet at Venice, where Milly arouses the resentment of Lord Mark, a British fortune-seeker, by refusing his proposal of marriage. Kate exposes her entire scheme to her lover, who weakly consents to go through with it if she will give herself to him at once. She fulfills her part of the bargain and returns to London. Lord Mark, who knows the relations of Kate and Densher, vents his spite by divulging the plot to Milly, and the dying girl, deprived of hope, quickly declines. Mrs. Stringham asks Densher to save Milly by telling her he is not engaged to Kate, but this he will not do. He returns to London, and after Milly's death receives a large legacy. He offers to marry Kate if she will consent to destroy the check, and she replies that she will if he can swear that he is "not in love with her memory." He cannot, for, as Kate realizes, they are now separated by the barriers of Densher's conscience and their tragic memories.

Winner Take Nothing, 14 stories by Hemingway,♦ published in 1933.

"The Light of the World," set in a small town in the Middle West, has for its chief character a fat, blonde prostitute, who recalls nostalgically the prizefighter who furnished the one rudimentary romantic episode of her life. "A Clean, Well-Lighted Place"♦ portrays the desolate lives of a waiter and a customer of a Spanish café. "The Sea Change" tells of the tragic separation of a young couple, when the girl drifts into a homosexual relation with another woman. "A Way You'll Never Be" describes the hysterical reaction of a young American officer in the Italian army, when he is relieved from active duty and thus has time to become aware of the significance of the war. "Homage to Switzerland" contains three vignettes of fatuous middle-class American tourists in Europe. "A Natural History of the Dead" is a bitter satire on the results of modern warfare. "The Gambler, the Nun, and the Radio" is concerned with two hospital patients, a Mexican gambler and an author, and the way in which the writer cynically plays upon the phrase "the opium of the people."

Winning of the West, The, historical study by Theodore Roosevelt,♦ published in four volumes (1889–96).

WINTERS, [ARTHUR] YVOR (1900–1968), born in Chicago, was a member of the Department of English, Stanford University, from 1928. There he edited *The Gyroscope* (1929–31), and was the Western editor of *Hound and Horn* (1932–34). His poetry, published in *The Immobile Wind* (1921), *The Magpie's Shadow* (1922), and *The Bare Hills* (1927)—all collected in *The Early Poems* (1966)—*The Proof* (1930), *The Journey* (1931), *Before Disaster* (1934), *Poems* (1940), and *The Giant Weapon* (1943), is marked by those qualities he asks for as a critic: classical order, dignity, restraint, and moral judgment. His *Collected Poems* (1952) was revised and enlarged (1960) and at that time was awarded a Bollingen Prize. His critical works are *Primitivism and Decadence* (1937), showing the obscurity of modern American poetry as the result of romanticism qualified by certain aspects of American history, *Maule's Curse* (1938), on obscurantism in 19th-century American authors, and *The Anatomy of Non-*

sense (1943), on 20th-century poets and critics—all three books collected in *In Defense of Reason* (1947); *Edwin Arlington Robinson* (1946); *The Function of Criticism: Problems and Exercises* (1957); *Forms of Discovery* (1967); and *Uncollected Essays* (1973).

Winterset, verse play by Maxwell Anderson,♦ produced and published in 1935. Its theme was suggested by the Sacco-Vanzetti case. ♦

WINTHROP, JOHN (1588–1649), a member of an English upper-class family, attended Cambridge and took his position in the English social scheme as lord of the manor at Groton and as an important lawyer. His Puritan sympathies worked against his success, however, and he determined to join the Massachusetts Bay Company. Selected as governor, he sailed on the *Arbella* (1630), affirming belief in Puritanism, and disclaiming any intention of separating from the Established Church. For nine of his remaining years he was governor, and during the other ten deputy-governor.

Since the charter of the company had been transferred to New England, and was not, as in other colonies, held by an English corporation, this Puritan commonwealth had in it the seeds of democracy. Winthrop and the other upper-class leaders, however, had their own ideas on how a democracy should operate, and they attempted to create a sort of benevolent despotism. Because of John Cotton,♦ the company became increasingly an aristocratic theocracy. Winthrop indicated his views by proclaiming, "If we should change from a mixt aristocratie to a mere Democratie, first we should have no warrant in scripture for it: there is no such government in Israel . . . a Democratie is, amongst most civil nations, accounted the meanest and worst forms of government."

His most famous piece of writing is his *Journal,* of which the first two parts were published in 1790, and the complete work as *The History of New England* (2 vols., 1825–26). This important source book, begun on the *Arbella* voyage and continued intermittently until his death, is composed of brief jottings. It records not only the great events but also the minute happenings, for as a Puritan he conceived of formal history as specific and concrete anecdotes, all equally important, since all occur through the will of God. The *Winthrop Papers,* a scholarly edition of his *Journal* was published by the Massachusetts Historical Society (5 vols., 1929–47). Winthrop figures frequently in literature, as in Hawthorne's *The Scarlet Letter,* "Howe's Masquerade," and "Endicott and the Red Cross."

WISE, JOHN (1652–1725), born at Roxbury, Mass., was minister of the Second Church of Ipswich (1680–1725), except for a brief period (1687) when Governor Andros deprived him of his ministry and jailed him for leading his townsmen in refusing to pay taxes that violated their charter rights. His pamphlets *The Churches Quarrel Espoused* (1710) and *A Vindication of the Government of New-England Churches* (1717) opposed the attempts of the Mathers to establish a centralized association for regulating the churches. Their underlying ideas of democracy caused them to be reissued and widely read before the revolution and the Civil War.

Wise Blood, novel by Flannery O'Connor, ♦ published in 1952.

A 22-year-old soldier, Hazel Motes, upon being released from the army because of a wound, makes his way to his home state of Tennessee. There he founds a Church Without Christ, not only in revolt against his grandfather, a preacher, but in opposition to Asa Hawkes, a religious charlatan who pretends to be blind. Hazel's follower, Hoover Shoates, who calls himself Onnie Jay Holy, comes to champion a rival prophet of the Church Without Christ. After killing the false prophet by running him down with an auto, Hazel blinds himself, stops preaching, tortures himself, sickens, and dies.

WISTER, OWEN (1860–1938), member of a distinguished Pennsylvania family and a grandson of Fanny Kemble, graduated from Harvard (1882), and found the subject matter for a literary career when ill health caused his doctor to advise him to follow the example of his classmate Theodore Roosevelt and go West. Out of summer trips to Wyoming ranches came the material for *Red Men and White* (1896), stories of the Western cattle country; *Lin McLean* (1898), another collection but more unified; *The Jimmyjohn Boss* (1900), a final collection of stories; and the extremely popular novel *The Virginian* ♦ (1902), about Wyoming cowpunchers during the 1870s and '80s, which established many of the patterns of fiction about the West and created a native mythology. Later works include *Philosophy 4* (1903), a tale about Harvard undergraduate life, and *Lady Baltimore* (1906), a romantic novel of life in Charleston.

Wizard of Oz, character in children's books by L. Frank Baum. ♦

WOIWODE, LARRY [ALFRED] (1941–), North Dakota-born author whose novels, set in the Midwest, are *What I'm Going To Do, I Think* (1969), a bittersweet tale of a young couple's romance and their return to the site of their honeymoon two years later; *Beyond the Bedroom Wall: A Family Album* (1975), a portrayal of several generations of a North Dakota family; and *Poppa John* (1981), about an aging television character actor who preaches religious platitudes. *Even Tide* (1977) collects poems.

WOLFE, THOMAS [CLAYTON] (1900–1938), was born and reared in Asheville, N.C. (the "Altamont, Old Catawba" of his fiction). His father, a powerful stonecutter from the North, is the prototype of Oliver Gant, and his mother, a member of a typical puritanical mountain family, is the original of the mother of Eugene Gant, whose drab life and eventual escape parallels the author's own youth. The lifelong influence of his mother is shown in his *Letters to His Mother* (1943).

After graduation from the University of North Carolina (1920), where he wrote and acted for the Carolina Playmakers, he studied playwriting at Harvard and received an M.A. (1922). One of his early plays, *Mannerhouse,* was published posthumously in 1945. He returned from a period abroad to teach English at New York University (1924–30) but after the publication of *Look Homeward, Angel* ♦ (1929) devoted his full time to writing. This strongly autobiographical novel, displaying originality and intensity as well as debts to Dreiser, Lewis, Joyce, and other contemporary novelists, was continued in a sequel, *Of Time and the River* ♦ (1935), incorporating a short novel, "A Portrait of Bascom Hawke," previously printed in *Scribner's* in 1932.

A posthumous novel, *The Web and the Rock* ♦ (1939), has as its central character George Webber, apparently the Eugene Gant of the previous books. Despite the author's claim that "It is the most objective novel that I have written," the first half of the book closely parallels the material of *Look Homeward, Angel,* and the second part serves as a sequel to *Of Time and the River.* The title indicates symbolically the problem of his first book: the web of experience, environment, and ancestry, in which the hero is snared; and his attempt to escape by finding the rock, which is the original strength and beauty of vision of his father. He concludes that "you can't go home again," that you must go forward, you can't return to a dead past. The sequel, *You Can't Go Home Again*♦ (1940), deals with George's life after his return to the U.S.: his continued unsatisfactory romance; his success in writing novels reminiscent of Wolfe's own; his kindly relation and later dissatisfaction with an internationally famous but disillusioned novelist and with his editor, who fatalistically accepts the sickness of civilization; his unsuccessful attempt to return to the roots of his hometown, whose morality has become shoddy during the prosperous decade of the '20s; and his horrid discovery of the destruction of the Germany he had once loved. It is the story of a man who recognizes that a corrupt society destroys each individual in it, but nevertheless believes that "the true fulfillment of our spirit, of our people, of our mighty and immortal land is yet to come."

In addition to his lengthy fiction, Wolfe published short stories, *From Death to Morning* (1935), and a critical examination of his own work, *The Story of a Novel* (1936). Volumes that appeared after his death include *The Hills Beyond* (1941), an unfinished novel and some short stories, the latter separately issued as *The Lost Boy* (1965); two plays, *Gentlemen of the Press* (1942) and *Mannerhouse* (1948); *A Western Journal . . . of the Great Parks Trip . . . 1938* (1951); a collection of *Letters* (1956); *Letters . . . to His Mother* (1968); and his *Notebooks* (2 vols., 1970). "Poetical Passages" from his novels have been collected in *The Face of a Nation* (1939) and *A Stone, a Leaf, a Door* (1945), the latter arranged as verse.

Throughout his fiction there is a self-fascination and self-torment that endow his writing now with a lofty romantic quality, now with the prosaic quality of literal reporting of the hero's life. His intensity results in both a powerful emotional evocation and a sprawling unrestrained formlessness. His prose is sometimes highly lyrical, but there are many passages characterized by swollen, frenzied rhetoric. His books cling always to the story of his life; however, he rises above egocentricity in his mystical, patriotic belief that there is something great in America that haunts and kindles the imaginations of its young men.

WOLFE, TOM (THOMAS KENNERLY WOLFE, JR.) (1931–), Virginia-born journalist, known for his treatment of contemporary American culture from its popular heroes to its alternative life-styles, a jet-set sociology

written in a baroque pop style. His collections of articles include *The Kandy-Kolored Tangerine-Flake Streamline Baby* (1965), *The Pump House Gang* (1968), and *Radical Chic and Mau-Mauing the Flak Catchers* (1970). Other books include *The Electric Kool-Aid Acid Test* (1968), partly about Ken Kesey♦ and his Merry Pranksters; *The New Journalism* (1973); *The Painted Word* (1975), commentary on the current art world's pretensions; *Mauve Gloves and Madmen* (1976), stories, essays, and sketches; *The Right Stuff* (1979), about U.S. astronauts, "gods for a day"; and *From Bauhaus to Our House* (1981), a satirical view of contemporary U.S architecture. *In Our Time* (1980) collects his drawings, and *The Purple Decades* (1982) collects 20 essays from previous books.

Women at Point Sur, *The,* free-verse narrative by Jeffers,♦ published in 1927. A "Prelude" reveals the author's personal philosophy, which in this narrative, as in "Tamar"♦ and "Roan Stallion,"♦ reasserts the need "to uncenter the human mind from itself." It also constitutes a "warning" against abuses or irrelevant applications of such an idea.

Dr. Barclay, a preacher in a California coast town, after learning of the death of his son in the World War, announces to his congregation that "Christianity is false," and that he is leaving them to create a new religion based on energy and violence. He goes to a farm near Point Lobos, where he elaborates his mystical faith, preaching to the trees and stones of the desolate mountainside, and "breaking from the mold" of his former gentleness and continence. Convinced that

All the relations of the world have changed in a moment.
If there was anything forbidden you may do it,

he sleeps with the Indian serving-woman Maruca, and then, having achieved "deliverance," goes mad with an indiscriminate lust that causes him to rape his daughter April and infects all the residents of the Morhaus farm, including the daughter Natalia, who murders her child to rectify the "sin" of bearing it; Randal, Natalia's husband, and Faith Heriot, her lesbian lover, whom Randal has previously possessed; and even crippled old Morhaus. The insane liberation of evil impulses that Barclay's nihilism has effected ends with April's suicide and her father's escape to starve to death in the hills, where he thinks "on the nothing Outside the stars, the other shore of me, there's peace."

Wonder-Book, A, tales for children adapted from Greek myths by Hawthorne, ♦ published in 1852. *Tanglewood Tales* (1853) is a similar collection.

Wonder-Working Providence of Sions Saviour in New England, The, chronicle of 17th-century New England by Edward Johnson, ♦ first published anonymously at London (1653, dated 1654) with the title *A History of New England.*

Wonderful One-Hoss Shay, see *Deacon's Masterpiece.*

WOODHULL, VICTORIA [CLAFLIN] (1838–1927), born in Ohio, during her early years figured with her mother and her sister Tennessee Celeste Claflin (1846–1923) in spiritualistic and mesmeric exhibitions. In 1868 the sisters went to New York City, where the elder Cornelius Vanderbilt set them up as "lady brokers" in Wall Street. With the aid of Stephen P. Andrews, they inaugurated *Woodhull and Claflin's Weekly* (1870–76), a journal advocating socialism, woman suffrage, free love, birth control, and vegetarianism. It published the scandalous Beecher-Tilton story that occasioned the trial of Henry Ward Beecher, and in the same year (1872) printed the first English translation of the *Communist Manifesto.* Victoria was nominated for President by the Equal Rights party (1872), with Frederick Douglass for Vice-President. The sisters moved to England (1877), where they each got married. Together they wrote *The Human Body as the Temple of God* (1890). Victoria's principal works were *Origin, Tendencies, and Principles of Government* (1871), *Stirpiculture* (1888), and *Humanitarian Money* (1892).

Wood-Pile, The, blank-verse poem by Robert Frost, ♦ published in *North of Boston* (1914).

The poet suggests a cosmic symbol in his discovery of a weathered, long-abandoned cord of maple, "cut and split and piled," held from being scattered by a growing tree on one side and on the other "a stake and prop, these latter about to fall." This wasted labor can be the work only of "someone who lived in turning to fresh tasks," and could leave his creation "To warm the frozen swamp as best it could With the slow smokeless burning of decay."

WOOLLCOTT, ALEXANDER [HUMPHREYS] (1887–1943), New York dramatic and literary critic, and whimsical, gossipy essayist.

WOOLMAN, JOHN (1720–72), New Jersey-born Quaker, had little formal education, and was a tailor's apprentice, baker, and shopkeeper until age 26, when he felt the presence of God in his heart commanding him to preach the gospel. As a preacher and leader of his faith, he began the long series of journeys which, with intermittent schoolteaching, occupied the rest of his life. His ardent humanitarianism aroused his interest in the problems of black slavery and the distribution of wealth. His two essays entitled *Some Considerations on the Keeping of Negroes* (1754, 1762) are among the earliest American antislavery works, and his other pamphlets include *Considerations on Pure Wisdom and Human Policy* (1758), on labor, education, and "the right use of the Lord's outward gifts"; *Considerations on the True Harmony of Mankind* (1770); *A Plea for the Poor* (written 1763), first published (1793) under the title "A Word of Remembrance and Caution to the Rich"; and *An Epistle* (1772), setting forth his religious belief in a farewell to friends before his departure for England, where he died. Woolman was consistently interested in social problems, but, when in opposition to the prevailing ideas of this world, governed himself by a principle of "passive obedience," obeying the letter of the law but not its spirit, for though he "studied to be quiet" and live according to his own views, he reasonably accepted that which was required of him. Although having frequently to bow to external authority, in personal matters he did what he wished, giving up dyed clothes because he knew dyes were harmful to workers and giving up sugar because of conditions among plantation slaves. He is best known for his lengthy *Journal* (1774), a classic document of the inner life characterized by a crystal-pure style, of which Whittier in his edition of 1871 said "it has a sweetness as of violets." Others have paid similar tributes, Channing finding it "beyond comparison the sweetest and purest autobiography in the language," and Charles Lamb exhorting his readers to "get the writings of John Woolman by heart."

WOOLSON, CONSTANCE FENIMORE (1840–94), New Hampshire-born grandniece of Cooper, spent her youth mainly in Ohio, of which she wrote in her early local-color stories and novels. *Castle Nowhere* (1875) collects stories dealing chiefly with the primitive French inhabitants near the Great Lakes. Later, as in the title story of *Rodman the Keeper: Southern Sketches* (1880), she wrote of the contrasts between the prewar South and its life during Reconstruction, which she studied at first hand during her residence in the Carolinas and Florida (1873–79). *The Front Yard* (1895) and *Dorothy* (1896) are collections of tales presenting character studies of Americans in Italy, where the author lived after 1879. Her five novels, written while she was abroad, use American settings. *Anne* (1882) deals with a simple Mackinac Island girl, thrown into the social life of New York; *For the Major* (1883), set in North Carolina, is a study of a woman's self-sacrifice for her husband to preserve his cherished illusions of the Old South; *East Angels* (1886) is a study of moral contrasts with a lush Florida background; *Jupiter Lights* (1889) is a story of the conflict between sisters-in-law representative of the Southern and Northern characters. Her last novel, *Horace Chase* (1894), is about a self-made man and his wife, who looks down upon him until she discovers his true character.

WORCESTER, Joseph Emerson (1784–1865), New England lexicographer, graduated from Yale (1811) and for five years taught at Salem, Mass., where, while writing his early textbooks, he had Hawthorne as one of his students. After moving to Cambridge (1819) he began his long series of dictionaries, first editing Dr. Johnson's, then Webster's, and finally compiling his own *Comprehensive Pronouncing and Explanatory Dictionary of the English Language* (1830). This led Webster to charge his rival with plagiarism, and precipitated the long "War of Dictionaries," intermittently intensified when each philologist followed the other in publishing new editions, and causing such by-products as Worcester's pamphlet *A Gross Literary Fraud Exposed* (1835), an invidious denial of his dependence upon Webster. Worcester was an uncompromising advocate of philological orthodoxy and English examples, zealously and consistently combating Webster's attempts at national independence. His conservatism in pronunciation and purism in spelling were accepted at Harvard and the University of Virginia, but elsewhere Webster prevailed, although Holmes was speaking for the best New England writers when he declared in favor of "Mr. Worcester's Dictionary, on which as is well known, the literary men of this metropolis are by special statutes allowed to be sworn in place of the Bible." Worcester's last great revision appeared as *A Dictionary of the English Language* (1860), but, with the 1864

revision of Webster by a company of scholars, the Webster supremacy was definitely established.

World According to Garp, The, novel by John Irving,♦ published in 1978.

Jenny Fields, a dedicated New England heiress, drops out of Wellesley College to nurse war-shattered soldiers in a Boston hospital during World War II. There she quixotically decides to have a child and therefore gives herself to a dying, brain-damaged airplane gunner who can only shout the meaningless exclamation, "Garp." Therefore she calls their child T.S. (for Technical Sergeant) Garp. In time he goes to a New England preparatory school, where she serves as a nurse and writes the book *A Sexual Suspect,* a statement on women's sensibilities and rights. Garp too becomes an author, matures to marry a bookish woman, Helen, and fathers two children, Duncan and Walt, while his mother becomes a leader of the women's rights movement. In an auto accident, while Garp is driving, Walt is killed, Duncan loses an eye, and Helen is severely injured. With his remaining family Garp then goes to live in a home for battered women run by his mother, which houses a cult of Ellen Jamesians, named for a folk hero, an 11-year-old girl who was raped. There he writes a novel, *The World According to Bensenhaver,* a tale of ghastly happenings and some compassionate people. Violent tragedy occurs in real life too as Jenny is killed by a demented man and Garp is later shot down by a woman who mistakenly believes he raped her sister. Although mother and son are murdered, their ideas, respectively about women and about people of sensitivity, continue to affect followers.

WOUK, Herman (1915–   ), New York City author, after graduation from Columbia and navy service in World War II published *Aurora Dawn* (1947), a mannered satire on the advertising business; *The City Boy* (1948), sympathetically and humorously describing a New York boy's life in the 1920s; *The Caine Mutiny*♦ (1951, Pulitzer Prize), about cruelties and cowardice on a minesweeper in the Pacific war, adapted by him as the play *The Caine Mutiny Court-Martial* (1954); *Marjorie Morningstar* (1955), about a Jewish girl's quest for romance and a stage career until she settles down as a New Jersey matron; *Youngblood Hawke* (1962), about a young Kentucky author (perhaps partly suggested by Thomas Wolfe), who is commercially successful but destroyed as artist and person in New York; and *Don't Stop the Carnival* (1965), a comic novel about a resort in the Caribbean. *The Winds of War* (1971) and *War and Remembrance* (1978) are two lengthy novels comprising a saga of World World War II in its vast scope, often concentrating on Pacific operations but also vividly depicting the Holocaust. Morally serious and documented by thorough research, the novels are also popular presentations of fictive characters mingling with great historic figures and situations. *The Traitor* (1949) and *Nature's Way* (1957) are plays. *The "Lomokome" Papers* (1968) is a brief and minor work of science fiction, written in 1949. *This Is My God* (1959) is about Judaism.

Wreck of the Hesperus, The, literary ballad by Longfellow, ♦ published in *Ballads and Other Poems* (1841).

Based on the actual wreck of the *Hesperus,* in which one body was found lashed to a piece of wreckage, the poem tells of the ill-fated voyage of the schooner, whose skipper refuses to head for port despite an approaching hurricane. When the gale descends, he wraps his little daughter in a seaman's coat, lashes her to the mast, and remains at the helm until he is overcome by the cold. The ship is shattered upon the reef of Norman's Woe near Gloucester, and at dawn a fisherman finds the child's body near the shore, still lashed to the mast.

WRIGHT, FRANCES (1795–1852), Scottish-born free-thinker and author, who spent two years in the U.S. (1818–20), where she produced her play *Altorf* (1819), about the Swiss fight for independence, and toured the country as reported in her enthusiastic *Views of Society and Manners in America* (1821). While abroad she wrote *A Few Days in Athens* (1822), fiction about a young disciple of Epicurus, which Whitman later called his "daily food." Returning to the U.S. (1824), she founded the Nashoba Community (1825–28) in Tennessee as part of her plan for gradual emancipation of blacks. Influenced by Robert Dale Owen, she joined him in editing *The New-Harmony Gazette* (1828–29), meanwhile giving public talks on women's rights, free education, birth control, equitable distribution of wealth, and errors of organized religion. These and later talks, given after an absence abroad (1830–35), were published as *Course of Popular Lectures* (2 vols., 1829, 1836).

WRIGHT, HAROLD BELL (1872–1944), popular novelist whose works include *The Shepherd of the Hills* (1907), *The Calling of Dan Matthews* (1909), and *When a Man's a Man* (1916). His stories, set in the great open spaces of the Southwest, are concerned with love and adventure, and emphasize an incredibly wholesome morality and the superiority of the rugged natural man. His books had a tremendous sale; *The Winning of Barbara Worth* (1911) sold 1,500,000 copies in 25 years.

WRIGHT, JAMES [ARLINGTON] (1927–80), Ohio-born poet, graduated from Kenyon College, received a Ph.D. from the University of Washington, and from 1966 on taught at Hunter College. His first book, *The Green Wall* (1957), in the Yale Series of Younger Poets, was followed by *Saint Judas* (1959), *The Lion's Tail and Eyes* (1962), *The Branch Will Not Break* (1963), *Shall We Gather at the River?* (1968), *Collected Poems* (1971, Pulitzer Prize), *Two Citizens* (1973), *Moments of the Italian Summer* (1976), *To a Blossoming Pear Tree* (1977), and *This Journey* (1982), whose poems are heavily imaged and often formal.

WRIGHT, RICHARD [NATHANIEL] (1908–60), self-educated black author, born near Natchez, Miss., and reared in Memphis. After many menial jobs there and in Chicago, to which he migrated at age 19, he had to go on relief during the Depression. During the 1930s he joined the Communist party but left it in the 1940s, as recorded in the anthology *The God That Failed* (1950). His *Uncle Tom's Children* (1938, enlarged 1940), a collection of four long stories, received the *Story* prize for the best book submitted by anyone associated with the Federal Writers' Project. ♦ The stories tell of race prejudice in the South and contain graphic descriptions of lynchings. With the publication in 1940 of *Native Son,* ♦ Wright was considered not only the leading black author of the U.S. but also a major heir of the naturalistic tradition in his story of the tragedy of a black boy reared in the Chicago slums. The novel was successfully dramatized (1941) by Wright and Paul Green, and in 1950 the author made a film of it in Argentina, with himself in the lead role. After his major novel, Wright participated in the creation of *12 Million Black Voices* (1941), a text and photo folk history of American blacks, and wrote *Black Boy* ♦ (1945), an autobiography of his childhood and youth. After World War II he became an expatriate in Paris and while there wrote *The Outsider*♦ (1953), a sensational novel of a black man's life in Chicago and New York City and his fatal involvement with the Communist party, and *The Long Dream* (1958), a novel about a black boy in Mississippi and his father's corrupt business dealings with both blacks and whites. Other books include *Black Power* (1954), his reactions to "a land of pathos," Africa's Gold Coast; *The Color Curtain* (1956), reporting the Bandung Conference of Asian and African nations; and *Pagan Spain* (1957), his bitter personal observations of Spain. Posthumously issued works include *Eight Men* (1961), stories, *Lawd Today* (1963), a novel written prior to *Native Son* and dealing in great detail with one unhappy day—February 12, 1936—in the life of a black postal clerk in Chicago, and *American Hunger* (1977), an autobiographical account written as a sequel to *Black Boy*.

WYLIE, ELINOR [HOYT] (1885–1928), born in New Jersey, published her first collection of poems in England, the anonymous, privately issued *Incidental Numbers* (1912). Her brilliant though brief literary career began with the publication of *Nets To Catch the Wind* (1921), highly polished verse influenced by the metaphysical poets, whose emotion has been described as "a passion frozen at its source." This was followed by a similar collection, *Black Armour* (1923). Her four novels are distinguished by very mannered craftmanship and a juxtaposition of artificial formality and fantasy like that of her verse. *Jennifer Lorn* (1923), subtitled "A Sedate Extravaganza," deals with 18th-century aristocrats in England and colonial India. *The Venetian Glass Nephew* (1925) has the same delicate color and fragility, which caused Cabell to characterize the author as a "Dresden china shepherdess." *The Orphan Angel* (1926), which appeared in England as *Mortal Image* (1927), is an imaginative story of Shelley, who, instead of being drowned, is picked up by a Yankee ship and brought to America, where his character is contrasted with the pioneer environment. *Mr. Hodge & Mr. Hazard* (1928) is a more realistic tale of English life during the 1830s, after the departure of such romantic figures as Byron and Shelley, whose spirits hover over the prosaic period. *One Person* (1928), a passionately intense sonnet sequence, was republished in *Angels and Earthly Creatures* (1929). *Trivial Breath* (1928) is a final selection of the poems after *Black Armour* which she wished to preserve. Her *Collected Poems* (1932) and *Collected Prose* (1933) were edited by her husband William Rose Benét, and *Last Poems* appeared in 1943.

X - Y

Xingu, and Other Stories, eight tales by Edith Wharton,♦ published in 1916.

"Xingu" is a witty account of the Hillbridge Lunch Club, a gathering of "indomitable huntresses of erudition"—hypocrites and snobs, with the single exception of a newcomer, Mrs. Roby—who entertain a famous woman author. Her indifference to the "topics" advanced for discussion ends only when Mrs. Roby refers familiarly to "Xingu," an esoteric subject that she and the other members then pretend to know thoroughly. The ladies of the Lunch Club discover the Xingu to be a Brazilian river, and, crestfallen and indignant, expel Mrs. Roby. "Coming Home," a story of the World War, is concerned with a young Frenchwoman who gives herself to a German officer to save her fiancé's home and family from destruction. The fiancé takes revenge by murdering the German, now a wounded prisoner, who is entrusted to his care. "Autres Temps . . ." is a poignant tale of a woman's personal tragedy, contrasting the attitudes toward divorce of two generations of New York society. "Kerfol" and "The Triumph of Night" are subtle delineations of ghosts, mystery, and terror. "Bunner Sisters," a novelette, tells of the lives of two commonplace spinsters who operate a small shop near Stuyvesant Square, in 19th-century New York City.

Yale Series of Younger Poets, volumes issued annually since 1919 by Yale University Press to print the work of promising American poets under 40 who have not previously published a book of poetry. Stephen Vincent Benét, MacLeish, Auden, and Dudley Fitts have been judges of manuscripts submitted for this literary award and editors of the published books. Winners have included Hervey Allen (1921), Paul Engle (1932), James Agee (1934), Muriel Rukeyser (1935), Adrienne Rich (1951), John Ashbery (1956), John Hollander (1958), Alan Dugan (1961), and James Tate (1967).

Yamasee Indians, war-like tribe in South Carolina and Georgia during colonial times. After 1715 reduced to a small number, they took refuge mainly in Florida. They are often referred to by Southern authors, notably in Simms's *The Yemassee,* ♦ which deals with their attempt to massacre the English of South Carolina, when incited by the Spanish of Florida (1715).

Yankee, term of unknown origin, applied during the 18th century to New Englanders. One hypothetical origin is an attempt by the Indians to pronounce either *English* or *Anglais.* This seems unlikely, since the word was first applied to the Dutch in the 17th century and may have been derived from *Janke,* diminutive of the common Dutch name *Jan,* or from *Jankees,* a blend of *Jan* and *Cornelis.* At some time in the 18th century the name began to be applied to the English colonists rather than the Dutch. The song "Yankee Doodle" did much to establish the name, which was adopted by the Americans after it had been contemptuously applied by the British in the Revolution. During the Civil War it was invidiously applied to Northerners, usually as "damn Yankee." During World War I it had mainly a kindly, facetious connotation, and long before that it was applied to Americans generally, although it is more properly restricted to the typical New England native and associated with the Down East character. The Yankee has long been a stock comic figure, and some of the notable characters of this type are Royall Tyler's Jonathan in *The Contrast,* Seba Smith's Major Jack Downing, T.C. Haliburton's Sam Slick, and Lowell's Hosea Biglow. Irving's Ichabod Crane, although he has some of the usual characteristics, lacks the conventional acuteness. The figure is usually marked by shrewd, homespun wit, caution, ability in trading, and taciturnity. When he speaks, it is frequently to ask a dry but astute question, or to make a striking understatement in his famous nasal twang. Later examples of the type include the title characters of Mark Twain's *Connecticut Yankee in King Arthur's Court* and E.N. Westcott's *David Harum.*

Yankee in Canada, A, travel narrative by Thoreau,♦ partly published in *Putnam's Monthly Magazine* (1853), and issued posthumously in a volume with his "Anti-Slavery and Reform Papers" (1866). Derived from his journal notes during a week's trip (Sept.

25–Oct. 3, 1850) from his home in Concord to Montreal and Quebec, the narrative presents homely impressions of the farmers and townspeople, and the intimate details of travel and scenery, with digressions of literary criticism and comments on fortresses, Roman Catholicism, the railroad, and comparative manners in Canada and New England.

YATES, RICHARD (1926–), New York-born author whose novels, generally perceptive and despairing views of commonplace people, include *Revolutionary Road* (1961), *A Special Providence* (1969), *Disturbing the Peace* (1975), *The Easter Parade* (1976), *A Good School* (1978), and *Young Hearts Crying* (1984). Stories are collected in *Eleven Kinds of Loneliness* (1962) and *Liars in Love* (1981).

Yearling, The, novel by Marjorie K. Rawlings. ♦

Yellow press, term applied to unscrupulously sensational newspapers. In 1894 the New York *World* printed the first colored comic strip, "Hogan's Alley," by R.F. Outcault, whose "bad boy" hero, the Yellow Kid, attracted subscribers by the cartoon and the novelty of color printing. Hearst's New York *Journal* employed Outcault (1896ff.), and from the sensational controversy between the two papers, both of which printed Yellow Kid serials, the term originated.

YERBY, FRANK [GARVIN] (1916–), Georgia-born black author, after receiving an M.A. from Fisk (1938) taught briefly at Southern universities but has concentrated on the writing of historical romances after the great success of his *The Foxes of Harrow* (1946), set in the pre-Civil War South. He has continued to write such popular fiction, some in part concerned with black people. His novels include *A Woman Called Fancy* (1951), *The Garfield Honor* (1961), *An Odor of Sanctity* (1965), *Goat Song: A Novel of Ancient Greece* (1967), *Judas, My Brother* (1968), *A Darkness at Ingraham's Crest* (1979), and *Western: A Saga of the Great Plains* (1982). In 1959 he became expatriated in Spain.

Yes Is for a Very Young Man, play by Gertrude Stein♦ (produced 1946, published 1947), about life and loyalties in World War II France under German occupation, drawing

upon her *Wars I Have Seen.* It was titled *In Savoy* in England.

YEZIERSKA, ANZIA (1885–1970), born in Russia, came to New York City (1901), whose sweatshops and ghetto life she described in tales, *Hungry Hearts* (1920), and novels, *Salome of the Tenements* (1922), *Children of Loneliness* (1923), *Arrogant Beggar* (1927), and *All I Could Never Be* (1932). *Red Ribbon on a White Horse* (1950) is her autobiography. A selection of her work, some previously unpublished, appeared as *The Open Cage* (1979).

Yoknapatawpha County, fictional setting in northern Mississippi for the saga of 14 novels and many stories by William Faulkner.♦ Based on Lafayette County and its capital, Oxford, Faulkner's mythical land, whose capital is called Jefferson, has an area of 2400 square miles and a population of 6298 whites and 9313 blacks, according to the map that its creator printed in the 1951 edition of *Absalom, Absalom!* The name of the county is presumably of Chickasaw derivation, for these Indians, such as Ikkemotubbe, are presented as the original possessors of the land. In order of their publication, the novels set in whole or in part in this land are *Sartoris, The Sound and the Fury, As I Lay Dying, Sanctuary, Light in August, Absalom, Absalom!, The Unvanquished, The Hamlet, Intruder in the Dust, Knight's Gambit, Requiem for a Nun, The Town, The Mansion,* and *The Reivers,* and the stories set there include "The Bear" and other tales in *Go Down, Moses.* The characters involved in the life of this land include the Benbow, Compson, De Spain, McCaslin, Sartoris, Snopes, Stevens, Sutpen, and Varner families. (See also *individual entries for titles and characters.*)

You Can't Go Home Again, novel by Thomas Wolfe,♦ published in 1940. It is a sequel to *The Web and the Rock.* ♦

George Webber, aged 29, returns to New York City from his emotional residence in Germany to resume his love affair with Esther Jack, the older, married, wealthy society woman who is an acclaimed stage designer. George also returns to an earlier life when he revisits his hometown of Libya Hill in the Southern state of Old Catawba to attend the funeral of his Aunt Joyner, who reared him after his father deserted the family and his mother died. But he sees how much his childhood world has changed as the townspeople are intent on making money during boom times to such an extent that even a leading citizen like Judge Rumford Bland takes usurious advantage of black people to become rich but morally bankrupt. Returning to New York, George falls prey to social lion hunters when his novel is published as a great success. Disaffected by both worlds, he becomes a recluse in Brooklyn, trying unsuccessfully to write a second novel, then flees to London and to Germany. But everywhere George is disillusioned, by contemporary values in the U.S., by the sterility and frustration of its most famous author, and by the evil he discerns in the rise of Nazism. Even upon his return to New York George can find no surcease and breaks with Fox Edwards, the brilliant editor who had helped to shape his novel, accusing him of fatalistically accepting the world as it is, while George declares that although "I believe that we are lost here in America, . . . I believe we shall be found."

You Can't Take It with You, comedy by Moss Hart♦ and George S. Kaufman,♦ produced in 1936 and published in 1937, when it was awarded a Pulitzer Prize.

You Know Me, Al, stories by Ring Lardner. ♦

YOUNG, AL[BERT JAMES] (1939–   ), Mississippi-born novelist and poet, long resident in California, a graduate of the University of California, Berkeley (1969), and a teacher of creative writing at Stanford. His first, brief novel, *Snakes* (1970), is the story of a black jazz musician; *Who Is Angelina?* (1975) depicts a young black woman in quest of herself; *Sitting Pretty* (1976) is the autobiographical recollection of a black man, told in the vernacular and ostensibly into a tape recorder; and *Ask Me Now* (1980) presents an overage black professional basketball player in retirement. Young's poems, also drawing on the experiences and attitudes of his race, and obviously influenced by Whitman, appear in *Dancing* (1969), *The Song Turning Back into Itself* (1971), *Geography of the Near Past* (1976), and *The Blues Don't Change* (1982). *Bodies & Soul* (1981) is an anecdotal memoir.

Young Goodman Brown, allegorical tale by Hawthorne,♦ published in *The New England Magazine* (1835) and in *Mosses from an Old Manse* (1846).

Goodman Brown, a Puritan of early Salem, leaves his young wife Faith, who pleads with him not to go, to attend a witches' sabbath in the woods. Among the congregation are many prominent people of the village and church. At the climax of the ceremonies, he and a young woman are about to be confirmed into the group, but he finds she is Faith, and cries to her to "look up to heaven, and resist the wicked one." Immediately he is alone in the forest, and all the fearful, flaming spectacle has disappeared. He returns to his home, but lives a dismal, gloomy life, doomed to skeptical doubt of all about him, and never able to believe in goodness or piety.

Young Lions, The, novel by Irwin Shaw. ♦

Young Lonigan: A Boyhood in Chicago Streets, novel by James T. Farrell,♦ published in 1932. This naturalistic study of the mind of a 15-year-old boy, utilizing a stream-of-consciousness technique, is the first part of the Studs Lonigan trilogy, which includes *The Young Manhood of Studs Lonigan*♦ and *Judgment Day.* ♦

The son of a lower-class Catholic family, William Lonigan, nicknamed Studs, is depicted in the common experiences of a boyhood on the South Side of Chicago. He smokes secretly, plays baseball and basketball, experiments with sex, fights, swims, enjoys his first familiarity with the older toughs he admires, and participates in Jew-baiting, shoplifting, and other activities of the youthful gang. Lucy Scanlan, a girl of his own age, provides his first romantic affair; he has a comradely friendship with the tomboy Helen Shires; and shares with other boys the attentions of Iris, a 14-year-old exponent of "free love." Other characters include Studs's father and mother; his sister Frances; the priest, Father Gilhooley; Leon, a middle-aged homosexual; Davey Cohen, who deserts the gang when Iris refuses him because he is a Jew; and such intimates of Studs as "Weary" Reilley, Paulie Haggerty, and Kenny Killarney. The boy is shown throughout to have healthy impulses and attitudes, but these are perverted by his environment and partially repressed in order that he may display the hard, unsentimental exterior prevalent among his fellows.

Young Manhood of Studs Lonigan, The, novel by James T. Farrell,♦ published in 1934. The second part of his Studs Lonigan trilogy, it follows *Young Lonigan*♦ and precedes *Judgment Day.* ♦

Continuing his naturalistic study of the

experiences of a Chicago youth, the author follows young Lonigan from the end of his schooling, during World War I, to a New Year's Eve celebration of a decade later. Studs tries to join the army but fails because of his youth; attempts a holdup; goes to work with his father as a house painter; helps his gang to torture a black child during race riots; plays football in a rough game that ends in a gang fight; frequently becomes drunk; learns to dance; joins the YMCA but gives it up because the "joint looks phony"; has various experiences with girls, including his early sweetheart Lucy, who rejects him after he contracts a venereal disease from a "pickup"; is impressed by the dedication ceremonies of a new church and is nearly persuaded by his mother to undertake a mission; but reverts to hard drinking and narrowly escapes incrimination in his friend Weary's rape of a pickup during a New Year's Eve party. Brief alternating chapters show the universality of the main narrative, by presenting the similar experiences of Stud's younger brother Martin and of a black boy; the love affair of Phil Rolfe, a Jew who accepts Catholicism because he wishes to marry Loretta Lonigan; the dreary lives of Studs's parents; the communistic ideas of the waiter Christy; Davey Cohen's degradation and beggary; and the views of Danny O'Neill, a university student and gas-station attendant, who seems to express the author's own commentary on these events.

Youth's Companion, The (1827–1929), Boston weekly magazine, of which Nathaniel Willis was a founder, provided an amusing and instructive children's periodical unconnected with Sunday schools. Early contributors included the editor's son N.P. Willis, Felicia Hemans, and Lydia Huntley Sigourney. In 1857 it was purchased by Daniel Sharp Ford, who raised the circulation from 4000 to 500,000 before his death (1899), and began to print material for adult reading. The authors included Harriet Beecher Stowe, Gladstone, Tennyson, Whittier, Sarah Orne Jewett, Hardy, Kipling, T.H. Huxley, C.E. Craddock, James Bryce, Louisa May Alcott, and Rebecca Harding Davis. Before the turn of the century, the list of contributors included Howells, J.T. Trowbridge, Stevenson, Theodore Roosevelt, Jules Verne, Cleveland, Jack London, Aldrich, Garland, and Woodrow Wilson. In 1929 the magazine was merged with *The American Boy,* suspended in 1941. An anthology of selections was issued in 1954.

Z

ZATURENSKA, MARYA (1902–82), Russian-born poet, educated at the University of Wisconsin, whose verse is collected in *Cold Morning Sky* (1937, Pulitzer Prize), *The Listening Landscape* (1941), *The Golden Mirror* (1944), *Selected Poems* (1954), *Terraces of Light* (1960), *Collected Poems* (1965), and *The Hidden Waterfall* (1974). She also wrote *Christina Rossetti* (1949), a biography, and, with her husband, Horace Gregory, *A History of American Poetry, 1900–1940* (1946).

ZENGER, JOHN PETER (1697–1746), German-born printer and journalist in New York, served as an apprentice to William Bradford, and established the *New-York Weekly Journal*♦ (1733) to oppose Bradford's *New York Gazette* and assail the administration of the provincial governor. His polemical articles and rhymes caused him to be arrested and tried for criminal libel (1735). Despite the opposition of the judge, the jury found him not guilty, and his acquittal has been considered instrumental in establishing American freedom of the press. He published a verbatim account of the trial as *A Brief Narrative of the Case and Tryal of John Peter Zenger* (1736), and continued to edit the *Journal* until his death.

ZINDEL, PAUL (1936–   ), New York-born dramatist whose *The Effect of Gamma Rays on Man-in-the-Moon Marigolds* (1970), about the relationship of a teenage girl and her unhappy mother and sister, won a Pulitzer Prize. He has also written fiction and plays for children and for teenagers.

ZUGSMITH, LEANE (1903–69), Kentucky-born proletarian author, whose novels include *All Victories Are Alike* (1929), the story of a newspaper columnist's loss of ideals; *Goodbye and Tomorrow* (1931), about a romantic spinster who seeks happiness by patronizing artists; *Never Enough* (1932), a panorama of American life during the 1920s; *The Reckoning* (1934), the story of a New York slum boy; *A Time To Remember* (1936), concerned with labor troubles and unionization in a New York department store; and *The Summer Soldier* (1938), about 20th-century injustices to blacks. *Home Is Where You Hang Your Childhood* (1937) and *Hard Times with Easy Payments* (1941) are collections of short stories.

ZUKOFSKY, LOUIS (1904–78), born of Russian immigrant parents on New York's Lower East Side, has come to be recognized as a major poet although his work was not commercially printed in a book until he was in his fifties. His lyric poems, spare, precise, and powerful, were first gathered from little magazines and booklets when he was in his sixties into *All the Collected Short Poems, 1923–1958* (1965) and *All the Collected Short Poems, 1956–1964* (1966). His works are marked by organic form, sharp observation, and verbal association with the object with which the poem began, and he was considered a leader of the Objectivist♦ school. In 1927 he started his great poem *"A,"* presenting in diverse forms his experience of art and life, of personal and public events, that began in *"A" 1–12* (1959) and *"A" 13–21* (1969) and was finally completed with the publication in 832 pages of *"A"* (1979). His poetic theories and other critical concepts are found in *Le Style Apollinaire* (Paris, 1934), *A Test of Poetry* (1948), *Prepositions* (1967), and *The Gas Age* (1969). His aesthetic views are also to be found in *Bottom: On Shakespeare* (2 vols., 1963), whose second part contains his wife Celia's musical setting for *Pericles*. With her he translated Catullus (1969), and to the poetic personal statements that make up his *Autobiography* (1970) she contributed musical settings for his lyrics. He also published works of fiction: *It Was* (1961), revised as *Ferdinand* (1968), and *Little; for Careenagers* (1970), a comic tale of a prodigy violinist from his birth to age 12. Zukofsky was a professor of English at various institutions, notably Polytechnic Institute, Brooklyn, and the University of Connecticut.

Zuñi Indians, agricultural tribe of western New Mexico, was visited by early Spanish explorers of the region. Incited by glowing accounts of the wealth of their seven pueblos, Coronado led an expedition against them in 1540, only to find that the "Seven Cities of

Cibola" were ordinary Indian villages. The tribe is now concentrated in a single town, Zuñi, noted for its preservation of aboriginal pueblo customs and religion. F.H. Cushing, ♦ who lived among the Zuñi, published several volumes dealing with their life, and Edmund Wilson wrote of them in *Red, Black, Blond and Olive*.

Chronological Index

This is a year-by-year outline in parallel sequence of the social and literary history summarized in *The Oxford Companion to American Literature*. While only the most significant events and writings are mentioned, the selection has not always been in accordance with conventional standards. The literary index attempts to include not only the leading authors, books, and periodicals, but also those less distinguished writers and works whose qualities make them noteworthy as representative of their time. In the social-historical index, each event and personality in some way constitutes a milestone in the progress of the American nation and its culture.

Since they are intended merely for reference to the discussions and summaries in the text, titles are not given in full. Plays and playwrights are included in the literary outline, the former under the date of first production. Only a few actors, painters, and other artists are included, and they are arbitrarily placed in the index of social history. In general terms, the index provides a means of ready comparison of the political, economic, religious, scientific, and aesthetic background of a given period with the chief literary events and personalities which it produced.

LITERARY HISTORY	SOCIAL HISTORY
	1577—Drake takes possession of New Albion
1578—Nathaniel Ward (*c.*1578–1652); Sandys (1578–1644)	
1580—John Smith (1580–1631)	
1584—John Cotton (1584–1652)	1584—Roanoke founded; Myles Standish (*c.*1584–1656)
1586—Thomas Hooker (1586–1647)	1587—Virginia Dare (1587–?)
1588—Hariot, *Briefe and True Report*; John Winthrop (1588–1649)	
1589—Hakluyt, *The Principal Navigations*	
1590—William Bradford (1590–1657); Thomas Morton (1590?–1647)	
1595—Edward Winslow (1595–1655)	
1596—Richard Mather (1596–1669)	
1603—Roger William (*c.*1603–83)	
1604—John Eliot (1604–90)	
1605—Thomas Shepard (1605–49)	
	1606—Virginia and Plymouth Companies chartered
	1607—Jamestown founded
1608—Smith, *A True Relation*	1608—Pocahontas "saves" Smith
1609—Gray, *Good Speed to Virginia*	1609—Hudson discovers Hudson River, claims New Netherland
1610—Rich, *Newes from Virginia*	
1612—Smith, *A Map of Virginia*; Anne Bradstreet (*c.*1612–72)	
1613—*Purchas His Pilgrimage;* Whitaker, *Good News from Virginia*	1613—Sir Henry Vane (1613–62)

459

1616—Smith, *A Description of New-England* Steendam (*c.*1616–*c.*1672)	1614—John Smith explores New England
	1619—Black slavery introduced in Virginia
	1620—Council for New England Voyage of *Mayflower* Plymouth founded
	1621—New Amsterdam founded
1622—*Mourt's Relation*	
1624—Smith, *Generall Historie;* Winslow, *Good News from New England*	1623—Dorchester Company of Adventurers
	1624—Virginia becomes royal colony
1625—Morrell, *Nova Anglia;* Purchas, *Hakluytus Posthumus*	1625—Merry Mount settled
1626—Sandys, *Ovid*	1626—Minuit director of New Netherland (1626–31); purchase of Manhattan
	1627—Suppression of Merry Mount
	1629—Massachusetts Bay Company chartered (Endecott governor, 1629–30)
1630—Smith, *The True Travels;* Cotton, *God's Promise to His Plantation;* Bradford, *History of Plimmoth Plantation* (1630–51); Winthrop, *Journals* (1630–49)	1630—Voyage of *Arbella* Massachusetts Bay Colony
1631—Wigglesworth (1631–1705)	
	1633—Van Twiller, director of New Netherland (1633–37)
1634—Wood, *New Englands Prospect*	
	1635—Boston Latin School
	1636—Roger Williams at Providence Harvard College founded
1637—Morton, *New English Canaan*	1637—Pequot War
	1638—Anne Hutchinson banished New Sweden founded
1639—Daye's press founded; first American almanac Increase Mather (1639–1723)	1639—*Oath of a Free-man*
1640—*Bay Psalm Book*	1640—Population of colonies, *c.*27,950
	1641—*Body of Liberties*
1642—Shepard, *The Sincere Convert*	1642—Sir William Berkeley governor of Virginia (1642–52, 1660–77)
1643—*New Englands First Fruits;* Williams, *A Key into the Language*	1643—New England Confederation (1643–84)
1644—Williams, *Bloudy Tenent of Persecution* Cotton, *Keys of the Kingdom of Heaven* Edward Taylor (*c.*1644–1729)	1644—William Penn (1644–1718)
	1645—Roxbury Latin School
1646—Cotton, *Milk for Babes*	
1647—Ward, *Simple Cobler;* Cotton, *The Bloudy Tenent Washed*	1647—Stuyvesant director of New Netherland (1647–64)
1648—Hooker, *Summe of Church Discipline*	1648—Cambridge Platform
1649—*Platform of Church-Discipline*	1649—Society for the Propagation of the Gospel in Foreign Parts
1650—Bradstreet, *The Tenth Muse*	1650—Population, 51,700
	1651—First Navigation Act

1652—Samuel Sewall (1652–1730)
1653—Johnson, *Wonder-Working Providence*

                                     1655—Dutch take New Sweden

1656—Hammond, *Leah and Rachel*

                                     1660—Population, 84,800
                                                    Second Navigation Act

1661—Eliot's translation of New Testament
      into Algonquin
1662—Wigglesworth, *Day of Doom*   1662—Half-Way Convenant
1663—Davenport, *Discourse about Civil
      Government*
      Cotton Mather (1663–1728)

                                       1664—English seize New Amsterdam (now
                                                  New York)

1665—*Ye Beare and Ye Club*
1666—Pain, *Daily Meditations*
1669—Wigglesworth, *Meat Out of the Eater;*
      Eliot, *The Indian Primer*

                                       1670—Population, 114,500
                                                  Hudson's Bay Company chartered
                                                  Charleston founded
                                      1671—Sir Henry Morgan captures Panama
                                      1672—Frontenac governor of New France
                                                  (1672–82, 1689–98)
                                      1673—Jolliet and Marquette explore upper
                                                  Mississippi

1674—Sewall's diary (1674–1729)
      William Byrd (1674–1744)

                                       1675—King Philip's War (1675–76)
1676—Tompson, *New Englands Crisis*   1676—Bacon's Rebellion
1677—Mather, *A Relation of the Troubles*
1678—Bradstreet, *Poems*
                                       1678—Duluth claims upper Mississippi for
                                                  France
                                      1680—Population, 155,600
1682—Rowlandson, *Captivity and Restaura-* 1682—Penn settles Pennsylvania; La Salle
      tion   explores Louisiana
                                                  Philadelphia founded
1683—*New England Primer* (1683?)
1684—Mather, *Remarkable Providences*   1684—Massachusetts charter revoked
                                      1686—Andros governor of consolidated
                                                  northern colonies
1687—Tulley's almanacs (1687–1701)

                                      1688—Smibert (1688–1751)
1689—Mather, *Memorable Providences*   1689—Andros overthrown; Leisler's revolt
                                                  King William's War (1689–97)
1690—*Publick Occurrences*   1690—Population, 213,500
                                        1692—Salem witchcraft trials
                                                  Massachusetts under new charter;
                                                  Phips governor (1692–95)
1693—Mather, *Wonders of the Invisible*   1693—William and Mary College founded
      World; Mather, *Cases of Conscience
      Concerning Evil Spirits*
1700—Sewall, *The Selling of Joseph;* Calef, 1700—Population, 275,000
      *More Wonders of the Invisible
      World*

	1701—Captain Kidd hanged Detroit founded; Yale College founded
1702—Mather, *Magnalia Christi Americana*	1702—Queen Anne's War (1702–13)
1703—Jonathan Edwards (1703–58)	
1704—Sarah Knight's diary (1704–5); *Boston News Letter* (1704–76)	
1705—Beverley, *History of Virginia*	
1706—Benjamin Franklin (1706–90)	
1708—Cook, *Sot-Weed Factor*	1708—Saybrook Platform
1710—Mather, *Bonifacius* ("Essays To Do Good") Wise, *The Churches Quarrel Espoused*	1710—Population, 375,500
	1713—Treaty of Utrecht
1714—*Androboros*	
1717—Wise, *Vindication of the Government of New England Churches*	1717—Mississippi Bubble (1717–20)
	1718—New Orleans founded Israel Putnam (1718–90)
1719—*Songs for the Nursery* *Boston Gazette* (1719–41)	
1720—John Woolman (1720–72)	1720—Population, 474,400
1721—Mather, *The Christian Philosopher* *New England Courant* (1721–26) Hell-Fire Club (1721–24)	
1722—Franklin, "Dogood Papers"	1722—Samuel Adams (1722–1803)
1724—Mather, *Parentator*	
1725—Ames almanacs (1725–75)	1725—Lovewell's Fight James Otis (1725–83)
1726—Mather, *Manuductio ad Ministerium*	
1727—Colden, *History of the Five Indian Nations* Junto Club founded Ezra Stiles (1727–95)	
1728—*Pennsylvania Gazette* (1728–1815); Byrd runs dividing line	
1729—Franklin, "Busy-Body Papers" Samuel Seabury (1729–96)	1729—Berkeley comes to America Baltimore founded
	1730—Population, 654,950
	1731—Robert Rogers (1731?–95)
1732—John Dickinson (1732–1808)	1732—Ephrata Community Washington (1732–99); R.H. Lee (1732–94)
1733—Franklin, *Poor Richard's Almanack* (1733–58); Byrd, *Journey to the Land of Eden*	1733—Oglethorpe settles Georgia Molasses Act Richmond founded
	1734—Great Awakening (*c*.1734ff.) Daniel Boone (1734–1820); Robert Morris (1734–1806)
1735—Crèvecœur (1735–1813)	1735—Zenger trial John Adams (1735–1826); Paul Revere (1735–1818)
	1736—Patrick Henry (1736–99)
1737—Paine (1737–1809); Hopkinson (1737–91); Jonathan Odell (1737–1818)	
	1738—Whitefield's first visit to America (1738–39)

Literary History	Social History
	Copley (1738?–1815); Benjamin West (1738–1820)
1740—Tailfer, *Narrative of the Colony of Georgia*	1740—Population, 889,000 Faneuil Hall erected
1741—Edwards, *Sinners in the Hands of an Angry God* Bradford, *The American Magazine;* Franklin, *The General Magazine*	1741—C.W. Peale (1741–1827)
1743—Sower's German Bible American Philosophical Society founded	1743—Jefferson (1743–1826)
	1745—King George's War (1745–48); capture of Louisburg Anthony Wayne (1745–96); John Jay (1745–1829); Benjamin Rush (1745–1813)
1746—Shirley, *Siege of Louisburg*	1746—College of New Jersey founded (now Princeton University) C.C. Pinckney (1746–1825)
1747—Stith, *Settlement of Virginia*	1747—John Paul Jones (1747–92)
1748—Brackenridge (1748–1816)	1748—Treaty of Aix-la-Chapelle
1749—First dramatic company in America at Philadelphia (later moved to New York)	1749—First Ohio Company chartered
1750—John Trumbull (1750–1831)	1750—Population, 1,207,000
	1751—Philadelphia Academy founded (now University of Pennsylvania) Madison (1751–1836)
1752—Freneau (1752–1832); Timothy Dwight (1752–1817)	1752—George Rogers Clark (1752–1818); Gouverneur Morris (1752–1816)
	1753—Edmund Randolph (1753–1813); Benjamin Thompson (1753–1814)
1754—Edwards, *Freedom of Will* Barlow (1754–1812)	1754—Albany Congress French and Indian War (1754–63); Braddock commander in chief of British forces (1754–55) King's College founded (now Columbia University)
	1755—Acadians deported John Marshall (1755–1835); Gilbert Stuart (1755–1828)
1756—Woolman's *Journal* (1756–72)	1756—John Trumbull (1756–1843); Aaron Burr (1756–1836); "Light-Horse Harry" Lee (1756–1818)
1757—*The American Magazine and Monthly Chronicle* (1757–58) Royall Tyler (1757–1826)	1757—Hamilton (1757–1804); Charles Pinckney (1757–1824)
1758-Franklin, "The Way to Wealth"; Maylem, *Conquest of Louisburg;* Prince, *Psalms, Hymns, and Spiritual Songs* Noah Webster (1758–1843)	1758—Mary Jemison captured Pittsburgh founded Monroe (1758–1831)
	1760—Population, 1,610,000
	1761—Gallatin (1761–1849)
1762—Susanna Rowson (*c.*1762–1824)	1762—Louisiana secretly transferred by France to Spain St. Louis founded

Literary History	Social History
	1763—Pontiac's Conspiracy (1763–65) Gage commander in chief of British forces (1763–75) Treaty of Paris Mason-Dixon survey (1763–67) Astor (1763–1848); Charles Bulfinch (1763–1844); James Kent (1763–1847)
1764—Otis, *Rights of British Colonies;* Hutchinson, *History of Massachusetts Bay*	1764—Sugar Act; Colonial Currency Act Brown University founded
1765—Godfrey, *Prince of Parthia;* Samuel Adams, *Resolutions*	1765—Stamp Act; Patrick Henry's resolutions; Stamp Act Congress, *Declaration of Rights;* Quartering Act; Regulators (1765–71) Robert Fulton (1765–1815)
1766—Rogers, *Ponteach* William Dunlap (1766–1839)	1766—Stamp Act repealed; Westmoreland Association Queen's College founded (now Rutgers University)
	1767—Townshend acts; Nonimportation agreements Monticello erected Andrew Jackson (1767–1845); John Quincy Adams (1767–1848); Black Hawk (1767–1838)
1768—Dickinson, *Letters from a Farmer in Pennsylvania*	1768—Troops sent to Boston
	1769—Portolá's expedition to California (1769ff.); Serra's first mission Dartmouth College founded DeWitt Clinton (1769–1828)
1770—*Massachusetts Spy* (1770–1904)	1770—Population 2,205,000 Boston Massacre Watauga Association
1771—Franklin begins autobiography C.B. Brown (1771–1810)	
1772—Freneau and Brackenridge, *Rising Glory of America;* Trumbull, *Progress of Dulness* (1772–73)	1772—First Committees of Correspondence
1773—Wheatley, *Poems;* Warren, *The Adulateur;* Franklin, "Edict of the King of Prussia" and "Rules by Which a Great Empire May Be Reduced to a Small One" *Rivington's New-York Gazetteer* (1773–83)	1773—Boston Tea Party Boone settles in Kentucky John Randolph (1773–1833); W.H. Harrison (1773–1841)
1774—Hopkinson, *A Pretty Story;* Duché, *Caspipina's Letters*	1774—First Continental Congress; Burke's speech on taxation; Dunmore's War; second Quartering Act Shakers in America Meriwether Lewis (1774–1809)
1775—Burgoyne, *The Blockade;* Burke, *On Conciliation;* Warren, *The Group;* Freneau, "A Political Litany"; Trumbull, *M'Fingal* (1775–82)	1775—Second Continental Congress Revolutionary War (1775–83); battles of Lexington and Concord; Arnold and Allen capture Ticonderoga and Crown Point; unsuccessful campaign against Canada; Washington commander in chief of Continental army; Siege of Boston; Battle of Bunker Hill

1776—Paine, *Common Sense;* Brackenridge, *Battle of Bunkers-Hill;* Leacock, *Fall of British Tyranny;* Freneau, "The Beauties of Santa Cruz"; Munford, *The Patriots*
Paine, *The American Crisis* (1776–83)

1777—Hopkinson, *A Political Catechism;* Burke, *Letter to the Sheriffs of Bristol*

1778—Hopkinson, "The Battle of the Kegs"
J.K. Paulding (1778–1860)

1779—Freneau, "The House of Night"
United States Magazine
Francis Scott Key (1779–1843)

1781—Freneau, *The British Prison Ship*

1782—Crèvecœur, *Letters from an American Farmer;* Aitken Bible (first complete English Bible printed in America)
1783—Webster, *Spelling Book*
Irving (1783–1859)
1784—Allen, *Reason the Only Oracle of Man*
Massachusetts Centinel (1784–1840)
Joseph Worcester (1784–1865)
1785—Dwight, *Conquest of Canaan;* Webster, *Sketches of American Policy*
Friendly Club of Hartford (c.1785–1807)
1786—Freneau, *Poems; The Anarchiad* (1786–87)
Columbian Magazine (1786–92)

1787—Jefferson, *Notes on Virginia;* Barlow, *The Vision of Columbus;* Tyler, *The Contract;* Adams, *Defence of the Constitutions; The Federalist* (1787–88)

1776—Declaration of Independence; Virginia Bill of Rights; Boston Port bill; separation from England; Nathan Hale executed; Battles of Trenton and Long Island
San Francisco mission and presidio founded
Phi Beta Kappa founded
1777—Stars and Stripes adopted as national flag
Battles of Princeton, Brandywine, Germantown, and Saratoga; Valley Forge (1777–78); Conway Cabal
Henry Clay (1777–1852); R.B. Taney (1777–1864)
1778—Alliance with France
Wyoming Valley massacre; Battle of Monmouth
1779—*Bonhomme Richard* vs. *Serapis;* Vincennes captured; Battle of Stony Point
University of Pennsylvania founded
Decatur (1779–1820); Joseph Story (1779–1845)
1780—Population, 2,781,000
Benedict Arnold's treason discovered, André captured; battles of Camden and King's Mountain; Rochambeau arrives with French troops
David Porter (1780–1843)
1781—Battle of Eutaw Springs; Cornwallis surrenders at Yorktown
Articles of Confederation (1781–89)
James Lawrence (1781–1813)
1782—Lewis Cass (1782–1866); Calhoun (1782–1850); Van Buren (1782–1862); Webster (1782–1852); T.H. Benton (1782–1858)
1783—Treaty of Paris

1784—Zachary Taylor (1784–1850)

1785—Audubon (1785–1851); O.H. Perry (1785–1819)

1786—Annapolis Convention
Shays's Rebellion (1786–87)
Ohio Company of Associates; Tammany Society
Nicholas Biddle (1786–1844); Crockett (1786–1836); W.L. Marcy (1786–1857); Winfield Scott (1786–1866)
1787—Federal Constitutional Convention
Ordinance of 1787
Emma Willard (1787–1870)

1788—Freneau, *Miscellaneous Works*	1788—Constitution ratified First settlement by Ohio Company
1789—Dunlap, *The Father;* Webster, *Dissertations on the English Language;* Brown, *The Power of Sympathy* *Gazette of the United States* (1789–1847) Cooper (1789–1851)	1789—Washington's administration (1789–97) First Congress University of North Carolina founded
1790—Webster, *Essays* Halleck (1790–1867)	1790—Population according to first national census, 3,929,214 John Tyler (1790–1862)
1791—Hamilton, *Report on Manufactures;* Adams, *Discourses of Davila;* Bartram, *Travels;* Paine, *Rights of Man* (1791–92); *The Echo* (1791–1805) J.H. Payne (1791–1852)	1791—Bill of Rights Bank of the U.S. Vermont admitted as 14th state Williams College founded Peter Cooper (1791–1883); James Buchanan (1791–1868)
1792—Barlow, *Advice to the Privileged Orders;* Hopkinson, *Essays;* Odiorne, *Progress of Refinement;* Brackenridge, *Modern Chivalry* (1792–1815) Seba Smith (1792–1868)	1792—White House cornerstone laid Thaddeus Stevens (1792–1868); Francis M. Drexel (1792–1863)
1793—*The Hapless Orphan* *Farmer's Almanack* (1793–) John Neal (1793–1876)	1793—Genêt mission Fugitive Slave Law Capitol cornerstone laid Cotton gin Houston (1793–1863)
1794—Dwight, *Greenfield Hill;* Rowson, *Charlotte Temple* and *Slaves in Algiers;* Paine, *The Age of Reason* (1794–95) Bryant (1794–1878)	1794—Whiskey Rebellion Jay's Treaty; Neutrality Act Bowdoin College founded Edward Everett (1794–1865); Matthew Perry (1794–1858); Vanderbilt (1794–1877)
1795—Freneau, *Poems* J.R. Drake (1795–1820); J.P. Kennedy (1795–1870); J.G. Percival (1795–1856)	1795—Yazoo frauds Pinckney's Treaty Boston State House erected First American circus Polk (1795–1849)
1796—Washington, "Farewell Address"; Barlow, *Hasty Pudding;* first of Dennie's "Lay Preacher" essays T.C. Haliburton (1796–1865); W.H. Prescott (1796–1859)	1796—Greek Revival introduced in U.S. Horace Mann (1796–1859)
1797—Foster, *The Coquette;* Burk, *Bunker Hill;* Tyler, *The Algerine Captive;* Dwight, *The Triumph of Infidelity* *Porcupine's Gazette* (1797–99)	1797—John Adams's administration (1797–1801) XYZ Affair (1797–98) Daniel Drew (1797–1879)
1798—Brown, *Wieland;* Dunlap, *André;* "Hail Columbia"	1798—Alien and Sedition acts; Kentucky and Virginia Resolutions Jedediah Smith (1798–1831)
1799—Brown, *Edgar Huntly* and *Ormond* and *Arthur Mervyn; The Political Greenhouse* Bronson Alcott (1799–1889); R.P. Smith (1799–1854)	
1800—Weems, *Life of Washington* (1800?); Wood, *Julia and the Illuminated Baron*	1800—Population, 5,308,483 Washington, D.C., becomes capital

Library of Congress founded; Tuesday Club of Philadelphia (1800–?); *National Intelligencer* (1800–1870) George Bancroft (1800–1891)

1801—Brown, *Clara Howard* and *Jane Talbot;* Chateaubriand, *Atala;* Tenney, *Female Quixotism*
New York *Evening Post* (1801–   ); *The Port Folio* (1801–27)

1803—Wirt, *Letters of the British Spy;* Fessenden, *Terrible Tractoration*
Emerson (1803–82)

1804—Marshall, *Life of Washington* Anthology Club (*c.*1804–11) Hawthorne (1804–64)

1805—Boston Athenaeum (1805–   )

1806—Webster, *Compendious Dictionary* R.M. Bird (1806–54); W.G. Simms (1806–70); N.P. Willis (1806–67)

1807—Barlow, *The Columbiad;* Irving and Paulding, *Salmagundi* (1807–8) Longfellow (1807–82); Whittier (1807–92)

1809—Irving, *History of New York;* Campbell, *Gertrude of Wyoming* Holmes (1809–94); Poe (1809–49)

1810—Ingersoll, *Inchiquin;* Thomas, *History of Printing in America* Margaret Fuller (1810–50); Theodore Parker (1810–60)

1811—Mitchell, *The Asylum* Greeley (1811–72); Henry James, Sr. (1811–82); Harriet Beecher Stowe (1811–96)

1812—Barker, *Marmion;* Paulding, *John Bull and Brother Jonathan;* Melish, *Travels in the United States* American Antiquarian Society (1812–   )

1813—Taylor, *Arator* *Boston Daily Advertiser* (1813–1929) Jones Very (1813–80)

1814—Key, "Star-Spangled Banner"; Humphreys, *Yankey in England; History of the Expedition of Captains Lewis and Clark*

Gothic Revival introduced in U.S. John Brown (1800–1859); Caleb Cushing (1800–1879); Fillmore (1800–1874)

1801—Jefferson's administration (1801–9) Barbary Wars (1801–5) W.H. Seward (1801–72); Brigham Young (1801–77)

1802—U.S. Military Academy founded Dorothea Dix (1802–87)

1803—Louisiana Purchase *Marbury* vs. *Madison*

1804—Lewis and Clark expedition (1804–6) Burr-Hamilton duel Harmony Society founded Franklin Pierce (1804–69)

1805—Garrison (1805–79); Joseph Smith (1805–44)

1806—Nonimportation Act Edwin Forrest (1806–72); J.A. Roebling (1806–69)

1807—Embargo Act Burr tried for treason *Clermont*'s first voyage Agassiz (1807–73); R.E. Lee (1807–70)

1808—Importation of slaves prohibited Salmon P. Chase (1808–73); Jefferson Davis (1808–89); Andrew Johnson (1808–75)

1809—Madison's administration (1809–17) Repeal of Embargo Act; Nonintercourse Act Lincoln (1809–65); Kit Carson (1809–68); Albert Brisbane (1809–90)

1810—Population, 7,239,881 P.T. Barnum (1810–91)

1811—Steamboats on the Mississippi Battle of Tippecanoe G.C. Bingham (1811–79); Charles Sumner (1811–74)

1812—War of 1812 (1812–15); *Constitution* vs. *Guerrière* "Gerrymander" A.H. Stephens (1812–83)

1813—Battle of Lake Erie Frémont (1813–90); Stephen Douglas (1813–61); H.W. Beecher (1813–87)

1814—Hartford Convention (1814–15) British invade Washington; Battle of Lake Champlain; Creek Indians defeated; Treaty of Ghent

	W.L. Yancey (1814–63); Stanton (1814–69); Tilden (1814–86)
1815—Freneau, *Poems* *North American Review* (1815–1939) R.H. Dana, Jr. (1815–82)	1815—Battle of New Orleans Tripolitan War
1816—Drake, "The Culprit Fay"; Woodworth, *Champions of Freedom* *The Portico* (1816–18) Parke Godwin (1816–1904)	1816—Second Bank of the U.S. Regular transatlantic shipping inaugurated
1817—Bryant, "Thanatopsis"; Barker, *How To Try a Lover;* Neal, *Keep Cool* Thoreau (1817–62)	1817—Monroe's administration (1817–25) First Seminole War (1817–18) University of Michigan founded
1818—Payne, *Brutus;* Bryant, "To a Waterfowl"	1818—Northern boundary (to Rocky Mountains) fixed at 49th parallel Lucy Stone (1818–93)
1819—Drake and Halleck, "Croaker Papers"; Noah, *She Would Be A Soldier;* Channing, *Baltimore Sermon;* Irving, *The Sketch Book* (1819–20) Lowell (1819–91); Melville (1819–91); Whitman (1819–92)	1819—Transatlantic voyage of the *Savannah* Purchase of Florida Dartmouth College case University of Virginia founded
1820—Cooper, *Precaution;* Eastburn and Sands, *Yamoyden;* Sydney Smith, "Who reads an American book?" Boucicault (1820–90)	1820—Population, 9,638,453 Missouri Compromise First American missionaries in Hawaii Susan B. Anthony (1820–1906); Sherman (1820–91)
1821—Cooper, *The Spy;* Bryant, *Poems;* Percival, *Poems;* Wright, *Views of Society and Manners in America;* Dwight, *Travels* (1821–22) *The Saturday Evening Post* (1821–1969); *Genius of Universal Emancipation* (1821–39)	1821—Santa Fe Trail James Longstreet (1821–1904); Mary Baker Eddy (1821–1910); Jay Cooke (1821–1905); C.P. Huntington (1821–1900); Clara Barton (1821–1912)
1822—Irving, *Bracebridge Hall;* Neal, *Logan;* Halleck, "Alnwick Castle"; Trumbull, *Works* Bread and Cheese Club (*c.*1822–27) E.E. Hale (1822–1909)	1822—Grant (1822–85); Hayes (1822–93)
1823—Cooper, *The Pioneers* and *The Pilot;* Paulding, *Koningsmarke;* Neal, *Seventy-Six;* Moore, "A Visit from St. Nicholas" *New-York Mirror* (1823–60) G.H. Boker (1823–90)	1823—Monroe Doctrine
1824—Irving, *Tales of a Traveller;* Payne, *Charles the Second;* Barker, *Superstition;* Neal, "American Writers" (1824–25) *Springfield Republican* (1824–) G.W. Curtis (1824–92)	1824—National Republican party (1824–32) Tour of Lafayette "Stonewall" Jackson (1824–63)
1825—Halleck, "Marco Bozzaris"; Webster, Bunker Hill oration; Bryant, "A Forest Hymn"; Woodworth, *The Widow's Son* *Atlantic Souvenir* (1825–32) R.H. Stoddard (1825–1903); Bayard Taylor (1825–78)	1825—John Quincy Adams's administration (1825–29) Erie Canal opened Nashoba Community (1825–28); New Harmony (1825–28) Rutgers College founded

1826—Cooper, *Last of the Mohicans;* Woodworth, *Ballads;* Payne, *Richelieu;* Kent, *Commentaries;* Flint, *Recollections of the Last Ten Years* Graham's Magazine (1826–58) De Forest (1826–1906); Stephen Foster (1826–64)	1826—First lyceum McCellan (1826–85)
1827—Poe, *Tamerlane and Other Poems;* Cooper, *The Prairie;* Sedgwick, *Hope Leslie;* Tucker, *A Voyage to the Moon;* Simms, *Poems* The Token (1827–42); Youth's Companion (1827–1929)	
1828—Hawthorne, *Fanshawe;* Webster, *American Dictionary of the English Language;* Cooper, *Red Rover;* Irving, *Columbus;* Sealsfield, *Americans as They Are;* Calhoun, "South Carolina Exposition"	1828—Tariff of Abominations American Peace Society
1829—Poe, *Al Aaraaf, Tamerlane, and Other Poems;* Irving, *Conquest of Granada;* Stone, *Metamora;* Smith, *Eighth of January;* Cooper, *Wept of Wish-ton-Wish;* Knapp, *Lectures on American Literature;* Kettell, *Specimens of American Poetry* S. Weir Mitchell (1829–1914); C.D. Warner (1829–1900)	1829—Andrew Jackson's administration (1829–37) *Tom Thumb,* first steam locomotive in U.S. Workingmen's party Roscoe Conkling (1829–88); Carl Schurz (1829–1906)
1830—Holmes, "Old Ironsides"; Paulding, *Lion of the West; Book of Mormon;* Smith, *Triumph at Plattsburg;* Worcester, *Dictionary;* Seba Smith begins "Jack Downing" letters; Hale, "Mary Had a Little Lamb" Godey's Lady's Book (1830–98); Boston Daily Evening Transcript (1830–1941) J.E. Cooke (1830–86); Emily Dickinson (1830–86); P.H. Hayne (1830–86)	1830—Population, 12,866,020 Mormon church Blaine (1830–93)
1831—Poe, *Poems;* Bird, *The Gladiator;* Whittier, *Legends of New England;* Smith, "America"; Paulding, *Dutchman's Fireside* Liberator (1831–65); Spirit of the Times (1831–58) Rebecca H. Davis (1831–1910)	1831—Southampton Insurrection New England Anti-Slavery Society New York University founded Garfield (1831–81); Sheridan (1831–88)
1832—Bryant, *Poems;* Kennedy, *Swallow Barn;* Mason, *The Choir;* Bird, *Oralloossa;* Irving, *The Alhambra;* Trollope, *Domestic Manners of the Americans;* Hawthorne, "Roger Malvin's Burial"; Dunlap, *History of the American Theatre;* Story, *Commentaries* (1832–45) Louisa May Alcott (1832–88); H.H. Bancroft (1832–1918)	1832—Ordinance of Nullification; beginning of U.S. Bank controversy

1833—Longfellow, *Outre-Mer;* Simms, *Martin Faber;* Neal, *The Down-Easters;* Poe, "MS. Found in a Bottle" *Knickerbocker Magazine* (1833–65); New York *Sun* (1833–1966); *Parley's Magazine* (1833–41)

1834—*Life of David Crockett;* Simms, *Guy Rivers;* Abbott, first of the Rollo books; Bancroft, *History of the United States* (1834–76) *Southern Literary Messenger* (1834–64) Frank Stockton (1834–1902); Horatio Alger (1834–99)

1835—Longstreet, *Georgia Scenes;* Simms, *The Yemassee* and *The Partisan;* Hawthorne, "Young Goodman Brown"; Sparks, *Life of Washington;* Irving, *Tour on the Prairies;* Drake, *The Culprit Fay;* Poe, "Berenice" and "Morella"; Bird, *The Hawks of Hawk-Hollow;* Kennedy, *Horse-Shoe Robinson* Crockett almanacs (1835–56); New York *Herald* (1835–1966); *Western Messenger* (1835–41) Clemens (1835–1910)

1836—Emerson, *Nature;* Haliburton, *The Clockmaker;* Hildreth, *The Slave;* Holmes, *Poems;* Tucker, *Partisan Leader;* McGuffey, *Eclectic Readers* (1836–57) Transcendental Club (1836–*c.*1844) Aldrich (1836–1907); Bret Harte (1836–1902)

1837—Hawthorne, *Twice-Told Tales;* Emerson, *The American Scholar;* Carey, *Principles of Political Economy;* Willis, *Bianca Visconti;* Bird, *Nick of the Woods;* Prescott, *Ferdinand and Isabella;* Cooper, *Gleanings in Europe* (1837–38) Baltimore *Sun* (1837–   ); *New Orleans Picayune* (1837–   ); *United States Magazine and Democratic Review* (1837–49); *Burton's Gentleman's Magazine* (1837–40) Burroughs (1837–1921); Howells (1837–1920); Edward Eggleston (1837–1902)

1838—Emerson, "Divinity School Address;" Cooper, *American Democrat;* Kennedy, *Rob of the Bowl;* Whittier, *Ballads and Anti-Slavery Poems;* Martineau, *Retrospect of Western Travel;* Neal, *Charcoal Sketches;* Tocqueville, *Democracy in Amer-*

1833—American Anti-Slavery Society Haverford College founded; Oberlin College founded Chicago incorporated Benjamin Harrison (1833–1901); R.G. Ingersoll (1833–99); J.E.B. Stuart (1833–64)

1834—McCormick reaper Whistler (1834–1903); Langley (1834–1906); James Fisk (1834–72)

1835—Locofocos (*c.*1835–40) Second Seminole War (1835–42) Adah Menken (1835–68); Carnegie (1835–1919); John La Farge (1835–1910)

1836—Lone Star Republic (1836–45); Battle of the Alamo Whig party Colt revolver Mt. Holyoke Seminary (first women's college) Jay Gould (1836–92); Winslow Homer (1836–1910)

1837—Van Buren's administration (1837–41) Caroline Affair Financial panic Cleveland (1837–1908); Mark Hanna (1837–1904); J.P. Morgan (1837–1913)

1838—Underground Railroad established J.J. Hill (1838–1916); H.H. Richardson (1838–86)

ica; Poe, "Silence" and "Ligeia"
and *Narrative of A. Gordon Pym*
Henry Adams (1838–1918); John Hay
(1838–1905); Muir (1838–1914);
F.H. Smith (1838–1915); Tourgée
(1838–1905)

1839—Longfellow, *Hyperion* and *Voices of the Night;* Very, *Essays and Poems;* Willis, *Tortesa;* Marryat, *Diary in America;* Kirkland, *A New Home;* Poe, *Tales of the Grotesque and Arabesque;* Thompson, *The Green Mountain Boys*
Liberty Bell (1839–58)
Henry George (1839–97)

1839—Aroostook War
Rockefeller (1839–1937)

1840—Dana, *Two Years Before the Mast;* Cooper, *The Pathfinder;* Alcott, "Orphic Sayings"; Simms, *Border Beagles;* Hoffman, *Greyslaer*
The Dial (1840–44)

1840—Population, 17,069,453
Chardon Street Convention (1840–41)
Thomas Nast (1840–1902)

1841—Emerson, *Essays, First Series;* Cooper, *The Deerslayer;* Lowell, *A Year's Life;* Thorpe, "Big Bear of Arkansas"; Catlin, *North American Indians;* Poe, "Murders in the Rue Morgue"; Longfellow, *Ballads and Other Poems*
New-York Tribune (1841–1966)
Joaquin Miller (1841?–1913)

1841—Harrison's administration (1841); Tyler's administration (1841–45)
Dorr's Rebellion
Brook Farm (1841–47)

1842—Hawthorne, *Twice-Told Tales* (enlarged); Simms, *Beauchampe;* Dickens, *American Notes;* Whittier, "Massachusetts to Virginia"; Cooper, *Wing-and-Wing;* Poe, "Eleonora" and "Masque of the Red Death"; Griswold, *Poets and Poetry of America*
Lanier (1842–81); William James (1842–1910); Bronson Howard (1842–1908); Bierce (1842–1914?)

1842—Amana Community; Fruitlands (1842–43); Hopedale (1842–56)
Webster-Ashburton Treaty
Barnum's American Museum

1843—Prescott, *Conquest of Mexico;* Webster, second Bunker Hill oration; Pierpont, *Anti-Slavery Poems:* Thompson, *Major Jones's Courtship;* Poe, "The Gold Bug" and "The Black Cat"
Henry James, Jr. (1843–1916)

1843—North American Phalanx (1843–54)
Barnburners (1843–48)
McKinley (1843–1901)

1844—Emerson, *Essays, Second Series;* Cooper, *Afloat and Ashore;* Whittier, *Voices of Freedom;* Smith, *The Drunkard;* Dickens, *Martin Chuzzlewit*
Littell's Living Age (1844–1941); *Brownson's Quarterly Review* (1844–75)
G.W. Cable (1844–1925)

1844—"Fifty-four forty or fight"
Hunkers (1844–52)
Vulcanizing process patented; Morse demonstrates telegraph
Bethel Community (1844–80)
Eakins (1844–1916); Comstock (1844–1915)

1845—Poe, *The Raven and Other Poems* and "The Literati"; Mowatt, *Fashion;* *Life of Frederick Douglass;* Fuller, *Woman in the Nineteenth Century;*

1845—Polk's administration (1845–49)
Texas annexed
U.S. Naval Academy founded
Elihu Root (1845–1937)

Judd, *Margaret;* Cooper, *Satanstoe;* Hooper, *Simon Suggs*
Broadway Journal (1845–46); *Harbinger* (1845–49)

1846—Melville, *Typee;* Hawthorne, *Mosses from an Old Manse;* Holmes, *Poems;* Emerson, *Poems;* Mathews, *Witchcraft;* Poe, "Cask of Amontillado" and "The Philosophy of Composition"
DeBow's Review (1846–80)

1846—Mexican War (1846–48); Oregon acquired; Bear Flag War; Wilmot Proviso
Hoe rotary press; Morton's use of ether as anaesthetic; Howe sewing machine
Donner Party
Smithsonian Institution
Carry Nation (1846–1911); Elbert Gary (1846–1927); W.F. Cody (1846–1917)

1847—Longfellow, *Evangeline;* Melville, *Omoo;* Field, *The Drama in Pokerville;* Prescott, *Conquest of Peru;* Paulding, *The Bucktails;* Griswold, *Prose Writers of America*
Union Magazine (1847–52)

1847—Free Soil party (1847–54)
Mormons in Utah
Edison (1847–1931); Jesse James (1847–82); C.F. McKim (1847–1909); Alexander G. Bell (1847–1922)

1848—Lowell, *Biglow Papers* and *Fable for Critics* and *Vision of Sir Launfal;* Poe, *Eureka;* Foster, *Songs of the Sable Harmonists*
The Independent (1848–1928)
H.H. Boyesen (1848–95); J.C. Harris (1848–1908)

1848—Gold discovered in California
Treaty of Guadalupe Hidalgo
Oneida Community (1848–79)
College of the City of New York founded; University of Wisconsin founded
Seneca Falls woman suffrage meeting
Saint-Gaudens (1848–1907); Harriman (1848–1909)

1849—Parkman, *Oregon Trail;* Melville, *Mardi* and *Redburn;* Longfellow, *Kavanagh;* Thoreau, *Week on the Concord and Merrimack* and "Civil Disobedience"; Whittier, *Margaret Smith's Journal;* Southworth, *Retribution;* Paulding, *The Puritan and His Daughter;* Poe, "Annabel Lee" and "The Bells" and "Eldorado"; Griswold, *Female Poets of America*
Sarah Orne Jewett (1849–1909); J.L. Allen (1849–1925); J.W. Riley (1849–1916)

1849—Taylor's administration (1849–50)
California gold rush
Astor Place riot
Burbank (1849–1926)

1850—Hawthorne, *The Scarlet Letter;* Taylor, *Eldorado;* Mitchell, *Reveries of a Bachelor;* Melville, *White-Jacket;* Garrard, *Wah-tó-yah;* Emerson, *Representative Men;* Whittier, "Ichabod," *Songs of Labor;* Calhoun, "Fourth of March" speech; Webster, "Seventh of March" speech
Bellamy (1850–98); Eugene Field (1850–1902); Hearn (1850–1904)

1850—Fillmore's administration (1850–53)
Population, 23,191,876
Clayton-Bulwer Treaty; Fugitive Slave Law; Compromise of 1850
Currier and Ives partnership established
Jenny Lind's tour (1850–52)
Gompers (1850–1924); H.C. Lodge (1850–1924); Seth Low (1850–1916)

1851—Melville, *Moby-Dick;* Parkman, *Conspiracy of Pontiac;* Simms, *Katharine Walton;* Hawthorne, *The Snow-Image* and *The House of the Seven Gables;* Mitchell, *Dream*

1851—"Go West, young man"
Maine becomes first state with long-term "dry" law
Northwestern University founded

Life; Foster, "Old Folks at
Home"; Morgan, *League of the
Ho-dé-no-sau-nee;* Schoolcraft, *Indian Tribes* (1851–57)
Kate Chopin (1851–1904)

1852—Stowe, *Uncle Tom's Cabin* (the novel
and the Aiken dramatization);
Hawthorne, *The Blithedale Romance;* Melville, *Pierre*
San Francisco *Golden Era* (1852–93)
Mary Wilkins Freeman (1852–1930)

1853—Baldwin, *Flush Times;* Curtis, *Potiphar Papers;* Simms, *The Sword and
the Distaff*
Putnam's Monthly Magazine (1853–
1910)
E.W. Howe (1853–1937); T.N. Page
(1853–1922)

1853—Pierce's administration (1853–57)
Gadsden Purchase; Perry's voyage to
Japan
Kane's Arctic expedition (1853–55)
Rail connection, New York to Chicago
Antioch College founded

1854—Thoreau, *Walden;* Arthur, *Ten Nights
in a Barroom;* Cooke, *Leather
Stocking and Silk* and *The Virginia
Comedians;* Melville, "The Encantadas"; Grayson, *The Hireling and
the Slave;* Shillaber, *Mrs. Partington;* Thorpe, *Hive of the Bee
Hunter;* Cummins, *The Lamplighter*
F.M. Crawford (1854–1909)

1854—Trade treaty with Japan; Ostend
Manifesto
Kansas-Nebraska Act; Emigrant Aid
Company

1855—Whitman, *Leaves of Grass;* Longfellow, *Hiawatha;* Melville, "Benito
Cereno"; Simms, *The Forayers;*
Bartlett, *Familiar Quotations;* Boker, *Francesca da Rimini;* Bulfinch, *Age of Fable;* Thomson, *Doesticks;* Parton, *Horace Greeley;* Duyckinck, *Cyclopaedia of American Literature;* Irving, *Life of Washington
(1855–59)*
Saturday Club of Boston (1855–　);
New York Ledger (1855–1903)
Belasco (1855?–1931); Bunner (1855–
96); Royce (1855–1916); Saltus
(1855?–1921); Woodberry (1855–
1930)

1855—Mellon (1855–1937); Debs (1855–
1926); La Follette (1855–1925);
W.H. Page (1855–1918)

1856—Stowe, *Dred;* Motley, *Rise of the
Dutch Republic;* Simms, *Eutaw;*
Emerson, *English Traits;* Curtis,
Prue and I; Reid, *The Quadroon;*
Bateman, *Self;* Thomson, *Pluribus-tah;* Whitcher, *Widow Bedott
Papers; Sabin's Dictionary* (1856–
1936)
Copyright law
Lizette Reese (1856–1935)

1856—Know-Nothing movement; national
organization of Republican party
Wilson (1856–1924); Brandeis (1856–
1941); J.S. Sargent (1856–1925);
L.H. Sullivan (1856–1924)

1857—Bunce, *Love in '76;* Butler, "Nothing
To Wear"; Helper, *Impending Crisis of the South;* Boucicault, *The
Poor of New York;* Trowbridge,
Neighbor Jackwood
Atlantic Monthly (1857–　); *Harper's*

1857—Buchanan's administration (1857–61)
Dred Scott decision
Financial panic
First Otis elevator
Clarence Darrow (1857–1938); Pennell (1857–1926); Taft (1857–1930)

Weekly (1857–1916); *Russell's Magazine* (1857–60)

Gertrude Atherton (1857–1948); Margaret Deland (1857–1945); H.B. Fuller (1857–1929); Veblen (1857–1929)

1858—Longfellow, *Courtship of Miles Standish;* Holmes, *Autocrat of the Breakfast-Table;* O'Brien, "The Diamond Lens"; Taylor, *Our American Cousin;* Allibone, *British and American Authors* (1858–71)

C.W. Chesnutt (1858–1932); Agnes Repplier (1858–1950)

1859—Stowe, *The Minister's Wooing;* Boucicault, *The Octoroon;* Simms, *The Cassique of Kiawah;* "Dixie"; Thackeray, *The Virginians Vanity Fair* (1859–63)

John Dewey (1859–1952)

1860—Hawthorne, *The Marble Faun;* Holmes, *Professor at the Breakfast-Table;* Timrod, *Poems;* Emerson, *Conduct of Life;* Boucicault, *The Colleen Bawn;* Whittier, *Home Ballads;* Tuckerman, *Poems;* Stephens, *Malaeska* (first dime novel)

Huneker (1860–1921); Garland (1860–1940)

1861—Holmes, *Elsie Venner;* Timrod, "Ethnogenesis"; Longfellow, "Paul Revere's Ride"

1862—Browne, *Artemus Ward;* Howe, "Battle Hymn of the Republic"; Davis, *Margaret Howth;* Winthrop, *John Brent;* Stowe, *The Pearl of Orr's Island;* Newell, *The Orpheus C. Kerr Papers* (1862–71)

Edith Wharton (1862–1937); W.S. Porter (1862–1910)

1863—Longfellow, *Tales of a Wayside Inn;* Lincoln, "Gettysburg Address"; Thoreau, *Excursions;* Hawthorne, *Our Old Home;* Hale, "The Man Without a Country"

Santayana (1863–1952); John Fox, Jr. (1863–1919)

1864—Boker, *Poems of the War;* Trowbridge, *Cudjo's Cave;* Halpine, *Pri-*

1858—Lincoln-Douglas debates
First transatlantic cable
Theodore Roosevelt (1858–1919); E.M. House (1858–1938)

1859—Brown's raid on Harpers Ferry
First commercial production of petroleum
Cooper Union founded

1860—Population, 31,443,321
Tweed Ring (c.1860–71)
Pony Express (1860–61)
Crittenden Resolutions; South Carolina secedes
Bryan (1860–1925); Pershing (1860–1948)

1861—Lincoln's administration (1861–65)
Secession of Mississippi, Florida, Alabama, Georgia, Louisiana, Texas, Virginia, Tennessee, Arkansas, and North Carolina; Jefferson Davis president of Confederate States of America; attack on Fort Sumter begins Civil War; first Battle of Bull Run; Trent Affair
Gatling machine gun
Vassar College founded
Alfred North Whitehead (1861–1947)

1862—Lee in command of Confederate army; *Monitor* vs. *Merrimac;* Peninsular campaign; battles of Shiloh, Antietam, second Bull Run; Siege of Vicksburg (1862–63)
Homestead Act
Union and Central Pacific railways chartered
C.E. Hughes (1862–1948)

1863—Battles of Chancellorsville, Gettysburg, and Chattanooga
Emancipation Proclamation
National Banking Act
Henry Ford (1863–1947); W.R. Hearst (1863–1951)

1864—Maximilian's regime in Mexico (1864–67)

vate *Miles O'Reilly;* Locke, *The Nasby Papers*
Richard H. Davis (1864–1916); Richard Hovey (1864–1900); P.E. More (1864–1937)

1865—Whitman, *Drum-Taps;* Clemens, "The Celebrated Jumping Frog"; Thoreau, *Cape Cod;* Parkman, *Pioneers of France in the New World;* Boucicault and Jefferson, *Rip Van Winkle;* Dodge, *Hans Brinker;* Shaw, *Josh Billings*
The Nation (1865–)
Irving Babbitt (1865–1933); P.L. Ford (1865–1902)

1866—Whittier, *Snow-Bound;* Howells, *Venetian Life;* Emerson, "Terminus"; Smith, *Bill Arp;* Cooke, *Surry of Eagle's Nest*
New York *World* (1866–1931); *Galaxy* (1866–78)
George Ade (1866–1944); Steffens (1866–1936)

1867—Harte, *Condensed Novels;* Harris, *Sut Lovingood Yarns;* De Forest, *Miss Ravenel's Conversion;* Longfellow, translation of the *Divine Comedy;* Parkman, *The Jesuits in North America;* Timrod, "Ode"; Daly, *Under the Gaslight;* Evans, *St. Elmo;* Burroughs, *Notes on Walt Whitman;* Whittier, *The Tent on the Beach;* Lowell, *Biglow Papers* (second series); Emerson, *May-Day and Other Poems*
Journal of Speculative Philosophy (1867–93); Radical Club (1867–80); *Oliver Optic's Magazine* (1867–75)
D.G. Phillips (1867–1911)

1868—Harte, "The Luck of Roaring Camp"; Ward, *The Gates Ajar;* Holmes, *The Guardian Angel;* Alcott, *Tablets;* Louisa May Alcott, *Little Women* (1868–69)
Hearth and Home (1868–75); *Lippincott's Magazine* (1868–1916); *Overland Monthly* (1868–1933); *Vanity Fair* (1868–1936)
Mary Austin (1868–1934); W.E.B. DuBois (1868–1963); Robert Herrick (1868–1938); W.A. White (1868–1944); Masters (1868–1950)

1869—Clemens, *Innocents Abroad;* Stowe, *Oldtown Folks;* Harte, "Tennessee's Partner" and "Outcasts of Poker Flat"; Parkman, *La Salle;*

Grant in command of Union army; Sherman's march to the sea; *Alabama* vs. *Kearsarge;* battle of Wilderness, Spotsylvania, and Mobile Bay
First Pullman car
Stieglitz (1864–1946)

1865—Johnson's administration (1865–69)
Lee's surrender at Appomattox ends war
Lincoln assassinated
13th Amendment outlaws slavery
Molly Maguires (1865–67); first Ku Klux Klan organization
Cornell University founded
Harding (1865–1923); Steinmetz (1865–1923)

1866—Civil Rights bill
Grand Army of the Republic
Second Atlantic cable

1867—National Ku Klux Klan
Reconstruction Act; purchase of Alaska
Granger movement
Howard University founded
J.P. Morgan, Jr. (1867–1943)

1868—14th Amendment: rights of citizenship
Johnson impeached, acquitted

1869—Grant's administration (1869–77)
15th Amendment: right to vote
Knights of Labor; Prohibition party
Union Pacific railroad completed

Aldrich, *Story of a Bad Boy;* Lowell, "The Cathedral"
Appleton's Journal (1869–81)
Herbert Croly (1869–1930); Stephen Leacock (1869–1944); W.V. Moody (1869–1910); E.A. Robinson (1869–1935); George Sterling (1869–1926); Tarkington (1869–1946)

1870—Harte, "Plain Language from Truthful James"; Emerson, *Society and Solitude;* Howard, *Saratoga;* Bryant, translation of the *Iliad*
Scribner's Monthly (1870–81)
Frank Norris (1870–1902); Ray S. Baker (1870–1946)

1871—James, "A Passionate Pilgrim"; Burroughs, *Wake-Robin;* Harte, *East and West Poems;* Hay, *Pike County Ballads;* Eggleston, *Hoosier Schoolmaster;* Lowell, *My Study Windows;* Miller, *Songs of the Sierras;* Johnston, *Dukesborough Tales;* Howells, *Their Wedding Journey;* Whitman, *Democratic Vistas* and *Passage to India;* Bryant, translation of the *Odyssey* (1871–72); Furness, *New Variorum Shakespeare* (1871–1913)
Winston Churchill (1871–1947); Stephen Crane (1871–1900); Dreiser (1871–1945)

1872—Clemens, *Roughing It;* Hayne, *Legends and Lyrics;* Stanley, *How I Found Livingstone;* King, *Mountaineering in the Sierra Nevada;* Murdoch and Mayo, *Davy Crockett;* Roe, *Barriers Burned Away;* Holmes, *Poet at the Breakfast-Table*
Congressional Record (1872–   )
P.L. Dunbar (1872–1906)

1873—Howells, *A Chance Acquaintance;* Clemens and Warner, *The Gilded Age;* Aldrich, "Marjorie Daw"; Wallace, *The Fair God;* Timrod, *The Cotton Boll*
Delineator (1873–1937); *St. Nicholas* (1873–1940); *Woman's Home Companion* (1873–1957)
Anne D. Sedgwick (1873–1935); Willa Cather (1873–1947)

1874—Eggleston, *The Circuit Rider;* Fiske, *Outlines of Cosmic Philosophy*
Ellen Glasgow (1874–1945); Charles Beard (1874–1948); Owen Davis (1874–1956); Clarence Day (1874–1935); Zona Gale (1874–1938); Amy Lowell (1874–1925); Gertrude Stein (1874–1946); Frost (1874–1963)

"Black Friday"
C.W. Eliot president of Harvard (1869–1909)
Brady's *National Photographic Collection of War Views*
Frank Lloyd Wright (1869–1959)

1870—Population, 38,818,449
Standard Oil Company founded
Moody and Sankey begin revivalist campaign
Cardozo (1870–1938)

1871—Tweed Ring overthrown
Treaty of Washington
Chicago fire
Smith College founded
Barnum opens circus

1872—Crédit Mobilier scandal (1872–73)
Muybridge's pictures of movement
Coolidge (1872–1933)

1873—Financial panic
Slaughterhouse cases
Nevada silver rush
Alfred E. Smith (1873–1944)

1874—Women's Christian Temperance Union
Massachusetts legalizes ten-hour work day for women
Hoover (1874–1964)

1875—Eddy, *Science and Health;* Howells, *A Foregone Conclusion;* Holland, *Sevenoaks*
Chicago Daily News (1875–1978)
Lambs Club (1875–)

1876—Clemens, *Tom Sawyer;* James, *Roderick Hudson;* Whitman, *Leaves of Grass* (Centennial Edition); Moore, *Sweet Singer of Michigan;* Julian Hawthorne, *Garth;* Melville, *Clarel*
Frank Leslie's Popular Monthly (1876–1906)
Sherwood Anderson (1876–1941); Jack London (1876–1916); Rölvaag (1876–1931)

1877—Jewett, *Deephaven;* James, *The American;* Lanier, *Poems;* Morgan, *Ancient Society;* Burroughs, *Birds and Poets;* Parkman, *Count Frontenac*
Puck (1877–1918)
William Beebe (1877–1962)

1878—James, *Daisy Miller* and *The Europeans;* Eggleston, *Roxy;* Green, *Leavenworth Case;* Lanier, "The Marshes of Glynn"; Tyler, *American Literature, 1607–1765*
Upton Sinclair (1878–1968); Sandburg (1878–1967); Don Marquis (1878–1937)

1879—George, *Progress and Poverty;* Cable, *Old Creole Days;* Tourgée, *A Fool's Errand;* Burroughs, *Locusts and Wild Honey;* Herne and Belasco, *Hearts of Oak;* Stockton, *Rudder Grange;* Howells, *Lady of the Aroostook*
Cabell (1879–1955); Vachel Lindsay (1879–1931); Dorothy Canfield Fisher (1879–1958); Wallace Stevens (1879–1955)

1880—Adams, *Democracy;* Cable, *The Grandissimes;* Wallace, *Ben-Hur;* Aldrich, *Stillwater Tragedy;* Tourgée, *Bricks Without Straw;* Clemens, *A Tramp Abroad;* MacKaye, *Hazel Kirke*
The Dial (1880–1929)
Sholem Asch (1880–1957); Hergesheimer (1880–1954); Mencken (1880–1956); Julia Peterkin (1880–1961); Ernest Poole (1880–1950); Van Vechten (1880–1964); Channing Pollock (1880–1946)

1881—James, *Washington Square* and *The Portrait of a Lady;* Harris, *Uncle Remus;* Lothrop, *Five Little Peppers*
Century (1881–1930); *Judge* (1881–1939)

1875—Greenback party
Brigham Young University founded
Arbor Day

1876—Bell telephone; barbed wire
Battle of Little Big Horn
Centennial Exposition
Johns Hopkins opened
University of Texas founded
Socialist-Labor party
Disputed election of Tilden and Hayes

1877—Hayes's administration (1877–81)
End of Reconstruction
Chief Joseph's revolt
Railroad and coal strikes
Edison's phonograph

1878—"Solid South"
Bland-Allison silver act
Arc light
Isadora Duncan (1878–1927)

1879—Edison's incandescent lamp
First Madison Square Garden
Chicago Art Institute founded

1880—Population, 50,155,783
Bryn Mawr College founded

1881—Garfield's administration (1881); Arthur's administration (1881–85)
Greely's Arctic expedition (1881–83)
Standard Oil incorporated
American Federation of Labor

Literary History	Social History
William McFee (1881–1966); Neihardt (1881–1973); Stribling (1881–1965)	Tuskegee Institute founded
1882—Clemens, *Prince and the Pauper;* Crawford, *Mr. Isaacs;* Stockton, "The Lady or the Tiger?"; Howard, *Young Mrs. Winthrop;* Whitman, *Specimen Days and Collect;* Howells, *A Modern Instance* Susan Glaspell (1882–1948); G.J. Nathan (1882–1958)	1882—Immigration of Chinese labor suspended Knights of Columbus W.H. Vanderbilt: "The public be damned" Jesse James shot to death F.D. Roosevelt (1882–1945); Frankfurter (1882–1965)
1883—Clemens, *Life on the Mississippi;* Howe, *Story of a Country Town;* James, *Siege of London;* Stevenson, *Silverado Squatters;* Riley, *Old Swimmin'-Hole;* Peck, *Peck's Bad Boy;* Rives, *Quick or the Dead?;* Grant, *An Average Man;* Wilcox, *Poems of Passion;* Eggleston, *Hoosier Schoolboy* *Ladies' Home Journal* (1883–); *Life* (1883–1936) Max Eastman (1883–1969)	1883—Civil Service Reform Act Brooklyn Bridge completed New steel navy begun Maxim machine gun Pulitzer buys the New York *World* Metropolitan Opera founded
1884—Clemens, *Huckleberry Finn;* Murfree, *In the Tennessee Mountains;* Parkman, *Montcalm and Wolfe;* Harris, *Mingo;* Jackson, *Ramona;* Jewett, *A Country Doctor;* Lowell, "On Democracy"; Hay, *Bread-Winners* Damon Runyon (1884–1946); Sara Teasdale (1884–1933)	1884—National Bureau of Labor "Mugwumps" "Rum, Romanism, and Rebellion" Norman Thomas (1884–1969) Truman (1884–1972)
1885—Howells, *Rise of Silas Lapham;* Janvier, *Color Studies;* Keenan, *Money-Makers;* Royce, *Religious Aspect of Philosophy;* Grant, *Personal Memoirs* (1885–86) DuBose Heyward (1885–1940); Lardner (1885–1933); Sinclair Lewis (1885–1951); Ezra Pound (1885–1972); Elinor Wylie (1885–1928)	1885—Cleveland's first administration (1885–89) Statue of Liberty; Washington Monument dedicated Stanford University founded
1886—James, *The Bostonians* and *The Princess Casamassima;* Jewett, *A White Heron;* Burnett, *Little Lord Fauntleroy;* Grady, "The New South"; Howells, *Indian Summer;* Carnegie, *Triumphant Democracy;* Thompson, *The Old Homestead* *Cosmopolitan* (1886–); *Forum* (1886–1950) Van Wyck Brooks (1886–1963); Elizabeth M. Roberts (1886–1941)	1886—Haymarket Riot Mergenthaler linotype first used Presidential succession law Statue of Liberty dedicated Last major war with Indians ends with Geronimo's capture Sears Roebuck founded Coca-Cola put on sale
1887—Page, *In Ole Virginia;* Howard, *The Henrietta;* Kirkland, *Zury;* French, *Knitters in the Sun;* Freeman, *A Humble Romance;* Wiggin, *Birds' Christmas Carol;* Crawford, *Saracinesca;* Frederic, *Seth's Brother's Wife;* Robinson, *Uncle Lisha's Shop*	1887—Interstate Commerce Act First electric streetcar First U.S. social register

Scribner's Magazine (1887–1939)
Floyd Dell (1887–1969); Edna Ferber
(1887–1968); Jeffers (1887–1962);
John Reed (1887–1920)

1888—Whitman, *November Boughs;* Bellamy, *Looking Backward;* Howard,
Shenandoah; Lowell, *Political Essays;* Bryce, *American Commonwealth;* James, *Aspern Papers;* Conwell, *Acres of Diamonds;* Whitman,
Complete Poems and Prose (1888–
89); Stedman, *Library of American
Literature* (1888–90)
Collier's (1888–1957); American
Folk-Lore Society (1888–   )
T.S. Eliot (1888–1965); O'Neill
(1888–1953); Maxwell Anderson
(1888–1959)

1888—Department of Labor
National Geographic founded
Irving Berlin (1888–   )

1889—Howells, *Annie Kilburn;* Field, *A
Little Book of Western Verse;* Cle-
mens, *A Connecticut Yankee;* Car-
negie, *Gospel of Wealth;* Hearn,
Chita; Smith, *A White Umbrella in
Mexico;* Adams, *History of the
United States* (1889–91); Roosevelt,
Winning of the West (1889–96)
Munsey's (1889–1929)
Conrad Aiken (1889–1973); Hervey
Allen (1889–1949); Waldo Frank
(1889–1967); George S. Kaufman
(1889–1961)

1889—Harrison's administration (1889–93)
Australian ballot system adopted in
ten states
Department of Agriculture
Barnard College founded
Oklahoma opened for settlement
Johnstown flood
First Pan-American Congress
Samoan treaty

1890—Dickinson, *Poems;* William James,
Principles of Psychology; Riis, *How
the Other Half Lives;* Mahan, *Influ-
ence of Sea Power;* Nicolay and
Hay, *Abraham Lincoln;* Howells, *A
Hazard of New Fortunes;* Hearn,
Youma; James, *The Tragic Muse;*
Woodberry, *Poems*
Literary Digest (1890–1938); *Smart
Set* (1890–1930)
Marc Connelly (1890–1980); Chris-
topher Morley (1890–1957); Kath-
erine Anne Porter (1890–1980);
Conrad Richter (1890–1968)

1890—Population, 62,947,714
Sherman Anti-Trust and Silver Pur-
chase acts
Nelly Bly completes 72-day tour of the
world
Daughters of the American Revolu-
tion organized
New Madison Square Garden
Dwight D. Eisenhower (1890–1969)

1891—Bierce, *Tales of Soldiers and Civilians;*
Garland, *Main-Travelled Roads;*
Howells, *Criticism and Fiction;*
Freeman, *A New England Nun;*
Smith, *Colonel Carter of Carters-
ville,* Dickinson, *Poems: Second
Series;* Fiske, *The American Revolu-
tion;* Cooke, *Huckleberries
Gathered from New England Hills;*
Allen, *Flute and Violin;* Hoyt, *A
Trip to Chinatown;* Norton, transla-
tion of *Divine Comedy* (1891–92)
First international copyright law
Review of Reviews (1891–1937)

1891—Forest Reserve Act (beginning of con-
servation movement)
Populist party
Basketball game invented
Thomas's Chicago Orchestra (1891–
1905)

Sidney Howard (1891–1939); Henry Miller (1891–1980)	
1892—Herne, *Shore Acres;* Page, *The Old South* *Sewanee Review* (1892–1973) Pearl Buck (1892–1973); MacLeish (1892–1982); Edna St. Vincent Millay (1892–1950); Elmer Rice (1892–1967); R.P.T. Coffin (1892–1955)	1892—Coeur d'Alene and Homestead strikes Ellis Island becomes immigrant station Lizzie Borden case Ward McCallister: "The Four Hundred" University of Chicago founded Wendell Willkie (1892–1944)
1893—Fuller, *The Cliff-Dwellers;* Crane, *Maggie;* Turner, "Significance of the Frontier" *McClure's Magazine* (1893–1929); *Outlook* (1893–1915) Dorothy Parker (1893–1967); S.N. Behrman (1893–1973)	1893—Cleveland's second administration (1893–97) Gold Panic Chicago World Fair Anti-Saloon League Treaty of annexation of Hawaii signed, then withdrawn Huey Long (1893–1935)
1894—Carman and Hovey, *Songs from Vagabondia;* Muir, *Mountains of California;* Clemens, *Pudd'nhead Wilson;* Santayana, *Sonnets;* Warner, *Golden House;* Allen, *Kentucky Cardinal;* Chopin, *Bayou Folk;* Tabb, *Poems;* Ford, *Honorable Peter Stirling;* Howells, *A Traveler from Altruria* *Chap Book* (1894–98) E.E. Cummings (1894–1962); Paul Green (1894–1981); Robert Nathan (1894–); James Thurber (1894–1961)	1894—Coxey's army; Pullman, coal, and American Railway Union strikes U.S. recognizes Republic of Hawaii First U.S. open golf tournament
1895—Crane, *Red Badge of Courage* and *Black Riders;* Gillette, *Secret Service;* Mitchell, *Amos Judd;* Garland, *Rose of Dutcher's Coolly;* Fuller, *With the Procession;* Bates, "America the Beautiful" *Bookman* (1895–1933); White's Emporia *Gazette* (1895–); *Collier's Weekly* (1895–1957) Vardis Fisher (1895–1968); Edmund Wilson (1895–1972)	1895—Cuban rebellion; Venezuela affair Income Tax Law declared unconstitutional New York Public Library
1896—Clemens, *Joan of Arc;* Dickinson, *Poems: Third Series;* Jewett, *Country of the Pointed Firs;* Robinson, *Torrent and the Night Before;* Van Dyke, *Story of the Other Wise Man;* Santayana, *The Sense of Beauty;* Bangs, *Houseboat on the Styx;* Frederic, *Damnation of Theron Ware;* Parker, *Seats of the Mighty;* Patten, first of the "Frank Merriwell" books; Sheldon, *In His Steps* Philip Barry (1896–1949); Bromfield (1896–1956); Dos Passos (1896–1970); Fitzgerald (1896–1940); Sherwood (1896–1955)	1896—Klondike gold rush (1896ff.) Bryan's "Cross of Gold" speech Rural free delivery Edison introduces motion pictures in U.S. Princeton University given present name

1897—James, *What Maisie Knew* and *The Spoils of Poynton;* Allen, *The Choir Invisible;* Mitchell, *Hugh Wynne;* Kipling, *Captains Courageous;* Davis, *Soldiers of Fortune;* Freeman, *Jerome;* Lewis, *Wolfville;* Robinson, *Children of the Night;* Tyler, *Literary History of the American Revolution;* William James, *The Will To Believe*
   Survey Graphic (1897–1944)
   Faulkner (1897–1962); Thornton Wilder (1897–1975); Lillian Smith (1897–1967)

1897—McKinley's administration (1897–1901)
   Sousa, "The Stars and Stripes Forever"
   Library of Congress building

1898—Dunne, *Mr. Dooley in Peace and War;* Rosenfeld, *Songs from the Ghetto;* Crane, *The Open Boat;* Johnston, *Prisoners of Hope;* Westcott, *David Harum;* Major, *When Knighthood Was in Flower;* Mitchell, *Adventures of François;* James, "Turn of the Screw"
   Stephen Benét (1898–1943); Hemingway (1898–1961)

1898—Spanish-American War; *Maine* incident; Battle of Manila Bay; Treaty of Paris
   Annexation of Hawaii
   Uniform Bankruptcy law
   Gershwin (1898–1937)

1899—Crane, *The Monster* and *War Is Kind;* Gillette, *Sherlock Holmes;* Ade, *Fables in Slang;* Markham, "The Man with the Hoe"; Hubbard, *Message to Garcia;* Norris, *McTeague;* Churchill, *Richard Carvel;* Veblen, *Theory of the Leisure Class;* Ford, *Janice Meredith;* James, *The Awkward Age;* Chesnutt, *The Conjure Woman;* Tarkington, *Gentleman from Indiana*
   Everybody's (1899–1928); *Pearson's* (1899–1925); *American Boy* (1899–1941)
   Hart Crane (1899–1932); Vincent Sheean (1899–1975); E.B. White (1899–)

1899—Philippine insurrection (1899–1902)
   First Hague conference
   "Open Door" policy in China
   United Mine Workers organized
   Carnegie Steel Company created

1900—London, *Son of the Wolf;* Roosevelt, *The Strenuous Life;* Crane, *Whilomville Stories;* Grant, *Unleavened Bread;* Dreiser, *Sister Carrie;* Belasco and Long, *Madame Butterfly;* Bacheller, *Eben Holden;* Thompson, *Alice of Old Vincennes;* Johnston, *To Have and To Hold;* Tarkington, *Monsieur Beaucaire;* Stedman, *An American Anthology;* Howells, *Literary Friends and Acquaintances;* Wendell, *Literary History of America;* Baum, *Wonderful Wizard of Oz;* Royce, *The World and the Individual* (1900–1901)
   World's Work (1900–1932); *Who's Who in America* (1900–)
   Thomas Wolfe (1900–1938); V.F. Calverton (1900–1940)

1900—Population, 75,994,575
   Galveston tornado
   Socialist party
   College Entrance Aptitude Tests
   Carnegie Institute of Technology
   First U.S. national automobile show
   Aaron Copland (1900–); Helen Hayes (1900–)

1901—Norris, *The Octopus;* Moody, *Poems;* Fitch, *The Climbers;* Churchill, *The Crisis;* McCutcheon, *Graustark;* Rice, *Mrs. Wiggs of the Cabbage Patch;* Riis, *Making of an American;* James, *Sacred Fount;* Washington, *Up from Slavery;* Muir, *Our National Parks*
    Granville Hicks (1901–82); Glenway Wescott (1901–)

1902—Robinson, *Captain Craig;* William James, *Varieties of Religious Experience;* Riis, *The Battle with the Slum;* Wilson, *History of the American People;* Wister, *The Virginian;* James, *Wings of the Dove;* Fitch, *Girl with the Green Eyes;* Wharton, *Valley of Decision;* Glasgow, *The Battle Ground;* White, *The Blazed Trail;* Davis, *Ranson's Folly*
    South Atlantic Quarterly (1902–)
    Langston Hughes (1902–67); Steinbeck (1902–67); Ogden Nash (1902–71)

1903—London, *Call of the Wild;* Norris, *The Pit;* Adams, *Log of a Cowboy;* Austin, *Land of Little Rain;* DuBois, *Souls of Black Folk;* James, *The Ambassadors;* Wiggin, *Rebecca of Sunnybrook Farm;* Trent, *History of American Literature;* Woodberry, *America in Literature;* Sterling, *Testimony of the Suns;* Fox, *Little Shepherd of Kingdom Come*
    Kay Boyle (1903–); Erskine Caldwell (1903–); James Gould Cozzens (1903–78); Countee Cullen (1903–46); Nathanael West (1903–40)

1904—James, *The Golden Bowl;* London, *The Sea-Wolf;* Cabell, *The Eagle's Shadow;* Tarbell, *History of the Standard Oil Company;* Porter, *Cabbages and Kings;* Stratton-Porter, *Freckles;* Steffens, *Shame of the Cities;* Belasco, *Girl of the Golden West;* Glasgow, *Deliverance;* Churchill, *The Crossing;* Howells, *Son of Royal Langbrith;* More, *Shelburne Essays* (1904–35); Adams, *Mont-Saint-Michel and Chartres*
    American Academy of Arts and Letters (1904–)
    James T. Farrell (1904–79); Louis Zukofsky (1904–78)

1905—De Leon, *Socialist Reconstruction of Society;* London, *War of the Classes;* Dixon, *The Clansman;* Austin, *Isidro;* Wharton, *House of Mirth;*

1901—Theodore Roosevelt's administration (1901–9)
    Hay-Pauncefote Treaty (Panama Canal)
    Northern Pacific panic
    First transatlantic radio
    Consolidation of U.S. Steel Corporation and of Union, Central, and Southern Pacific railroads

1902—Reclamation Act; Isthmian Canal Act
    Anthracite coal strike
    Maryland enacts first state workmen's compensation law; Oregon adopts first state initiative and referendum laws
    Lindberg (1902–74)

1903—Department of Commerce and Labor
    Wisconsin enacts first state direct primary law
    Postal scandal
    Pacific cable from San Francisco to Manila
    Revolt of Panama from Colombia; independence of Panama recognized by U.S.
    Wright brothers' airplane
    Rhodes Scholarships

1904—Pacific cable completed; Panama Canal begun
    Northern Securities case
    Chicago meat packers strike

1905—Insurance companies investigated
    Rotary clubs; I.W.W.

Royle, *Squaw Man;* Santayana, *Life of Reason* (1905–6)
Variety (1905–   )
Harvard's 47 Workshop
Jesse Stuart (1905–   ); R.P. Warren (1905–   ); Lillian Hellman (1905–84)

1906—Austin, *The Flock;* Porter, *The Four Million;* Sinclair, *The Jungle;* Mitchell, *The New York Idea;* Churchill, *Coniston;* Deland, *Awakening of Helena Ritchie;* Traubel, *With Walt Whitman in Camden* (1906–82)
Clifford Odets (1906–63)

1906—San Francisco earthquake and fire
Pure Food and Drug Act; Meat Inspection Act
Helicon Home Colony (1906–7)

1907—*Education of Henry Adams;* Sumner, *Folkways;* James, *The American Scene;* William James, *Pragmatism;* Porter, *Trimmed Lamp;* Fitch, *The Truth;* Thomas, *Witching Hour;* Wharton, *Madame de Treymes;* Jesse Stuart (1907–84); Jessamyn West (1907–84)

1907—Second Hague Conference
Georgia and Alabama adopt prohibition
First Ziegfeld Follies
De Forest's vacuum tube

1908—Herrick, *Together* and *Master of the Inn;* Royce, *Philosophy of Loyalty;* Fox, *Trail of the Lonesome Pine;* Gale, *Friendship Village;* MacKaye, *The Scarecrow;* London, *The Iron Heel*
Paul Engle (1908–   ); Theodore Roethke (1908–63); Saroyan (1908–81); Richard Wright (1908–60)

1908—"Gentlemen's agreement" with Japan restricts immigration
Lyndon B. Johnson (1908–73)

1909—Stein, *Three Lives;* Croly, *The Promise of American Life;* White, *A Certain Rich Man;* Crothers, *A Man's World;* Porter, *Roads of Destiny;* Stratton-Porter, *Girl of the Limberlost;* London, *Martin Eden;* Moody, *Great Divide* and *Faith Healer;* Pound, *Personae;* Sheldon, *The Nigger*
James Agee (1909–55); Wallace Stegner (1909–   ); Eudora Welty (1909–   )

1909—Taft's administration (1909–13)
Peary's last North Pole expedition
Rise of "Progressive" movement
"Dollar diplomacy"
Model T Ford marks first mass production of automobiles

1910—Robinson, *Town Down the River;* Myers, *History of the Great American Fortunes;* Peabody, *The Piper;* Lomax, *Cowboy Songs;* Addams, *Twenty Years at Hull-House;* Harvard Classics; Huneker, *Promenades of an Impressionist*
Peter De Vries (1910–   )

1910—Population, 91,972,266
First long-distance flight, from Albany to New York City
NAACP founded
Boy Scouts of America founded

1911—Dreiser, *Jennie Gerhardt;* Wharton, *Ethan Frome;* Belasco, *Return of Peter Grimm;* Spingarn, *The New Criticism;* Sheldon, *The Boss;* Wright, *Winning of Barbara Worth;* Harrison, *Queed;* Bierce, *Devil's Dictionary;* Johnston, *Long Roll;* Sedgwick, *Tante*
Masses, later *New Masses* (1911–53)

1911—La Follette forms National Republic Progressive League
Standard Oil and American Tobacco trusts dissolved
First flight across U.S. (68 landings during 49 days)

1912—Johnson, *Autobiography of an Ex-Colored Man;* Dreiser, *The Financier;* Antin, *Promised Land;* Grey, *Riders of the Purple Sage;* Millay, "Renascence"; London, *Smoke Bellew;* Lowell, *Dome of Many-Coloured Glass*
Poetry: A Magizine of Verse (1912–)
John Cheever (1912–82); William Everson (1912–)

1913—Cather, *O Pioneers!;* Frost, *A Boy's Will;* Wilson, *The New Freedom;* Sheldon, *Romance;* Glasgow, *Virginia;* Beard, *Economic Interpretation of the Constitution;* London, *Valley of the Moon;* Lindsay, *General William Booth Enters into Heaven;* Churchill, *Inside of the Cup;* Eastman, *Enjoyment of Poetry;* Herrick, *One Woman's Life;* James, *A Small Boy and Others;* Macy, *Spirit of American Literature*
Reedy's Mirror (1913–20)
Karl Shapiro (1913–)

1914—Dickinson, *Single Hound;* Ficke, *Sonnets of a Portrait Painter;* Frost, *North of Boston;* Lowell, *Sword Blades and Poppy Seed;* Tarkington, *Penrod;* Oppenheim, *Songs for the New Age;* Brandeis, *Other People's Money;* Lindsay, *The Congo;* Herrick, *Clark's Field;* Giovannitti, *Arrows in the Gale*
New Republic (1914–); *Little Review* (1914–29)
Ralph Ellison (1914–); Howard Fast (1914–); Hersey (1914–); Malamud (1914–); Irwin Shaw (1914–); Tennessee Williams (1914–); John Berryman (1914–72)

1915—Widdemer, *Factories;* Brooks, *America's Coming-of-Age; Some Imagist Poets;* Masters, *Spoon River Anthology;* Teasdale, *Rivers to the Sea;* Dreiser, *The "Genius";* Poole, *The Harbor;* Neihardt, *Song of Hugh Glass;* Cather, *Song of the Lark;* Pattee, *History of American Literature Since 1870*
Provincetown and Washington Square Players
Saul Bellow (1915–); Alfred Kazin (1915–); Herman Wouk (1915–)

1916—Frost, *Mountain Interval;* Sandburg, *Chicago Poems;* Clemens, *Mysterious Stranger;* Tarkington, *Seventeen;* Robinson, *Man Against the Sky;* McFee, *Casuals of the Sea;*

1912—Progressive party (1912–46)
Massachusetts establishes first minimum wage for women and children
Stokowski leader of Philadelphia Orchestra (1912–36)

1913—Wilson's administration (1913–21)
16th and 17th Amendments; Federal Reserve Bank Act; Parcel Post system; Department of Labor
Armory Show of modern art
Ludlow strike (1913–14)
Richard Nixon (1913–)

1914—Panama Canal opened
Financial crisis
Federal Trade Commission; Clayton Anti-Trust Act
U.S. fleet in Vera Cruz; protest against British interference with American shipping
Kiwanis clubs

1915—*Lusitania* sunk; Ford's "Peace Ship"
Wilson: "Too proud to fight"
1,000,000th Ford auto
Widener Library opened at Harvard
Revival of Ku Klux Klan

1916—American punitive expedition in Mexico
U.S. Shipping Board; Federal Farm Loan Bank Act; 17th Amendment:

Lowell, *Men, Women and Ghosts;* O'Neill, *Bound East for Cardiff;* Dewey, *Democracy and Education;* Wharton, *Xingu;* Bynner and Ficke, *Spectra;* Glasgow, *Life and Gabriella;* Lardner, *You Know Me, Al* Seven Arts (1916–17); *Theatre Arts Magazine* (1916–64) Walker Percy (1916–)	San Francisco Preparedness Day bombing

1917—Eliot, *Prufrock;* Garland, *Son of the Middle Border;* Teasdale, *Love Songs;* Robinson, *Merlin;* Moeller, *Madame Sand;* Morley, *Parnassus on Wheels;* Cabell, *Cream of the Jest;* Williams, *Why Marry?;* Lindsay, *Chinese Nightingale;* Austin, *The Ford;* Hergesheimer, *Three Black Pennys;* Phillips, *Susan Lenox;* Poole, *His Family;* Smith, *Trivia; Cambridge History of American Literature* (1917–20)
Pulitzer Prizes (1917–)
The Dial (1917–29)
Gwendolyn Brooks (1917–); Carson McCullers (1917–67); Robert Lowell (1917–77)

1917—Germans renew unrestricted submarine warfare; U.S. enters World War I; draft; AEF in France; Espionage Act; War Industries Board; food production and control bills; government control of railroads
Prohibition amendment submitted to states
Lansing-Ishii Agreement
Rosenwald Fund
Lions clubs
John F. Kennedy (1917–63)

1918—Sandburg, *Cornhuskers;* Gale, *Birth;* Wharton, *The Marne;* Tarkington, *Magnificent Ambersons;* O'Neill, *Moon of the Caribbees;* Beebe, *Jungle Peace;* Ridge, *The Ghetto;* Smith and Bacon, *Lightnin';* Streeter, *Dere Mable!;* Cather, *My Ántonia; I.W.W. Songs;* Perry, *American Spirit in Literature*
Theatre Guild (1918–); Carolina Playmakers (1918–)

1918—Battles of Belleau Wood and Château-Thierry; Argonne and St. Mihiel offensives; second Battle of the Marne
"Fourteen points"; armistice; Wilson at peace conference

1919—Anderson, *Winesburg, Ohio;* Mencken, *The American Language;* Veblen, *Higher Learning in America;* Moeller, *Molière* and *Sophie;* Reed, *Ten Days That Shook the World;* Frank, *Our America;* Untermeyer, *Modern American Poetry;* Cabell, *Jurgen* and *Beyond Life;* Hergesheimer, *Linda Condon;* O'Brien, *White Shadows in the South Seas;* Mencken, *Prejudices* (1919–27)

1919—Treaty of Versailles (not signed by U.S.)
18th Amendment: prohibition of liquor; Volstead Act
Steel strike; National Industrial Conference
American Legion; Communist party

1920—Eliot, *Poems;* Lewis, *Main Street;* Sandburg, *Smoke and Steel;* Huneker, *Painted Veils;* Wharton, *Age of Innocence;* Robinson, *Lancelot;* Brooks, *Ordeal of Mark Twain;* Gale, *Miss Lulu Bett;* O'Neill, *Emperor Jones* and *Beyond the Horizon;* Anderson, *Poor White;* Dell, *Moon-Calf;* Sinclair, *The Brass Check;* Millay, *A Few Figs from*

1920—Population, 105,710,620
19th Amendment: woman suffrage
Transcontinental airmail; first commercial radio broadcasting
Transportation, Merchant Marine, and Water-Power acts
Socialists poll 919,799 votes in presidential election

Thistles; Fitzgerald, *This Side of Paradise;* Yezierska, *Hungry Hearts*
Frontier (1920–39)

1921—Dos Passos, *Three Soldiers;* O'Neill, "Anna Christie"; Robinson, *Collected Poems;* Tarkington, *Alice Adams;* Davis, *The Detour;* McFee, *Harbours of Memory;* Marquis, *The Old Soak;* Anderson, *Triumph of the Egg;* Adams, *Founding of New England;* Hecht, *Erik Dorn;* Donn-Byrne, *Messer Marco Polo;* Cabell, *Figures of Earth;* Wylie, *Nets To Catch the Wind;* Kaufman and Connelly, *Dulcy;* C. Van Doren, *The American Novel*
Richard Wilbur (1921–   )

1922—Eliot, *The Waste Land;* Lewis, *Babbitt;* Cummings, *The Enormous Room;* Santayana, *Soliloquies in England;* Van Vechten, *Peter Whiffle;* Quick, *Vandemark's Folly;* Cather, *One of Ours; Civilization in the United States;* Sedgwick, *Adrienne Toner;* Colton, *Rain;* O'Neill, "The Hairy Ape"; Lowell, *Critical Fable;* Hough, *Covered Wagon;* Pound, *American Songs and Ballads*
Secession (1922–24); *The Fugitive* (1922–25); *Reader's Digest* (1922–)
Kurt Vonnegut (1922–   )

1923—Millay, *Harp-Weaver;* Cather, *A Lost Lady;* Davis, *Icebound;* Leonard, *Two Lives;* Sinclair, *Goose Step;* Bradford, *Damaged Souls;* Wylie, *Black Armour* and *Jennifer Lorn;* Frost, *New Hampshire;* Atherton, *Black Oxen;* Rice, *Adding Machine;* Stevens, *Harmonium;* D.H. Lawrence, *Studies in Classic American Literature;* Quinn, *History of American Drama* (1923–27); Santayana, *Realms of Being* (1923–40)
Time (1923–   )
Norman Mailer (1923–   ); James Purdy (1923–   )

1924—Jeffers, *Tamar;* Lardner, *How To Write Short Stories;* Seldes, *Seven Lively Arts;* Anderson, *Story Teller's Story;* Dickinson, *Complete Poems;* Clemens, *Autobiography;* O'Neill, *All God's Chillun* and *Desire Under the Elms;* Anderson and Stallings, *What Price Glory?;* Kaufman and Connelly, *Beggar on Horseback;* Howard, *They Knew What They Wanted;* Melville, *Billy Budd;* Bromfield, *Green Bay Tree;*

1921—Harding's administration (1921–23)
Industrial depression (nearly 6,000,000 unemployed)
Emergency Tariff Act; immigration quotas
First Sacco-Vanzetti trial
Separate peace with Germany; Washington Armament Limitation Conference

1922—Coal and railway strikes
Fordney-McCumber tariff, higher than any before
Nine-Power Treaty concerning China
First one-day coast-to-coast flight

1923—Coolidge's administration (1923–29)
Minimum wage law held unconstitutional
Teapot Dome scandal (1923–24)

1924—Industrial depression
Soldiers' bonus passed over veto; new immigration quotas, with exclusion of Japanese; child labor amendment submitted
Second Progressive party
London reparations conference ("Dawes Plan")

Hemingway, *in our time;* Wharton, "Old New York"; Sedgwick, *Little French Girl*

James Baldwin (1924–   ); Truman Capote (1924–84)

1925—Dos Passos, *Manhattan Transfer;* Anderson, *Dark Laughter;* Dreiser, *An American Tragedy;* Lewis, *Arrowsmith;* Cather, *Professor's House;* Heyward, *Porgy;* Kelly, *Craig's Wife;* Glasgow, *Barren Ground;* H.D., *Collected Poems;* Boyd, *Drums;* Fitzgerald, *The Great Gatsby;* Jeffers, *Roan Stallion;* Neihardt, *Song of the Indian Wars;* Loos, *Gentlemen Prefer Blondes;* Green, *In Abraham's Bosom;* Sullivan, *Our Times* (1926–36); Pound, *Cantos* (1925–70)

American Speech (1925–   ); *New Yorker* (1925–   )

Guggenheim Fellowships (1925–   )

John Hawkes (1925–   ); William Styron (1925–   ); Gore Vidal (1925–   )

1926—Hemingway, *The Sun Also Rises;* Sandburg, *Abraham Lincoln: The Prairie Years;* O'Neill, *The Great God Brown;* Hughes, *The Weary Blues;* Van Vechten, *Nigger Heaven;* Parker, *Enough Rope;* Stribling, *Teeftallow;* Roberts, *Time of Man;* Cabell, *Silver Stallion;* Howard, *Silver Cord;* Beer, *Mauve Decade;* De Kruif, *Microbe Hunters;* Faulkner, *Soldiers' Pay*

Book-of-the-Month Club founded

Allen Ginsberg (1926–   )

1927—Robinson, *Tristram;* Sinclair, *Oil!;* Cather, *Death Comes for the Archbishop;* Peterkin, *Black April;* Aiken, *Blue Voyage;* Rourke, *Trumpets of Jubilee;* Marquis, *archy and mehitabel;* Wescott, *The Grandmothers;* Rölvaag, *Giants in the Earth;* Sandburg, *American Songbag;* Parrington, *Main Currents in American Thought* (vols. I, II); Beard, *Rise of American Civilization;* Wilder, *Bridge of San Luis Rey;* Hemingway, *Men Without Women;* O'Neill, *Marco Millions*

Hound and Horn (1927–34); *American Caravan* (1927–36); *transition* (1927–38)

Literary Guild founded

John Ashbery (1927–   )

1928—O'Neill, *Strange Interlude;* MacLeish, *Hamlet of A. MacLeish;* Benét,

1925—Scopes trial

Trinity College becomes Duke University

U.S. initiates air freight service

Standard Oil Co. adopts eight-hour day

1926—Transatlantic wireless telephone

Byrd flies over North Pole

Army Air Corps created

1927—Lindbergh flight, New York to Paris

Transatlantic telephone

Sacco and Vanzetti executed

U.S. Marines in Nicaragua (1927–33)

1928—Pan-American Conference; Kellogg Pact to outlaw war

John Brown's Body; Sandburg, *Good Morning, America;* Sinclair, *Boston;* Peterkin, *Scarlet Sister Mary;* Frost, *West-Running Brook;* Bradford, *Ol' Man Adam an' His Chillun;* Foerster, *American Criticism;* Whipple, *Spokesmen; Dictionary of American Biography* (1928–36) *American Literature* (1928–) Edward Albee (1928–)	First Byrd explorations of Antarctica from Little America Talking pictures; first Mickey Mouse cartoon
1929—Hemingway, *Farewell to Arms;* Krutch, *Modern Temper;* Wolfe, *Look Homeward, Angel;* Faulkner, *Sound and the Fury;* Frank, *Re-Discovery of America;* Aiken, *Selected Poems;* Lewis, *Dodsworth;* Rölvaag, *Peder Victorious;* Rice, *Street Scene;* La Farge, *Laughing Boy;* Lynd, *Middletown;* Lippmann, *Preface to Morals;* Glasgow, *They Stooped to Folly* John Hollander (1929–)	1929—Hoover's administration (1929–33) Stock market collapse begins Depression; Gastonia strike; Agricultural Marketing Act Byrd flies over South Pole Museum of Modern Art founded Martin Luther King, Jr. (1929–68)
1930—Eliot, *Ash-Wednesday;* Crane, *The Bridge;* Faulkner, *As I Lay Dying;* MacLeish, *New Found Land; I'll Take My Stand; Humanism and America;* Connelly, *Green Pastures;* Gold, *Jews Without Money;* Barry, *Hotel Universe;* Glaspell, *Alison's House;* Dos Passos, *42nd Parallel;* Roberts, *Great Meadow;* Gregory, *Chelsea Rooming House;* Porter, *Flowering Judas;* Roberts, *Arundel;* Mott, *History of American Magazines* (1930–38); *Encyclopaedia of the Social Sciences* (1930–35) Lewis receives Nobel Prize *Fortune* (1930–) John Barth (1930–); Gary Snyder (1930–)	1930—Population, 122,775,046 London Naval Treaty; Smoot-Hawley high tariff Institute for Advanced Study (Princeton) First supermarket
1931—O'Neill, *Mourning Becomes Electra;* Steffens, *Autobiography;* Cather, *Shadows on the Rock;* Wilson, *Axel's Castle;* Stribling, *The Forge;* Aiken, *Preludes for Memnon;* Allen, *Only Yesterday;* Buck, *Good Earth;* Rölvaag, *Their Fathers' God;* Kaufman and Ryskind, *Of Thee I Sing;* Faulkner, *Sanctuary;* Riggs, *Green Grow the Lilacs;* Canby, *Classic Americans* *Story* (1931–53) Group Theatre (1931–41) Tom Wolfe (1931–)	1931—Debt and reparations moratorium; Norris Anti-Injunction Act Ford's 20-millionth automobile First Scottsboro trial
1932—Caldwell, *Tobacco Road;* Farrell, *Young Lonigan;* Glasgow, *Sheltered Life;* Austin, *Earth Horizon;* Calverton, *Liberation of American Lit-*	1932—Reconstruction Finance Corporation War veterans' bonus march on Washington St. Lawrence Waterway Treaty signed

erature; MacLeish, *Conquistador;*
De Voto, *Mark Twain's America;*
Dos Passos, *1919;* Fisher, *In Tragic
Life;* Anderson, *Night Over Taos;*
Nordhoff and Hall, *Mutiny on the
Bounty;* Jeffers, *Thurso's Landing;*
Faulkner, *Light in August;* Stong,
State Fair
Common Sense (1932–46)
John Updike (1932–   ); Robert
Coover (1932–   )

1933—Stein, *Autobiography of Alice B. Tok-
las;* Caldwell, *God's Little Acre;*
Allen, *Anthony Adverse;* O'Neill,
Ah, Wilderness!; Hicks, *Great Tra-
dition;* MacLeish, *Frescoes;*
Hemingway, *Winner Take Nothing;*
Howard, *Alien Corn;* Kingsley, *Men
in White;* Nathan, *One More Spring;*
Robinson, *Talifer;* Kirkland and
Caldwell, *Tobacco Road* (1933–41)
Philip Roth (1933–   ); John Gardner
(1933–82)

1934—Saroyan, *Daring Young Man on the
Flying Trapeze;* Adamic, *Native's
Return;* Fitzgerald, *Tender Is the
Night;* Cantwell, *Land of Plenty;*
Hellman, *Children's Hour;* Sher-
wood, *Petrified Forest;* Farrell, *Yo-
ung Manhood of Studs Lonigan;*
Suckow, *The Folks;* Anderson,
Valley Forge; Millay, *Wine from
These Grapes;* Young, *So Red the
Rose;* Lomax, *American Ballads
and Folk Songs;* Stuart, *Man with
a Bull-Tongue Plow;* Miller, *Tropic
of Cancer*
Partisan Review (1934–   )
Joan Didion (1934–   ); Le Roi Jones
(1934–   ); N. Scott Momaday
(1934–   )

1935—Lewis, *It Can't Happen Here;* MacLe-
ish, *Panic;* Wolfe, *Of Time and the
River;* Sheean, *Personal History;*
Steinbeck, *Tortilla Flat;* Freeman,
R.E. Lee; Perry, *William James;*
Day, *Life with Father;* Glasgow,
Vein of Iron; Anderson, *Winterset;*
Odets, *Waiting for Lefty* and *Awake
and Sing;* Kingsley, *Dead End*
Federal Writers' Project (1935–39);
American Writers Congress
Southern Review (1935–42)
Richard Brautigan (1935–84); Ken
Kesey (1935–   )

1936—Brooks, *Flowering of New England;*
Dos Passos, *The Big Money;* Santayana, *The Last Puritan;* Faulkner,

Charles A. Lindbergh, Jr., kidnap-
murder

1933—Franklin Roosevelt's administration
(1933–45)
Bank "holidays"; National Industrial
Recovery Act; Civilian Conservation Corps; Tennessee Valley power
project; Home Owners' Loan Act;
Agricultural Adjustment and Farm
Credit acts; Banking and Gold Reserve acts; Emergency Relief Act
U.S. recognizes U.S.S.R.
20th and 21st Amendments
Einstein and other German émigrés
come to U.S.

1934—Reciprocal trade treaties
Securities Exchange Act; National
Housing Act; Tyding-McDuffie In-
dependence Act grants autonomy to
Philippines in 1946
Federal Communications Commission
Upton Sinclair's EPIC campaign in
California

1935—Works Progress Administration
("work relief"); NRA declared unconstitutional; Social Security Act;
Agricultural Adjustment Act; National Labor Relations Act; first
Neutrality Act; Public Utility Holding Company Act; National Youth
Administration
Congress of Industrial Organizations
founded
Regular trans-Pacific air service

1936—Rural electrification act; AAA declared unconstitutional; Merchant
Marine Act; Soil Conservation and

Absalom, Absalom!; Frost, *A Further Range;* MacLeish, *Public Speech;* Sandburg, *The People, Yes;* Mitchell, *Gone with the Wind;* Steinbeck, *In Dubious Battle;* Jeffers, *Solstice;* Eliot, *Collected Poems;* Sherwood, *Idiot's Delight;* Shaw, *Bury the Dead*
O'Neill receives Nobel Prize
Federal Theatre Project (1936–39)
New *Life* (1936–   ); *New Directions* (1936–   )
Tom Robbins (1936–   )

Domestic Allotment Act; Roosevelt reelected, winning electoral votes of all but two states
CIO expelled from AFL
Inter-American Peace Conference

1937—Hemingway, *To Have and Have Not;* Roberts, *Northwest Passage;* MacLeish, *The Fall of the City;* Marquand, *The Late George Apley;* Zaturenska, *Cold Morning Sky;* Blitzstein, *The Cradle Will Rock;* Millay, *Conversation at Midnight;* Steinbeck, *Of Mice and Men* and *The Red Pony;* Paul, *Life and Death of a Spanish Town;* Anderson, *High Tor;* Jeffers, *Such Counsels You Gave to Me*
Thomas Pynchon (1937–   )

1937—CIO "sit-down" strikes in glass and automotive industries
Roosevelt asks for reorganization of federal judiciary; Supreme Court validates National Labor Relations Act
"Quarantine aggressors" speech of Roosevelt; third Neutrality Act
Business recession; migrant labor problem increased by drought
Bonneville dam project; U.S. Housing Authority

1938—Sherwood, *Abe Lincoln in Illinois;* Wilder, *Our Town;* C. Van Doren, *Benjamin Franklin;* Rawlings, *The Yearling;* Hemingway, *The Fifth Column;* Peattie, *Prairie Grove;* Dictionary of American English (1938–44)
Pearl Buck receives Nobel Prize
Rocky Mountain Review (1938–59); *Twice a Year* (1938–48)
Joyce Carol Oates (1938–   )

1938—Naval bill larger than any previous peacetime bill; Lima Conference
Wages and Hours Law
Mexico expropriates foreign oil holdings
Howard Hughes flies around world in 91 hours

1939—Steinbeck, *The Grapes of Wrath;* Edward Taylor, *Poetical Works;* Nathanael West, *The Day of the Locust;* Beard, *America in Midpassage;* Dos Passos, *Adventures of a Young Man;* Fisher, *Children of God;* Frank, *The Bridegroom Cometh;* Frost, *Collected Poems;* Shaw, *The Gentle People* and *Sailor Off the Bremen;* Marquand, *Wickford Point;* Parker, *Here Lies;* Sandburg, *Abraham Lincoln: The War Years;* Saroyan, *The Time of Your Life;* Thurber, *The Last Flower;* M. Van Doren, *Collected Poems;* Wolfe, *The Web and the Rock;* Benét, *The Devil and Daniel Webster;* Crouse and Lindsay, *Life with Father*
Kenyon Review (1939–   )

1939—Regular trans-Atlantic air service
King George and Queen Elizabeth tour U.S. and Canada
Neutrality Act amended, repealing arms embargo
Hatch Act forbids political activity by government employees
Tom Mooney pardoned

1940—*Dictionary of American History;* Brooks, *New England Indian Summer;* Hansen, *The Atlantic Migra-*

1940—Population, 131,669,275
Limited national emergency declared; first peacetime conscription; Na-

tion; Josephson, *The President
Makers;* Lindbergh, *The Wave of
the Future;* MacLeish, *The Irrespon-
sibles;* Wright, *Native Son;*
McCullers, *The Heart Is a Lonely
Hunter;* Clark, *The Ox-Bow Inci-
dent;* Wolfe, *You Can't Go Home
Again;* Sinclair, *World's End;*
Hemingway, *For Whom the Bell
Tolls;* Saroyan, *My Name is Aram;*
Sherwood, *There Shall Be No Night;*
Cather, *Sapphira and the Slave Girl;*
Roberts, *Oliver Wiswell;* Wescott,
The Pilgrim Hawk; Anderson,
Journey to Jerusalem; Bacon, *Sun-
derland Capture*
PM (1940–48)

1941—Fast, *The Last Frontier;* Adamic,
Two-Way Passage; Marquand,
H.M. Pulham, Esq.; Benét, *The
Dust Which Is God;* MacLeish, *A
Time To Speak;* Brooks, *On Litera-
ture Today;* Sinclair, *Between Two
Worlds;* Glasgow, *In This Our Life;*
Saroyan, *The Beautiful People;*
Hellman, *Watch on the Rhine;* Na-
than, *They Went On Together;* Fitz-
gerald, *The Last Tycoon;* Millay,
Collected Sonnets; Stewart, *Storm;*
M. Van Doren, *The Mayfield Deer;*
C. Van Doren, *Secret History of the
American Revolution;* Wilson, *The
Wound and the Bow*

1942—Anderson, *Eve of St. Mark;* Berlin,
This Is the Army; Faulkner, *Go
Down, Moses;* Freeman, *Lee's
Lieutenants;* Paul, *Last Time I Saw
Paris;* Sinclair, *Dragon's Teeth;*
Wilder, *Skin of Our Teeth;* E.B.
White, *One Man's Meat;* W.L.
White, *They Were Expendable*
John Irving (1942–   )
Yank (1942–45)

1943—Allen, *Forest and the Fort;* Benét,
Western Star; De Voto, *Year of
Decision;* Dos Passos, *Number One;*
Fast, *Citizen Tom Paine;* Flavin,
Journey in the Dark; Rodgers and
Hammerstein, *Oklahoma!;* Santay-

tional Guard, naval and marine re-
serves called to active duty; bases
acquired in British possessions;
"two-ocean" navy; joint defense
with Canada; aid to Great Britain
"short of war"; transfer of warships
to Britain
Refugee children from Europe admitted to U.S. as "visitors"; aliens
required to register; Communist
party ends affiliation with Communist International

1941—Roosevelt inaugurated for third term
"Lend-lease" bill to aid anti-Axis
powers; Greenland bases acquired
to maintain "present status"; unli-
mited national emergency declared;
Axis ships seized; Nazi consulates
closed; U.S. becomes "arsenal of
democracy"; Iceland occupied; Atlantic Charter; U.S. enters "shooting war" in Atlantic; Roosevelt's
"Four Freedoms" speech
Japanese attack Pearl Harbor; U.S. at
war with Japan, Germany, Italy,
and Axis satellites; Japanese capture Guam and Wake, and invade
Philippines
Hoover Library on War, Revolution,
and Peace opened at Stanford; National Gallery of Art opened

1942—U.S. and Philippine forces surrender
after battles of Bataan and Corregi-
dor; General MacArthur commands
forces in southwest Pacific; Doolittle fliers bomb Tokyo; naval battles
of Coral Sea, Midway, Santa Cruz,
Solomons; battle of Guadalcanal;
U.S. air forces begin European
bombing raids; American and British troops land in North Africa
War Manpower Commission, Office
of War Information, War Production Board, Office of Civilian Defense, War Labor Board formed;
price control and rationing
Twenty-six signatories to "Declaration by United Nations"

1943—General Eisenhower leads forces in
driving Germans from North Africa, invading Sicily and Italy, and is
made supreme Allied commander in
Europe; Japanese offensive power
destroyed in southwest Pacific and

ana, *Persons and Places;* Smith, *A Tree Grows in Brooklyn;* Thurber, *Men, Women, and Dogs;* Willkie, *One World;* T.S. Eliot, *Four Quartets*
James Tate (1943–　)

1944—Hersey, *A Bell for Adano;* Brown, *A Walk in the Sun;* Brooks, *The World of Washington Irving;* Chase, *Harvey;* Hellman, *The Searching Wind;* Jackson, *The Lost Weekend;* Pyle, *Brave Men;* Shapiro, *V-Letter;* Smith, *Strange Fruit;* Bellow, *Dangling Man*
Alice Walker (1944–　)

1945—Frost, *Masque of Reason;* Crouse and Lindsay, *State of the Union;* Mauldin, *Up Front;* Mencken, *The American Language: Supplement I;* Schlesinger, *The Age of Jackson;* Shapiro, *Essay on Rime;* Stein, *Wars I Have Seen;* Stewart, *Names on the Land;* Wescott, *Apartment in Athens;* Williams, *The Glass Menagerie;* Wright, *Black Boy*
Commentary (1945–　)

1946—Dreiser, *The Bulwark;* Fast, *The American;* Hersey, *Hiroshima;* La Farge, *The Sudden Guest;* Williams, *Paterson;* McCullers, *The Member of the Wedding;* W.A. White, *Autobiography;* R.P. Warren, *All the King's Men;* Welty, *Delta Wedding;* Stein, *Brewsie and Willie;* Jeffers, *Medea;* Lowell, *Lord Weary's Castle;* Vidal, *Williwaw*

1947—Anderson, *Joan of Lorraine;* Brooks, *The Times of Melville and Whitman;* Canby, *American Memoir;* De Voto, *Across the Wide Missouri;* Frost, *Masque of Mercy;* James, *Notebooks;* Lewis, *Kingsblood Royal;* Nevins, *Ordeal of the Union;* Steinbeck, *The Wayward Bus;* Michener, *Tales of the South Pacific;* Williams, *A Streetcar Named Desire*
Ann Beattie (1947–　)

1948—Faulkner, *Intruder in the Dust;* Mailer, *The Naked and the Dead;* Cozzens, *Guard of Honor;* Literary

Aleutians; Italian armistice; Roosevelt and Churchill meet at Casablanca, decide on "unconditional surrender" of Axis as war aim; Roosevelt, Churchill, Stalin meet at Teheran
United Nations Relief and Rehabilitation Administration organized

1944—U.S. forces return to Philippines, begin air bombardment of Japan; D-Day invasion of western Europe, battles from Normandy beachhead to German frontiers; "round-the-clock" bombing of German military and industrial installations
Servicemen's Readjustment Act (G.I. Bill of Rights)
Dumbarton Oaks conference plans United Nations organization; Bretton Woods conference plans World Bank and International Monetary Fund

1945—Roosevelt inaugurated for fourth term; "Big Three" confer at Yalta
Truman's administration (1945–53)
Invaded Germany capitulates on V-E Day; battles of Iwo Jima and Okinawa; atomic bombs dropped on Hiroshima and Nagasaki; Japan surrenders on V-J Day
United Nations charter written at San Francisco
Rationing, wartime controls relaxed or abandoned

1946—First meetings of United Nations; Paris Conference plans peace treaty with Axis satellite nations
Lewis and United Mine Workers return to AFL; price controls relaxed; coal, railroad, maritime, and other major strikes
Atomic bomb tests in Pacific; United Nations commission considers international control of atomic energy

1947—Truman Doctrine aiding foreign nations "to maintain independence"; Marshall Plan offering cooperation for economic reconstruction; Western Hemisphere Mutual Defense Treaty; Armed Forces under a secretary of defense; Air Forces co-equal with Army and Navy; U.S. Trusteeship of 625 Pacific isles; Taft-Hartley Labor Relations Act

1948—Truman elected to full term; first peacetime selective service act; Berlin blockade and airlift; many inves-

History of the United States; Pound, *Pisan Cantos;* Capote, *Other Voices, Other Rooms;* Auden, *Age of Anxiety;* Sandburg, *Remembrance Rock*
T.S. Eliot receives Nobel Prize

1949—Clark, *Track of the Cat;* Miller, *Death of a Salesman;* Lewis, *Kingsblood Royal;* Buechner, *A Long Day's Dying;* Bowles, *The Sheltering Sky*

1950—Eliot, *The Cocktail Party;* Hemingway, *Across the River and into the Trees;* Schulberg, *The Disenchanted*
Faulkner receives Nobel Prize
National Book Awards (1950–   )

1951—Carson, *The Sea Around Us;* Faulkner, *Requiem for a Nun;* Jones, *From Here to Eternity;* McCullers, *Ballad of the Sad Café;* Moore, *Collected Poems;* Salinger, *Catcher in the Rye;* Saroyan, *Rock Wagram;* Styron, *Lie Down in Darkness;* Wouk, *The Caine Mutiny*

1952—Hemingway, *The Old Man and the Sea;* Davis, *Winds of Morning;* De Voto, *Course of Empire;* MacLeish, *Collected Poems;* Steinbeck, *East of Eden*

1953—Eliot, *The Confidential Clerk;* Warren, *Brother to Dragons;* Roethke, *The Waking;* Bellow, *Adventures of Augie March;* Wright, *The Outsider;* Stewart, *U.S. 40*

1954—Welty, *The Ponder Heart;* Hecht, *A Child of the Century;* Steinbeck, *Sweet Thursday;* Faulkner, *A Fable;* Glasgow, *The Woman Within;* Jeffers, *Hungerfield;* Wallace Stevens, *Collected Poems*
Hemingway receives Nobel Prize

1955—Anderson, *The Bad Seed;* Bishop, *North & South;* Inge, *Bus Stop;* Mailer, *Deer Park;* Miller, *A View from the Bridge;* O'Hara, *Ten North Frederick;* Williams, *Cat on a Hot Tin Roof*

1956—Algren, *A Walk on the Wild Side;* Berryman, *Homage to Mistress Bradstreet;* Ginsberg, *Howl;* Kennedy, *Profiles in Courage;* O'Connor, *The Last Hurrah;* O'Neill, *Long Day's Journey into Night;* Thurber, *Fables for Our Time*

tigations by House Committee on Un-American Activities; Organization of American States created

1949—American Communist party leaders convicted of conspiracy
U.S. nuclear monopoly ended as U.S.S.R. explodes atom bomb
North Atlantic Defense Pact signed

1950—Population, 150,597,361
Peace treaty with Japan; South Korea invaded by forces from north, including Chinese "volunteers"; U.N. sends troops and support to South Korea; U.S. proclaims state of national emergency

1951—22nd Amendment: President limited to two terms; Puerto Rico becomes a commonwealth; Truman relieves MacArthur of Far East command; Japanese Peace Treaty signed

1952—Eisenhower elected President; strong wave of anti-communism; investigations into "un-American" activities; increasing sweep to "loyalty" oaths

1953—Truce in Korea; U.S. pledges atomic aid to NATO forces; Eisenhower creates Health, Education, Welfare cabinet post

1954—Supreme Court rules racial segregation in schools unconstitutional; McCarthy censured by Senate
St. Lawrence Seaway construction begins
Southeast Asia Treaty Organization

1955—"Big Four" confer at Geneva
AFL and CIO merge
Salk antipolio vaccine developed
Supreme Court orders reasonable speed in implementation of 1954 decision on racial desegregation in schools

1956—Eisenhower reelected

1957—Agee, *A Death in the Family;*
    Cheever, *Wapshot Chronicle;* Coz-
    zens, *By Love Possessed;* Faulkner,
    The Town; Kerouac, *On the Road;*
    Malamud, *The Assistant;* Wilbur,
    Poems
1958—Eliot, *The Elder Statesman;* MacLe-
    ish, *J.B.;* Nabokov, *Lolita;* Ro-
    ethke, *Words for the Wind;* Willi-
    ams, *Suddenly Last Summer*
1959—Bellow, *Henderson the Rain King;*
    Hansberry, *A Raisin in the Sun;*
    Lowell, *Life Studies;* Pound,
    Thrones; Roth, *Goodbye, Colum-
    bus;* Snodgrass, *Heart's Needle;*
    Warren, *The Cave*
1960—Faulkner, *The Mansion;* Jarrell, *The
    Woman at the Washington Zoo;*
    Morris, *Ceremony in Lone Tree;*
    Styron, *Set This House on Fire;*
    Updike, *Rabbit, Run*

1961—Baldwin, *Nobody Knows My Name;*
    Dugan, *Poems;* Heinlein, *Stranger
    in a Strange Land;* Heller, *Catch-
    22;* McCullers, *Clock Without
    Hands;* Salinger, *Franny and
    Zooey;* Schorer, *Sinclair Lewis;*
    Steinbeck, *The Winter of Our Dis-
    content*
1962—Albee, *Who's Afraid of Virginia
    Woolfe?;* Auden, *The Dyer's Hand;*
    Faulkner, *The Reivers;* Nabokov,
    Pale Fire; Porter, *Ship of Fools;*
    Saroyan, *Here Comes, There Goes,
    You Know Who;* Williams, *The
    Night of the Iguana;* Wilson, *Patri-
    otic Gore*
    Steinbeck receives Nobel Prize
1963—Jeffers, *The Beginning and the End;*
    McCarthy, *The Group;* Malamud,
    Idiots First; Pynchon, *V.;* Updike,
    The Centaur; Williams, *Pictures
    from Brueghel*
    New York Review of Books (1963–)

1964—Bellow, *Herzog;* Berryman, *77 Dream
    Songs;* Hemingway, *A Moveable
    Feast;* Vidal, *Julian;* Warren, *Flood*

1965—Albee, *Tiny Alice;* Ammons, *Tape for
    the Turn of the Year;* Haley, *The
    Autobiography of Malcolm X;*
    Mailer, *American Dream*
    Wilder receives first National Medal
    for Literature
1966—Alfred, *Hogan's Goat;* Barth, *Giles
    Goat-Boy;* Capote, *In Cold Blood;*
    Malamud, *The Fixer;* Merrill,

1957—International Geophysical Year be-
    gins
    Eisenhower sends National Guard to
    Little Rock, Ark., in school integra-
    tion crisis
    Truman Library dedicated
1958—Alaska admitted as 49th state
    U.S. launches earth satellite
    U.S. inaugurates jet airline service

1959—Hawaii admitted as 50th state
    St. Lawrence Seaway opened
    Antarctica designated scientific pre-
    serve by international treaty

1960—Kennedy elected President
    Population, 170,323,175; New York,
    7,781,984; Chicago, 3,550,404; Los
    Angeles, 2,479,015
    U.S. and Japan sign treaty of mutual
    security and cooperation
1961—Peace Corps created
    U.S. severs relations with Cuba; Cuba
    invasion fails
    First U.S. manned suborbital space
    flight

1962—Two Americans and two Russians
    orbit the earth
    Soviet arming of Cuba causes crisis
    Telstar, first private communications
    satellite

1963—Kennedy assassinated (Nov. 22);
    Johnson becomes President
    California most populous state
    Widespread civil rights demonstra-
    tions
    "Big Three" sign limited nuclear test
    ban
1964—Antipoverty and civil rights legisla-
    tion; Johnson elected President
    Martin Luther King, Jr., receives No-
    bel Peace Prize
1965—Military support of South Vietnam
    Intervention in Dominican Republic
    revolt
    25th Amendment: presidential succes-
    sion stipulated
1966—Medicare established
    U.S. planes begin bombing North
    Vietnam; antiwar protests

Nights and Days; Pynchon, *The Crying of Lot 49*

1967—Brautigan, *Trout Fishing in America;* Kelley, *dem;* Podhoretz, *Making It;* Styron, *The Confessions of Nat Turner;* Wilder, *The Eighth Day*

1968—Didion, *Slouching Towards Bethlehem;* Mailer, *The Armies of the Night;* Miller, *The Price;* Updike, *Couples;* Vidal, *Myra Breckenridge*

1969—Bishop, *Complete Poems;* Hellman, *An Unfinished Woman;* Howard, *Untitled Subjects;* Momaday, *House Made of Dawn;* Roth, *Portnoy's Complaint*

1970—Dickey, *Deliverance;* Didion, *Play It as It Lays;* Hemingway, *Islands in the Stream;* Pound, *Cantos* (collected); Wolfe, *Radical Chic and Mau-Mauing the Flak Catchers*

1971—Ammons, *Collected Poems;* DeVries, *Into Your Tent I'll Creep;* Doctorow, *The Book of Daniel;* Gaines, *The Autobiography of Miss Jane Pitman;* Malamud, *Tenants;* Stegner, *Angle of Repose;* E. Wilson, *Upstate*

1972—Barth, *Chimera;* Oates, *Marriages and Infidelities;* Purdy, *I Am Elijah Thrush;* Reed, *Mumbo-Jumbo;* Welty, *Optimist's Daughter;* T. Williams, *Small Craft Warnings*

1973—Ginsberg, *The Fall of America;* Hellman, *Pentimento;* Lowell, *The Dolphin;* Pynchon, *Gravity's Rainbow;* Vidal, *Burr;* Vonnegut, *Breakfast of Champions;* Wilder, *Theophilus North*

1974—Connell, *The Connoisseur;* Everson, *Man-Fate;* Lurie, *The War Between the Tates;* Olson, *Yonnondio;* Snyder, *Turtle Island*

Racial riot in Watts, Cal.

1967—Vietnam War intensified; 475,000 U.S. troops in South Vietnam; protests against war increased
Racial disturbances in U.S. cities

1968—*Pueblo* seized by North Korea, crew later released
Martin Luther King, Jr., assassinated
American astronauts orbit moon
Nixon elected President

1969—Large-scale anti-Vietnam-War demonstrations
Peace talks with Vietnam begun
Limited military withdrawal from Vietnam
Astronauts Neil A. Armstrong and Colonel Edwin E. Aldrin, Jr., are first men to walk on the moon

1970—Population, 203,235,298: New York, 7,895,563; Chicago, 3,369,357; Los Angeles, 2,811,801
Four Kent State University students protesting Vietnam War shot to death by National Guardsmen
Independent U.S. Postal Service created

1971—26th Amendment lowers voting age to 18
New national railway system, Amtrak, inaugurated

1972—President Nixon visits China
U.S. troops leave Vietnam
Nixon visits Moscow, signs strategic arms limitation treaty
Democratic National Committee headquarters in Watergate building (Washington, D.C.) broken into by people associated with Republican party's committee to reelect Nixon
Nixon reelected

1973—Vietnam War ended
Military draft ended
Watergate and allied scandals involve Nixon administration; several chief administrators resign
Vice-President Agnew sentenced to probation and fine for evading taxes on undercover payments
Agnew resigns

1974—Nixon impeachment hearings begun
Watergate scandals spread
Nixon resigns
Ford succeeds to presidency, grants unconditional pardon to Nixon

1975—Albee, *Seascape;* Ashbery, *Self-Portrait in a Convex Mirror;* Bellow, *Humboldt's Gift;* Doctorow, *Ragtime;* R.W.B. Lewis, *Edith Wharton;* Sexton, *The Awful Rowing Toward God*

1975—U.S. merchant ship *Mayaguez* seized by Cambodia; 38 of the 39 crewmen freed by U.S. marines are killed in rescue

1976—D.L. Coburn, *The Gin Game;* Everson, *River-Root;* Gass, *On Being Blue;* Haley, *Roots;* Hawkes, *Travesty;* Hellman, *Scoundrel Time;* Isherwood, *Christopher and His Kind;* Stegner, *The Spectator Bird*
Saul Bellow awarded Nobel Prize

1976—U.S. celebrates Bicentennial
Viking II lands on Mars
Carter elected President

1977—Coover, *The Public Burning;* Dunne, *True Confessions;* Percy, *Lancelot;* Perelman, *Eastward Ha!*

1977—Most Vietnam War draft evaders pardoned by Carter
First National Women's Conference drafts women's rights program

1978—Cowley, *And I Worked at the Writer's Trade;* Gardner, *On Moral Fiction;* Irving, *The World According to Garp;* Kazin, *New York Jew;* Tuchman, *A Distant Mirror;* Warren, *Now and Then;* Wouk, *The Winds of War*
I.B. Singer awarded Nobel Prize

1978—Panama Canal turned over to Panama
Mass suicide of over 900 persons in People's Temple cult
Carter promotes peace treaty between Israel and Egypt

1979—Barth, *Letters;* Didion, *The White Album;* Justice, *Selected Poems;* Mailer, *The Executioner's Song;* Maxwell, *So Long, See You Tomorrow;* Roth, *The Ghost Writer;* Styron, *Sophie's Choice;* Zukofsky, *A*

1979—American citizens taken hostage by Iran
Last Watergate convict (former Attorney General Mitchell) released
U.S. and China establish formal diplomatic relations
Large antinuclear demonstration in Washington, D.C.

1980—Ferlinghetti and Peters, *Literary San Francisco;* Gold, *He/She;* Kinnell, *Mortal Acts, Mortal Words;* Morris, *Plains Song;* Oates, *Bellefleur;* Percy, *The Second Coming;* Robbins, *Still Life with Woodpecker*
Milosz awarded Nobel Prize

1980—Population, 224,599,260: New York, 7,035,348; Chicago, 3,005,072; Los Angeles, 2,952,511
Miami race riots
Reagan elected President

1981—Ashbery, *Shadow Train;* Hemingway, *Letters;* Roth, *Zuckerman Unbound;* Vidal, *Creation;* Tuchman, *Practicing History;* Updike, *Rabbit Is Rich*

1981—American hostages released by Iran
Severe federal budget cuts
Reagan assassination attempt

1982—Bellow, *The Dean's December;* Dunne, *Dutch Shea, Jr.;* Stegner, *One Way To Spell Man;* Theroux, *The Mosquito Coast;* Walker, *The Color Purple; The Library of America* begun

1982—Increased concern with Central American civil strife
Economic recession
12,000,000 unemployed (10.8 per cent of work force)

1983—Adler, *Pitch Dark;* Dickey, *The Central Motion;* Gaines, *A Gathering of Old Men;* Holander, *Power of Thirteen;* Maller, *Ancient Evenings;* Roth, *The Anatomy Lesson*

1983—U.S. invades Grenada because of communist threat; U.S. embassy and marine compound in Beirut bombed by terrorists, causing many deaths; Reagan calls for "Star Wars" defense system

1984—Ashbery, *A Wave;* Bellow, *Him With His Foot in His Mouth;* Didion,

1984—Reagan reelected for second term; Olympic Games held in Los Angeles

Democracy; LeRoi Jones, *Autobiography;* Kazin, *An American Procession;* Pynchon, *Slow Learner;*
Snyder, *Axe Handles*

1985—Baldwin, *The Evidence of Things Not
Seen;* Hawkes, Adventures in the
Alaska Skin Trade; Irving, *The
Cider House Rules;* Jarrell, *Letters;*
Roth, *Zuckerman Bound*

1985—Deficit in national budget exceeds
$200 billion; stock market reaches
new highs; several U.S. spies for
USSR arrested; auto sales of
15,600,000 vehicles sets record